The 109th Congressional District Atlas

The 109th Congressional District Atlas

Editors
Deirdre A. Gaquin
Katherine A. DeBrandt

BERNAN PRESS
Lanham, MD

ISBN: 1-886222-28-2

Printed by Automated Graphic Systems, Inc., White Plains, MD, on acid-free paper that meets the American National Standards Institute Z39-48 standard.

2006 2005   4 3 2 1

BERNAN PRESS
4611-F Assembly Drive
Lanham, MD 20706
800-274-4447
email: info@bernan.com
www.bernanpress.com

Contents

Preface

The 109th Congressional District Atlas is the first print edition of the *Atlas* since the 103rd Congress. Unless a state initiative or court-ordered redistricting requires a change, these boundaries will be in effect until the 113th Congress.

Deirdre A. Gaquin and Katherine A. DeBrandt have edited this edition of *The 109th Congressional District Atlas*. Ms. Gaquin has been a data use consultant to private organizations, government agencies, and universities for over 20 years. Prior to that, she was Director of Data Access Services at Data Use & Access Laboratories, a pioneer in private sector distribution of federal statistical data. A former president of the Association of Public Data Users, Ms. Gaquin has served on numerous boards, panels, and task forces concerned with federal statistical data and has worked on four decennial censuses. She holds a Master of Urban Planning degree from Hunter College. Ms. Gaquin is also an editor of Bernan Press' *The Who, What, and Where of America: Understanding the Census Results*; *County and City Extra: Annual Metro, City, and County Data Book*; and *Places, Towns and Townships*.

Ms. DeBrandt is a data analyst team leader with Bernan Press. She received her B.A. in political science from Colgate University. She is also a co-editor of *The Almanac of American Education*; *State Profiles: The Population and Economy of Each U.S. State*; and *Social Change in America: The Historical Handbook*, all published by Bernan Press.

We are extremely grateful to Kara Prezocki, Bernan Press' production team leader, for capably managing the production aspects of this volume as well as for preparing the graphics and cover design. Production assistant Rebecca Zayas assisted Kara in coordinating this project. With support from Director of Publishing Tamera Wells-Lee; Automated Graphics Systems; and Publications Professionals, Kara and Rebecca assisted the editors tremendously with finalizing this special edition.

Responsibility of the editors and publisher of this publication is limited to reasonable care in the reproduction and presentation of data obtained from sources believed to be reliable.

As always, we are especially grateful to the many federal agency personnel who assisted us in obtaining the data, provided excellent resources on their Web sites, and patiently answered our questions.

Introduction

The Atlas is organized into two sections—Part I: Maps and Part II: Tables. The maps are presented on the national and state level and detail the districts of the 109th Congress. The 108th Congress was the first to reflect the reapportionment and district boundary changes established by the states based on the results of the 2000 census. For just three states—Maine, Pennsylvania, and Texas—changes have occurred from the 108th Congress to the 109th Congress. For these three states, two sets of maps have been included, one of the 109th congressional districts and one of the 108th districts. The United States congressional districts map reflects the 108th district boundaries.

As required by Article 1, Section 2 of the Constitution, a census is conducted every 10 years for the purpose of reapportioning the seats of the House of Representatives among the 50 states (the District of Columbia and the territories have no voting representation). The number of representatives has been set at 435 since the 1910 census, except for a brief period with 437 representatives to account for the new states of Alaska and Hawaii in the 1950s.

California has the most seats in the House of Representatives with 53, followed by Texas (32) and New York (29). Arizona, Florida, Georgia, and Texas all gained two seats from 1990 to 2000. New York and Pennsylvania each lost two seats as a result of the census count. Another 12 states lost or gained one seat, primarily reflecting the higher population growth in southern and western states. There are six states—Alaska, Delaware, Montana, North Dakota, South Dakota, and Wyoming—with just one "At Large" representative. Montana has the largest population among the six states with about 900,000, which is too small to earn a second representative.

The total U.S. population exceeded 280,000,000 in 2000, giving the average congressional district a population of about 645,000 people. The census population counts are used by states to create new boundaries for congressional districts that must be equal in population. This redistricting can be a contentious issue, as in some states the political party with the majority can design districts to suit its own interests.

The state-based tables show the relationship between the congressional districts and counties or county equivalents. Data from the 2000 census have been retabulated for the 109th districts. Data from the 2002 Census of Agriculture were tabulated for the 108th Congress, so they do not reflect the boundary changes in Maine, Pennsylvania, and Texas. Complete source information is included in the notes and definitions on page 479.

Number of Representatives by State, 1890–2000

State	2000	1990	1980	1970	1960	1950	1940	1930	1920	1910	1900	1890
United States Total	435	435	435	435	435	437	435	435	435	435	391	357
Alabama	7	7	7	7	8	9	9	9	10	10	9	9
Alaska	1	1	1	1	1	1	X	X	X	X	X	X
Arizona	8	6	5	4	3	2	2	1	1	1	X	X
Arkansas	4	4	4	4	4	6	7	7	7	7	8	7
California	53	52	45	43	38	30	23	20	11	11	8	7
Colorado	7	6	6	5	4	4	4	4	4	4	3	2
Connecticut	5	6	6	6	6	6	6	6	5	5	5	4
Delaware	1	1	1	1	1	1	1	1	1	1	1	1
Florida	25	23	19	15	12	8	6	5	4	4	3	2
Georgia	13	11	10	10	10	10	10	10	12	12	11	11
Hawaii	2	2	2	2	2	1	X	X	X	X	X	X
Idaho	2	2	2	2	2	2	2	2	2	2	1	1
Illinois	19	20	22	24	24	25	26	27	27	27	25	22
Indiana	9	10	10	11	11	11	11	12	13	13	13	13
Iowa	5	5	6	6	7	8	8	9	11	11	11	11
Kansas	4	4	5	5	5	6	6	7	8	8	8	8
Kentucky	6	6	7	7	7	8	9	9	11	11	11	11
Louisiana	7	7	8	8	8	8	8	8	8	8	7	6
Maine	2	2	2	2	2	3	3	3	4	4	4	4
Maryland	8	8	8	8	8	7	6	6	6	6	6	6
Massachusetts	10	10	11	12	12	14	14	15	16	16	14	13
Michigan	15	16	18	19	19	18	17	17	13	13	12	12
Minnesota	8	8	8	8	8	9	9	9	10	10	9	7
Mississippi	4	5	5	5	5	6	7	7	8	8	8	7
Missouri	9	9	9	10	10	11	13	13	16	16	16	15
Montana	1	1	2	2	2	2	2	2	2	2	1	1
Nebraska	3	3	3	3	3	4	4	5	6	6	6	6
Nevada	3	2	2	1	1	1	1	1	1	1	1	1
New Hampshire	2	2	2	2	2	2	2	2	2	2	2	2
New Jersey	13	13	14	15	15	14	14	14	12	12	10	8
New Mexico	3	3	3	2	2	2	2	1	1	1	X	X
New York	29	31	34	39	41	43	45	45	43	43	37	34
North Carolina	13	12	11	11	11	12	12	11	10	10	10	9
North Dakota	1	1	1	1	2	2	2	2	3	3	2	1
Ohio	18	19	21	23	24	23	23	24	22	22	21	21
Oklahoma	5	6	6	6	6	6	8	9	8	8	5	X
Oregon	5	5	5	4	4	4	4	3	3	3	2	2
Pennsylvania	19	21	23	25	27	30	33	34	36	36	32	30
Rhode Island	2	2	2	2	2	2	2	2	3	3	2	2
South Carolina	6	6	6	6	6	6	6	6	7	7	7	7
South Dakota	1	1	1	2	2	2	2	2	3	3	2	2
Tennessee	9	9	9	8	9	9	10	9	10	10	10	10
Texas	32	30	27	24	23	22	21	21	18	18	16	13
Utah	3	3	3	2	2	2	2	2	2	2	1	1
Vermont	1	1	1	1	1	1	1	1	2	2	2	2
Virginia	11	11	10	10	10	10	9	9	10	10	10	10
Washington	9	9	8	7	7	7	6	6	5	5	3	2
West Virginia	3	3	4	4	5	6	6	6	6	6	5	4
Wisconsin	8	9	9	9	10	10	10	10	11	11	11	10
Wyoming	1	1	1	1	1	1	1	1	1	1	1	1

Note: American Samoa, District of Columbia, Guam, Puerto Rico, and Virgin Islands have nonvoting delegates to the House of Representatives.
X = Not applicable.

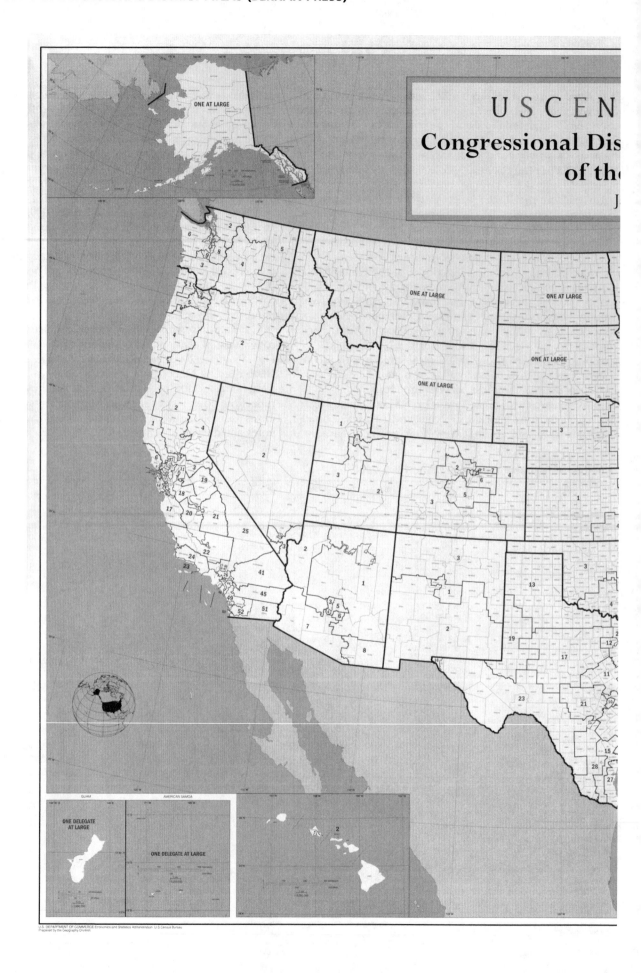

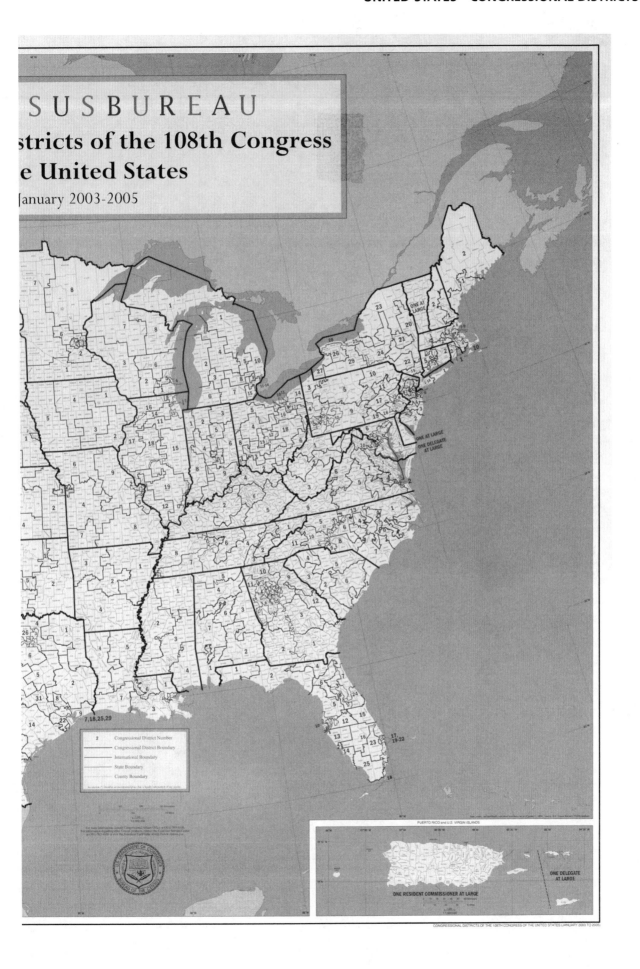

SUSBUREAU

stricts of the 108th Congress
e United States

January 2003-2005

PART I: MAPS

Alabama Congressional Districts — 7 Districts Total

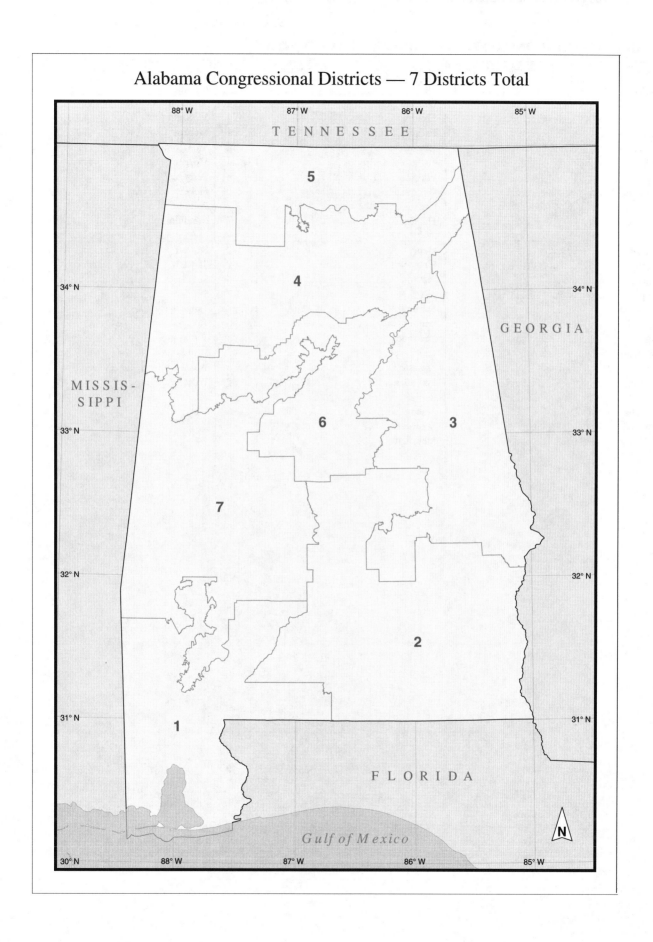

ALABAMA—109th CONGRESSIONAL DISTRICTS BY COUNTIES

County	Congressional District
Autauga	2
Baldwin	1
Barbour	2
Bibb	6
Blount	4
Bullock	2
Butler	2
Calhoun	3
Chambers	3
Cherokee	3
Chilton	6
Choctaw	7
Clarke	1, 7
Clay	3
Cleburne	3
Coffee	2
Colbert	5
Conecuh	2
Coosa	3, 6
Covington	2
Crenshaw	2
Cullman	4
Dale	2

County	Congressional District
Dallas	7
DeKalb	4
Elmore	2
Escambia	1
Etowah	4
Fayette	4
Franklin	4
Geneva	2
Greene	7
Hale	7
Henry	2
Houston	2
Jackson	5
Jefferson	6, 7
Lamar	4
Lauderdale	5
Lawrence	5
Lee	3
Limestone	5
Lowndes	2
Macon	3
Madison	5
Marengo	7

County	Congressional District
Marion	4
Marshall	4
Mobile	1
Monroe	1
Montgomery	2, 3
Morgan	4, 5
Perry	7
Pickens	4, 7
Pike	2
Randolph	3
Russell	3
St. Clair	4, 6
Shelby	6
Sumter	7
Talladega	3
Tallapoosa	3
Tuscaloosa	6, 7
Walker	4
Washington	1
Wilcox	7
Winston	4

Congressional District 1

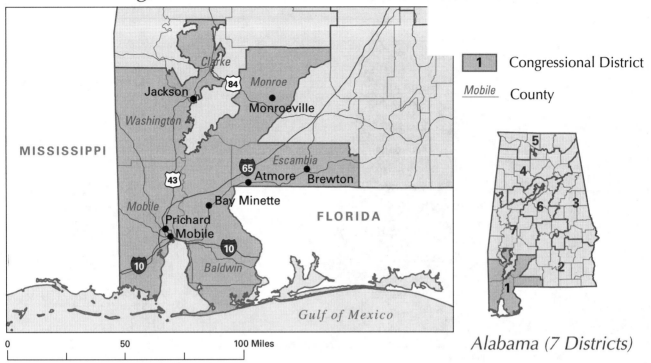

1 Congressional District
Mobile County

Alabama (7 Districts)

Congressional District 2

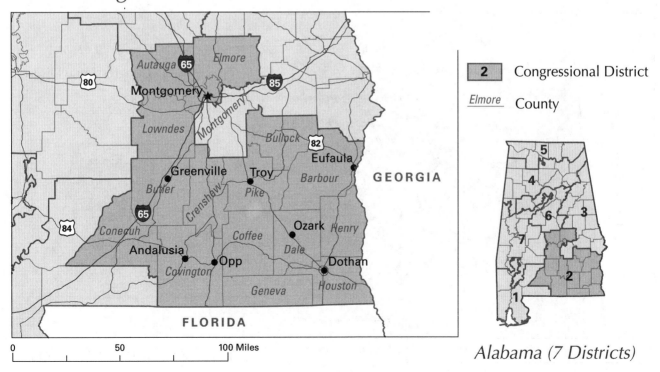

2 Congressional District
Elmore County

Alabama (7 Districts)

Congressional District 3

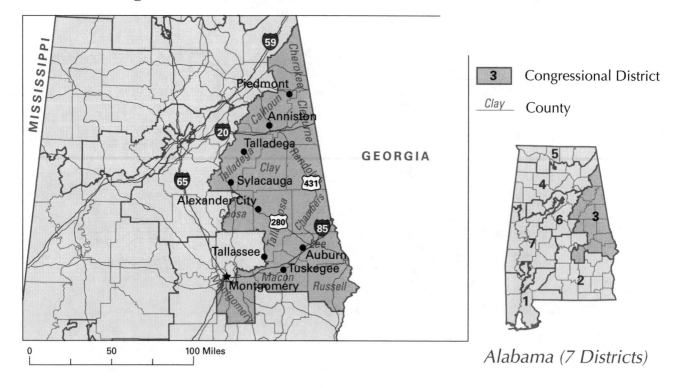

Alabama (7 Districts)

Congressional District 4

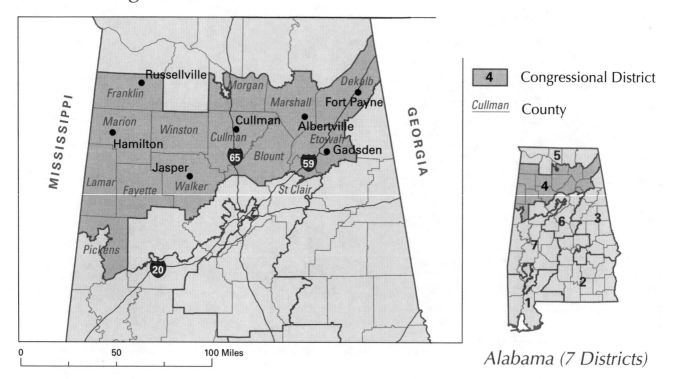

Alabama (7 Districts)

Congressional District 5

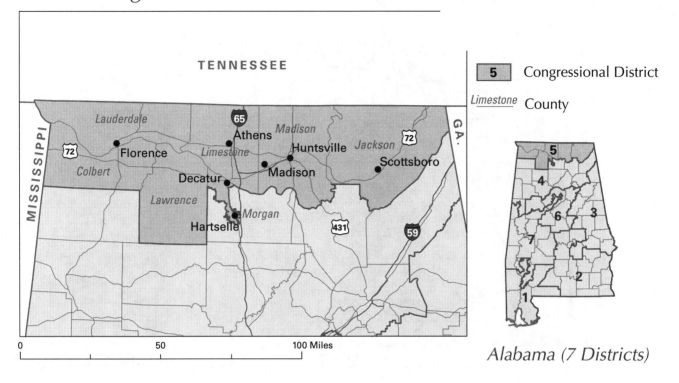

Alabama (7 Districts)

Congressional District 6

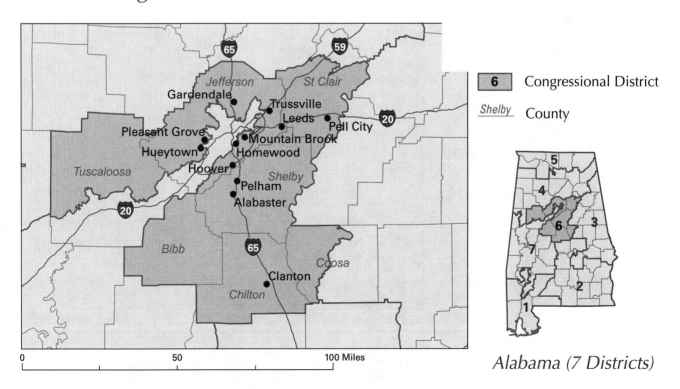

Alabama (7 Districts)

Congressional District 7

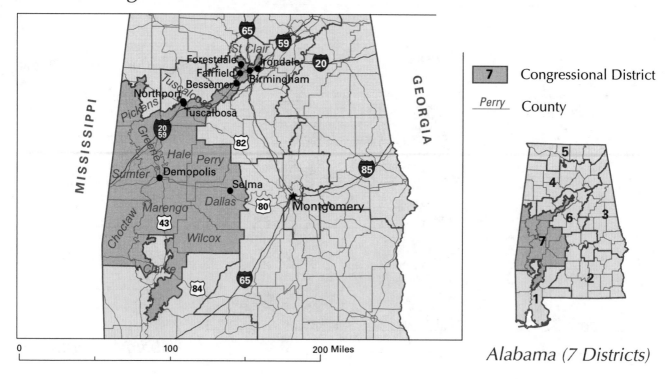

Alabama (7 Districts)

Alaska–
Congressional District: At large

Congressional District

Denali Borough

0 200 400 Miles

Alaska (1 district)

ALASKA—109th CONGRESSIONAL DISTRICTS BY COUNTIES

County	Congressional District
Aleutians East Borough	1
Aleutians West Census Area	1
Anchorage	1
Bethel	1
Bristol Bay	1
Denali Borough	1
Dillingham	1
Fairbanks North Star	1
Haines	1
Juneau	1

County	Congressional District
Kenai Peninsula	1
Ketchikan Gateway	1
Kodiak Island	1
Lake and Peninsula Borough	1
Matanuska-Susitna	1
Nome	1
North Slope	1
Northwest Arctic Borough	1
Prince of Wales-Outer Ketchikan	1
Sitka	1

County	Congressional District
Skagway-Hoonah-Angoon	1
Southeast Fairbanks	1
Valdez-Cordova	1
Wade Hampton	1
Wrangell-Petersburg	1
Yakutat Borough	1
Yukon-Koyukuk	1

Arizona Congressional Districts — 8 Districts Total

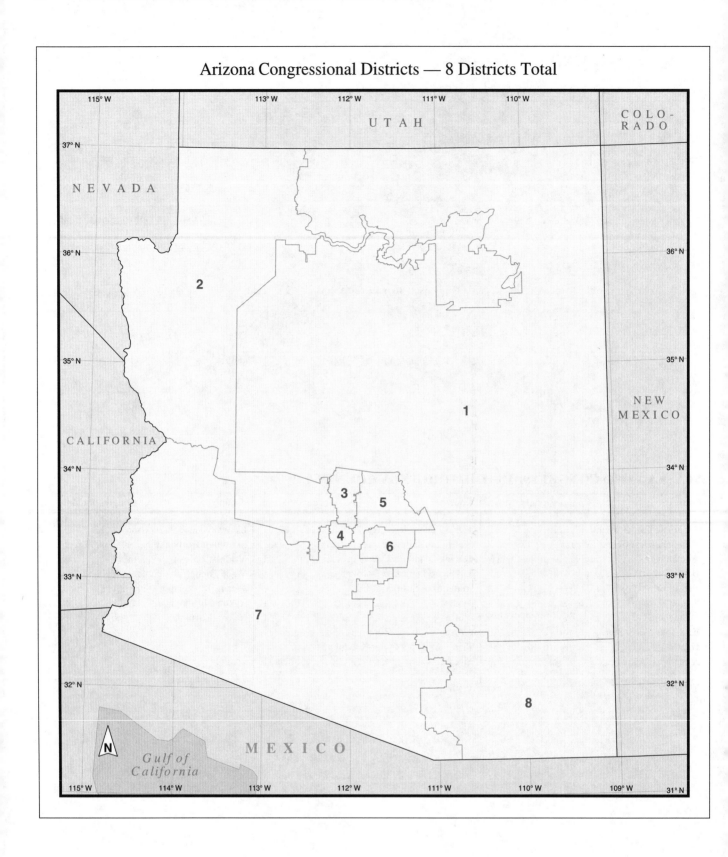

ARIZONA—109th CONGRESSIONAL DISTRICTS BY COUNTIES

County	Congressional District	County	Congressional District	County	Congressional District
Apache	1	Greenlee	1	Pima	7,8
Cochise	8	La Paz	2,7	Pinal	1,6–8
Coconino	1,2	Maricopa	2–7	Santa Cruz	7,8
Gila	1	Mohave	2	Yavapai	1,2
Graham	1	Navajo	1,2	Yuma	7

Congressional District 1

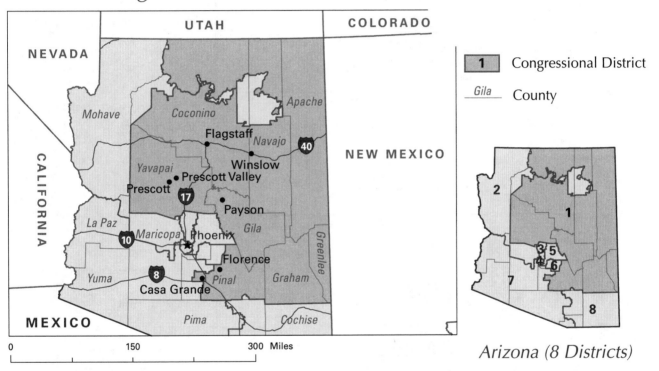

Arizona (8 Districts)

Congressional District 2

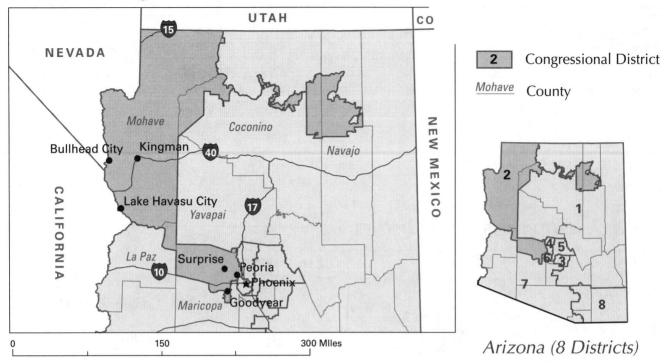

Arizona (8 Districts)

Congressional District 3

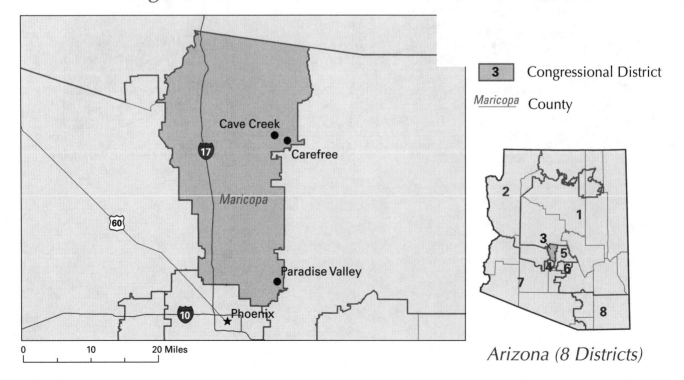

Arizona (8 Districts)

Congressional District 4

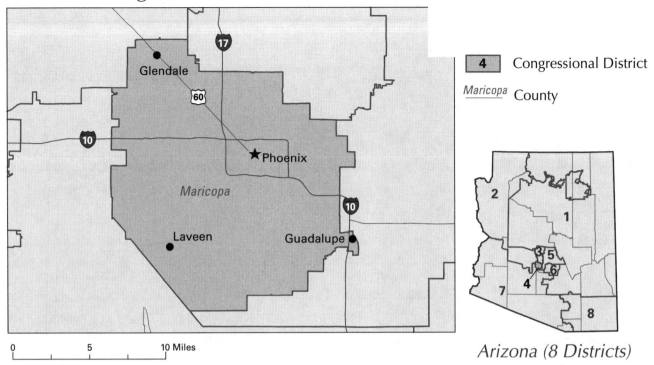

4 ▮ Congressional District
Maricopa County

Arizona (8 Districts)

Congressional District 5

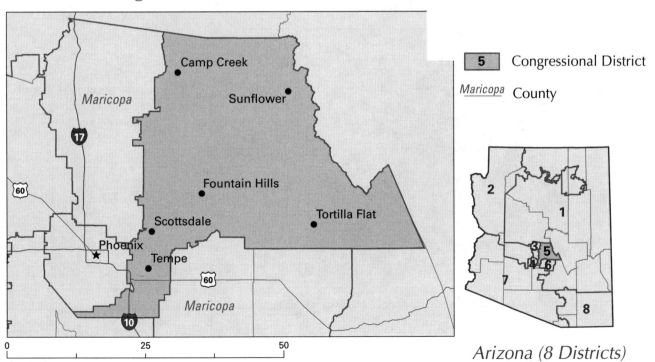

5 ▮ Congressional District
Maricopa County

Arizona (8 Districts)

Congressional District 6

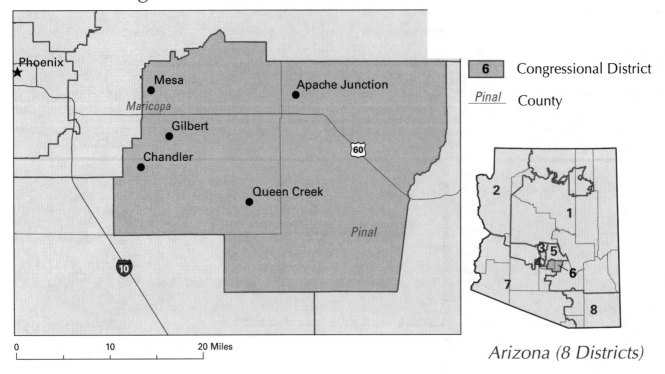

0   10   20 Miles

Arizona (8 Districts)

Congressional District 7

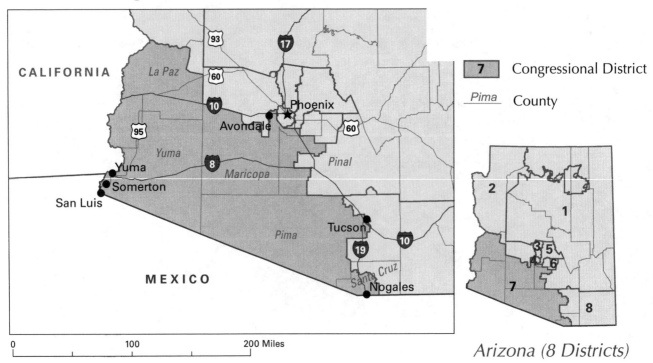

0   100   200 Miles

Arizona (8 Districts)

Congressional District 8

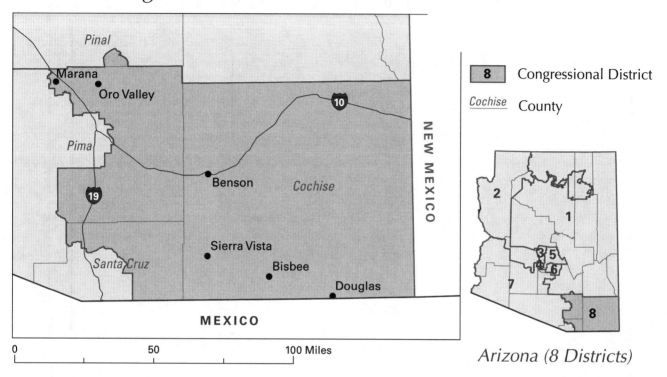

0   50   100 Miles

8 Congressional District

Cochise County

Arizona (8 Districts)

Arkansas Congressional Districts — 4 Districts Total

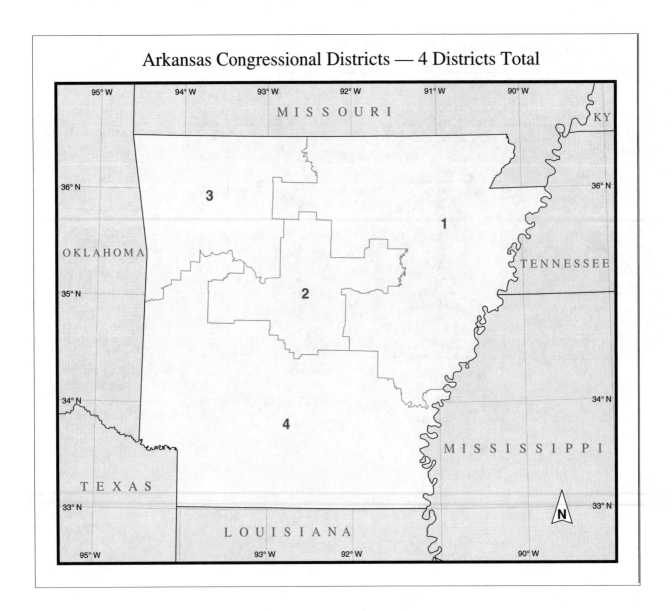

ARKANSAS—109th CONGRESSIONAL DISTRICTS BY COUNTIES

County	Congressional District	County	Congressional District	County	Congressional District
Arkansas	1	Garland	4	Newton	3
Ashley	4	Grant	4	Ouachita	4
Baxter	1	Greene	1	Perry	2
Benton	3	Hempstead	4	Phillips	1
Boone	3	Hot Spring	4	Pike	4
Bradley	4	Howard	4	Poinsett	1
Calhoun	4	Independence	1	Polk	4
Carroll	3	Izard	1	Pope	3
Chicot	4	Jackson	1	Prairie	1
Clark	4	Jefferson	4	Pulaski	2
Clay	1	Johnson	3	Randolph	1
Cleburne	1	Lafayette	4	St. Francis	1
Cleveland	4	Lawrence	1	Saline	2
Columbia	4	Lee	1	Scott	4
Conway	2	Lincoln	4	Searcy	1
Craighead	1	Little River	4	Sebastian	3
Crawford	3	Logan	4	Sevier	4
Crittenden	1	Lonoke	1	Sharp	1
Cross	1	Madison	3	Stone	1
Dallas	4	Marion	3	Union	4
Desha	4	Miller	4	Van Buren	2
Drew	4	Mississippi	1	Washington	3
Faulkner	2	Monroe	1	White	2
Franklin	3	Montgomery	4	Woodruff	1
Fulton	1	Nevada	4	Yell	2

Congressional District 1

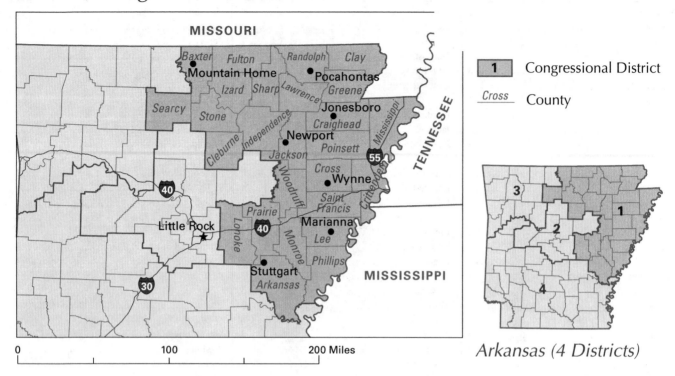

Arkansas (4 Districts)

Congressional District 2

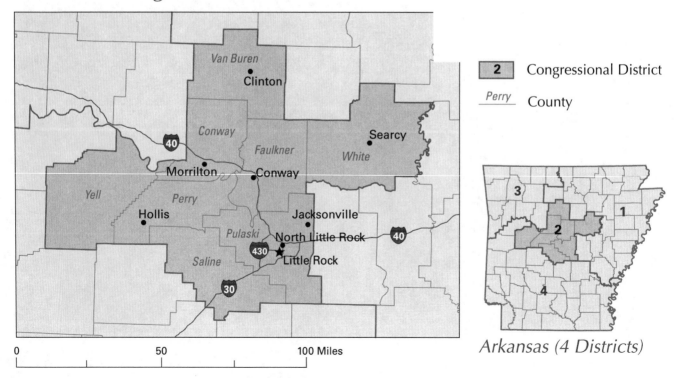

Arkansas (4 Districts)

Congressional District 3

3	Congressional District
Franklin	County

Arkansas (4 Districts)

Congressional District 4

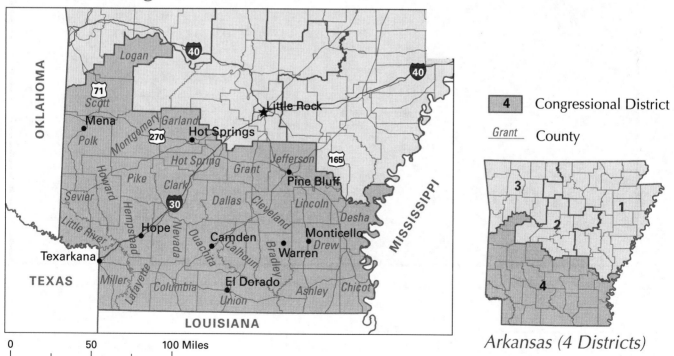

4	Congressional District
Grant	County

Arkansas (4 Districts)

California Congressional Districts — 53 Districts Total

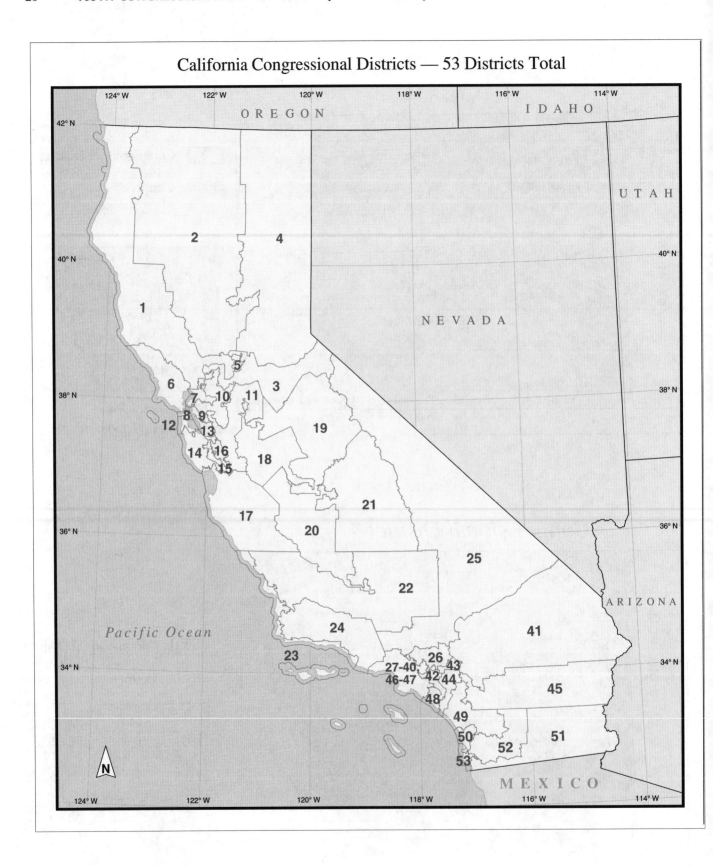

CALIFORNIA—109th CONGRESSIONAL DISTRICTS BY COUNTIES

County	Congressional District	County	Congressional District	County	Congressional District
Alameda	9–11, 13	Marin	6	San Mateo	12, 14
Alpine	3	Mariposa	19	Santa Barbara	23, 24
Amador	3	Mendocino	1	Santa Clara	11, 14–16
Butte	2, 4	Merced	18	Santa Cruz	14, 17
Calaveras	3	Modoc	4	Shasta	2
Colusa	2	Mono	25	Sierra	4
Contra Costa	7, 10, 11	Monterey	17	Siskiyou	2
Del Norte	1	Napa	1	Solano	3, 7, 10
El Dorado	4	Nevada	4	Sonoma	1, 6
Fresno	18–21	Orange	40, 42, 44, 46–48	Stanislaus	18, 19
Glenn	2	Placer	4	Sutter	2
Humboldt	1	Plumas	4	Tehama	2
Imperial	51	Riverside	41, 44, 45, 49	Trinity	2
Inyo	25	Sacramento	3–5, 10	Tulare	21
Kern	20, 22	San Benito	17	Tuolumne	19
Kings	20	San Bernardino	25, 26, 41–43	Ventura	23, 24
Lake	1	San Diego	49-53	Yolo	1, 2
Lassen	4	San Francisco	8, 12	Yuba	2
Los Angeles	22, 25–39, 42, 46	San Joaquin	11, 18		
Madera	18, 19	San Luis Obispo	22, 23		

Congressional District 1

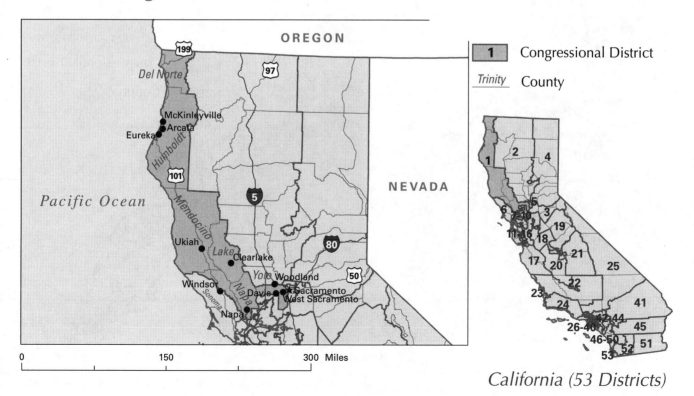

California (53 Districts)

Congressional District 2

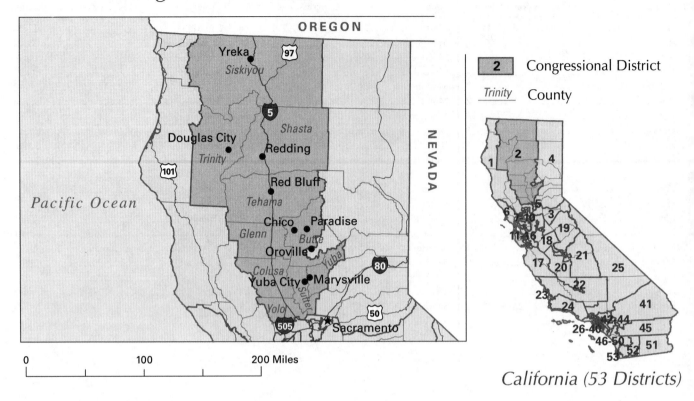

California (53 Districts)

Congressional District 3

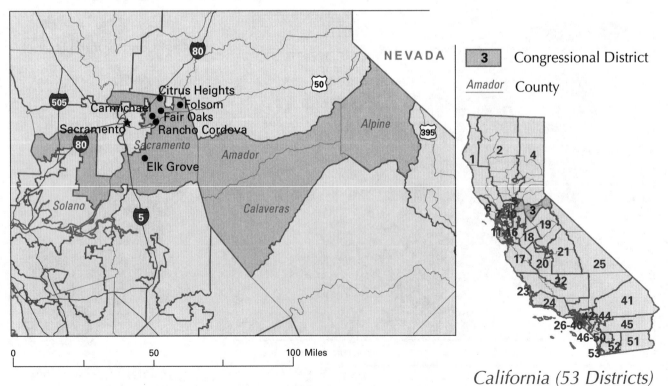

California (53 Districts)

Congressional District 4

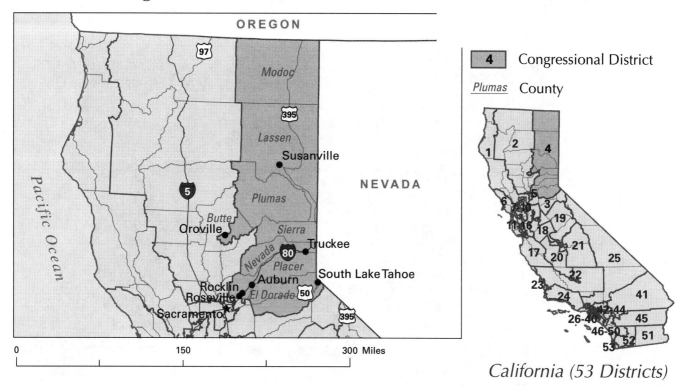

California (53 Districts)

Congressional District 5

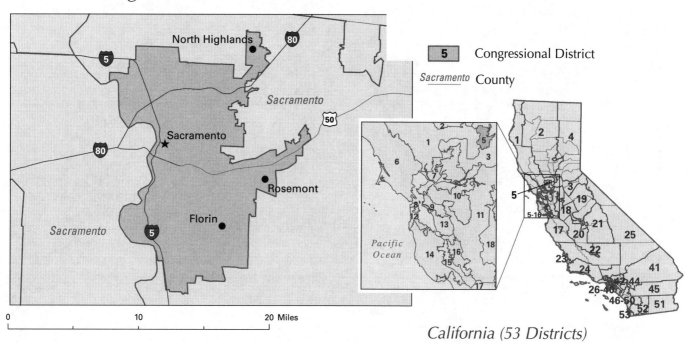

California (53 Districts)

Congressional District 6

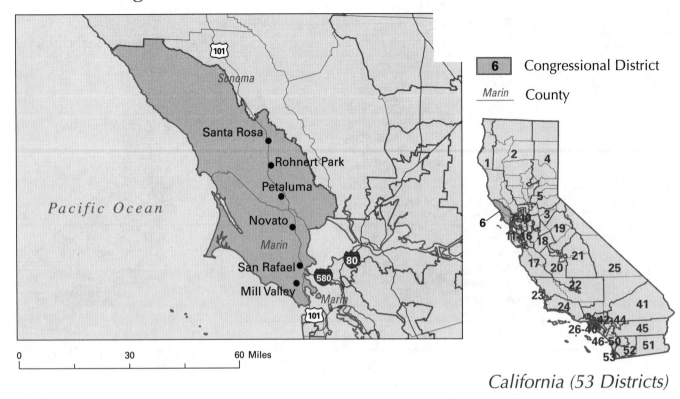

0   30   60 Miles

6   Congressional District
Marin   County

California (53 Districts)

Congressional District 7

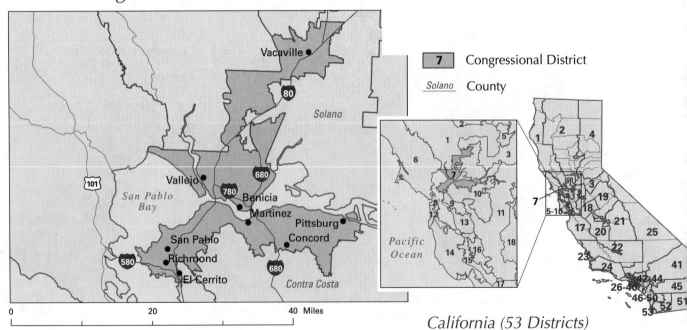

0   20   40 Miles

7   Congressional District
Solano   County

California (53 Districts)

Congressional District 8

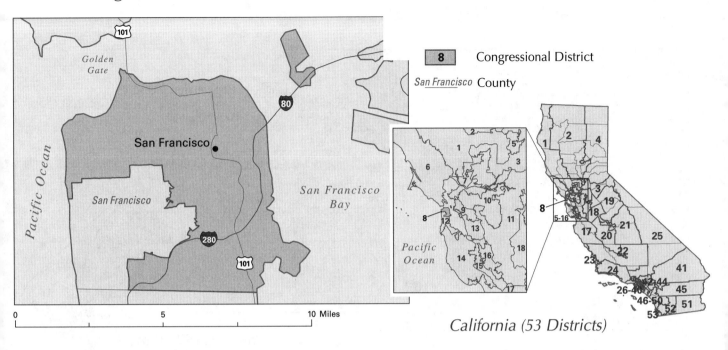

California (53 Districts)

Congressional District 9

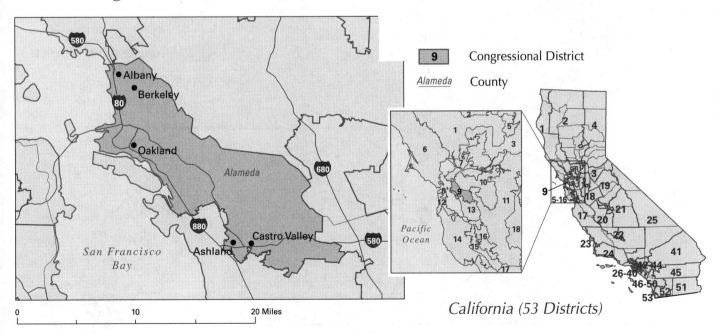

California (53 Districts)

Congressional District 10

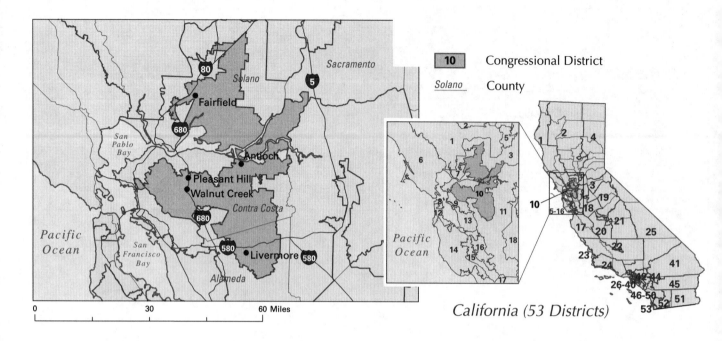

California (53 Districts)

Congressional District 11

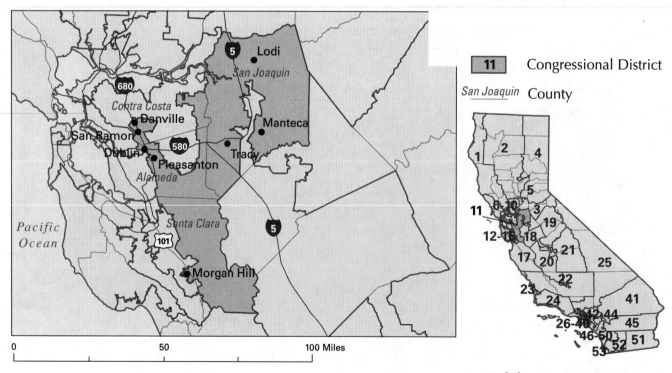

California (53 Districts)

Congressional District 12

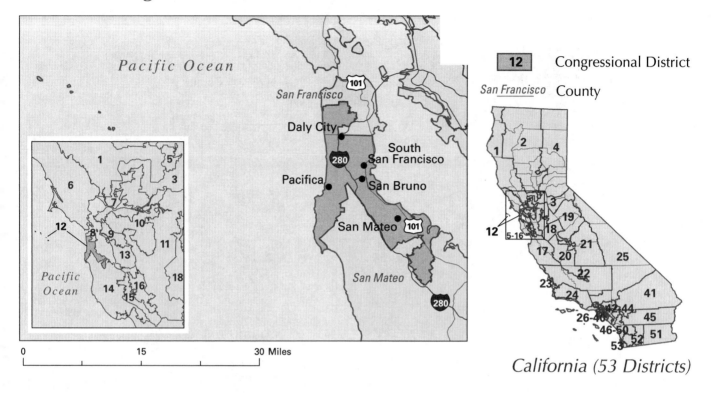

12 Congressional District
San Francisco County

California (53 Districts)

Congressional District 13

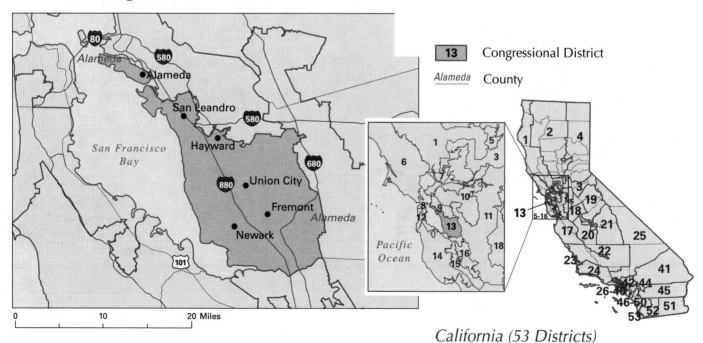

13 Congressional District
Alameda County

California (53 Districts)

Congressional District 14

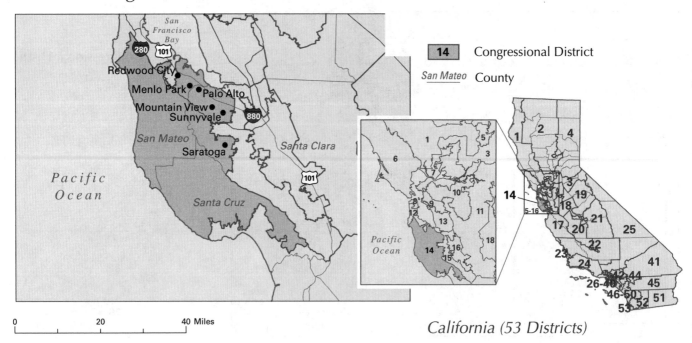

California (53 Districts)

Congressional District 15

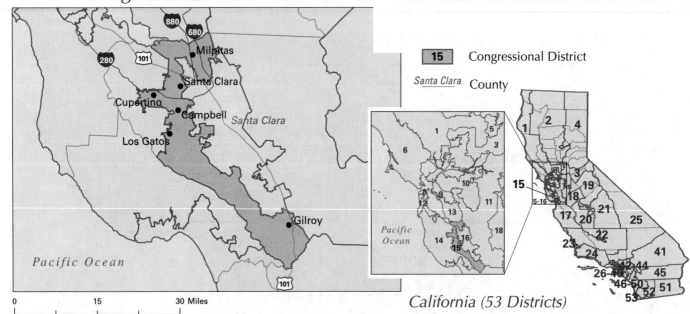

California (53 Districts)

Congressional District 16

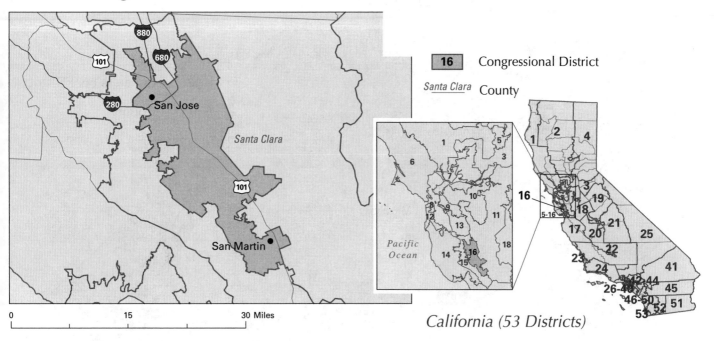

California (53 Districts)

Congressional District 17

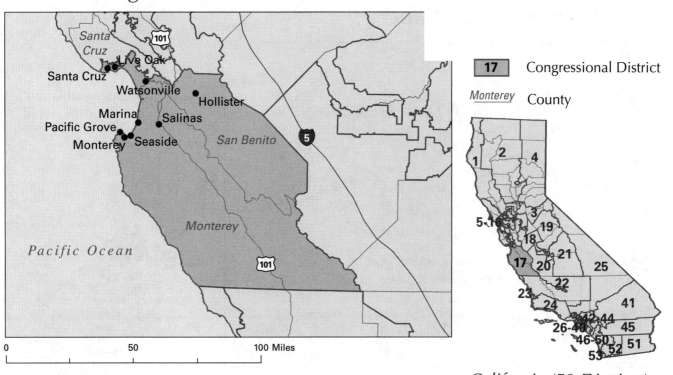

California (53 Districts)

Congressional District 18

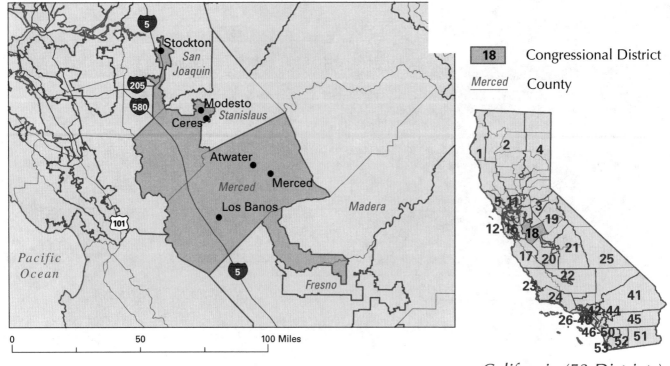

18 Congressional District

Merced County

California (53 Districts)

Congressional District 19

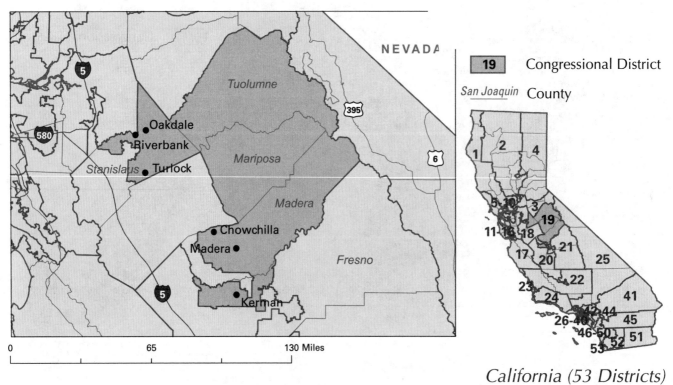

19 Congressional District

San Joaquin County

California (53 Districts)

Congressional District 20

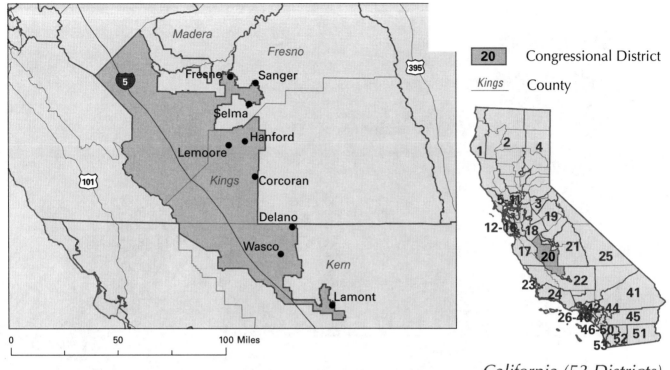

California (53 Districts)

Congressional District 21

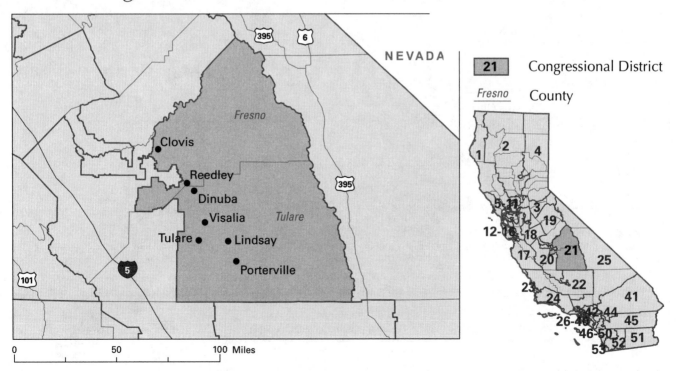

California (53 Districts)

Congressional District 22

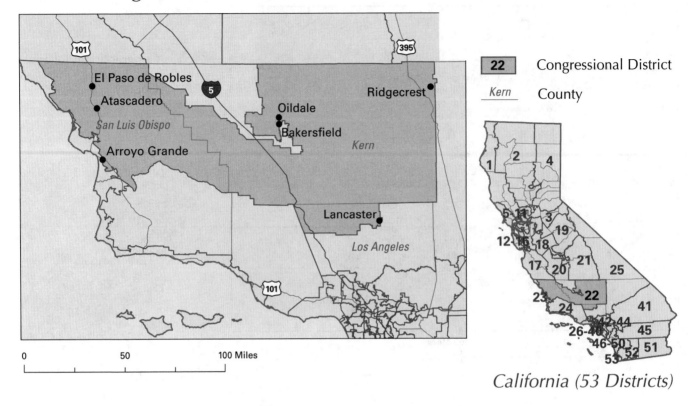

0   50   100 Miles

22   Congressional District

Kern   County

California (53 Districts)

Congressional District 23

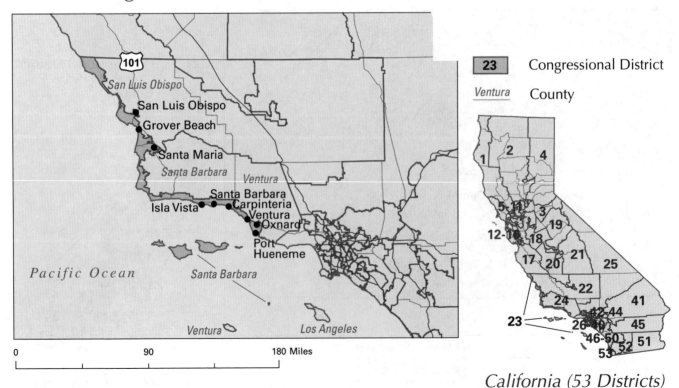

0   90   180 Miles

23   Congressional District

Ventura   County

California (53 Districts)

Congressional District 24

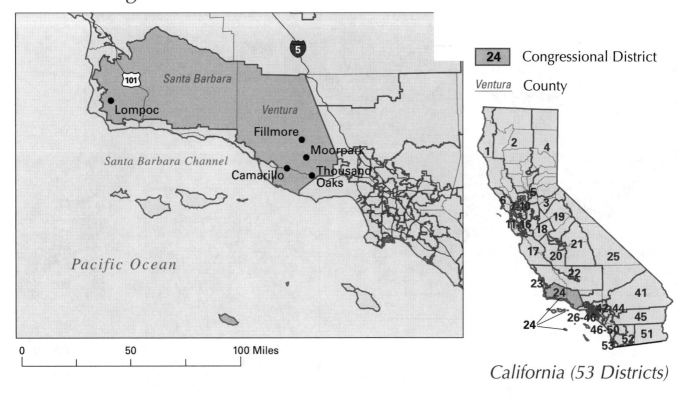

California (53 Districts)

Congressional District 25

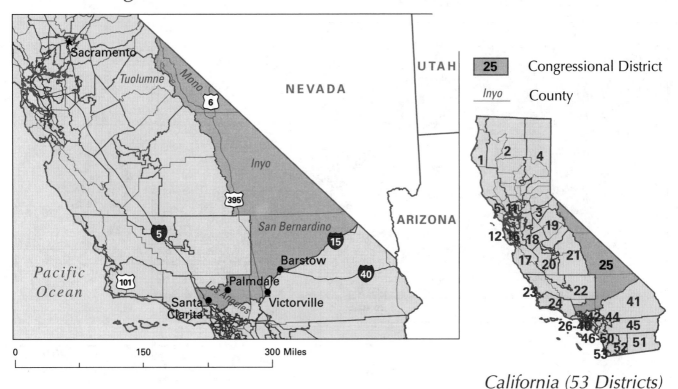

California (53 Districts)

Congressional District 26

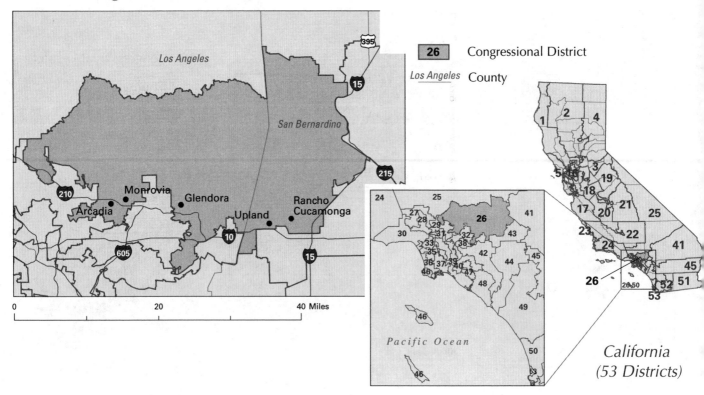

Congressional District 27

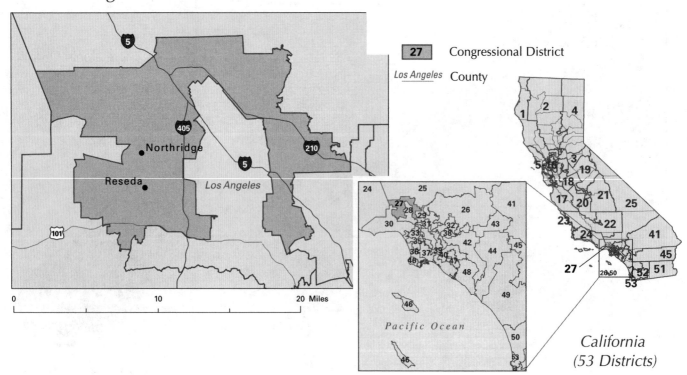

Congressional District 28

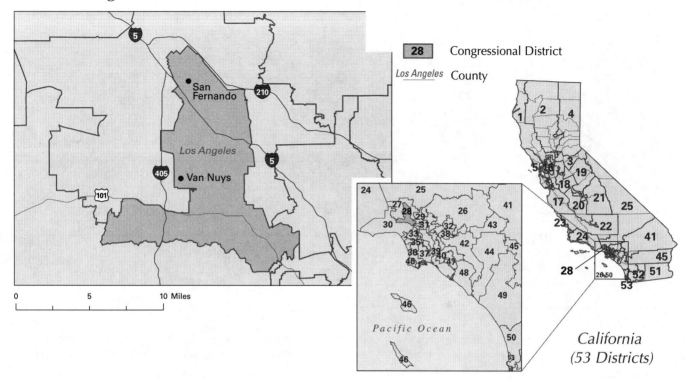

Congressional District 29

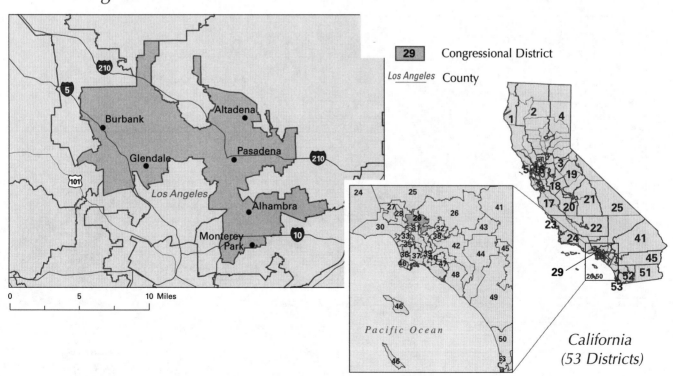

Congressional District 30

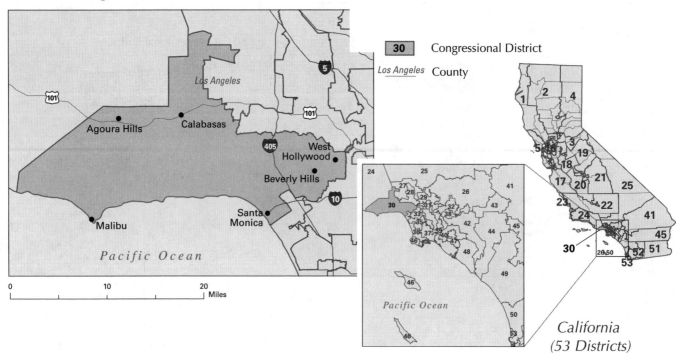

Congressional District 31

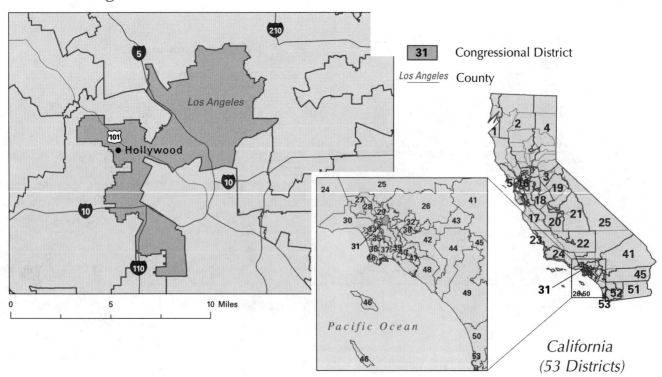

Congressional District 32

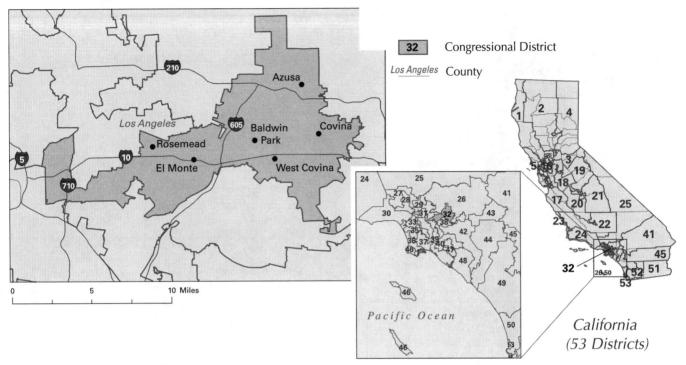

Congressional District 33

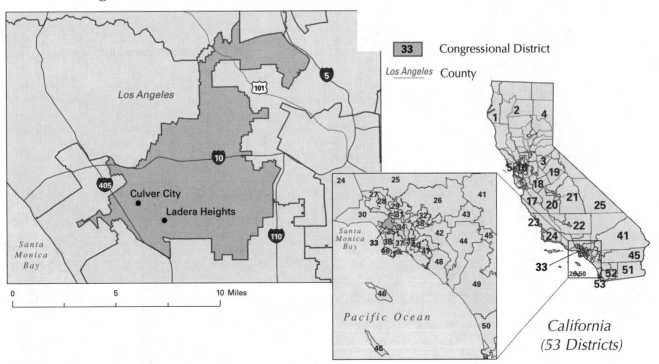

Congressional District 34

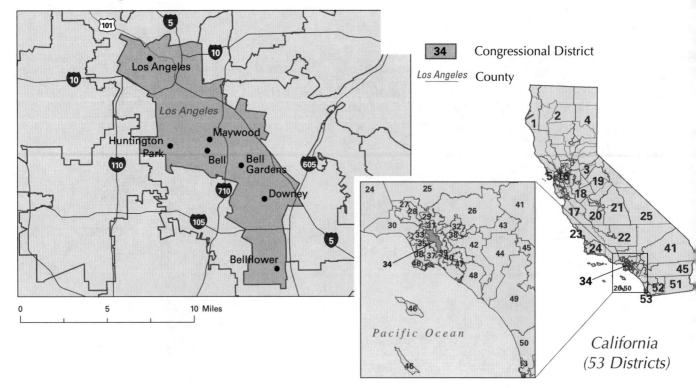

0   5   10 Miles

Congressional District 35

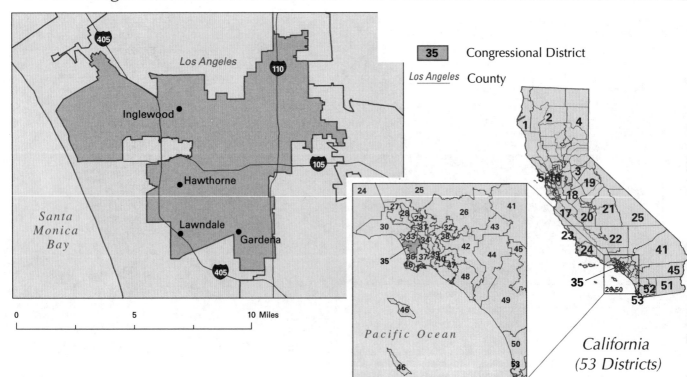

0   5   10 Miles

Congressional District 36

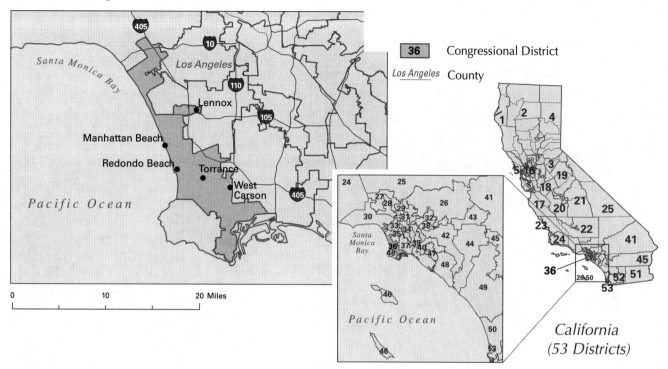

Congressional District 37

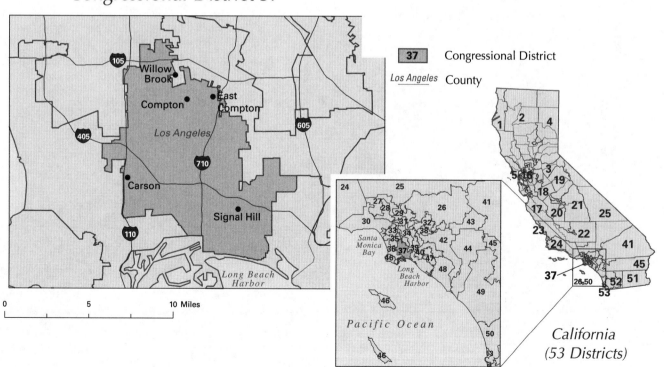

Congressional District 38

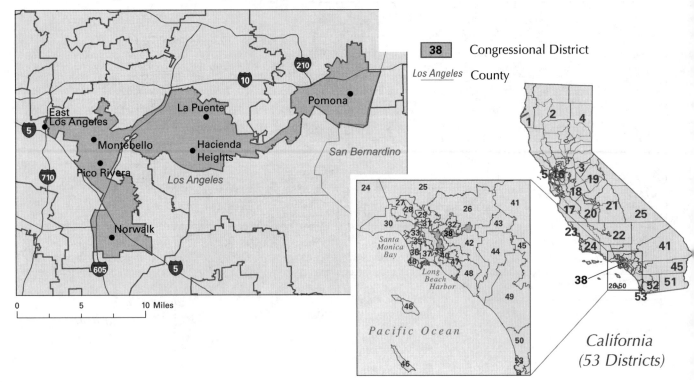

Congressional District 39

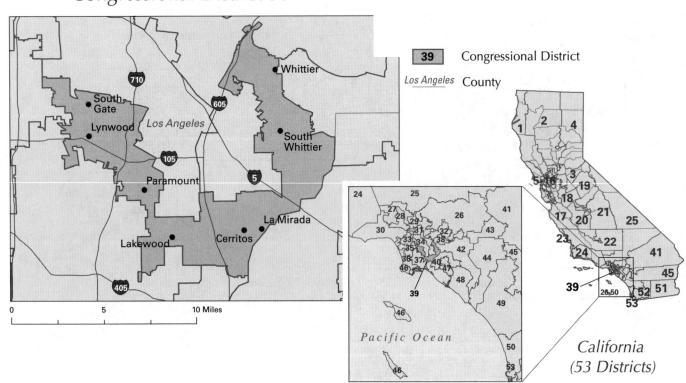

Congressional District 40

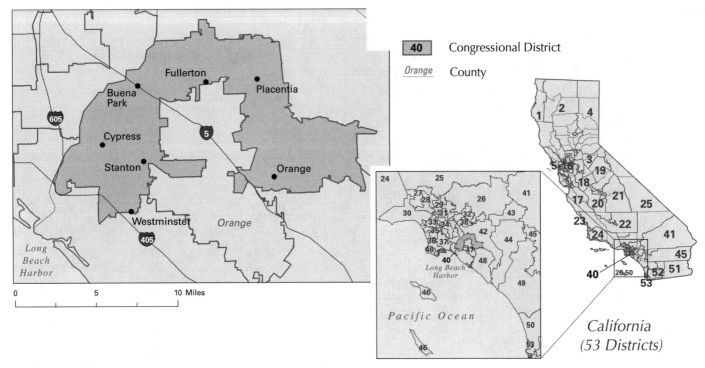

Congressional District 41

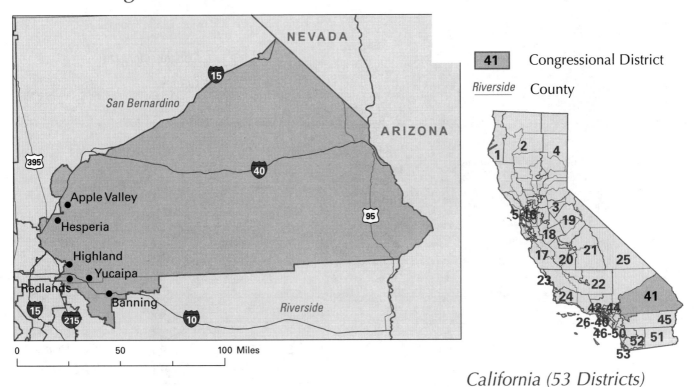

Congressional District 42

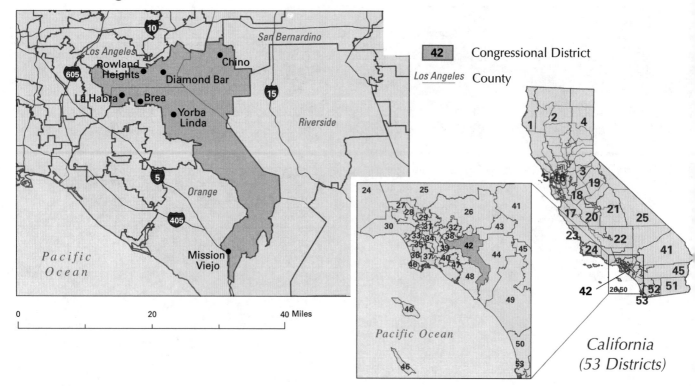

Congressional District 43

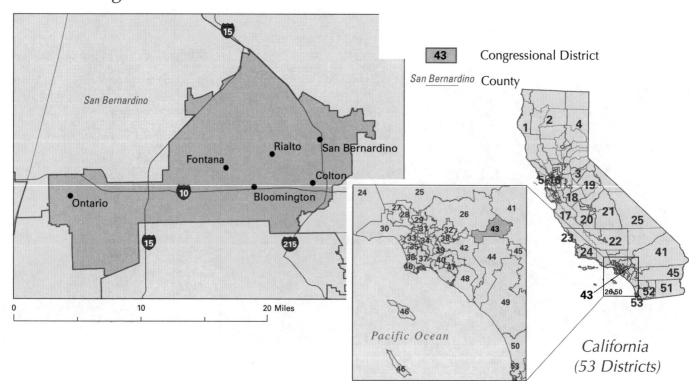

Congressional District 44

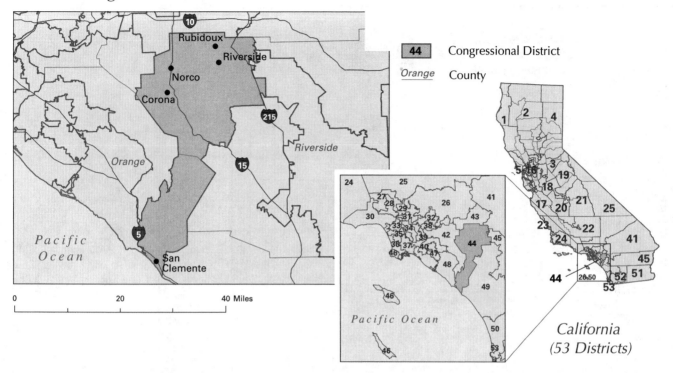

Congressional District 45

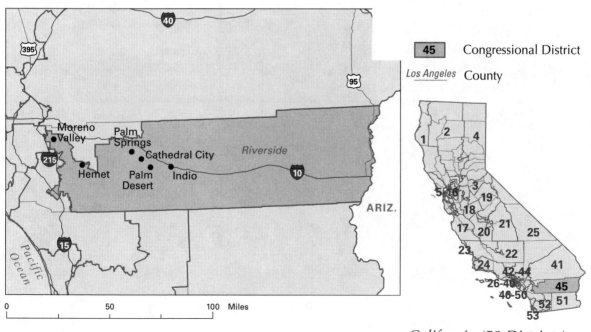

California (53 Districts)

Congressional District 46

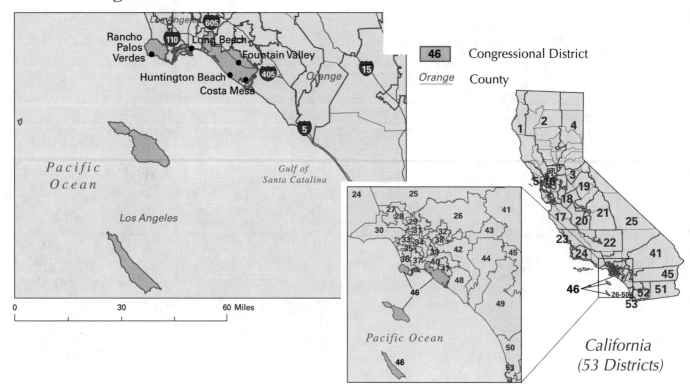

Congressional District 47

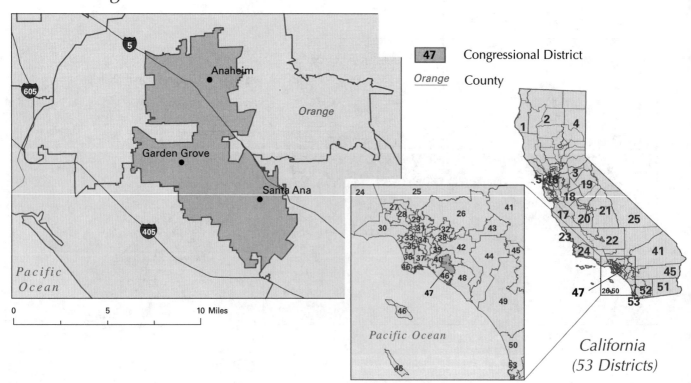

Congressional District 48

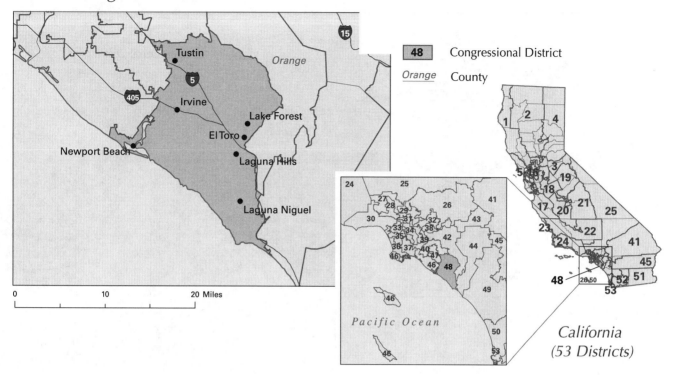

48	Congressional District
Orange	County

California
(53 Districts)

Congressional District 49

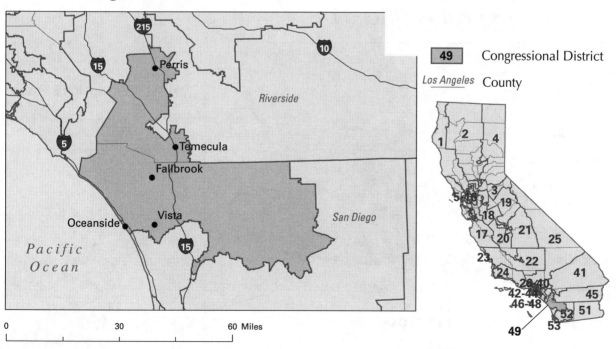

49	Congressional District
Los Angeles	County

California (53 Districts)

Congressional District 50

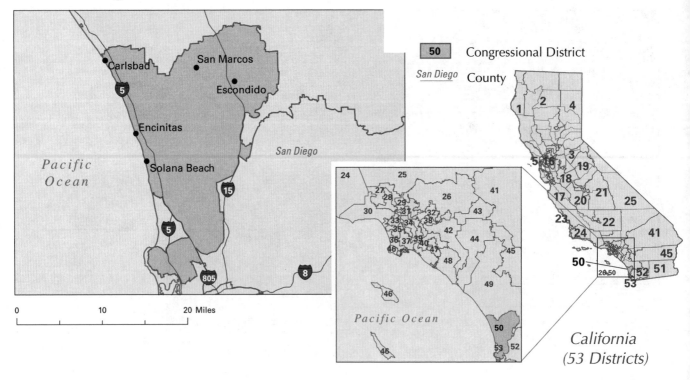

Congressional District 51

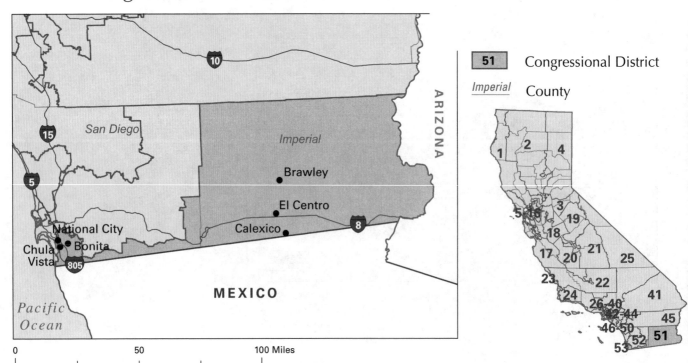

Congressional District 52

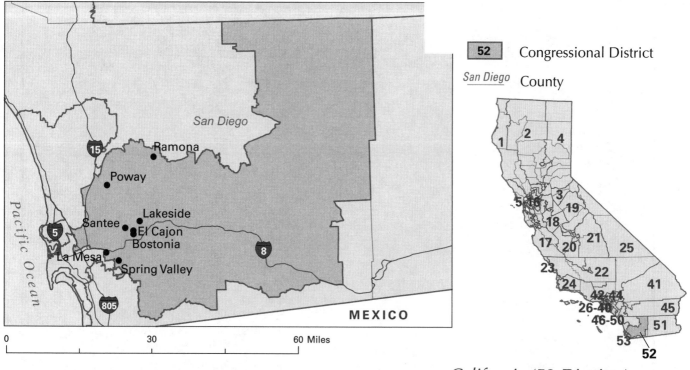

California (53 Districts)

Congressional District 53

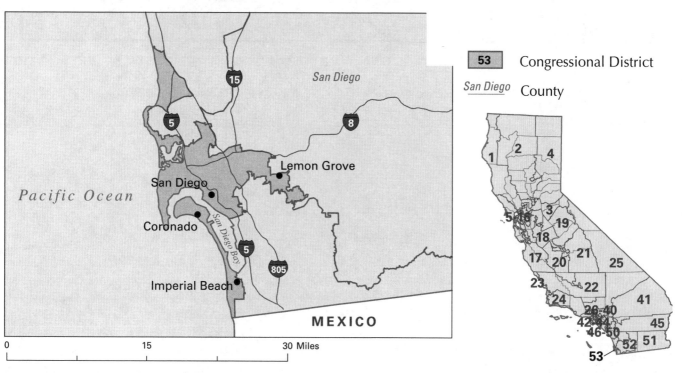

California (53 Districts)

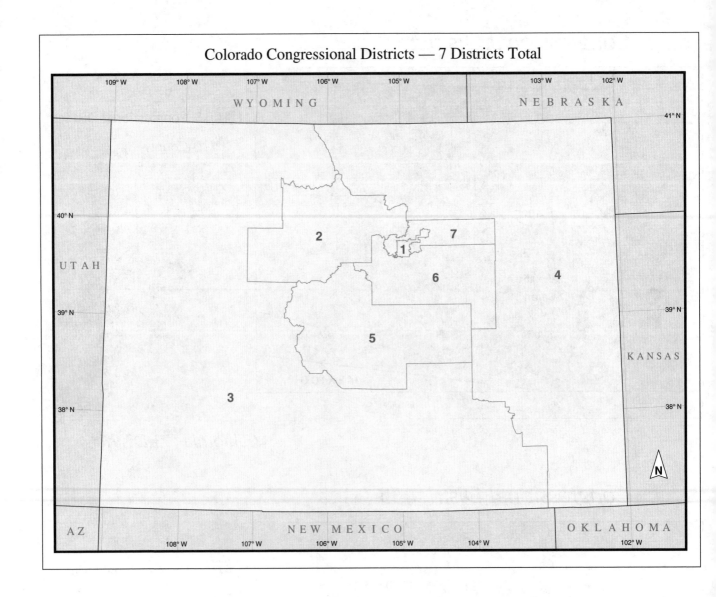

Colorado Congressional Districts — 7 Districts Total

COLORADO—109th CONGRESSIONAL DISTRICTS BY COUNTIES

County	Congressional District	County	Congressional District	County	Congressional District
Adams	1, 2, 7	Garfield	3	Otero	3, 4
Alamosa	3	Gilpin	2	Ouray	3
Arapahoe	1, 6, 7	Grand	2	Park	5, 6
Archuleta	3	Gunnison	3	Phillips	4
Baca	4	Hinsdale	3	Pitkin	3
Bent	4	Huerfano	3	Prowers	4
Boulder	2, 4	Jackson	3	Pueblo	3
Chaffee	5	Jefferson	1, 2, 6, 7	Rio Blanco	3
Cheyenne	4	Kiowa	4	Rio Grande	3
Clear Creek	2	Kit Carson	4	Routt	3
Conejos	3	Lake	5	Saguache	3
Costilla	3	La Plata	3	San Juan	3
Crowley	4	Larimer	4	San Miguel	3
Custer	3	Las Animas	3	Sedgwick	4
Delta	3	Lincoln	4	Summit	2
Denver	1	Logan	4	Teller	5
Dolores	3	Mesa	3	Washington	4
Douglas	6	Mineral	3	Weld	2, 4
Eagle	2	Moffat	3	Yuma	4
Elbert	6	Montezuma	3		
El Paso	5	Montrose	3		
Fremont	5	Morgan	4		

Congressional District 1

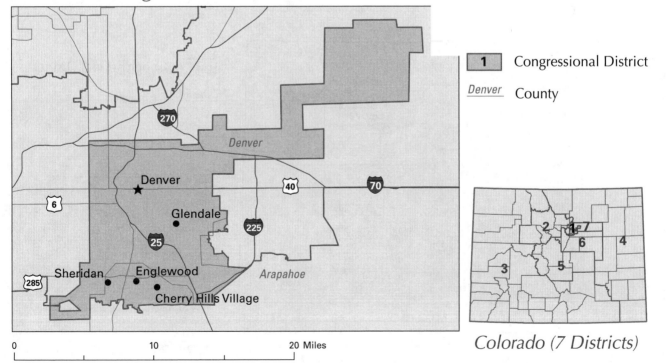

| 1 | Congressional District |
| *Denver* | County |

Colorado (7 Districts)

Congressional District 2

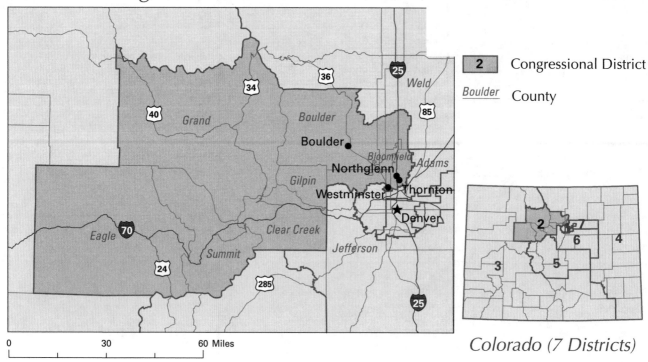

0   30   60 Miles

2 — Congressional District
Boulder — County

Colorado (7 Districts)

Congressional District 3

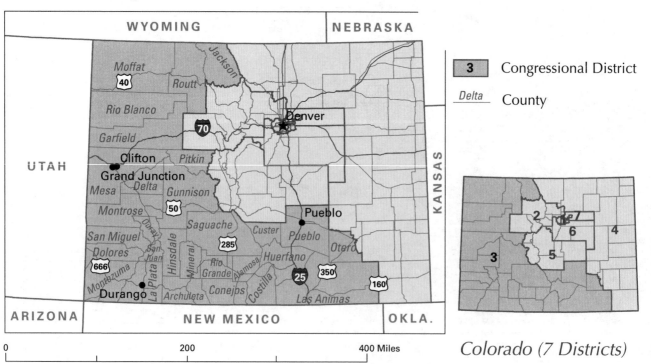

0   200   400 Miles

3 — Congressional District
Delta — County

Colorado (7 Districts)

Congressional District 4

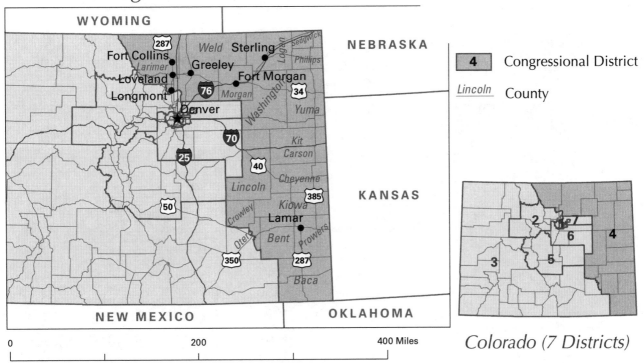

4	Congressional District
Lincoln	County

Colorado (7 Districts)

Congressional District 5

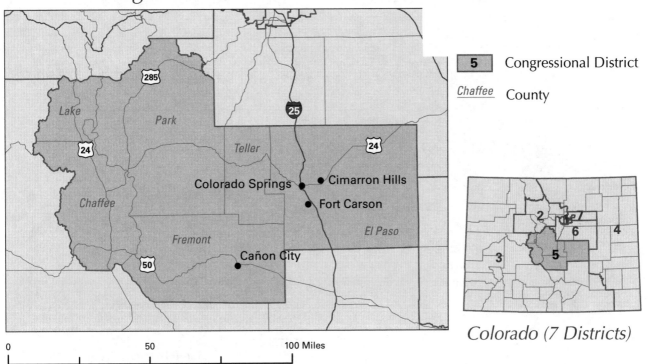

5	Congressional District
Chaffee	County

Colorado (7 Districts)

Congressional District 6

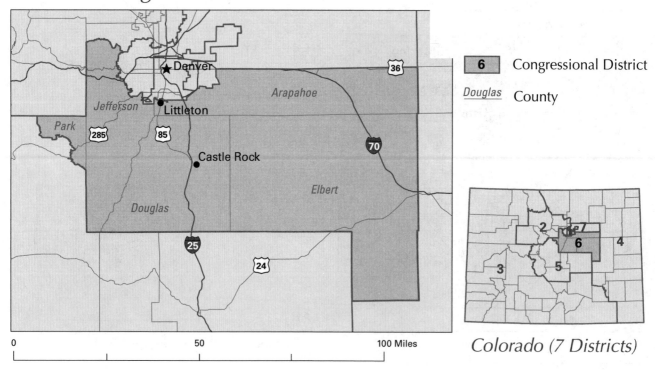

Colorado (7 Districts)

Congressional District 7

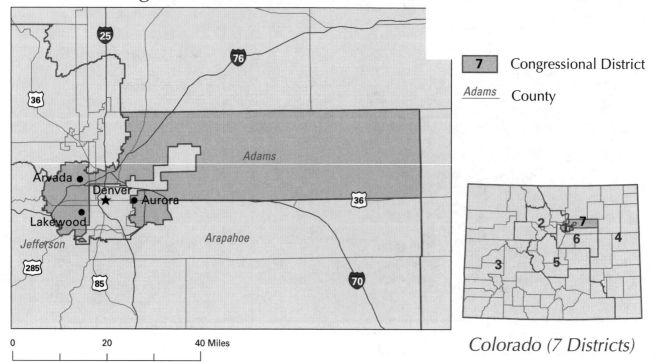

Colorado (7 Districts)

Connecticut Congressional Districts — 5 Districts Total

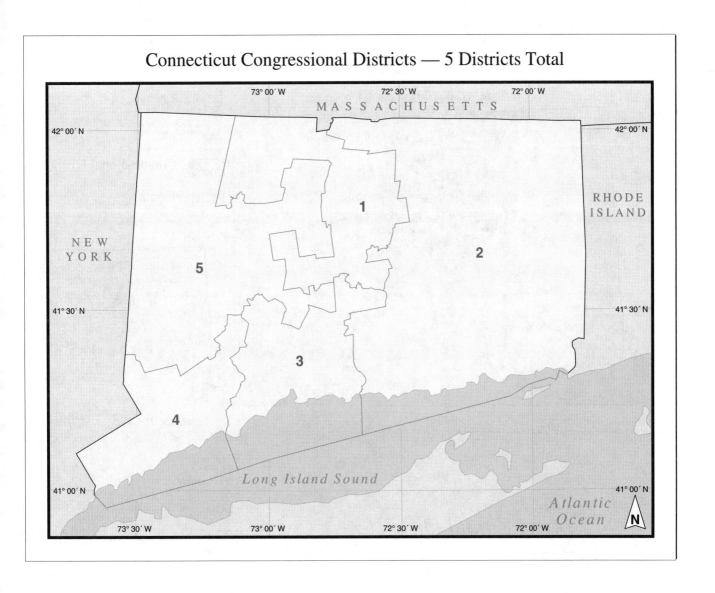

CONNECTICUT—109th CONGRESSIONAL DISTRICTS BY COUNTIES

County	Congressional District
Fairfield	3–5
Hartford	1, 2, 5
Litchfield	1, 5
Middlesex	1–3
New Haven	2–5
New London	2
Tolland	2
Windham	2

Congressional District 1

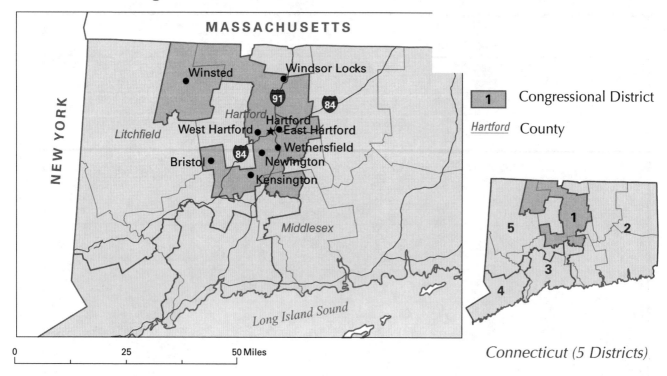

Connecticut (5 Districts)

Congressional District 2

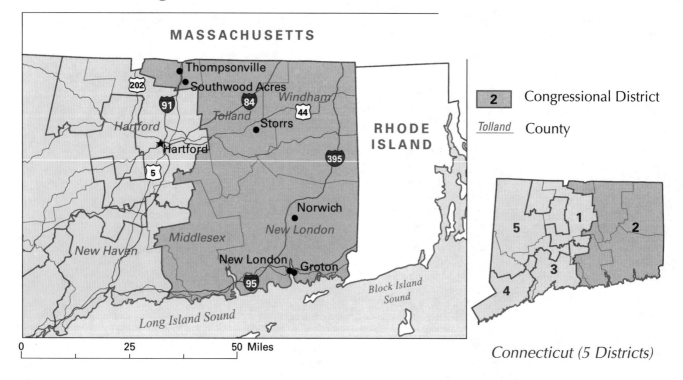

Connecticut (5 Districts)

Congressional District 3

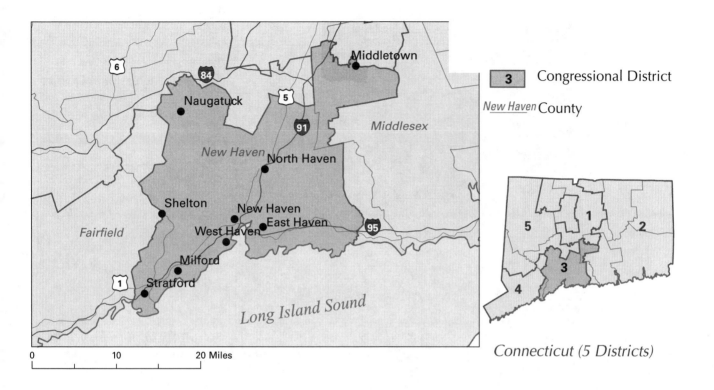

Congressional District 4

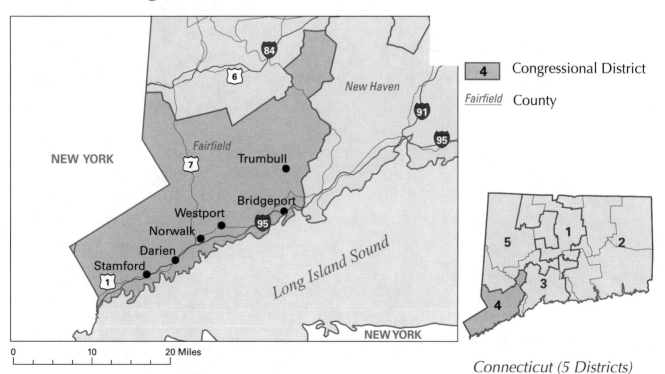

Congressional District 5

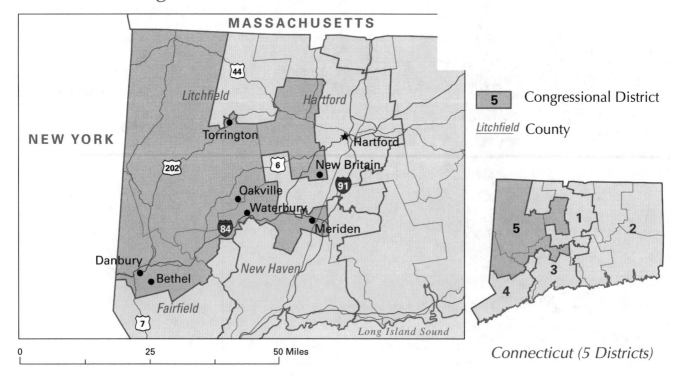

Connecticut (5 Districts)

Delaware—
Congressional District: At large

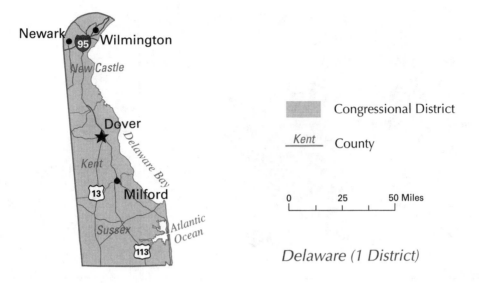

Congressional District

Kent County

0   25   50 Miles

Delaware (1 District)

DELAWARE—109th CONGRESSIONAL DISTRICTS BY COUNTIES

County	Congressional District
Kent	1
New Castle	1
Sussex	1

District of Columbia—*Delegate District*

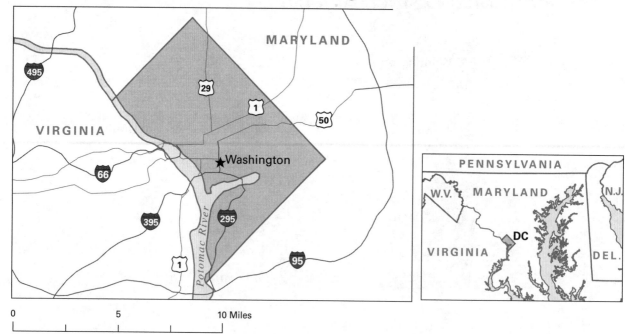

0   5   10 Miles

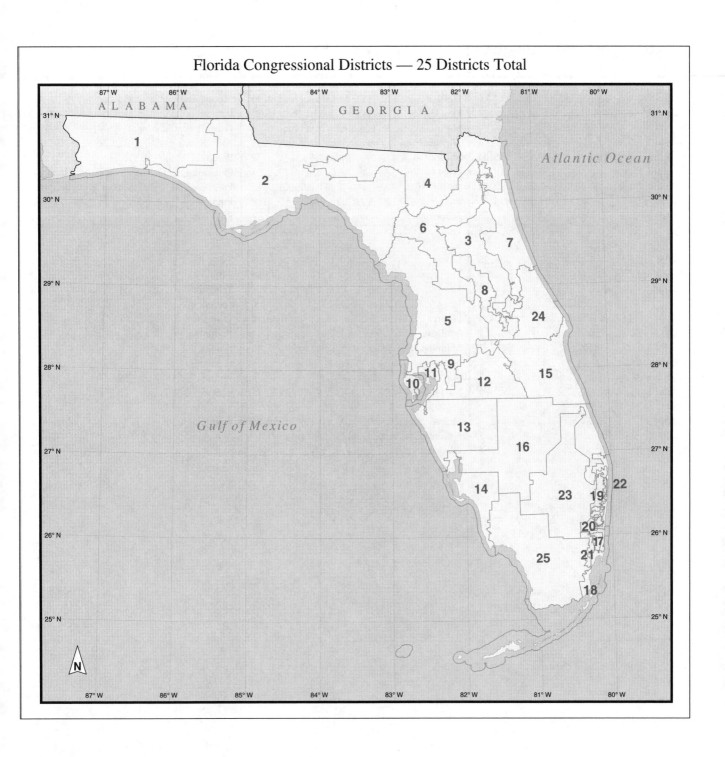

Florida Congressional Districts — 25 Districts Total

FLORIDA—109th CONGRESSIONAL DISTRICTS BY COUNTIES

County	Congressional District
Alachua	3, 6
Baker	4
Bay	2
Bradford	6
Brevard	15, 24
Broward	17, 19–23
Calhoun	2
Charlotte	13, 14, 16
Citrus	5
Clay	3, 6
Collier	14, 25
Columbia	4
DeSoto	13
Dixie	2
Duval	3, 4, 6
Escambia	1
Flagler	7
Franklin	2
Gadsden	2
Gilchrist	6
Glades	16
Gulf	2
Hamilton	4

County	Congressional District
Hardee	13
Hendry	16, 23
Hernando	5
Highlands	16
Hillsborough	9, 11, 12
Holmes	1
Indian River	15
Jackson	2
Jefferson	2, 4
Lafayette	2
Lake	3, 5, 6, 8
Lee	14
Leon	2, 4
Levy	5, 6
Liberty	2
Madison	4
Manatee	11, 13
Marion	3, 5, 6, 8
Martin	16, 23
Miami-Dade	17, 18, 20, 21, 25
Monroe	18, 25
Nassau	4
Okaloosa	1, 2

County	Congressional District
Okeechobee	16
Orange	3, 7, 8, 24
Osceola	8, 12, 15
Palm Beach	16, 19, 22, 23
Pasco	5, 9
Pinellas	9–11
Polk	5, 12, 15
Putnam	3, 7
St. Johns	7
St. Lucie	16, 23
Santa Rosa	1
Sarasota	13
Seminole	3, 7, 24
Sumter	5
Suwannee	2
Taylor	2
Union	4
Volusia	3, 7, 24
Wakulla	2
Walton	1, 2
Washington	1

Congressional District 1

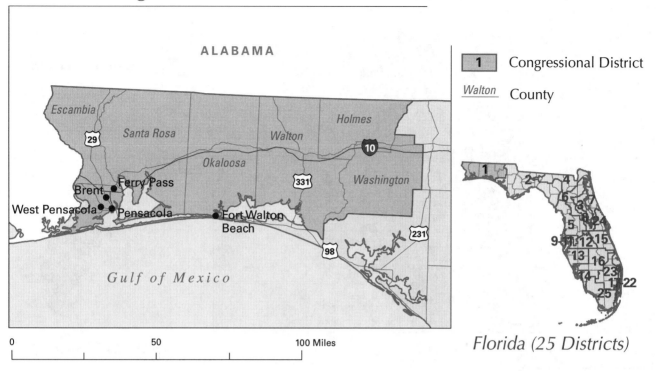

Florida (25 Districts)

Congressional District 2

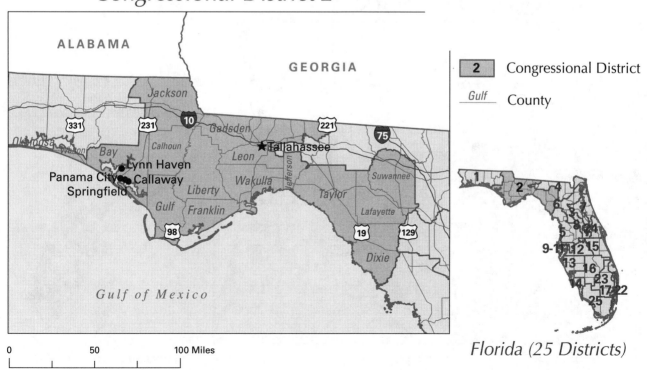

Florida (25 Districts)

Congressional District 3

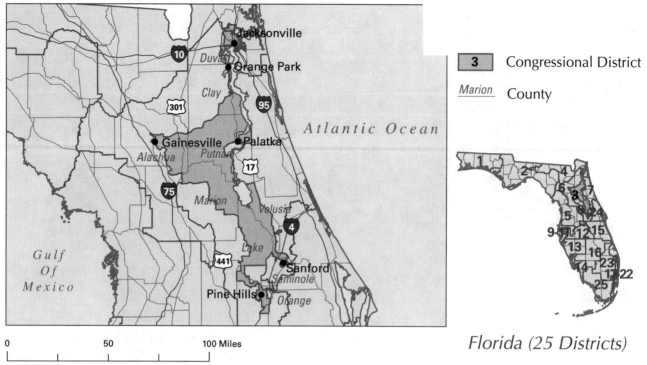

3 Congressional District

Marion County

Atlantic Ocean

Gulf Of Mexico

0   50   100 Miles

Florida (25 Districts)

Congressional District 4

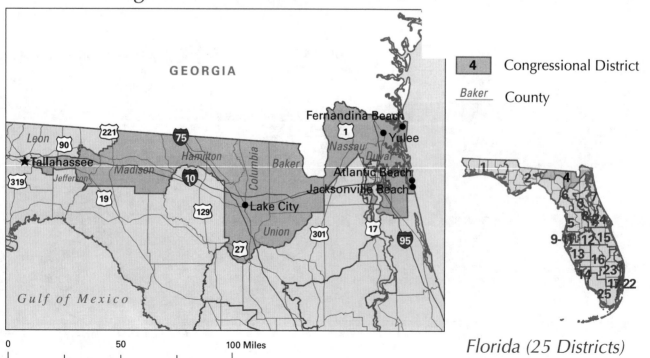

4 Congressional District

Baker County

GEORGIA

Gulf of Mexico

0   50   100 Miles

Florida (25 Districts)

Congressional District 5

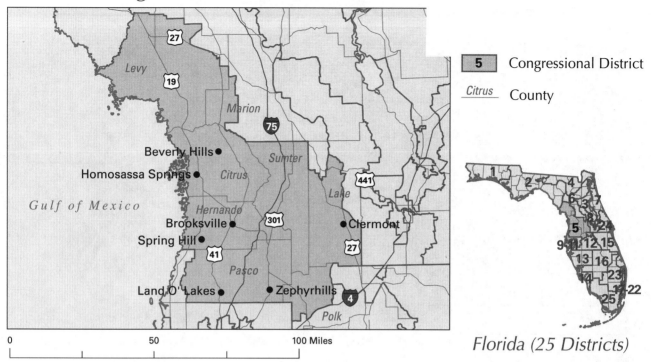

Florida (25 Districts)

Congressional District 6

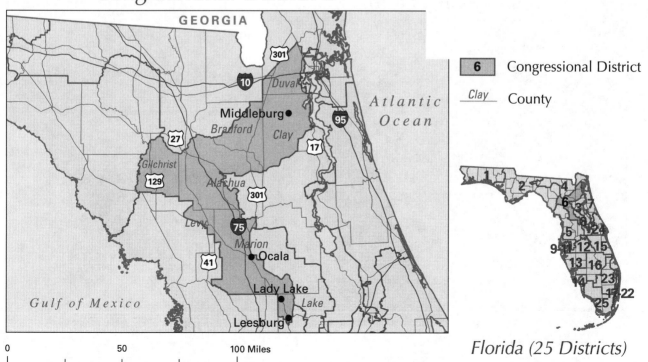

Florida (25 Districts)

Congressional District 7

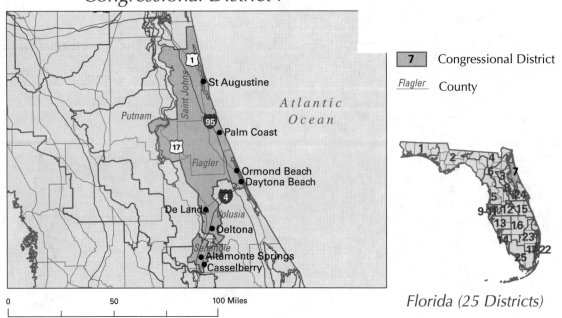

7 Congressional District

Flagler County

Florida (25 Districts)

Congressional District 8

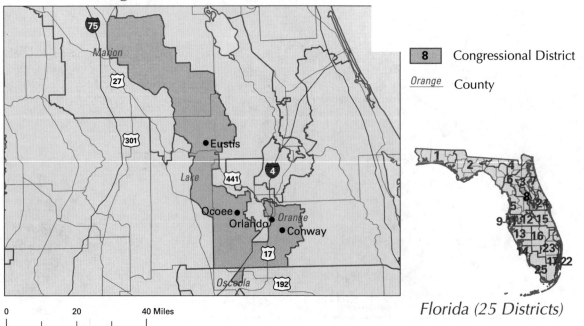

8 Congressional District

Orange County

Florida (25 Districts)

Congressional District 9

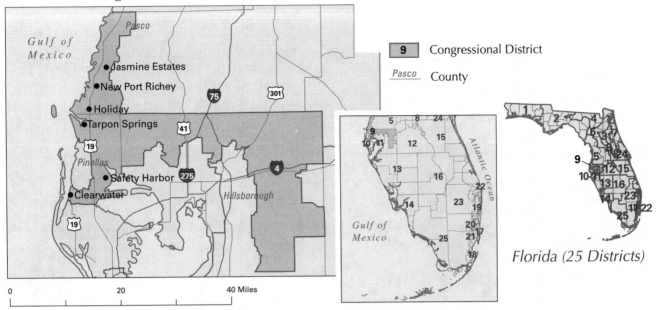

9 Congressional District

Pasco County

Florida (25 Districts)

Congressional District 10

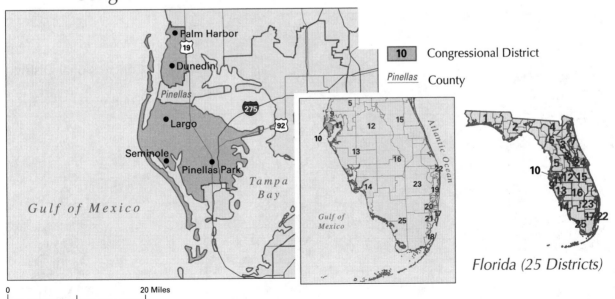

10 Congressional District

Pinellas County

Florida (25 Districts)

Congressional District 11

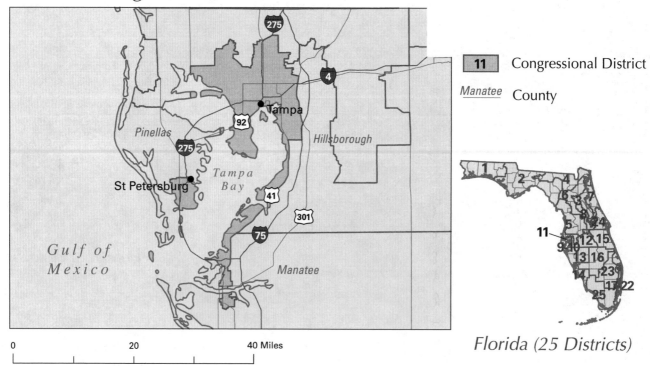

Florida (25 Districts)

Congressional District 12

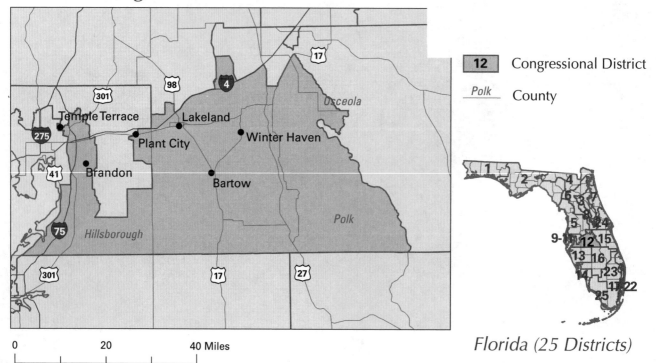

Florida (25 Districts)

Congressional District 13

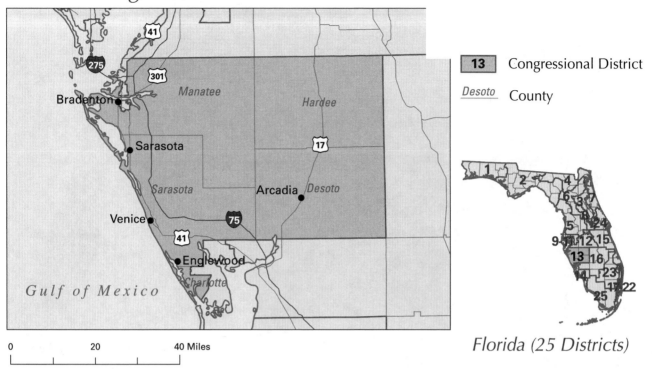

13   Congressional District

Desoto   County

Florida (25 Districts)

Congressional District 14

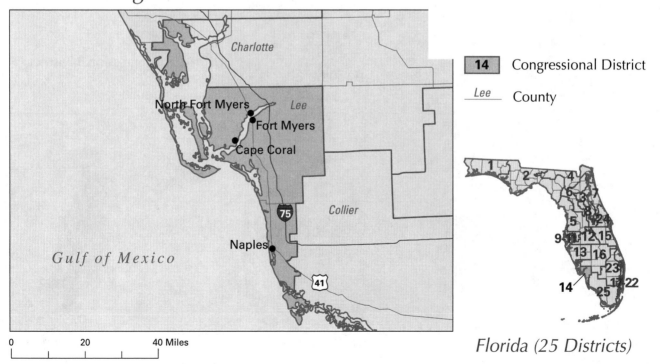

14   Congressional District

Lee   County

Florida (25 Districts)

Congressional District 15

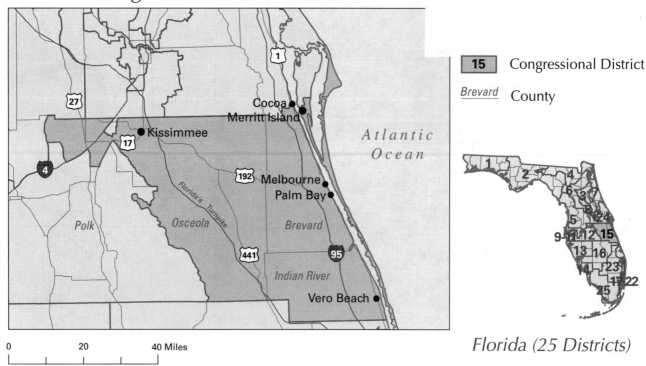

15	Congressional District
Brevard	County

Florida (25 Districts)

Congressional District 16

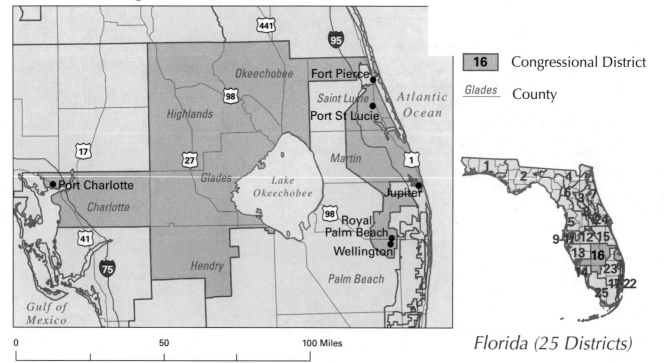

16	Congressional District
Glades	County

Florida (25 Districts)

Congressional District 17

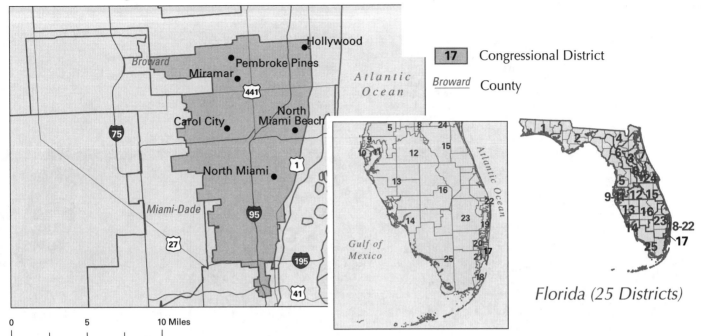

17 Congressional District
Broward County

Florida (25 Districts)

Congressional District 18

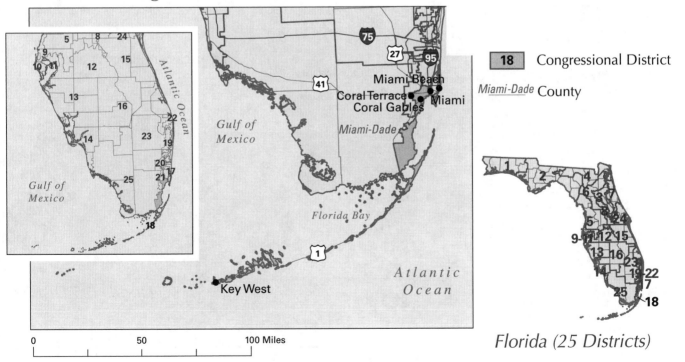

18 Congressional District
Miami-Dade County

Florida (25 Districts)

Congressional District 19

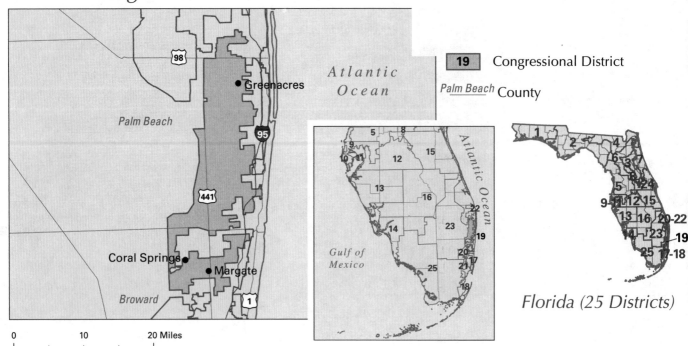

Congressional District 20

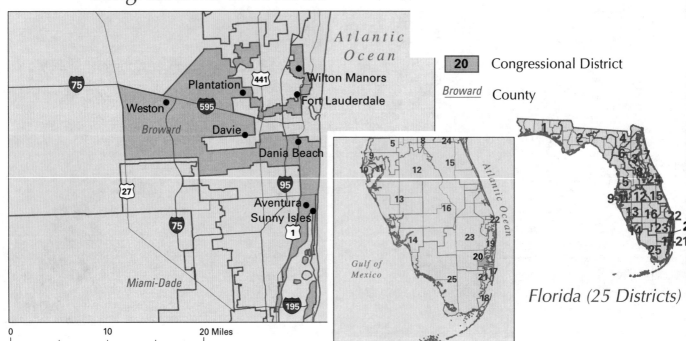

Congressional District 21

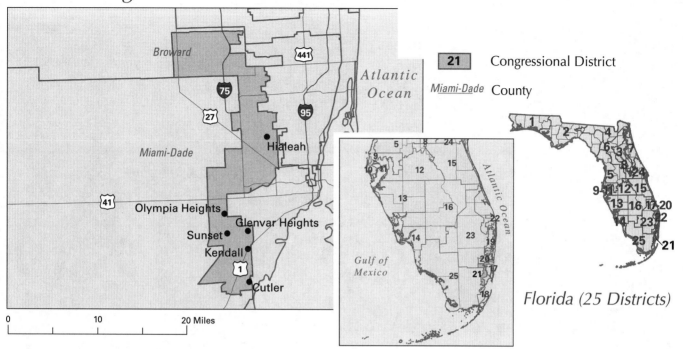

21	Congressional District
Miami-Dade	County

Florida (25 Districts)

Congressional District 22

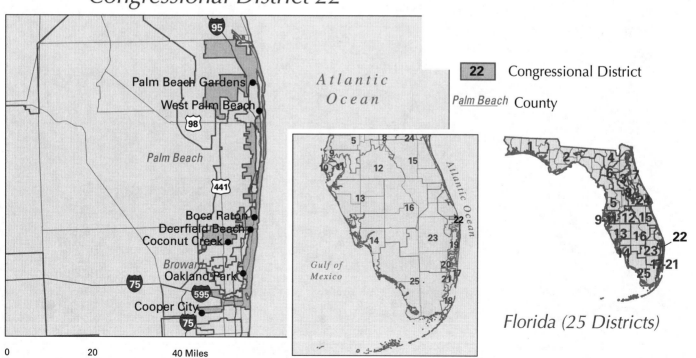

22	Congressional District
Palm Beach	County

Florida (25 Districts)

Congressional District 23

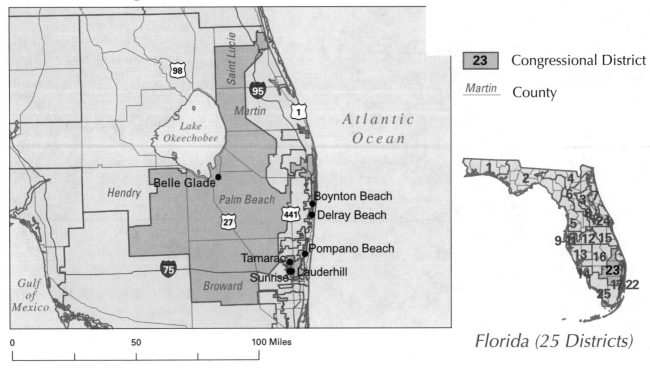

23	Congressional District
Martin	County

Florida (25 Districts)

Congressional District 24

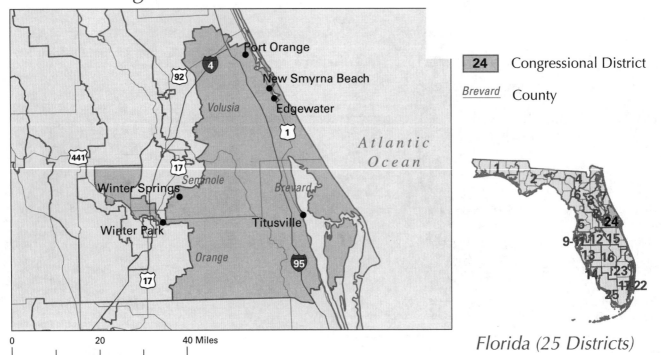

24	Congressional District
Brevard	County

Florida (25 Districts)

Congressional District 25

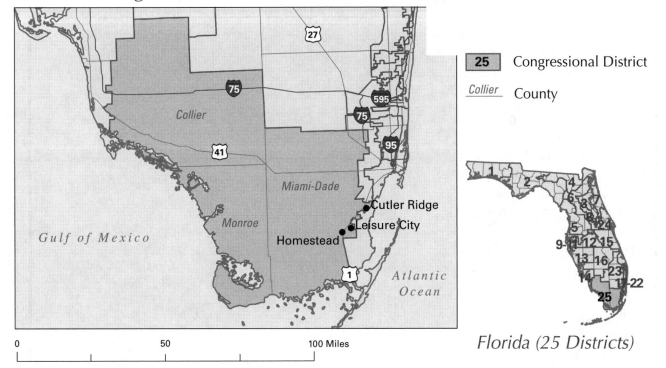

25 Congressional District

Collier County

Florida (25 Districts)

Georgia Congressional Districts — 13 Districts Total

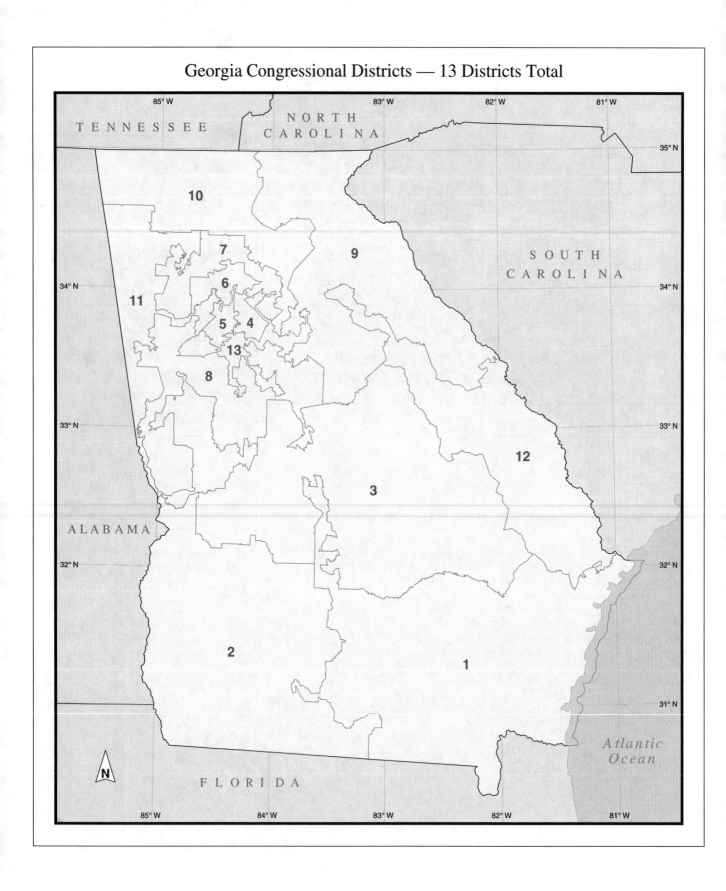

GEORGIA—109th CONGRESSIONAL DISTRICTS BY COUNTIES

County	Congressional District	County	Congressional District	County	Congressional District
Appling	1	Dade	10	Jefferson	12
Atkinson	1	Dawson	10	Jenkins	12
Bacon	1	Decatur	2	Johnson	3
Baker	2	DeKalb	4, 5, 13	Jones	3, 8
Baldwin	3	Dodge	3	Lamar	8
Banks	9	Dooly	3	Lanier	1
Barrow	9	Dougherty	2	Laurens	3
Bartow	7, 11	Douglas	8, 11	Lee	2
Ben Hill	1	Early	2	Liberty	1
Berrien	1	Echols	1	Lincoln	9
Bibb	3, 8	Effingham	12	Long	1
Bleckley	3	Elbert	9	Lowndes	1, 2
Brantley	1	Emanuel	3	Lumpkin	9
Brooks	2	Evans	3	McDuffie	9
Bryan	1, 12	Fannin	10	McIntosh	1
Bulloch	12	Fayette	8, 13	Macon	3
Burke	12	Floyd	11	Madison	9
Butts	8, 13	Forsyth	7, 10	Marion	3
Calhoun	2	Franklin	9	Meriwether	11
Camden	1	Fulton	5, 6, 13	Miller	2
Candler	3	Gilmer	10	Mitchell	2
Carroll	8, 11	Glascock	12	Monroe	3
Catoosa	10	Glynn	1	Montgomery	3
Charlton	1	Gordon	10	Morgan	9
Chatham	1, 12	Grady	2	Murray	10
Chattahoochee	2	Greene	9	Muscogee	2, 8, 11
Chattooga	11	Gwinnett	4, 7, 10, 13	Newton	8, 9, 13
Cherokee	6, 7	Habersham	9	Oconee	9
Clarke	12	Hall	10	Oglethorpe	9, 12
Clay	2	Hancock	3	Paulding	7, 11
Clayton	5, 13	Haralson	11	Peach	3
Clinch	1	Harris	8, 11	Pickens	10
Cobb	5, 6, 11	Hart	9	Pierce	1
Coffee	1	Heard	11	Pike	8
Colquitt	1, 2	Henry	8, 13	Polk	11
Columbia	9	Houston	1, 3	Pulaski	1, 3
Cook	1	Irwin	1	Putnam	9
Coweta	8, 11	Jackson	9	Quitman	2
Crawford	3	Jasper	8	Rabun	9
Crisp	2	Jeff Davis	1	Randolph	2

GEORGIA—109th CONGRESSIONAL DISTRICTS BY COUNTIES

County	Congressional District
Richmond	9, 12
Rockdale	8, 10, 13
Schley	3
Screven	12
Seminole	2
Spalding	8, 13
Stephens	9
Stewart	2
Sumter	2
Talbot	11
Taliaferro	12
Tattnall	3
Taylor	3

County	Congressional District
Telfair	3
Terrell	2
Thomas	2
Tift	2
Toombs	3
Towns	9
Treutlen	3
Troup	8, 11
Turner	2
Twiggs	3
Union	9
Upson	8, 11
Walker	10

County	Congressional District
Walton	9, 10, 13
Ware	1
Warren	12
Washington	3
Wayne	1
Webster	2
Wheeler	3
White	9
Whitfield	10
Wilcox	1, 3
Wilkes	9
Wilkinson	3
Worth	2

Congressional District 1

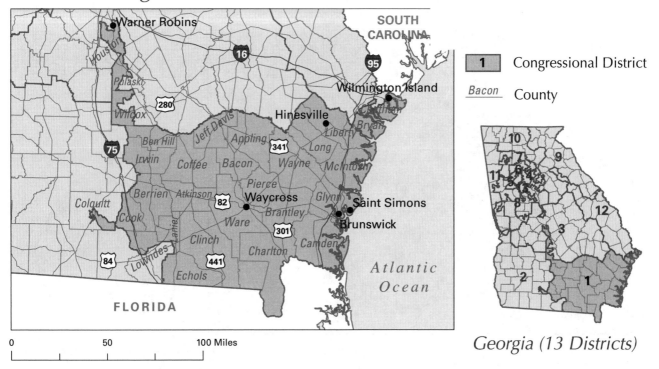

Georgia (13 Districts)

Congressional District 2

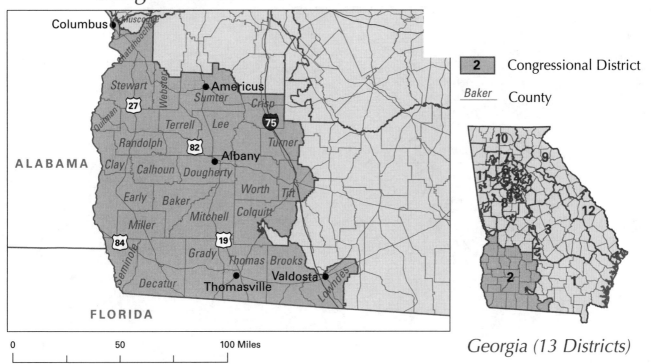

Georgia (13 Districts)

Congressional District 3

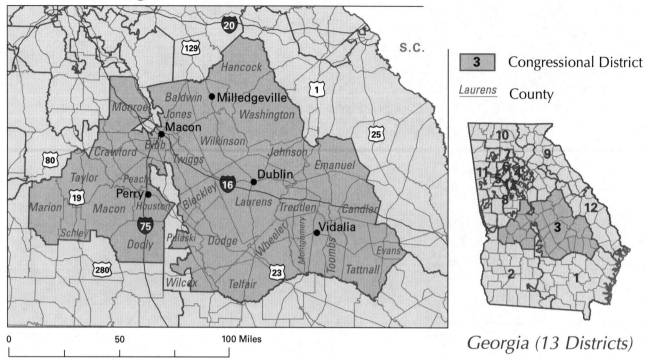

0   50   100 Miles

3   Congressional District

Laurens   County

Georgia (13 Districts)

Congressional District 4

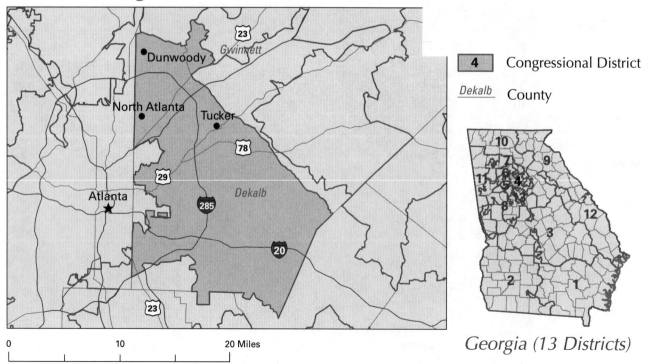

0   10   20 Miles

4   Congressional District

Dekalb   County

Georgia (13 Districts)

Congressional District 5

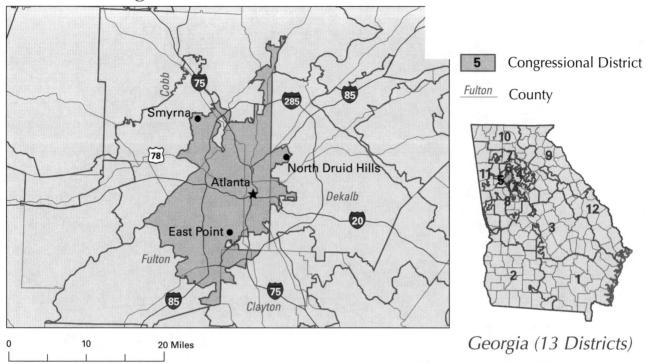

5 Congressional District
Fulton County

Georgia (13 Districts)

0   10   20 Miles

Congressional District 6

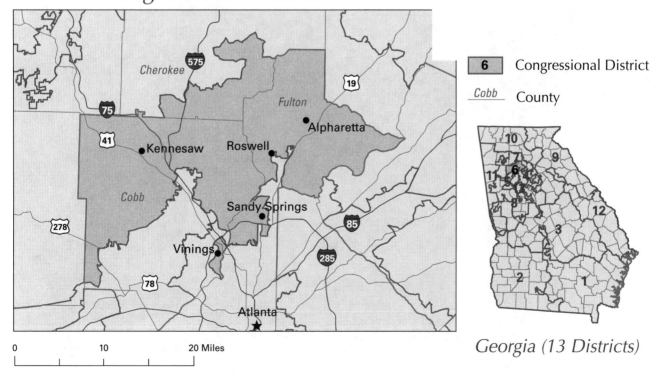

6 Congressional District
Cobb County

Georgia (13 Districts)

0   10   20 Miles

Congressional District 7

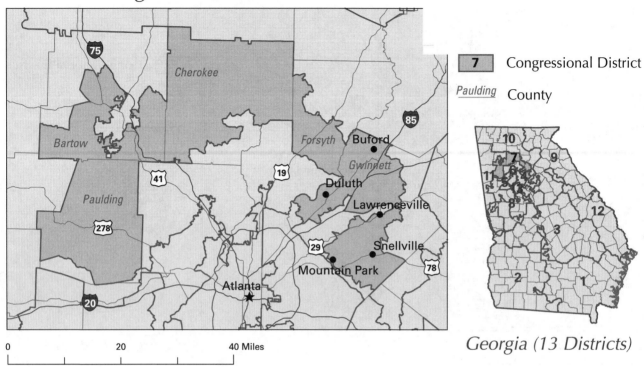

Georgia (13 Districts)

Congressional District 8

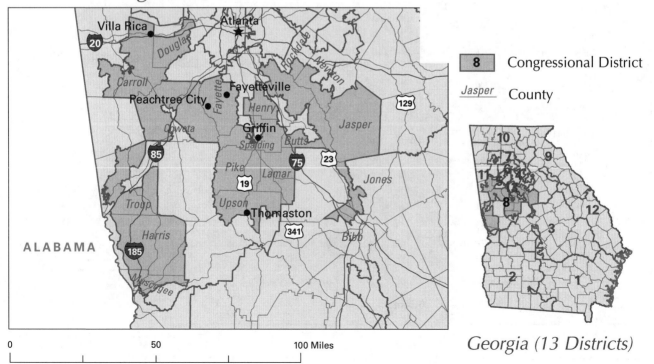

Georgia (13 Districts)

Congressional District 9

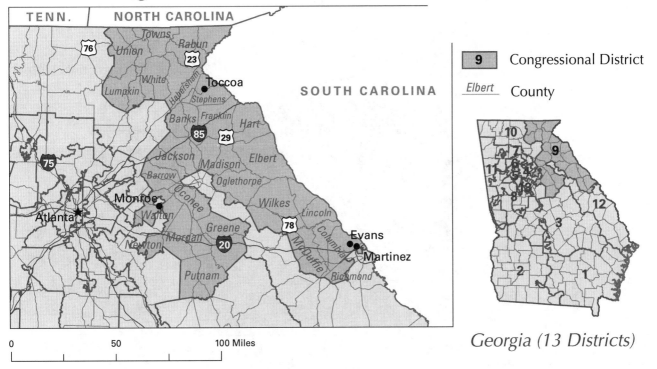

9 Congressional District
Elbert County

Georgia (13 Districts)

Congressional District 10

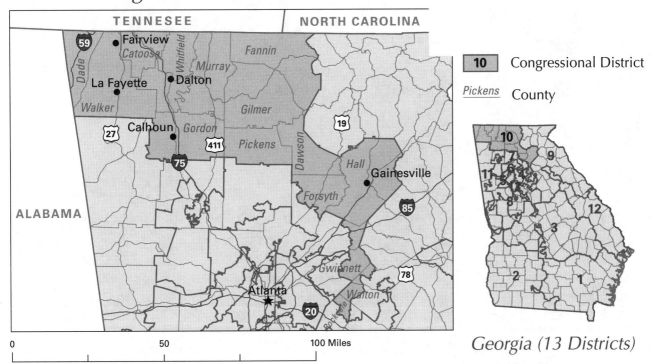

10 Congressional District
Pickens County

Georgia (13 Districts)

Congressional District 11

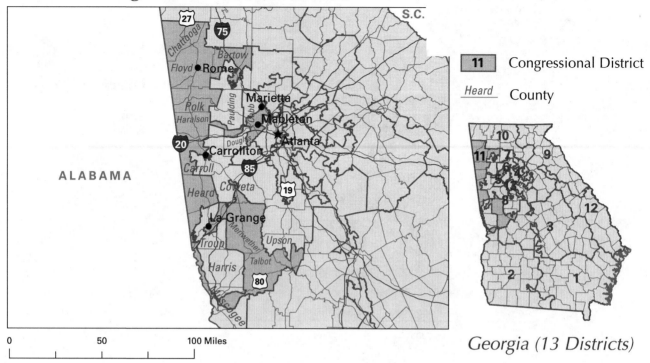

Georgia (13 Districts)

Congressional District 12

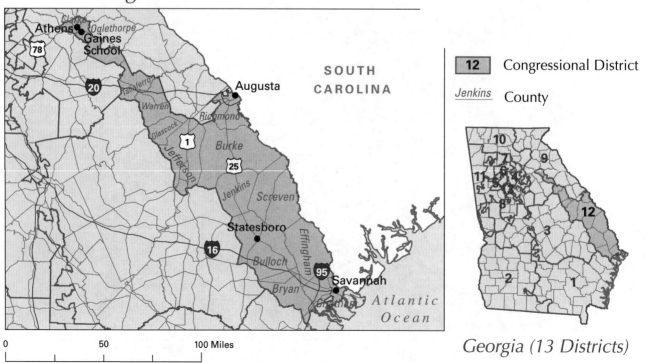

Georgia (13 Districts)

Congressional District 13

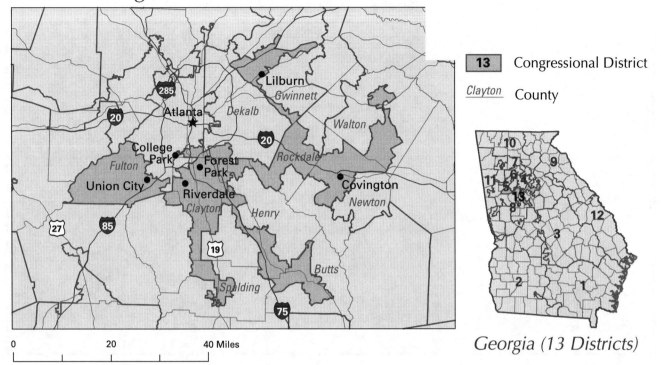

13 Congressional District

Clayton County

Georgia (13 Districts)

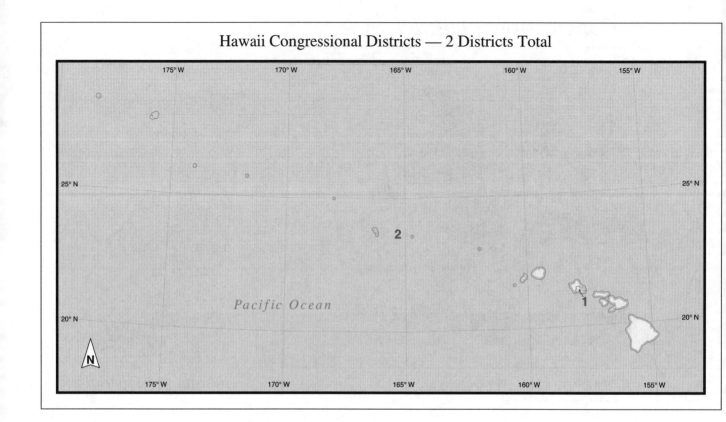

HAWAII—109th CONGRESSIONAL DISTRICTS BY COUNTIES

County	Congressional District
Hawaii	2
Honolulu	1, 2
Kalawao	2
Kauai	2
Maui	2

Congressional District 1

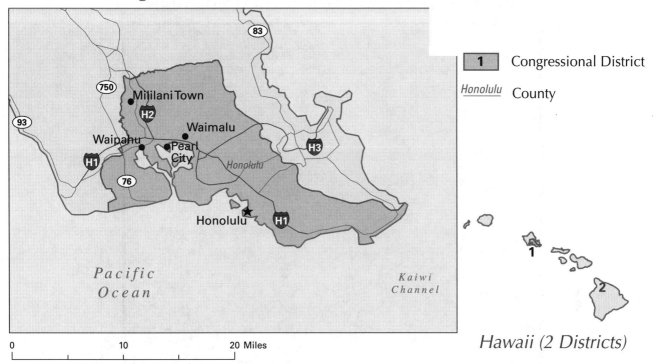

Hawaii (2 Districts)

Congressional District 2

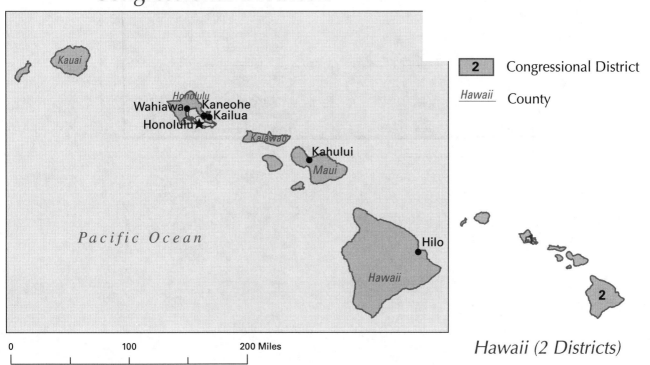

Hawaii (2 Districts)

Idaho Congressional Districts — 2 Districts Total

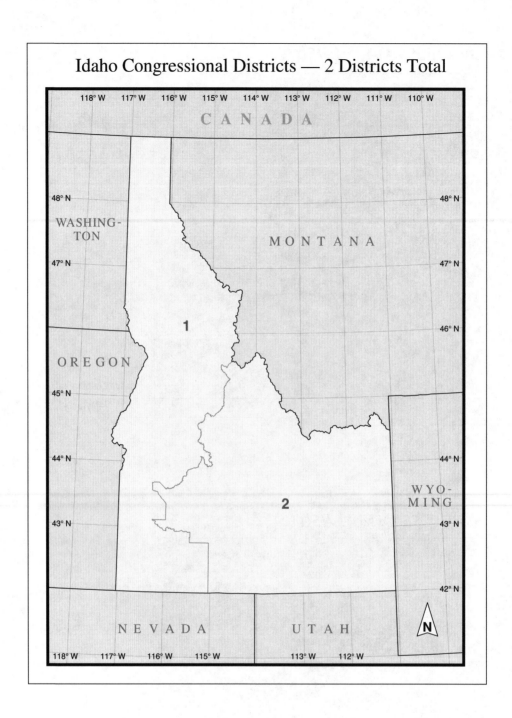

IDAHO—109th CONGRESSIONAL DISTRICTS BY COUNTIES

County	Congressional District	County	Congressional District	County	Congressional District
Ada	1, 2	Cassia	2	Lewis	1
Adams	1	Clark	2	Lincoln	2
Bannock	2	Clearwater	1	Madison	2
Bear Lake	2	Custer	2	Minidoka	2
Benewah	1	Elmore	2	Nez Perce	1
Bingham	2	Franklin	2	Oneida	2
Blaine	2	Fremont	2	Owyhee	1
Boise	1	Gem	1	Payette	1
Bonner	1	Gooding	2	Power	2
Bonneville	2	Idaho	1	Shoshone	1
Boundary	1	Jefferson	2	Teton	2
Butte	2	Jerome	2	Twin Falls	2
Camas	2	Kootenai	1	Valley	1
Canyon	1	Latah	1	Washington	1
Caribou	2	Lemhi	2		

Congressional District 1

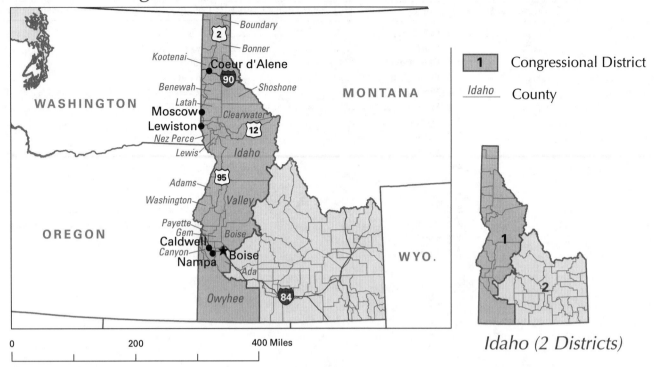

Idaho (2 Districts)

Congressional District 2

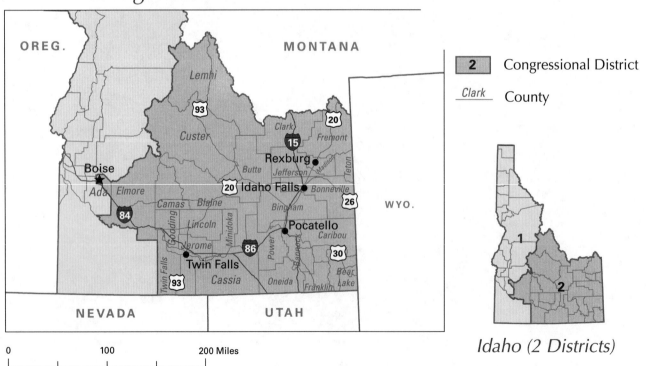

Idaho (2 Districts)

Illinois Congressional Districts — 19 Districts Total

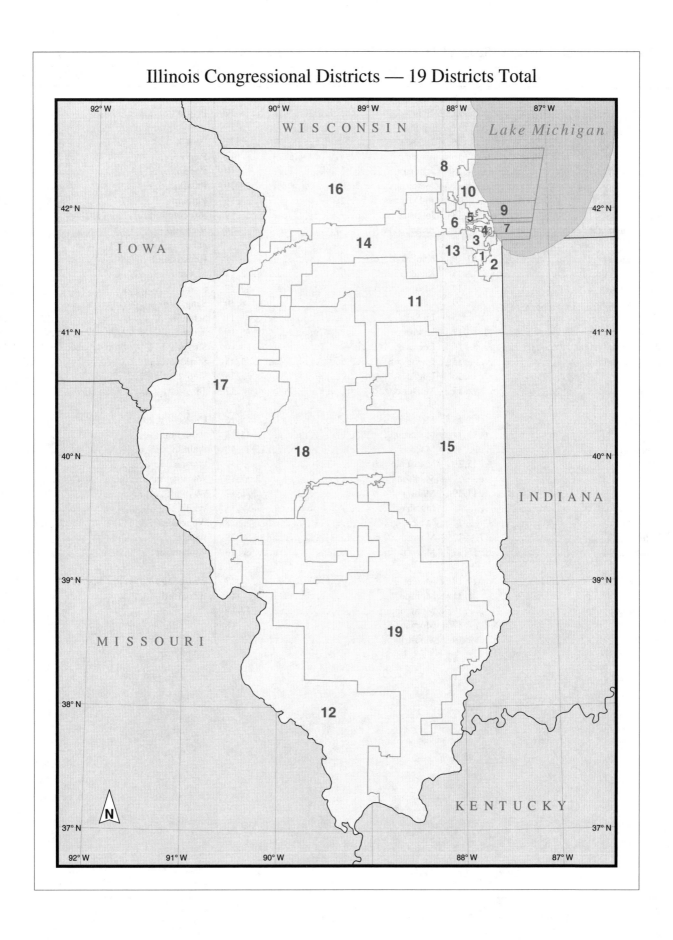

ILLINOIS—109th CONGRESSIONAL DISTRICTS BY COUNTIES

County	Congressional District	County	Congressional District	County	Congressional District
Adams	17, 18	Henderson	17	Ogle	16
Alexander	12	Henry	14, 17	Peoria	18
Bond	19	Iroquois	15	Perry	12
Boone	16	Jackson	12	Piatt	15
Brown	18	Jasper	19	Pike	17, 18
Bureau	11, 14, 18	Jefferson	19	Pope	19
Calhoun	17	Jersey	17, 19	Pulaski	12
Carroll	16	Jo Daviess	16	Putnam	18
Cass	18	Johnson	19	Randolph	12
Champaign	15	Kane	14	Richland	19
Christian	17, 19	Kankakee	11	Rock Island	17
Clark	15	Kendall	14	St. Clair	12
Clay	19	Knox	17, 18	Saline	15, 19
Clinton	19	Lake	8, 10	Sangamon	17–19
Coles	15	La Salle	11	Schuyler	18
Cook	1–10, 13	Lawrence	15, 19	Scott	18
Crawford	15	Lee	14	Shelby	17, 19
Cumberland	15	Livingston	11, 15	Stark	18
DeKalb	14, 16	Logan	18	Stephenson	16
De Witt	15	McDonough	17	Tazewell	18
Douglas	15	McHenry	8, 16	Union	12
DuPage	6, 13, 14	McLean	11, 15	Vermilion	15
Edgar	15	Macon	15, 17, 18	Wabash	15, 19
Edwards	15, 19	Macoupin	17	Warren	17
Effingham	19	Madison	12, 17, 19	Washington	19
Fayette	17, 19	Marion	19	Wayne	19
Ford	15	Marshall	18	White	15, 19
Franklin	12	Mason	18	Whiteside	14, 16, 17
Fulton	17	Massac	19	Will	2, 11, 13
Gallatin	15, 19	Menard	18	Williamson	12, 19
Greene	17, 19	Mercer	17	Winnebago	16
Grundy	11	Monroe	12	Woodford	11, 18
Hamilton	19	Montgomery	17, 19		
Hancock	17	Morgan	18		
Hardin	19	Moultrie	15		

Congressional District 1

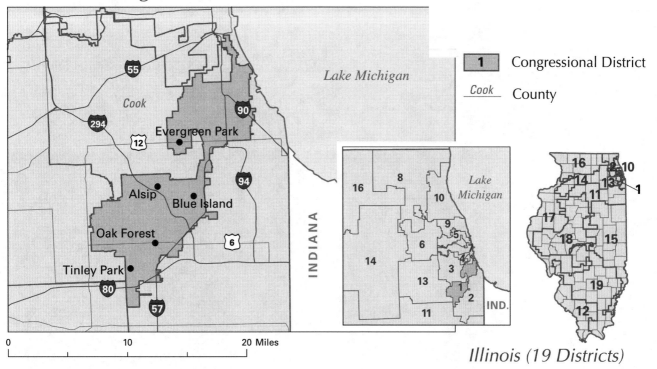

Congressional District 2

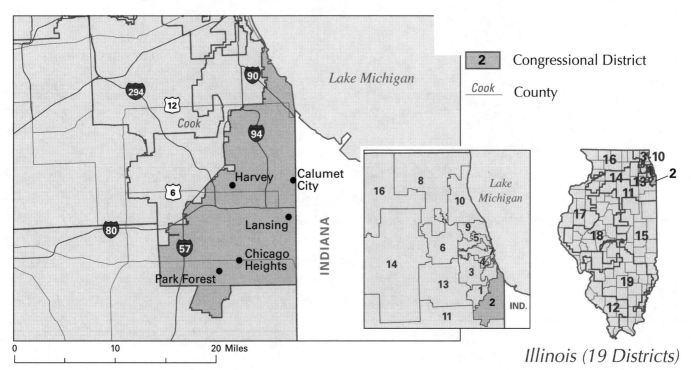

Congressional District 3

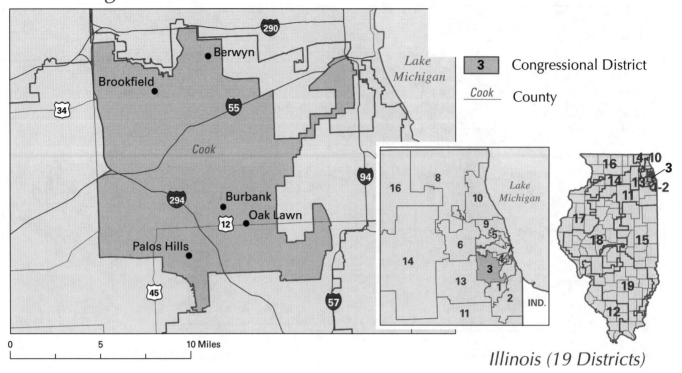

3 Congressional District
Cook County

Illinois (19 Districts)

Congressional District 4

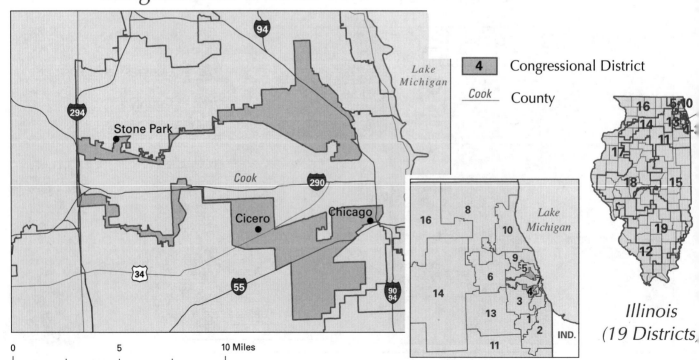

4 Congressional District
Cook County

Illinois (19 Districts)

Congressional District 5

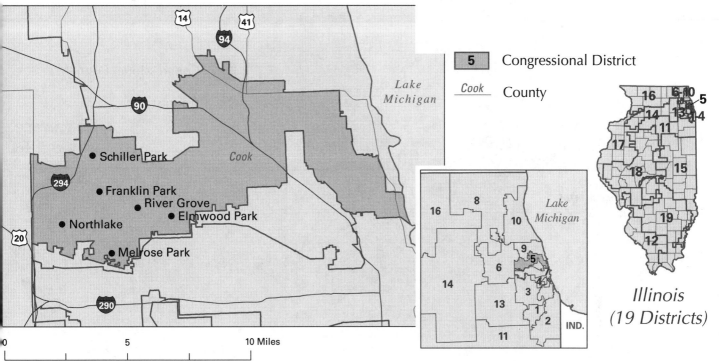

Congressional District 6

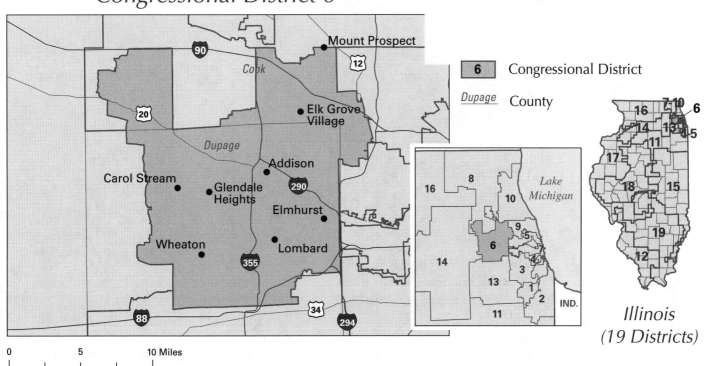

Congressional District 7

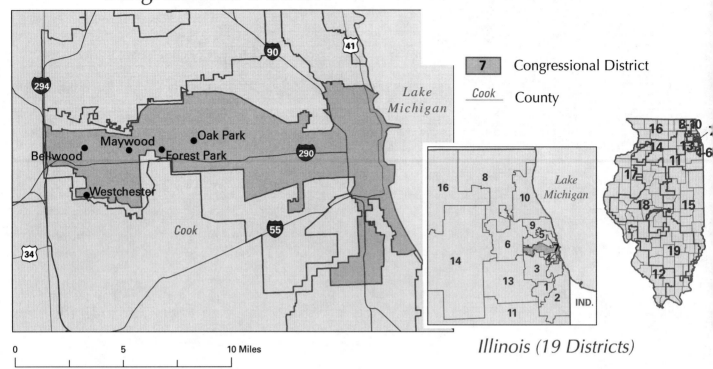

0   5   10 Miles

7	Congressional District
Cook	County

Illinois (19 Districts)

Congressional District 8

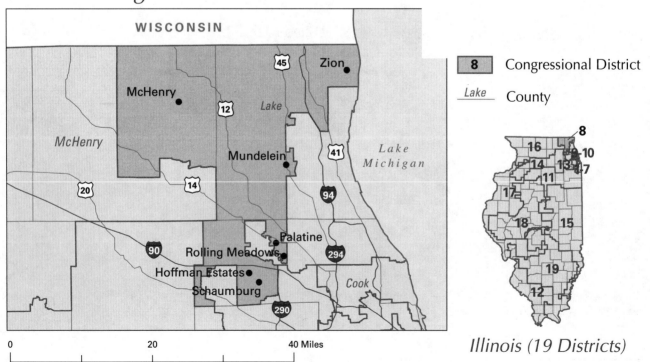

0   20   40 Miles

8	Congressional District
Lake	County

Illinois (19 Districts)

Congressional District 9

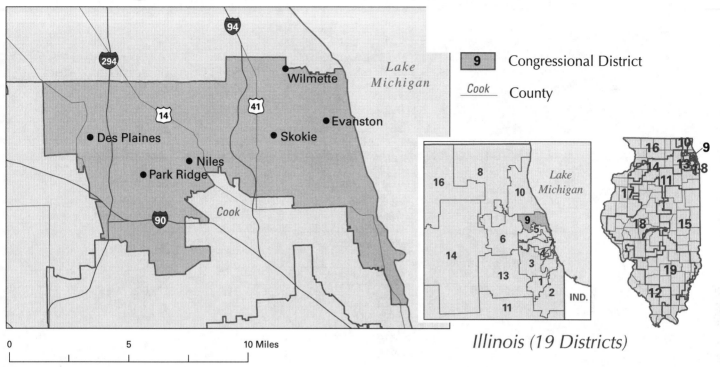

Illinois (19 Districts)

Congressional District 10

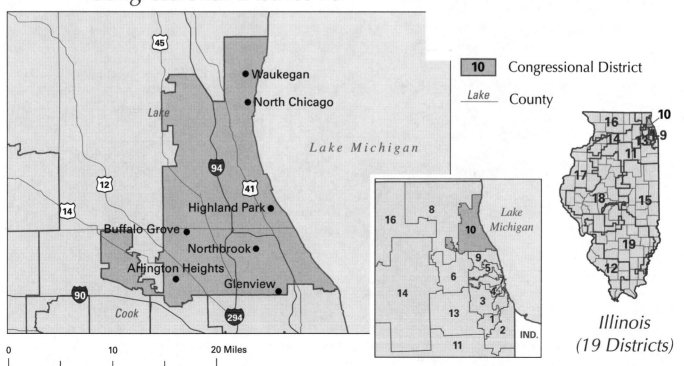

Illinois
(19 Districts)

Congressional District 11

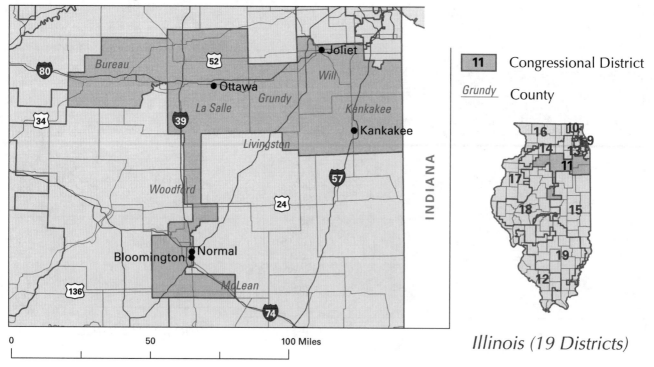

Illinois (19 Districts)

Congressional District 12

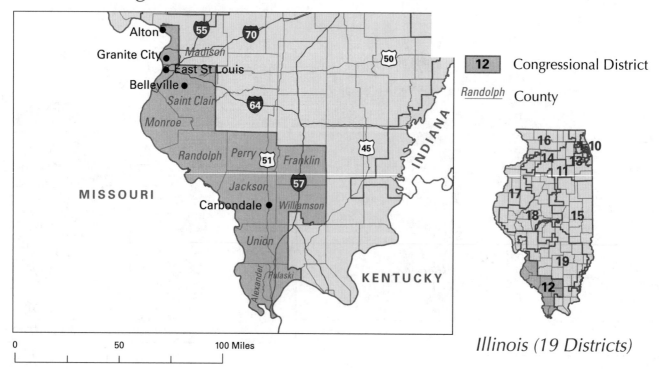

Illinois (19 Districts)

Congressional District 13

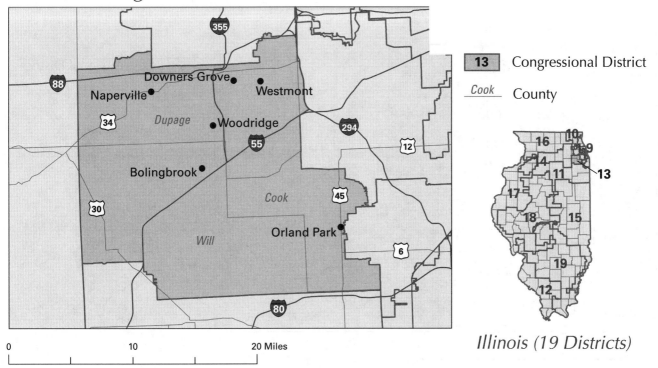

13	Congressional District
Cook	County

Illinois (19 Districts)

Congressional District 14

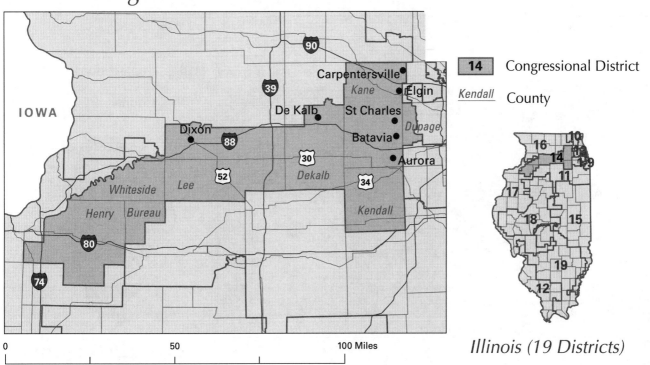

14	Congressional District
Kendall	County

Illinois (19 Districts)

Congressional District 15

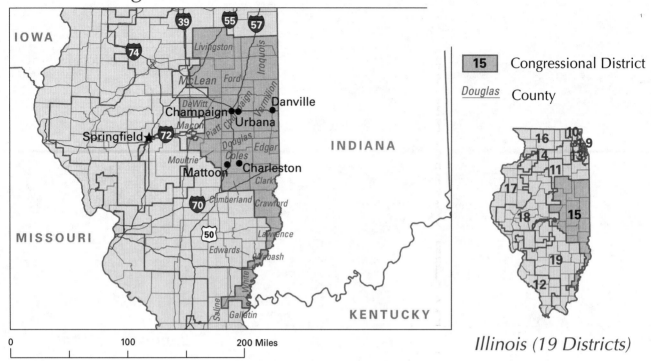

Illinois (19 Districts)

Congressional District 16

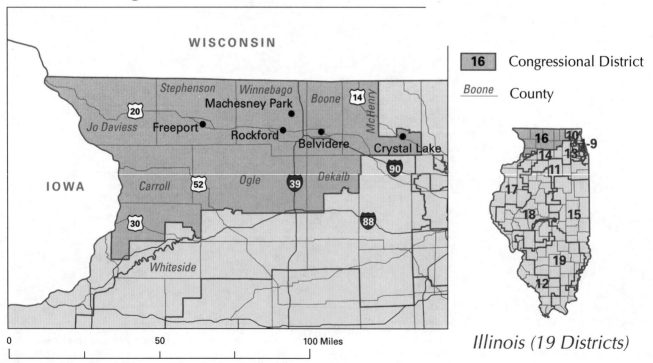

Illinois (19 Districts)

Congressional District 17

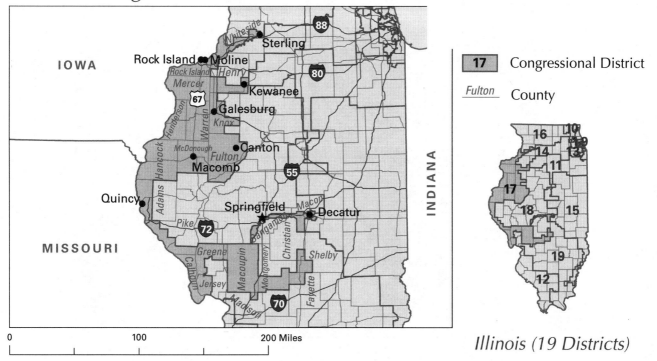

17 Congressional District
Fulton County

Illinois (19 Districts)

Congressional District 18

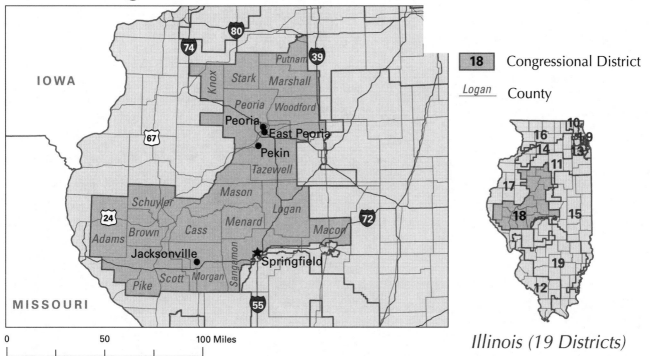

18 Congressional District
Logan County

Illinois (19 Districts)

Congressional District 19

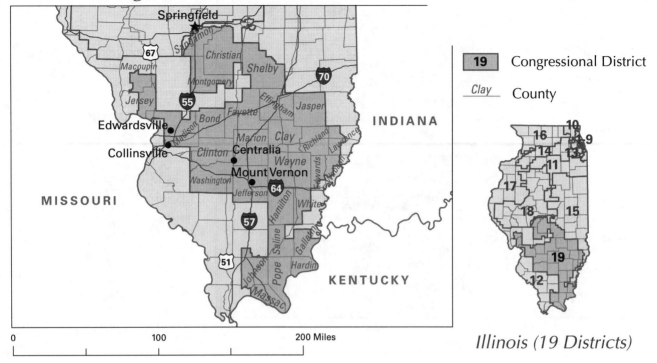

0   100   200 Miles

Illinois (19 Districts)

Indiana Congressional Districts — 9 Districts Total

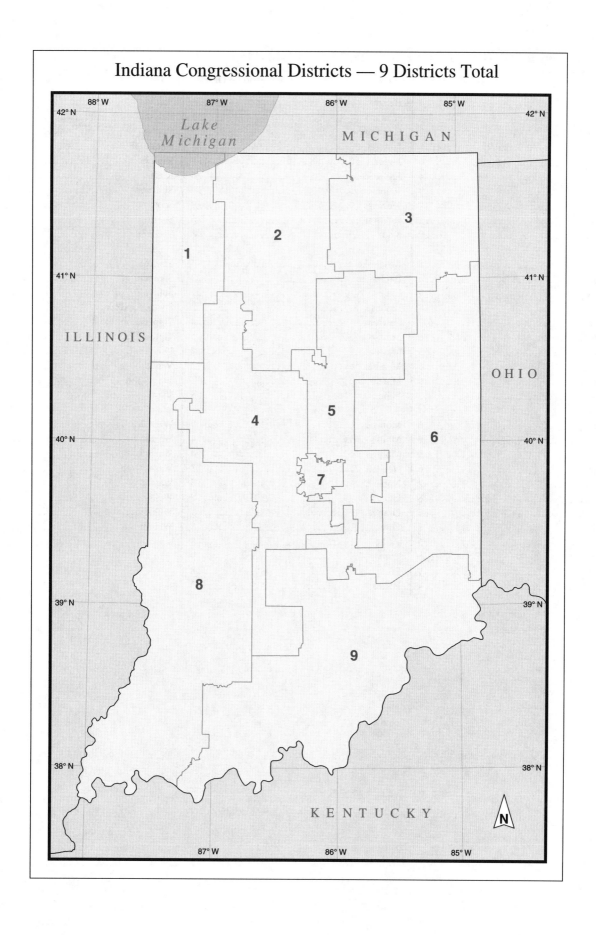

INDIANA — 109th CONGRESSIONAL DISTRICTS BY COUNTIES

County	Congressional District	County	Congressional District	County	Congressional District
Adams	6	Henry	6	Posey	8
Allen	3, 6	Howard	2, 5	Pulaski	2
Bartholomew	6, 9	Huntington	5	Putnam	8
Benton	1	Jackson	9	Randolph	6
Blackford	6	Jasper	1	Ripley	9
Boone	4	Jay	6	Rush	6
Brown	9	Jefferson	9	St. Joseph	2
Carroll	2	Jennings	9	Scott	9
Cass	2	Johnson	4–6	Shelby	5, 6
Clark	9	Knox	8	Spencer	9
Clay	8	Kosciusko	3	Starke	2
Clinton	4	LaGrange	3	Steuben	3
Crawford	9	Lake	1	Sullivan	8
Daviess	8	LaPorte	2	Switzerland	9
Dearborn	6, 9	Lawrence	4	Tippecanoe	4
Decatur	6	Madison	6	Tipton	5
DeKalb	3	Marion	4, 5, 7	Union	6
Delaware	6	Marshall	2	Vanderburgh	8
Dubois	9	Martin	8	Vermillion	8
Elkhart	2, 3	Miami	5	Vigo	8
Fayette	6	Monroe	4, 9	Wabash	5
Floyd	9	Montgomery	4	Warren	8
Fountain	4, 8	Morgan	4	Warrick	8
Franklin	6	Newton	1	Washington	9
Fulton	2	Noble	3	Wayne	6
Gibson	8	Ohio	9	Wells	6
Grant	5	Orange	9	White	2, 4
Greene	8	Owen	8	Whitley	3
Hamilton	5	Parke	8		
Hancock	5	Perry	9		
Harrison	9	Pike	8		
Hendricks	4	Porter	1, 2		

Congressional District 1

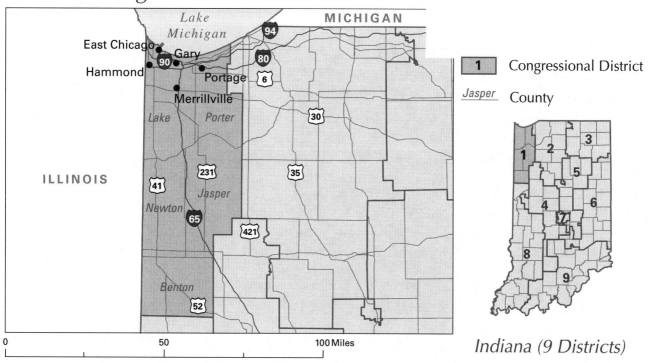

1	Congressional District
Jasper	County

Indiana (9 Districts)

Congressional District 2

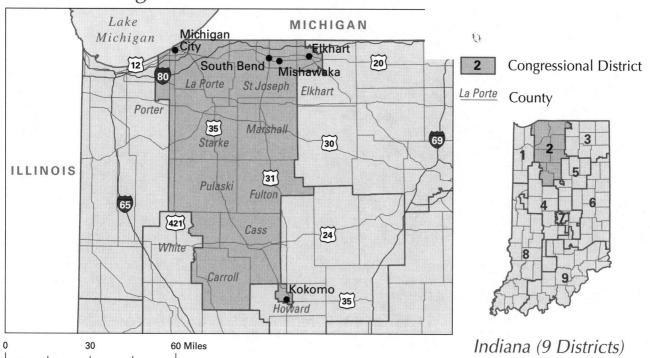

2	Congressional District
La Porte	County

Indiana (9 Districts)

Congressional District 3

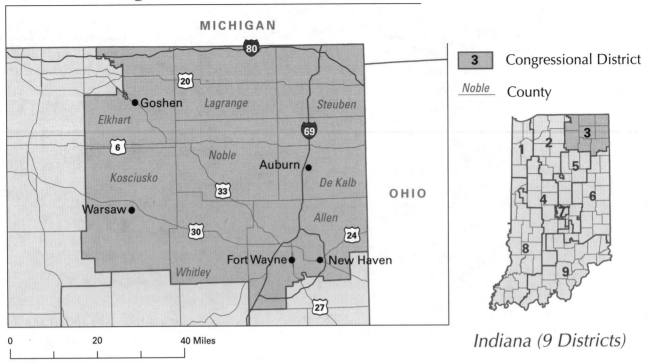

Indiana (9 Districts)

Congressional District 4

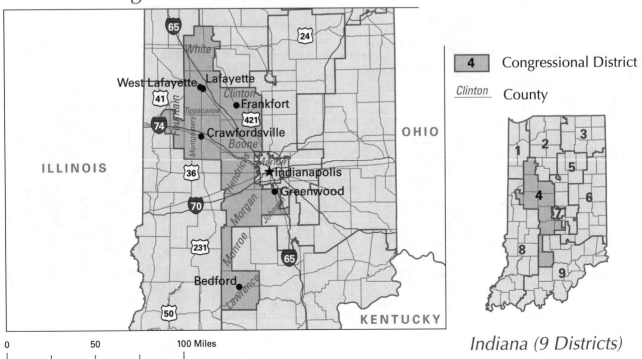

Indiana (9 Districts)

Congressional District 5

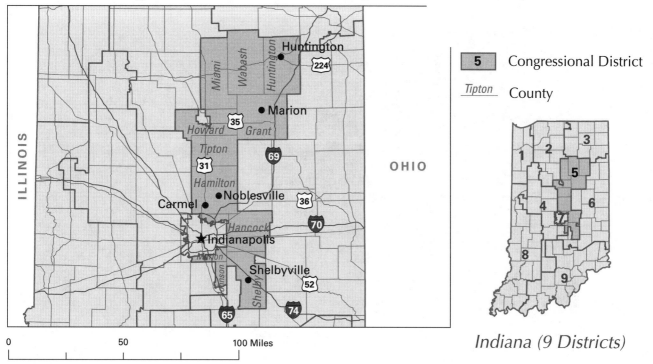

Indiana (9 Districts)

Congressional District 6

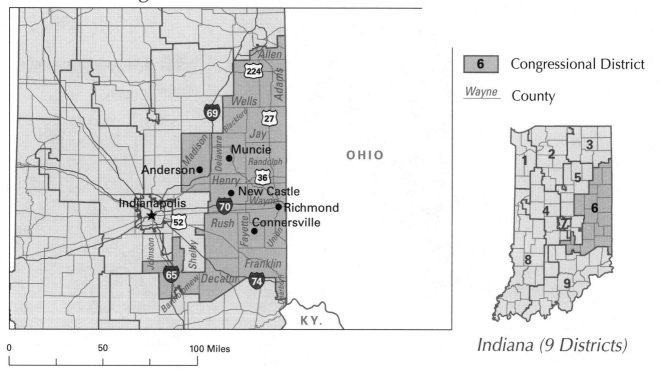

Indiana (9 Districts)

Congressional District 7

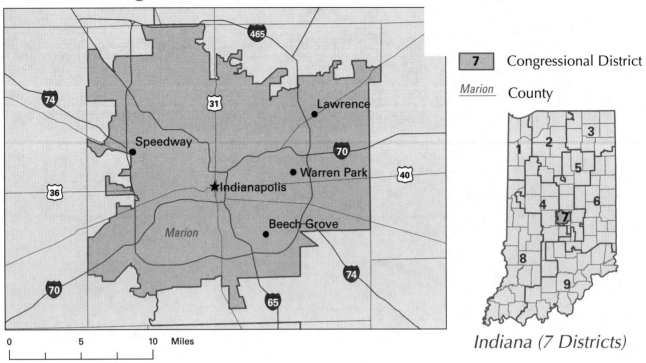

0   5   10   Miles

7   Congressional District

Marion   County

Indiana (7 Districts)

Congressional District 8

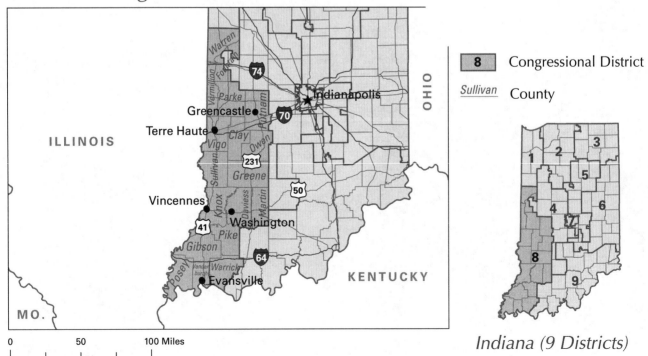

0   50   100 Miles

8   Congressional District

Sullivan   County

Indiana (9 Districts)

Congressional District 9

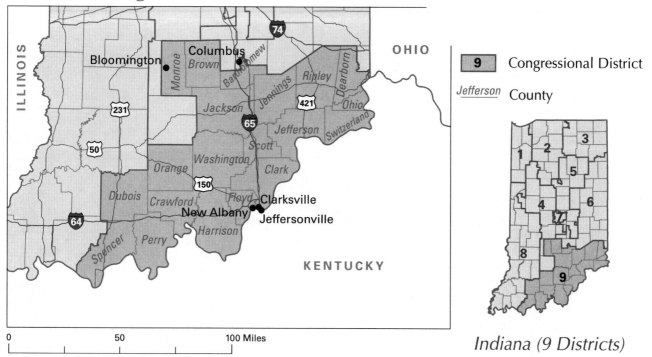

9 Congressional District

Jefferson County

Indiana (9 Districts)

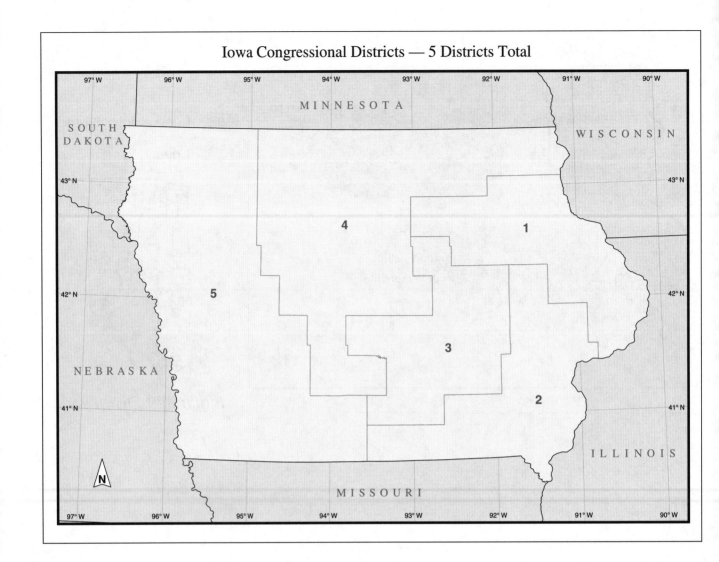

Iowa Congressional Districts — 5 Districts Total

IOWA—109th CONGRESSIONAL DISTRICTS BY COUNTIES

County	Congressional District	County	Congressional District	County	Congressional District
Adair	5	Floyd	4	Monona	5
Adams	5	Franklin	4	Monroe	3
Allamakee	4	Fremont	5	Montgomery	5
Appanoose	2	Greene	4	Muscatine	2
Audubon	5	Grundy	3	O'Brien	5
Benton	3	Guthrie	5	Osceola	5
Black Hawk	1	Hamilton	4	Page	5
Boone	4	Hancock	4	Palo Alto	4
Bremer	1	Hardin	4	Plymouth	5
Buchanan	1	Harrison	5	Pocahontas	4
Buena Vista	5	Henry	2	Polk	3
Butler	1	Howard	4	Pottawattamie	5
Calhoun	4	Humboldt	4	Poweshiek	3
Carroll	5	Ida	5	Ringgold	5
Cass	5	Iowa	3	Sac	5
Cedar	2	Jackson	1	Scott	1
Cerro Gordo	4	Jasper	3	Shelby	5
Cherokee	5	Jefferson	2	Sioux	5
Chickasaw	4	Johnson	2	Story	4
Clarke	5	Jones	1	Tama	3
Clay	5	Keokuk	3	Taylor	5
Clayton	1	Kossuth	4	Union	5
Clinton	1	Lee	2	Van Buren	2
Crawford	5	Linn	2	Wapello	2
Dallas	4	Louisa	2	Warren	4
Davis	2	Lucas	3	Washington	2
Decatur	5	Lyon	5	Wayne	2
Delaware	1	Madison	4	Webster	4
Des Moines	2	Mahaska	3	Winnebago	4
Dickinson	5	Marion	3	Winneshiek	4
Dubuque	1	Marshall	4	Woodbury	5
Emmet	4	Mills	5	Worth	4
Fayette	1	Mitchell	4	Wright	4

Congressional District 1

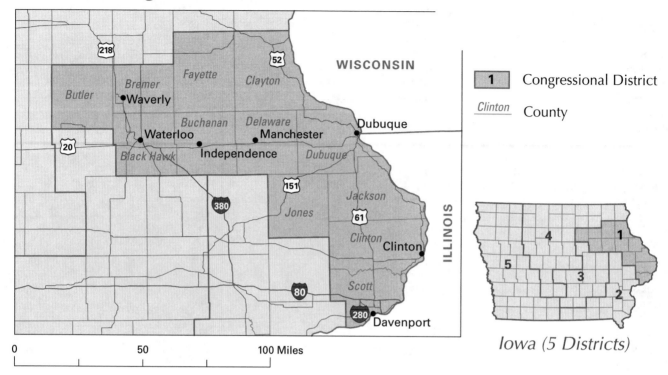

1 Congressional District
Clinton County

Iowa (5 Districts)

Congressional District 2

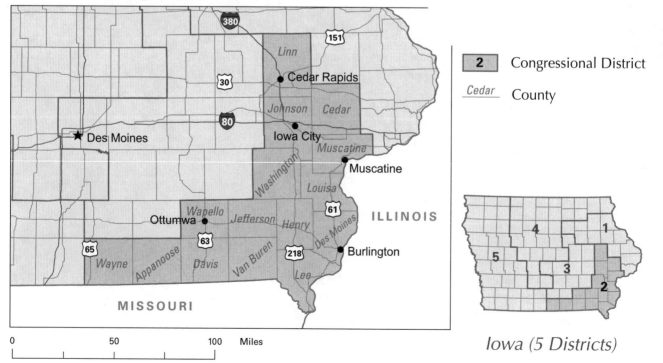

2 Congressional District
Cedar County

Iowa (5 Districts)

Congressional District 3

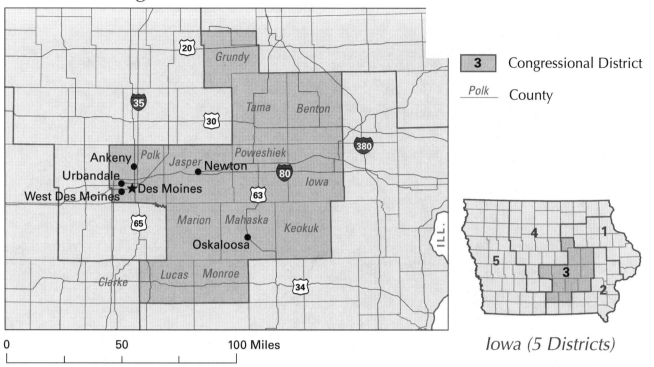

3	Congressional District
Polk	County

Iowa (5 Districts)

Congressional District 4

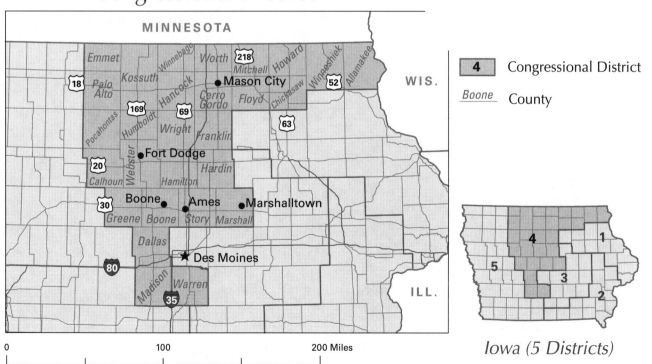

4	Congressional District
Boone	County

Iowa (5 Districts)

Congressional District 5

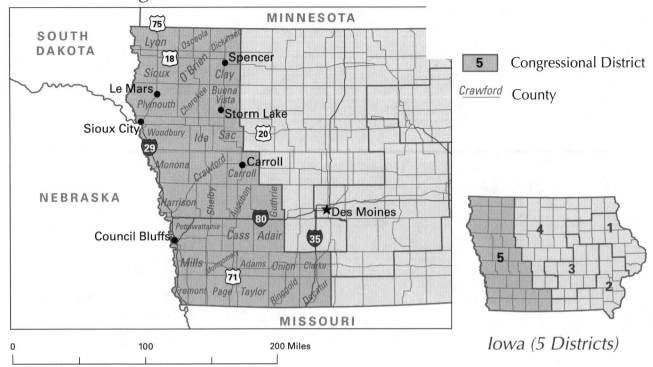

Iowa (5 Districts)

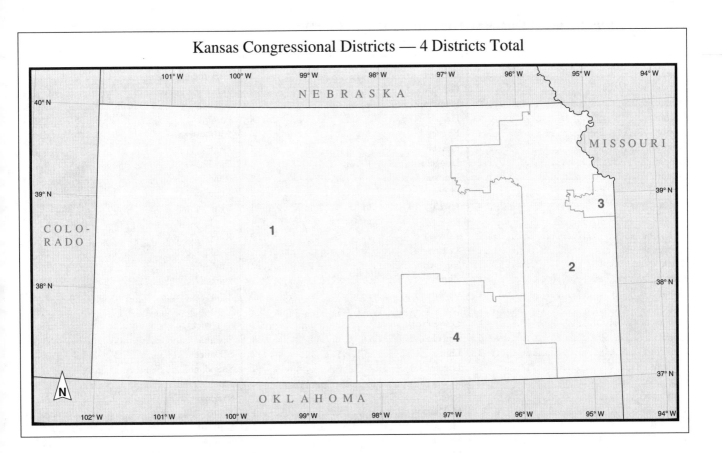

Kansas Congressional Districts — 4 Districts Total

KANSAS—109th CONGRESSIONAL DISTRICTS BY COUNTIES

County	Congressional District
Allen	2
Anderson	2
Atchison	2
Barber	1
Barton	1
Bourbon	2
Brown	2
Butler	4
Chase	1
Chautauqua	4
Cherokee	2
Cheyenne	1
Clark	1
Clay	1
Cloud	1
Coffey	2
Comanche	1
Cowley	4
Crawford	2
Decatur	1
Dickinson	1
Doniphan	2
Douglas	2, 3
Edwards	1
Elk	4
Ellis	1
Ellsworth	1
Finney	1
Ford	1
Franklin	2
Geary	1, 2
Gove	1
Graham	1
Grant	1
Gray	1

County	Congressional District
Greeley	1
Greenwood	1, 4
Hamilton	1
Harper	4
Harvey	4
Haskell	1
Hodgeman	1
Jackson	2
Jefferson	2
Jewell	1
Johnson	3
Kearny	1
Kingman	4
Kiowa	1
Labette	2
Lane	1
Leavenworth	2
Lincoln	1
Linn	2
Logan	1
Lyon	1
McPherson	1
Marion	1
Marshall	1
Meade	1
Miami	2
Mitchell	1
Montgomery	4
Morris	1
Morton	1
Nemaha	1, 2
Neosho	2
Ness	1
Norton	1
Osage	2

County	Congressional District
Osborne	1
Ottawa	1
Pawnee	1
Phillips	1
Pottawatomie	2
Pratt	1
Rawlins	1
Reno	1
Republic	1
Rice	1
Riley	2
Rooks	1
Rush	1
Russell	1
Saline	1
Scott	1
Sedgwick	4
Seward	1
Shawnee	2
Sheridan	1
Sherman	1
Smith	1
Stafford	1
Stanton	1
Stevens	1
Sumner	4
Thomas	1
Trego	1
Wabaunsee	1
Wallace	1
Washington	1
Wichita	1
Wilson	2
Woodson	2
Wyandotte	3

Congressional District 1

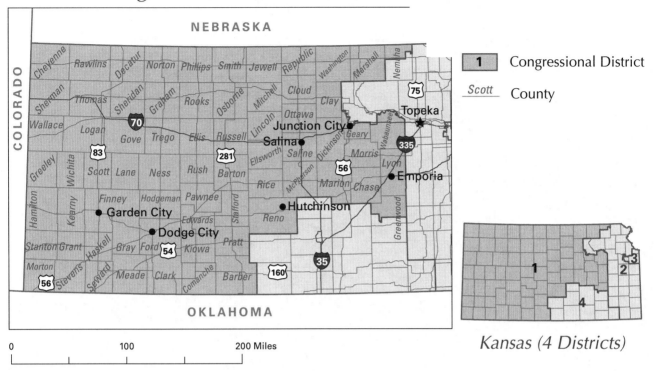

Kansas (4 Districts)

Congressional District 2

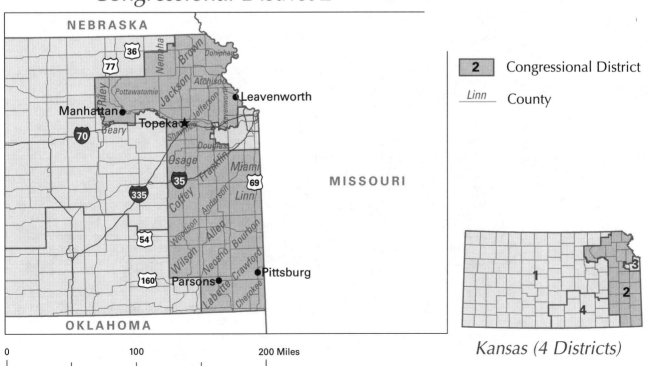

Kansas (4 Districts)

Congressional District 3

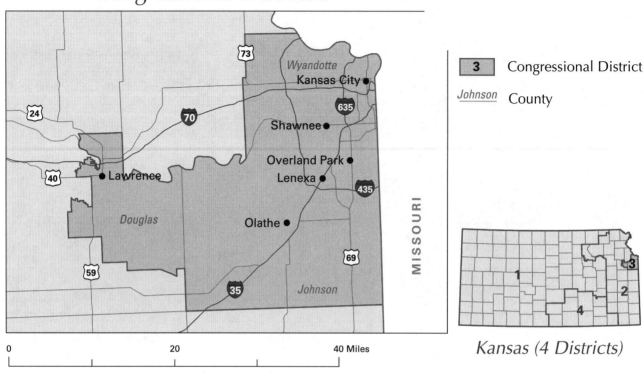

3 Congressional District
Johnson County

Kansas (4 Districts)

Congressional District 4

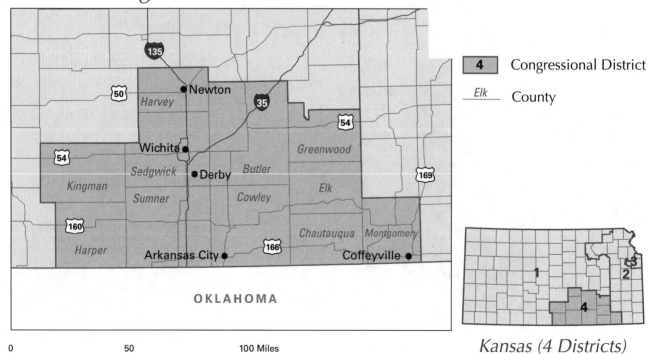

4 Congressional District
Elk County

Kansas (4 Districts)

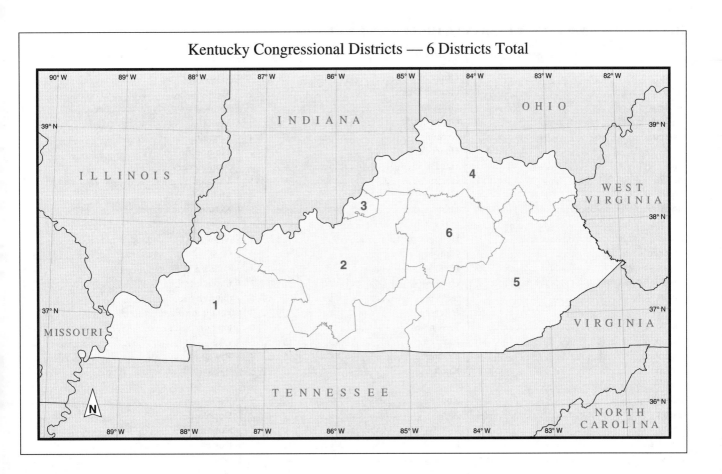

Kentucky Congressional Districts — 6 Districts Total

KENTUCKY—109th CONGRESSIONAL DISTRICTS BY COUNTIES

County	Congressional District	County	Congressional District	County	Congressional District
Adair	1	Grant	4	Mason	4
Allen	1	Graves	1	Meade	2
Anderson	6	Grayson	2	Menifee	5
Ballard	1	Green	2	Mercer	6
Barren	2	Greenup	4	Metcalfe	1
Bath	4, 5	Hancock	2	Monroe	1
Bell	5	Hardin	2	Montgomery	6
Boone	4	Harlan	5	Morgan	5
Bourbon	6	Harrison	4	Muhlenberg	1
Boyd	4	Hart	2	Nelson	2
Boyle	6	Henderson	1	Nicholas	4
Bracken	4	Henry	4	Ohio	1, 2
Breathitt	5	Hickman	1	Oldham	4
Breckinridge	2	Hopkins	1	Owen	4
Bullitt	2	Jackson	5	Owsley	5
Butler	1	Jefferson	2, 3	Pendleton	4
Caldwell	1	Jessamine	6	Perry	5
Calloway	1	Johnson	5	Pike	5
Campbell	4	Kenton	4	Powell	6
Carlisle	1	Knott	5	Pulaski	5
Carroll	4	Knox	5	Robertson	4
Carter	4	Larue	2	Rockcastle	5
Casey	1	Laurel	5	Rowan	5
Christian	1	Lawrence	5	Russell	1
Clark	6	Lee	5	Scott	4, 6
Clay	5	Leslie	5	Shelby	2
Clinton	1	Letcher	5	Simpson	1
Crittenden	1	Lewis	4	Spencer	2
Cumberland	1	Lincoln	1, 6	Taylor	2
Daviess	2	Livingston	1	Todd	1
Edmonson	2	Logan	1	Trigg	1
Elliott	4	Lyon	1	Trimble	4
Estill	6	McCracken	1	Union	1
Fayette	6	McCreary	5	Warren	2
Fleming	4	McLean	1	Washington	2
Floyd	5	Madison	6	Wayne	5
Franklin	6	Magoffin	5	Webster	1
Fulton	1	Marion	2	Whitley	5
Gallatin	4	Marshall	1	Wolfe	5
Garrard	6	Martin	5	Woodford	6

Congressional District 1

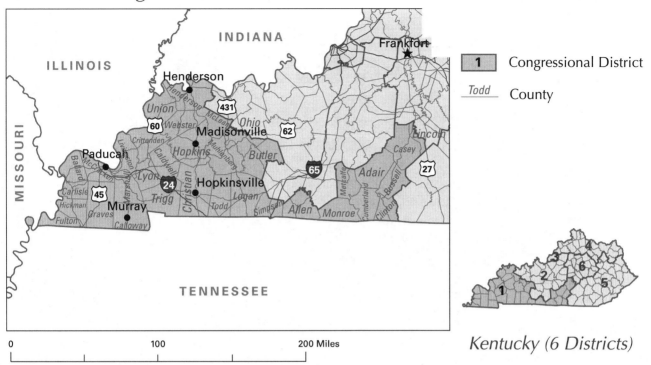

1	Congressional District
Todd	County

Kentucky (6 Districts)

Congressional District 2

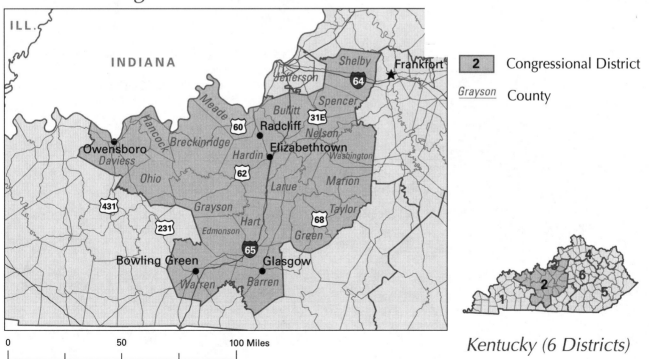

2	Congressional District
Grayson	County

Kentucky (6 Districts)

Congressional District 3

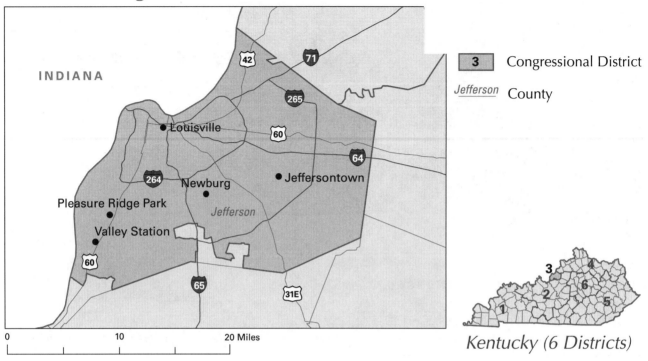

Kentucky (6 Districts)

Congressional District 4

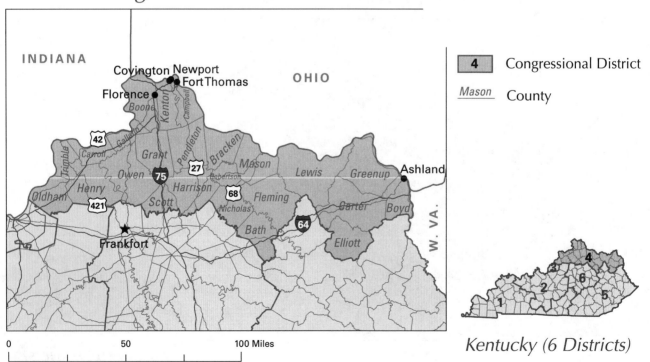

Kentucky (6 Districts)

Congressional District 5

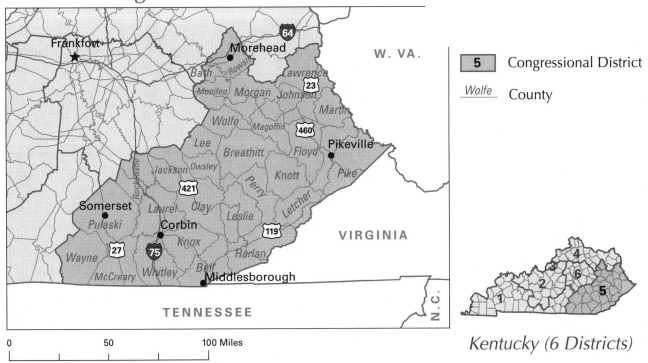

Kentucky (6 Districts)

Congressional District 6

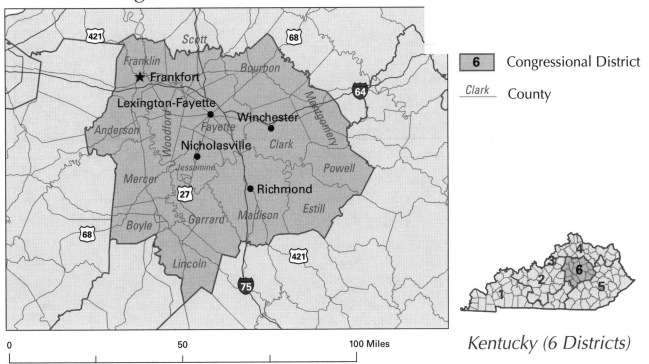

Kentucky (6 Districts)

Louisiana Congressional Districts — 7 Districts Total

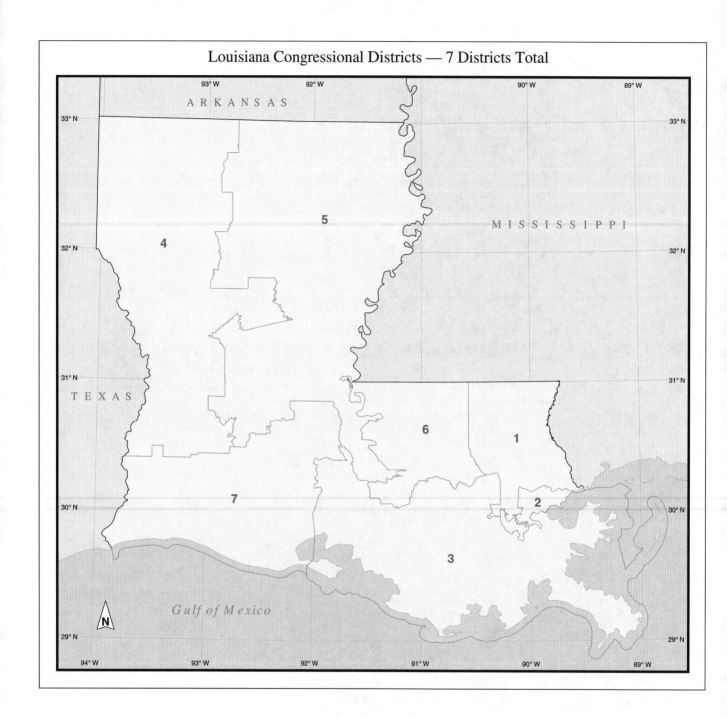

LOUISIANA—109th CONGRESSIONAL DISTRICTS BY COUNTIES

County	Congressional District
Acadia	7
Allen	4, 5
Ascension	3, 6
Assumption	3
Avoyelles	5
Beauregard	4
Bienville	4
Bossier	4
Caddo	4
Calcasieu	7
Caldwell	5
Cameron	7
Catahoula	5
Claiborne	4
Concordia	5
De Soto	4
East Baton Rouge	6
East Carroll	5
East Feliciana	6
Evangeline	5, 7
Franklin	5
Grant	4

County	Congressional District
Iberia	3
Iberville	5, 6
Jackson	5
Jefferson	1–3
Jefferson Davis	7
Lafayette	7
Lafourche	3
La Salle	5
Lincoln	5
Livingston	6
Madison	5
Morehouse	5
Natchitoches	4
Orleans	1, 2
Ouachita	5
Plaquemines	3
Pointe Coupee	5, 6
Rapides	5
Red River	4
Richland	5
Sabine	4
St. Bernard	3

County	Congressional District
St. Charles	1, 3
St. Helena	6
St. James	3
St. John the Baptist	3
St. Landry	7
St. Martin	3
St. Mary	3
St. Tammany	1
Tangipahoa	1
Tensas	5
Terrebonne	3
Union	5
Vermilion	7
Vernon	4
Washington	1
Webster	4
West Baton Rouge	6
West Carroll	5
West Feliciana	6
Winn	5

Congressional District 1

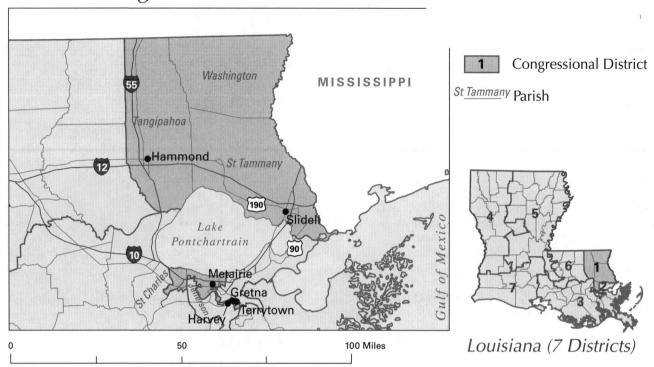

Louisiana (7 Districts)

Congressional District 2

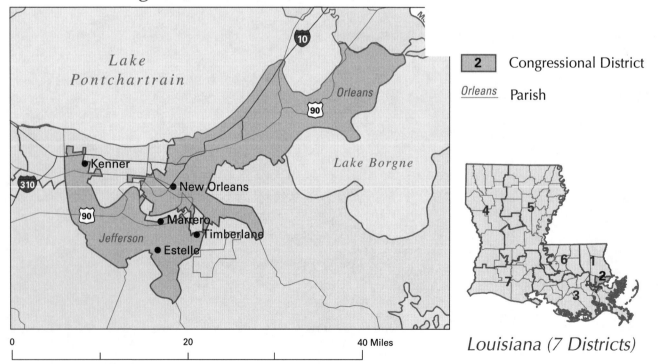

Louisiana (7 Districts)

Congressional District 3

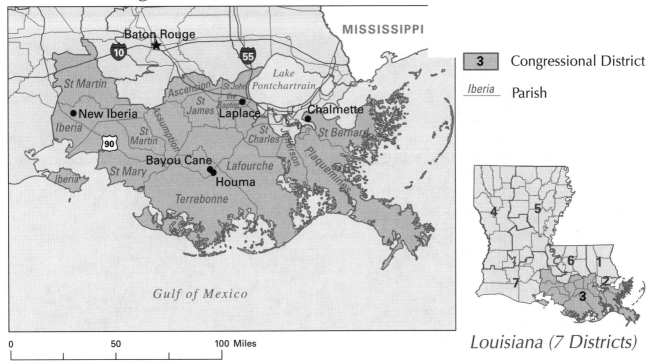

3 Congressional District

Iberia Parish

Louisiana (7 Districts)

Congressional District 4

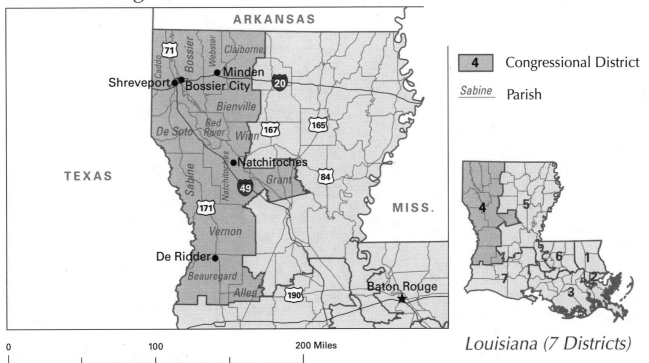

4 Congressional District

Sabine Parish

Louisiana (7 Districts)

Congressional District 5

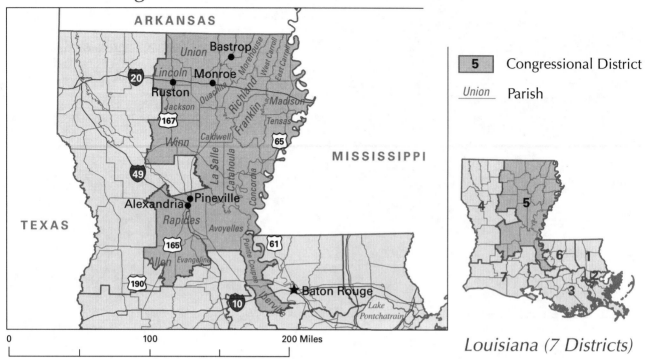

Louisiana (7 Districts)

Congressional District 6

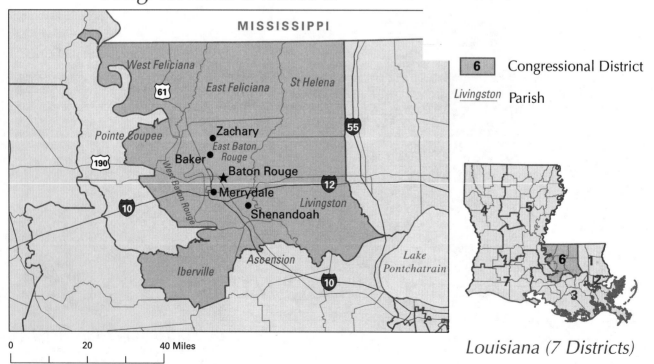

Louisiana (7 Districts)

Congressional District 7

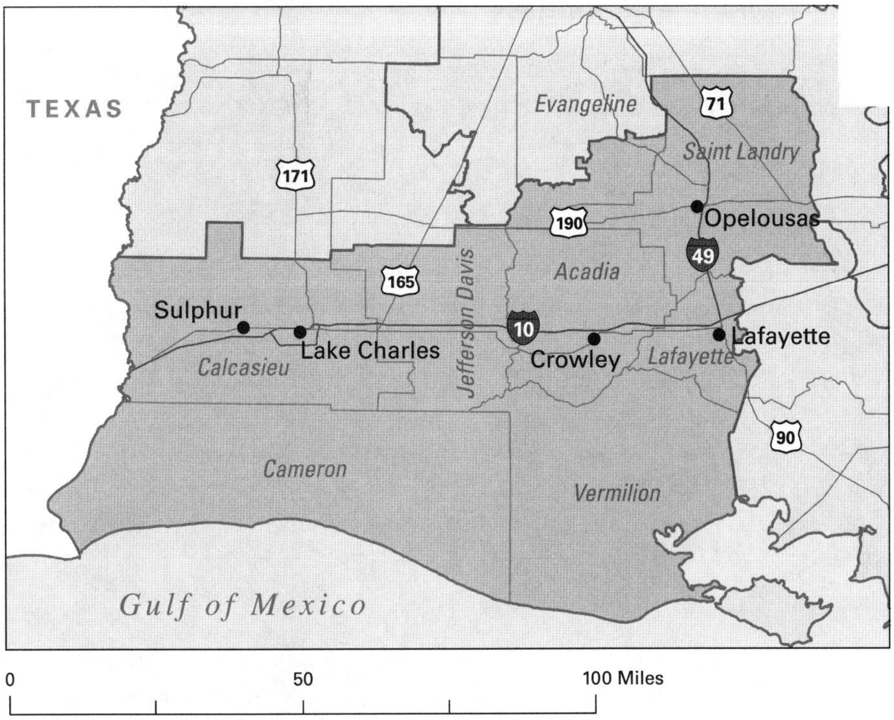

TEXAS

Evangeline

71

Saint Landry

171

Opelousas

190

49

Acadia

165

Sulphur

Jefferson Davis

10

Lafayette

Lake Charles

Crowley

Lafayette

Calcasieu

90

Cameron

Vermilion

Gulf of Mexico

0   50   100 Miles

7 Congressional District

Cameron Parish

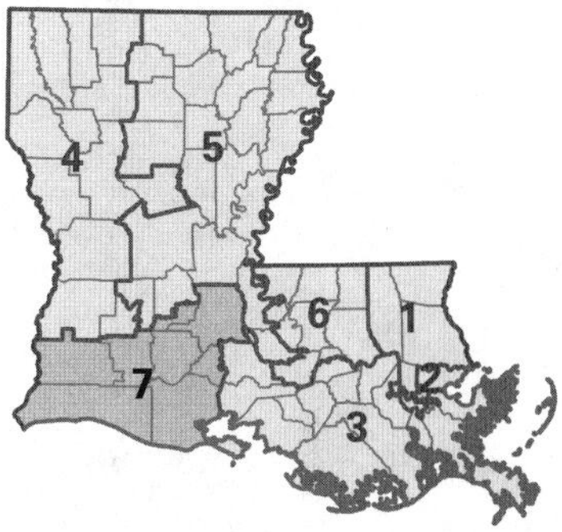

4

5

7

6

1

2

3

Louisiana (7 Districts)

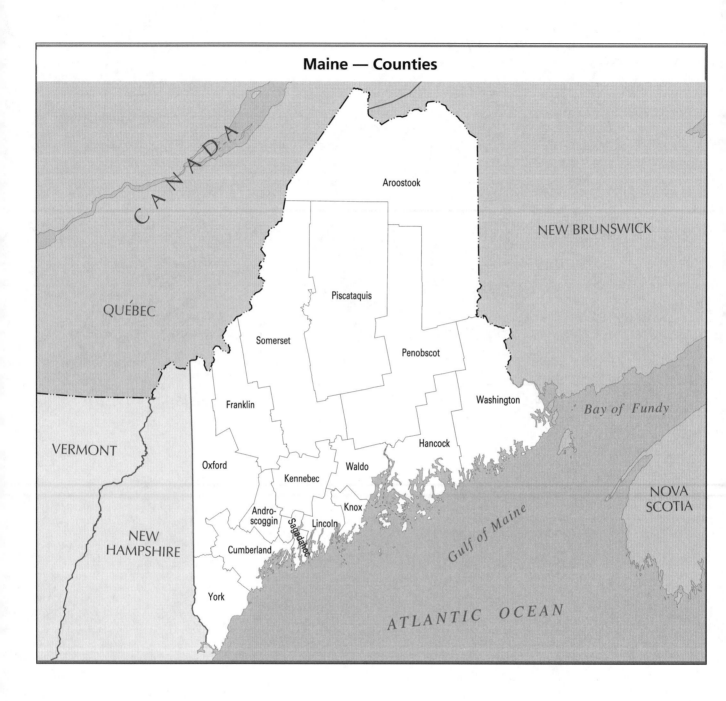

Maine — Counties

MAINE—109th CONGRESSIONAL DISTRICTS BY COUNTIES

County	Congressional District
Androscoggin	2
Aroostook	2
Cumberland	1
Franklin	2
Hancock	2
Kennebec	1, 2
Knox	1
Lincoln	1
Oxford	2

County	Congressional District
Penobscot	2
Piscataquis	2
Sagadahoc	1
Somerset	2
Waldo	2
Washington	2
York	1

Congressional District 1

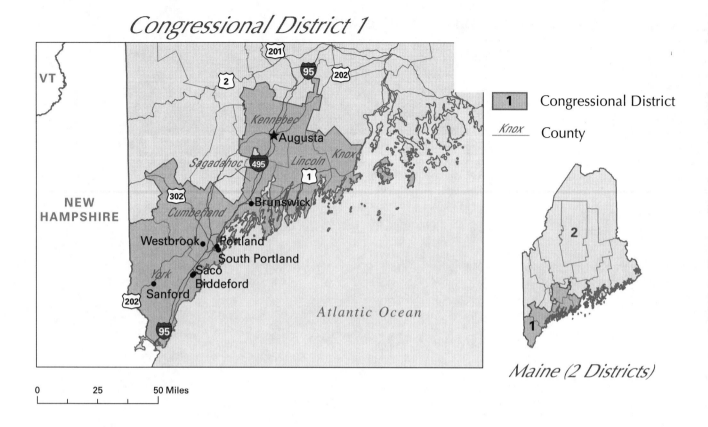

Congressional District 2

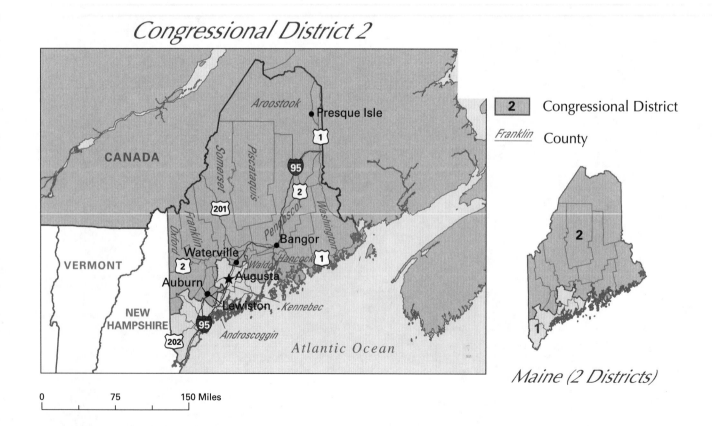

Maine 108th Congressional Districts — 2 Districts Total

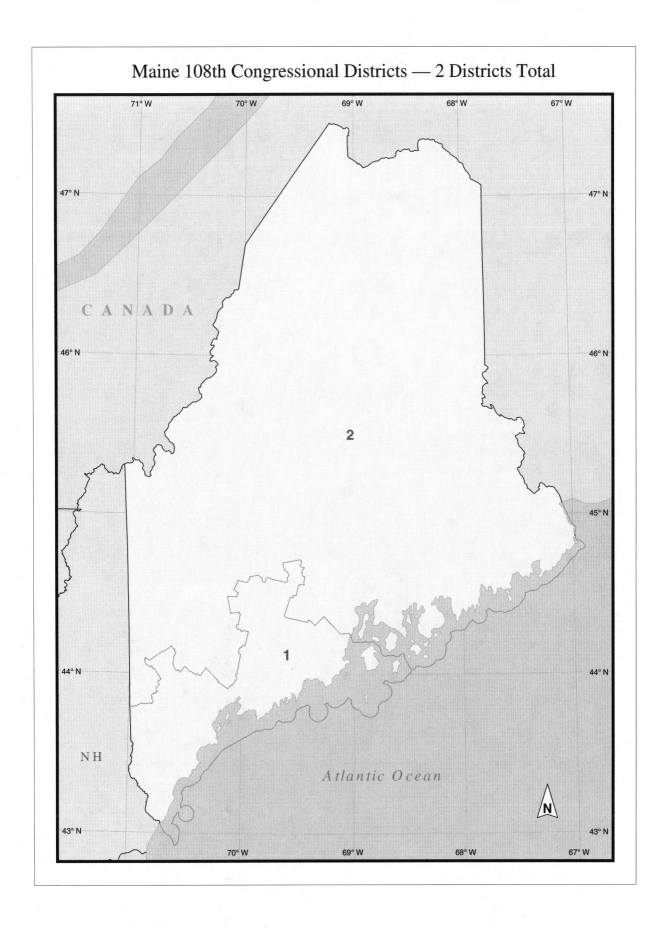

MAINE—108th CONGRESSIONAL DISTRICTS BY COUNTIES

County	Congressional District
Androscoggin	2
Aroostook	2
Cumberland	1, 2
Franklin	2
Hancock	2
Kennebec	1, 2
Knox	1
Lincoln	1
Oxford	2

County	Congressional District
Penobscot	2
Piscataquis	2
Sagadahoc	1
Somerset	2
Waldo	2
Washington	2
York	1

Congressional District 1

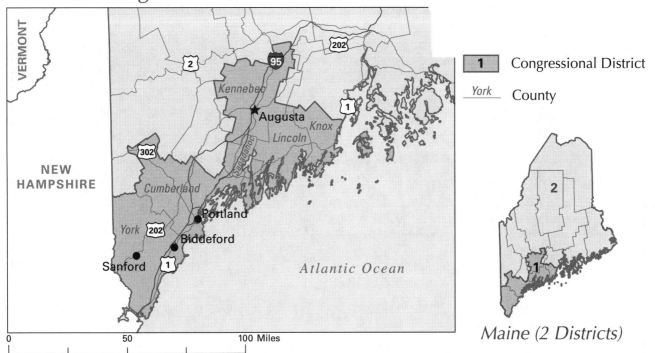

1	Congressional District
York	County

Maine (2 Districts)

Congressional District 2

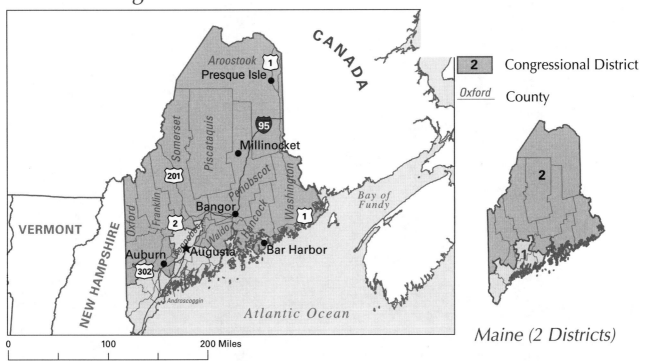

2	Congressional District
Oxford	County

Maine (2 Districts)

Maryland Congressional Districts — 8 Districts Total

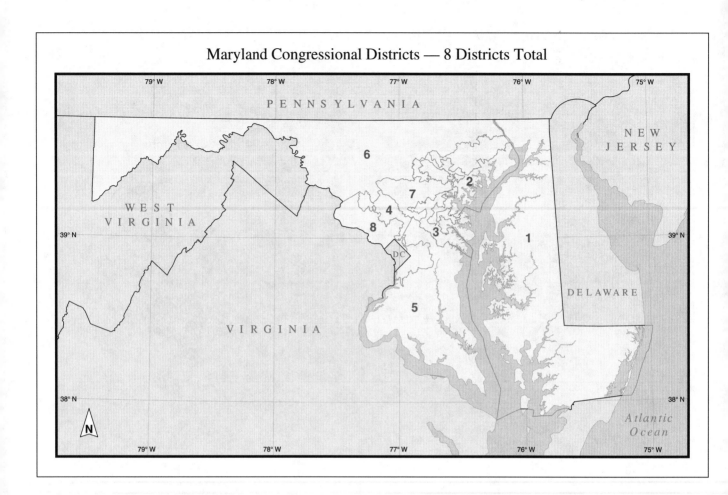

MARYLAND—109th CONGRESSIONAL DISTRICTS BY COUNTIES AND INDEPENDENT CITIES

County	Congressional District
Allegany	6
Anne Arundel	1–3, 5
Baltimore	1–3, 6, 7
Calvert	5
Caroline	1
Carroll	6
Cecil	1
Charles	5
Dorchester	1
Frederick	6
Garrett	6

County	Congressional District
Harford	1, 2, 6
Howard	3, 7
Kent	1
Montgomery	4, 6, 8
Prince George's	4, 5, 8
Queen Anne's	1
St. Mary's	5
Somerset	1
Talbot	1
Washington	6
Wicomico	1

County	Congressional District
Worcester	1
Baltimore city	2, 3, 7

Congressional District 1

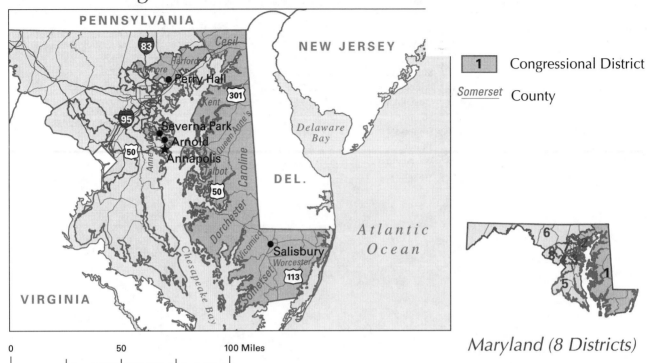

1 Congressional District
Somerset County

Maryland (8 Districts)

Congressional District 2

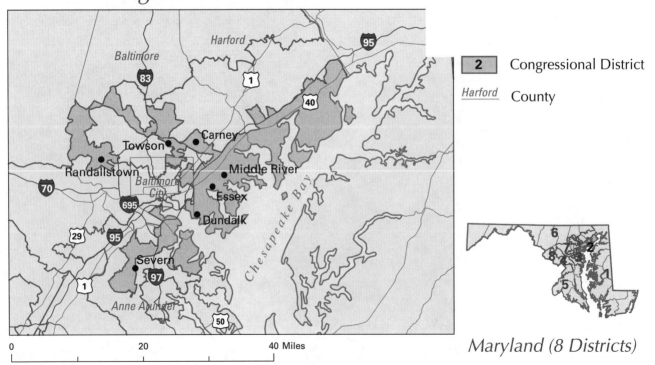

2 Congressional District
Harford County

Maryland (8 Districts)

Congressional District 3

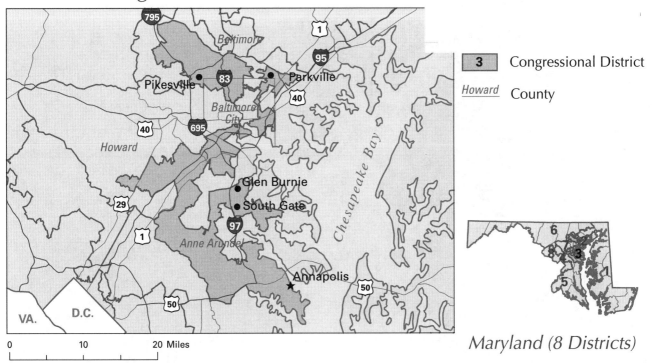

3 Congressional District

Howard County

Maryland (8 Districts)

Congressional District 4

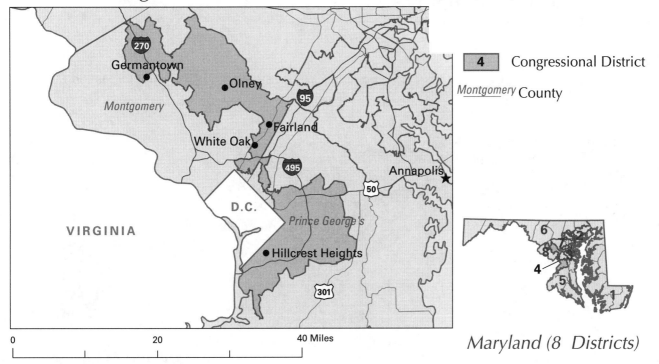

4 Congressional District

Montgomery County

Maryland (8 Districts)

Congressional District 5

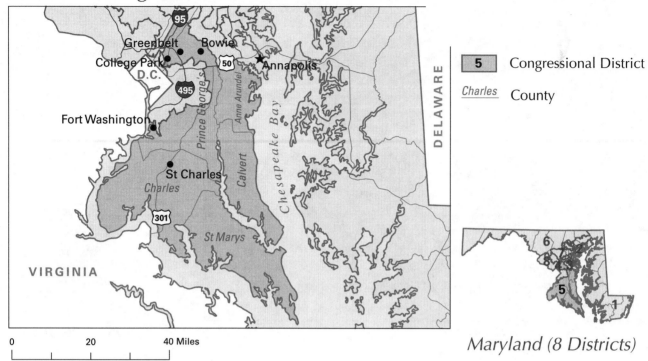

| 5 | Congressional District |
| *Charles* | County |

Maryland (8 Districts)

Congressional District 6

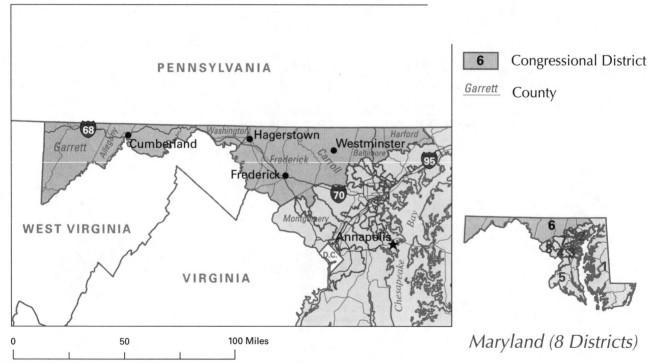

| 6 | Congressional District |
| *Garrett* | County |

Maryland (8 Districts)

Congressional District 7

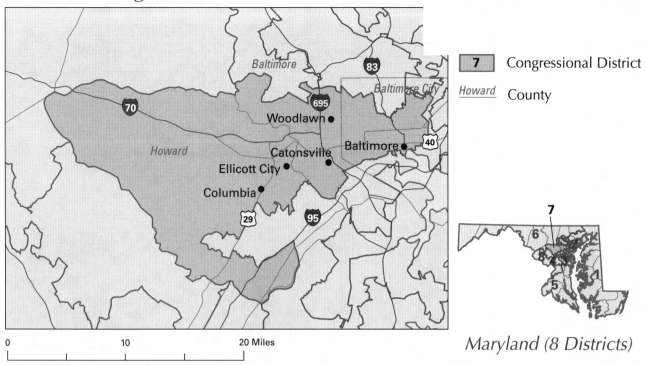

7 Congressional District

Howard County

7

Maryland (8 Districts)

Congressional District 8

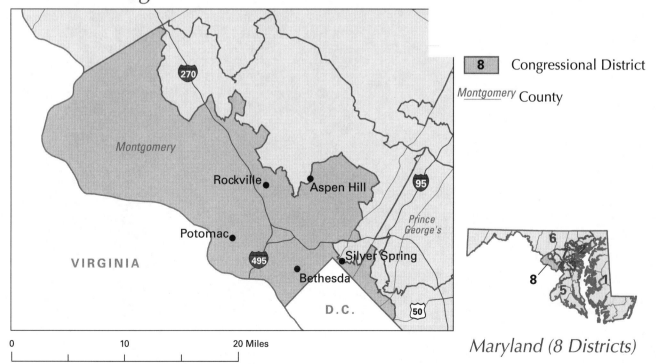

8 Congressional District

Montgomery County

8

Maryland (8 Districts)

Massachusetts Congressional Districts — 10 Districts Total

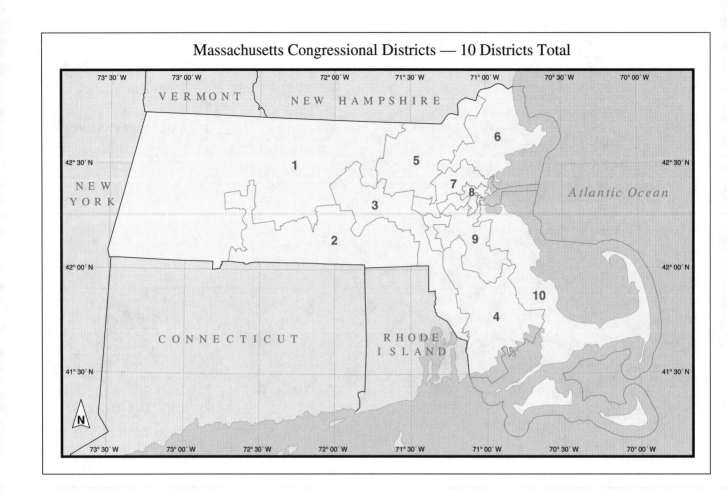

MASSACHUSETTS—109th CONGRESSIONAL DISTRICTS BY COUNTIES

County	Congressional District
Barnstable	10
Berkshire	1
Bristol	3, 4, 9, 10
Dukes	10
Essex	5, 6
Franklin	1
Hampden	1, 2
Hampshire	1, 2

County	Congressional District
Middlesex	1, 3–8
Nantucket	10
Norfolk	2–4, 9, 10
Plymouth	4, 9, 10
Suffolk	7–9
Worcester	1–3, 5

Congressional District 1

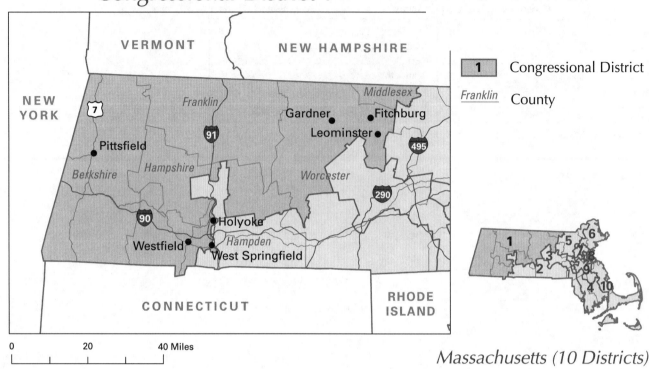

Congressional District 2

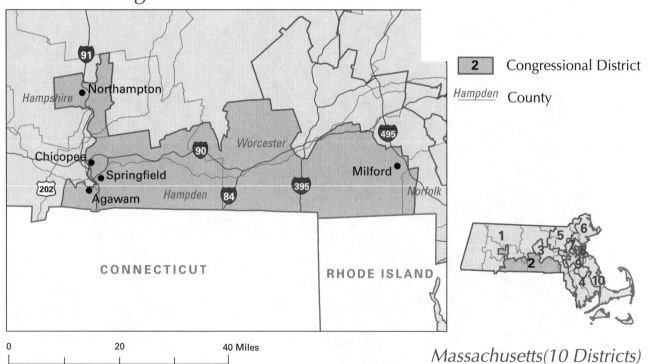

Congressional District 3

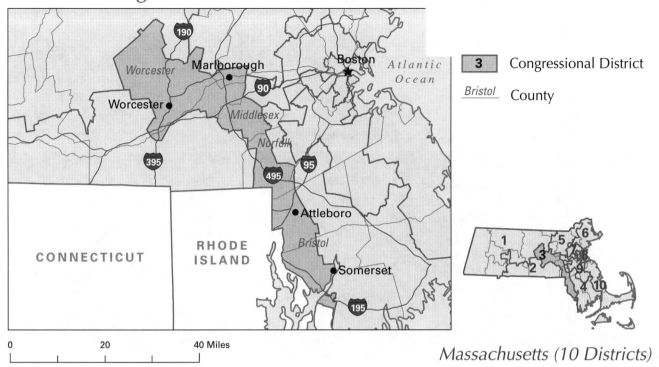

3 Congressional District

Bristol County

Massachusetts (10 Districts)

Congressional District 4

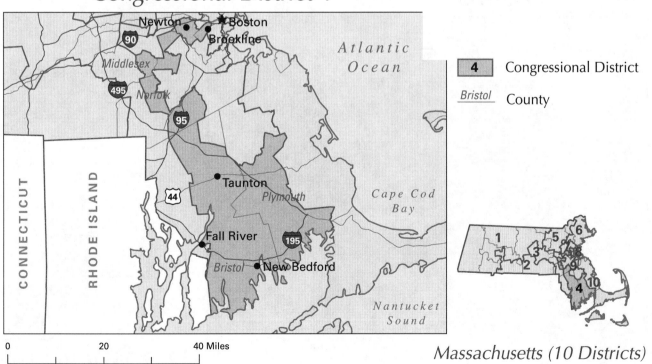

4 Congressional District

Bristol County

Massachusetts (10 Districts)

Congressional District 5

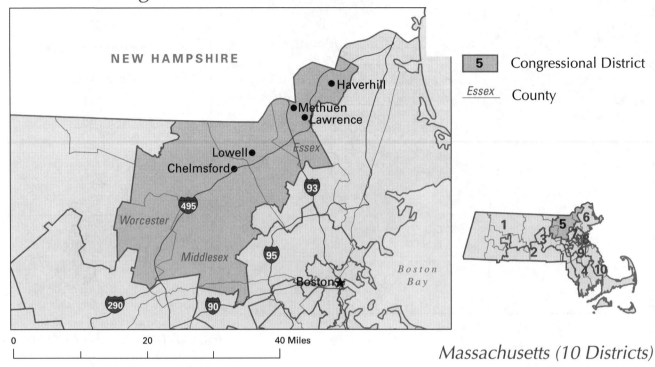

Massachusetts (10 Districts)

Congressional District 6

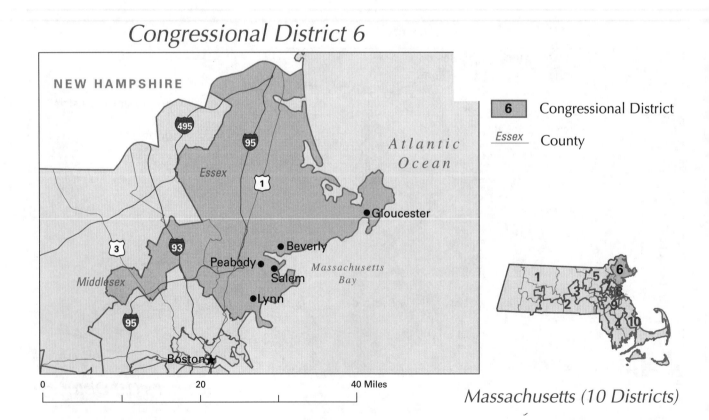

Massachusetts (10 Districts)

Congressional District 7

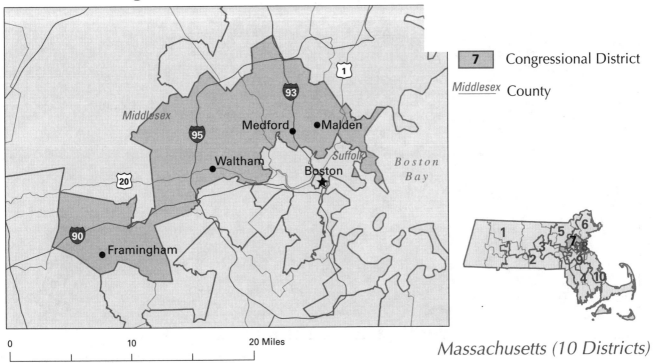

7   Congressional District

Middlesex   County

0   10   20 Miles

Massachusetts (10 Districts)

Congressional District 8

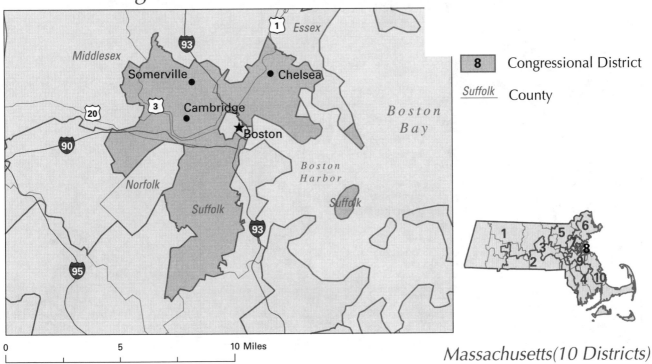

8   Congressional District

Suffolk   County

0   5   10 Miles

Massachusetts(10 Districts)

Congressional District 9

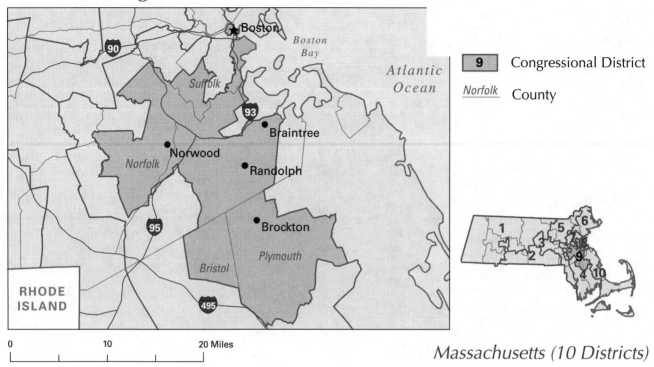

Massachusetts (10 Districts)

Congressional District 10

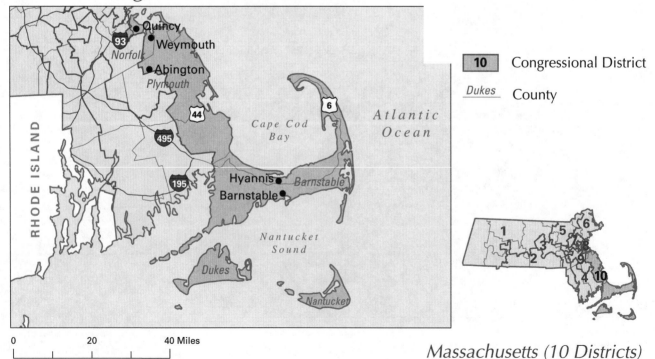

Massachusetts (10 Districts)

Michigan Congressional Districts — 15 Districts Total

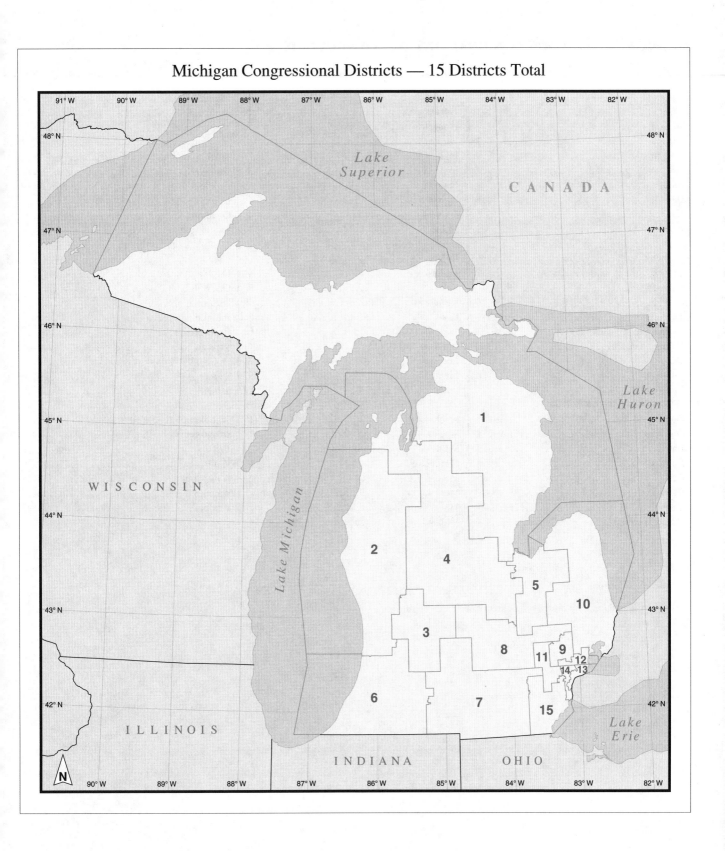

MICHIGAN—109th CONGRESSIONAL DISTRICTS BY COUNTIES

County	Congressional District
Alcona	1
Alger	1
Allegan	2, 6
Alpena	1
Antrim	1
Arenac	1
Baraga	1
Barry	3
Bay	1, 5
Benzie	2
Berrien	6
Branch	7
Calhoun	6, 7
Cass	6
Charlevoix	1
Cheboygan	1
Chippewa	1
Clare	4
Clinton	8
Crawford	1
Delta	1
Dickinson	1
Eaton	7
Emmet	1
Genesee	5
Gladwin	1
Gogebic	1
Grand Traverse	4

County	Congressional District
Gratiot	4
Hillsdale	7
Houghton	1
Huron	10
Ingham	8
Ionia	3
Iosco	1
Iron	1
Isabella	4
Jackson	7
Kalamazoo	6
Kalkaska	4
Kent	2, 3
Keweenaw	1
Lake	2
Lapeer	10
Leelanau	4
Lenawee	7
Livingston	8
Luce	1
Mackinac	1
Macomb	10, 12
Manistee	2
Marquette	1
Mason	2
Mecosta	4
Menominee	1
Midland	4

County	Congressional District
Missaukee	4
Monroe	15
Montcalm	4
Montmorency	1
Muskegon	2
Newaygo	2
Oakland	8, 9, 11, 12
Oceana	2
Ogemaw	1
Ontonagon	1
Osceola	4
Oscoda	1
Otsego	1
Ottawa	2
Presque Isle	1
Roscommon	4
Saginaw	4, 5
St. Clair	10
St. Joseph	6
Sanilac	10
Schoolcraft	1
Shiawassee	4, 8
Tuscola	5
Van Buren	6
Washtenaw	7, 15
Wayne	11, 13–15
Wexford	2

Congressional District 1

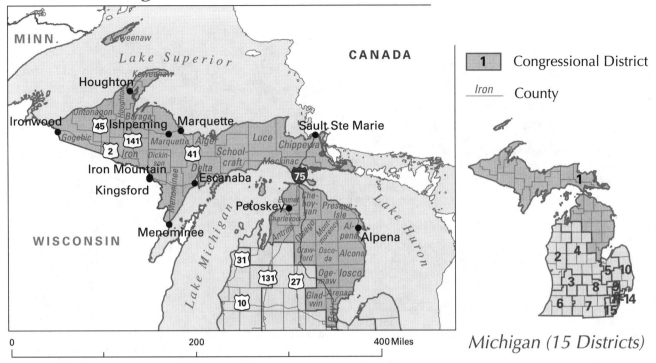

Michigan (15 Districts)

Congressional District 2

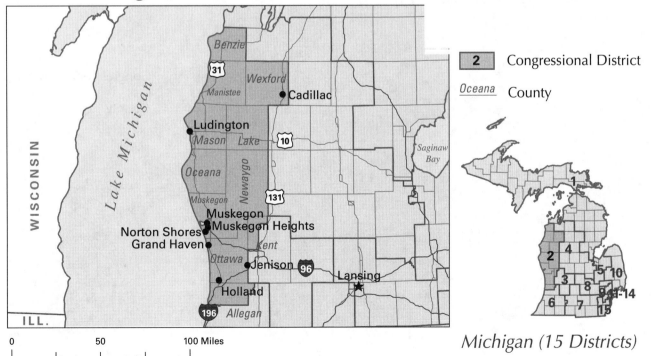

Michigan (15 Districts)

Congressional District 3

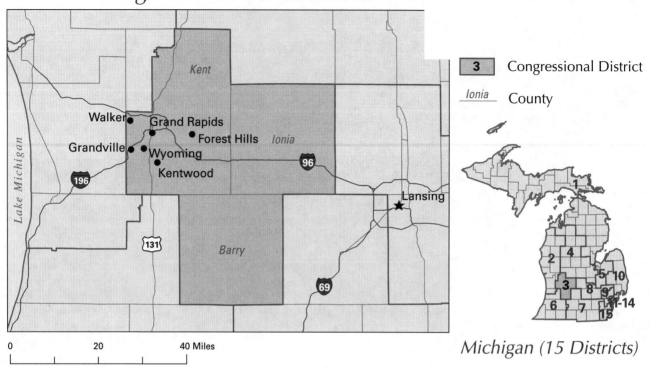

Michigan (15 Districts)

Congressional District 4

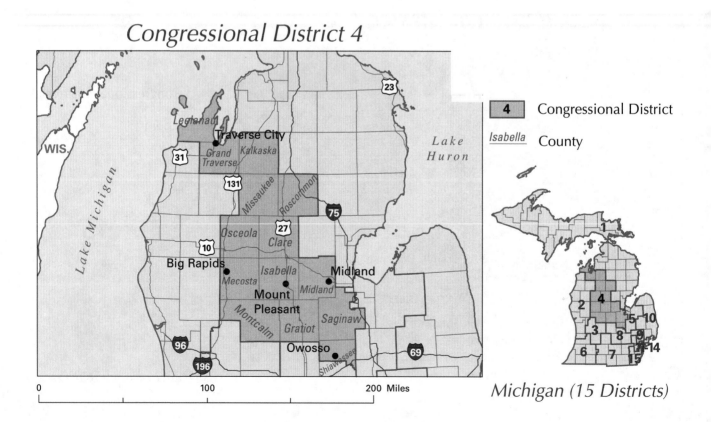

Michigan (15 Districts)

Congressional District 5

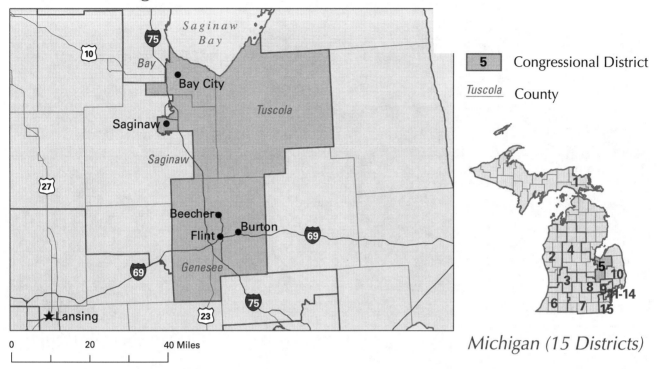

5	Congressional District
Tuscola	County

Michigan (15 Districts)

Congressional District 6

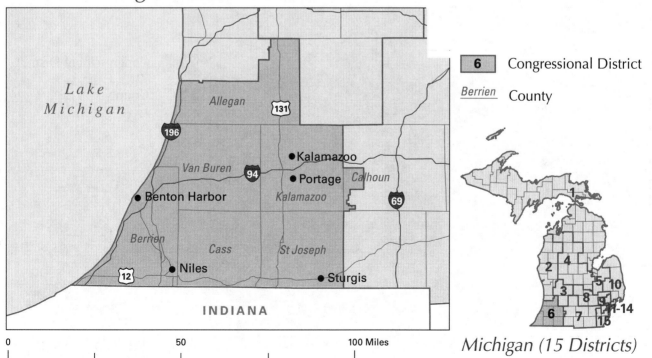

6	Congressional District
Berrien	County

Michigan (15 Districts)

Congressional District 7

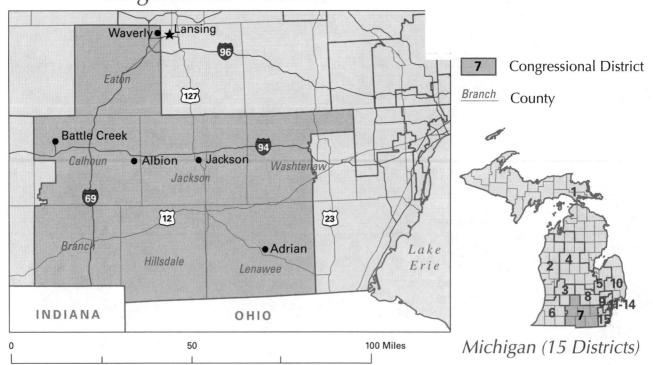

7 Congressional District
Branch County

Michigan (15 Districts)

Congressional District 8

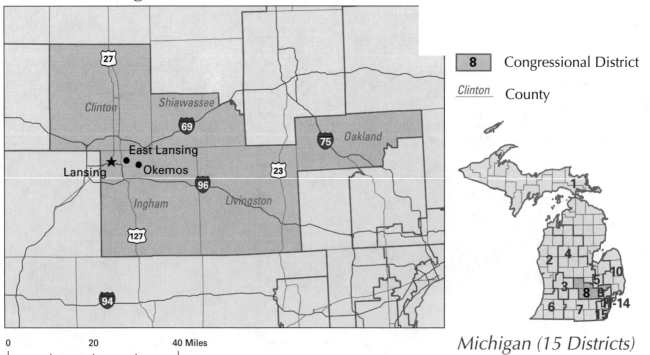

8 Congressional District
Clinton County

Michigan (15 Districts)

Congressional District 9

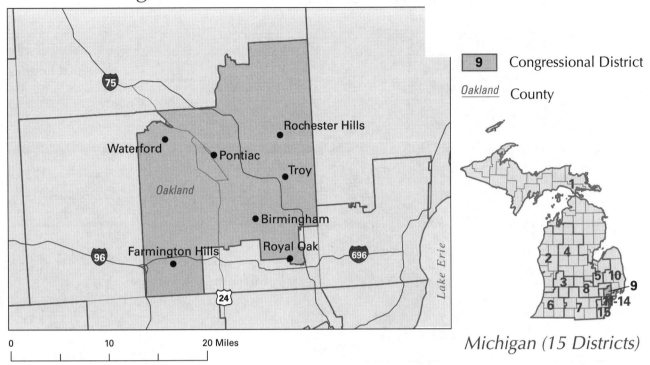

| 9 | Congressional District |
| *Oakland* | County |

Michigan (15 Districts)

Congressional District 10

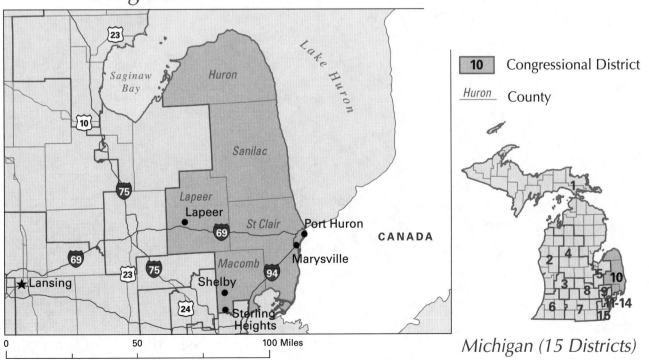

| 10 | Congressional District |
| *Huron* | County |

Michigan (15 Districts)

Congressional District 11

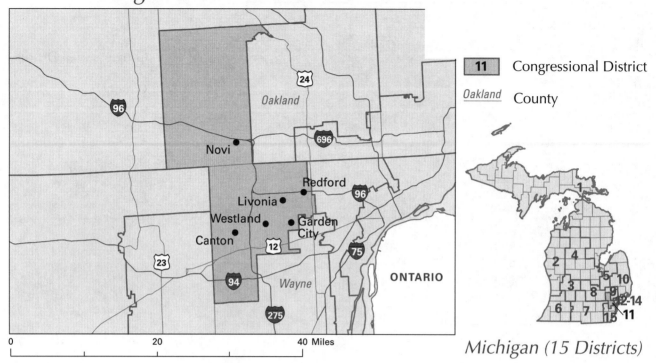

Michigan (15 Districts)

Congressional District 12

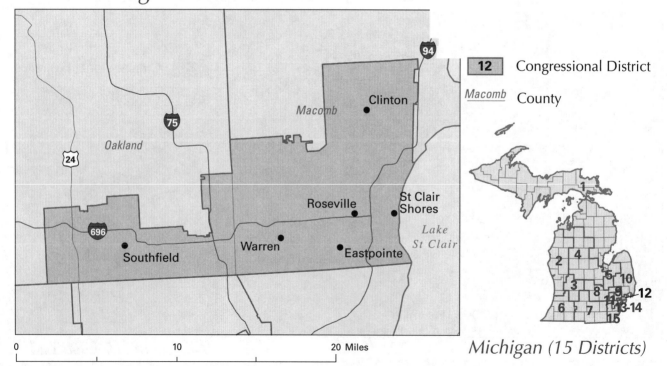

Michigan (15 Districts)

Congressional District 13

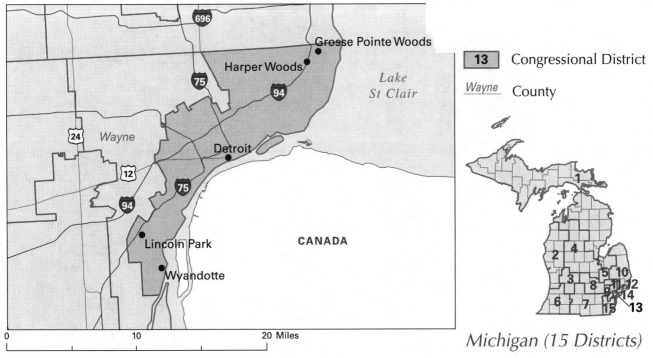

| 13 | Congressional District |
| *Wayne* | County |

Michigan (15 Districts)

Congressional District 14

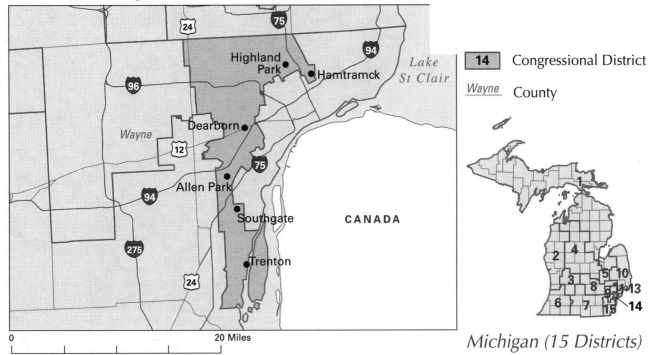

| 14 | Congressional District |
| *Wayne* | County |

Michigan (15 Districts)

Congressional District 15

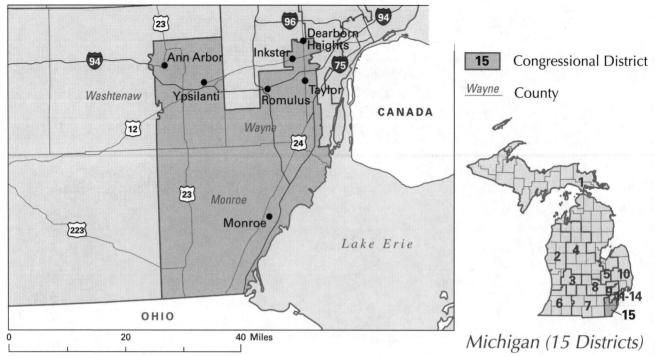

Michigan (15 Districts)

Minnesota Congressional Districts — 8 Districts Total

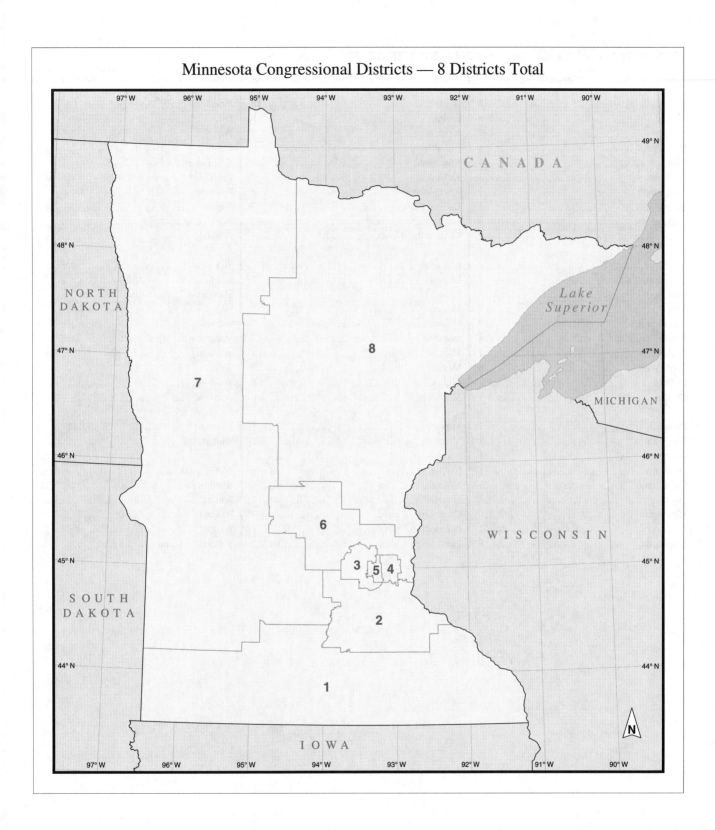

MINNESOTA—109th CONGRESSIONAL DISTRICTS BY COUNTIES

County	Congressional District	County	Congressional District	County	Congressional District
Aitkin	8	Isanti	8	Pipestone	1
Anoka	3, 5, 6	Itasca	8	Polk	7
Becker	7	Jackson	1	Pope	7
Beltrami	7, 8	Kanabec	8	Ramsey	4–6
Benton	6	Kandiyohi	7	Red Lake	7
Big Stone	7	Kittson	7	Redwood	7
Blue Earth	1	Koochiching	8	Renville	7
Brown	1	Lac qui Parle	7	Rice	2
Carlton	8	Lake	8	Rock	1
Carver	2	Lake of the Woods	7	Roseau	7
Cass	8	Le Sueur	1, 2	St. Louis	8
Chippewa	7	Lincoln	7	Scott	2
Chisago	8	Lyon	7	Sherburne	6
Clay	7	McLeod	7	Sibley	7
Clearwater	7	Mahnomen	7	Stearns	6, 7
Cook	8	Marshall	7	Steele	1
Cottonwood	1	Martin	1	Stevens	7
Crow Wing	8	Meeker	7	Swift	7
Dakota	2, 4	Mille Lacs	8	Todd	7
Dodge	1	Morrison	8	Traverse	7
Douglas	7	Mower	1	Wabasha	1
Faribault	1	Murray	1	Wadena	8
Fillmore	1	Nicollet	1	Waseca	1
Freeborn	1	Nobles	1	Washington	2, 4, 6
Goodhue	2	Norman	7	Watonwan	1
Grant	7	Olmsted	1	Wilkin	7
Hennepin	2, 3, 5, 6	Otter Tail	7	Winona	1
Houston	1	Pennington	7	Wright	6
Hubbard	8	Pine	8	Yellow Medicine	7

Congressional District 1

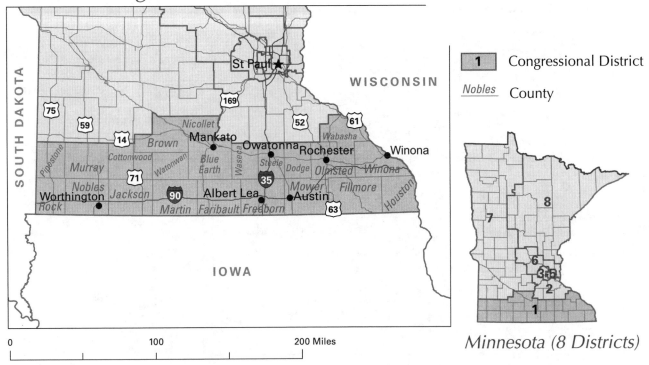

| 1 | Congressional District |
| *Nobles* | County |

Minnesota (8 Districts)

Congressional District 2

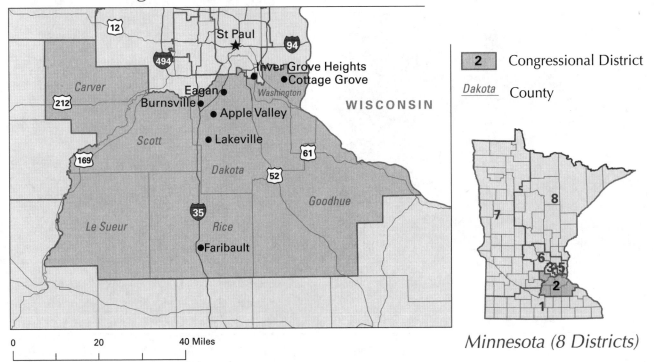

| 2 | Congressional District |
| *Dakota* | County |

Minnesota (8 Districts)

Congressional District 3

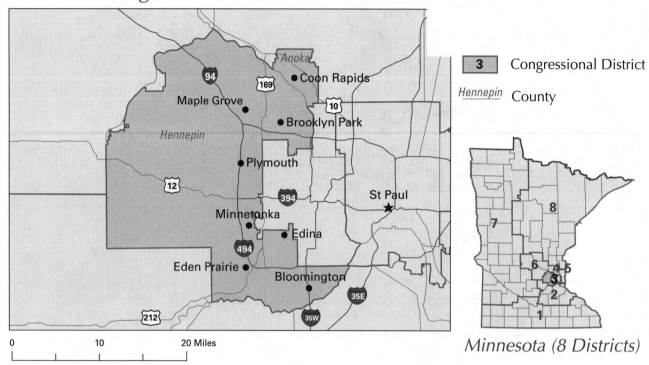

3 Congressional District

Hennepin County

Minnesota (8 Districts)

Congressional District 4

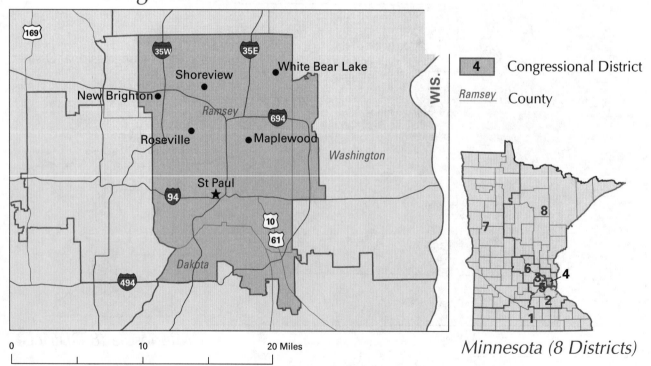

4 Congressional District

Ramsey County

Minnesota (8 Districts)

Congressional District 5

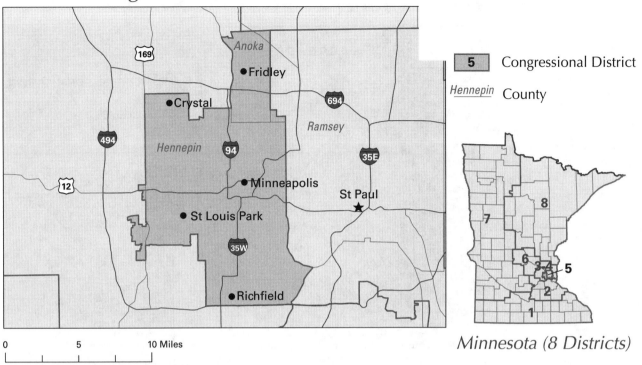

5 Congressional District
Hennepin County

Minnesota (8 Districts)

Congressional District 6

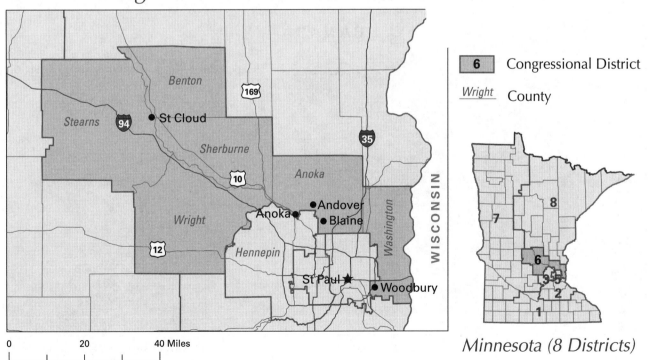

6 Congressional District
Wright County

Minnesota (8 Districts)

Congressional District 7

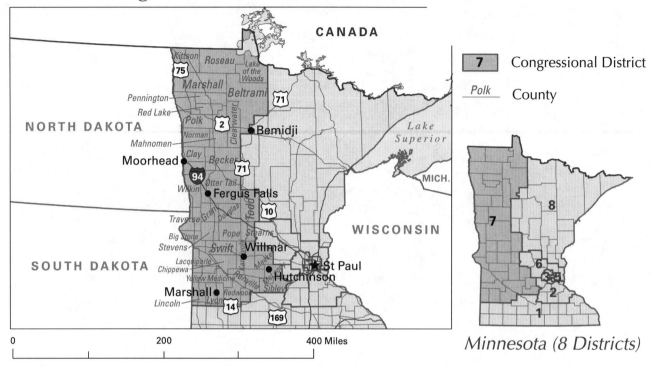

Minnesota (8 Districts)

Congressional District 8

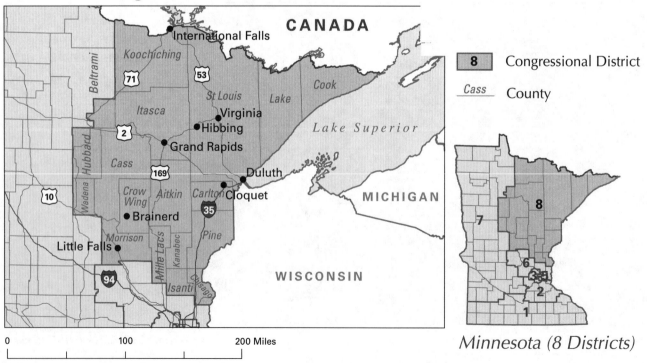

Minnesota (8 Districts)

Mississippi Congressional Districts — 4 Districts Total

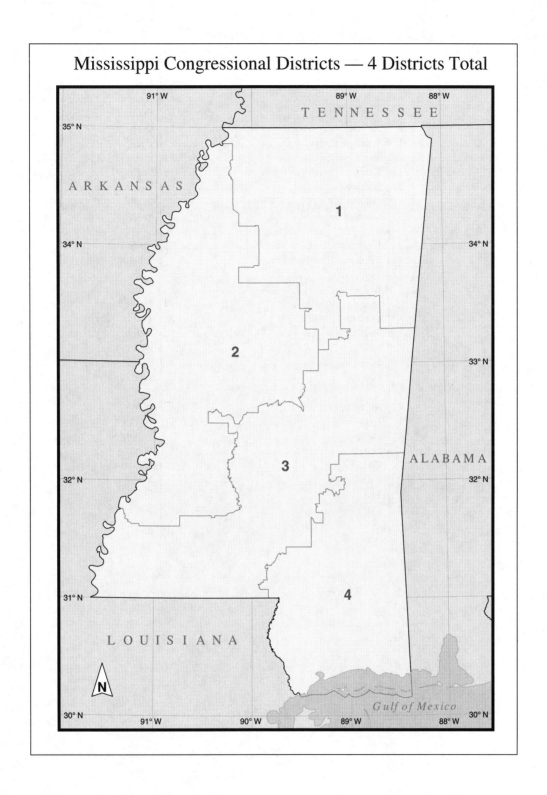

MISSISSIPPI—109th CONGRESSIONAL DISTRICTS BY COUNTIES

County	Congressional District	County	Congressional District	County	Congressional District
Adams	3	Itawamba	1	Pike	3
Alcorn	1	Jackson	4	Pontotoc	1
Amite	3	Jasper	3, 4	Prentiss	1
Attala	2	Jefferson	2	Quitman	2
Benton	1	Jefferson Davis	3	Rankin	3
Bolivar	2	Jones	3, 4	Scott	3
Calhoun	1	Kemper	3	Sharkey	2
Carroll	2	Lafayette	1	Simpson	3
Chickasaw	1	Lamar	4	Smith	3
Choctaw	1	Lauderdale	3	Stone	4
Claiborne	2	Lawrence	3	Sunflower	2
Clarke	4	Leake	2, 3	Tallahatchie	2
Clay	1	Lee	1	Tate	1
Coahoma	2	Leflore	2	Tippah	1
Copiah	2	Lincoln	3	Tishomingo	1
Covington	3	Lowndes	1	Tunica	2
DeSoto	1	Madison	2, 3	Union	1
Forrest	4	Marion	3, 4	Walthall	3
Franklin	3	Marshall	1	Warren	2
George	4	Monroe	1	Washington	2
Greene	4	Montgomery	2	Wayne	4
Grenada	1	Neshoba	3	Webster	1, 3
Hancock	4	Newton	3	Wilkinson	3
Harrison	4	Noxubee	3	Winston	1, 3
Hinds	2, 3	Oktibbeha	3	Yalobusha	1
Holmes	2	Panola	1	Yazoo	2
Humphreys	2	Pearl River	4		
Issaquena	2	Perry	4		

Congressional District 1

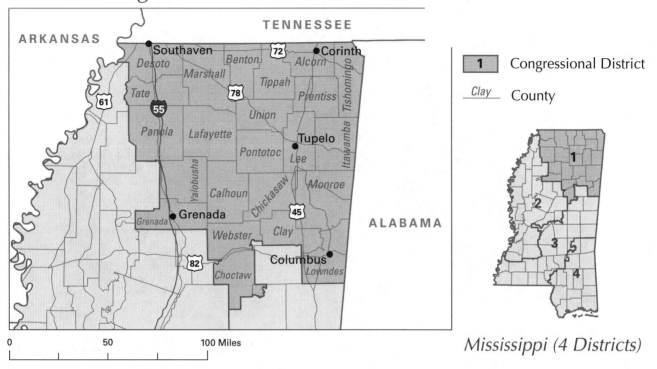

Mississippi (4 Districts)

Congressional District 2

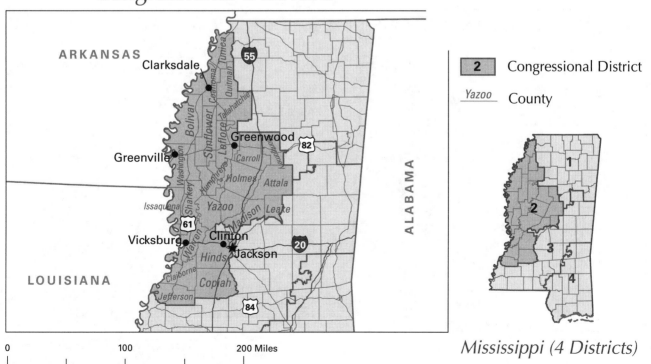

Mississippi (4 Districts)

Congressional District 3

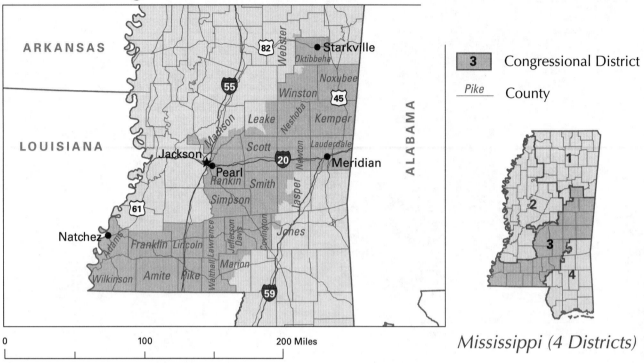

Mississippi (4 Districts)

Congressional District 4

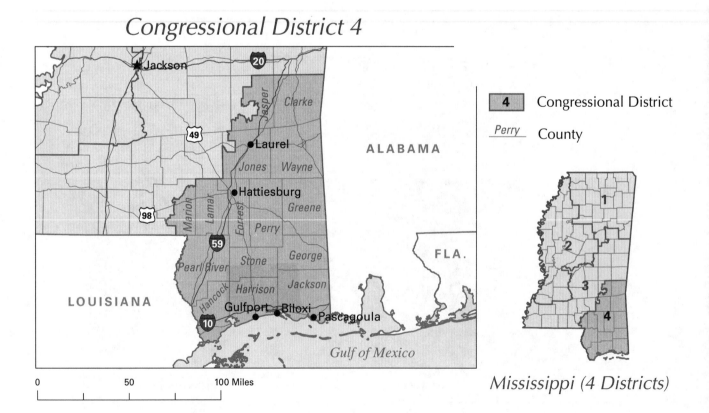

Mississippi (4 Districts)

Missouri Congressional Districts — 9 Districts Total

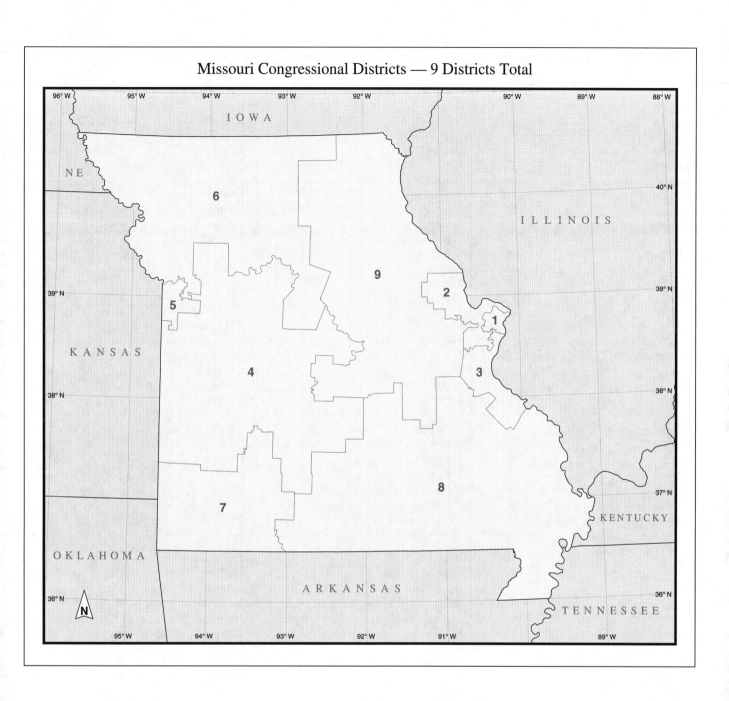

MISSOURI—109th CONGRESSIONAL DISTRICTS BY COUNTIES AND INDEPENDENT CITIES

County	Congressional District	County	Congressional District	County	Congressional District
Adair	9	Grundy	6	Perry	8
Andrew	6	Harrison	6	Pettis	4
Atchison	6	Henry	4	Phelps	8
Audrain	9	Hickory	4	Pike	9
Barry	7	Holt	6	Platte	6
Barton	4	Howard	6	Polk	4, 7
Bates	4	Howell	8	Pulaski	4
Benton	4	Iron	8	Putnam	6
Bollinger	8	Jackson	4–6	Ralls	9
Boone	9	Jasper	7	Randolph	9
Buchanan	6	Jefferson	3	Ray	4
Butler	8	Johnson	4	Reynolds	8
Caldwell	6	Knox	9	Ripley	8
Callaway	9	Laclede	4	St. Charles	2, 9
Camden	4, 9	Lafayette	4	St. Clair	4
Cape Girardeau	8	Lawrence	7	Ste. Genevieve	3
Carroll	6	Lewis	9	St. Francois	8
Carter	8	Lincoln	2	St. Louis	1–3
Cass	4, 5	Linn	6	Saline	4
Cedar	4	Livingston	6	Schuyler	6
Chariton	6	McDonald	7	Scotland	9
Christian	7	Macon	9	Scott	8
Clark	9	Madison	8	Shannon	8
Clay	6	Maries	9	Shelby	9
Clinton	6	Marion	9	Stoddard	8
Cole	4	Mercer	6	Stone	7
Cooper	6	Miller	9	Sullivan	6
Crawford	9	Mississippi	8	Taney	7, 8
Dade	4	Moniteau	4	Texas	8
Dallas	4	Monroe	9	Vernon	4
Daviess	6	Montgomery	9	Warren	9
DeKalb	6	Morgan	4	Washington	8
Dent	8	New Madrid	8	Wayne	8
Douglas	8	Newton	7	Webster	4
Dunklin	8	Nodaway	6	Worth	6
Franklin	9	Oregon	8	Wright	8
Gasconade	9	Osage	9	St. Louis city	1, 3
Gentry	6	Ozark	8		
Greene	7	Pemiscot	8		

Congressional District 1

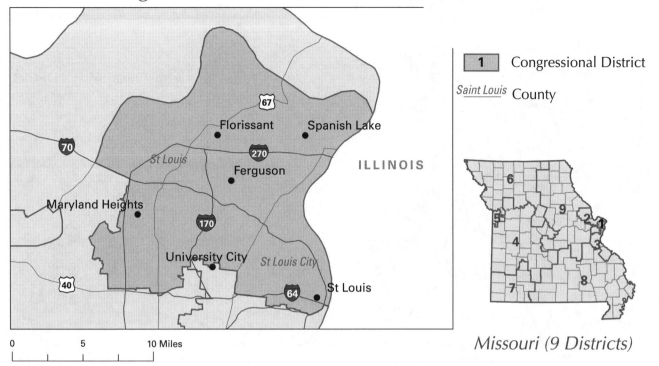

1 Congressional District
Saint Louis County

Missouri (9 Districts)

0 5 10 Miles

Congressional District 2

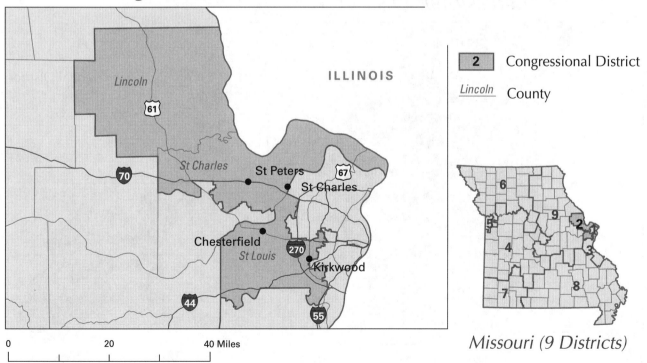

2 Congressional District
Lincoln County

Missouri (9 Districts)

0 20 40 Miles

Congressional District 3

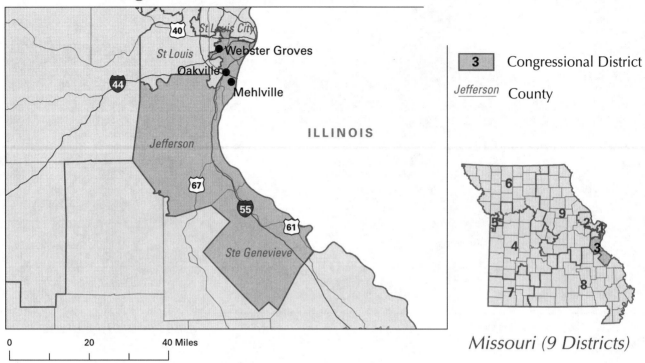

0   20   40 Miles

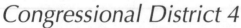

Missouri (9 Districts)

Congressional District 4

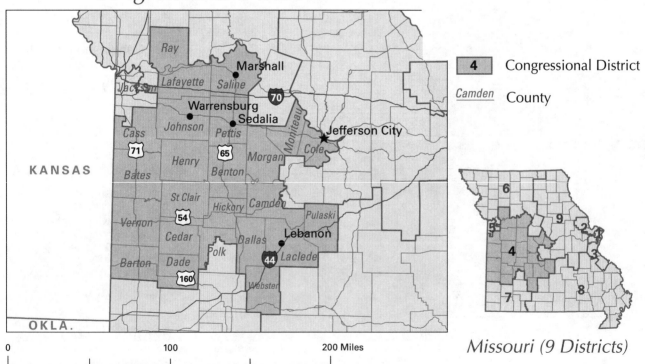

0   100   200 Miles

Missouri (9 Districts)

Congressional District 5

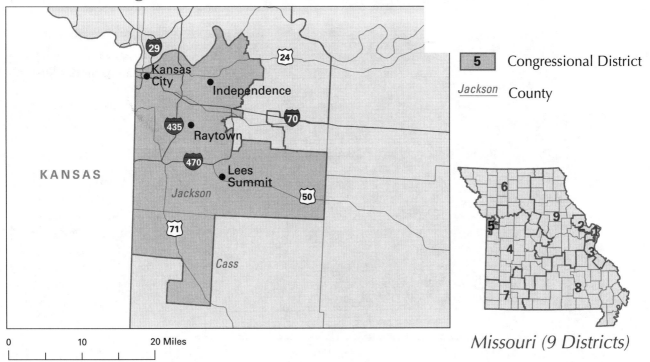

Missouri (9 Districts)

Congressional District 6

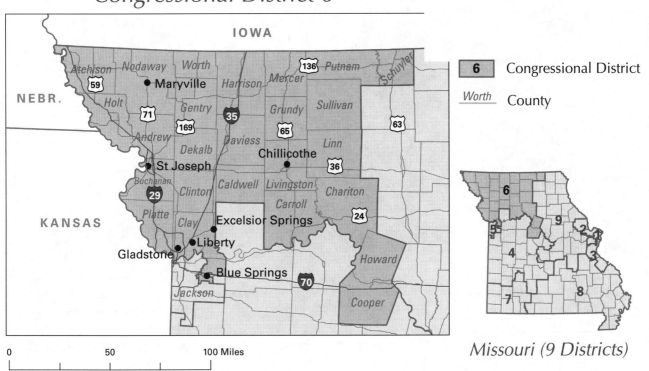

Missouri (9 Districts)

Congressional District 7

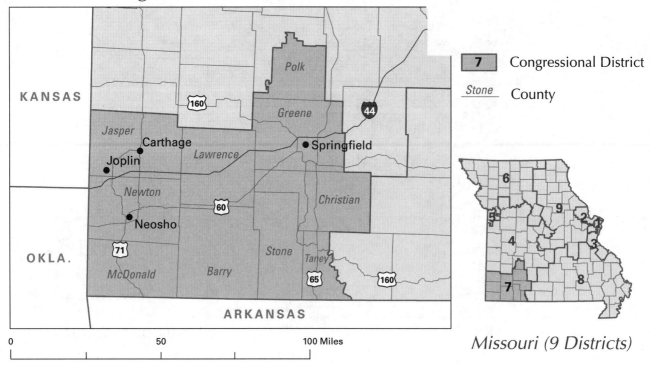

Missouri (9 Districts)

Congressional District 8

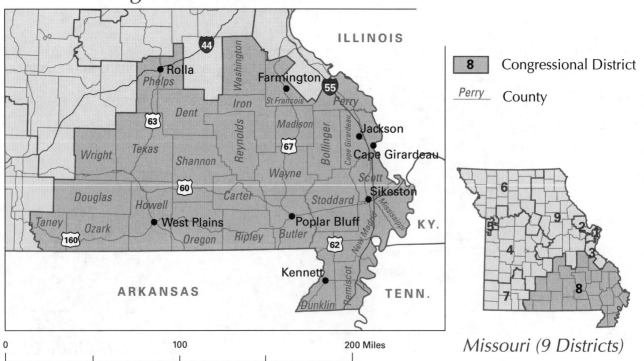

Missouri (9 Districts)

Congressional District 9

Missouri (9 Districts)

Montana—
Congressional District: At large

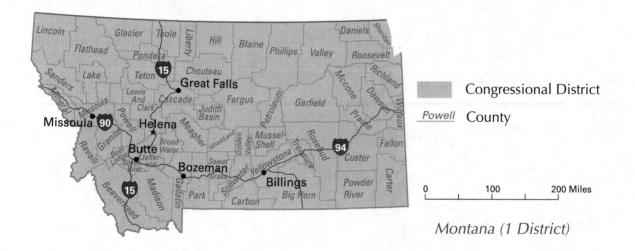

Montana (1 District)

MONTANA—109th CONGRESSIONAL DISTRICTS BY COUNTIES

County	Congressional District	County	Congressional District	County	Congressional District
Beaverhead	1	Granite	1	Powell	1
Big Horn	1	Hill	1	Prairie	1
Blaine	1	Jefferson	1	Ravalli	1
Broadwater	1	Judith Basin	1	Richland	1
Carbon	1	Lake	1	Roosevelt	1
Carter	1	Lewis and Clark	1	Rosebud	1
Cascade	1	Liberty	1	Sanders	1
Chouteau	1	Lincoln	1	Sheridan	1
Custer	1	McCone	1	Silver Bow	1
Daniels	1	Madison	1	Stillwater	1
Dawson	1	Meagher	1	Sweet Grass	1
Deer Lodge	1	Mineral	1	Teton	1
Fallon	1	Missoula	1	Toole	1
Fergus	1	Musselshell	1	Treasure	1
Flathead	1	Park	1	Valley	1
Gallatin	1	Petroleum	1	Wheatland	1
Garfield	1	Phillips	1	Wibaux	1
Glacier	1	Pondera	1	Yellowstone	1
Golden Valley	1	Powder River	1		

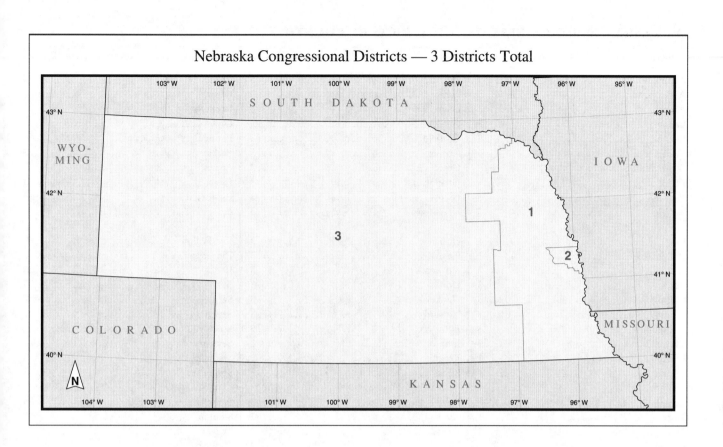

Nebraska Congressional Districts — 3 Districts Total

NEBRASKA—109th CONGRESSIONAL DISTRICTS BY COUNTIES

County	Congressional District	County	Congressional District	County	Congressional District
Adams	3	Frontier	3	Nance	3
Antelope	3	Furnas	3	Nemaha	1
Arthur	3	Gage	1	Nuckolls	3
Banner	3	Garden	3	Otoe	1
Blaine	3	Garfield	3	Pawnee	1
Boone	3	Gosper	3	Perkins	3
Box Butte	3	Grant	3	Phelps	3
Boyd	3	Greeley	3	Pierce	3
Brown	3	Hall	3	Platte	3
Buffalo	3	Hamilton	3	Polk	3
Burt	1	Harlan	3	Red Willow	3
Butler	1	Hayes	3	Richardson	1
Cass	1	Hitchcock	3	Rock	3
Cedar	1, 3	Holt	3	Saline	3
Chase	3	Hooker	3	Sarpy	1, 2
Cherry	3	Howard	3	Saunders	1
Cheyenne	3	Jefferson	3	Scotts Bluff	3
Clay	3	Johnson	1	Seward	1
Colfax	1	Kearney	3	Sheridan	3
Cuming	1	Keith	3	Sherman	3
Custer	3	Keya Paha	3	Sioux	3
Dakota	1	Kimball	3	Stanton	1
Dawes	3	Knox	3	Thayer	3
Dawson	3	Lancaster	1	Thomas	3
Deuel	3	Lincoln	3	Thurston	1
Dixon	1	Logan	3	Valley	3
Dodge	1	Loup	3	Washington	1
Douglas	2	McPherson	3	Wayne	1
Dundy	3	Madison	1	Webster	3
Fillmore	3	Merrick	3	Wheeler	3
Franklin	3	Morrill	3	York	3

Congressional District 1

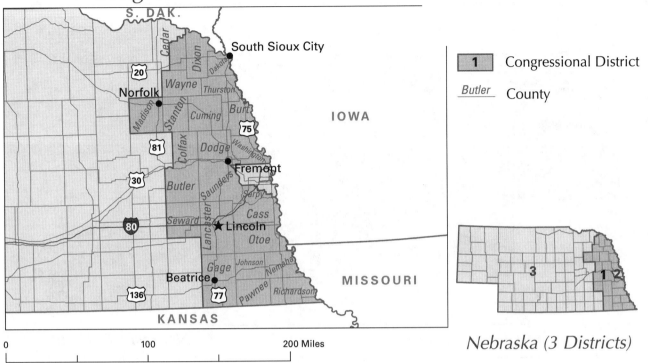

| 1 | Congressional District |
| *Butler* | County |

Nebraska (3 Districts)

Congressional District 2

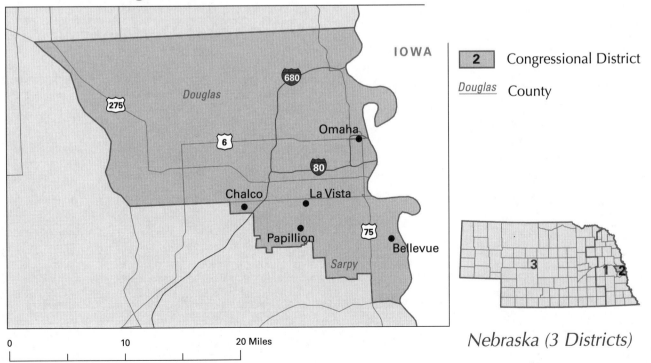

| 2 | Congressional District |
| *Douglas* | County |

Nebraska (3 Districts)

Congressional District 3

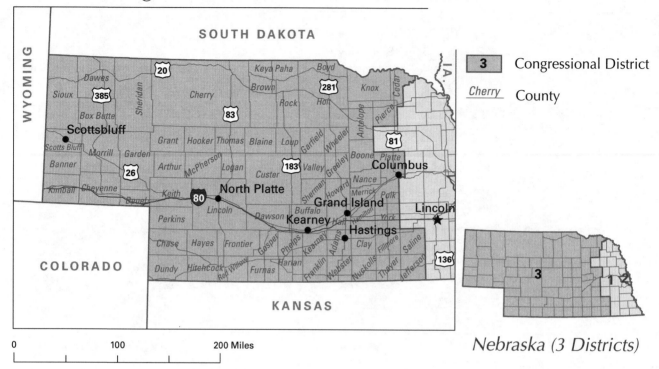

Nebraska (3 Districts)

Nevada Congressional Districts — 3 Districts Total

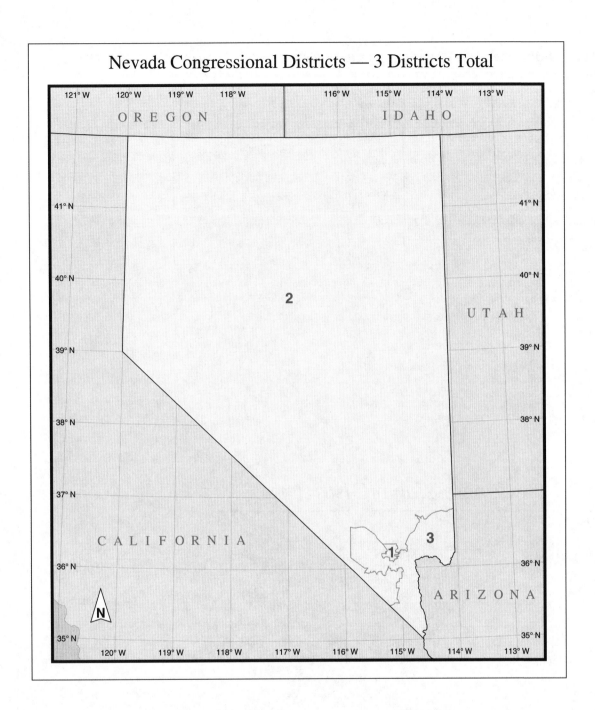

NEVADA — 109th CONGRESSIONAL DISTRICTS BY COUNTIES AND INDEPENDENT CITIES

County	Congressional District	County	Congressional District
Churchill	2	Mineral	2
Clark	1–3	Nye	2
Douglas	2	Pershing	2
Elko	2	Storey	2
Esmeralda	2	Washoe	2
Eureka	2	White Pine	2
Humboldt	2	Carson City	2
Lander	2		
Lincoln	2		
Lyon	2		

Congressional District 1

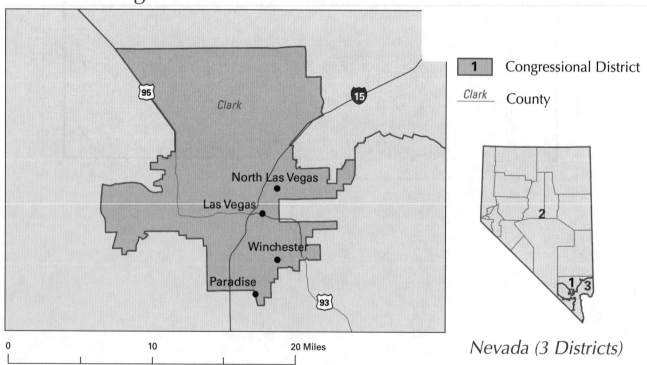

Nevada (3 Districts)

Congressional District 2

| 2 | Congressional District |
| *Eureka* | County |

Nevada (3 Districts)

Congressional District 3

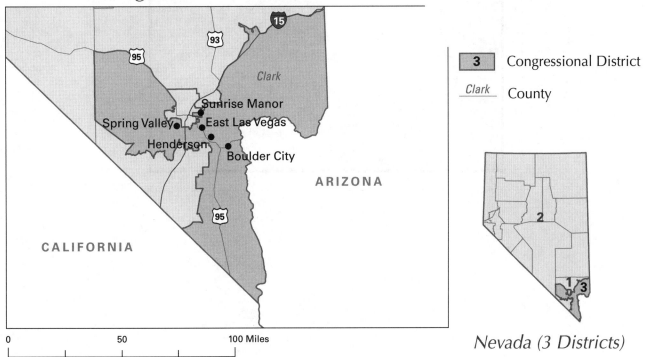

| 3 | Congressional District |
| *Clark* | County |

Nevada (3 Districts)

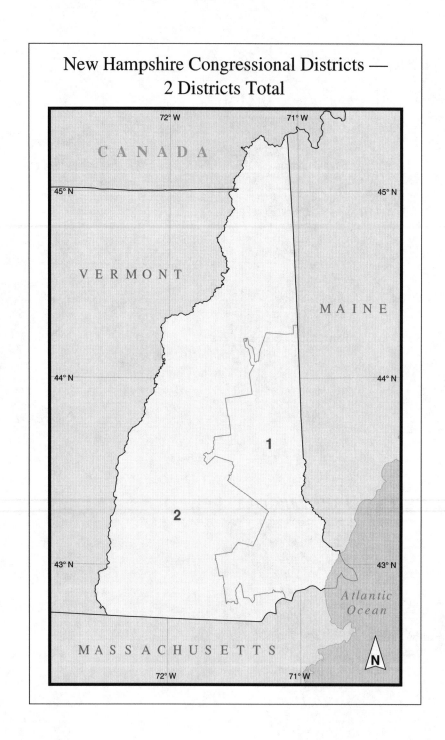

New Hampshire Congressional Districts —
2 Districts Total

NEW HAMPSHIRE—109th CONGRESSIONAL DISTRICTS BY COUNTIES

County	Congressional District
Belknap	1, 2
Carroll	1, 2
Cheshire	2
Coos	2
Grafton	2
Hillsborough	1, 2
Merrimack	1, 2
Rockingham	1, 2

County	Congressional District
Strafford	1
Sullivan	2

Congressional District 1

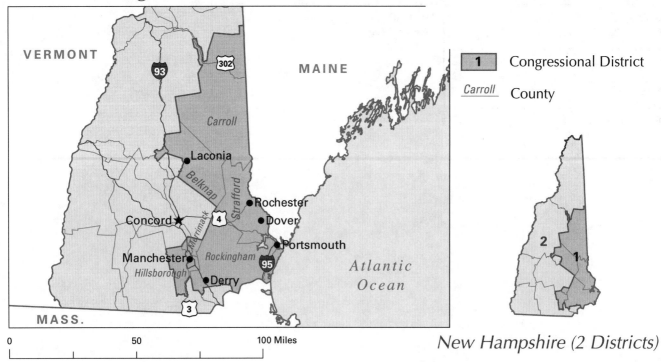

Congressional District

Carroll County

New Hampshire (2 Districts)

Congressional District 2

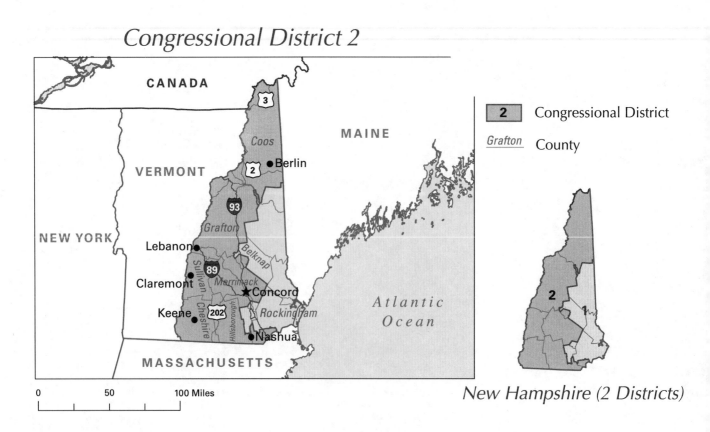

2 Congressional District

Grafton County

New Hampshire (2 Districts)

New Jersey Congressional Districts — 13 Districts Total

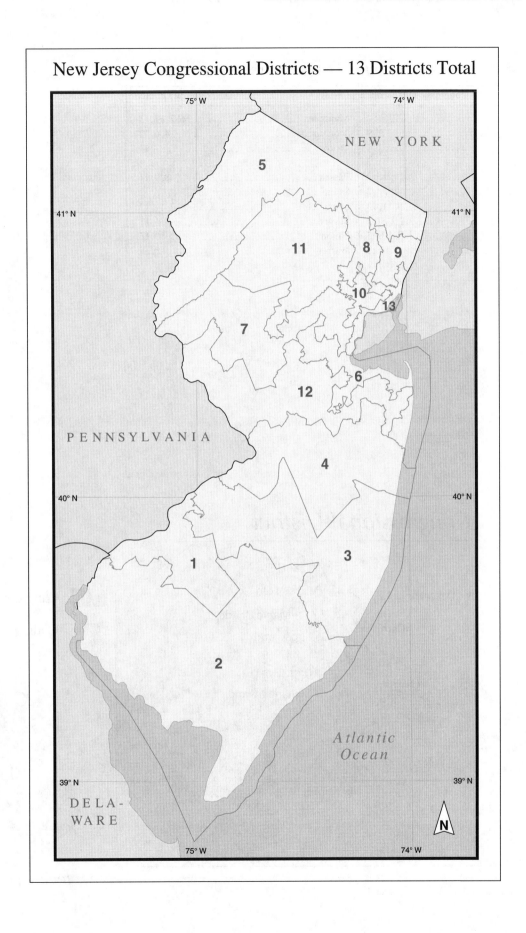

NEW JERSEY—109th CONGRESSIONAL DISTRICTS BY COUNTIES

County	Congressional District
Atlantic	2
Bergen	5, 9
Burlington	1–4
Camden	1–3
Cape May	2
Cumberland	2
Essex	8, 10, 11, 13
Gloucester	1, 2
Hudson	9, 10, 13
Hunterdon	7, 12
Mercer	4, 12

County	Congressional District
Middlesex	6, 7, 12, 13
Monmouth	4, 6, 12
Morris	11
Ocean	3, 4
Passaic	5, 8, 9, 11
Salem	2
Somerset	6, 7, 11, 12
Sussex	5, 11
Union	6, 7, 10, 13
Warren	5

Congressional District 1

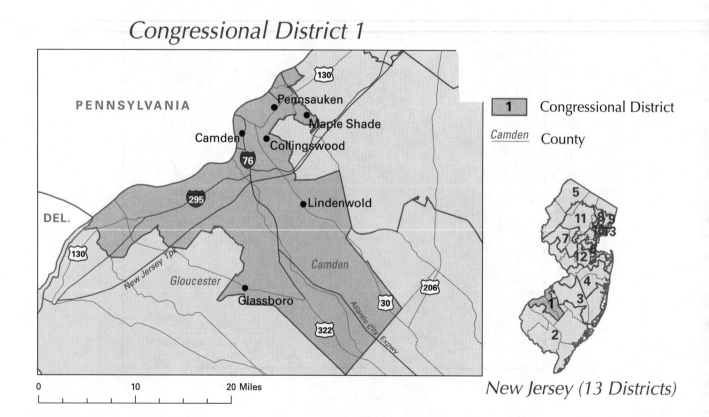

New Jersey (13 Districts)

Congressional District 2

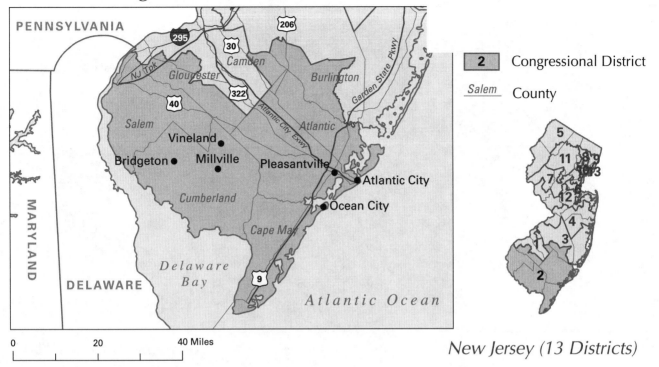

Congressional District 3

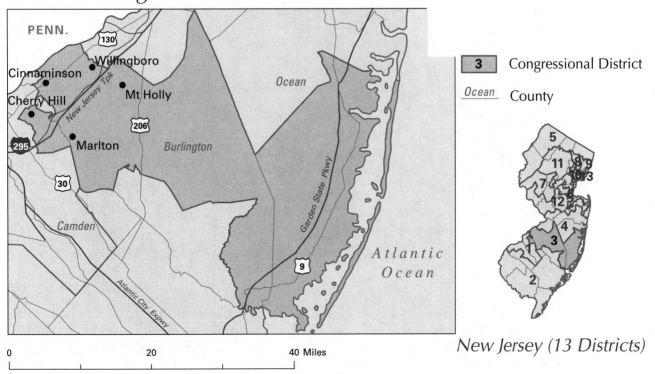

Congressional District 4

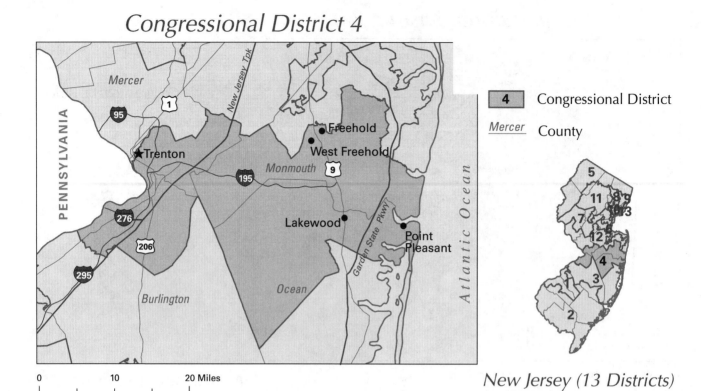

New Jersey (13 Districts)

Congressional District 5

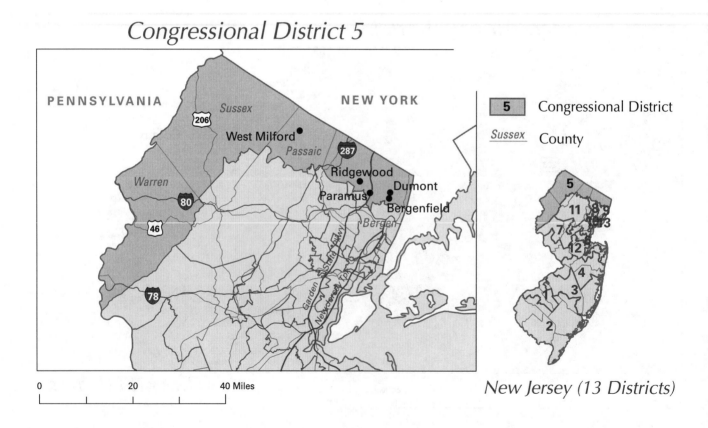

New Jersey (13 Districts)

Congressional District 6

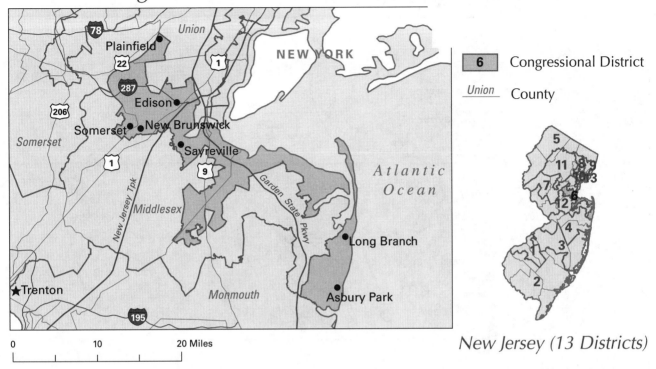

6 Congressional District

Union County

New Jersey (13 Districts)

Congressional District 7

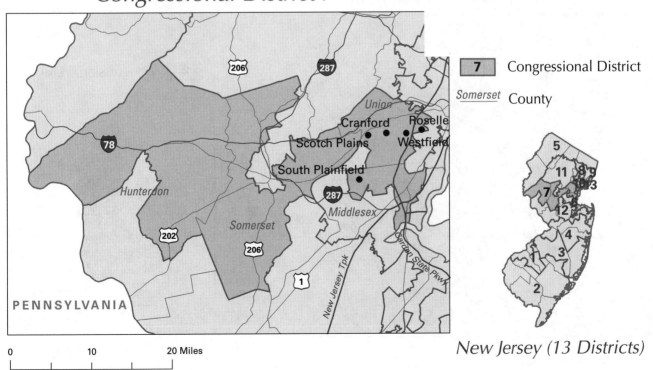

7 Congressional District

Somerset County

New Jersey (13 Districts)

Congressional District 8

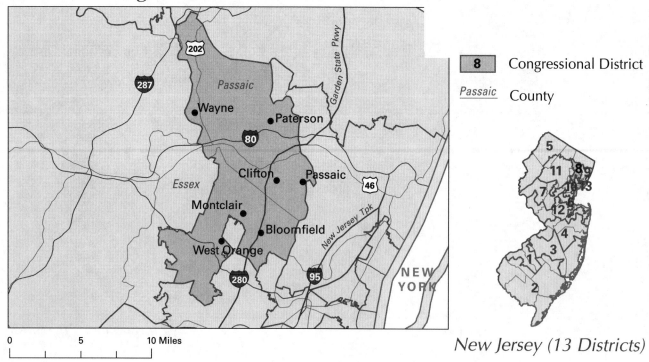

8   Congressional District

Passaic   County

New Jersey (13 Districts)

Congressional District 9

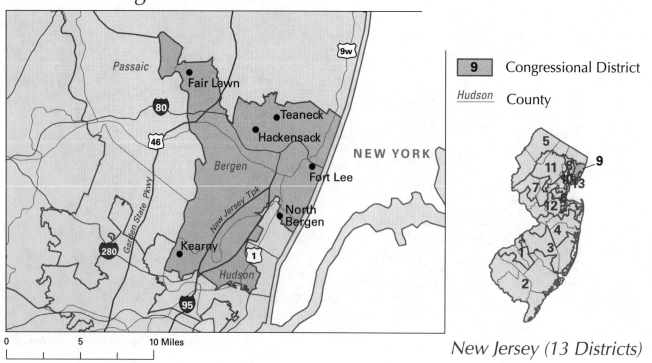

9   Congressional District

Hudson   County

New Jersey (13 Districts)

Congressional District 10

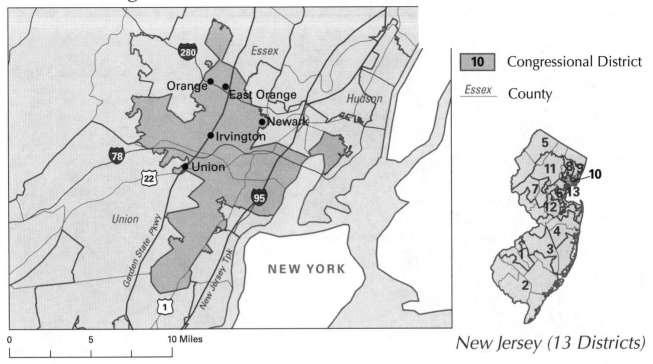

New Jersey (13 Districts)

Congressional District 11

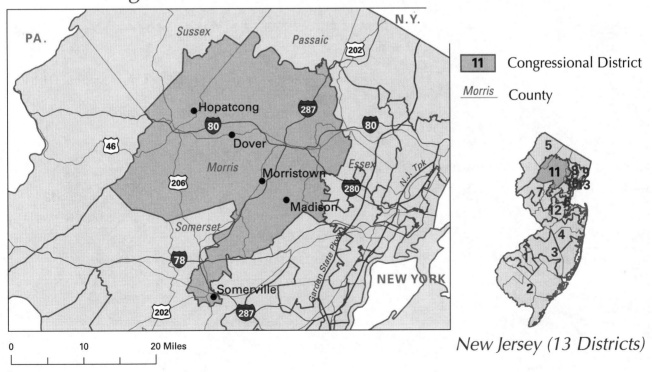

New Jersey (13 Districts)

Congressional District 12

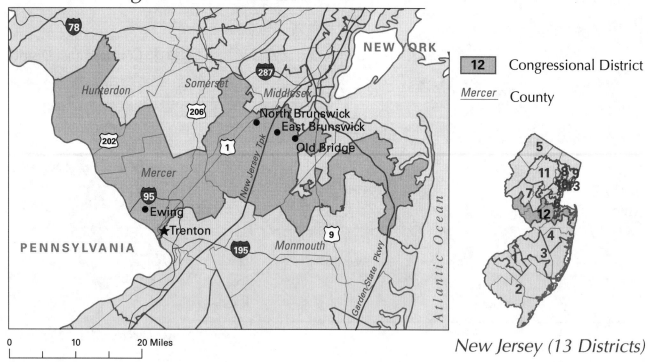

New Jersey (13 Districts)

Congressional District 13

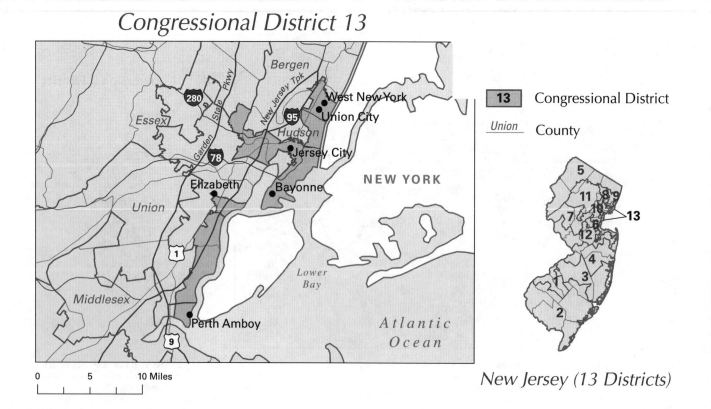

New Jersey (13 Districts)

New Mexico Congressional Districts — 3 Districts Total

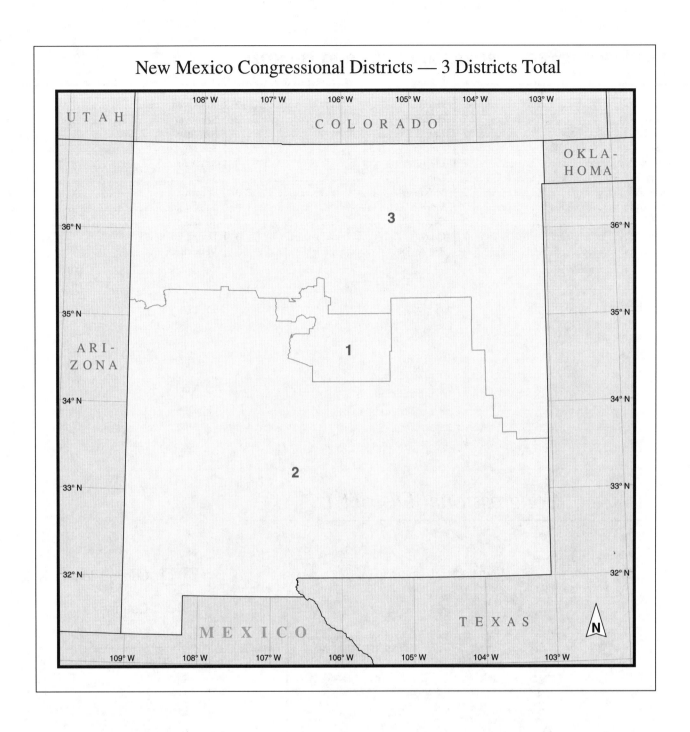

NEW MEXICO — 109th CONGRESSIONAL DISTRICTS BY COUNTIES

County	Congressional District	County	Congressional District	County	Congressional District
Bernalillo	1–3	Harding	3	Roosevelt	3
Catron	2	Hidalgo	2	Sandoval	1, 3
Chaves	2	Lea	2	San Juan	3
Cibola	2	Lincoln	2	San Miguel	3
Colfax	3	Los Alamos	3	Santa Fe	1, 3
Curry	3	Luna	2	Sierra	2
De Baca	2	McKinley	2, 3	Socorro	2
Dona Ana	2	Mora	3	Taos	3
Eddy	2	Otero	2	Torrance	1
Grant	2	Quay	3	Union	3
Guadalupe	2	Rio Arriba	3	Valencia	1, 2

Congressional District 1

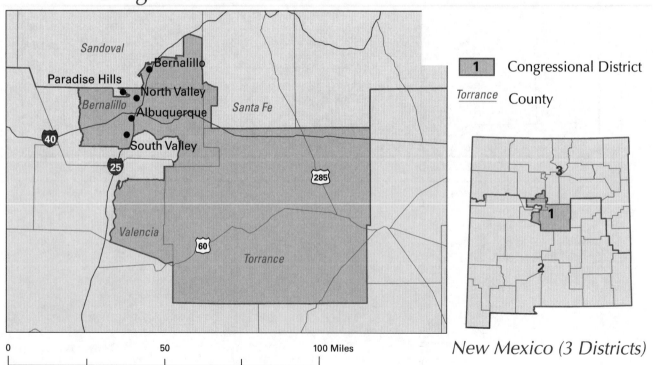

New Mexico (3 Districts)

Congressional District 2

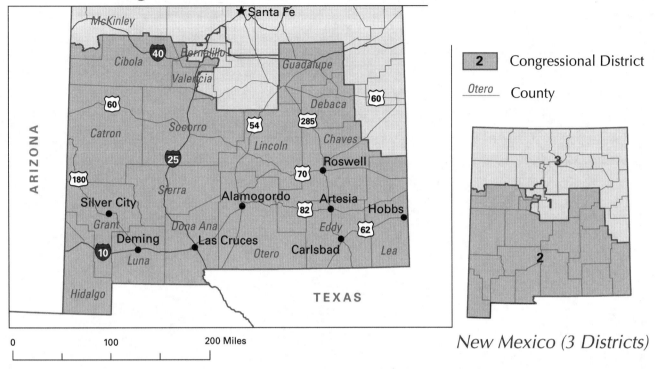

New Mexico (3 Districts)

Congressional District 3

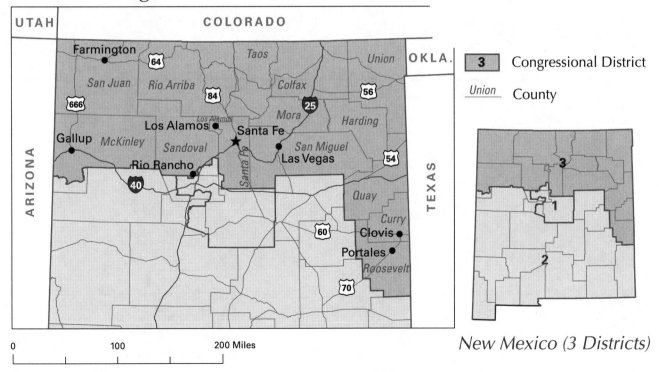

New Mexico (3 Districts)

New York Congressional Districts — 29 Districts Total

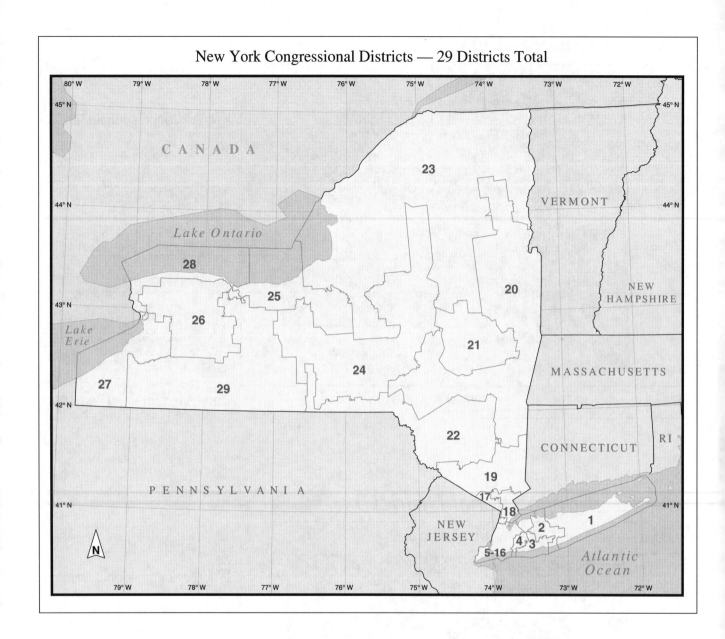

NEW YORK—109th CONGRESSIONAL DISTRICTS BY COUNTIES

County	Congressional District
Albany	21
Allegany	29
Bronx	7, 15–17
Broome	22, 24
Cattaraugus	29
Cayuga	24, 25
Chautauqua	27
Chemung	29
Chenango	24
Clinton	23
Columbia	20
Cortland	24
Delaware	20, 22
Dutchess	19, 20, 22
Erie	26–28
Essex	20, 23
Franklin	23
Fulton	21, 23
Genesee	26
Greene	20
Hamilton	23

County	Congressional District
Herkimer	24
Jefferson	23
Kings	8–13
Lewis	23
Livingston	26
Madison	23
Monroe	25, 26, 28, 29
Montgomery	21
Nassau	2–5
New York	8, 12, 14, 15
Niagara	26, 28
Oneida	23, 24
Onondaga	25
Ontario	24, 29
Orange	19, 22
Orleans	26, 28
Oswego	23
Otsego	20, 24
Putnam	19
Queens	5–7, 9, 12, 14, 15
Rensselaer	20, 21

County	Congressional District
Richmond	13
Rockland	17–19
St. Lawrence	23
Saratoga	20, 21
Schenectady	21
Schoharie	21
Schuyler	29
Seneca	24
Steuben	29
Suffolk	1–3
Sullivan	22
Tioga	22, 24
Tompkins	22, 24
Ulster	22
Warren	20
Washington	20
Wayne	25
Westchester	17–19
Wyoming	26
Yates	29

Congressional District 1

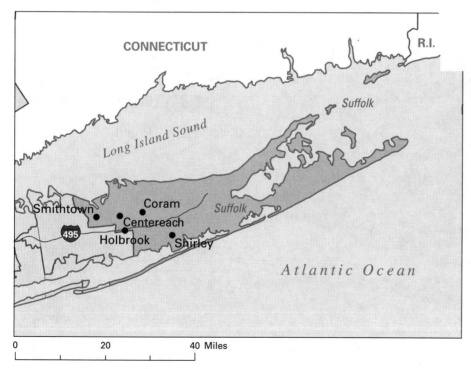

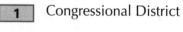

New York (29 Districts)

Congressional District 2

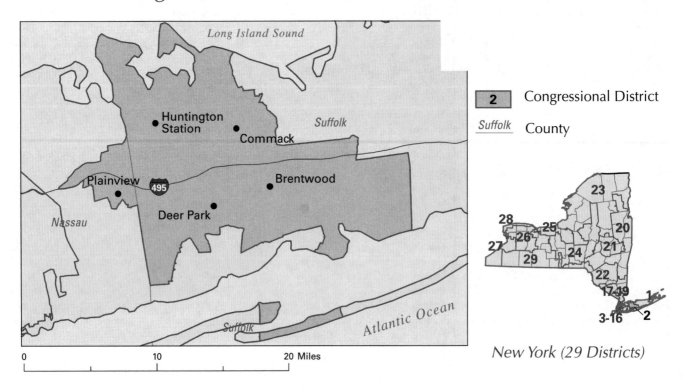

Congressional District
County

New York (29 Districts)

Congressional District 3

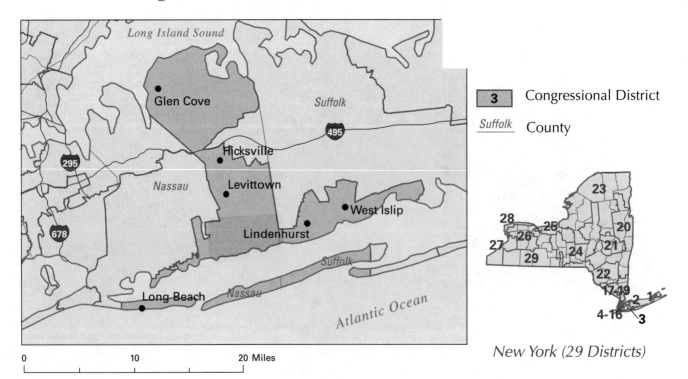

Congressional District
County

New York (29 Districts)

Congressional District 4

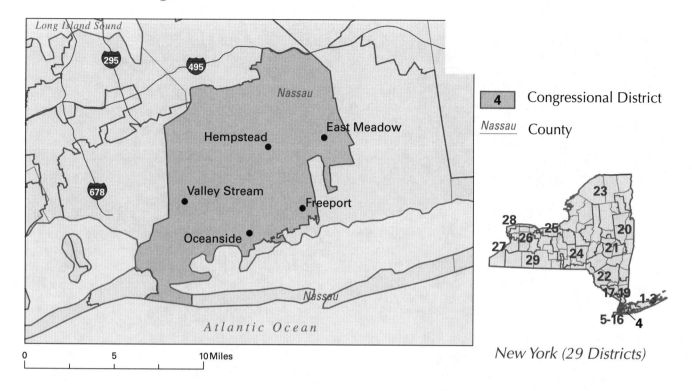

0   5   10 Miles

New York (29 Districts)

Congressional District 5

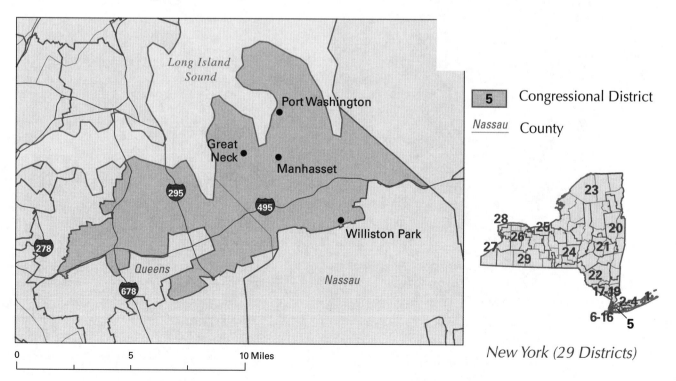

0   5   10 Miles

New York (29 Districts)

Congressional District 6

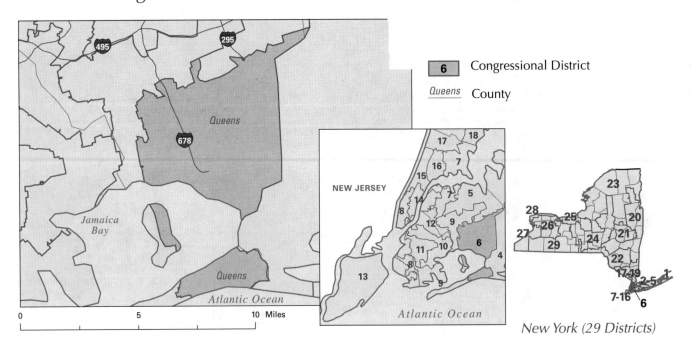

Congressional District 7

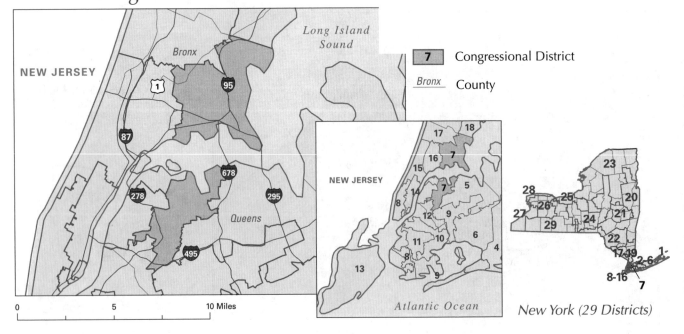

Congressional District 8

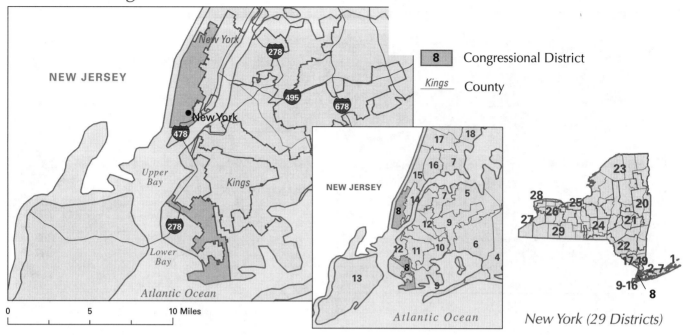

0   5   10 Miles

New York (29 Districts)

Congressional District 9

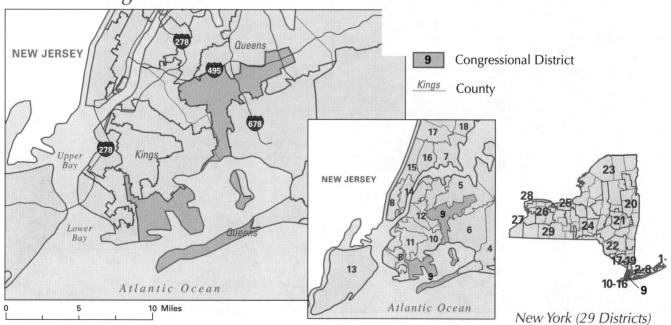

0   5   10 Miles

New York (29 Districts)

Congressional District 10

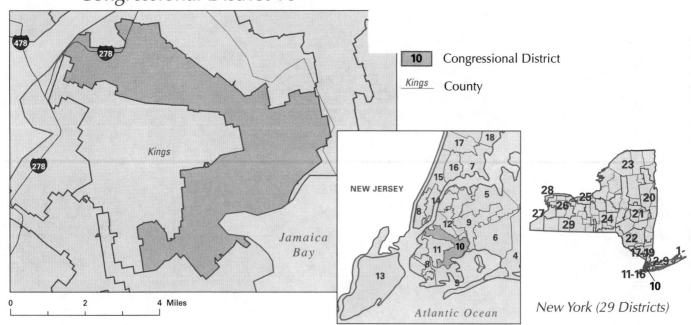

10 Congressional District

Kings County

0   2   4 Miles

New York (29 Districts)

Congressional District 11

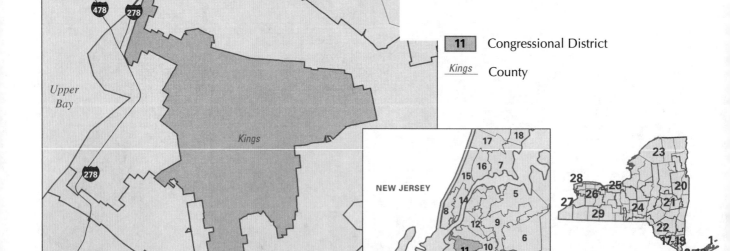

11 Congressional District

Kings County

0   2   4 Miles

New York (29 Districts)

Congressional District 12

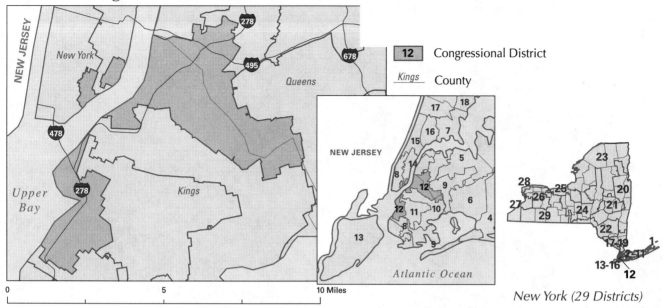

Congressional District 13

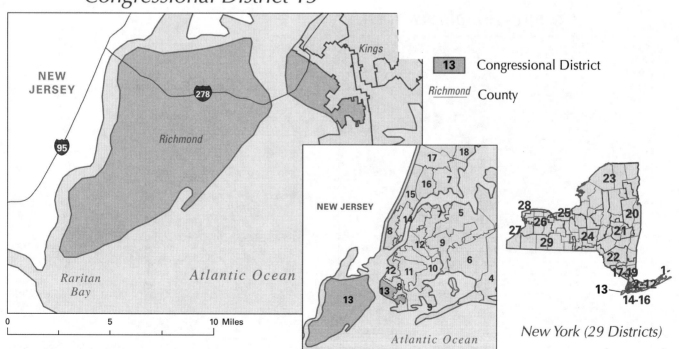

Congressional District 14

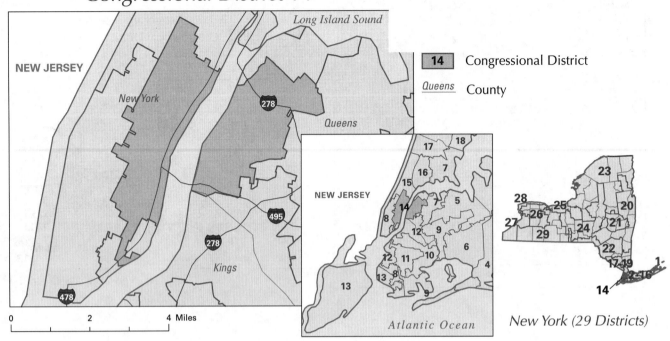

Congressional District 15

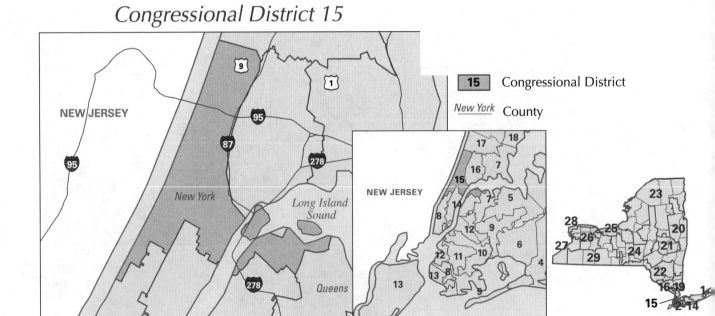

Congressional District 16

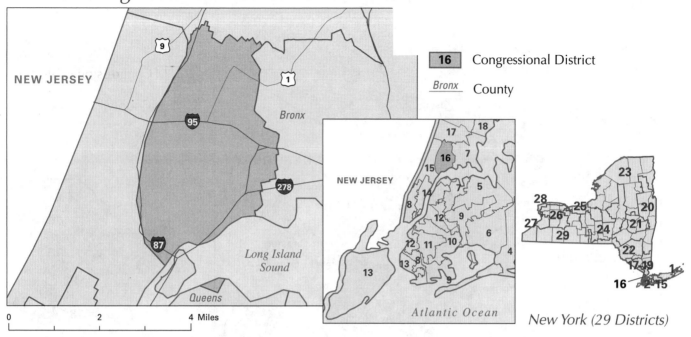

16 Congressional District

Bronx County

New York (29 Districts)

Congressional District 17

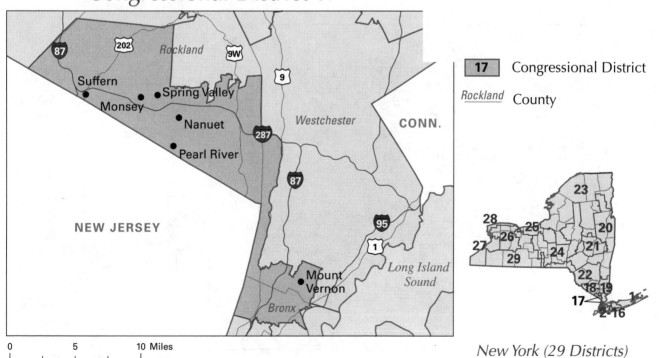

17 Congressional District

Rockland County

New York (29 Districts)

Congressional District 18

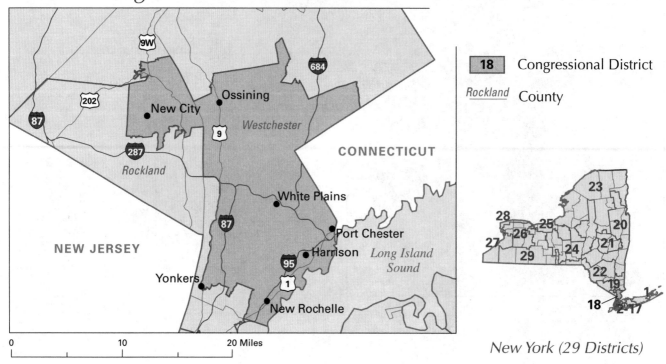

18	Congressional District
Rockland	County

New York (29 Districts)

Congressional District 19

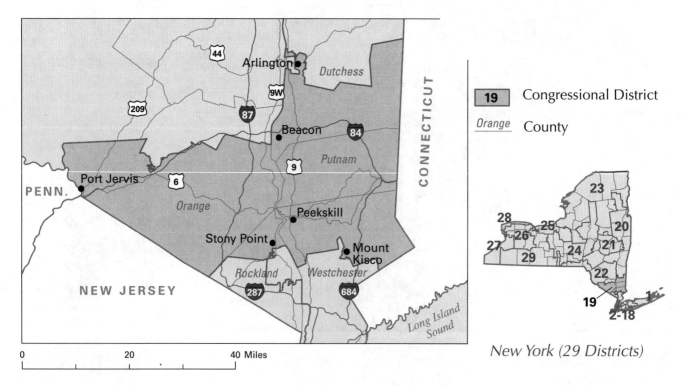

19	Congressional District
Orange	County

New York (29 Districts)

Congressional District 20

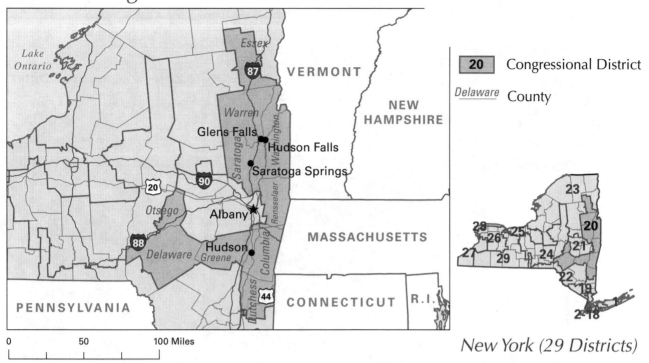

20	Congressional District
Delaware	County

New York (29 Districts)

Congressional District 21

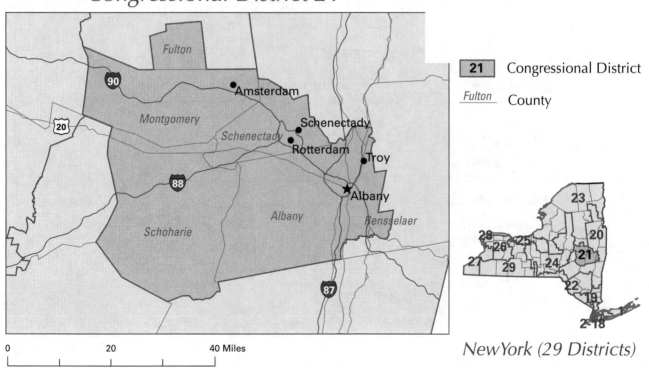

21	Congressional District
Fulton	County

New York (29 Districts)

Congressional District 22

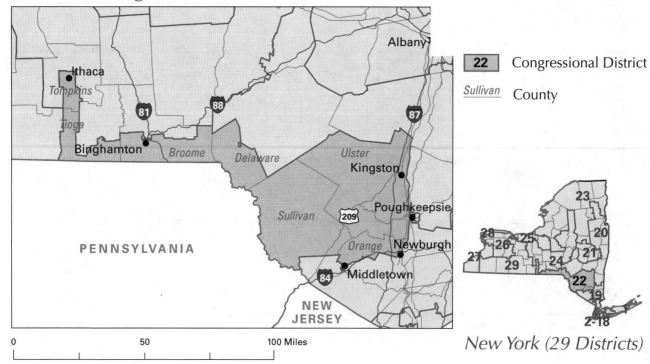

22	Congressional District
Sullivan	County

New York (29 Districts)

Congressional District 23

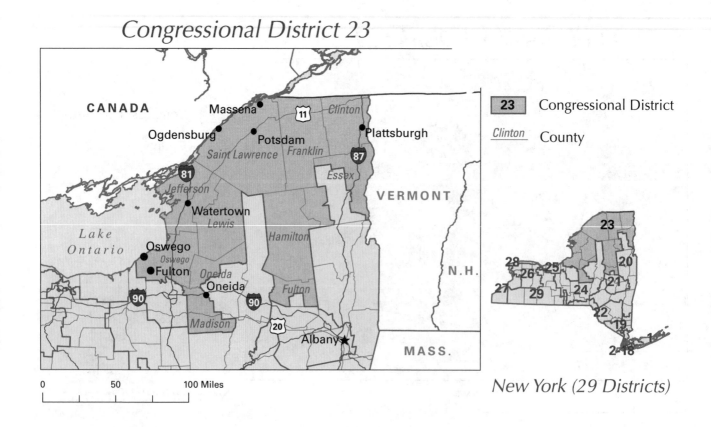

23	Congressional District
Clinton	County

New York (29 Districts)

Congressional District 24

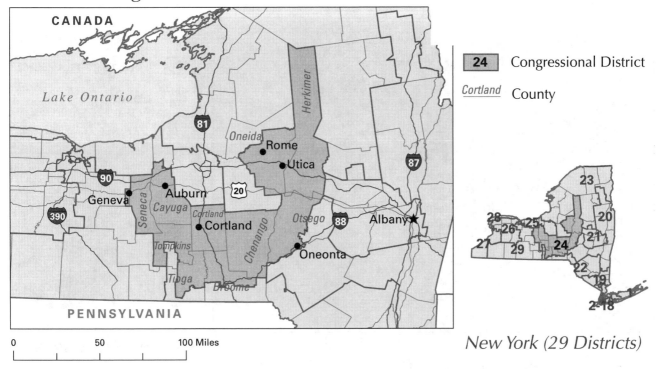

24 Congressional District
Cortland County

New York (29 Districts)

Congressional District 25

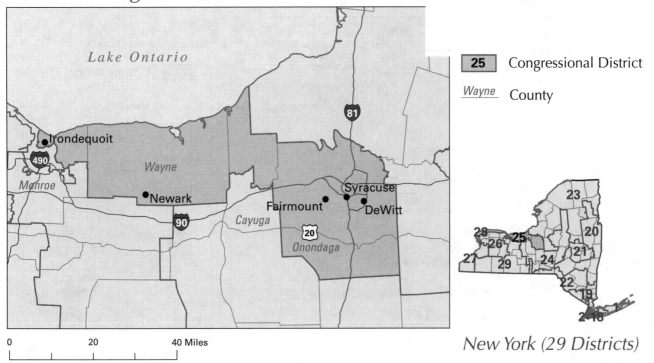

25 Congressional District
Wayne County

New York (29 Districts)

Congressional District 26

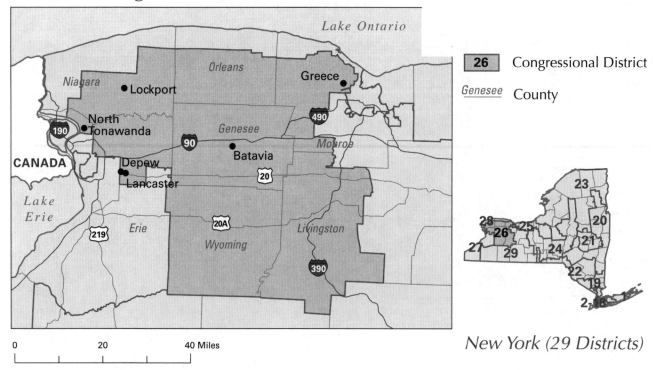

26   Congressional District

Genesee   County

New York (29 Districts)

Congressional District 27

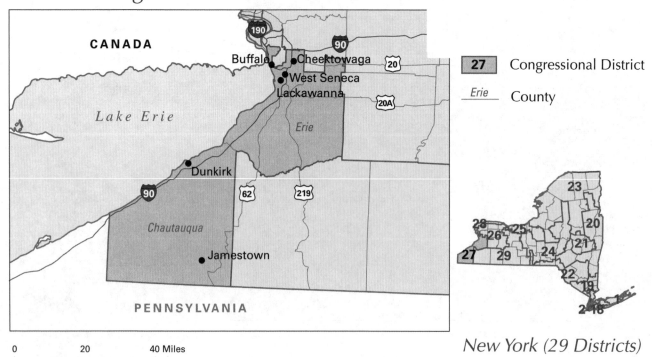

27   Congressional District

Erie   County

New York (29 Districts)

Congressional District 28

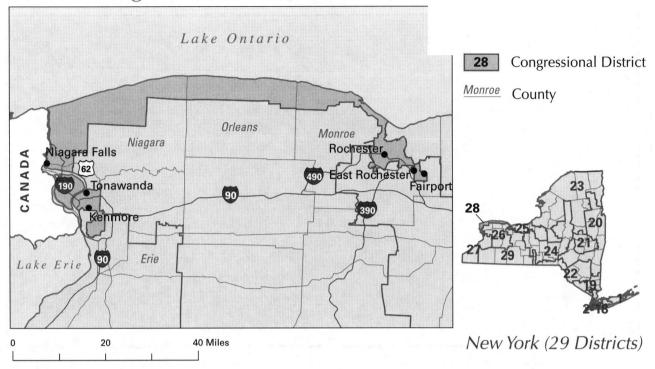

28 Congressional District

Monroe County

New York (29 Districts)

Congressional District 29

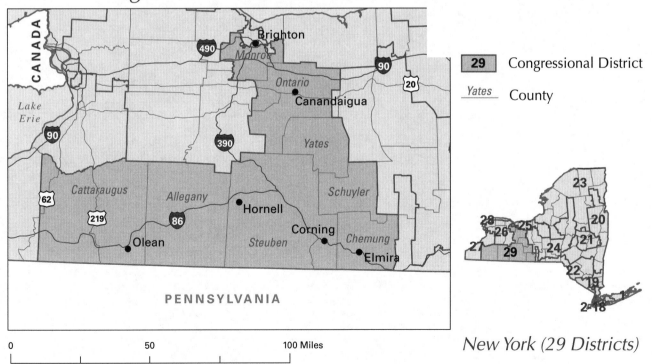

29 Congressional District

Yates County

New York (29 Districts)

North Carolina Congressional Districts — 13 Districts Total

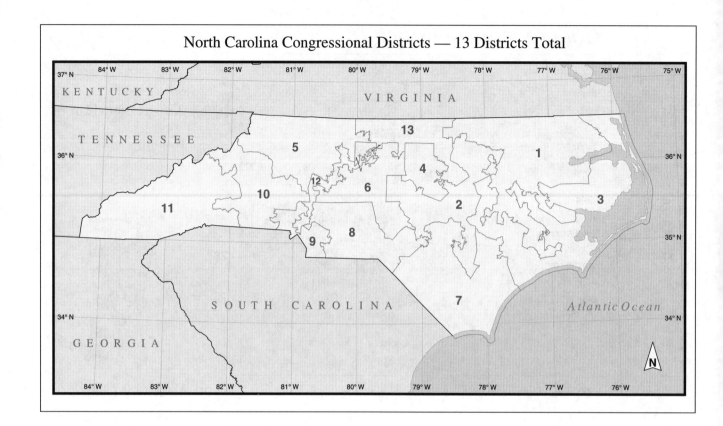

NORTH CAROLINA—109th CONGRESSIONAL DISTRICTS BY COUNTIES

County	Congressional District	County	Congressional District	County	Congressional District
Alamance	6, 13	Franklin	2	Pamlico	3
Alexander	5	Gaston	9, 10	Pasquotank	1
Alleghany	5	Gates	1	Pender	7
Anson	8	Graham	11	Perquimans	1
Ashe	5	Granville	1, 13	Person	13
Avery	10	Greene	1	Pitt	1, 3
Beaufort	1, 3	Guilford	6, 12, 13	Polk	11
Bertie	1	Halifax	1	Randolph	6
Bladen	7	Harnett	2	Richmond	8
Brunswick	7	Haywood	11	Robeson	7
Buncombe	11	Henderson	11	Rockingham	5, 13
Burke	10	Hertford	1	Rowan	6, 12
Cabarrus	8, 12	Hoke	8	Rutherford	10, 11
Caldwell	10	Hyde	3	Sampson	2, 7
Camden	3	Iredell	5, 10	Scotland	7, 8
Carteret	3	Jackson	11	Stanly	8
Caswell	13	Johnston	2	Stokes	5
Catawba	10	Jones	1, 3	Surry	5
Chatham	2, 4	Lee	2	Swain	11
Cherokee	11	Lenoir	1, 3	Transylvania	11
Chowan	1	Lincoln	10	Tyrrell	3
Clay	11	McDowell	11	Union	8, 9
Cleveland	10	Macon	11	Vance	1, 2
Columbus	7	Madison	11	Wake	2, 4, 13
Craven	1, 3	Martin	1	Warren	1
Cumberland	2, 7, 8	Mecklenburg	8, 9, 12	Washington	1
Currituck	3	Mitchell	10	Watauga	5
Dare	3	Montgomery	8	Wayne	1, 3
Davidson	6, 12	Moore	6	Wilkes	5
Davie	5	Nash	1–3	Wilson	1, 3
Duplin	3, 7	New Hanover	7	Yadkin	5
Durham	4	Northampton	1	Yancey	11
Edgecombe	1	Onslow	3		
Forsyth	5, 12	Orange	4		

Congressional District 1

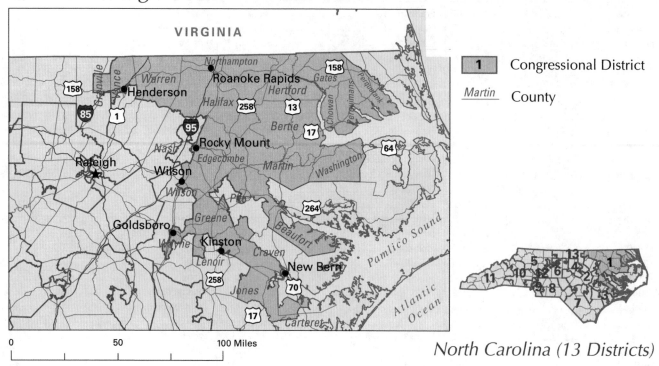

North Carolina (13 Districts)

Congressional District 2

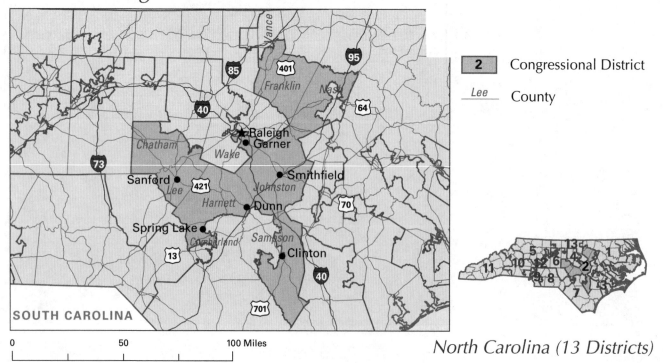

North Carolina (13 Districts)

Congressional District 3

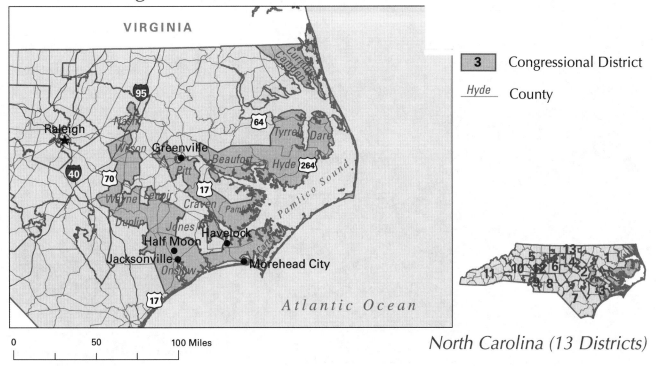

North Carolina (13 Districts)

Congressional District 4

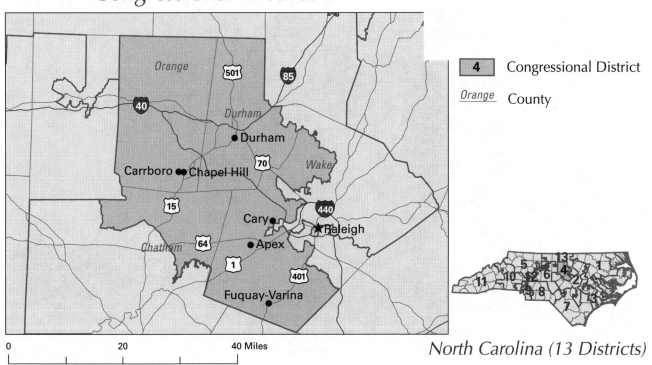

North Carolina (13 Districts)

Congressional District 5

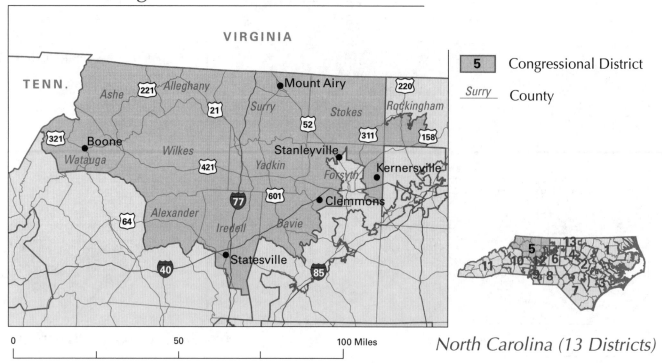

North Carolina (13 Districts)

Congressional District 6

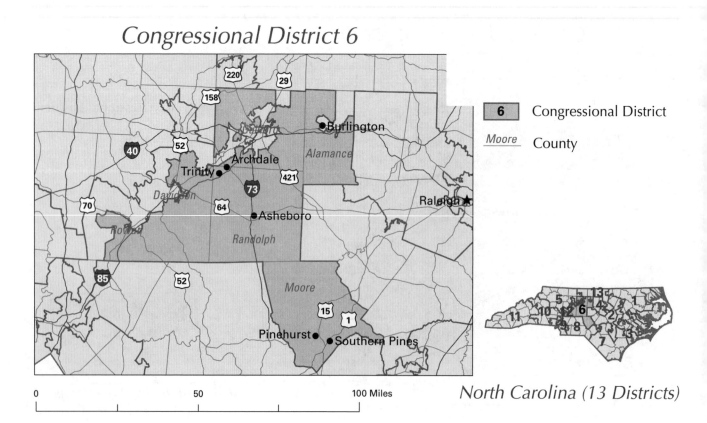

North Carolina (13 Districts)

Congressional District 7

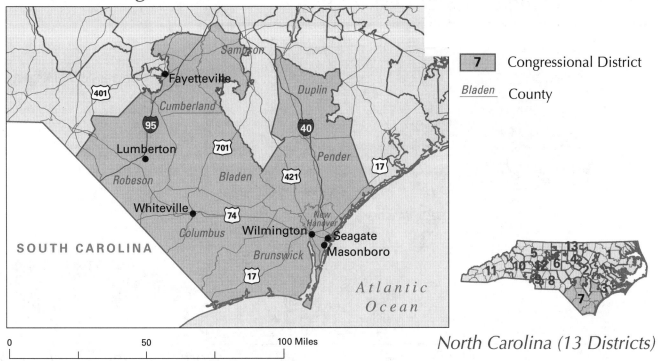

North Carolina (13 Districts)

Congressional District 8

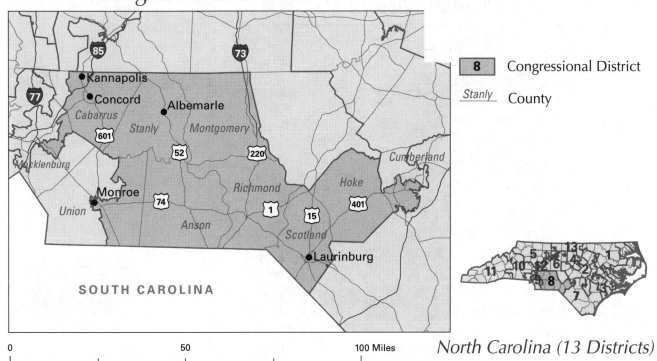

North Carolina (13 Districts)

Congressional District 9

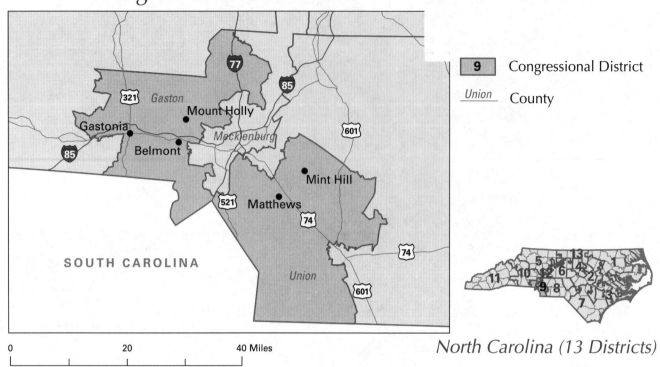

9 Congressional District
Union County

North Carolina (13 Districts)

Congressional District 10

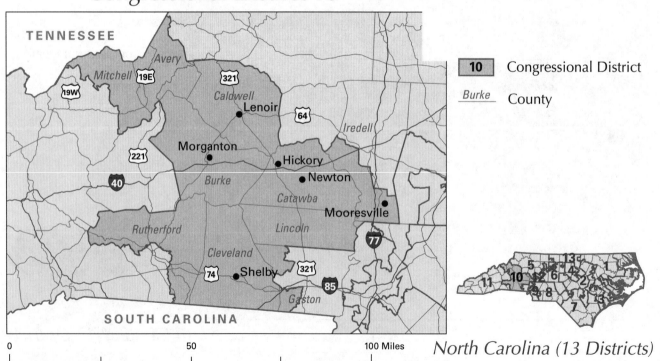

10 Congressional District
Burke County

North Carolina (13 Districts)

Congressional District 11

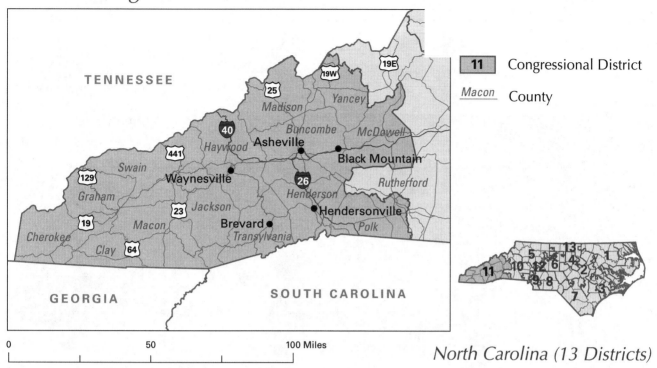

North Carolina (13 Districts)

Congressional District 12

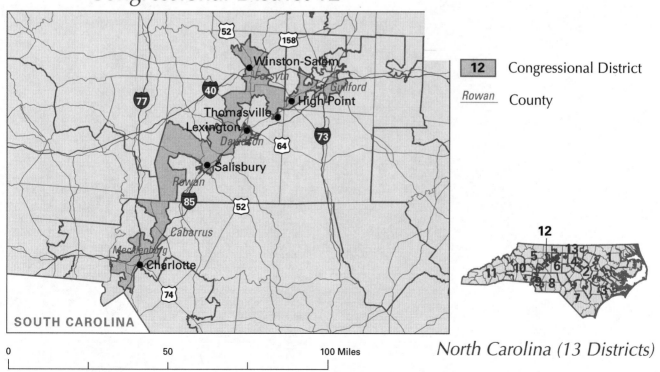

North Carolina (13 Districts)

Congressional District 13

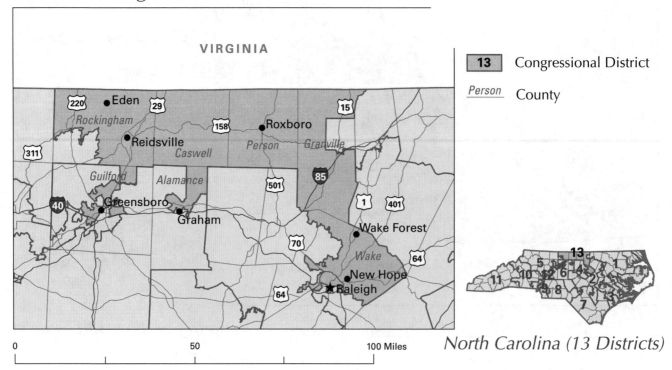

North Carolina (13 Districts)

North Dakota—

Congressional District: At large

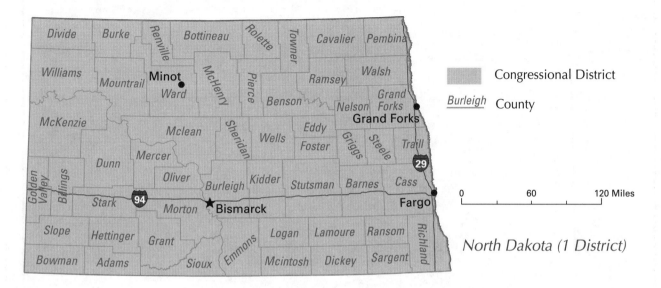

Congressional District

Burleigh County

North Dakota (1 District)

NORTH DAKOTA—109th CONGRESSIONAL DISTRICTS BY COUNTIES

County	Congressional District	County	Congressional District	County	Congressional District
Adams	1	Grant	1	Ransom	1
Barnes	1	Griggs	1	Renville	1
Benson	1	Hettinger	1	Richland	1
Billings	1	Kidder	1	Rolette	1
Bottineau	1	La Moure	1	Sargent	1
Bowman	1	Logan	1	Sheridan	1
Burke	1	McHenry	1	Sioux	1
Burleigh	1	McIntosh	1	Slope	1
Cass	1	McKenzie	1	Stark	1
Cavalier	1	McLean	1	Steele	1
Dickey	1	Mercer	1	Stutsman	1
Divide	1	Morton	1	Towner	1
Dunn	1	Mountrail	1	Traill	1
Eddy	1	Nelson	1	Walsh	1
Emmons	1	Oliver	1	Ward	1
Foster	1	Pembina	1	Wells	1
Golden Valley	1	Pierce	1	Williams	1
Grand Forks	1	Ramsey	1		

Ohio Congressional Districts — 18 Districts Total

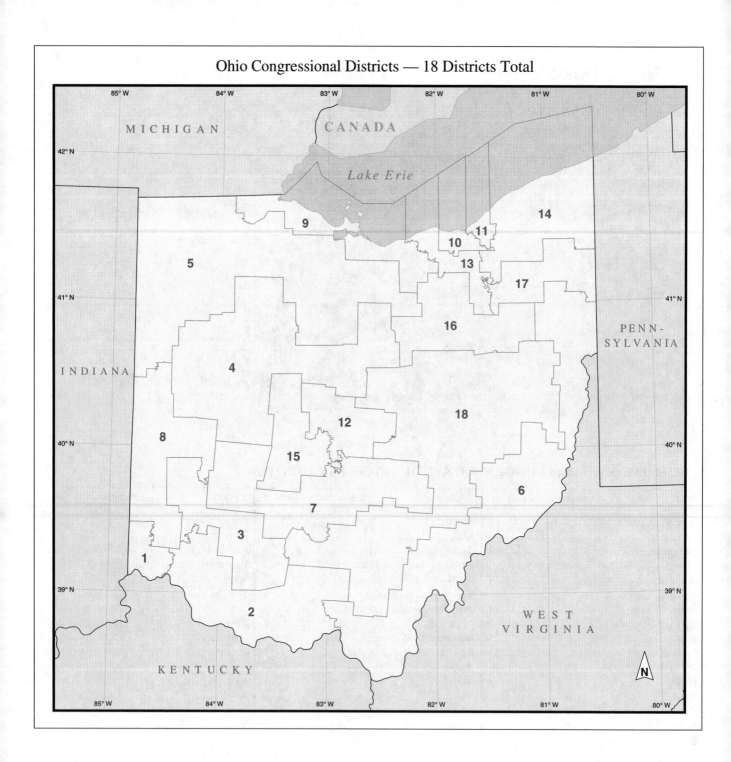

OHIO—109th CONGRESSIONAL DISTRICTS BY COUNTIES

County	Congressional District	County	Congressional District	County	Congressional District
Adams	2	Hamilton	1, 2	Noble	6
Allen	4	Hancock	4	Ottawa	9
Ashland	5, 16	Hardin	4	Paulding	5
Ashtabula	14	Harrison	18	Perry	7
Athens	6, 18	Henry	5	Pickaway	7
Auglaize	4	Highland	3	Pike	2
Belmont	6, 18	Hocking	18	Portage	14, 17
Brown	2	Holmes	18	Preble	8
Butler	1, 8	Huron	5	Putnam	5
Carroll	18	Jackson	18	Richland	4
Champaign	4	Jefferson	6	Ross	7, 18
Clark	7	Knox	12, 18	Sandusky	5
Clermont	2	Lake	14	Scioto	2, 6
Clinton	3	Lawrence	6	Seneca	5
Columbiana	6	Licking	12, 18	Shelby	4
Coshocton	18	Logan	4	Stark	16
Crawford	5	Lorain	9, 13	Summit	13, 14, 17
Cuyahoga	10, 11, 13, 14	Lucas	5, 9	Trumbull	14, 17
Darke	8	Madison	15	Tuscarawas	18
Defiance	5	Mahoning	6, 17	Union	15
Delaware	12	Marion	4	Van Wert	5
Erie	9	Medina	13, 16	Vinton	18
Fairfield	7	Meigs	6	Warren	2, 3
Fayette	7	Mercer	5, 8	Washington	6
Franklin	7, 12, 15	Miami	8	Wayne	16
Fulton	5	Monroe	6	Williams	5
Gallia	6	Montgomery	3, 8	Wood	5
Geauga	14	Morgan	18	Wyandot	4, 5
Greene	7	Morrow	4		
Guernsey	18	Muskingum	18		

Congressional District 1

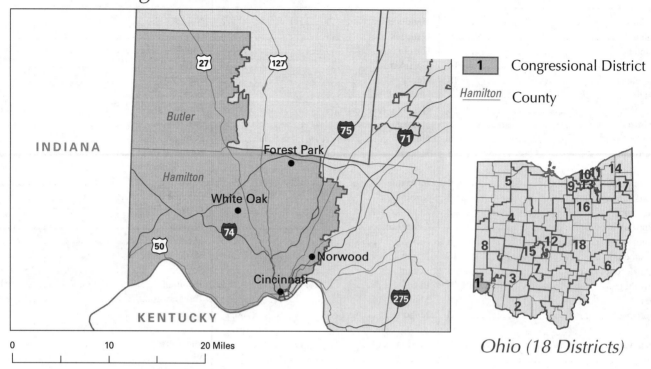

Ohio (18 Districts)

Congressional District 2

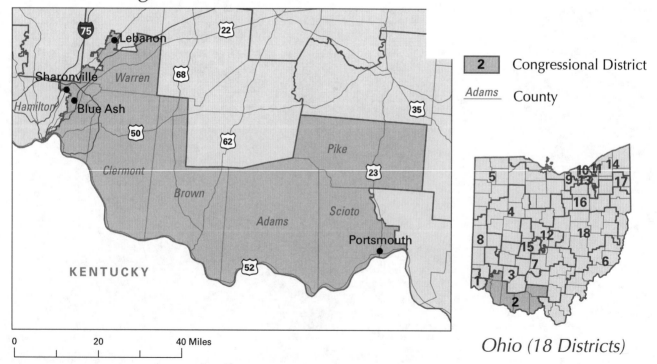

Ohio (18 Districts)

Congressional District 3

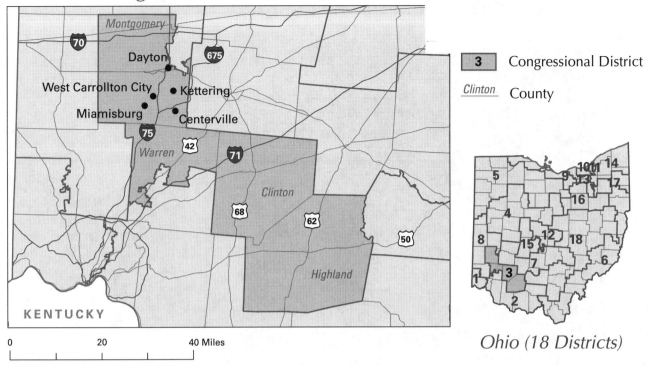

3	Congressional District
Clinton	County

Ohio (18 Districts)

Congressional District 4

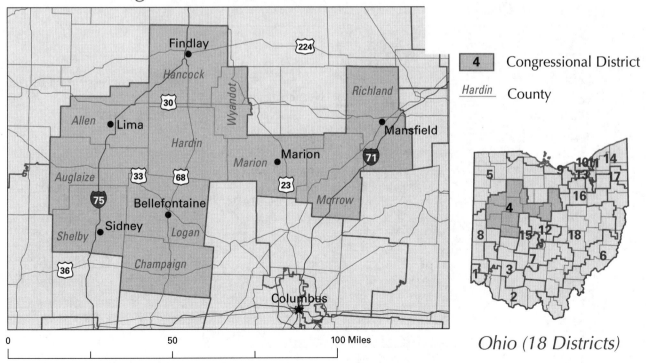

4	Congressional District
Hardin	County

Ohio (18 Districts)

Congressional District 5

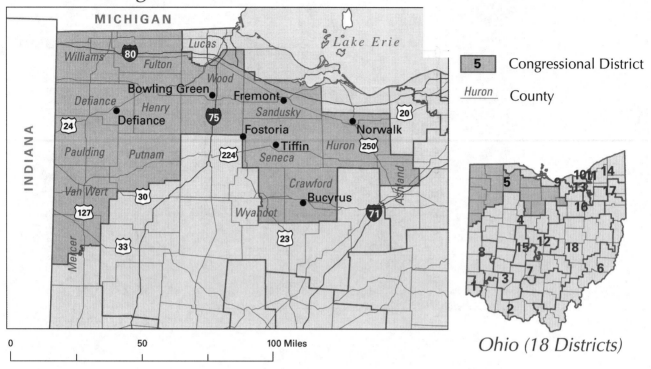

Ohio (18 Districts)

Congressional District 6

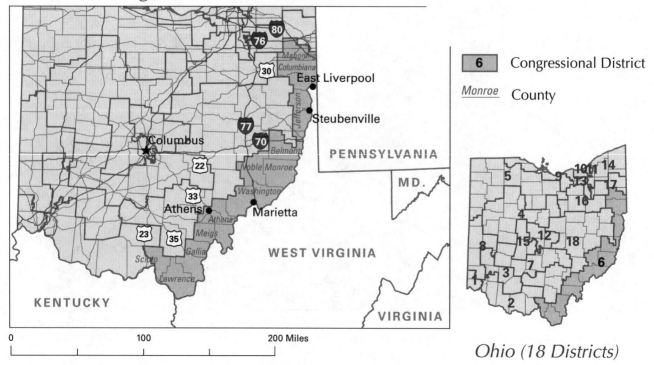

Ohio (18 Districts)

Congressional District 7

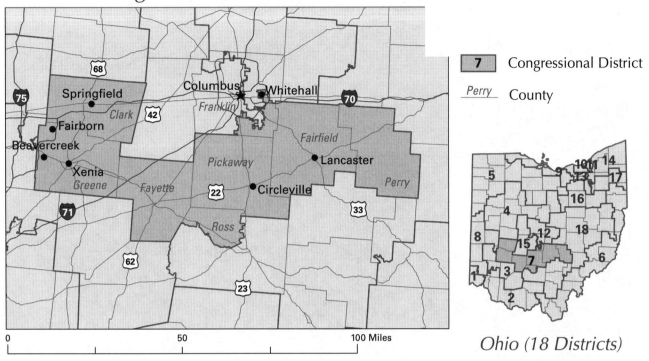

7	Congressional District
Perry	County

Ohio (18 Districts)

Congressional District 8

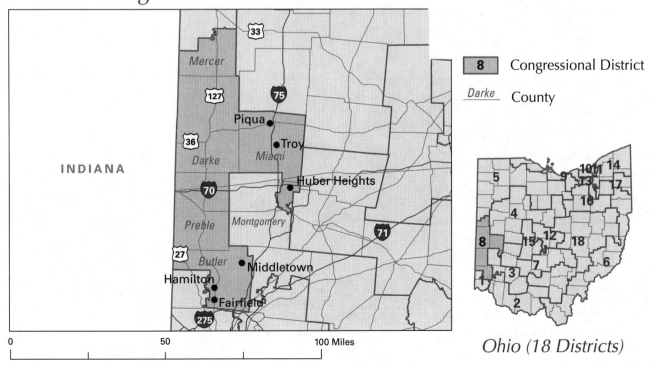

8	Congressional District
Darke	County

Ohio (18 Districts)

Congressional District 9

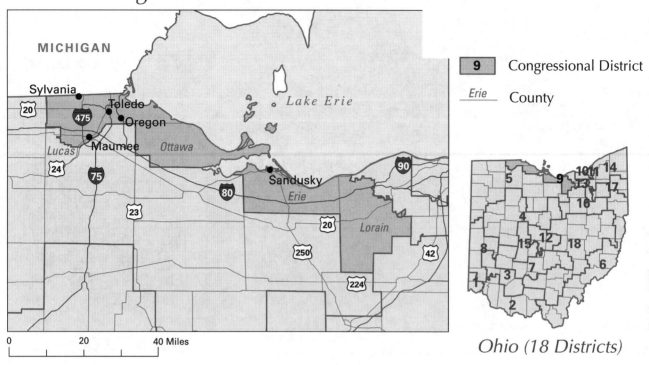

9 Congressional District

Erie County

Ohio (18 Districts)

Congressional District 10

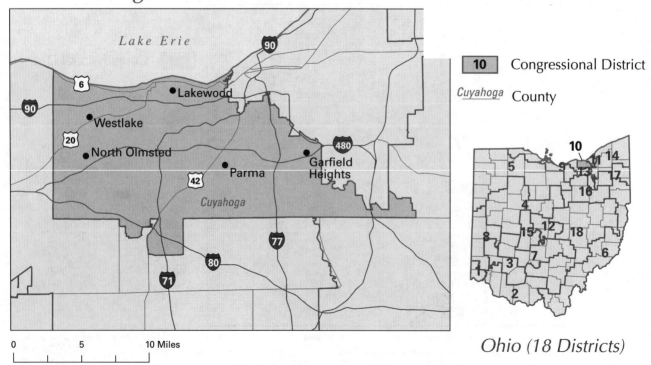

10 Congressional District

Cuyahoga County

Ohio (18 Districts)

Congressional District 11

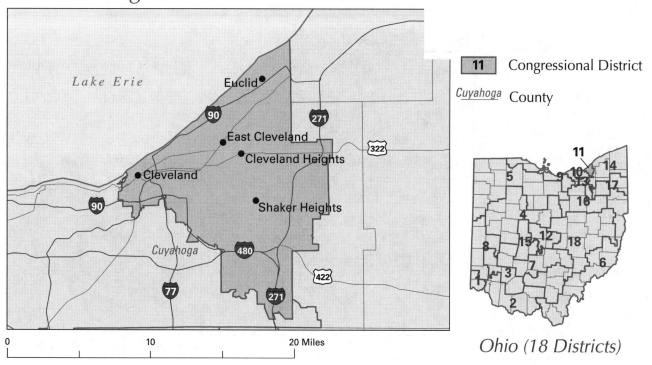

11 Congressional District

Cuyahoga County

Ohio (18 Districts)

Congressional District 12

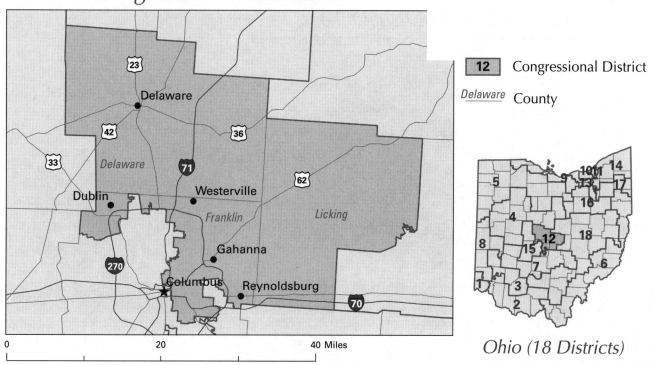

12 Congressional District

Delaware County

Ohio (18 Districts)

Congressional District 13

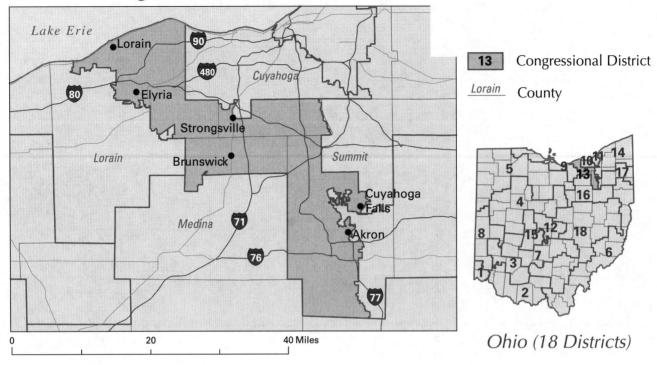

13 Congressional District
Lorain County

Ohio (18 Districts)

Congressional District 14

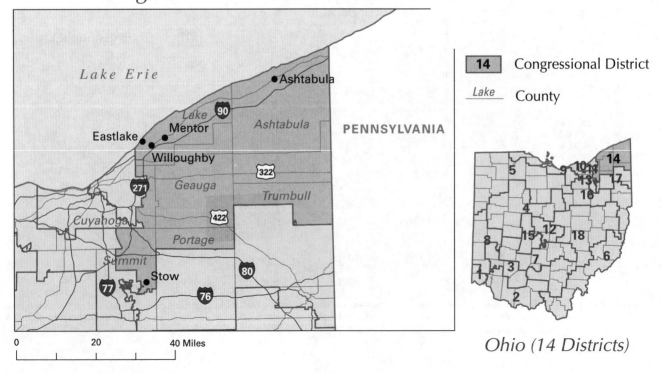

14 Congressional District
Lake County

Ohio (14 Districts)

Congressional District 15

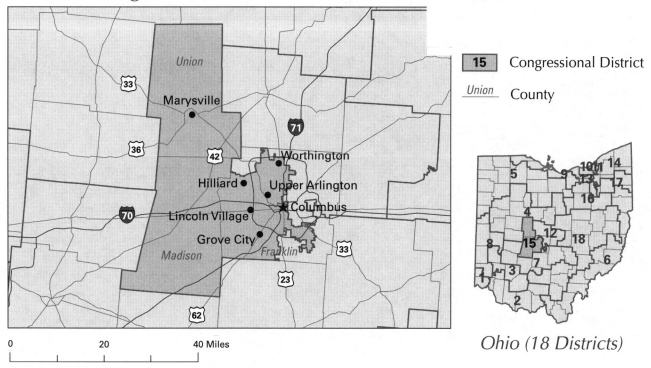

15 Congressional District
Union County

Ohio (18 Districts)

Congressional District 16

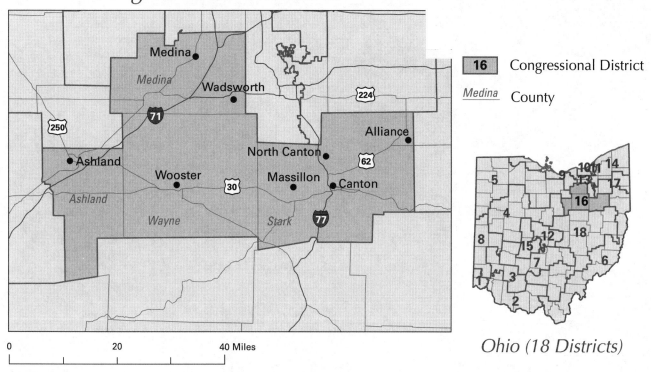

16 Congressional District
Medina County

Ohio (18 Districts)

Congressional District 17

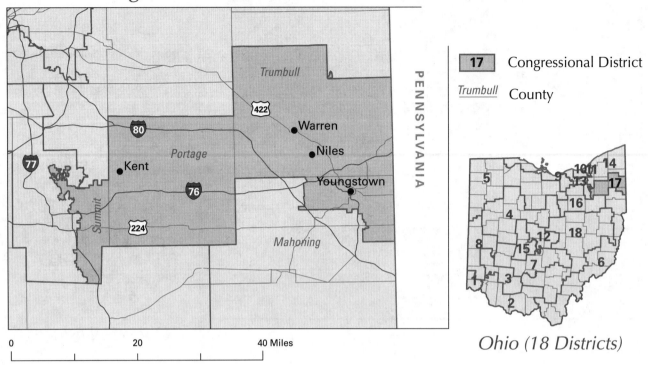

Ohio (18 Districts)

Congressional District 18

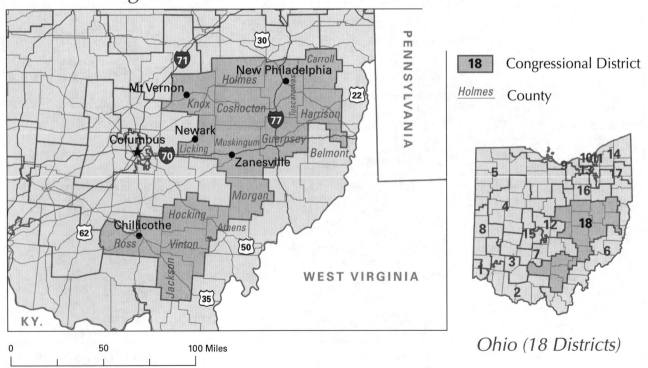

Ohio (18 Districts)

Oklahoma Congressional Districts — 5 Districts Total

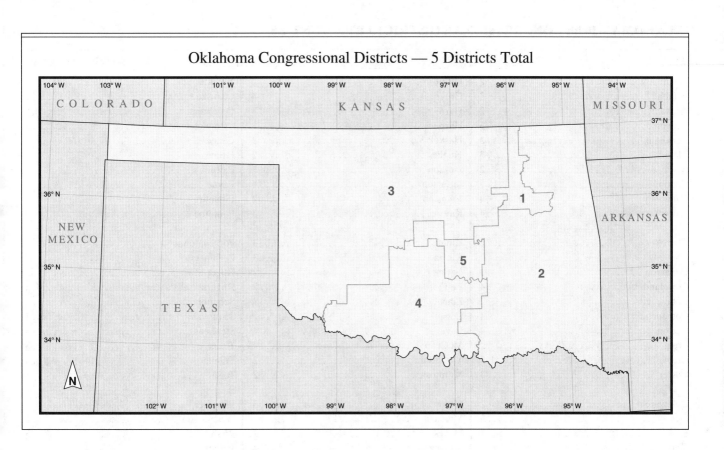

OKLAHOMA—109th CONGRESSIONAL DISTRICTS BY COUNTIES

County	Congressional District	County	Congressional District	County	Congressional District
Adair	2	Grant	3	Nowata	2
Alfalfa	3	Greer	3	Okfuskee	2
Atoka	2	Harmon	3	Oklahoma	4, 5
Beaver	3	Harper	3	Okmulgee	2
Beckham	3	Haskell	2	Osage	3
Blaine	3	Hughes	2	Ottawa	2
Bryan	2	Jackson	3	Pawnee	3
Caddo	3	Jefferson	4	Payne	3
Canadian	3, 4	Johnston	2	Pittsburg	2
Carter	4	Kay	3	Pontotoc	4
Cherokee	2	Kingfisher	3	Pottawatomie	5
Choctaw	2	Kiowa	3	Pushmataha	2
Cimarron	3	Latimer	2	Roger Mills	3
Cleveland	4	Le Flore	2	Rogers	1, 2
Coal	2	Lincoln	3	Seminole	5
Comanche	4	Logan	3	Sequoyah	2
Cotton	4	Love	4	Stephens	4
Craig	2	McClain	4	Texas	3
Creek	1, 3	McCurtain	2	Tillman	4
Custer	3	McIntosh	2	Tulsa	1
Delaware	2	Major	3	Wagoner	1
Dewey	3	Marshall	4	Washington	1
Ellis	3	Mayes	2	Washita	3
Garfield	3	Murray	4	Woods	3
Garvin	4	Muskogee	2	Woodward	3
Grady	4	Noble	3		

Congressional District 1

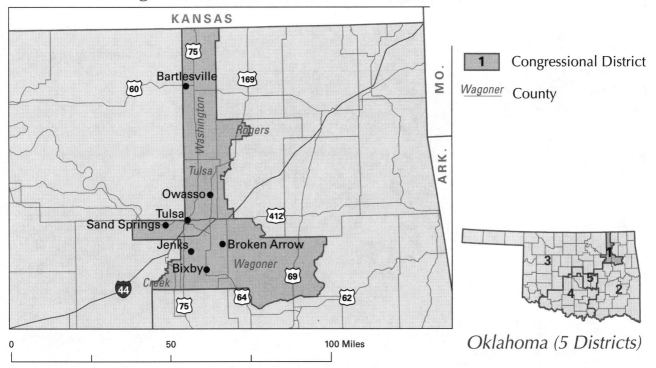

1 Congressional District
Wagoner County

Oklahoma (5 Districts)

Congressional District 2

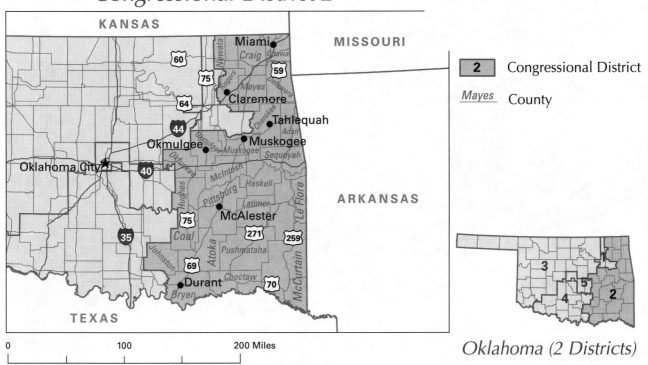

2 Congressional District
Mayes County

Oklahoma (2 Districts)

Congressional District 3

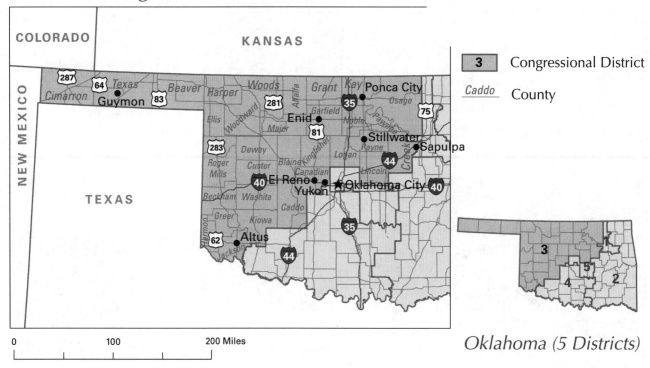

3 Congressional District
Caddo County

0   100   200 Miles

Oklahoma (5 Districts)

Congressional District 4

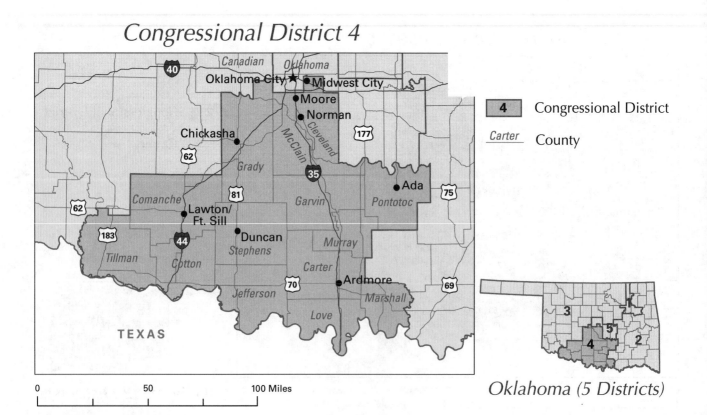

4 Congressional District
Carter County

0   50   100 Miles

Oklahoma (5 Districts)

Congressional District 5

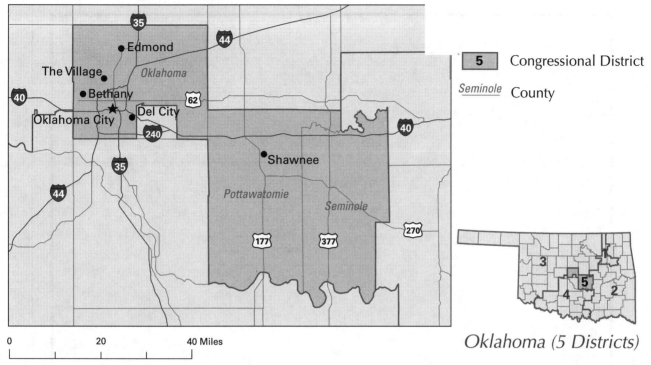

0   20   40 Miles

5 Congressional District

Seminole County

Oklahoma (5 Districts)

Oregon Congressional Districts — 5 Districts Total

OREGON—109th CONGRESSIONAL DISTRICTS BY COUNTIES

County	Congressional District	County	Congressional District	County	Congressional District
Baker	2	Harney	2	Morrow	2
Benton	4,5	Hood River	2	Multnomah	1,3,5
Clackamas	3,5	Jackson	2	Polk	5
Clatsop	1	Jefferson	2	Sherman	2
Columbia	1	Josephine	2,4	Tillamook	5
Coos	4	Klamath	2	Umatilla	2
Crook	2	Lake	2	Union	2
Curry	4	Lane	4	Wallowa	2
Deschutes	2	Lincoln	5	Wasco	2
Douglas	4	Linn	4	Washington	1
Gilliam	2	Malheur	2	Wheeler	2
Grant	2	Marion	5	Yamhill	1

Congressional District 1

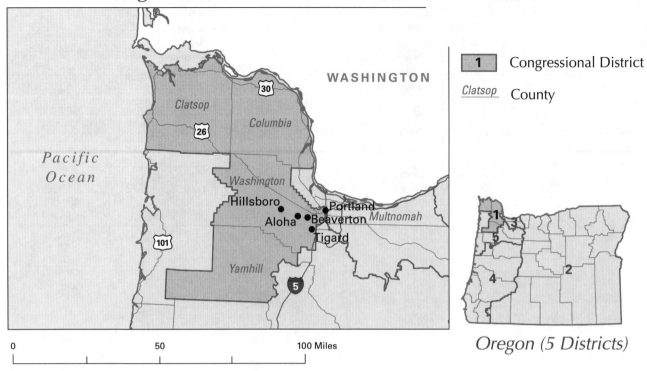

Oregon (5 Districts)

Congressional District 2

Oregon (5 Districts)

Congressional District 3

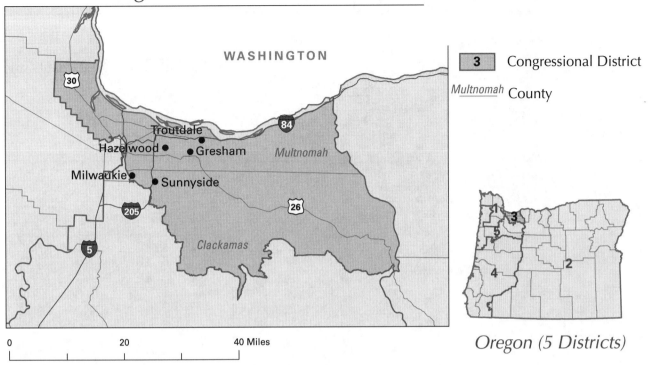

Oregon (5 Districts)

Congressional District 4

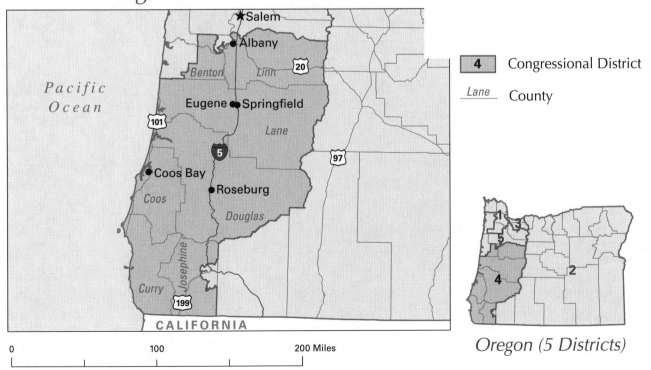

Oregon (5 Districts)

Congressional District 5

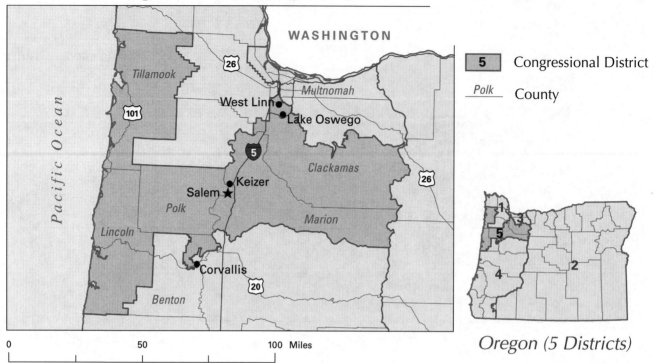

Oregon (5 Districts)

Pennsylvania — Counties

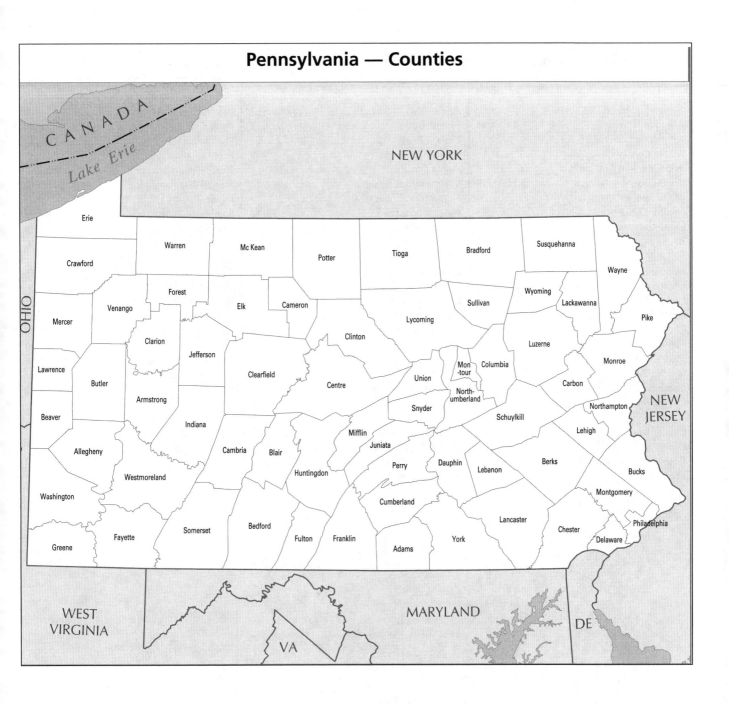

PENNSYLVANIA—109th CONGRESSIONAL DISTRICTS BY COUNTIES

County	Congressional District
Adams County	19
Allegheny County	4, 12, 14, 18
Armstrong County	3, 12
Beaver County	4, 18
Bedford County	9
Berks County	6, 15, 16, 17
Blair County	9
Bradford County	10
Bucks County	8
Butler County	3, 4
Cambria County	9, 12
Cameron County	5
Carbon County	11
Centre County	5, 10
Chester County	6, 7, 16
Clarion County	5
Clearfield County	5, 9
Clinton County	5
Columbia County	11
Crawford County	3, 5
Cumberland County	9, 19
Dauphin County	17
Delaware County	1, 7
Elk County	5

County	Congressional District
Erie County	3
Fayette County	9, 12
Forest County	5
Franklin County	9, 19
Fulton County	9
Greene County	12
Huntingdon County	9
Indiana County	9, 12
Jefferson County	5
Juniata County	5, 9
Lackawanna County	10, 11
Lancaster County	16
Lawrence County	4
Lebanon County	17
Lehigh County	6, 8, 15
Luzerne County	10, 11
Lycoming County	5, 10, 11
McKean County	5
Mercer County	3, 4
Mifflin County	5, 9
Monroe County	11
Montgomery County	2, 6, 7, 8, 13, 15
Montour County	10
Northampton County	15

County	Congressional District
Northumberland County	10
Perry County	9, 17
Philadelphia County	1, 2, 8, 13
Pike County	10
Potter County	5
Schuylkill County	17
Snyder County	10
Somerset County	9, 12
Sullivan County	10
Susquehanna County	10
Tioga County	5, 10
Union County	10
Venango County	3, 5
Warren County	3, 5
Washington County	12, 18
Wayne County	10
Westmoreland County	4, 9, 12, 18
Wyoming County	10
York County	19

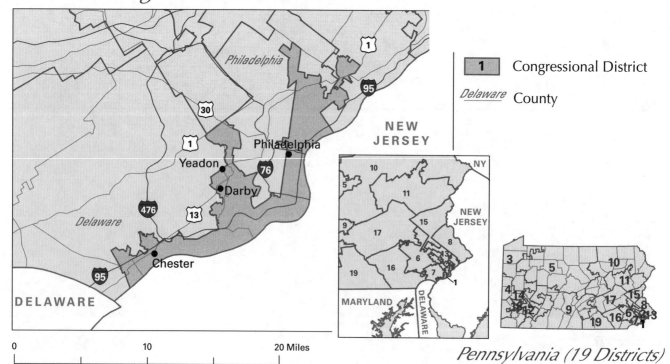

Congressional District 1

Pennsylvania (19 Districts)

Congressional District 2

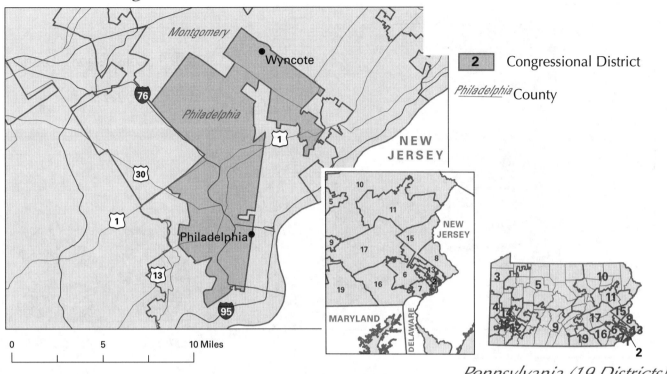

Pennsylvania (19 Districts)

Congressional District 3

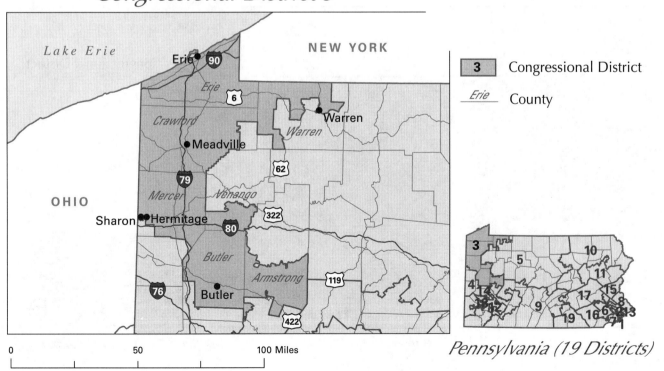

Pennsylvania (19 Districts)

Congressional District 4

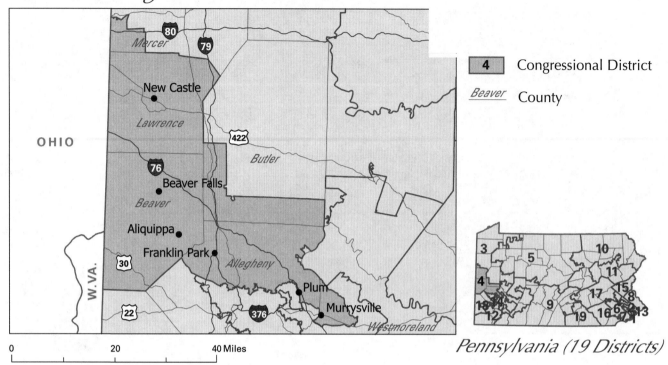

4	Congressional District
Beaver	County

Pennsylvania (19 Districts)

Congressional District 5

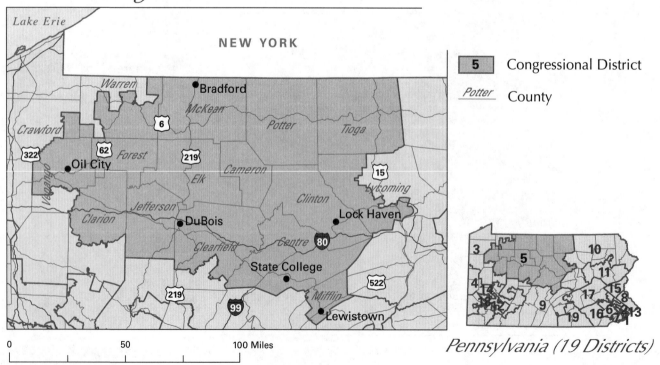

5	Congressional District
Potter	County

Pennsylvania (19 Districts)

Congressional District 6

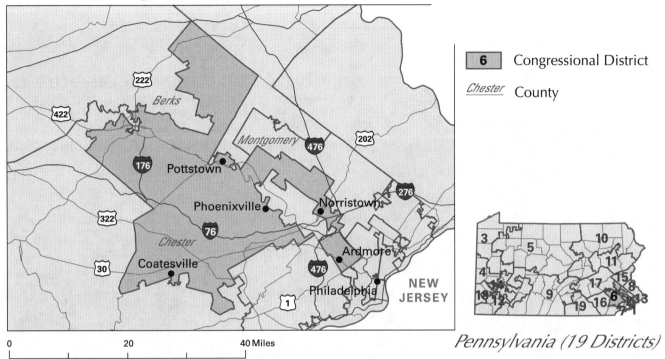

Pennsylvania (19 Districts)

Congressional District 7

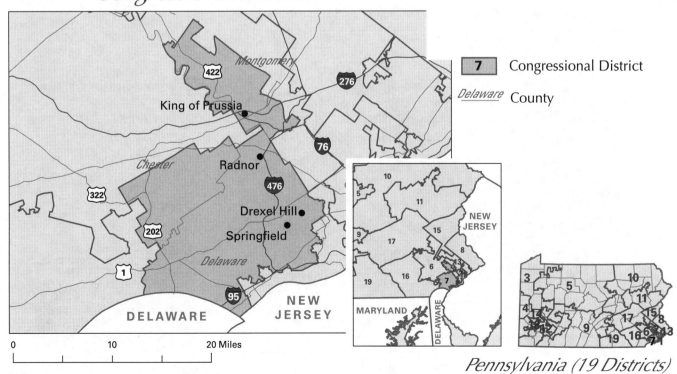

Pennsylvania (19 Districts)

Congressional District 8

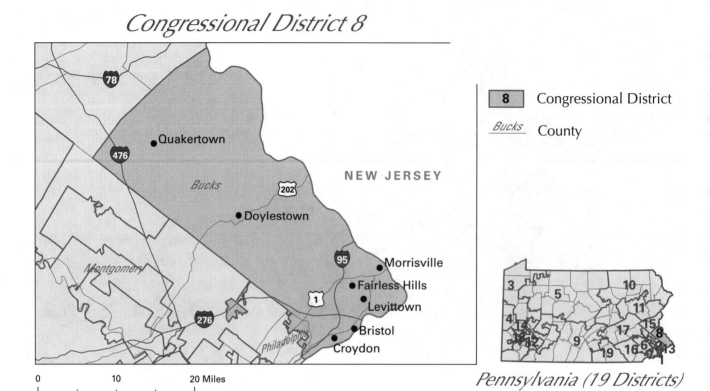

Pennsylvania (19 Districts)

Congressional District 9

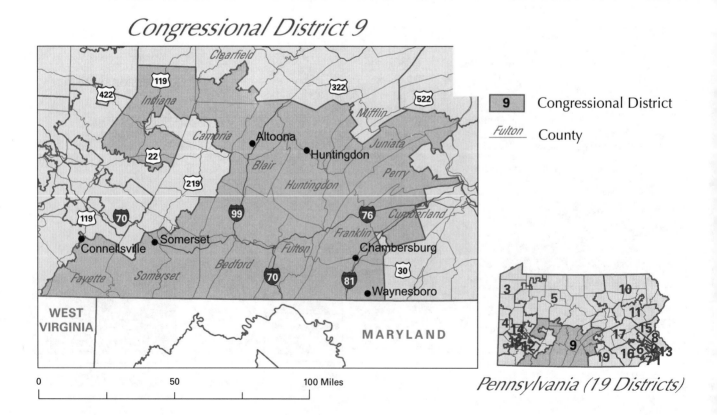

Pennsylvania (19 Districts)

Congressional District 10

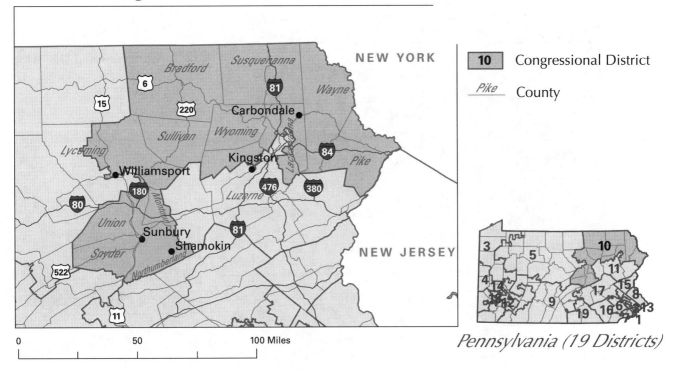

Pennsylvania (19 Districts)

Congressional District 11

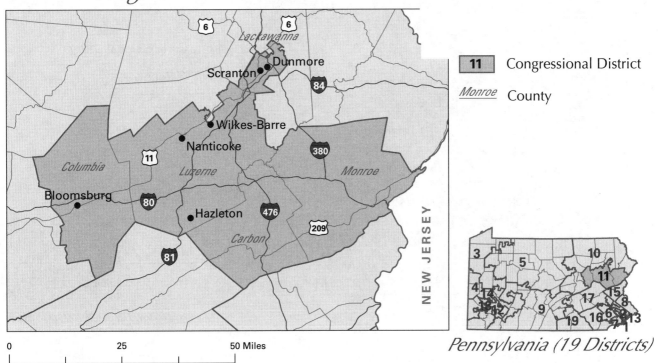

Pennsylvania (19 Districts)

Congressional District 12

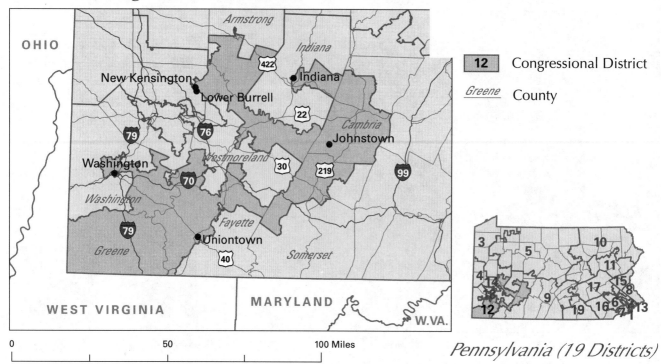

12	Congressional District
Greene	County

Pennsylvania (19 Districts)

Congressional District 13

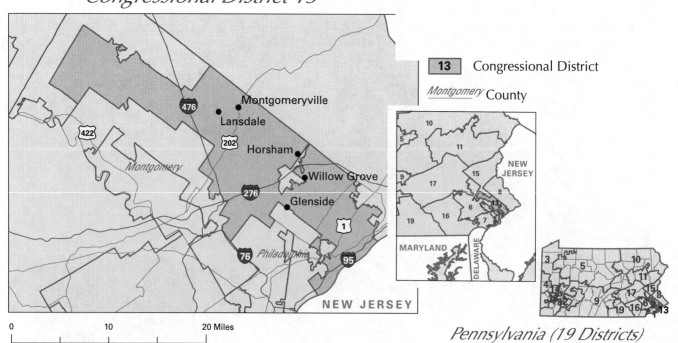

13	Congressional District
Montgomery	County

Pennsylvania (19 Districts)

Congressional District 14

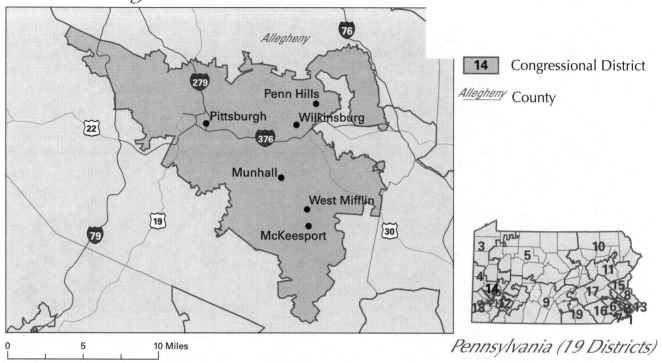

14	Congressional District
Allegheny	County

Pennsylvania (19 Districts)

Congressional District 15

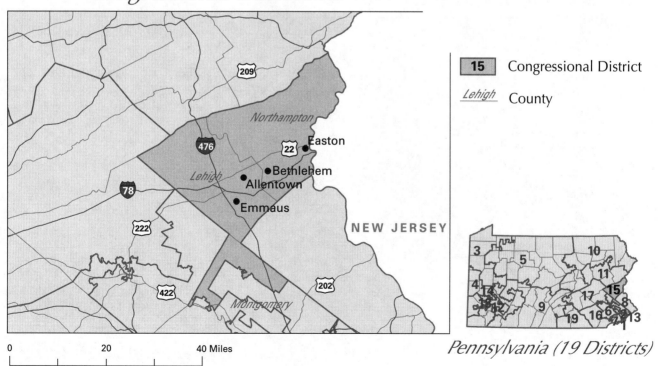

15	Congressional District
Lehigh	County

Pennsylvania (19 Districts)

Congressional District 16

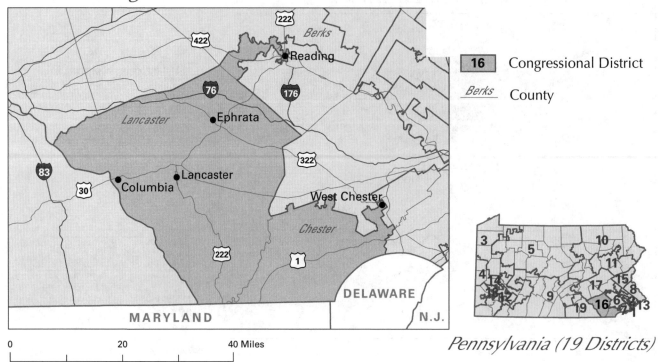

16   Congressional District

Berks   County

Pennsylvania (19 Districts)

0   20   40 Miles

Congressional District 17

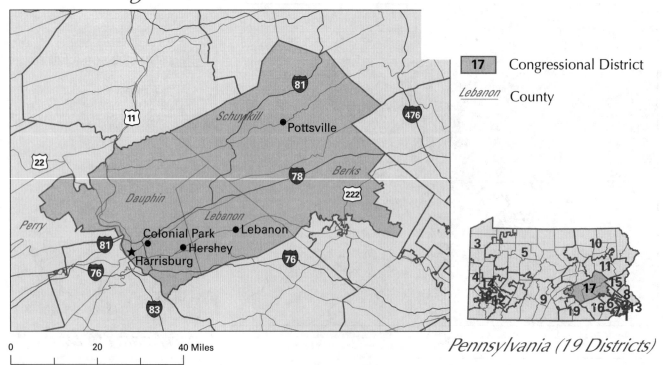

17   Congressional District

Lebanon   County

Pennsylvania (19 Districts)

0   20   40 Miles

Congressional District 18

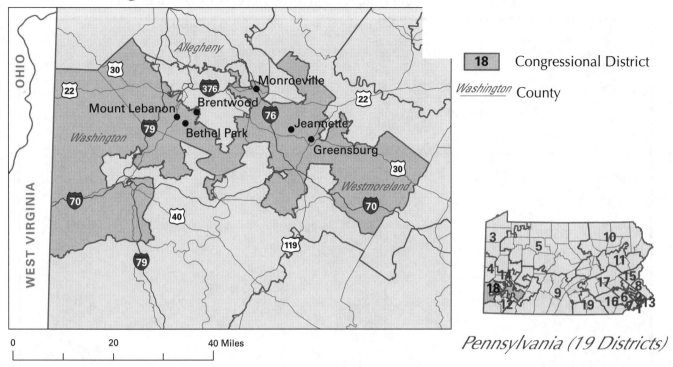

18	Congressional District
Washington	County

Pennsylvania (19 Districts)

0   20   40 Miles

Congressional District 19

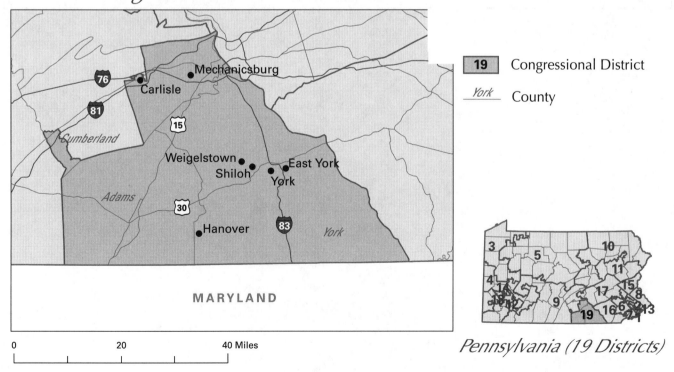

19	Congressional District
York	County

Pennsylvania (19 Districts)

0   20   40 Miles

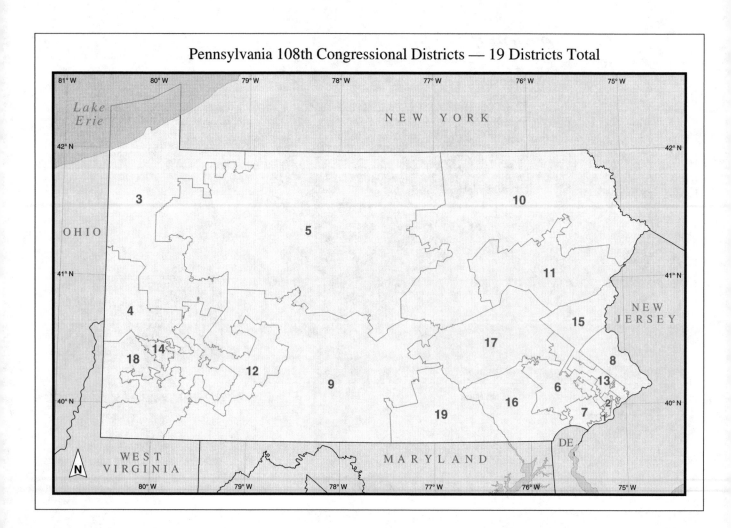

Pennsylvania 108th Congressional Districts — 19 Districts Total

PENNSYLVANIA—108th CONGRESSIONAL DISTRICTS BY COUNTIES

County	Congressional District	County	Congressional District	County	Congressional District
Adams	19	Elk	5	Montour	10
Allegheny	4, 12, 14, 18	Erie	3	Northampton	15
Armstrong	3, 12	Fayette	9, 12	Northumberland	10
Beaver	4	Forest	5	Perry	9, 17
Bedford	9	Franklin	9	Philadelphia	1, 2, 8, 13
Berks	6, 16, 17	Fulton	9	Pike	10
Blair	9	Greene	12	Potter	5
Bradford	10	Huntingdon	9	Schuylkill	17
Bucks	8	Indiana	9, 12	Snyder	10
Butler	3, 4	Jefferson	5	Somerset	9, 12
Cambria	9, 12	Juniata	9	Sullivan	10
Cameron	5	Lackawanna	10, 11	Susquehanna	10
Carbon	11	Lancaster	16	Tioga	5
Centre	5	Lawrence	4	Union	10
Chester	6, 7, 16	Lebanon	17	Venango	3, 5
Clarion	5	Lehigh	15	Warren	3, 5
Clearfield	5, 9	Luzerne	10, 11	Washington	12, 18
Clinton	5	Lycoming	5, 10	Wayne	10
Columbia	11	McKean	5	Westmoreland	4, 12, 18
Crawford	3, 5	Mercer	3, 4	Wyoming	10
Cumberland	9, 19	Mifflin	5, 9	York	19
Dauphin	17	Monroe	11		
Delaware	1, 7	Montgomery	2, 6–8, 13, 15		

Congressional District 1

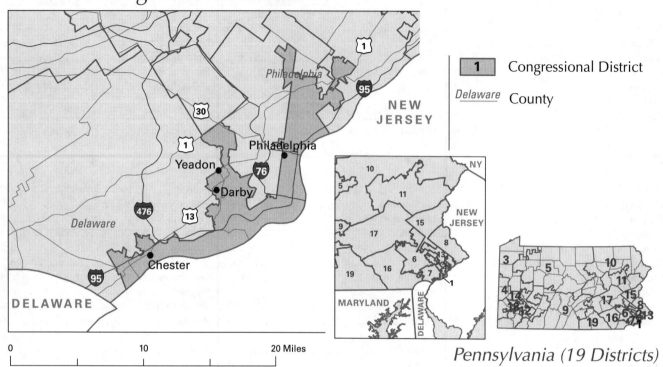

Pennsylvania (19 Districts)

Congressional District 2

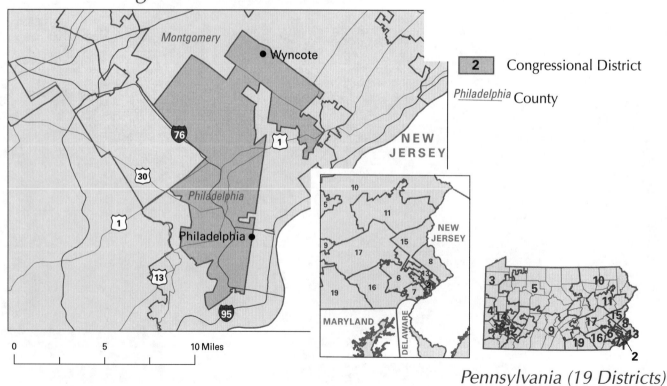

Pennsylvania (19 Districts)

Congressional District 3

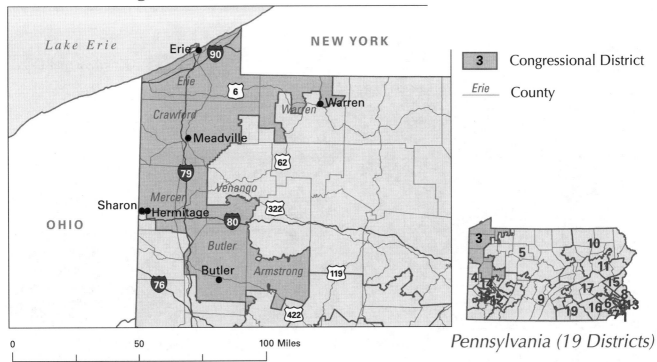

Pennsylvania (19 Districts)

Congressional District 4

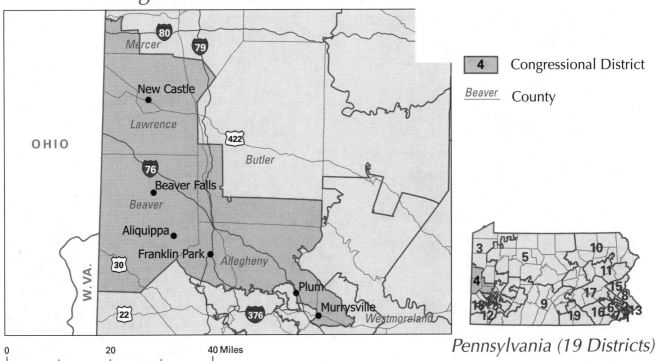

Pennsylvania (19 Districts)

Congressional District 5

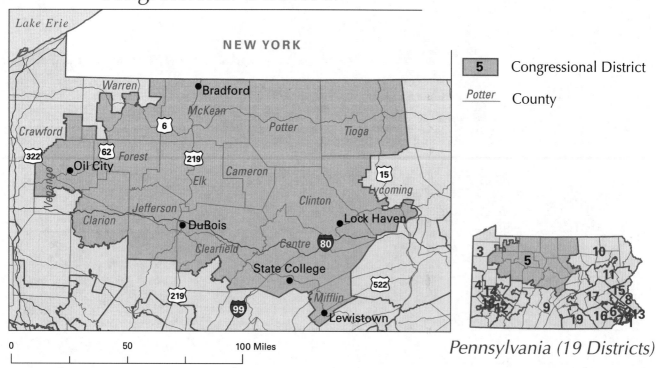

Pennsylvania (19 Districts)

Congressional District 6

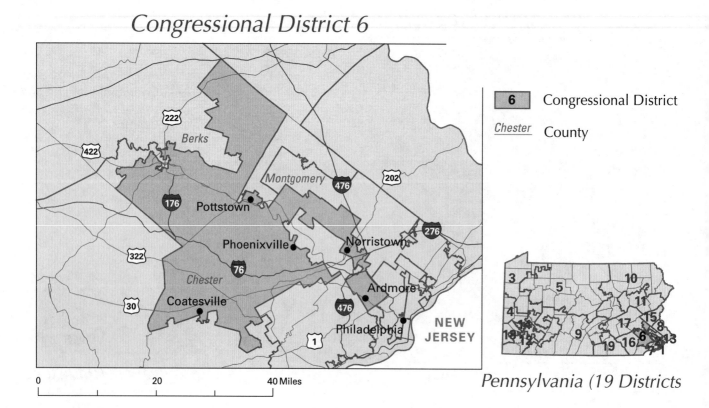

Pennsylvania (19 Districts

Congressional District 7

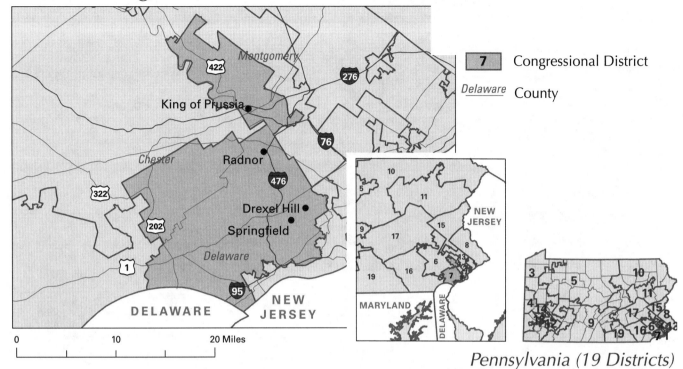

Pennsylvania (19 Districts)

Congressional District 8

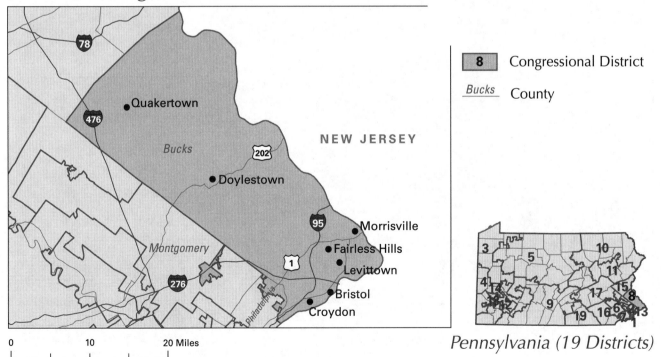

Pennsylvania (19 Districts)

Congressional District 9

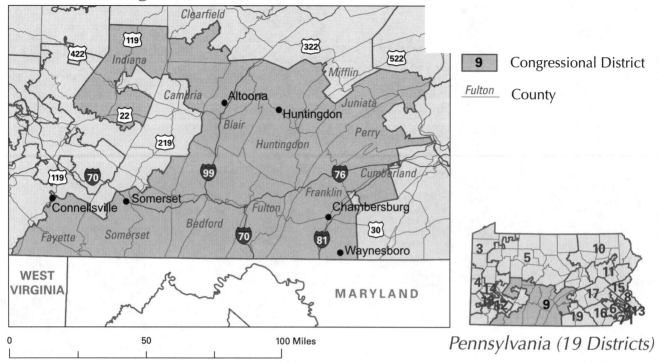

9	Congressional District
Fulton	County

Pennsylvania (19 Districts)

Congressional District 10

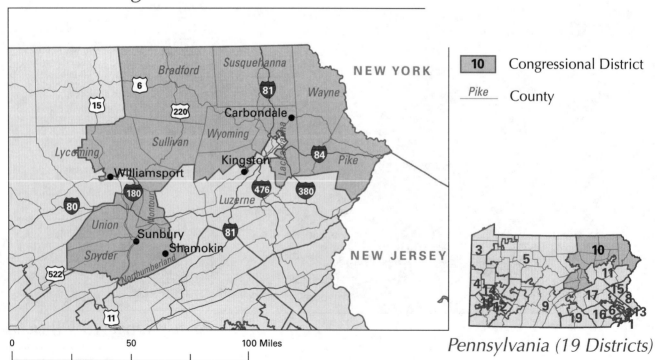

10	Congressional District
Pike	County

Pennsylvania (19 Districts)

Congressional District 11

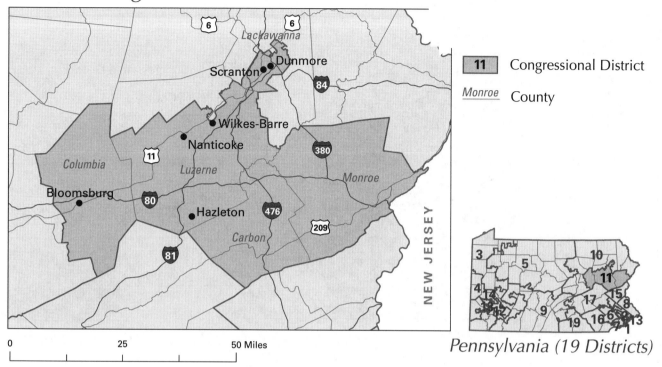

11 Congressional District

Monroe County

Pennsylvania (19 Districts)

Congressional District 12

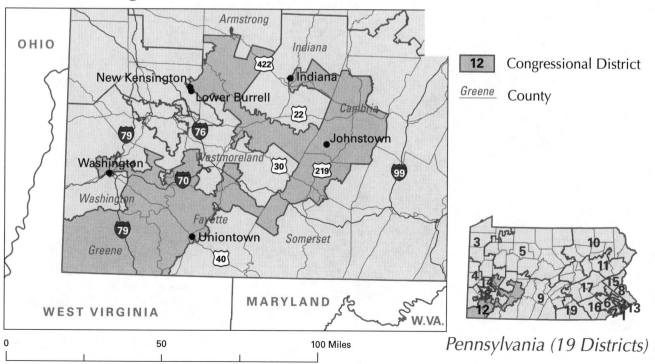

12 Congressional District

Greene County

Pennsylvania (19 Districts)

Congressional District 13

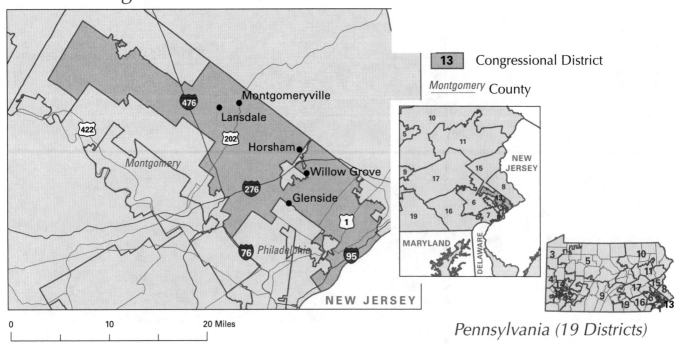

13   Congressional District

Montgomery County

Pennsylvania (19 Districts)

Congressional District 14

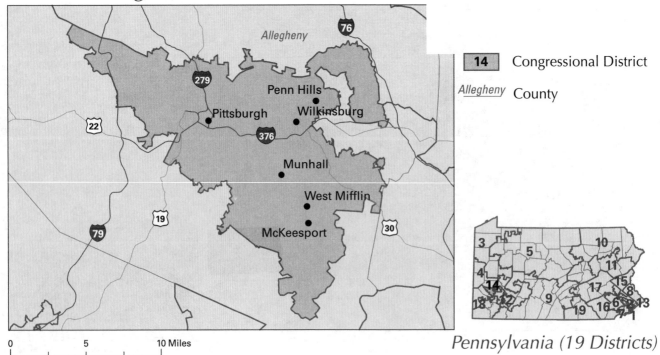

14   Congressional District

Allegheny County

Pennsylvania (19 Districts)

Congressional District 15

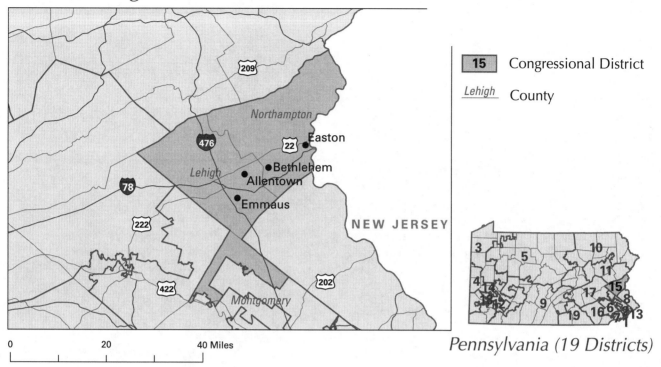

Pennsylvania (19 Districts)

Congressional District 16

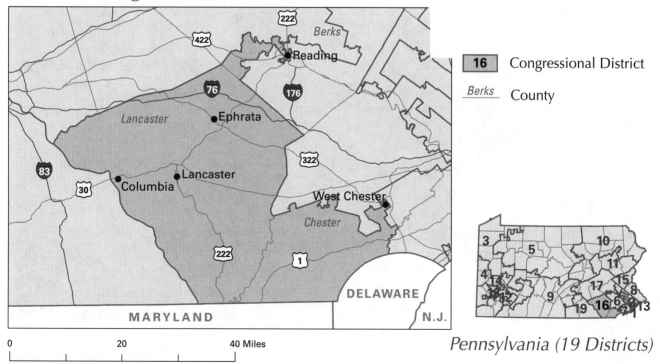

Pennsylvania (19 Districts)

Congressional District 17

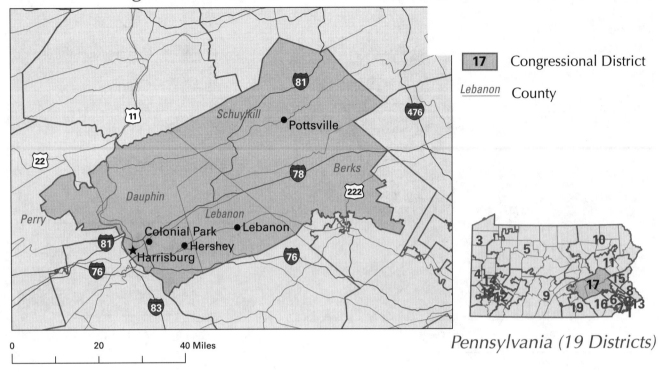

17 Congressional District
Lebanon County

Pennsylvania (19 Districts)

Congressional District 18

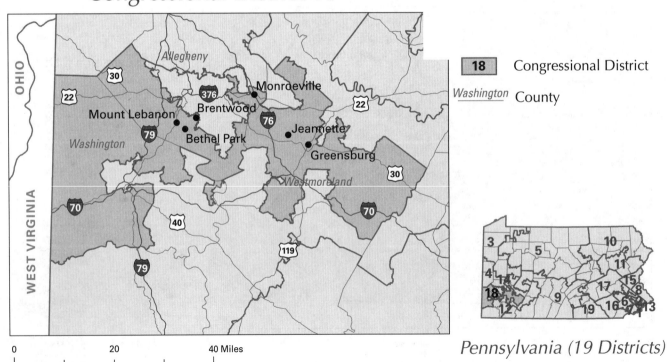

18 Congressional District
Washington County

Pennsylvania (19 Districts)

Congressional District 19

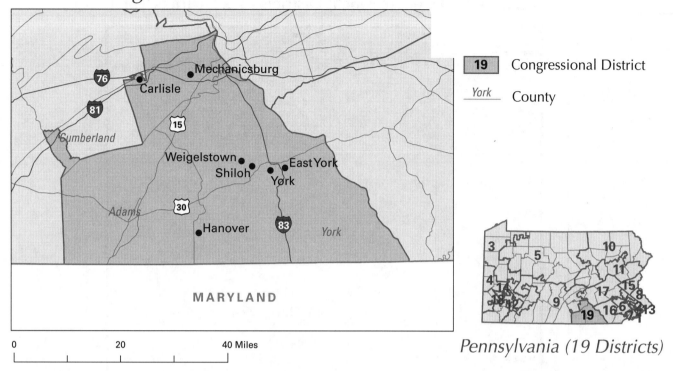

19	Congressional District
York	County

Pennsylvania (19 Districts)

Rhode Island Congressional Districts — 2 Districts Total

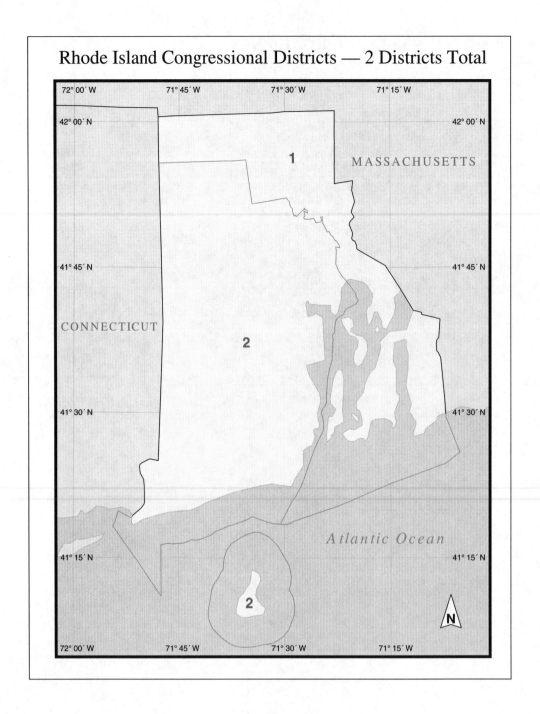

RHODE ISLAND—109th CONGRESSIONAL DISTRICTS BY COUNTIES

County	Congressional District
Bristol	1
Kent	2
Newport	1
Providence	1, 2
Washington	2

Congressional District 1

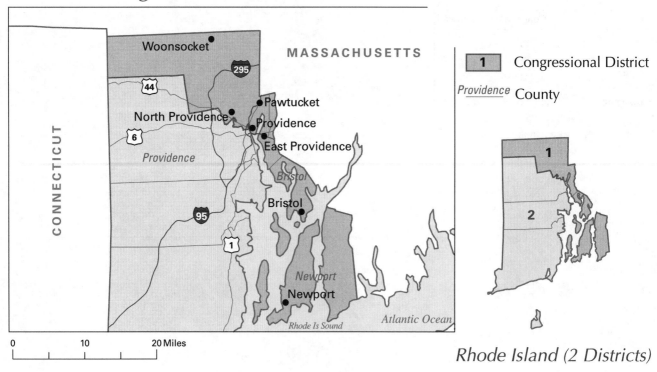

Rhode Island (2 Districts)

Congressional District 2

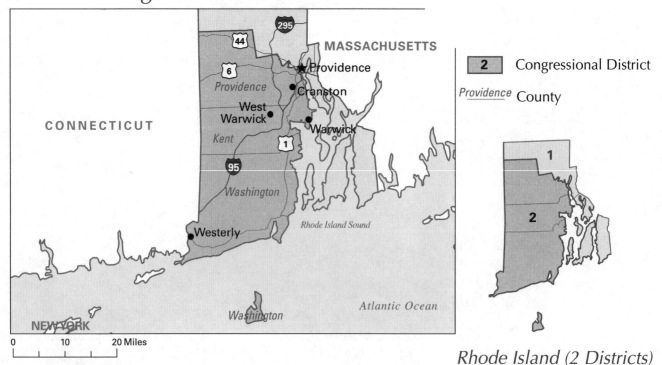

Rhode Island (2 Districts)

South Carolina Congressional Districts — 6 Districts Total

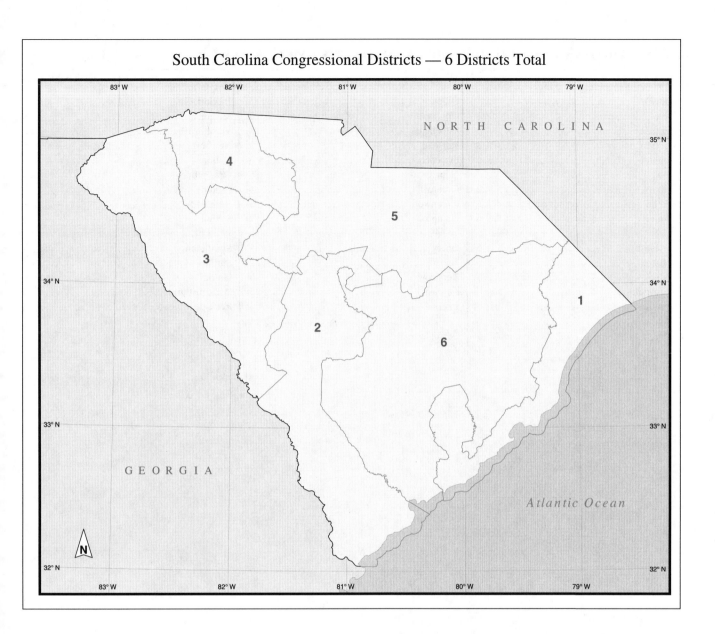

SOUTH CAROLINA—109th CONGRESSIONAL DISTRICTS BY COUNTIES

County	Congressional District
Abbeville	3
Aiken	2, 3
Allendale	2
Anderson	3
Bamberg	6
Barnwell	2
Beaufort	2
Berkeley	1, 6
Calhoun	2, 6
Charleston	1, 6
Cherokee	5
Chester	5
Chesterfield	5
Clarendon	6
Colleton	6
Darlington	5

County	Congressional District
Dillon	5
Dorchester	1, 6
Edgefield	3
Fairfield	5
Florence	5, 6
Georgetown	1, 6
Greenville	4
Greenwood	3
Hampton	2
Horry	1
Jasper	2
Kershaw	5
Lancaster	5
Laurens	3, 4
Lee	5, 6
Lexington	2

County	Congressional District
McCormick	3
Marion	6
Marlboro	5
Newberry	5
Oconee	3
Orangeburg	2, 6
Pickens	3
Richland	2, 6
Saluda	3
Spartanburg	4
Sumter	5, 6
Union	4
Williamsburg	6
York	5

Congressional District 1

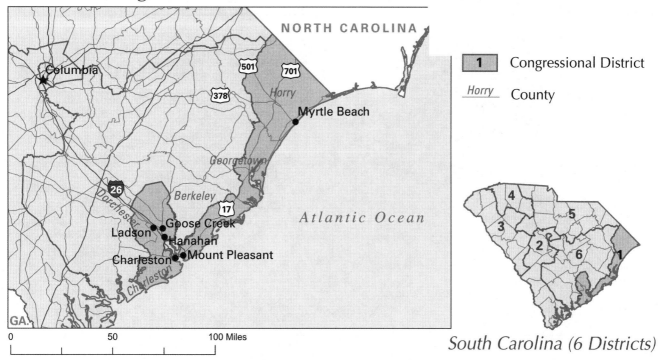

South Carolina (6 Districts)

Congressional District 2

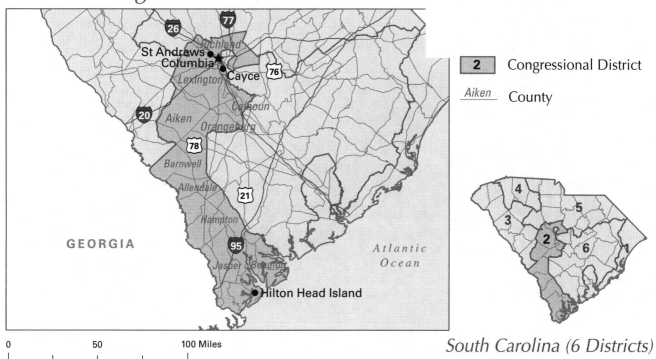

South Carolina (6 Districts)

Congressional District 3

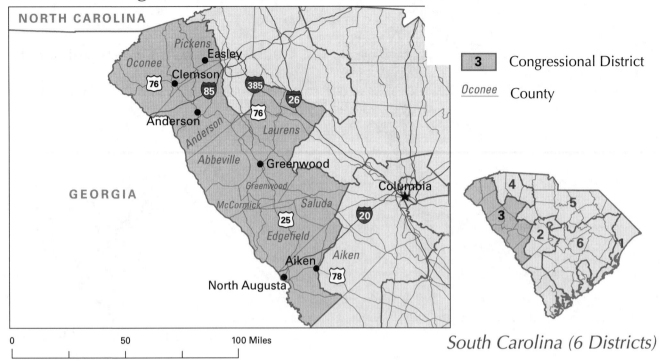

South Carolina (6 Districts)

Congressional District 4

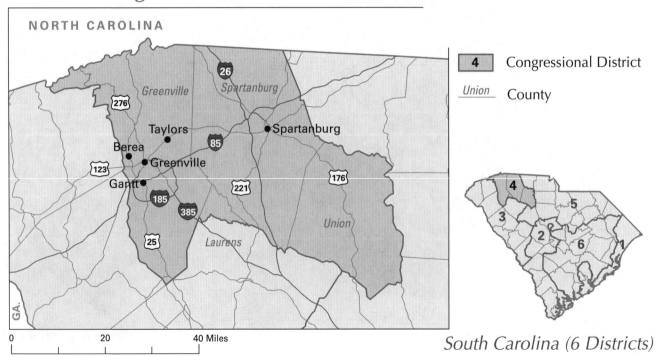

South Carolina (6 Districts)

Congressional District 5

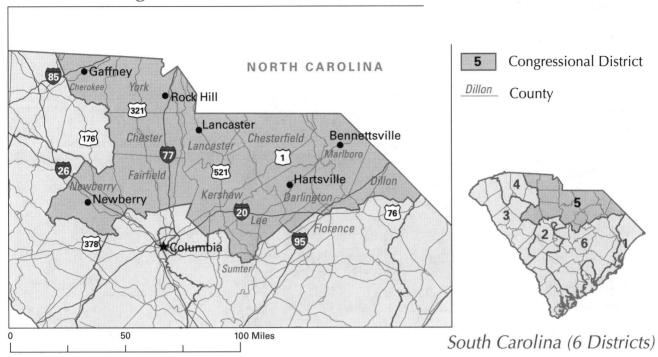

South Carolina (6 Districts)

Congressional District 6

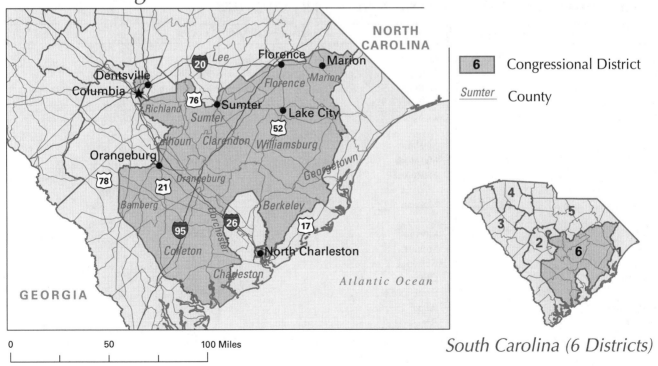

South Carolina (6 Districts)

South Dakota—
Congressional District: At large

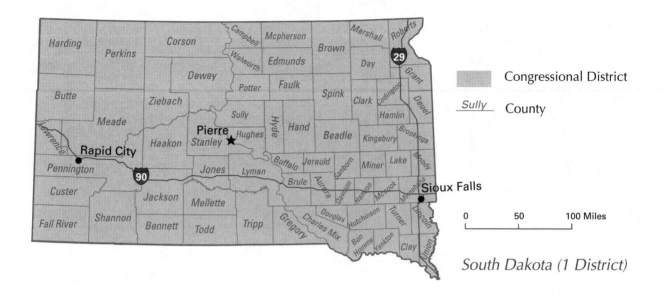

Congressional District

Sully County

South Dakota (1 District)

SOUTH DAKOTA—109th CONGRESSIONAL DISTRICTS BY COUNTIES

County	Congressional District	County	Congressional District	County	Congressional District
Adams	1	Grant	1	Ransom	1
Barnes	1	Griggs	1	Renville	1
Benson	1	Hettinger	1	Richland	1
Billings	1	Kidder	1	Rolette	1
Bottineau	1	La Moure	1	Sargent	1
Bowman	1	Logan	1	Sheridan	1
Burke	1	McHenry	1	Sioux	1
Burleigh	1	McIntosh	1	Slope	1
Cass	1	McKenzie	1	Stark	1
Cavalier	1	McLean	1	Steele	1
Dickey	1	Mercer	1	Stutsman	1
Divide	1	Morton	1	Towner	1
Dunn	1	Mountrail	1	Traill	1
Eddy	1	Nelson	1	Walsh	1
Emmons	1	Oliver	1	Ward	1
Foster	1	Pembina	1	Wells	1
Golden Valley	1	Pierce	1	Williams	1
Grand Forks	1	Ramsey	1		

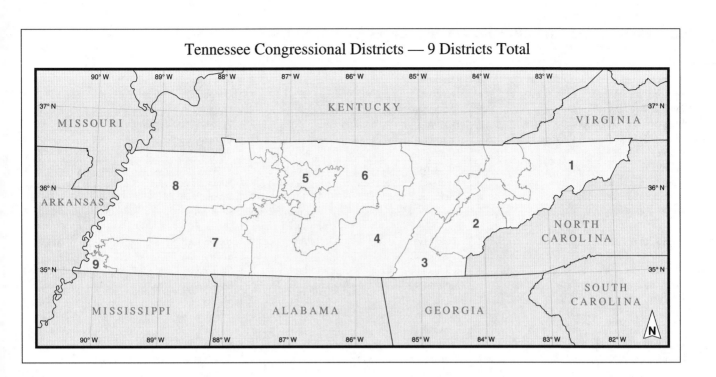

Tennessee Congressional Districts — 9 Districts Total

TENNESSEE—109th CONGRESSIONAL DISTRICTS BY COUNTIES

County	Congressional District	County	Congressional District	County	Congressional District
Anderson	3	Hamilton	3	Morgan	4
Bedford	6	Hancock	1	Obion	8
Benton	8	Hardeman	7	Overton	6
Bledsoe	4	Hardin	7	Perry	7
Blount	2	Hawkins	1	Pickett	4
Bradley	3	Haywood	8	Polk	3
Campbell	4	Henderson	7	Putnam	6
Cannon	6	Henry	8	Rhea	3
Carroll	8	Hickman	4, 7	Roane	3, 4
Carter	1	Houston	8	Robertson	6
Cheatham	5, 7	Humphreys	8	Rutherford	6
Chester	7	Jackson	6	Scott	4
Claiborne	3	Jefferson	1, 3	Sequatchie	4
Clay	6	Johnson	1	Sevier	1, 2
Cocke	1	Knox	2	Shelby	7–9
Coffee	4	Lake	8	Smith	6
Crockett	8	Lauderdale	8	Stewart	8
Cumberland	4	Lawrence	4	Sullivan	1
Davidson	5, 7	Lewis	4	Sumner	6
Decatur	7	Lincoln	4	Tipton	8
DeKalb	6	Loudon	2	Trousdale	6
Dickson	7, 8	McMinn	2	Unicoi	1
Dyer	8	McNairy	7	Union	3
Fayette	7	Macon	6	Van Buren	4
Fentress	4	Madison	8	Warren	4
Franklin	4	Marion	4	Washington	1
Gibson	8	Marshall	6	Wayne	7
Giles	4	Maury	4	Weakley	8
Grainger	3	Meigs	3	White	4
Greene	1	Monroe	2	Williamson	4, 7
Grundy	4	Montgomery	7, 8	Wilson	5, 6
Hamblen	1	Moore	4		

Congressional District 1

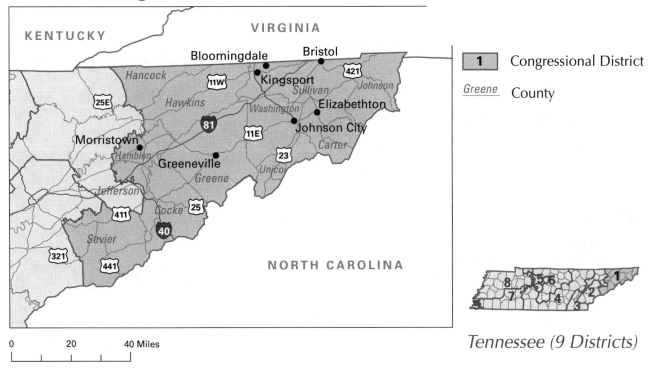

1	Congressional District
Greene	County

Tennessee (9 Districts)

0   20   40 Miles

Congressional District 2

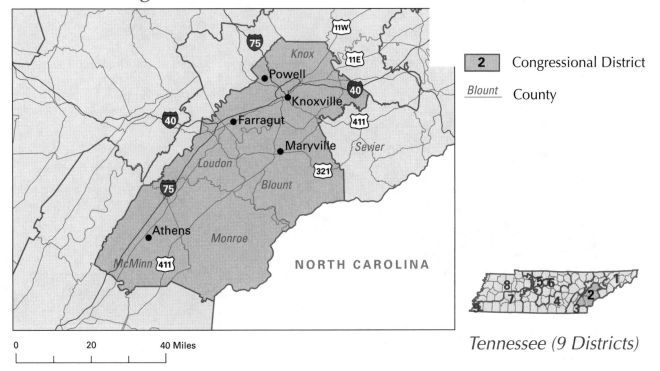

2	Congressional District
Blount	County

Tennessee (9 Districts)

0   20   40 Miles

Congressional District 3

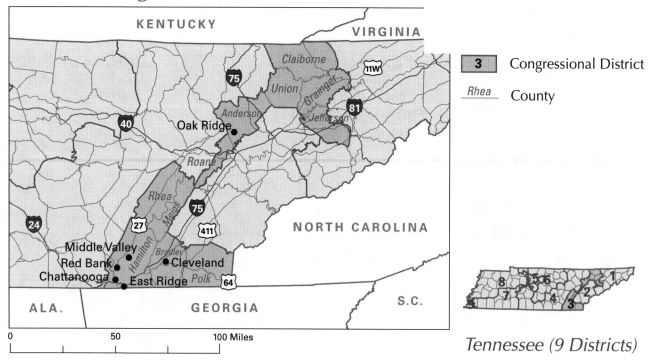

Tennessee (9 Districts)

Congressional District 4

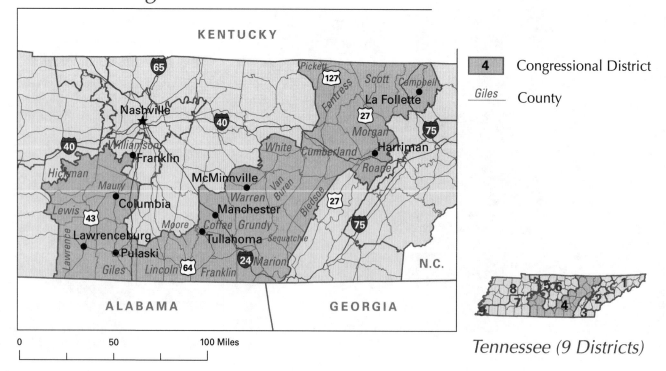

Tennessee (9 Districts)

Congressional District 5

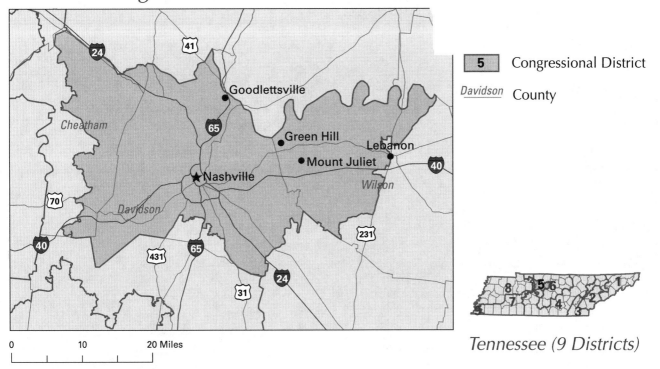

| 5 | Congressional District |
| *Davidson* | County |

Tennessee (9 Districts)

0   10   20 Miles

Congressional District 6

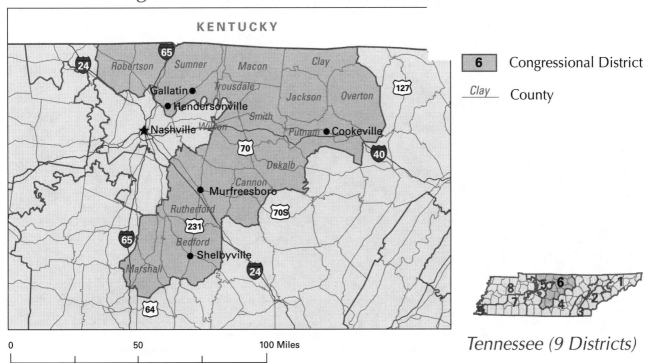

| 6 | Congressional District |
| *Clay* | County |

Tennessee (9 Districts)

0   50   100 Miles

Congressional District 7

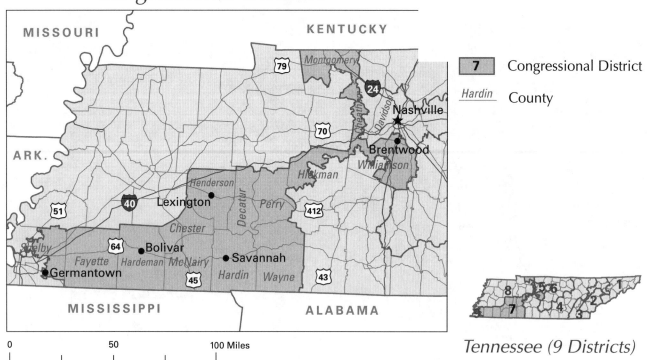

Tennessee (9 Districts)

Congressional District 8

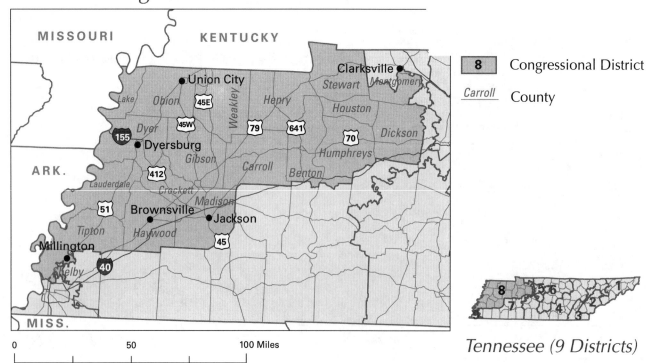

Tennessee (9 Districts)

Congressional District 9

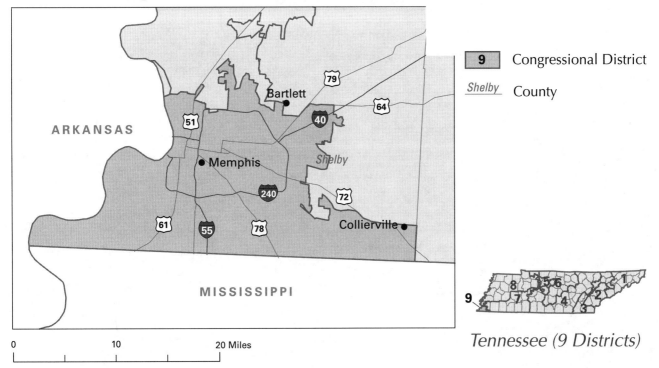

ARKANSAS

Bartlett

Memphis

Shelby

Collierville

MISSISSIPPI

9 Congressional District

Shelby County

0   10   20 Miles

Tennessee (9 Districts)

Texas — Counties

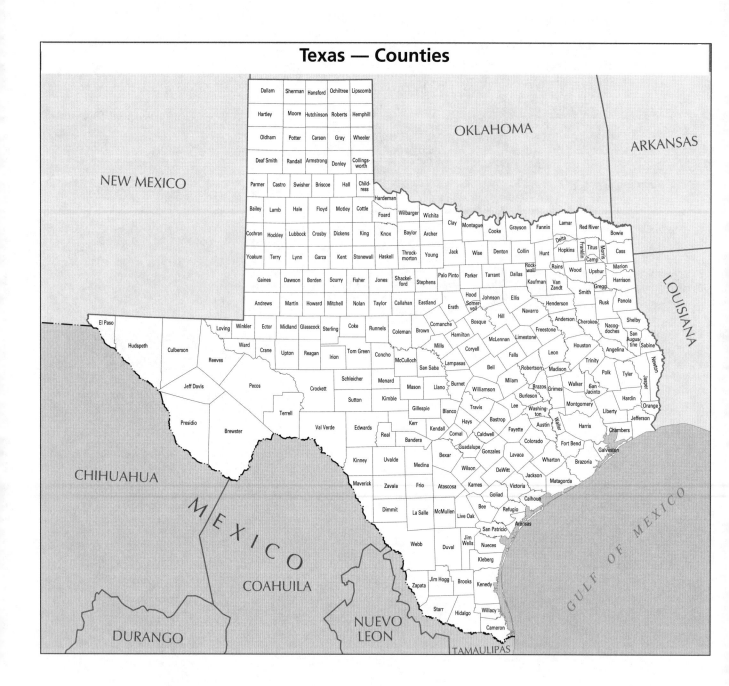

TEXAS—109th CONGRESSIONAL DISTRICTS BY COUNTIES

County	Congressional District
Anderson County	5
Andrews County	11
Angelina County	1
Aransas County	14
Archer County	13, 19
Armstrong County	13
Atascosa County	28
Austin County	10
Bailey County	19
Bandera County	23
Bastrop County	10, 15
Baylor County	13
Bee County	15
Bell County	31
Bexar County	20, 21, 23, 28
Blanco County	21
Borden County	19
Bosque County	17
Bowie County	4
Brazoria County	14, 22
Brazos County	17
Brewster County	23
Briscoe County	13
Brooks County	15
Brown County	11
Burleson County	10, 17
Burnet County	11
Caldwell County	25
Calhoun County	14
Callahan County	19
Cameron County	15, 27
Camp County	4
Carson County	13
Cass County	1, 4
Castro County	19
Chambers County	14
Cherokee County	5
Childress County	13
Clay County	13
Cochran County	19
Coke County	11
Coleman County	11
Collin County	3, 4
Collingsworth County	13
Colorado County	15
Comal County	21, 28
Comanche County	11
Concho County	11
Cooke County	13, 26
Coryell County	31

County	Congressional District
Cottle County	13
Crane County	11
Crockett County	23
Crosby County	13
Culberson County	23
Dallam County	13
Dallas County	3, 5, 24, 26, 30, 32
Dawson County	11
Deaf Smith County	19
Delta County	4
Denton County	24, 26
DeWitt County	15
Dickens County	13
Dimmit County	23
Donley County	13
Duval County	25
Eastland County	19
Ector County	11
Edwards County	23
El Paso County	16, 23
Ellis County	6
Erath County	31
Falls County	31
Fannin County	4
Fayette County	15
Fisher County	19
Floyd County	19
Foard County	13
Fort Bend County	9, 14, 22
Franklin County	4
Freestone County	6
Frio County	28
Gaines County	19
Galveston County	14, 22
Garza County	19
Gillespie County	11
Glasscock County	11
Goliad County	15
Gonzales County	25
Gray County	13
Grayson County	4
Gregg County	1
Grimes County	17
Guadalupe County	28
Hale County	19
Hall County	13
Hamilton County	31
Hansford County	13
Hardeman County	13
Hardin County	8

County	Congressional District
Harris County	2, 7, 9, 10, 18, 22, 29
Harrison County	1
Hartley County	13
Haskell County	13
Hays County	21, 28
Hemphill County	13
Henderson County	5
Hidalgo County	15, 25
Hill County	17
Hockley County	19
Hood County	17
Hopkins County	4
Houston County	6
Howard County	19
Hudspeth County	23
Hunt County	4
Hutchinson County	13
Irion County	11
Jack County	13
Jackson County	14
Jasper County	8
Jeff Davis County	23
Jefferson County	2
Jim Hogg County	25
Jim Wells County	15
Johnson County	17
Jones County	13
Karnes County	25
Kaufman County	5
Kendall County	23
Kenedy County	27
Kent County	19
Kerr County	23
Kimble County	11
King County	13
Kinney County	23
Kleberg County	27
Knox County	13
La Salle County	28
Lamar County	4
Lamb County	19
Lampasas County	11
Lavaca County	15
Lee County	10
Leon County	6
Liberty County	2, 8
Limestone County	6, 17
Lipscomb County	13
Live Oak County	25
Llano County	11

TEXAS—109th CONGRESSIONAL DISTRICTS BY COUNTIES

County	Congressional District
Loving County	11
Lubbock County	19
Lynn County	19
Madison County	17
Marion County	1
Martin County	11
Mason County	11
Matagorda County	14
Maverick County	23
McCulloch County	11
McLennan County	17
McMullen County	28
Medina County	23
Menard County	11
Midland County	11
Milam County	31
Mills County	11
Mitchell County	11
Montague County	13
Montgomery County	8
Moore County	13
Morris County	4
Motley County	13
Nacogdoches County	1
Navarro County	6
Newton County	8
Nolan County	11, 19
Nueces County	27
Ochiltree County	13
Oldham County	13
Orange County	8
Palo Pinto County	13
Panola County	1
Parker County	12
Parmer County	19

County	Congressional District
Pecos County	23
Polk County	8
Potter County	13
Presidio County	23
Rains County	4
Randall County	13
Reagan County	11
Real County	23
Red River County	4
Reeves County	23
Refugio County	15
Roberts County	13
Robertson County	17, 31
Rockwall County	4
Runnels County	11
Rusk County	1
Sabine County	1
San Augustine County	1
San Jacinto County	8
San Patricio County	15, 27
San Saba County	11
Schleicher County	11
Scurry County	11
Shackelford County	19
Shelby County	1
Sherman County	13
Smith County	1
Somervell County	17
Starr County	25
Stephens County	19
Sterling County	11
Stonewall County	13
Sutton County	11, 23
Swisher County	13
Tarrant County	6, 12, 24, 26

County	Congressional District
Taylor County	19
Terrell County	23
Terry County	19
Throckmorton County	13
Titus County	4
Tom Green County	11
Travis County	10, 21, 25
Trinity County	6, 8
Tyler County	8
Upshur County	1
Upton County	11
Uvalde County	23
Val Verde County	23
Van Zandt County	5
Victoria County	14
Walker County	8
Waller County	10
Ward County	11
Washington County	10
Webb County	23, 28
Wharton County	14
Wheeler County	13
Wichita County	13
Wilbarger County	13
Willacy County	27
Williamson County	31
Wilson County	28
Winkler County	11
Wise County	12
Wood County	5
Yoakum County	19
Young County	19
Zapata County	28
Zavala County	23

Congressional District 1

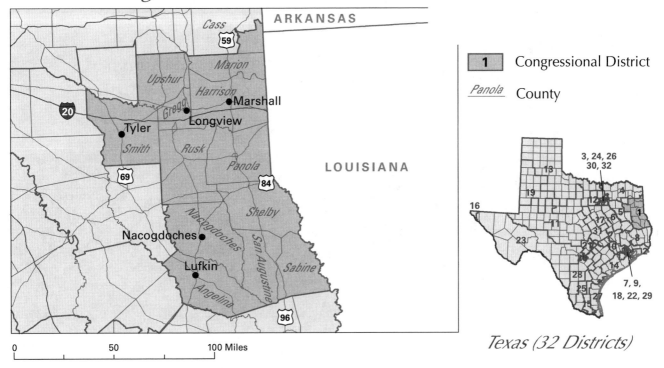

1	Congressional District
Panola	County

Texas (32 Districts)

Congressional District 2

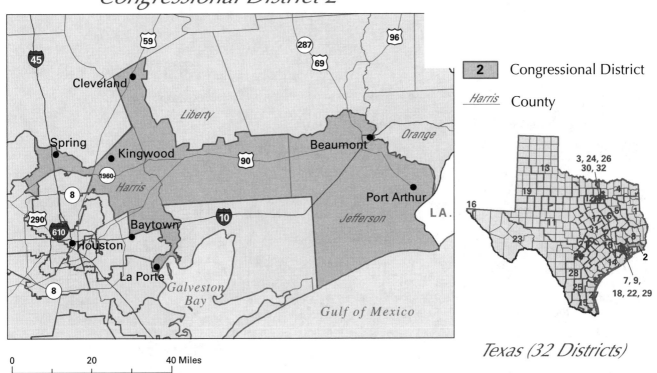

2	Congressional District
Harris	County

Texas (32 Districts)

Congressional District 3

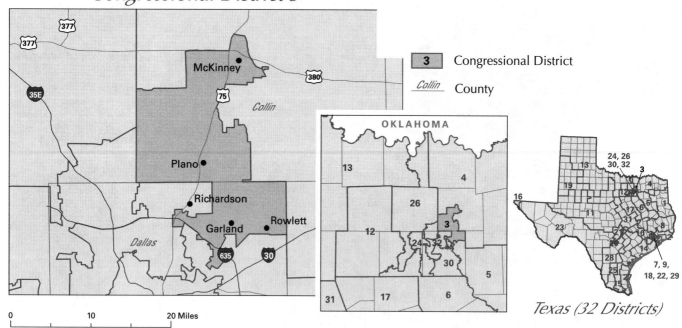

Congressional District 4

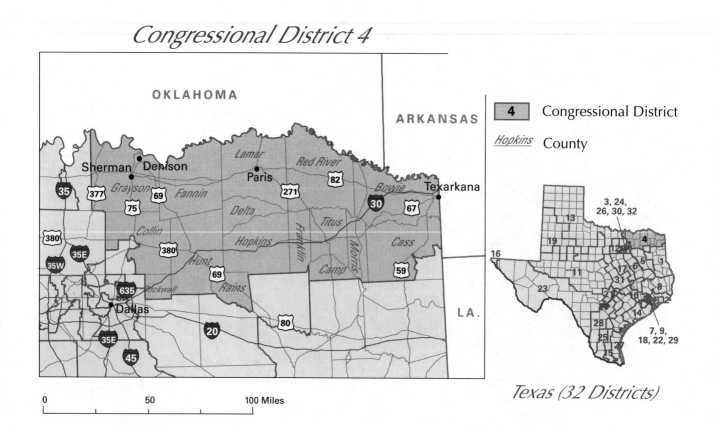

Congressional District 5

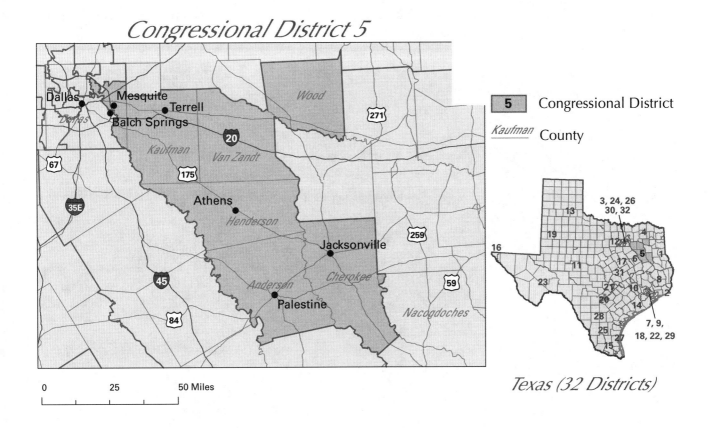

5 Congressional District
Kaufman County

Texas (32 Districts)

Congressional District 6

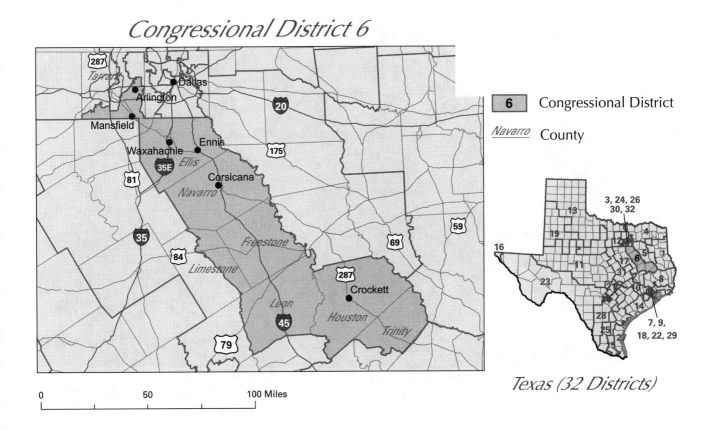

6 Congressional District
Navarro County

Texas (32 Districts)

Congressional District 7

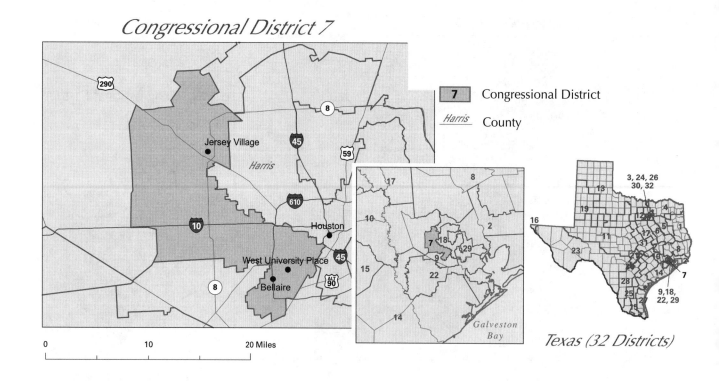

Congressional District 8

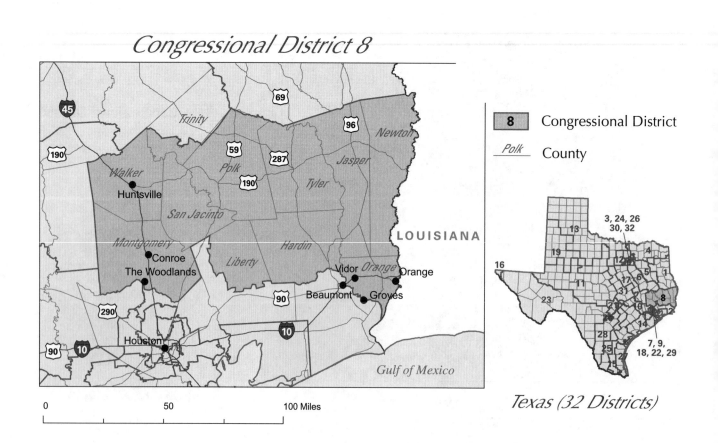

Congressional District 9

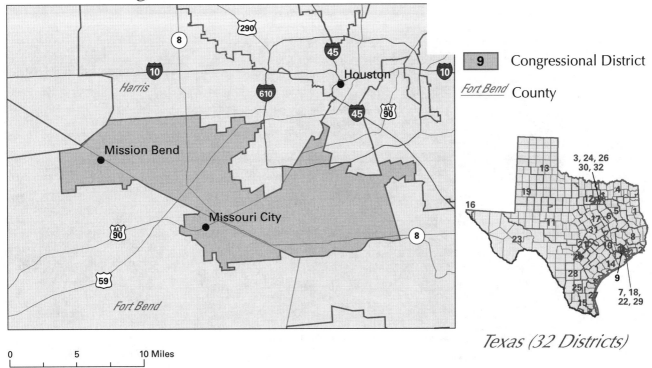

9 Congressional District

Fort Bend County

Texas (32 Districts)

Congressional District 10

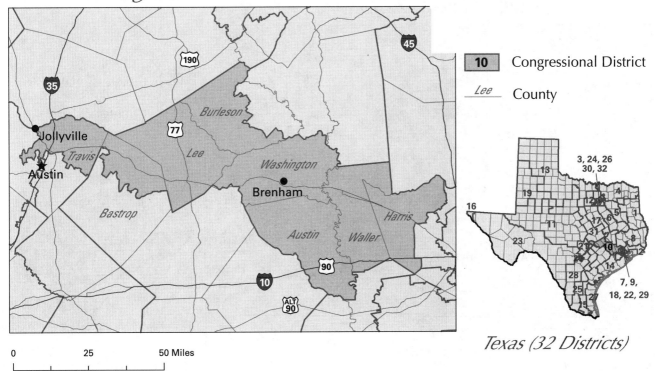

10 Congressional District

Lee County

Texas (32 Districts)

Congressional District 11

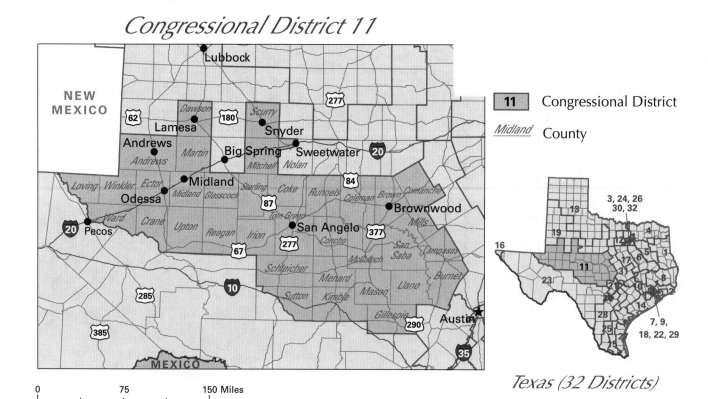

11	Congressional District
Midland	County

Texas (32 Districts)

Congressional District 12

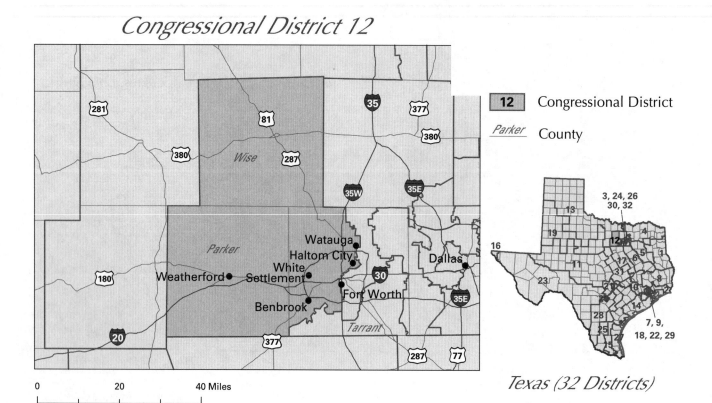

12	Congressional District
Parker	County

Texas (32 Districts)

Congressional District 13

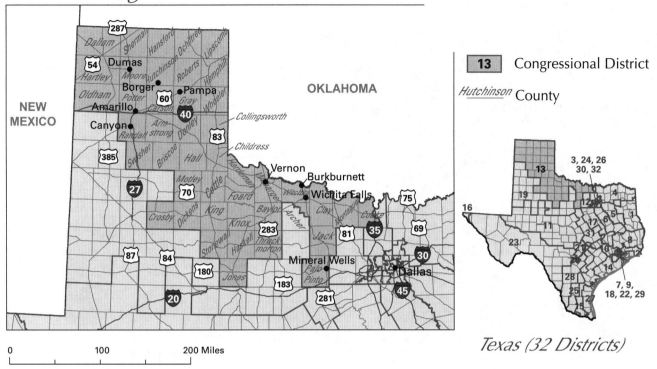

13 Congressional District

Hutchinson County

Texas (32 Districts)

Congressional District 14

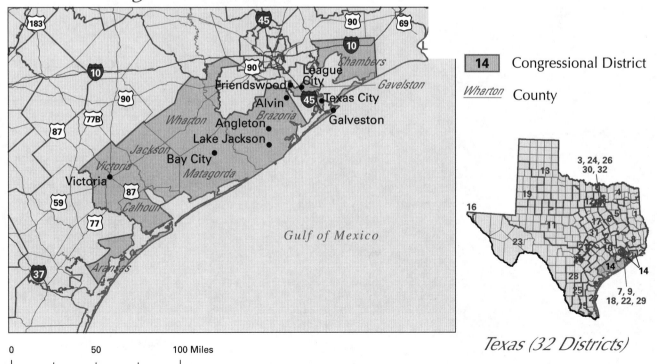

14 Congressional District

Wharton County

Texas (32 Districts)

Congressional District 15

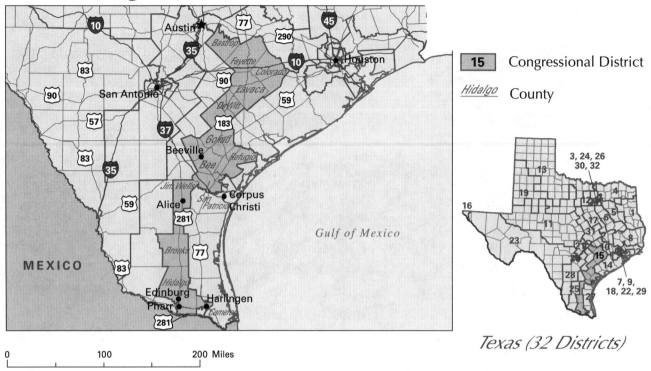

15	Congressional District
Hidalgo	County

Texas (32 Districts)

Congressional District 16

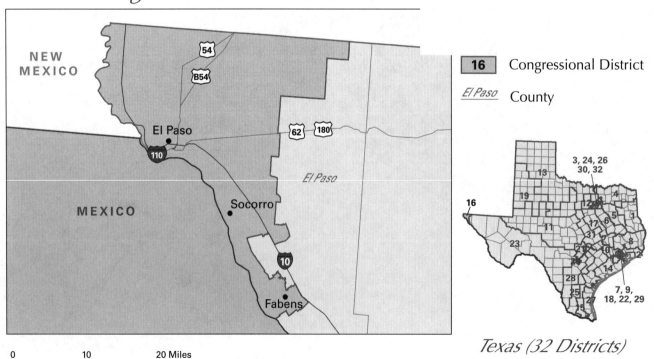

16	Congressional District
El Paso	County

Texas (32 Districts)

Congressional District 17

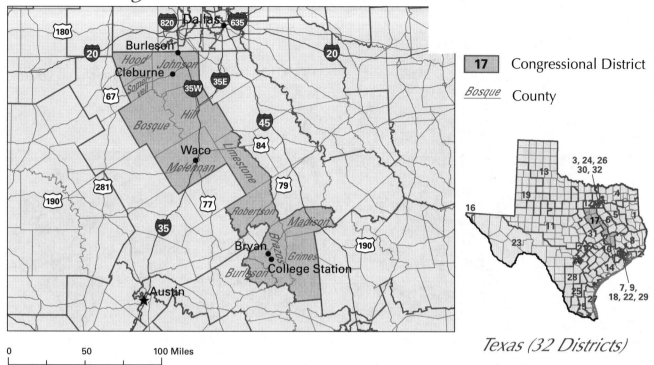

17	Congressional District
Bosque	County

Texas (32 Districts)

Congressional District 18

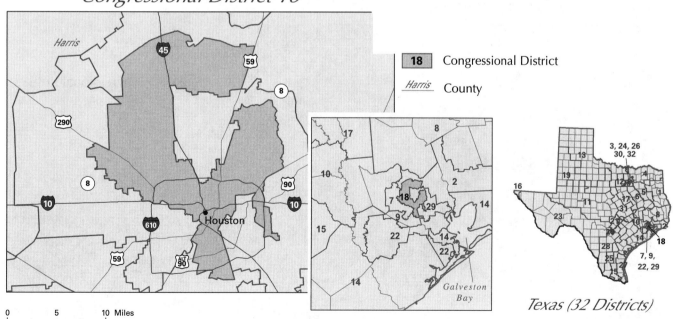

18	Congressional District
Harris	County

Texas (32 Districts)

Congressional District 19

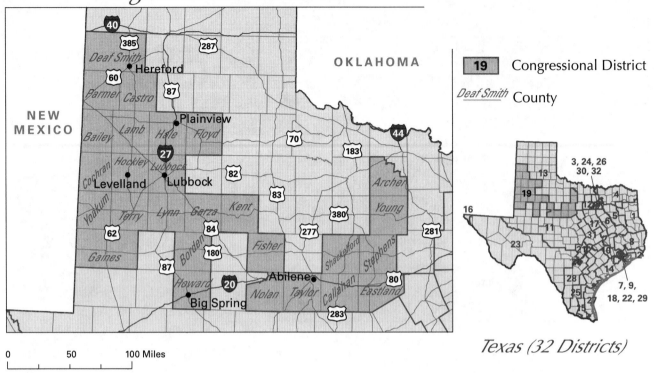

Texas (32 Districts)

Congressional District 20

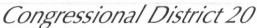

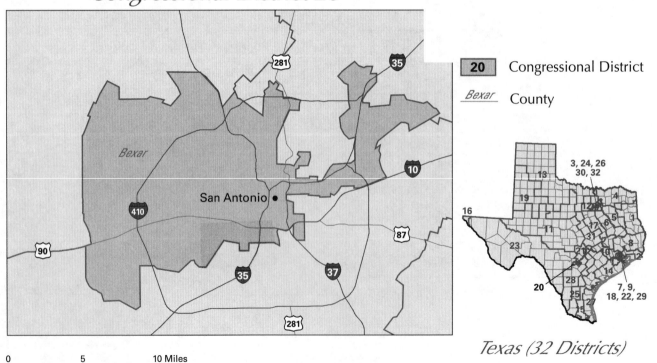

Texas (32 Districts)

Congressional District 21

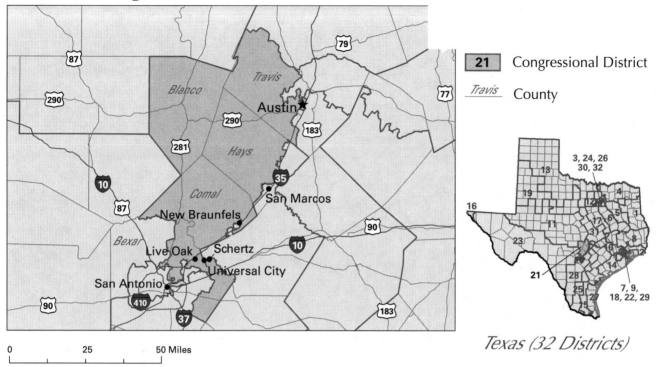

0   25   50 Miles

Texas (32 Districts)

21 Congressional District

Travis County

Congressional District 22

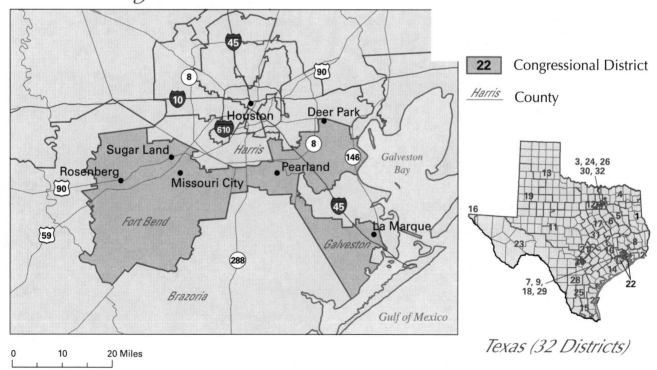

0   10   20 Miles

Texas (32 Districts)

22 Congressional District

Harris County

Congressional District 23

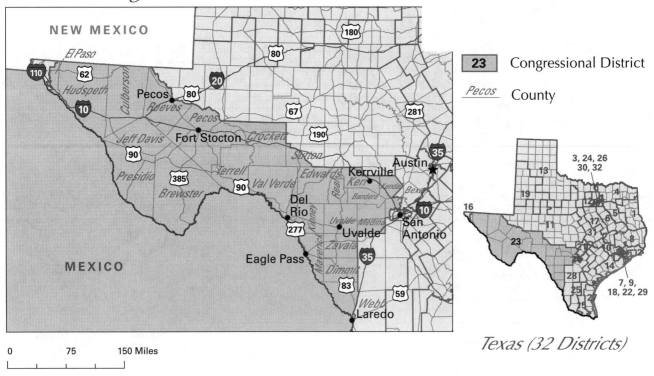

23 Congressional District
Pecos County

Texas (32 Districts)

Congressional District 24

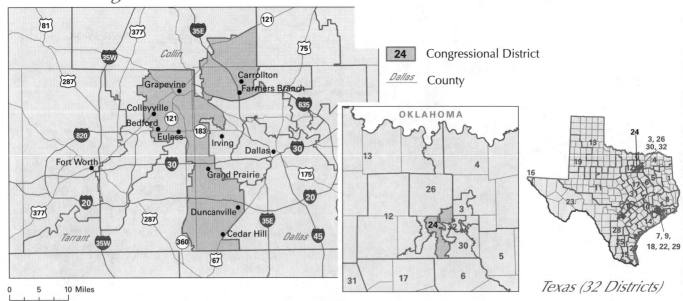

24 Congressional District
Dallas County

Texas (32 Districts)

Congressional District 25

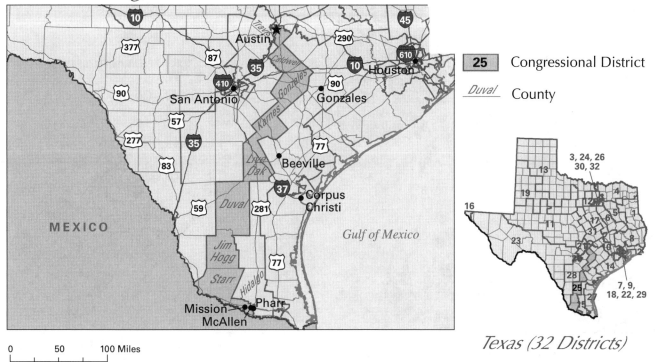

25	Congressional District
Duval	County

Texas (32 Districts)

Congressional District 26

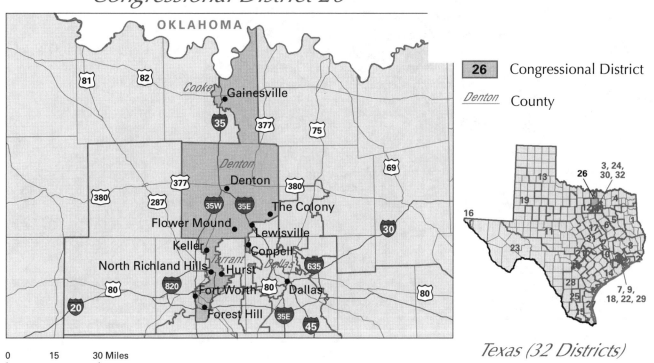

26	Congressional District
Denton	County

Texas (32 Districts)

Congressional District 27

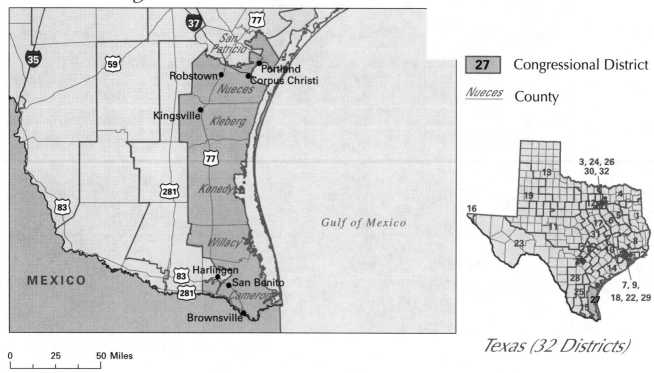

27 Congressional District
Nueces County

Texas (32 Districts)

Congressional District 28

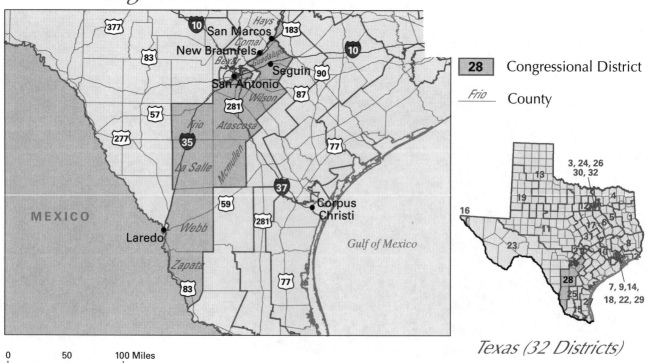

28 Congressional District
Frio County

Texas (32 Districts)

Congressional District 29

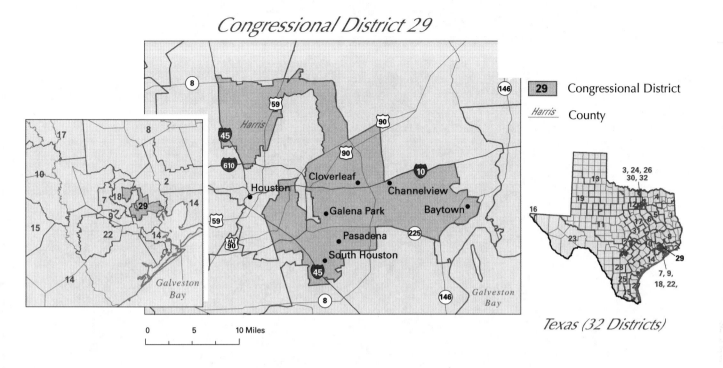

29 Congressional District
Harris County

Texas (32 Districts)

Congressional District 30

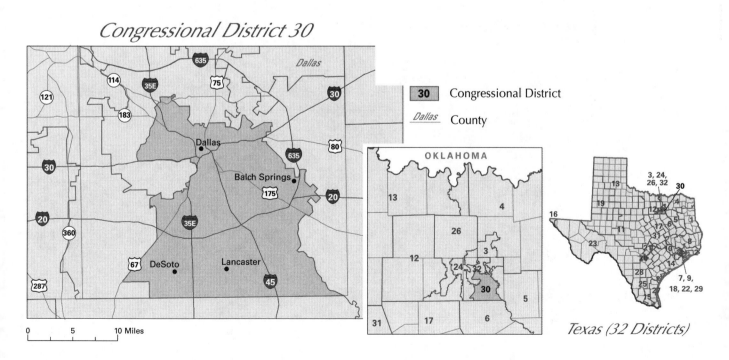

30 Congressional District
Dallas County

Texas (32 Districts)

Congressional District 31

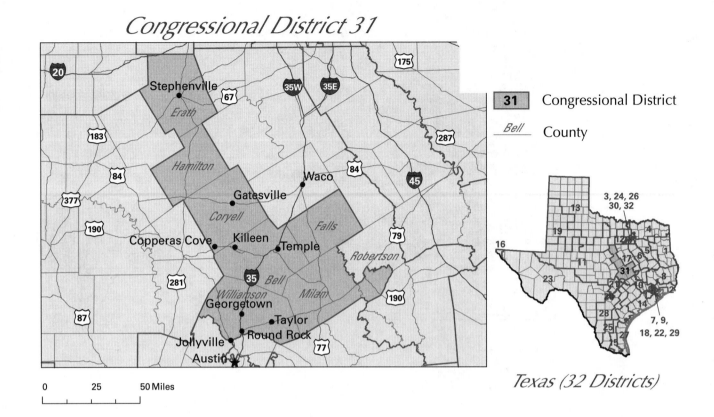

Texas (32 Districts)

Congressional District 32

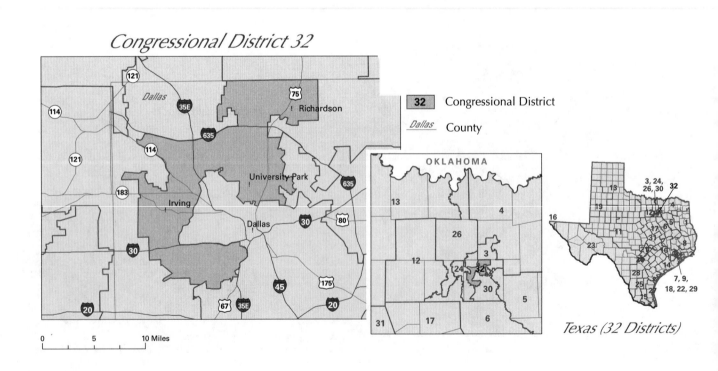

Texas (32 Districts)

Texas 108th Congressional Districts — 32 Districts Total

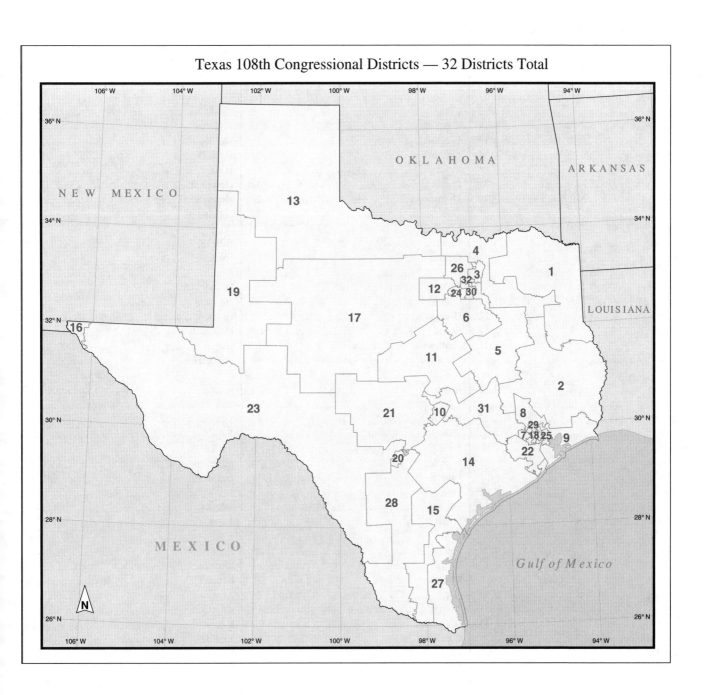

TEXAS—108th CONGRESSIONAL DISTRICTS BY COUNTIES

County	Congressional District	County	Congressional District	County	Congressional District
Anderson	5	Coryell	11	Hardeman	13
Andrews	19	Cottle	13	Hardin	2
Angelina	2	Crane	19	Harris	7–9, 18, 22, 25, 29, 31
Aransas	14	Crockett	23	Harrison	1
Archer	13	Crosby	13	Hartley	13
Armstrong	13	Culberson	23	Haskell	17
Atascosa	28	Dallam	13	Hays	14, 21
Austin	31	Dallas	3, 5, 24, 30, 32	Hemphill	13
Bailey	19	Dawson	17	Henderson	5
Bandera	21	Deaf Smith	13	Hidalgo	15, 28
Bastrop	14, 31	Delta	1	Hill	6
Baylor	13	Denton	26	Hockley	19
Bee	15	DeWitt	14	Hood	17
Bell	11	Dickens	13	Hopkins	1
Bexar	20, 21, 23, 28	Dimmit	23	Houston	2
Blanco	21	Donley	13	Howard	19
Borden	17	Duval	28	Hudspeth	23
Bosque	11	Eastland	17	Hunt	1, 4
Bowie	1	Ector	19	Hutchinson	13
Brazoria	14, 22	Edwards	23	Irion	17
Brazos	31	Ellis	6	Jack	17
Brewster	23	El Paso	16, 23	Jackson	14
Briscoe	13	Erath	17	Jasper	2
Brooks	15	Falls	5	Jeff Davis	23
Brown	17	Fannin	4	Jefferson	9
Burleson	31	Fayette	14	Jim Hogg	28
Burnet	21	Fisher	17	Jim Wells	28
Caldwell	14	Floyd	13	Johnson	6
Calhoun	14	Foard	13	Jones	17
Callahan	17	Fort Bend	22, 25	Karnes	14
Cameron	27	Franklin	1	Kaufman	4, 5
Camp	1	Freestone	5	Kendall	21
Carson	13	Frio	28	Kenedy	27
Cass	1	Gaines	19	Kent	17
Castro	13	Galveston	9	Kerr	21
Chambers	9	Garza	13, 17	Kimble	21
Cherokee	2	Gillespie	21	King	13
Childress	13	Glasscock	17	Kinney	23
Clay	13	Goliad	15	Kleberg	15, 27
Cochran	19	Gonzales	14	Knox	13
Coke	17	Gray	13	Lamar	1
Coleman	17	Grayson	4	Lamb	13, 19
Collin	3, 4, 26	Gregg	4	Lampasas	11
Collingsworth	13	Grimes	2	La Salle	28
Colorado	14	Guadalupe	14	Lavaca	14
Comal	21	Hale	13	Lee	31
Comanche	17	Hall	13	Leon	5
Concho	17	Hamilton	11	Liberty	2
Cooke	4	Hansford	13	Limestone	5

TEXAS—108th CONGRESSIONAL DISTRICTS BY COUNTIES

County	Congressional District	County	Congressional District	County	Congressional District
Lipscomb	13	Parker	12	Tarrant	6, 12, 24, 26
Live Oak	15	Parmer	19	Taylor	17
Llano	21	Pecos	23	Terrell	23
Loving	19	Polk	2	Terry	19
Lubbock	19	Potter	13	Throckmorton	17
Lynn	19	Presidio	23	Titus	1
McCulloch	17	Rains	4	Tom Green	17
McLennan	5, 11	Randall	13	Travis	10, 21
McMullen	28	Reagan	23	Trinity	2
Madison	5	Real	23	Tyler	2
Marion	1	Red River	1	Upshur	1
Martin	19	Reeves	23	Upton	23
Mason	21	Refugio	14	Uvalde	23
Matagorda	14	Roberts	13	Val Verde	23
Maverick	23	Robertson	5	Van Zandt	4
Medina	23	Rockwall	4	Victoria	14
Menard	21	Runnels	17	Walker	2
Midland	19	Rusk	1	Waller	31
Milam	11	Sabine	2	Ward	19
Mills	11	San Augustine	2	Washington	31
Mitchell	17	San Jacinto	2	Webb	23
Montague	13	San Patricio	15	Wharton	14
Montgomery	2, 8	San Saba	11	Wheeler	13
Moore	13	Schleicher	17	Wichita	13
Morris	1	Scurry	17	Wilbarger	13
Motley	13	Shackelford	17	Willacy	27
Nacogdoches	1, 2	Shelby	1	Williamson	11, 31
Navarro	6	Sherman	13	Wilson	14
Newton	2	Smith	4	Winkler	19
Nolan	17	Somervell	17	Wise	17, 26
Nueces	15, 27	Starr	28	Wood	1
Ochiltree	13	Stephens	17	Yoakum	19
Oldham	13	Sterling	17	Young	17
Orange	2	Stonewall	17	Zapata	28
Palo Pinto	17	Sutton	23	Zavala	23
Panola	1	Swisher	13		

Congressional District 1

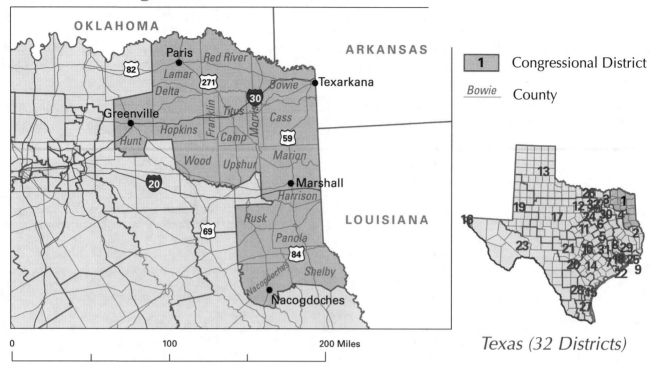

1 Congressional District
Bowie County

Texas (32 Districts)

Congressional District 2

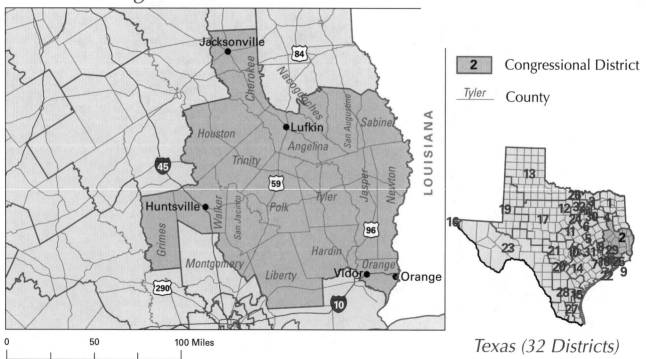

2 Congressional District
Tyler County

Texas (32 Districts)

Congressional District 3

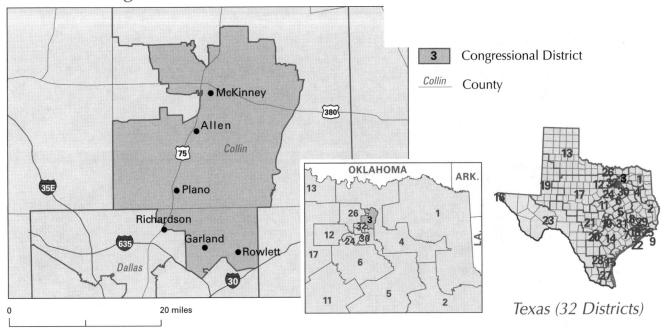

3 Congressional District
Collin County

Texas (32 Districts)

Congressional District 4

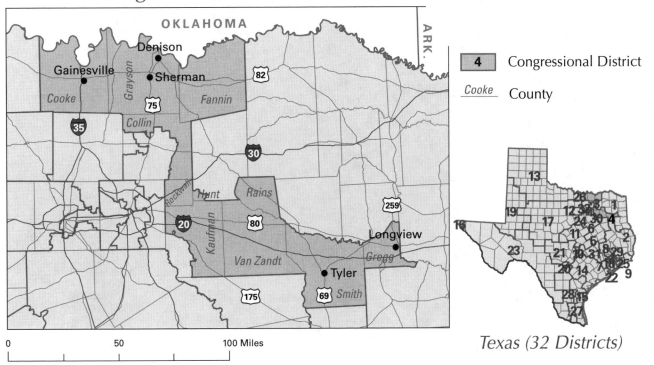

4 Congressional District
Cooke County

Texas (32 Districts)

Congressional District 5

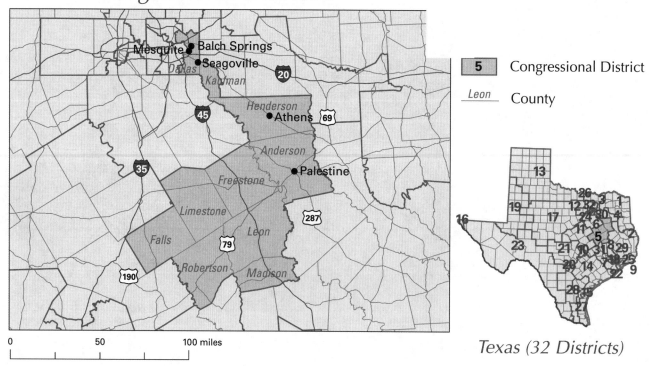

0   50   100 miles

5   Congressional District
Leon   County

Texas (32 Districts)

Congressional District 6

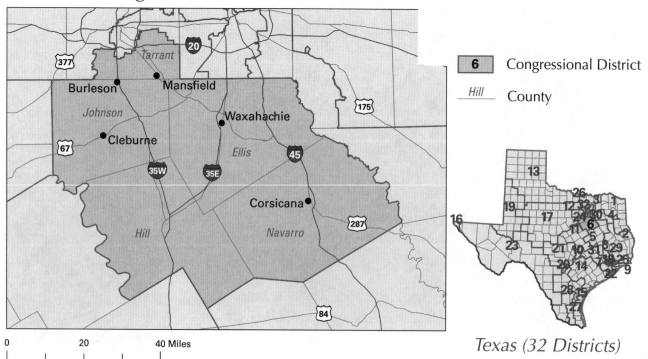

0   20   40 Miles

6   Congressional District
Hill   County

Texas (32 Districts)

Congressional District 7

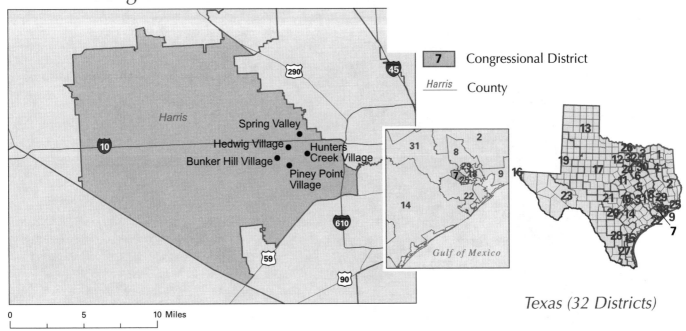

| 7 | Congressional District |
| *Harris* | County |

Texas (32 Districts)

Congressional District 8

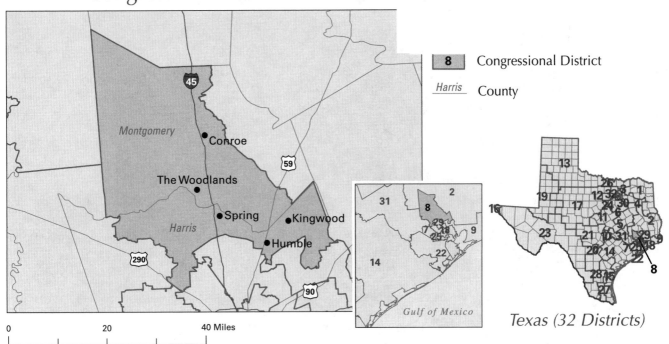

| 8 | Congressional District |
| *Harris* | County |

Texas (32 Districts)

Congressional District 9

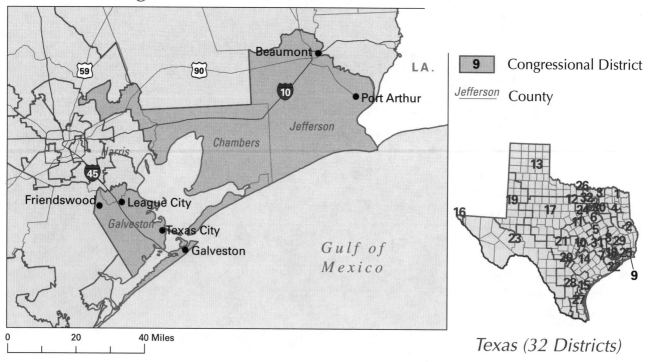

0   20   40 Miles

9 Congressional District

Jefferson County

Texas (32 Districts)

Congressional District 10

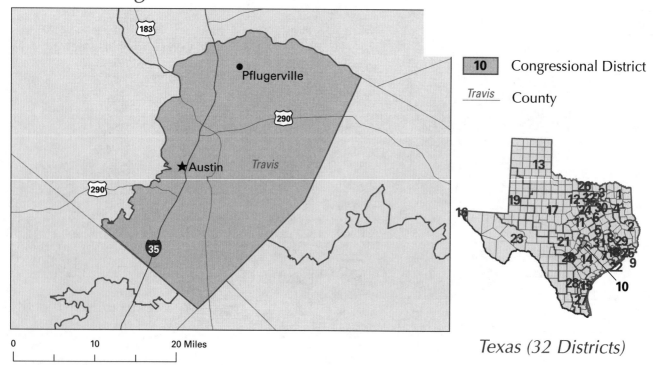

0   10   20 Miles

10 Congressional District

Travis County

Texas (32 Districts)

Congressional District 11

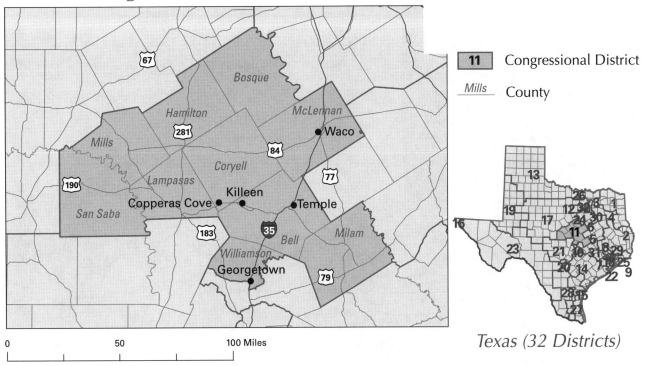

11	Congressional District
Mills	County

Texas (32 Districts)

Congressional District 12

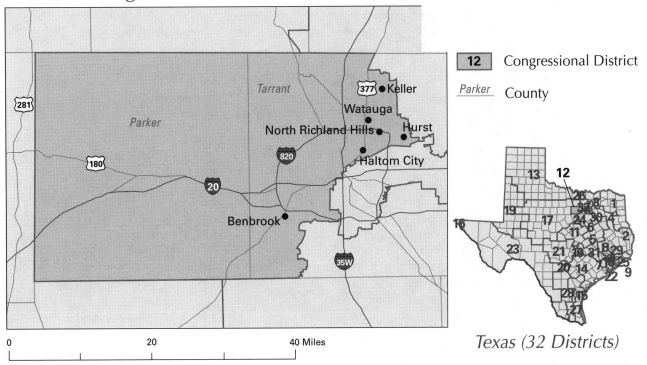

12	Congressional District
Parker	County

Texas (32 Districts)

Congressional District 13

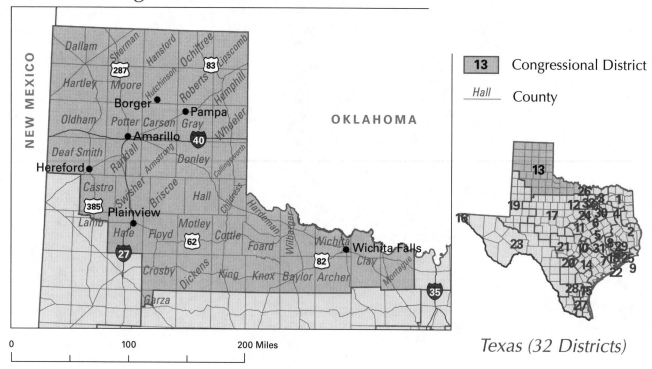

Texas (32 Districts)

Congressional District 14

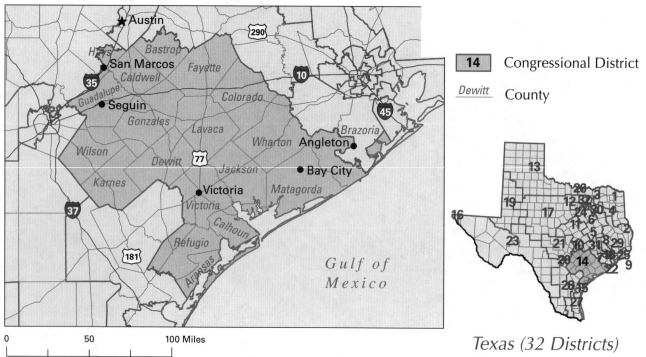

Texas (32 Districts)

Congressional District 15

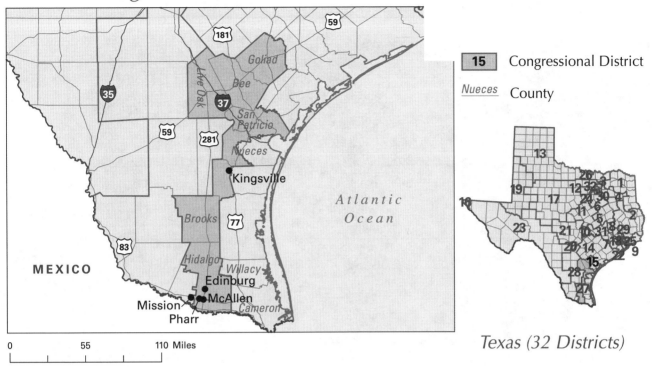

15 Congressional District
Nueces County

Texas (32 Districts)

Congressional District 16

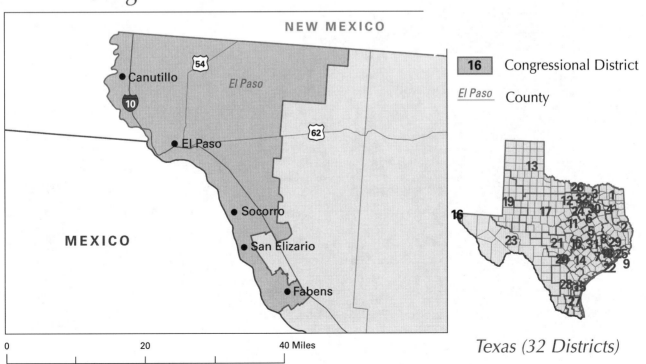

16 Congressional District
El Paso County

Texas (32 Districts)

Congressional District 17

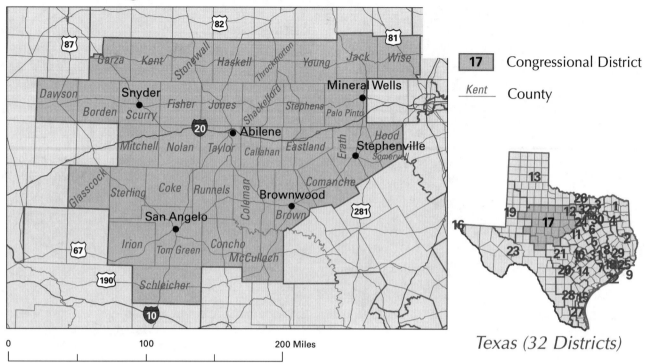

17 Congressional District

Kent County

Texas (32 Districts)

Congressional District 18

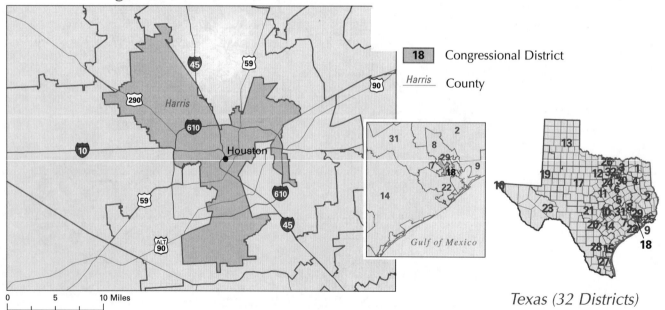

18 Congressional District

Harris County

Texas (32 Districts)

Congressional District 19

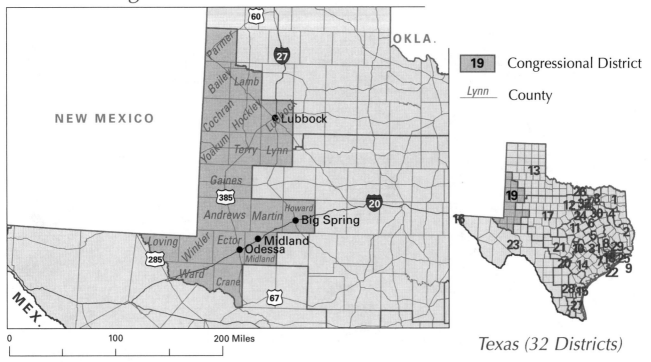

Texas (32 Districts)

Congressional District 20

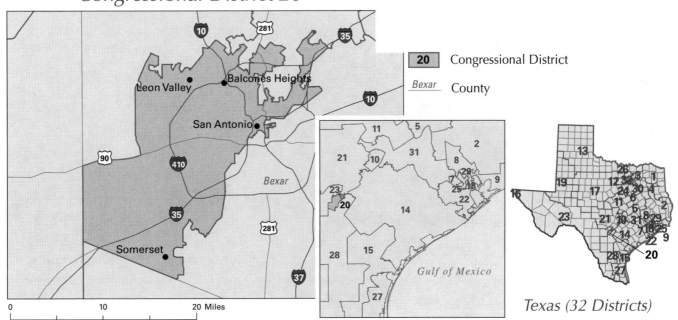

Texas (32 Districts)

Congressional District 21

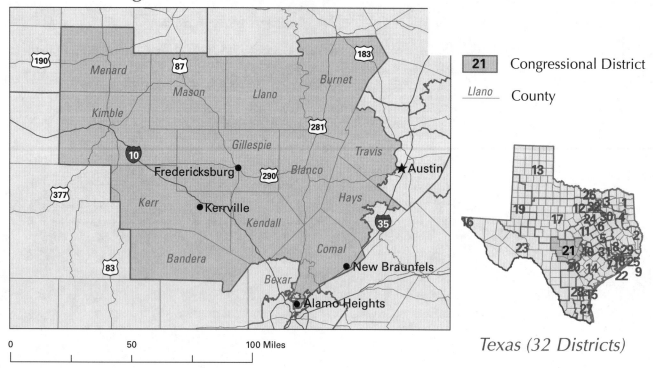

0   50   100 Miles

21 Congressional District

Llano County

Texas (32 Districts)

Congressional District 22

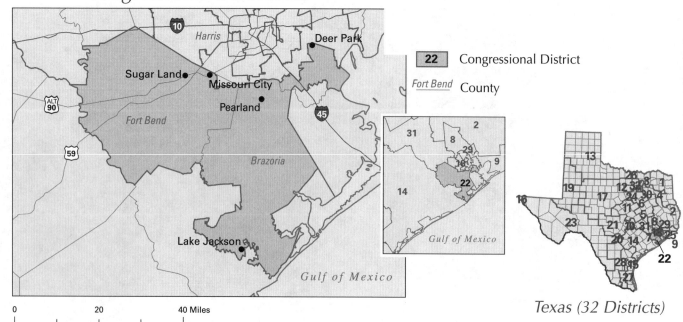

0   20   40 Miles

22 Congressional District

Fort Bend County

Texas (32 Districts)

Congressional District 23

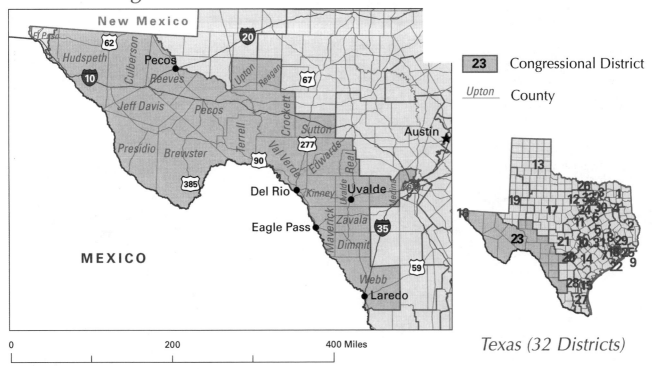

Texas (32 Districts)

Congressional District 24

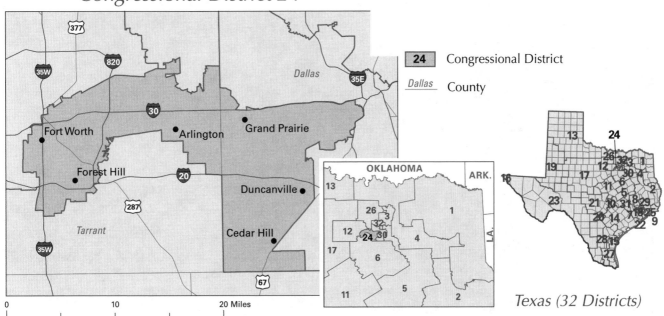

Texas (32 Districts)

Congressional District 25

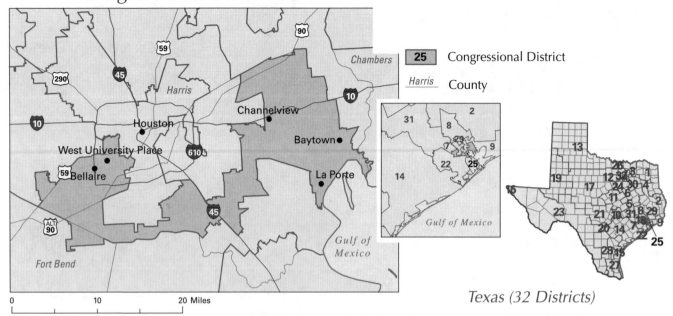

25   Congressional District

Harris   County

Texas (32 Districts)

Congressional District 26

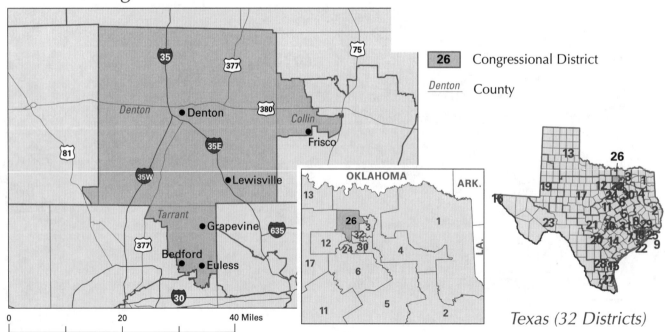

26   Congressional District

Denton   County

Texas (32 Districts)

Congressional District 27

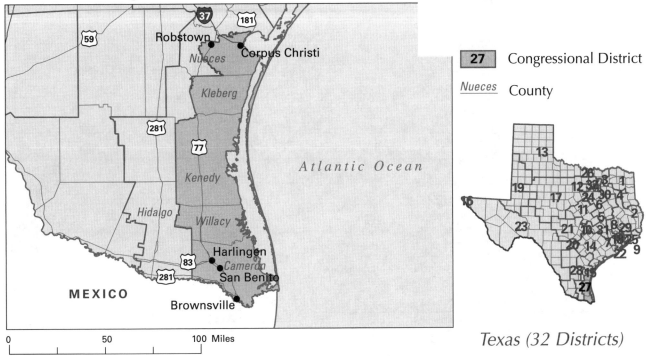

27 Congressional District

Nueces County

Texas (32 Districts)

Congressional District 28

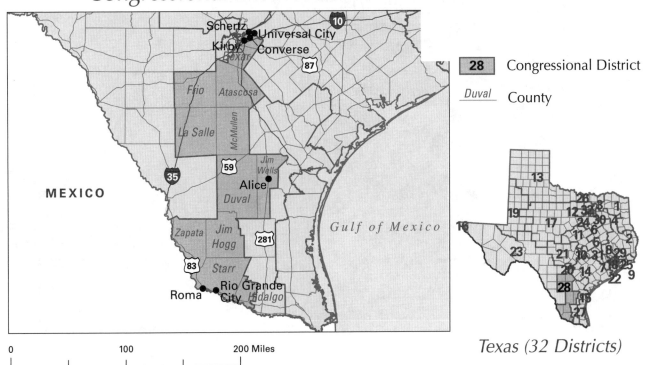

28 Congressional District

Duval County

Texas (32 Districts)

Congressional District 29

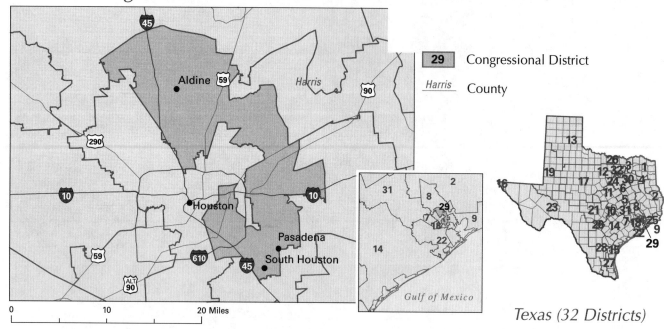

29 Congressional District

Harris County

Texas (32 Districts)

Congressional District 30

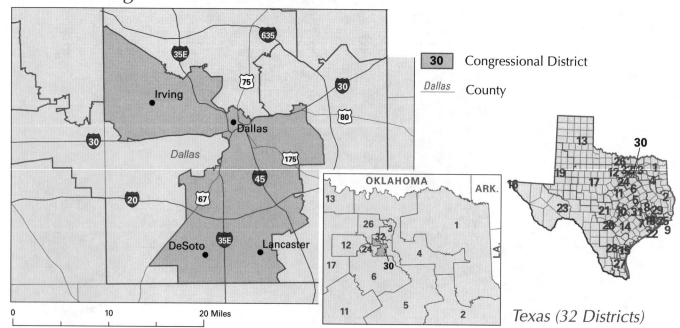

30 Congressional District

Dallas County

Texas (32 Districts)

Congressional District 31

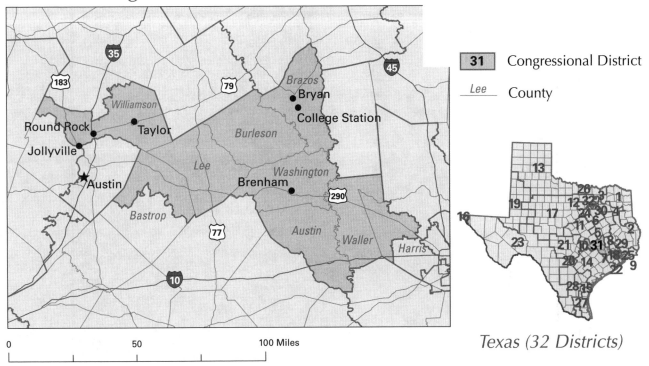

Texas (32 Districts)

Congressional District 32

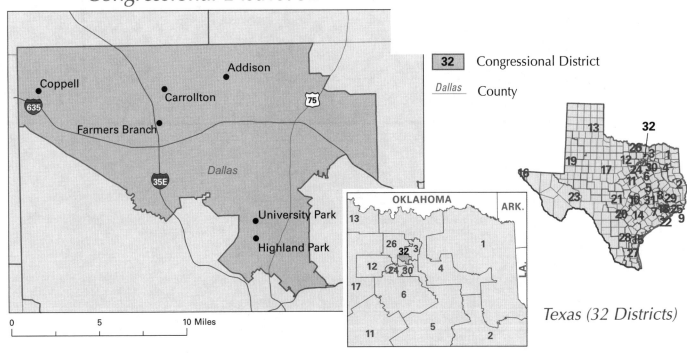

Texas (32 Districts)

Utah Congressional Districts — 3 Districts Total

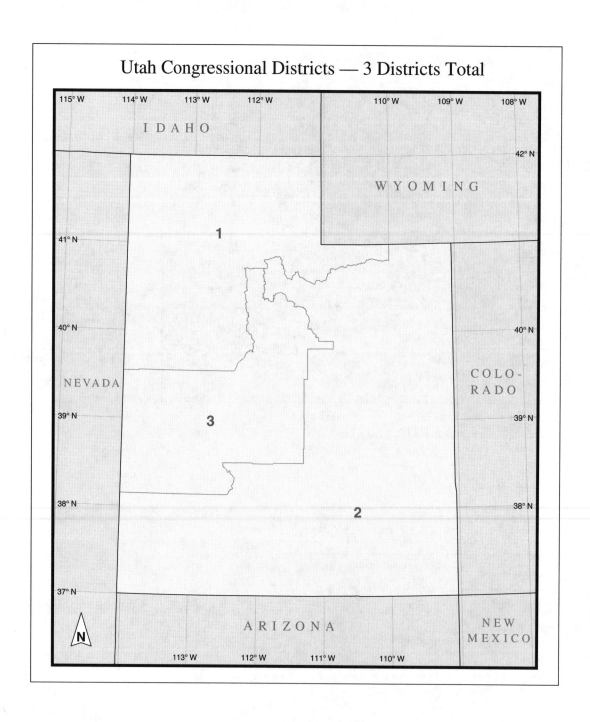

UTAH—109th CONGRESSIONAL DISTRICTS BY COUNTIES

County	Congressional District	County	Congressional District	County	Congressional District
Beaver	3	Iron	2	Sevier	3
Box Elder	1	Juab	1, 3	Summit	1
Cache	1	Kane	2	Tooele	1
Carbon	2	Millard	3	Uintah	2
Daggett	2	Morgan	1	Utah	2, 3
Davis	1	Piute	2	Wasatch	2
Duchesne	2	Rich	1	Washington	2
Emery	2	Salt Lake	1–3	Wayne	2
Garfield	2	San Juan	2	Weber	1
Grand	2	Sanpete	3		

Congressional District 1

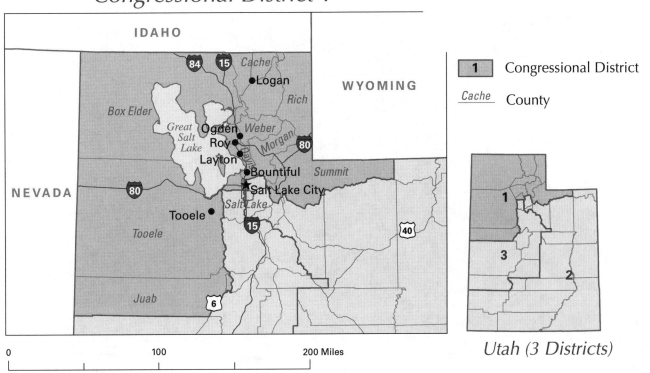

Utah (3 Districts)

Congressional District 2

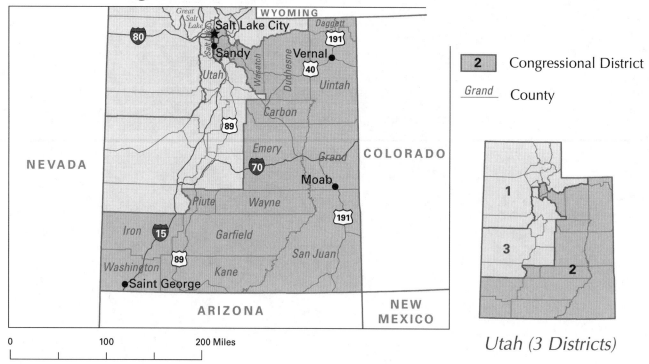

Utah (3 Districts)

Congressional District 3

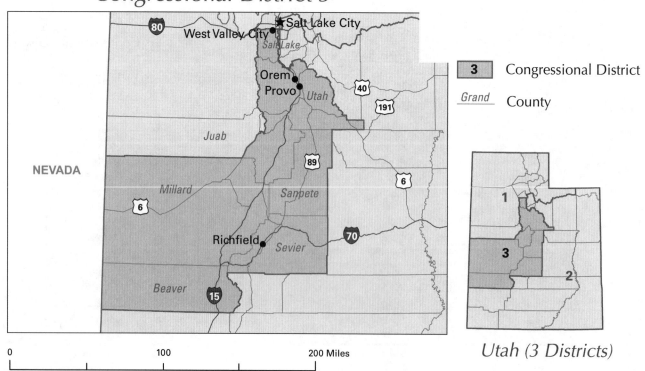

Utah (3 Districts)

Vermont—

Congressional District: At large

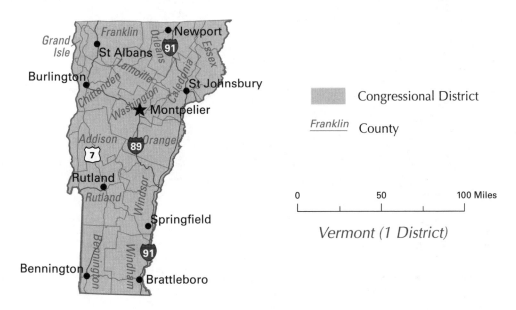

Congressional District

Franklin County

0   50   100 Miles

Vermont (1 District)

VERMONT—109th CONGRESSIONAL DISTRICTS BY COUNTIES

County	Congressional District	County	Congressional District
Addison	1	Lamoille	1
Bennington	1	Orange	1
Caledonia	1	Orleans	1
Chittenden	1	Rutland	1
Essex	1	Washington	1
Franklin	1	Windham	1
Grand Isle	1	Windsor	1

Virginia Congressional Districts — 11 Districts Total

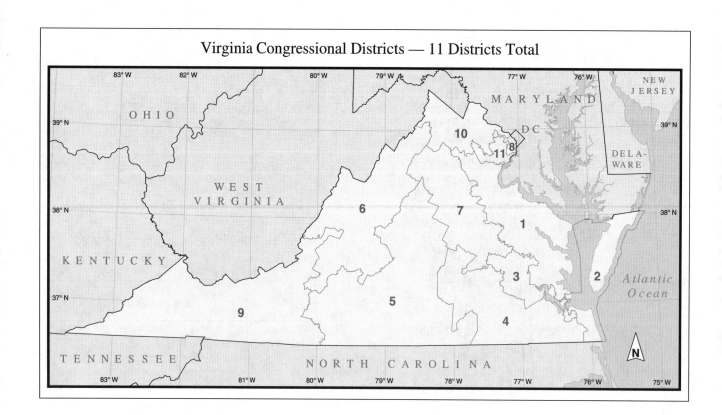

VIRGINIA—109th CONGRESSIONAL DISTRICTS BY COUNTIES AND INDEPENDENT CITIES

County	Congressional District	County	Congressional District	County	Congressional District
Accomack	2	James City	1, 3	Wise	9
Albemarle	5	King and Queen	1	Wythe	9
Alleghany	6, 9	King George	1	York	1
Amelia	4	King William	1	Alexandria city	8
Amherst	6	Lancaster	1	Bedford city	5
Appomattox	5	Lee	9	Bristol city	9
Arlington	8	Loudoun	10	Buena Vista city	6
Augusta	6	Louisa	7	Charlottesville city	5
Bath	6	Lunenburg	5	Chesapeake city	4
Bedford	5, 6	Madison	7	Clifton Forge city	9
Bland	9	Mathews	1	Colonial Heights city	4
Botetourt	6	Mecklenburg	5	Covington city	6, 9
Brunswick	4, 5	Middlesex	1	Danville city	5
Buchanan	9	Montgomery	9	Emporia city	4
Buckingham	5	Nelson	5	Fairfax city	11
Campbell	5	New Kent	3	Falls Church city	8
Caroline	1, 7	Northampton	2	Franklin city	4
Carroll	9	Northumberland	1	Fredericksburg city	1
Charles City	3	Nottoway	4	Galax city	9
Charlotte	5	Orange	7	Hampton city	1–3
Chesterfield	4, 7	Page	7	Harrisonburg city	6
Clarke	10	Patrick	9	Hopewell city	4
Craig	9	Pittsylvania	5	Lexington city	6
Culpeper	7	Powhatan	4	Lynchburg city	6
Cumberland	5	Prince Edward	5	Manassas city	10
Dickenson	9	Prince George	3, 4	Manassas Park city	10
Dinwiddie	4	Prince William	1, 10, 11	Martinsville city	5
Essex	1	Pulaski	9	Newport News city	1, 3
Fairfax	8, 10, 11	Rappahannock	7	Norfolk city	2, 3
Fauquier	1, 10	Richmond	1	Norton city	9
Floyd	9	Roanoke	6, 9	Petersburg city	4
Fluvanna	5	Rockbridge	6	Poquoson city	1
Franklin	5	Rockingham	6	Portsmouth city	3
Frederick	10	Russell	9	Radford city	9
Giles	9	Scott	9	Richmond city	3, 7
Gloucester	1	Shenandoah	6	Roanoke city	6
Goochland	7	Smyth	9	Salem city	6
Grayson	9	Southampton	4	Staunton city	6
Greene	5	Spotsylvania	1, 7	Suffolk city	4
Greensville	4	Stafford	1	Virginia Beach city	2
Halifax	5	Surry	3	Waynesboro city	6
Hanover	7	Sussex	4	Williamsburg city	1
Henrico	3, 7	Tazewell	9	Winchester city	10
Henry	5, 9	Warren	10		
Highland	6	Washington	9		
Isle of Wight	3, 4	Westmoreland	1		

Congressional District 1

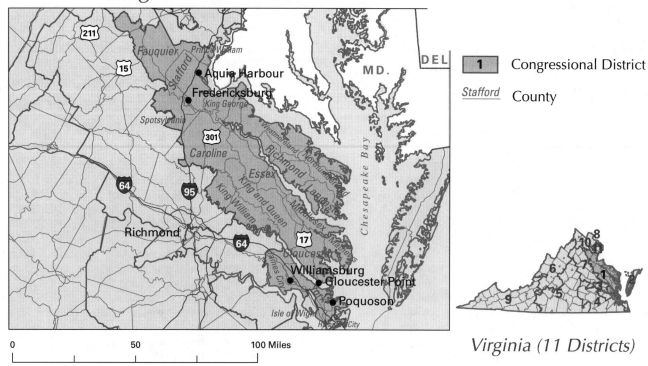

1	Congressional District
Stafford	County

Virginia (11 Districts)

Congressional District 2

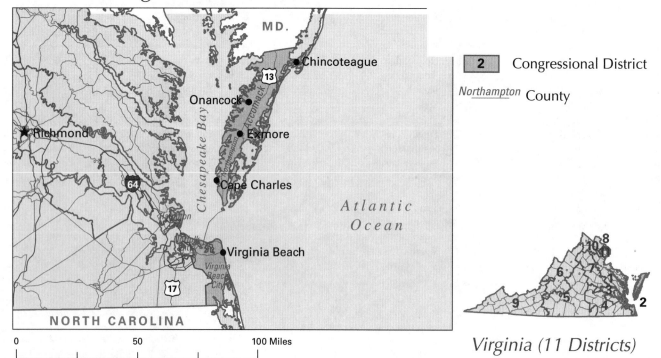

2	Congressional District
Northampton	County

Virginia (11 Districts)

Congressional District 3

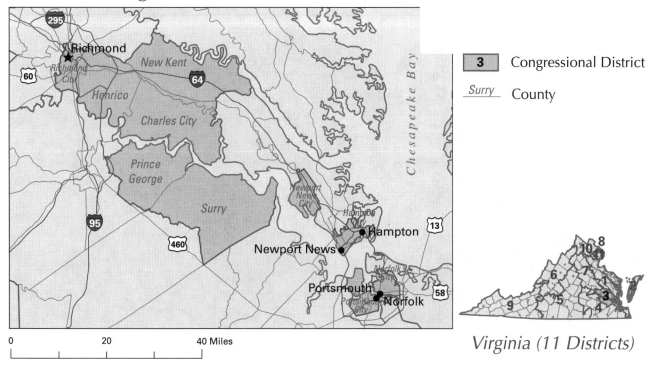

3	Congressional District
Surry	County

Virginia (11 Districts)

Congressional District 4

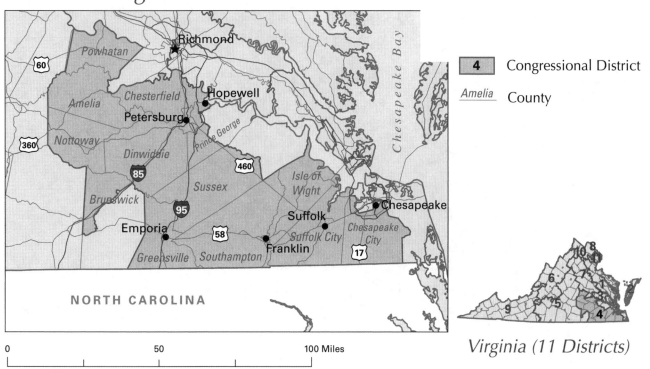

4	Congressional District
Amelia	County

Virginia (11 Districts)

Congressional District 5

Virginia (11 Districts)

Congressional District 6

Virginia (11 Districts)

Congressional District 7

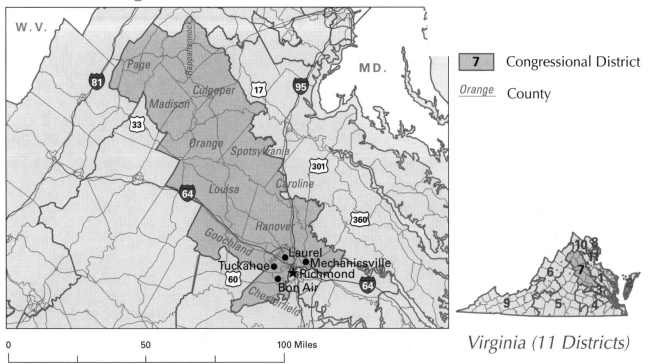

7 Congressional District
Orange County

0   50   100 Miles

Virginia (11 Districts)

Congressional District 8

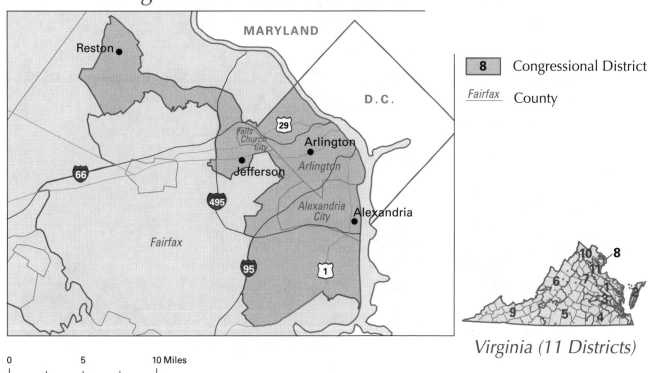

8 Congressional District
Fairfax County

0   5   10 Miles

Virginia (11 Districts)

Congressional District 9

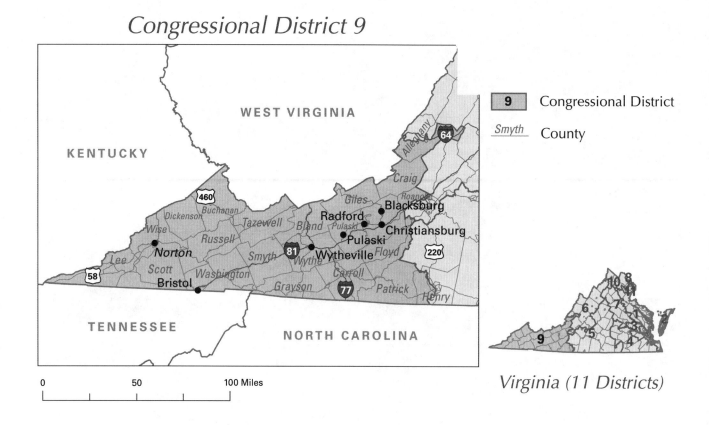

Congressional District 10

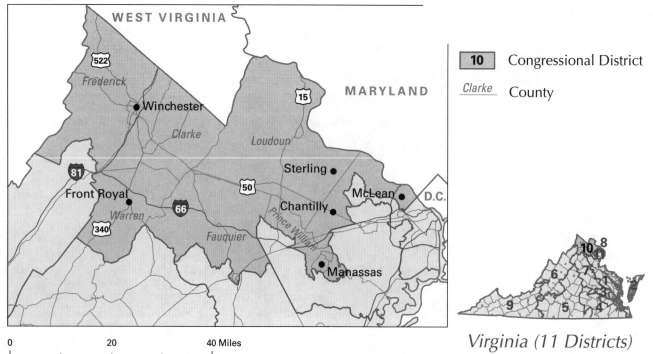

Congressional District 11

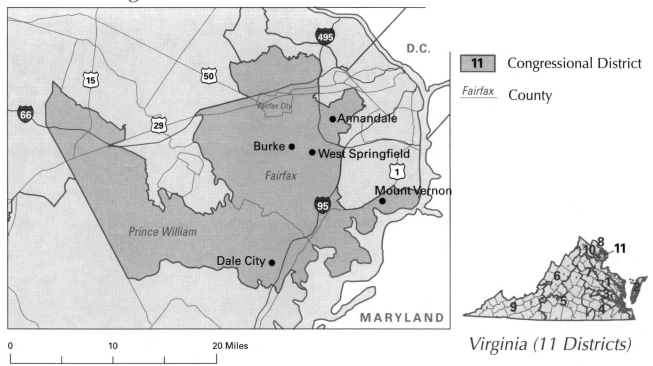

| 11 | Congressional District |
| *Fairfax* | County |

D.C.

Fairfax City

● Annandale

Burke ● ● West Springfield

Fairfax

● Mount Vernon

Prince William

Dale City ●

MARYLAND

0   10   20 Miles

Virginia (11 Districts)

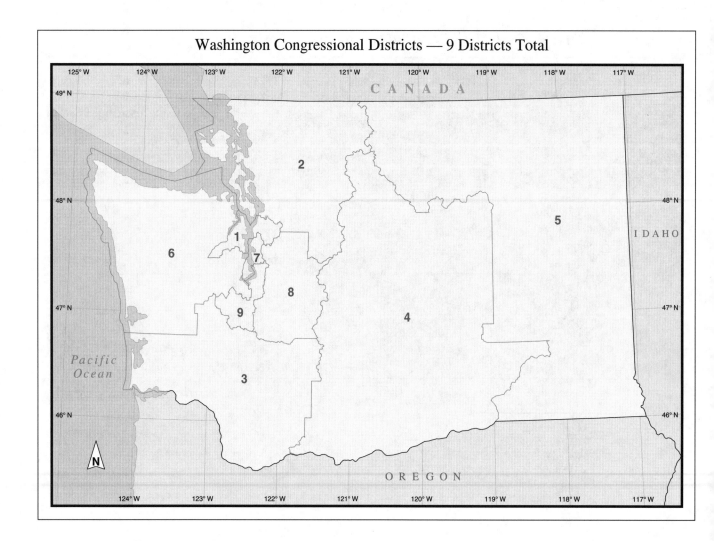

Washington Congressional Districts — 9 Districts Total

WASHINGTON—109th CONGRESSIONAL DISTRICTS BY COUNTIES

County	Congressional District	County	Congressional District	County	Congressional District
Adams	4, 5	Grays Harbor	6	Pierce	6, 8, 9
Asotin	5	Island	2	San Juan	2
Benton	4	Jefferson	6	Skagit	2
Chelan	4	King	1, 2, 7–9	Skamania	3, 4
Clallam	6	Kitsap	1, 6	Snohomish	1,2
Clark	3	Kittitas	4	Spokane	5
Columbia	5	Klickitat	4	Stevens	5
Cowlitz	3	Lewis	3	Thurston	3, 9
Douglas	4	Lincoln	5	Wahkiakum	3
Ferry	5	Mason	6	Walla Walla	5
Franklin	4	Okanogan	5	Whatcom	2
Garfield	5	Pacific	3	Whitman	5
Grant	4	Pend Oreille	5	Yakima	4

Congressional District 1

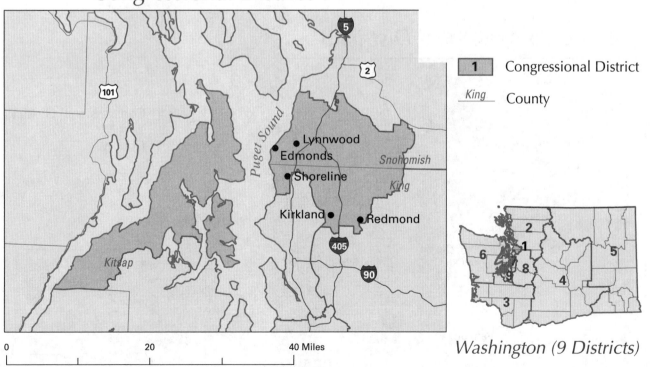

1	Congressional District
King	County

Washington (9 Districts)

0 20 40 Miles

Congressional District 2

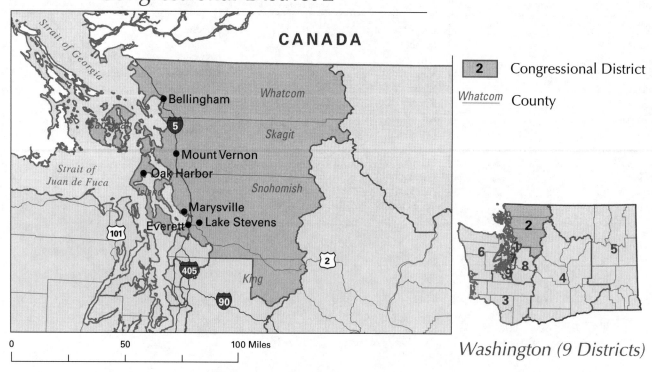

Washington (9 Districts)

Congressional District 3

Washington (9 Districts)

Congressional District 4

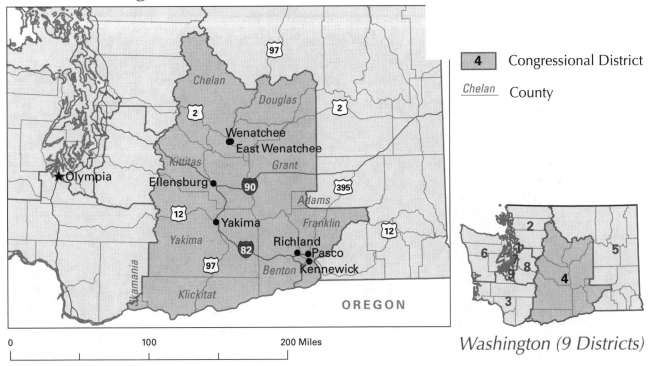

Congressional District 5

Congressional District 6

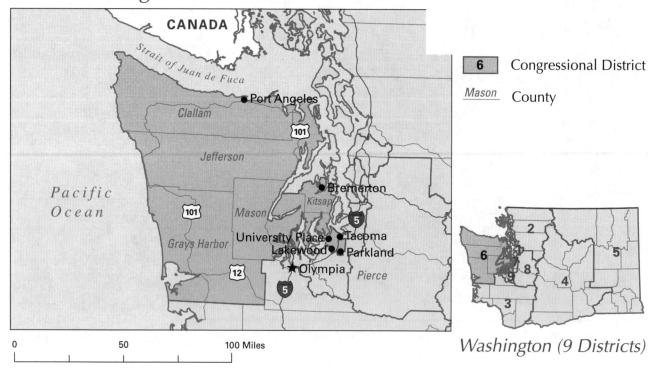

| 6 | Congressional District |
| *Mason* | County |

Washington (9 Districts)

Congressional District 7

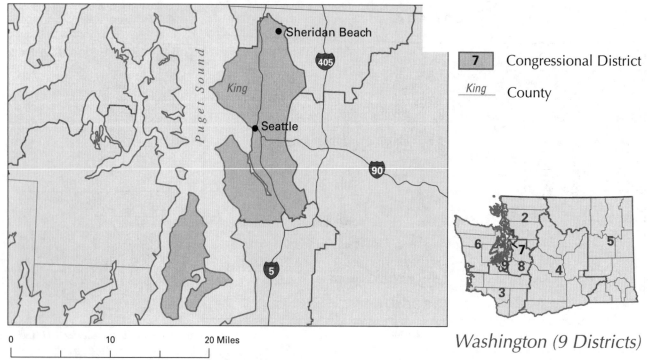

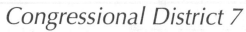

| 7 | Congressional District |
| *King* | County |

Washington (9 Districts)

Congressional District 8

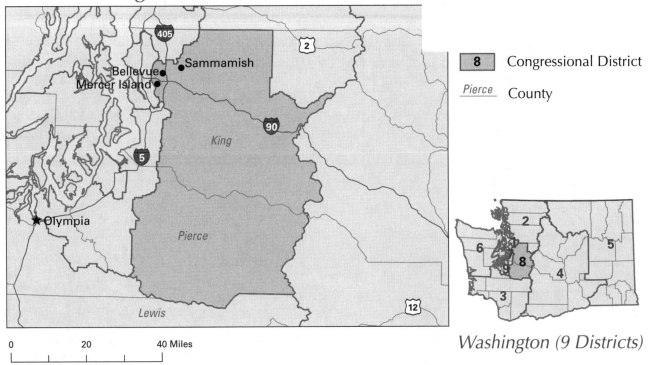

8 Congressional District

Pierce County

Washington (9 Districts)

Congressional District 9

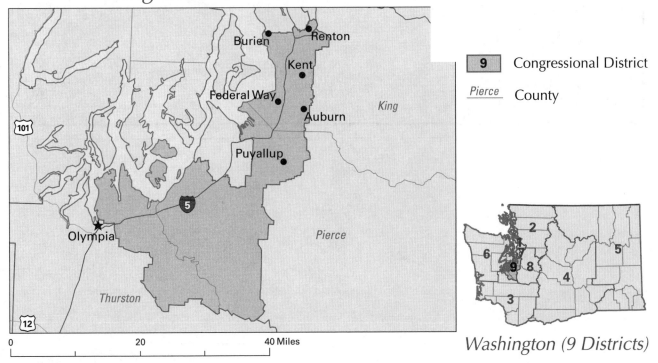

9 Congressional District

Pierce County

Washington (9 Districts)

West Virginia Congressional Districts — 3 Districts Total

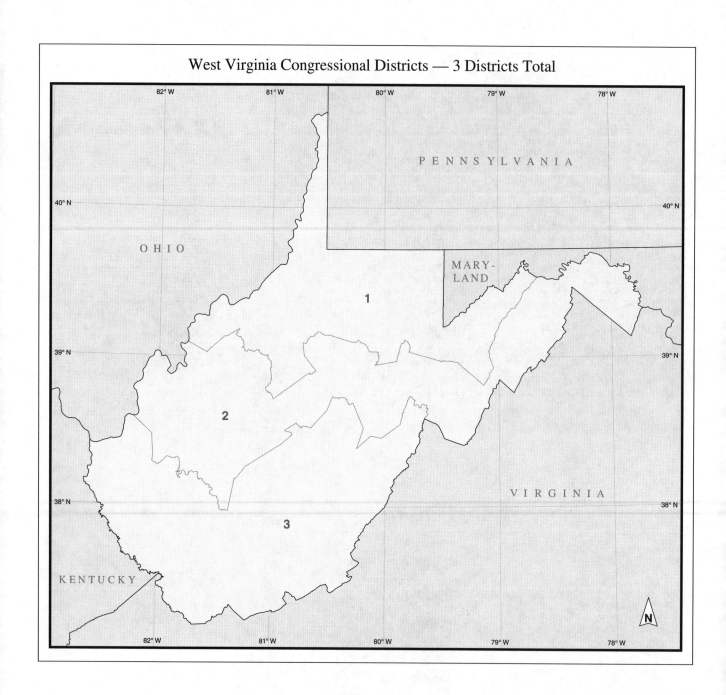

WEST VIRGINIA—109th CONGRESSIONAL DISTRICTS BY COUNTIES

County	Congressional District
Barbour	1
Berkeley	2
Boone	3
Braxton	2
Brooke	1
Cabell	3
Calhoun	2
Clay	2
Doddridge	1
Fayette	3
Gilmer	1
Grant	1
Greenbrier	3
Hampshire	2
Hancock	1
Hardy	2
Harrison	1
Jackson	2
Jefferson	2

County	Congressional District
Kanawha	2
Lewis	2
Lincoln	3
Logan	3
McDowell	3
Marion	1
Marshall	1
Mason	2
Mercer	3
Mineral	1
Mingo	3
Monongalia	1
Monroe	3
Morgan	2
Nicholas	3
Ohio	1
Pendleton	2
Pleasants	1
Pocahontas	3

County	Congressional District
Preston	1
Putnam	2
Raleigh	3
Randolph	2
Ritchie	1
Roane	2
Summers	3
Taylor	1
Tucker	1
Tyler	1
Upshur	2
Wayne	3
Webster	3
Wetzel	1
Wirt	2
Wood	1
Wyoming	3

Congressional District 1

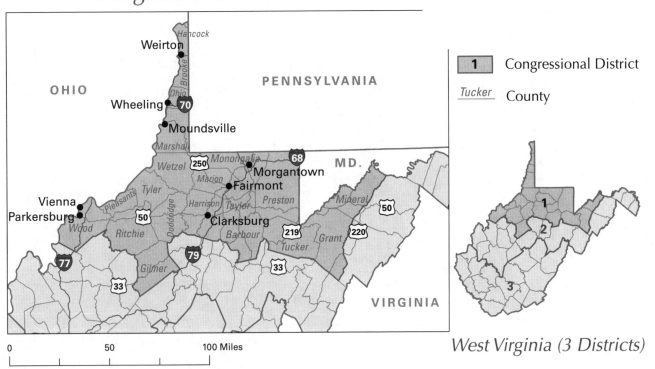

West Virginia (3 Districts)

Congressional District 2

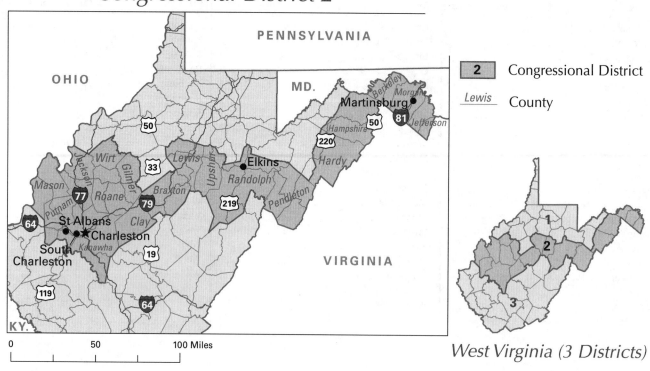

West Virginia (3 Districts)

Congressional District 3

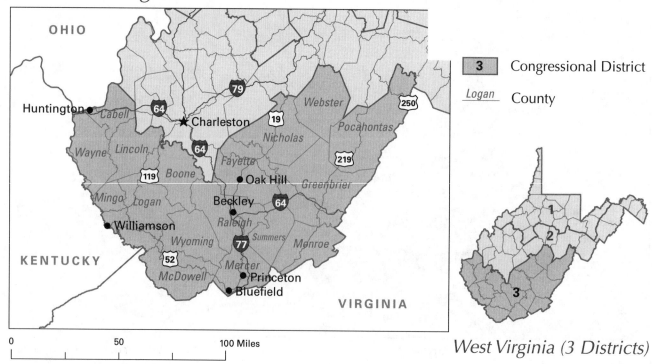

West Virginia (3 Districts)

Wisconsin Congressional Districts — 8 Districts Total

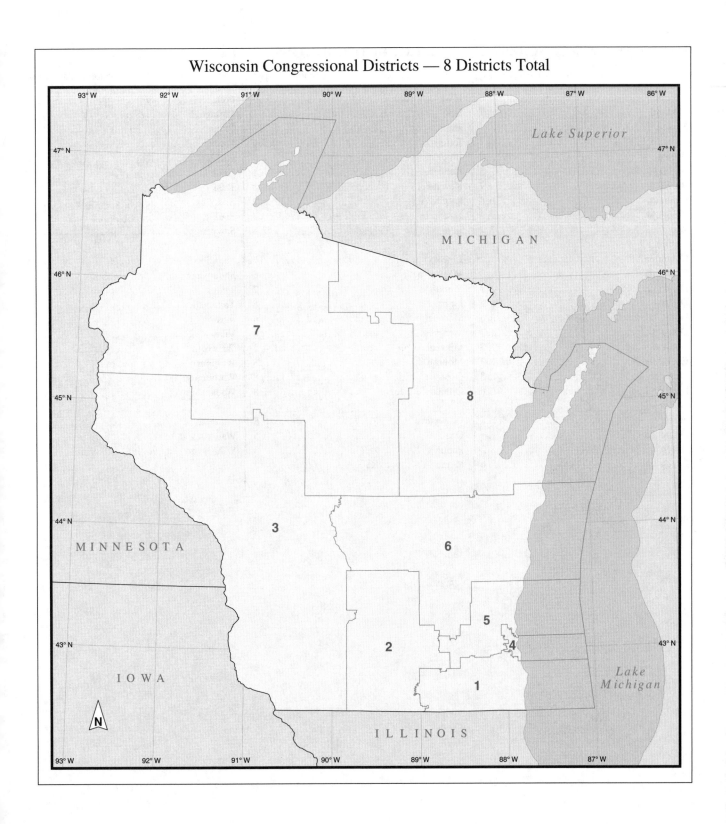

WISCONSIN—109th CONGRESSIONAL DISTRICTS BY COUNTIES

County	Congressional District	County	Congressional District	County	Congressional District
Adams	6	Iowa	3	Polk	7
Ashland	7	Iron	7	Portage	7
Barron	7	Jackson	3	Price	7
Bayfield	7	Jefferson	2, 5, 6	Racine	1
Brown	8	Juneau	3	Richland	3
Buffalo	3	Kenosha	1	Rock	1, 2
Burnett	7	Kewaunee	8	Rusk	7
Calumet	6, 8	La Crosse	3	St. Croix	3
Chippewa	7	Lafayette	3	Sauk	2, 3
Clark	3, 7	Langlade	7, 8	Sawyer	7
Columbia	2	Lincoln	7	Shawano	8
Crawford	3	Manitowoc	6	Sheboygan	6
Dane	2	Marathon	7	Taylor	7
Dodge	6	Marinette	8	Trempealeau	3
Door	8	Marquette	6	Vernon	3
Douglas	7	Menominee	8	Vilas	8
Dunn	3	Milwaukee	1, 4, 5	Walworth	1, 2
Eau Claire	3	Monroe	3	Washburn	7
Florence	8	Oconto	8	Washington	5
Fond du Lac	6	Oneida	7, 8	Waukesha	1, 5
Forest	8	Outagamie	6, 8	Waupaca	8
Grant	3	Ozaukee	5	Waushara	6
Green	2	Pepin	3	Winnebago	6
Green Lake	6	Pierce	3	Wood	7

Congressional District 1

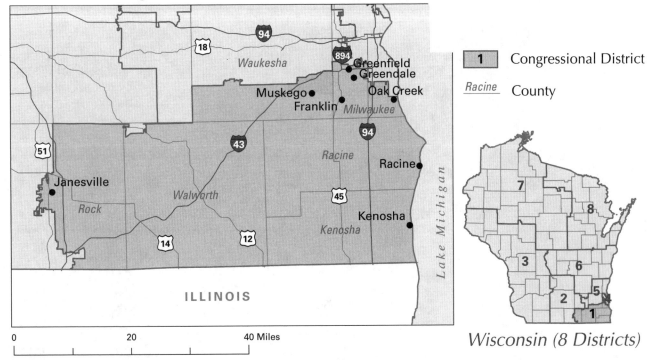

	Congressional District
Racine	County

Wisconsin (8 Districts)

Congressional District 2

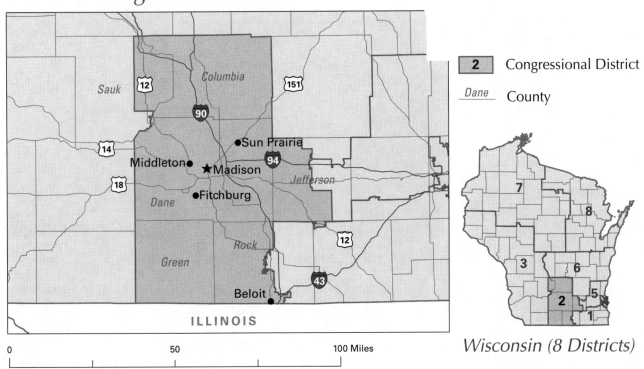

	Congressional District
Dane	County

Wisconsin (8 Districts)

Congressional District 3

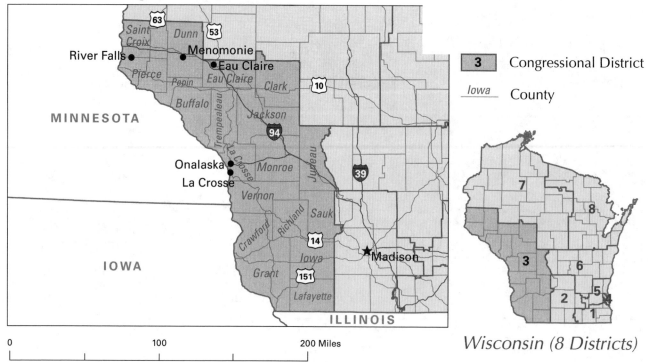

0   100   200 Miles

3 Congressional District

Iowa County

Wisconsin (8 Districts)

Congressional District 4

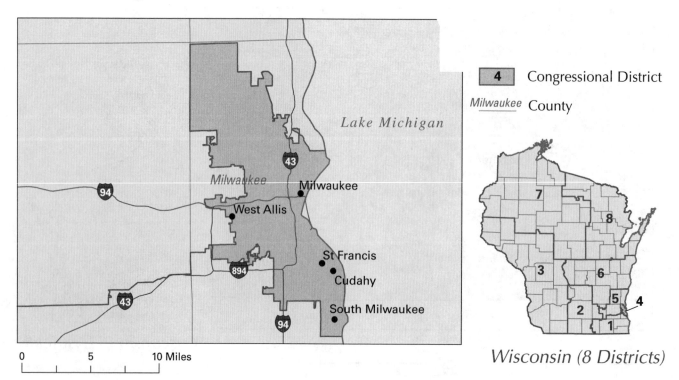

0   5   10 Miles

4 Congressional District

Milwaukee County

Wisconsin (8 Districts)

Congressional District 5

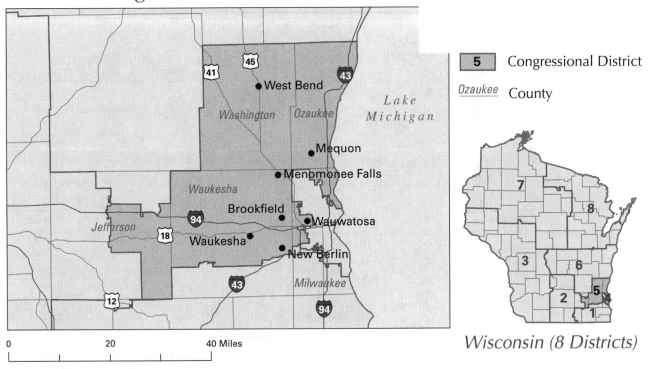

5	Congressional District
Ozaukee	County

Wisconsin (8 Districts)

Congressional District 6

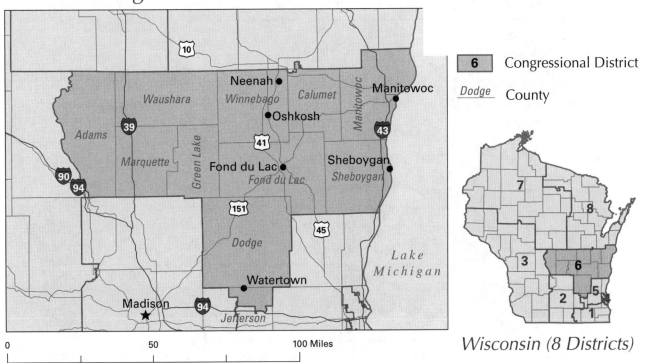

6	Congressional District
Dodge	County

Wisconsin (8 Districts)

Congressional District 7

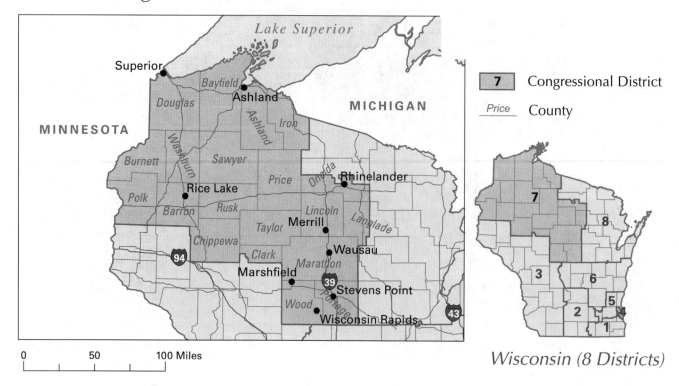

Wisconsin (8 Districts)

Congressional District 8

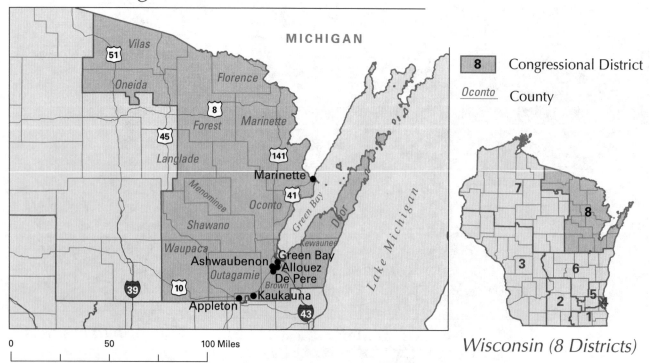

Wisconsin (8 Districts)

Wyoming—
Congressional District: At large

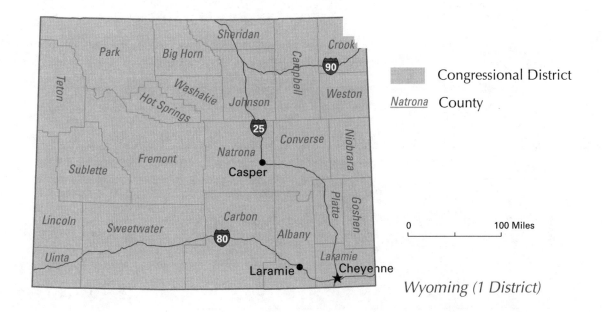

■ Congressional District

Natrona County

0   100 Miles

Wyoming (1 District)

WYOMING—109th CONGRESSIONAL DISTRICTS BY COUNTIES

County	Congressional District	County	Congressional District
Albany	1	Natrona	1
Big Horn	1	Niobrara	1
Campbell	1	Park	1
Carbon	1	Platte	1
Converse	1	Sheridan	1
Crook	1	Sublette	1
Fremont	1	Sweetwater	1
Goshen	1	Teton	1
Hot Springs	1	Uinta	1
Johnson	1	Washakie	1
Laramie	1	Weston	1
Lincoln	1		

American Samoa—Delegate District
Congressional District: At large

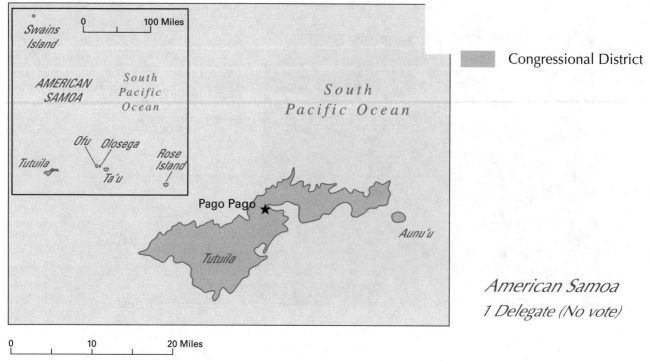

Congressional District

American Samoa
1 Delegate (No vote)

AMERICAN SAMOA—109th DELEGATE DISTRICTS BY COUNTIES

County	Delegate District
Eastern District	1
Manu'a District	1
Rose Island	1
Swains Island	1
Western District	1

Guam—Delegate District

Congressional District: At large

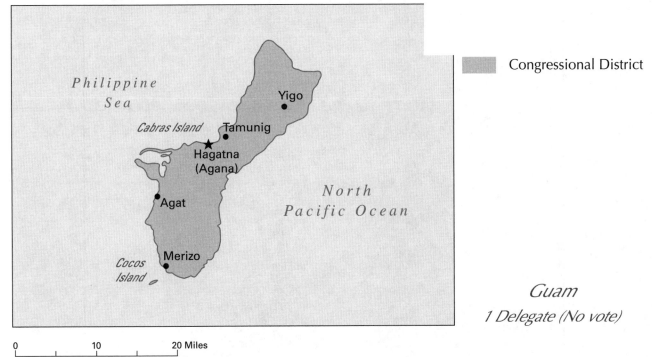

Congressional District

Guam
1 Delegate (No vote)

0   10   20 Miles

Northern Mariana Islands—Resident Representative District

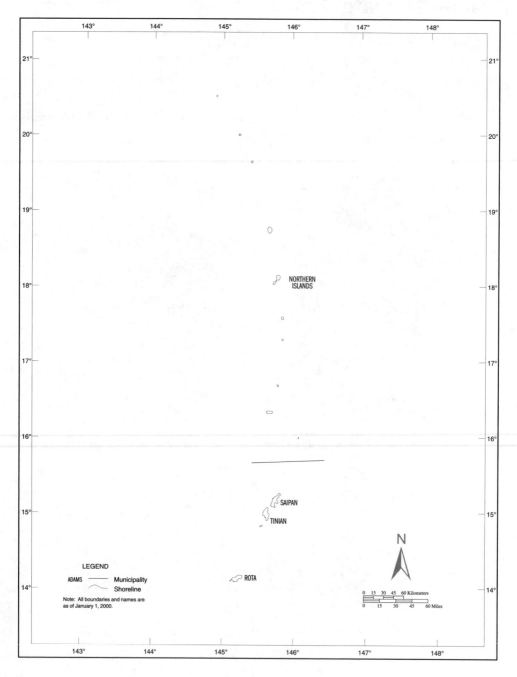

NORTHERN MARIANA ISLANDS—109th REPRESENTATIVE DISTRICT BY COUNTIES

County	Representative District
Northern Islands Municipality	1
Rota Municipality	1
Saipan Municipality	1
Tinian Municipality	1

Commonwealth of Puerto Rico—*Delegate District*

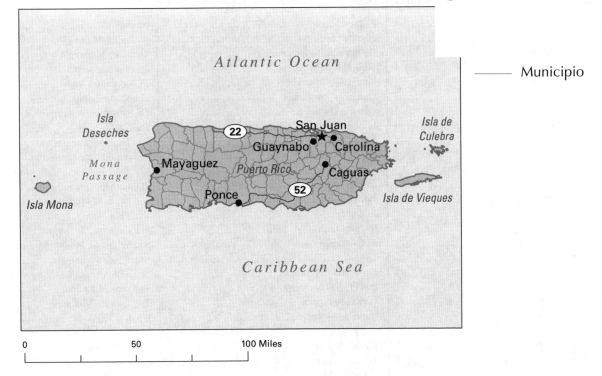

—— Municipio

PUERTO RICO—109th DELEGATE DISTRICTS BY COUNTIES

County	Delegate District	County	Delegate District	County	Delegate District
Adjuntas Municipio	1	Fajardo Municipio	1	Naguabo Municipio	1
Aguada Municipio	1	Florida Municipio	1	Naranjito Municipio	1
Aguadilla Municipio	1	Guánica Municipio	1	Orocovis Municipio	1
Aguas Buenas Municipio	1	Guayama Municipio	1	Patillas Municipio	1
Aibonito Municipio	1	Guayanilla Municipio	1	Peñuelas Municipio	1
Añasco Municipio	1	Guaynabo Municipio	1	Ponce Municipio	1
Arecibo Municipio	1	Gurabo Municipio	1	Quebradillas Municipio	1
Arroyo Municipio	1	Hatillo Municipio	1	Rincón Municipio	1
Barceloneta Municipio	1	Hormigueros Municipio	1	Río Grande Municipio	1
Barranquitas Municipio	1	Humacao Municipio	1	Sabana Grande Municipio	1
Bayamón Municipio	1	Isabela Municipio	1	Salinas Municipio	1
Cabo Rojo Municipio	1	Jayuya Municipio	1	San Germán Municipio	1
Caguas Municipio	1	Juana Díaz Municipio	1	San Juan Municipio	1
Camuy Municipio	1	Juncos Municipio	1	San Lorenzo Municipio	1
Canóvanas Municipio	1	Lajas Municipio	1	San Sebastián Municipio	1
Carolina Municipio	1	Lares Municipio	1	Santa Isabel Municipio	1
Cataño Municipio	1	Las Marías Municipio	1	Toa Alta Municipio	1
Cayey Municipio	1	Las Piedras Municipio	1	Toa Baja Municipio	1
Ceiba Municipio	1	Loíza Municipio	1	Trujillo Alto Municipio	1
Ciales Municipio	1	Luquillo Municipio	1	Utuado Municipio	1
Cidra Municipio	1	Manatí Municipio	1	Vega Alta Municipio	1
Coamo Municipio	1	Maricao Municipio	1	Vega Baja Municipio	1
Comerío Municipio	1	Maunabo Municipio	1	Vieques Municipio	1
Corozal Municipio	1	Mayagüez Municipio	1	Villalba Municipio	1
Culebra Municipio	1	Moca Municipio	1	Yabucoa Municipio	1
Dorado Municipio	1	Morovis Municipio	1	Yauco Municipio	1

United States Virgin Islands—Delegate District

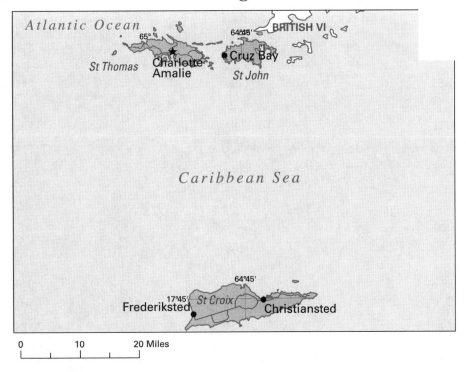

0   10   20 Miles

VIRGIN ISLANDS—109th DELEGATE DISTRICTS BY COUNTIES

County	Delegate District
Northern Islands Municipality	1
St. Croix Island	1
St. John Island	1
St. Thomas Island	1

PART II: TABLES

109th Congressional District Rankings[1]

(Top 30 districts and lowest 30 districts by rank.)

Largest Land Area, 2000			Most Densely Populated, 2000		
Rank	Congressional district	Land area[2] (square kilometers)	Rank	Congressional district	Population density (persons per square kilometer)
1	Congressional District (At Large), Alaska	1 481 347	1	Congressional District 15, New York	24 235.4
2	Congressional District (At Large), Montana	376 979	2	Congressional District 16, New York	21 109.7
3	Congressional District 2, Nevada	272 153	3	Congressional District 11, New York	21 101.1
4	Delegate District (At Large), Wyoming	251 489	4	Congressional District 14, New York	19 823.2
5	Congressional District (At Large), South Dakota	196 540	5	Congressional District 8, New York	16 780.2
6	Congressional District 2, New Mexico	179 986	6	Congressional District 10, New York	14 253.7
7	Congressional District 2, Oregon	179 982	7	Congressional District 12, New York	13 333.6
8	Congressional District (At Large), North Dakota	178 647	8	Congressional District 7, New York	9 602.1
9	Congressional District 3, Nebraska	167 083	9	Congressional District 8, California	6 949.6
10	Congressional District 1, Arizona	151 795	10	Congressional District 9, New York	6 822.0
11	Congressional District 1, Kansas	148 596	11	Congressional District 4, Illinois	6 471.8
12	Congressional District 3, Colorado	139 765	12	Congressional District 6, New York	6 421.0
13	Congressional District 23, Texas	136 287	13	Congressional District 31, California	6 267.1
14	Congressional District 3, New Mexico	122 108	14	Congressional District 8, Massachusetts	6 049.4
15	Congressional District 2, Utah	118 166	15	Congressional District 33, California	5 109.2
16	Congressional District 2, Idaho	111 946	16	Congressional District 47, California	4 501.7
17	Congressional District 13, Texas	104 110	17	Congressional District 7, Illinois	4 476.2
18	Congressional District 1, Idaho	102 369	18	Congressional District 35, California	4 436.5
19	Congressional District 11, Texas	90 636	19	Congressional District 5, Illinois	4 419.7
20	Congressional District 3, Oklahoma	88 289	20	Congressional District 13, New Jersey	4 404.1
21	Congressional District 7, Minnesota	82 353	21	Congressional District 2, Pennsylvania	4 258.9
22	Congressional District 4, Colorado	80 025	22	Congressional District 1, Pennsylvania	4 246.2
23	Congressional District 8, Minnesota	71 439	23	Congressional District 34, California	4 230.5
24	Congressional District 2, Maine	70 775	24	Congressional District 13, New York	3 896.5
25	Congressional District 19, Texas	65 445	25	Congressional District 39, California	3 806.7
26	Congressional District 1, Michigan	64 458	26	Congressional District 5, New York	3 803.8
27	Congressional District 7, Arizona	59 240	27	Congressional District 10, New Jersey	3 784.3
28	Congressional District 5, Washington	59 217	28	Delegate District (At Large), District of Columbia	3 597.9
29	Congressional District 2, California	56 353	29	Congressional District 9, Illinois	3 349.3
30	Congressional District 25, California	55 644	30	Congressional District 37, California	3 309.4

Smallest Land Area, 2000			Least Densely Populated, 2000		
Rank	Congressional district	Land area[2] (square kilometers)	Rank	Congressional district	Population density (persons per square kilometer)
407	Congressional District 36, California	194	407	Congressional District 25, California	11.5
408	Congressional District 37, California	193	408	Congressional District 2, California	11.3
409	Congressional District 5, New York	172	409	Congressional District 5, Washington	11.1
410	Congressional District 10, New Jersey	171	410	Congressional District 7, Arizona	10.8
411	Congressional District 39, California	168	411	Congressional District 1, Michigan	10.3
411	Congressional District 13, New York	168	412	Congressional District 19, Texas	10.0
413	Delegate District (At Large), District of Columbia	159	413	Congressional District 2, Maine	9.0
414	Congressional District 1, Pennsylvania	152	414	Congressional District 8, Minnesota	8.6
414	Congressional District 2, Pennsylvania	152	415	Congressional District 3, Oklahoma	7.8
416	Congressional District 34, California	151	416	Congressional District 4, Colorado	7.7
417	Congressional District 5, Illinois	148	417	Congressional District 7, Minnesota	7.5
418	Congressional District 13, New Jersey	147	418	Congressional District 11, Texas	7.2
419	Congressional District 7, Illinois	146	419	Congressional District 1, Idaho	6.3
420	Congressional District 35, California	144	419	Congressional District 13, Texas	6.3
421	Congressional District 47, California	142	419	Congressional District 2, Utah	6.3
422	Congressional District 33, California	125	422	Congressional District 2, Idaho	5.8
423	Congressional District 8, Massachusetts	105	423	Congressional District 3, New Mexico	5.0
424	Congressional District 31, California	102	424	Congressional District 23, Texas	4.8
424	Congressional District 6, New York	102	425	Congressional District 1, Kansas	4.5
426	Congressional District 4, Illinois	101	426	Congressional District 3, Colorado	4.4
427	Congressional District 9, New York	96	427	Congressional District 1, Arizona	4.2
428	Congressional District 8, California	92	428	Congressional District 2, Oregon	3.8
429	Congressional District 7, New York	68	428	Congressional District (At Large), South Dakota	3.8
430	Congressional District 12, New York	49	430	Congressional District (At Large), North Dakota	3.6
431	Congressional District 10, New York	46	431	Congressional District 3, Nebraska	3.4
432	Congressional District 8, New York	39	431	Congressional District 2, New Mexico	3.4
433	Congressional District 14, New York	33	433	Congressional District (At Large), Montana	2.4
434	Congressional District 11, New York	31	433	Congressional District 2, Nevada	2.4
434	Congressional District 16, New York	31	435	Congressional District (At Large), Wyoming	2.0
436	Congressional District 15, New York	27	436	Congressional District (At Large), Alaska	0.4

[1] Includes 435 state congressional districts and the District of Columbia.
[2] Dry land or land partially or temporarily covered by water.

109th Congressional District Rankings[1]—*Continued*

(Top 30 districts and lowest 30 districts by rank.)

Highest Proportion of Minority Population, 2000			Highest Proportion of Foreign-Born Population, 2000		
Rank	Congressional district	Percent minority[3]	Rank	Congressional district	Percent foreign born
1	Congressional District 16, New York	97.1	1	Congressional District 21, Florida	56.6
2	Congressional District 31, California	90.3	2	Congressional District 31, California	56.3
3	Congressional District 35, California	89.6	3	Congressional District 18, Florida	54.0
4	Congressional District 34, California	88.6	4	Congressional District 47, California	50.7
5	Congressional District 6, New York	87.2	5	Congressional District 34, California	47.2
6	Congressional District 38, California	86.6	6	Congressional District 25, Florida	46.5
7	Congressional District 32, California	85.2	7	Congressional District 5, New York	45.6
8	Congressional District 10, New York	83.7	8	Congressional District 28, California	44.0
8	Congressional District 15, New York	83.7	9	Congressional District 29, California	43.8
10	Congressional District 37, California	83.4	10	Congressional District 11, New York	41.7
11	Congressional District 16, Texas	82.7	11	Congressional District 32, California	41.6
11	Congressional District 47, California	82.7	12	Congressional District 12, New York	41.4
13	Congressional District 9, Texas	82.6	13	Congressional District 4, Illinois	40.6
14	Congressional District 1, Hawaii	82.3	14	Congressional District 9, New York	40.1
15	Congressional District 17, Florida	81.5	15	Congressional District 13, New Jersey	39.6
16	Congressional District 4, Illinois	81.4	16	Congressional District 6, New York	39.5
17	Congressional District 18, Texas	80.2	17	Congressional District 7, New York	38.7
17	Congressional District 33, California	80.2	18	Congressional District 38, California	38.3
19	Congressional District 39, California	79.2	19	Congressional District 33, California	37.5
20	Congressional District 21, Florida	79.0	20	Congressional District 16, California	37.0
21	Congressional District 51, California	78.8	21	Congressional District 8, California	36.7
22	Congressional District 20, California	78.7	22	Congressional District 27, California	35.8
23	Congressional District 10, New Jersey	78.6	23	Congressional District 39, California	35.5
24	Congressional District 11, New York	78.5	24	Congressional District 12, California	34.3
25	Congressional District 29, Texas	78.2	25	Congressional District 17, Florida	34.1
25	Congressional District 25, Texas	78.2	26	Congressional District 15, California	33.8
27	Congressional District 30, Texas	78.1	27	Congressional District 13, California	33.7
28	Congressional District 12, New York	76.9	28	Congressional District 15, New York	33.6
29	Congressional District 43, California	76.8	29	Congressional District 8, New York	33.2
30	Congressional District 20, Texas	76.7	30	Congressional District 51, California	32.7
			30	Congressional District 9, Texas	32.7

Lowest Proportion of Minority Population, 2000			Lowest Proportion of Foreign-Born Population, 2000		
Rank	Congressional district	Percent minority[3]	Rank	Congressional district	Percent foreign born
407	Congressional District 5, Iowa	6.1	404	Congressional District 7, Alabama	1.6
407	Congressional District 2, West Virginia	6.1	404	Congressional District 4, Louisiana	1.6
409	Congressional District 5, Wisconsin	6.0	404	Congressional District 1, Tennessee	1.6
409	Congressional District 3, West Virginia	6.0	404	Congressional District 9, Virginia	1.6
409	Congressional District 14, Ohio	6.0	408	Congressional District 3, Alabama	1.5
409	Congressional District 19, Illinois	6.0	408	Congressional District 7, Louisiana	1.5
413	Congressional District 9, Indiana	5.9	408	Congressional District 8, Minnesota	1.5
414	Congressional District 4, Pennsylvania	5.8	408	Congressional District 8, Tennessee	1.5
414	Congressional District 6, Wisconsin	5.8	408	Congressional District 3, Wisconsin	1.5
416	Congressional District 8, Minnesota	5.4	413	Congressional District 4, Kentucky	1.4
417	Congressional District 4, Iowa	5.2	413	Congressional District 1, Michigan	1.4
418	Congressional District 6, Minnesota	5.1	413	Congressional District 3, Mississipi	1.4
419	Congressional District 12, Pennsylvania	5.0	413	Congressional District 5, Ohio	1.4
419	Congressional District 1, Tennessee	5.0	413	Congressional District 2, Oklahoma	1.4
419	Congressional District 1, New Hampshire	5.0	413	Congressional District 1, West Virginia	1.4
422	Congressional District 6, Ohio	4.9	419	Congressional District 4, Ohio	1.3
422	Congressional District 4, Kentucky	4.9	419	Congressional District 6, Ohio	1.3
422	Congressional District 2, New Hampshire	4.9	419	Congressional District 4, Tennessee	1.3
425	Congressional District 7, Wisconsin	4.8	422	Congressional District 6, Indiana	1.2
426	Congressional District 18, Pennsylvania	4.6	422	Congressional District 8, Indiana	1.2
427	Congressional District 10, Pennsylvania	4.4	422	Congressional District 1, Kentucky	1.2
428	Congressional District 1, West Virginia	4.3	422	Congressional District 1, Mississipi	1.2
429	Congressional District 18, Ohio	4.2	422	Congressional District 9, Pennsylvania	1.2
430	Congressional District 5, Pennsylvania	3.9	427	Congressional District 19, Illinois	1.1
430	Congressional District (At Large), Vermont	3.9	427	Congressional District 8, Missouri	1.1
432	Congressional District 3, Wisconsin	3.8	427	Congressional District 2, West Virginia	1.1
433	Congressional District 9, Pennsylvania	3.6	430	Congressional District 1, Arkansas	1.0
433	Congressional District 1, Maine	3.6	430	Congressional District 5, Louisiana	1.0
435	Congressional District 2, Maine	3.3	430	Congressional District 12, Pennsylvania	1.0
436	Congressional District 5, Kentucky	2.9	433	Congressional District 2, Mississipi	0.9
			433	Congressional District 18, Ohio	0.9
			435	Congressional District 3, West Virginia	0.7
			436	Congressional District 5, Kentucky	0.6

[1]Includes 435 state congressional districts and the District of Columbia.
[3]Persons who do not identify themselves as White alone, not of Hispanic origin.

109th Congressional District Rankings[1]—Continued

(Top 30 districts and lowest 30 districts by rank.)

Highest Proportion with a Bachelor's Degree, 2000			Highest Median Household Income, 1999		
Rank	Congressional district	Percent with bachelor's degree or more[4]	Rank	Congressional district	Median household income (dollars)
1	Congressional District 14, New York	56.9	1	Congressional District 11, Virginia	80 397
2	Congressional District 8, Virginia	53.8	2	Congressional District 11, New Jersey	79 009
3	Congressional District 8, Maryland	53.7	3	Congressional District 14, California	77 985
4	Congressional District 30, California	53.5	4	Congressional District 6, Georgia	75 611
5	Congressional District 14, California	52.2	5	Congressional District 15, California	74 947
6	Congressional District 6, Georgia	50.7	6	Congressional District 7, New Jersey	74 823
7	Congressional District 7, Texas	50.0	7	Congressional District 6, Colorado	73 393
8	Congressional District 11, Virginia	48.9	8	Congressional District 5, New Jersey	72 781
9	Congressional District 4, North Carolina	48.0	9	Congressional District 13, Illinois	71 686
10	Congressional District 8, New York	47.8	10	Congressional District 10, Illinois	71 663
11	Congressional District 10, Illinois	47.5	11	Congressional District 10, Virginia	71 560
12	Congressional District 6, Colorado	46.8	12	Congressional District 2, New York	71 147
13	Congressional District 48, California	46.5	13	Congressional District 3, New York	70 561
14	Congressional District 11, New Jersey	45.2	14	Congressional District 42, California	70 463
15	Congressional District 7, Washington	44.1	15	Congressional District 12, California	70 307
16	Congressional District 8, California	44.0	16	Congressional District 12, New Jersey	69 668
17	Congressional District 18, New York	43.8	17	Congressional District 48, California	69 663
18	Congressional District 9, Michigan	43.5	18	Congressional District 18, New York	68 887
19	Congressional District 21, Texas	43.1	19	Congressional District 8, Maryland	68 306
19	Congressional District 10, Virginia	43.1	20	Congressional District 16, California	67 689
21	Congressional District 13, Illinois	42.4	21	Congressional District 4, New York	66 799
22	Congressional District 12, New Jersey	42.3	22	Congressional District 4, Connecticut	66 598
23	Congressional District 4, Connecticut	42.2	23	Congressional District 9, Michigan	65 358
24	Congressional District 15, California	41.6	24	Congressional District 10, California	65 245
25	Congressional District 7, New Jersey	41.5	25	Congressional District 19, New York	64 337
26	Congressional District 3, Texas	41.4	26	Congressional District 8, Washington	63 854
27	Congressional District 12, California	40.7	27	Congressional District 3, Minnesota	63 816
28	Congressional District 3, Minnesota	40.1	28	Congressional District 7, Georgia	63 455
29	Congressional District 50, California	40.0	29	Congressional District 8, Virginia	63 430
30	Congressional District 8, Massachusetts	39.8	30	Congressional District 8, Illinois	62 762

Lowest Proportion with a Bachelor's Degree, 2000			Lowest Median Household Income, 1999		
Rank	Congressional district	Percent with bachelor's degree or more[4]	Rank	Congressional district	Median household income (dollars)
406	Congressional District 7, Arizona	13.3	407	Congressional District 17, Florida	30 426
406	Congressional District 4, Arkansas	13.3	408	Congressional District 1, Kentucky	30 360
406	Congressional District 35, California	13.3	409	Congressional District 1, West Virginia	30 303
406	Congressional District 15, Texas	13.3	410	Congressional District 10, New York	30 212
410	Congressional District 2, Oklahoma	13.2	411	Congressional District 14, Pennsylvania	30 139
		13.1			
411	Congressional District 4, Ohio		412	Congressional District 34, California	29 863
412	Congressional District 9, Pennsylvania	13.0	413	Congressional District 3, Florida	29 785
413	Congressional District 3, Florida	12.9	414	Congressional District 9, Virginia	29 783
414	Congressional District 23, Florida	12.8	415	Congressional District 4, Arkansas	29 675
414	Congressional District 3, Georgia	12.8	416	Congressional District 2, Georgia	29 354
		12.5			
416	Congressional District 38, California		417	Congressional District 2, New Mexico	29 269
416	Congressional District 8, Tennessee	12.5	418	Congressional District 12, New York	29 195
418	Congressional District 1, Arkansas	12.3	419	Congressional District 6, South Carolina	28 967
419	Congressional District 1, North Carolina	12.0	420	Congressional District 1, Arkansas	28 940
419	Congressional District 3, West Virginia	12.0	421	Congressional District 1, North Carolina	28 410
		11.9			
421	Congressional District 8, Missouri		422	Congressional District 25, Texas	28 348
422	Congressional District 1, Kentucky	11.8	423	Congressional District 1, Pennsylvania	28 261
423	Congressional District 4, Alabama	11.3	424	Congressional District 15, Texas	28 061
423	Congressional District 18, Ohio	11.3	425	Congressional District 15, New York	27 934
423	Congressional District 4, Tennessee	11.3	426	Congressional District 2, Oklahoma	27 885
		10.9			
426	Congressional District 28, Texas		427	Congressional District 8, Missouri	27 865
427	Congressional District 3, Louisiana	10.8	428	Congressional District 2, Louisiana	27 514
428	Congressional District 4, Arizona	10.2	429	Congressional District 5, Louisiana	27 453
429	Congressional District 47, California	10.0	430	Congressional District 2, Mississipi	26 894
430	Congressional District 18, California	9.7	431	Congressional District 20, California	26 800
431	Congressional District 5, Kentucky	9.6	432	Congressional District 7, Alabama	26 672
432	Congressional District 43, California	8.8	433	Congressional District 31, California	26 093
433	Congressional District 34, California	8.7	434	Congressional District 3, West Virginia	25 630
434	Congressional District 16, New York	7.8	435	Congressional District 5, Kentucky	21 915
435	Congressional District 29, Texas	6.5	436	Congressional District 16, New York	19 311
436	Congressional District 20, California	6.3			

[1]Includes 435 state congressional districts and the District of Columbia.
[4]Persons 25 years old and over.

109th Congressional District Rankings[1]—*Continued*

(Top 30 districts and lowest 30 districts by rank.)

Rank	Highest Poverty Rate, 2000 Congressional district	Persons in poverty (percent)	Rank	Highest Unemployment Rate, 2000 Congressional district	Unemployment rate[5]
1	Congressional District 16, New York	42.2	1	Congressional District 16, New York	20.3
2	Congressional District 20, California	32.2	2	Congressional District 20, California	19.0
3	Congressional District 15, New York	30.5	3	Congressional District 15, New York	14.4
4	Congressional District 31, California	30.1	4	Congressional District 18, California	14.3
5	Congressional District 10, New York	29.0	5	Congressional District 10, New York	13.5
6	Congressional District 25, Texas	28.8	6	Congressional District 13, Michigan	12.9
7	Congressional District 15, Texas	28.7	7	Congressional District 1, Illinois	12.8
8	Congressional District 12, New York	28.3	8	Congressional District 1, Pennsylvania	12.7
9	Congressional District 5, Kentucky	28.1	9	Congressional District 7, Illinois	12.2
10	Congressional District 2, Mississipi	27.3	10	Congressional District 2, Pennsylvania	11.7
11	Congressional District 1, Pennsylvania	26.9	11	Congressional District 11, New York	11.6
12	Congressional District 2, Louisiana	26.8	12	Congressional District 21, California	11.4
13	Congressional District 35, California	26.4	12	Congressional District 34, California	11.4
14	Congressional District 34, California	26.0	14	Congressional District 31, California	11.2
15	Congressional District 4, Arizona	25.6	14	Congressional District 35, California	11.2
16	Congressional District 27, Texas	25.3	14	Congressional District 37, California	11.2
17	Congressional District 37, California	25.2	17	Congressional District 17, Florida	11.1
18	Congressional District 7, Alabama	24.7	18	Congressional District 10, New Jersey	10.9
19	Congressional District 13, Michigan	24.4	18	Congressional District 12, New York	10.9
20	Congressional District 7, Illinois	24.0	20	Delegate District (At Large), District of Columbia	10.7
21	Congressional District 2, Pennsylvania	23.8	21	Congressional District 5, Georgia	10.6
22	Congressional District 5, Louisiana	23.6	22	Congressional District 33, California	10.4
22	Congressional District 16, Texas	23.6	22	Congressional District 43, California	10.4
24	Congressional District 33, California	23.5	22	Congressional District 2, Illinois	10.4
25	Congressional District 17, Florida	23.3	22	Congressional District 2, Mississipi	10.4
25	Congressional District 18, Texas	23.3	26	Congressional District 14, Michigan	9.8
27	Congressional District 11, New York	23.2	27	Congressional District 4, Washington	9.7
28	Congressional District 18, California	22.7	28	Congressional District 7, Alabama	9.5
29	Congressional District 28, Texas	22.6	28	Congressional District 2, Louisiana	9.5
30	Congressional District 2, Georgia	22.5	28	Congressional District 13, New Jersey	9.5
			28	Congressional District 6, New York	9.5

Rank	Lowest Poverty Rate, 2000 Congressional district	Persons in poverty (percent)	Rank	Lowest Unemployment Rate, 2000 Congressional district	Unemployment rate[5]
407	Congressional District 14, Ohio	5.7	404	Congressional District 15, California	3.5
408	Congressional District 5, Maryland	5.6	404	Congressional District 8, Georgia	3.5
408	Congressional District 1, Washington	5.6	404	Congressional District 7, Massachusetts	3.5
410	Congressional District 12, California	5.4	404	Congressional District 14, Ohio	3.5
410	Congressional District 9, Michigan	5.4	404	Congressional District 8, Pennsylvania	3.5
410	Congressional District 7, Pennsylvania	5.4	409	Congressional District 6, Alabama	3.4
413	Congressional District 5, Indiana	5.2	409	Congressional District 14, Florida	3.4
413	Congressional District 12, New Jersey	5.2	409	Congressional District 10, Georgia	3.4
415	Congressional District 3, New Jersey	5.1	409	Congressional District 8, Illinois	3.4
415	Congressional District 8, Washington	5.1	409	Congressional District 11, Michigan	3.4
417	Congressional District 10, Illinois	4.8	409	Congressional District 1, New Hampshire	3.4
418	Congressional District 6, Minnesota	4.7	409	Congressional District 11, New Jersey	3.4
419	Congressional District 7, Georgia	4.5	409	Congressional District 3, New York	3.4
419	Congressional District 8, Pennsylvania	4.5	417	Congressional District 5, Indiana	3.3
421	Congressional District 8, Illinois	4.4	417	Congressional District 3, Nebraska	3.3
421	Congressional District 10, Virginia	4.4	417	Congressional District 5, New Jersey	3.3
423	Congressional District 6, Illinois	4.3	417	Congressional District 21, Texas	3.3
423	Congressional District 11, Michigan	4.3	417	Congressional District 24, Texas	3.3
423	Congressional District 3, New York	4.3	422	Congressional District 13, Illinois	3.2
426	Congressional District 2, Minnesota	3.9	422	Congressional District 7, New Jersey	3.2
427	Congressional District 11, Virginia	3.8	424	Congressional District 12, California	3.1
428	Congressional District 6, Georgia	3.7	424	Congressional District 2, Missouri	3.1
429	Congressional District 2, Missouri	3.6	426	Congressional District 2, Minnesota	3.0
429	Congressional District 5, New Jersey	3.6	426	Congressional District 6, Minnesota	3.0
431	Congressional District 3, Minnesota	3.5	428	Congressional District 8, Virginia	2.9
431	Congressional District 11, New Jersey	3.5	429	Congressional District 3, Minnesota	2.8
433	Congressional District 7, New Jersey	3.4	429	Congressional District 7, Virginia	2.8
433	Congressional District 5, Wisconsin	3.4	431	Congressional District 6, Georgia	2.7
435	Congressional District 13, Illinois	2.9	431	Congressional District 7, Georgia	2.7
436	Congressional District 6, Colorado	2.7	431	Congressional District 5, Wisconsin	2.7
			434	Congressional District 11, Virginia	2.6
			435	Congressional District 10, Virginia	2.3
			436	Congressional District 6, Colorado	2.2

[1]Includes 435 state congressional districts and the District of Columbia.
[5]Percent of civilian labor force.

109th Congressional District Rankings[1]—Continued

(Top 75 districts by rank.)

	Highest Number of Farms, 2002			Highest Value of Agricultural Products Sold, 2002	
Rank	Congressional district	Number of farms	Rank	Congressional district	Market value of agricultural products sold ($1,000)
1	Congressional District 1, Kansas	34 746	1	Congressional District 1, Kansas	7 176 335
2	Congressional District 7, Minnesota	32 629	2	Congressional District 3, Nebraska	7 174 525
3	Congressional District 3, Nebraska	31 774	3	Congressional District 13, Texas	5 656 446
4	Congressional District (At Large), South Dakota	31 736	4	Congressional District 5, Iowa	4 480 496
5	Congressional District (At Large), North Dakota	30 619	5	Congressional District (At Large), South Dakota	3 834 625
6	Congressional District 3, Oklahoma	30 462	6	Congressional District 4, Iowa	3 813 075
7	Congressional District 2, Oklahoma	30 416	7	Congressional District 7, Minnesota	3 792 754
8	Congressional District (At Large), Montana	27 870	8	Congressional District 4, Colorado	3 456 724
9	Congressional District 3, Wisconsin	27 124	9	Congressional District 21, California	3 282 057
10	Congressional District 5, Iowa	26 562	10	Congressional District (At Large), North Dakota	3 233 366
11	Congressional District 4, Missouri	26 556	11	Congressional District 1, Minnesota	3 186 486
12	Congressional District 14, Texas	26 242	12	Congressional District 20, California	3 022 243
13	Congressional District 17, Texas	25 433	13	Congressional District 2, Idaho	3 011 342
14	Congressional District 4, Iowa	24 501	14	Congressional District 4, Washington	2 924 142
15	Congressional District 1, Kentucky	24 157	15	Congressional District 17, California	2 627 098
16	Congressional District 2, Kentucky	23 291	16	Congressional District 3, Oklahoma	2 528 847
17	Congressional District 9, Missouri	22 595	17	Congressional District 1, Nebraska	2 489 414
18	Congressional District 1, Minnesota	21 384	18	Congressional District 18, California	2 011 986
19	Congressional District 1, Texas	21 053	19	Congressional District (At Large), Montana	1 882 114
20	Congressional District 6, Missouri	20 879	20	Congressional District 19, California	1 867 389
21	Congressional District 8, Missouri	19 816	21	Congressional District 3, Wisconsin	1 649 004
22	Congressional District 2, Kansas	19 459	22	Congressional District 1, Iowa	1 642 021
23	Congressional District 4, Tennessee	19 059	23	Congressional District 7, North Carolina	1 641 469
24	Congressional District 19, Illinois	18 783	24	Congressional District 1, Arkansas	1 574 413
25	Congressional District 6, Tennessee	17 959	25	Congressional District 4, Arkansas	1 566 116
26	Congressional District 13, Texas	17 197	26	Congressional District 22, California	1 556 281
27	Congressional District 1, Nebraska	17 159	27	Congressional District 15, Illinois	1 533 084
28	Congressional District 7, Wisconsin	16 407	28	Congressional District 3, Arkansas	1 454 448
29	Congressional District 4, Texas	16 085	29	Congressional District 2, California	1 450 753
30	Congressional District 4, Kentucky	15 394	30	Congressional District 19, Texas	1 427 265
31	Congressional District 4, Oklahoma	14 907	31	Congressional District 4, Alabama	1 384 212
32	Congressional District 2, Oregon	14 768	32	Congressional District 19, Illinois	1 374 345
33	Congressional District 1, Arkansas	14 524	33	Congressional District 9, Georgia	1 330 465
34	Congressional District 3, Arkansas	14 277	34	Congressional District 3, Mississipi	1 308 446
35	Congressional District 9, Virginia	14 103	35	Congressional District 2, Oregon	1 302 248
36	Congressional District 2, Texas	14 099	36	Congressional District 1, Kentucky	1 289 939
37	Congressional District 1, Iowa	14 046	37	Congressional District 2, Oklahoma	1 289 267
38	Congressional District 2, Iowa	13 904	38	Congressional District 3, Iowa	1 245 663
39	Congressional District 2, Idaho	13 757	39	Congressional District 18, Illinois	1 222 379
40	Congressional District 4, Alabama	13 754	40	Congressional District 11, California	1 206 548
41	Congressional District 31, Texas	13 511	41	Congressional District 7, Arizona	1 195 488
42	Congressional District 11, Texas	13 461	42	Congressional District 4, Missouri	1 169 374
43	Congressional District 1, Tennessee	13 428	43	Congressional District 1, Texas	1 136 605
44	Congressional District 3, Mississipi	13 241	44	Congressional District 17, Illinois	1 133 509
45	Congressional District 7, Missouri	13 028	45	Congressional District 16, Pennsylvania	1 121 589
46	Congressional District 1, Mississipi	12 947	46	Congressional District 16, Florida	1 093 314
47	Congressional District 5, Texas	12 764	47	Congressional District 2, Iowa	1 092 379
48	Congressional District 8, Tennessee	12 620	48	Congressional District 1, North Carolina	1 083 751
49	Congressional District 8, Minnesota	12 619	49	Congressional District 1, California	1 081 764
50	Congressional District 6, Kentucky	12 448	50	Congressional District 5, Washington	1 081 288
51	Congressional District 5, Ohio	12 354	51	Congressional District 23, California	1 078 883
52	Congressional District 4, Colorado	12 156	52	Congressional District 2, Mississipi	1 066 712
53	Congressional District 3, Colorado	12 015	53	Congressional District 51, California	1 066 057
54	Congressional District 4, Arkansas	11 944	54	Congressional District 6, Missouri	1 061 393
55	Congressional District 4, Washington	11 752	55	Congressional District 7, Wisconsin	1 048 406
56	Congressional District 18, Ohio	11 737	56	Congressional District 17, Texas	1 036 036
57	Congressional District 3, Iowa	11 642	57	Congressional District 14, Texas	995 563
58	Congressional District 15, Illinois	11 576	58	Congressional District 6, Wisconsin	981 682
59	Congressional District 9, Indiana	11 428	59	Congressional District 3, North Carolina	981 552
60	Congressional District 1, Idaho	11 260	60	Congressional District 2, Georgia	944 223
61	Congressional District 21, Texas	11 022	61	Congressional District 8, Missouri	943 180
62	Congressional District 6, Indiana	10 845	62	Congressional District 9, Missouri	924 717
63	Congressional District 5, Kentucky	10 761	63	Congressional District 2, New Mexico	914 991
64	Congressional District 6, Wisconsin	10 625	64	Congressional District 1, Idaho	896 919
65	Congressional District 17, Illinois	10 613	65	Congressional District 2, North Carolina	892 784
66	Congressional District 2, California	10 253	66	Congressional District 2, Kansas	887 080
67	Congressional District 5, North Carolina	10 156	67	Congressional District 1, Maryland	875 979
68	Congressional District 18, Illinois	10 105	68	Congressional District (At Large), Wyoming	863 887
69	Congressional District 5, Virginia	10 059	69	Congressional District 5, Ohio	859 731
70	Congressional District 9, Georgia	10 034	70	Congressional District 6, Indiana	859 457
71	Congressional District 8, Wisconsin	9 853	71	Congressional District 8, Wisconsin	830 563
72	Congressional District 4, Ohio	9 610	72	Congressional District 2, Alabama	802 683
73	Congressional District (At Large), Wyoming	9 422	73	Congressional District 5, Oregon	796 286
74	Congressional District 5, Washington	9 367	74	Congressional District 3, Colorado	781 245
75	Congressional District 4, Kansas	9 168	75	Congressional District 24, California	777 345

[1] Includes 435 state congressional districts and the District of Columbia.

Table A. 109th Congressional Districts, 2000

(Number, percent.)

STATE Congressional district	Representative	Land area,[1] (sq km)	Total population	Persons per square kilometer	White	Black	American Indian/Alaska Native	Asian and Pacific Islander	Other race	Hispanic or Latino[2] (percent)	Non-Hispanic White (percent)	Two or more races (percent)
					Race alone or in combination (percent)							
	1	2	3	4	5	6	7	8	9	10	11	12
UNITED STATES		9 161 924	281 421 906	30.7	77.1	12.9	1.5	4.5	6.6	12.5	69.1	2.4
ALABAMA		131 426	4 447 100	33.8	72.0	26.3	1.0	1.0	0.9	1.7	70.3	1.0
Congressional District 1	Jo Bonner (R)	16 361	635 498	38.8	69.3	28.4	1.5	1.3	0.6	1.3	67.8	1.0
Congressional District 2	Terry Everett (R)	27 199	635 311	23.4	68.6	30.0	0.9	0.9	0.7	1.5	67.0	1.0
Congressional District 3	Mike Rogers (R)	20 290	635 374	31.3	66.2	32.7	0.6	0.9	0.5	1.2	64.9	0.8
Congressional District 4	Robert B. Aderholt (R)	21 684	635 365	29.3	92.6	5.3	1.0	0.4	1.7	3.0	90.4	1.0
Congressional District 5	Robert E. (Bud) Cramer Jr. (D)	11 618	635 179	54.7	80.2	17.4	1.9	1.3	0.9	2.0	77.7	1.6
Congressional District 6	Spencer Bachus (R)	11 821	634 742	53.7	90.4	7.9	0.6	1.1	0.8	1.6	88.8	0.8
Congressional District 7	Artur Davis (D)	22 453	635 631	28.3	36.5	62.4	0.5	0.8	0.7	1.3	35.5	0.7
ALASKA		1 481 347	626 932	0.4	74.0	4.3	19.0	6.1	2.4	4.1	67.6	5.4
Congressional District (At Large)	Don Young (R)	1 481 347	626 932	0.4	74.0	4.3	19.0	6.1	2.4	4.1	67.6	5.4
ARIZONA		294 312	5 130 632	17.4	77.9	3.6	5.7	2.6	13.2	25.3	63.8	2.9
Congressional District 1	Rick Renzi (R)	151 795	641 710	4.2	67.7	1.5	23.5	0.9	8.6	16.4	58.4	2.2
Congressional District 2	Trent Franks (R)	52 369	641 435	12.2	87.5	2.6	2.8	2.5	7.0	14.2	78.4	2.3
Congressional District 3	John B. Shadegg (R)	1 550	640 898	413.5	87.9	2.9	1.9	2.9	7.0	14.1	78.5	2.5
Congressional District 4	Ed Pastor (D)	516	641 430	1 243.1	57.6	8.7	4.0	2.1	32.0	58.0	29.3	4.2
Congressional District 5	J. D. Hayworth (R)	3 641	641 348	176.1	85.2	3.3	2.7	4.4	7.2	13.3	76.8	2.7
Congressional District 6	Jeff Flake (R)	1 874	641 360	342.2	86.4	2.5	1.6	2.7	9.5	17.2	76.6	2.5
Congressional District 7	Raúl M. Grijalva (D)	59 240	640 996	10.8	64.9	3.5	7.2	2.0	26.0	50.6	38.6	3.5
Congressional District 8	Jim Kolbe (R)	23 327	641 455	27.5	86.3	3.8	1.8	3.1	8.2	18.2	73.9	3.0
ARKANSAS		134 856	2 673 400	19.8	81.2	16.0	1.4	1.1	1.8	3.2	78.6	1.3
Congressional District 1	Marion Berry (D)	44 422	668 360	15.0	81.9	17.0	1.0	0.5	0.7	1.6	80.2	1.0
Congressional District 2	Vic Snyder (D)	15 338	666 058	43.4	77.8	19.9	1.0	1.2	1.4	2.4	75.6	1.3
Congressional District 3	John Boozman (R)	21 989	672 756	30.6	91.9	2.3	2.4	1.9	3.5	6.3	87.3	1.9
Congressional District 4	Mike Ross (D)	53 107	666 226	12.5	73.1	24.9	1.1	0.6	1.6	2.7	71.0	1.1
CALIFORNIA		403 933	33 871 648	83.9	63.4	7.4	1.9	13.0	19.4	32.4	46.7	4.7
Congressional District 1	Mike Thompson (D)	28 505	639 275	22.4	82.5	1.9	4.5	5.4	10.3	17.9	71.2	4.2
Congressional District 2	Wally Herger (R)	56 353	638 921	11.3	85.1	1.7	4.0	4.8	8.7	14.0	76.2	4.0
Congressional District 3	Dan Lungren (R)	8 739	639 374	73.2	83.2	5.3	2.3	8.2	6.1	10.7	74.4	4.7
Congressional District 4	John T. Doolittle (R)	42 614	639 071	15.0	91.5	1.5	2.7	3.6	4.1	8.9	83.8	3.2
Congressional District 5	Vacant	381	638 837	1 676.7	55.6	16.7	2.8	19.0	13.2	20.8	43.4	6.7
Congressional District 6	Lynn C. Woolsey (D)	4 208	638 970	151.8	85.9	2.7	1.9	5.4	8.3	14.5	76.1	3.9
Congressional District 7	George Miller (D)	904	639 791	707.7	56.3	18.6	1.9	16.8	12.8	21.4	43.2	5.9
Congressional District 8	Nancy Pelosi (D)	92	639 362	6 949.6	52.7	9.7	1.2	31.5	9.5	15.7	42.9	4.4
Congressional District 9	Barbara Lee (D)	343	639 426	1 864.2	46.1	28.2	1.7	18.1	11.8	18.7	35.2	5.2
Congressional District 10	Ellen O. Tauscher (D)	2 624	638 238	243.2	76.7	6.8	1.6	12.3	8.5	15.0	65.4	5.4
Congressional District 11	Richard W. Pombo (R)	5 897	639 625	108.5	76.3	4.1	1.7	11.5	11.7	19.7	64.1	5.0
Congressional District 12	Tom Lantos (D)	303	638 598	2 107.6	59.6	3.2	1.0	32.7	9.1	15.7	48.2	5.1
Congressional District 13	Fortney Pete Stark (D)	573	638 708	1 114.7	52.4	7.5	1.6	33.0	12.5	21.1	38.4	6.4
Congressional District 14	Anna G. Eshoo (D)	2 138	639 953	299.3	70.6	3.6	1.1	18.8	10.0	17.5	59.6	3.8
Congressional District 15	Michael M. Honda (D)	741	639 090	862.5	58.5	3.1	1.3	32.2	9.9	17.2	47.1	4.6
Congressional District 16	Zoe Lofgren (D)	595	638 760	1 073.5	49.9	4.2	1.6	26.3	23.5	37.6	31.9	5.2
Congressional District 17	Sam Farr (D)	12 484	638 519	51.1	65.0	3.4	2.0	7.2	27.6	42.9	46.3	4.9
Congressional District 18	Dennis A. Cardoza (D)	7 906	639 004	80.8	57.9	6.8	2.6	11.7	27.4	41.9	39.1	6.1
Congressional District 19	George Radanovich (R)	17 333	638 975	36.9	74.7	4.1	2.7	5.9	17.5	28.2	59.9	4.7
Congressional District 20	Jim Costa (D)	12 904	639 705	49.6	43.7	8.1	2.6	6.9	43.5	63.1	21.4	4.6
Congressional District 21	Devin Nunes (R)	20 787	639 755	30.8	64.6	2.7	2.6	6.2	28.7	43.4	46.4	4.6
Congressional District 22	William M. Thomas (R)	26 980	638 514	23.7	78.7	6.5	2.5	4.2	12.3	21.0	66.8	4.0
Congressional District 23	Lois Capps (D)	2 698	638 854	236.8	69.0	2.7	2.1	6.6	24.2	41.7	48.7	4.3
Congressional District 24	Elton Gallegly (R)	10 057	639 060	63.5	82.4	2.2	1.7	6.1	11.6	22.3	68.6	3.7
Congressional District 25	Howard P. "Buck" McKeon (R)	55 644	638 768	11.5	72.7	9.1	2.3	5.4	15.5	27.1	57.2	4.7
Congressional District 26	David Dreier (R)	1 947	639 913	328.7	67.8	5.2	1.4	17.2	13.1	24.4	52.7	4.4
Congressional District 27	Brad Sherman (D)	390	638 532	1 637.3	65.3	5.4	1.4	12.3	21.3	36.5	44.9	5.4
Congressional District 28	Howard L. Berman (D)	200	639 364	3 196.8	58.0	5.0	1.4	7.1	34.1	55.6	31.4	5.4
Congressional District 29	Adam B. Schiff (D)	263	638 899	2 429.3	56.9	6.8	1.1	25.7	16.4	26.1	39.1	6.5
Congressional District 30	Henry A. Waxman (D)	740	639 700	864.5	84.6	3.3	0.8	10.6	4.9	8.3	76.4	3.9
Congressional District 31	Xavier Becerra (D)	102	639 248	6 267.1	38.9	5.2	1.8	15.2	44.9	70.2	9.8	5.8
Congressional District 32	Hilda L. Solis (D)	238	638 579	2 683.1	44.9	3.2	1.8	20.0	34.9	62.3	14.8	4.5
Congressional District 33	Diane E. Watson (D)	125	638 655	5 109.2	35.3	32.1	1.4	13.5	23.2	34.6	19.9	5.1
Congressional District 34	Lucille Roybal-Allard (D)	151	638 807	4 230.5	45.6	5.2	1.7	6.4	46.0	77.2	11.4	4.8
Congressional District 35	Maxine Waters (D)	144	638 851	4 436.5	29.3	35.8	1.3	7.1	31.2	47.4	10.4	4.5
Congressional District 36	Jane Harman (D)	194	639 168	3 294.7	65.5	4.9	1.4	16.2	17.4	30.3	48.4	5.0
Congressional District 37	Juanita Millender-McDonald (D)	193	638 722	3 309.4	33.7	26.4	1.6	14.5	29.2	43.2	16.6	5.0
Congressional District 38	Grace F. Napolitano (D)	269	639 334	2 376.7	47.6	4.3	1.8	11.7	39.6	70.6	13.6	4.9
Congressional District 39	Linda T. Sánchez (D)	168	639 529	3 806.7	48.9	6.8	1.6	11.2	36.4	61.2	21.0	4.7
Congressional District 40	Edward R. Royce (R)	259	638 671	2 465.9	66.5	2.9	1.4	17.9	15.9	29.6	49.3	4.3

[1]Dry land or land partially or temporarily covered by water.
[2]Hispanic or Latino persons may be of any race.

Table A. 109th Congressional Districts, 2000—*Continued*

(Number, percent.)

STATE Congressional district	Foreign born (percent)	Under 5 years	5 to 17 years	18 to 24 years	25 to 34 years	35 to 44 years	45 to 54 years	55 to 64 years	65 to 74 years	75 years and over	Percent female	Number	Persons per household	Female-family householder[3]	One-person households
					Age (percent)									Percent	
	13	14	15	16	17	18	19	20	21	22	23	24	25	26	27
UNITED STATES	11.1	6.8	18.9	9.7	14.2	16.0	13.4	8.6	6.5	5.9	50.9	105 480 101	2.59	12.2	25.8
ALABAMA	2.0	6.7	18.6	9.9	13.6	15.4	13.5	9.3	7.1	5.9	51.7	1 737 080	2.49	14.2	26.1
Congressional District 1	2.0	7.0	19.7	9.3	13.0	15.3	13.3	9.4	7.1	5.8	51.7	241 376	2.57	15.5	24.5
Congressional District 2	1.7	6.6	18.9	9.7	13.7	15.3	13.2	9.3	7.1	6.2	51.5	246 607	2.48	15.0	26.5
Congressional District 3	1.5	6.4	18.2	12.1	13.3	14.6	13.2	9.2	7.1	5.8	51.9	248 618	2.47	15.2	27.0
Congressional District 4	2.2	6.5	17.8	8.6	13.4	15.0	13.7	10.5	8.0	6.5	51.2	251 477	2.49	10.3	24.4
Congressional District 5	2.6	6.5	18.4	9.1	13.8	16.6	13.6	9.7	7.0	5.3	51.3	252 819	2.46	11.6	26.3
Congressional District 6	2.3	6.5	18.0	8.5	14.6	16.6	14.5	9.2	6.7	5.6	51.2	249 318	2.50	9.0	24.6
Congressional District 7	1.6	7.0	19.3	11.9	13.3	14.5	12.8	8.1	6.8	6.2	53.5	246 865	2.49	22.9	29.6
ALASKA	5.9	7.6	22.8	9.1	14.3	18.2	15.1	7.1	3.6	2.1	48.3	221 600	2.74	10.8	23.5
Congressional District (At Large)	5.9	7.6	22.8	9.1	14.3	18.2	15.1	7.1	3.6	2.1	48.3	221 600	2.74	10.8	23.5
ARIZONA	12.8	7.5	19.2	10.0	14.5	15.0	12.2	8.6	7.1	5.9	50.1	1 901 327	2.64	11.1	24.8
Congressional District 1	4.9	7.0	21.2	9.6	11.8	14.1	12.8	9.7	7.9	5.8	49.2	223 831	2.74	12.2	23.3
Congressional District 2	7.4	6.4	17.6	7.2	11.9	14.0	11.0	10.5	10.5	9.9	51.1	249 882	2.52	8.5	23.3
Congressional District 3	11.0	7.1	17.9	9.2	15.8	16.9	14.1	8.7	5.5	4.8	50.2	254 358	2.50	10.5	27.0
Congressional District 4	29.7	10.4	22.6	13.0	18.0	14.1	9.6	5.7	3.8	2.9	48.0	196 214	3.18	16.9	24.1
Congressional District 5	10.7	6.3	16.3	12.0	16.8	16.4	13.4	8.4	5.7	4.5	50.2	261 912	2.42	9.2	27.4
Congressional District 6	9.8	8.4	19.5	8.4	15.0	15.2	11.0	8.0	7.6	6.9	50.7	233 971	2.72	9.0	21.1
Congressional District 7	20.1	8.2	21.5	12.0	14.0	14.0	11.2	7.8	6.6	4.7	50.3	216 299	2.88	14.7	22.4
Congressional District 8	8.8	5.9	17.0	8.7	12.5	15.1	13.9	10.1	8.9	7.9	51.0	264 860	2.36	9.6	28.6
ARKANSAS	2.8	6.8	18.7	9.8	13.2	14.9	13.1	9.6	7.4	6.6	51.2	1 042 696	2.49	12.1	25.6
Congressional District 1	1.0	6.7	19.0	9.2	12.3	14.5	13.0	10.2	8.1	7.0	51.5	260 695	2.50	12.8	25.1
Congressional District 2	2.6	6.8	18.3	10.2	14.4	15.6	13.5	8.9	6.5	5.7	51.5	263 453	2.46	12.8	26.7
Congressional District 3	5.3	7.1	18.6	10.4	13.8	15.0	12.7	9.2	7.0	6.0	50.6	259 465	2.54	9.5	24.2
Congressional District 4	2.1	6.5	18.7	9.4	12.2	14.4	13.1	10.0	8.1	7.5	51.2	259 083	2.48	13.5	26.3
CALIFORNIA	26.2	7.3	20.0	9.9	15.4	16.2	12.8	7.7	5.6	5.0	50.2	11 502 870	2.87	12.6	23.5
Congressional District 1	13.1	6.0	18.5	11.4	12.5	14.9	14.6	8.9	6.6	6.6	50.4	240 438	2.56	11.0	26.4
Congressional District 2	9.6	6.3	20.1	10.2	11.3	14.5	13.7	9.4	7.5	7.1	50.7	241 216	2.59	11.2	24.8
Congressional District 3	10.6	6.7	19.5	7.9	13.2	17.2	14.3	8.9	6.6	5.6	50.3	237 600	2.61	11.2	23.2
Congressional District 4	6.3	5.8	19.8	7.0	10.9	16.8	16.0	9.8	7.4	6.4	49.8	240 821	2.59	9.5	22.1
Congressional District 5	20.5	7.6	20.7	10.7	15.6	15.1	12.3	7.2	5.5	5.3	51.4	237 330	2.65	16.3	29.9
Congressional District 6	15.2	5.8	17.0	7.7	13.0	17.1	17.0	9.7	6.2	6.6	50.6	248 221	2.49	9.8	27.5
Congressional District 7	21.1	7.2	20.2	9.0	14.5	17.0	14.3	8.0	5.2	4.6	50.4	218 697	2.85	15.3	22.5
Congressional District 8	36.7	4.1	10.2	9.1	24.4	17.4	13.6	8.2	6.7	6.3	48.6	276 619	2.25	8.7	40.9
Congressional District 9	24.4	6.5	16.7	11.2	17.3	15.8	14.0	7.7	5.3	5.6	51.5	247 822	2.52	15.1	32.1
Congressional District 10	15.9	6.9	19.6	7.8	13.2	17.4	14.6	8.7	6.0	5.9	51.0	232 855	2.70	10.0	22.3
Congressional District 11	14.7	7.3	21.4	8.2	13.0	17.5	14.3	8.4	5.2	4.6	50.5	219 211	2.84	10.2	19.5
Congressional District 12	34.3	5.7	15.1	7.9	16.0	17.2	15.0	9.3	7.0	6.9	51.2	235 831	2.67	10.0	25.0
Congressional District 13	33.7	7.1	18.3	8.7	16.5	17.7	13.5	7.8	5.5	4.9	50.5	217 121	2.91	11.7	20.8
Congressional District 14	28.3	6.4	16.1	8.5	16.9	17.5	14.3	8.8	5.9	5.7	49.4	240 550	2.59	7.9	26.0
Congressional District 15	33.8	7.0	17.2	8.5	18.0	18.6	13.2	8.0	5.2	4.3	49.6	222 685	2.82	10.3	21.4
Congressional District 16	37.0	7.8	19.5	10.6	17.6	16.7	12.3	7.4	4.5	3.5	48.9	186 226	3.38	12.1	17.5
Congressional District 17	26.0	7.4	19.9	11.3	15.7	15.6	12.9	7.1	5.1	4.8	49.0	202 490	3.01	11.4	22.5
Congressional District 18	24.2	8.7	24.8	10.4	14.0	14.8	11.0	6.7	5.1	4.5	49.9	193 379	3.22	15.9	19.2
Congressional District 19	14.5	7.3	21.1	9.6	13.2	15.2	13.3	8.4	6.4	5.5	51.1	220 020	2.82	12.3	21.4
Congressional District 20	28.9	9.5	25.4	12.0	15.8	14.7	9.6	5.6	4.0	3.5	46.2	163 634	3.61	18.7	16.1
Congressional District 21	19.7	8.5	23.9	10.7	13.3	14.4	11.7	7.2	5.4	4.9	50.4	200 404	3.14	13.8	18.5
Congressional District 22	9.2	7.1	21.5	9.5	13.0	16.6	13.3	8.1	6.0	5.0	49.0	221 297	2.73	12.4	22.7
Congressional District 23	24.6	6.8	18.4	14.4	14.6	15.4	12.1	7.4	6.0	5.8	49.8	213 124	2.91	10.8	24.3
Congressional District 24	15.1	6.9	20.7	7.8	12.7	17.5	14.4	8.7	5.8	5.5	50.3	218 748	2.86	10.0	19.4
Congressional District 25	15.2	8.1	24.1	8.7	13.4	18.1	12.6	6.9	4.6	3.4	49.6	206 878	3.01	12.5	18.7
Congressional District 26	22.2	6.3	20.7	9.2	12.6	16.7	15.0	8.6	5.7	5.2	51.4	215 713	2.89	12.1	19.7
Congressional District 27	35.8	7.2	18.3	9.8	16.5	16.7	12.9	7.9	5.5	5.1	50.5	221 666	2.83	12.4	24.5
Congressional District 28	44.0	8.4	20.2	10.5	18.5	16.0	11.3	6.4	4.5	4.1	49.7	207 748	3.06	13.0	25.9
Congressional District 29	43.8	6.1	16.9	8.6	16.2	16.9	13.6	8.6	6.6	6.6	52.1	233 307	2.69	13.2	26.8
Congressional District 30	26.4	4.5	12.4	9.0	17.5	17.3	14.9	9.6	7.1	7.5	51.2	291 562	2.12	7.0	39.0
Congressional District 31	56.3	9.1	20.9	12.1	19.1	15.0	10.4	5.9	4.1	3.3	49.2	191 693	3.29	17.7	22.3
Congressional District 32	41.6	8.6	22.4	11.2	16.2	14.7	11.0	6.9	5.1	3.9	50.6	170 640	3.70	17.3	14.2
Congressional District 33	37.5	6.9	17.5	11.2	18.5	16.3	11.9	7.5	5.4	4.9	51.5	246 077	2.54	17.3	34.5
Congressional District 34	47.2	9.5	22.9	12.1	18.1	14.2	9.8	5.6	4.0	3.6	48.9	172 589	3.55	17.8	19.8
Congressional District 35	32.6	9.4	23.4	10.9	16.6	15.0	10.4	6.5	4.4	3.4	51.7	198 116	3.19	23.5	22.8
Congressional District 36	28.3	6.7	16.5	8.5	18.9	17.9	13.2	8.0	5.6	4.7	50.1	255 157	2.49	10.8	31.2
Congressional District 37	31.6	9.1	23.9	11.1	16.3	14.8	10.5	6.3	4.3	3.7	51.2	193 764	3.25	20.8	23.3
Congressional District 38	38.3	8.5	23.2	11.3	15.7	14.4	10.9	6.9	5.2	3.8	50.4	166 175	3.80	17.0	13.5
Congressional District 39	35.5	8.8	23.7	11.0	15.7	14.9	11.1	6.7	4.4	3.7	50.6	173 625	3.64	16.3	14.3
Congressional District 40	28.2	7.3	19.6	9.7	15.7	16.3	12.4	8.3	5.9	4.7	50.4	205 968	3.04	12.4	18.8

[3]No spouse present.

Table A. 109th Congressional Districts, 2000—*Continued*

(Number, percent.)

STATE Congressional district	Group quarters — Persons in correctional institutions	Persons in nursing homes	Persons in college dormitories	Persons in military quarters	Education — School enrollment[4] Public	Private	Attainment level[5] H.S. graduate or more	Bachelor's degree or more	Money income, 1999 — Per capita income[6]	Households Median income	Percent with income over $100,000	Percent below poverty level, 1999 Persons	Families
	28	29	30	31	32	33	34	35	36	37	38	39	40
UNITED STATES	1 976 019	1 720 500	2 064 128	355 155	64 083 103	12 549 824	80.4	24.4	21 587	41 994	12.3	12.4	9.2
ALABAMA	33 542	26 697	31 086	5 370	994 978	160 526	75.3	19.0	18 189	34 135	7.6	16.1	12.5
Congressional District 1	3 825	3 113	3 083	61	134 546	31 235	77.0	18.5	17 622	34 739	7.0	16.9	13.7
Congressional District 2	11 533	3 833	1 765	4 715	139 694	23 795	74.3	18.0	17 139	32 460	6.6	17.2	13.6
Congressional District 3	4 965	4 446	9 213	4	157 300	21 391	71.9	16.7	16 363	30 806	5.8	14.8	13.8
Congressional District 4	2 019	4 856	409	0	130 650	11 491	68.9	11.3	16 456	31 344	5.3	14.7	11.4
Congressional District 5	4 268	2 892	4 792	587	142 029	21 923	78.5	23.5	20 060	38 054	9.5	12.5	9.7
Congressional District 6	4 223	3 220	2 749	0	130 201	28 798	82.9	29.6	25 007	46 946	14.8	8.1	5.9
Congressional District 7	2 709	4 337	9 075	3	160 558	21 893	73.2	15.1	14 684	26 672	4.2	24.7	20.4
ALASKA	3 331	803	1 748	3 970	166 991	18 769	88.3	24.7	22 660	51 571	16.1	9.4	6.7
Congressional District (At Large)	3 331	803	1 748	3 970	166 991	18 769	88.3	24.7	22 660	51 571	16.1	9.4	6.7
ARIZONA	45 783	13 607	17 340	5 256	1 253 669	148 171	81.0	23.5	20 275	40 558	10.8	13.9	9.9
Congressional District 1	19 019	2 410	4 248	0	175 286	13 636	77.3	17.5	15 357	32 979	6.1	20.3	15.0
Congressional District 2	4 316	3 160	573	681	134 625	17 906	84.1	19.3	20 896	42 432	9.7	8.9	5.9
Congressional District 3	1 229	408	137	0	138 815	28 443	87.8	30.3	26 923	48 108	16.1	8.7	5.7
Congressional District 4	8 656	1 421	491	0	166 830	12 618	59.1	10.2	12 205	30 624	4.2	25.6	21.1
Congressional District 5	60	1 169	4 600	0	158 737	23 865	91.7	39.6	29 141	51 780	19.2	8.4	4.8
Congressional District 6	0	2 073	69	0	153 836	17 895	85.4	23.6	21 312	47 976	12.2	7.7	5.4
Congressional District 7	4 758	875	7 094	1 677	182 080	12 548	68.0	13.3	13 756	30 828	4.9	21.8	17.2
Congressional District 8	7 745	2 091	128	2 898	143 460	21 260	88.5	30.6	22 614	40 656	10.8	10.5	7.3
ARKANSAS	20 565	21 379	18 280	1 290	602 713	72 396	75.3	16.7	16 904	32 182	6.0	15.8	12.0
Congressional District 1	7 787	6 049	2 150	0	152 187	12 780	70.4	12.3	15 170	28 940	4.4	18.5	14.4
Congressional District 2	2 763	4 460	5 950	1 246	144 462	31 091	81.3	23.2	19 615	37 221	8.3	12.7	9.5
Congressional District 3	1 416	4 407	5 863	27	153 695	16 217	76.8	17.9	17 269	33 915	6.5	13.7	9.9
Congressional District 4	8 599	6 463	4 317	17	152 369	12 308	72.7	13.3	15 564	29 675	4.7	18.5	14.2
CALIFORNIA	248 516	120 724	126 715	58 810	8 703 390	1 426 600	76.8	26.6	22 711	47 493	17.3	14.2	10.6
Congressional District 1	5 410	2 903	7 287	1	173 606	19 617	81.0	25.0	20 615	38 918	11.7	15.3	9.7
Congressional District 2	2 366	2 760	3 270	512	173 877	15 331	79.4	17.4	17 185	33 559	6.9	17.0	12.0
Congressional District 3	8 143	2 934	6	235	154 567	25 194	88.3	27.0	24 527	49 387	16.1	8.5	5.8
Congressional District 4	10 152	2 551	224	0	156 515	18 803	88.1	25.2	24 527	49 387	16.0	8.7	6.1
Congressional District 5	2 104	2 649	907	104	177 822	20 229	77.8	21.4	17 871	36 719	8.3	19.7	15.3
Congressional District 6	7 730	2 994	1 892	331	135 840	28 866	87.7	37.9	33 036	59 115	24.7	7.7	4.4
Congressional District 7	10 352	2 143	0	25	159 666	27 220	81.4	22.4	22 016	52 778	16.4	10.0	7.5
Congressional District 8	1 369	1 582	2 428	36	108 543	37 938	79.8	44.0	34 552	52 322	23.5	12.2	8.8
Congressional District 9	979	2 595	5 116	0	159 469	32 944	79.6	37.4	25 201	44 314	17.6	16.9	12.3
Congressional District 10	1 109	2 967	1 473	2 019	152 487	29 212	89.3	36.2	31 093	65 245	26.5	6.3	4.3
Congressional District 11	7 216	2 622	1 854	15	159 708	30 278	83.8	29.1	28 420	61 996	26.5	8.8	6.2
Congressional District 12	20	2 670	1 498	0	126 264	40 564	87.3	40.7	34 448	70 307	31.3	5.4	3.2
Congressional District 13	40	2 327	636	224	147 480	30 747	82.9	31.8	26 076	62 415	23.8	7.1	5.0
Congressional District 14	2 019	2 684	8 309	281	123 435	47 314	88.5	52.2	43 063	77 985	38.4	6.4	3.8
Congressional District 15	3 112	2 810	2 075	0	142 153	35 632	86.8	41.6	32 617	74 947	34.2	6.6	4.4
Congressional District 16	1 255	1 102	2 294	0	165 509	25 132	73.8	26.9	25 064	67 689	29.6	9.8	6.7
Congressional District 17	12 888	2 009	4 644	2 478	168 208	20 777	72.3	24.9	21 244	49 234	16.4	13.3	9.0
Congressional District 18	6 821	2 373	26	3	190 670	14 788	62.4	9.7	13 564	34 211	6.0	22.7	18.1
Congressional District 19	11 476	1 649	630	0	173 681	17 949	76.8	20.3	19 280	41 225	11.1	14.8	11.0
Congressional District 20	39 151	2 157	118	1 085	197 981	10 133	50.2	6.3	10 968	26 800	4.1	32.2	27.4
Congressional District 21	1 222	3 039	1 420	0	191 635	15 878	67.8	15.0	15 175	36 047	8.4	20.7	15.8
Congressional District 22	22 515	2 213	3 032	742	172 164	21 600	79.9	18.3	19 263	41 801	10.7	13.7	10.8
Congressional District 23	959	2 098	7 604	892	180 804	22 299	74.9	26.2	20 747	44 874	14.1	15.7	9.4
Congressional District 24	5 466	1 896	1 266	1 029	159 696	30 243	85.9	30.0	26 998	61 453	24.3	7.2	5.0
Congressional District 25	9 342	1 288	925	1 632	180 773	25 660	80.8	18.8	20 175	49 002	15.1	12.6	9.9
Congressional District 26	1 971	2 861	5 279	0	161 834	42 411	85.8	32.4	26 699	58 968	23.1	8.4	6.2
Congressional District 27	24	4 155	2 352	0	147 272	37 300	76.3	25.8	21 578	46 781	15.4	13.4	10.1
Congressional District 28	144	1 088	16	0	157 864	27 501	63.0	23.7	20 611	40 439	14.6	19.1	16.0
Congressional District 29	42	5 296	1 395	0	144 779	40 449	78.4	33.4	22 880	43 895	15.7	14.5	11.6
Congressional District 30	107	3 205	12 709	0	111 237	50 007	92.5	53.5	47 498	60 713	30.1	9.0	4.8
Congressional District 31	367	2 359	1 397	0	177 542	21 474	47.5	13.7	11 702	26 093	5.3	30.1	27.5
Congressional District 32	102	2 023	1 738	0	182 946	24 710	59.1	13.6	14 150	41 394	9.9	18.0	14.6
Congressional District 33	190	1 919	5 356	0	150 618	42 911	71.5	26.9	19 250	31 655	10.1	23.5	19.9
Congressional District 34	11 903	1 817	0	0	188 072	16 982	46.3	8.7	11 816	29 863	6.0	26.0	22.1
Congressional District 35	185	1 279	2 251	0	185 434	27 973	60.7	13.3	14 041	32 156	7.6	26.4	23.2
Congressional District 36	8	1 894	361	44	142 602	29 469	81.9	36.9	28 962	51 633	21.1	12.7	9.7
Congressional District 37	52	2 604	930	0	196 498	20 442	63.5	15.2	14 286	34 006	8.2	25.2	22.1
Congressional District 38	45	2 300	2 349	0	190 326	21 334	58.4	12.5	14 021	42 488	10.2	16.3	13.3
Congressional District 39	1 205	1 955	1 417	0	188 519	26 120	62.9	14.7	15 250	45 307	11.7	15.7	12.5
Congressional District 40	2 446	2 872	1 775	0	162 946	29 701	79.9	26.4	22 434	54 356	18.9	10.2	7.1

[4]All persons 3 years old and over enrolled in nursery school through college.
[5]Persons 25 years old and over.
[6]Based on the population enumerated as of April 1, 2000.

Table A. 109th Congressional Districts, 2000—*Continued*

(Number, percent.)

STATE Congressional district	Housing units									Civilian labor force		
	Total	Total occupied units	Owner occupied		Median owner costs as a percent of income		Renter occupied		Sub-standard housing units (percent)[9]	Total	Unemployment	
			Percent	Median value[7] (dollars)	With a mortgage	Without a mortgage[8]	Median rent (dollars)	Median rent as a percent of income			Total	Rate[10]
	41	42	43	44	45	46	47	48	49	50	51	52
UNITED STATES	115 904 641	105 480 101	66.2	119 600	21.7	10.5	602	25.5	6.3	137 668 798	7 947 286	5.8
ALABAMA	1 963 711	1 737 080	72.5	85 100	19.8	9.9	447	24.8	3.5	2 047 100	126 911	6.2
Congressional District 1	281 766	241 434	73.1	85 300	20.1	9.9	474	26.0	4.4	283 003	19 249	6.8
Congressional District 2	281 153	246 539	71.6	79 100	19.3	9.9	437	24.2	3.8	282 546	18 140	6.2
Congressional District 3	286 195	248 689	71.0	76 400	20.0	9.9	412	26.7	3.7	285 817	19 177	6.7
Congressional District 4	282 789	251 545	78.0	75 000	20.1	9.9	380	22.7	2.9	290 954	16 368	5.6
Congressional District 5	278 611	252 745	72.5	90 500	19.0	9.9	449	23.9	2.6	311 310	17 169	5.5
Congressional District 6	271 053	249 160	78.0	129 100	19.5	9.9	593	22.6	2.1	320 823	10 906	3.4
Congressional District 7	282 144	246 968	62.8	68 100	21.4	11.0	432	26.9	5.2	272 647	25 902	9.5
ALASKA	260 978	221 600	62.5	144 200	22.3	9.9	720	24.8	13.0	309 485	27 953	9.0
Congressional District (At Large)	260 978	221 600	62.5	144 200	22.3	9.9	720	24.8	13.0	309 485	27 953	8.6
ARIZONA	2 189 189	1 901 327	68.0	121 300	22.1	9.9	619	26.6	9.3	2 366 372	133 368	5.6
Congressional District 1	294 076	223 930	71.5	103 500	22.4	9.9	537	25.2	13.9	256 697	22 875	8.9
Congressional District 2	287 509	249 789	79.3	118 000	22.3	9.9	661	26.8	5.2	275 469	13 789	4.9
Congressional District 3	271 256	254 432	66.4	140 400	21.7	9.9	675	26.2	6.1	349 589	14 073	4.0
Congressional District 4	210 341	196 221	50.8	80 300	23.0	11.6	546	27.3	23.9	265 410	22 244	8.4
Congressional District 5	289 251	261 936	62.9	160 500	21.1	9.9	760	26.4	4.7	360 594	13 550	3.8
Congressional District 6	282 933	233 942	77.5	135 200	22.4	9.9	686	26.2	6.3	300 849	11 470	3.8
Congressional District 7	258 674	216 094	66.1	85 800	22.7	9.9	483	27.4	14.9	260 671	21 793	8.2
Congressional District 8	295 149	264 983	67.1	124 600	22.1	9.9	577	26.8	4.3	297 093	13 574	4.4
ARKANSAS	1 173 043	1 042 696	69.4	72 800	19.4	9.9	453	24.4	4.4	1 249 546	76 147	6.1
Congressional District 1	297 612	260 695	69.6	63 600	19.7	10.6	410	25.1	3.9	295 920	18 884	6.4
Congressional District 2	289 170	263 453	67.1	83 800	19.3	9.9	517	24.7	3.8	332 428	19 860	5.9
Congressional District 3	286 029	259 465	68.7	82 200	19.4	9.9	460	23.7	5.4	328 381	18 168	5.5
Congressional District 4	300 232	259 083	72.2	59 300	19.0	10.5	411	24.4	4.4	292 817	19 235	6.6
CALIFORNIA	12 214 549	11 502 870	56.9	211 500	25.3	9.9	747	27.7	15.6	15 829 202	1 110 274	7.0
Congressional District 1	265 209	240 381	60.7	182 600	24.8	10.0	653	29.4	8.7	303 818	21 112	6.9
Congressional District 2	264 086	241 200	63.1	120 600	24.2	10.5	537	28.7	7.8	281 395	26 830	9.4
Congressional District 3	255 289	237 926	68.6	162 500	23.6	9.9	705	25.6	5.4	316 253	16 878	5.3
Congressional District 4	285 140	240 815	73.1	191 500	24.8	10.4	704	27.3	4.9	303 767	16 568	5.4
Congressional District 5	250 299	237 038	49.6	120 300	24.0	9.9	626	27.7	12.1	289 249	23 577	8.1
Congressional District 6	261 732	248 258	63.3	352 800	25.6	9.9	956	27.9	6.3	337 888	12 840	3.8
Congressional District 7	225 452	218 711	64.0	190 100	24.6	9.9	810	27.0	11.2	307 841	18 804	6.1
Congressional District 8	291 782	276 659	30.2	367 300	25.4	9.9	902	24.5	14.9	372 676	17 831	4.8
Congressional District 9	257 897	247 798	45.6	286 300	25.3	9.9	734	27.9	13.4	320 654	21 919	6.8
Congressional District 10	239 406	232 728	69.8	274 300	24.8	9.9	923	26.8	5.8	317 796	14 449	4.5
Congressional District 11	227 383	219 367	69.0	254 500	24.6	9.9	771	26.3	7.7	311 562	18 560	6.0
Congressional District 12	241 909	235 780	62.3	443 400	25.6	9.9	1 160	26.1	11.1	343 505	10 656	3.1
Congressional District 13	222 084	217 139	60.7	295 000	24.9	9.9	992	25.6	14.0	323 905	15 679	4.8
Congressional District 14	248 923	240 537	58.5	626 500	24.2	9.9	1 189	24.9	10.4	343 485	12 323	3.6
Congressional District 15	227 632	222 721	57.9	432 400	24.0	9.9	1 218	25.4	12.8	342 084	11 947	3.5
Congressional District 16	190 099	186 227	64.1	376 700	25.0	9.9	1 059	27.9	21.6	316 431	15 059	4.8
Congressional District 17	219 297	202 486	55.5	298 100	26.8	9.9	812	27.6	18.0	302 767	23 707	7.7
Congressional District 18	203 794	193 333	56.8	108 100	25.0	10.2	554	28.5	20.3	259 784	37 096	14.3
Congressional District 19	240 410	219 833	64.5	131 900	24.0	10.1	609	27.5	10.4	288 191	25 900	9.0
Congressional District 20	176 521	163 772	50.1	79 600	25.8	11.5	478	29.4	30.0	224 015	43 225	19.0
Congressional District 21	217 492	200 508	61.6	105 400	24.2	10.1	526	27.8	16.6	276 915	31 566	11.4
Congressional District 22	244 865	221 335	65.2	115 100	23.3	9.9	587	27.6	7.9	274 850	21 088	7.6
Congressional District 23	227 233	213 117	53.7	248 600	26.7	9.9	806	30.3	16.3	310 505	21 040	6.7
Congressional District 24	225 876	218 728	71.0	256 400	25.1	9.9	917	27.1	7.9	313 594	14 839	4.7
Congressional District 25	231 023	206 818	70.0	147 600	24.7	10.3	697	27.9	10.4	281 740	22 100	7.7
Congressional District 26	223 632	215 830	68.7	238 300	25.3	9.9	794	26.8	9.4	314 001	16 751	5.3
Congressional District 27	228 377	221 730	54.1	211 300	26.8	10.8	735	28.1	18.2	316 511	23 208	7.3
Congressional District 28	215 465	207 603	43.8	195 400	28.2	10.5	703	28.2	28.9	292 738	25 604	8.7
Congressional District 29	240 997	233 376	44.0	270 000	26.6	9.9	752	28.1	19.9	308 152	20 336	6.6
Congressional District 30	306 458	291 693	47.7	490 000	26.7	9.9	961	27.3	5.4	361 708	20 287	5.6
Congressional District 31	202 112	191 535	23.0	173 300	27.9	10.8	567	29.3	46.7	262 801	29 380	11.2
Congressional District 32	175 435	170 594	55.9	169 500	26.3	9.9	713	28.5	32.6	266 931	21 933	8.2
Congressional District 33	259 389	246 339	30.4	228 200	28.6	10.3	658	29.8	23.8	297 523	30 816	10.4
Congressional District 34	180 836	172 533	30.6	178 300	29.1	9.9	604	28.7	44.1	241 969	27 549	11.4
Congressional District 35	210 133	198 170	39.5	169 800	29.1	9.9	643	30.1	30.6	255 704	28 574	11.2
Congressional District 36	265 808	255 228	44.8	320 200	25.6	9.9	851	25.8	13.8	337 513	18 790	5.6
Congressional District 37	204 212	193 734	44.1	163 200	27.4	9.9	615	29.3	29.6	260 489	29 199	11.2
Congressional District 38	171 000	166 057	62.5	162 500	26.5	9.9	698	28.7	31.9	258 529	22 286	8.6
Congressional District 39	179 021	173 624	59.5	184 600	26.5	9.9	709	27.8	30.4	267 612	22 185	8.3
Congressional District 40	210 896	205 982	60.0	238 700	24.6	9.9	851	27.5	16.2	313 482	16 991	5.4

[7]Specified owner-occupied units.
[8]Median monthly owner costs is often in the minimum category—9.9 percent or less, which is indicated as 9.9 percent.
[9]Overcrowded or lacking complete plumbing facilities.
[10]Percent of civilian labor force.

Table A. 109th Congressional Districts, 2000—*Continued*

(Number, percent.)

STATE Congressional district	Civilian employment and occupations				Total farms, 2002	Farms by size, 2002 (percent)			Land in farms, 2002		Cropland harvested, 2002		Farm's principal operator's primary occupation is farming, 2002 (percent)
	Total	Management, professional, and related (percent)	Service, sales, and office (percent)	Construction and production (percent)		1 to 49 acres	50 to 999 acres	1,000 acres or more	Acreage	Average size of farms (acres)	Acreage	Farms	
	53	54	55	56	57	58	59	60	61	62	63	64	65
UNITED STATES	129 721 512	33.6	41.5	24.1	2 128 982	34.9	56.8	8.3	938 279 056	441	302 697 252	1 362 608	57.5
ALABAMA	1 920 189	29.5	39.4	30.3	45 126	37.1	59.6	3.3	8 904 387	197	1 995 139	23 327	53.1
Congressional District 1	263 754	28.2	41.2	29.7	3 275	44.0	52.9	3.1	605 168	185	169 737	1 975	54.1
Congressional District 2	264 406	28.9	40.6	29.5	8 885	26.7	68.0	5.3	2 434 064	274	563 407	4 421	52.3
Congressional District 3	266 640	26.9	39.3	33.1	5 370	31.2	65.0	3.8	1 178 279	219	180 345	2 617	53.7
Congressional District 4	274 586	23.2	34.7	40.8	13 754	43.3	55.8	1.0	1 656 852	120	353 300	7 221	54.2
Congressional District 5	294 141	33.3	36.6	29.6	7 592	43.8	53.6	2.7	1 241 928	164	503 485	4 090	50.8
Congressional District 6	309 917	38.5	39.0	22.1	2 518	42.2	56.2	1.6	364 603	145	66 495	1 253	52.0
Congressional District 7	246 745	25.4	45.3	28.6	3 732	24.8	66.0	9.3	1 423 493	381	158 370	1 750	54.3
ALASKA	281 532	34.4	41.7	22.4	609	42.0	48.6	9.4	900 715	1 479	31 824	393	60.8
Congressional District (At Large)	281 532	34.4	41.7	22.4	609	42.0	48.6	9.4	900 715	1 479	31 824	393	60.8
ARIZONA	2 233 004	32.7	44.8	21.9	7 294	58.0	30.5	11.5	26 586 577	3 645	887 966	3 139	58.9
Congressional District 1	233 822	28.5	44.7	25.6	2 441	51.7	35.2	13.1	19 310 231	7 911	190 799	929	58.9
Congressional District 2	261 680	30.0	47.3	22.2	769	61.0	26.3	12.7	2 040 011	2 653	128 066	307	62.7
Congressional District 3	335 516	37.4	44.7	17.7	364	89.8	8.0	2.2	100 362	276	8 862	77	49.2
Congressional District 4	243 166	18.3	45.5	35.7	183	76.5	19.7	3.8	27 243	149	21 803	94	62.3
Congressional District 5	347 044	42.4	43.3	14.2	182	74.2	22.0	3.8	180 266	990	12 989	69	55.5
Congressional District 6	289 379	33.8	43.2	22.6	778	82.6	15.6	1.8	64 320	83	34 058	419	53.3
Congressional District 7	238 878	25.1	45.9	26.8	1 201	55.7	30.6	13.7	1 223 087	1 018	412 571	740	59.2
Congressional District 8	283 519	38.8	44.4	16.5	1 376	42.5	41.5	16.0	3 641 057	2 646	78 818	504	62.3
ARKANSAS	1 173 399	27.7	39.2	31.6	47 483	27.3	65.7	7.0	14 502 793	305	7 457 599	29 466	57.7
Congressional District 1	277 036	24.9	37.9	35.0	14 524	20.0	65.3	14.7	7 268 862	500	4 965 282	9 811	61.8
Congressional District 2	312 568	32.3	42.1	25.0	6 738	32.0	65.1	2.9	1 347 815	200	449 647	4 013	53.7
Congressional District 3	310 213	27.9	38.9	32.0	14 277	32.3	65.4	2.3	2 537 053	178	533 965	8 347	54.6
Congressional District 4	273 582	25.1	37.5	34.9	11 944	27.5	66.8	5.7	3 349 063	280	1 508 705	7 295	58.7
CALIFORNIA	14 718 928	36.0	41.5	21.2	79 631	61.7	32.3	6.0	27 589 027	346	8 466 321	54 115	61.7
Congressional District 1	282 706	34.5	41.6	20.9	6 057	58.9	34.0	7.0	2 248 591	371	346 944	4 373	58.1
Congressional District 2	254 565	29.6	43.6	23.2	10 253	48.8	44.1	7.1	4 125 002	402	1 412 319	6 953	63.1
Congressional District 3	299 375	38.4	42.5	18.4	2 676	60.7	32.1	7.1	866 501	324	140 743	1 036	58.3
Congressional District 4	287 199	36.5	43.0	19.6	4 579	67.1	27.0	5.9	1 674 734	366	207 162	1 934	56.6
Congressional District 5	265 672	33.1	46.4	20.1	114	63.2	30.7	6.1	20 613	181	12 330	72	63.2
Congressional District 6	325 048	41.9	40.1	17.2	2 836	69.6	26.4	4.0	560 354	198	68 544	1 677	55.3
Congressional District 7	289 037	31.8	45.2	22.7	416	69.7	27.6	2.6	61 199	147	19 387	181	53.6
Congressional District 8	354 845	47.4	40.5	11.9	8	100.0	0.0	0.0	D	D	D	7	37.5
Congressional District 9	298 735	44.4	38.2	17.3	72	66.7	33.3	0.0	7 300	101	660	28	52.8
Congressional District 10	303 347	41.7	40.2	17.8	784	52.2	36.4	11.5	434 222	554	111 036	456	58.4
Congressional District 11	293 002	39.7	39.3	19.1	4 438	64.5	31.2	4.3	953 808	215	474 116	3 350	66.1
Congressional District 12	332 849	44.2	41.0	14.6	64	87.5	12.5	0.0	1 915	30	563	36	54.7
Congressional District 13	308 226	39.2	38.4	22.3	94	52.1	42.6	5.3	31 270	333	2 090	27	40.4
Congressional District 14	331 162	57.2	30.1	12.1	799	69.6	27.9	2.5	92 324	116	18 283	566	63.0
Congressional District 15	330 137	50.0	32.7	16.9	204	65.7	29.9	4.4	26 740	131	7 444	123	55.4
Congressional District 16	301 372	36.3	38.5	24.7	372	79.8	15.1	5.1	123 660	332	5 676	225	55.1
Congressional District 17	279 060	31.9	40.0	19.7	2 199	49.5	37.7	12.8	1 863 180	847	308 995	1 376	65.0
Congressional District 18	222 688	21.9	40.6	31.0	4 566	51.8	41.9	6.3	1 429 594	313	765 331	3 557	71.3
Congressional District 19	262 291	32.3	42.2	22.0	6 521	59.0	36.3	4.6	1 718 145	263	638 131	4 342	65.9
Congressional District 20	180 790	17.7	39.3	27.2	3 719	46.4	42.0	11.6	2 046 714	550	1 258 343	3 077	73.1
Congressional District 21	245 349	28.1	40.6	22.0	8 787	62.1	33.8	4.1	2 170 193	247	1 034 716	7 123	66.0
Congressional District 22	253 762	32.0	43.2	23.1	3 621	49.1	39.2	11.7	3 426 156	946	588 909	2 022	61.9
Congressional District 23	289 465	31.9	42.3	20.3	1 368	63.7	29.9	6.4	481 690	352	96 105	1 102	65.0
Congressional District 24	298 755	40.1	41.2	17.1	2 815	69.3	25.6	5.0	770 148	274	122 289	2 173	57.3
Congressional District 25	259 640	33.3	42.9	23.6	858	77.4	17.9	4.7	373 393	435	29 128	294	58.4
Congressional District 26	297 250	42.0	40.5	17.3	277	87.7	10.5	1.8	21 992	79	7 489	122	53.4
Congressional District 27	293 303	35.8	44.2	19.9	117	90.6	6.8	2.6	9 244	79	902	50	48.7
Congressional District 28	267 134	32.3	41.3	26.2	52	78.8	21.2	0.0	3 702	71	479	20	59.6
Congressional District 29	287 816	42.1	41.8	16.0	39	92.3	7.7	0.0	565	14	147	17	43.6
Congressional District 30	341 421	58.2	34.9	6.9	148	84.5	14.9	0.7	8 367	57	1 428	66	51.4
Congressional District 31	233 421	20.1	46.0	33.7	4	75.0	25.0	0.0	D	D	D	1	25.0
Congressional District 32	244 998	23.2	43.8	32.7	50	82.0	18.0	0.0	1 896	38	894	40	78.0
Congressional District 33	266 707	35.3	46.8	17.8	12	91.7	8.3	0.0	127	11	81	8	50.0
Congressional District 34	214 420	17.6	42.1	40.0	14	85.7	14.3	0.0	387	28	340	9	57.1
Congressional District 35	227 130	24.1	47.4	28.3	40	100.0	0.0	0.0	311	8	274	37	77.5
Congressional District 36	318 723	44.3	39.5	16.1	54	74.1	25.9	0.0	2 806	52	297	41	48.1
Congressional District 37	231 290	25.9	45.0	29.0	24	87.5	12.5	0.0	344	14	267	18	75.0
Congressional District 38	236 243	22.5	43.2	34.1	56	87.5	8.9	3.6	3 862	69	454	37	58.9
Congressional District 39	245 427	25.4	43.3	31.2	34	91.2	8.8	0.0	715	21	97	20	47.1
Congressional District 40	296 491	34.9	42.8	22.1	62	83.9	16.1	0.0	3 117	50	1 291	43	53.2

D = Suppressed to avoid disclosure.

Table A. 109th Congressional Districts, 2000—*Continued*

(Number, percent.)

STATE Congressional district	Farm's principal operator is full owner, 2002 (percent)	Type of organization, 2002 (percent) Family or individual	Partner-ship	Corpo-ration	Value of all agricultural products sold, 2002 Total ($1,000)	Percent of farms Less than $50,000	$50,000 to $249,999	$250,000 or more	Payments received from federal farm programs, 2002 Total payments ($1,000)	Farms receiving payments Number	Percent	Percent of farms receiving Less than $50,000	$50,000 to $249,999	$250,000 or more
	66	67	68	69	70	72	73	74	75	76	77	78	79	80
UNITED STATES	67.1	89.7	6.1	3.5	200 646 355	78.8	14.1	7.2	6 545 679	707 596	33.2	97.1	2.8	0.1
ALABAMA	71.3	93.9	4.2	1.5	3 264 949	86.9	5.6	7.5	77 930	12 863	28.5	97.7	2.2	0.1
Congressional District 1	71.0	91.2	5.6	2.5	203 142	87.8	8.0	4.2	7 550	840	25.6	96.1	3.8	0.1
Congressional District 2	71.9	92.7	4.9	1.7	802 683	84.2	7.3	8.5	31 990	3 855	43.4	96.8	3.1	0.1
Congressional District 3	74.7	94.3	3.9	1.3	301 216	90.1	5.0	4.9	6 376	1 267	23.6	97.9	2.1	0.0
Congressional District 4	71.5	95.9	2.9	0.8	1 384 212	83.0	4.7	12.2	6 457	2 967	21.6	99.7	0.3	0.0
Congressional District 5	69.2	93.8	4.7	1.0	321 987	91.2	4.3	4.5	16 061	2 360	31.1	97.1	2.8	0.1
Congressional District 6	72.8	94.4	3.0	2.1	80 085	93.6	4.1	2.3	1 317	326	12.9	98.5	1.5	0.0
Congressional District 7	67.3	90.5	5.9	2.8	171 623	88.7	7.0	4.3	8 179	1 248	33.4	98.1	1.9	0.0
ALASKA	70.8	81.6	4.9	5.9	46 143	82.8	11.0	6.2	1 765	72	11.8	87.5	12.5	0.0
Congressional District (At Large)	70.8	81.6	4.9	5.9	46 143	82.8	11.0	6.2	1 765	72	11.8	87.5	12.5	0.0
ARIZONA	78.5	78.1	11.5	8.1	2 395 447	79.4	8.6	12.0	31 760	833	11.4	80.0	18.0	2.0
Congressional District 1	79.1	79.4	10.7	6.9	493 023	82.3	8.8	8.9	8 156	298	12.2	81.2	18.1	0.7
Congressional District 2	74.3	78.7	11.4	7.5	243 542	77.9	7.8	14.3	5 103	106	13.8	74.5	21.7	3.8
Congressional District 3	94.0	81.9	6.9	10.7	36 952	91.2	4.4	4.4	572	6	1.6	50.0	50.0	0.0
Congressional District 4	77.0	70.5	8.7	20.8	99 751	66.1	7.7	26.2	318	12	6.6	75.0	25.0	0.0
Congressional District 5	83.5	63.7	20.9	13.2	17 186	87.9	7.7	4.4	483	8	4.4	62.5	37.5	0.0
Congressional District 6	84.8	85.1	8.6	5.9	191 311	85.6	5.4	9.0	1 725	40	5.1	80.0	17.5	2.5
Congressional District 7	69.2	71.1	17.0	8.9	1 195 488	64.5	10.4	25.1	11 937	166	13.8	68.1	27.1	4.8
Congressional District 8	79.5	79.4	10.4	8.2	118 194	82.3	10.2	7.4	3 465	197	14.3	92.9	6.1	1.0
ARKANSAS	66.4	91.5	5.5	2.5	4 950 397	78.1	9.5	12.3	238 577	7 811	16.5	82.0	16.6	1.5
Congressional District 1	57.7	87.3	8.9	3.3	1 574 413	72.4	14.2	13.4	181 865	4 706	32.4	76.4	21.6	2.0
Congressional District 2	72.0	94.0	3.7	2.0	355 420	87.3	6.2	6.4	7 958	745	11.1	94.2	5.8	0.0
Congressional District 3	72.3	94.7	3.0	1.9	1 454 448	82.7	6.4	10.9	3 884	970	6.8	99.9	0.1	0.0
Congressional District 4	66.7	91.5	5.5	2.6	1 566 116	74.5	9.4	16.1	44 870	1 390	11.6	81.7	16.6	1.7
CALIFORNIA	76.5	80.9	11.2	6.4	25 737 173	66.9	17.7	15.5	168 698	7 228	9.1	86.1	13.7	0.2
Congressional District 1	79.9	80.3	10.9	6.7	1 081 764	70.3	18.6	11.0	6 745	414	6.8	93.5	6.5	0.0
Congressional District 2	70.2	81.6	11.8	5.3	1 450 753	66.5	21.2	12.3	50 553	1 896	18.5	82.4	17.4	0.2
Congressional District 3	75.8	87.6	7.8	3.6	284 961	81.7	11.0	7.3	3 320	210	7.8	93.8	6.2	0.0
Congressional District 4	81.9	92.2	5.3	1.8	159 450	89.4	7.6	3.0	3 718	338	7.4	94.4	5.6	0.0
Congressional District 5	60.5	76.3	8.8	11.4	14 352	74.6	14.9	10.5	419	19	16.7	94.7	5.3	0.0
Congressional District 6	78.4	83.7	9.4	5.3	428 735	74.8	14.8	10.4	2 247	172	6.1	95.9	4.1	0.0
Congressional District 7	75.0	80.5	14.2	3.6	89 897	85.3	9.9	4.8	328	22	5.3	95.5	4.5	0.0
Congressional District 8	87.5	87.5	0.0	12.5	1 012	62.5	12.5	25.0	D	D	D	D	D	D
Congressional District 9	75.0	81.9	15.3	2.8	2 436	87.5	8.3	4.2	D	1	1.4	100.0	0.0	0.0
Congressional District 10	61.9	81.9	9.8	5.5	159 248	69.3	13.5	17.2	2 066	109	13.9	87.2	12.8	0.0
Congressional District 11	75.8	81.2	11.7	6.4	1 206 548	62.7	19.3	18.1	6 548	325	7.3	87.4	12.6	0.0
Congressional District 12	53.1	75.0	12.5	12.5	10 702	71.9	17.2	10.9	D	D	D	D	D	D
Congressional District 13	47.9	81.9	8.5	7.4	21 234	75.5	10.6	13.8	51	7	7.4	100.0	0.0	0.0
Congressional District 14	74.1	75.3	11.5	11.8	295 179	68.3	16.3	15.4	174	24	3.0	100.0	0.0	0.0
Congressional District 15	74.0	84.3	4.4	8.3	63 826	84.8	3.9	11.3	24	7	3.4	100.0	0.0	0.0
Congressional District 16	78.5	85.5	8.6	4.6	64 604	81.2	14.0	4.8	31	4	1.1	100.0	0.0	0.0
Congressional District 17	59.5	71.3	14.4	12.8	2 627 098	58.3	12.9	28.8	1 511	157	11.7	96.2	3.8	0.0
Congressional District 18	68.9	78.8	14.2	6.2	2 011 986	52.9	23.5	23.7	15 117	597	13.1	82.9	17.1	0.0
Congressional District 19	75.9	83.2	11.0	4.7	1 867 389	63.6	20.0	16.4	13 170	485	7.4	81.6	18.4	0.0
Congressional District 20	69.3	71.0	19.2	8.0	3 022 243	44.7	23.3	32.0	26 257	690	18.6	74.8	24.3	0.9
Congressional District 21	81.4	78.1	14.3	6.1	3 282 057	56.4	24.9	18.7	17 745	692	7.9	86.7	12.9	0.4
Congressional District 22	76.0	78.7	13.3	6.5	1 556 281	69.6	13.9	16.5	9 323	435	12.0	89.0	11.0	0.0
Congressional District 23	68.3	71.3	11.3	15.4	1 078 883	56.1	16.7	27.2	546	77	5.6	98.7	1.3	0.0
Congressional District 24	84.7	75.8	11.8	9.3	777 345	65.0	19.7	15.3	1 549	129	4.6	98.4	1.6	0.0
Congressional District 25	80.0	86.1	7.5	3.7	178 809	85.2	6.5	8.3	168	14	1.6	92.9	7.1	0.0
Congressional District 26	81.2	88.1	5.8	5.1	31 824	81.2	9.0	9.7	85	8	2.9	100.0	0.0	0.0
Congressional District 27	66.7	88.9	0.9	9.4	18 358	81.2	10.3	8.5	D	D	D	D	D	D
Congressional District 28	53.8	86.5	9.6	3.8	3 617	84.6	7.7	7.7	D	2	3.8	100.0	0.0	0.0
Congressional District 29	61.5	76.9	0.0	23.1	2 417	87.2	2.6	10.3	D	1	2.6	100.0	0.0	0.0
Congressional District 30	88.5	74.3	14.9	8.8	10 649	85.8	8.1	6.1	D	2	1.4	100.0	0.0	0.0
Congressional District 31	100.0	75.0	25.0	0.0	8	100.0	0.0	0.0	D	1	25.0	100.0	0.0	0.0
Congressional District 32	54.0	60.0	8.0	32.0	83 532	48.0	8.0	44.0	D	D	D	D	D	D
Congressional District 33	58.3	75.0	8.3	16.7	733	58.3	41.7	0.0	D	D	D	D	D	D
Congressional District 34	64.3	85.7	0.0	14.3	6 831	50.0	35.7	14.3	D	1	7.1	100.0	0.0	0.0
Congressional District 35	52.5	60.0	25.0	15.0	13 719	27.5	52.5	20.0	D	D	D	D	D	D
Congressional District 36	59.3	68.5	0.0	31.5	24 909	61.1	11.1	27.8	3	4	7.4	100.0	0.0	0.0
Congressional District 37	25.0	75.0	0.0	25.0	22 312	54.2	12.5	33.3	D	1	4.2	100.0	0.0	0.0
Congressional District 38	48.2	78.6	7.1	7.1	7 319	58.9	21.4	19.6	D	D	D	D	D	D
Congressional District 39	64.7	61.8	14.7	20.6	2 975	55.9	20.6	23.5	D	2	5.9	100.0	0.0	0.0
Congressional District 40	53.2	72.6	3.2	17.7	31 072	58.1	14.5	27.4	1	3	4.8	100.0	0.0	0.0

D = Suppressed to avoid disclosure.

Table A. 109th Congressional Districts, 2000—*Continued*

(Number, percent.)

STATE Congressional district	Representative	Land area,[1] (sq km)	Total population	Persons per square kilometer	White	Black	American Indian/Alaska Native	Asian and Pacific Islander	Other race	Hispanic or Latino[2] (percent)	Non-Hispanic White (percent)	Two or more races (percent)
	1	2	3	4	5	6	7	8	9	10	11	12
CALIFORNIA—*Continued*												
Congressional District 41	Jerry Lewis (R)	34 484	639 935	18.6	77.6	6.3	2.7	5.2	13.1	23.4	63.5	4.5
Congressional District 42	Gary G. Miller (R)	813	640 090	787.3	69.5	3.4	1.1	18.0	12.3	23.8	54.4	4.1
Congressional District 43	Joe Baca (D)	494	637 764	1 291.0	48.1	13.9	2.2	4.6	36.8	58.3	23.4	5.3
Congressional District 44	Ken Calvert (R)	1 352	639 008	472.6	69.1	6.5	1.9	6.5	20.9	35.0	51.3	4.6
Congressional District 45	Mary Bono (R)	15 488	638 553	41.2	68.9	7.3	1.8	4.2	22.0	38.0	50.1	3.9
Congressional District 46	Dana Rohrabacher (R)	683	639 245	935.9	74.1	1.9	1.3	17.6	9.1	16.9	62.8	3.9
Congressional District 47	Loretta Sanchez (D)	142	639 242	4 501.7	47.3	2.2	1.7	15.4	38.3	65.3	17.3	4.7
Congressional District 48	Christopher Cox (R)	550	638 848	1 161.5	78.6	1.9	0.9	14.8	7.9	14.7	68.0	3.8
Congressional District 49	Darrell E. Issa (R)	4 378	639 380	146.0	73.7	6.1	2.3	5.8	16.9	29.5	57.9	4.4
Congressional District 50	Randy "Duke" Cunningham (R)	778	639 437	821.9	77.6	2.5	1.3	12.5	10.4	18.8	65.8	4.0
Congressional District 51	Bob Filner (D)	11 868	638 989	53.8	47.4	10.8	1.7	15.5	30.2	53.3	21.3	5.2
Congressional District 52	Duncan Hunter (R)	5 473	639 329	116.8	83.6	4.6	1.7	7.8	7.2	13.7	72.9	4.5
Congressional District 53	Susan A. Davis (D)	246	638 703	2 596.4	67.1	8.6	1.6	10.8	17.3	29.4	51.0	5.0
COLORADO		268 627	4 301 261	16.0	85.2	4.4	1.9	3.0	8.5	17.1	74.5	2.8
Congressional District 1	Diana DeGette (D)	444	614 139	1 383.2	70.1	11.4	2.2	3.7	16.7	30.0	54.3	3.7
Congressional District 2	Mark Udall (D)	14 542	614 289	42.2	88.5	1.4	1.4	4.1	7.3	14.7	78.9	2.5
Congressional District 3	John T. Salazar (D)	139 765	614 494	4.4	88.6	1.0	2.9	0.9	9.2	21.5	74.6	2.5
Congressional District 4	Marilyn N. Musgrave (R)	80 025	614 571	7.7	89.0	1.0	1.5	1.7	9.1	17.0	79.4	2.3
Congressional District 5	Joel Hefley (R)	19 963	614 668	30.8	85.7	7.0	2.1	3.6	5.6	11.1	77.4	3.6
Congressional District 6	Thomas G. Tancredo (R)	10 629	614 491	57.8	93.0	2.4	1.0	3.5	2.3	5.8	87.7	2.0
Congressional District 7	Bob Beauprez (R)	3 259	614 609	188.6	81.7	6.9	1.9	3.8	9.2	19.6	68.9	3.3
CONNECTICUT		12 548	3 405 565	271.4	83.3	10.0	0.7	2.9	5.5	9.4	77.5	2.2
Congressional District 1	John B. Larson (D)	1 691	680 851	402.6	76.8	14.2	0.7	3.0	7.9	11.4	71.6	2.4
Congressional District 2	Rob Simmons (R)	5 253	681 092	129.7	92.1	4.2	1.2	2.2	2.4	4.3	88.6	1.9
Congressional District 3	Rosa L. DeLauro (D)	1 189	681 085	572.8	81.4	12.7	0.7	3.0	4.4	8.0	76.1	2.0
Congressional District 4	Christopher Shays (R)	1 183	681 176	575.8	79.4	12.3	0.5	3.8	6.7	12.8	70.9	2.5
Congressional District 5	Nancy L. Johnson (R)	3 231	681 361	210.9	86.8	6.3	0.6	2.6	6.0	10.5	80.2	2.2
DELAWARE		5 060	783 600	154.9	75.9	20.1	0.8	2.5	2.6	4.8	72.5	1.7
Congressional District (At Large)	Michael N. Castle (R)	5 060	783 600	154.9	75.9	20.1	0.8	2.5	2.6	4.8	72.5	1.7
DISTRICT OF COLUMBIA		159	572 059	3 597.9	32.2	61.3	0.8	3.2	5.0	7.9	27.8	2.4
Delegate District (At Large)	Eleanor Holmes Norton (D)	159	572 059	3 597.9	32.2	61.3	0.8	3.3	5.0	7.9	27.8	2.4
FLORIDA		139 670	15 982 378	114.4	79.7	15.5	0.7	2.3	4.4	16.8	65.4	2.4
Congressional District 1	Jeff Miller (R)	12 022	639 335	53.2	81.7	14.7	1.8	2.9	1.4	3.0	78.0	2.3
Congressional District 2	Allen Boyd (D)	24 410	639 190	26.2	74.7	22.8	1.1	1.7	1.3	3.3	71.5	1.5
Congressional District 3	Corrine Brown (D)	4 652	640 123	137.6	43.9	51.4	0.8	2.3	4.5	8.0	38.4	2.7
Congressional District 4	Ander Crenshaw (R)	10 665	638 922	59.9	81.9	14.2	0.9	3.1	1.8	4.2	77.8	1.8
Congressional District 5	Ginny Brown-Waite (R)	10 474	639 719	61.1	92.5	4.9	0.9	1.1	1.9	5.6	87.7	1.3
Congressional District 6	Cliff Stearns (R)	7 541	638 952	84.7	83.6	12.5	0.9	2.9	2.0	5.2	78.9	1.8
Congressional District 7	John L. Mica (R)	4 654	639 140	137.3	87.1	9.4	0.7	1.9	2.5	6.9	81.3	1.5
Congressional District 8	Ric Keller (R)	2 556	639 026	250.0	82.8	8.5	0.8	3.8	7.0	17.6	69.9	2.8
Congressional District 9	Michael Bilirakis (R)	1 642	638 563	388.9	91.9	4.0	0.7	2.3	2.8	7.9	85.2	1.6
Congressional District 10	C. W. Bill Young (R)	452	639 428	1 414.7	92.3	4.1	0.8	2.8	1.7	4.4	88.0	1.6
Congressional District 11	Jim Davis (D)	632	639 059	1 011.2	63.8	29.3	0.9	2.8	6.4	20.0	48.3	2.9
Congressional District 12	Adam H. Putnam (R)	5 066	640 090	126.4	80.1	13.9	0.9	1.5	5.6	12.0	72.1	1.9
Congressional District 13	Katherine Harris (R)	6 732	639 216	95.0	91.5	4.9	0.6	1.1	3.1	7.7	86.0	1.2
Congressional District 14	Connie Mack (R)	2 736	639 298	233.7	90.7	5.8	0.5	1.1	3.5	9.0	83.8	1.5
Congressional District 15	Dave Weldon (R)	6 591	639 133	97.0	86.5	8.3	0.8	2.3	4.4	11.3	77.8	2.1
Congressional District 16	Mark Foley (R)	11 755	638 817	54.3	89.1	6.4	0.7	1.4	4.1	10.1	81.8	1.5
Congressional District 17	Kendrick B. Meek (D)	250	639 593	2 558.4	34.8	60.0	0.6	2.4	7.1	21.2	18.4	4.7
Congressional District 18	Ileana Ros-Lehtinen (R)	919	639 753	696.1	86.7	7.8	0.5	1.4	7.0	62.7	29.7	3.2
Congressional District 19	Robert Wexler (D)	598	638 503	1 067.7	88.1	7.0	0.4	2.5	4.2	12.7	77.5	2.1
Congressional District 20	Debbie Wasserman Schultz (D)	416	639 795	1 538.0	85.5	9.2	0.5	3.0	4.6	20.6	66.9	2.7
Congressional District 21	Lincoln Diaz-Balart (R)	349	639 005	1 831.0	85.0	8.3	0.3	2.4	7.6	69.7	21.0	3.5
Congressional District 22	E. Clay Shaw Jr. (R)	694	640 100	922.3	91.7	4.5	0.4	2.2	3.1	10.7	82.3	1.8
Congressional District 23	Alcee L. Hastings (D)	8 708	639 781	73.5	39.1	55.5	0.7	2.0	7.8	13.7	29.4	4.9
Congressional District 24	Tom Feeney (R)	4 101	639 516	155.9	87.9	7.1	0.8	2.7	3.6	9.8	80.0	2.0
Congressional District 25	Mario Diaz-Balart (R)	11 054	638 315	57.7	79.2	12.0	0.5	2.3	10.1	62.4	24.3	3.9
GEORGIA		149 976	8 186 453	54.6	66.1	29.2	0.6	2.5	2.9	5.3	62.6	1.4
Congressional District 1	Jack Kingston (R)	29 092	628 453	21.6	73.7	23.2	0.7	1.4	2.4	4.1	71.0	1.3
Congressional District 2	Sanford D. Bishop Jr. (D)	25 185	630 481	25.0	52.2	45.2	0.7	0.9	2.1	3.5	50.3	1.0
Congressional District 3	Jim Marshall (D)	28 269	630 000	22.3	57.7	40.3	0.5	0.8	1.6	2.6	56.2	0.8
Congressional District 4	Cynthia Ann McKinney (D)	650	629 896	969.1	37.1	54.7	0.7	4.9	5.1	8.5	32.0	2.2
Congressional District 5	John Lewis (D)	652	629 839	966.0	38.0	56.9	0.6	2.7	3.5	6.1	34.4	1.5

[1]Dry land or land partially or temporarily covered by water.
[2]Hispanic or Latino persons may be of any race.

Table A. 109th Congressional Districts, 2000—*Continued*

(Number, percent.)

| STATE Congressional district | Foreign born (percent) | Age (percent) | | | | | | | | | Percent female | Households | | Percent | |
		Under 5 years	5 to 17 years	18 to 24 years	25 to 34 years	35 to 44 years	45 to 54 years	55 to 64 years	65 to 74 years	75 years and over		Number	Persons per household	Female-family householder[3]	One-person households
	13	14	15	16	17	18	19	20	21	22	23	24	25	26	27
CALIFORNIA—*Continued*															
Congressional District 41	11.6	7.0	21.4	9.7	12.1	15.1	12.7	8.4	7.1	6.4	50.6	226 250	2.74	13.1	23.3
Congressional District 42	22.8	7.2	21.1	8.3	13.7	18.5	14.8	8.1	4.6	3.7	50.4	205 634	3.05	10.0	15.8
Congressional District 43	26.4	10.0	26.6	10.9	15.6	15.2	10.1	5.3	3.5	2.8	50.3	174 806	3.60	18.2	15.4
Congressional District 44	19.0	8.2	22.5	10.3	14.6	16.7	12.4	7.0	4.5	3.9	50.0	200 177	3.12	12.1	18.2
Congressional District 45	20.5	7.5	21.6	8.6	12.3	14.9	11.2	8.2	8.2	7.5	49.9	218 502	2.85	11.4	23.1
Congressional District 46	23.8	6.0	15.9	8.3	16.1	16.8	14.0	9.9	6.9	6.0	50.3	241 993	2.60	9.1	26.3
Congressional District 47	50.7	10.0	23.2	11.9	18.9	14.9	9.2	5.3	3.6	2.8	48.6	150 284	4.20	13.8	13.8
Congressional District 48	22.5	6.5	16.9	8.5	15.6	17.7	14.4	8.6	5.6	6.2	51.4	247 176	2.53	8.8	26.4
Congressional District 49	17.5	7.9	21.2	11.4	13.6	15.6	11.0	6.8	6.4	6.2	49.3	209 018	2.95	10.4	19.2
Congressional District 50	21.0	6.9	18.4	8.4	14.3	17.3	14.3	8.1	6.1	6.2	50.3	231 839	2.72	9.3	22.4
Congressional District 51	32.7	7.8	22.9	10.5	14.7	15.6	11.5	7.1	5.7	4.2	49.9	184 751	3.33	17.7	15.9
Congressional District 52	12.5	7.0	19.6	8.5	14.0	17.6	14.1	8.1	5.9	5.2	51.0	232 804	2.71	11.2	21.0
Congressional District 53	24.0	6.2	14.6	16.1	20.8	15.3	10.9	6.1	4.7	5.2	48.1	252 619	2.34	11.2	35.6
COLORADO	8.6	6.9	18.7	10.0	15.4	17.1	14.3	7.9	5.3	4.4	49.6	1 658 238	2.53	9.6	26.3
Congressional District 1	16.8	6.7	15.1	10.7	20.4	15.7	12.9	7.2	5.5	5.8	49.5	266 388	2.26	10.8	39.2
Congressional District 2	9.1	6.8	17.9	11.8	17.6	17.9	14.3	7.0	4.0	2.7	48.9	233 172	2.59	8.5	23.5
Congressional District 3	4.2	6.3	18.8	9.4	12.4	15.6	14.9	9.3	7.2	6.2	50.0	240 903	2.48	9.9	25.9
Congressional District 4	7.0	6.9	19.2	12.2	14.0	16.1	13.4	7.8	5.4	5.0	49.6	227 615	2.61	8.6	23.4
Congressional District 5	5.9	7.2	19.5	10.0	14.7	17.7	13.8	7.7	5.3	4.0	49.1	228 136	2.58	9.8	24.1
Congressional District 6	5.7	7.4	22.1	5.9	13.3	20.2	16.9	7.8	3.9	2.7	50.3	221 373	2.76	7.2	17.7
Congressional District 7	11.6	7.2	18.0	10.0	15.8	16.7	13.8	8.4	5.6	4.5	50.1	240 651	2.51	11.8	27.8
CONNECTICUT	10.9	6.6	18.2	8.0	13.3	17.1	14.1	9.1	6.8	7.0	51.6	1 301 670	2.53	12.1	26.4
Congressional District 1	11.7	6.4	18.0	7.7	13.3	16.5	14.1	9.2	7.1	7.7	52.3	269 019	2.46	14.0	28.4
Congressional District 2	5.1	6.2	18.1	9.1	12.9	17.9	14.5	9.1	6.4	5.9	50.2	255 449	2.53	9.7	24.4
Congressional District 3	9.3	6.2	17.4	8.9	14.0	16.4	13.6	8.8	7.0	7.7	52.1	267 124	2.47	13.2	28.8
Congressional District 4	17.2	7.4	18.6	6.9	13.2	17.4	13.9	9.2	6.8	6.5	51.8	250 190	2.67	12.0	24.1
Congressional District 5	10.9	6.6	18.7	7.3	12.9	17.2	14.5	9.1	6.6	7.2	51.4	259 888	2.55	11.3	26.2
DELAWARE	5.7	6.6	18.3	9.6	13.9	16.3	13.3	9.1	7.2	5.8	51.4	298 736	2.54	13.1	25.0
Congressional District (At Large)	5.7	6.6	18.3	9.6	13.9	16.3	13.3	9.1	7.2	5.8	51.4	298 736	2.54	13.1	25.0
DISTRICT OF COLUMBIA	12.9	5.7	14.4	12.7	17.8	15.3	13.2	8.7	6.3	5.9	52.9	248 338	2.16	18.9	43.8
Delegate District (At Large)	12.9	5.7	14.4	12.7	17.8	15.3	13.2	8.7	6.3	5.9	52.9	248 338	2.16	18.9	43.8
FLORIDA	16.7	5.9	16.9	8.3	13.0	15.5	12.9	9.8	9.1	8.5	51.2	6 337 929	2.46	12.0	26.6
Congressional District 1	3.9	6.2	18.1	10.3	13.6	16.3	13.2	9.5	7.3	5.4	49.8	242 609	2.49	12.7	24.7
Congressional District 2	3.7	5.8	17.0	13.4	13.7	15.4	13.6	9.2	6.8	5.2	50.3	248 654	2.42	12.9	26.9
Congressional District 3	8.8	7.5	20.8	10.7	14.7	15.4	12.1	7.9	6.0	4.8	51.5	236 230	2.63	22.4	26.7
Congressional District 4	5.8	6.6	17.7	9.2	15.6	17.2	14.1	8.5	6.0	5.1	50.1	246 192	2.49	11.2	25.2
Congressional District 5	5.3	5.0	15.3	5.7	10.0	13.4	12.3	12.8	14.3	11.3	51.1	263 158	2.37	8.4	23.1
Congressional District 6	5.6	5.7	17.2	12.2	12.5	14.8	12.7	9.4	8.6	6.8	51.0	247 842	2.48	10.9	23.4
Congressional District 7	7.1	5.4	16.7	7.9	11.3	15.5	14.3	10.6	9.6	8.6	51.5	259 246	2.41	10.7	25.9
Congressional District 8	12.0	6.2	17.2	9.0	15.4	16.9	13.0	8.6	7.3	6.5	51.0	254 707	2.47	11.0	25.9
Congressional District 9	9.6	5.7	16.2	6.5	11.8	15.7	13.7	9.9	9.8	10.7	52.0	267 147	2.36	9.0	27.5
Congressional District 10	9.5	4.6	13.4	6.2	11.8	15.7	14.2	10.7	10.8	12.5	52.1	294 543	2.12	9.4	35.1
Congressional District 11	12.8	6.9	18.3	10.3	15.8	15.9	12.6	8.2	6.3	5.7	51.5	257 416	2.42	17.1	31.4
Congressional District 12	7.7	6.7	18.6	8.5	12.8	14.7	12.3	9.5	9.0	8.1	50.9	243 066	2.56	12.3	23.7
Congressional District 13	9.5	4.6	13.4	5.9	10.0	13.0	12.5	12.1	14.2	14.3	51.6	281 888	2.21	7.9	29.1
Congressional District 14	10.0	4.8	13.5	5.7	10.0	13.0	12.4	13.2	15.0	12.3	51.3	279 349	2.26	7.8	26.1
Congressional District 15	9.1	5.4	16.7	7.1	11.4	15.6	12.9	10.6	10.8	9.4	51.2	262 084	2.40	10.3	25.9
Congressional District 16	10.1	5.1	16.0	6.0	9.7	14.0	12.4	11.3	13.4	12.1	50.8	262 499	2.39	8.3	24.5
Congressional District 17	34.1	7.4	21.9	10.1	14.0	15.5	12.4	7.9	5.7	5.1	52.3	213 262	2.94	24.0	24.3
Congressional District 18	54.0	5.2	14.2	8.2	15.0	16.0	13.2	10.5	9.2	8.6	50.6	254 897	2.45	12.9	31.3
Congressional District 19	18.0	5.1	13.8	5.8	11.4	13.8	11.3	9.1	12.7	17.0	53.1	283 779	2.23	8.3	30.6
Congressional District 20	26.7	5.8	15.5	6.6	14.5	17.5	13.8	9.0	7.8	9.6	51.7	275 076	2.30	10.3	32.3
Congressional District 21	56.6	6.5	17.9	8.5	15.2	16.7	12.6	9.7	7.4	5.5	52.1	211 124	2.99	15.6	17.0
Congressional District 22	16.7	4.9	13.9	5.7	12.0	16.8	14.8	11.0	10.0	10.8	51.2	285 462	2.22	7.5	32.5
Congressional District 23	26.9	7.5	20.7	9.9	14.8	15.9	11.6	7.4	5.8	6.3	50.6	224 179	2.74	20.5	27.2
Congressional District 24	7.9	5.7	17.4	9.4	13.2	16.8	13.4	9.4	8.2	6.5	50.5	249 141	2.51	10.1	23.3
Congressional District 25	46.5	7.6	21.0	9.5	15.8	17.3	12.3	7.8	5.1	3.5	50.5	194 419	3.21	16.0	13.7
GEORGIA	7.1	7.3	19.2	10.2	15.9	16.5	13.2	8.1	5.3	4.3	50.8	3 006 369	2.65	14.5	23.6
Congressional District 1	3.5	7.5	20.1	10.4	14.6	15.8	12.7	8.5	6.0	4.6	49.9	228 671	2.64	12.9	22.3
Congressional District 2	2.7	7.5	20.2	11.6	13.9	14.3	12.3	8.2	6.4	5.6	51.6	228 845	2.62	20.2	25.3
Congressional District 3	2.2	6.8	19.5	10.2	13.7	15.6	13.1	9.0	6.5	5.6	50.9	229 679	2.58	18.3	25.8
Congressional District 4	16.2	7.3	17.7	11.0	19.5	17.2	12.8	6.9	4.2	3.5	51.4	234 065	2.63	17.6	26.3
Congressional District 5	9.2	6.4	15.4	13.1	21.6	15.7	12.0	6.9	4.5	4.3	50.7	261 651	2.29	18.3	37.6

[3]No spouse present.

Table A. 109th Congressional Districts, 2000—*Continued*

(Number, percent.)

STATE Congressional district	Persons in correctional institutions	Persons in nursing homes	Persons in college dormitories	Persons in military quarters	Public	Private	H.S. graduate or more	Bachelor's degree or more	Per capita income[6]	Median income	Percent with income over $100,000	Persons	Families
	Group quarters				**Education**				**Money income, 1999**			**Percent below poverty level, 1999**	
					School enrollment[4]		Attainment level[5]			Households			
	28	29	30	31	32	33	34	35	36	37	38	39	40
CALIFORNIA—*Continued*													
Congressional District 41	2 019	2 290	1 590	5 583	164 932	26 251	80.2	18.1	18 201	38 721	9.5	15.2	11.8
Congressional District 42	9 726	569	714	0	166 860	36 806	87.5	34.8	27 572	70 463	29.6	6.0	4.2
Congressional District 43	2 257	1 703	0	0	201 258	16 025	61.7	8.8	12 861	37 390	6.8	20.7	17.4
Congressional District 44	5 968	2 049	2 814	1	177 293	27 518	77.2	21.1	21 335	51 578	17.5	12.1	8.7
Congressional District 45	9 748	1 971	0	0	162 474	17 140	74.3	17.4	19 423	40 468	11.9	15.0	11.3
Congressional District 46	1 375	1 618	2 617	154	144 105	30 223	86.7	36.4	30 942	61 567	25.5	7.8	5.0
Congressional District 47	2 473	1 653	28	0	185 943	14 857	50.4	10.0	12 541	41 618	8.8	19.1	15.4
Congressional District 48	944	1 850	7 122	0	151 703	32 394	91.8	46.5	37 242	69 663	31.6	6.3	3.7
Congressional District 49	1 141	1 026	497	15 770	161 177	21 277	80.1	20.7	19 659	46 445	13.1	11.9	8.7
Congressional District 50	148	2 512	36	4 114	149 416	28 869	87.1	40.0	29 877	59 813	24.5	8.1	5.0
Congressional District 51	17 028	942	0	2 700	193 636	17 650	69.0	15.2	14 923	39 243	8.9	16.3	13.8
Congressional District 52	1 280	3 288	400	0	160 389	26 772	88.5	28.6	24 544	52 940	17.7	8.1	5.7
Congressional District 53	2 402	2 611	12 638	18 800	163 162	27 686	80.1	32.2	21 715	36 637	10.6	20.2	15.4
COLORADO	30 136	18 495	23 631	8 512	1 003 508	162 496	86.9	32.7	24 049	47 203	14.2	9.3	6.2
Congressional District 1	3 059	3 257	2 027	0	116 233	28 477	79.6	34.3	24 622	39 658	11.5	13.7	10.1
Congressional District 2	782	1 579	6 125	0	149 615	22 921	89.7	39.3	26 544	55 204	18.0	7.4	4.0
Congressional District 3	3 787	3 290	4 715	0	143 752	14 767	83.8	23.8	19 148	35 970	7.6	12.8	9.2
Congressional District 4	6 726	3 667	7 976	0	166 081	17 938	85.3	28.7	20 836	43 389	11.2	10.9	6.7
Congressional District 5	11 375	2 477	1 817	8 321	142 277	26 608	90.2	29.8	21 605	45 454	11.5	8.3	5.9
Congressional District 6	1 260	1 357	39	0	151 091	29 660	95.6	46.8	33 175	73 393	30.1	2.7	1.9
Congressional District 7	3 147	2 868	932	191	134 459	22 125	84.6	26.0	22 412	46 149	11.3	8.9	6.4
CONNECTICUT	20 023	32 223	38 051	2 097	731 418	179 451	84.0	31.4	28 766	53 935	20.2	7.9	5.6
Congressional District 1	1 055	9 159	5 310	0	149 877	27 218	82.2	28.2	25 084	50 227	16.0	9.6	7.3
Congressional District 2	11 896	4 781	14 476	2 081	158 447	28 479	86.7	28.8	25 548	54 498	17.2	5.8	3.7
Congressional District 3	1 365	6 254	10 882	16	139 264	46 966	83.6	28.0	24 655	49 752	15.6	8.8	6.4
Congressional District 4	880	4 982	4 524	0	136 317	46 114	84.6	42.2	41 147	66 598	33.2	7.4	5.4
Congressional District 5	4 827	7 047	2 859	0	147 513	30 674	82.9	29.9	27 396	53 118	19.5	7.7	5.5
DELAWARE	5 965	4 852	9 394	381	164 193	45 786	82.6	25.0	23 305	47 381	14.0	9.2	6.5
Congressional District (At Large)	5 965	4 852	9 394	381	164 193	45 786	82.6	25.0	23 305	47 381	14.0	9.2	6.5
DISTRICT OF COLUMBIA	2 838	3 759	19 322	927	105 998	51 477	77.8	39.1	28 659	40 127	16.4	20.2	16.7
Delegate District (At Large)	2 838	3 759	19 322	927	105 998	51 477	77.8	39.1	28 659	40 127	16.4	20.2	16.7
FLORIDA	139 148	88 828	54 085	13 457	3 257 226	676 053	79.9	22.3	21 557	38 819	10.4	12.5	9.0
Congressional District 1	15 657	4 065	4 412	7 702	142 370	23 571	82.5	20.2	18 814	36 738	7.3	13.1	10.3
Congressional District 2	19 044	3 904	8 907	527	170 884	18 564	80.1	24.1	18 462	34 718	7.8	16.5	11.1
Congressional District 3	8 532	2 292	1 572	0	165 629	20 284	71.3	12.9	14 473	29 785	4.2	21.5	17.4
Congressional District 4	14 104	3 651	1 265	4 036	130 604	30 773	84.7	24.4	22 332	43 947	11.6	9.1	6.6
Congressional District 5	8 846	3 476	464	0	108 408	16 602	78.8	14.3	18 631	34 815	6.0	10.6	7.6
Congressional District 6	8 762	3 756	8 349	4	162 669	22 598	82.8	21.4	18 983	36 846	8.0	13.4	8.3
Congressional District 7	1 636	4 702	5 127	0	121 149	33 012	84.5	24.5	23 153	40 525	12.0	10.1	7.0
Congressional District 8	879	3 301	1 083	0	128 221	30 451	83.7	25.9	22 292	41 568	10.9	9.4	6.9
Congressional District 9	81	5 265	452	0	118 002	26 627	83.6	24.6	23 837	40 742	12.5	8.6	6.0
Congressional District 10	3 269	5 370	1 346	56	96 176	28 403	84.3	22.6	24 045	37 168	9.3	8.9	5.8
Congressional District 11	3 076	3 095	3 786	412	145 529	28 211	76.5	21.2	19 149	33 559	7.8	17.5	13.4
Congressional District 12	5 835	3 901	2 392	0	132 778	24 155	76.3	16.6	18 544	37 769	7.2	12.4	9.0
Congressional District 13	4 010	5 854	756	13	96 375	18 497	83.8	23.7	25 055	40 187	10.9	9.4	6.1
Congressional District 14	1 709	4 190	238	16	93 605	17 944	84.2	24.4	28 159	42 541	13.4	8.8	5.9
Congressional District 15	1 621	3 084	1 388	215	120 917	25 992	83.8	22.3	21 721	39 397	9.2	9.8	7.1
Congressional District 16	4 212	3 995	267	7	114 240	19 682	81.0	20.0	22 996	39 408	11.0	10.0	6.7
Congressional District 17	4 154	3 635	1 653	262	181 897	28 392	66.5	13.5	13 676	30 426	5.3	23.3	20.0
Congressional District 18	2 509	2 504	3 594	179	113 955	35 304	67.1	25.6	22 786	32 298	12.5	19.3	14.5
Congressional District 19	382	2 370	1 356	0	102 259	26 631	85.7	25.7	26 810	42 237	13.4	7.7	5.2
Congressional District 20	91	2 130	617	0	112 060	40 711	85.3	29.6	26 845	44 034	15.2	9.6	6.8
Congressional District 21	1 148	2 602	825	11	142 986	35 479	68.8	22.9	18 829	41 426	12.4	13.0	10.6
Congressional District 22	0	3 667	1 779	11	94 283	38 953	88.6	34.1	35 484	51 200	21.0	7.1	4.6
Congressional District 23	13 767	3 442	0	0	163 803	20 256	66.5	12.8	14 715	31 309	5.0	21.9	18.3
Congressional District 24	7 132	2 691	2 457	5	139 918	29 237	86.4	25.5	22 114	43 954	11.4	8.7	5.5
Congressional District 25	8 692	1 886	0	1	158 514	35 724	72.4	20.3	17 030	44 489	11.4	13.7	11.0
GEORGIA	81 773	34 812	47 910	25 461	1 892 188	319 500	78.6	24.3	21 154	42 433	12.3	13.0	9.9
Congressional District 1	10 727	3 625	167	8 840	148 035	18 173	77.2	17.9	18 080	36 158	8.3	14.8	11.7
Congressional District 2	7 617	4 275	3 879	9 816	160 701	16 661	70.3	13.9	15 128	29 354	5.6	22.5	18.3
Congressional District 3	23 414	6 075	3 900	0	148 511	20 862	70.6	12.8	15 532	31 433	5.6	19.9	15.9
Congressional District 4	3 181	1 881	4 086	0	135 039	38 076	85.4	35.9	23 851	49 307	15.6	10.5	7.6
Congressional District 5	7 705	1 683	13 612	88	126 564	37 689	80.8	37.3	26 024	39 725	14.6	19.7	16.5

[4]All persons 3 years old and over enrolled in nursery school through college.
[5]Persons 25 years old and over.
[6]Based on the population enumerated as of April 1, 2000.

Table A. 109th Congressional Districts, 2000—*Continued*

(Number, percent.)

STATE Congressional district	Housing units									Civilian labor force		
	Total	Total occupied units	Owner occupied		Median owner costs as a percent of income		Renter occupied		Sub-standard housing units (percent)[9]	Total	Unemployment	
			Percent	Median value[7] (dollars)	With a mortgage	Without a mortgage[8]	Median rent (dollars)	Median rent as a percent of income			Total	Rate[10]
	41	42	43	44	45	46	47	48	49	50	51	52
CALIFORNIA—*Continued*												
Congressional District 41	279 801	226 258	66.9	119 100	23.7	10.9	609	27.7	9.3	268 848	21 411	7.7
Congressional District 42	210 169	205 667	76.4	262 500	25.4	9.9	956	27.6	8.9	321 090	13 938	4.3
Congressional District 43	188 160	174 721	59.9	118 200	26.3	9.9	625	30.1	25.3	251 321	26 054	10.4
Congressional District 44	209 646	200 212	65.8	175 300	25.2	9.9	727	28.2	13.3	294 136	19 434	6.6
Congressional District 45	277 924	218 350	69.2	138 400	25.5	11.4	644	28.6	12.7	258 909	19 777	7.6
Congressional District 46	250 875	241 898	61.6	305 000	24.6	9.9	963	25.5	9.1	338 212	14 022	4.1
Congressional District 47	153 604	150 209	47.4	183 600	26.8	9.9	787	29.0	44.6	266 300	20 797	7.8
Congressional District 48	263 140	247 151	65.1	338 100	25.3	9.9	1 151	27.0	7.4	341 555	13 621	4.0
Congressional District 49	222 746	209 193	66.8	187 600	26.6	9.9	774	28.8	12.2	264 780	17 020	5.8
Congressional District 50	241 828	231 948	65.9	282 000	25.0	9.9	907	27.4	8.5	318 693	13 853	4.2
Congressional District 51	193 365	184 647	56.7	158 500	26.0	9.9	638	28.5	22.4	251 072	21 965	8.4
Congressional District 52	241 079	232 585	63.9	232 300	25.3	9.9	785	27.1	6.7	317 273	15 442	4.7
Congressional District 53	267 628	252 788	34.4	218 700	26.3	9.9	709	28.7	14.5	316 680	23 458	6.8
COLORADO	1 808 037	1 658 238	67.3	166 600	22.6	9.9	671	26.4	4.9	2 304 454	99 260	4.3
Congressional District 1	279 512	266 247	52.2	164 800	23.2	9.9	634	26.1	7.9	335 614	18 454	5.5
Congressional District 2	270 701	233 172	69.2	196 500	22.9	9.9	817	26.9	4.4	361 893	14 225	3.9
Congressional District 3	284 939	240 911	70.4	116 000	22.9	9.9	529	27.0	4.6	305 359	16 902	5.5
Congressional District 4	245 330	227 695	68.0	151 800	22.8	9.9	619	26.8	4.7	323 987	14 066	4.3
Congressional District 5	249 339	228 166	66.5	145 100	22.7	9.9	648	26.2	3.9	300 659	13 848	4.3
Congressional District 6	229 852	221 355	84.9	214 200	21.9	9.9	931	25.2	1.8	344 973	7 625	2.2
Congressional District 7	248 364	240 692	63.2	161 200	22.5	9.9	698	26.4	6.5	331 969	14 140	4.2
CONNECTICUT	1 385 975	1 301 670	66.8	166 900	22.4	13.1	681	25.4	3.2	1 757 108	92 668	5.3
Congressional District 1	284 006	268 880	63.6	145 100	22.0	12.8	651	25.0	3.7	351 736	22 373	6.4
Congressional District 2	277 472	255 470	72.0	147 000	21.7	11.9	645	24.0	1.8	358 658	15 678	4.3
Congressional District 3	283 405	267 105	63.6	155 000	23.1	14.1	695	26.3	2.9	354 342	20 702	5.8
Congressional District 4	262 030	250 230	67.8	347 200	23.1	13.7	844	26.5	4.4	340 503	17 539	5.1
Congressional District 5	279 062	259 985	67.5	167 000	22.3	13.2	637	25.0	3.2	351 869	16 376	4.7
DELAWARE	343 072	298 736	72.3	130 400	20.8	9.9	639	24.3	3.1	397 360	20 549	5.2
Congressional District (At Large)	343 072	298 736	72.3	130 400	20.8	9.9	639	24.3	3.1	397 360	20 549	5.1
DISTRICT OF COLUMBIA	274 845	248 338	40.8	157 200	22.2	9.9	618	24.8	9.5	294 952	31 844	10.8
Delegate District (At Large)	274 845	248 338	40.8	157 200	22.2	9.9	618	24.8	9.5	294 952	31 844	10.7
FLORIDA	7 302 947	6 337 929	70.1	105 500	22.8	10.5	641	27.5	6.8	7 407 458	412 411	5.6
Congressional District 1	275 465	242 696	70.6	91 200	21.2	9.9	540	25.7	3.5	279 915	16 334	5.4
Congressional District 2	309 440	248 547	68.4	95 600	21.1	9.9	550	28.6	4.2	305 536	20 586	6.6
Congressional District 3	265 805	236 276	55.6	69 300	22.8	10.2	546	27.5	9.3	289 439	22 454	7.7
Congressional District 4	267 576	246 246	69.4	104 200	20.4	9.9	648	24.3	3.7	320 152	13 143	3.9
Congressional District 5	306 839	263 218	85.2	94 800	22.0	9.9	512	25.2	2.7	250 766	12 323	4.9
Congressional District 6	272 176	247 789	72.9	93 300	21.0	9.9	571	27.9	3.4	295 340	15 720	5.3
Congressional District 7	290 241	259 281	74.1	106 400	22.2	9.9	643	27.3	3.2	307 532	15 453	5.0
Congressional District 8	280 066	254 858	66.4	107 900	22.5	10.2	710	26.1	5.5	330 246	14 205	4.3
Congressional District 9	301 330	266 733	76.3	107 000	22.1	10.8	653	26.2	3.1	298 490	11 536	3.9
Congressional District 10	344 300	294 533	71.7	94 400	22.3	11.4	611	26.3	2.6	313 336	12 402	3.9
Congressional District 11	283 139	257 770	55.4	81 000	22.3	11.6	588	27.0	8.4	316 564	23 135	7.2
Congressional District 12	283 384	243 267	72.7	87 600	21.1	9.9	540	24.1	5.5	292 604	16 122	5.5
Congressional District 13	347 408	281 788	77.5	119 400	23.2	10.6	666	26.9	3.4	275 829	10 573	3.8
Congressional District 14	375 871	279 398	77.3	128 000	23.4	10.5	690	26.2	3.6	276 619	9 522	3.4
Congressional District 15	305 171	261 939	73.2	99 200	22.3	9.9	639	27.1	4.0	293 120	14 023	4.7
Congressional District 16	316 665	262 341	81.7	103 500	22.7	10.3	630	26.5	4.0	268 557	11 056	4.1
Congressional District 17	236 208	213 285	57.4	89 600	27.0	13.5	587	30.0	21.2	274 068	30 476	11.1
Congressional District 18	300 681	255 055	47.9	161 500	27.3	14.1	617	30.7	18.9	292 745	22 905	7.8
Congressional District 19	326 763	283 625	79.1	134 300	23.4	11.3	828	28.0	4.2	273 756	13 022	4.8
Congressional District 20	318 402	275 276	69.9	138 600	24.0	12.9	807	28.7	6.4	325 891	15 662	4.8
Congressional District 21	220 530	211 014	61.9	139 800	25.7	13.1	711	29.8	20.4	297 583	21 490	7.2
Congressional District 22	343 482	285 359	74.3	165 200	23.7	12.2	798	27.6	3.2	321 652	11 924	3.7
Congressional District 23	250 339	224 530	56.5	85 400	24.8	12.7	627	29.5	15.6	288 291	23 996	8.3
Congressional District 24	273 700	248 930	74.3	105 800	21.9	9.9	694	26.5	3.3	322 757	13 635	4.2
Congressional District 25	207 966	194 175	72.7	126 200	25.7	12.3	726	29.1	18.4	296 670	20 714	7.0
GEORGIA	3 281 737	3 006 369	67.5	111 200	20.8	9.9	613	24.9	5.3	4 062 808	223 052	5.5
Congressional District 1	262 476	228 520	71.4	89 400	20.5	10.3	476	23.7	4.5	274 508	14 289	4.8
Congressional District 2	260 043	228 773	62.5	71 200	20.4	10.6	418	25.0	6.7	270 954	20 632	7.2
Congressional District 3	262 560	229 691	69.0	71 000	20.0	9.9	418	24.9	5.2	271 328	18 533	6.8
Congressional District 4	244 845	234 301	57.7	135 000	21.3	9.9	769	25.6	7.9	348 009	18 985	5.4
Congressional District 5	287 599	261 795	42.1	132 700	22.6	10.8	705	26.0	7.4	343 563	36 463	10.6

[7]Specified owner-occupied units.
[8]Median monthly owner costs is often in the minimum category—9.9 percent or less, which is indicated as 9.9 percent.
[9]Overcrowded or lacking complete plumbing facilities.
[10]Percent of civilian labor force.

Table A. 109th Congressional Districts, 2000—Continued

(Number, percent.)

STATE Congressional district	Civilian employment and occupations				Total farms, 2002	Farms by size, 2002 (percent)			Land in farms, 2002		Cropland harvested, 2002		Farm's principal operator's primary occupation is farming, 2002 (percent)
	Total	Management, professional, and related (percent)	Service, sales, and office (percent)	Construction and production (percent)		1 to 49 acres	50 to 999 acres	1,000 acres or more	Acreage	Average size of farms (acres)	Acreage	Farms	
	53	54	55	56	57	58	59	60	61	62	63	64	65
CALIFORNIA—*Continued*													
Congressional District 41	247 437	31.4	43.3	25.0	1 061	76.1	21.2	2.7	493 098	465	42 123	625	50.8
Congressional District 42	307 152	43.5	41.0	15.2	242	84.7	13.2	2.1	16 154	67	2 146	120	51.2
Congressional District 43	225 267	19.2	43.8	36.2	223	76.2	22.9	0.9	17 463	78	2 421	82	67.7
Congressional District 44	274 702	31.9	41.5	26.0	962	88.7	10.3	1.0	38 917	40	15 206	405	45.8
Congressional District 45	239 132	26.5	47.3	23.1	1 379	74.5	20.4	5.0	408 381	296	151 898	923	54.6
Congressional District 46	324 190	44.1	40.3	15.4	57	77.2	22.8	0.0	1 963	34	993	34	57.9
Congressional District 47	245 503	17.2	43.9	37.9	31	80.6	19.4	0.0	855	28	459	23	41.9
Congressional District 48	327 934	50.1	39.7	10.1	106	70.8	26.4	2.8	60 185	568	6 825	67	49.1
Congressional District 49	247 760	30.9	43.5	24.4	3 694	90.0	8.9	1.1	273 023	74	56 281	3 205	52.5
Congressional District 50	304 840	45.2	38.6	15.7	912	90.0	9.2	0.8	41 120	45	11 225	795	52.3
Congressional District 51	229 107	26.4	48.1	23.5	663	33.3	42.7	24.0	548 162	827	478 705	518	74.8
Congressional District 52	301 831	38.8	42.8	18.2	1 037	85.8	12.2	1.9	121 241	117	13 663	640	45.9
Congressional District 53	293 222	38.6	44.8	16.3	61	80.3	19.7	0.0	3 493	57	683	39	36.1
COLORADO	2 205 194	37.4	41.1	21.0	31 369	32.8	47.7	19.5	31 093 336	991	4 346 955	14 655	58.4
Congressional District 1	317 160	37.7	41.8	20.4	21	61.9	33.3	4.8	3 466	165	75	9	57.1
Congressional District 2	347 668	39.9	39.6	20.2	1 158	49.2	41.3	9.5	517 949	447	69 347	591	50.7
Congressional District 3	288 457	30.2	43.3	25.0	12 015	36.8	48.7	14.5	11 532 734	960	853 599	6 398	57.2
Congressional District 4	309 921	35.2	39.0	24.0	12 156	22.2	48.9	28.9	15 135 952	1 245	2 996 506	6 158	62.9
Congressional District 5	286 811	36.2	42.4	21.3	2 418	42.2	45.3	12.5	1 516 812	627	37 155	647	53.8
Congressional District 6	337 348	48.0	38.6	13.2	2 754	42.1	46.9	10.9	1 676 376	609	131 317	480	51.9
Congressional District 7	317 829	32.6	43.4	23.8	847	47.3	35.7	17.0	710 047	838	258 956	372	57.1
CONNECTICUT	1 664 440	39.1	40.7	19.9	4 191	62.3	37.1	0.6	357 154	85	131 248	3 000	49.6
Congressional District 1	329 363	38.0	42.2	19.7	579	67.9	31.4	0.7	39 192	68	17 408	447	49.4
Congressional District 2	342 980	37.4	41.3	20.9	2 011	57.9	41.3	0.8	183 720	91	66 358	1 407	48.8
Congressional District 3	333 640	37.5	41.3	21.1	389	71.5	28.3	0.3	21 617	56	8 557	293	55.3
Congressional District 4	322 964	45.3	39.2	15.5	201	76.6	23.4	0.0	7 711	38	2 145	143	45.8
Congressional District 5	335 493	37.7	39.7	22.4	1 011	61.3	38.1	0.6	104 914	104	36 780	710	49.8
DELAWARE	376 811	35.3	42.2	22.0	2 391	52.3	41.8	5.9	540 080	226	433 105	1 548	69.4
Congressional District (At Large)	376 811	35.3	42.2	22.0	2 391	52.3	41.8	5.9	540 080	226	433 105	1 548	69.4
DISTRICT OF COLUMBIA	263 108	51.1	38.9	10.0	0	X	X	X	X	X	X	X	X
Delegate District (At Large)	263 108	51.1	38.9	10.0	0	X	X	X	X	X	X	X	X
FLORIDA	6 995 047	31.5	46.5	21.1	44 081	64.9	31.3	3.8	10 414 877	236	2 313 537	20 495	52.2
Congressional District 1	263 581	29.8	45.2	24.4	3 230	47.6	50.9	1.5	417 786	129	121 703	1 440	50.3
Congressional District 2	284 950	34.8	44.6	19.3	3 857	45.7	50.4	3.9	899 330	233	171 073	1 550	51.7
Congressional District 3	266 985	22.6	50.0	26.6	1 280	70.5	27.8	1.7	233 062	182	18 688	692	54.1
Congressional District 4	307 009	34.5	44.3	20.6	2 615	51.0	46.1	2.9	480 130	184	57 362	1 002	49.1
Congressional District 5	238 443	26.8	45.8	26.1	5 182	68.6	28.7	2.7	807 182	156	122 144	1 845	51.9
Congressional District 6	279 620	33.1	44.3	21.7	5 073	68.7	29.3	2.0	622 805	123	85 924	1 461	54.1
Congressional District 7	292 079	33.4	45.6	20.3	1 102	73.2	23.4	3.4	187 718	170	37 131	537	45.2
Congressional District 8	316 041	34.1	46.2	19.3	1 403	77.4	21.2	1.4	98 812	70	21 778	656	52.0
Congressional District 9	286 954	36.7	45.2	17.6	1 826	81.8	17.3	1.0	132 013	72	24 179	829	52.8
Congressional District 10	300 934	33.9	46.0	19.9	78	94.9	5.1	0.0	D	D	139	50	43.6
Congressional District 11	293 429	30.0	48.4	21.2	290	74.8	24.1	1.0	28 538	98	7 581	136	51.4
Congressional District 12	276 482	27.3	44.6	26.1	3 690	67.4	29.0	3.6	700 744	190	157 101	2 279	53.4
Congressional District 13	265 256	30.2	46.3	21.0	3 502	57.9	35.4	6.7	1 156 599	330	225 009	1 913	52.4
Congressional District 14	267 097	29.6	48.6	21.1	730	74.5	20.3	5.2	162 548	223	38 653	338	50.3
Congressional District 15	279 097	30.7	47.1	21.5	1 359	65.2	26.6	8.2	1 015 972	748	105 053	708	55.3
Congressional District 16	257 501	29.5	45.3	21.8	3 409	58.3	31.7	10.1	2 338 369	686	593 917	1 352	54.2
Congressional District 17	243 592	23.3	52.4	24.0	5	100.0	0.0	0.0	D	D	19	5	20.0
Congressional District 18	269 840	32.3	46.3	20.6	505	90.7	8.9	0.4	15 368	30	9 332	446	52.1
Congressional District 19	260 734	34.3	48.2	17.1	261	89.3	9.2	1.5	21 560	83	17 075	185	52.1
Congressional District 20	310 229	38.2	45.6	16.0	271	93.7	5.9	0.4	8 047	30	2 537	133	47.2
Congressional District 21	276 093	31.2	46.0	22.6	46	95.7	4.3	0.0	871	19	228	38	78.3
Congressional District 22	309 728	39.6	44.2	16.0	324	87.7	12.3	0.0	8 916	28	3 118	159	53.4
Congressional District 23	264 295	21.6	50.9	25.8	828	55.7	30.7	13.6	730 595	882	387 555	449	58.9
Congressional District 24	309 122	35.5	44.7	19.4	1 285	81.9	16.0	2.0	126 714	99	17 044	622	47.9
Congressional District 25	275 956	29.5	47.5	20.8	1 930	85.5	12.3	2.1	220 096	114	89 194	1 670	51.1
GEORGIA	3 839 756	32.7	40.2	26.5	49 311	39.2	56.5	4.3	10 744 239	218	3 245 784	24 424	50.9
Congressional District 1	260 219	28.4	39.7	30.2	5 943	34.7	59.9	5.4	1 498 461	252	541 383	3 735	51.8
Congressional District 2	250 322	25.9	41.0	31.1	6 925	29.5	59.3	11.2	2 973 040	429	1 282 406	4 086	53.4
Congressional District 3	252 795	25.2	40.6	32.5	8 461	27.4	66.8	5.8	2 284 878	270	626 223	4 432	47.7
Congressional District 4	329 024	38.8	41.4	19.6	39	82.1	17.9	0.0	1 108	28	114	14	48.7
Congressional District 5	307 100	41.2	41.9	16.7	38	71.1	28.9	0.0	2 554	67	73	5	65.8

X = Not applicable.
D = Suppressed to avoid disclosure.

Table A. 109th Congressional Districts, 2000—*Continued*

(Number, percent.)

STATE / Congressional district	Farm's principal operator is full owner, 2002 (percent)	Type of organization, 2002 (percent) Family or individual	Partnership	Corporation	Value of all agricultural products sold, 2002 Total ($1,000)	Percent of farms Less than $50,000	$50,000 to $249,999	$250,000 or more	Payments received from federal farm programs, 2002 Total payments ($1,000)	Farms receiving payments Number	Percent	Percent of farms receiving Less than $50,000	$50,000 to $249,999	$250,000 or more
	66	67	68	69	70	72	73	74	75	76	77	78	79	80
CALIFORNIA—*Continued*														
Congressional District 41	89.0	85.0	7.1	5.3	296 111	79.8	11.1	9.0	459	31	2.9	90.3	9.7	0.0
Congressional District 42	76.4	79.3	10.3	7.9	125 169	68.2	11.2	20.7	409	17	7.0	94.1	5.9	0.0
Congressional District 43	62.3	76.2	17.0	5.8	243 456	46.6	9.4	43.9	753	29	13.0	96.6	3.4	0.0
Congressional District 44	88.8	87.7	6.7	4.9	188 940	84.3	6.4	9.3	411	19	2.0	94.7	5.3	0.0
Congressional District 45	83.2	78.4	11.5	7.8	601 166	70.3	14.7	15.0	991	52	3.8	88.5	11.5	0.0
Congressional District 46	59.6	61.4	19.3	19.3	26 226	57.9	17.5	24.6	D	2	3.5	100.0	0.0	0.0
Congressional District 47	61.3	74.2	9.7	16.1	15 819	71.0	9.7	19.4	21	3	9.7	100.0	0.0	0.0
Congressional District 48	74.5	66.0	10.4	18.9	190 295	67.0	5.7	27.4	D	2	1.9	100.0	0.0	0.0
Congressional District 49	91.9	89.2	5.3	4.3	664 262	79.5	13.7	6.8	452	33	0.9	97.0	3.0	0.0
Congressional District 50	84.9	81.9	5.7	11.0	212 248	73.2	13.4	13.4	74	5	0.5	100.0	0.0	0.0
Congressional District 51	51.3	66.4	11.8	19.6	1 066 057	35.4	16.4	48.1	3 301	174	26.2	87.9	12.1	0.0
Congressional District 52	89.3	87.6	6.6	4.4	103 665	83.3	10.7	6.0	76	10	1.0	100.0	0.0	0.0
Congressional District 53	82.0	78.7	11.5	9.8	6 695	90.2	4.9	4.9	D	2	3.3	100.0	0.0	0.0
COLORADO	66.3	87.0	6.7	5.2	4 525 196	80.5	13.5	5.9	125 774	10 163	32.4	95.5	4.4	0.1
Congressional District 1	81.0	57.1	9.5	33.3	D	71.4	14.3	14.3	D	4	19.0	100.0	0.0	0.0
Congressional District 2	71.0	85.4	6.0	7.5	58 154	88.8	7.6	3.6	D	141	12.2	97.2	2.8	0.0
Congressional District 3	68.5	88.0	6.5	4.4	781 245	84.1	11.5	4.4	18 330	2 659	22.1	98.6	1.4	0.0
Congressional District 4	60.8	85.2	7.7	5.7	3 456 724	70.9	19.6	9.5	97 872	6 317	52.0	93.7	6.1	0.1
Congressional District 5	70.2	90.8	4.4	4.0	61 158	92.4	5.6	2.0	998	320	13.2	99.7	0.3	0.0
Congressional District 6	74.1	88.1	5.9	5.4	D	93.4	5.3	1.3	3 701	463	16.8	98.3	1.7	0.0
Congressional District 7	71.8	85.0	6.6	7.8	106 077	80.8	12.4	6.8	3 840	259	30.6	95.0	4.6	0.4
CONNECTICUT	68.9	82.0	8.1	8.1	470 637	85.0	9.1	5.8	3 681	254	6.1	92.9	7.1	0.0
Congressional District 1	65.1	81.7	7.3	9.8	79 971	82.9	9.8	7.3	305	20	3.5	95.0	5.0	0.0
Congressional District 2	71.2	85.1	7.2	6.3	267 705	85.5	8.7	5.9	2 208	147	7.3	93.2	6.8	0.0
Congressional District 3	69.7	71.5	14.7	9.8	20 755	85.3	8.7	5.9	324	19	4.9	89.5	10.5	0.0
Congressional District 4	73.6	71.6	11.4	12.9	24 218	82.1	10.0	8.0	4	3	1.5	100.0	0.0	0.0
Congressional District 5	65.2	82.0	7.4	8.9	77 988	85.9	9.7	4.5	840	65	6.4	92.3	7.7	0.0
DELAWARE	66.8	84.3	5.7	8.9	618 853	49.6	15.7	34.7	8 643	617	25.8	93.2	6.8	0.0
Congressional District (At Large)	66.8	84.3	5.7	8.9	618 853	49.6	15.7	34.7	8 643	617	25.8	93.2	6.8	0.0
DISTRICT OF COLUMBIA	X	X	X	X	X	X	X	X	X	X	X	X	X	X
Delegate District (At Large)	X	X	X	X	X	X	X	X	X	X	X	X	X	X
FLORIDA	83.0	84.2	5.5	9.2	6 242 272	82.8	10.4	6.8	21 818	2 554	5.8	96.7	3.0	0.3
Congressional District 1	83.4	95.9	2.6	1.2	98 006	90.9	6.0	3.1	6 933	809	25.0	96.3	3.2	0.5
Congressional District 2	80.8	90.2	5.7	3.5	376 327	87.2	6.3	6.5	6 744	741	19.2	97.0	2.4	0.5
Congressional District 3	83.8	84.6	5.5	8.6	177 597	79.8	11.0	9.2	156	28	2.2	100.0	0.0	0.0
Congressional District 4	86.7	91.7	5.1	2.9	160 033	89.5	5.5	5.0	1 346	317	12.1	99.1	0.9	0.0
Congressional District 5	80.7	89.7	3.9	5.7	272 377	89.8	7.2	3.0	1 512	138	2.7	94.9	5.1	0.0
Congressional District 6	84.1	90.1	4.0	5.1	247 344	91.9	4.9	3.1	1 326	199	3.9	98.0	2.0	0.0
Congressional District 7	80.8	84.8	5.5	9.2	161 400	81.3	9.2	9.5	102	16	1.5	93.8	6.3	0.0
Congressional District 8	88.2	82.7	4.3	12.3	138 264	85.9	9.4	4.7	134	22	1.6	100.0	0.0	0.0
Congressional District 9	80.5	87.6	3.3	8.2	199 927	85.0	8.9	6.1	115	22	1.2	95.5	4.5	0.0
Congressional District 10	88.5	79.5	2.6	16.7	7 007	88.5	7.7	3.8	18	4	5.1	100.0	0.0	0.0
Congressional District 11	82.1	76.9	9.0	13.8	72 008	82.4	10.7	6.9	26	3	1.0	100.0	0.0	0.0
Congressional District 12	85.6	76.6	8.6	11.3	422 102	72.4	20.4	7.3	531	42	1.1	97.6	2.4	0.0
Congressional District 13	82.3	78.7	9.2	10.8	632 290	75.9	15.6	8.5	409	38	1.1	94.7	5.3	0.0
Congressional District 14	77.8	78.6	6.4	13.3	201 688	82.5	9.6	7.9	D	16	2.2	100.0	0.0	0.0
Congressional District 15	80.9	80.8	6.5	11.8	218 552	75.7	14.9	9.4	304	27	2.0	96.3	3.7	0.0
Congressional District 16	81.5	77.1	6.3	15.7	1 093 314	74.5	14.7	10.8	884	58	1.7	89.7	10.3	0.0
Congressional District 17	80.0	20.0	0.0	80.0	649	20.0	60.0	20.0	D	D	D	D	D	D
Congressional District 18	84.2	77.2	2.8	19.0	88 195	76.8	12.7	10.5	D	9	1.8	88.9	11.1	0.0
Congressional District 19	80.8	51.0	9.2	39.1	163 438	67.4	11.5	21.1	D	4	1.5	100.0	0.0	0.0
Congressional District 20	79.3	67.9	2.2	28.0	25 943	83.4	10.3	6.3	163	8	3.0	100.0	0.0	0.0
Congressional District 21	80.4	73.9	10.9	15.2	3 950	78.3	15.2	6.5	D	D	D	D	D	D
Congressional District 22	84.9	67.6	4.6	27.2	31 439	79.9	12.0	8.0	D	D	D	D	D	D
Congressional District 23	80.4	64.1	10.6	23.1	622 969	62.2	19.3	18.5	838	20	2.4	70.0	30.0	0.0
Congressional District 24	86.8	83.1	4.0	12.2	155 873	81.6	11.2	7.2	44	16	1.2	100.0	0.0	0.0
Congressional District 25	86.1	73.8	5.7	19.6	671 577	72.4	13.2	14.4	84	17	0.9	100.0	0.0	0.0
GEORGIA	75.8	91.4	5.0	3.0	4 911 752	84.1	6.9	9.1	118 535	15 510	31.5	96.9	3.0	0.1
Congressional District 1	72.7	91.9	5.4	2.4	585 126	81.8	9.7	8.4	18 045	2 179	36.7	96.7	3.3	0.0
Congressional District 2	70.3	86.4	8.0	4.7	944 223	76.3	12.3	11.4	50 009	3 382	48.8	92.9	6.9	0.3
Congressional District 3	76.4	91.0	5.9	2.6	671 779	86.7	6.6	6.7	24 369	3 535	41.8	97.0	3.0	0.0
Congressional District 4	69.2	87.2	2.6	10.3	857	89.7	7.7	2.6	2	4	10.3	100.0	0.0	0.0
Congressional District 5	63.2	65.8	10.5	23.7	16	100.0	0.0	0.0	29	4	10.5	100.0	0.0	0.0

X = Not applicable.
D = Suppressed to avoid disclosure.

Table A. 109th Congressional Districts, 2000—*Continued*

(Number, percent.)

STATE Congressional district	Representative	Land area,[1] (sq km)	Total population	Persons per square kilometer	Race alone or in combination (percent)					Hispanic or Latino[2] (percent)	Non-Hispanic White (percent)	Two or more races (percent)
					White	Black	American Indian/Alaska Native	Asian and Pacific Islander	Other race			
1		2	3	4	5	6	7	8	9	10	11	12
GEORGIA—*Continued*												
Congressional District 6	Thomas Edmunds Price (R)	1 127	630 087	559.1	86.9	7.4	0.5	4.6	2.3	4.5	83.0	1.5
Congressional District 7	John Linder (R)	3 095	629 851	203.5	86.4	7.4	0.6	4.3	2.8	5.4	82.4	1.4
Congressional District 8	Lynn A. Westmoreland (R)	9 097	627 870	69.0	84.9	12.9	0.6	1.6	1.0	2.1	82.8	1.0
Congressional District 9	Charlie Norwood (R)	17 992	630 036	35.0	83.5	14.1	0.7	1.6	1.3	2.6	81.2	1.1
Congressional District 10	Nathan Deal (R)	9 690	628 794	64.9	90.8	3.6	0.7	1.0	5.1	9.4	85.4	1.2
Congressional District 11	Phil Gingrey (R)	9 585	630 176	65.7	66.0	29.1	0.7	1.7	4.2	7.2	61.7	1.6
Congressional District 12	John Jenkins Barrow (D)	13 530	630 405	46.6	54.1	43.2	0.6	2.0	1.6	2.9	51.9	1.3
Congressional District 13	David Scott (D)	2 014	630 565	313.1	48.4	42.0	0.8	5.8	5.3	10.2	42.1	2.1
HAWAII		16 635	1 211 537	72.8	39.3	2.8	2.1	81.3	3.9	7.2	22.9	21.4
Congressional District 1	Neil Abercrombie (D)	494	606 610	1 228.0	30.5	2.9	1.5	84.8	3.0	5.4	17.7	16.9
Congressional District 2	Ed Case (D)	16 140	604 927	37.5	48.2	2.6	2.6	78.0	4.9	9.0	28.0	26.0
IDAHO		214 314	1 293 953	6.0	92.8	0.6	2.1	1.5	5.0	7.9	88.0	2.0
Congressional District 1	C. L. "Butch" Otter (R)	102 369	648 922	6.3	93.5	0.5	2.2	1.6	4.4	6.8	89.0	2.0
Congressional District 2	Michael K. Simpson (R)	111 946	645 031	5.8	92.2	0.8	2.0	1.5	5.6	8.9	87.1	2.0
ILLINOIS		143 961	12 419 293	86.3	75.1	15.6	0.6	3.9	6.8	12.3	67.8	1.9
Congressional District 1	Bobby L. Rush (D)	253	654 203	2 585.8	30.4	66.2	0.5	1.8	2.6	4.8	27.3	1.4
Congressional District 2	Jesse L. Jackson Jr. (D)	478	654 078	1 368.4	30.9	63.4	0.7	0.9	6.1	10.4	25.6	1.8
Congressional District 3	Daniel Lipinski (D)	322	653 292	2 028.9	80.4	6.1	0.6	3.3	12.4	21.3	68.2	2.7
Congressional District 4	Luis V. Gutierrez (D)	101	653 654	6 471.8	50.4	4.9	1.1	2.4	46.0	74.5	18.4	4.5
Congressional District 5	Rahm Emanuel (D)	148	654 116	4 419.7	80.5	2.7	0.7	7.5	12.2	23.0	65.9	3.5
Congressional District 6	Henry J. Hyde (R)	553	654 549	1 183.6	84.0	3.1	0.5	8.8	5.7	12.5	75.3	2.0
Congressional District 7	Danny K. Davis (D)	146	653 521	4 476.2	30.9	62.8	0.5	4.3	3.3	5.8	27.3	1.5
Congressional District 8	Melissa Bean (D)	1 600	652 805	408.0	86.0	3.7	0.6	6.3	5.3	10.8	78.8	1.8
Congressional District 9	Janice D. Schakowsky (D)	195	653 117	3 349.3	71.0	11.7	0.7	13.6	6.5	11.5	62.5	3.3
Congressional District 10	Mark Steven Kirk (R)	646	654 062	1 012.5	82.7	5.8	0.4	6.6	6.3	12.3	75.2	1.7
Congressional District 11	Jerry Weller (R)	10 984	653 861	59.5	88.2	8.3	0.5	1.1	3.3	6.7	83.7	1.3
Congressional District 12	Jerry F. Costello (D)	11 460	653 456	57.0	81.7	16.8	0.7	1.2	0.9	1.8	79.7	1.2
Congressional District 13	Judy Biggert (R)	918	652 879	711.2	86.2	5.4	0.4	7.3	2.4	5.5	81.6	1.5
Congressional District 14	J. Dennis Hastert (R)	7 386	654 031	88.6	85.1	5.2	0.6	2.2	9.0	18.5	74.0	1.9
Congressional District 15	Timothy V. Johnson (R)	26 088	653 618	25.1	90.6	6.2	0.5	2.7	1.3	2.2	88.5	1.2
Congressional District 16	Donald A. Manzullo (R)	10 614	653 467	61.6	90.2	5.8	0.6	1.7	3.3	6.5	85.7	1.4
Congressional District 17	Lane Evans (D)	21 031	653 531	31.1	90.2	7.8	0.6	0.8	2.0	3.7	87.3	1.3
Congressional District 18	Ray LaHood (R)	21 202	653 426	30.8	91.8	6.9	0.5	1.1	0.8	1.5	90.0	1.0
Congressional District 19	John Shimkus (R)	29 833	653 627	21.9	95.3	3.8	0.6	0.7	0.5	1.1	94.0	0.8
INDIANA		92 895	6 080 485	65.5	88.6	8.8	0.6	1.3	2.0	3.5	85.8	1.2
Congressional District 1	Peter J. Visclosky (D)	5 722	675 541	118.1	76.4	18.8	0.7	1.1	4.8	10.0	69.8	1.7
Congressional District 2	Chris Chocola (R)	9 529	675 685	70.9	87.9	8.8	0.8	1.2	3.1	5.0	84.4	1.7
Congressional District 3	Mark E. Souder (R)	8 391	675 533	80.5	90.6	6.1	0.7	1.2	2.8	4.5	87.6	1.4
Congressional District 4	Steve Buyer (R)	10 403	675 272	64.9	95.7	1.6	0.6	1.8	1.4	2.6	93.6	0.9
Congressional District 5	Dan Burton (R)	8 459	675 753	79.9	95.0	2.9	0.6	1.7	0.8	1.6	93.2	1.0
Congressional District 6	Mike Pence (R)	14 375	675 819	47.0	94.9	4.1	0.5	0.7	0.7	1.3	93.4	0.9
Congressional District 7	Julia Carson (D)	677	675 804	998.2	66.2	30.5	0.7	1.7	2.7	4.4	63.0	1.8
Congressional District 8	John N. Hostettler (R)	18 238	675 693	37.0	95.0	4.1	0.6	0.8	0.5	0.9	93.7	0.9
Congressional District 9	Michael Sodrel (R)	17 101	675 385	39.5	95.7	2.6	0.6	1.2	0.9	1.5	94.0	1.0
IOWA		144 701	2 926 324	20.2	94.9	2.5	0.6	1.6	1.6	2.8	92.6	1.1
Congressional District 1	Jim Nussle (R)	18 691	585 302	31.3	94.2	4.3	0.5	1.1	1.1	2.0	92.1	1.2
Congressional District 2	James A. Leach (R)	19 595	585 241	29.9	94.9	2.5	0.6	1.9	1.5	2.7	92.4	1.2
Congressional District 3	Leonard L. Boswell (D)	18 076	585 305	32.4	92.7	3.7	0.8	2.3	2.0	3.2	90.1	1.3
Congressional District 4	Tom Latham (R)	40 818	585 305	14.3	96.5	1.0	0.4	1.4	1.5	2.5	94.7	0.8
Congressional District 5	Steve King (R)	47 520	585 171	12.3	96.3	0.9	0.8	1.1	1.9	3.6	93.7	0.9
KANSAS		211 900	2 688 418	12.7	87.9	6.3	1.8	2.2	4.0	7.0	83.1	2.1
Congressional District 1	Jerry Moran (R)	148 596	672 051	4.5	90.5	2.6	1.1	1.3	6.3	10.9	84.5	1.7
Congressional District 2	Jim Ryun (R)	36 606	672 302	18.4	90.9	5.7	2.2	1.4	2.0	3.8	87.3	2.1
Congressional District 3	Dennis Moore (D)	2 014	671 981	333.7	84.4	9.5	1.3	3.1	3.7	6.8	79.6	2.0
Congressional District 4	Todd Tiahrt (R)	24 684	672 084	27.2	85.8	7.6	2.4	3.0	4.0	6.6	81.0	2.6
KENTUCKY		102 896	4 041 769	39.3	91.0	7.7	0.6	1.0	0.8	1.5	89.3	1.1
Congressional District 1	Ed Whitfield (R)	30 259	673 723	22.3	91.4	7.7	0.6	0.6	0.8	1.5	89.7	1.0
Congressional District 2	Ron Lewis (R)	19 598	673 201	34.4	92.5	6.1	0.7	1.0	1.0	1.7	90.6	1.2
Congressional District 3	Anne M. Northup (R)	950	674 011	709.5	78.2	19.9	0.6	1.8	1.1	1.8	76.0	1.4
Congressional District 4	Geoffrey C. Davis (R)	14 707	673 619	45.8	96.5	2.5	0.5	0.7	0.6	1.1	95.1	0.8
Congressional District 5	Harold Rogers (R)	27 652	673 654	24.4	98.2	1.3	0.6	0.4	0.2	0.7	97.1	0.7
Congressional District 6	Ben Chandler (D)	9 729	673 561	69.2	89.4	8.8	0.6	1.5	1.1	2.1	87.1	1.2

[1]Dry land or land partially or temporarily covered by water.
[2]Hispanic or Latino persons may be of any race.

Table A. 109th Congressional Districts, 2000—Continued

(Number, percent.)

STATE Congressional district	Foreign born (percent)	Under 5 years	5 to 17 years	18 to 24 years	25 to 34 years	35 to 44 years	45 to 54 years	55 to 64 years	65 to 74 years	75 years and over	Percent female	Number	Persons per household	Female-family householder[3]	One-person households
					Age (percent)									Households Percent	
	13	14	15	16	17	18	19	20	21	22	23	24	25	26	27
GEORGIA—*Continued*															
Congressional District 6	9.6	7.3	20.3	6.8	14.8	19.7	16.3	8.0	3.9	2.9	50.6	229 908	2.73	7.6	19.3
Congressional District 7	8.7	8.4	21.0	7.2	16.0	20.0	14.2	7.1	3.6	2.4	50.0	213 686	2.92	8.6	14.8
Congressional District 8	3.2	6.9	20.4	8.3	13.8	17.4	14.8	9.0	5.5	3.9	50.8	225 113	2.75	10.1	17.9
Congressional District 9	3.1	6.8	19.0	8.8	13.7	15.8	13.8	9.9	6.9	5.3	50.9	235 853	2.62	11.3	21.4
Congressional District 10	7.8	7.5	18.8	9.0	15.3	16.3	13.3	9.2	6.2	4.3	50.0	228 012	2.72	10.1	19.7
Congressional District 11	7.9	7.3	18.8	10.2	16.5	16.0	12.2	8.1	6.0	5.0	50.9	233 574	2.62	15.7	24.5
Congressional District 12	3.7	6.7	18.6	15.8	14.3	14.3	11.9	7.6	5.6	5.0	51.7	235 441	2.55	18.3	26.9
Congressional District 13	13.9	8.1	20.3	10.5	18.5	16.8	12.1	6.7	3.9	3.0	50.9	221 871	2.80	18.2	22.6
HAWAII	17.5	6.5	18.0	9.5	14.1	15.8	14.1	8.8	7.0	6.2	49.8	403 240	2.92	12.4	21.9
Congressional District 1	22.9	5.8	15.9	9.2	15.0	15.9	13.9	9.2	7.8	7.3	50.1	209 875	2.80	11.9	24.7
Congressional District 2	12.2	7.1	20.0	9.8	13.3	15.7	14.4	8.5	6.2	5.2	49.4	193 365	3.04	12.9	18.7
IDAHO	5.0	7.5	21.0	10.7	13.1	14.9	13.2	8.3	5.9	5.4	49.9	469 645	2.69	8.7	22.4
Congressional District 1	4.3	7.4	20.7	9.3	13.0	15.3	13.8	8.9	6.1	5.5	49.9	237 250	2.67	8.6	21.2
Congressional District 2	5.6	7.7	21.2	12.1	13.2	14.5	12.5	7.8	5.6	5.4	49.8	232 395	2.71	8.8	23.6
ILLINOIS	12.3	7.1	19.1	9.8	14.6	16.0	13.1	8.4	6.2	5.9	51.0	4 591 779	2.63	12.3	26.8
Congressional District 1	5.1	7.4	21.0	9.9	13.4	14.8	12.3	8.5	6.9	5.8	53.8	233 410	2.75	26.3	28.4
Congressional District 2	6.4	7.6	21.8	9.0	13.1	15.0	12.7	9.1	6.5	5.1	53.5	228 212	2.84	24.2	24.8
Congressional District 3	19.0	7.1	18.6	8.9	14.1	15.5	12.9	8.4	7.1	7.4	51.5	236 988	2.73	12.6	26.5
Congressional District 4	40.6	9.7	22.1	13.2	20.2	14.1	9.2	5.3	3.4	2.7	48.3	192 910	3.37	15.7	21.1
Congressional District 5	29.3	6.1	13.7	10.6	22.0	15.8	12.2	7.8	5.8	6.0	50.7	266 778	2.42	9.5	34.8
Congressional District 6	18.8	7.2	18.9	8.8	15.4	17.4	13.7	8.3	5.5	4.9	50.4	232 594	2.77	8.5	22.9
Congressional District 7	7.9	7.3	19.5	10.8	17.5	15.4	12.2	7.8	5.4	4.3	52.7	250 404	2.50	22.6	37.2
Congressional District 8	13.8	7.8	20.4	7.7	15.4	18.6	14.1	7.9	4.5	3.6	50.2	234 791	2.77	8.8	21.9
Congressional District 9	30.6	5.8	14.8	9.7	16.0	15.8	13.5	8.9	7.4	8.1	51.4	268 439	2.35	9.7	35.8
Congressional District 10	18.4	7.1	20.0	8.3	11.9	16.5	14.8	9.1	6.6	5.7	50.5	229 497	2.75	7.9	22.3
Congressional District 11	4.2	7.1	19.7	10.7	13.3	16.2	12.9	8.2	6.0	5.9	50.7	236 451	2.66	10.3	23.8
Congressional District 12	1.8	6.3	18.8	10.3	13.0	15.5	12.9	8.7	7.4	7.1	51.3	255 607	2.47	13.7	28.1
Congressional District 13	11.1	7.7	20.6	7.4	14.3	18.5	14.7	7.9	4.6	4.3	50.7	230 971	2.78	7.6	21.0
Congressional District 14	12.7	8.1	20.6	10.6	14.5	16.6	13.1	7.5	4.7	4.3	49.8	220 852	2.88	9.2	20.4
Congressional District 15	3.5	6.1	17.4	13.5	12.8	14.8	12.9	8.6	7.0	7.0	50.8	257 370	2.41	8.9	28.5
Congressional District 16	5.6	7.3	20.3	7.6	13.3	17.0	13.7	8.8	6.3	5.8	50.6	244 763	2.64	9.6	23.4
Congressional District 17	2.1	6.1	17.9	10.4	12.0	14.6	13.4	9.4	7.9	8.3	51.4	260 837	2.40	11.2	29.3
Congressional District 18	2.0	6.2	18.1	8.9	12.6	15.4	14.2	9.5	7.5	7.5	51.2	257 277	2.44	9.8	27.5
Congressional District 19	1.1	6.0	18.3	8.8	12.4	15.9	13.6	9.6	7.7	7.6	50.4	253 628	2.47	9.0	26.1
INDIANA	3.1	7.0	18.9	10.1	13.7	15.8	13.4	8.7	6.5	5.9	51.0	2 336 306	2.53	11.1	25.9
Congressional District 1	4.6	7.0	19.6	9.4	12.7	15.7	14.0	9.0	6.8	5.9	51.6	252 318	2.64	14.5	24.8
Congressional District 2	4.2	7.1	19.1	9.9	13.4	15.3	13.4	8.6	6.8	6.5	50.7	256 547	2.54	11.4	26.3
Congressional District 3	3.7	7.7	20.5	9.3	13.8	15.6	13.4	8.2	6.0	5.5	50.4	252 897	2.63	10.0	24.6
Congressional District 4	3.3	6.9	18.9	11.6	13.8	16.0	13.3	8.5	5.8	5.2	50.3	252 434	2.57	8.6	22.9
Congressional District 5	2.6	7.2	19.6	7.9	13.7	17.2	14.2	8.8	6.1	5.3	51.0	258 353	2.56	8.3	23.5
Congressional District 6	1.2	6.6	18.6	9.9	12.7	15.0	13.5	9.7	7.4	6.7	51.1	262 404	2.50	10.0	25.3
Congressional District 7	4.7	7.6	18.2	10.6	16.8	16.2	12.1	7.4	5.8	5.3	51.7	277 370	2.37	16.8	33.0
Congressional District 8	1.2	6.3	18.1	10.4	12.5	15.6	13.6	9.3	7.3	7.0	50.9	263 004	2.46	10.0	26.9
Congressional District 9	2.1	6.4	17.8	12.0	13.6	15.6	13.5	9.0	6.5	5.6	50.7	260 979	2.49	9.9	25.4
IOWA	3.1	6.4	18.6	10.2	12.4	15.2	13.4	8.8	7.2	7.7	50.9	1 149 276	2.46	8.6	27.2
Congressional District 1	2.3	6.4	18.9	10.4	12.1	15.0	13.7	9.0	7.1	7.3	51.2	227 405	2.48	9.5	26.6
Congressional District 2	3.2	6.4	17.8	11.7	13.4	15.2	13.7	8.5	6.5	6.8	50.8	232 880	2.42	8.5	27.8
Congressional District 3	4.3	7.0	18.6	9.0	14.2	16.0	13.3	8.5	6.6	6.7	51.2	231 632	2.46	9.1	27.4
Congressional District 4	2.8	6.0	18.4	11.1	11.2	14.8	13.1	8.9	7.7	8.7	50.6	229 320	2.43	7.4	27.4
Congressional District 5	3.0	6.3	19.4	8.7	11.2	15.0	13.3	9.0	8.3	8.8	51.0	228 039	2.48	8.2	26.9
KANSAS	5.0	7.0	19.5	10.3	13.0	15.6	13.2	8.2	6.5	6.7	50.6	1 037 891	2.51	9.3	27.0
Congressional District 1	6.2	6.7	19.7	9.5	11.4	14.9	12.7	8.7	7.8	8.6	50.4	260 490	2.49	7.7	27.6
Congressional District 2	2.3	6.5	18.8	11.9	12.3	15.2	13.1	8.6	6.7	6.9	50.2	257 856	2.49	9.2	26.7
Congressional District 3	6.5	7.4	19.2	10.5	15.0	16.6	13.7	7.5	5.2	4.9	51.1	258 439	2.54	10.3	26.1
Congressional District 4	5.0	7.4	20.3	9.1	13.1	15.9	13.2	8.0	6.5	6.5	50.7	261 106	2.52	10.1	27.6
KENTUCKY	2.0	6.6	18.0	9.9	14.1	15.9	13.8	9.2	6.8	5.7	51.1	1 590 647	2.47	11.8	26.0
Congressional District 1	1.2	6.5	17.6	9.8	13.2	14.8	13.4	10.1	7.7	7.0	51.1	267 254	2.44	10.7	26.0
Congressional District 2	2.1	6.8	18.9	10.1	13.7	16.2	13.5	9.2	6.5	5.1	50.7	255 503	2.56	11.0	23.3
Congressional District 3	3.5	6.7	17.5	8.9	14.1	16.3	14.2	8.7	7.3	6.5	52.3	280 037	2.36	14.7	30.8
Congressional District 4	1.4	6.9	19.1	8.8	14.2	16.7	13.9	9.0	6.4	5.2	50.7	257 362	2.56	10.9	24.2
Congressional District 5	0.6	6.2	18.4	9.7	13.7	15.5	14.2	9.8	6.9	5.5	50.9	262 131	2.50	12.0	24.2
Congressional District 6	3.2	6.4	16.7	12.4	15.5	15.9	13.6	8.5	5.9	5.1	51.2	268 360	2.41	11.4	27.2

[3]No spouse present.

Table A. 109th Congressional Districts, 2000—*Continued*

(Number, percent.)

STATE Congressional district	Group quarters				Education				Money income, 1999			Percent below poverty level, 1999	
	Persons in correctional institutions	Persons in nursing homes	Persons in college dormitories	Persons in military quarters	School enrollment[4]		Attainment level[5]		Per capita income[6]	Households		Persons	Families
					Public	Private	H.S. graduate or more	Bachelor's degree or more		Median income	Percent with income over $100,000		
	28	29	30	31	32	33	34	35	36	37	38	39	40
GEORGIA—*Continued*													
Congressional District 6	34	1 063	0	0	137 490	38 019	93.9	50.7	35 781	75 611	33.9	3.7	2.4
Congressional District 7	2 167	900	356	0	147 768	24 878	86.8	31.9	25 773	63 455	21.9	4.5	3.2
Congressional District 8	4 105	1 473	3 727	0	144 846	26 082	83.0	23.4	23 202	52 406	15.0	6.3	4.6
Congressional District 9	3 361	2 586	2 954	1 084	136 231	21 106	75.4	18.5	19 475	39 987	9.0	11.2	8.6
Congressional District 10	3 271	2 393	956	0	132 916	15 143	71.4	15.9	19 331	42 037	9.4	10.3	7.5
Congressional District 11	7 428	3 903	2 026	159	141 697	20 461	72.6	16.9	17 953	37 582	7.1	13.8	10.7
Congressional District 12	6 328	2 226	11 704	4 657	180 710	21 582	74.9	19.3	16 295	31 108	6.2	21.7	15.9
Congressional District 13	2 435	2 729	543	817	151 680	20 768	77.8	19.4	18 590	43 429	8.7	11.2	8.8
HAWAII	3 233	2 949	4 716	13 992	255 215	65 627	84.6	26.2	21 525	49 820	16.6	10.7	7.6
Congressional District 1	2 302	1 799	2 984	5 063	118 992	36 574	84.1	28.9	23 028	50 798	18.0	9.7	6.6
Congressional District 2	931	1 150	1 732	8 929	136 223	29 053	85.1	23.1	20 018	48 686	15.0	11.7	8.7
IDAHO	7 401	5 735	8 006	673	323 683	44 896	84.7	21.7	17 841	37 572	7.3	11.8	8.3
Congressional District 1	4 341	3 233	4 716	0	154 730	21 377	84.3	20.3	17 861	38 364	7.2	11.0	7.9
Congressional District 2	3 060	2 502	3 290	673	168 953	23 519	85.2	23.1	17 820	36 934	7.5	12.6	8.7
ILLINOIS	67 820	91 887	90 463	10 865	2 787 463	663 141	81.4	26.1	23 104	46 590	14.4	10.7	7.8
Congressional District 1	0	3 128	4 853	0	158 357	42 717	77.5	18.7	17 352	37 222	9.0	19.7	15.9
Congressional District 2	81	3 092	911	0	165 960	35 717	79.3	18.1	18 280	41 330	9.7	15.2	12.3
Congressional District 3	0	3 828	327	0	120 554	48 674	77.3	20.5	21 785	48 048	13.5	8.3	6.4
Congressional District 4	0	831	308	0	161 776	29 064	51.7	13.6	13 833	35 935	7.3	20.2	17.8
Congressional District 5	0	3 551	2 893	0	96 279	56 358	79.3	33.9	26 689	48 531	15.8	8.5	6.2
Congressional District 6	718	4 828	3 481	0	139 389	38 691	86.7	34.6	27 669	62 640	22.6	4.3	3.0
Congressional District 7	11 587	3 450	5 910	0	152 579	41 131	76.1	32.1	25 329	40 361	16.6	24.0	20.5
Congressional District 8	307	2 385	151	0	150 233	31 203	88.0	32.1	28 215	62 762	22.5	4.4	3.2
Congressional District 9	35	8 800	7 395	0	113 374	58 798	84.0	39.6	26 344	46 531	16.2	11.0	7.7
Congressional District 10	846	4 643	2 076	10 432	142 666	37 846	88.7	47.5	38 722	71 663	34.6	4.8	3.1
Congressional District 11	3 972	5 718	11 025	0	158 151	29 070	84.0	18.5	20 906	47 800	11.7	8.4	5.7
Congressional District 12	7 433	6 193	5 284	427	161 424	21 885	79.5	16.8	17 821	35 198	6.4	15.0	11.4
Congressional District 13	2 691	4 007	2 336	0	148 844	40 767	91.9	42.4	32 321	71 686	30.1	2.9	1.9
Congressional District 14	3 274	4 110	7 676	0	164 054	29 395	82.1	26.3	23 406	56 314	17.8	7.0	4.6
Congressional District 15	6 999	6 814	16 496	0	180 828	16 300	84.8	23.2	19 524	38 583	8.1	11.7	6.6
Congressional District 16	1 104	4 659	443	0	147 034	29 443	84.2	21.1	22 606	48 960	13.0	7.3	5.2
Congressional District 17	5 788	8 296	10 275	0	144 964	24 426	81.3	14.7	17 894	35 066	5.5	12.5	9.0
Congressional District 18	9 157	6 874	4 950	6	134 871	31 038	84.5	20.7	20 936	41 934	8.9	8.9	6.2
Congressional District 19	13 828	6 680	3 673	0	146 126	20 618	81.5	17.1	19 356	38 955	7.5	9.1	6.6
INDIANA	34 676	48 745	69 147	7	1 337 569	265 985	82.1	19.4	20 397	41 567	9.2	9.5	6.7
Congressional District 1	1 124	4 161	3 285	0	152 617	29 589	82.3	17.1	20 374	44 087	9.8	10.5	8.1
Congressional District 2	6 561	4 992	8 879	4	139 474	37 119	80.3	17.2	19 231	40 381	7.8	9.5	6.9
Congressional District 3	1 952	5 022	1 980	0	141 191	35 029	82.1	18.4	20 606	44 013	9.2	7.8	5.5
Congressional District 4	3 643	6 127	14 022	0	168 145	22 506	85.6	22.1	21 198	45 947	10.9	8.0	4.9
Congressional District 5	2 248	4 907	5 001	0	140 332	35 883	88.4	30.6	26 186	52 800	16.9	5.2	3.5
Congressional District 6	4 086	5 861	6 997	0	150 726	21 088	80.6	14.7	19 160	39 002	7.3	9.7	6.7
Congressional District 7	4 361	4 955	3 634	0	135 407	35 907	78.5	21.2	19 559	36 522	7.2	13.5	10.6
Congressional District 8	8 089	7 194	11 492	3	147 802	26 962	81.3	15.9	18 467	36 732	6.6	10.7	7.7
Congressional District 9	2 612	5 526	13 857	0	161 875	21 902	80.1	17.3	18 796	39 011	7.1	10.5	6.7
IOWA	11 771	33 428	41 171	4	669 809	122 248	86.1	21.2	19 674	39 469	7.3	9.1	6.0
Congressional District 1	2 158	5 532	8 724	1	132 760	31 341	85.6	20.0	19 236	38 727	6.9	10.1	6.9
Congressional District 2	3 579	5 256	9 314	3	143 323	22 092	87.5	25.0	20 515	40 121	8.1	9.9	6.0
Congressional District 3	2 260	5 534	5 113	0	123 395	26 479	87.2	24.6	21 777	43 176	9.4	8.0	5.4
Congressional District 4	2 182	9 081	12 969	0	144 643	18 617	86.7	20.4	18 869	38 242	6.4	8.9	5.5
Congressional District 5	1 592	8 025	5 051	0	125 688	23 719	83.6	16.1	17 976	36 773	5.6	8.9	6.3
KANSAS	16 703	25 248	24 492	4 580	654 604	102 356	86.0	25.8	20 506	40 624	9.3	9.9	6.7
Congressional District 1	4 964	9 184	5 934	0	163 192	15 858	82.3	18.0	17 255	34 869	5.2	11.0	7.8
Congressional District 2	7 674	6 723	8 500	4 067	171 476	22 213	86.9	23.2	18 595	37 855	6.7	11.2	7.1
Congressional District 3	544	4 101	7 978	0	161 511	34 170	89.9	39.1	26 133	51 118	17.1	7.8	4.9
Congressional District 4	3 521	5 240	2 080	513	158 425	30 115	85.0	23.0	20 041	40 917	8.1	9.6	7.0
KENTUCKY	28 388	29 266	31 883	7 277	859 020	148 432	74.1	17.1	18 093	33 672	7.2	15.8	12.7
Congressional District 1	4 931	6 788	2 980	4 648	142 717	14 871	71.3	11.8	16 269	30 360	4.7	16.5	12.7
Congressional District 2	4 027	4 667	5 123	2 629	148 745	21 348	75.5	13.9	17 413	35 724	6.0	13.3	10.3
Congressional District 3	1 169	5 182	2 592	0	127 624	42 579	82.1	25.3	22 514	39 468	10.9	12.4	9.5
Congressional District 4	6 191	4 284	1 326	0	138 117	30 323	77.4	17.5	19 722	40 150	9.3	11.4	9.1
Congressional District 5	6 288	4 609	4 446	0	147 377	11 893	59.2	9.6	12 513	21 915	3.0	28.1	24.0
Congressional District 6	5 776	3 736	15 416	0	154 440	27 418	79.1	24.6	20 124	37 544	8.9	13.2	9.6

[4]All persons 3 years old and over enrolled in nursery school through college.
[5]Persons 25 years old and over.
[6]Based on the population enumerated as of April 1, 2000.

Table A. 109th Congressional Districts, 2000—*Continued*

(Number, percent.)

STATE Congressional district	Housing units									Civilian labor force		
	Total	Total occupied units	Owner occupied		Median owner costs as a percent of income		Renter occupied		Sub-standard housing units (percent)[9]	Total	Unemployment	
			Percent	Median value[7] (dollars)	With a mortgage	Without a mortgage[8]	Median rent (dollars)	Median rent as a percent of income			Total	Rate[10]
	41	42	43	44	45	46	47	48	49	50	51	52
GEORGIA—*Continued*												
Congressional District 6	238 911	229 887	79.2	185 100	20.1	9.9	903	24.3	2.1	347 255	9 336	2.7
Congressional District 7	221 709	213 675	85.0	143 600	20.7	9.9	775	24.0	3.2	338 850	9 092	2.7
Congressional District 8	238 114	224 673	80.6	120 300	20.6	9.9	631	23.4	2.7	321 890	11 332	3.5
Congressional District 9	271 087	235 801	77.0	103 200	21.2	9.9	497	23.4	3.6	305 969	12 747	4.1
Congressional District 10	249 452	227 841	76.3	108 200	20.5	9.9	523	22.8	5.3	316 568	10 830	3.4
Congressional District 11	250 821	233 726	64.1	89 300	20.9	9.9	600	24.7	6.1	309 823	18 005	5.8
Congressional District 12	260 150	235 515	58.3	80 900	21.3	10.2	508	28.2	5.7	291 280	25 441	8.4
Congressional District 13	233 970	222 171	59.3	99 800	21.7	9.9	720	24.9	8.4	322 811	17 367	5.4
HAWAII	460 542	403 240	56.5	272 700	26.3	9.9	779	27.2	16.1	573 795	35 886	6.3
Congressional District 1	232 123	209 847	53.1	328 900	26.3	9.9	787	27.3	16.2	291 195	16 765	5.4
Congressional District 2	228 419	193 393	60.2	227 600	26.3	9.9	768	26.9	16.1	282 600	19 121	6.3
IDAHO	527 824	469 645	72.4	106 300	21.5	9.9	515	25.3	5.4	636 237	36 784	5.8
Congressional District 1	268 105	237 288	75.7	113 500	22.2	9.9	524	25.9	4.9	317 934	19 640	6.2
Congressional District 2	259 719	232 357	69.0	97 700	20.6	9.9	507	24.8	5.9	318 303	17 144	5.3
ILLINOIS	4 885 615	4 591 779	67.3	130 800	21.7	11.1	605	24.4	5.3	6 208 597	375 412	6.0
Congressional District 1	255 239	233 426	54.4	118 900	23.3	12.1	570	27.2	7.1	288 919	37 143	12.8
Congressional District 2	243 842	228 365	66.2	96 700	22.8	11.6	598	27.1	6.7	296 330	30 819	10.4
Congressional District 3	246 359	236 791	72.6	145 600	23.0	12.2	632	23.4	6.3	314 037	17 796	5.7
Congressional District 4	209 122	193 008	39.2	124 000	25.4	13.0	576	24.2	21.5	278 214	25 883	9.3
Congressional District 5	276 961	266 664	49.8	173 800	24.0	13.0	705	23.0	7.2	367 505	17 490	4.8
Congressional District 6	238 588	232 718	75.8	181 700	22.7	11.7	817	23.8	5.4	357 017	13 009	3.6
Congressional District 7	280 068	250 442	41.9	144 900	23.1	12.1	640	26.2	8.3	303 554	37 018	12.2
Congressional District 8	244 381	234 592	77.6	170 400	23.2	11.6	830	24.5	4.1	355 245	12 152	3.4
Congressional District 9	279 286	268 430	54.7	222 100	23.8	11.8	693	26.2	8.2	339 586	18 159	5.3
Congressional District 10	237 268	229 591	78.7	268 100	22.3	11.6	805	24.5	4.5	326 047	12 254	3.6
Congressional District 11	250 441	236 533	74.6	117 600	21.5	11.0	534	23.2	2.8	334 528	19 130	5.7
Congressional District 12	278 744	255 599	69.4	67 300	19.4	11.0	451	25.3	2.8	306 474	21 439	6.9
Congressional District 13	239 908	230 918	80.7	203 000	22.2	10.8	840	23.6	2.2	347 465	11 102	3.2
Congressional District 14	230 015	220 953	74.8	150 000	22.8	11.5	651	24.3	5.8	338 820	15 807	4.7
Congressional District 15	277 086	257 248	68.8	79 200	18.9	9.9	488	25.0	2.3	336 264	16 825	5.0
Congressional District 16	261 363	244 751	75.5	112 900	21.5	11.3	522	23.1	2.8	338 929	16 732	4.9
Congressional District 17	284 459	260 924	71.0	66 100	18.6	10.4	423	23.5	2.1	324 396	22 143	6.8
Congressional District 18	276 707	257 236	73.6	85 000	19.0	9.9	472	22.1	1.7	330 607	15 282	4.6
Congressional District 19	275 778	253 590	78.1	76 100	19.2	10.4	434	22.2	1.8	324 660	15 229	4.7
INDIANA	2 532 319	2 336 306	71.4	94 300	19.3	9.9	521	23.9	2.7	3 117 897	152 723	4.9
Congressional District 1	269 564	252 348	71.0	102 800	19.8	10.6	558	24.3	3.9	329 270	21 566	6.5
Congressional District 2	279 059	256 650	72.8	85 700	19.0	9.9	510	23.3	3.2	339 374	16 950	5.0
Congressional District 3	278 774	252 847	75.0	93 600	18.7	9.9	505	22.1	2.9	355 352	13 987	3.9
Congressional District 4	268 781	252 284	73.5	112 600	19.6	9.9	557	24.7	2.3	357 594	14 987	4.2
Congressional District 5	275 191	258 319	76.0	122 000	19.1	9.9	592	22.5	1.4	359 982	11 796	3.3
Congressional District 6	280 989	262 371	74.3	83 200	18.8	9.9	459	23.5	2.1	338 364	17 603	5.2
Congressional District 7	307 853	277 502	55.8	87 600	20.4	9.9	549	24.6	4.0	350 697	22 003	6.3
Congressional District 8	288 683	263 037	73.9	77 900	18.8	9.9	435	23.8	2.2	336 951	18 758	5.6
Congressional District 9	283 425	260 948	71.7	92 600	19.4	9.9	507	25.1	2.4	350 313	15 073	4.3
IOWA	1 232 511	1 149 276	72.3	82 500	19.1	9.9	470	23.2	2.3	1 554 722	64 906	4.2
Congressional District 1	241 991	227 405	72.6	82 500	18.9	9.9	447	23.5	2.1	306 491	14 426	4.7
Congressional District 2	248 194	232 880	70.8	89 500	19.2	9.9	488	24.4	2.3	317 969	13 139	4.1
Congressional District 3	245 617	231 632	71.5	93 100	19.7	10.5	535	23.4	2.9	319 004	13 902	4.4
Congressional District 4	247 124	229 320	73.3	75 200	18.8	9.9	437	22.7	1.8	308 531	12 018	3.9
Congressional District 5	249 585	228 039	73.6	71 900	18.9	10.1	427	21.9	2.6	302 727	11 421	3.8
KANSAS	1 131 200	1 037 891	69.2	83 500	19.3	9.9	498	23.4	3.4	1 374 698	58 415	4.2
Congressional District 1	292 411	260 475	71.4	63 100	19.0	9.9	413	22.1	4.0	336 551	13 804	4.1
Congressional District 2	280 217	257 846	69.0	74 900	19.0	10.0	472	24.2	2.7	337 216	14 531	4.2
Congressional District 3	272 728	258 464	67.7	131 600	19.7	9.9	624	24.0	3.2	364 189	13 988	3.8
Congressional District 4	285 844	261 106	68.9	76 800	19.2	9.9	489	23.0	3.7	336 742	16 092	4.7
KENTUCKY	1 750 927	1 590 647	70.8	86 700	19.6	9.9	445	24.0	2.9	1 907 614	109 350	5.7
Congressional District 1	302 464	267 297	74.0	66 900	19.2	9.9	387	23.6	2.8	305 242	19 375	6.1
Congressional District 2	282 795	255 468	73.5	85 900	19.5	9.9	432	23.0	3.0	327 050	17 267	5.2
Congressional District 3	298 505	280 034	64.7	104 500	19.7	9.9	492	23.9	2.6	343 087	17 366	5.1
Congressional District 4	280 795	257 417	73.4	96 100	19.6	9.9	477	23.5	2.5	331 098	15 536	4.7
Congressional District 5	297 355	262 110	76.3	58 300	21.3	9.9	331	26.4	4.0	247 286	22 129	8.9
Congressional District 6	289 013	268 321	63.2	97 200	19.2	9.9	487	24.3	2.6	353 851	17 677	5.0

[7]Specified owner-occupied units.
[8]Median monthly owner costs is often in the minimum category—9.9 percent or less, which is indicated as 9.9 percent.
[9]Overcrowded or lacking complete plumbing facilities.
[10]Percent of civilian labor force.

Table A. 109th Congressional Districts, 2000—*Continued*

(Number, percent.)

STATE Congressional district	Civilian employment and occupations				Total farms, 2002	Farms by size, 2002 (percent)			Land in farms, 2002		Cropland harvested, 2002		Farm's principal operator's primary occupation is farming, 2002 (percent)
	Total	Management, professional, and related (percent)	Service, sales, and office (percent)	Construction and production (percent)		1 to 49 acres	50 to 999 acres	1,000 acres or more	Acreage	Average size of farms (acres)	Acreage	Farms	
	53	54	55	56	57	58	59	60	61	62	63	64	65
GEORGIA—*Continued*													
Congressional District 6	337 919	50.1	38.6	11.2	443	78.3	21.7	0.0	25 429	57	2 426	129	47.9
Congressional District 7	329 758	39.5	39.7	20.6	1 211	64.3	35.0	0.7	89 612	74	15 089	430	51.1
Congressional District 8	310 558	33.1	39.1	27.5	3 700	45.4	52.1	2.5	521 089	141	67 443	1 540	47.3
Congressional District 9	293 222	28.6	37.6	32.8	10 034	46.3	52.6	1.1	1 197 699	119	200 314	4 364	54.5
Congressional District 10	305 738	25.9	36.6	36.9	5 150	53.0	46.4	0.5	478 437	93	94 218	2 088	50.4
Congressional District 11	291 818	26.1	40.1	33.4	3 537	38.8	59.4	1.8	544 987	154	76 620	1 555	49.3
Congressional District 12	265 839	28.6	42.7	28.0	3 081	27.5	65.0	7.5	1 043 618	339	324 975	1 693	48.9
Congressional District 13	305 444	26.6	43.6	29.6	749	58.6	40.7	0.7	83 327	111	14 500	353	44.5
HAWAII	537 909	32.2	49.0	17.5	5 398	88.0	10.0	2.0	1 300 499	241	109 461	4 522	57.9
Congressional District 1	274 430	34.0	49.8	15.7	208	91.3	8.2	0.5	7 200	35	1 479	183	65.9
Congressional District 2	263 479	30.4	48.2	19.3	5 190	87.8	10.1	2.0	1 293 299	249	107 982	4 339	57.6
IDAHO	599 453	31.4	40.9	25.0	25 017	49.2	40.2	10.5	11 767 294	470	4 313 288	13 444	55.4
Congressional District 1	298 294	30.5	41.1	26.2	11 260	54.1	37.9	8.0	4 242 845	377	1 316 384	5 852	53.6
Congressional District 2	301 159	32.3	40.7	23.8	13 757	45.2	42.2	12.6	7 524 449	547	2 996 904	7 592	56.9
ILLINOIS	5 833 185	34.2	41.5	24.0	73 027	26.9	62.6	10.5	27 310 833	374	22 562 904	56 083	64.1
Congressional District 1	251 776	30.3	48.1	21.6	0	X	X	X	X	X	X	X	X
Congressional District 2	265 511	29.6	46.6	23.8	211	60.7	37.9	1.4	23 836	113	14 969	131	52.6
Congressional District 3	296 241	28.6	43.7	27.6	0	X	X	X	X	X	X	X	X
Congressional District 4	252 331	19.7	40.8	39.2	0	X	X	X	X	X	X	X	X
Congressional District 5	350 015	38.2	40.3	21.5	0	X	X	X	X	X	X	X	X
Congressional District 6	344 008	38.2	41.5	20.2	24	70.8	25.0	4.2	2 956	123	2 135	16	50.0
Congressional District 7	266 536	42.2	42.2	15.5	0	X	X	X	X	X	X	X	X
Congressional District 8	343 093	37.8	40.3	21.8	531	61.0	35.0	4.0	92 926	175	79 598	418	51.8
Congressional District 9	321 427	42.6	41.2	16.1	0	X	X	X	X	X	X	X	X
Congressional District 10	313 793	47.3	38.2	14.4	57	59.6	36.8	3.5	7 390	130	5 202	40	47.4
Congressional District 11	315 398	28.4	41.8	29.4	5 022	22.6	65.1	12.3	2 158 549	430	1 982 699	4 432	71.3
Congressional District 12	285 035	28.4	44.9	26.2	5 847	29.9	62.8	7.3	1 707 050	292	1 222 253	3 961	55.4
Congressional District 13	336 363	45.6	38.5	15.8	148	44.6	52.0	3.4	31 388	212	27 756	117	54.7
Congressional District 14	323 013	32.5	40.3	26.8	3 518	26.3	62.5	11.2	1 435 883	408	1 313 971	3 011	73.7
Congressional District 15	319 439	33.0	39.9	26.3	11 576	23.8	61.6	14.6	5 336 908	461	4 870 852	9 687	70.1
Congressional District 16	322 197	31.0	38.7	29.7	6 592	31.5	61.0	7.5	2 069 669	314	1 675 417	4 970	65.7
Congressional District 17	302 253	26.4	43.0	29.9	10 613	24.0	65.3	10.7	4 059 056	382	3 124 950	8 249	65.4
Congressional District 18	315 325	32.6	41.9	24.7	10 105	23.9	63.8	12.3	4 157 816	411	3 354 613	7 943	65.3
Congressional District 19	309 431	30.5	40.5	28.2	18 783	29.3	62.1	8.6	6 227 406	332	4 888 489	13 108	58.1
INDIANA	2 965 174	28.7	39.5	31.4	60 296	39.9	53.8	6.3	15 058 670	250	11 937 370	44 298	55.7
Congressional District 1	307 704	26.8	41.8	31.2	2 336	37.2	48.9	13.9	963 515	412	872 298	1 795	61.4
Congressional District 2	322 424	26.6	38.3	34.7	5 909	40.4	52.0	7.6	1 677 432	284	1 431 767	4 434	58.1
Congressional District 3	341 365	27.3	36.4	35.9	8 831	43.9	52.8	3.3	1 467 409	166	1 100 249	6 001	53.7
Congressional District 4	342 607	31.1	38.8	29.6	6 110	44.5	46.8	8.7	1 818 133	298	1 511 653	4 320	54.8
Congressional District 5	348 186	37.0	38.2	24.4	5 694	42.3	50.3	7.5	1 593 566	280	1 413 496	4 301	58.0
Congressional District 6	320 761	25.7	38.9	35.0	10 845	38.6	55.0	6.4	2 823 497	260	2 367 982	8 429	58.5
Congressional District 7	328 694	29.5	44.2	26.2	149	80.5	18.1	1.3	9 716	65	6 697	94	42.3
Congressional District 8	318 193	26.6	40.9	31.9	8 994	36.8	54.6	8.6	2 686 375	299	2 074 435	6 703	54.7
Congressional District 9	335 240	26.9	38.1	34.4	11 428	36.4	60.7	2.9	2 019 027	177	1 158 793	8 221	52.7
IOWA	1 489 816	31.3	40.7	27.0	90 655	23.3	68.4	8.3	31 729 490	350	23 994 343	67 338	68.3
Congressional District 1	292 065	29.7	41.1	28.3	14 046	23.6	71.3	5.1	3 983 519	284	2 992 347	10 367	68.6
Congressional District 2	304 830	32.8	39.9	26.5	13 904	24.1	70.2	5.6	3 980 560	286	2 525 744	9 836	61.6
Congressional District 3	305 102	33.4	42.5	23.5	11 642	23.9	68.8	7.3	3 889 325	334	2 714 384	8 299	65.8
Congressional District 4	296 513	32.0	39.2	27.2	24 501	25.7	64.4	10.0	9 100 488	371	7 581 558	18 513	69.6
Congressional District 5	291 306	28.3	40.5	29.5	26 562	20.1	69.5	10.3	10 775 598	406	8 180 310	20 323	71.6
KANSAS	1 316 283	33.9	40.3	24.9	64 414	17.4	61.4	21.2	47 227 944	733	18 976 719	44 073	63.1
Congressional District 1	322 747	29.4	39.5	28.5	34 746	12.6	58.3	29.1	33 928 632	976	12 966 721	23 013	67.3
Congressional District 2	322 685	32.3	40.9	26.1	19 459	22.8	67.3	10.0	7 472 712	384	3 460 293	13 860	58.1
Congressional District 3	350 201	41.5	41.0	17.3	1 041	47.6	47.6	4.7	217 874	209	105 627	692	48.2
Congressional District 4	320 650	31.5	39.7	28.3	9 168	20.7	62.5	16.8	5 608 726	612	2 444 078	6 508	59.6
KENTUCKY	1 798 264	28.7	39.7	30.7	86 541	34.8	63.3	2.0	13 843 706	160	4 978 994	65 815	54.2
Congressional District 1	285 867	24.2	37.0	37.3	24 157	32.2	63.9	3.8	5 020 379	208	2 389 031	16 784	54.7
Congressional District 2	309 783	25.2	38.5	35.2	23 291	36.9	61.7	1.4	3 338 827	143	1 265 735	18 006	54.9
Congressional District 3	325 721	33.4	42.8	23.7	490	63.9	35.9	0.2	38 251	78	11 626	296	49.4
Congressional District 4	315 562	29.1	40.6	29.6	15 394	30.7	68.3	1.1	2 243 996	146	546 534	12 612	53.2
Congressional District 5	225 157	24.5	39.1	35.3	10 761	35.5	63.8	0.8	1 383 891	129	273 979	8 874	52.2
Congressional District 6	336 174	33.4	39.7	25.8	12 448	39.1	59.3	1.6	1 818 362	146	492 089	9 243	55.4

X = Not applicable.

Table A. 109th Congressional Districts, 2000—*Continued*

(Number, percent.)

STATE Congressional district	Farm's principal operator is full owner, 2002 (percent)	Type of organization, 2002 (percent) Family or individual	Partnership	Corporation	Value of all agricultural products sold, 2002 Total ($1,000)	Percent of farms Less than $50,000	$50,000 to $249,999	$250,000 or more	Payments received from federal farm programs, 2002 Total payments ($1,000)	Farms receiving payments Number	Percent	Percent of farms receiving Less than $50,000	$50,000 to $249,999	$250,000 or more
	66	67	68	69	70	72	73	74	75	76	77	78	79	80
GEORGIA—*Continued*														
Congressional District 6	86.9	88.3	6.3	4.7	16 697	93.5	3.6	2.9	62	67	15.1	100.0	0.0	0.0
Congressional District 7	78.7	91.3	3.7	4.2	87 424	88.3	2.6	9.1	367	213	17.6	100.0	0.0	0.0
Congressional District 8	79.3	92.9	3.4	3.3	145 135	94.4	2.4	3.2	2 253	720	19.5	99.6	0.4	0.0
Congressional District 9	77.8	93.0	3.6	2.8	1 330 465	80.5	5.8	13.7	7 362	2 455	24.5	99.8	0.2	0.0
Congressional District 10	78.0	93.6	3.6	2.4	697 426	82.4	5.6	12.0	2 229	837	16.3	99.9	0.1	0.0
Congressional District 11	77.7	94.0	3.5	1.8	208 400	91.3	3.4	5.3	1 678	637	18.0	99.7	0.3	0.0
Congressional District 12	73.4	89.9	6.1	3.1	206 660	86.1	8.0	5.8	11 844	1 351	43.8	96.4	3.4	0.1
Congressional District 13	78.4	88.9	5.6	4.5	17 544	94.5	3.3	2.1	285	126	16.8	99.2	0.8	0.0
HAWAII	59.3	D	D	D	533 423	85.2	10.4	4.4	886	113	2.1	98.2	1.8	0.0
Congressional District 1	45.7	81.3	3.4	13.0	21 128	80.8	10.1	9.1	D	3	1.4	100.0	0.0	0.0
Congressional District 2	59.9	85.9	4.2	8.6	512 294	85.4	10.4	4.2	D	110	2.1	98.2	1.8	0.0
IDAHO	71.3	88.1	6.2	4.9	3 908 262	79.0	12.2	8.8	93 934	7 098	28.4	94.7	5.1	0.2
Congressional District 1	72.9	90.6	4.9	3.7	896 919	84.7	9.3	6.0	22 450	2 435	21.6	97.1	2.9	0.0
Congressional District 2	70.1	86.1	7.2	5.8	3 011 342	74.3	14.6	11.2	71 484	4 663	33.9	93.4	6.3	0.3
ILLINOIS	54.2	88.3	7.3	3.5	7 676 239	62.3	26.0	11.7	412 636	47 857	65.5	97.9	2.0	0.0
Congressional District 1	X	X	X	X	X	X	X	X	X	X	X	X	X	X
Congressional District 2	73.9	81.5	6.6	10.0	21 283	78.2	13.7	8.1	263	60	28.4	100.0	0.0	0.0
Congressional District 3	X	X	X	X	X	X	X	X	X	X	X	X	X	X
Congressional District 4	X	X	X	X	X	X	X	X	X	X	X	X	X	X
Congressional District 5	X	X	X	X	X	X	X	X	X	X	X	X	X	X
Congressional District 6	66.7	37.5	16.7	37.5	4 991	58.3	16.7	25.0	51	4	16.7	100.0	0.0	0.0
Congressional District 7	X	X	X	X	X	X	X	X	X	X	X	X	X	X
Congressional District 8	63.8	79.3	6.8	11.9	39 358	73.6	19.0	7.3	1 316	139	26.2	97.1	2.9	0.0
Congressional District 9	X	X	X	X	X	X	X	X	X	X	X	X	X	X
Congressional District 10	71.9	66.7	0.0	28.1	8 749	75.4	17.5	7.0	132	12	21.1	100.0	0.0	0.0
Congressional District 11	40.2	87.5	7.9	3.7	674 408	49.9	35.2	14.9	34 079	3 364	67.0	97.7	2.3	0.0
Congressional District 12	63.9	89.4	7.2	2.5	287 086	80.0	14.8	5.2	22 438	3 407	58.3	98.2	1.8	0.0
Congressional District 13	55.4	82.4	5.4	10.1	16 707	75.7	17.6	6.8	418	52	35.1	100.0	0.0	0.0
Congressional District 14	44.1	86.8	8.0	4.5	589 287	47.3	35.4	17.3	24 703	2 232	63.4	97.2	2.8	0.0
Congressional District 15	45.2	88.5	6.9	3.7	1 533 084	51.4	32.5	16.1	80 689	8 142	70.3	97.3	2.6	0.0
Congressional District 16	56.6	88.4	7.0	3.6	771 054	60.2	27.4	12.5	41 434	4 054	61.5	97.2	2.8	0.0
Congressional District 17	57.1	88.4	7.3	3.5	1 133 509	62.1	25.6	12.2	59 894	6 861	64.6	98.0	2.0	0.0
Congressional District 18	53.0	86.7	8.4	4.1	1 222 379	58.6	27.0	14.4	58 813	6 749	66.8	98.4	1.6	0.0
Congressional District 19	59.8	89.5	6.7	2.8	1 374 345	71.9	20.8	7.3	88 404	12 781	68.0	98.4	1.6	0.0
INDIANA	64.8	89.3	5.7	4.4	4 783 158	74.6	17.6	7.8	224 701	26 841	44.5	97.5	2.4	0.0
Congressional District 1	51.8	86.3	6.0	6.8	392 965	56.5	27.0	16.6	14 393	1 289	55.2	97.1	2.9	0.0
Congressional District 2	59.8	88.7	5.7	5.1	562 141	69.4	20.8	9.8	28 134	3 043	51.5	97.1	2.9	0.0
Congressional District 3	72.0	90.6	5.5	3.4	567 371	76.7	17.6	5.7	24 283	3 712	42.0	98.4	1.6	0.0
Congressional District 4	63.2	88.0	5.8	5.4	597 015	73.0	16.8	10.2	28 439	2 469	40.4	95.7	4.2	0.1
Congressional District 5	58.3	86.7	6.0	6.8	547 120	68.8	21.4	9.9	27 365	2 769	48.6	96.4	3.6	0.0
Congressional District 6	61.7	88.9	6.2	4.5	859 457	71.5	21.0	7.5	43 180	5 350	49.3	97.9	2.1	0.0
Congressional District 7	76.5	77.9	6.7	13.4	29 117	69.1	20.8	10.1	93	22	14.8	100.0	0.0	0.0
Congressional District 8	64.3	88.7	6.4	4.4	716 990	74.0	16.9	9.1	36 797	3 840	42.7	97.0	3.0	0.1
Congressional District 9	71.9	92.4	4.9	2.3	510 981	86.8	9.7	3.6	22 018	4 347	38.0	99.0	1.0	0.0
IOWA	55.0	86.8	6.4	5.8	12 273 634	56.8	29.4	13.8	538 896	63 074	69.6	98.6	1.4	0.0
Congressional District 1	56.8	87.4	7.0	5.0	1 642 021	55.3	31.8	12.9	84 588	9 759	69.5	99.0	1.0	0.0
Congressional District 2	64.3	87.1	5.9	5.8	1 092 379	69.4	22.6	8.0	77 593	9 388	67.5	98.5	1.5	0.0
Congressional District 3	59.2	86.4	6.4	6.0	1 245 663	62.3	26.3	11.4	70 023	8 091	69.5	98.6	1.3	0.0
Congressional District 4	52.1	86.4	6.4	6.2	3 813 075	53.4	30.7	16.0	146 304	17 439	71.2	98.5	1.5	0.0
Congressional District 5	50.1	87.0	6.3	5.9	4 480 496	51.9	31.8	16.3	160 387	18 397	69.3	98.5	1.5	0.0
KANSAS	57.3	88.9	6.3	3.5	8 746 244	73.1	19.9	7.0	328 244	39 191	60.8	98.1	1.9	0.0
Congressional District 1	53.4	86.3	7.3	4.6	7 176 335	66.6	24.1	9.3	251 017	25 088	72.2	97.4	2.5	0.0
Congressional District 2	63.6	92.2	5.0	2.0	887 080	82.7	13.6	3.7	48 070	9 274	47.7	99.4	0.6	0.0
Congressional District 3	72.8	89.8	4.5	3.9	39 596	89.0	8.5	2.5	1 462	279	26.8	98.2	1.8	0.0
Congressional District 4	57.3	91.4	5.6	2.2	643 234	75.9	18.5	5.6	27 694	4 550	49.6	99.2	0.8	0.0
KENTUCKY	76.8	91.6	6.7	1.3	3 080 080	90.1	7.4	2.5	94 053	22 825	26.4	98.9	1.1	0.0
Congressional District 1	74.8	91.8	6.7	1.0	1 289 939	86.6	8.6	4.7	57 210	9 826	40.7	98.1	1.9	0.0
Congressional District 2	79.0	92.0	6.5	1.1	600 353	90.8	7.0	2.2	23 064	6 403	27.5	99.3	0.7	0.0
Congressional District 3	81.0	90.8	4.1	4.5	12 039	90.8	6.3	2.9	79	30	6.1	100.0	0.0	0.0
Congressional District 4	76.9	91.6	6.6	1.3	278 945	93.1	6.0	0.8	5 682	2 740	17.8	99.7	0.3	0.0
Congressional District 5	74.9	94.3	4.7	0.6	153 909	95.7	3.8	0.5	2 543	1 600	14.9	99.9	0.1	0.0
Congressional District 6	78.0	88.4	8.6	2.5	744 895	86.6	10.6	2.9	5 475	2 226	17.9	99.9	0.1	0.0

X = Not applicable.
D = Suppressed to avoid disclosure.

Table A. 109th Congressional Districts, 2000—*Continued*

(Number, percent.)

STATE Congressional district	Representative	Land area,[1] (sq km)	Total population	Persons per square kilo- meter	Race alone or in combination (percent)					Hispanic or Latino[2] (percent)	Non- Hispanic White (percent)	Two or more races (percent)
					White	Black	American Indian/Alaska Native	Asian and Pacific Islander	Other race			
1	2	3	4	5	6	7	8	9	10	11	12
LOUISIANA		112 825	4 468 976	39.6	64.8	32.9	1.0	1.5	1.1	2.4	62.5	1.1
Congressional District 1	Bobby Jindal (R)	6 221	637 543	102.5	83.8	13.2	0.7	1.9	1.8	4.7	79.6	1.3
Congressional District 2	William J. Jefferson (D)	689	639 048	927.5	31.2	64.8	0.7	3.0	1.8	3.8	28.3	1.4
Congressional District 3	Charles Melacon (D)	18 157	638 674	35.2	71.9	25.0	2.1	1.3	1.0	2.1	69.7	1.1
Congressional District 4	Jim McCrery (R)	27 881	638 366	22.9	64.0	33.9	1.4	1.1	1.0	2.0	62.0	1.3
Congressional District 5	Rodney Alexander (D)	35 677	638 726	17.9	64.7	34.1	0.7	0.7	0.5	1.3	63.4	0.7
Congressional District 6	Richard H. Baker (R)	7 966	638 209	80.1	64.4	33.6	0.5	1.7	0.7	1.6	62.7	0.8
Congressional District 7	Charles Boustany (R)	16 234	638 410	39.3	73.5	25.3	0.6	0.9	0.6	1.4	72.0	0.8
MAINE		79 931	1 274 923	16.0	97.9	0.7	1.0	1.0	0.4	0.7	96.5	1.0
Congressional District 1	Thomas H. Allen (D)	9 156	637 450	69.6	97.7	0.9	0.7	1.3	0.4	0.8	96.3	1.0
Congressional District 2	Michael H. Michaud (D)	70 775	637 473	9.0	98.0	0.6	1.4	0.7	0.4	0.7	96.7	1.0
MARYLAND		25 314	5 296 486	209.2	65.4	28.8	0.7	4.6	2.5	4.3	62.1	2.0
Congressional District 1	Wayne T. Gilchrest (R)	9 461	663 097	70.1	86.4	11.6	0.6	1.7	0.8	1.6	84.7	1.1
Congressional District 2	C. A. Dutch Ruppersberger (D)	919	661 945	720.3	68.6	28.2	0.8	3.0	1.3	2.2	66.3	1.8
Congressional District 3	Benjamin L. Cardin (D)	758	661 068	872.1	78.7	17.1	0.7	3.8	1.7	2.9	75.7	1.8
Congressional District 4	Albert Russell Wynn (D)	816	661 651	810.8	31.9	58.8	0.9	6.5	5.0	7.5	27.6	2.7
Congressional District 5	Steny H. Hoyer (D)	3 896	662 203	170.0	63.5	31.4	1.0	4.4	2.0	3.5	60.4	2.2
Congressional District 6	Roscoe G. Bartlett (R)	7 931	661 559	83.4	93.3	5.3	0.5	1.4	0.7	1.4	91.5	1.0
Congressional District 7	Elijah E. Cummings (D)	762	662 615	869.6	35.9	60.0	0.7	4.1	1.0	1.7	34.2	1.5
Congressional District 8	Chris Van Hollen (D)	769	662 348	861.3	65.1	18.0	0.8	12.1	7.8	13.7	56.1	3.6
MASSACHUSETTS		20 306	6 349 097	312.7	86.2	6.3	0.6	4.3	5.1	6.8	81.9	2.3
Congressional District 1	John W. Olver (D)	8 032	634 484	79.0	92.8	2.4	0.7	2.1	3.8	6.3	88.8	1.7
Congressional District 2	Richard E. Neal (D)	2 387	634 444	265.8	87.1	6.6	0.6	1.8	6.0	9.2	82.5	1.9
Congressional District 3	James P. McGovern (D)	1 505	634 466	421.6	90.6	3.4	0.6	3.7	3.8	6.0	86.2	2.0
Congressional District 4	Barney Frank (D)	1 895	634 697	334.9	91.1	3.0	0.6	3.7	3.9	3.3	87.9	2.2
Congressional District 5	Martin T. Meehan (D)	1 465	635 223	433.6	85.4	2.9	0.5	5.9	7.6	11.6	79.7	2.3
Congressional District 6	John F. Tierney (D)	1 244	636 554	511.7	92.6	2.7	0.4	3.0	2.9	4.4	89.8	1.5
Congressional District 7	Edward J. Markey (D)	441	634 381	1 438.5	87.9	4.2	0.4	6.4	3.6	4.8	83.5	2.3
Congressional District 8	Michael E. Capuano (D)	105	635 185	6 049.4	57.7	25.5	0.9	9.2	11.9	15.9	48.9	4.9
Congressional District 9	Stephen F. Lynch (D)	811	633 846	781.6	82.7	10.0	0.6	4.2	5.4	4.6	79.3	2.8
Congressional District 10	William D. Delahunt (D)	2 420	635 813	262.7	94.2	2.1	0.7	3.1	1.5	1.3	92.2	1.4
MICHIGAN		147 121	9 938 444	67.6	81.8	14.8	1.3	2.2	2.0	3.3	78.6	1.9
Congressional District 1	Bart Stupak (D)	64 458	662 583	10.3	95.8	1.2	3.6	0.6	0.4	0.9	93.8	1.5
Congressional District 2	Peter Hoekstra (R)	13 895	663 003	47.7	91.2	5.0	1.3	1.3	2.8	5.2	87.5	1.6
Congressional District 3	Vernon J. Ehlers (R)	4 803	662 354	137.9	86.5	8.9	1.1	2.0	3.7	6.2	82.2	2.0
Congressional District 4	Dave Camp (R)	19 299	662 497	34.3	95.4	2.4	1.5	1.0	1.1	2.4	92.8	1.3
Congressional District 5	Dale E. Kildee (D)	4 543	662 584	145.8	78.5	19.5	1.4	0.9	1.9	3.6	75.0	2.1
Congressional District 6	Fred Upton (R)	8 628	662 305	76.8	87.6	9.7	1.3	1.4	2.1	3.6	84.3	1.9
Congressional District 7	Joe Schwarz (R)	11 125	662 535	59.6	91.6	6.3	1.1	1.1	1.7	3.2	88.5	1.7
Congressional District 8	Mike Rogers (R)	5 837	662 349	113.5	91.2	5.6	1.1	2.3	1.8	3.5	87.7	1.9
Congressional District 9	Joe Knollenberg (R)	806	662 892	822.4	84.7	8.6	0.7	6.2	1.8	3.0	81.4	1.8
Congressional District 10	Candice S. Miller (R)	9 193	662 510	72.1	96.2	1.8	0.8	1.5	1.1	2.1	93.6	1.4
Congressional District 11	Thaddeus G. McCotter (R)	1 032	662 505	642.0	92.3	4.0	0.8	3.5	0.9	2.0	89.5	1.5
Congressional District 12	Sander M. Levin (D)	415	662 559	1 596.5	84.6	12.7	1.0	2.9	1.2	1.5	81.7	2.2
Congressional District 13	Carolyn C. Kilpatrick (D)	280	662 844	2 367.3	33.5	61.8	1.0	1.6	4.6	7.2	28.9	2.3
Congressional District 14	John Conyers Jr. (D)	318	662 468	2 083.2	35.9	62.3	0.9	1.8	2.7	1.8	32.1	3.5
Congressional District 15	John D. Dingell (D)	2 490	662 456	266.0	82.8	12.6	1.1	4.3	1.6	2.8	79.2	2.3
MINNESOTA		206 189	4 919 479	23.9	90.8	4.1	1.6	3.4	1.8	2.9	88.2	1.7
Congressional District 1	Gil Gutknecht (R)	34 503	614 952	17.8	95.3	1.3	0.5	2.1	1.8	3.0	93.2	1.0
Congressional District 2	John Kline (R)	7 861	615 117	78.2	94.4	2.1	0.8	2.8	1.4	2.6	91.8	1.4
Congressional District 3	Jim Ramstad (R)	1 211	614 979	507.8	90.8	4.5	0.7	4.6	1.1	1.8	88.6	1.6
Congressional District 4	Betty McCollum (D)	523	614 911	1 175.7	81.9	7.8	1.4	8.6	3.3	5.2	77.7	2.7
Congressional District 5	Martin Olav Sabo (D)	321	614 874	1 915.5	75.9	14.8	2.5	6.1	4.4	6.0	71.2	3.6
Congressional District 6	Mark R. Kennedy (R)	7 979	614 793	77.1	96.7	1.3	0.8	1.8	0.6	1.3	94.9	1.1
Congressional District 7	Collin C. Peterson (D)	82 353	615 129	7.5	95.2	0.5	3.1	0.8	1.5	2.6	93.1	1.0
Congressional District 8	James L. Oberstar (D)	71 439	614 724	8.6	96.1	0.8	3.3	0.7	0.3	0.8	94.6	1.1
MISSISSIPPI		121 488	2 844 658	23.4	61.9	36.6	0.7	0.9	0.7	1.4	60.7	0.7
Congressional District 1	Roger F. Wicker (R)	29 559	711 113	24.1	72.4	26.5	0.4	0.6	0.7	1.4	71.3	0.6
Congressional District 2	Bennie G. Thompson (D)	35 288	710 996	20.1	35.3	63.9	0.4	0.6	0.5	1.2	34.5	0.6
Congressional District 3	Charles W. "Chip" Pickering (R)	34 106	711 409	20.9	64.7	33.5	1.2	0.8	0.5	1.2	63.7	0.6
Congressional District 4	Gene Taylor (D)	22 535	711 140	31.6	75.3	22.6	0.8	1.6	0.9	1.8	73.5	1.0
MISSOURI		178 414	5 595 211	31.4	86.1	11.7	1.1	1.5	1.2	2.1	83.8	1.5
Congressional District 1	Wm. Lacy Clay (D)	562	621 497	1 105.9	47.5	50.7	0.6	1.9	0.8	1.3	45.8	1.4
Congressional District 2	W. Todd Akin (R)	3 232	621 422	192.3	95.1	2.5	0.5	2.4	0.6	1.4	93.2	1.0
Congressional District 3	Russ Carnahan (D)	3 230	622 148	192.6	88.0	9.7	0.7	2.1	1.1	1.8	85.7	1.5
Congressional District 4	Ike Skelton (D)	37 669	621 882	16.5	94.7	3.6	1.3	1.0	1.1	1.9	92.4	1.5
Congressional District 5	Emanuel Cleaver (D)	1 325	621 496	469.1	70.7	25.3	1.3	1.9	3.3	5.6	66.3	2.3

[1] Dry land or land partially or temporarily covered by water.
[2] Hispanic or Latino persons may be of any race.

Table A. 109th Congressional Districts, 2000—*Continued*

(Number, percent.)

STATE Congressional district	Foreign born (percent)	Age (percent) Under 5 years	5 to 17 years	18 to 24 years	25 to 34 years	35 to 44 years	45 to 54 years	55 to 64 years	65 to 74 years	75 years and over	Percent female	Households Number	Persons per household	Percent Female-family householder[3]	One-person households
	13	14	15	16	17	18	19	20	21	22	23	24	25	26	27
LOUISIANA	2.6	7.1	20.2	10.6	13.5	15.5	13.1	8.5	6.3	5.2	51.6	1 656 053	2.62	16.6	25.3
Congressional District 1	4.7	6.5	18.4	8.8	13.4	16.4	14.7	9.1	6.8	5.9	51.6	251 124	2.50	12.1	27.0
Congressional District 2	4.8	7.3	21.0	11.2	14.3	15.1	13.0	7.9	5.6	4.7	52.9	235 765	2.63	25.1	29.0
Congressional District 3	1.8	7.3	21.5	9.7	13.3	16.2	12.9	8.4	6.1	4.6	51.3	223 828	2.81	15.3	20.2
Congressional District 4	1.6	7.2	20.0	10.4	13.2	14.7	12.7	8.9	6.9	6.0	51.5	241 334	2.56	16.6	26.3
Congressional District 5	1.0	7.0	20.1	11.2	12.7	14.6	12.5	8.8	7.0	6.1	51.5	233 462	2.59	17.0	25.4
Congressional District 6	2.8	7.1	19.7	12.6	14.3	15.7	13.3	7.9	5.3	4.3	51.0	232 972	2.62	15.6	24.5
Congressional District 7	1.5	7.4	20.7	10.3	13.1	15.8	12.7	8.3	6.5	5.1	51.5	237 568	2.63	14.8	24.4
MAINE	2.9	5.5	18.1	8.1	12.4	16.7	15.1	9.7	7.5	6.8	51.3	518 200	2.39	9.5	27.0
Congressional District 1	3.0	5.7	18.2	7.4	12.8	17.3	15.3	9.4	7.2	6.7	51.4	258 917	2.41	9.4	27.0
Congressional District 2	2.7	5.4	18.0	8.9	11.9	16.1	14.9	9.9	7.9	7.0	51.3	259 283	2.38	9.5	27.0
MARYLAND	9.8	6.7	18.9	8.5	14.1	17.3	14.3	8.9	6.1	5.2	51.7	1 980 859	2.61	14.1	25.0
Congressional District 1	3.2	6.0	19.1	7.5	11.5	17.0	15.1	10.4	7.5	5.9	51.1	248 464	2.60	10.4	21.6
Congressional District 2	5.4	6.9	18.8	8.9	14.8	16.9	13.3	8.2	6.4	5.9	52.5	260 345	2.51	16.2	27.1
Congressional District 3	8.1	6.4	16.6	9.1	16.0	16.8	13.9	8.7	6.4	6.2	51.4	262 561	2.42	11.9	29.1
Congressional District 4	15.6	7.6	20.8	8.4	15.5	17.7	14.4	8.3	4.3	2.9	52.6	236 346	2.78	19.9	22.7
Congressional District 5	8.3	6.8	19.5	9.5	14.3	18.2	14.2	8.8	5.0	3.7	51.0	234 254	2.75	12.5	20.9
Congressional District 6	2.6	6.5	19.5	7.7	12.8	17.8	14.6	9.1	6.4	5.7	50.3	240 846	2.65	9.2	21.7
Congressional District 7	5.9	6.5	19.6	9.8	13.4	16.7	13.7	8.6	6.3	5.4	52.7	247 804	2.56	22.5	29.8
Congressional District 8	29.2	6.7	17.7	7.2	14.8	17.2	14.9	9.1	6.2	6.3	52.0	250 239	2.61	10.6	26.5
MASSACHUSETTS	12.2	6.3	17.4	9.1	14.6	16.7	13.8	8.6	6.7	6.8	51.8	2 443 580	2.51	11.9	28.0
Congressional District 1	5.5	5.8	18.4	10.5	12.1	16.3	14.5	8.5	6.8	7.2	51.5	245 033	2.47	11.5	27.8
Congressional District 2	6.1	6.5	19.1	8.6	13.1	16.7	13.8	8.4	6.6	7.1	52.2	242 706	2.53	13.6	26.8
Congressional District 3	10.8	6.9	18.6	8.3	14.0	17.5	13.6	8.2	6.4	6.6	51.5	240 487	2.56	11.4	26.3
Congressional District 4	12.9	6.3	17.7	8.8	13.8	16.6	14.3	8.9	6.6	7.1	52.4	241 809	2.53	11.2	26.5
Congressional District 5	13.0	7.3	20.0	7.6	13.8	18.0	13.9	8.4	5.7	5.4	51.0	227 369	2.72	12.5	23.1
Congressional District 6	8.9	6.5	17.7	6.9	12.6	17.7	15.0	9.3	7.3	7.1	51.9	243 310	2.55	10.5	26.4
Congressional District 7	16.6	5.9	14.7	8.2	16.4	16.8	13.6	8.9	7.7	7.9	52.4	255 231	2.41	10.3	29.9
Congressional District 8	28.1	5.1	13.3	18.7	22.7	14.2	10.2	6.5	4.8	4.5	51.4	254 393	2.31	15.3	36.9
Congressional District 9	13.4	6.4	17.4	7.9	14.8	16.9	13.7	8.8	7.0	7.2	51.9	238 795	2.57	12.7	27.6
Congressional District 10	6.5	5.9	16.8	6.0	12.6	16.8	14.9	10.1	8.6	8.2	52.0	254 447	2.45	9.7	27.9
MICHIGAN	5.3	6.8	19.4	9.4	13.7	16.1	13.8	8.7	6.5	5.8	51.0	3 785 661	2.56	12.5	26.2
Congressional District 1	1.4	5.4	17.7	8.4	10.8	15.3	14.3	11.1	9.1	7.9	49.6	266 138	2.39	8.5	27.4
Congressional District 2	3.2	7.0	20.6	9.6	12.7	15.9	13.2	8.6	6.5	5.9	50.4	241 996	2.66	9.8	22.7
Congressional District 3	5.8	7.6	20.5	10.2	14.7	16.3	12.9	7.3	5.4	5.1	50.4	243 190	2.65	11.1	24.9
Congressional District 4	2.0	6.0	18.6	11.1	11.9	15.4	13.7	9.8	7.3	6.3	50.6	252 123	2.52	9.2	24.1
Congressional District 5	1.9	7.1	20.2	8.8	13.3	15.8	13.7	8.8	6.7	5.6	51.9	257 344	2.54	16.1	26.7
Congressional District 6	3.8	6.6	19.3	10.7	12.7	15.5	13.8	8.9	6.6	5.9	51.1	253 972	2.53	11.3	25.5
Congressional District 7	2.1	6.5	19.6	8.5	12.8	16.3	14.7	9.2	6.6	5.9	50.3	248 443	2.56	10.8	24.4
Congressional District 8	4.2	6.9	19.5	11.8	13.5	17.0	14.4	8.1	4.8	4.0	50.6	245 198	2.62	9.6	23.4
Congressional District 9	11.7	6.6	17.9	7.0	14.5	17.1	15.3	9.3	6.4	6.0	51.1	263 960	2.47	8.7	28.1
Congressional District 10	5.5	6.8	19.8	7.9	13.5	17.3	14.4	9.2	6.0	5.1	50.2	244 586	2.67	8.7	22.0
Congressional District 11	6.7	7.0	18.5	7.4	14.8	18.2	14.3	8.3	6.2	5.4	51.0	257 798	2.54	9.4	25.8
Congressional District 12	9.8	6.1	16.6	7.9	15.4	16.1	13.3	8.9	7.8	7.8	51.9	274 665	2.39	12.2	31.4
Congressional District 13	5.9	7.8	22.2	9.4	14.9	15.0	12.3	6.9	5.8	5.7	51.9	239 672	2.70	26.5	31.1
Congressional District 14	7.9	7.5	21.5	9.0	14.6	14.5	12.7	8.0	6.5	5.8	52.9	243 508	2.69	25.1	28.4
Congressional District 15	7.2	6.7	17.9	12.9	15.5	15.7	13.5	7.9	5.5	4.5	50.8	253 067	2.52	11.9	26.9
MINNESOTA	5.3	6.7	19.5	9.6	13.7	16.8	13.5	8.2	6.0	6.1	50.5	1 895 127	2.52	8.9	26.9
Congressional District 1	3.8	6.2	19.3	10.4	11.8	15.5	13.1	8.6	7.1	8.0	50.6	237 884	2.49	7.4	26.8
Congressional District 2	4.2	7.9	21.9	8.1	14.6	19.2	13.4	7.3	4.2	3.4	50.1	217 579	2.77	8.2	19.5
Congressional District 3	6.8	6.8	19.8	7.3	13.6	18.3	15.4	8.7	5.6	4.6	51.1	237 636	2.56	8.5	24.2
Congressional District 4	9.5	6.9	18.9	10.8	14.7	16.1	13.3	7.7	5.7	6.0	51.8	242 053	2.46	11.7	31.1
Congressional District 5	12.2	6.4	15.1	12.2	19.2	16.0	12.4	7.0	5.3	6.4	50.5	263 538	2.25	11.4	37.6
Congressional District 6	2.4	7.6	21.6	9.7	14.2	18.4	13.4	7.3	4.2	3.5	49.4	214 096	2.80	7.9	18.8
Congressional District 7	2.0	6.1	20.0	9.3	10.6	14.9	13.0	9.3	7.9	8.9	50.3	238 482	2.49	7.3	27.2
Congressional District 8	1.5	5.7	19.1	8.6	10.8	15.7	14.3	10.1	8.1	7.7	50.1	243 859	2.45	8.5	27.1
MISSISSIPPI	1.4	7.2	20.1	10.9	13.4	15.0	12.7	8.6	6.5	5.5	51.7	1 046 434	2.63	17.3	24.6
Congressional District 1	1.2	7.1	19.6	10.4	13.7	15.0	12.7	9.1	6.7	5.7	51.7	267 660	2.59	14.7	23.9
Congressional District 2	0.9	7.6	21.8	11.8	13.0	14.4	12.2	7.7	5.9	5.5	52.4	245 889	2.76	24.9	25.1
Congressional District 3	1.4	7.0	19.4	10.6	13.4	15.0	13.1	8.7	6.9	6.0	51.9	268 942	2.56	15.6	25.6
Congressional District 4	2.2	7.1	19.5	10.9	13.6	15.4	12.9	9.0	6.7	5.0	50.9	263 943	2.61	14.6	23.9
MISSOURI	2.7	6.6	18.9	9.6	13.2	15.9	13.3	9.1	7.0	6.5	51.4	2 194 594	2.48	11.6	27.3
Congressional District 1	3.2	6.5	19.9	9.5	13.4	15.4	12.8	8.5	7.2	6.6	53.5	249 047	2.44	20.9	32.0
Congressional District 2	3.5	7.0	20.3	7.4	12.5	17.7	14.8	9.0	6.2	5.2	51.2	230 645	2.65	8.2	21.7
Congressional District 3	4.5	6.5	18.2	9.3	14.7	16.8	13.3	8.1	6.4	6.6	51.7	251 971	2.42	11.8	31.1
Congressional District 4	1.8	6.5	19.0	9.6	12.4	15.3	12.9	10.0	7.8	6.7	50.1	238 395	2.50	8.8	24.8
Congressional District 5	4.5	7.0	18.6	9.1	14.8	16.2	12.9	8.4	6.7	6.3	51.9	254 600	2.39	15.0	32.0

[3]No spouse present.

Table A. 109th Congressional Districts, 2000—*Continued*

(Number, percent.)

STATE Congressional district	Group quarters: Persons in correctional institutions	Persons in nursing homes	Persons in college dormitories	Persons in military quarters	Education: School enrollment[4] Public	Private	Attainment level[5] H.S. graduate or more	Bachelor's degree or more	Money income, 1999 Per capita income[6]	Households Median income	Percent with income over $100,000	Percent below poverty level, 1999 Persons	Families
	28	29	30	31	32	33	34	35	36	37	38	39	40
LOUISIANA	49 854	31 521	26 959	3 877	1 030 634	240 665	74.8	18.7	16 912	32 566	7.4	19.6	15.8
Congressional District 1	3 084	3 563	1 363	0	114 676	55 156	82.4	27.4	22 255	40 948	12.2	12.1	9.1
Congressional District 2	6 160	3 214	4 726	284	149 580	48 961	72.1	19.4	15 183	27 514	5.9	26.8	22.8
Congressional District 3	3 168	3 435	744	30	145 546	32 082	68.9	10.8	15 336	34 463	5.8	18.6	15.6
Congressional District 4	6 708	5 441	2 714	3 563	157 460	16 642	76.5	16.7	16 284	31 085	6.2	20.0	16.0
Congressional District 5	15 020	7 007	6 863	0	157 398	20 261	70.5	15.5	14 462	27 453	5.3	23.6	18.7
Congressional District 6	11 998	3 924	7 713	0	155 796	39 126	80.3	24.1	18 650	37 931	9.7	16.6	12.5
Congressional District 7	3 716	4 937	2 836	0	150 178	28 437	72.3	16.6	16 228	31 453	6.7	19.9	16.2
MAINE	2 864	9 339	13 793	688	275 158	45 883	85.4	22.9	19 533	37 240	7.1	10.9	7.8
Congressional District 1	1 957	3 934	3 880	547	133 788	25 250	88.1	27.9	21 939	42 044	9.4	8.6	6.0
Congressional District 2	907	5 405	9 913	141	141 370	20 633	82.6	17.7	17 126	32 600	4.8	13.3	9.5
MARYLAND	35 698	26 716	35 371	7 412	1 174 026	301 458	83.8	31.4	25 614	52 868	18.1	8.5	6.1
Congressional District 1	4 635	3 870	3 929	263	142 945	32 374	84.2	27.3	25 197	51 918	17.0	7.3	5.2
Congressional District 2	1 179	2 908	772	1 570	146 111	31 482	79.8	20.3	21 211	44 309	9.6	9.8	7.5
Congressional District 3	7 924	3 034	6 918	3 427	126 399	49 346	84.1	36.5	27 694	52 906	18.2	7.7	5.2
Congressional District 4	1 283	1 196	19	892	163 739	38 080	86.3	32.7	25 134	57 727	20.2	7.3	5.5
Congressional District 5	846	3 012	10 469	612	160 274	39 963	87.7	28.7	25 744	62 661	21.0	5.6	3.4
Congressional District 6	11 658	4 591	4 333	254	145 541	27 553	83.8	23.7	23 014	50 957	14.7	6.7	4.6
Congressional District 7	7 523	3 934	8 590	0	159 077	36 487	76.2	27.5	20 676	38 885	13.4	17.6	13.6
Congressional District 8	650	4 171	341	394	129 940	46 173	88.4	53.7	36 245	68 306	31.3	6.2	4.2
MASSACHUSETTS	23 513	55 837	103 583	472	1 276 945	449 166	84.8	33.2	25 952	50 502	17.7	9.3	6.7
Congressional District 1	1 441	6 041	18 017	0	154 478	28 608	84.4	25.4	20 758	42 570	10.0	10.5	7.3
Congressional District 2	2 133	5 649	8 196	0	137 807	35 230	81.9	23.1	21 312	44 386	11.7	10.8	8.2
Congressional District 3	1 220	5 999	7 870	0	133 149	39 532	82.4	30.8	24 429	50 223	17.1	9.0	6.6
Congressional District 4	2 824	6 020	12 003	55	125 355	46 339	82.1	36.9	29 388	53 169	21.2	8.4	6.2
Congressional District 5	5 521	4 844	2 528	0	143 930	32 990	83.6	33.6	27 215	56 217	22.6	8.9	6.7
Congressional District 6	1 340	6 165	5 175	21	128 869	36 893	88.4	35.1	28 560	57 826	22.3	6.3	4.3
Congressional District 7	812	5 748	8 695	163	103 883	48 721	87.5	39.5	30 381	56 110	21.8	6.7	4.6
Congressional District 8	2 088	3 652	35 216	79	108 106	104 678	78.4	39.8	23 274	39 300	13.1	19.9	15.6
Congressional District 9	4 330	6 207	4 673	97	121 970	46 350	86.9	33.8	27 287	55 407	20.3	7.5	5.4
Congressional District 10	1 804	5 512	1 210	57	119 398	29 825	90.8	33.5	26 907	51 928	17.3	5.9	4.1
MICHIGAN	65 330	50 113	69 854	112	2 397 577	382 801	83.4	21.8	22 168	44 667	12.7	10.5	7.4
Congressional District 1	11 355	5 196	5 138	63	149 681	13 402	83.0	15.6	17 700	34 076	5.3	11.2	7.8
Congressional District 2	5 672	3 948	5 207	7	156 168	28 525	83.6	18.3	19 325	42 589	8.5	8.9	6.3
Congressional District 3	6 740	4 455	3 792	0	150 575	37 470	84.7	23.9	21 265	45 936	11.1	8.6	6.2
Congressional District 4	7 806	3 769	11 009	0	165 753	21 584	84.5	18.6	19 347	39 020	8.6	10.5	6.6
Congressional District 5	1 699	2 695	497	0	160 802	21 049	82.0	15.1	19 823	39 675	9.5	13.7	10.6
Congressional District 6	1 645	3 305	7 998	4	162 977	25 427	83.5	21.1	20 031	40 943	9.0	11.4	7.5
Congressional District 7	13 350	4 017	4 350	0	151 371	24 734	85.3	19.1	21 216	45 181	10.8	7.9	5.4
Congressional District 8	1 037	2 127	13 876	0	188 217	23 619	89.5	29.0	24 409	52 510	17.4	8.4	4.9
Congressional District 9	1 813	2 729	1 554	0	144 608	33 792	90.1	43.5	36 072	65 358	28.5	5.4	3.5
Congressional District 10	2 717	2 451	0	34	157 631	21 038	84.6	16.9	23 597	52 690	16.2	6.0	4.3
Congressional District 11	1 953	2 931	77	0	150 122	27 279	88.0	28.5	27 921	59 177	20.5	4.3	3.0
Congressional District 12	1 316	3 695	283	0	137 583	25 994	81.4	19.5	23 560	46 784	11.8	7.3	5.4
Congressional District 13	4 151	2 891	193	4	171 810	24 593	69.4	14.1	17 078	31 165	8.5	24.4	19.8
Congressional District 14	884	3 648	891	0	169 630	27 968	75.6	14.2	17 546	36 099	8.9	19.7	15.9
Congressional District 15	3 192	2 256	14 989	0	180 649	26 327	84.7	27.5	23 628	48 963	14.9	10.3	6.3
MINNESOTA	16 999	40 506	44 835	12	1 146 595	215 912	87.9	27.4	23 198	47 111	12.6	7.9	5.1
Congressional District 1	2 467	6 343	8 756	0	144 359	26 119	85.1	21.6	19 889	40 941	7.7	8.5	5.3
Congressional District 2	1 894	2 405	4 690	0	148 006	32 210	91.6	31.2	25 718	61 344	19.1	3.9	2.5
Congressional District 3	792	2 219	252	0	136 977	28 868	94.0	40.1	32 594	63 816	24.4	3.5	2.3
Congressional District 4	590	4 701	8 402	0	132 764	43 616	88.1	33.0	23 853	46 811	13.4	9.6	6.6
Congressional District 5	804	7 481	7 523	0	132 535	28 174	87.0	34.9	23 798	41 569	10.7	12.7	8.2
Congressional District 6	4 633	2 713	5 261	0	157 176	26 846	90.6	24.5	23 533	56 862	15.5	4.7	2.8
Congressional District 7	2 092	8 798	6 223	0	149 637	16 121	82.1	16.4	17 603	36 453	5.3	10.3	6.8
Congressional District 8	3 727	5 846	3 728	12	145 141	13 958	85.2	17.7	18 596	37 911	6.1	10.4	6.9
MISSISSIPPI	25 778	18 382	29 238	5 722	688 942	100 961	72.9	16.9	15 853	31 330	6.0	19.9	16.0
Congressional District 1	2 631	4 876	7 377	247	168 199	20 127	70.4	13.9	16 156	32 535	5.5	16.4	12.9
Congressional District 2	12 515	4 798	11 263	4	188 818	29 675	68.6	16.8	13 616	26 894	5.0	27.3	22.7
Congressional District 3	5 653	5 092	5 647	628	163 508	30 405	74.8	20.2	17 218	31 907	7.5	19.2	15.4
Congressional District 4	4 979	3 616	4 951	4 843	168 417	20 754	77.4	16.7	16 422	33 023	6.0	16.9	13.4
MISSOURI	35 206	48 708	44 587	5 435	1 205 378	274 195	81.3	21.6	19 936	37 934	8.8	11.7	8.6
Congressional District 1	1 113	4 782	3 306	0	139 258	39 987	80.0	22.4	19 888	36 314	8.4	15.8	12.4
Congressional District 2	1 441	4 897	1 950	0	123 821	51 235	90.8	38.3	29 668	61 416	22.6	3.6	2.5
Congressional District 3	1 386	4 780	3 879	6	113 062	51 249	80.4	23.2	21 338	41 091	9.2	10.1	7.4
Congressional District 4	7 065	5 827	4 154	5 429	135 471	19 548	79.6	15.6	17 127	34 541	5.4	12.1	8.9
Congressional District 5	1 602	4 319	1 383	0	131 792	29 142	82.8	22.9	20 465	38 311	8.3	12.4	9.4

[4]All persons 3 years old and over enrolled in nursery school through college.
[5]Persons 25 years old and over.
[6]Based on the population enumerated as of April 1, 2000.

Table A. 109th Congressional Districts, 2000—*Continued*

(Number, percent.)

STATE Congressional district	Housing units									Civilian labor force		
	Total	Total occupied units	Owner occupied		Median owner costs as a percent of income		Renter occupied		Sub-standard housing units (percent)[9]	Total	Unemployment	
			Percent	Median value[7] (dollars)	With a mortgage	Without a mortgage[8]	Median rent (dollars)	Median rent as a percent of income			Total	Rate[10]
	41	42	43	44	45	46	47	48	49	50	51	52
LOUISIANA	1 847 181	1 656 053	67.9	85 000	19.6	9.9	466	25.8	5.8	1 997 995	146 218	7.3
Congressional District 1	271 455	250 838	70.3	123 800	20.2	9.9	558	24.4	3.6	312 697	14 881	4.7
Congressional District 2	265 540	236 008	50.4	80 100	22.5	11.0	481	28.6	9.0	277 929	26 580	9.5
Congressional District 3	248 866	223 921	77.5	81 700	19.0	9.9	431	23.2	6.5	275 775	19 525	7.1
Congressional District 4	277 422	241 288	68.5	71 400	19.2	9.9	435	24.9	5.2	274 658	22 872	8.0
Congressional District 5	264 786	233 533	70.3	65 500	19.7	10.1	396	26.7	5.3	268 061	22 970	8.6
Congressional District 6	255 900	232 902	68.7	98 100	19.2	9.9	498	25.7	5.3	305 823	18 429	6.0
Congressional District 7	263 212	237 563	70.3	78 100	18.5	9.9	420	24.8	5.8	283 052	20 961	7.4
MAINE	651 901	518 200	71.6	98 700	21.4	12.1	497	25.3	2.1	655 176	31 165	4.8
Congressional District 1	313 375	258 917	70.8	120 700	21.9	12.2	570	25.3	1.7	337 544	12 444	3.7
Congressional District 2	338 526	259 283	72.4	80 800	20.8	12.1	435	25.3	2.5	317 632	18 721	5.9
MARYLAND	2 145 283	1 980 859	67.7	146 000	22.2	9.9	689	24.7	4.0	2 737 359	128 902	4.7
Congressional District 1	294 477	248 619	78.5	148 900	21.9	9.9	598	24.6	2.0	344 194	13 505	3.9
Congressional District 2	277 503	260 455	62.4	110 500	22.0	10.8	617	24.6	3.1	335 143	16 657	4.9
Congressional District 3	278 634	262 186	67.5	134 600	21.7	10.4	713	24.3	2.7	349 405	14 060	4.0
Congressional District 4	247 974	236 464	62.8	154 500	23.3	9.9	753	25.0	7.7	349 641	18 452	5.2
Congressional District 5	248 393	234 188	74.8	158 100	22.8	9.9	804	24.3	3.8	357 211	14 580	4.0
Congressional District 6	258 584	240 769	75.7	144 900	22.2	9.9	559	23.5	1.5	339 226	12 219	3.6
Congressional District 7	280 527	247 981	55.5	104 300	22.4	10.9	545	26.6	4.7	309 164	26 645	8.6
Congressional District 8	259 191	250 197	65.3	229 000	21.5	9.9	888	24.5	6.7	353 375	12 784	3.6
MASSACHUSETTS	2 621 989	2 443 580	61.7	185 700	21.9	12.4	684	25.5	3.4	3 312 039	150 952	4.6
Congressional District 1	267 098	245 029	65.5	127 200	21.4	12.0	545	25.4	2.7	330 011	16 564	5.0
Congressional District 2	255 284	242 706	65.8	132 900	21.5	12.7	559	25.2	2.7	322 084	15 004	4.7
Congressional District 3	250 037	240 491	62.9	168 800	21.3	11.8	584	23.8	2.9	326 531	14 238	4.4
Congressional District 4	256 725	241 784	65.1	187 900	21.4	12.1	603	24.7	2.1	332 139	16 341	4.9
Congressional District 5	234 489	227 344	67.2	206 900	21.6	12.2	656	25.3	4.1	320 718	12 504	3.9
Congressional District 6	253 272	243 310	68.9	239 800	22.2	12.3	704	25.2	2.5	335 384	13 491	4.0
Congressional District 7	262 059	255 260	57.1	251 600	22.3	12.7	842	24.8	3.1	344 427	11 937	3.5
Congressional District 8	266 874	254 471	28.4	200 900	22.7	12.6	829	27.5	8.7	342 061	24 301	7.1
Congressional District 9	246 374	238 738	64.4	200 600	22.0	12.2	759	25.5	3.1	329 389	13 712	4.2
Congressional District 10	329 777	254 447	73.6	194 600	22.9	12.8	768	25.9	1.9	329 295	12 860	3.9
MICHIGAN	4 234 279	3 785 661	73.8	115 600	19.6	9.9	546	24.4	3.4	4 922 453	284 992	5.8
Congressional District 1	390 612	266 115	80.1	79 600	19.6	9.9	405	24.4	2.5	303 731	24 237	8.0
Congressional District 2	290 266	242 071	80.0	107 900	19.6	9.9	511	23.3	3.1	332 577	16 546	5.0
Congressional District 3	257 959	243 184	72.5	112 800	19.5	9.9	544	23.4	3.5	342 955	15 258	4.4
Congressional District 4	311 787	252 141	77.8	95 900	19.3	9.9	495	25.0	2.6	323 137	20 049	6.2
Congressional District 5	278 094	257 373	73.8	87 200	18.8	9.9	488	25.9	3.3	312 205	23 261	7.4
Congressional District 6	286 433	253 892	72.9	98 100	19.3	9.9	497	24.5	3.1	341 751	19 970	5.8
Congressional District 7	271 467	248 411	76.7	103 400	19.3	9.9	516	23.4	2.3	332 697	16 145	4.8
Congressional District 8	258 901	245 099	75.2	144 600	19.7	9.9	568	25.6	2.4	355 162	15 499	4.4
Congressional District 9	275 826	264 060	74.3	198 000	19.9	9.9	714	23.2	2.7	350 327	12 581	3.6
Congressional District 10	266 814	244 523	82.1	152 000	19.8	9.9	579	23.2	2.4	339 023	15 124	4.4
Congressional District 11	266 952	257 783	78.5	153 700	19.6	10.0	656	22.4	2.4	352 653	11 858	3.4
Congressional District 12	284 081	274 732	73.0	121 400	19.9	10.9	629	24.0	3.3	339 775	15 837	4.7
Congressional District 13	268 682	239 745	55.7	71 600	20.5	11.8	474	26.1	7.4	272 991	35 350	12.9
Congressional District 14	261 483	243 452	64.9	84 500	20.4	11.4	525	26.5	6.8	281 728	27 739	9.8
Congressional District 15	264 897	253 080	68.4	130 500	19.6	9.9	630	25.3	3.7	341 741	15 538	4.5
MINNESOTA	2 065 946	1 895 127	74.6	122 400	20.0	9.9	566	24.7	3.3	2 689 115	109 069	4.1
Congressional District 1	251 372	237 886	76.9	89 300	18.9	9.9	439	23.1	2.5	333 528	13 247	4.0
Congressional District 2	224 502	217 641	82.2	149 900	20.7	9.9	672	24.1	2.3	350 641	10 498	3.0
Congressional District 3	242 991	237 651	77.4	159 000	20.0	9.9	773	24.5	2.7	352 017	9 737	2.8
Congressional District 4	248 060	242 046	65.3	127 800	19.9	9.9	611	25.5	4.9	334 376	13 904	4.2
Congressional District 5	271 454	263 486	57.2	121 300	20.2	9.9	605	25.5	5.8	354 730	17 078	4.8
Congressional District 6	223 746	214 072	82.8	137 500	20.7	9.9	544	23.7	2.2	345 494	10 489	3.0
Congressional District 7	283 889	238 530	77.8	77 100	19.2	9.9	401	24.4	2.6	313 071	15 728	5.0
Congressional District 8	319 932	243 815	80.1	87 100	19.9	9.9	417	25.4	3.3	305 258	18 388	6.0
MISSISSIPPI	1 161 953	1 046 434	72.3	71 400	20.4	9.9	439	25.0	5.7	1 267 092	93 778	7.4
Congressional District 1	294 875	267 649	75.1	74 000	20.2	9.9	417	24.0	4.3	329 209	19 955	6.0
Congressional District 2	271 770	245 770	65.7	58 700	21.3	11.0	409	26.4	8.5	297 585	30 984	10.4
Congressional District 3	299 863	269 154	75.7	74 900	19.9	9.9	451	24.7	5.2	321 173	21 409	6.6
Congressional District 4	295 445	263 861	72.4	78 000	20.2	9.9	485	25.0	4.9	319 125	21 430	6.5
MISSOURI	2 442 017	2 194 594	70.3	89 900	19.5	9.9	484	24.0	2.9	2 806 718	148 794	5.3
Congressional District 1	277 454	249 256	62.1	73 200	19.9	9.9	522	25.8	3.8	301 078	25 018	8.3
Congressional District 2	239 814	230 452	81.6	147 900	19.2	9.9	662	22.7	1.4	332 595	10 385	3.1
Congressional District 3	273 566	251 895	68.9	97 500	19.2	9.9	492	23.4	3.0	327 327	18 419	5.6
Congressional District 4	289 512	238 497	73.5	80 200	19.6	9.9	425	22.5	2.9	292 747	13 481	4.4
Congressional District 5	276 309	254 560	62.3	83 100	19.8	10.6	532	24.5	3.8	315 116	18 479	5.9

[7]Specified owner-occupied units.
[8]Median monthly owner costs is often in the minimum category—9.9 percent or less, which is indicated as 9.9 percent.
[9]Overcrowded or lacking complete plumbing facilities.
[10]Percent of civilian labor force.

Table A. 109th Congressional Districts, 2000—*Continued*

(Number, percent.)

STATE Congressional district	Civilian employment and occupations				Total farms, 2002	Farms by size, 2002 (percent)			Land in farms, 2002		Cropland harvested, 2002		Farm's principal operator's primary occupation is farming, 2002 (percent)
	Total	Management, professional, and related (percent)	Service, sales, and office (percent)	Construction and production (percent)		1 to 49 acres	50 to 999 acres	1,000 acres or more	Acreage	Average size of farms (acres)	Acreage	Farms	
	53	54	55	56	57	58	59	60	61	62	63	64	65
LOUISIANA	1 851 777	29.9	43.5	25.8	27 413	41.2	51.5	7.3	7 830 664	286	3 332 146	14 017	54.0
Congressional District 1	297 816	37.2	42.2	20.2	2 509	52.4	47.1	0.5	D	D	63 045	1 221	51.3
Congressional District 2	251 349	29.2	49.2	21.4	60	48.3	50.0	1.7	D	D	1 722	31	51.7
Congressional District 3	256 250	23.8	41.1	33.6	1 917	48.7	40.6	10.7	687 309	359	324 737	1 087	57.7
Congressional District 4	251 786	27.2	43.4	28.5	5 480	37.1	58.5	4.4	1 260 290	230	288 605	2 679	51.0
Congressional District 5	245 091	28.0	43.3	26.9	8 422	32.0	58.2	9.8	2 956 790	351	1 690 535	4 711	57.6
Congressional District 6	287 394	33.3	42.8	23.6	2 826	47.5	47.1	5.4	651 500	231	242 700	1 397	44.6
Congressional District 7	262 091	28.7	42.6	27.9	6 199	47.4	43.6	9.0	1 995 170	322	720 802	2 891	56.1
MAINE[11]	624 011	31.5	41.2	25.6	7 196	38.6	58.8	2.6	1 369 768	190	394 121	4 869	47.4
Congressional District 1	325 100	34.7	41.2	23.0	2 572	50.0	49.3	0.7	276 575	108	86 056	1 760	48.5
Congressional District 2	298 911	28.1	41.2	28.5	4 624	32.3	64.1	3.6	1 093 193	236	308 065	3 109	46.8
MARYLAND	2 608 457	41.3	40.4	18.1	12 198	47.8	49.0	3.2	2 077 630	170	1 282 004	8 335	57.2
Congressional District 1	330 689	37.0	40.1	21.9	4 051	44.5	48.8	6.7	1 010 337	249	703 604	2 547	60.1
Congressional District 2	318 486	31.8	45.0	23.0	166	61.4	38.0	0.6	12 557	76	4 914	97	54.8
Congressional District 3	335 345	44.8	39.4	15.7	119	73.9	26.1	0.0	6 107	51	2 337	71	47.9
Congressional District 4	331 189	42.6	42.4	15.0	261	61.7	36.0	2.3	34 207	131	19 898	169	49.0
Congressional District 5	342 631	41.4	39.6	18.8	2 033	53.0	45.9	1.1	216 320	106	99 960	1 515	57.5
Congressional District 6	327 007	35.5	40.1	23.9	4 922	44.8	53.8	1.4	717 861	146	406 462	3 584	56.2
Congressional District 7	282 519	40.4	43.3	16.2	353	63.7	33.4	2.8	38 504	109	20 938	194	51.0
Congressional District 8	340 591	55.6	33.7	10.6	293	57.7	40.3	2.0	41 737	142	23 891	158	51.2
MASSACHUSETTS	3 161 087	41.1	40.0	18.7	6 075	60.0	39.4	0.5	518 570	85	159 253	4 210	54.0
Congressional District 1	313 447	34.8	40.9	23.9	2 160	45.2	54.0	0.7	263 787	122	75 570	1 565	52.5
Congressional District 2	307 080	34.2	41.5	24.1	730	52.2	47.8	0.0	58 060	80	23 137	536	52.5
Congressional District 3	312 293	39.6	39.7	20.6	371	64.2	35.6	0.3	23 482	63	7 688	279	49.6
Congressional District 4	315 798	43.5	37.0	19.2	798	67.0	32.5	0.5	54 843	69	17 689	542	58.5
Congressional District 5	308 214	42.5	36.5	20.9	532	65.4	34.4	0.2	31 987	60	12 381	372	58.3
Congressional District 6	321 893	42.4	40.0	17.2	366	73.2	26.5	0.3	24 873	68	7 198	233	51.1
Congressional District 7	332 490	46.8	38.8	14.3	68	79.4	20.6	0.0	2 873	42	890	48	58.8
Congressional District 8	317 760	46.9	40.6	12.4	6	66.7	33.3	0.0	281	47	14	5	66.7
Congressional District 9	315 677	41.3	41.3	17.3	81	70.4	28.4	1.2	4 913	61	1 938	56	44.4
Congressional District 10	316 435	38.3	43.2	18.1	963	81.4	17.7	0.9	53 471	56	12 748	574	55.9
MICHIGAN	4 637 461	31.5	40.4	27.6	53 315	41.1	55.2	3.7	10 142 958	190	6 827 903	38 244	54.5
Congressional District 1	279 494	26.3	43.9	28.8	6 783	29.4	67.5	3.1	1 356 992	200	621 831	5 122	53.6
Congressional District 2	316 031	27.3	38.5	33.1	5 704	43.4	54.5	2.1	855 633	150	508 700	4 316	52.4
Congressional District 3	327 697	30.4	39.6	29.5	3 167	45.0	51.7	3.4	537 901	170	347 334	2 113	52.6
Congressional District 4	303 088	28.4	42.1	28.7	8 597	34.2	61.9	3.9	1 789 857	208	1 194 306	6 344	56.0
Congressional District 5	288 944	26.3	42.0	31.4	2 827	44.7	50.3	5.0	599 039	212	478 403	2 013	59.5
Congressional District 6	321 781	29.0	38.6	31.3	5 831	47.1	49.0	3.9	1 084 879	186	768 130	4 401	56.5
Congressional District 7	316 552	29.2	39.0	31.3	8 580	40.4	55.5	4.1	1 655 008	193	1 158 768	5 636	50.8
Congressional District 8	339 663	36.4	40.3	23.0	3 916	51.5	45.4	3.1	639 493	163	468 934	2 678	49.7
Congressional District 9	337 746	48.7	36.5	14.7	82	67.1	30.5	2.4	7 280	89	3 436	47	43.9
Congressional District 10	323 899	30.3	37.8	31.5	5 743	40.1	54.9	5.0	1 306 071	227	1 023 580	4 113	61.1
Congressional District 11	340 795	37.5	39.0	23.4	335	79.4	19.7	0.9	18 835	56	11 150	160	51.9
Congressional District 12	323 938	31.2	42.0	26.7	10	70.0	30.0	0.0	325	33	138	6	60.0
Congressional District 13	237 641	24.8	45.7	29.3	17	76.5	23.5	0.0	815	48	D	10	11.8
Congressional District 14	253 989	25.2	46.3	28.4	18	66.7	33.3	0.0	701	39	D	2	27.8
Congressional District 15	326 203	34.9	38.6	26.2	1 705	53.5	42.9	3.6	290 129	170	243 003	1 283	55.1
MINNESOTA	2 580 046	35.8	40.2	23.3	80 839	24.9	67.2	7.9	27 512 270	340	19 398 309	57 323	62.9
Congressional District 1	320 281	32.9	38.8	26.8	21 384	25.7	66.5	7.8	7 417 386	347	6 058 721	15 897	69.7
Congressional District 2	340 143	37.2	40.0	22.3	6 784	39.3	56.8	3.9	1 424 134	210	1 081 859	4 751	57.5
Congressional District 3	342 280	43.2	40.0	16.7	600	60.5	38.2	1.3	64 222	107	43 980	437	51.8
Congressional District 4	320 472	39.1	41.5	19.2	111	74.8	25.2	0.0	4 653	42	1 784	76	53.2
Congressional District 5	337 652	39.7	42.3	17.9	21	61.9	38.1	0.0	1 020	49	146	12	28.6
Congressional District 6	335 005	33.4	39.2	26.9	6 691	38.1	59.9	2.0	1 130 137	169	726 486	4 882	56.9
Congressional District 7	297 343	30.4	38.5	29.2	32 629	18.2	69.4	12.4	14 848 949	455	10 401 069	21 592	64.8
Congressional District 8	286 870	28.6	41.5	28.9	12 619	24.0	73.9	2.1	2 621 769	208	1 084 264	9 676	53.0
MISSISSIPPI	1 173 314	27.4	39.8	31.6	42 186	30.0	65.1	5.0	11 097 543	263	4 139 341	19 405	48.8
Congressional District 1	309 254	24.0	36.6	38.6	12 947	28.3	67.5	4.1	3 023 453	234	943 682	6 002	44.1
Congressional District 2	266 601	27.2	42.3	28.8	8 847	21.8	64.8	13.4	4 637 093	524	2 698 889	4 287	53.9
Congressional District 3	299 764	31.3	38.3	28.9	13 241	29.5	68.2	2.2	2 531 167	191	378 213	5 813	50.8
Congressional District 4	297 695	27.0	42.3	29.7	7 151	42.9	55.1	1.0	905 830	127	118 557	3 303	47.2
MISSOURI	2 657 924	31.5	41.9	26.0	106 797	23.1	71.5	5.4	29 946 035	280	13 137 184	71 698	57.2
Congressional District 1	276 060	32.7	46.5	20.7	103	52.4	45.6	1.9	13 159	128	6 394	54	57.3
Congressional District 2	322 210	42.2	40.1	17.5	1 735	34.2	61.4	4.4	391 538	226	236 947	1 206	51.8
Congressional District 3	308 908	32.6	43.1	24.2	1 491	27.6	69.2	3.2	317 404	213	108 133	1 073	51.3
Congressional District 4	279 266	26.9	40.0	31.9	26 556	23.7	71.6	4.7	6 986 378	263	2 976 880	18 378	58.5
Congressional District 5	296 637	32.7	44.5	22.7	594	55.6	41.6	2.9	94 515	159	51 190	338	47.5

[11]Agriculture data were tabulated for the 108th Congress and some boundary changes have occurred.
D = Suppressed to avoid disclosure.

Table A. 109th Congressional Districts, 2000—*Continued*

(Number, percent.)

STATE Congressional district	Farm's principal operator is full owner, 2002 (percent)	Type of organization, 2002 (percent)			Value of all agricultural products sold, 2002				Payments received from federal farm programs, 2002					
		Family or individual	Partner-ship	Corpo-ration	Total ($1,000)	Percent of farms			Total payments ($1,000)	Farms receiving payments		Percent of farms receiving		
						Less than $50,000	$50,000 to $249,999	$250,000 or more		Number	Percent	Less than $50,000	$50,000 to $249,999	$250,000 or more
	66	67	68	69	70	72	73	74	75	76	77	78	79	80
LOUISIANA	62.7	90.9	4.8	3.8	1 815 803	82.8	10.3	6.9	123 599	7 562	27.6	90.9	8.8	0.3
Congressional District 1	72.4	92.5	3.8	3.2	104 569	83.9	11.4	4.8	3 588	486	19.4	99.2	0.8	0.0
Congressional District 2	68.3	76.7	5.0	18.3	1 722	93.3	3.3	3.3	D	4	6.7	100.0	0.0	0.0
Congressional District 3	50.7	81.1	5.8	12.3	255 549	76.6	8.8	14.7	D	250	13.0	99.6	0.4	0.0
Congressional District 4	69.6	94.0	3.4	2.3	299 063	88.4	6.2	5.4	11 320	1 175	21.4	95.3	4.5	0.2
Congressional District 5	60.8	90.5	5.7	3.3	753 248	76.4	13.2	10.4	58 650	3 385	40.2	91.0	8.5	0.4
Congressional District 6	64.7	91.2	4.1	3.9	171 815	87.3	7.9	4.7	5 427	590	20.9	98.5	1.2	0.3
Congressional District 7	58.0	91.1	5.3	3.2	229 837	85.9	11.1	3.0	43 633	1 672	27.0	81.1	18.5	0.4
MAINE[11]	72.8	88.6	4.5	5.9	463 603	86.3	9.2	4.6	8 664	1 244	17.3	97.3	2.7	0.0
Congressional District 1	72.1	88.6	3.7	6.5	83 295	88.8	8.7	2.5	1 757	221	8.6	96.8	3.2	0.0
Congressional District 2	73.2	88.6	4.9	5.5	380 307	84.8	9.5	5.7	6 907	1 023	22.1	97.5	2.5	0.0
MARYLAND	69.5	86.7	6.3	6.0	1 293 303	77.3	12.2	10.5	33 131	3 372	27.6	95.9	4.0	0.0
Congressional District 1	69.7	83.4	7.0	8.0	875 979	63.4	14.6	22.0	18 892	1 748	43.1	95.2	4.8	0.0
Congressional District 2	74.7	77.1	7.2	15.7	8 882	78.9	15.7	5.4	77	16	9.6	100.0	0.0	0.0
Congressional District 3	75.6	79.8	6.7	13.4	8 824	85.7	10.9	3.4	7	8	6.7	100.0	0.0	0.0
Congressional District 4	75.5	85.8	5.7	6.5	31 598	83.9	8.8	7.3	318	32	12.3	90.6	9.4	0.0
Congressional District 5	69.9	90.2	5.0	3.3	39 341	92.5	6.4	1.1	1 583	299	14.7	98.0	2.0	0.0
Congressional District 6	67.7	88.7	6.1	4.6	296 508	80.5	13.2	6.3	10 977	1 151	23.4	96.6	3.3	0.1
Congressional District 7	77.3	84.4	7.1	8.2	21 903	87.5	7.6	4.8	571	66	18.7	97.0	3.0	0.0
Congressional District 8	73.7	86.0	5.8	6.1	10 267	88.1	8.2	3.8	706	52	17.7	94.2	5.8	0.0
MASSACHUSETTS	71.7	82.6	6.2	9.2	384 314	82.3	12.6	5.1	4 268	415	6.8	96.6	3.4	0.0
Congressional District 1	65.5	87.0	6.9	4.7	127 425	83.8	10.6	5.6	2 304	192	8.9	95.8	4.2	0.0
Congressional District 2	69.7	87.1	5.3	5.8	34 833	83.4	11.5	5.1	527	63	8.6	96.8	3.2	0.0
Congressional District 3	73.6	84.1	4.6	10.0	35 570	83.6	12.1	4.3	81	16	4.3	100.0	0.0	0.0
Congressional District 4	81.7	77.7	5.9	14.9	45 590	81.2	14.0	4.8	488	52	6.5	96.2	3.8	0.0
Congressional District 5	72.0	82.1	4.5	11.8	42 027	81.2	12.4	6.4	366	37	7.0	97.3	2.7	0.0
Congressional District 6	77.3	81.1	7.4	8.5	27 513	79.8	15.8	4.4	146	12	3.3	100.0	0.0	0.0
Congressional District 7	72.1	66.2	2.9	22.1	22 884	67.6	16.2	16.2	D	1	1.5	100.0	0.0	0.0
Congressional District 8	100.0	50.0	16.7	16.7	297	66.7	33.3	0.0	D	D	D	D	D	D
Congressional District 9	82.7	74.1	6.2	13.6	5 055	81.5	13.6	4.9	D	5	6.2	100.0	0.0	0.0
Congressional District 10	74.6	75.9	6.9	14.4	43 120	81.3	15.2	3.5	335	37	3.8	97.3	2.7	0.0
MICHIGAN	69.6	90.2	5.9	3.4	3 772 435	81.8	12.1	6.1	144 771	18 133	34.0	97.1	2.9	0.0
Congressional District 1	69.8	91.7	5.4	2.6	239 550	86.6	9.8	3.5	9 995	1 766	26.0	98.6	1.4	0.0
Congressional District 2	71.9	88.8	6.4	4.5	642 326	80.1	11.5	8.3	12 819	1 330	23.3	95.6	4.4	0.0
Congressional District 3	72.5	91.5	5.0	2.6	277 796	84.1	9.9	6.0	8 931	1 115	35.2	96.3	3.6	0.1
Congressional District 4	69.8	91.4	5.7	2.4	521 445	82.0	12.4	5.6	23 631	3 351	39.0	97.7	2.3	0.0
Congressional District 5	63.8	87.8	6.5	5.0	169 889	78.3	14.8	7.0	8 100	1 091	38.6	97.6	2.4	0.0
Congressional District 6	71.3	89.2	6.4	3.9	621 052	78.2	13.1	8.7	16 545	1 798	30.8	97.0	2.8	0.2
Congressional District 7	70.8	91.3	5.5	2.7	444 832	84.4	11.2	4.4	28 753	3 729	43.5	97.0	3.0	0.0
Congressional District 8	72.2	89.6	6.5	3.3	199 167	85.1	10.0	4.9	9 997	1 084	27.7	96.0	4.0	0.0
Congressional District 9	84.1	75.6	6.1	17.1	27 125	85.4	6.1	8.5	24	6	7.3	100.0	0.0	0.0
Congressional District 10	64.0	89.8	5.9	4.1	482 026	75.2	16.0	8.8	20 900	2 336	40.7	97.1	2.9	0.0
Congressional District 11	80.6	79.7	10.7	8.7	19 333	87.2	8.4	4.5	139	24	7.2	100.0	0.0	0.0
Congressional District 12	100.0	20.0	60.0	20.0	D	100.0	0.0	0.0	D	D	D	D	D	D
Congressional District 13	94.1	47.1	11.8	11.8	546	76.5	23.5	0.0	D	3	17.6	100.0	0.0	0.0
Congressional District 14	66.7	83.3	5.6	5.6	D	94.4	5.6	0.0	D	5	27.8	100.0	0.0	0.0
Congressional District 15	60.6	87.2	6.7	5.4	127 090	79.9	15.4	4.8	4 932	495	29.0	96.2	3.8	0.0
MINNESOTA	63.5	90.3	6.3	2.9	8 575 627	67.1	22.2	10.7	350 709	43 927	54.3	98.5	1.5	0.0
Congressional District 1	55.6	89.4	7.1	3.1	3 186 486	53.8	30.3	15.9	108 132	13 291	62.2	98.5	1.5	0.0
Congressional District 2	65.0	90.6	6.1	3.0	569 025	70.7	20.6	8.6	21 459	3 360	49.5	99.3	0.7	0.0
Congressional District 3	75.2	86.7	5.0	7.8	54 034	81.2	13.5	5.3	883	153	25.5	99.3	0.7	0.0
Congressional District 4	77.5	75.7	7.2	10.8	D	73.9	16.2	9.9	19	5	4.5	100.0	0.0	0.0
Congressional District 5	85.7	81.0	4.8	14.3	D	95.2	0.0	4.8	6	4	19.0	100.0	0.0	0.0
Congressional District 6	70.8	90.8	5.8	2.9	522 287	77.2	16.5	6.3	14 165	2 525	37.7	99.5	0.5	0.0
Congressional District 7	63.1	89.3	6.8	3.3	3 792 754	64.8	23.2	11.9	193 524	21 762	66.7	98.0	2.0	0.0
Congressional District 8	72.4	94.6	3.7	1.2	432 003	87.7	9.9	2.4	12 521	2 827	22.4	99.5	0.5	0.0
MISSISSIPPI	74.1	92.5	5.1	1.7	3 116 295	87.1	5.4	7.5	145 508	12 383	29.4	94.6	4.8	0.6
Congressional District 1	75.3	93.4	5.0	1.0	370 633	93.1	4.4	2.5	28 559	5 210	40.2	98.4	1.5	0.1
Congressional District 2	65.9	84.6	11.0	3.6	1 066 712	80.1	8.2	11.7	102 209	3 626	41.0	84.6	13.6	1.8
Congressional District 3	74.9	95.1	3.0	1.3	1 308 446	84.9	4.7	10.4	12 280	2 779	21.0	99.1	0.9	0.0
Congressional District 4	80.3	96.0	2.2	1.2	370 504	89.1	5.0	5.9	2 460	768	10.7	99.6	0.4	0.0
MISSOURI	70.7	92.2	5.2	2.0	4 983 255	84.7	11.4	3.9	264 475	43 379	40.6	98.7	1.3	0.0
Congressional District 1	77.7	70.9	19.4	8.7	4 488	86.4	6.8	6.8	153	25	24.3	100.0	0.0	0.0
Congressional District 2	68.4	84.6	8.5	6.1	85 698	82.3	14.1	3.6	4 575	749	43.2	98.5	1.5	0.0
Congressional District 3	69.3	90.5	6.0	2.7	31 389	92.2	6.1	1.7	1 402	383	25.7	99.2	0.8	0.0
Congressional District 4	70.4	93.6	4.7	1.4	1 169 374	85.0	11.5	3.4	45 830	9 741	36.7	99.4	0.6	0.0
Congressional District 5	77.4	88.7	6.7	4.2	14 868	92.3	5.2	2.5	533	136	22.9	99.3	0.7	0.0

[11]Agriculture data were tabulated for the 108th Congress and some boundary changes have occurred.

D = Suppressed to avoid disclosure.

Table A. 109th Congressional Districts, 2000—*Continued*

(Number, percent.)

STATE Congressional district	Representative	Land area,[1] (sq km)	Total population	Persons per square kilometer	White	Black	American Indian/Alaska Native	Asian and Pacific Islander	Other race	Hispanic or Latino[2] (percent)	Non-Hispanic White (percent)	Two or more races (percent)
	1	2	3	4	5	6	7	8	9	10	11	12
MISSOURI—*Continued*												
Congressional District 6	Sam Graves (R)	33 753	621 790	18.4	95.0	3.2	1.0	1.2	1.1	2.4	92.4	1.4
Congressional District 7	Roy Blunt (R)	14 192	621 746	43.8	95.8	1.6	2.1	1.0	1.4	2.6	92.9	1.7
Congressional District 8	Jo Ann Emerson (R)	48 384	621 746	12.9	94.2	4.6	1.4	0.6	0.5	1.0	92.5	1.2
Congressional District 9	Kenny C. Hulshof (R)	36 067	621 484	17.2	94.3	4.3	0.9	1.2	0.5	1.1	92.6	1.2
MONTANA		376 979	902 195	2.4	92.2	0.5	7.4	0.9	0.9	2.0	89.5	1.7
Congressional District (At Large)	Dennis R. Rehberg (R)	376 979	902 195	2.4	92.2	0.5	7.4	0.9	0.9	2.0	89.5	1.7
NEBRASKA		199 099	1 711 263	8.6	90.8	4.4	1.3	1.7	3.3	5.5	87.3	1.4
Congressional District 1	Jeff Fortenberry (R)	30 952	570 423	18.4	93.4	1.8	1.7	1.9	2.7	4.2	90.5	1.4
Congressional District 2	Lee Terry (R)	1 063	570 308	536.5	83.8	11.0	1.1	2.4	3.7	6.3	79.6	1.9
Congressional District 3	Tom Osborne (R)	167 083	570 532	3.4	95.3	0.4	1.1	0.7	3.5	6.0	91.9	1.0
NEVADA		284 448	1 998 257	7.0	78.4	7.5	2.1	6.4	9.7	19.7	65.2	3.8
Congressional District 1	Shelley Berkley (D)	459	666 442	1 451.9	69.5	13.2	1.6	6.9	13.6	28.2	51.5	4.5
Congressional District 2	Jim Gibbons (R)	272 153	666 470	2.4	84.6	2.9	3.4	4.2	8.2	15.3	74.8	3.1
Congressional District 3	Jon C. Porter (R)	11 836	665 345	56.2	80.9	6.4	1.4	8.2	7.3	15.6	69.3	3.9
NEW HAMPSHIRE		23 227	1 235 786	53.2	97.0	1.0	0.6	1.7	0.9	1.7	95.1	1.1
Congressional District 1	Jeb Bradley (R)	6 342	617 575	97.4	97.1	1.1	0.6	1.6	0.8	1.6	95.1	1.1
Congressional District 2	Charles F. Bass (R)	16 885	618 211	36.6	96.9	0.9	0.7	1.7	0.9	1.7	95.1	1.1
NEW JERSEY		19 211	8 414 350	438.0	74.4	14.4	0.6	6.3	6.9	13.3	66.0	2.5
Congressional District 1	Robert E. Andrews (D)	867	647 392	746.7	75.3	17.9	0.6	3.2	5.0	8.2	71.2	1.8
Congressional District 2	Frank A. LoBiondo (R)	5 133	647 080	126.1	77.2	15.3	0.9	2.9	5.9	10.3	71.7	2.1
Congressional District 3	Jim Saxton (R)	2 397	647 300	270.0	86.9	9.4	0.5	3.3	1.6	3.8	83.4	1.6
Congressional District 4	Christopher H. Smith (R)	1 862	647 357	347.7	86.6	8.4	0.5	2.7	3.6	7.6	81.3	1.7
Congressional District 5	Scott Garrett (R)	2 846	647 338	227.5	90.3	1.8	0.4	7.1	1.6	4.5	86.3	1.3
Congressional District 6	Frank Pallone Jr. (D)	509	647 121	1 271.4	69.3	17.8	0.6	9.1	5.9	11.7	61.7	2.6
Congressional District 7	Mike Ferguson (R)	1 541	647 269	420.0	84.7	4.9	0.4	8.9	2.9	6.9	79.0	1.6
Congressional District 8	Bill Pascrell Jr. (D)	277	647 130	2 336.2	66.3	14.4	0.6	6.1	16.5	25.8	53.7	3.8
Congressional District 9	Steven R. Rothman (D)	241	647 477	2 686.6	74.2	7.9	0.6	11.7	9.4	18.8	61.3	3.5
Congressional District 10	Donald M. Payne (D)	171	647 109	3 784.3	30.2	59.9	0.8	4.4	8.9	15.0	21.4	3.9
Congressional District 11	Rodney P. Frelinghuysen (R)	1 580	647 127	409.6	88.7	3.1	0.3	7.0	2.4	6.8	82.9	1.5
Congressional District 12	Rush D. Holt (D)	1 640	647 253	394.7	76.7	12.3	0.4	9.8	2.7	5.5	72.4	1.8
Congressional District 13	Robert Menendez (D)	147	647 397	4 404.1	60.7	14.1	0.9	6.5	23.9	47.6	32.3	5.8
NEW MEXICO		314 309	1 819 046	5.8	69.9	2.3	10.5	1.7	19.4	42.1	44.7	3.6
Congressional District 1	Heather Wilson (R)	12 216	606 729	49.7	74.7	3.3	4.5	2.6	19.4	42.6	48.5	4.2
Congressional District 2	Stevan Pearce (R)	179 986	606 110	3.4	71.8	2.2	6.3	1.0	22.1	47.3	44.3	3.3
Congressional District 3	Tom Udall (D)	122 108	606 207	5.0	63.3	1.5	20.7	1.3	16.7	36.3	41.4	3.4
NEW YORK		122 283	18 976 457	155.2	70.0	17.0	0.9	6.4	9.1	15.1	62.0	3.1
Congressional District 1	Timothy H. Bishop (D)	1 674	654 458	391.0	90.6	4.9	0.7	2.9	2.8	7.5	84.5	1.7
Congressional District 2	Steve Israel (D)	620	654 346	1 055.4	80.1	11.3	0.6	3.6	7.0	13.9	71.5	2.4
Congressional District 3	Peter T. King (R)	475	653 934	1 376.7	92.4	2.6	0.3	3.5	2.7	6.9	86.9	1.5
Congressional District 4	Carolyn McCarthy (D)	233	654 691	2 809.8	70.6	19.3	0.6	5.2	7.3	13.6	62.3	2.8
Congressional District 5	Gary L. Ackerman (D)	172	654 253	3 803.8	58.4	6.5	0.7	26.0	12.4	23.5	44.2	3.9
Congressional District 6	Gregory W. Meeks (D)	102	654 946	6 421.0	20.9	57.8	2.1	12.0	15.4	16.9	12.8	7.7
Congressional District 7	Joseph Crowley (D)	68	652 943	9 602.1	48.8	20.3	1.2	14.4	21.3	39.5	27.6	5.6
Congressional District 8	Jerrold Nadler (D)	39	654 429	16780.2	77.2	6.8	0.6	12.2	6.9	11.7	68.7	3.3
Congressional District 9	Anthony D. Weiner (D)	96	654 916	6 822.0	73.7	5.2	0.6	16.0	8.6	13.6	64.0	3.9
Congressional District 10	Edolphus Towns (D)	46	655 668	14253.7	22.7	65.3	0.9	3.6	11.7	17.2	16.2	4.0
Congressional District 11	Major R. Owens (D)	31	654 134	21101.1	26.5	63.6	0.8	5.3	8.1	12.1	21.4	4.1
Congressional District 12	Nydia M. Velázquez (D)	49	653 346	13333.6	43.7	12.4	1.3	17.3	31.5	48.5	23.3	5.9
Congressional District 13	Vito Fossella (R)	168	654 619	3 896.5	79.3	7.5	0.5	10.0	5.9	11.0	70.9	3.1
Congressional District 14	Carolyn B. Maloney (D)	33	654 165	19823.2	76.4	6.0	0.6	12.9	8.6	14.0	65.9	4.3
Congressional District 15	Charles B. Rangel (D)	27	654 355	24235.4	31.8	37.3	1.7	3.8	31.8	47.9	16.4	5.9
Congressional District 16	José E. Serrano (D)	31	654 400	21109.7	24.0	39.1	2.0	2.6	39.2	62.8	2.9	6.6
Congressional District 17	Eliot L. Engel (D)	328	654 283	1 994.8	51.2	34.4	0.9	5.5	12.4	20.4	41.3	4.2
Congressional District 18	Nita M. Lowey (D)	575	654 696	1 138.6	77.1	10.8	0.5	6.0	8.7	16.2	67.1	2.9
Congressional District 19	Sue W. Kelly (R)	3 629	653 397	180.0	89.5	6.0	0.6	2.7	3.1	7.7	83.5	1.7
Congressional District 20	John E. Sweeney (R)	18 176	655 277	36.1	95.6	2.8	0.6	1.1	1.0	2.2	93.4	1.1
Congressional District 21	Michael R. McNulty (D)	5 012	654 374	130.6	88.4	8.6	0.6	2.5	1.7	3.2	85.5	1.7
Congressional District 22	Maurice D. Hinchey (D)	8 407	654 522	77.9	85.5	9.2	0.8	3.1	3.9	7.8	79.9	2.3
Congressional District 23	John M. McHugh (R)	34 278	654 216	19.1	94.7	3.0	1.4	0.8	1.2	2.1	92.9	1.0
Congressional District 24	Sherwood Boehlert (R)	15 964	654 390	41.0	94.5	3.9	0.6	1.2	1.2	2.3	92.2	1.3
Congressional District 25	James T. Walsh (R)	4 195	654 484	156.0	89.2	8.1	1.2	2.1	1.2	2.3	86.6	1.7
Congressional District 26	Thomas M. Reynolds (R)	7 073	654 343	92.5	94.2	3.5	0.6	1.8	0.9	1.9	92.3	1.0
Congressional District 27	Brian Higgins (D)	4 740	654 200	138.0	92.0	4.7	1.2	0.9	2.6	4.6	88.8	1.4
Congressional District 28	Louise McIntosh Slaughter (D)	1 383	654 464	473.2	65.5	30.4	1.1	1.9	3.5	5.5	62.0	2.2
Congressional District 29	John R. Kuhl (R)	14 660	654 208	44.6	94.3	3.1	0.9	2.1	0.7	1.4	92.5	1.1

[1] Dry land or land partially or temporarily covered by water.
[2] Hispanic or Latino persons may be of any race.

Table A. 109th Congressional Districts, 2000—*Continued*

(Number, percent.)

STATE Congressional district	Foreign born (percent)	Under 5 years	5 to 17 years	18 to 24 years	25 to 34 years	35 to 44 years	45 to 54 years	55 to 64 years	65 to 74 years	75 years and over	Percent female	Number	Persons per household	Female-family householder[3]	One-person households
														Percent	
	13	14	15	16	17	18	19	20	21	22	23	24	25	26	27
MISSOURI—*Continued*															
Congressional District 6	1.9	6.6	18.8	9.3	13.3	16.2	13.6	9.0	6.7	6.6	50.8	241 518	2.49	9.3	25.8
Congressional District 7	2.1	6.7	17.8	11.1	13.1	14.9	13.0	9.4	7.3	6.6	51.3	246 019	2.45	9.6	26.0
Congressional District 8	1.1	6.3	18.8	9.2	11.9	14.6	13.1	10.3	8.3	7.5	51.2	245 479	2.46	10.6	26.2
Congressional District 9	1.8	6.4	18.7	11.6	12.7	15.7	13.0	8.9	6.7	6.3	50.8	236 920	2.50	9.1	25.6
MONTANA	1.8	6.1	19.4	9.5	11.4	15.7	15.0	9.4	6.9	6.5	50.2	358 667	2.45	8.9	27.4
Congressional District (At Large)	1.8	6.1	19.4	9.5	11.4	15.7	15.0	9.4	6.9	6.5	50.2	358 667	2.45	8.9	27.4
NEBRASKA	4.4	6.8	19.5	10.2	13.0	15.4	13.2	8.3	6.8	6.8	50.7	666 184	2.49	9.1	27.6
Congressional District 1	4.4	6.6	18.7	11.9	12.9	15.3	13.1	8.1	6.6	6.8	50.4	220 837	2.48	8.3	27.1
Congressional District 2	5.5	7.6	19.8	10.2	15.4	16.3	13.1	7.5	5.4	4.7	50.9	219 997	2.53	11.7	27.9
Congressional District 3	3.2	6.3	19.9	8.5	10.8	14.7	13.4	9.2	8.3	9.0	50.8	225 350	2.46	7.2	27.6
NEVADA	15.8	7.3	18.3	9.0	15.3	16.1	13.5	9.5	6.6	4.4	49.1	751 165	2.62	11.1	24.9
Congressional District 1	22.2	8.2	18.5	9.8	17.1	15.9	12.0	8.6	6.0	4.0	48.5	244 497	2.68	13.0	27.2
Congressional District 2	11.2	7.0	18.9	8.8	13.6	16.3	14.4	9.7	6.6	4.7	48.7	253 325	2.56	9.8	25.4
Congressional District 3	14.1	6.7	17.6	8.4	15.3	16.1	14.0	10.3	7.2	4.4	50.0	253 343	2.61	10.6	22.1
NEW HAMPSHIRE	4.4	6.1	18.9	8.4	13.0	17.9	14.9	8.9	6.3	5.6	50.8	474 606	2.53	9.1	24.4
Congressional District 1	4.4	6.2	18.8	8.4	13.5	18.2	14.7	8.6	6.2	5.5	50.9	238 422	2.52	9.2	24.6
Congressional District 2	4.4	6.0	19.1	8.3	12.5	17.6	15.1	9.1	6.5	5.8	50.7	236 184	2.53	8.9	24.3
NEW JERSEY	17.5	6.7	18.1	8.0	14.1	17.1	13.8	9.0	6.8	6.4	51.5	3 064 645	2.68	12.6	24.5
Congressional District 1	5.4	6.7	19.8	8.8	14.1	16.9	13.5	8.2	6.3	5.7	51.7	236 866	2.68	15.0	25.1
Congressional District 2	7.1	6.3	19.0	7.8	13.0	16.8	13.8	9.3	7.3	6.8	51.0	238 555	2.61	13.9	25.5
Congressional District 3	6.5	5.9	18.1	6.6	11.8	16.6	14.1	9.9	9.0	8.0	51.5	243 882	2.60	9.9	23.3
Congressional District 4	9.4	7.1	18.0	7.3	12.8	16.7	13.1	8.8	7.8	8.5	51.7	241 143	2.63	10.2	25.5
Congressional District 5	12.9	6.8	19.3	5.8	11.2	18.3	15.4	9.8	6.9	6.4	51.4	229 151	2.78	8.1	19.5
Congressional District 6	19.2	6.7	17.1	10.4	15.5	16.9	13.4	8.4	6.1	5.6	51.3	234 153	2.69	12.6	25.6
Congressional District 7	16.4	6.9	18.0	5.9	13.2	18.6	15.1	9.2	6.8	6.3	51.2	233 323	2.72	8.5	21.1
Congressional District 8	26.1	7.1	18.0	8.8	14.8	16.2	13.2	8.6	6.6	6.8	52.0	225 635	2.81	14.8	24.1
Congressional District 9	32.4	5.9	15.3	7.9	16.1	16.8	13.8	9.4	7.5	7.3	51.8	251 137	2.55	11.8	28.5
Congressional District 10	22.7	7.4	19.7	10.2	15.4	15.8	12.3	8.4	5.8	5.1	53.0	228 446	2.76	24.7	27.7
Congressional District 11	14.7	7.1	18.0	6.1	13.2	18.5	15.2	9.9	6.4	5.5	51.1	233 288	2.72	7.7	21.3
Congressional District 12	15.6	6.5	18.4	7.9	13.1	17.8	14.8	8.8	6.6	6.0	51.3	232 923	2.67	9.8	23.0
Congressional District 13	39.6	6.7	16.7	11.1	19.5	15.9	11.5	7.8	5.7	5.0	50.2	236 143	2.68	17.5	28.2
NEW MEXICO	8.2	7.2	20.8	9.8	12.9	15.5	13.5	8.7	6.5	5.2	50.8	677 971	2.63	13.2	25.4
Congressional District 1	8.6	6.9	18.8	10.1	14.0	16.2	14.1	8.5	6.1	5.3	51.0	238 282	2.50	12.7	27.8
Congressional District 2	11.2	7.3	21.6	10.2	11.9	14.5	12.5	9.0	7.4	5.6	50.6	218 601	2.70	13.4	23.5
Congressional District 3	4.9	7.3	21.9	9.0	12.7	15.8	13.9	8.8	6.0	4.7	50.9	221 088	2.70	13.6	24.7
NEW YORK	20.4	6.5	18.2	9.3	14.5	16.2	13.5	8.9	6.7	6.2	51.8	7 056 860	2.61	14.7	28.1
Congressional District 1	9.0	6.9	18.8	8.1	13.3	17.4	14.3	9.3	6.3	5.9	50.9	223 857	2.84	9.9	20.1
Congressional District 2	14.0	7.3	19.4	7.3	13.4	17.7	13.8	9.6	6.7	4.8	51.1	206 786	3.12	11.5	15.7
Congressional District 3	11.2	6.6	17.8	6.4	12.6	18.0	14.6	9.4	8.0	6.6	51.5	225 363	2.87	9.9	18.7
Congressional District 4	21.7	6.6	18.6	8.3	12.8	16.3	14.1	9.0	7.4	7.0	52.1	212 500	3.03	13.0	19.4
Congressional District 5	45.6	6.0	15.7	8.8	15.2	16.2	13.9	9.4	7.5	7.3	51.4	228 353	2.82	11.8	23.6
Congressional District 6	39.5	7.1	19.9	10.0	14.9	16.1	12.6	8.8	5.9	4.7	53.3	204 346	3.15	23.9	20.7
Congressional District 7	38.7	6.6	17.0	9.5	16.8	15.9	12.5	8.9	6.7	6.1	52.3	239 163	2.69	19.6	27.8
Congressional District 8	33.2	5.5	12.4	9.6	20.1	16.2	13.7	8.7	6.9	6.9	50.7	303 231	2.08	8.0	45.8
Congressional District 9	40.1	5.9	15.3	8.2	14.9	15.4	14.1	9.5	8.2	8.6	52.4	256 229	2.53	11.5	29.9
Congressional District 10	28.3	8.0	22.2	10.6	14.9	14.8	11.9	8.0	5.4	4.2	54.4	225 520	2.83	29.7	27.2
Congressional District 11	41.7	7.4	19.7	10.4	16.5	15.8	12.7	8.1	5.2	4.0	54.5	238 136	2.71	26.6	28.2
Congressional District 12	41.4	7.2	18.5	11.5	18.6	15.5	11.7	7.6	5.4	4.1	50.9	225 095	2.87	21.3	26.4
Congressional District 13	23.9	6.4	17.3	8.4	15.1	16.3	14.0	9.2	7.0	6.4	51.8	240 922	2.68	13.0	26.3
Congressional District 14	31.9	4.5	8.8	9.4	24.2	16.7	13.3	9.8	6.9	6.4	52.9	340 074	1.88	6.8	49.6
Congressional District 15	33.6	6.4	17.6	11.7	17.5	15.9	12.1	8.1	5.7	5.0	52.2	247 307	2.49	25.6	36.3
Congressional District 16	30.2	9.6	24.9	11.7	15.6	14.6	10.2	6.7	4.0	2.8	53.5	211 326	3.01	38.2	24.2
Congressional District 17	28.6	7.4	19.2	8.9	14.7	15.4	12.7	9.0	6.5	6.2	53.3	235 573	2.71	19.3	27.7
Congressional District 18	22.8	6.8	17.9	7.2	13.1	16.8	14.2	9.6	7.5	6.8	51.9	235 481	2.70	10.9	24.6
Congressional District 19	9.4	7.1	19.9	7.7	12.2	18.5	14.8	9.0	5.9	5.0	50.1	223 760	2.79	8.9	21.0
Congressional District 20	3.7	5.8	18.7	7.7	12.2	16.9	15.0	10.0	7.3	6.4	50.1	250 202	2.50	9.4	25.1
Congressional District 21	5.3	5.9	17.5	10.2	12.9	15.5	14.0	8.6	7.4	8.1	51.9	265 363	2.35	12.3	31.6
Congressional District 22	8.1	6.0	17.8	12.0	12.5	15.7	13.5	8.9	6.9	6.7	51.0	248 889	2.47	11.9	29.3
Congressional District 23	2.8	5.9	19.2	11.1	13.0	16.3	13.3	8.8	6.7	5.7	49.2	240 469	2.54	10.1	25.2
Congressional District 24	3.6	5.7	18.7	9.5	12.0	15.7	13.9	9.3	7.4	7.7	50.7	251 338	2.46	10.9	27.7
Congressional District 25	5.3	6.4	19.5	8.5	12.5	16.5	14.1	8.7	7.1	6.8	51.8	255 854	2.50	11.9	27.5
Congressional District 26	4.5	5.8	18.8	9.2	12.0	16.8	14.4	8.9	7.0	7.0	51.0	243 470	2.56	9.5	25.1
Congressional District 27	3.6	6.0	18.0	8.6	12.8	15.9	13.7	9.3	8.0	7.8	51.6	261 667	2.42	12.3	29.8
Congressional District 28	5.4	6.7	19.3	9.8	13.7	15.3	12.7	8.1	6.9	7.3	52.7	268 208	2.37	18.8	33.9
Congressional District 29	4.2	6.0	19.1	9.4	11.5	15.8	14.5	9.6	7.3	6.8	50.8	248 381	2.52	9.8	25.4

[3]No spouse present.

Table A. 109th Congressional Districts, 2000—*Continued*

(Number, percent.)

STATE Congressional district	Group quarters				Education				Money income, 1999			Percent below poverty level, 1999	
					School enrollment[4]		Attainment level[5]			Households			
	Persons in correctional institutions	Persons in nursing homes	Persons in college dormitories	Persons in military quarters	Public	Private	H.S. graduate or more	Bachelor's degree or more	Per capita income[6]	Median income	Percent with income over $100,000	Persons	Families
	28	29	30	31	32	33	34	35	36	37	38	39	40
MISSOURI—*Continued*													
Congressional District 6	7 902	5 672	4 520	0	139 330	21 503	85.7	21.2	20 307	41 225	8.9	8.7	6.2
Congressional District 7	1 910	5 090	10 022	0	136 492	23 827	81.7	18.8	17 508	32 929	5.7	13.0	9.0
Congressional District 8	4 486	7 332	3 641	0	138 289	13 318	70.4	11.9	14 862	27 865	3.8	18.2	13.7
Congressional District 9	8 301	6 009	11 732	0	147 863	24 386	80.5	19.9	18 262	36 693	7.2	11.8	7.7
MONTANA	4 124	6 470	7 035	404	217 183	24 571	87.2	24.4	17 151	33 024	5.6	14.6	10.5
Congressional District (At Large)	4 124	6 470	7 035	404	217 183	24 571	87.2	24.4	17 151	33 024	5.6	14.6	10.5
NEBRASKA	6 060	16 195	18 376	590	398 031	82 674	86.6	23.7	19 613	39 250	8.1	9.7	6.7
Congressional District 1	3 142	5 242	10 724	0	137 120	27 009	86.8	23.9	19 268	40 021	7.5	9.2	5.9
Congressional District 2	1 847	3 430	2 836	590	128 681	37 989	88.4	30.5	22 610	45 235	11.9	8.8	6.0
Congressional District 3	1 071	7 523	4 816	0	132 230	17 676	84.7	17.1	16 962	33 866	5.0	11.1	8.1
NEVADA	15 940	4 895	2 498	1 312	448 044	44 841	80.7	18.2	21 989	44 581	11.3	10.5	7.5
Congressional District 1	4 811	1 918	1 042	0	146 221	13 985	74.3	14.6	19 240	39 480	8.8	13.9	10.3
Congressional District 2	9 188	2 039	1 456	945	159 032	14 759	82.8	19.3	21 988	43 879	10.5	10.1	7.1
Congressional District 3	1 941	938	0	367	142 791	16 097	84.6	20.4	24 743	50 749	14.5	7.5	5.4
NEW HAMPSHIRE	3 468	9 316	17 574	95	264 403	68 485	87.4	28.7	23 844	49 467	13.8	6.5	4.3
Congressional District 1	1 422	4 224	7 544	89	133 348	32 440	87.5	28.5	23 943	50 135	13.7	6.7	4.4
Congressional District 2	2 046	5 092	10 030	6	131 055	36 045	87.3	28.9	23 744	48 762	13.9	6.4	4.2
NEW JERSEY	47 941	51 493	45 222	3 291	1 735 248	482 584	82.1	29.8	27 006	55 146	21.3	8.5	6.3
Congressional District 1	3 610	3 678	2 781	0	149 773	32 224	80.2	20.7	21 419	47 473	12.8	9.9	7.6
Congressional District 2	10 556	4 555	2 017	355	141 894	24 853	77.6	17.9	20 964	44 173	11.3	10.3	7.6
Congressional District 3	5 637	4 410	4	1 229	133 018	28 056	86.3	27.2	26 248	55 282	18.8	5.1	3.5
Congressional District 4	4 396	5 554	796	1 409	122 774	39 957	83.8	25.4	25 475	54 073	18.8	6.6	4.5
Congressional District 5	267	6 190	1 650	0	136 077	36 953	90.1	38.6	34 617	72 781	32.5	3.6	2.3
Congressional District 6	19	3 879	10 850	23	143 880	35 234	83.4	29.7	25 410	55 681	20.0	9.1	6.2
Congressional District 7	5 226	2 852	0	0	128 324	35 677	89.1	41.5	35 692	74 823	34.2	3.4	2.2
Congressional District 8	1 921	3 653	2 708	0	129 617	40 084	76.8	28.0	25 253	51 954	20.9	10.7	8.1
Congressional District 9	980	1 609	933	0	111 061	44 091	80.6	29.5	26 887	52 437	18.9	7.6	5.6
Congressional District 10	4 594	3 038	5 488	0	147 289	41 996	72.7	18.3	18 804	38 177	11.0	17.5	14.9
Congressional District 11	1 669	4 444	3 187	10	126 603	41 863	90.9	45.2	38 244	79 009	36.9	3.5	2.2
Congressional District 12	5 240	3 810	12 248	255	134 303	44 733	88.8	42.3	33 047	69 668	31.0	5.2	3.4
Congressional District 13	3 826	3 821	2 560	10	130 635	36 863	64.6	20.5	19 019	37 129	11.2	18.0	15.6
NEW MEXICO	10 940	6 810	7 921	1 827	476 022	57 764	78.9	23.5	17 261	34 133	7.6	18.4	14.5
Congressional District 1	2 444	1 835	2 377	431	145 845	24 287	83.9	29.5	20 348	38 413	10.0	14.0	10.4
Congressional District 2	6 324	2 729	3 530	834	168 380	13 396	73.1	16.9	14 239	29 269	4.5	22.4	17.9
Congressional District 3	2 172	2 246	2 014	562	161 797	20 081	79.3	23.7	17 193	35 058	8.2	19.0	15.2
NEW YORK	108 088	123 852	174 111	8 598	3 987 395	1 229 635	79.1	27.4	23 389	43 393	15.3	14.6	11.5
Congressional District 1	1 471	4 450	6 959	21	151 000	28 355	87.2	27.2	26 080	61 884	23.3	6.0	4.0
Congressional District 2	0	3 867	1 406	18	147 062	32 952	85.6	30.6	28 129	71 147	30.1	5.9	3.9
Congressional District 3	0	3 039	151	4	126 603	41 204	88.5	31.3	30 955	70 561	29.9	4.3	2.8
Congressional District 4	1 423	3 214	4 142	0	133 768	47 163	83.3	31.0	27 633	66 799	28.1	6.4	4.4
Congressional District 5	0	4 694	2 566	0	124 307	42 197	77.9	33.6	26 526	51 156	21.3	12.1	9.4
Congressional District 6	0	4 814	954	0	154 071	43 372	73.0	18.0	17 048	43 546	12.1	14.5	12.1
Congressional District 7	0	5 561	1 490	0	124 509	50 116	71.6	19.8	17 305	36 990	8.4	17.7	14.9
Congressional District 8	2 517	2 669	10 558	0	77 585	75 030	81.8	47.8	39 901	47 061	23.8	18.7	15.5
Congressional District 9	467	2 869	65	0	106 560	54 482	80.7	31.0	22 680	45 426	14.4	12.2	9.9
Congressional District 10	695	2 710	1 815	0	162 700	52 555	67.6	17.5	14 771	30 212	8.1	29.0	25.8
Congressional District 11	141	2 198	768	0	155 014	49 339	72.2	25.0	18 119	34 082	10.2	23.2	21.1
Congressional District 12	1 421	1 306	449	0	149 632	31 545	56.4	17.1	14 812	29 195	6.9	28.3	25.5
Congressional District 13	944	4 108	1 048	230	118 999	51 261	79.4	24.0	23 208	50 092	17.0	11.9	9.6
Congressional District 14	620	2 532	5 920	0	64 413	59 717	86.6	56.9	53 752	57 152	27.9	12.4	9.4
Congressional District 15	13 642	3 176	10 564	0	142 337	52 438	63.1	25.0	18 094	27 934	9.3	30.5	27.6
Congressional District 16	955	2 669	2 442	0	194 810	31 948	50.5	7.8	9 803	19 311	2.8	42.2	39.9
Congressional District 17	9	6 659	4 458	0	126 423	64 076	77.7	28.5	22 364	44 868	16.8	16.0	13.4
Congressional District 18	3 735	5 336	4 292	0	122 625	51 069	84.3	43.8	39 446	68 887	34.0	7.8	5.5
Congressional District 19	8 686	3 946	6 861	3 695	140 351	43 790	86.4	32.3	28 488	64 337	26.2	6.4	4.2
Congressional District 20	11 583	4 962	5 126	0	139 575	25 873	84.4	24.7	21 891	44 239	11.2	7.9	5.5
Congressional District 21	2 318	7 427	14 507	0	139 587	37 827	84.1	27.0	21 493	40 254	10.4	11.2	7.8
Congressional District 22	5 924	4 959	18 576	1	151 455	40 743	81.4	23.9	19 490	38 586	9.6	14.3	9.3
Congressional District 23	15 753	4 102	15 623	4 616	157 625	21 504	79.6	16.0	16 862	35 434	5.7	13.5	9.5
Congressional District 24	11 480	5 614	11 474	13	153 660	23 141	80.9	19.3	17 979	36 082	6.5	12.6	8.8
Congressional District 25	1 418	4 167	7 028	0	144 471	39 465	85.8	27.8	21 692	43 188	11.5	10.4	7.2
Congressional District 26	11 383	6 652	10 445	0	150 070	32 038	85.7	25.5	21 731	46 653	11.6	6.9	4.7
Congressional District 27	6 647	4 623	4 324	0	138 615	29 571	81.3	19.9	18 916	36 884	7.3	12.0	8.8
Congressional District 28	939	6 330	6 754	0	148 304	37 558	79.2	21.2	17 872	31 751	6.4	18.7	15.3
Congressional District 29	3 917	5 199	14 356	0	141 264	39 306	85.6	26.1	21 255	41 875	11.2	9.9	6.8

[4]All persons 3 years old and over enrolled in nursery school through college.
[5]Persons 25 years old and over.
[6]Based on the population enumerated as of April 1, 2000.

Table A. 109th Congressional Districts, 2000—*Continued*

(Number, percent.)

STATE Congressional district	Housing units									Civilian labor force		
	Total	Total occupied units	Owner occupied		Median owner costs as a percent of income		Renter occupied		Sub-standard housing units (percent)9	Total	Unemployment	
			Percent	Median value7 (dollars)	With a mortgage	Without a mortgage8	Median rent (dollars)	Median rent as a percent of income			Total	Rate10
	41	42	43	44	45	46	47	48	49	50	51	52
MISSOURI—*Continued*												
Congressional District 6	263 824	241 504	72.0	92 100	19.3	9.9	502	22.3	2.1	322 893	12 240	3.8
Congressional District 7	272 549	246 008	68.9	83 200	20.0	9.9	450	24.6	3.0	317 094	17 855	5.6
Congressional District 8	280 076	245 519	72.0	64 100	19.1	9.9	366	24.7	3.3	280 264	18 269	6.5
Congressional District 9	268 913	236 903	72.6	87 800	19.2	9.9	448	24.1	2.7	317 604	14 648	4.6
MONTANA	412 633	358 667	69.1	99 500	22.2	10.4	447	25.3	3.8	454 687	28 710	6.3
Congressional District (At Large)	412 633	358 667	69.1	99 500	22.2	10.4	447	25.3	3.8	454 687	28 710	6.3
NEBRASKA	722 668	666 184	67.4	88 000	19.7	10.5	491	23.0	3.0	909 524	32 287	3.5
Congressional District 1	236 798	220 835	67.4	92 100	19.9	10.0	486	23.3	2.9	312 761	11 167	3.6
Congressional District 2	231 658	219 999	63.8	103 300	19.8	10.4	551	23.5	3.4	303 619	11 474	3.7
Congressional District 3	254 212	225 350	71.0	66 700	19.2	11.0	416	22.0	2.8	293 144	9 646	3.3
NEVADA	827 457	751 165	60.9	142 000	23.8	9.9	699	26.5	8.9	995 200	61 920	6.2
Congressional District 1	266 871	244 538	51.8	126 000	24.0	9.9	655	27.6	13.1	319 873	25 015	7.8
Congressional District 2	284 431	253 503	63.6	147 300	23.5	9.9	650	25.4	7.9	331 001	18 435	5.5
Congressional District 3	276 155	253 124	66.9	150 500	23.8	9.9	806	26.2	5.9	344 326	18 470	5.3
NEW HAMPSHIRE	547 024	474 606	69.7	133 300	22.3	13.6	646	24.2	2.1	676 371	25 500	3.8
Congressional District 1	276 597	238 422	68.6	139 000	22.6	13.8	658	24.2	2.1	340 399	11 524	3.4
Congressional District 2	270 427	236 184	70.9	127 000	22.0	13.5	630	24.2	2.0	335 972	13 976	4.2
NEW JERSEY	3 310 275	3 064 645	65.6	170 800	23.7	15.3	751	25.5	5.4	4 193 145	243 116	5.8
Congressional District 1	253 871	236 875	70.0	108 600	23.4	15.6	640	26.2	4.2	324 364	20 137	6.2
Congressional District 2	313 352	238 517	71.1	116 000	23.9	14.9	649	27.3	4.4	313 837	24 255	7.7
Congressional District 3	288 042	243 939	82.4	137 300	23.7	15.3	790	26.7	1.8	312 554	13 753	4.3
Congressional District 4	259 219	241 042	77.7	145 800	23.8	16.1	781	27.0	3.3	308 687	13 845	4.4
Congressional District 5	239 813	229 150	81.6	238 400	24.3	14.8	855	25.8	1.9	331 568	11 018	3.3
Congressional District 6	248 934	234 071	61.3	164 000	23.9	15.0	785	25.2	6.2	339 656	19 637	5.8
Congressional District 7	239 147	233 383	78.7	224 300	22.9	14.7	906	23.5	3.0	338 393	10 908	3.2
Congressional District 8	232 789	225 542	56.7	200 700	24.4	16.8	759	25.8	8.1	312 967	20 487	6.5
Congressional District 9	259 372	251 055	52.8	198 100	25.2	16.9	825	24.8	7.2	334 581	17 983	5.4
Congressional District 10	244 845	228 419	38.6	144 000	25.6	17.3	664	26.4	11.1	296 420	32 443	10.9
Congressional District 11	240 079	233 258	77.9	256 900	22.9	13.8	891	23.8	2.6	343 993	11 666	3.4
Congressional District 12	242 926	233 010	75.1	206 000	22.7	14.5	825	23.9	3.2	332 225	18 141	5.4
Congressional District 13	247 886	236 384	28.9	140 100	26.2	17.1	685	25.4	13.9	303 900	28 843	9.5
NEW MEXICO	780 579	677 971	70.0	108 100	22.2	9.9	503	26.6	8.7	823 440	60 324	7.3
Congressional District 1	258 471	238 379	65.4	127 100	23.0	9.9	557	27.7	6.1	300 737	17 578	5.8
Congressional District 2	261 040	218 546	72.0	76 900	20.6	9.9	417	26.0	9.0	248 877	21 767	8.6
Congressional District 3	261 068	221 046	72.9	114 100	22.3	9.9	521	25.4	11.1	273 826	20 979	7.6
NEW YORK	7 679 307	7 056 860	53.0	148 700	23.2	13.6	672	26.8	8.4	9 023 096	640 108	7.1
Congressional District 1	267 522	223 885	79.4	176 700	25.0	15.9	925	28.9	3.0	329 050	13 638	4.1
Congressional District 2	214 835	206 854	81.7	204 200	25.3	15.8	991	27.8	4.2	325 702	12 272	3.8
Congressional District 3	231 017	225 221	81.7	224 500	24.8	16.1	989	26.6	2.3	328 676	11 058	3.4
Congressional District 4	217 425	212 562	77.3	224 700	25.6	16.5	905	27.3	6.1	317 441	12 831	4.0
Congressional District 5	236 258	228 362	53.3	341 000	25.3	13.6	838	27.3	16.9	309 459	18 428	6.0
Congressional District 6	216 196	204 235	52.7	180 000	28.5	12.9	730	26.7	15.5	296 869	28 139	9.5
Congressional District 7	249 742	238 573	32.3	204 900	28.3	13.9	705	25.9	18.1	286 792	25 160	8.8
Congressional District 8	322 443	303 343	26.1	260 000	29.1	13.4	817	25.6	11.5	341 751	22 980	6.7
Congressional District 9	268 219	255 970	46.2	246 000	25.6	12.2	770	25.7	11.3	299 639	17 728	5.9
Congressional District 10	245 526	226 363	28.6	193 900	28.4	12.7	606	27.9	15.1	260 646	35 297	13.5
Congressional District 11	249 952	238 213	21.6	214 800	26.0	12.2	689	27.2	17.5	302 527	35 141	11.6
Congressional District 12	237 484	224 653	18.8	189 700	29.4	13.6	645	27.7	21.2	281 025	30 782	10.9
Congressional District 13	250 914	240 389	54.0	217 800	23.6	12.0	745	25.6	7.4	301 859	18 446	6.1
Congressional District 14	367 464	340 543	26.8	252 500	29.2	14.0	993	24.4	8.3	390 942	20 278	5.2
Congressional District 15	265 077	247 218	10.0	314 700	30.1	10.9	586	26.2	18.7	273 272	39 498	14.4
Congressional District 16	226 095	211 904	7.1	155 600	30.8	15.0	564	30.0	28.7	215 754	43 819	20.3
Congressional District 17	245 266	235 347	41.2	230 600	25.4	14.6	737	26.8	12.2	302 608	22 939	7.6
Congressional District 18	242 797	235 623	63.7	346 500	23.9	15.2	881	26.1	6.3	321 066	12 441	3.9
Congressional District 19	236 035	223 647	75.2	188 800	23.6	13.6	796	25.8	2.8	323 292	13 673	4.2
Congressional District 20	304 081	250 312	73.8	110 600	22.1	12.5	582	24.9	1.8	328 986	15 412	4.7
Congressional District 21	292 459	265 380	60.8	100 500	21.4	12.3	567	25.7	2.0	331 000	21 354	6.4
Congressional District 22	290 868	248 893	61.2	98 500	21.9	12.8	572	28.2	3.5	317 043	20 451	6.4
Congressional District 23	306 262	240 431	71.0	71 900	20.1	12.3	470	26.3	2.4	300 553	24 688	7.9
Congressional District 24	286 416	251 360	69.8	75 300	20.9	12.8	477	26.6	1.8	317 059	20 585	6.5
Congressional District 25	277 435	255 813	69.1	89 000	21.2	13.1	557	27.1	2.0	328 395	16 577	5.0
Congressional District 26	257 287	243 482	75.0	97 600	21.7	13.0	569	26.3	1.6	333 782	19 081	5.7
Congressional District 27	289 471	261 614	66.2	84 500	21.7	13.7	496	27.1	2.2	319 934	20 108	6.3
Congressional District 28	301 352	268 193	55.4	76 900	21.6	13.5	528	30.3	3.0	308 311	26 719	8.7
Congressional District 29	283 409	248 477	74.0	87 700	20.8	12.0	543	25.8	1.9	329 663	20 585	6.2

7Specified owner-occupied units.
8Median monthly owner costs is often in the minimum category—9.9 percent or less, which is indicated as 9.9 percent.
9Overcrowded or lacking complete plumbing facilities.
10Percent of civilian labor force.

Table A. 109th Congressional Districts, 2000—*Continued*

(Number, percent.)

STATE Congressional district	Civilian employment and occupations				Total farms, 2002	Farms by size, 2002 (percent)			Land in farms, 2002		Cropland harvested, 2002		Farm's principal operator's primary occupation is farming, 2002 (percent)
	Total	Management, professional, and related (percent)	Service, sales, and office (percent)	Construction and production (percent)		1 to 49 acres	50 to 999 acres	1,000 acres or more	Acreage	Average size of farms (acres)	Acreage	Farms	
	53	54	55	56	57	58	59	60	61	62	63	64	65
MISSOURI—*Continued*													
Congressional District 6	310 653	31.7	41.5	25.9	20 879	20.0	72.8	7.3	6 933 337	332	3 362 093	14 281	57.3
Congressional District 7	299 239	27.6	43.1	28.5	13 028	33.3	64.9	1.8	2 301 046	177	679 816	7 677	55.8
Congressional District 8	261 995	24.7	39.0	34.5	19 816	19.8	73.2	7.0	6 445 021	325	2 838 744	13 033	59.0
Congressional District 9	302 956	30.1	39.3	29.7	22 595	20.3	74.3	5.4	6 463 637	286	2 876 987	15 658	55.6
MONTANA	425 977	33.1	42.8	22.0	27 870	23.3	40.3	36.4	59 612 403	2 139	8 742 111	16 543	63.5
Congressional District (At Large)	425 977	33.1	42.8	22.0	27 870	23.3	40.3	36.4	59 612 403	2 139	8 742 111	16 543	63.5
NEBRASKA	877 237	33.0	41.0	24.4	49 355	14.8	61.9	23.3	45 903 116	930	17 336 624	37 143	73.0
Congressional District 1	301 594	32.1	40.6	26.2	17 159	21.2	67.2	11.7	7 176 787	418	5 197 652	12 722	67.2
Congressional District 2	292 145	36.5	43.8	19.5	422	45.7	45.0	9.2	112 806	267	89 516	311	54.7
Congressional District 3	283 498	30.2	38.6	27.6	31 774	11.0	59.2	29.8	38 613 523	1 215	12 049 456	24 110	76.4
NEVADA	933 280	25.7	52.2	21.8	2 989	46.7	36.3	17.0	6 330 622	2 118	549 076	1 521	58.7
Congressional District 1	294 858	21.3	55.7	23.0	69	81.2	18.8	0.0	2 326	34	258	18	49.3
Congressional District 2	312 566	27.8	47.3	24.3	2 789	44.3	37.6	18.1	6 266 999	2 247	545 669	1 462	59.8
Congressional District 3	325 856	27.6	53.9	18.4	131	80.2	16.8	3.1	61 297	468	3 149	41	38.9
NEW HAMPSHIRE	650 871	35.8	39.6	24.1	3 363	45.9	53.0	1.2	444 879	132	95 983	2 043	48.6
Congressional District 1	328 875	35.2	40.8	23.6	1 196	51.6	47.9	0.5	119 603	100	24 863	753	49.2
Congressional District 2	321 996	36.4	38.4	24.7	2 167	42.7	55.7	1.6	325 276	150	71 120	1 290	48.3
NEW JERSEY	3 950 029	38.0	42.1	19.7	9 924	70.5	28.4	1.2	805 682	81	444 670	7 230	52.3
Congressional District 1	304 227	32.8	44.3	22.8	418	74.6	24.6	0.7	23 707	57	12 927	311	50.7
Congressional District 2	289 582	27.9	48.3	23.0	2 585	65.7	32.7	1.5	250 568	97	162 608	2 060	58.8
Congressional District 3	298 801	38.1	43.1	18.6	691	69.6	26.8	3.6	84 923	123	36 826	500	55.7
Congressional District 4	294 842	36.4	43.2	20.1	1 099	77.1	21.9	1.0	78 343	71	47 765	686	55.8
Congressional District 5	320 550	44.0	39.6	16.3	1 975	67.5	31.9	0.6	153 759	78	73 615	1 433	48.5
Congressional District 6	320 019	37.4	42.4	20.1	97	83.5	16.5	0.0	3 544	37	D	73	62.9
Congressional District 7	327 485	47.5	36.7	15.7	1 352	72.6	26.8	0.6	91 772	68	41 144	913	45.6
Congressional District 8	292 480	35.5	42.0	22.4	0	X	X	X	X	X	X	X	X
Congressional District 9	316 598	36.0	43.6	20.3	0	X	X	X	X	X	X	X	X
Congressional District 10	263 977	27.7	48.7	23.6	15	100.0	0.0	0.0	153	10	D	11	53.3
Congressional District 11	332 327	48.6	37.3	14.0	466	76.0	23.6	0.4	24 184	52	9 033	335	43.3
Congressional District 12	314 084	48.8	37.3	13.8	1 208	72.0	26.7	1.3	94 547	78	58 939	896	50.2
Congressional District 13	275 057	28.2	43.3	28.4	18	100.0	0.0	0.0	182	10	104	12	66.7
NEW MEXICO	763 116	34.0	42.8	22.2	15 170	44.7	33.2	22.1	44 810 083	2 954	856 166	7 204	55.9
Congressional District 1	283 159	37.3	43.7	18.9	1 400	62.7	24.2	13.1	2 059 643	1 471	25 431	619	50.6
Congressional District 2	227 110	28.9	42.4	26.7	6 724	51.3	27.2	21.5	24 480 558	3 641	310 575	3 654	54.2
Congressional District 3	252 847	34.9	42.3	21.7	7 046	34.8	40.6	24.6	18 269 882	2 593	520 160	2 931	58.6
NEW YORK	8 382 988	36.7	43.7	19.3	37 255	30.4	66.9	2.8	7 660 969	206	3 846 368	29 162	60.8
Congressional District 1	315 412	36.0	43.3	20.3	550	74.0	25.8	0.2	28 100	51	18 042	397	62.5
Congressional District 2	313 430	37.3	42.5	20.1	98	89.8	8.2	2.0	5 956	61	3 679	73	63.3
Congressional District 3	317 618	38.6	44.2	17.0	46	87.0	13.0	0.0	832	18	291	23	47.8
Congressional District 4	304 610	37.6	45.7	16.6	18	83.3	16.7	0.0	353	20	254	15	61.1
Congressional District 5	291 031	36.9	44.9	18.2	4	100.0	0.0	0.0	D	D	4	4	D
Congressional District 6	268 730	27.2	52.2	20.5	0	X	X	X	X	X	X	X	X
Congressional District 7	261 632	27.9	51.0	21.1	0	X	X	X	X	X	X	X	X
Congressional District 8	318 771	55.0	34.8	10.1	0	X	X	X	X	X	X	X	X
Congressional District 9	281 911	39.0	43.3	17.6	3	100.0	0.0	0.0	D	D	D	3	D
Congressional District 10	225 349	31.0	51.4	17.5	0	X	X	X	X	X	X	X	X
Congressional District 11	267 386	35.1	49.2	15.7	0	X	X	X	X	X	X	X	X
Congressional District 12	250 243	25.9	46.5	27.5	4	100.0	0.0	0.0	D	D	4	4	D
Congressional District 13	283 413	34.9	46.7	18.3	16	100.0	0.0	0.0	44	3	D	9	6.3
Congressional District 14	370 664	57.7	34.5	7.8	0	X	X	X	X	X	X	X	X
Congressional District 15	233 774	38.1	47.1	14.8	0	X	X	X	X	X	X	X	X
Congressional District 16	171 935	18.2	58.0	23.6	0	X	X	X	X	X	X	X	X
Congressional District 17	279 669	37.8	46.1	16.0	29	65.5	34.5	0.0	1 076	37	272	23	69.0
Congressional District 18	308 625	47.5	39.6	12.8	50	70.0	30.0	0.0	3 270	65	500	31	64.0
Congressional District 19	309 619	40.6	40.7	18.5	788	46.2	52.0	1.8	112 781	143	49 540	539	67.3
Congressional District 20	313 574	35.7	40.7	22.7	4 193	33.0	64.4	2.6	840 858	201	377 214	3 093	61.1
Congressional District 21	309 646	37.8	43.0	18.9	2 127	30.7	67.7	1.6	386 117	182	205 197	1 715	59.1
Congressional District 22	296 592	35.0	43.1	21.4	1 784	34.6	64.0	1.3	297 391	167	119 560	1 357	60.1
Congressional District 23	275 865	28.4	42.8	27.4	6 327	19.0	78.1	2.9	1 624 632	257	750 745	5 109	64.3
Congressional District 24	296 474	32.5	42.0	24.4	6 405	25.0	72.3	2.6	1 398 291	218	706 598	5 111	60.8
Congressional District 25	311 818	37.7	41.1	20.8	1 856	39.0	57.1	4.0	358 638	193	217 917	1 472	63.5
Congressional District 26	314 701	35.6	40.3	23.4	3 486	37.3	57.5	5.1	870 106	250	561 290	2 624	60.5
Congressional District 27	299 826	30.8	43.5	25.3	2 767	39.5	58.9	1.5	389 152	141	186 031	2 181	59.7
Congressional District 28	281 592	31.9	44.7	23.2	595	43.4	52.1	4.5	113 437	191	71 941	438	60.0
Congressional District 29	309 078	36.8	39.3	23.0	6 109	24.3	72.9	2.8	1 229 921	201	577 263	4 941	57.1

X = Not applicable.
D = Suppressed to avoid disclosure.

Table A. 109th Congressional Districts, 2000—*Continued*

(Number, percent.)

STATE Congressional district	Farm's principal operator is full owner, 2002 (percent)	Type of organization, 2002 (percent)			Value of all agricultural products sold, 2002				Payments received from federal farm programs, 2002					
		Family or individual	Partner-ship	Corpo-ration	Total ($1,000)	Percent of farms			Total payments ($1,000)	Farms receiving payments		Percent of farms receiving		
						Less than $50,000	$50,000 to $249,999	$250,000 or more		Number	Percent	Less than $50,000	$50,000 to $249,999	$250,000 or more
	66	67	68	69	70	72	73	74	75	76	77	78	79	80
MISSOURI—*Continued*														
Congressional District 6	70.1	90.6	5.9	2.7	1 061 393	82.0	14.1	3.9	87 794	12 467	59.7	98.8	1.2	0.0
Congressional District 7	72.2	94.7	3.5	1.5	748 148	87.8	7.9	4.3	9 687	3 139	24.1	99.9	0.1	0.0
Congressional District 8	70.5	92.9	4.9	1.7	943 180	84.7	10.5	4.8	51 686	6 226	31.4	96.6	3.3	0.1
Congressional District 9	71.1	90.8	6.1	2.4	924 717	84.5	12.0	3.5	62 814	10 513	46.5	98.9	1.1	0.0
MONTANA	61.0	80.5	7.9	9.8	1 882 114	71.1	23.1	5.8	210 749	12 389	44.5	92.5	7.4	0.1
Congressional District (At Large)	61.0	80.5	7.9	9.8	1 882 114	71.1	23.1	5.8	210 749	12 389	44.5	92.5	7.4	0.1
NEBRASKA	49.0	86.8	6.2	6.2	9 703 657	54.6	31.3	14.1	347 517	32 007	64.9	97.4	2.6	0.0
Congressional District 1	54.1	89.3	5.6	4.2	2 489 414	62.5	27.9	9.6	104 813	11 727	68.3	98.6	1.4	0.0
Congressional District 2	62.3	85.5	7.1	6.4	39 718	71.3	20.4	8.3	1 488	181	42.9	98.3	1.7	0.0
Congressional District 3	46.1	85.4	6.6	7.3	7 174 525	50.1	33.3	16.6	241 217	20 099	63.3	96.7	3.2	0.0
NEVADA	78.8	83.6	6.9	6.7	446 989	73.0	16.8	10.2	4 322	439	14.7	96.6	3.2	0.2
Congressional District 1	87.0	87.0	1.4	5.8	5 204	91.3	2.9	5.8	9	6	8.7	100.0	0.0	0.0
Congressional District 2	78.5	83.4	7.0	6.8	431 493	71.6	17.7	10.7	4 301	428	15.3	96.5	3.3	0.2
Congressional District 3	80.9	87.0	6.1	5.3	10 293	91.6	6.1	2.3	13	5	3.8	100.0	0.0	0.0
NEW HAMPSHIRE	73.6	86.7	6.1	4.7	144 835	88.6	7.7	3.7	3 823	359	10.7	96.7	3.3	0.0
Congressional District 1	80.5	85.5	6.5	5.4	37 468	90.5	5.9	3.6	802	84	7.0	97.6	2.4	0.0
Congressional District 2	69.7	87.4	5.9	4.3	107 367	87.6	8.7	3.7	3 021	275	12.7	96.4	3.6	0.0
NEW JERSEY	80.5	86.4	5.8	7.1	749 872	85.5	8.5	6.0	4 441	582	5.9	98.5	1.4	0.2
Congressional District 1	78.5	87.8	6.0	6.2	29 770	85.9	7.4	6.7	195	12	2.9	91.7	8.3	0.0
Congressional District 2	75.2	88.3	5.2	6.1	343 077	78.9	9.7	11.4	1 517	187	7.2	97.9	1.6	0.5
Congressional District 3	78.6	80.6	6.7	12.0	64 385	79.0	13.9	7.1	427	32	4.6	96.9	3.1	0.0
Congressional District 4	82.1	82.7	6.3	10.5	95 925	84.6	8.6	6.8	326	44	4.0	97.7	2.3	0.0
Congressional District 5	82.0	88.9	6.1	4.6	67 729	89.4	7.9	2.7	D	126	6.4	100.0	0.0	0.0
Congressional District 6	85.6	83.5	6.2	6.2	11 987	85.6	9.3	5.2	D	1	1.0	100.0	0.0	0.0
Congressional District 7	86.3	87.6	4.9	6.5	29 565	92.5	5.8	1.7	470	82	6.1	98.8	1.2	0.0
Congressional District 8	X	X	X	X	X	X	X	X	X	X	X	X	X	X
Congressional District 9	X	X	X	X	X	X	X	X	X	X	X	X	X	X
Congressional District 10	100.0	40.0	6.7	53.3	737	73.3	20.0	6.7	X	X	X	X	X	X
Congressional District 11	87.1	82.0	7.7	7.7	42 397	90.1	5.4	4.5	54	13	2.8	100.0	0.0	0.0
Congressional District 12	80.1	86.2	5.8	7.4	57 551	88.2	8.4	3.4	483	85	7.0	98.8	1.2	0.0
Congressional District 13	83.3	66.7	11.1	16.7	6 750	72.2	5.6	22.2	D	D	D	D	D	D
NEW MEXICO	70.3	88.7	5.8	4.2	1 700 030	84.7	10.0	5.4	50 201	3 246	21.4	92.9	6.8	0.3
Congressional District 1	75.5	91.6	4.9	2.9	65 761	92.5	4.7	2.8	1 209	153	10.9	98.7	1.3	0.0
Congressional District 2	72.4	88.0	6.6	4.5	914 991	81.5	12.3	6.2	14 241	1 057	15.7	93.9	5.8	0.3
Congressional District 3	67.3	88.8	5.3	4.1	719 279	86.1	8.8	5.1	34 751	2 036	28.9	91.9	7.8	0.3
NEW YORK	66.4	87.6	7.6	4.2	3 117 834	74.4	18.7	6.9	110 234	9 896	26.6	96.0	4.0	0.0
Congressional District 1	67.8	61.1	12.5	26.0	163 986	59.8	21.1	19.1	147	37	6.7	100.0	0.0	0.0
Congressional District 2	66.3	60.2	3.1	36.7	37 016	70.4	13.3	16.3	D	D	D	D	D	D
Congressional District 3	87.0	67.4	8.7	23.9	3 939	73.9	21.7	4.3	D	D	D	D	D	D
Congressional District 4	61.1	44.4	11.1	44.4	4 141	61.1	16.7	22.2	D	D	D	D	D	D
Congressional District 5	100.0	25.0	75.0	0.0	350	0.0	100.0	0.0	D	D	D	D	D	D
Congressional District 6	X	X	X	X	X	X	X	X	X	X	X	X	X	X
Congressional District 7	X	X	X	X	X	X	X	X	X	X	X	X	X	X
Congressional District 8	X	X	X	X	X	X	X	X	X	X	X	X	X	X
Congressional District 9	100.0	33.3	0.0	33.3	78	100.0	0.0	0.0	D	D	D	D	D	D
Congressional District 10	X	X	X	X	X	X	X	X	X	X	X	X	X	X
Congressional District 11	X	X	X	X	X	X	X	X	X	X	X	X	X	X
Congressional District 12	100.0	0.0	0.0	100.0	390	0.0	100.0	0.0	D	D	D	D	D	D
Congressional District 13	75.0	56.3	0.0	25.0	1 720	81.3	6.3	12.5	D	D	D	D	D	D
Congressional District 14	X	X	X	X	X	X	X	X	X	X	X	X	X	X
Congressional District 15	X	X	X	X	X	X	X	X	X	X	X	X	X	X
Congressional District 16	X	X	X	X	X	X	X	X	X	X	X	X	X	X
Congressional District 17	48.3	55.2	10.3	13.8	3 130	65.5	27.6	6.9	D	D	D	D	D	D
Congressional District 18	74.0	50.0	14.0	36.0	6 700	56.0	34.0	10.0	D	2	4.0	100.0	0.0	0.0
Congressional District 19	67.6	73.4	8.9	15.7	63 726	75.4	17.0	7.6	D	121	15.4	95.9	4.1	0.0
Congressional District 20	64.3	83.5	10.0	6.0	293 186	77.2	15.8	7.0	11 873	967	23.1	95.7	4.3	0.0
Congressional District 21	66.9	89.5	7.1	2.8	110 513	79.0	15.7	5.4	5 315	561	26.4	97.7	2.3	0.0
Congressional District 22	66.8	83.7	8.2	6.6	113 170	80.6	14.2	5.2	3 139	291	16.3	95.5	4.5	0.0
Congressional District 23	65.7	90.8	7.3	1.6	509 814	70.0	23.1	6.9	23 560	1 845	29.2	95.8	4.2	0.0
Congressional District 24	64.5	89.1	8.2	2.5	495 145	70.8	22.6	6.6	20 476	1 984	31.0	97.1	2.9	0.0
Congressional District 25	65.8	86.9	8.1	5.0	202 074	70.9	19.2	9.9	7 178	525	28.3	92.2	7.8	0.0
Congressional District 26	64.2	87.5	7.6	4.5	518 978	74.7	15.0	10.3	16 824	1 234	35.4	93.8	6.1	0.1
Congressional District 27	71.2	90.2	5.9	3.8	166 089	77.7	17.4	4.9	5 426	552	19.9	96.6	3.4	0.0
Congressional District 28	72.1	89.4	5.9	4.7	60 527	81.3	11.1	7.6	1 584	168	28.2	94.0	6.0	0.0
Congressional District 29	68.2	90.9	6.1	2.6	363 162	77.9	17.3	4.8	13 288	1 609	26.3	97.5	2.5	0.0

X = Not applicable.
D = Suppressed to avoid disclosure.

Table A. 109th Congressional Districts, 2000—*Continued*

(Number, percent.)

STATE Congressional district	Representative	Land area,[1] (sq km)	Total population	Persons per square kilometer	Race alone or in combination (percent) White	Black	American Indian/Alaska Native	Asian and Pacific Islander	Other race	Hispanic or Latino[2] (percent)	Non-Hispanic White (percent)	Two or more races (percent)
	1	2	3	4	5	6	7	8	9	10	11	12
NORTH CAROLINA		126 161	8 049 313	63.8	73.1	22.1	1.6	1.8	2.8	4.7	70.2	1.3
Congressional District 1	Frank W. Ballance Jr. (D)	18 645	619 249	33.2	46.1	51.2	1.1	0.7	2.0	3.1	44.4	1.0
Congressional District 2	Bob Etheridge (D)	10 246	618 753	60.4	63.0	31.1	1.1	1.5	5.1	7.9	59.1	1.7
Congressional District 3	Walter B. Jones (R)	16 037	618 810	38.6	79.1	17.3	0.9	1.5	2.8	4.4	76.3	1.5
Congressional District 4	David E. Price (D)	3 246	619 432	190.8	72.2	21.3	0.8	4.5	3.0	5.0	68.8	1.6
Congressional District 5	Virginia Ann Foxx (R)	11 401	619 433	54.3	90.3	7.1	0.5	1.0	2.1	3.6	87.9	0.9
Congressional District 6	Howard Coble (R)	7 624	619 228	81.2	88.0	9.0	0.7	1.2	2.1	3.9	85.3	0.9
Congressional District 7	Mike McIntyre (D)	15 766	619 603	39.3	65.3	23.6	9.1	0.8	2.4	3.9	63.0	1.1
Congressional District 8	Robin Hayes (R)	8 502	618 465	72.7	66.0	27.6	2.3	2.3	3.7	6.6	61.8	1.8
Congressional District 9	Sue Wilkins Myrick (R)	2 566	619 705	241.5	85.7	10.8	0.6	2.4	1.7	3.5	82.9	1.1
Congressional District 10	Patrick T. McHenry (R)	8 552	618 943	72.4	87.3	9.5	0.5	1.8	1.8	3.5	84.9	0.9
Congressional District 11	Charles H. Taylor (R)	15 605	619 224	39.7	92.1	4.9	2.1	0.7	1.3	2.6	89.8	1.0
Congressional District 12	Melvin L. Watt (D)	2 127	619 269	291.1	48.3	45.8	0.8	2.5	4.4	7.1	44.6	1.6
Congressional District 13	Brad Miller (D)	5 842	619 199	106.0	67.1	27.7	0.8	2.5	3.7	6.0	63.3	1.6
NORTH DAKOTA		178 647	642 200	3.6	93.4	0.8	5.5	0.9	0.6	1.2	91.7	1.2
Congressional District (At Large)	Earl Pomeroy (D)	178 647	642 200	3.6	93.4	0.8	5.5	0.8	0.6	1.2	91.7	1.2
OHIO		106 056	11 353 140	107.0	86.1	12.1	0.7	1.5	1.1	1.9	84.0	1.4
Congressional District 1	Steve Chabot (R)	1 078	630 545	584.9	70.2	28.3	0.6	1.6	0.8	1.1	68.6	1.4
Congressional District 2	Rob Portman (R)	6 764	630 893	93.3	93.3	5.1	0.7	1.6	0.5	1.0	91.7	1.0
Congressional District 3	Michael R. Turner (R)	4 132	630 804	152.7	81.1	17.6	0.7	1.4	0.6	1.1	79.5	1.3
Congressional District 4	Michael G. Oxley (R)	11 966	630 549	52.7	93.4	5.7	0.6	0.8	0.7	1.2	91.7	1.1
Congressional District 5	Paul E. Gillmor (R)	15 872	630 826	39.7	96.5	1.4	0.5	0.6	2.1	3.8	93.7	1.1
Congressional District 6	Ted Strickland (D)	13 461	630 529	46.8	96.6	2.8	0.6	0.6	0.3	0.8	95.2	0.9
Congressional District 7	David L. Hobson (R)	7 377	630 805	85.5	90.6	8.2	0.9	1.3	0.7	1.1	88.7	1.5
Congressional District 8	John A. Boehner (R)	5 216	630 795	120.9	93.5	4.9	0.6	1.5	0.7	1.3	91.8	1.2
Congressional District 9	Marcy Kaptur (D)	2 853	630 711	221.1	83.2	14.6	0.8	1.3	2.2	4.0	79.6	2.0
Congressional District 10	Dennis J. Kucinich (D)	506	631 003	1 247.0	91.1	4.9	0.6	2.1	3.2	5.0	87.2	1.9
Congressional District 11	Stephanie Tubbs Jones (D)	348	630 668	1 812.3	40.8	56.9	0.7	2.0	1.5	2.3	38.8	1.6
Congressional District 12	Patrick J. Tiberi (R)	2 632	630 744	239.6	74.3	23.2	0.8	2.6	1.4	1.7	72.1	2.0
Congressional District 13	Sherrod Brown (D)	1 374	630 928	459.2	84.7	13.1	0.7	1.4	1.9	3.5	81.5	1.7
Congressional District 14	Steven C. LaTourette (R)	4 654	630 655	135.5	95.7	2.8	0.4	1.4	0.7	1.3	94.0	0.9
Congressional District 15	Deborah Pryce (R)	3 052	630 607	206.6	87.8	8.1	0.8	3.8	1.6	2.3	85.2	1.9
Congressional District 16	Ralph Regula (R)	4 486	630 710	140.6	94.0	5.4	0.6	0.8	0.4	0.9	92.4	1.2
Congressional District 17	Tim Ryan (D)	2 604	630 316	242.1	86.5	12.4	0.7	1.0	0.9	1.6	84.5	1.4
Congressional District 18	Robert W. Ney (R)	17 680	631 052	35.7	97.3	2.4	0.8	0.4	0.3	0.6	95.9	1.0
OKLAHOMA		177 847	3 450 654	19.4	80.3	8.3	11.4	1.8	3.0	5.2	74.1	4.5
Congressional District 1	John Sullivan (R)	4 498	690 419	153.5	80.3	10.2	9.4	1.9	3.0	5.3	73.8	4.6
Congressional District 2	Daniel David Boren (D)	53 258	689 974	13.0	77.2	4.6	23.0	0.5	1.3	2.4	70.2	6.5
Congressional District 3	Frank D. Lucas (R)	88 289	689 994	7.8	86.2	4.3	8.8	1.2	3.1	5.2	81.0	3.5
Congressional District 4	Tom Cole (R)	26 449	690 400	26.1	83.4	7.5	8.4	2.4	2.5	4.8	77.6	4.1
Congressional District 5	Ernest J. Istook Jr. (R)	5 353	689 867	128.9	74.3	14.7	7.1	3.2	4.9	8.3	67.7	4.0
OREGON		248 631	3 421 399	13.8	89.3	2.1	2.5	4.2	5.2	8.0	83.5	3.1
Congressional District 1	David Wu (D)	7 618	684 351	89.8	87.6	1.6	1.7	6.6	5.7	9.4	81.1	3.0
Congressional District 2	Greg Walden (R)	179 982	684 184	3.8	91.5	0.7	3.3	1.5	5.7	8.8	86.1	2.5
Congressional District 3	Earl Blumenauer (D)	2 644	684 502	258.9	83.2	6.3	2.2	7.2	5.4	7.6	77.2	4.0
Congressional District 4	Peter A. DeFazio (D)	44 498	684 512	15.4	94.6	0.9	2.9	2.5	2.3	4.2	89.7	3.0
Congressional District 5	Darlene Hooley (D)	13 889	683 850	49.2	89.8	1.1	2.3	3.1	6.8	10.3	83.6	2.9
PENNSYLVANIA		116 074	12 281 054	105.8	86.3	10.5	0.4	2.1	1.9	3.2	84.1	1.2
Congressional District 1	Robert A. Brady (D)	152	645 422	4 246.2	38.8	47.2	0.8	5.5	10.6	15.0	33.0	2.7
Congressional District 2	Chaka Fattah (D)	152	647 350	4 258.9	31.9	62.5	0.8	4.9	2.2	3.0	29.9	2.0
Congressional District 3	Phil English (R)	10 280	646 332	62.9	95.3	3.9	0.4	0.7	0.7	1.3	93.7	0.9
Congressional District 4	Melissa A. Hart (R)	3 373	646 555	191.7	95.4	3.7	0.3	1.1	0.3	0.6	94.3	0.7
Congressional District 5	John E. Peterson (R)	28 598	646 326	22.6	97.1	1.5	0.4	1.3	0.4	0.8	96.0	0.6
Congressional District 6	Jim Gerlach (R)	2 107	645 741	306.5	89.0	7.5	0.4	2.4	2.1	3.7	86.3	1.3
Congressional District 7	Curt Weldon (R)	751	646 355	860.7	90.0	5.9	0.3	4.1	0.7	1.3	88.4	1.0
Congressional District 8	Mike Fitzpatrick (R)	1 603	644 798	402.2	93.0	3.9	0.4	2.8	1.2	2.3	90.8	1.0
Congressional District 9	Bill Shuster (R)	18 543	647 032	34.9	97.5	1.9	0.3	0.5	0.5	0.9	96.4	0.6
Congressional District 10	Don Sherwood (R)	16 985	646 627	38.1	97.0	2.2	0.4	0.7	0.5	1.4	95.5	0.7
Congressional District 11	Paul E. Kanjorski (D)	5 744	646 148	112.5	95.4	3.0	0.4	0.9	1.3	2.5	93.3	1.0
Congressional District 12	John P. Murtha (D)	7 127	646 419	90.7	96.0	3.7	0.3	0.4	0.3	0.6	95.0	0.7
Congressional District 13	Allyson Y. Schwartz (D)	660	647 976	981.8	88.1	6.5	0.4	4.5	1.8	3.1	85.7	1.2
Congressional District 14	Michael F. Doyle (D)	419	645 809	1 541.3	74.6	23.6	0.6	2.0	0.8	1.1	72.9	1.5
Congressional District 15	Charlie Wieder Dent (R)	2 189	646 544	295.4	90.9	3.7	0.4	2.0	4.6	7.9	86.4	1.6
Congressional District 16	Joseph R. Pitts (R)	3 341	646 602	193.5	89.1	5.0	0.5	1.7	5.3	9.0	84.5	1.5
Congressional District 17	Tim Holden (D)	6 048	646 550	106.9	89.7	8.1	0.4	1.4	1.8	3.2	87.3	1.1
Congressional District 18	Tim Murphy (R)	3 708	646 325	174.3	96.4	2.3	0.2	1.5	0.3	0.6	95.4	0.7
Congressional District 19	Todd Russell Platts (R)	4 294	646 143	150.5	94.4	3.5	0.4	1.4	1.5	2.7	92.2	1.1

[1]Dry land or land partially or temporarily covered by water.
[2]Hispanic or Latino persons may be of any race.

Table A. 109th Congressional Districts, 2000—*Continued*

(Number, percent.)

STATE Congressional district	Foreign born (percent)	Age (percent)									Percent female	Households			
		Under 5 years	5 to 17 years	18 to 24 years	25 to 34 years	35 to 44 years	45 to 54 years	55 to 64 years	65 to 74 years	75 years and over		Number	Persons per household	Percent	
														Female-family householder[3]	One-person households
	13	14	15	16	17	18	19	20	21	22	23	24	25	26	27
NORTH CAROLINA	5.3	6.7	17.7	10.0	15.1	16.0	13.5	9.0	6.6	5.4	51.0	3 132 013	2.49	12.5	25.4
Congressional District 1	2.6	6.7	19.3	9.6	12.8	15.1	13.3	9.2	7.6	6.5	52.4	236 609	2.52	19.4	26.9
Congressional District 2	6.2	7.4	18.1	12.8	16.5	15.5	12.1	7.8	5.5	4.3	49.7	223 225	2.60	14.1	23.9
Congressional District 3	3.5	6.6	17.2	13.3	13.8	15.3	13.0	9.2	6.9	4.7	49.4	234 242	2.50	10.7	23.2
Congressional District 4	9.5	6.9	17.7	11.4	17.2	17.8	13.8	7.1	4.3	3.8	51.3	240 138	2.49	10.2	25.7
Congressional District 5	3.7	6.3	16.9	8.7	13.9	16.1	14.5	10.3	7.4	6.0	51.1	249 380	2.43	9.3	25.0
Congressional District 6	4.2	6.3	17.5	7.9	14.0	16.4	14.3	9.9	7.5	6.2	51.0	246 125	2.48	9.4	23.5
Congressional District 7	3.7	6.6	17.9	9.6	13.9	15.3	13.9	10.1	7.4	5.3	51.2	243 125	2.49	14.0	25.3
Congressional District 8	6.8	7.4	18.7	10.6	16.7	15.9	12.3	7.9	5.8	4.8	50.9	233 428	2.58	14.2	24.9
Congressional District 9	5.8	7.2	18.1	7.1	16.7	18.1	14.4	8.4	5.5	4.4	51.2	243 745	2.52	9.1	24.2
Congressional District 10	3.7	6.4	17.8	8.3	14.4	15.9	14.1	10.1	7.3	5.8	50.7	241 093	2.51	11.0	23.6
Congressional District 11	3.2	5.5	15.8	8.1	12.5	14.6	14.4	11.3	9.4	8.4	51.7	257 353	2.33	9.8	27.1
Congressional District 12	8.1	7.1	18.5	11.6	16.2	15.7	12.3	7.8	5.8	5.1	51.6	235 544	2.52	18.9	27.8
Congressional District 13	8.4	6.6	16.5	11.2	17.4	16.4	13.0	8.0	5.9	4.9	50.9	248 006	2.42	12.6	28.9
NORTH DAKOTA	1.9	6.1	18.9	11.4	12.0	15.3	13.3	8.3	7.1	7.6	50.1	257 152	2.41	7.8	29.3
Congressional District (At Large)	1.9	6.1	18.9	11.4	12.0	15.3	13.3	8.3	7.1	7.6	50.1	257 152	2.41	7.8	29.3
OHIO	3.0	6.6	18.8	9.3	13.4	15.9	13.8	8.9	7.0	6.3	51.4	4 445 773	2.49	12.1	27.3
Congressional District 1	2.8	6.8	19.5	10.5	13.7	15.6	12.7	8.1	6.8	6.2	52.2	254 959	2.42	16.0	32.3
Congressional District 2	2.6	6.9	19.3	7.8	14.1	16.8	14.1	8.7	6.4	5.8	51.5	247 211	2.51	9.9	26.6
Congressional District 3	2.1	6.7	18.3	9.2	13.4	15.8	13.8	9.2	7.2	6.4	51.6	252 366	2.42	12.6	28.8
Congressional District 4	1.3	6.6	19.3	9.0	12.8	15.7	13.8	9.2	7.1	6.5	50.2	238 947	2.54	10.2	25.0
Congressional District 5	1.4	6.6	19.8	10.1	12.2	15.6	13.8	8.9	6.8	6.3	51.0	237 931	2.58	9.1	23.8
Congressional District 6	1.3	5.5	17.4	10.2	11.9	15.1	14.4	9.9	8.1	7.4	51.3	246 785	2.46	10.2	26.1
Congressional District 7	2.0	6.6	18.8	9.9	13.4	16.0	14.0	9.3	6.6	5.4	50.3	236 211	2.56	11.1	23.5
Congressional District 8	2.2	7.0	19.3	10.3	13.3	16.0	13.6	8.7	6.5	5.3	51.1	238 796	2.58	10.7	23.5
Congressional District 9	2.7	6.5	19.1	9.5	13.1	15.4	13.9	8.8	7.0	6.6	51.7	251 012	2.46	13.4	28.7
Congressional District 10	7.1	6.3	17.1	7.7	14.4	16.2	13.3	8.8	7.8	8.3	52.0	262 996	2.36	11.5	32.8
Congressional District 11	5.3	6.9	19.3	8.7	13.5	14.9	12.7	8.4	7.7	7.8	53.8	258 872	2.36	21.7	35.0
Congressional District 12	4.8	7.5	19.7	9.2	14.9	16.6	14.0	8.1	5.4	4.4	51.9	248 553	2.49	13.7	27.2
Congressional District 13	3.6	6.8	19.0	7.7	12.9	16.5	14.6	9.0	7.1	6.5	51.6	244 603	2.53	12.9	26.1
Congressional District 14	3.7	6.4	19.6	6.9	11.8	16.9	15.3	9.8	7.2	6.2	51.2	238 693	2.61	9.1	23.0
Congressional District 15	5.7	6.9	16.6	13.0	17.9	16.2	12.4	7.1	5.3	4.7	50.5	256 769	2.37	10.2	30.8
Congressional District 16	1.8	6.6	19.1	8.5	12.2	15.9	14.4	9.3	7.2	6.8	51.2	240 988	2.55	10.3	24.6
Congressional District 17	2.3	6.2	17.7	10.3	12.9	15.2	13.9	9.0	7.8	7.0	51.6	249 485	2.45	13.5	28.0
Congressional District 18	0.9	6.7	19.3	9.0	12.5	15.5	13.6	9.6	7.4	6.3	51.0	240 596	2.56	10.2	24.5
OKLAHOMA	3.8	6.8	19.0	10.3	13.1	15.2	13.1	9.2	7.0	6.2	50.9	1 342 293	2.49	11.4	26.7
Congressional District 1	4.7	7.2	19.2	9.6	14.1	15.7	13.6	8.6	6.4	5.6	51.4	275 234	2.46	11.6	28.2
Congressional District 2	1.4	6.6	19.4	9.0	11.9	14.3	13.1	10.5	8.2	7.0	50.8	264 439	2.52	11.3	25.2
Congressional District 3	2.8	6.4	19.1	10.9	11.9	15.1	13.0	9.4	7.3	6.9	50.2	263 375	2.51	9.6	25.6
Congressional District 4	3.5	6.8	19.0	11.4	13.3	15.5	13.0	8.9	6.6	5.5	50.3	262 122	2.53	10.9	24.4
Congressional District 5	6.8	7.3	18.3	10.9	14.4	15.2	13.0	8.5	6.6	5.9	51.5	277 123	2.42	13.3	29.9
OREGON	8.5	6.5	18.2	9.6	13.8	15.4	14.8	8.9	6.4	6.4	50.4	1 333 723	2.51	9.8	26.1
Congressional District 1	11.7	7.1	18.2	9.6	16.3	16.5	14.4	7.8	5.0	5.1	49.9	268 476	2.49	8.5	28.1
Congressional District 2	5.2	6.4	19.2	8.3	11.6	14.6	14.8	10.0	7.8	7.4	50.3	264 607	2.52	9.7	24.3
Congressional District 3	12.2	6.8	17.2	9.8	16.3	16.4	14.7	7.8	5.2	5.7	50.7	268 508	2.50	11.6	27.9
Congressional District 4	4.2	5.7	17.6	10.0	11.8	14.4	15.3	10.0	7.8	7.4	50.7	275 617	2.44	9.7	25.7
Congressional District 5	9.0	6.6	19.0	10.2	12.6	15.0	14.9	8.9	6.3	6.4	50.4	256 515	2.58	9.5	24.3
PENNSYLVANIA	4.1	5.9	17.9	8.9	12.7	15.9	13.9	9.2	7.9	7.7	51.7	4 777 003	2.48	11.6	27.7
Congressional District 1	9.2	7.3	21.2	10.8	14.7	14.7	11.7	7.7	6.2	5.7	53.3	238 559	2.63	26.0	31.0
Congressional District 2	7.1	6.1	18.1	12.4	14.9	14.2	12.2	8.3	6.9	6.9	54.5	259 983	2.38	23.2	37.1
Congressional District 3	1.9	5.9	18.3	9.9	12.1	15.2	13.9	9.3	7.7	7.7	51.2	247 365	2.49	10.4	26.6
Congressional District 4	2.3	5.8	18.0	6.5	11.1	16.7	14.9	9.7	8.8	8.5	52.1	254 224	2.49	9.6	25.7
Congressional District 5	1.9	5.4	16.9	12.5	12.3	14.8	13.1	9.6	8.1	7.3	50.5	250 257	2.45	8.5	26.5
Congressional District 6	5.0	6.4	18.2	8.1	13.3	16.9	14.3	8.9	7.1	6.8	51.4	244 929	2.53	9.3	25.4
Congressional District 7	6.9	6.1	17.8	8.1	13.1	16.7	13.9	8.9	7.8	7.6	51.8	246 467	2.53	9.8	27.0
Congressional District 8	6.0	6.4	19.1	7.0	12.7	17.9	15.0	9.3	6.8	5.8	51.0	236 439	2.69	9.0	21.6
Congressional District 9	1.2	5.9	17.7	8.4	12.6	15.4	14.1	10.0	8.3	7.6	50.7	249 948	2.50	8.8	24.6
Congressional District 10	1.9	5.4	18.1	8.0	11.7	15.7	14.3	10.2	8.5	8.1	50.7	250 604	2.47	9.1	26.3
Congressional District 11	2.8	5.2	17.0	9.2	11.9	15.4	13.7	9.7	8.9	9.1	51.8	256 256	2.42	11.1	29.2
Congressional District 12	1.0	5.2	16.1	9.0	11.7	14.9	14.3	9.7	9.3	9.7	52.0	262 421	2.38	11.1	29.2
Congressional District 13	9.6	6.1	17.4	7.2	13.0	16.2	13.7	9.2	8.2	9.1	52.1	250 845	2.51	10.8	27.9
Congressional District 14	3.9	5.5	15.5	11.2	13.6	15.4	13.1	8.6	8.7	9.3	53.0	280 332	2.21	16.0	37.3
Congressional District 15	5.2	5.9	18.1	8.4	12.5	16.6	14.1	9.0	7.7	7.8	51.5	248 052	2.52	10.0	25.4
Congressional District 16	4.5	7.0	19.8	9.9	12.6	15.9	13.1	8.4	6.6	6.7	51.1	233 569	2.67	9.5	23.3
Congressional District 17	2.6	5.8	17.6	7.5	13.0	16.3	14.6	9.4	8.1	7.8	51.0	255 916	2.44	10.5	27.4
Congressional District 18	2.8	5.5	16.9	6.4	11.7	16.6	15.3	10.1	8.9	8.8	52.0	260 803	2.42	8.6	27.3
Congressional District 19	2.7	5.8	17.9	8.8	12.9	16.7	14.5	9.4	7.3	6.8	51.0	250 034	2.48	8.7	24.5

[3]No spouse present.

Table A. 109th Congressional Districts, 2000—*Continued*

(Number, percent.)

STATE Congressional district	Group quarters				Education				Money income, 1999			Percent below poverty level, 1999	
	Persons in correctional institutions	Persons in nursing homes	Persons in college dormitories	Persons in military quarters	School enrollment[4]		Attainment level[5]		Per capita income[6]	Households		Persons	Families
					Public	Private	H.S. graduate or more	Bachelor's degree or more		Median income	Percent with income over $100,000		
	28	29	30	31	32	33	34	35	36	37	38	39	40
NORTH CAROLINA	46 614	50 892	76 018	37 022	1 762 124	281 101	78.1	22.5	20 307	39 184	9.4	12.3	9.0
Congressional District 1	6 678	5 476	1 749	4 016	146 886	15 287	69.2	12.0	14 864	28 410	4.2	21.1	17.1
Congressional District 2	6 490	3 414	11 930	13 857	145 416	20 412	76.3	15.9	17 046	36 510	6.2	14.3	10.9
Congressional District 3	3 660	2 148	4 877	18 531	139 481	17 580	81.4	20.1	18 799	37 510	7.4	12.4	8.8
Congressional District 4	958	3 566	14 866	0	147 471	37 238	88.4	48.0	27 508	53 847	20.7	9.2	5.7
Congressional District 5	731	4 931	4 742	0	127 634	18 514	76.4	20.1	21 041	39 710	9.0	9.5	6.5
Congressional District 6	1 576	3 267	1 914	0	121 984	23 176	79.1	22.7	22 561	43 503	10.9	8.2	5.8
Congressional District 7	5 092	2 654	2 627	244	141 922	14 249	75.6	17.8	17 874	33 998	7.1	16.7	12.7
Congressional District 8	5 094	4 180	5 042	374	146 372	18 557	77.5	18.2	18 201	38 390	7.1	12.4	9.7
Congressional District 9	556	2 751	796	0	118 781	34 525	86.3	35.9	29 290	55 059	19.6	6.2	4.3
Congressional District 10	3 898	4 254	2 066	0	127 199	15 148	71.9	14.1	18 640	37 649	6.8	10.6	7.8
Congressional District 11	2 927	5 871	5 294	0	119 793	16 426	78.5	20.5	19 005	34 720	6.4	12.0	8.4
Congressional District 12	4 210	4 922	12 876	0	142 495	26 505	74.7	19.2	17 901	35 775	6.9	15.9	12.4
Congressional District 13	4 744	3 458	7 239	0	136 690	23 484	80.4	27.3	21 244	41 060	9.7	11.6	8.1
NORTH DAKOTA	1 518	7 254	10 137	1 244	163 677	15 990	83.9	22.0	17 769	34 604	5.7	11.9	8.3
Congressional District (At Large)	1 518	7 254	10 137	1 244	163 677	15 990	83.9	22.0	17 769	34 604	5.7	11.9	8.3
OHIO	68 873	93 157	91 713	369	2 475 221	539 239	83.0	21.1	21 003	40 956	9.8	10.6	7.8
Congressional District 1	1 251	5 363	4 916	0	134 625	44 791	80.1	22.3	20 427	37 414	9.2	13.9	10.5
Congressional District 2	3 152	5 563	221	0	127 648	32 863	83.3	29.0	25 560	46 813	15.4	8.4	6.3
Congressional District 3	5 432	5 814	7 028	0	133 689	34 735	83.8	22.7	22 147	41 591	10.8	10.2	7.4
Congressional District 4	12 856	5 856	3 697	0	135 706	24 623	82.4	13.1	18 732	40 100	6.9	9.4	7.1
Congressional District 5	1 141	5 073	7 398	0	151 298	22 806	84.2	14.6	19 031	41 701	6.9	7.6	5.2
Congressional District 6	6 504	5 373	9 291	0	144 325	18 334	81.2	14.2	17 039	32 888	5.5	14.0	10.2
Congressional District 7	12 404	4 694	7 026	341	141 780	27 411	83.5	18.7	20 194	43 248	9.4	8.8	6.4
Congressional District 8	878	4 323	7 571	0	147 930	22 872	82.5	18.7	20 725	43 753	10.0	8.8	6.0
Congressional District 9	679	5 772	4 354	17	139 391	34 537	83.3	19.8	20 885	40 265	9.4	12.0	8.9
Congressional District 10	58	5 422	1 890	0	109 689	41 193	82.7	23.3	22 455	41 841	9.6	9.1	6.7
Congressional District 11	3 075	6 048	4 755	5	139 432	38 478	78.2	23.4	19 510	31 998	8.3	19.5	16.0
Congressional District 12	276	4 265	5 748	0	140 539	37 377	87.5	32.1	24 958	47 289	15.4	10.0	7.8
Congressional District 13	5 007	4 800	554	1	133 517	29 021	84.6	22.3	22 631	44 524	12.1	9.4	7.2
Congressional District 14	481	4 607	982	5	130 858	32 040	87.2	27.1	25 423	51 304	16.2	5.7	4.0
Congressional District 15	6 635	3 183	9 531	0	154 172	27 265	85.5	32.1	22 680	43 885	10.9	10.8	6.7
Congressional District 16	844	6 369	5 438	0	131 704	29 616	83.9	19.2	20 529	41 801	9.2	8.3	6.1
Congressional District 17	4 629	4 526	7 470	0	145 470	20 851	82.2	15.8	18 531	36 705	6.4	12.3	9.2
Congressional District 18	3 571	6 106	3 843	0	133 448	20 426	77.5	11.3	16 603	34 462	4.9	12.6	9.7
OKLAHOMA	33 919	28 021	26 643	7 616	832 166	98 699	80.6	20.3	17 646	33 400	6.6	14.7	11.2
Congressional District 1	1 303	4 163	3 870	0	151 619	34 791	84.7	25.6	20 780	38 610	9.6	11.3	8.5
Congressional District 2	9 036	6 779	3 457	4	165 416	8 481	73.8	13.2	14 491	27 885	3.9	18.5	14.6
Congressional District 3	11 514	6 585	8 180	510	178 021	12 304	80.5	18.1	16 350	32 098	5.4	15.0	10.9
Congressional District 4	5 969	5 677	6 115	7 102	180 322	14 682	82.5	20.2	17 507	35 510	6.5	13.1	9.7
Congressional District 5	6 097	4 817	5 021	0	156 788	28 441	81.5	24.5	19 100	33 893	7.7	15.8	12.2
OREGON	19 523	14 677	18 831	95	753 762	122 730	85.1	25.1	20 940	40 916	10.0	11.6	7.9
Congressional District 1	3 805	2 305	3 262	45	144 551	31 980	88.4	33.3	24 667	48 464	14.6	8.7	5.4
Congressional District 2	6 665	3 438	1 748	0	151 787	16 856	82.7	19.0	18 218	35 600	6.9	13.0	9.4
Congressional District 3	1 953	3 000	3 118	0	139 148	29 645	84.5	24.8	20 835	42 063	9.3	11.7	8.1
Congressional District 4	1 732	2 524	3 523	33	161 815	17 536	84.9	21.4	18 674	35 796	6.9	13.7	9.4
Congressional District 5	5 368	3 410	7 180	17	156 461	26 713	85.1	27.0	22 307	44 409	12.5	10.9	7.2
PENNSYLVANIA	76 553	114 113	147 542	758	2 398 189	737 745	81.9	22.4	20 880	40 106	10.3	11.0	7.8
Congressional District 1	1 222	2 710	7 746	531	146 218	46 956	66.7	13.9	14 422	28 261	4.9	26.9	22.8
Congressional District 2	369	5 347	15 317	0	132 218	70 511	74.3	24.2	18 109	30 646	7.9	23.8	18.5
Congressional District 3	4 627	7 193	12 362	0	133 787	34 335	83.7	18.0	17 642	35 884	5.9	11.6	8.1
Congressional District 4	534	6 217	2 540	0	127 596	28 399	87.1	27.1	23 467	43 547	12.8	7.5	5.6
Congressional District 5	8 054	5 425	16 788	0	158 740	17 665	82.1	16.9	16 688	33 254	5.0	13.5	8.3
Congressional District 6	4 165	5 855	9 730	0	119 847	49 770	85.8	34.2	29 460	55 611	21.0	6.1	3.9
Congressional District 7	2 820	5 374	8 161	0	107 535	66 161	89.1	36.1	28 391	56 126	20.7	5.4	3.6
Congressional District 8	917	4 424	1 203	0	120 101	49 243	88.3	30.7	27 220	59 207	21.2	4.5	3.2
Congressional District 9	7 081	6 748	3 435	32	125 368	19 675	79.0	13.0	16 830	34 910	4.8	11.1	8.0
Congressional District 10	9 206	6 216	7 177	0	124 418	30 694	81.6	17.1	18 191	35 996	6.7	10.3	7.2
Congressional District 11	4 921	6 679	8 669	3	125 965	33 648	80.4	15.9	17 920	34 979	6.3	11.3	7.8
Congressional District 12	4 379	4 296	8 055	0	129 125	19 725	80.2	13.7	16 416	30 612	4.5	13.6	9.9
Congressional District 13	6 359	7 933	754	159	98 963	61 237	83.3	28.6	25 053	49 319	16.3	7.1	5.1
Congressional District 14	4 713	4 657	12 335	0	124 033	45 150	82.3	21.4	18 244	30 139	5.7	17.1	12.7
Congressional District 15	1 989	6 881	8 732	0	123 616	41 901	81.2	22.2	21 792	45 330	11.7	8.2	5.9
Congressional District 16	1 029	6 742	10 109	0	131 341	36 671	77.6	22.8	21 161	45 934	11.9	9.4	6.3
Congressional District 17	7 633	7 733	1 998	0	121 144	24 544	80.1	17.4	20 405	40 473	8.0	8.4	6.1
Congressional District 18	1 252	6 735	2 811	3	121 263	29 460	88.5	29.3	23 708	44 938	12.5	6.3	4.4
Congressional District 19	5 283	6 948	9 620	30	126 911	32 000	82.3	21.3	21 613	45 345	9.7	6.8	4.4

[4]All persons 3 years old and over enrolled in nursery school through college.
[5]Persons 25 years old and over.
[6]Based on the population enumerated as of April 1, 2000.

Table A. 109th Congressional Districts, 2000—*Continued*

(Number, percent.)

STATE Congressional district	Total	Total occupied units	Owner occupied Percent	Owner occupied Median value[7] (dollars)	Median owner costs as a percent of income With a mortgage	Median owner costs as a percent of income Without a mortgage[8]	Renter occupied Median rent (dollars)	Renter occupied Median rent as a percent of income	Sub-standard housing units (percent)[9]	Civilian labor force Total	Unemployment Total	Unemployment Rate[10]
	41	42	43	44	45	46	47	48	49	50	51	52
NORTH CAROLINA	3 523 944	3 132 013	69.4	108 300	21.3	9.9	548	24.3	4.0	4 039 732	214 991	5.3
Congressional District 1	271 651	236 646	63.4	73 500	22.0	12.3	428	26.4	5.7	265 000	22 468	8.2
Congressional District 2	246 261	223 122	66.5	96 400	21.8	10.8	521	24.8	5.3	288 777	21 420	6.8
Congressional District 3	292 135	234 158	70.9	100 700	21.6	9.9	502	23.6	3.2	284 966	14 831	4.6
Congressional District 4	257 494	240 099	64.1	167 300	21.0	9.9	717	25.8	3.9	341 867	12 514	3.7
Congressional District 5	278 140	249 357	76.8	109 800	20.3	9.9	493	22.6	2.6	323 785	12 693	3.9
Congressional District 6	266 193	246 278	76.7	117 200	20.7	9.9	563	22.2	2.9	327 799	11 928	3.6
Congressional District 7	295 338	243 322	73.1	98 900	22.6	11.1	508	26.7	4.1	291 882	19 513	6.6
Congressional District 8	256 664	233 377	66.2	93 200	21.9	10.9	579	24.0	5.0	303 822	18 335	5.8
Congressional District 9	259 490	243 854	72.8	146 200	20.9	9.9	703	23.3	2.6	341 928	12 758	3.7
Congressional District 10	269 326	241 060	75.1	93 500	20.8	9.9	474	21.8	3.3	320 051	13 167	4.1
Congressional District 11	310 361	257 331	75.4	107 700	21.5	9.9	486	24.4	2.7	299 108	15 534	5.2
Congressional District 12	254 245	235 533	56.8	93 000	22.1	9.9	533	24.7	6.1	314 800	24 272	7.7
Congressional District 13	266 646	247 876	62.4	117 500	21.4	9.9	620	24.8	4.5	335 947	15 558	4.6
NORTH DAKOTA	289 677	257 152	66.6	74 400	19.4	10.2	412	22.3	2.5	331 889	15 257	4.6
Congressional District (At Large)	289 677	257 152	66.6	74 400	19.4	10.2	412	22.3	2.5	331 889	15 257	4.5
OHIO	4 783 051	4 445 773	69.1	103 700	20.6	10.6	515	24.2	2.1	5 684 790	282 615	5.0
Congressional District 1	276 443	254 914	57.6	100 000	20.8	11.1	459	24.6	3.0	313 585	17 766	5.7
Congressional District 2	263 542	247 290	71.5	124 000	20.6	10.5	544	23.2	1.8	318 645	13 205	4.1
Congressional District 3	273 270	252 297	67.4	102 800	20.8	11.0	522	24.3	1.9	311 924	15 182	4.8
Congressional District 4	258 216	238 920	73.9	88 300	19.3	9.9	463	22.6	1.8	311 153	13 123	4.2
Congressional District 5	251 969	237 945	76.5	92 800	19.3	9.9	465	21.6	1.8	327 661	14 927	4.6
Congressional District 6	270 497	246 659	75.1	78 400	19.8	10.1	420	25.3	2.0	287 781	19 869	6.9
Congressional District 7	251 457	236 171	71.1	103 600	20.6	9.9	540	23.9	1.8	314 800	14 545	4.6
Congressional District 8	253 359	238 870	71.2	105 500	20.3	10.1	537	23.6	1.7	321 752	13 643	4.2
Congressional District 9	278 469	250 985	68.4	97 900	20.1	11.2	489	24.4	2.0	314 321	17 789	5.7
Congressional District 10	277 699	262 940	68.0	116 000	21.8	12.3	550	23.9	1.9	319 123	14 524	4.5
Congressional District 11	287 518	258 965	54.2	92 300	22.7	12.8	523	27.3	2.9	286 988	25 127	8.7
Congressional District 12	268 159	248 615	62.5	131 800	20.9	10.3	590	24.0	2.5	335 819	14 903	4.4
Congressional District 13	258 456	244 563	72.7	117 700	21.2	11.1	538	24.7	1.7	317 370	15 568	4.9
Congressional District 14	251 490	238 653	79.6	142 300	21.3	11.0	613	23.5	1.5	329 023	11 469	3.5
Congressional District 15	272 972	256 778	59.1	119 500	21.2	11.0	596	24.4	2.4	348 605	12 910	3.7
Congressional District 16	254 335	241 013	73.6	108 600	20.4	9.9	498	23.2	1.7	320 035	13 091	4.1
Congressional District 17	268 811	249 550	70.1	85 800	20.0	10.8	482	24.9	1.9	308 423	18 369	6.0
Congressional District 18	266 389	240 645	74.3	83 800	20.0	9.9	421	23.1	2.6	297 782	16 605	5.6
OKLAHOMA	1 514 400	1 342 293	68.4	70 700	19.2	9.9	456	24.3	4.2	1 632 128	86 832	5.3
Congressional District 1	297 040	275 329	64.8	85 800	19.0	9.9	511	24.0	4.2	350 799	16 359	4.7
Congressional District 2	314 070	264 390	74.3	56 400	19.3	10.2	370	23.9	4.6	297 761	19 426	6.5
Congressional District 3	301 441	263 332	72.5	60 800	18.8	9.9	414	24.0	3.6	325 743	16 530	5.0
Congressional District 4	294 055	262 143	69.7	73 200	19.2	9.9	466	24.5	3.6	323 272	16 467	4.8
Congressional District 5	307 794	277 099	61.3	73 600	19.8	9.9	477	24.6	5.0	334 553	18 050	5.3
OREGON	1 452 709	1 333 723	64.3	152 100	23.2	10.5	620	26.9	5.3	1 740 298	112 529	6.5
Congressional District 1	288 911	268 505	59.6	180 800	22.7	10.0	678	25.9	5.2	370 323	19 393	5.2
Congressional District 2	296 970	264 616	68.2	121 900	22.6	10.3	543	26.7	5.3	323 084	25 160	7.8
Congressional District 3	285 436	268 551	61.3	156 300	24.1	11.8	643	27.0	6.1	370 033	23 570	6.4
Congressional District 4	297 801	275 607	65.7	132 200	22.9	10.2	575	28.7	4.3	333 311	23 091	6.9
Congressional District 5	283 591	256 444	66.5	163 800	23.2	10.1	625	26.5	5.5	343 547	21 315	6.2
PENNSYLVANIA	5 249 750	4 777 003	71.3	97 000	21.6	12.2	531	25.0	2.4	5 992 886	339 386	5.7
Congressional District 1	271 703	238 648	60.3	51 500	22.7	13.8	546	28.8	8.0	266 435	33 996	12.7
Congressional District 2	296 380	259 903	53.4	58 200	21.6	13.2	585	28.5	5.4	288 372	33 814	11.7
Congressional District 3	273 364	247 374	73.5	83 100	20.3	11.5	436	24.5	2.0	310 372	17 819	5.7
Congressional District 4	269 138	254 233	78.4	99 300	21.1	12.5	510	23.7	1.2	315 769	13 824	4.4
Congressional District 5	305 281	250 231	72.9	73 800	20.6	11.1	442	26.2	2.2	306 818	17 900	5.8
Congressional District 6	256 582	245 016	73.7	143 400	21.5	12.2	686	23.9	1.8	340 544	16 908	5.0
Congressional District 7	256 204	246 445	74.3	148 200	22.0	13.2	727	24.6	1.7	332 072	11 967	3.6
Congressional District 8	243 403	236 264	77.5	158 300	22.9	12.9	738	24.2	1.9	344 005	12 060	3.5
Congressional District 9	279 544	250 103	76.6	83 000	20.9	10.7	417	23.1	2.0	306 934	16 270	5.3
Congressional District 10	311 979	250 693	75.7	91 400	21.8	11.9	448	24.2	1.6	305 433	16 030	5.2
Congressional District 11	300 757	256 175	70.2	90 100	22.3	13.2	453	24.9	1.4	309 003	18 917	6.1
Congressional District 12	287 528	262 370	73.4	68 500	20.6	11.9	386	24.8	1.5	290 018	21 365	7.4
Congressional District 13	261 150	251 044	72.3	122 300	21.5	13.0	652	25.3	2.6	321 133	14 683	4.6
Congressional District 14	313 828	280 228	57.9	61 300	20.8	13.4	480	26.6	2.0	309 028	25 825	8.3
Congressional District 15	261 019	248 049	71.6	119 400	22.2	12.5	585	25.1	2.1	327 938	14 436	4.4
Congressional District 16	245 468	233 454	69.9	123 400	22.1	10.5	571	24.2	3.4	329 909	12 358	3.7
Congressional District 17	276 909	255 934	72.7	94 400	21.1	11.7	501	22.9	2.1	324 829	14 917	4.6
Congressional District 18	275 560	260 857	77.3	101 800	20.7	11.8	544	23.7	1.0	323 719	13 961	4.3
Congressional District 19	263 953	249 982	74.8	113 500	21.9	10.3	542	23.1	1.6	340 555	12 336	3.6

[7]Specified owner-occupied units.
[8]Median monthly owner costs is often in the minimum category—9.9 percent or less, which is indicated as 9.9 percent.
[9]Overcrowded or lacking complete plumbing facilities.
[10]Percent of civilian labor force.

Table A. 109th Congressional Districts, 2000—*Continued*

(Number, percent.)

STATE Congressional district	Civilian employment and occupations				Total farms, 2002	Farms by size, 2002 (percent)			Land in farms, 2002		Cropland harvested, 2002		Farm's principal operator's primary occupation is farming, 2002 (percent)
	Total	Management, professional, and related (percent)	Service, sales, and office (percent)	Construction and production (percent)		1 to 49 acres	50 to 999 acres	1,000 acres or more	Acreage	Average size of farms (acres)	Acreage	Farms	
	53	54	55	56	57	58	59	60	61	62	63	64	65
NORTH CAROLINA	3 824 741	31.2	38.3	29.7	53 930	45.6	51.1	3.3	9 079 001	168	4 308 209	36 622	58.7
Congressional District 1	242 532	23.3	40.2	34.8	4 356	29.3	58.0	12.7	1 843 684	423	1 188 879	3 000	69.0
Congressional District 2	267 357	27.5	38.7	32.6	4 961	43.9	52.4	3.7	901 841	182	395 324	3 138	63.4
Congressional District 3	270 135	30.5	40.3	27.3	3 206	39.2	50.1	10.7	1 131 915	353	852 877	2 269	67.9
Congressional District 4	329 353	51.1	34.4	14.3	1 447	50.6	48.5	0.9	154 398	107	38 080	887	56.9
Congressional District 5	311 092	30.0	36.0	33.2	10 156	48.9	50.2	0.8	1 038 572	102	303 083	7 333	56.0
Congressional District 6	315 871	30.4	36.9	32.3	5 227	46.9	52.5	0.6	553 268	106	157 154	3 323	56.8
Congressional District 7	272 369	26.9	39.2	32.4	4 701	42.1	52.6	5.4	1 100 034	234	653 793	3 442	64.4
Congressional District 8	285 487	27.8	39.7	31.8	3 320	41.2	55.4	3.3	583 995	176	241 913	1 806	56.3
Congressional District 9	329 170	40.4	39.1	20.4	1 246	55.2	42.9	1.9	155 208	125	75 895	691	53.0
Congressional District 10	306 884	23.0	34.5	41.9	5 126	49.4	50.1	0.5	475 329	93	144 361	3 377	53.0
Congressional District 11	283 574	28.3	39.4	31.5	6 305	58.0	41.6	0.4	504 064	80	105 687	4 585	53.6
Congressional District 12	290 528	25.7	42.0	32.1	1 261	50.4	48.5	1.1	126 959	101	50 575	935	53.9
Congressional District 13	320 389	34.7	39.2	25.7	2 618	34.3	62.1	3.6	509 734	195	100 588	1 836	58.6
NORTH DAKOTA	316 632	33.3	42.8	22.2	30 619	6.7	52.6	40.8	39 294 879	1 283	19 908 697	20 789	70.7
Congressional District (At Large)	316 632	33.3	42.8	22.2	30 619	6.7	52.6	40.8	39 294 879	1 283	19 908 697	20 789	70.7
OHIO	5 402 175	31.0	40.9	27.8	77 797	39.5	57.0	3.5	14 583 435	187	10 041 416	58 577	55.9
Congressional District 1	295 819	31.8	45.0	23.1	654	61.9	36.9	1.2	58 769	90	31 978	441	49.2
Congressional District 2	305 440	37.4	39.2	23.2	5 048	43.2	54.9	1.9	714 003	141	333 037	3 666	53.2
Congressional District 3	296 742	33.5	40.3	26.0	3 518	46.5	49.3	4.2	689 433	196	487 061	2 519	53.0
Congressional District 4	298 030	24.5	37.5	37.5	9 610	35.9	59.0	5.0	2 197 740	229	1 797 411	7 291	58.0
Congressional District 5	312 734	24.6	34.9	39.8	12 354	33.7	60.0	6.3	3 234 851	262	2 762 464	9 572	59.4
Congressional District 6	267 912	26.2	41.9	31.3	8 234	30.9	68.3	0.8	1 170 630	142	374 629	6 350	51.5
Congressional District 7	300 255	29.9	41.7	28.1	4 909	45.7	47.8	6.5	1 187 634	242	924 568	3 553	56.2
Congressional District 8	308 109	30.0	39.7	29.9	5 434	44.7	52.1	3.2	968 735	178	806 078	4 293	58.6
Congressional District 9	296 532	29.2	41.3	29.2	1 877	46.0	48.8	5.2	393 275	210	314 819	1 444	55.9
Congressional District 10	304 599	32.6	43.9	23.3	89	87.6	12.4	0.0	2 128	24	389	49	53.9
Congressional District 11	261 861	34.2	44.4	21.3	16	81.3	18.8	0.0	553	35	26	5	25.0
Congressional District 12	320 916	38.9	42.9	18.0	1 832	54.0	42.8	3.2	325 618	178	235 499	1 258	54.0
Congressional District 13	301 802	31.6	41.9	26.3	761	68.9	30.7	0.4	59 820	79	35 751	498	49.7
Congressional District 14	317 554	35.4	39.1	25.1	3 267	49.7	49.6	0.7	334 704	102	167 457	2 498	55.6
Congressional District 15	335 695	37.7	42.4	19.8	2 078	45.0	47.7	7.2	552 482	266	466 635	1 522	59.8
Congressional District 16	306 944	29.0	40.0	30.5	4 893	47.1	51.3	1.6	621 510	127	419 666	3 617	57.9
Congressional District 17	290 054	25.2	42.8	31.8	1 486	49.3	49.8	0.9	155 079	104	88 095	1 077	50.4
Congressional District 18	281 177	23.4	38.3	37.5	11 737	30.8	67.4	1.8	1 916 471	163	795 853	8 924	54.6
OKLAHOMA	1 545 296	30.3	42.1	26.7	83 300	24.2	67.0	8.8	33 661 826	404	7 705 860	43 930	55.3
Congressional District 1	334 440	33.5	43.2	23.2	3 542	45.1	51.8	3.2	688 644	194	198 884	1 863	48.3
Congressional District 2	278 335	25.5	39.5	33.2	30 416	26.8	69.0	4.2	8 021 017	264	1 483 385	16 521	55.5
Congressional District 3	309 213	29.3	40.9	28.2	30 462	16.8	67.6	15.6	19 093 990	627	4 861 261	16 442	57.4
Congressional District 4	306 805	30.6	42.3	26.4	14 907	26.8	65.9	7.3	5 083 348	341	1 011 856	7 299	54.1
Congressional District 5	316 503	31.8	44.3	23.6	3 973	33.1	64.4	2.5	774 827	195	150 474	1 805	48.4
OREGON	1 627 769	33.1	41.4	23.9	40 033	62.5	31.2	6.4	17 080 422	427	3 119 384	23 013	53.9
Congressional District 1	350 930	39.1	39.2	20.6	5 357	72.9	26.1	1.0	411 634	77	207 955	3 458	48.1
Congressional District 2	297 924	29.2	41.7	26.3	14 768	49.3	36.3	14.4	14 461 305	979	2 024 634	8 078	57.7
Congressional District 3	346 463	31.6	43.3	24.6	2 648	83.8	15.9	0.3	108 249	41	43 094	1 690	46.8
Congressional District 4	310 220	30.5	41.2	26.3	9 086	62.6	34.5	2.8	1 356 038	149	447 076	4 917	54.8
Congressional District 5	322 232	34.1	41.4	22.1	8 174	72.3	26.4	1.3	743 196	91	396 625	4 870	52.2
PENNSYLVANIA[11]	5 653 500	32.6	41.8	25.2	58 105	37.8	61.1	1.1	7 745 336	133	4 079 276	45 374	56.7
Congressional District 1	232 439	27.3	51.3	21.2	9	88.9	11.1	0.0	D	D	D	9	66.7
Congressional District 2	254 558	37.8	47.5	14.6	2	100.0	0.0	0.0	D	D	D	2	50.0
Congressional District 3	292 553	27.7	40.9	30.7	5 612	30.3	68.6	1.1	810 906	144	401 585	4 543	55.4
Congressional District 4	301 945	36.2	41.2	22.4	2 037	40.4	59.2	0.5	213 169	105	102 940	1 591	55.2
Congressional District 5	288 918	27.9	38.6	32.5	6 507	28.0	70.8	1.2	1 010 615	155	440 960	5 273	52.8
Congressional District 6	323 636	41.1	38.6	20.0	1 662	57.8	41.8	0.4	142 425	86	87 229	1 196	56.9
Congressional District 7	320 105	43.3	40.5	16.1	179	73.2	26.8	0.0	8 822	49	3 634	98	45.8
Congressional District 8	331 945	38.2	40.7	20.9	919	70.2	28.7	1.1	76 851	84	50 013	638	54.8
Congressional District 9	290 664	25.1	39.4	34.2	8 719	28.0	70.9	1.2	1 435 257	165	748 184	6 970	61.1
Congressional District 10	289 403	28.1	39.9	31.1	7 354	28.5	70.2	1.2	1 191 928	162	563 496	5 796	56.9
Congressional District 11	290 086	26.4	43.5	29.8	1 858	39.8	59.0	1.2	236 805	127	118 597	1 336	48.7
Congressional District 12	268 653	25.7	43.3	30.5	4 456	31.1	67.8	1.1	612 558	137	254 778	3 494	48.0
Congressional District 13	306 450	38.0	42.6	19.3	291	71.8	28.2	0.0	16 482	57	7 814	187	51.2
Congressional District 14	283 203	32.7	48.6	18.6	34	97.1	2.9	0.0	414	12	83	27	20.6
Congressional District 15	313 502	32.4	40.9	26.5	1 353	60.8	36.5	2.7	185 234	137	136 944	1 052	56.8
Congressional District 16	317 551	29.9	38.9	29.7	6 315	46.9	52.7	0.4	512 384	81	362 318	5 120	72.0
Congressional District 17	309 912	29.1	40.1	30.2	4 150	44.2	54.9	0.9	518 343	125	351 052	3 121	58.9
Congressional District 18	309 758	38.0	41.9	20.0	2 309	41.6	58.3	0.2	242 174	105	87 513	1 722	43.9
Congressional District 19	328 219	30.1	40.1	29.3	4 339	55.3	43.0	1.7	530 682	122	362 066	3 199	51.9

[11]Agriculture data were tabulated for the 108th Congress and some boundary changes have occurred.
D = Suppressed to avoid disclosure.

Table A. 109th Congressional Districts, 2000—*Continued*

(Number, percent.)

STATE Congressional district	Farm's principal operator is full owner, 2002 (percent)	Type of organization, 2002 (percent)			Value of all agricultural products sold, 2002				Payments received from federal farm programs, 2002					
		Family or individual	Partnership	Corporation	Total ($1,000)	Percent of farms			Total payments ($1,000)	Farms receiving payments		Percent of farms receiving		
						Less than $50,000	$50,000 to $249,999	$250,000 or more		Number	Percent	Less than $50,000	$50,000 to $249,999	$250,000 or more
	66	67	68	69	70	72	73	74	75	76	77	78	79	80
NORTH CAROLINA	64.0	90.3	6.0	3.4	6 961 686	79.6	9.0	11.4	97 696	12 312	22.8	96.1	3.8	0.1
Congressional District 1	49.3	83.4	9.2	6.7	1 083 751	57.9	18.9	23.2	34 323	1 992	45.7	89.0	10.8	0.2
Congressional District 2	64.7	89.1	6.9	3.5	892 784	73.4	10.3	16.4	8 571	1 328	26.8	97.6	2.2	0.2
Congressional District 3	56.1	84.4	8.1	6.9	981 552	58.0	14.2	27.8	17 564	1 131	35.3	91.4	8.4	0.2
Congressional District 4	69.8	87.8	5.7	5.9	62 326	88.1	7.5	4.4	864	255	17.6	99.2	0.8	0.0
Congressional District 5	64.4	93.0	5.2	1.5	613 366	84.5	8.6	6.8	5 100	1 493	14.7	99.4	0.5	0.1
Congressional District 6	68.7	93.2	4.6	1.7	339 241	85.1	6.6	8.4	2 923	857	16.4	99.5	0.5	0.0
Congressional District 7	57.3	86.8	7.0	5.6	1 641 469	65.8	11.4	22.8	11 603	1 339	28.5	95.8	4.1	0.1
Congressional District 8	72.2	91.2	4.5	4.2	551 749	77.3	5.9	16.8	6 466	921	27.7	96.5	3.1	0.3
Congressional District 9	72.0	91.5	5.5	2.8	196 494	81.4	4.7	14.0	1 283	236	18.9	97.0	3.0	0.0
Congressional District 10	67.5	91.6	5.7	2.5	252 553	91.2	4.9	3.9	2 843	1 051	20.5	99.6	0.4	0.0
Congressional District 11	67.9	92.8	4.5	2.4	184 021	93.4	5.0	1.6	3 740	849	13.5	98.4	1.6	0.0
Congressional District 12	67.4	91.3	6.3	1.8	46 637	92.6	4.5	2.9	807	233	18.5	98.3	1.7	0.0
Congressional District 13	61.6	90.9	5.8	2.7	115 744	83.9	12.0	4.1	1 608	627	23.9	99.4	0.6	0.0
NORTH DAKOTA	47.4	90.1	7.5	1.5	3 233 366	58.6	29.6	11.8	293 067	23 892	78.0	96.9	3.1	0.0
Congressional District (At Large)	47.4	90.1	7.5	1.5	3 233 366	58.6	29.6	11.8	293 067	23 892	78.0	96.9	3.1	0.0
OHIO	67.1	91.1	5.8	2.4	4 263 549	81.8	13.7	4.5	197 425	28 851	37.1	98.4	1.6	0.0
Congressional District 1	78.0	92.2	3.5	3.7	22 965	88.5	6.9	4.6	563	99	15.1	100.0	0.0	0.0
Congressional District 2	78.0	91.9	5.7	1.7	103 156	91.3	7.4	1.3	5 301	1 416	28.1	99.7	0.3	0.0
Congressional District 3	71.3	92.1	5.8	1.6	144 037	83.1	13.2	3.7	11 635	1 585	45.1	98.0	2.0	0.0
Congressional District 4	60.8	90.6	7.0	1.6	598 361	77.0	17.7	5.3	36 471	5 010	52.1	98.3	1.7	0.0
Congressional District 5	56.4	89.5	7.1	2.7	859 731	73.5	20.3	6.2	50 501	7 340	59.4	98.6	1.4	0.0
Congressional District 6	73.3	94.5	4.0	1.1	174 070	91.7	6.7	1.6	6 333	1 621	19.7	99.6	0.4	0.0
Congressional District 7	65.9	89.5	6.4	3.3	304 200	79.1	14.3	6.6	17 338	1 997	40.7	97.1	2.9	0.0
Congressional District 8	65.1	90.8	6.6	2.0	652 468	74.6	16.3	9.1	18 392	2 291	42.2	97.9	2.1	0.0
Congressional District 9	58.3	87.1	7.2	5.0	153 463	76.9	17.2	5.9	5 069	754	40.2	98.0	2.0	0.0
Congressional District 10	85.4	71.9	7.9	19.1	D	76.4	12.4	11.2	D	2	2.2	100.0	0.0	0.0
Congressional District 11	81.3	81.3	0.0	18.8	D	93.8	0.0	6.3	D	D	D	D	D	D
Congressional District 12	73.7	89.9	5.2	4.0	142 861	85.4	10.5	4.1	4 685	519	28.3	97.5	2.3	0.2
Congressional District 13	71.0	86.9	6.0	5.3	46 111	84.2	12.1	3.7	D	103	13.5	100.0	0.0	0.0
Congressional District 14	72.8	89.2	5.2	4.9	160 057	87.6	9.8	2.6	3 234	566	17.3	98.9	1.1	0.0
Congressional District 15	62.5	88.6	6.4	3.1	167 896	75.4	17.4	7.2	9 516	960	46.2	96.7	3.3	0.0
Congressional District 16	66.8	90.7	5.7	3.2	296 288	80.2	14.8	5.0	10 265	1 272	26.0	97.9	2.1	0.0
Congressional District 17	71.5	92.0	4.6	3.1	38 159	88.8	9.1	2.1	1 439	283	19.0	98.9	1.1	0.0
Congressional District 18	72.5	93.3	4.7	1.5	386 443	86.5	10.9	2.5	16 270	3 033	25.8	98.8	1.1	0.1
OKLAHOMA	63.4	93.9	4.1	1.3	4 456 404	87.0	9.6	3.4	149 942	24 316	29.2	98.7	1.3	0.0
Congressional District 1	67.9	94.7	2.9	1.8	82 443	92.9	5.5	1.6	1 705	572	16.1	99.5	0.5	0.0
Congressional District 2	68.9	95.7	3.1	0.8	1 289 267	90.1	6.5	3.4	14 807	5 127	16.9	99.7	0.3	0.0
Congressional District 3	56.7	91.7	5.4	1.8	2 528 847	81.3	14.3	4.3	113 436	14 227	46.7	98.2	1.8	0.0
Congressional District 4	63.8	94.2	3.9	1.3	495 593	89.0	8.7	2.4	18 656	3 739	25.1	99.3	0.7	0.0
Congressional District 5	67.3	94.5	3.2	1.5	60 254	95.0	4.3	0.8	1 338	651	16.4	99.7	0.3	0.0
OREGON	78.1	88.4	5.7	5.2	3 195 497	84.9	9.5	5.6	52 085	4 430	11.1	95.0	4.9	0.1
Congressional District 1	81.6	89.6	4.3	5.3	476 529	88.1	7.1	4.8	D	453	8.5	98.7	1.3	0.0
Congressional District 2	73.8	87.2	7.0	4.9	1 302 248	80.2	13.3	6.5	43 311	2 970	20.1	93.2	6.6	0.2
Congressional District 3	82.8	89.4	4.2	5.7	226 687	88.7	7.1	4.3	D	33	1.2	100.0	0.0	0.0
Congressional District 4	81.2	89.9	5.3	4.1	393 747	90.2	6.3	3.5	2 710	448	4.9	97.5	2.5	0.0
Congressional District 5	78.7	87.6	5.3	6.4	796 286	83.9	8.6	7.5	3 680	526	6.4	99.8	0.2	0.0
PENNSYLVANIA[11]	68.4	91.6	5.9	2.1	4 256 959	76.9	17.2	5.9	85 794	11 991	20.6	98.7	1.3	0.0
Congressional District 1	88.9	88.9	0.0	0.0	363	66.7	33.3	0.0	D	D	D	D	D	D
Congressional District 2	100.0	100.0	0.0	0.0	D	50.0	50.0	0.0	D	1	50.0	100.0	0.0	0.0
Congressional District 3	67.4	92.1	6.1	1.4	245 974	82.6	14.4	3.0	6 583	1 162	20.7	99.7	0.3	0.0
Congressional District 4	70.8	92.8	4.6	2.6	52 295	87.6	10.3	2.1	1 660	333	16.3	99.4	0.6	0.0
Congressional District 5	70.0	92.5	5.9	1.1	247 496	82.9	14.2	2.9	7 707	1 237	19.0	98.9	1.1	0.0
Congressional District 6	66.5	88.3	6.6	4.7	92 995	74.7	20.4	4.9	2 021	247	14.9	99.6	0.4	0.0
Congressional District 7	81.0	77.7	3.9	14.0	20 185	85.5	10.6	3.9	D	12	6.7	100.0	0.0	0.0
Congressional District 8	68.8	84.3	6.4	8.8	61 640	82.8	11.1	6.1	773	114	12.4	99.1	0.9	0.0
Congressional District 9	67.0	91.5	7.0	1.3	718 203	72.2	19.5	8.3	22 122	2 427	27.8	98.0	2.0	0.0
Congressional District 10	68.0	92.3	5.7	1.4	495 114	75.5	19.4	5.2	12 031	1 837	25.0	99.0	1.0	0.0
Congressional District 11	71.3	91.4	5.9	2.4	68 839	86.4	10.7	2.9	2 248	584	31.4	99.7	0.3	0.0
Congressional District 12	74.3	93.2	5.1	1.4	101 852	91.8	6.2	2.0	3 557	720	16.2	99.0	1.0	0.0
Congressional District 13	77.0	84.5	5.8	8.2	18 588	84.5	9.6	5.8	152	36	12.4	100.0	0.0	0.0
Congressional District 14	67.6	85.3	0.0	11.8	D	91.2	8.8	0.0	D	1	2.9	100.0	0.0	0.0
Congressional District 15	70.4	86.5	8.0	5.1	80 875	82.1	13.2	4.7	2 618	282	20.8	96.8	2.8	0.4
Congressional District 16	60.6	91.5	5.1	3.1	1 121 589	50.6	37.9	11.5	8 168	737	11.7	97.8	2.2	0.0
Congressional District 17	63.7	91.1	6.1	2.3	564 994	69.9	18.5	11.6	8 347	1 065	25.7	99.0	1.0	0.0
Congressional District 18	81.2	94.0	4.4	1.0	32 312	95.2	3.8	1.0	942	335	14.5	99.7	0.3	0.0
Congressional District 19	70.2	90.7	6.1	2.8	332 956	80.4	12.8	6.8	6 830	861	19.8	97.9	2.1	0.0

[11]Agriculture data were tabulated for the 108th Congress and some boundary changes have occurred.
D = Suppressed to avoid disclosure.

Table A. 109th Congressional Districts, 2000—*Continued*

(Number, percent.)

STATE Congressional district	Representative	Land area,[1] (sq km)	Total population	Persons per square kilo-meter	Race alone or in combination (percent)					Hispanic or Latino[2] (percent)	Non-Hispanic White (percent)	Two or more races (percent)
					White	Black	American Indian/Alaska Native	Asian and Pacific Islander	Other race			
	1	2	3	4	5	6	7	8	9	10	11	12
RHODE ISLAND		2 706	1 048 319	387.4	86.9	5.5	1.0	2.9	6.6	8.7	81.9	2.7
Congressional District 1	Patrick J. Kennedy (D)	841	524 189	623.3	87.8	5.6	0.8	2.5	6.4	7.5	82.6	2.9
Congressional District 2	James R. Langevin (D)	1 865	524 130	281.0	86.0	5.5	1.2	3.2	6.8	9.8	81.2	2.5
SOUTH CAROLINA		77 983	4 012 012	51.4	68.0	29.9	0.7	1.2	1.3	2.4	66.1	1.0
Congressional District 1	Henry E. Brown Jr. (R)	6 849	668 462	97.6	75.9	21.5	0.8	1.8	1.4	2.5	73.7	1.3
Congressional District 2	Joe Wilson (R)	12 347	668 374	54.1	70.4	26.9	0.7	1.6	1.8	3.3	68.0	1.2
Congressional District 3	J. Gresham Barrett (R)	13 966	668 657	47.9	77.6	20.9	0.6	0.8	1.0	1.9	76.0	0.8
Congressional District 4	Bob Inglis (R)	5 570	668 706	120.1	77.1	20.2	0.5	1.6	1.7	3.2	74.6	1.1
Congressional District 5	John M. Spratt Jr. (D)	18 221	668 451	36.7	65.5	32.7	1.0	0.8	1.0	1.8	64.1	0.8
Congressional District 6	James E. Clyburn (D)	21 030	669 362	31.8	41.3	57.4	0.6	0.8	0.8	1.5	40.3	0.8
SOUTH DAKOTA		196 540	754 844	3.8	89.9	0.9	9.0	0.9	0.7	1.4	88.0	1.3
Congressional District (At Large)	Stephanie M. Herseth (D)	196 540	754 844	3.8	89.9	0.9	9.0	0.9	0.7	1.4	88.0	1.3
TENNESSEE		106 752	5 689 283	53.3	81.2	16.8	0.7	1.3	1.3	2.2	79.2	1.1
Congressional District 1	William L. Jenkins (R)	10 601	632 216	59.6	96.5	2.4	0.6	0.6	0.8	1.5	95.0	0.8
Congressional District 2	John J. Duncan Jr. (R)	6 285	632 112	100.6	91.8	6.6	0.8	1.2	0.8	1.3	90.1	1.1
Congressional District 3	Zach Wamp (R)	8 834	632 100	71.6	86.9	11.5	0.8	1.1	0.9	1.6	85.2	1.1
Congressional District 4	Lincoln Davis (D)	25 999	631 842	24.3	94.2	4.7	0.8	0.4	0.9	1.6	92.6	0.9
Congressional District 5	Jim Cooper (D)	2 315	632 173	273.1	71.4	24.2	0.7	2.6	3.0	4.2	68.2	1.8
Congressional District 6	Bart Gordon (D)	14 194	632 118	44.5	91.2	6.7	0.7	1.1	1.4	2.6	89.0	1.0
Congressional District 7	Marsha Blackburn (R)	16 296	632 793	38.8	85.7	11.9	0.7	2.0	1.2	2.2	83.5	1.2
Congressional District 8	John S. Tanner (D)	21 398	632 189	29.5	76.0	22.8	0.7	0.7	0.9	1.6	74.4	0.9
Congressional District 9	Harold E. Ford Jr. (D)	830	631 740	761.1	36.8	60.2	0.5	1.9	1.8	3.0	34.9	1.0
TEXAS		678 051	20 851 820	30.8	73.1	12.0	1.0	3.2	13.3	32.0	52.4	2.5
Congressional District 1	Louie B. Gohmert (R)	22 036	651 562	29.6	75.6	18.8	0.9	0.8	5.4	9.3	70.6	1.3
Congressional District 2	Ted Poe (R)	5 016	651 605	129.9	72.5	19.5	0.8	3.1	6.0	12.6	64.2	1.8
Congressional District 3	Sam Johnson (R)	686	651 782	950.1	73.8	9.9	0.9	9.2	8.8	16.9	63.3	2.5
Congressional District 4	Ralph M. Hall (D)	24 694	651 500	26.4	84.4	10.8	1.5	0.9	4.1	7.9	79.2	1.6
Congressional District 5	Jeb Hensarling (R)	14 061	651 919	46.4	79.1	12.9	1.1	1.9	6.9	12.9	71.5	1.8
Congressional District 6	Joe Barton (R)	16 053	651 691	40.6	75.0	13.5	1.1	4.1	8.7	15.9	65.8	2.3
Congressional District 7	John Abney Culberson (R)	512	651 682	1 272.8	79.9	6.1	0.7	7.8	8.2	18.0	67.5	2.7
Congressional District 8	Kevin Brady (R)	21 108	651 755	30.9	86.4	9.0	1.1	1.0	4.1	9.0	80.1	1.4
Congressional District 9	Al Green (D)	399	651 086	1 631.8	35.6	38.3	0.7	11.7	17.5	32.8	17.4	3.7
Congressional District 10	Michael McCaul (R)	9 851	651 523	66.1	77.4	9.7	0.9	4.6	9.8	18.7	66.5	2.3
Congressional District 11	Mike Conaway (R)	90 636	651 590	7.2	82.2	4.4	1.1	0.8	13.5	29.6	64.6	2.1
Congressional District 12	Kay Granger (R)	5 615	651 770	116.1	79.8	6.1	1.3	2.9	12.5	23.7	66.5	2.4
Congressional District 13	Mac Thornberry (R)	104 101	651 665	6.3	82.9	6.2	1.5	1.5	10.1	17.6	73.7	2.1
Congressional District 14	Ron Paul (R)	18 376	651 837	35.5	77.2	10.3	1.0	2.1	11.7	24.9	62.1	2.2
Congressional District 15	Rubén Hinojosa (D)	27 696	651 202	23.5	80.0	3.1	0.7	0.7	17.7	69.0	27.2	2.1
Congressional District 16	Silvestre Reyes (D)	1 504	652 363	433.8	76.8	3.6	1.1	1.6	20.3	77.7	17.4	3.2
Congressional District 17	Chet Edwards (D)	19 921	651 509	32.7	80.2	10.8	1.0	1.8	8.1	15.4	71.4	1.8
Congressional District 18	Sheila Jackson Lee (D)	589	651 789	1 106.6	39.1	41.0	0.8	3.9	18.1	35.6	19.7	2.7
Congressional District 19	Randy Neugebauer (R)	65 445	651 610	10.0	79.0	5.9	1.1	1.2	15.0	29.0	63.6	2.1
Congressional District 20	Charles A. Gonzalez (D)	476	651 603	1 368.9	68.7	7.5	1.5	2.2	24.4	67.1	23.4	4.1
Congressional District 21	Lamar S. Smith (R)	6 687	651 297	97.4	86.2	4.3	1.0	3.9	7.2	18.1	73.1	2.5
Congressional District 22	Tom DeLay (R)	2 516	651 657	259.0	73.3	9.8	0.8	8.8	9.8	20.3	60.6	2.5
Congressional District 23	Henry Bonilla (R)	136 287	651 707	4.8	83.1	2.0	1.0	1.6	14.9	55.1	41.0	2.5
Congressional District 24	Kenny Marchant (R)	866	651 137	751.9	75.2	10.3	1.1	7.2	8.9	17.9	63.9	2.5
Congressional District 25	Lloyd Doggett (D)	20 759	651 894	31.4	68.8	8.0	0.9	1.5	23.5	68.6	21.9	2.7
Congressional District 26	Michael C. Burgess (R)	3 346	651 858	194.8	74.7	16.1	1.2	2.7	7.5	14.3	66.1	2.1
Congressional District 27	Solomon P. Ortiz (D)	12 225	651 843	53.3	78.3	2.9	0.9	1.2	19.5	68.1	27.6	2.8
Congressional District 28	Henry Roberto Cuellar (D)	26 259	651 295	24.8	71.3	6.6	1.2	0.9	23.4	64.5	27.9	3.3
Congressional District 29	Gene Green (D)	611	651 406	1 066.1	58.3	10.4	1.0	1.7	32.3	66.1	21.9	3.7
Congressional District 30	Eddie Bernice Johnson (D)	822	652 261	793.5	38.6	42.3	1.0	1.7	19.0	34.2	21.9	2.4
Congressional District 31	John R. Carter (R)	18 476	651 868	35.3	75.5	14.2	1.2	3.3	8.8	16.3	66.1	2.8
Congressional District 32	Pete Sessions (R)	413	650 555	1 575.2	70.1	8.3	1.0	4.9	18.8	36.2	50.1	2.9
UTAH		212 751	2 233 169	10.5	91.1	1.1	1.8	3.2	5.1	9.0	85.3	2.1
Congressional District 1	Rob Bishop (R)	53 790	744 337	13.8	89.9	1.6	1.4	3.0	6.4	11.1	83.3	2.3
Congressional District 2	Jim Matheson (D)	118 166	744 287	6.3	92.6	0.9	2.8	2.6	3.2	5.9	88.0	1.9
Congressional District 3	Chris Cannon (R)	40 795	744 545	18.3	90.8	0.8	1.2	3.8	5.7	10.0	84.5	2.2
VERMONT		23 956	608 827	25.4	97.9	0.7	1.1	1.2	0.4	0.9	96.2	1.2
Congressional District (At Large)	Bernard Sanders (I)	23 956	608 827	25.4	97.9	0.7	1.1	1.1	0.4	0.9	96.2	1.2

[1]Dry land or land partially or temporarily covered by water.
[2]Hispanic or Latino persons may be of any race.

Table A. 109th Congressional Districts, 2000—*Continued*

(Number, percent.)

STATE Congressional district	Foreign born (percent)	Age (percent)									Percent female	Households			
		Under 5 years	5 to 17 years	18 to 24 years	25 to 34 years	35 to 44 years	45 to 54 years	55 to 64 years	65 to 74 years	75 years and over		Number	Persons per household	Female-family householder[3]	One-person households
	13	14	15	16	17	18	19	20	21	22	23	24	25	26	27
RHODE ISLAND	11.4	6.1	17.5	10.2	13.4	16.2	13.5	8.5	7.0	7.5	52.0	408 424	2.47	12.9	28.6
Congressional District 1	12.3	5.9	16.8	10.8	13.6	15.8	13.2	8.5	7.3	8.1	52.3	208 431	2.41	12.7	30.2
Congressional District 2	10.5	6.3	18.3	9.5	13.2	16.6	13.9	8.5	6.8	6.9	51.6	199 993	2.54	13.1	26.8
SOUTH CAROLINA	2.9	6.6	18.6	10.2	14.0	15.6	13.7	9.3	6.7	5.4	51.4	1 533 854	2.53	14.8	25.0
Congressional District 1	3.8	6.4	17.7	10.5	14.7	15.8	13.6	9.5	7.0	4.8	51.1	263 903	2.48	12.6	24.7
Congressional District 2	3.8	6.7	18.6	10.1	14.8	16.2	13.7	8.8	6.3	4.9	50.7	254 612	2.52	12.7	24.6
Congressional District 3	2.2	6.4	17.9	10.3	13.3	15.1	13.6	9.9	7.4	6.0	51.3	258 762	2.50	13.0	24.6
Congressional District 4	4.2	6.7	18.0	9.4	14.7	16.0	13.9	9.3	6.5	5.6	51.4	261 279	2.49	13.1	26.0
Congressional District 5	1.8	6.8	19.5	9.1	13.7	15.7	14.0	9.2	6.5	5.4	51.7	251 331	2.59	16.4	23.9
Congressional District 6	1.7	6.5	19.8	11.6	12.8	14.7	13.6	9.0	6.6	5.4	52.4	243 967	2.60	21.4	26.1
SOUTH DAKOTA	1.8	6.8	20.1	10.3	12.1	15.3	12.9	8.3	7.0	7.3	50.4	290 245	2.50	9.0	27.6
Congressional District (At Large)	1.8	6.8	20.1	10.3	12.1	15.3	12.9	8.3	7.0	7.3	50.4	290 245	2.50	9.0	27.6
TENNESSEE	2.8	6.6	18.0	9.6	14.3	15.9	13.8	9.4	6.7	5.6	51.3	2 232 905	2.48	12.9	25.8
Congressional District 1	1.6	5.8	16.2	8.5	13.8	15.3	14.5	11.2	8.0	6.5	51.2	259 346	2.38	10.6	25.9
Congressional District 2	2.1	6.1	16.6	10.3	14.0	15.8	14.2	9.8	7.2	6.1	51.6	258 081	2.39	10.5	27.2
Congressional District 3	2.3	6.1	17.3	9.5	13.5	15.4	14.4	10.2	7.4	6.2	51.7	253 062	2.44	12.0	25.9
Congressional District 4	1.3	6.3	17.9	8.5	13.0	15.2	13.9	10.7	8.1	6.4	51.0	248 333	2.49	11.2	23.9
Congressional District 5	6.2	6.7	16.2	11.3	17.1	16.7	13.3	8.0	5.7	5.0	51.4	258 297	2.35	14.0	31.5
Congressional District 6	2.8	6.9	18.6	10.4	14.5	16.3	13.4	9.0	6.0	4.9	50.6	238 955	2.59	10.8	22.1
Congressional District 7	3.1	7.0	20.2	8.1	13.7	17.5	15.0	8.8	5.6	4.2	50.4	229 626	2.69	9.5	19.6
Congressional District 8	1.5	6.8	19.1	9.6	13.3	15.4	13.2	9.3	7.0	6.2	51.5	242 532	2.53	14.7	24.8
Congressional District 9	4.1	7.7	19.8	10.7	16.0	15.2	12.6	7.2	5.5	5.2	52.5	244 673	2.51	22.7	30.5
TEXAS	13.9	7.8	20.4	10.5	15.2	15.9	12.5	7.7	5.5	4.5	50.4	7 393 354	2.74	12.7	23.7
Congressional District 1	5.3	6.8	19.4	10.4	12.4	14.6	13.0	9.3	7.5	6.6	51.5	245 091	2.57	12.4	24.9
Congressional District 2	7.9	7.0	20.5	9.3	13.8	16.7	14.5	8.4	5.5	4.4	50.2	233 046	2.69	12.8	22.3
Congressional District 3	18.9	8.7	19.9	8.7	18.6	19.1	13.0	6.6	3.2	2.2	50.0	239 989	2.70	9.5	24.0
Congressional District 4	4.5	6.9	19.9	8.5	12.9	16.0	13.2	9.4	6.9	6.4	50.5	241 417	2.61	11.3	23.0
Congressional District 5	7.5	7.1	19.6	8.6	14.2	16.6	13.1	8.8	6.7	5.4	50.1	237 751	2.63	12.2	23.4
Congressional District 6	10.9	7.7	20.5	9.8	15.7	16.8	12.8	7.6	5.0	4.0	50.1	236 958	2.69	11.5	22.8
Congressional District 7	18.8	6.8	16.8	8.1	18.0	17.9	14.9	8.0	5.0	4.4	50.7	277 063	2.33	8.0	34.0
Congressional District 8	5.3	6.9	20.0	9.5	13.0	16.1	13.7	9.4	6.7	4.7	49.3	232 227	2.69	10.4	21.0
Congressional District 9	32.7	8.9	20.8	11.6	19.1	16.2	11.7	6.0	3.5	2.3	50.9	229 479	2.82	18.3	26.1
Congressional District 10	12.3	7.6	19.9	9.9	17.1	17.9	13.4	6.6	4.1	3.5	49.9	241 666	2.65	9.6	24.4
Congressional District 11	6.9	6.8	20.5	9.3	11.7	14.8	12.9	9.2	8.0	6.9	50.9	243 505	2.58	10.9	25.2
Congressional District 12	12.3	7.7	19.9	10.1	15.5	16.5	12.6	7.7	5.4	4.6	50.1	236 586	2.68	11.0	25.0
Congressional District 13	5.7	6.9	19.5	10.3	12.7	15.2	12.5	8.9	7.5	6.6	49.7	243 077	2.53	10.6	26.2
Congressional District 14	7.9	7.2	20.9	8.7	12.9	16.8	13.9	8.6	6.2	4.7	49.9	234 341	2.70	11.6	22.8
Congressional District 15	17.2	8.8	23.2	10.2	13.7	13.7	11.1	7.3	6.5	5.6	50.5	200 869	3.15	14.1	18.2
Congressional District 16	27.0	8.6	23.0	10.6	14.5	14.8	11.4	7.2	5.9	4.1	51.8	203 028	3.15	18.2	18.2
Congressional District 17	6.5	6.7	18.7	15.9	13.0	14.1	11.7	8.1	6.2	5.6	50.2	236 208	2.61	11.3	23.8
Congressional District 18	20.4	8.3	20.6	11.7	16.8	15.6	11.7	6.9	4.8	3.5	50.0	222 415	2.84	20.2	26.6
Congressional District 19	5.4	7.2	20.0	12.7	12.7	14.4	11.8	8.3	6.9	6.1	50.7	239 854	2.60	11.4	25.1
Congressional District 20	13.3	8.3	20.5	12.1	15.9	14.8	11.2	6.9	5.6	4.8	51.2	223 152	2.82	18.1	25.2
Congressional District 21	7.2	6.4	17.8	10.4	14.6	17.5	14.9	8.1	5.4	4.8	50.6	254 508	2.48	8.5	25.9
Congressional District 22	14.0	7.6	21.5	8.4	14.5	18.4	14.6	7.7	4.4	2.9	50.2	226 576	2.84	10.4	19.1
Congressional District 23	15.8	7.8	21.9	9.4	13.6	15.0	12.9	8.4	6.2	4.8	51.0	222 085	2.87	11.5	20.6
Congressional District 24	14.4	7.7	19.7	9.3	17.9	18.8	13.8	7.1	3.5	2.3	50.6	249 158	2.60	10.3	25.7
Congressional District 25	24.4	8.9	21.4	13.8	17.0	13.6	10.1	6.2	5.0	4.0	49.7	207 047	3.07	15.4	21.6
Congressional District 26	9.0	8.2	20.5	10.4	15.6	17.5	12.7	7.2	4.4	3.5	50.7	232 117	2.74	12.4	21.3
Congressional District 27	14.9	8.5	22.5	10.9	13.7	14.4	11.9	7.6	6.0	4.5	51.2	208 900	3.06	15.9	19.3
Congressional District 28	12.3	8.5	22.9	11.9	14.2	14.2	11.2	7.2	5.5	4.3	50.8	203 313	3.11	16.5	18.6
Congressional District 29	31.9	9.9	23.5	12.4	16.5	14.4	10.4	6.0	4.1	2.9	49.2	193 168	3.35	15.7	17.9
Congressional District 30	20.5	8.6	21.0	11.5	17.7	15.5	11.2	6.6	4.4	3.5	49.9	220 558	2.87	20.8	26.6
Congressional District 31	6.9	8.3	20.3	11.5	16.6	16.4	11.3	6.7	4.7	4.2	50.1	225 585	2.73	10.9	20.7
Congressional District 32	27.0	7.9	17.4	11.5	19.2	15.7	11.7	7.1	4.8	4.7	49.2	252 617	2.55	10.0	31.9
UTAH	7.1	9.4	22.8	14.2	14.6	13.4	10.6	6.4	4.5	4.0	49.9	701 281	3.13	9.4	17.8
Congressional District 1	7.8	9.4	22.9	13.5	14.7	13.9	10.7	6.3	4.6	4.0	49.7	238 393	3.07	9.5	19.0
Congressional District 2	5.8	8.3	21.3	12.6	14.0	13.7	11.8	7.4	5.6	5.2	50.0	252 582	2.89	9.2	20.9
Congressional District 3	7.7	10.4	24.1	16.6	15.3	12.6	9.5	5.4	3.4	2.7	50.0	210 306	3.48	9.5	12.6
VERMONT	3.8	5.6	18.6	9.3	12.2	16.7	15.4	9.3	6.7	6.0	51.0	240 634	2.44	9.3	26.2
Congressional District (At Large)	3.8	5.6	18.6	9.3	12.2	16.7	15.4	9.3	6.7	6.0	51.0	240 634	2.44	9.3	26.2

[3]No spouse present.

Table A. 109th Congressional Districts, 2000—*Continued*

(Number, percent.)

STATE Congressional district	Group quarters				Education				Money income, 1999			Percent below poverty level, 1999	
	Persons in correctional institutions	Persons in nursing homes	Persons in college dormitories	Persons in military quarters	School enrollment[4]		Attainment level[5]		Per capita income[6]	Households		Persons	Families
					Public	Private	H.S. graduate or more	Bachelor's degree or more		Median income	Percent with income over $100,000		
	28	29	30	31	32	33	34	35	36	37	38	39	40
RHODE ISLAND	3 576	9 222	20 551	870	219 700	70 905	78.0	25.6	21 688	42 090	11.5	11.9	8.9
Congressional District 1	324	5 800	13 308	867	100 168	44 329	76.3	26.0	21 885	40 616	11.4	11.9	8.9
Congressional District 2	3 252	3 422	7 243	3	119 532	26 576	79.6	25.2	21 491	44 129	11.6	11.9	8.8
SOUTH CAROLINA	34 909	20 867	39 360	17 102	905 055	148 097	76.3	20.4	18 795	37 082	8.1	14.1	10.7
Congressional District 1	1 488	2 952	3 678	3 350	144 325	28 952	83.8	25.4	21 130	40 713	9.7	11.5	8.2
Congressional District 2	8 651	2 923	0	12 829	149 785	24 567	83.6	28.5	21 892	42 915	11.4	11.0	8.1
Congressional District 3	5 285	4 060	9 450	0	151 317	20 850	73.2	17.1	17 710	36 092	6.6	13.3	9.6
Congressional District 4	4 309	2 994	7 700	0	134 941	32 145	76.4	22.3	20 487	39 417	9.7	11.4	8.6
Congressional District 5	5 802	4 501	2 978	830	151 513	19 192	71.0	14.8	17 101	35 416	6.4	15.2	11.9
Congressional District 6	9 374	3 437	15 554	93	173 174	22 391	69.6	14.1	14 453	28 967	4.6	22.4	18.4
SOUTH DAKOTA	4 479	7 791	8 998	566	184 458	23 771	84.6	21.5	17 562	35 282	5.9	13.2	9.3
Congressional District (At Large)	4 479	7 791	8 998	566	184 458	23 771	84.6	21.5	17 562	35 282	5.9	13.2	9.3
TENNESSEE	38 481	36 994	45 030	2 593	1 203 685	211 420	75.9	19.6	19 393	36 360	8.3	13.5	10.3
Congressional District 1	3 381	4 982	3 142	0	123 907	12 335	71.8	15.0	17 231	31 228	5.2	14.8	11.3
Congressional District 2	1 241	3 855	8 716	1	136 801	20 767	79.2	23.3	20 502	36 796	8.8	12.2	8.5
Congressional District 3	1 599	4 293	5 799	10	125 685	27 188	75.2	18.9	19 205	35 434	7.8	13.4	10.4
Congressional District 4	4 242	5 132	1 494	45	126 886	13 931	69.0	11.3	16 592	31 645	5.3	15.2	11.9
Congressional District 5	5 947	2 507	11 691	0	114 497	43 099	80.9	27.9	22 303	40 419	10.0	12.2	9.3
Congressional District 6	1 695	3 978	5 035	0	146 196	15 961	74.7	16.3	18 698	39 721	7.5	11.1	7.9
Congressional District 7	6 801	3 398	935	2 287	134 750	33 508	83.7	29.2	24 839	50 090	17.6	8.0	6.2
Congressional District 8	7 198	5 826	4 623	250	141 723	18 150	71.8	12.5	16 475	33 001	5.3	15.0	11.9
Congressional District 9	6 377	3 023	3 595	0	153 240	26 481	77.3	22.1	18 687	33 806	8.0	19.4	16.1
TEXAS	244 363	105 052	92 246	34 056	5 268 790	679 470	75.7	23.2	19 617	39 927	11.5	15.4	12.0
Congressional District 1	5 488	5 548	6 945	0	156 927	17 534	76.4	17.6	17 219	33 461	6.9	16.0	12.1
Congressional District 2	19 334	2 498	596	0	161 649	20 597	82.6	23.2	22 016	47 029	15.1	11.4	9.0
Congressional District 3	162	1 713	245	0	150 400	29 477	87.2	41.4	29 193	60 878	24.4	7.0	5.0
Congressional District 4	9 930	6 287	2 268	0	153 853	15 700	78.1	18.0	19 160	38 276	9.4	12.8	9.8
Congressional District 5	17 903	4 522	1 039	0	143 693	20 748	77.4	18.6	19 950	41 007	10.5	11.0	8.4
Congressional District 6	4 814	3 255	2 283	0	159 907	24 960	81.5	24.4	21 078	45 857	12.2	10.4	7.9
Congressional District 7	16	2 689	1 310	0	126 514	39 522	90.0	50.0	36 627	57 846	25.7	7.4	5.2
Congressional District 8	20 710	2 829	2 303	0	156 529	17 265	77.7	17.7	19 962	40 459	11.8	12.6	9.7
Congressional District 9	0	1 433	220	0	175 069	22 035	72.1	24.2	15 998	34 870	7.0	18.4	15.7
Congressional District 10	2 017	2 473	3 450	0	161 736	22 788	85.6	35.2	25 217	52 465	17.6	8.2	5.8
Congressional District 11	10 589	5 952	2 272	1 416	161 921	13 578	73.8	17.0	17 076	32 711	6.8	15.8	12.6
Congressional District 12	8 635	4 006	3 010	271	144 042	27 948	76.2	21.1	20 183	41 735	10.2	11.3	8.4
Congressional District 13	20 933	5 237	2 237	4 696	159 850	13 973	76.4	17.2	16 965	33 501	6.1	14.0	10.7
Congressional District 14	11 781	3 464	903	36	163 363	19 387	77.5	19.3	19 632	41 335	11.8	13.3	10.5
Congressional District 15	12 575	3 953	902	0	185 154	10 826	60.6	13.3	12 228	28 061	5.4	28.7	23.5
Congressional District 16	6 220	1 329	179	2 833	197 987	17 943	66.4	17.0	13 624	31 245	6.5	23.6	20.2
Congressional District 17	10 323	5 249	15 407	0	185 943	27 956	77.1	20.0	17 203	35 253	7.8	17.0	11.0
Congressional District 18	10 085	1 788	2 599	0	169 236	15 216	64.0	14.4	14 584	31 291	6.2	23.3	19.8
Congressional District 19	10 077	4 591	9 093	897	174 663	21 679	74.1	18.7	16 105	31 575	6.1	17.5	13.0
Congressional District 20	4 208	3 176	2 109	7 449	166 657	24 045	70.6	15.4	14 273	31 937	4.6	19.9	16.5
Congressional District 21	467	3 009	10 030	2 532	157 905	30 353	92.4	43.1	29 207	55 609	20.7	7.0	3.9
Congressional District 22	4 083	2 161	17	0	167 249	26 351	85.1	32.4	25 110	57 932	21.0	7.3	5.6
Congressional District 23	6 381	2 425	1 734	271	174 619	21 379	73.3	25.9	18 814	38 081	12.6	18.4	14.6
Congressional District 24	50	1 817	897	0	150 025	29 950	87.2	36.2	27 880	56 098	20.9	6.3	4.6
Congressional District 25	9 895	2 891	1 067	0	189 773	11 127	57.9	15.0	12 375	28 348	4.6	28.8	24.6
Congressional District 26	2 612	2 800	5 435	0	167 625	22 203	83.1	26.9	22 627	48 714	16.3	11.0	8.0
Congressional District 27	3 472	2 451	1 593	1 307	189 501	14 449	65.6	16.2	13 975	31 327	6.4	25.3	21.1
Congressional District 28	6 614	3 164	5 238	86	188 925	15 402	63.8	10.9	13 017	31 355	4.8	22.6	18.3
Congressional District 29	969	1 278	176	0	180 994	11 169	50.2	6.5	12 119	31 751	4.4	21.9	19.2
Congressional District 30	10 955	2 711	558	0	158 490	18 335	63.6	16.0	15 970	33 505	7.3	21.4	18.4
Congressional District 31	13 001	4 716	3 105	12 262	160 181	21 444	84.2	24.1	19 551	43 381	10.9	9.6	7.4
Congressional District 32	64	3 637	3 026	0	128 410	34 131	76.3	36.4	28 843	45 725	18.0	12.5	9.4
UTAH	9 921	6 853	9 837	1 760	645 683	95 841	87.7	26.1	18 185	45 726	11.2	9.4	6.5
Congressional District 1	1 483	2 417	2 157	1 760	222 739	17 214	86.7	24.7	18 151	45 058	10.4	9.5	6.6
Congressional District 2	6 732	3 113	2 466	0	206 225	25 703	89.4	30.9	20 725	45 583	13.5	9.0	6.6
Congressional District 3	1 706	1 323	5 214	0	216 719	52 924	86.9	22.1	15 679	46 568	9.2	9.7	6.2
VERMONT	1 219	4 037	12 863	22	134 366	29 790	86.4	29.4	20 625	40 856	8.7	9.4	6.3
Congressional District (At Large)	1 219	4 037	12 863	22	134 366	29 790	86.4	29.4	20 625	40 856	8.7	9.4	6.3

[4]All persons 3 years old and over enrolled in nursery school through college.
[5]Persons 25 years old and over.
[6]Based on the population enumerated as of April 1, 2000.

Table A. 109th Congressional Districts, 2000—*Continued*

(Number, percent.)

STATE Congressional district	Housing units Total	Total occupied units	Owner occupied Percent	Owner occupied Median value[7] (dollars)	Median owner costs as a percent of income With a mortgage	Median owner costs as a percent of income Without a mortgage[8]	Renter occupied Median rent (dollars)	Renter occupied Median rent as a percent of income	Sub-standard housing units (percent)[9]	Civilian labor force Total	Unemployment Total	Unemployment Rate[10]
	41	42	43	44	45	46	47	48	49	50	51	52
RHODE ISLAND	439 837	408 424	60.0	133 000	22.7	13.4	553	25.7	3.3	530 590	29 859	5.6
Congressional District 1	221 562	208 498	55.7	136 500	22.5	13.5	544	25.2	3.0	265 772	14 685	5.5
Congressional District 2	218 275	199 926	64.6	129 700	23.0	13.3	567	26.2	3.6	264 818	15 174	5.7
SOUTH CAROLINA	1 753 670	1 533 854	72.2	94 900	20.5	9.9	510	24.4	3.8	1 938 195	113 495	5.9
Congressional District 1	328 019	263 896	69.4	120 800	21.4	9.9	616	25.1	3.3	337 031	15 643	4.5
Congressional District 2	289 163	254 578	73.4	113 900	20.5	9.9	583	24.1	3.5	324 336	13 804	4.0
Congressional District 3	292 411	258 800	75.5	86 900	19.6	9.9	449	24.2	3.1	322 296	17 345	5.4
Congressional District 4	285 122	261 236	70.1	99 500	20.3	9.9	519	23.6	3.2	340 960	17 262	5.1
Congressional District 5	279 347	251 219	74.7	83 200	19.9	9.9	442	23.4	4.2	319 317	21 953	6.8
Congressional District 6	279 608	244 125	70.2	73 000	20.8	10.8	430	26.1	5.6	294 255	27 488	9.3
SOUTH DAKOTA	323 208	290 245	68.2	79 600	19.7	10.5	426	22.9	3.6	391 594	17 221	4.4
Congressional District (At Large)	323 208	290 245	68.2	79 600	19.7	10.5	426	22.9	3.6	391 594	17 221	4.4
TENNESSEE	2 439 443	2 232 905	69.9	93 000	21.1	9.9	505	24.8	3.3	2 805 234	153 596	5.5
Congressional District 1	290 169	259 389	74.2	86 900	20.6	9.9	418	24.1	2.5	303 462	16 675	5.5
Congressional District 2	281 771	258 049	70.9	97 300	20.7	9.9	475	25.1	2.0	317 938	15 617	4.9
Congressional District 3	277 832	253 042	70.5	90 300	20.2	9.9	472	24.2	2.7	311 075	16 946	5.4
Congressional District 4	276 267	248 234	76.7	78 400	21.0	9.9	413	23.7	3.0	292 189	16 460	5.6
Congressional District 5	275 000	258 235	58.1	115 600	21.7	9.9	611	25.2	4.0	340 143	17 078	5.0
Congressional District 6	257 966	238 975	73.3	102 900	21.2	9.9	520	25.4	3.1	329 537	15 172	4.6
Congressional District 7	248 645	229 831	79.3	137 900	21.1	9.9	607	23.4	2.6	310 785	11 719	3.6
Congressional District 8	267 299	242 466	70.3	74 100	20.4	9.9	443	24.2	3.6	296 911	19 265	6.4
Congressional District 9	264 494	244 684	56.9	77 600	22.2	11.3	553	26.3	6.4	303 194	24 664	8.1
TEXAS	8 157 575	7 393 354	63.8	82 500	20.1	10.9	574	24.4	10.0	9 830 559	596 187	6.1
Congressional District 1	279 811	245 088	71.9	70 900	19.4	10.3	467	24.9	6.3	296 949	20 429	6.9
Congressional District 2	251 743	233 043	70.1	84 200	19.0	10.5	563	23.6	5.9	308 795	17 829	5.8
Congressional District 3	254 342	239 947	61.3	137 600	20.5	10.9	738	23.4	7.6	359 510	13 390	3.7
Congressional District 4	270 630	241 494	74.5	73 900	19.7	11.5	477	23.7	5.1	304 641	14 884	4.9
Congressional District 5	263 744	237 891	70.7	85 600	20.1	11.3	607	23.9	6.7	311 326	15 902	5.1
Congressional District 6	255 923	237 167	64.9	90 900	20.0	11.1	606	23.8	8.0	335 109	15 513	4.6
Congressional District 7	299 318	277 148	55.1	145 300	19.4	9.9	720	22.5	5.8	366 238	13 798	3.8
Congressional District 8	269 248	232 204	78.4	85 200	19.2	10.1	525	24.2	6.2	291 913	17 560	6.0
Congressional District 9	246 597	229 350	42.0	72 700	20.7	10.2	570	25.0	20.0	319 347	23 897	7.5
Congressional District 10	257 333	241 672	66.1	116 500	20.0	9.9	731	24.4	6.5	354 194	14 434	4.1
Congressional District 11	290 786	243 501	71.6	57 200	19.3	10.9	431	23.7	6.5	289 427	17 609	6.0
Congressional District 12	254 303	236 645	65.1	79 100	20.1	11.5	571	23.6	8.2	320 892	15 084	4.7
Congressional District 13	278 741	243 086	69.4	58 400	19.0	10.7	449	23.5	5.2	297 881	15 648	5.1
Congressional District 14	276 022	234 340	69.3	79 800	19.1	10.7	519	23.4	7.6	303 271	18 625	6.1
Congressional District 15	243 382	200 663	73.8	53 300	21.0	11.4	410	24.0	17.0	248 541	22 713	9.1
Congressional District 16	216 878	203 161	62.8	70 000	21.8	10.0	469	27.2	14.5	256 006	24 126	9.1
Congressional District 17	261 560	236 230	64.5	76 900	19.5	11.3	531	28.6	6.6	311 112	20 901	6.7
Congressional District 18	244 258	222 454	48.8	65 500	21.0	11.9	522	24.8	17.0	289 443	27 354	9.4
Congressional District 19	271 318	239 851	65.3	56 500	19.2	10.6	462	25.3	6.9	302 203	19 718	6.4
Congressional District 20	238 026	223 059	54.3	59 500	20.8	10.1	519	25.2	12.9	283 158	19 992	6.7
Congressional District 21	272 395	254 482	67.1	134 200	20.5	9.9	737	25.5	3.7	347 970	11 720	3.3
Congressional District 22	239 483	226 585	72.0	105 800	19.6	10.1	654	22.7	6.5	334 086	15 986	4.8
Congressional District 23	252 449	222 061	70.3	93 500	20.6	11.1	532	24.1	10.5	286 045	18 570	6.4
Congressional District 24	261 182	248 764	57.1	121 200	20.4	10.2	736	23.0	7.1	371 017	12 357	3.3
Congressional District 25	237 773	207 233	58.7	61 900	22.7	11.8	574	28.0	18.9	277 880	24 030	8.6
Congressional District 26	247 734	232 209	67.7	103 100	20.6	11.4	611	25.5	6.7	337 849	17 316	5.1
Congressional District 27	241 660	209 011	63.9	62 500	21.8	12.3	496	26.1	15.5	268 953	25 371	9.2
Congressional District 28	224 159	203 302	69.4	56 000	20.8	10.8	478	26.7	15.7	271 363	21 196	7.7
Congressional District 29	207 843	193 092	55.3	55 000	20.3	11.1	491	24.0	25.1	259 838	24 168	9.3
Congressional District 30	238 005	220 701	49.1	66 800	21.7	12.5	571	25.4	18.1	292 751	25 877	8.8
Congressional District 31	244 295	225 600	64.8	95 000	20.6	10.2	590	23.9	6.0	292 332	14 769	4.5
Congressional District 32	266 634	252 320	46.5	133 200	19.9	11.0	667	23.6	13.9	340 519	15 451	4.5
UTAH	768 594	701 281	71.5	146 100	22.9	9.9	597	24.9	6.3	1 098 923	54 561	5.0
Congressional District 1	261 924	238 384	70.8	137 800	22.6	9.9	563	25.2	6.2	367 461	19 934	5.4
Congressional District 2	285 032	252 500	70.6	164 500	22.5	9.9	621	24.4	5.2	368 080	16 879	4.6
Congressional District 3	221 638	210 397	73.5	140 700	23.5	9.9	613	25.5	7.7	363 382	17 748	4.9
VERMONT	294 382	240 634	70.6	111 500	22.4	13.9	553	26.2	2.0	331 131	13 997	4.2
Congressional District (At Large)	294 382	240 634	70.6	111 500	22.4	13.9	553	26.2	2.0	331 131	13 997	4.2

[7]Specified owner-occupied units.
[8]Median monthly owner costs is often in the minimum category—9.9 percent or less, which is indicated as 9.9 percent.
[9]Overcrowded or lacking complete plumbing facilities.
[10]Percent of civilian labor force.

Table A. 109th Congressional Districts, 2000—*Continued*

(Number, percent.)

STATE Congressional district	Civilian employment and occupations				Total farms, 2002	Farms by size, 2002 (percent)			Land in farms, 2002		Cropland harvested, 2002		Farm's princi-pal operator's primary occupation is farming, 2002 (percent)
	Total	Management, professional, and related (percent)	Service, sales, and office (percent)	Construc-tion and production (percent)		1 to 49 acres	50 to 999 acres	1,000 acres or more	Acreage	Average size of farms (acres)	Acreage	Farms	
	53	54	55	56	57	58	59	60	61	62	63	64	65
RHODE ISLAND	500 731	33.9	42.8	22.9	858	59.8	39.6	0.6	61 223	71	17 820	628	51.5
Congressional District 1	251 087	34.5	42.0	23.2	308	62.3	37.3	0.3	19 589	64	7 292	245	53.2
Congressional District 2	249 644	33.4	43.6	22.6	550	58.4	40.9	0.7	41 634	76	10 528	383	50.5
SOUTH CAROLINA	1 824 700	29.1	39.9	30.4	24 541	41.7	54.4	3.8	4 845 923	197	1 374 617	13 321	46.4
Congressional District 1	321 388	32.0	44.5	23.0	1 591	48.7	48.0	3.3	277 012	174	78 694	966	50.6
Congressional District 2	310 532	35.9	41.0	22.6	3 216	42.1	53.9	4.0	731 148	227	162 374	1 729	44.4
Congressional District 3	304 951	26.6	36.0	36.8	6 543	45.1	53.0	1.9	902 892	138	165 820	3 494	45.3
Congressional District 4	323 698	30.1	38.7	30.8	2 687	53.1	46.1	0.8	273 197	102	54 141	1 449	45.2
Congressional District 5	297 364	24.4	37.4	37.5	5 549	35.6	59.7	4.7	1 252 899	226	404 643	2 949	47.2
Congressional District 6	266 767	24.2	41.8	33.0	4 955	35.5	57.4	7.1	1 408 775	284	508 945	2 734	47.4
SOUTH DAKOTA	374 373	32.6	42.1	23.3	31 736	13.6	54.2	32.2	43 785 079	1 380	13 492 286	22 931	72.6
Congressional District (At Large)	374 373	32.6	42.1	23.3	31 736	13.6	54.2	32.2	43 785 079	1 380	13 492 286	22 931	72.6
TENNESSEE	2 651 638	29.5	39.8	30.2	87 595	43.6	54.9	1.5	11 681 533	133	4 365 360	56 316	50.3
Congressional District 1	286 787	25.4	39.7	34.4	13 428	55.1	44.7	0.2	1 029 733	77	301 163	10 410	52.8
Congressional District 2	302 321	32.4	41.3	25.9	6 064	53.2	46.3	0.5	526 333	87	168 514	4 039	47.7
Congressional District 3	294 129	29.1	38.8	31.7	7 607	47.7	51.9	0.4	730 080	96	179 797	5 406	51.3
Congressional District 4	275 729	23.0	35.3	40.4	19 059	39.4	59.4	1.2	2 513 707	132	747 877	12 040	50.0
Congressional District 5	323 065	35.6	42.4	21.9	1 974	48.8	50.8	0.4	181 721	92	42 513	1 054	46.5
Congressional District 6	314 365	26.9	38.4	33.9	17 959	43.3	55.7	0.9	2 124 154	118	589 026	10 992	50.5
Congressional District 7	299 066	37.2	38.3	24.0	8 728	33.1	64.6	2.3	1 573 162	180	502 970	4 912	49.0
Congressional District 8	277 646	23.8	38.5	37.0	12 620	37.4	57.6	5.1	2 983 641	236	1 826 394	7 377	50.5
Congressional District 9	278 530	30.5	45.3	24.0	156	48.7	48.7	2.6	19 002	122	7 106	86	37.8
TEXAS[11]	9 234 372	33.3	41.9	24.1	228 926	32.6	57.5	9.9	129 877 666	567	17 750 938	106 827	53.6
Congressional District 1	276 520	27.8	40.8	30.3	21 053	33.4	63.2	3.4	4 468 828	212	847 889	11 349	54.0
Congressional District 2	290 966	34.4	42.0	23.4	14 099	43.0	53.9	3.1	2 698 951	191	355 328	6 792	51.3
Congressional District 3	346 120	46.4	38.3	15.2	925	63.5	33.9	2.6	114 125	123	54 673	470	43.6
Congressional District 4	289 787	30.5	40.2	28.3	16 085	45.7	51.1	3.2	2 786 930	173	702 711	8 351	49.5
Congressional District 5	295 424	30.3	42.8	26.0	12 764	29.7	65.1	5.2	3 522 032	276	527 362	6 514	53.7
Congressional District 6	319 596	33.7	41.8	24.1	8 951	43.2	52.8	4.0	1 903 872	213	570 614	4 351	48.8
Congressional District 7	352 440	52.2	36.5	11.2	223	52.5	46.6	0.9	22 740	102	3 294	74	30.5
Congressional District 8	274 353	29.4	41.0	28.7	1 989	64.4	34.5	1.1	196 716	99	23 235	728	44.2
Congressional District 9	295 450	30.5	46.7	22.7	2 398	51.5	40.6	7.9	834 325	348	89 858	915	54.3
Congressional District 10	339 760	42.3	38.7	18.6	970	47.3	48.8	3.9	211 359	218	47 536	409	50.9
Congressional District 11	271 818	28.8	43.0	26.8	13 461	31.0	61.3	7.8	4 835 760	359	741 131	6 273	52.1
Congressional District 12	305 808	30.2	41.6	28.0	3 797	60.0	37.6	2.4	594 681	157	71 828	1 722	43.4
Congressional District 13	282 233	28.6	42.5	27.1	17 197	12.6	60.2	27.1	22 993 010	1 337	4 153 835	7 837	62.6
Congressional District 14	284 646	32.0	39.1	27.8	26 242	30.1	63.5	6.4	8 239 677	314	1 460 613	12 555	54.4
Congressional District 15	225 828	27.6	42.2	27.7	5 690	34.4	54.5	11.1	3 798 707	668	707 606	2 652	55.2
Congressional District 16	231 880	29.7	45.3	24.7	423	75.7	22.2	2.1	57 753	137	22 261	351	49.6
Congressional District 17	290 211	30.9	41.8	26.5	25 433	22.7	62.5	14.8	18 712 734	736	2 534 838	12 101	54.6
Congressional District 18	262 089	24.0	45.8	30.0	154	50.0	49.4	0.6	17 265	112	1 595	61	39.6
Congressional District 19	282 485	30.9	43.1	23.8	7 958	18.6	55.4	26.0	9 682 524	1 217	2 486 528	4 051	63.1
Congressional District 20	263 166	26.9	48.9	24.0	519	50.5	47.0	2.5	81 035	156	23 504	262	56.1
Congressional District 21	336 250	47.6	38.7	13.4	11 022	27.8	60.5	11.7	5 615 781	510	148 902	3 279	51.8
Congressional District 22	318 100	42.0	38.0	19.8	3 177	52.9	41.8	5.3	808 135	254	190 453	1 349	48.8
Congressional District 23	267 475	36.8	41.7	20.1	7 145	19.8	49.9	30.3	27 065 473	3 788	395 942	2 095	57.9
Congressional District 24	358 660	41.7	41.2	17.0	146	66.4	32.9	0.7	12 279	84	2 049	52	45.2
Congressional District 25	253 850	26.5	44.2	27.7	319	56.4	42.3	1.3	40 680	128	4 055	101	42.9
Congressional District 26	320 533	35.1	42.6	22.1	2 628	62.2	35.3	2.5	396 781	151	110 133	1 262	45.3
Congressional District 27	243 582	28.8	44.8	25.4	2 227	47.0	38.8	14.2	1 801 602	809	557 174	1 374	60.3
Congressional District 28	250 167	22.5	46.1	30.7	7 955	23.7	62.0	14.3	5 624 041	707	369 848	2 535	54.5
Congressional District 29	235 670	14.8	41.8	43.1	145	53.1	44.1	2.8	18 061	125	1 621	53	37.2
Congressional District 30	266 874	25.0	44.1	30.7	220	62.3	35.0	2.7	30 336	138	14 586	78	57.3
Congressional District 31	277 563	35.6	40.9	22.7	13 511	38.8	57.7	3.4	2 672 962	198	527 684	6 793	50.2
Congressional District 32	325 068	38.2	40.3	21.3	100	43.0	54.0	3.0	18 511	185	2 252	38	39.0
UTAH	1 044 362	32.5	42.8	24.1	15 282	54.8	36.8	8.4	11 731 228	768	961 037	9 661	48.7
Congressional District 1	347 527	31.3	41.9	26.2	5 334	57.6	34.3	8.1	3 413 726	640	375 393	3 519	47.8
Congressional District 2	351 201	36.0	43.5	20.1	5 394	50.4	40.0	9.5	6 721 729	1 246	279 135	3 198	49.2
Congressional District 3	345 634	30.1	43.2	26.2	4 554	56.6	35.9	7.5	1 595 773	350	306 509	2 944	49.3
VERMONT	317 134	36.3	39.1	23.3	6 571	33.7	64.0	2.3	1 244 909	189	454 699	4 373	53.1
Congressional District (At Large)	317 134	36.3	39.1	23.3	6 571	33.7	64.0	2.3	1 244 909	189	454 699	4 373	53.1

[11]Agriculture data were tabulated for the 108th Congress and some boundary changes have occurred.

Table A. 109th Congressional Districts, 2000—*Continued*

(Number, percent.)

STATE Congressional district	Farm's principal operator is full owner, 2002 (percent)	Type of organization, 2002 (percent)			Value of all agricultural products sold, 2002				Payments received from federal farm programs, 2002					
		Family or individual	Partner-ship	Corpo-ration	Total ($1,000)	Percent of farms			Total payments ($1,000)	Farms receiving payments		Percent of farms receiving		
						Less than $50,000	$50,000 to $249,999	$250,000 or more		Number	Percent	Less than $50,000	$50,000 to $249,999	$250,000 or more
	66	67	68	69	70	72	73	74	75	76	77	78	79	80
RHODE ISLAND	71.1	81.5	6.1	10.5	55 546	80.4	14.1	5.5	528	52	6.1	96.2	3.8	0.0
Congressional District 1	63.3	78.6	7.1	13.0	22 947	77.6	16.6	5.8	211	17	5.5	94.1	5.9	0.0
Congressional District 2	75.5	83.1	5.5	9.1	32 599	82.0	12.7	5.3	317	35	6.4	97.1	2.9	0.0
SOUTH CAROLINA	75.3	92.7	4.3	2.3	1 489 750	90.8	4.8	4.4	38 384	6 112	24.9	97.1	2.9	0.0
Congressional District 1	75.3	88.9	6.6	4.0	99 925	87.6	7.4	5.0	1 916	332	20.9	97.3	2.7	0.0
Congressional District 2	78.1	92.1	4.2	3.0	182 062	91.0	4.4	4.6	4 714	820	25.5	97.8	2.1	0.1
Congressional District 3	76.7	95.3	2.7	1.4	266 512	94.0	3.1	2.8	3 345	1 103	16.9	99.5	0.5	0.0
Congressional District 4	79.2	94.2	3.2	1.9	45 459	96.1	2.3	1.6	605	273	10.2	99.6	0.4	0.0
Congressional District 5	73.9	91.9	4.5	2.5	568 374	88.9	5.0	6.1	11 874	1 576	28.4	95.8	4.2	0.0
Congressional District 6	71.0	91.0	5.9	2.3	327 419	86.7	7.4	5.9	15 931	2 008	40.5	96.1	3.9	0.0
SOUTH DAKOTA	50.1	88.8	6.8	3.4	3 834 625	55.2	33.7	11.2	215 084	20 259	63.8	97.5	2.4	0.0
Congressional District (At Large)	50.1	88.8	6.8	3.4	3 834 625	55.2	33.7	11.2	215 084	20 259	63.8	97.5	2.4	0.0
TENNESSEE	73.4	94.6	4.6	0.5	2 199 814	93.2	4.6	2.2	59 231	16 034	18.3	99.2	0.8	0.0
Congressional District 1	71.5	95.3	4.0	0.4	211 833	95.6	3.3	1.1	2 397	1 154	8.6	99.6	0.4	0.0
Congressional District 2	71.2	95.1	3.6	0.9	154 262	95.1	3.1	1.8	2 166	428	7.1	97.9	2.1	0.0
Congressional District 3	74.1	94.9	4.2	0.6	171 995	94.4	3.5	2.1	2 060	857	11.3	99.5	0.5	0.0
Congressional District 4	72.9	94.6	4.6	0.5	541 272	91.9	5.6	2.4	9 881	3 678	19.3	99.6	0.4	0.0
Congressional District 5	76.3	94.7	4.0	1.0	24 291	97.2	2.2	0.6	179	138	7.0	100.0	0.0	0.0
Congressional District 6	75.4	95.1	4.3	0.3	375 843	93.9	4.4	1.6	6 513	2 502	13.9	99.8	0.2	0.0
Congressional District 7	75.0	93.5	5.6	0.5	166 601	94.0	4.2	1.8	8 821	2 700	30.9	99.4	0.6	0.0
Congressional District 8	72.1	93.5	5.6	0.6	549 892	88.6	6.8	4.7	27 067	4 538	36.0	98.2	1.7	0.1
Congressional District 9	85.9	87.8	1.9	5.8	3 824	93.6	4.5	1.9	146	39	25.0	100.0	0.0	0.0
TEXAS[11]	67.7	91.9	5.6	1.9	14 134 744	89.8	7.1	3.1	528 979	42 217	18.4	94.9	4.9	0.2
Congressional District 1	69.5	95.6	3.0	0.9	1 136 605	90.5	5.2	4.3	10 511	1 389	6.6	98.3	1.7	0.0
Congressional District 2	71.1	95.6	3.0	1.1	365 351	94.9	3.7	1.4	4 518	250	1.8	89.6	9.2	1.2
Congressional District 3	76.8	94.1	3.0	2.3	22 197	95.5	2.2	2.4	433	52	5.6	96.2	3.8	0.0
Congressional District 4	71.5	95.0	3.5	1.1	337 993	94.4	4.2	1.3	5 464	1 096	6.8	99.3	0.7	0.0
Congressional District 5	65.7	95.1	3.6	0.8	397 387	92.6	5.7	1.7	3 929	571	4.5	98.2	1.6	0.2
Congressional District 6	70.6	94.7	4.0	1.1	181 361	93.7	4.9	1.5	9 107	1 248	13.9	96.5	3.5	0.0
Congressional District 7	83.0	84.3	9.0	4.5	6 708	97.3	1.3	1.3	43	17	7.6	100.0	0.0	0.0
Congressional District 8	74.5	92.3	4.2	2.7	31 080	97.2	2.1	0.7	135	36	1.8	100.0	0.0	0.0
Congressional District 9	60.9	91.8	5.4	2.5	47 493	90.4	8.3	1.3	6 829	244	10.2	80.3	19.7	0.0
Congressional District 10	71.1	92.6	4.2	1.6	13 561	93.8	4.9	1.2	628	141	14.5	99.3	0.7	0.0
Congressional District 11	71.0	93.8	4.7	1.0	359 118	93.0	5.1	1.8	10 645	2 272	16.9	99.0	0.9	0.0
Congressional District 12	78.6	94.3	3.5	1.9	69 160	96.6	2.4	1.0	377	172	4.5	99.4	0.6	0.0
Congressional District 13	60.1	84.8	9.7	3.9	5 656 446	72.5	16.7	10.8	158 262	9 679	56.3	92.7	7.1	0.1
Congressional District 14	62.9	92.1	6.1	1.3	995 563	91.2	6.5	2.3	44 012	3 833	14.6	94.2	5.5	0.3
Congressional District 15	67.0	89.1	7.0	3.1	359 252	87.7	7.6	4.8	14 844	1 199	21.1	95.2	4.5	0.3
Congressional District 16	76.4	89.4	4.3	5.9	26 747	85.6	9.5	5.0	136	25	5.9	100.0	0.0	0.0
Congressional District 17	68.3	91.4	6.3	1.6	1 036 036	88.8	8.7	2.4	76 111	8 264	32.5	97.4	2.6	0.1
Congressional District 18	59.7	88.3	6.5	5.2	7 212	95.5	2.6	1.9	29	5	3.2	100.0	0.0	0.0
Congressional District 19	61.9	84.3	8.0	6.1	1 427 265	69.6	19.2	11.1	113 793	5 011	63.0	89.9	9.5	0.6
Congressional District 20	75.0	94.2	4.0	1.7	47 818	92.5	5.8	1.7	213	57	11.0	100.0	0.0	0.0
Congressional District 21	73.4	90.4	6.8	2.2	162 249	95.8	3.7	0.5	4 192	1 368	12.4	99.7	0.3	0.0
Congressional District 22	60.3	92.3	4.8	2.0	82 406	91.1	6.9	2.0	6 847	370	11.6	90.3	9.7	0.0
Congressional District 23	67.4	85.7	10.4	3.2	522 302	85.2	10.5	4.3	19 466	1 429	20.0	94.8	5.2	0.1
Congressional District 24	82.9	89.0	6.2	2.7	3 132	92.5	6.2	1.4	D	4	2.7	100.0	0.0	0.0
Congressional District 25	64.9	90.0	6.0	3.4	1 981	98.4	1.6	0.0	293	10	3.1	80.0	20.0	0.0
Congressional District 26	77.1	91.5	4.8	2.9	53 596	95.2	4.0	0.8	1 069	182	6.9	98.9	1.1	0.0
Congressional District 27	60.6	84.5	9.6	4.8	171 477	79.4	13.2	7.4	10 755	684	30.7	90.9	8.9	0.1
Congressional District 28	67.4	89.8	7.1	2.2	342 195	93.1	5.0	1.9	18 138	1 651	20.8	97.6	1.6	0.8
Congressional District 29	63.4	91.7	1.4	4.1	940	98.6	1.4	0.0	D	2	1.4	100.0	0.0	0.0
Congressional District 30	69.1	93.2	2.7	1.8	6 073	94.1	3.2	2.7	204	15	6.8	86.7	13.3	0.0
Congressional District 31	67.7	93.4	5.0	1.1	258 218	94.2	4.8	1.0	7 975	930	6.9	95.9	4.0	0.1
Congressional District 32	83.0	85.0	7.0	7.0	5 823	93.0	3.0	4.0	17	11	11.0	100.0	0.0	0.0
UTAH	68.7	85.8	8.6	4.1	1 115 898	84.5	10.3	5.2	26 669	2 987	19.5	96.8	3.1	0.0
Congressional District 1	65.2	83.5	10.6	4.5	327 278	83.4	11.1	5.4	11 413	1 176	22.0	96.3	3.7	0.0
Congressional District 2	72.7	87.2	7.7	3.4	254 272	87.5	9.2	3.3	8 057	939	17.4	96.7	3.2	0.1
Congressional District 3	68.2	86.8	7.4	4.6	534 347	82.0	10.7	7.3	7 199	872	19.1	97.7	2.3	0.0
VERMONT	61.0	87.0	7.4	4.3	473 065	76.3	16.9	6.9	24 377	1 296	19.7	90.0	10.0	0.1
Congressional District (At Large)	61.0	87.0	7.4	4.3	473 065	76.3	16.9	6.9	24 377	1 296	19.7	90.0	10.0	0.1

[11]Agriculture data were tabulated for the 108th Congress and some boundary changes have occurred.
D = Suppressed to avoid disclosure.

Table A. 109th Congressional Districts, 2000—*Continued*

(Number, percent.)

STATE Congressional district	Representative	Land area,[1] (sq km)	Total population	Persons per square kilometer	Race alone or in combination (percent) White	Black	American Indian/Alaska Native	Asian and Pacific Islander	Other race	Hispanic or Latino[2] (percent)	Non-Hispanic White (percent)	Two or more races (percent)
	1	2	3	4	5	6	7	8	9	10	11	12
VIRGINIA		102 548	7 078 515	69.0	73.9	20.4	0.7	4.4	2.7	4.7	70.2	2.0
Congressional District 1	Jo Ann Davis (R)	9 771	642 404	65.7	77.7	19.5	1.0	2.4	1.5	3.0	74.7	2.0
Congressional District 2	Thelma D. Drake (R)	2 489	643 367	258.5	71.3	22.8	1.1	5.3	2.4	4.4	67.4	2.6
Congressional District 3	Robert C. Scott (D)	2 895	643 917	222.4	39.8	57.5	1.1	2.0	1.7	2.6	37.7	1.9
Congressional District 4	J. Randy Forbes (R)	11 626	643 670	55.4	63.9	33.9	0.7	1.8	1.1	2.0	62.0	1.3
Congressional District 5	Virgil H. Goode Jr. (R)	23 108	643 323	27.8	74.0	24.5	0.5	1.2	0.8	1.6	72.4	1.0
Congressional District 6	Bob Goodlatte (R)	14 625	643 630	44.0	86.9	11.5	0.6	1.3	1.1	2.0	84.8	1.2
Congressional District 7	Eric Cantor (R)	9 102	643 583	70.7	80.1	16.7	0.6	2.7	1.2	2.0	78.2	1.2
Congressional District 8	James P. Moran (D)	319	643 764	2 018.1	67.9	14.8	0.8	11.1	10.0	16.4	57.1	4.4
Congressional District 9	Rick Boucher (D)	22 801	643 561	28.2	94.7	4.1	0.5	1.0	0.6	1.1	93.3	0.8
Congressional District 10	Frank R. Wolf (R)	4 808	643 714	133.9	82.8	7.5	0.6	7.7	4.1	7.1	77.2	2.5
Congressional District 11	Tom Davis (R)	1 004	643 582	641.0	74.2	11.1	0.7	12.5	5.0	9.1	66.8	3.4
WASHINGTON		172 348	5 894 121	34.2	84.9	4.0	2.7	7.4	4.9	7.5	78.9	3.6
Congressional District 1	Jay Inslee (D)	1 138	654 799	575.4	86.8	2.5	1.8	10.2	2.5	4.3	81.6	3.5
Congressional District 2	Rick Larsen (D)	17 002	654 984	38.5	90.6	1.6	3.1	4.3	3.6	5.8	85.6	2.9
Congressional District 3	Brian Baird (D)	19 465	654 992	33.6	92.5	1.7	2.3	4.0	2.7	4.6	87.7	2.9
Congressional District 4	Doc Hastings (R)	49 343	654 851	13.3	78.4	1.3	3.1	2.0	18.4	26.4	67.8	3.0
Congressional District 5	Cathy Anne McMorris (R)	59 217	654 935	11.1	92.2	1.8	3.5	2.7	2.7	4.5	87.7	2.7
Congressional District 6	Norman D. Dicks (D)	17 564	655 068	37.3	83.8	7.0	4.0	7.2	3.1	5.1	77.7	4.8
Congressional District 7	Jim McDermott (D)	366	655 016	1 789.7	72.6	9.9	2.2	16.2	4.1	5.8	66.9	4.6
Congressional District 8	David G. Reichert (R)	6 680	655 029	98.1	86.9	2.7	1.7	9.8	2.4	4.0	82.1	3.2
Congressional District 9	Adam Smith (D)	1 574	654 447	415.8	80.1	7.9	2.6	10.6	4.3	6.7	73.3	5.0
WEST VIRGINIA		62 361	1 808 344	29.0	95.9	3.5	0.6	0.7	0.3	0.7	94.6	0.9
Congressional District 1	Alan B. Mollohan (D)	16 281	602 545	37.0	97.1	2.0	0.5	0.9	0.3	0.7	95.8	0.8
Congressional District 2	Shelley Moore Capito (R)	21 909	602 243	27.5	95.3	4.0	0.6	0.7	0.4	0.8	93.9	1.0
Congressional District 3	Nick J. Rahall II (D)	24 170	603 556	25.0	95.1	4.4	0.6	0.5	0.2	0.6	93.9	0.8
WISCONSIN		140 663	5 363 675	38.1	90.0	6.1	1.3	2.0	2.0	3.6	87.3	1.2
Congressional District 1	Paul Ryan (R)	4 351	670 359	154.1	91.4	5.2	0.7	1.3	3.0	5.7	87.4	1.4
Congressional District 2	Tammy Baldwin (D)	9 095	670 670	73.7	92.0	4.2	0.8	2.8	1.8	3.4	89.0	1.6
Congressional District 3	Ron Kind (D)	35 134	670 473	19.1	97.3	0.7	0.9	1.5	0.5	0.9	96.1	0.8
Congressional District 4	Gwendolynn Moore (D)	290	670 373	2 311.6	56.8	34.6	1.5	3.3	6.7	11.2	50.4	2.6
Congressional District 5	F. James Sensenbrenner Jr. (R)	3 298	670 392	203.3	96.1	1.6	0.5	1.8	1.0	2.2	94.0	0.9
Congressional District 6	Thomas E. Petri (R)	14 611	670 609	45.9	96.1	1.2	0.7	1.8	1.1	2.3	94.1	0.8
Congressional District 7	David R. Obey (D)	48 657	670 432	13.8	96.3	0.4	2.0	1.8	0.4	0.9	95.1	0.8
Congressional District 8	Mark Green (R)	25 228	670 367	26.6	94.1	0.9	3.3	1.7	1.2	2.2	92.2	1.0
WYOMING		251 489	493 782	2.0	93.7	1.0	3.0	0.9	3.2	6.4	88.9	1.8
Congressional District (At Large)	Barbara Cubin (R)	251 489	493 782	2.0	93.7	1.0	3.0	1.0	3.2	6.4	88.9	1.8
NONVOTING DELEGATES												
AMERICAN SAMOA		200	57 291	286.5	2.3	0.0	...	98.5	0.2	...	...	2.8
Delegate District (At Large)	Eni F. H. Faleomavaega (D)	200	57 291	286.5	2.3	0.0	...	98.5	0.2	...	...	2.8
GUAM		544	154 805	284.6	8.5	1.0	...	90.4	1.2	...	...	8.8
Delegate District (At Large)	Madeleine Bordallo (D)	544	154 805	284.6	8.5	1.0	...	90.4	1.2	...	...	8.8
COMMONWEALTH OF THE NORTHERN MARIANA ISLANDS		464	69 221	149.2	2.6	0.0	...	97.2	0.7	...	...	4.8
Resident Representative District	Pete A. Tenorio (R)	464	69 221	149.2	2.6	0.0	...	97.2	0.7	...	...	4.8
PUERTO RICO		8 870	3 808 610	429.4	84.0	10.9	0.7	0.5	8.3	98.8	0.9	4.2
Delegate District (At Large)	Luis G. Fortuno (R)	8 870	3 808 610	429.4	84.0	10.9	0.7	0.5	8.3	98.8	0.9	4.2
VIRGIN ISLANDS		346	108 612	313.9	14.4	78.3	0.3	1.1	5.8	14.0	11.3	3.5
Delegate District (At Large)	Donna M. Christian-Christensen (D)	346	108 612	313.9	14.4	78.3	0.3	1.1	5.8	14.0	11.3	3.5

[1]Dry land or land partially or temporarily covered by water.
[2]Hispanic or Latino persons may be of any race.
. . . = Not available.

Table A. 109th Congressional Districts, 2000—*Continued*

(Number, percent.)

STATE Congressional district	Foreign born (percent)	Age (percent) Under 5 years	5 to 17 years	18 to 24 years	25 to 34 years	35 to 44 years	45 to 54 years	55 to 64 years	65 to 74 years	75 years and over	Percent female	Households Number	Persons per household	Percent Female-family householder[3]	One-person households
	13	14	15	16	17	18	19	20	21	22	23	24	25	26	27
VIRGINIA	8.1	6.5	18.0	9.6	14.6	17.0	14.1	8.9	6.1	5.1	51.0	2 699 173	2.54	11.9	25.1
Congressional District 1	4.0	6.8	19.7	9.1	13.2	17.3	13.6	9.0	6.2	5.0	51.0	237 802	2.63	10.7	21.6
Congressional District 2	6.2	6.9	18.8	12.3	16.0	17.2	12.2	7.3	5.3	4.1	49.2	231 695	2.62	12.8	22.7
Congressional District 3	3.2	7.0	18.9	11.9	14.9	15.6	12.5	7.8	6.1	5.5	52.3	250 285	2.46	21.7	29.6
Congressional District 4	2.8	6.7	20.0	8.4	13.5	17.8	14.0	8.9	6.0	4.7	50.8	231 868	2.67	14.8	20.9
Congressional District 5	2.5	5.7	16.9	9.7	12.7	15.6	14.3	10.4	8.1	6.7	51.5	253 987	2.42	12.5	26.5
Congressional District 6	3.0	5.7	16.6	11.0	12.5	15.3	14.1	9.8	7.8	7.2	51.9	254 318	2.40	11.2	27.4
Congressional District 7	4.8	6.4	18.6	7.6	13.8	17.4	15.1	9.0	6.5	5.6	51.8	252 155	2.49	10.5	25.1
Congressional District 8	27.9	6.4	13.3	8.9	22.0	18.0	14.3	8.2	4.6	4.3	50.6	277 891	2.29	8.8	36.0
Congressional District 9	1.6	5.3	15.5	11.9	13.1	14.7	14.3	10.7	8.0	6.6	50.8	259 819	2.38	10.0	26.0
Congressional District 10	13.6	8.0	20.2	7.1	15.4	19.3	14.6	8.0	4.2	3.2	50.3	228 147	2.80	8.6	19.3
Congressional District 11	19.0	7.0	20.0	7.6	14.1	18.4	16.3	9.1	4.5	3.1	50.4	221 206	2.87	8.9	17.2
WASHINGTON	10.4	6.7	19.0	9.5	14.3	16.5	14.4	8.4	5.7	5.5	50.2	2 271 398	2.53	9.9	26.2
Congressional District 1	12.0	6.5	19.0	8.2	14.6	18.1	15.7	8.3	4.9	4.6	50.3	250 896	2.57	8.7	23.7
Congressional District 2	7.9	6.8	19.7	9.9	13.3	16.3	14.1	8.3	5.9	5.7	50.1	247 485	2.59	9.4	23.7
Congressional District 3	6.6	7.0	20.2	8.6	13.0	16.1	14.8	9.0	6.0	5.5	50.4	249 440	2.59	10.2	23.6
Congressional District 4	14.4	8.1	22.3	9.9	12.8	14.7	12.9	8.1	5.8	5.4	49.8	228 850	2.82	10.6	22.3
Congressional District 5	5.1	6.3	19.1	11.4	12.3	15.2	14.1	8.7	6.4	6.5	50.6	253 206	2.48	10.3	27.4
Congressional District 6	7.6	6.4	18.6	9.4	12.7	15.5	14.2	9.3	7.1	6.8	50.7	259 477	2.45	11.7	27.7
Congressional District 7	17.2	4.9	12.1	11.3	20.6	17.0	14.6	7.6	5.3	6.5	50.1	292 364	2.15	8.7	38.9
Congressional District 8	11.6	6.9	20.8	7.0	13.7	19.1	15.2	8.4	4.8	4.0	50.0	240 770	2.70	8.3	20.0
Congressional District 9	11.4	7.2	19.1	9.7	15.3	17.0	13.6	8.1	5.3	4.7	49.9	248 910	2.56	11.3	25.5
WEST VIRGINIA	1.1	5.6	16.6	9.5	12.7	15.1	15.0	10.2	8.2	7.1	51.4	736 481	2.40	10.7	27.1
Congressional District 1	1.4	5.4	16.4	10.6	12.4	14.7	14.5	10.2	8.2	7.6	51.5	245 352	2.38	10.2	27.7
Congressional District 2	1.1	5.9	17.2	8.4	12.8	15.8	15.0	10.3	8.0	6.6	51.2	244 587	2.42	10.6	26.5
Congressional District 3	0.7	5.6	16.3	9.6	12.7	14.7	15.3	10.2	8.5	7.1	51.5	246 542	2.39	11.5	27.1
WISCONSIN	3.6	6.4	19.1	9.7	13.2	16.3	13.7	8.5	6.6	6.5	50.6	2 084 544	2.50	9.6	26.8
Congressional District 1	4.2	6.6	19.5	8.2	13.2	17.3	14.1	8.7	6.4	5.9	50.5	254 833	2.57	10.0	24.6
Congressional District 2	5.0	6.1	17.3	12.8	14.8	16.3	13.9	7.7	5.5	5.4	50.6	267 178	2.42	8.3	28.1
Congressional District 3	1.5	6.1	19.2	11.9	12.1	15.4	13.4	8.4	6.7	6.8	50.3	254 507	2.53	7.8	25.6
Congressional District 4	7.3	7.8	20.2	11.8	15.7	14.7	11.6	6.7	5.7	5.7	52.1	264 201	2.47	19.9	33.7
Congressional District 5	3.9	6.3	19.1	6.8	12.2	17.5	15.2	9.3	7.0	6.7	51.2	261 618	2.52	7.2	24.6
Congressional District 6	2.5	6.0	18.8	9.0	12.8	16.6	13.6	8.9	7.2	7.1	49.9	258 247	2.49	7.6	25.8
Congressional District 7	1.8	5.9	19.4	8.5	11.6	16.0	13.9	9.5	7.6	7.6	50.3	263 671	2.49	8.0	26.0
Congressional District 8	2.6	6.3	19.5	8.5	13.0	16.7	13.5	9.0	6.9	6.6	50.2	260 289	2.51	8.0	25.5
WYOMING	2.3	6.3	19.8	10.1	12.1	16.0	15.0	9.0	6.3	5.3	49.7	193 608	2.48	8.7	26.3
Congressional District (At Large)	2.3	6.3	19.8	10.1	12.1	16.0	15.0	9.0	6.3	5.3	49.7	193 608	2.48	8.7	26.3
NONVOTING DELEGATES															
AMERICAN SAMOA	36.1	13.6	30.9	11.1	15.2	12.8	8.3	4.7	2.3	1.0	48.9	9 349	6.05	15.0	5.7
Delegate District (At Large)	36.1	13.6	30.9	11.1	15.2	12.8	8.3	4.7	2.3	1.0	48.9	9 349	6.05	15.0	5.7
GUAM	32.1	10.8	24.6	10.8	16.7	14.9	10.7	6.2	3.8	1.5	48.9	38 769	3.89	16.2	13.1
Delegate District (At Large)	32.1	10.8	24.6	10.8	16.7	14.9	10.7	6.2	3.8	1.5	48.9	38 769	3.89	16.2	13.1
COMMONWEALTH OF THE NORTHERN MARIANA ISLANDS	58.0	8.4	17.3	13.5	29.2	18.3	9.0	2.9	1.1	0.4	53.8	14 055	3.66	11.8	19.2
Resident Representative District	58.0	8.4	17.3	13.5	29.2	18.3	9.0	2.9	1.1	0.4	53.8	14 055	3.66	11.8	19.2
PUERTO RICO	2.9	7.8	20.9	11.3	14.0	13.5	12.2	9.2	6.3	4.8	51.9	1 261 325	2.98	21.3	18.4
Delegate District (At Large)	2.9	7.8	20.9	11.3	14.0	13.5	12.2	9.2	6.3	4.8	51.9	1 261 325	2.98	21.3	18.4
VIRGIN ISLANDS	33.2	7.9	23.7	8.0	12.6	14.5	14.3	10.6	5.4	3.0	52.2	40 648	2.64	24.9	30.2
Delegate District (At Large)	33.2	7.9	23.7	8.0	12.6	14.5	14.3	10.6	5.4	3.0	52.2	40 648	2.64	24.9	30.2

[3]No spouse present.

Table A. 109th Congressional Districts, 2000—*Continued*

(Number, percent.)

STATE Congressional district	Group quarters Persons in correctional institutions	Persons in nursing homes	Persons in college dormitories	Persons in military quarters	Education School enrollment[4] Public	Private	Attainment level[5] H.S. graduate or more	Bachelor's degree or more	Money income, 1999 Per capita income[6]	Households Median income	Percent with income over $100,000	Percent below poverty level, 1999 Persons	Families
	28	29	30	31	32	33	34	35	36	37	38	39	40
VIRGINIA	64 036	38 865	65 557	33 752	1 566 180	301 921	81.5	29.5	23 975	46 677	15.1	9.6	7.0
Congressional District 1	2 627	3 397	7 075	2 927	152 979	25 224	84.6	26.8	22 918	50 257	13.7	6.7	4.8
Congressional District 2	9 271	2 664	1 924	20 694	147 310	27 570	87.5	25.5	21 371	44 193	10.5	8.7	6.6
Congressional District 3	7 809	3 562	6 926	5 185	156 845	23 205	75.1	17.2	16 870	32 238	5.5	18.9	15.3
Congressional District 4	14 067	3 133	1 846	3 008	150 300	23 228	78.5	19.6	20 085	45 249	10.2	9.5	7.6
Congressional District 5	10 311	4 415	10 633	0	141 252	20 110	72.4	19.0	18 919	35 739	7.2	13.2	9.2
Congressional District 6	4 458	6 376	16 797	0	132 731	31 676	77.6	20.8	19 544	37 773	7.7	11.0	7.3
Congressional District 7	3 854	4 265	3 712	0	134 185	30 232	84.9	33.2	25 861	50 990	15.9	6.1	4.4
Congressional District 8	926	2 774	641	1 795	109 080	38 856	87.1	53.8	35 613	63 430	26.1	7.5	5.2
Congressional District 9	5 731	3 874	12 690	2	149 387	11 468	68.7	14.0	16 336	29 783	4.5	16.2	11.2
Congressional District 10	1 222	2 381	816	77	140 401	35 406	88.2	43.1	32 933	71 560	31.0	4.4	2.8
Congressional District 11	3 760	2 024	2 497	64	151 710	34 946	91.7	48.9	33 268	80 397	36.3	3.8	2.5
WASHINGTON	28 871	23 275	30 858	13 868	1 368 232	216 469	87.1	27.7	22 973	45 776	12.6	10.6	7.3
Congressional District 1	3 679	1 858	489	879	148 527	26 913	92.8	36.4	28 011	58 565	19.3	5.6	3.8
Congressional District 2	1 119	2 115	3 339	3 365	158 437	19 155	87.3	22.4	21 331	45 441	10.3	10.0	6.6
Congressional District 3	2 290	2 405	637	13	153 377	19 443	86.4	21.4	20 718	44 426	10.1	10.5	7.7
Congressional District 4	2 498	2 657	2 103	9	172 943	15 545	75.2	18.7	17 355	37 764	8.1	16.2	12.0
Congressional District 5	6 122	3 706	10 644	698	164 605	27 026	87.1	23.8	18 086	35 720	7.0	14.4	9.6
Congressional District 6	6 116	3 235	2 797	2 049	144 753	23 212	85.8	20.1	19 740	39 205	7.9	13.2	9.5
Congressional District 7	3 394	3 074	10 642	232	124 602	35 784	88.5	44.1	29 099	45 864	15.3	11.5	7.0
Congressional District 8	36	1 158	101	0	153 370	27 219	92.1	37.4	30 536	63 854	24.0	5.1	3.5
Congressional District 9	3 617	3 067	106	6 623	147 618	22 172	87.4	22.3	21 879	46 495	10.8	9.2	6.7
WEST VIRGINIA	10 505	11 601	14 300	59	380 827	37 726	75.2	14.8	16 477	29 696	5.0	17.9	13.9
Congressional District 1	2 416	4 578	8 236	0	135 371	14 451	79.4	16.3	16 511	30 303	5.0	17.0	12.3
Congressional District 2	2 212	3 380	3 020	59	120 399	13 844	76.9	16.2	17 872	33 198	6.2	14.8	11.6
Congressional District 3	5 877	3 643	3 044	0	125 057	9 431	69.4	12.0	15 053	25 630	3.9	21.9	17.7
WISCONSIN	31 068	41 370	51 397	82	1 209 333	253 705	85.1	22.4	21 271	43 791	9.4	8.7	5.6
Congressional District 1	5 713	4 116	1 745	5	144 956	33 764	85.4	21.5	22 730	50 372	11.8	6.3	4.3
Congressional District 2	3 069	3 941	13 483	0	175 523	22 211	89.1	32.1	23 246	46 979	11.2	8.7	4.2
Congressional District 3	2 696	6 088	13 562	52	168 635	23 061	85.5	19.5	18 786	40 006	7.0	9.8	5.6
Congressional District 4	2 152	4 151	6 745	13	155 651	46 756	75.8	17.8	16 607	33 121	4.8	19.8	15.9
Congressional District 5	1 053	5 384	2 063	0	131 661	44 848	90.9	35.0	29 064	58 594	19.3	3.4	2.2
Congressional District 6	11 286	5 797	5 306	3	138 927	32 289	84.0	17.1	20 506	44 242	7.1	6.1	3.8
Congressional District 7	1 484	5 985	4 088	2	150 432	21 256	83.8	16.6	18 749	39 026	6.1	8.6	5.7
Congressional District 8	3 615	5 908	4 405	7	143 548	29 520	85.3	19.1	20 480	43 274	8.1	6.8	4.6
WYOMING	4 176	2 869	3 850	545	126 439	9 700	87.9	21.9	19 134	37 892	6.7	11.4	8.0
Congressional District (At Large)	4 176	2 869	3 850	545	126 439	9 700	87.9	21.9	19 134	37 892	6.7	11.4	8.0
NONVOTING DELEGATES													
AMERICAN SAMOA	99	13	0	0	18 649	2 181	66.1	7.4	4 357	1 821	1.8	61.0	58.3
Delegate District (At Large)	99	13	0	0	18 649	2 181	66.1	7.4	4 357	1 821	1.8	61.0	58.3
GUAM	852	54	65	1 710	39 102	7 726	76.3	20.0	12 722	39 317	10.2	23.0	20.0
Delegate District (At Large)	852	54	65	1 710	39 102	7 726	76.3	20.0	12 722	39 317	10.2	23.0	20.0
COMMONWEALTH OF THE NORTHERN MARIANA ISLANDS	84	0	0	0	10 475	2 914	69.2	15.5	9 151	22 898	5.4	46.0	30.6
Resident Representative District	84	0	0	0	10 475	2 914	69.2	15.5	9 151	22 898	5.4	46.0	30.6
PUERTO RICO	17 283	7 311	2 174	1 199	817 987	312 327	60.0	18.3	8 185	14 412	2.4	48.2	44.6
Delegate District (At Large)	17 283	7 311	2 174	1 199	817 987	312 327	60.0	18.3	8 185	14 412	2.4	48.2	44.6
VIRGIN ISLANDS	428	168	160	0	24 806	7 313	60.6	16.8	13 139	24 704	5.0	32.5	28.7
Delegate District (At Large)	428	168	160	0	24 806	7 313	60.6	16.8	13 139	24 704	5.0	32.5	28.7

[4]All persons 3 years old and over enrolled in nursery school through college.
[5]Persons 25 years old and over.
[6]Based on the population enumerated as of April 1, 2000.

Table A. 109th Congressional Districts, 2000—*Continued*

(Number, percent.)

STATE Congressional district	Housing units									Civilian labor force		
	Total	Total occupied units	Owner occupied		Median owner costs as a percent of income		Renter occupied		Sub-standard housing units (percent)[9]	Total	Unemployment	
			Percent	Median value[7] (dollars)	With a mortgage	Without a mortgage[8]	Median rent (dollars)	Median rent as a percent of income			Total	Rate[10]
	41	42	43	44	45	46	47	48	49	50	51	52
VIRGINIA	2 904 192	2 699 173	68.1	125 400	21.4	9.9	650	24.5	3.9	3 563 772	151 125	4.2
Congressional District 1	261 274	237 490	72.7	131 400	21.9	9.9	671	24.4	2.9	316 021	14 531	4.3
Congressional District 2	249 974	231 653	63.5	113 900	23.6	10.7	677	26.1	3.8	293 350	14 711	4.2
Congressional District 3	272 393	250 417	52.1	83 600	23.1	11.9	535	27.4	4.9	295 625	23 330	7.4
Congressional District 4	246 708	231 889	73.5	105 700	22.1	9.9	568	24.9	3.2	305 287	13 428	4.2
Congressional District 5	287 824	253 996	72.4	92 900	20.3	9.9	469	24.0	3.4	308 990	15 727	5.1
Congressional District 6	275 233	254 321	69.2	99 500	20.5	9.9	478	23.4	2.5	325 347	14 280	4.4
Congressional District 7	267 603	252 282	72.9	128 800	20.8	9.9	667	23.9	2.4	342 769	9 501	2.8
Congressional District 8	288 518	277 916	50.1	227 500	20.6	9.9	899	23.4	8.5	381 816	11 499	2.9
Congressional District 9	290 823	259 829	74.2	75 700	19.7	9.9	403	24.7	2.6	291 961	16 508	5.6
Congressional District 10	237 718	228 202	75.4	189 900	21.3	9.9	883	23.8	3.4	354 174	8 374	2.3
Congressional District 11	226 124	221 178	76.6	210 300	20.9	9.9	988	23.5	4.4	348 432	9 236	2.6
WASHINGTON	2 451 075	2 271 398	64.6	168 300	23.8	10.4	663	26.5	5.5	2 979 824	186 102	6.2
Congressional District 1	261 755	250 775	67.9	229 300	24.2	10.6	841	25.4	3.9	351 321	13 377	3.7
Congressional District 2	275 776	247 566	67.2	170 900	24.9	10.9	675	27.5	5.2	324 602	20 927	6.2
Congressional District 3	271 140	249 432	67.9	147 400	23.7	9.9	634	26.6	4.6	322 188	20 812	6.4
Congressional District 4	253 496	228 819	66.0	119 200	21.9	9.9	527	26.3	11.1	304 106	29 402	9.7
Congressional District 5	279 929	253 204	66.0	110 800	22.7	9.9	509	27.7	4.4	316 391	26 851	8.4
Congressional District 6	290 072	259 518	63.5	133 300	23.8	11.0	589	27.3	5.1	300 480	22 484	7.3
Congressional District 7	306 270	292 385	50.5	242 800	24.2	11.3	718	26.6	6.0	385 486	19 970	5.2
Congressional District 8	251 820	240 810	75.6	237 700	24.0	10.2	848	25.2	3.7	347 381	13 906	4.0
Congressional District 9	260 817	248 889	59.6	160 500	23.7	10.5	690	25.8	6.2	327 869	18 373	5.4
WEST VIRGINIA	844 623	736 481	75.2	72 800	19.5	9.9	401	25.8	2.3	790 694	58 021	7.3
Congressional District 1	277 962	245 352	74.0	71 000	19.3	9.9	402	26.8	1.9	274 428	20 115	7.3
Congressional District 2	280 581	244 587	75.5	83 900	19.2	9.9	430	23.9	2.4	279 072	16 512	5.9
Congressional District 3	286 080	246 542	76.0	63 300	20.0	9.9	374	27.1	2.6	237 194	21 394	9.0
WISCONSIN	2 321 144	2 084 544	68.4	112 200	20.9	11.2	540	23.4	2.8	2 869 236	134 311	4.7
Congressional District 1	275 803	254 793	70.8	127 100	21.3	11.8	602	23.4	2.6	358 046	16 558	4.6
Congressional District 2	281 861	267 211	62.3	134 600	22.1	11.0	614	24.9	2.8	389 553	16 797	4.3
Congressional District 3	276 415	254 520	72.1	91 400	20.3	10.9	464	22.7	2.6	364 522	16 358	4.5
Congressional District 4	282 789	264 190	46.6	84 200	21.0	12.5	529	25.3	6.2	322 788	28 492	8.8
Congressional District 5	271 508	261 626	73.4	161 700	21.4	11.6	674	22.7	1.5	368 809	9 976	2.7
Congressional District 6	287 252	258 274	73.4	99 100	20.4	11.1	490	21.0	2.0	359 115	13 403	3.7
Congressional District 7	323 266	263 682	76.1	86 100	19.5	10.5	439	22.7	2.6	350 415	18 474	5.3
Congressional District 8	322 250	260 248	73.4	103 600	20.4	11.0	498	21.8	2.4	355 988	14 253	4.0
WYOMING	223 854	193 608	70.0	96 600	19.7	9.9	437	22.5	3.2	254 508	13 453	5.3
Congressional District (At Large)	223 854	193 608	70.0	96 600	19.7	9.9	437	22.5	3.2	254 508	13 453	5.2
NONVOTING DELEGATES												
AMERICAN SAMOA	10 052	9 349	77.2	44 800	20.3	9.9	361	19.9	73.0	17 627	909	5.2
Delegate District (At Large)	10 052	9 349	77.2	44 800	20.3	9.9	361	19.9	73.0	17 627	909	5.2
GUAM	47 677	38 769	48.4	171 900	23.9	9.9	774	28.8	38.7	64 452	7 399	11.5
Delegate District (At Large)	47 677	38 769	48.4	171 900	23.9	9.9	774	28.8	38.7	64 452	7 399	11.5
COMMONWEALTH OF THE NORTHERN MARIANA ISLANDS	17 566	14 055	32.4	159 800	20.2	9.9	373	18.7	51.7	44 465	1 712	3.9
Resident Representative District	17 566	14 055	32.4	159 800	20.2	9.9	373	18.7	51.7	44 465	1 712	3.9
PUERTO RICO	1 418 476	1 261 325	72.9	75 100	27.9	12.5	297	27.0	23.2	1 151 863	220 998	19.2
Delegate District (At Large)	1 418 476	1 261 325	72.9	75 100	27.9	12.5	297	27.0	23.2	1 151 863	220 998	19.2
VIRGIN ISLANDS	50 202	40 648	46.0	149 118	26.3	9.9	530	26.7	16.6	50 933	4 368	8.6
Delegate District (At Large)	50 202	40 648	46.0	149 118	26.3	9.9	530	26.7	16.6	50 933	4 368	8.6

[7]Specified owner-occupied units.
[8]Median monthly owner costs is often in the minimum category—9.9 percent or less, which is indicated as 9.9 percent.
[9]Overcrowded or lacking complete plumbing facilities.
[10]Percent of civilian labor force.

Table A. 109th Congressional Districts, 2000—*Continued*

(Number, percent.)

STATE Congressional district	Civilian employment and occupations — Total	Management, professional, and related (percent)	Service, sales, and office (percent)	Construction and production (percent)	Total farms, 2002	Farms by size, 2002 (percent) — 1 to 49 acres	50 to 999 acres	1,000 acres or more	Land in farms, 2002 — Acreage	Average size of farms (acres)	Cropland harvested, 2002 — Acreage	Farms	Farm's principal operator's primary occupation is farming, 2002 (percent)
	53	54	55	56	57	58	59	60	61	62	63	64	65
VIRGINIA	3 412 647	38.2	39.2	22.1	47 606	35.9	61.1	2.9	8 624 829	181	2 623 776	33 791	53.6
Congressional District 1	301 490	36.7	40.5	22.1	2 827	40.9	53.6	5.6	667 153	236	355 314	1 833	53.2
Congressional District 2	278 639	34.0	44.3	21.1	675	48.9	44.3	6.8	171 745	254	130 740	467	60.3
Congressional District 3	272 295	27.8	46.2	25.8	577	36.0	57.4	6.6	160 326	278	88 802	381	52.9
Congressional District 4	291 859	31.4	40.5	27.6	3 062	33.7	58.8	7.6	878 218	287	405 467	2 023	59.5
Congressional District 5	293 263	29.3	38.1	31.7	10 059	24.2	72.9	2.9	2 099 927	209	461 906	7 359	54.8
Congressional District 6	311 067	29.3	41.4	28.5	7 634	36.0	61.7	2.3	1 278 792	168	343 619	5 375	55.7
Congressional District 7	333 268	39.8	40.4	19.4	4 539	40.6	56.7	2.8	767 654	169	255 073	3 027	52.5
Congressional District 8	370 317	55.9	33.3	10.7	17	70.6	29.4	0.0	578	34	180	10	35.3
Congressional District 9	275 453	26.2	37.5	35.3	14 103	37.0	61.3	1.8	2 050 132	145	402 805	10 979	51.7
Congressional District 10	345 800	48.2	35.6	15.9	3 736	51.0	47.0	2.0	516 614	138	164 775	2 118	49.4
Congressional District 11	339 196	52.1	36.1	11.7	377	59.2	40.1	0.8	33 690	89	15 095	219	45.9
WASHINGTON	2 793 722	35.6	40.8	22.1	35 939	57.5	34.2	8.3	15 318 008	426	4 894 634	21 802	58.5
Congressional District 1	337 944	42.5	39.2	18.0	727	87.3	12.5	0.1	20 984	29	5 224	330	54.1
Congressional District 2	303 675	30.0	40.8	27.6	4 258	68.9	30.2	0.9	353 378	83	165 246	2 405	55.1
Congressional District 3	301 376	30.9	40.9	26.8	4 829	68.0	31.2	0.7	363 097	75	93 687	2 472	51.8
Congressional District 4	274 704	30.1	38.4	23.7	11 752	55.2	36.8	8.0	5 904 194	502	1 859 402	8 374	63.6
Congressional District 5	289 540	33.5	43.7	21.1	9 367	35.8	43.5	20.7	8 443 095	901	2 709 040	6 077	60.8
Congressional District 6	277 996	29.5	43.8	25.3	1 976	73.5	25.9	0.7	123 993	63	33 360	963	50.3
Congressional District 7	365 516	46.3	38.7	14.7	116	90.5	9.5	0.0	2 115	18	633	88	59.5
Congressional District 8	333 475	41.7	38.2	19.7	1 782	84.2	15.7	0.1	61 064	34	13 633	623	52.5
Congressional District 9	309 496	30.6	44.2	24.7	1 132	80.9	18.8	0.3	46 088	41	14 409	470	53.6
WEST VIRGINIA	732 673	27.9	42.6	28.7	20 812	27.3	71.0	1.7	3 584 668	172	648 635	15 827	50.5
Congressional District 1	254 313	28.4	42.6	28.5	8 127	25.7	73.3	1.0	1 296 090	159	237 224	6 258	50.5
Congressional District 2	262 560	29.1	41.3	28.9	8 207	28.9	68.9	2.2	1 480 527	180	290 633	6 222	50.7
Congressional District 3	215 800	25.9	44.4	28.8	4 478	27.1	70.9	2.1	808 051	180	120 778	3 347	50.0
WISCONSIN	2 734 925	31.3	39.3	28.4	77 131	27.6	69.9	2.5	15 741 552	204	8 928 083	54 741	59.4
Congressional District 1	341 488	31.0	39.3	29.4	2 966	47.5	48.0	4.6	621 006	209	500 209	2 101	55.9
Congressional District 2	372 756	37.9	39.2	22.3	7 821	36.7	60.3	3.1	1 546 841	198	1 081 803	5 374	58.1
Congressional District 3	348 164	29.6	39.3	29.2	27 124	22.7	75.0	2.3	5 714 323	211	2 729 038	17 994	57.7
Congressional District 4	294 296	27.5	44.6	27.8	0	X	X	X	X	X	X	X	X
Congressional District 5	358 833	40.9	37.6	21.3	2 335	43.3	54.5	2.2	350 259	150	248 157	1 639	57.9
Congressional District 6	345 712	26.4	37.0	35.4	10 625	31.3	65.9	2.8	2 175 334	205	1 536 397	7 604	63.0
Congressional District 7	331 941	27.3	39.1	31.8	16 407	21.7	76.2	2.1	3 491 740	213	1 701 896	12 856	60.2
Congressional District 8	341 735	28.6	38.8	31.3	9 853	30.0	67.9	2.1	1 842 049	187	1 130 583	7 173	61.0
WYOMING	241 055	30.0	40.9	27.5	9 422	21.4	44.3	34.3	34 402 726	3 651	1 298 709	5 003	61.1
Congressional District (At Large)	241 055	30.0	40.9	27.5	9 422	21.4	44.3	34.3	34 402 726	3 651	1 298 709	5 003	61.1
NONVOTING DELEGATES													
AMERICAN SAMOA	16 718	24.8	28.6	43.4	. . .	. . .	. . .	. . .	. . .	. . .	. . .	. . .	. . .
Delegate District (At Large)	16 718	24.8	28.6	43.4	. . .	. . .	. . .	. . .	. . .	. . .	. . .	. . .	. . .
GUAM	57 053	27.8	50.3	21.6	153	95.4	D	D	1 648	11	744	141	87.6
Delegate District (At Large)	57 053	27.8	50.3	21.6	153	95.4	D	D	1 648	11	744	141	87.6
COMMONWEALTH OF THE NORTHERN MARIANA ISLANDS	42 753	15.8	31.4	51.4	214	93.5	D	D	2 353	11	529	189	43.0
Resident Representative District	42 753	15.8	31.4	51.4	214	93.5	D	D	2 353	11	529	189	43.0
PUERTO RICO	930 865	27.4	44.1	22.7	17 659	85.0	D	D	670 743	38	195 625	15 284	49.3
Delegate District (At Large)	930 865	27.4	44.1	22.7	17 659	85.0	D	D	670 743	38	195 625	15 284	49.3
VIRGIN ISLANDS	46 565	24.5	50.2	24.7	191	86.4	12.6	2.0	9 168	48	602	129	41.4
Delegate District (At Large)	46 565	24.5	50.2	24.7	191	86.4	12.6	2.0	9 168	48	602	129	41.4

X = Not applicable.
D = Suppressed to avoid disclosure.
. . . = Not available.

Table A. 109th Congressional Districts, 2000—*Continued*

(Number, percent.)

STATE Congressional district	Farm's principal operator is full owner, 2002 (percent)	Type of organization, 2002 (percent)			Value of all agricultural products sold, 2002				Payments received from federal farm programs, 2002					
		Family or individual	Partner-ship	Corpo-ration	Total ($1,000)	Percent of farms			Total payments ($1,000)	Farms receiving payments		Percent of farms receiving		
						Less than $50,000	$50,000 to $249,999	$250,000 or more		Number	Percent	Less than $50,000	$50,000 to $249,999	$250,000 or more
	66	67	68	69	70	72	73	74	75	76	77	78	79	80
VIRGINIA	66.8	90.0	5.8	3.6	2 360 911	87.9	7.5	4.6	54 677	9 206	19.3	98.0	2.0	0.0
Congressional District 1	64.3	87.1	5.6	6.5	137 491	86.2	9.4	4.4	7 710	828	29.3	96.3	3.7	0.0
Congressional District 2	54.5	81.5	7.7	10.2	162 985	64.4	16.9	18.7	1 863	182	27.0	96.2	3.8	0.0
Congressional District 3	60.7	86.0	8.3	5.0	36 772	82.7	12.0	5.4	2 732	200	34.7	91.0	9.0	0.0
Congressional District 4	61.7	88.6	5.4	5.2	290 385	80.3	10.9	8.7	12 061	1 090	35.6	94.7	5.2	0.1
Congressional District 5	64.5	91.4	5.5	2.3	317 554	90.1	6.9	3.0	8 290	2 587	25.7	99.3	0.7	0.0
Congressional District 6	65.7	88.6	6.9	4.0	718 577	79.9	9.3	10.8	9 742	1 358	17.8	98.9	1.0	0.1
Congressional District 7	68.5	89.0	5.2	5.3	265 184	87.7	7.0	5.3	4 539	842	18.6	98.3	1.7	0.0
Congressional District 8	82.4	88.2	5.9	5.9	950	94.1	0.0	5.9	D	D	D	D	D	D
Congressional District 9	68.8	92.5	5.6	1.6	324 654	92.5	5.9	1.6	5 691	1 760	12.5	99.3	0.7	0.0
Congressional District 10	74.4	87.3	5.4	6.4	95 434	92.7	5.4	1.9	1 814	319	8.5	95.9	4.1	0.0
Congressional District 11	75.6	83.0	4.5	11.4	10 926	93.6	4.0	2.4	234	40	10.6	97.5	2.5	0.0
WASHINGTON	73.0	84.9	6.3	7.6	5 330 740	75.6	14.1	10.3	133 763	7 332	20.4	91.1	8.8	0.1
Congressional District 1	83.9	85.1	5.2	8.4	86 434	88.7	5.1	6.2	230	24	3.3	95.8	4.2	0.0
Congressional District 2	73.7	85.6	5.7	7.8	609 838	79.9	9.2	10.8	6 947	422	9.9	93.1	6.9	0.0
Congressional District 3	80.9	91.6	3.9	3.6	279 750	90.2	5.5	4.3	1 584	179	3.7	98.9	1.1	0.0
Congressional District 4	71.7	82.1	7.7	9.4	2 924 142	63.5	20.5	16.0	54 917	3 026	25.7	90.4	9.5	0.1
Congressional District 5	64.8	82.0	7.6	9.1	1 081 288	72.4	18.0	9.6	68 578	3 504	37.4	90.6	9.3	0.1
Congressional District 6	80.8	90.6	3.3	3.8	127 490	91.4	5.0	3.6	504	65	3.3	98.5	1.5	0.0
Congressional District 7	82.8	83.6	9.5	5.2	9 274	88.8	6.9	4.3	8	12	10.3	100.0	0.0	0.0
Congressional District 8	84.2	91.6	3.6	4.0	96 645	91.1	4.7	4.2	941	73	4.1	98.6	1.4	0.0
Congressional District 9	79.3	88.3	4.7	6.1	115 879	89.1	5.7	5.1	54	27	2.4	100.0	0.0	0.0
WEST VIRGINIA	74.6	95.4	3.1	1.1	482 814	94.8	3.3	1.9	5 180	1 675	8.0	99.6	0.4	0.0
Congressional District 1	76.8	96.2	2.5	0.8	100 866	97.0	2.1	0.9	971	426	5.2	100.0	0.0	0.0
Congressional District 2	72.8	94.6	3.6	1.4	305 038	92.6	4.0	3.4	3 116	814	9.9	99.3	0.7	0.0
Congressional District 3	74.1	95.6	3.1	0.9	76 910	94.9	4.1	1.0	1 093	435	9.7	100.0	0.0	0.0
WISCONSIN	67.9	89.1	6.9	3.5	5 623 275	72.6	21.4	6.1	247 942	37 234	48.3	98.9	1.1	0.0
Congressional District 1	62.5	82.6	8.1	8.2	269 672	73.2	18.4	8.5	11 025	1 277	43.1	97.0	3.0	0.0
Congressional District 2	68.3	86.9	8.7	3.8	678 738	71.9	20.9	7.2	31 962	4 275	54.7	98.5	1.5	0.0
Congressional District 3	72.0	89.5	7.4	2.6	1 649 004	74.2	20.7	5.1	87 439	14 812	54.6	99.3	0.7	0.0
Congressional District 4	X	X	X	X	X	X	X	X	X	X	X	X	X	X
Congressional District 5	64.8	86.7	7.5	5.5	165 210	75.8	18.0	6.2	6 520	1 001	42.9	98.5	1.5	0.0
Congressional District 6	63.7	87.7	7.5	4.4	981 682	68.4	23.2	8.4	41 084	5 560	52.3	98.6	1.3	0.0
Congressional District 7	66.2	91.5	4.9	3.4	1 048 406	73.2	22.3	4.4	37 761	5 685	34.6	99.1	0.9	0.1
Congressional District 8	66.1	89.9	6.5	3.4	830 563	70.8	21.8	7.3	32 151	4 624	46.9	98.8	1.2	0.0
WYOMING	59.0	80.3	9.8	7.9	863 887	70.2	21.9	7.8	37 913	3 163	33.6	95.4	4.6	0.1
Congressional District (At Large)	59.0	80.3	9.8	7.9	863 887	70.2	21.9	7.8	37 913	3 163	33.6	95.4	4.6	0.1
NONVOTING DELEGATES														
AMERICAN SAMOA	...	...	...	...	...	...	...	...	...	...	...	...	...	...
Delegate District (At Large)	...	...	...	...	...	...	...	...	...	...	...	...	...	...
GUAM	49.0	88.2	7.2	4.6	4 198	...	...	...	...	...	...	...	...	...
Delegate District (At Large)	49.0	88.2	7.2	4.6	4 198	...	...	...	...	...	...	...	...	...
COMMONWEALTH OF THE NORTHERN MARIANA ISLANDS	72.0	86.4	2.3	6.5	2 287	...	...	...	...	...	...	...	...	...
Resident Representative District	72.0	86.4	2.3	6.5	2 287	...	...	...	...	...	...	...	...	...
PUERTO RICO	77.5	89.7	0.9	3.4	581 544	91.5	D	D	56 294	6 051	34.3	D	D	D
Delegate District (At Large)	77.5	89.7	0.9	3.4	581 544	91.5	D	D	56 294	6 051	34.3	D	D	D
VIRGIN ISLANDS	59.2	88.0	4.7	5.8	3 019	...	...	...	...	...	...	...	...	...
Delegate District (At Large)	59.2	88.0	4.7	5.8	3 019	...	...	...	...	...	...	...	...	...

X = Not applicable.
D = Suppressed to avoid disclosure.
. . . = Not available.

Table B. 109th Congressional Districts by Counties, 2000

(Number, percent.)

STATE Congressional district County	Land area,[1] (sq km)	Population				Percent with bachelor's degree or more[3]	Median income, 1999 (dollars)	Percent living in poverty	Percent unem- ployed	Households	
		Total	Percent minority[2]	Percent under 18 years old	Percent 65 years old and over					Total	Percent owner occupied
	1	2	3	4	5	6	7	8	9	10	11
UNITED STATES	9 161 923	281 421 906	30.9	25.6	12.4	24.4	41 994	12.4	5.8	105 480 101	66.2
ALABAMA	131 426	4 447 100	29.7	25.2	13.0	19.0	34 135	16.1	6.2	1 737 080	72.5
Congressional District 1, Alabama	16 361	635 498	32.2	26.7	13.0	18.5	34 739	16.9	6.8	241 434	73.1
Baldwin County	4 135	140 415	13.9	24.4	15.4	23.1	40 250	10.1	4.3	55 336	79.6
Clarke County (part)	1 123	14 379	30.2	27.0	14.0	14.1	33 537	18.8	6.6	5 534	81.5
Escambia County	2 454	38 440	36.2	24.2	13.4	10.6	28 319	20.9	7.0	14 297	77.1
Mobile County	3 194	399 843	37.5	27.5	12.0	18.6	33 710	18.5	7.6	150 179	68.9
Monroe County	2 657	24 324	42.7	28.2	13.9	11.8	29 093	21.3	8.4	9 383	80.4
Washington County	2 799	18 097	35.4	28.8	12.7	8.6	30 815	18.5	7.7	6 705	88.2
Congressional District 2, Alabama	27 199	635 311	32.9	25.5	13.3	18.0	32 460	17.2	6.4	246 539	71.6
Autauga County	1 544	43 671	20.4	28.6	10.2	18.0	42 013	10.9	4.9	16 003	80.8
Barbour County	2 292	29 038	49.1	25.4	13.5	10.9	25 101	26.8	5.7	10 409	73.2
Bullock County	1 619	11 714	76.1	25.7	12.9	7.7	20 605	33.5	8.6	3 986	74.4
Butler County	2 012	21 399	42.0	26.9	16.4	10.4	24 791	24.6	10.6	8 398	76.2
Coffee County	1 759	43 615	24.1	24.7	14.3	19.3	33 664	14.7	5.7	17 421	71.4
Conecuh County	2 204	14 089	44.8	25.8	15.8	9.2	22 111	26.6	9.8	5 792	81.1
Covington County	2 678	37 631	14.4	23.6	17.9	12.2	26 336	18.4	7.6	15 640	77.7
Crenshaw County	1 579	13 665	26.7	24.7	17.3	11.2	26 054	22.1	5.4	5 577	76.6
Dale County	1 453	49 129	27.2	26.7	11.7	14.0	31 998	15.1	7.7	18 878	64.2
Elmore County	1 609	65 874	23.5	25.6	10.9	16.6	41 243	10.2	5.0	22 737	81.4
Geneva County	1 493	25 764	13.8	24.0	16.3	8.7	26 448	19.6	8.0	10 477	80.6
Henry County	1 455	16 310	34.3	24.2	16.2	14.1	30 353	19.1	6.3	6 525	80.9
Houston County	1 503	88 787	27.1	25.9	13.6	18.4	34 431	15.0	5.2	35 834	69.5
Lowndes County	1 859	13 473	74.2	30.0	12.4	11.0	23 050	31.4	11.9	4 909	83.4
Montgomery County (part)	404	131 547	44.3	24.8	12.3	29.8	36 905	15.9	5.7	52 020	61.0
Pike County	1 738	29 605	39.8	24.2	12.5	18.4	25 551	23.1	9.3	11 933	67.2
Congressional District 3, Alabama	20 290	635 374	35.1	24.6	12.9	16.7	30 806	18.8	6.7	248 689	71.0
Calhoun County	1 576	112 249	21.9	23.6	14.1	15.2	31 768	16.1	6.6	45 307	72.5
Chambers County	1 547	36 583	39.6	24.7	16.1	9.5	29 667	17.0	6.5	14 522	75.7
Cherokee County	1 433	23 988	7.3	22.1	16.0	9.7	30 874	15.6	3.9	9 719	81.7
Clay County	1 567	14 254	18.7	23.8	16.7	7.8	27 885	17.1	5.5	5 765	77.2
Cleburne County	1 451	14 123	6.4	24.2	13.8	9.2	30 820	13.9	5.3	5 590	80.4
Coosa County (part)	976	9 085	47.8	24.4	13.7	8.3	29 900	16.5	7.1	3 373	83.4
Lee County	1 577	115 092	26.8	23.2	8.1	27.9	30 952	21.8	5.8	45 702	62.1
Macon County	1 581	24 105	86.3	25.2	14.0	18.8	21 180	32.8	12.3	8 950	67.3
Montgomery County (part)	1 642	91 963	62.2	27.1	11.1	26.6	34 248	19.4	8.0	34 048	68.7
Randolph County	1 505	22 380	24.3	25.1	15.8	10.0	28 675	17.0	5.3	8 642	79.1
Russell County	1 661	49 756	44.4	26.5	13.1	9.7	27 492	19.9	6.3	19 741	62.4
Talladega County	1 915	80 321	33.6	25.0	13.4	11.2	31 628	17.6	7.7	30 674	76.4
Tallapoosa County	1 859	41 475	26.7	24.1	16.5	14.1	30 745	16.6	6.1	16 656	76.3
Congressional District 4, Alabama	21 684	635 365	9.5	24.2	14.5	11.3	31 344	14.7	5.6	251 545	78.0
Blount County	1 672	51 024	7.6	25.6	12.7	9.6	35 241	11.7	4.8	19 265	83.5
Cullman County	1 913	77 483	4.8	24.2	14.6	11.9	32 256	13.0	4.1	30 706	78.1
DeKalb County	2 015	64 452	9.3	24.7	13.8	8.3	30 137	15.4	5.1	25 113	78.7
Etowah County	1 385	103 459	17.8	23.9	16.0	13.4	31 170	15.7	6.0	41 615	74.4
Fayette County	1 626	18 495	13.5	23.9	16.2	9.2	28 539	17.3	7.7	7 493	77.2
Franklin County	1 646	31 223	12.5	24.2	14.9	9.7	27 177	18.9	5.6	12 259	74.3
Lamar County	1 567	15 904	13.4	23.6	15.9	7.8	28 059	16.1	7.1	6 468	76.9
Marion County	1 920	31 214	5.7	22.5	15.8	8.0	27 475	15.6	8.1	12 697	77.9
Marshall County	1 469	82 231	8.0	24.8	14.3	13.9	32 167	14.7	5.7	32 547	74.7
Morgan County (part)	1 309	49 940	5.4	25.1	12.1	17.5	40 615	9.5	4.8	19 202	83.4
Pickens County (part)	1 215	9 365	18.9	24.1	17.1	9.5	30 841	16.6	4.6	3 759	81.1
St. Clair County (part)	300	5 019	6.4	24.0	12.9	12.6	34 317	11.6	6.0	1 950	82.8
Walker County	2 057	70 713	8.5	23.5	14.7	9.1	29 076	16.5	6.4	28 364	80.0
Winston County	1 591	24 843	3.3	23.7	14.2	8.3	28 435	17.1	6.3	10 107	80.0
Congressional District 5, Alabama	11 618	635 179	22.3	24.9	12.3	23.5	38 054	12.5	5.5	252 745	72.5
Colbert County	1 540	54 984	19.0	23.8	15.4	14.1	31 954	14.0	5.2	22 461	75.7
Jackson County	2 794	53 926	8.7	24.1	13.3	10.4	32 020	13.7	5.1	21 615	77.9
Lauderdale County	1 734	87 966	12.3	23.0	15.1	18.5	33 354	14.4	5.6	36 088	73.2
Lawrence County	1 796	34 803	22.7	25.6	12.1	7.5	31 549	15.3	6.2	13 538	83.1
Limestone County	1 471	65 676	17.5	24.8	11.2	16.9	37 405	12.3	4.3	24 688	77.3
Madison County	2 085	276 700	29.0	25.5	10.8	34.3	44 704	10.5	5.7	109 955	69.9
Morgan County (part)	199	61 124	26.2	25.7	12.4	19.2	35 416	14.6	5.9	24 400	65.1
Congressional District 6, Alabama	11 821	634 742	11.2	24.4	12.3	29.6	46 946	8.1	3.4	249 160	78.0
Bibb County	1 614	20 826	23.8	25.4	11.6	7.1	31 420	20.6	6.2	7 421	80.2
Chilton County	1 797	39 593	14.5	25.7	12.8	9.9	32 588	15.7	4.3	15 287	82.2
Coosa County (part)	713	3 117	2.9	21.7	15.7	7.4	29 776	10.6	7.2	1 309	88.5
Jefferson County (part)	2 205	326 606	10.4	23.3	14.2	33.6	48 878	6.3	3.2	132 030	74.8
St. Clair County (part)	1 341	59 723	10.8	25.5	11.5	11.0	37 642	12.1	4.0	22 193	83.8

[1]Dry land or land partially or temporarily covered by water.
[2]Persons who do not identify themselves as White alone, not of Hispanic origin.
[3]Persons 25 years old and over.

Table B. 109th Congressional Districts by Counties, 2000—*Continued*

(Number, percent.)

STATE Congressional district County	Land area,[1] (sq km)	Population Total	Population Percent minority[2]	Population Percent under 18 years old	Population Percent 65 years old and over	Percent with bachelor's degree or more[3]	Median income, 1999 (dollars)	Percent living in poverty	Percent unemployed	Households Total	Households Percent owner occupied
	1	2	3	4	5	6	7	8	9	10	11
Congressional District 6, Alabama—*Continued*											
Shelby County	2 058	143 293	11.3	26.2	8.4	36.8	55 440	6.3	3.0	54 631	80.9
Tuscaloosa County (part)	2 092	41 584	9.0	24.7	11.3	31.6	47 231	8.4	4.0	16 289	80.5
Congressional District 7, Alabama	22 453	635 631	64.5	26.3	13.0	15.1	26 672	24.7	9.5	246 968	62.8
Choctaw County	2 366	15 922	45.4	25.9	14.4	9.6	24 749	24.5	8.8	6 363	86.3
Clarke County (part)	2 084	13 488	58.9	29.1	12.8	9.8	23 692	26.6	11.6	5 044	80.7
Dallas County	2 540	46 365	64.7	28.5	13.9	13.9	23 370	31.1	11.2	17 841	65.7
Greene County	1 673	9 974	81.4	29.1	15.0	10.5	19 819	34.3	13.1	3 931	75.6
Hale County	1 667	17 185	60.5	29.4	13.6	8.1	25 807	26.9	8.0	6 415	80.2
Jefferson County (part)	677	335 441	73.9	26.3	13.2	15.1	27 298	23.1	9.9	131 235	58.1
Marengo County	2 531	22 539	53.1	28.4	14.8	12.1	27 025	25.9	8.7	8 767	79.2
Perry County	1 863	11 861	69.3	29.8	15.1	10.0	20 200	35.4	14.7	4 333	73.8
Pickens County (part)	1 068	11 584	64.0	29.9	13.6	10.1	23 413	31.7	11.6	4 327	77.5
Sumter County	2 344	14 798	74.3	29.1	13.9	12.4	18 911	38.7	11.5	5 708	72.3
Tuscaloosa County (part)	1 338	123 291	40.5	23.0	11.2	21.1	30 658	20.1	6.9	48 228	57.7
Wilcox County	2 302	13 183	72.7	30.4	13.8	10.1	16 646	39.9	15.2	4 776	83.3
ALASKA	1 481 347	626 932	32.4	30.4	5.6	24.7	51 571	9.4	9.0	221 600	62.5
Congressional District (At Large), Alaska	1 481 347	626 932	32.4	30.4	5.6	24.7	51 571	9.4	9.0	221 600	62.5
Aleutians East Borough	18 099	2 697	80.8	16.1	2.3	4.9	47 875	21.8	41.4	526	58.4
Aleutians West Census Area	11 388	5 465	62.3	17.1	1.7	11.0	61 406	11.9	12.7	1 270	27.8
Anchorage Municipality	4 396	260 283	30.1	29.1	5.3	28.9	55 546	7.3	6.8	94 822	60.0
Bethel Census Area	105 240	16 006	87.9	39.9	5.3	13.1	35 701	20.6	14.6	4 226	60.9
Bristol Bay Borough	1 308	1 258	47.6	31.2	5.0	21.1	52 167	9.5	10.5	490	51.0
Denali Borough	33 021	1 893	15.2	24.0	3.1	22.7	53 654	7.9	11.6	785	64.7
Dillingham Census Area	48 367	4 922	79.0	38.5	5.6	16.4	43 079	21.4	11.5	1 529	60.6
Fairbanks North Star Borough	19 078	82 840	23.9	30.0	4.7	27.0	49 076	7.8	9.1	29 777	54.0
Haines Borough	6 070	2 392	18.5	25.9	10.7	23.8	40 772	10.7	13.7	991	69.7
Juneau City and Borough	7 036	30 711	26.7	27.6	6.2	36.0	62 034	6.0	5.4	11 543	63.8
Kenai Peninsula Borough	41 474	49 691	14.9	30.0	7.3	20.3	46 397	10.0	11.4	18 438	73.7
Ketchikan Gateway Borough	3 194	14 070	27.1	28.2	7.5	20.2	51 344	6.5	7.6	5 399	60.7
Kodiak Island Borough	16 990	13 913	42.9	32.5	4.6	18.7	54 636	6.6	5.2	4 424	54.8
Lake and Peninsula Borough	61 595	1 823	81.0	38.0	5.7	12.4	36 442	18.9	14.3	588	67.5
Matanuska-Susitna Borough	63 925	59 322	13.8	32.2	5.8	18.3	51 221	11.0	10.3	20 556	78.8
Nome Census Area	59 572	9 196	81.1	37.0	6.0	14.7	41 250	17.4	16.4	2 693	58.2
North Slope Borough	230 035	7 385	83.2	38.2	4.2	17.0	63 173	9.1	14.9	2 109	48.8
Northwest Arctic Borough	92 976	7 208	87.9	41.4	5.2	12.7	45 976	17.4	15.0	1 780	56.3
Prince of Wales-Outer Ketchikan Census Area ...	19 193	6 146	48.0	30.9	5.7	14.2	40 636	12.1	15.0	2 262	70.1
Sitka City and Borough	7 444	8 835	33.5	26.8	7.6	29.5	51 901	7.8	7.8	3 278	58.1
Skagway-Hoonah-Angoon Census Area	20 452	3 436	42.6	26.8	7.1	21.6	40 879	12.8	15.7	1 369	63.6
Southeast Fairbanks Census Area	64 270	6 174	22.0	32.8	6.1	18.2	38 776	18.9	17.7	2 098	69.1
Valdez-Cordova Census Area	88 886	10 195	25.5	29.7	5.7	21.2	48 734	9.8	9.6	3 884	67.8
Wade Hampton Census Area	44 531	7 028	95.1	46.7	5.1	9.1	30 184	26.2	23.9	1 602	66.4
Wrangell-Petersburg Census Area	15 112	6 684	27.5	29.7	9.7	16.3	46 434	7.9	11.0	2 587	70.4
Yakutat City and Borough	19 815	808	50.7	27.5	4.5	17.6	46 786	13.5	7.8	265	59.6
Yukon-Koyukuk Census Area	377 878	6 551	75.7	35.1	7.2	14.2	28 666	23.8	19.9	2 309	67.2
ARIZONA	294 312	5 130 632	36.2	26.6	13.0	23.5	40 558	13.9	5.6	1 901 327	68.0
Congressional District 1, Arizona	151 795	641 710	41.6	28.1	13.7	17.5	32 979	20.3	8.9	223 930	71.5
Apache County	29 021	69 423	82.5	38.4	8.4	11.3	23 344	37.8	21.8	19 971	74.3
Coconino County (part)	41 706	114 993	41.7	28.5	6.8	30.2	38 313	18.1	6.9	40 092	61.4
Gila County	12 348	51 335	31.0	25.1	20.0	13.9	30 917	17.4	9.7	20 140	78.7
Graham County	11 990	33 489	44.8	30.1	11.7	11.8	29 668	23.0	11.6	10 116	73.2
Greenlee County	4 784	8 547	46.7	31.8	9.8	12.2	39 384	9.9	6.3	3 117	51.0
Navajo County (part)	21 487	91 658	55.4	35.5	10.0	12.4	29 115	28.5	11.9	28 381	75.4
Pinal County (part)	9 474	104 748	51.0	26.2	12.7	10.0	34 563	18.2	8.7	31 942	71.7
Yavapai County (part)	20 985	167 517	13.5	21.1	21.9	21.1	34 901	11.9	5.0	70 171	73.4
Congressional District 2, Arizona	52 369	641 435	21.6	23.9	20.5	19.3	42 432	8.9	5.0	249 789	79.3
Coconino County (part)	6 513	1 327	96.6	38.4	9.6	7.4	35 655	27.9	15.6	356	57.3
La Paz County (part)	858	58	0.0	12.1	25.9	9.8	25 972	15.5	0.0	28	67.9
Maricopa County (part)	6 176	479 206	22.3	24.0	20.7	22.5	47 498	6.7	4.3	184 934	81.3
Mohave County	34 477	155 032	16.0	23.0	20.4	9.9	31 521	13.9	7.0	62 809	73.6
Navajo County (part)	4 292	5 812	95.8	36.2	8.8	10.6	20 308	44.6	18.0	1 662	77.3
Yavapai County (part)	54	0	X	X	X	X	X	X	X	0	X
Congressional District 3, Arizona	1 550	640 898	21.4	24.9	10.3	30.3	48 108	8.7	4.0	254 432	66.4
Maricopa County (part)	1 550	640 898	21.4	24.9	10.3	30.3	48 108	8.7	4.0	254 432	66.4
Congressional District 4, Arizona	516	641 430	70.8	32.9	6.8	10.2	30 624	25.6	8.4	196 221	50.8
Maricopa County (part)	516	641 430	70.8	32.9	6.8	10.2	30 624	25.6	8.4	196 221	50.8

[1]Dry land or land partially or temporarily covered by water.
[2]Persons who do not identify themselves as White alone, not of Hispanic origin.
[3]Persons 25 years old and over.

Table B. 109th Congressional Districts by Counties, 2000—*Continued*

(Number, percent.)

STATE Congressional district County	Land area,[1] (sq km)	Population Total	Percent minority[2]	Percent under 18 years old	Percent 65 years old and over	Percent with bachelor's degree or more[3]	Median income, 1999 (dollars)	Percent living in poverty	Percent unemployed	Households Total	Percent owner occupied
	1	2	3	4	5	6	7	8	9	10	11
Congressional District 5, Arizona	3 641	641 348	23.2	22.5	10.3	39.6	51 780	8.4	3.8	261 936	62.9
Maricopa County (part)	3 641	641 348	23.2	22.5	10.3	39.6	51 780	8.4	3.8	261 936	62.9
Congressional District 6, Arizona	1 874	641 360	23.5	27.9	14.4	23.6	47 976	7.7	3.8	233 942	77.5
Maricopa County (part)	810	588 712	24.5	28.5	13.6	24.7	49 375	7.4	3.7	211 750	76.7
Pinal County (part)	1 064	52 648	13.1	20.7	23.6	12.9	37 260	10.6	5.7	22 192	85.0
Congressional District 7, Arizona	59 240	640 996	61.5	29.6	11.4	13.3	30 828	21.8	8.4	216 094	66.1
La Paz County (part)	10 796	19 657	36.4	21.0	26.1	8.7	25 836	19.6	8.0	8 334	78.1
Maricopa County (part)	11 143	80 555	58.7	34.9	5.1	12.0	45 216	15.0	5.6	23 613	77.7
Pima County (part)	18 455	328 825	62.8	28.2	10.0	15.2	28 421	23.8	7.4	115 545	59.9
Pinal County (part)	3 266	17 604	77.0	37.6	6.8	4.0	26 705	33.6	13.9	4 825	71.3
Santa Cruz County (part)	1 297	34 329	89.6	35.5	8.8	11.9	28 658	25.9	8.3	9 929	65.7
Yuma County	14 281	160 026	55.6	28.8	16.6	11.8	32 182	19.2	12.1	53 848	72.2
Congressional District 8, Arizona	23 327	641 455	26.1	22.7	16.7	30.6	40 656	10.5	4.6	264 983	67.1
Cochise County	15 979	117 755	40.0	26.2	14.6	18.8	32 105	17.7	6.7	43 893	67.3
Pima County (part)	5 337	514 921	23.2	22.2	16.8	32.9	42 045	8.9	4.2	216 805	66.6
Pinal County (part)	103	4 727	2.7	1.7	49.9	48.3	62 282	1.5	4.8	2 405	96.5
Santa Cruz County (part)	1 908	4 052	24.8	17.4	25.7	34.7	40 859	12.2	4.1	1 880	80.3
ARKANSAS	134 856	2 673 400	21.4	25.4	14.0	16.7	32 182	15.8	6.1	1 042 696	69.4
Congressional District 1, Arkansas	44 422	668 360	19.8	25.7	15.2	12.3	28 940	18.5	6.4	260 695	69.6
Arkansas County	2 560	20 749	25.1	24.9	15.9	12.2	30 316	17.8	6.2	8 457	67.8
Baxter County	1 436	38 386	2.9	18.9	26.8	12.8	29 106	11.1	4.0	17 052	79.7
Clay County	1 656	17 609	2.0	23.1	19.4	7.4	25 345	17.5	5.6	7 417	74.9
Cleburne County	1 432	24 046	2.6	21.4	21.1	13.9	31 531	13.1	4.9	10 190	80.6
Craighead County	1 841	82 148	11.6	24.2	11.7	20.9	32 425	15.4	5.7	32 301	63.9
Crittenden County	1 580	50 866	49.6	31.1	9.9	12.8	30 109	25.3	6.9	18 471	60.3
Cross County	1 595	19 526	25.7	27.8	13.7	9.9	29 362	19.9	7.6	7 391	70.7
Fulton County	1 601	11 642	2.4	22.8	20.1	10.5	25 529	16.3	5.9	4 810	81.1
Greene County	1 496	37 331	3.3	25.0	14.1	10.9	30 828	13.3	5.6	14 750	71.3
Independence County	1 978	34 233	5.7	24.5	14.5	13.7	31 920	13.0	5.9	13 467	74.4
Izard County	1 504	13 249	4.3	21.0	21.1	11.7	25 670	17.2	4.1	5 440	80.1
Jackson County	1 641	18 418	19.9	22.3	16.2	10.3	25 081	17.4	6.9	6 971	69.6
Lawrence County	1 519	17 774	2.8	23.9	17.5	8.5	27 139	18.4	5.6	7 108	71.2
Lee County	1 558	12 580	59.7	26.2	14.1	7.3	20 510	29.9	13.3	4 182	63.6
Lonoke County	1 984	52 828	9.9	28.8	10.4	14.6	40 314	10.5	3.9	19 262	75.9
Mississippi County	2 326	51 979	36.2	29.6	12.6	11.3	27 479	23.0	8.8	19 349	58.9
Monroe County	1 571	10 254	41.3	28.2	17.7	8.4	22 632	27.5	5.3	4 105	64.9
Phillips County	1 794	26 445	61.3	32.2	13.9	12.4	22 231	32.7	11.3	9 711	56.3
Poinsett County	1 963	25 614	9.9	26.0	14.2	6.3	26 558	21.2	6.3	10 026	66.8
Prairie County	1 673	9 539	15.6	23.9	17.3	9.0	29 990	15.5	4.5	3 894	72.8
Randolph County	1 688	18 195	3.5	24.5	17.1	10.6	27 583	15.3	6.4	7 265	74.5
St. Francis County	1 642	29 329	54.9	27.9	12.1	9.6	26 146	27.5	11.8	10 043	63.2
Searcy County	1 728	8 261	2.9	22.8	19.1	8.4	21 397	23.8	4.7	3 523	77.7
Sharp County	1 565	17 119	3.6	21.7	23.6	10.3	25 152	18.2	6.4	7 211	80.1
Stone County	1 571	11 499	3.0	22.2	18.8	9.8	22 209	18.9	4.4	4 768	77.9
Woodruff County	1 519	8 741	32.1	25.9	16.8	8.0	22 099	27.0	8.0	3 531	65.6
Congressional District 2, Arkansas	15 338	666 058	24.4	25.1	12.1	23.2	37 221	12.7	6.0	263 453	67.1
Conway County	1 440	20 336	17.0	25.5	15.7	11.5	31 209	16.1	6.6	7 967	78.0
Faulkner County	1 677	86 014	12.7	25.6	9.5	25.2	38 204	12.5	6.8	31 882	68.6
Perry County	1 427	10 209	5.6	25.5	14.9	11.1	31 083	14.0	4.7	3 989	82.1
Pulaski County	1 996	361 474	37.1	25.2	11.5	28.1	38 120	13.3	5.3	147 942	60.9
Saline County	1 874	83 529	5.6	25.4	12.4	16.4	42 569	7.2	3.9	31 778	80.7
Van Buren County	1 843	16 192	4.3	21.6	23.4	11.5	27 004	15.4	6.7	6 825	81.1
White County	2 678	67 165	7.5	24.4	13.7	15.5	32 203	14.0	11.3	25 148	73.0
Yell County	2 403	21 139	16.5	26.5	14.5	10.9	28 916	15.4	5.2	7 922	72.9
Congressional District 3, Arkansas	21 989	672 756	12.7	25.7	13.1	17.9	33 915	13.7	5.5	259 465	68.7
Benton County	2 191	153 406	13.3	26.6	14.3	20.3	40 281	10.1	3.4	58 212	72.2
Boone County	1 531	33 948	3.3	23.9	16.6	12.7	29 988	14.8	5.0	13 851	73.3
Carroll County	1 632	25 357	12.4	23.9	15.8	13.8	27 924	15.5	5.5	10 189	73.0
Crawford County	1 542	53 247	9.1	28.2	11.3	9.7	32 871	14.2	6.1	19 702	75.9
Franklin County	1 579	17 771	5.8	25.8	15.7	11.0	30 848	15.2	5.9	6 882	78.0
Johnson County	1 715	22 781	9.8	25.1	14.9	13.1	27 910	16.4	7.8	8 738	73.0
Madison County	2 167	14 243	5.7	26.8	14.3	10.1	27 895	18.6	2.7	5 463	79.0
Marion County	1 548	16 140	3.2	22.2	20.1	10.4	26 737	15.2	5.1	6 776	80.0
Newton County	2 131	8 608	4.1	24.9	14.8	11.8	24 756	20.4	4.5	3 500	81.5
Pope County	2 103	54 469	7.1	25.6	12.7	19.0	32 069	15.2	5.8	20 701	71.2
Sebastian County	1 389	115 071	20.0	25.9	12.9	16.6	33 889	13.6	4.7	45 300	63.5
Washington County	2 460	157 715	15.5	25.0	9.9	24.5	34 691	14.6	7.9	60 151	59.4

[1]Dry land or land partially or temporarily covered by water.
[2]Persons who do not identify themselves as White alone, not of Hispanic origin.
[3]Persons 25 years old and over.

Table B. 109th Congressional Districts by Counties, 2000—*Continued*

(Number, percent.)

STATE Congressional district County	Land area,[1] (sq km)	Population Total	Population Percent minority[2]	Population Percent under 18 years old	Population Percent 65 years old and over	Percent with bachelor's degree or more[3]	Median income, 1999 (dollars)	Percent living in poverty	Percent unem-ployed	Households Total	Households Percent owner occupied
	1	2	3	4	5	6	7	8	9	10	11
Congressional District 4, Arkansas	53 107	666 226	28.9	25.2	15.7	13.3	29 675	18.5	6.6	259 083	72.2
Ashley County	2 386	24 209	31.3	26.9	13.8	10.1	31 758	17.5	6.9	9 384	76.2
Bradley County	1 685	12 600	37.6	23.5	17.8	11.9	24 821	26.3	10.8	4 834	72.5
Calhoun County	1 627	5 744	26.3	24.9	15.7	7.3	28 438	16.5	5.3	2 317	82.2
Chicot County	1 668	14 117	57.5	27.3	15.9	11.7	22 024	28.6	10.2	5 205	69.6
Clark County	2 241	23 546	26.4	21.8	14.7	19.8	28 845	19.1	4.7	8 912	65.6
Cleveland County	1 548	8 571	15.6	26.2	13.7	10.0	32 405	15.2	5.5	3 273	82.2
Columbia County	1 984	25 603	38.5	25.1	16.0	16.8	27 640	21.1	7.6	9 981	71.3
Dallas County	1 729	9 210	43.4	26.0	17.0	9.6	26 608	18.9	7.4	3 519	73.9
Desha County	1 981	15 341	50.2	28.9	14.3	11.1	24 121	28.9	8.8	5 922	63.5
Drew County	2 145	18 723	30.1	25.7	13.1	17.3	28 627	18.2	8.9	7 337	68.9
Garland County	1 754	88 068	12.7	21.5	21.4	18.0	31 724	14.6	5.1	37 813	71.2
Grant County	1 636	16 464	4.7	26.0	12.0	11.0	37 182	10.2	4.2	6 241	80.2
Hempstead County	1 888	23 587	40.3	27.3	14.2	11.0	28 622	20.3	6.5	8 959	69.3
Hot Spring County	1 593	30 353	13.3	25.0	15.7	11.2	31 543	14.0	4.9	12 004	78.0
Howard County	1 521	14 300	28.3	26.9	15.3	11.6	28 699	15.5	4.9	5 471	72.0
Jefferson County	2 292	84 278	52.0	26.1	12.8	15.7	31 327	20.5	8.3	30 555	66.1
Lafayette County	1 364	8 559	38.6	25.3	17.6	9.5	24 831	23.2	7.9	3 434	78.4
Lincoln County	1 454	14 492	35.4	22.0	12.0	7.6	29 607	19.5	7.0	4 265	76.2
Little River County	1 377	13 628	26.7	25.2	14.9	9.9	29 417	15.4	6.5	5 465	76.5
Logan County	1 839	22 486	4.5	25.9	16.0	9.4	28 344	15.4	5.3	8 693	77.2
Miller County	1 616	40 443	26.6	26.4	13.3	12.5	30 951	19.3	6.8	15 637	67.9
Montgomery County	2 023	9 245	4.6	23.7	18.9	8.8	28 421	17.0	6.3	3 785	82.8
Nevada County	1 606	9 955	33.3	25.4	15.9	10.7	26 962	22.8	6.3	3 893	74.8
Ouachita County	1 897	28 790	40.5	25.9	17.2	12.7	29 341	19.5	8.5	11 613	71.4
Pike County	1 562	11 303	8.2	24.9	17.1	10.1	27 695	16.8	4.3	4 504	78.6
Polk County	2 226	20 229	6.8	25.5	17.0	10.9	25 180	18.2	5.8	8 047	78.4
Scott County	2 315	10 996	9.3	26.6	14.7	8.4	26 412	18.2	3.9	4 323	74.2
Sevier County	1 461	15 757	27.5	28.2	13.2	9.2	30 144	19.2	4.7	5 708	74.2
Union County	2 691	45 629	34.4	25.9	16.2	14.9	29 809	18.7	6.9	17 989	72.9
CALIFORNIA	403 933	33 871 648	53.4	27.2	10.6	26.6	47 493	14.2	7.0	11 502 870	56.9
Congressional District 1, California	28 505	639 275	28.9	24.4	13.1	25.0	38 918	15.3	6.9	240 381	60.7
Del Norte County	2 610	27 507	29.9	25.1	12.6	11.0	29 642	20.2	10.7	9 170	63.8
Humboldt County	9 253	126 518	18.1	23.1	12.6	23.0	31 226	19.5	8.6	51 238	57.6
Lake County	3 258	58 309	19.4	23.9	19.4	12.1	29 627	17.6	11.0	23 974	70.5
Mendocino County	9 088	86 265	25.3	25.4	13.6	20.2	35 996	15.9	7.3	33 266	61.3
Napa County	1 952	124 279	31.1	24.2	15.3	26.4	51 738	8.3	4.3	45 402	65.1
Sonoma County (part)	1 220	66 933	26.1	25.1	14.2	29.2	55 790	6.4	3.9	24 795	69.9
Yolo County (part)	1 123	149 464	43.0	24.9	8.7	36.1	39 179	19.6	7.3	52 536	50.3
Congressional District 2, California	56 353	638 921	23.9	26.3	14.4	17.4	33 559	17.0	9.5	241 200	63.1
Butte County (part)	3 310	158 701	18.9	22.8	15.2	25.4	32 924	18.1	8.7	62 942	59.0
Colusa County	2 980	18 804	52.5	31.6	11.0	10.6	35 062	16.1	10.7	6 097	63.3
Glenn County	3 405	26 453	38.0	30.6	12.8	10.7	32 107	18.1	9.1	9 172	64.0
Shasta County	9 804	163 256	13.6	26.1	15.2	16.6	34 335	15.4	8.7	63 426	66.1
Siskiyou County	16 283	44 301	16.4	23.9	18.2	17.7	29 530	18.6	9.6	18 556	67.2
Sutter County	1 561	78 930	40.3	28.8	12.1	15.3	38 375	15.5	11.8	27 033	61.5
Tehama County	7 643	56 039	21.5	27.4	15.9	11.3	31 206	17.3	9.7	21 013	67.7
Trinity County	8 233	13 022	13.8	22.9	16.8	15.5	27 711	18.7	13.9	5 587	71.3
Yolo County (part)	1 501	19 196	35.9	27.0	13.4	21.2	51 238	9.2	5.8	6 839	74.6
Yuba County	1 633	60 219	34.5	30.9	10.2	10.3	30 460	20.8	11.3	20 535	54.0
Congressional District 3, California	8 739	639 374	25.7	26.1	12.2	27.0	51 313	8.5	5.3	237 926	68.6
Alpine County	1 913	1 208	28.0	22.8	9.9	28.2	41 875	19.5	8.1	483	67.9
Amador County	1 536	35 100	17.6	20.7	18.1	16.6	42 280	9.2	4.4	12 759	75.4
Calaveras County	2 642	40 554	12.4	22.7	18.0	17.1	41 022	11.8	7.7	16 469	78.7
Sacramento County (part)	1 875	551 128	27.2	26.7	11.4	28.6	52 462	8.1	5.2	204 130	67.3
Solano County (part)	773	11 384	28.3	25.8	12.4	21.3	53 299	9.7	6.9	4 085	71.5
Congressional District 4, California	42 614	639 071	16.3	25.5	13.8	25.2	49 387	8.7	5.5	240 815	73.1
Butte County (part)	936	44 470	24.9	28.0	17.5	9.5	28 635	25.9	12.1	16 624	67.3
El Dorado County	4 431	156 299	15.2	26.0	12.5	26.5	51 484	7.1	5.4	58 939	74.7
Lassen County	11 803	33 828	29.2	21.7	9.0	10.7	36 310	14.0	9.4	9 625	68.1
Modoc County	10 215	9 449	19.5	25.6	17.3	12.4	27 522	21.5	11.9	3 784	70.7
Nevada County	2 480	92 033	9.9	22.9	17.5	26.1	45 864	8.1	4.7	36 894	75.8
Placer County	3 637	248 399	16.6	26.3	13.1	30.3	57 535	5.8	4.0	93 382	73.2
Plumas County	6 614	20 824	11.2	22.7	17.9	17.5	36 351	13.1	9.5	9 000	70.1
Sacramento County (part)	28	30 214	15.7	26.6	11.6	23.5	54 207	6.4	4.7	11 047	72.3
Sierra County	2 469	3 555	10.5	23.4	17.3	17.2	35 827	11.3	9.4	1 520	70.9
Congressional District 5, California	381	638 837	56.6	28.3	10.8	21.4	36 719	19.7	8.2	237 038	49.6
Sacramento County (part)	381	638 837	56.6	28.3	10.8	21.4	36 719	19.7	8.2	237 038	49.6

[1]Dry land or land partially or temporarily covered by water.
[2]Persons who do not identify themselves as White alone, not of Hispanic origin.
[3]Persons 25 years old and over.

Table B. 109th Congressional Districts by Counties, 2000—*Continued*

(Number, percent.)

| STATE
Congressional district
County | Land
area,[1]
(sq km) | Population | | | | Percent
with
bachelor's
degree or
more[3] | Median
income,
1999
(dollars) | Percent
living in
poverty | Percent
unem-
ployed | Households | |
		Total	Percent minority[2]	Percent under 18 years old	Percent 65 years old and over					Total	Percent owner occupied
	1	2	3	4	5	6	7	8	9	10	11
Congressional District 6, California	4 208	638 970	24.0	22.6	12.8	37.9	59 115	7.7	3.8	248 258	63.3
Marin County	1 346	247 289	21.5	20.2	13.5	51.3	71 306	6.6	3.0	100 650	63.6
Sonoma County (part)	2 861	391 681	25.6	24.2	12.3	28.4	52 679	8.3	4.3	147 608	63.1
Congressional District 7, California	904	639 791	56.9	27.3	9.8	22.4	52 778	10.0	6.1	218 711	64.0
Contra Costa County (part)	404	399 619	60.0	27.4	9.7	22.3	51 901	11.2	6.2	138 011	63.1
Solano County (part)	500	240 172	51.7	27.2	9.9	22.5	54 596	8.1	6.0	80 700	65.4
Congressional District 8, California	92	639 362	57.1	14.1	13.2	44.0	52 322	12.2	4.8	276 659	30.2
San Francisco County (part)	92	639 362	57.1	14.1	13.2	44.0	52 322	12.2	4.8	276 659	30.2
Congressional District 9, California	343	639 426	65.0	23.1	10.8	37.4	44 314	16.9	6.8	247 798	45.6
Alameda County (part)	343	639 426	65.0	23.1	10.8	37.4	44 314	16.9	6.8	247 798	45.6
Congressional District 10, California	2 624	638 238	34.7	26.5	11.8	36.2	65 245	6.3	4.5	232 728	69.8
Alameda County (part)	350	75 174	25.2	28.0	7.6	31.7	75 133	5.3	3.4	26 763	72.4
Contra Costa County (part)	1 183	416 758	30.6	25.0	13.7	42.2	67 662	5.7	4.2	158 960	71.0
Sacramento County (part)	217	3 320	42.4	19.3	18.4	12.7	37 383	10.8	10.8	1 387	67.1
Solano County (part)	874	142 986	51.4	30.2	8.5	19.4	53 271	8.5	6.2	45 618	64.1
Congressional District 11, California	5 897	639 625	36.1	28.6	9.7	29.1	61 996	8.8	6.0	219 367	69.0
Alameda County (part)	644	90 433	29.0	25.5	6.7	42.0	84 925	2.7	2.8	31 666	69.9
Contra Costa County (part)	278	132 439	25.5	28.3	8.4	48.3	98 783	3.0	2.7	47 158	81.7
San Joaquin County (part)	3 347	373 958	41.2	29.4	11.2	17.9	47 142	12.8	8.2	127 027	63.6
Santa Clara County (part)	1 628	42 795	39.6	29.9	7.3	32.2	82 647	5.5	5.2	13 516	73.1
Congressional District 12, California	303	638 598	51.9	20.6	13.9	40.7	70 307	5.4	3.1	235 780	62.3
San Francisco County (part)	29	137 371	52.8	15.8	16.6	49.5	68 212	7.3	3.7	53 041	60.1
San Mateo County (part)	274	501 227	51.7	21.9	13.1	38.1	70 744	4.9	2.9	182 739	63.0
Congressional District 13, California	573	638 708	61.7	25.4	10.5	31.8	62 415	7.1	4.8	217 139	60.7
Alameda County (part)	573	638 708	61.7	25.4	10.5	31.8	62 415	7.1	4.8	217 139	60.7
Congressional District 14, California	2 138	639 953	40.4	22.4	11.5	52.2	77 985	6.4	3.6	240 537	58.5
San Mateo County (part)	889	205 934	46.9	25.0	10.9	41.4	71 030	8.0	4.1	71 364	57.7
Santa Clara County (part)	378	361 940	41.1	20.6	12.5	60.5	83 200	5.3	3.1	143 399	56.0
Santa Cruz County (part)	871	72 079	18.3	24.0	8.6	39.0	69 009	7.1	4.9	25 774	74.9
Congressional District 15, California	741	639 090	53.1	24.1	9.4	41.6	74 947	6.6	3.5	222 721	57.9
Santa Clara County (part)	741	639 090	53.1	24.1	9.4	41.6	74 947	6.6	3.5	222 721	57.9
Congressional District 16, California	595	638 760	68.4	27.2	8.0	26.9	67 689	9.8	4.8	186 227	64.1
Santa Clara County (part)	595	638 760	68.4	27.2	8.0	26.9	67 689	9.8	4.8	186 227	64.1
Congressional District 17, California	12 484	638 519	53.9	27.3	9.9	24.9	49 234	13.3	7.8	202 486	55.5
Monterey County	8 604	401 762	59.8	28.4	10.0	22.5	48 305	13.5	8.7	121 236	54.7
San Benito County	3 598	53 234	54.3	32.1	7.9	17.1	57 469	10.0	6.6	15 885	68.1
Santa Cruz County (part)	283	183 523	40.9	23.5	10.4	32.2	49 128	13.8	6.5	65 365	54.1
Congressional District 18, California	7 906	639 004	61.3	33.4	9.5	9.7	34 211	22.7	14.3	193 333	56.8
Fresno County (part)	103	3 109	58.7	25.4	16.1	7.4	37 500	15.7	8.9	935	69.8
Madera County (part)	626	2 843	72.8	33.0	6.8	3.8	30 801	19.4	17.7	765	38.8
Merced County	4 995	210 554	59.7	34.4	9.4	11.0	35 532	21.7	13.1	63 815	58.7
San Joaquin County (part)	277	189 640	75.8	33.9	9.2	7.3	30 201	27.7	15.5	54 602	52.9
Stanislaus County (part)	1 904	232 858	50.7	32.3	9.7	10.5	36 092	19.8	14.5	73 216	58.0
Congressional District 19, California	17 333	638 975	40.2	28.3	11.8	20.3	41 225	14.8	9.0	219 833	64.5
Fresno County (part)	914	232 939	46.5	28.7	10.9	28.0	41 918	14.9	7.3	84 896	60.1
Madera County (part)	4 906	120 266	52.7	29.4	10.8	12.2	36 416	21.4	13.1	35 390	66.8
Mariposa County	3 758	17 130	15.5	22.2	17.0	20.2	34 626	14.8	14.1	6 613	69.9
Stanislaus County (part)	1 965	214 139	34.7	29.7	11.2	17.7	44 710	11.9	8.8	71 930	66.0
Tuolumne County	5 790	54 501	15.2	20.7	18.5	16.1	38 725	11.4	7.7	21 004	71.2
Congressional District 20, California	12 904	639 705	78.7	34.8	7.4	6.3	26 800	32.2	19.3	163 772	50.1
Fresno County (part)	6 133	291 625	83.4	36.1	7.8	6.0	25 297	35.7	19.1	76 986	46.1
Kern County (part)	3 169	218 619	84.5	36.7	6.7	3.8	24 644	34.4	23.1	52 368	52.1
Kings County	3 603	129 461	58.5	28.8	7.5	10.4	35 749	19.5	13.6	34 418	55.9
Congressional District 21, California	20 787	639 755	53.8	32.3	10.3	15.0	36 047	20.7	11.4	200 508	61.6
Fresno County (part)	8 293	271 734	47.7	30.4	11.1	19.4	38 677	16.4	9.7	90 123	61.8
Tulare County	12 494	368 021	58.3	33.7	9.7	11.5	33 983	23.9	12.7	110 385	61.5
Congressional District 22, California	26 980	638 514	33.3	28.5	11.0	18.3	41 801	13.7	7.7	221 335	65.2
Kern County (part)	17 916	443 026	34.0	29.4	10.7	17.5	40 701	14.3	7.7	156 284	65.5
Los Angeles County (part)	1 392	74 177	44.6	30.0	9.4	16.8	41 018	16.8	10.5	24 301	57.1
San Luis Obispo County (part)	7 671	121 311	23.7	23.9	12.9	22.0	47 720	9.4	5.9	40 750	69.0
Congressional District 23, California	2 698	638 854	51.4	25.1	11.7	26.2	44 874	15.7	6.8	213 117	53.7
San Luis Obispo County (part)	887	125 370	24.2	19.2	16.0	31.3	38 897	15.8	6.0	51 989	55.5
Santa Barbara County (part)	1 590	286 840	46.7	23.4	12.4	32.0	46 455	16.2	6.8	97 861	52.3
Ventura County (part)	221	226 644	72.4	30.4	8.5	15.3	47 129	15.0	7.2	63 267	54.4

[1]Dry land or land partially or temporarily covered by water.
[2]Persons who do not identify themselves as White alone, not of Hispanic origin.
[3]Persons 25 years old and over.

Table B. 109th Congressional Districts by Counties, 2000—*Continued*

(Number, percent.)

STATE Congressional district County	Land area,[1] (sq km)	Population				Percent with bachelor's degree or more[3]	Median income, 1999 (dollars)	Percent living in poverty	Percent unemployed	Households	
		Total	Percent minority[2]	Percent under 18 years old	Percent 65 years old and over					Total	Percent owner occupied
	1	2	3	4	5	6	7	8	9	10	11
Congressional District 24, California	10 057	639 060	31.6	27.6	11.1	30.0	61 453	7.2	4.7	218 728	71.0
Santa Barbara County (part)	5 499	112 507	34.4	28.0	13.4	23.2	47 272	9.5	6.5	38 761	65.4
Ventura County (part)	4 558	526 553	31.0	27.5	10.7	31.5	65 251	6.8	4.4	179 967	72.2
Congressional District 25, California	55 644	638 768	43.0	32.0	8.2	18.8	49 002	12.6	7.8	206 818	70.0
Inyo County	26 426	17 945	25.9	24.5	19.3	17.1	35 006	12.6	5.9	7 703	65.9
Los Angeles County (part)	4 082	454 722	42.2	32.2	7.0	21.2	55 155	11.1	7.3	144 354	73.2
Mono County	7 885	12 853	23.7	22.6	7.3	28.9	44 992	11.5	5.8	5 137	60.1
San Bernardino County (part)	17 251	153 248	49.2	33.1	10.2	10.6	36 589	17.2	10.3	49 624	62.5
Congressional District 26, California	1 947	639 913	47.5	27.0	11.0	32.4	58 968	8.4	5.3	215 830	68.7
Los Angeles County (part)	1 266	388 410	46.5	25.3	13.0	38.5	62 136	7.0	5.0	134 453	70.3
San Bernardino County (part)	682	251 503	49.2	29.6	8.0	22.1	53 386	10.5	5.9	81 377	66.1
Congressional District 27, California	390	638 532	55.4	25.4	10.6	25.8	46 781	13.4	7.3	221 730	54.1
Los Angeles County (part)	390	638 532	55.4	25.4	10.6	25.8	46 781	13.4	7.3	221 730	54.1
Congressional District 28, California	200	639 364	68.9	28.6	8.6	23.7	40 439	19.1	8.7	207 603	43.8
Los Angeles County (part)	200	639 364	68.9	28.6	8.6	23.7	40 439	19.1	8.7	207 603	43.8
Congressional District 29, California	263	638 899	61.0	22.9	13.2	33.4	43 895	14.5	6.6	233 376	44.0
Los Angeles County (part)	263	638 899	61.0	22.9	13.2	33.4	43 895	14.5	6.6	233 376	44.0
Congressional District 30, California	740	639 700	23.9	16.8	14.6	53.5	60 713	9.0	5.6	291 693	47.7
Los Angeles County (part)	740	639 700	23.9	16.8	14.6	53.5	60 713	9.0	5.6	291 693	47.7
Congressional District 31, California	102	639 248	90.3	29.8	7.3	13.7	26 093	30.1	11.2	191 535	23.0
Los Angeles County (part)	102	639 248	90.3	29.8	7.3	13.7	26 093	30.1	11.2	191 535	23.0
Congressional District 32, California	238	638 579	85.2	30.9	9.0	13.6	41 394	18.0	8.2	170 594	55.9
Los Angeles County (part)	238	638 579	85.2	30.9	9.0	13.6	41 394	18.0	8.2	170 594	55.9
Congressional District 33, California	125	638 655	80.2	24.3	10.4	26.9	31 655	23.5	10.4	246 339	30.4
Los Angeles County (part)	125	638 655	80.2	24.3	10.4	26.9	31 655	23.5	10.4	246 339	30.4
Congressional District 34, California	151	638 807	88.6	32.3	7.6	8.7	29 863	26.0	11.4	172 533	30.6
Los Angeles County (part)	151	638 807	88.6	32.3	7.6	8.7	29 863	26.0	11.4	172 533	30.6
Congressional District 35, California	144	638 851	89.6	32.8	7.7	13.3	32 156	26.4	11.2	198 170	39.5
Los Angeles County (part)	144	638 851	89.6	32.8	7.7	13.3	32 156	26.4	11.2	198 170	39.5
Congressional District 36, California	194	639 168	51.7	23.1	10.3	36.9	51 633	12.7	5.6	255 228	44.8
Los Angeles County (part)	194	639 168	51.7	23.1	10.3	36.9	51 633	12.7	5.6	255 228	44.8
Congressional District 37, California	193	638 722	83.4	32.8	8.0	15.2	34 006	25.2	11.2	193 734	44.1
Los Angeles County (part)	193	638 722	83.4	32.8	8.0	15.2	34 006	25.2	11.2	193 734	44.1
Congressional District 38, California	269	639 334	86.6	31.8	9.2	12.5	42 488	16.3	8.6	166 057	62.5
Los Angeles County (part)	269	639 334	86.6	31.8	9.2	12.5	42 488	16.3	8.6	166 057	62.5
Congressional District 39, California	168	639 529	79.2	32.5	8.1	14.7	45 307	15.7	8.3	173 624	59.5
Los Angeles County (part)	168	639 529	79.2	32.5	8.1	14.7	45 307	15.7	8.3	173 624	59.5
Congressional District 40, California	259	638 671	50.9	26.9	10.5	26.4	54 356	10.2	5.4	205 982	60.0
Orange County (part)	259	638 671	50.9	26.9	10.5	26.4	54 356	10.2	5.4	205 982	60.0
Congressional District 41, California	34 484	639 935	36.6	28.4	13.4	18.1	38 721	15.2	8.0	226 258	66.9
Riverside County (part)	1 172	113 441	40.6	27.6	20.1	11.2	31 578	18.7	9.9	41 902	70.3
San Bernardino County (part)	33 311	526 494	35.7	28.6	12.0	19.7	40 525	14.5	7.6	184 356	66.1
Congressional District 42, California	813	640 090	45.8	28.2	8.2	34.8	70 463	6.0	4.3	205 667	76.4
Los Angeles County (part)	123	131 930	67.2	25.9	10.2	38.4	66 096	7.7	4.9	41 250	78.9
Orange County (part)	493	367 735	33.0	28.2	8.7	37.2	72 477	5.1	3.7	125 901	75.4
San Bernardino County (part)	197	140 425	59.2	30.3	4.9	24.5	67 067	6.6	5.6	38 516	77.1
Congressional District 43, California	494	637 764	76.8	36.5	6.2	8.8	37 390	20.7	10.4	174 721	59.9
San Bernardino County (part)	494	637 764	76.8	36.5	6.2	8.8	37 390	20.7	10.4	174 721	59.9
Congressional District 44, California	1 352	639 008	48.8	30.5	8.3	21.1	51 578	12.1	6.6	200 212	65.8
Orange County (part)	398	85 259	21.9	26.2	11.3	41.2	74 766	5.6	3.5	31 346	71.3
Riverside County (part)	954	553 749	53.0	31.2	7.8	17.5	48 484	13.2	7.1	168 866	64.8
Congressional District 45, California	15 488	638 553	50.0	29.0	15.6	17.4	40 468	15.0	7.6	218 350	69.2
Riverside County (part)	15 488	638 553	50.0	29.0	15.6	17.4	40 468	15.0	7.6	218 350	69.2
Congressional District 46, California	683	639 245	37.4	21.9	12.8	36.4	61 567	7.8	4.1	241 898	61.6
Los Angeles County (part)	480	162 711	28.8	19.7	16.8	50.7	73 726	4.1	3.5	67 200	71.3
Orange County (part)	203	476 534	40.3	22.7	11.5	31.2	57 601	9.0	4.3	174 698	57.9
Congressional District 47, California	142	639 242	82.7	33.2	6.4	10.0	41 618	19.1	7.8	150 209	47.4
Orange County (part)	142	639 242	82.7	33.2	6.4	10.0	41 618	19.1	7.8	150 209	47.4

[1]Dry land or land partially or temporarily covered by water.
[2]Persons who do not identify themselves as White alone, not of Hispanic origin.
[3]Persons 25 years old and over.

Table B. 109th Congressional Districts by Counties, 2000—*Continued*

(Number, percent.)

STATE Congressional district County	Land area,[1] (sq km)	Population Total	Population Percent minority[2]	Population Percent under 18 years old	Population Percent 65 years old and over	Percent with bachelor's degree or more[3]	Median income, 1999 (dollars)	Percent living in poverty	Percent unemployed	Households Total	Households Percent owner occupied
	1	2	3	4	5	6	7	8	9	10	11
Congressional District 48, California	550	638 848	32.1	23.3	11.7	46.5	69 663	6.3	4.0	247 151	65.1
Orange County (part)	550	638 848	32.1	23.3	11.7	46.5	69 663	6.3	4.0	247 151	65.1
Congressional District 49, California	4 378	639 380	42.1	29.0	12.6	20.7	46 445	11.9	6.4	209 193	66.8
Riverside County (part)	1 053	239 644	41.4	32.6	12.1	15.3	46 293	12.2	7.2	77 100	75.7
San Diego County (part)	3 326	399 736	42.5	26.8	13.0	23.8	46 543	11.7	6.0	132 093	61.6
Congressional District 50, California	778	639 437	34.3	25.2	12.3	40.0	59 813	8.1	4.3	231 948	65.9
San Diego County (part)	778	639 437	34.3	25.2	12.3	40.0	59 813	8.1	4.3	231 948	65.9
Congressional District 51, California	11 868	638 989	78.8	30.7	9.9	15.2	39 243	16.3	8.7	184 647	56.7
Imperial County	10 813	142 361	80.0	31.4	10.2	10.3	31 870	22.6	12.6	39 384	58.3
San Diego County (part)	1 055	496 628	78.4	30.5	9.8	16.6	41 049	14.6	7.8	145 263	56.3
Congressional District 52, California	5 473	639 329	27.6	26.4	11.1	28.6	52 940	8.1	4.9	232 585	63.9
San Diego County (part)	5 473	639 329	27.6	26.4	11.1	28.6	52 940	8.1	4.9	232 585	63.9
Congressional District 53, California	246	638 703	49.2	20.7	9.9	32.2	36 637	20.2	7.4	252 788	34.4
San Diego County (part)	246	638 703	49.2	20.7	9.9	32.2	36 637	20.2	7.4	252 788	34.4
COLORADO	268 627	4 301 261	25.6	25.5	9.7	32.7	47 203	9.3	4.3	1 658 238	67.3
Congressional District 1, Colorado	444	614 139	45.7	21.7	11.3	34.3	39 658	13.7	5.5	266 247	52.2
Adams County (part)	0	0	X	X	X	X	X	X	X	0	X
Arapahoe County (part)	47	59 503	23.5	21.1	11.9	33.2	40 763	8.7	4.0	27 012	49.0
Denver County	397	554 636	48.1	21.8	11.2	34.5	39 500	14.3	5.7	239 235	52.5
Jefferson County (part)	0	0	X	X	X	X	X	X	X	0	X
Congressional District 2, Colorado	14 542	614 289	21.2	24.7	6.6	39.3	55 204	7.4	3.9	233 172	69.2
Adams County (part)	223	239 887	29.7	27.9	7.5	21.1	51 236	6.0	3.9	87 047	72.6
Boulder County (part)	1 731	216 010	14.3	21.2	7.3	59.7	57 413	10.1	4.7	86 439	64.2
Clear Creek County	1 024	9 322	5.7	22.6	7.0	38.8	50 997	5.4	2.0	4 019	75.9
Eagle County	4 372	41 659	25.9	23.4	2.8	42.6	62 682	7.8	3.3	15 148	63.7
Gilpin County	388	4 757	8.0	21.2	6.6	31.2	51 942	4.0	2.1	2 043	78.5
Grand County	4 783	12 442	7.2	21.8	7.9	34.5	47 759	7.3	3.2	5 075	68.3
Jefferson County (part)	237	53 566	16.2	28.6	4.2	36.7	64 017	2.8	2.9	19 643	79.0
Summit County	1 575	23 548	13.9	17.4	3.2	48.3	56 587	9.0	2.8	9 120	59.0
Weld County (part)	210	13 098	26.0	28.5	6.7	19.2	50 590	6.3	4.1	4 638	85.4
Congressional District 3, Colorado	139 765	614 494	25.5	25.0	13.4	23.8	35 970	12.8	5.5	240 911	70.4
Alamosa County	1 872	14 966	45.6	27.4	9.6	27.0	29 447	21.3	8.8	5 467	64.0
Archuleta County	3 497	9 898	20.0	25.3	11.9	29.0	37 901	11.7	4.9	3 980	76.8
Conejos County	3 334	8 400	61.1	32.1	15.1	14.4	24 744	23.0	6.0	2 980	78.6
Costilla County	3 178	3 663	72.0	25.1	16.8	12.8	19 531	26.8	13.2	1 503	78.5
Custer County	1 914	3 503	5.6	22.3	15.0	26.7	34 731	13.3	3.7	1 480	78.9
Delta County	2 958	27 834	14.0	23.9	19.7	17.6	32 785	12.1	5.6	11 058	77.5
Dolores County	2 763	1 844	9.9	21.7	17.5	13.5	32 196	13.1	6.1	785	76.1
Garfield County	7 633	43 791	18.9	27.2	8.7	23.8	47 016	7.5	2.7	16 229	65.1
Gunnison County	8 388	13 956	7.3	18.0	6.7	43.6	36 916	15.0	5.3	5 649	58.4
Hinsdale County	2 895	790	4.3	19.7	11.5	34.9	37 279	7.2	2.2	359	64.9
Huerfano County	4 120	7 862	42.3	20.8	17.1	16.1	25 775	18.0	8.6	3 082	70.6
Jackson County	4 178	1 577	9.1	25.2	12.7	19.9	31 821	14.0	4.3	661	67.9
La Plata County	4 383	43 941	17.6	22.6	9.3	36.4	40 159	11.7	5.7	17 342	68.4
Las Animas County	12 361	15 207	44.9	24.2	18.8	16.2	28 273	17.3	5.7	6 173	70.4
Mesa County	8 619	116 255	13.1	24.9	15.1	22.0	35 864	10.2	5.7	45 823	72.7
Mineral County	2 268	831	5.3	20.0	17.0	31.2	34 844	10.2	2.8	377	73.2
Moffat County	12 282	13 184	11.7	28.2	9.3	12.5	41 528	8.3	5.5	4 983	72.0
Montezuma County	5 275	23 830	22.6	27.6	14.0	21.0	32 083	16.4	6.9	9 201	74.8
Montrose County	5 803	33 432	17.9	26.9	15.3	18.7	35 234	12.6	5.0	13 043	74.9
Otero County (part)	2 581	18 486	43.0	26.8	16.5	15.2	29 508	19.4	8.7	7 230	68.4
Ouray County	1 400	3 742	5.8	22.5	12.3	36.8	42 019	7.2	3.6	1 576	73.0
Pitkin County	2 513	14 872	9.7	16.5	6.7	57.1	59 375	6.2	3.2	6 807	59.1
Pueblo County	6 187	141 472	42.5	25.6	15.3	18.3	32 775	14.9	6.3	54 579	70.4
Rio Blanco County	8 342	5 986	7.4	26.7	11.2	19.5	37 711	9.6	6.0	2 306	70.4
Rio Grande County	2 361	12 413	43.6	28.2	14.9	18.8	31 836	14.5	6.1	4 701	70.8
Routt County	6 116	19 690	4.9	22.5	5.0	42.5	53 612	6.1	3.1	7 953	69.3
Saguache County	8 206	5 917	48.6	28.4	10.6	19.6	25 495	22.6	6.1	2 300	69.4
San Juan County	1 003	558	8.8	19.5	7.5	43.7	30 764	20.9	3.0	269	67.3
San Miguel County	3 332	6 594	9.3	17.7	3.4	48.5	48 514	10.4	2.6	3 015	51.6
Congressional District 4, Colorado	80 025	614 571	20.5	26.0	10.4	28.7	43 389	10.9	4.3	227 695	68.0
Baca County	6 619	4 517	9.3	24.5	22.3	14.0	28 099	16.9	2.4	1 905	76.5
Bent County	3 921	5 998	37.5	23.8	16.0	11.5	28 125	19.5	5.3	2 003	67.7
Boulder County (part)	192	75 278	22.6	27.6	9.2	31.4	51 709	7.7	3.5	28 241	66.5
Cheyenne County	4 614	2 231	8.9	28.6	16.5	14.2	37 054	11.1	1.1	880	75.0
Crowley County	2 043	5 518	33.4	18.8	10.9	11.9	26 803	18.5	5.7	1 358	72.9

[1]Dry land or land partially or temporarily covered by water.
[2]Persons who do not identify themselves as White alone, not of Hispanic origin.
[3]Persons 25 years old and over.

Table B. 109th Congressional Districts by Counties, 2000—*Continued*

(Number, percent.)

STATE Congressional district County	Land area,[1] (sq km)	Population Total	Percent minority[2]	Percent under 18 years old	Percent 65 years old and over	Percent with bachelor's degree or more[3]	Median income, 1999 (dollars)	Percent living in poverty	Percent unem- ployed	Households Total	Percent owner occupied
	1	2	3	4	5	6	7	8	9	10	11
Congressional District 4, Colorado—*Continued*											
Kiowa County	4 587	1 622	6.2	25.9	17.4	16.1	30 494	12.2	3.0	665	71.3
Kit Carson County	5 597	8 011	16.7	26.8	14.9	15.4	33 152	12.1	2.2	2 990	72.1
Larimer County	6 737	251 494	12.4	23.6	9.6	39.5	48 655	9.2	4.2	97 164	67.7
Lincoln County	6 698	6 087	16.4	23.8	14.1	13.2	31 914	11.7	2.3	2 058	68.9
Logan County	4 762	20 504	15.2	24.6	14.5	14.6	32 724	12.2	3.8	7 551	69.8
Morgan County	3 329	27 171	32.4	30.3	12.9	13.5	34 568	12.4	4.2	9 539	68.5
Otero County (part)	689	1 825	19.3	27.2	12.2	17.1	32 452	12.2	4.8	690	78.1
Phillips County	1 781	4 480	13.6	27.1	19.3	19.9	32 177	11.6	2.8	1 781	76.3
Prowers County	4 249	14 483	35.1	29.9	12.8	11.9	29 935	19.5	3.9	5 307	66.2
Sedgwick County	1 420	2 747	12.7	22.5	22.4	13.4	28 278	10.0	1.4	1 165	73.4
Washington County	6 529	4 926	6.6	26.4	18.3	14.3	32 431	11.4	1.6	1 989	73.7
Weld County (part)	10 130	167 838	30.4	28.2	9.2	21.9	41 720	13.0	5.6	58 609	67.3
Yuma County	6 127	9 841	14.0	28.4	16.0	15.5	33 169	12.9	2.4	3 800	71.1
Congressional District 5, Colorado	19 963	614 668	22.6	26.7	9.2	29.8	45 454	8.3	4.6	228 166	66.5
Chaffee County	2 625	16 242	13.0	19.6	16.9	24.3	34 368	11.7	4.7	6 584	73.3
El Paso County	5 507	516 929	23.8	27.5	8.6	31.8	46 844	8.0	4.7	192 409	64.7
Fremont County	3 970	46 145	18.9	20.6	14.5	13.5	34 150	11.7	4.1	15 232	76.0
Lake County	976	7 812	38.4	26.9	6.3	19.5	37 691	12.9	6.0	2 977	68.1
Park County (part)	5 442	6 985	8.2	22.3	8.8	27.5	42 764	8.3	3.8	2 971	83.2
Teller County	1 443	20 555	7.1	25.9	7.3	31.7	50 165	5.4	4.0	7 993	80.9
Congressional District 6, Colorado	10 629	614 491	12.4	29.2	6.5	46.8	73 393	2.7	2.2	221 355	84.9
Arapahoe County (part)	1 934	266 076	16.4	28.4	8.4	44.9	66 694	3.1	2.5	98 244	80.6
Douglas County	2 176	175 766	10.3	31.4	4.1	51.9	82 929	2.1	1.7	60 924	87.9
Elbert County	4 794	19 872	6.7	30.0	6.0	26.6	62 480	4.0	2.4	6 770	89.4
Jefferson County (part)	1 468	145 239	8.8	28.2	6.0	47.7	76 708	2.5	2.3	52 494	88.5
Park County (part)	258	7 538	6.4	24.9	6.2	32.9	60 078	3.1	2.0	2 923	92.4
Congressional District 7, Colorado	3 259	614 609	31.0	25.2	10.2	26.0	46 149	8.9	4.3	240 692	63.2
Adams County (part)	2 864	123 970	50.2	29.6	8.5	9.8	39 548	14.6	6.4	41 109	66.3
Arapahoe County (part)	100	162 388	43.2	25.8	7.7	25.4	43 912	9.1	4.2	65 653	57.1
Jefferson County (part)	295	328 251	17.8	23.4	12.1	31.7	49 966	6.7	3.6	133 930	65.3
CONNECTICUT	12 548	3 405 565	22.6	24.7	13.8	31.4	53 935	7.9	5.3	1 301 670	66.8
Congressional District 1, Connecticut	1 691	680 851	28.5	24.4	14.8	28.2	50 227	9.6	6.4	268 880	63.6
Hartford County (part)	1 145	613 977	30.6	24.5	14.9	28.1	49 310	10.2	6.7	241 956	62.6
Litchfield County (part)	442	36 498	5.4	24.5	13.9	25.1	55 233	4.2	3.6	14 205	77.4
Middlesex County (part)	104	30 376	12.6	22.5	13.6	33.8	58 871	3.9	3.1	12 719	66.8
Congressional District 2, Connecticut	5 253	681 092	11.4	24.2	12.3	28.8	54 498	5.8	4.4	255 470	72.0
Hartford County (part)	339	74 603	10.4	23.9	12.6	29.1	61 006	3.5	3.3	26 628	80.3
Middlesex County (part)	705	84 088	5.2	23.6	13.3	36.2	64 784	3.5	5.6	31 919	81.8
New Haven County (part)	94	17 858	4.6	28.1	14.3	57.2	87 497	1.3	2.1	6 515	88.3
New London County (part)	1 725	259 088	15.4	24.3	13.0	26.2	50 646	6.4	4.1	99 835	66.7
Tolland County	1 062	136 364	9.0	23.1	10.2	32.8	59 044	5.6	3.7	49 431	73.5
Windham County	1 328	109 091	11.5	25.1	12.3	19.0	45 115	8.5	5.8	41 142	67.4
Congressional District 3, Connecticut	1 189	681 085	24.0	23.7	14.7	28.0	49 752	8.8	5.8	267 105	63.6
Fairfield County (part)	60	59 822	17.7	23.1	19.0	24.9	54 125	4.8	4.3	23 688	79.3
Middlesex County (part)	147	40 607	19.6	23.0	14.2	29.0	48 509	7.5	4.5	16 703	57.5
New Haven County (part)	983	580 656	25.0	23.8	14.3	28.3	49 163	9.3	6.1	226 714	62.4
Congressional District 4, Connecticut	1 183	681 176	29.1	25.9	13.3	42.2	66 598	7.4	5.2	250 230	67.8
Fairfield County (part)	1 098	671 355	29.5	25.9	13.4	42.3	66 416	7.5	5.2	246 887	67.5
New Haven County (part)	85	9 821	3.7	27.3	8.8	32.2	77 126	2.1	3.1	3 343	91.1
Congressional District 5, Connecticut	3 231	681 361	19.8	25.1	13.8	29.9	53 118	7.7	4.7	259 985	67.5
Fairfield County (part)	463	151 390	19.5	25.0	10.4	35.3	66 004	5.2	3.2	53 657	72.8
Hartford County (part)	421	168 603	21.1	25.0	14.5	35.3	51 649	8.7	5.4	66 514	63.9
Litchfield County (part)	1 941	145 695	5.5	24.5	14.3	28.1	56 553	4.5	3.9	57 346	74.7
New Haven County (part)	407	215 673	28.6	25.7	15.3	23.1	44 840	11.0	5.8	82 468	62.0
DELAWARE	5 060	783 600	27.5	24.8	13.0	25.0	47 381	9.2	5.2	298 736	72.3
Congressional District (At Large), Delaware	5 060	783 600	27.5	24.8	13.0	25.0	47 381	9.2	5.2	298 736	72.3
Kent County	1 527	126 697	27.8	27.2	11.6	18.6	40 950	10.7	5.6	47 224	70.0
New Castle County	1 104	500 265	29.3	24.8	11.6	29.5	52 419	8.4	5.2	188 935	70.1
Sussex County	2 428	156 638	21.5	22.5	18.5	16.6	39 208	10.5	4.9	62 577	80.7
DISTRICT OF COLUMBIA	159	572 059	72.3	20.0	12.3	39.1	40 127	20.2	10.8	248 338	40.8
Delegate District (At Large), District of Columbia	159	572 059	72.3	20.0	12.3	39.1	40 127	20.2	10.8	248 338	40.8

[1]Dry land or land partially or temporarily covered by water.
[2]Persons who do not identify themselves as White alone, not of Hispanic origin.
[3]Persons 25 years old and over.

Table B. 109th Congressional Districts by Counties, 2000—*Continued*

(Number, percent.)

STATE Congressional district County	Land area,[1] (sq km)	Population Total	Population Percent minority[2]	Population Percent under 18 years old	Population Percent 65 years old and over	Percent with bachelor's degree or more[3]	Median income, 1999 (dollars)	Percent living in poverty	Percent unem-ployed	Households Total	Households Percent owner occupied
	1	2	3	4	5	6	7	8	9	10	11
FLORIDA	139 670	15 982 378	34.6	22.7	17.6	22.3	38 819	12.5	5.6	6 337 929	70.1
Congressional District 1, Florida	12 022	639 335	22.0	24.3	12.7	20.2	36 738	13.1	5.8	242 696	70.6
Escambia County	1 715	294 410	29.2	23.5	13.3	21.0	35 234	15.4	6.6	111 049	67.3
Holmes County	1 250	18 564	10.5	23.1	14.8	8.8	27 923	19.1	6.2	6 921	81.6
Okaloosa County (part)	2 390	156 781	20.0	24.5	11.8	21.9	40 108	9.3	4.9	60 973	65.2
Santa Rosa County	2 634	117 743	10.8	26.4	11.0	22.9	41 881	9.8	5.3	43 793	80.4
Walton County (part)	2 531	30 864	15.3	23.5	14.8	9.3	29 626	16.8	5.2	12 029	79.7
Washington County	1 502	20 973	19.7	23.5	15.2	9.2	27 922	19.2	5.5	7 931	81.9
Congressional District 2, Florida	24 410	639 190	28.5	22.8	12.0	24.1	34 718	16.5	6.7	248 547	68.4
Bay County	1 978	148 217	17.2	24.0	13.3	17.7	36 092	13.0	4.9	59 597	68.6
Calhoun County	1 469	13 017	23.1	23.0	13.8	7.7	26 575	20.0	6.5	4 468	80.2
Dixie County	1 823	13 827	11.7	22.0	17.0	6.8	26 082	19.1	7.4	5 205	86.5
Franklin County	1 410	11 057	20.3	18.1	16.0	12.4	26 756	17.7	3.6	4 096	79.2
Gadsden County	1 337	45 087	64.1	26.5	12.3	12.9	31 248	19.9	7.6	15 867	78.0
Gulf County	1 436	13 332	21.3	21.5	16.3	10.1	30 276	16.7	6.0	4 931	81.0
Jackson County	2 372	46 755	31.3	22.3	14.6	12.8	29 744	17.2	5.7	16 620	77.9
Jefferson County (part)	1 102	6 371	35.0	25.1	14.9	18.6	34 909	14.0	5.3	2 463	84.6
Lafayette County	1 406	7 022	24.6	21.5	12.1	7.2	30 651	17.5	4.5	2 142	80.4
Leon County (part)	1 620	227 067	35.7	21.2	8.4	42.5	36 946	18.9	8.6	92 035	55.8
Liberty County	2 165	7 021	25.6	21.9	10.4	7.4	28 840	19.9	5.0	2 222	81.7
Okaloosa County (part)	33	13 717	7.4	25.3	15.2	49.0	63 852	3.5	2.6	5 296	79.3
Suwannee County	1 781	34 844	19.1	24.0	16.9	10.5	29 963	18.5	7.3	13 460	81.0
Taylor County	2 699	19 256	22.6	24.7	13.8	8.9	30 032	18.0	5.5	7 176	79.8
Wakulla County	1 571	22 863	15.1	25.7	10.2	15.7	37 149	11.3	3.9	8 450	84.2
Walton County (part)	208	9 737	7.1	16.1	19.0	35.5	44 553	7.0	2.3	4 519	77.2
Congressional District 3, Florida	4 652	640 123	61.6	28.4	10.8	12.9	29 785	21.5	7.8	236 276	55.6
Alachua County (part)	473	47 695	52.2	24.2	9.5	22.3	23 443	30.4	10.6	18 732	48.6
Clay County (part)	253	14 486	19.2	23.6	16.2	21.2	43 711	9.7	7.3	5 396	67.0
Duval County (part)	230	252 271	67.4	29.2	11.4	11.6	29 373	21.4	7.8	96 547	53.8
Lake County (part)	776	19 591	16.8	26.8	13.3	9.9	33 942	14.5	4.3	7 410	82.9
Marion County (part)	883	8 774	6.0	21.5	21.8	6.3	27 095	18.5	8.0	3 809	88.1
Orange County (part)	251	218 791	73.3	29.7	7.8	13.7	31 445	20.7	7.4	74 557	49.4
Putnam County (part)	1 401	39 037	26.7	25.5	16.5	8.9	28 079	22.4	6.8	15 055	78.9
Seminole County (part)	25	25 033	60.8	28.2	12.5	10.5	26 503	23.7	7.7	9 488	50.6
Volusia County (part)	361	14 445	48.1	27.2	17.5	10.5	28 843	24.1	10.6	5 282	70.1
Congressional District 4, Florida	10 665	638 922	22.1	24.3	10.9	24.4	43 947	9.1	4.1	246 246	69.4
Baker County	1 516	22 259	17.7	27.5	9.0	8.2	40 035	14.7	4.5	7 043	81.3
Columbia County	2 064	56 513	22.0	25.3	14.0	10.9	30 881	15.0	6.0	20 925	77.1
Duval County (part)	1 098	438 069	21.1	24.0	10.4	29.3	47 091	6.9	3.7	175 423	65.5
Hamilton County	1 333	13 327	45.1	23.5	11.0	7.3	25 638	26.0	7.1	4 161	77.3
Jefferson County (part)	446	6 531	48.8	20.4	14.1	15.3	30 077	20.7	4.2	2 232	76.8
Leon County (part)	107	12 385	37.6	22.7	6.8	30.4	46 851	4.8	3.0	4 486	81.6
Madison County	1 792	18 733	44.3	25.4	14.6	10.2	26 533	23.1	5.4	6 629	78.4
Nassau County	1 688	57 663	11.1	25.0	12.6	18.9	46 022	9.1	4.8	21 980	80.7
Union County	622	13 442	28.3	21.9	7.3	7.5	34 563	14.0	4.0	3 367	74.5
Congressional District 5, Florida	10 474	639 719	12.4	20.2	25.7	14.3	34 815	10.6	4.9	263 218	85.2
Citrus County	1 512	118 085	7.1	17.1	32.3	13.2	31 001	11.7	6.7	52 634	85.6
Hernando County	1 239	130 802	10.9	18.8	30.9	12.7	32 572	10.3	5.2	55 425	86.5
Lake County (part)	1 020	78 316	16.1	20.3	23.9	18.9	41 313	7.2	3.2	31 977	83.6
Levy County (part)	2 677	26 669	11.9	22.9	18.8	10.4	26 860	17.9	5.8	10 935	84.7
Marion County (part)	345	14 138	10.9	18.3	30.3	14.1	32 725	12.2	6.8	6 209	88.0
Pasco County (part)	1 685	164 457	13.2	22.9	20.8	15.6	37 460	10.1	4.6	64 958	85.1
Polk County (part)	583	53 907	11.3	24.8	16.3	14.5	41 812	9.0	4.0	20 301	81.5
Sumter County	1 413	53 345	21.7	16.2	27.6	12.2	32 073	13.7	4.8	20 779	86.4
Congressional District 6, Florida	7 541	638 952	21.2	22.9	15.4	21.4	36 846	13.4	5.3	247 789	72.9
Alachua County (part)	1 792	170 260	24.2	18.9	9.5	43.4	34 620	20.6	6.1	68 777	56.7
Bradford County	759	26 088	24.9	21.8	12.9	8.4	33 140	14.6	4.8	8 497	79.0
Clay County (part)	1 304	126 328	14.8	28.4	9.0	19.9	49 578	6.5	4.4	44 847	79.2
Duval County (part)	676	88 539	23.9	29.2	7.7	11.6	42 658	9.6	4.2	31 777	78.2
Gilchrist County	904	14 437	11.1	24.3	13.6	9.4	30 328	14.1	4.4	5 021	86.2
Lake County (part)	149	44 429	17.7	17.9	35.8	13.4	32 133	11.8	4.8	19 983	80.6
Levy County (part)	220	7 781	33.9	26.0	15.0	11.5	27 276	20.9	7.3	2 932	79.3
Marion County (part)	1 738	161 090	22.2	20.6	25.7	14.8	32 225	13.3	6.1	65 955	78.8
Congressional District 7, Florida	4 654	639 140	18.5	22.0	18.2	24.5	40 525	10.1	5.0	259 281	74.1
Flagler County	1 256	49 832	16.5	17.9	28.6	21.2	40 214	8.7	4.3	21 294	84.1
Orange County (part)	8	9 641	6.2	27.1	15.0	61.7	75 016	1.5	2.5	3 625	90.9
Putnam County (part)	469	31 386	21.9	23.5	20.9	10.0	28 291	19.1	4.4	12 784	81.3
St. Johns County	1 577	123 135	11.0	23.0	15.9	33.1	50 099	8.0	3.3	49 614	76.4
Seminole County (part)	314	161 950	20.9	24.6	11.3	30.8	50 588	6.6	3.4	62 354	71.1
Volusia County (part)	1 029	263 196	21.0	20.3	21.4	17.8	33 328	12.8	7.3	109 610	71.5

[1]Dry land or land partially or temporarily covered by water.
[2]Persons who do not identify themselves as White alone, not of Hispanic origin.
[3]Persons 25 years old and over.

Table B. 109th Congressional Districts by Counties, 2000—*Continued*

(Number, percent.)

STATE Congressional district County	Land area,[1] (sq km)	Population Total	Population Percent minority[2]	Population Percent under 18 years old	Population Percent 65 years old and over	Percent with bachelor's degree or more[3]	Median income, 1999 (dollars)	Percent living in poverty	Percent unemployed	Households Total	Households Percent owner occupied
	1	2	3	4	5	6	7	8	9	10	11
Congressional District 8, Florida	2 556	639 026	30.0	23.2	13.9	25.9	41 568	9.4	4.3	254 858	66.4
Lake County (part)	524	68 192	14.0	19.9	26.9	17.8	36 428	9.6	4.1	29 043	79.5
Marion County (part)	1 123	74 914	17.2	23.6	21.3	12.0	31 793	12.1	4.9	30 782	79.3
Orange County (part)	884	492 684	34.3	23.6	11.0	29.2	43 958	9.0	4.3	193 759	62.4
Osceola County (part)	24	3 236	12.6	28.4	5.3	54.7	63 036	7.4	2.0	1 274	52.0
Congressional District 9, Florida	1 642	638 563	15.0	21.9	20.5	24.6	40 742	8.6	3.9	266 733	76.3
Hillsborough County (part)	1 165	245 935	20.8	26.8	9.6	34.7	55 352	6.4	3.4	91 295	76.6
Pasco County (part)	244	180 308	7.3	17.5	32.3	11.1	30 248	11.2	4.7	82 608	80.2
Pinellas County (part)	233	212 320	14.6	19.9	23.1	26.3	40 780	8.9	3.8	92 830	72.6
Congressional District 10, Florida	452	639 428	12.0	17.9	23.5	22.6	37 168	8.9	4.0	294 533	71.7
Pinellas County (part)	452	639 428	12.0	17.9	23.5	22.6	37 168	8.9	4.0	294 533	71.7
Congressional District 11, Florida	632	639 059	51.6	25.0	12.0	21.2	33 559	17.5	7.3	257 770	55.4
Hillsborough County (part)	544	541 862	47.7	24.2	11.9	22.6	35 009	16.3	7.2	221 799	55.4
Manatee County (part)	48	27 463	73.5	30.8	13.0	7.3	26 888	26.1	6.9	8 366	54.0
Pinellas County (part)	40	69 734	73.1	29.1	13.1	14.4	26 908	23.3	8.8	27 605	55.4
Congressional District 12, Florida	5 066	640 096	27.9	25.1	17.1	16.6	37 769	12.4	5.5	243 267	72.7
Hillsborough County (part)	1 014	211 151	27.0	26.0	15.0	20.2	43 831	9.9	4.4	78 263	74.3
Osceola County (part)	91	13 583	60.5	34.2	8.0	9.8	37 172	12.8	6.6	4 147	78.6
Polk County (part)	3 961	415 362	27.4	24.4	18.5	14.9	35 136	13.7	6.1	160 857	71.7
Congressional District 13, Florida	6 732	639 216	14.1	18.0	28.6	23.7	40 187	9.4	3.8	281 788	77.5
Charlotte County (part)	79	17 573	3.4	10.2	45.6	19.2	33 945	7.0	3.3	8 845	84.9
DeSoto County	1 651	32 209	38.9	22.5	19.4	8.4	30 714	23.6	5.3	10 746	74.7
Hardee County	1 651	26 938	44.9	27.6	13.6	8.4	30 183	24.6	9.7	8 166	73.4
Manatee County (part)	1 871	236 539	13.2	19.4	26.3	22.0	39 771	8.3	3.2	104 094	75.3
Sarasota County	1 480	325 957	10.4	16.2	31.4	27.4	41 957	7.8	3.7	149 937	79.1
Congressional District 14, Florida	2 736	639 298	16.2	18.2	27.3	24.4	42 541	8.8	3.4	279 398	77.3
Charlotte County (part)	236	26 680	7.7	18.3	26.4	14.5	38 312	8.1	3.2	11 378	86.2
Collier County (part)	420	171 730	12.9	14.8	32.3	33.8	51 155	6.4	2.7	79 421	77.9
Lee County	2 081	440 888	18.1	19.6	25.4	21.1	40 319	9.7	3.7	188 599	76.5
Congressional District 15, Florida	6 591	639 133	22.1	22.1	20.2	22.3	39 397	9.8	4.8	261 939	73.2
Brevard County (part)	1 669	355 857	16.6	21.3	21.0	24.9	39 781	9.3	4.9	151 171	73.3
Indian River County	1 303	112 947	16.5	19.2	29.2	23.1	39 635	9.3	4.5	49 137	77.6
Osceola County (part)	3 308	155 674	39.0	26.1	11.7	15.4	37 906	11.5	4.9	55 556	67.3
Polk County (part)	310	14 655	21.1	19.5	20.5	16.1	41 061	7.1	2.8	6 075	89.7
Congressional District 16, Florida	11 755	638 817	18.2	21.0	25.5	20.0	39 408	10.0	4.1	262 341	81.7
Charlotte County (part)	1 481	97 374	11.2	15.9	35.0	18.1	36 272	8.5	3.6	43 641	82.8
Glades County	2 004	10 576	31.5	22.1	19.2	9.8	30 774	15.2	8.8	3 852	81.6
Hendry County (part)	1 430	28 831	51.0	30.0	10.6	8.9	34 839	23.2	6.7	8 949	74.8
Highlands County	2 663	87 366	23.5	19.3	33.1	13.6	30 160	15.2	4.4	37 471	79.7
Martin County (part)	930	121 950	12.3	18.2	29.1	27.0	43 557	8.0	4.0	54 268	80.4
Okeechobee County	2 005	35 910	28.6	25.2	16.5	8.9	30 456	16.0	4.7	12 593	74.9
Palm Beach County (part)	467	102 406	18.1	27.1	13.8	32.6	61 841	4.6	3.2	37 484	84.9
St. Lucie County (part)	774	154 404	14.8	20.6	25.6	16.4	38 417	8.9	4.1	64 083	83.6
Congressional District 17, Florida	250	639 593	81.5	29.3	10.8	13.5	30 426	23.3	11.1	213 285	57.4
Broward County (part)	67	166 109	62.5	26.4	12.5	16.7	35 394	14.2	6.5	62 512	60.0
Miami-Dade County (part)	183	473 484	88.2	30.3	10.2	12.3	28 209	26.5	13.0	150 773	56.4
Congressional District 18, Florida	919	639 753	70.2	19.2	17.8	25.6	32 298	19.3	7.8	255 055	47.9
Miami-Dade County (part)	539	560 206	77.0	19.5	18.3	25.6	30 834	20.7	8.6	219 997	45.6
Monroe County (part)	381	79 547	22.7	16.9	14.6	25.4	42 319	10.2	3.2	35 058	62.5
Congressional District 19, Florida	598	638 503	22.5	18.9	29.7	25.7	42 237	7.7	4.8	283 625	79.1
Broward County (part)	123	209 314	25.2	19.5	25.6	23.5	40 010	8.2	4.6	93 096	73.6
Palm Beach County (part)	476	429 189	21.2	18.6	31.7	26.8	43 718	7.5	4.9	190 529	81.8
Congressional District 20, Florida	416	639 795	33.3	21.2	17.3	29.6	44 034	9.6	4.8	275 276	69.9
Broward County (part)	378	543 879	32.1	22.2	16.3	27.9	44 477	9.2	4.7	227 698	71.6
Miami-Dade County (part)	38	95 916	39.9	15.2	22.9	38.3	41 924	12.0	5.5	47 578	62.0
Congressional District 21, Florida	349	639 005	79.0	24.3	12.8	22.9	41 426	13.0	7.2	211 014	61.9
Broward County (part)	95	73 875	60.1	31.9	4.7	37.0	74 448	3.9	3.3	23 183	91.7
Miami-Dade County (part)	255	565 130	81.5	23.4	13.9	21.2	38 235	14.2	7.8	187 831	58.2
Congressional District 22, Florida	694	640 100	17.7	18.6	20.8	34.1	51 200	7.1	3.7	285 359	74.3
Broward County (part)	212	277 945	18.8	19.9	17.1	33.6	50 799	7.8	3.9	122 484	72.3
Palm Beach County (part)	481	362 155	16.8	17.7	23.6	34.5	51 517	6.5	3.6	162 875	75.7
Congressional District 23, Florida	8 708	639 781	70.7	28.1	12.2	12.8	31 309	21.9	8.3	224 530	56.5
Broward County (part)	2 247	351 896	72.3	27.5	13.1	12.2	31 597	20.4	8.2	125 472	60.4
Hendry County (part)	1 555	7 379	73.9	30.3	6.5	5.1	28 523	28.4	12.7	1 901	61.3
Martin County (part)	509	4 781	65.2	26.2	6.7	7.2	24 583	36.3	11.6	1 020	48.3
Palm Beach County (part)	3 688	237 434	68.4	28.5	11.3	14.6	31 817	22.2	8.2	83 287	51.6
St. Lucie County (part)	709	38 291	70.1	30.1	11.0	8.4	24 685	31.9	9.5	12 850	50.2

[1]Dry land or land partially or temporarily covered by water.
[2]Persons who do not identify themselves as White alone, not of Hispanic origin.
[3]Persons 25 years old and over.

Table B. 109th Congressional Districts by Counties, 2000—Continued

(Number, percent.)

STATE Congressional district County	Land area,[1] (sq km)	Population				Percent with bachelor's degree or more[3]	Median income, 1999 (dollars)	Percent living in poverty	Percent unem- ployed	Households	
		Total	Percent minority[2]	Percent under 18 years old	Percent 65 years old and over					Total	Percent owner occupied
	1	2	3	4	5	6	7	8	9	10	11
Congressional District 24, Florida	4 101	639 516	20.1	23.1	14.6	25.5	43 954	8.7	4.2	248 930	74.3
Brevard County (part)	968	120 373	15.7	23.7	16.6	19.3	40 980	10.0	5.0	47 024	78.8
Orange County (part)	1 207	175 228	28.7	23.9	9.8	29.6	45 075	10.7	4.7	64 345	67.1
Seminole County (part)	459	178 213	23.2	25.4	9.6	33.9	51 426	5.9	3.4	67 730	70.6
Volusia County (part)	1 467	165 702	10.7	19.3	23.7	18.0	38 467	8.6	4.1	69 831	81.6
Congressional District 25, Florida	11 054	638 315	75.8	28.6	8.6	20.3	44 489	13.7	7.0	194 175	72.7
Collier County (part)	4 826	79 647	55.5	30.6	7.4	10.4	41 234	18.7	5.5	23 552	67.8
Miami-Dade County (part)	4 027	558 626	78.7	28.3	8.7	21.6	45 147	12.9	7.2	170 595	73.4
Monroe County (part)	2 201	42	0.0	0.0	0.0	0.0	36 250	0.0	0.0	28	0.0
GEORGIA	149 976	8 186 453	37.3	26.5	9.6	24.3	42 433	13.0	5.5	3 006 369	67.5
Congressional District 1, Georgia	29 092	628 453	28.9	27.5	10.6	17.9	36 158	14.8	5.2	228 520	71.4
Appling County	1 317	17 419	24.9	27.3	12.0	8.4	30 266	18.6	4.8	6 606	79.0
Atkinson County	876	7 609	37.6	30.2	9.3	6.9	26 470	23.0	5.2	2 717	74.2
Bacon County	738	10 103	20.4	25.7	13.0	6.6	26 910	23.7	4.5	3 833	74.9
Ben Hill County	652	17 484	37.9	27.6	13.1	9.5	27 100	22.3	6.3	6 673	66.7
Berrien County	1 172	16 235	15.4	27.2	12.4	9.4	30 044	17.7	4.5	6 261	75.6
Brantley County	1 151	14 629	6.4	28.3	10.1	6.2	30 361	15.6	4.9	5 436	86.9
Bryan County (part)	242	7 278	8.8	31.2	7.0	33.6	69 692	6.1	1.4	2 437	86.3
Camden County	1 631	43 664	27.0	31.7	4.9	16.0	41 056	10.1	5.8	14 705	63.2
Charlton County	2 022	10 282	31.6	27.5	9.9	6.4	27 869	20.9	5.2	3 342	80.7
Chatham County (part)	532	51 863	13.5	23.4	15.0	43.2	63 376	3.6	2.6	20 505	81.6
Clinch County	2 096	6 878	31.9	28.0	12.2	10.4	26 755	23.4	4.2	2 512	72.4
Coffee County	1 551	37 413	33.9	28.1	9.7	10.0	30 710	19.1	6.4	13 354	74.4
Colquitt County (part)	179	14 316	33.1	26.2	15.4	15.3	28 030	20.2	6.5	5 590	57.7
Cook County	593	15 771	33.5	28.8	13.1	8.1	27 582	20.7	5.3	5 882	74.9
Echols County	1 047	3 754	28.9	29.7	9.0	8.4	25 851	28.7	3.7	1 264	75.7
Glynn County	1 094	67 568	31.0	25.3	14.6	23.8	38 765	15.1	5.6	27 208	65.5
Houston County (part)	353	45 723	22.5	29.7	5.9	26.3	54 695	4.9	3.9	15 534	79.3
Irwin County	924	9 931	28.2	29.0	14.4	9.9	30 257	17.8	6.0	3 644	76.8
Jeff Davis County	863	12 684	21.0	27.0	11.9	9.4	27 310	19.4	5.6	4 828	77.4
Lanier County	484	7 241	29.6	27.3	10.5	8.8	29 171	18.5	6.2	2 593	76.3
Liberty County	1 344	61 610	55.7	31.9	4.0	14.5	33 477	15.0	8.6	19 383	50.7
Long County	1 038	10 304	35.5	32.8	5.6	5.8	30 640	19.5	8.8	3 574	66.2
Lowndes County (part)	414	40 329	23.7	23.8	9.1	27.9	42 836	9.2	3.7	13 778	66.7
McIntosh County	1 123	10 847	38.9	28.2	11.4	11.1	30 102	18.7	5.7	4 202	83.5
Pierce County	889	15 636	13.9	26.3	12.3	10.1	29 895	18.4	4.0	5 958	80.7
Pulaski County (part)	282	6 285	37.2	25.8	16.4	15.9	31 417	18.6	6.0	2 512	72.3
Ware County	2 337	35 483	31.1	24.7	15.5	11.4	28 360	20.5	6.4	13 475	70.3
Wayne County	1 670	26 565	25.3	25.6	11.3	11.6	32 766	16.7	5.0	9 324	76.5
Wilcox County (part)	476	3 549	20.8	25.6	18.1	8.3	28 779	16.9	4.2	1 390	82.5
Congressional District 2, Georgia	25 185	630 481	49.7	27.8	12.0	13.9	29 354	22.5	7.6	228 773	62.5
Baker County	889	4 074	53.8	27.4	13.5	10.7	30 338	23.4	8.3	1 514	77.6
Brooks County	1 278	16 450	43.0	27.2	15.1	11.3	26 911	23.4	5.3	6 155	76.9
Calhoun County	726	6 320	62.1	22.0	12.8	11.7	24 588	26.5	5.6	1 962	71.6
Chattahoochee County	644	14 882	45.0	28.5	1.8	25.0	37 106	10.6	7.5	2 932	27.9
Clay County	506	3 357	61.7	25.7	19.5	10.1	21 448	31.3	6.8	1 347	74.2
Colquitt County (part)	1 251	27 737	36.0	27.9	11.7	9.3	28 857	19.7	6.2	9 905	71.8
Crisp County	709	21 996	46.4	29.1	12.8	12.8	26 547	29.3	7.0	8 337	60.5
Decatur County	1 546	28 240	44.1	28.6	13.3	12.1	28 820	22.7	6.5	10 380	72.5
Dougherty County	854	96 065	62.8	27.6	11.8	17.8	30 934	24.8	10.1	35 552	53.5
Early County	1 324	12 354	49.9	28.6	16.2	12.6	25 629	25.7	8.1	4 695	72.4
Grady County	1 187	23 659	36.8	27.3	13.2	10.6	28 656	21.3	7.4	8 797	73.3
Lee County	921	24 757	18.4	30.6	6.3	17.0	48 600	8.2	3.4	8 229	78.3
Lowndes County (part)	892	51 786	51.5	27.9	9.1	12.5	26 792	24.9	7.3	18 876	56.5
Miller County	733	6 383	30.4	26.3	17.2	11.3	27 335	21.2	4.0	2 487	76.9
Mitchell County	1 326	23 932	51.0	27.5	11.9	9.1	26 581	26.4	6.2	8 063	72.0
Muscogee County (part)	99	84 304	67.1	27.6	11.7	14.0	26 187	25.3	10.1	31 299	41.0
Quitman County	392	2 598	47.6	24.0	19.8	6.1	25 875	21.9	5.8	1 047	80.4
Randolph County	1 112	7 791	61.0	27.3	15.4	9.5	22 004	27.7	7.9	2 909	68.8
Seminole County	617	9 369	39.0	26.0	15.7	8.6	27 094	23.2	7.0	3 573	80.8
Stewart County	1 188	5 252	63.5	25.0	18.4	9.3	24 789	22.2	10.1	2 007	72.5
Sumter County	1 257	33 200	52.8	28.0	12.5	19.3	30 904	21.4	6.8	12 025	63.9
Terrell County	869	10 970	62.5	28.7	13.3	10.7	26 969	28.6	8.5	4 002	66.3
Thomas County	1 420	42 737	41.8	27.1	14.0	16.8	31 115	17.4	6.5	16 309	70.0
Tift County	686	38 407	37.1	27.4	11.6	15.6	32 616	19.9	6.8	13 919	67.2
Turner County	741	9 504	44.3	29.6	12.8	10.5	25 676	26.7	8.0	3 435	71.4
Webster County	543	2 390	50.6	24.8	14.7	9.1	27 992	19.3	7.5	911	81.4
Worth County	1 476	21 967	31.5	28.6	12.2	8.6	32 384	18.5	7.2	8 106	76.2

[1]Dry land or land partially or temporarily covered by water.
[2]Persons who do not identify themselves as White alone, not of Hispanic origin.
[3]Persons 25 years old and over.

Table B. 109th Congressional Districts by Counties, 2000—*Continued*

(Number, percent.)

STATE Congressional district County	Land area,[1] (sq km)	Population Total	Percent minority[2]	Percent under 18 years old	Percent 65 years old and over	Percent with bachelor's degree or more[3]	Median income, 1999 (dollars)	Percent living in poverty	Percent unem- ployed	Households Total	Percent owner occupied
	1	2	3	4	5	6	7	8	9	10	11
Congressional District 3, Georgia	28 269	630 000	43.8	26.2	12.2	12.8	31 433	19.9	6.8	229 691	69.0
Baldwin County	669	44 700	46.3	21.7	10.6	16.2	35 159	16.8	6.2	14 758	66.4
Bibb County (part)	551	127 566	56.8	27.0	12.9	15.3	30 475	22.1	8.5	48 992	57.0
Bleckley County	563	11 666	27.5	26.7	13.6	12.5	33 448	15.9	6.0	4 372	76.1
Candler County	639	9 577	37.3	26.8	15.1	10.2	25 022	26.1	7.2	3 375	73.2
Crawford County	842	12 495	27.5	27.5	9.1	6.8	37 848	15.4	4.6	4 461	84.8
Dodge County	1 296	19 171	31.5	26.0	13.3	11.6	27 607	17.4	5.4	7 062	73.8
Dooly County	1 018	11 525	55.1	25.5	11.5	9.6	27 980	22.1	6.4	3 909	71.4
Emanuel County	1 776	21 837	37.3	27.9	13.2	10.1	24 383	27.4	4.4	8 045	71.2
Evans County	479	10 495	39.8	27.8	12.3	9.0	25 447	27.0	8.1	3 778	71.4
Hancock County	1 226	10 076	78.8	24.3	12.2	9.8	22 003	29.4	13.7	3 237	76.5
Houston County (part)	623	65 042	37.1	27.0	11.8	15.4	37 563	13.8	5.6	25 377	61.9
Johnson County	788	8 560	37.9	30.2	15.6	7.8	23 848	22.6	5.5	3 130	79.8
Jones County (part)	882	21 406	26.2	27.2	10.5	13.0	42 175	10.6	4.7	7 820	85.4
Laurens County	2 104	44 874	37.1	26.8	13.2	14.4	32 010	18.4	5.2	17 083	71.3
Macon County	1 045	14 074	62.6	27.6	13.0	10.0	24 224	25.8	9.1	4 834	73.2
Marion County	951	7 144	41.7	28.5	10.8	8.9	29 145	22.4	3.6	2 668	78.1
Monroe County	1 025	21 757	30.3	26.2	10.0	17.1	44 195	9.8	3.4	7 719	79.4
Montgomery County	635	8 270	30.5	24.9	10.5	13.5	30 240	19.9	3.9	2 919	78.2
Peach County	391	23 668	51.0	25.9	9.8	16.8	34 453	20.2	12.9	8 436	68.4
Pulaski County (part)	359	3 303	40.6	18.0	7.2	7.4	34 018	10.4	4.2	895	77.7
Schley County	434	3 766	34.4	29.1	11.2	13.7	32 035	19.9	5.7	1 435	76.3
Tattnall County	1 253	22 305	40.6	23.1	11.3	7.9	28 664	23.9	6.8	7 057	70.5
Taylor County	978	8 815	45.2	26.9	13.1	8.5	25 148	26.0	8.0	3 281	76.8
Telfair County	1 142	11 794	40.6	22.5	15.1	8.3	26 097	21.2	6.5	4 140	78.3
Treutlen County	520	6 854	35.2	25.7	13.6	8.5	24 644	26.3	9.4	2 531	74.9
Twiggs County	933	10 590	46.2	27.0	11.7	5.4	31 608	19.7	8.3	3 832	82.7
Washington County	1 762	21 176	54.4	26.9	12.7	10.5	29 910	22.9	9.5	7 435	74.1
Wheeler County	771	6 179	37.7	22.3	12.6	7.1	24 053	25.3	5.0	2 011	77.4
Wilcox County (part)	509	5 028	50.9	21.0	10.4	6.0	26 525	24.9	5.6	1 395	77.2
Wilkinson County	1 157	10 220	42.8	27.1	13.3	9.6	32 723	17.9	6.7	3 827	82.3
Congressional District 4, Georgia	650	629 896	67.9	24.9	7.8	35.9	49 307	10.5	5.5	234 301	57.7
DeKalb County (part)	631	607 860	68.5	24.9	7.9	35.7	49 425	10.5	5.5	224 970	58.7
Gwinnett County (part)	20	22 036	52.7	23.5	4.4	41.0	46 739	10.3	5.5	9 331	34.2
Congressional District 5, Georgia	652	629 839	65.4	21.7	8.9	37.3	39 725	19.7	10.6	261 795	42.1
Clayton County (part)	28	9 175	93.4	29.5	3.3	20.7	38 021	8.0	5.5	3 510	28.0
Cobb County (part)	63	57 417	41.9	15.8	6.4	48.4	49 783	8.4	4.5	28 168	35.6
DeKalb County (part)	29	45 845	49.8	18.1	11.2	46.2	44 045	16.0	6.2	20 431	49.8
Fulton County (part)	532	517 402	69.0	22.6	9.1	35.3	37 343	21.5	12.0	209 686	42.4
Congressional District 6, Georgia	1 127	630 087	17.1	27.6	6.9	50.7	75 611	3.7	2.7	229 887	79.2
Cherokee County (part)	143	43 342	11.5	27.2	6.1	28.1	61 893	5.3	2.9	15 458	81.4
Cobb County (part)	565	347 307	16.1	27.8	6.8	46.9	72 864	3.3	2.6	124 539	83.1
Fulton County (part)	419	239 438	19.5	27.3	7.0	60.1	83 916	3.9	2.7	89 890	73.4
Congressional District 7, Georgia	3 095	629 851	17.7	29.3	6.0	31.9	63 455	4.5	2.7	213 675	85.0
Bartow County (part)	498	37 050	10.0	28.7	7.4	12.6	45 471	7.3	3.5	13 143	79.2
Cherokee County (part)	955	98 561	9.6	28.6	6.8	26.5	60 237	5.3	2.6	34 037	84.9
Forsyth County (part)	223	48 273	9.3	29.6	5.0	42.9	83 532	4.3	2.0	16 211	93.0
Gwinnett County (part)	669	366 954	23.3	29.1	5.8	37.2	68 225	3.9	2.7	123 165	84.1
Paulding County (part)	750	79 013	10.5	30.9	5.8	15.2	52 367	5.4	2.6	27 119	86.9
Congressional District 8, Georgia	9 097	627 870	17.3	27.2	9.4	23.4	52 406	6.3	3.5	224 673	80.6
Bibb County (part)	96	26 321	19.8	24.4	11.8	48.7	59 354	5.1	3.8	10 675	67.0
Butts County (part)	340	10 600	16.3	21.6	8.1	8.6	44 614	8.5	1.6	3 204	89.5
Carroll County (part)	857	58 276	16.4	26.4	8.7	16.7	42 030	12.1	4.7	20 300	76.8
Coweta County (part)	1 029	73 986	16.5	28.9	7.3	22.4	56 717	4.8	3.2	26 140	82.8
Douglas County (part)	327	58 647	17.3	27.3	8.2	19.7	52 926	5.7	3.7	20 544	79.8
Fayette County (part)	490	86 742	15.5	29.2	9.0	36.0	70 711	2.6	2.7	29 990	86.1
Harris County (part)	1 095	21 375	23.8	25.9	11.6	19.8	46 328	9.0	3.6	7 860	85.3
Henry County (part)	641	77 384	11.9	28.8	7.5	19.1	61 531	3.7	2.4	26 687	90.7
Jasper County	959	11 426	30.2	27.3	11.8	11.5	39 890	14.2	4.7	4 175	79.1
Jones County (part)	137	2 233	19.3	26.3	8.7	34.5	51 058	6.3	2.4	839	89.4
Lamar County	479	15 912	32.4	24.5	12.9	11.3	37 087	11.2	5.5	5 712	72.4
Muscogee County (part)	213	53 721	20.9	25.8	10.7	32.6	49 994	4.4	3.0	20 817	68.8
Newton County (part)	197	19 127	14.3	27.8	8.0	12.5	51 230	5.4	3.4	6 873	90.2
Pike County	566	13 688	17.2	27.6	11.0	14.0	44 370	9.6	3.4	4 755	81.5
Rockdale County (part)	54	18 678	12.6	28.0	8.1	24.4	65 399	3.0	3.2	6 206	92.0
Spalding County (part)	420	30 663	14.0	24.8	11.8	16.2	45 299	9.1	4.4	11 412	77.7
Troup County (part)	697	27 708	16.6	25.9	11.2	25.2	46 470	8.0	4.3	10 185	75.5
Upson County (part)	501	21 383	24.2	25.4	14.2	11.0	32 422	12.8	7.0	8 299	71.2

[1]Dry land or land partially or temporarily covered by water.
[2]Persons who do not identify themselves as White alone, not of Hispanic origin.
[3]Persons 25 years old and over.

Table B. 109th Congressional Districts by Counties, 2000—*Continued*

(Number, percent.)

STATE Congressional district County	Land area,[1] (sq km)	Population Total	Percent minority[2]	Percent under 18 years old	Percent 65 years old and over	Percent with bachelor's degree or more[3]	Median income, 1999 (dollars)	Percent living in poverty	Percent unem-ployed	Households Total	Percent owner occupied
	1	2	3	4	5	6	7	8	9	10	11
Congressional District 9, Georgia	17 992	630 036	18.7	25.8	12.3	18.5	39 987	11.2	4.2	235 801	77.0
Banks County	605	14 422	8.5	26.1	10.4	8.6	38 523	12.5	3.0	5 364	81.0
Barrow County	420	46 144	16.3	28.1	9.3	10.9	45 019	8.3	4.2	16 354	75.5
Columbia County	751	89 288	18.7	29.5	8.0	32.0	55 682	5.1	3.7	31 120	82.1
Elbert County	955	20 511	34.2	26.0	15.1	9.8	28 724	17.3	5.8	8 004	75.9
Franklin County	682	20 285	11.5	23.9	15.4	10.3	32 134	13.9	4.2	7 888	79.3
Greene County	1 006	14 406	47.9	25.0	14.4	17.6	33 479	22.3	6.7	5 477	76.2
Habersham County	720	35 902	15.2	23.3	13.8	15.8	36 321	12.2	4.2	13 259	76.2
Hart County	601	22 997	21.5	23.6	16.4	13.5	32 833	14.8	5.3	9 106	80.8
Jackson County	887	41 589	12.3	26.8	10.4	11.7	40 349	12.0	3.4	15 057	74.9
Lincoln County	547	8 348	36.1	24.4	14.9	10.1	31 952	15.3	6.0	3 251	81.8
Lumpkin County	737	21 016	7.6	24.2	9.8	17.6	39 167	13.2	4.0	7 537	72.3
McDuffie County	673	21 231	40.1	27.9	12.4	11.7	31 920	18.4	7.7	7 970	71.4
Madison County	735	25 730	12.1	26.3	10.9	10.9	36 347	11.6	2.7	9 800	80.2
Morgan County	906	15 457	31.7	26.6	12.5	18.7	40 249	10.9	5.1	5 558	77.6
Newton County (part)	283	11 643	10.3	27.5	8.6	17.5	51 563	9.6	3.1	3 910	89.5
Oconee County	481	26 225	12.1	30.3	8.5	39.8	55 211	6.5	3.7	9 051	80.2
Oglethorpe County (part)	751	10 417	20.9	25.1	12.3	15.4	35 094	13.2	3.0	4 029	82.1
Putnam County	892	18 812	33.5	23.2	14.4	14.4	36 956	14.6	3.8	7 402	79.5
Rabun County	961	15 050	7.0	22.0	18.1	17.6	33 899	11.1	4.9	6 279	79.4
Richmond County (part)	248	37 346	31.9	23.9	11.6	38.9	42 568	8.8	6.2	15 430	54.1
Stephens County	464	25 435	15.0	23.3	15.7	14.1	29 466	15.1	4.2	9 951	72.7
Towns County	432	9 319	2.8	16.2	25.9	17.4	31 950	11.8	3.8	3 998	85.2
Union County	835	17 289	2.5	19.7	21.6	12.5	31 893	12.5	3.2	7 159	82.3
Walton County (part)	574	30 543	10.4	27.2	9.8	13.0	47 560	7.6	2.6	10 802	82.1
White County	626	19 944	5.8	23.1	14.5	15.4	36 084	10.5	2.8	7 731	79.3
Wilkes County	1 221	10 687	45.9	24.0	17.5	12.0	27 644	17.5	4.4	4 314	75.5
Congressional District 10, Georgia	9 690	628 794	14.5	26.3	10.5	15.9	42 037	10.3	3.4	227 841	76.3
Catoosa County	420	53 282	4.5	25.8	11.8	13.8	39 998	9.4	3.3	20 425	77.0
Dade County	451	15 154	3.0	23.8	12.0	10.9	35 259	9.7	5.4	5 633	80.2
Dawson County	547	15 999	3.0	25.2	9.3	18.1	47 486	7.6	3.4	6 069	81.4
Fannin County	999	19 798	3.1	21.0	19.0	10.4	30 612	12.4	3.9	8 369	82.6
Forsyth County (part)	361	50 134	6.2	26.3	9.1	26.8	58 521	6.7	2.1	18 354	83.7
Gilmer County	1 105	23 456	8.8	24.2	13.2	12.9	35 140	12.5	4.2	9 071	78.1
Gordon County	921	44 104	12.5	26.1	10.4	10.6	38 831	9.9	3.5	16 173	71.7
Gwinnett County (part)	270	43 137	9.9	29.8	6.2	27.4	67 131	2.8	1.8	14 019	93.1
Hall County	1 020	139 277	28.9	26.9	9.4	18.7	44 908	12.4	3.8	47 381	71.1
Murray County	892	36 506	7.2	27.8	8.0	7.2	36 996	12.7	4.0	13 286	73.7
Pickens County	601	22 983	4.6	23.5	13.2	15.6	41 387	9.2	2.3	8 960	82.1
Rockdale County (part)	69	4 497	11.6	24.9	9.5	23.8	49 972	7.2	3.4	1 628	74.4
Walker County	1 157	61 053	6.2	24.6	13.8	10.2	32 406	12.5	4.3	23 605	77.0
Walton County (part)	126	15 889	5.9	29.6	7.5	16.4	57 105	7.7	2.2	5 483	85.0
Whitfield County	751	83 525	27.5	27.1	10.4	12.8	39 377	11.5	3.6	29 385	67.6
Congressional District 11, Georgia	9 585	630 176	38.3	26.0	11.0	16.9	37 582	13.8	5.8	233 726	64.1
Bartow County (part)	692	38 969	17.0	27.0	11.2	15.6	41 869	9.8	4.5	14 033	71.5
Carroll County (part)	436	28 992	29.5	24.9	12.6	16.1	32 348	16.9	5.1	11 268	59.2
Chattooga County	812	25 470	14.3	23.0	14.2	7.7	30 664	14.3	5.6	9 577	75.4
Cobb County (part)	253	203 027	54.1	25.7	7.3	24.3	43 675	11.4	5.6	74 780	55.6
Coweta County (part)	118	15 229	53.3	27.5	14.7	11.3	30 651	23.1	8.1	5 302	54.3
Douglas County (part)	189	33 527	36.3	28.2	6.6	18.4	42 904	11.4	4.1	12 278	66.5
Floyd County	1 329	90 565	21.0	24.5	13.9	15.8	35 615	14.4	6.7	34 028	66.8
Haralson County	731	25 690	7.4	26.1	13.2	9.0	31 656	15.5	4.1	9 826	75.2
Harris County (part)	106	2 320	10.0	20.3	15.5	32.5	59 508	1.4	1.8	962	92.6
Heard County	767	11 012	13.2	28.7	11.6	7.3	33 038	13.6	5.7	4 043	77.3
Meriwether County	1 303	22 534	44.4	26.9	13.8	10.8	31 870	17.8	7.0	8 248	74.1
Muscogee County (part)	247	48 266	58.0	26.5	12.8	16.3	36 100	12.4	7.3	17 703	69.1
Paulding County (part)	62	2 665	11.7	25.3	9.8	14.2	45 079	7.4	1.5	970	84.6
Polk County	806	38 127	22.0	25.9	13.2	8.0	32 328	15.5	6.0	14 012	71.3
Talbot County	1 018	6 498	63.9	24.1	14.4	7.9	26 611	24.2	8.7	2 538	82.7
Troup County (part)	375	31 071	51.3	29.6	13.8	11.1	28 825	20.8	6.1	11 735	54.9
Upson County (part)	342	6 214	50.4	26.1	17.0	13.1	27 305	21.6	7.3	2 423	65.3
Congressional District 12, Georgia	13 530	630 405	48.2	25.3	10.7	19.3	31 108	21.7	8.7	235 515	58.3
Bryan County (part)	902	16 139	22.5	31.1	7.4	12.6	38 226	14.2	3.8	5 652	74.5
Bulloch County	1 767	55 983	32.1	22.3	9.4	25.4	29 499	24.5	10.2	20 743	58.1
Burke County	2 151	22 243	53.2	31.3	11.0	9.5	27 877	28.7	9.3	7 934	76.0
Chatham County (part)	602	180 185	55.1	25.5	12.4	19.0	31 763	19.2	7.2	69 360	54.2
Clarke County	313	101 489	38.0	17.9	8.0	39.8	28 403	28.3	10.2	39 706	42.1

[1]Dry land or land partially or temporarily covered by water.
[2]Persons who do not identify themselves as White alone, not of Hispanic origin.
[3]Persons 25 years old and over.

Table B. 109th Congressional Districts by Counties, 2000—*Continued*

(Number, percent.)

STATE Congressional district County	Land area,[1] (sq km)	Population Total	Percent minority[2]	Percent under 18 years old	Percent 65 years old and over	Percent with bachelor's degree or more[3]	Median income, 1999 (dollars)	Percent living in poverty	Percent unemployed	Households Total	Percent owner occupied
	1	2	3	4	5	6	7	8	9	10	11
Congressional District 12, Georgia—*Continued*											
Effingham County	1 242	37 535	16.2	29.9	8.0	13.6	46 505	9.3	4.2	13 151	82.7
Glascock County	373	2 556	9.9	23.6	18.4	6.5	29 743	17.2	12.3	1 004	80.2
Jefferson County	1 367	17 266	58.0	28.5	13.7	9.1	26 120	23.0	11.8	6 339	72.2
Jenkins County	906	8 575	44.1	28.6	13.9	10.8	24 025	28.4	10.7	3 214	73.4
Oglethorpe County (part)	392	2 218	25.9	27.4	11.5	16.7	37 091	13.5	3.0	820	84.6
Richmond County (part)	591	162 429	61.1	27.5	10.8	13.8	30 887	22.1	10.0	58 490	58.9
Screven County	1 679	15 374	46.9	27.8	14.1	10.2	29 312	20.1	9.4	5 797	77.7
Taliaferro County	506	2 077	61.8	24.3	18.6	8.4	23 750	23.4	9.8	870	77.1
Warren County	739	6 336	60.6	26.5	16.1	8.0	27 366	27.0	9.4	2 435	76.8
Congressional District 13, Georgia	2 014	630 565	57.7	28.5	6.9	19.4	43 429	11.2	5.4	222 171	59.3
Butts County (part)	143	8 922	49.8	26.9	12.2	8.7	34 579	14.5	6.3	3 251	63.9
Clayton County (part)	342	227 342	63.8	29.9	6.0	16.5	43 064	10.2	5.5	78 733	62.1
DeKalb County (part)	35	12 160	93.2	30.8	3.7	24.3	53 581	6.6	6.5	3 938	90.7
Fayette County (part)	21	4 521	66.6	25.9	9.1	39.4	83 246	2.6	1.8	1 534	95.2
Fulton County (part)	418	59 166	71.7	28.4	10.0	14.9	36 760	15.1	6.9	21 666	56.1
Gwinnett County (part)	163	156 321	58.9	26.2	3.9	27.3	47 301	10.0	4.5	55 802	47.9
Henry County (part)	195	41 957	34.7	29.9	7.1	20.4	50 405	7.2	3.3	14 686	75.3
Newton County (part)	236	31 231	38.5	27.6	11.6	14.7	40 006	13.1	7.4	11 214	66.0
Rockdale County (part)	215	46 936	34.9	27.7	9.8	22.9	48 639	10.4	4.8	16 218	67.8
Spalding County (part)	93	27 754	57.1	29.9	11.4	7.9	27 635	22.5	8.6	10 107	46.1
Walton County (part)	153	14 255	46.7	29.8	11.3	9.2	33 750	16.7	6.8	5 022	55.4
HAWAII	16 635	1 211 537	77.2	24.3	13.3	26.2	49 820	10.7	6.3	403 240	56.5
Congressional District 1, Hawaii	494	606 610	82.3	21.6	15.2	28.9	50 798	9.7	5.8	209 847	53.1
Honolulu County (part)	494	606 610	82.3	21.6	15.2	28.9	50 798	9.7	5.8	209 847	53.1
Congressional District 2, Hawaii	16 140	604 927	72.1	27.0	11.4	23.1	48 686	11.7	6.8	193 393	60.2
Hawaii County	10 433	148 677	70.5	26.1	13.4	22.1	39 805	15.7	8.0	52 985	64.5
Honolulu County (part)	1 059	269 546	74.7	28.4	9.7	25.1	55 736	10.2	7.4	76 603	58.6
Kalawao County	34	147	90.5	0.0	49.7	10.2	9 333	40.1	0.0	115	0.0
Kauai County	1 612	58 463	72.3	26.4	13.9	19.4	45 020	10.5	5.3	20 183	61.3
Maui County	3 002	128 094	68.1	25.5	11.5	22.4	49 489	10.5	5.0	43 507	57.5
IDAHO	214 314	1 293 953	12.0	28.5	11.3	21.7	37 572	11.8	5.8	469 645	72.4
Congressional District 1, Idaho	102 369	648 922	11.1	28.1	11.6	20.3	38 364	11.0	6.2	237 288	75.7
Ada County (part)	2 261	164 438	8.4	30.7	7.8	28.5	52 281	5.5	3.6	56 010	83.2
Adams County	3 534	3 476	5.2	23.7	16.3	14.9	28 423	15.1	7.7	1 421	79.0
Benewah County	2 010	9 171	12.2	26.8	14.3	11.4	31 517	14.1	13.9	3 580	78.4
Boise County	4 927	6 670	6.2	27.0	11.1	19.9	38 651	12.9	7.2	2 616	83.3
Bonner County	4 501	36 835	4.6	25.4	13.2	16.9	32 803	15.5	7.3	14 693	77.8
Boundary County	3 286	9 871	6.6	29.2	13.4	14.7	31 250	15.7	10.0	3 707	78.4
Canyon County	1 527	131 441	22.4	31.0	10.9	14.9	35 884	12.0	5.9	45 018	73.3
Clearwater County	6 375	8 930	6.6	22.9	15.6	13.4	32 071	13.5	11.5	3 456	77.9
Gem County	1 457	15 181	9.9	28.0	15.7	11.4	34 460	13.1	5.1	5 539	79.9
Idaho County	21 976	15 511	6.6	25.0	16.7	14.4	29 515	16.3	10.2	6 084	77.0
Kootenai County	3 225	108 685	6.0	27.1	12.3	19.1	37 754	10.5	7.8	41 308	74.5
Latah County	2 789	34 935	7.5	20.3	9.4	41.0	32 524	16.7	7.6	13 059	58.7
Lewis County	1 241	3 747	8.9	25.1	18.4	14.8	31 413	12.0	8.6	1 554	74.5
Nez Perce County	2 199	37 410	9.0	23.7	16.8	18.9	36 282	12.2	4.6	15 286	68.7
Owyhee County	19 886	10 644	28.7	31.3	12.3	10.2	28 339	16.9	6.8	3 710	69.7
Payette County	1 055	20 578	15.4	30.3	13.3	10.6	33 046	13.2	6.2	7 371	74.2
Shoshone County	6 822	13 771	4.6	23.0	17.4	10.2	28 535	16.4	11.8	5 906	72.6
Valley County	9 526	7 651	4.0	23.7	14.7	26.3	36 927	9.3	6.1	3 208	79.1
Washington County	3 772	9 977	17.5	27.1	17.2	12.7	30 625	13.3	7.8	3 762	73.8
Congressional District 2, Idaho	111 946	645 031	12.9	28.8	11.0	23.1	36 934	12.6	5.4	232 357	69.0
Ada County (part)	471	136 466	10.7	22.9	10.7	34.2	40 077	10.3	4.3	57 398	58.4
Bannock County	2 883	75 565	10.4	28.0	10.3	24.9	36 683	13.9	6.9	27 192	70.6
Bear Lake County	2 516	6 411	3.6	32.8	15.8	11.7	32 162	9.6	7.2	2 259	83.2
Bingham County	5 425	41 735	21.1	35.0	10.4	14.4	36 423	12.4	5.8	13 317	79.4
Blaine County	6 850	18 991	13.2	23.9	7.7	43.1	50 496	7.8	4.2	7 780	68.7
Bonneville County	4 839	82 522	9.6	32.0	10.2	26.1	41 805	10.1	5.0	28 753	74.7
Butte County	5 783	2 899	9.6	28.9	14.9	13.0	30 473	18.2	5.8	1 089	77.1
Camas County	2 784	991	3.4	24.7	13.1	22.2	34 167	8.3	4.0	396	77.8
Caribou County	4 574	7 304	4.8	31.7	13.6	15.9	37 609	9.6	4.8	2 560	79.5
Cassia County	6 647	21 416	20.5	34.0	12.7	13.9	33 322	13.6	5.2	7 060	72.6
Clark County	4 570	1 022	37.4	34.8	9.2	12.6	31 576	19.9	6.1	340	68.2
Custer County	12 757	4 342	5.7	25.7	14.4	17.4	32 174	14.3	6.2	1 770	74.7
Elmore County	7 971	29 130	20.1	27.8	7.1	17.3	35 256	11.2	6.6	9 092	57.4
Franklin County	1 723	11 329	6.6	37.2	11.7	13.6	36 061	7.4	5.3	3 476	80.8
Fremont County	4 835	11 819	13.1	33.1	12.5	12.0	33 424	14.2	5.3	3 885	84.3

[1]Dry land or land partially or temporarily covered by water.
[2]Persons who do not identify themselves as White alone, not of Hispanic origin.
[3]Persons 25 years old and over.

Table B. 109th Congressional Districts by Counties, 2000—*Continued*

(Number, percent.)

STATE Congressional district County	Land area,[1] (sq km)	Population				Percent with bachelor's degree or more[3]	Median income, 1999 (dollars)	Percent living in poverty	Percent unem- ployed	Households	
		Total	Percent minority[2]	Percent under 18 years old	Percent 65 years old and over					Total	Percent owner occupied
	1	2	3	4	5	6	7	8	9	10	11
Congressional District 2, Idaho—*Continued*											
Gooding County	1 893	14 155	19.5	29.7	15.5	12.0	31 888	13.8	3.4	5 046	72.4
Jefferson County	2 836	19 155	11.6	36.2	9.3	15.2	37 737	10.4	4.4	5 901	84.7
Jerome County	1 554	18 342	19.9	31.6	12.3	14.0	34 696	13.9	5.9	6 298	70.0
Lemhi County	11 821	7 806	4.2	25.5	16.7	17.9	30 185	15.3	8.6	3 275	76.1
Lincoln County	3 122	4 044	17.0	30.5	13.2	13.0	32 484	13.1	3.9	1 447	74.4
Madison County	1 221	27 467	5.6	26.2	6.0	24.4	32 607	30.5	7.3	7 129	59.2
Minidoka County	1 967	20 174	27.8	31.6	13.1	10.1	32 021	14.8	6.5	6 973	76.9
Oneida County	3 109	4 125	3.9	32.0	16.0	15.0	34 309	10.8	4.3	1 430	82.3
Power County	3 640	7 538	25.5	33.8	10.2	14.3	32 226	16.1	4.7	2 560	74.5
Teton County	1 166	5 999	13.0	31.8	7.4	28.1	41 968	12.9	3.3	2 078	73.7
Twin Falls County	4 986	64 284	12.3	27.8	14.1	16.0	34 506	12.7	5.9	23 853	68.3
ILLINOIS	143 961	12 419 293	32.2	26.1	12.1	26.1	46 590	10.7	6.0	4 591 779	67.3
Congressional District 1, Illinois	253	654 203	72.6	28.3	12.6	18.7	37 222	19.7	12.9	233 426	54.4
Cook County (part)	253	654 203	72.6	28.3	12.6	18.7	37 222	19.7	12.9	233 426	54.4
Congressional District 2, Illinois	478	654 078	74.5	29.5	11.6	18.1	41 330	15.2	10.4	228 365	66.2
Cook County (part)	457	643 430	74.5	29.4	11.7	18.0	41 199	15.4	10.5	224 654	66.3
Will County (part)	21	10 648	72.8	33.0	6.5	25.5	51 516	7.0	5.9	3 711	60.3
Congressional District 3, Illinois	322	653 292	31.9	25.7	14.5	20.5	48 048	8.3	5.7	236 791	72.6
Cook County (part)	322	653 292	31.9	25.7	14.5	20.5	48 048	8.3	5.7	236 791	72.6
Congressional District 4, Illinois	101	653 654	81.4	31.7	6.2	13.6	35 935	20.2	9.3	193 008	39.2
Cook County (part)	101	653 654	81.4	31.7	6.2	13.6	35 935	20.2	9.3	193 008	39.2
Congressional District 5, Illinois	148	654 116	34.2	19.8	11.7	33.9	48 531	8.5	4.8	266 664	49.8
Cook County (part)	148	654 116	34.2	19.8	11.7	33.9	48 531	8.5	4.8	266 664	49.8
Congressional District 6, Illinois	553	654 549	24.8	26.0	10.3	34.6	62 640	4.3	3.6	232 718	75.8
Cook County (part)	158	165 297	32.7	24.9	9.9	28.8	57 218	5.0	4.0	60 049	71.6
DuPage County (part)	395	489 252	22.1	26.4	10.4	36.6	65 217	4.1	3.5	172 669	77.3
Congressional District 7, Illinois	146	653 521	72.7	26.6	9.6	32.1	40 361	24.0	12.2	250 442	41.9
Cook County (part)	146	653 521	72.7	26.6	9.6	32.1	40 361	24.0	12.2	250 442	41.9
Congressional District 8, Illinois	1 600	652 805	21.1	28.2	8.1	32.1	62 762	4.4	3.4	234 592	77.6
Cook County (part)	234	221 890	28.8	25.0	8.4	35.7	61 395	4.2	3.3	85 163	71.3
Lake County (part)	784	329 213	19.4	30.1	7.7	33.1	66 100	4.5	3.5	113 624	81.5
McHenry County (part)	582	101 702	9.8	28.9	8.9	20.9	58 300	4.5	3.4	35 805	80.5
Congressional District 9, Illinois	195	653 117	37.6	20.4	15.6	39.6	46 531	11.0	5.3	268 430	54.7
Cook County (part)	195	653 117	37.6	20.4	15.6	39.6	46 531	11.0	5.3	268 430	54.7
Congressional District 10, Illinois	646	654 062	24.9	27.0	12.3	47.5	71 663	4.8	3.8	229 591	78.7
Cook County (part)	271	338 919	16.3	25.5	15.0	49.9	74 472	2.7	2.5	126 918	82.6
Lake County (part)	375	315 143	34.1	28.5	9.4	44.6	68 514	7.0	5.2	102 673	73.7
Congressional District 11, Illinois	10 984	653 861	16.4	26.7	11.9	18.5	47 800	8.4	5.7	236 533	74.6
Bureau County (part)	1 794	28 108	6.5	24.9	17.7	15.6	40 353	7.3	4.3	11 280	76.5
Grundy County	1 088	37 535	6.1	26.8	12.2	15.2	51 719	4.8	4.6	14 293	72.3
Kankakee County	1 753	103 833	22.1	27.0	13.1	15.0	41 532	11.4	6.4	38 182	69.4
La Salle County	2 939	111 509	8.2	25.1	16.5	13.3	40 308	9.1	5.4	43 417	75.1
Livingston County (part)	94	399	2.3	24.6	10.0	10.6	48 304	1.8	1.8	145	82.1
McLean County (part)	1 351	81 911	13.1	21.3	9.1	27.6	39 534	14.1	9.3	29 316	61.8
Will County (part)	1 730	287 466	21.0	29.0	9.9	20.7	57 621	6.3	4.7	98 713	80.3
Woodford County (part)	236	3 100	1.3	27.9	19.0	15.5	45 564	7.5	3.7	1 187	80.1
Congressional District 12, Illinois	11 460	653 456	20.3	25.1	14.5	16.8	35 198	15.0	7.0	255 599	69.4
Alexander County	612	9 590	37.8	25.9	16.8	6.9	26 042	26.1	10.6	3 808	72.0
Franklin County	1 067	39 018	2.1	23.1	18.6	11.3	28 411	16.2	6.8	16 408	77.7
Jackson County	1 523	59 612	20.3	19.2	11.1	32.0	24 946	25.2	7.9	24 215	53.3
Madison County (part)	304	120 972	14.7	25.5	15.4	11.4	35 080	14.0	7.6	49 106	70.0
Monroe County	1 006	27 619	1.4	26.5	13.3	20.4	55 320	3.4	2.5	10 275	80.2
Perry County	1 142	23 094	10.7	21.9	16.1	10.1	33 281	13.2	8.0	8 504	78.6
Pulaski County	520	7 348	34.1	27.4	17.4	7.1	25 361	24.7	9.6	2 893	75.7
Randolph County	1 498	33 893	11.8	22.2	15.5	8.6	37 013	10.0	5.7	12 084	79.4
St. Clair County	1 719	256 082	33.1	27.7	13.1	19.3	39 148	14.5	6.8	96 810	67.0
Union County	1 078	18 293	5.1	23.2	17.5	15.8	30 994	16.5	10.7	7 290	75.4
Williamson County (part)	991	57 935	5.1	23.2	16.7	17.1	31 586	14.9	6.7	24 206	73.0
Congressional District 13, Illinois	918	652 879	18.5	28.2	8.8	42.4	71 686	2.9	3.2	230 918	80.7
Cook County (part)	164	85 302	7.8	28.0	12.4	33.3	74 639	2.9	2.9	28 636	91.5
DuPage County (part)	338	363 425	18.7	26.5	9.5	49.7	71 701	2.8	2.9	137 164	74.5
Will County (part)	416	204 152	22.5	31.2	6.0	32.5	70 750	2.9	3.8	65 118	88.9

[1]Dry land or land partially or temporarily covered by water.
[2]Persons who do not identify themselves as White alone, not of Hispanic origin.
[3]Persons 25 years old and over.

Table B. 109th Congressional Districts by Counties, 2000—*Continued*

(Number, percent.)

STATE Congressional district County	Land area,[1] (sq km)	Population Total	Percent minority[2]	Percent under 18 years old	Percent 65 years old and over	Percent with bachelor's degree or more[3]	Median income, 1999 (dollars)	Percent living in poverty	Percent unem-ployed	Households Total	Percent owner occupied
	1	2	3	4	5	6	7	8	9	10	11
Congressional District 14, Illinois	7 386	654 031	26.1	28.7	9.0	26.3	56 314	7.0	4.7	220 953	74.8
Bureau County (part)	282	923	2.4	29.6	14.4	8.7	32 241	13.8	3.4	331	68.0
DeKalb County (part)	1 011	73 039	16.5	22.0	9.7	28.8	43 323	13.1	6.6	25 958	55.3
DuPage County (part)	131	51 484	31.4	30.8	5.3	31.3	71 911	4.9	3.4	15 768	83.0
Henry County (part)	1 321	22 762	2.0	26.0	15.8	19.7	46 230	5.8	3.1	8 745	80.0
Kane County	1 348	404 119	32.4	30.3	8.3	27.7	59 351	6.7	4.7	133 901	76.0
Kendall County	830	54 544	11.5	29.5	8.4	25.3	64 625	3.0	2.9	18 798	84.1
Lee County	1 879	36 062	9.7	24.2	14.7	13.2	40 967	7.7	5.3	13 253	73.9
Whiteside County (part)	584	11 098	8.6	24.8	15.6	8.9	41 096	10.7	4.7	4 199	78.6
Congressional District 15, Illinois	26 088	653 618	11.5	23.5	14.0	23.2	38 583	11.7	5.0	257 248	68.8
Champaign County	2 582	179 669	22.3	21.0	9.8	38.0	37 780	16.1	5.5	70 597	55.7
Clark County	1 299	17 008	1.4	24.8	17.9	13.6	35 967	9.2	4.8	6 971	77.5
Coles County	1 316	53 196	5.4	19.7	13.3	20.8	32 286	17.5	5.5	21 043	61.9
Crawford County	1 149	20 452	8.0	22.8	16.7	10.3	32 531	11.2	5.4	7 842	80.2
Cumberland County	896	11 253	1.5	26.6	15.9	10.1	36 149	9.5	5.4	4 368	82.0
De Witt County	1 030	16 798	2.7	24.6	15.9	13.4	41 256	8.2	5.3	6 770	74.9
Douglas County	1 080	19 922	5.0	27.1	16.0	13.8	39 439	6.4	2.8	7 574	76.9
Edgar County	1 615	19 704	2.8	23.8	17.8	13.3	35 203	10.5	4.8	7 874	74.6
Edwards County (part)	68	1 115	1.6	24.3	15.8	6.7	30 185	6.5	4.9	474	75.7
Ford County	1 258	14 241	2.7	25.9	19.4	13.9	38 073	7.0	3.3	5 639	76.0
Gallatin County (part)	208	1 180	1.4	24.6	16.8	5.0	24 808	21.4	7.9	491	83.1
Iroquois County	2 892	31 334	5.6	25.5	18.1	11.8	38 071	8.7	3.8	12 220	76.4
Lawrence County (part)	516	8 709	2.5	21.9	22.9	11.9	28 838	14.3	6.3	3 614	74.8
Livingston County (part)	2 610	39 279	9.2	25.0	15.3	12.7	41 281	8.9	5.3	14 229	74.1
McLean County (part)	1 714	68 522	10.5	25.9	10.6	44.7	56 432	5.1	2.2	27 430	71.5
Macon County (part)	394	15 396	4.6	23.1	16.1	23.1	51 969	4.6	3.9	6 087	87.7
Moultrie County	869	14 287	1.8	25.5	17.7	14.7	40 084	7.8	3.3	5 405	78.4
Piatt County	1 140	16 365	2.3	25.2	15.4	21.0	45 752	5.0	2.9	6 475	80.3
Saline County (part)	142	6 468	1.6	24.4	21.8	9.6	26 118	18.7	9.6	2 722	75.2
Vermilion County	2 329	83 919	15.5	25.0	16.0	12.5	34 071	13.3	7.6	33 406	71.8
Wabash County (part)	303	10 773	2.8	24.1	17.8	12.6	34 525	14.1	6.7	4 344	73.1
White County (part)	680	4 028	2.6	22.2	18.9	7.3	34 222	12.6	4.1	1 673	79.1
Congressional District 16, Illinois	10 614	653 467	14.3	27.6	12.0	21.1	48 960	7.3	4.9	244 751	75.5
Boone County	728	41 786	14.9	29.8	10.7	14.5	52 397	7.0	4.4	14 597	78.6
Carroll County	1 151	16 674	3.8	24.4	19.2	13.1	37 148	9.6	6.9	6 794	76.7
DeKalb County (part)	631	15 930	6.5	28.8	10.0	19.1	55 225	4.0	3.5	5 716	79.4
Jo Daviess County	1 557	22 289	2.0	23.1	17.9	15.2	40 411	6.7	4.0	9 218	77.3
McHenry County (part)	981	158 375	10.6	31.1	7.4	32.2	69 221	3.1	3.5	53 598	84.9
Ogle County	1 965	51 032	7.7	27.4	13.4	17.0	45 448	7.1	4.6	19 278	74.5
Stephenson County	1 461	48 979	11.4	25.2	16.3	15.6	40 366	9.0	6.2	19 785	74.8
Whiteside County (part)	810	19 984	4.7	24.5	17.0	14.4	42 154	5.6	3.8	7 785	77.7
Winnebago County	1 331	278 418	20.7	26.4	12.7	19.4	43 886	9.6	5.8	107 980	70.1
Congressional District 17, Illinois	21 031	653 531	12.7	24.0	16.2	14.7	35 066	12.5	6.8	260 924	71.0
Adams County (part)	775	55 875	5.9	24.5	18.1	19.3	33 936	10.5	5.3	22 272	71.8
Calhoun County	657	5 084	1.6	23.0	19.1	9.4	34 375	9.0	4.9	2 046	80.8
Christian County (part)	127	6 892	1.3	24.6	20.7	7.3	30 553	15.5	4.9	2 800	73.2
Fayette County (part)	281	2 495	0.6	26.4	16.3	7.9	29 973	12.2	5.8	982	79.4
Fulton County	2 242	38 250	5.5	22.0	18.3	11.4	33 952	9.9	6.7	14 877	76.3
Greene County (part)	951	8 443	2.4	25.6	16.7	8.8	30 866	14.6	7.3	3 270	76.5
Hancock County	2 058	20 121	1.3	24.6	18.2	15.6	36 654	8.3	4.8	8 069	80.3
Henderson County	981	8 213	2.3	23.3	16.7	10.0	36 405	9.5	5.2	3 365	78.9
Henry County (part)	811	28 258	7.7	24.8	16.8	12.4	35 813	9.8	5.5	11 311	77.8
Jersey County (part)	419	3 736	3.1	26.8	11.7	11.6	42 354	7.1	8.0	1 369	80.6
Knox County (part)	1 029	49 414	13.0	21.7	17.5	14.7	34 940	11.8	7.0	19 462	70.2
McDonough County	1 526	32 913	7.5	17.7	14.1	26.9	32 141	19.8	11.1	12 360	63.1
Macon County (part)	374	69 874	23.2	24.9	15.3	13.5	31 915	18.1	9.6	28 742	64.7
Macoupin County	2 237	49 019	2.4	24.7	17.5	11.8	36 190	9.4	5.2	19 253	79.0
Madison County (part)	81	1 760	1.6	25.0	16.4	10.0	40 000	7.9	6.0	722	84.5
Mercer County	1 453	16 957	1.9	24.7	16.0	12.6	40 893	7.8	5.9	6 624	79.7
Montgomery County (part)	752	15 259	1.9	25.1	17.5	10.8	31 722	16.0	6.3	6 144	76.5
Pike County (part)	809	4 808	1.1	25.4	17.0	9.0	29 572	13.4	6.6	1 957	81.3
Rock Island County	1 105	149 374	18.5	23.8	15.0	17.1	38 608	10.7	6.3	60 712	69.7
Sangamon County (part)	298	36 546	36.7	28.3	13.7	12.7	27 308	24.0	9.5	14 993	52.2
Shelby County (part)	278	1 934	0.9	27.3	17.8	3.5	33 594	11.8	5.8	728	85.6
Warren County	1 405	18 735	5.6	23.1	16.4	15.8	36 224	9.2	6.5	7 166	74.4
Whiteside County (part)	380	29 571	17.0	25.7	15.8	10.1	38 760	9.5	5.7	11 700	70.8

[1]Dry land or land partially or temporarily covered by water.
[2]Persons who do not identify themselves as White alone, not of Hispanic origin.
[3]Persons 25 years old and over.

Table B. 109th Congressional Districts by Counties, 2000—*Continued*

(Number, percent.)

STATE Congressional district County	Land area,[1] (sq km)	Population Total	Population Percent minority[2]	Population Percent under 18 years old	Population Percent 65 years old and over	Percent with bachelor's degree or more[3]	Median income, 1999 (dollars)	Percent living in poverty	Percent unem- ployed	Households Total	Households Percent owner occupied
	1	2	3	4	5	6	7	8	9	10	11
Congressional District 18, Illinois	21 202	653 426	10.0	24.3	15.1	20.7	41 934	8.9	4.6	257 236	73.6
Adams County (part)	1 444	12 402	2.9	27.0	14.9	10.2	37 912	7.8	3.7	4 588	83.1
Brown County	792	6 950	22.1	17.7	12.7	9.2	35 445	8.5	3.5	2 108	74.1
Bureau County (part)	173	6 472	7.3	23.8	18.2	17.0	40 721	6.2	4.9	2 571	74.8
Cass County	974	13 695	10.0	25.3	15.6	12.6	35 243	12.0	5.8	5 347	75.2
Knox County (part)	826	6 422	1.9	23.4	17.4	13.9	38 376	6.3	2.8	2 594	81.5
Logan County	1 601	31 183	9.0	21.9	14.9	14.2	39 389	8.1	6.3	11 113	71.3
Macon County (part)	736	29 436	8.8	24.5	15.0	21.2	46 234	5.3	3.5	11 732	80.6
Marshall County	1 000	13 180	2.3	23.4	18.8	14.5	41 576	5.6	3.7	5 225	80.2
Mason County	1 396	16 038	1.9	24.3	17.2	11.2	35 985	9.7	6.1	6 389	76.7
Menard County	814	12 486	2.3	26.6	13.3	20.5	46 596	8.2	3.9	4 873	78.9
Morgan County	1 473	36 616	8.1	22.7	15.7	19.9	36 933	9.7	6.1	14 039	70.3
Peoria County	1 605	183 433	21.5	25.1	14.1	23.3	39 978	13.7	5.8	72 733	67.8
Pike County (part)	1 341	12 576	3.5	23.6	20.1	10.3	31 755	12.0	6.1	4 919	75.6
Putnam County	414	6 086	4.8	25.1	16.0	12.1	45 492	5.5	4.9	2 415	82.3
Sangamon County (part)	1 274	86 539	7.7	23.1	14.8	31.8	46 424	5.8	2.9	36 931	72.3
Schuyler County	1 133	7 189	1.5	23.2	19.3	11.7	35 233	10.1	5.7	2 975	79.0
Scott County	650	5 537	0.8	24.9	16.5	12.1	36 566	9.7	4.6	2 222	77.6
Stark County	746	6 332	2.4	25.1	19.1	13.4	35 826	8.6	6.9	2 525	77.4
Tazewell County	1 681	128 485	3.2	24.3	14.9	18.1	45 250	6.3	4.0	50 327	76.1
Woodford County (part)	1 132	32 369	2.2	26.6	14.5	21.7	52 071	4.0	2.6	11 610	83.0
Congressional District 19, Illinois	29 833	653 627	6.0	24.3	15.3	17.1	38 955	9.1	4.7	253 590	78.1
Bond County	985	17 633	10.2	21.9	14.6	15.0	37 680	9.3	5.3	6 155	79.6
Christian County (part)	1 709	28 480	4.9	23.9	16.5	11.3	38 342	8.1	4.9	11 121	77.0
Clay County	1 215	14 560	1.3	23.9	19.2	9.7	30 599	11.8	5.6	5 839	79.8
Clinton County	1 228	35 535	6.4	24.9	14.5	13.0	44 618	6.4	3.3	12 754	80.3
Edwards County (part)	508	5 856	1.8	22.8	19.0	10.4	32 102	10.4	3.7	2 431	82.3
Effingham County	1 240	34 264	2.0	28.6	13.9	15.1	39 379	8.1	4.5	13 001	76.0
Fayette County (part)	1 574	19 307	7.2	23.3	15.9	9.2	32 025	12.2	5.8	7 164	79.8
Gallatin County (part)	631	5 265	2.9	21.7	18.3	8.3	26 269	20.5	6.7	2 235	80.6
Greene County (part)	455	6 318	1.7	25.1	18.6	11.8	32 702	9.5	3.5	2 487	76.3
Hamilton County	1 127	8 621	2.5	24.0	19.2	10.5	30 496	12.9	4.6	3 462	81.5
Hardin County	462	4 800	5.6	20.5	18.6	9.6	27 693	18.6	5.9	1 987	80.5
Jasper County	1 280	10 117	0.8	25.9	16.5	11.2	34 721	9.9	3.5	3 930	83.2
Jefferson County	1 479	40 045	11.2	24.3	15.3	13.7	33 555	12.3	5.6	15 374	74.4
Jersey County (part)	537	17 932	2.4	25.2	14.9	12.8	42 003	7.1	5.5	6 727	77.1
Johnson County	893	12 878	17.1	18.6	13.5	11.7	33 326	11.3	7.5	4 183	84.9
Lawrence County (part)	448	6 743	1.9	23.7	16.7	6.8	31 836	12.8	6.2	2 695	79.9
Madison County (part)	1 493	136 209	7.5	24.4	13.2	26.3	50 207	6.0	3.5	52 125	77.3
Marion County	1 482	41 691	6.2	25.5	16.6	12.1	35 227	11.3	7.0	16 619	76.6
Massac County	619	15 161	7.9	22.9	17.8	10.7	31 498	13.5	5.9	6 261	78.6
Montgomery County (part)	1 071	15 393	9.0	22.1	16.4	11.6	34 783	10.5	4.8	5 363	80.4
Pope County	961	4 413	7.0	21.5	17.7	10.5	30 048	18.2	11.2	1 769	82.1
Richland County	933	16 149	1.9	24.5	17.6	15.2	31 185	12.9	7.4	6 660	76.4
Saline County (part)	851	20 265	7.5	23.9	17.9	12.9	29 869	12.8	7.3	8 270	76.9
Sangamon County (part)	676	65 866	6.6	25.4	12.1	32.2	49 174	5.8	3.0	26 798	76.8
Shelby County (part)	1 686	20 959	1.2	24.7	17.7	12.2	37 762	8.9	3.5	8 328	80.6
Wabash County (part)	276	2 164	1.4	24.7	13.0	12.0	34 325	14.3	5.9	848	85.8
Washington County	1 457	15 148	1.7	25.3	16.7	13.4	40 932	6.0	3.2	5 848	81.0
Wayne County	1 849	17 151	2.2	23.8	18.8	10.0	30 481	12.4	6.6	7 143	79.6
White County (part)	602	11 343	1.7	21.2	21.6	11.6	28 301	12.5	6.3	4 861	77.6
Williamson County (part)	106	3 361	13.1	18.5	14.0	17.9	46 033	9.0	7.2	1 152	87.8
INDIANA	92 895	6 080 485	14.1	25.9	12.4	19.4	41 567	9.5	4.9	2 336 306	71.4
Congressional District 1, Indiana	5 722	675 541	30.3	26.6	12.6	17.1	44 087	10.5	6.5	252 348	71.0
Benton County	1 052	9 421	4.7	27.5	15.8	13.0	39 813	5.5	3.3	3 558	75.8
Jasper County	1 450	30 043	4.2	27.5	12.4	13.0	43 369	6.7	6.0	10 686	77.5
Lake County	1 287	484 564	39.5	26.8	13.0	16.2	41 829	12.2	7.5	181 633	69.0
Newton County	1 041	14 566	4.5	26.5	13.0	9.6	40 944	6.9	4.4	5 340	80.0
Porter County (part)	892	136 947	8.2	25.6	10.9	22.2	52 345	6.1	4.0	51 131	75.6
Congressional District 2, Indiana	9 529	675 685	15.5	26.1	13.3	17.2	40 381	9.5	5.0	256 650	72.8
Carroll County	964	20 165	3.8	26.3	14.0	12.9	42 677	6.8	3.9	7 718	79.7
Cass County	1 069	40 930	9.5	25.8	14.4	12.0	39 193	7.6	4.0	15 715	73.6
Elkhart County (part)	189	85 958	23.8	28.4	10.8	13.5	40 139	10.1	4.6	32 282	66.2
Fulton County	954	20 511	5.0	25.8	15.3	10.3	38 290	7.6	4.7	8 082	78.3
Howard County (part)	76	35 837	16.2	25.3	14.4	12.7	34 063	14.2	6.7	15 454	64.1
LaPorte County	1 549	110 106	15.1	24.5	13.6	14.0	41 430	8.7	4.3	41 050	75.2
Marshall County	1 151	45 128	7.7	28.0	13.2	14.9	42 581	6.8	4.2	16 519	76.8
Porter County (part)	191	9 851	3.2	26.3	9.8	27.3	64 091	4.1	3.4	3 518	90.9
Pulaski County	1 123	13 755	3.9	26.9	15.3	10.3	35 422	8.3	4.3	5 170	80.7
St. Joseph County	1 185	265 559	19.2	25.7	13.6	23.6	40 420	10.4	5.6	100 743	71.7

[1] Dry land or land partially or temporarily covered by water.
[2] Persons who do not identify themselves as White alone, not of Hispanic origin.
[3] Persons 25 years old and over.

Table B. 109th Congressional Districts by Counties, 2000—*Continued*

(Number, percent.)

STATE Congressional district County	Land area,[1] (sq km)	Population Total	Population Percent minority[2]	Population Percent under 18 years old	Population Percent 65 years old and over	Percent with bachelor's degree or more[3]	Median income, 1999 (dollars)	Percent living in poverty	Percent unem-ployed	Households Total	Households Percent owner occupied
	1	2	3	4	5	6	7	8	9	10	11
Congressional District 2, Indiana—*Continued*											
Starke County	801	23 556	3.5	26.7	13.8	8.4	37 243	11.1	6.2	8 740	80.8
White County (part)	276	4 329	3.3	26.0	14.2	7.2	41 684	5.0	3.2	1 659	82.2
Congressional District 3, Indiana	8 391	675 533	12.3	28.2	11.4	18.4	44 013	7.8	3.9	252 847	75.0
Allen County (part)	1 330	319 253	18.6	27.6	11.4	23.1	42 472	9.3	4.7	124 188	70.4
DeKalb County	940	40 285	2.9	28.2	11.4	12.4	44 909	5.9	4.2	15 134	81.5
Elkhart County (part)	1 013	96 833	10.3	29.2	11.0	17.3	49 089	5.8	2.6	33 872	78.0
Kosciusko County	1 392	74 057	7.1	27.7	12.0	14.9	43 939	6.4	3.4	27 283	78.9
LaGrange County	983	34 909	4.3	33.7	10.0	8.9	42 848	7.7	2.5	11 225	81.4
Noble County	1 065	46 275	8.6	28.9	11.0	11.1	42 700	7.9	3.3	16 696	78.0
Steuben County	800	33 214	3.8	25.6	11.9	15.5	44 089	6.7	4.5	12 738	78.3
Whitley County	869	30 707	1.9	26.8	13.1	13.3	45 503	4.9	2.5	11 711	83.3
Congressional District 4, Indiana	10 403	675 272	6.5	25.7	11.0	22.1	45 947	8.0	4.2	252 284	73.5
Boone County	1 095	46 107	2.6	28.3	11.7	27.6	49 632	5.2	3.0	17 081	78.7
Clinton County	1 049	33 866	8.0	27.3	14.6	10.1	40 759	8.6	5.4	12 545	72.9
Fountain County (part)	442	5 974	1.9	27.6	13.7	8.9	39 539	7.4	4.4	2 322	81.5
Hendricks County	1 058	104 093	4.3	28.0	9.7	23.1	55 208	3.6	2.1	37 275	82.9
Johnson County (part)	442	96 991	3.4	27.6	11.1	24.6	53 705	5.2	3.3	36 112	76.1
Lawrence County	1 162	45 922	2.9	24.5	14.8	10.7	36 280	9.8	5.7	18 535	78.9
Marion County (part)	101	40 056	12.0	26.7	9.7	28.7	56 744	4.5	3.3	15 130	83.7
Monroe County (part)	367	28 052	5.0	27.1	10.2	19.7	41 720	7.0	4.0	10 958	75.4
Montgomery County	1 307	37 629	3.6	25.9	13.9	14.7	41 297	8.3	3.9	14 595	73.3
Morgan County	1 053	66 689	2.1	27.2	10.7	12.6	47 739	6.6	3.0	24 437	79.7
Tippecanoe County	1 294	148 955	13.5	20.9	9.0	33.2	38 652	15.4	6.9	55 226	55.9
White County (part)	1 032	20 938	7.9	25.6	15.0	11.1	40 403	7.4	3.5	8 068	75.4
Congressional District 5, Indiana	8 459	675 753	6.7	26.8	11.3	30.6	52 800	5.2	3.3	258 319	76.0
Grant County	1 072	73 403	11.9	23.7	14.9	14.1	36 162	11.8	7.3	28 319	73.2
Hamilton County	1 031	182 740	6.6	30.7	7.5	48.9	71 026	2.9	2.3	65 933	80.9
Hancock County	793	55 391	2.0	26.4	11.3	22.2	56 416	3.0	3.0	20 718	81.4
Howard County (part)	683	49 127	7.3	25.8	12.7	21.9	51 630	6.1	3.6	19 346	77.8
Huntington County	991	38 075	2.8	26.2	14.0	14.2	41 620	5.5	3.8	14 242	77.0
Johnson County (part)	137	5 985	2.3	23.2	9.9	23.0	57 470	3.2	2.8	1 957	76.9
Marion County (part)	248	144 594	9.3	25.1	11.2	43.0	58 597	3.7	2.2	59 532	69.6
Miami County	973	36 082	7.0	26.0	12.9	10.4	39 184	8.0	3.7	13 716	76.0
Shelby County (part)	787	38 819	3.5	26.5	12.0	12.5	43 191	7.8	3.6	14 872	72.1
Tipton County	674	16 577	2.3	25.0	14.6	12.4	48 546	5.1	2.6	6 469	79.9
Wabash County	1 070	34 960	3.5	24.5	15.6	13.7	40 413	6.9	4.5	13 215	75.9
Congressional District 6, Indiana	14 375	675 819	6.6	25.1	14.1	14.7	39 002	9.7	5.2	262 371	74.3
Adams County	879	33 625	4.0	31.2	13.5	10.7	40 625	9.1	2.9	11 818	77.0
Allen County (part)	372	12 596	17.3	27.6	11.3	11.7	48 620	5.9	3.4	4 557	86.6
Bartholomew County (part)	631	37 641	5.1	27.4	11.5	27.7	50 570	5.7	3.4	14 261	80.1
Blackford County	428	14 048	2.4	24.7	15.4	10.3	34 760	8.7	4.4	5 690	78.6
Dearborn County (part)	159	14 607	1.5	30.0	7.3	21.7	61 711	3.4	2.5	4 937	89.4
Decatur County	965	24 555	2.7	26.3	13.3	11.5	40 401	9.3	3.8	9 389	73.2
Delaware County	1 019	118 769	9.8	22.1	13.5	20.4	34 659	15.1	7.1	47 131	67.2
Fayette County	557	25 588	2.8	24.4	15.6	7.8	38 840	7.9	6.4	10 199	71.6
Franklin County	1 000	22 151	1.5	28.1	12.7	12.5	43 530	7.1	4.0	7 868	81.4
Henry County	1 018	48 508	2.2	24.1	15.7	11.7	38 150	7.8	4.9	19 486	77.1
Jay County	994	21 806	3.3	26.9	14.7	9.9	35 700	9.1	4.2	8 405	77.8
Johnson County (part)	251	12 233	5.5	26.1	10.2	11.3	44 550	9.8	4.5	4 365	79.9
Madison County	1 171	133 358	10.8	23.8	14.9	14.4	38 925	9.3	5.7	53 052	74.2
Randolph County	1 173	27 401	2.2	25.3	15.8	9.9	34 544	11.1	5.5	10 937	75.9
Rush County	1 057	18 261	3.3	26.7	14.8	10.3	38 152	7.3	3.7	6 923	74.1
Shelby County (part)	282	4 626	0.9	27.3	13.6	14.3	49 549	5.6	4.0	1 689	85.0
Union County	418	7 349	1.5	27.2	12.9	11.1	36 672	9.7	5.2	2 793	75.0
Wayne County	1 045	71 097	8.5	24.2	15.9	13.7	34 885	11.4	6.5	28 469	68.7
Wells County	958	27 600	2.9	27.4	14.1	14.3	43 934	5.9	3.0	10 402	80.8
Congressional District 7, Indiana	677	675 804	36.9	25.8	11.2	21.2	36 522	13.5	6.3	277 502	55.8
Marion County (part)	677	675 804	36.9	25.8	11.2	21.2	36 522	13.5	6.3	277 502	55.8
Congressional District 8, Indiana	18 238	675 693	6.4	24.4	14.4	15.9	36 732	10.7	5.6	263 037	73.9
Clay County	926	26 556	2.0	26.2	15.1	12.8	36 865	8.7	5.2	10 216	79.1
Daviess County	1 115	29 820	3.4	29.0	14.6	9.7	34 064	13.8	4.3	10 894	78.6
Fountain County (part)	583	11 980	1.5	25.6	16.5	10.6	37 149	9.1	5.1	4 719	76.2
Gibson County	1 266	32 500	4.0	24.8	15.6	12.4	37 515	8.2	5.0	12 847	77.9
Greene County	1 403	33 157	2.0	24.7	15.3	10.5	33 998	11.0	5.4	13 372	80.0

[1]Dry land or land partially or temporarily covered by water.
[2]Persons who do not identify themselves as White alone, not of Hispanic origin.
[3]Persons 25 years old and over.

Table B. 109th Congressional Districts by Counties, 2000—*Continued*

(Number, percent.)

STATE Congressional district County	Land area,[1] (sq km)	Population				Percent with bachelor's degree or more[3]	Median income, 1999 (dollars)	Percent living in poverty	Percent unemployed	Households	
		Total	Percent minority[2]	Percent under 18 years old	Percent 65 years old and over					Total	Percent owner occupied
	1	2	3	4	5	6	7	8	9	10	11
Congressional District 8, Indiana—*Continued*											
Knox County	1 336	39 256	4.3	23.0	15.3	14.4	31 362	16.0	8.7	15 552	68.9
Martin County	871	10 369	1.1	25.2	14.3	8.8	36 411	11.2	5.8	4 183	81.3
Owen County	998	21 786	2.6	26.7	12.8	9.2	36 529	9.4	4.5	8 282	81.6
Parke County	1 152	17 241	3.6	24.0	14.7	11.6	35 724	11.5	4.1	6 415	80.3
Pike County	871	12 837	2.0	24.0	15.3	8.4	34 759	8.0	5.4	5 119	82.7
Posey County	1 058	27 061	2.4	27.3	12.4	14.8	44 209	7.4	4.1	10 205	81.9
Putnam County	1 244	36 019	6.1	23.7	12.4	13.1	38 882	8.0	4.8	12 374	78.6
Sullivan County	1 158	21 751	6.6	22.6	14.1	9.4	32 976	10.9	6.9	7 819	79.8
Vanderburgh County	608	171 922	11.3	23.1	15.3	19.3	36 823	11.2	5.6	70 623	66.8
Vermillion County	665	16 788	2.5	23.8	15.9	11.2	34 837	9.5	5.4	6 762	79.2
Vigo County	1 045	105 848	10.1	22.8	14.3	21.4	33 184	14.1	7.1	40 998	67.4
Warren County	945	8 419	1.4	26.3	14.0	14.0	41 825	6.5	2.9	3 219	80.9
Warrick County	995	52 383	2.3	26.8	10.8	21.8	48 814	5.3	3.8	19 438	83.3
Congressional District 9, Indiana	17 101	675 385	5.9	24.2	12.1	17.3	39 011	10.5	4.3	260 948	71.7
Bartholomew County (part)	423	33 794	9.3	25.3	13.0	15.8	38 426	9.2	4.0	13 675	68.1
Brown County	809	14 957	3.0	23.3	12.9	18.5	43 708	8.9	3.6	5 897	85.0
Clark County	971	96 472	10.5	24.2	12.4	14.3	40 111	8.1	4.5	38 751	70.0
Crawford County	792	10 743	1.3	25.6	12.8	8.4	32 646	16.8	5.3	4 181	82.9
Dearborn County (part)	632	31 502	2.6	26.5	12.9	12.6	42 795	8.1	3.7	11 895	74.1
Dubois County	1 114	39 674	3.2	27.4	12.9	14.5	44 169	5.3	2.5	14 813	78.0
Floyd County	383	70 823	7.3	25.8	12.2	20.4	44 022	8.7	3.9	27 511	72.5
Harrison County	1 257	34 325	2.4	26.0	11.4	13.1	43 423	6.4	4.0	12 917	84.1
Jackson County	1 319	41 335	4.7	25.6	13.3	11.5	39 401	8.5	3.3	16 052	74.2
Jefferson County	936	31 705	4.6	24.4	13.1	16.4	38 189	9.6	5.6	12 148	74.6
Jennings County	977	27 554	3.5	27.7	10.7	8.4	39 402	9.2	7.3	10 134	79.1
Monroe County (part)	654	92 511	11.6	15.1	8.8	47.3	30 632	23.2	4.2	35 940	47.4
Ohio County	225	5 623	1.6	24.8	13.8	11.6	41 348	7.1	4.8	2 201	77.6
Orange County	1 035	19 306	2.4	25.7	14.8	10.2	31 564	12.4	5.1	7 621	79.2
Perry County	988	18 899	2.6	23.0	14.9	9.6	36 246	9.4	4.9	7 270	79.2
Ripley County	1 156	26 523	1.7	28.1	13.4	11.5	41 426	7.5	3.3	9 842	76.9
Scott County	493	22 960	2.3	26.2	11.1	8.8	34 656	13.1	4.5	8 832	75.8
Spencer County	1 033	20 391	2.5	26.5	12.9	13.0	42 451	6.9	4.6	7 569	83.4
Switzerland County	573	9 065	1.5	26.2	12.7	7.6	37 092	13.9	7.7	3 435	77.8
Washington County	1 332	27 223	1.6	26.5	12.1	10.2	36 630	10.6	4.4	10 264	81.1
IOWA	144 701	2 926 324	7.3	25.0	14.9	21.2	39 469	9.1	4.2	1 149 276	72.3
Congressional District 1, Iowa	18 691	585 302	7.8	25.3	14.5	20.0	38 727	10.1	4.7	227 405	72.6
Black Hawk County	1 469	128 012	12.3	23.1	14.0	23.0	37 266	13.1	4.8	49 683	68.9
Bremer County	1 134	23 325	2.3	24.1	15.9	21.5	40 826	5.1	5.8	8 860	78.1
Buchanan County	1 480	21 093	2.5	28.5	14.5	12.7	38 036	9.4	4.3	7 933	78.1
Butler County	1 503	15 305	1.1	24.6	20.2	12.4	35 883	8.0	3.1	6 175	80.4
Clayton County	2 017	18 678	1.8	25.3	18.6	12.8	34 068	8.6	3.7	7 375	76.6
Clinton County	1 800	50 149	4.6	25.6	15.8	14.4	37 423	10.2	5.0	20 105	72.9
Delaware County	1 497	18 404	1.4	29.0	15.0	13.0	37 168	7.9	3.4	6 834	78.0
Dubuque County	1 575	89 143	3.3	25.5	14.8	21.3	39 582	7.8	4.5	33 690	73.5
Fayette County	1 893	22 008	3.1	25.0	19.0	13.8	32 453	10.8	4.6	8 778	75.6
Jackson County	1 647	20 296	1.1	26.0	17.3	12.1	34 529	10.3	3.7	8 078	75.8
Jones County	1 490	20 221	4.3	24.2	15.8	12.7	37 449	8.6	3.9	7 560	75.8
Scott County	1 186	158 668	13.2	26.3	11.9	24.9	42 701	10.5	5.2	62 334	70.5
Congressional District 2, Iowa	19 595	585 241	7.5	24.1	13.3	25.0	40 121	9.9	4.1	232 880	70.8
Appanoose County	1 285	13 721	3.0	23.8	20.0	12.2	28 612	14.5	5.9	5 779	74.1
Cedar County	1 501	18 187	2.0	25.3	16.2	16.3	42 198	5.5	2.3	7 147	76.9
Davis County	1 303	8 541	1.7	27.2	17.4	11.4	32 864	11.9	3.6	3 207	79.8
Des Moines County	1 078	42 351	6.8	24.3	16.7	16.0	36 790	10.7	5.5	17 270	74.2
Henry County	1 125	20 336	6.5	24.6	14.8	16.2	39 087	8.8	4.4	7 626	73.1
Jefferson County	1 128	16 181	4.5	24.5	13.7	31.2	33 851	10.9	4.1	6 649	67.4
Johnson County	1 591	111 006	11.0	20.0	7.5	47.6	40 060	15.0	3.9	44 080	56.7
Lee County	1 340	38 052	7.0	24.3	16.5	12.5	36 193	9.7	5.8	15 161	75.5
Linn County	1 858	191 701	6.8	25.2	12.2	27.7	46 206	6.5	3.5	76 753	72.7
Louisa County	1 041	12 183	13.6	27.7	13.9	12.7	39 086	9.3	4.3	4 519	77.3
Muscatine County	1 136	41 722	14.4	26.9	12.9	17.2	41 803	8.9	3.9	15 847	75.4
Van Buren County	1 256	7 809	1.0	24.7	18.9	11.8	31 094	12.7	3.7	3 181	79.3
Wapello County	1 118	36 051	4.8	23.2	17.8	14.6	32 188	13.2	6.7	14 784	75.6
Washington County	1 473	20 670	3.7	26.1	17.8	16.4	39 103	7.6	2.6	8 056	75.3
Wayne County	1 361	6 730	1.9	23.8	23.6	12.1	29 380	14.0	4.0	2 821	79.5

[1] Dry land or land partially or temporarily covered by water.
[2] Persons who do not identify themselves as White alone, not of Hispanic origin.
[3] Persons 25 years old and over.

Table B. 109th Congressional Districts by Counties, 2000—*Continued*

(Number, percent.)

STATE Congressional district County	Land area,[1] (sq km)	Population				Percent with bachelor's degree or more[3]	Median income, 1999 (dollars)	Percent living in poverty	Percent unem- ployed	Households	
		Total	Percent minority[2]	Percent under 18 years old	Percent 65 years old and over					Total	Percent owner occupied
	1	2	3	4	5	6	7	8	9	10	11
Congressional District 3, Iowa	18 076	585 305	9.8	25.5	13.3	24.6	43 176	8.0	4.4	231 632	71.5
Benton County	1 855	25 308	1.3	27.3	15.4	13.9	42 427	6.1	2.9	9 746	79.4
Grundy County	1 302	12 369	1.4	25.2	19.3	17.2	39 396	4.6	3.6	4 984	79.7
Iowa County	1 519	15 671	1.4	26.3	17.1	15.8	41 222	5.0	2.3	6 163	77.9
Jasper County	1 891	37 213	3.2	24.6	16.0	15.9	41 683	6.5	3.1	14 689	75.7
Keokuk County	1 500	11 400	1.4	25.8	20.2	11.6	34 025	10.1	3.9	4 586	78.8
Lucas County	1 115	9 422	1.8	25.4	19.3	11.1	30 876	13.7	4.9	3 811	78.4
Mahaska County	1 479	22 335	3.7	25.7	16.3	16.5	37 314	9.8	4.5	8 880	71.1
Marion County	1 435	32 052	2.9	25.4	16.0	18.9	42 401	7.6	3.4	12 017	75.5
Monroe County	1 123	8 016	2.0	25.4	19.6	12.6	34 877	9.0	3.7	3 228	78.5
Polk County	1 475	374 601	13.5	25.6	11.1	29.7	46 116	7.9	4.7	149 112	68.8
Poweshiek County	1 515	18 815	3.6	22.6	17.6	18.5	37 836	9.8	5.0	7 398	71.9
Tama County	1 868	18 103	10.1	26.6	18.7	12.9	37 419	10.5	4.0	7 018	77.6
Congressional District 4, Iowa	40 818	585 305	5.2	24.4	16.4	20.4	38 242	8.9	3.9	229 320	73.3
Allamakee County	1 656	14 675	5.1	25.5	18.4	14.4	33 967	9.6	3.9	5 722	76.5
Boone County	1 480	26 224	2.0	24.8	16.4	18.8	40 763	7.6	2.6	10 374	75.6
Calhoun County	1 477	11 115	2.3	22.9	22.1	15.4	33 286	10.1	3.3	4 513	77.4
Cerro Gordo County	1 472	46 447	5.1	24.0	17.7	20.3	35 867	8.5	4.7	19 374	71.5
Chickasaw County	1 307	13 095	1.5	26.0	17.9	12.2	37 649	8.3	6.4	5 192	80.4
Dallas County	1 519	40 750	7.5	28.2	11.1	26.8	48 528	5.6	2.6	15 584	76.4
Emmet County	1 025	11 027	5.1	23.8	19.2	13.0	33 305	8.2	4.7	4 450	75.2
Floyd County	1 296	16 900	2.0	25.2	19.1	14.8	35 237	9.3	4.5	6 828	74.1
Franklin County	1 508	10 704	6.9	24.2	20.5	14.5	36 042	8.0	4.1	4 356	74.8
Greene County	1 472	10 366	2.5	25.6	21.7	14.6	33 883	8.1	4.8	4 205	75.6
Hamilton County	1 494	16 438	3.4	25.5	18.0	17.5	38 658	6.3	2.5	6 692	72.8
Hancock County	1 479	12 100	3.7	26.7	17.8	15.4	37 703	6.0	2.7	4 795	78.2
Hardin County	1 474	18 812	3.5	24.5	20.7	17.1	35 429	8.0	4.4	7 628	74.6
Howard County	1 226	9 932	0.7	26.2	20.0	12.6	34 641	9.3	3.4	3 974	79.2
Humboldt County	1 125	10 381	2.9	24.8	21.0	15.4	38 201	8.3	3.5	4 295	75.9
Kossuth County	2 520	17 163	1.8	25.7	20.1	13.6	34 562	10.2	3.8	6 974	77.6
Madison County	1 453	14 019	2.0	27.0	15.2	14.4	41 845	6.7	4.2	5 326	78.0
Marshall County	1 482	39 311	11.8	25.3	16.6	17.0	38 268	10.2	4.4	15 338	73.8
Mitchell County	1 215	10 874	0.2	26.4	21.5	12.8	34 843	10.7	3.1	4 294	81.5
Palo Alto County	1 460	10 147	2.0	24.2	21.4	13.9	32 409	10.6	2.1	4 119	74.0
Pocahontas County	1 496	8 662	1.0	25.5	21.7	15.0	33 362	9.1	3.3	3 617	79.2
Story County	1 484	79 981	9.6	19.0	9.7	44.5	40 442	14.1	4.4	29 383	58.3
Warren County	1 481	40 671	2.8	27.0	11.8	21.2	50 349	5.1	3.5	14 708	79.9
Webster County	1 852	40 235	7.5	24.5	17.4	16.9	35 334	10.0	4.3	15 878	71.2
Winnebago County	1 037	11 723	3.3	23.9	18.9	16.5	38 381	8.4	3.0	4 749	76.1
Winneshiek County	1 786	21 310	2.9	22.7	15.8	20.5	38 908	8.0	4.5	7 734	73.6
Worth County	1 036	7 909	3.0	24.1	19.4	12.7	36 444	8.3	3.8	3 278	79.0
Wright County	1 504	14 334	5.5	24.5	21.1	13.5	36 197	7.0	3.7	5 940	74.1
Congressional District 5, Iowa	47 520	585 171	6.1	25.7	17.1	16.1	36 773	8.9	3.8	228 039	73.6
Adair County	1 474	8 243	1.3	24.0	22.1	11.2	35 179	7.6	3.4	3 398	75.3
Adams County	1 097	4 482	1.0	23.8	21.3	12.0	30 453	9.3	4.9	1 867	74.8
Audubon County	1 148	6 830	1.2	25.8	23.6	12.3	32 215	7.7	4.1	2 773	79.0
Buena Vista County	1 489	20 411	18.4	25.3	16.8	18.7	35 300	10.5	3.8	7 499	70.5
Carroll County	1 475	21 421	1.4	27.0	18.7	16.0	37 275	6.5	2.4	8 486	74.3
Cass County	1 462	14 684	1.8	23.7	20.8	16.6	32 922	11.1	5.0	6 120	74.6
Cherokee County	1 495	13 035	1.9	24.5	20.3	15.2	35 142	7.3	3.6	5 378	73.5
Clarke County	1 117	9 133	5.0	26.2	17.0	12.1	34 474	8.5	5.9	3 584	72.3
Clay County	1 473	17 372	2.9	24.7	18.0	16.3	35 799	8.2	3.8	7 259	69.2
Crawford County	1 850	16 942	10.8	26.6	17.3	12.4	33 922	11.1	3.6	6 441	73.1
Decatur County	1 377	8 689	3.5	23.1	17.6	15.1	27 343	15.5	7.5	3 337	71.1
Dickinson County	987	16 424	1.6	21.9	20.6	21.3	39 020	6.0	2.8	7 103	78.0
Fremont County	1 324	8 010	3.1	24.9	19.8	14.0	38 345	9.5	2.8	3 199	74.5
Guthrie County	1 530	11 353	2.4	23.5	20.6	14.9	36 495	8.0	3.8	4 641	79.6
Harrison County	1 805	15 666	1.6	26.2	17.7	12.7	38 141	7.1	4.3	6 115	76.6
Ida County	1 118	7 837	1.4	25.5	21.6	13.6	34 805	8.8	3.9	3 213	73.2
Lyon County	1 522	11 763	0.8	28.1	18.7	14.2	36 878	7.0	2.4	4 428	81.7
Mills County	1 131	14 547	2.8	26.7	12.6	16.3	42 428	8.3	4.9	5 324	79.5
Monona County	1 795	10 020	1.7	23.3	23.9	13.4	33 235	9.4	3.8	4 211	76.2
Montgomery County	1 098	11 771	2.3	24.7	20.2	12.9	33 214	9.1	5.0	4 886	73.2
O'Brien County	1 484	15 102	3.0	24.9	21.2	14.7	35 758	7.3	3.0	6 001	76.8
Osceola County	1 033	7 003	3.0	26.0	19.1	13.4	34 274	7.0	3.3	2 778	77.8
Page County	1 385	16 976	4.1	23.3	19.7	16.6	35 466	12.5	6.0	6 708	71.7
Plymouth County	2 237	24 849	2.0	28.3	15.9	19.3	41 638	6.0	1.9	9 372	77.4
Pottawattamie County	2 472	87 704	5.7	25.8	13.8	15.0	40 089	8.4	4.1	33 844	71.1

[1]Dry land or land partially or temporarily covered by water.
[2]Persons who do not identify themselves as White alone, not of Hispanic origin.
[3]Persons 25 years old and over.

Table B. 109th Congressional Districts by Counties, 2000—*Continued*

(Number, percent.)

STATE Congressional district County	Land area,[1] (sq km)	Population				Percent with bachelor's degree or more[3]	Median income, 1999 (dollars)	Percent living in poverty	Percent unem- ployed	Households	
		Total	Percent minority[2]	Percent under 18 years old	Percent 65 years old and over					Total	Percent owner occupied
	1	2	3	4	5	6	7	8	9	10	11
Congressional District 5, Iowa—*Continued*											
Ringgold County	1 393	5 469	1.4	24.0	24.1	13.4	29 110	14.3	4.1	2 245	75.5
Sac County	1 491	11 529	2.6	24.1	22.7	13.6	32 874	9.9	3.1	4 746	76.8
Shelby County	1 530	13 173	1.6	26.3	20.5	15.3	37 442	6.0	2.6	5 173	77.1
Sioux County	1 989	31 589	3.6	27.2	15.0	19.8	40 536	6.4	1.8	10 693	80.4
Taylor County	1 383	6 958	4.6	24.0	22.1	12.0	31 297	12.1	3.9	2 824	76.6
Union County	1 099	12 309	2.4	23.4	18.7	14.7	31 905	11.4	3.9	5 242	72.0
Woodbury County	2 260	103 877	16.2	27.3	13.4	18.9	38 509	10.3	4.2	39 151	68.6
KANSAS	211 900	2 688 418	16.9	26.5	13.2	25.8	40 624	9.9	4.2	1 037 891	69.3
Congressional District 1, Kansas	148 596	672 051	15.4	26.4	16.3	18.0	34 869	11.0	4.1	260 475	71.4
Barber County	2 937	5 307	3.4	24.9	21.5	21.0	33 407	10.1	2.0	2 235	75.3
Barton County	2 315	28 205	11.2	26.0	17.9	16.6	32 176	12.9	5.3	11 393	72.0
Chase County	2 010	3 030	3.7	24.1	18.7	19.6	32 656	8.6	2.7	1 246	73.5
Cheyenne County	2 641	3 165	3.2	23.6	26.6	16.0	30 599	9.4	2.8	1 360	77.4
Clark County	2 524	2 390	6.0	26.3	21.6	22.1	33 857	12.7	2.6	979	76.5
Clay County	1 668	8 822	3.2	24.9	20.8	16.5	33 965	10.1	3.5	3 617	77.0
Cloud County	1 853	10 268	2.5	22.3	23.2	18.0	31 758	10.8	4.3	4 163	74.4
Comanche County	2 042	1 967	2.8	22.3	25.7	15.1	29 415	10.2	0.2	872	73.5
Decatur County	2 314	3 472	3.1	23.6	26.3	15.4	30 257	11.6	1.1	1 494	76.0
Dickinson County	2 196	19 344	5.2	25.8	18.6	15.2	35 975	7.5	3.2	7 903	74.8
Edwards County	1 611	3 449	12.2	24.6	21.3	16.3	30 530	10.4	2.7	1 455	77.5
Ellis County	2 331	27 507	3.9	22.2	14.3	29.2	32 339	12.9	4.1	11 193	63.3
Ellsworth County	1 854	6 525	9.2	20.8	20.2	16.4	35 772	7.2	3.5	2 481	79.6
Finney County	3 372	40 523	48.3	34.3	6.7	14.3	38 474	14.2	4.9	12 948	64.8
Ford County	2 845	32 458	42.8	30.9	11.0	16.4	37 860	12.4	4.9	10 852	64.8
Geary County (part)	927	23 682	38.1	27.7	11.1	15.8	31 837	12.3	5.5	9 377	56.1
Gove County	2 775	3 068	2.9	25.7	22.8	18.4	33 510	10.3	1.9	1 245	79.7
Graham County	2 327	2 946	5.4	22.4	23.5	17.4	31 286	11.5	2.7	1 263	79.3
Grant County	1 489	7 909	36.7	32.7	9.4	15.2	39 854	10.1	4.7	2 742	74.7
Gray County	2 250	5 904	11.1	31.6	12.4	16.3	40 000	9.1	3.2	2 045	72.7
Greeley County	2 015	1 534	12.1	28.7	18.1	17.4	34 605	11.6	2.5	602	75.1
Greenwood County (part)	1 250	2 127	4.7	26.2	20.9	16.3	30 734	14.6	3.6	862	75.4
Hamilton County	2 581	2 670	22.5	28.0	18.2	17.4	32 033	15.7	2.0	1 054	69.7
Haskell County	1 495	4 307	26.7	32.9	10.6	17.5	38 634	11.6	2.9	1 481	72.2
Hodgeman County	2 227	2 085	4.8	29.1	19.0	19.7	35 994	11.5	1.4	796	78.4
Jewell County	2 355	3 791	2.4	21.8	26.0	13.8	30 538	11.6	2.3	1 695	79.9
Kearny County	2 256	4 531	28.7	34.4	11.4	15.0	40 149	11.7	2.9	1 542	73.5
Kiowa County	1 871	3 278	3.7	23.8	21.3	18.9	31 576	10.8	3.4	1 365	71.8
Lane County	1 858	2 155	4.0	25.3	20.6	18.5	36 047	8.2	1.9	910	77.0
Lincoln County	1 862	3 578	2.3	23.1	23.4	17.4	30 893	9.7	2.4	1 529	78.7
Logan County	2 779	3 046	3.0	25.3	20.8	17.5	32 131	7.3	3.8	1 243	76.3
Lyon County	2 204	35 935	22.7	25.8	11.5	23.0	32 819	14.5	6.0	13 691	60.9
McPherson County	2 330	29 554	4.3	25.3	17.3	22.2	41 138	6.6	4.1	11 205	73.9
Marion County	2 443	13 361	3.5	24.9	21.1	17.9	34 500	8.3	2.9	5 114	79.9
Marshall County	2 338	10 965	2.6	25.0	22.1	13.2	32 089	9.2	3.5	4 458	79.7
Meade County	2 534	4 631	13.7	29.7	17.8	19.6	36 761	9.3	2.9	1 728	73.9
Mitchell County	1 813	6 932	2.7	24.6	21.3	16.9	33 385	9.5	4.2	2 850	74.7
Morris County	1 806	6 104	5.0	25.1	21.0	16.0	32 163	9.0	2.9	2 539	78.2
Morton County	1 890	3 496	18.0	29.6	13.8	17.6	37 232	10.5	3.8	1 306	71.6
Nemaha County (part)	655	7 028	2.5	27.4	23.7	16.6	35 794	7.3	1.7	2 625	78.2
Ness County	2 784	3 454	2.6	22.8	24.2	17.9	32 340	8.7	1.8	1 516	76.1
Norton County	2 274	5 953	8.0	21.9	19.5	15.4	31 050	10.5	4.0	2 266	77.9
Osborne County	2 311	4 452	2.4	23.9	25.8	15.5	29 145	10.4	3.7	1 940	78.6
Ottawa County	1 868	6 163	2.4	25.6	17.6	16.3	38 009	8.6	4.4	2 430	82.2
Pawnee County	1 953	7 233	10.8	24.1	18.7	21.8	35 175	11.8	12.0	2 739	74.4
Phillips County	2 295	6 001	2.0	24.7	21.9	16.1	35 013	10.0	2.1	2 496	77.9
Pratt County	1 904	9 647	5.4	24.8	19.3	21.0	35 529	9.4	4.6	3 963	73.4
Rawlins County	2 770	2 966	4.0	23.9	26.0	15.9	32 105	12.5	2.0	1 269	76.8
Reno County	3 249	64 790	10.9	24.4	16.3	17.3	35 510	10.9	4.6	25 498	70.7
Republic County	1 855	5 835	2.4	22.3	26.2	14.9	30 494	9.1	2.4	2 557	78.9
Rice County	1 882	10 761	8.2	24.6	18.1	17.5	35 671	10.7	5.8	4 050	76.6
Rooks County	2 301	5 685	3.6	25.2	21.5	15.4	30 457	9.8	4.1	2 362	77.1
Rush County	1 860	3 551	1.5	22.2	25.5	16.4	31 268	9.7	2.7	1 548	82.4
Russell County	2 291	7 370	2.7	22.0	24.3	16.7	29 284	12.0	4.2	3 207	75.2
Saline County	1 864	53 597	12.9	26.2	13.8	20.4	37 308	8.8	3.4	21 436	69.0

[1]Dry land or land partially or temporarily covered by water.
[2]Persons who do not identify themselves as White alone, not of Hispanic origin.
[3]Persons 25 years old and over.

Table B. 109th Congressional Districts by Counties, 2000—*Continued*

(Number, percent.)

STATE Congressional district County	Land area,[1] (sq km)	Population				Percent with bachelor's degree or more[3]	Median income, 1999 (dollars)	Percent living in poverty	Percent unem- ployed	Households	
		Total	Percent minority[2]	Percent under 18 years old	Percent 65 years old and over					Total	Percent owner occupied
	1	2	3	4	5	6	7	8	9	10	11
Congressional District 1, Kansas—*Continued*											
Scott County	1 858	5 120	7.5	26.9	16.4	23.0	40 534	5.1	2.2	2 045	74.4
Seward County	1 656	22 510	50.5	32.0	8.4	13.6	36 752	16.9	4.9	7 419	64.1
Sheridan County	2 322	2 813	1.1	26.4	20.2	15.9	33 547	15.7	0.6	1 124	82.3
Sherman County	2 735	6 760	10.0	24.5	17.0	15.0	32 684	12.9	3.1	2 758	68.9
Smith County	2 319	4 536	2.2	21.8	27.6	16.7	28 486	10.7	2.3	1 953	79.7
Stafford County	2 051	4 789	7.5	26.5	21.0	18.4	31 107	11.8	3.5	2 010	77.7
Stanton County	1 761	2 406	25.5	30.8	13.3	16.9	40 172	14.9	2.8	858	67.8
Stevens County	1 884	5 463	25.1	31.1	13.4	17.5	41 830	10.3	3.8	1 988	75.4
Thomas County	2 784	8 180	3.2	26.1	14.7	25.0	37 034	9.7	5.8	3 226	69.0
Trego County	2 301	3 319	0.8	24.0	24.3	14.0	29 677	12.3	1.8	1 412	81.4
Wabaunsee County	2 065	6 885	2.6	26.6	15.6	17.3	41 710	7.3	2.7	2 633	82.9
Wallace County	2 367	1 749	7.8	28.9	18.1	17.2	33 000	16.1	1.5	674	76.6
Washington County	2 327	6 483	1.5	23.7	25.0	15.2	29 363	10.1	2.2	2 673	79.5
Wichita County	1 861	2 531	20.5	28.5	16.2	15.5	33 462	14.8	3.0	967	74.3
Congressional District 2, Kansas	36 606	672 302	12.7	25.3	13.5	23.2	37 855	11.2	4.3	257 846	69.0
Allen County	1 303	14 385	6.2	25.4	18.0	15.2	31 481	14.9	4.3	5 775	74.9
Anderson County	1 510	8 110	2.8	25.6	20.2	11.7	33 244	12.8	3.7	3 221	80.0
Atchison County	1 120	16 774	10.3	26.7	16.3	18.0	34 355	13.3	6.2	6 275	73.5
Bourbon County	1 650	15 379	6.2	25.8	18.2	17.8	31 199	13.5	3.9	6 161	74.1
Brown County	1 478	10 724	14.1	26.4	19.8	19.0	31 971	12.9	5.8	4 318	71.3
Cherokee County	1 521	22 605	8.6	26.5	15.2	11.3	30 505	14.3	5.5	8 875	76.2
Coffey County	1 631	8 865	4.5	26.8	16.3	20.1	37 839	6.6	4.4	3 489	78.3
Crawford County	1 536	38 242	7.8	22.8	15.5	23.9	29 409	16.0	4.9	15 504	64.3
Doniphan County	1 016	8 249	5.1	25.2	16.1	14.8	32 537	11.9	7.0	3 173	74.6
Douglas County (part)	796	36 949	11.7	24.0	9.7	45.7	48 804	11.6	3.1	14 292	61.3
Franklin County	1 486	24 784	6.0	27.5	13.9	16.5	39 052	7.7	3.5	9 452	73.5
Geary County (part)	69	4 265	40.0	40.3	0.2	29.0	32 480	10.8	18.5	1 081	0.8
Jackson County	1 698	12 657	10.4	28.3	14.9	15.4	40 451	8.8	3.4	4 727	80.6
Jefferson County	1 389	18 426	3.6	27.3	12.8	17.9	45 535	6.7	3.4	6 830	85.1
Labette County	1 680	22 835	12.3	25.5	17.5	15.9	30 875	12.7	3.6	9 194	73.3
Leavenworth County	1 200	68 691	18.1	26.6	9.9	23.1	48 114	6.7	3.4	23 071	67.0
Linn County	1 551	9 570	3.5	24.9	18.3	12.7	35 906	11.0	5.5	3 807	82.5
Miami County	1 494	28 351	5.1	27.9	11.9	19.4	46 665	5.5	2.5	10 365	78.5
Nemaha County (part)	1 205	3 689	1.4	30.3	18.7	10.6	31 632	12.3	2.2	1 334	84.9
Neosho County	1 481	16 997	6.8	25.6	17.3	15.0	32 167	13.0	4.9	6 739	74.5
Osage County	1 822	16 712	3.1	27.0	15.8	14.3	37 928	8.4	3.5	6 490	79.8
Pottawatomie County	2 187	18 209	4.7	29.2	13.4	22.7	40 176	9.7	3.1	6 771	78.5
Riley County	1 579	62 843	17.0	18.7	7.5	40.5	32 042	20.6	7.0	22 137	47.3
Shawnee County	1 424	169 871	20.0	25.2	13.7	26.0	40 988	9.6	4.0	68 920	67.5
Wilson County	1 486	10 332	3.7	25.4	19.9	10.9	29 747	11.3	4.2	4 203	78.1
Woodson County	1 297	3 788	3.6	21.8	24.8	11.4	25 335	13.2	3.6	1 642	81.4
Congressional District 3, Kansas	2 014	671 981	20.4	26.5	10.1	39.1	51 118	7.8	3.8	258 464	67.7
Douglas County (part)	387	63 013	17.5	18.2	6.9	40.6	33 224	18.7	5.5	24 194	46.4
Johnson County	1 235	451 086	11.0	27.0	10.0	47.7	61 455	3.4	2.3	174 570	72.3
Wyandotte County	392	157 882	48.4	28.4	11.7	12.0	33 784	16.5	8.2	59 700	62.9
Congressional District 4, Kansas	24 684	672 084	19.0	27.6	13.0	23.0	40 917	9.6	4.8	261 106	68.9
Butler County	3 698	59 482	6.4	28.6	12.5	20.4	45 474	7.3	3.6	21 527	77.7
Chautauqua County	1 662	4 359	7.1	23.4	24.4	12.3	28 717	12.2	4.8	1 796	81.8
Cowley County	2 917	36 291	11.9	25.9	15.9	18.3	34 406	12.9	7.8	14 039	70.9
Elk County	1 676	3 261	5.4	22.5	25.6	10.6	27 267	13.8	4.7	1 412	80.8
Greenwood County (part)	1 702	5 546	4.5	22.9	23.4	13.8	29 948	11.7	4.6	2 372	75.2
Harper County	2 076	6 536	3.3	24.6	23.1	14.0	29 776	11.6	3.8	2 773	74.6
Harvey County	1 397	32 869	11.8	26.0	17.0	23.0	40 907	6.4	3.7	12 581	71.9
Kingman County	2 236	8 673	3.3	27.4	19.6	17.8	37 790	10.6	1.4	3 371	78.1
Montgomery County	1 671	36 252	15.9	25.0	18.3	16.0	30 997	12.6	4.7	14 903	71.7
Sedgwick County	2 588	452 869	23.6	28.1	11.4	25.4	42 485	9.5	4.8	176 444	66.2
Sumner County	3 061	25 946	7.5	28.5	15.4	15.7	39 415	9.5	5.0	9 888	76.7
KENTUCKY	102 896	4 041 769	10.7	24.6	12.5	17.1	33 672	15.8	5.7	1 590 647	70.7
Congressional District 1, Kentucky	30 259	673 723	10.3	24.1	14.6	11.8	30 360	16.5	6.3	267 297	74.0
Adair County	1 054	17 244	4.3	23.5	14.6	10.9	24 055	24.0	10.8	6 747	80.1
Allen County	896	17 800	2.4	25.9	13.7	9.1	31 238	17.3	4.9	6 910	79.0
Ballard County	651	8 286	6.4	23.0	16.1	10.6	32 130	13.6	4.2	3 395	81.9
Butler County	1 109	13 010	2.7	25.3	12.9	6.4	29 405	16.0	4.8	5 059	79.5
Caldwell County	899	13 060	6.5	22.4	18.0	10.0	28 686	15.9	5.5	5 431	77.4
Calloway County	1 000	34 177	7.2	18.8	14.9	24.0	30 134	16.6	9.6	13 862	68.3
Carlisle County	499	5 351	2.3	23.3	18.3	10.6	30 087	13.1	6.2	2 208	84.0
Casey County	1 154	15 447	3.1	24.4	15.2	7.4	21 580	25.5	5.9	6 260	81.1
Christian County	1 868	72 265	31.6	28.2	9.7	12.5	31 177	15.0	6.8	24 857	55.3
Clinton County	511	9 634	2.8	22.8	15.0	8.0	19 563	25.8	6.1	4 086	77.2

[1]Dry land or land partially or temporarily covered by water.
[2]Persons who do not identify themselves as White alone, not of Hispanic origin.
[3]Persons 25 years old and over.

Table B. 109th Congressional Districts by Counties, 2000—*Continued*

(Number, percent.)

STATE Congressional district County	Land area,[1] (sq km)	Population Total	Percent minority[2]	Percent under 18 years old	Percent 65 years old and over	Percent with bachelor's degree or more[3]	Median income, 1999 (dollars)	Percent living in poverty	Percent unemployed	Households Total	Percent owner occupied
	1	2	3	4	5	6	7	8	9	10	11
Congressional District 1, Kentucky—*Continued*											
Crittenden County	938	9 384	1.7	23.2	16.3	7.3	29 060	19.1	6.7	3 829	80.3
Cumberland County	792	7 147	4.9	23.6	17.8	7.1	21 572	23.8	6.5	2 976	77.6
Fulton County	541	7 752	25.3	24.9	17.4	11.5	24 382	23.1	8.6	3 237	64.2
Graves County	1 439	37 028	7.9	24.4	16.2	12.6	30 874	16.4	5.5	14 841	77.9
Henderson County	1 140	44 829	9.7	24.7	13.2	13.8	35 892	12.3	5.4	18 095	67.3
Hickman County	633	5 262	12.0	22.0	18.7	8.8	31 615	17.4	6.5	2 188	81.4
Hopkins County	1 426	46 519	8.6	24.1	14.7	10.6	30 868	16.5	7.0	18 820	74.7
Lincoln County (part)	222	5 942	1.2	24.8	13.6	5.9	28 088	16.2	5.0	2 341	80.4
Livingston County	819	9 804	1.7	22.5	15.0	8.4	31 776	10.3	4.7	3 996	85.2
Logan County	1 439	26 573	10.1	25.7	13.9	9.6	32 474	15.5	4.2	10 506	75.2
Lyon County	559	8 080	8.3	15.6	16.9	10.1	31 694	12.7	5.5	2 898	82.2
McCracken County	650	65 514	13.6	23.3	15.9	18.1	33 865	15.1	6.0	27 736	68.7
McLean County	659	9 938	2.8	24.3	14.4	8.7	29 675	16.0	6.1	3 984	80.3
Marshall County	790	30 125	2.4	21.7	17.5	13.7	35 573	9.5	4.2	12 412	82.6
Metcalfe County	753	10 037	3.6	24.7	15.0	6.6	23 540	23.6	6.5	4 016	79.3
Monroe County	857	11 756	5.1	24.0	15.2	8.4	22 356	23.4	10.1	4 741	75.1
Muhlenberg County	1 230	31 839	6.1	22.6	15.3	8.1	28 566	19.7	7.6	12 357	82.9
Ohio County (part)	581	12 875	3.6	24.5	15.7	8.2	28 994	17.4	5.6	5 099	74.1
Russell County	657	16 315	2.1	22.4	16.5	9.6	22 042	24.3	6.5	6 941	79.4
Simpson County	612	16 405	12.3	26.2	13.3	11.9	36 432	11.6	3.2	6 415	71.8
Todd County	975	11 971	11.2	26.6	14.0	9.2	29 718	17.2	4.4	4 569	76.5
Trigg County	1 148	12 597	12.3	22.7	16.8	12.0	33 002	12.3	4.9	5 215	81.3
Union County	894	15 637	15.7	25.2	12.8	10.9	35 018	17.7	12.8	5 710	77.9
Webster County	867	14 120	8.1	24.2	14.9	7.1	31 529	15.4	4.7	5 560	78.0
Congressional District 2, Kentucky	19 598	673 201	9.2	25.7	11.5	13.9	35 724	13.3	5.3	255 468	73.5
Barren County	1 272	38 033	6.0	24.1	14.9	11.1	31 240	15.6	5.4	15 346	72.3
Breckinridge County	1 483	18 648	4.4	24.9	14.2	7.4	30 554	15.8	6.0	7 324	81.9
Bullitt County	775	61 236	2.4	27.2	7.8	9.2	45 106	7.9	3.2	22 171	83.9
Daviess County	1 198	91 545	6.5	25.7	13.9	17.0	36 813	12.3	5.8	36 033	70.3
Edmonson County	784	11 644	1.9	23.5	14.4	4.9	25 413	18.4	6.9	4 648	85.6
Grayson County	1 305	24 053	2.2	24.6	14.0	7.7	27 639	18.1	5.7	9 596	77.3
Green County	748	11 518	3.3	22.7	16.9	9.1	25 463	18.4	5.1	4 706	78.4
Hancock County	489	8 392	3.2	26.8	10.9	8.1	36 914	13.6	5.1	3 215	82.5
Hardin County	1 626	94 174	19.2	27.5	9.7	15.4	37 744	10.0	5.7	34 497	66.9
Hart County	1 077	17 445	7.5	25.7	13.8	7.0	25 378	22.4	6.6	6 769	77.3
Jefferson County (part)	48	19 593	9.5	28.3	7.1	7.3	39 060	12.1	4.4	6 978	72.3
Larue County	682	13 373	6.4	25.0	15.1	10.9	32 056	15.4	4.8	5 275	80.3
Marion County	897	18 212	11.3	25.2	12.9	9.1	30 387	18.6	5.9	6 613	78.2
Meade County	799	26 349	8.4	29.7	8.2	11.3	36 966	11.3	7.2	9 470	73.9
Nelson County	1 095	37 477	7.4	27.6	10.6	13.4	39 010	12.2	3.7	13 953	78.0
Ohio County (part)	957	10 041	1.0	25.2	12.8	6.5	30 494	17.1	5.0	3 800	88.5
Shelby County	995	33 337	15.0	25.4	10.6	18.7	45 534	9.9	3.9	12 104	72.7
Spencer County	481	11 766	3.2	27.1	9.1	11.1	47 042	8.8	4.1	4 251	82.6
Taylor County	699	22 927	7.3	23.4	15.3	12.2	28 089	17.5	7.3	9 233	72.3
Warren County	1 412	92 522	13.9	23.1	10.4	24.7	36 151	15.4	5.8	35 365	64.0
Washington County	779	10 916	10.1	25.5	14.8	13.3	33 136	13.5	4.6	4 121	79.9
Congressional District 3, Kentucky	950	674 011	23.9	24.1	13.7	25.3	39 468	12.4	5.1	280 034	64.7
Jefferson County (part)	950	674 011	23.9	24.1	13.7	25.3	39 468	12.4	5.1	280 034	64.7
Congressional District 4, Kentucky	14 707	673 619	4.9	25.9	11.6	17.5	40 150	11.4	4.7	257 417	73.4
Bath County (part)	544	8 276	3.9	24.6	15.1	10.5	25 856	22.5	6.4	3 316	78.3
Boone County	638	85 991	6.0	28.4	8.1	22.8	53 593	5.6	3.1	31 258	74.2
Boyd County	415	49 752	5.0	21.8	15.6	14.1	32 749	15.5	8.5	20 010	72.9
Bracken County	526	8 279	1.4	25.5	13.5	9.5	34 823	10.8	4.9	3 228	76.9
Campbell County	393	88 616	4.1	25.6	12.6	20.5	41 903	9.3	3.9	34 742	69.0
Carroll County	337	10 155	6.8	25.0	12.8	8.3	35 925	14.9	6.7	3 940	66.8
Carter County	1 063	26 889	1.3	24.6	12.5	8.9	26 427	22.3	8.2	10 342	81.0
Elliott County	606	6 748	0.6	25.2	13.4	7.8	21 014	25.9	10.5	2 638	82.3
Fleming County	909	13 792	3.0	25.3	13.4	8.8	27 990	18.6	6.7	5 367	78.8
Gallatin County	256	7 870	2.5	28.6	10.3	6.9	36 422	13.4	3.5	2 902	77.0
Grant County	673	22 384	2.0	28.6	9.5	9.4	38 438	11.1	5.4	8 175	74.1
Greenup County	896	36 891	2.8	23.6	14.6	11.5	32 142	14.1	7.3	14 536	81.8
Harrison County	802	17 983	5.0	25.1	13.4	10.6	36 210	12.0	3.6	7 012	70.5
Henry County	749	15 060	6.9	25.5	12.2	9.8	37 263	13.7	3.7	5 844	77.4
Kenton County	419	151 464	6.6	26.3	11.0	22.9	43 906	9.0	3.5	59 444	66.4
Lewis County	1 255	14 092	1.4	25.2	12.5	6.4	22 208	28.5	11.7	5 422	81.2
Mason County	624	16 800	9.9	24.2	15.4	14.4	30 195	16.8	5.4	6 847	67.4
Nicholas County	509	6 813	2.5	23.5	15.5	7.5	29 886	13.2	9.6	2 710	74.8
Oldham County	490	46 178	7.0	27.4	7.0	30.6	63 229	4.1	2.5	14 856	86.8
Owen County	912	10 547	3.5	25.4	14.0	9.1	33 310	15.5	5.3	4 086	78.2

[1]Dry land or land partially or temporarily covered by water.
[2]Persons who do not identify themselves as White alone, not of Hispanic origin.
[3]Persons 25 years old and over.

Table B. 109th Congressional Districts by Counties, 2000—*Continued*

(Number, percent.)

STATE Congressional district County	Land area,[1] (sq km)	Population Total	Population Percent minority[2]	Population Percent under 18 years old	Population Percent 65 years old and over	Percent with bachelor's degree or more[3]	Median income, 1999 (dollars)	Percent living in poverty	Percent unemployed	Households Total	Households Percent owner occupied
	1	2	3	4	5	6	7	8	9	10	11
Congressional District 4, Kentucky—*Continued*											
Pendleton County	727	14 390	1.7	28.3	10.4	9.7	38 125	11.4	5.0	5 170	77.9
Robertson County	259	2 266	1.8	24.1	16.9	8.7	30 581	22.2	5.7	866	77.9
Scott County (part)	319	4 258	2.1	26.2	8.7	13.7	51 705	9.4	2.6	1 569	84.8
Trimble County	386	8 125	2.7	26.5	11.4	7.6	36 192	13.6	5.2	3 137	80.6
Congressional District 5, Kentucky	27 652	673 654	2.9	24.6	12.4	9.6	21 915	28.1	8.9	262 110	76.3
Bath County (part)	180	2 809	1.4	23.9	12.9	8.6	26 563	20.1	7.2	1 129	84.2
Bell County	934	30 060	4.2	24.4	13.4	9.0	19 057	31.1	11.1	12 004	67.5
Breathitt County	1 283	16 100	1.9	25.5	11.6	10.0	19 155	33.2	10.1	6 170	76.5
Clay County	1 220	24 556	7.2	25.4	10.3	8.0	16 271	39.7	10.7	8 556	74.8
Floyd County	1 021	42 441	2.9	23.6	12.2	9.7	21 168	30.3	10.0	16 881	76.2
Harlan County	1 210	33 202	4.7	25.0	13.9	8.9	18 665	32.5	13.2	13 291	73.5
Jackson County	897	13 495	1.3	26.0	11.9	6.8	20 177	30.2	8.8	5 307	80.2
Johnson County	677	23 445	1.5	23.9	12.7	9.3	24 911	26.6	8.4	9 103	76.4
Knott County	912	17 649	2.7	24.6	11.4	10.2	20 373	31.1	15.6	6 717	79.6
Knox County	1 004	31 795	2.5	26.1	12.7	8.8	18 294	34.8	8.9	12 416	71.4
Laurel County	1 128	52 715	2.8	25.4	11.4	10.6	27 015	21.3	5.4	20 353	77.0
Lawrence County	1 085	15 569	0.7	25.2	12.3	6.6	21 610	30.7	11.5	5 954	78.0
Lee County	544	7 916	4.3	22.6	14.4	6.3	18 544	30.4	9.4	2 985	76.8
Leslie County	1 046	12 401	1.4	24.6	11.5	6.3	18 546	32.7	10.2	4 885	82.1
Letcher County	878	25 277	1.7	23.8	12.5	7.7	21 110	27.1	11.0	10 085	80.8
McCreary County	1 108	17 080	2.6	27.4	10.5	6.7	19 348	32.2	11.3	6 520	75.6
Magoffin County	801	13 332	0.6	26.7	10.5	6.3	19 421	36.6	12.8	5 024	81.9
Martin County	598	12 578	1.1	28.1	9.7	9.0	18 279	37.0	12.8	4 776	79.3
Menifee County	528	6 556	2.7	24.9	11.7	8.4	22 064	29.6	8.3	2 537	81.2
Morgan County	987	13 948	6.0	22.4	11.8	7.7	21 869	27.2	8.4	4 752	79.9
Owsley County	513	4 858	1.2	24.3	15.3	7.7	15 805	45.4	8.8	1 894	78.4
Perry County	886	29 390	3.0	24.3	11.3	8.9	22 089	29.1	11.6	11 460	77.4
Pike County	2 040	68 736	1.9	23.7	12.4	9.9	23 930	23.4	9.0	27 612	78.7
Pulaski County	1 714	56 217	3.2	23.5	15.0	10.5	27 370	19.1	5.1	22 719	76.0
Rockcastle County	822	16 582	1.5	24.3	13.3	8.3	23 475	23.1	6.7	6 544	79.6
Rowan County	727	22 094	4.9	20.3	10.4	21.9	28 055	21.3	8.1	7 927	69.7
Wayne County	1 190	19 923	4.4	25.4	13.4	7.2	20 863	29.4	7.9	7 913	76.4
Whitley County	1 140	35 865	2.4	25.7	12.9	13.4	22 075	26.4	6.7	13 780	72.7
Wolfe County	577	7 065	0.7	26.0	12.7	10.6	19 310	35.9	9.1	2 816	73.8
Congressional District 6, Kentucky	9 729	673 561	12.9	23.1	10.9	24.6	37 544	13.2	5.0	268 321	63.2
Anderson County	525	19 111	4.1	26.6	10.6	12.0	45 433	7.5	4.0	7 320	79.8
Bourbon County	755	19 360	10.4	25.0	13.4	13.5	35 038	14.0	3.8	7 681	65.5
Boyle County	471	27 697	13.0	22.7	14.2	19.3	35 241	11.9	4.3	10 574	69.3
Clark County	659	33 144	7.2	24.7	12.4	15.6	39 946	10.6	4.6	13 015	68.6
Estill County	658	15 307	1.0	24.3	13.5	6.9	23 318	26.4	7.4	6 108	73.9
Fayette County	737	260 512	20.8	21.3	10.0	35.6	39 813	12.9	5.4	108 288	55.3
Franklin County	545	47 687	12.5	22.8	12.3	23.8	40 011	10.2	6.2	19 907	64.8
Garrard County	599	14 792	6.0	24.4	13.1	10.5	34 284	14.7	5.1	5 741	76.4
Jessamine County	448	39 041	6.4	26.3	9.5	21.5	40 096	10.5	4.3	13 867	67.1
Lincoln County (part)	648	17 419	5.2	26.1	13.0	9.3	26 099	22.8	5.0	6 865	78.4
Madison County	1 141	70 872	7.6	21.8	9.8	21.8	32 861	16.8	5.0	27 152	59.7
Mercer County	650	20 817	7.1	24.4	14.6	13.5	35 555	12.9	3.6	8 423	74.5
Montgomery County	514	22 554	5.8	24.8	12.8	13.4	31 746	15.2	5.9	8 902	71.5
Powell County	467	13 237	1.8	26.6	10.6	6.5	25 515	23.5	5.6	5 044	74.0
Scott County (part)	419	28 803	9.5	26.3	9.0	21.4	46 740	8.7	3.9	10 541	67.5
Woodford County	494	23 208	9.1	25.3	10.4	25.9	49 491	7.3	2.6	8 893	72.4
LOUISIANA	112 825	4 468 976	37.5	27.3	11.6	18.7	32 566	19.6	7.3	1 656 053	67.9
Congressional District 1, Louisiana	6 221	637 543	20.4	24.8	12.7	27.4	40 948	12.1	4.8	250 838	70.3
Jefferson Parish (part)	120	252 900	19.6	21.2	14.8	28.4	42 274	8.6	4.1	106 874	62.2
Orleans Parish (part)	25	37 501	10.4	18.5	18.5	54.7	49 898	7.7	2.9	17 927	63.0
St. Charles Parish (part)	83	11 360	18.8	32.8	5.4	34.6	61 142	5.6	2.5	3 759	87.2
St. Tammany Parish	2 212	191 268	15.0	28.4	10.0	28.3	47 883	9.7	3.8	69 253	80.5
Tangipahoa Parish	2 047	100 588	31.3	27.7	10.6	16.3	29 412	22.7	8.6	36 558	73.3
Washington Parish	1 734	43 926	33.2	26.8	14.8	10.9	24 264	24.7	8.2	16 467	76.5
Congressional District 2, Louisiana	689	639 048	71.6	28.3	10.3	19.4	27 514	26.8	9.6	236 008	50.4
Jefferson Parish (part)	246	191 875	55.4	30.4	8.3	11.4	32 628	20.4	8.1	65 684	65.1
Orleans Parish (part)	442	447 173	78.6	27.3	11.1	22.8	25 782	29.7	10.2	170 324	44.8
Congressional District 3, Louisiana	18 157	638 674	30.3	28.8	10.7	10.8	34 463	18.6	7.1	223 921	77.5
Ascension Parish (part)	551	39 811	35.6	29.3	9.7	10.3	36 045	18.3	7.0	14 008	76.1
Assumption Parish	877	23 388	33.8	28.4	11.0	7.4	31 168	21.8	9.3	8 239	84.1
Iberia Parish	1 490	73 266	35.7	30.0	11.4	11.2	31 204	23.6	9.2	25 381	73.4
Jefferson Parish (part)	427	10 691	13.1	27.2	9.0	9.2	40 083	12.9	4.2	3 676	87.6
Lafourche Parish	2 809	89 974	17.8	27.3	11.2	12.4	34 910	16.5	5.9	32 057	77.9

[1] Dry land or land partially or temporarily covered by water.
[2] Persons who do not identify themselves as White alone, not of Hispanic origin.
[3] Persons 25 years old and over.

Table B. 109th Congressional Districts by Counties, 2000—*Continued*

(Number, percent.)

STATE Congressional district County	Land area,[1] (sq km)	Population				Percent with bachelor's degree or more[3]	Median income, 1999 (dollars)	Percent living in poverty	Percent unemployed	Households	
		Total	Percent minority[2]	Percent under 18 years old	Percent 65 years old and over					Total	Percent owner occupied
	1	2	3	4	5	6	7	8	9	10	11
Congressional District 3, Louisiana—*Continued*											
Plaquemines Parish	2 187	26 757	31.2	29.3	9.9	10.8	38 173	18.0	6.7	9 021	78.9
St. Bernard Parish	1 204	67 229	15.4	25.2	13.7	8.9	35 939	13.1	5.8	25 123	74.7
St. Charles Parish (part)	652	36 712	32.6	29.6	10.2	12.2	40 727	13.2	6.2	12 663	79.7
St. James Parish	637	21 216	50.3	29.5	11.3	10.1	35 277	20.7	10.2	6 992	85.6
St. John the Baptist Parish	567	43 044	49.1	31.1	8.1	12.9	39 456	16.7	6.9	14 283	81.0
St. Martin Parish	1 916	48 583	34.6	29.5	10.1	8.5	30 701	21.5	8.6	17 164	81.7
St. Mary Parish	1 587	53 500	38.2	29.6	11.1	9.4	28 072	23.6	8.6	19 317	73.9
Terrebonne Parish	3 250	104 503	26.9	29.1	9.6	12.3	35 235	19.1	5.9	35 997	75.5
Congressional District 4, Louisiana	27 881	638 366	38.0	27.1	13.0	16.7	31 085	20.0	8.3	241 288	68.5
Allen Parish (part)	938	11 591	28.4	24.6	11.6	8.3	31 453	17.8	5.8	3 781	77.8
Beauregard Parish	3 005	32 986	16.5	27.4	11.8	13.8	32 582	15.6	7.2	12 104	79.8
Bienville Parish	2 100	15 752	45.5	27.2	17.7	11.5	23 663	26.1	10.0	6 108	77.8
Bossier Parish	2 174	98 310	27.0	28.0	10.5	18.1	39 203	13.7	5.6	36 628	69.5
Caddo Parish	2 284	252 161	47.8	26.8	13.7	20.6	31 467	21.1	9.3	97 974	63.8
Claiborne Parish	1 955	16 851	48.5	25.5	17.4	12.4	25 344	26.5	9.4	6 270	75.8
De Soto Parish	2 272	25 494	44.9	28.4	14.5	10.2	28 252	25.1	8.1	9 691	76.6
Grant Parish	1 671	18 698	14.8	28.2	12.8	9.8	29 622	21.5	7.0	7 073	81.7
Natchitoches Parish	3 252	39 080	42.8	25.9	12.2	18.4	25 722	26.5	9.9	14 263	64.5
Red River Parish	1 008	9 622	42.7	30.1	14.5	8.7	23 153	29.9	11.9	3 414	76.2
Sabine Parish	2 241	23 459	28.9	26.2	16.5	11.1	26 655	21.5	8.2	9 221	81.0
Vernon Parish	3 441	52 531	28.5	29.1	8.0	13.5	31 216	15.3	8.5	18 260	56.7
Webster Parish	1 542	41 831	34.8	25.7	16.3	12.6	28 408	20.2	8.1	16 501	74.5
Congressional District 5, Louisiana	35 677	638 726	36.6	27.0	13.2	15.5	27 453	23.6	8.6	233 533	70.3
Allen Parish (part)	1 042	13 849	34.9	24.7	11.7	10.0	24 897	21.7	8.8	4 321	74.5
Avoyelles Parish	2 156	41 481	32.2	26.8	13.8	8.3	23 851	25.9	8.1	14 736	74.4
Caldwell Parish	1 371	10 560	20.5	24.9	13.8	8.8	26 972	21.2	7.4	3 941	79.2
Catahoula Parish	1 822	10 920	28.6	25.8	14.2	9.4	22 528	28.1	8.6	4 082	83.0
Concordia Parish	1 802	20 247	40.1	27.7	14.8	9.6	22 742	29.1	9.9	7 521	76.1
East Carroll Parish	1 092	9 421	69.0	30.4	13.0	12.3	20 723	40.5	15.0	2 969	62.1
Evangeline Parish (part)	1 192	12 898	12.0	29.3	10.8	10.3	27 547	21.2	3.9	4 532	83.1
Franklin Parish	1 615	21 263	33.4	28.0	15.7	9.8	22 964	28.4	8.3	7 754	76.2
Iberville Parish (part)	761	15 204	58.0	30.0	11.2	10.3	26 040	26.7	9.1	5 212	73.9
Jackson Parish	1 476	15 397	29.3	25.3	16.4	12.9	28 352	19.8	5.4	6 086	77.3
La Salle Parish	1 616	14 282	14.6	26.1	14.6	11.2	28 189	18.7	5.5	5 291	83.5
Lincoln Parish	1 221	42 509	43.0	22.2	11.4	31.8	26 977	26.5	13.3	15 235	59.9
Madison Parish	1 616	13 728	63.4	33.0	11.4	11.0	20 509	36.7	12.5	4 469	61.9
Morehouse Parish	2 057	31 021	44.6	27.5	15.4	9.7	25 124	26.8	11.1	11 382	71.6
Ouachita Parish	1 581	147 250	36.2	27.8	11.8	22.7	32 047	20.7	8.2	55 216	64.1
Pointe Coupee Parish (part)	1 158	12 749	56.0	29.5	12.3	8.1	25 048	29.4	10.5	4 515	76.6
Rapides Parish	3 425	126 337	34.3	27.3	13.0	16.5	29 856	20.5	7.1	47 120	68.0
Richland Parish	1 446	20 981	39.5	27.2	15.2	12.8	23 668	27.9	6.9	7 490	72.3
Tensas Parish	1 560	6 618	57.0	26.4	15.5	14.8	19 799	36.3	11.6	2 416	69.4
Union Parish	2 273	22 803	30.6	25.7	14.8	11.8	29 061	18.6	7.0	8 857	81.2
West Carroll Parish	931	12 314	20.8	25.6	15.5	9.5	24 637	23.4	12.2	4 458	79.0
Winn Parish	2 462	16 894	34.0	24.8	14.4	9.4	25 462	21.5	7.7	5 930	74.7
Congressional District 6, Louisiana	7 966	638 209	37.2	26.7	9.6	24.1	37 931	16.6	6.0	232 902	68.7
Ascension Parish (part)	204	36 816	10.8	30.9	5.4	19.1	53 728	7.3	3.9	12 683	89.1
East Baton Rouge Parish	1 180	412 852	44.9	26.1	9.9	30.8	37 224	17.9	6.3	156 365	61.6
East Feliciana Parish	1 174	21 360	48.6	25.7	11.1	11.3	31 631	23.0	11.2	6 699	82.4
Iberville Parish (part)	841	18 116	45.6	23.0	10.8	9.0	31 764	19.6	5.7	5 462	80.5
Livingston Parish	1 678	91 814	6.6	29.4	8.7	11.4	38 887	11.4	4.8	32 630	83.8
Pointe Coupee Parish (part)	285	10 014	18.7	24.2	15.5	18.1	37 561	15.0	3.7	3 882	79.0
St. Helena Parish	1 058	10 525	53.8	29.0	12.5	11.2	24 970	26.8	9.5	3 873	85.0
West Baton Rouge Parish	495	21 601	37.9	28.0	9.8	11.1	37 117	17.0	5.6	7 663	78.8
West Feliciana Parish	1 052	15 111	52.0	20.4	7.0	10.6	39 667	19.9	5.6	3 645	74.5
Congressional District 7, Louisiana	16 234	638 410	28.0	28.1	11.7	16.6	31 453	19.9	7.4	237 563	70.3
Acadia Parish	1 697	58 861	20.0	29.8	12.3	9.4	26 684	24.5	7.1	21 142	72.2
Calcasieu Parish	2 774	183 577	27.2	27.4	11.9	16.9	35 372	15.4	6.9	68 613	71.5
Cameron Parish	3 401	9 991	7.3	28.3	10.5	7.9	34 232	12.3	4.6	3 592	85.2
Evangeline Parish (part)	528	22 536	40.5	29.6	13.9	9.0	17 101	38.7	9.6	8 204	61.8
Jefferson Davis Parish	1 689	31 435	20.1	29.4	13.2	9.9	27 736	20.9	7.9	11 480	74.9
Lafayette Parish	699	190 503	27.6	27.3	9.5	25.5	36 518	15.7	6.9	72 372	66.1
St. Landry Parish	2 405	87 700	44.0	29.4	13.5	10.7	22 855	29.3	10.4	32 328	70.7
Vermilion Parish	3 040	53 807	18.2	28.2	13.6	10.7	29 500	22.1	7.0	19 832	77.0

[1]Dry land or land partially or temporarily covered by water.
[2]Persons who do not identify themselves as White alone, not of Hispanic origin.
[3]Persons 25 years old and over.

Table B. 109th Congressional Districts by Counties, 2000—*Continued*

(Number, percent.)

STATE Congressional district County	Land area,[1] (sq km)	Population				Percent with bachelor's degree or more[3]	Median income, 1999 (dollars)	Percent living in poverty	Percent unemployed	Households	
		Total	Percent minority[2]	Percent under 18 years old	Percent 65 years old and over					Total	Percent owner occupied
	1	2	3	4	5	6	7	8	9	10	11
MAINE	79 931	1 274 923	3.5	23.6	14.4	22.9	37 240	10.9	4.8	518 200	71.6
Congressional District 1, Maine	9 156	637 450	3.6	23.9	13.9	27.9	42 044	8.6	3.7	258 917	70.8
Cumberland County	2 164	265 612	4.7	23.3	13.3	34.2	44 048	7.9	3.7	107 989	66.7
Kennebec County (part)	1 640	76 648	2.9	24.2	13.7	21.3	37 577	10.4	4.3	31 482	72.6
Knox County	947	39 618	2.0	22.4	17.3	26.2	36 774	10.1	3.4	16 608	74.0
Lincoln County	1 181	33 616	1.9	22.6	18.1	26.6	38 686	10.1	4.3	14 158	83.1
Sagadahoc County	658	35 214	3.9	25.7	12.3	25.0	41 908	8.6	3.3	14 117	72.0
York County	2 566	186 742	2.9	24.7	13.6	22.9	43 630	8.2	3.5	74 563	72.6
Congressional District 2, Maine	70 775	637 473	3.3	23.3	14.9	17.7	32 600	13.3	5.9	259 283	72.4
Androscoggin County	1 218	103 793	3.7	23.8	14.4	14.4	35 793	11.1	5.1	42 028	63.4
Aroostook County	17 279	73 938	3.4	22.6	17.0	14.6	28 837	14.3	6.5	30 356	73.1
Franklin County	4 397	29 467	2.3	23.7	14.2	20.9	31 459	14.6	7.3	11 806	76.0
Hancock County	4 112	51 791	2.9	22.3	15.9	27.1	35 811	10.2	5.4	21 864	75.6
Kennebec County (part)	607	40 466	3.2	23.1	15.2	19.3	33 929	12.6	5.4	16 201	68.5
Oxford County	5 382	54 755	2.5	24.1	16.1	15.7	33 435	11.8	5.3	22 314	77.0
Penobscot County	8 795	144 919	3.7	22.8	13.1	20.3	34 274	13.7	5.6	58 096	69.8
Piscataquis County	10 272	17 235	2.4	23.3	17.3	13.3	28 250	14.8	8.0	7 278	79.4
Somerset County	10 170	50 888	2.1	24.7	14.3	11.8	30 731	14.9	6.3	20 496	77.9
Waldo County	1 890	36 280	2.7	24.2	13.5	22.3	33 986	13.9	5.7	14 726	79.8
Washington County	6 652	33 941	6.9	22.9	17.3	14.7	25 869	19.0	8.5	14 118	77.6
MARYLAND	25 314	5 296 486	37.9	25.6	11.3	31.4	52 868	8.5	4.7	1 980 859	67.7
Congressional District 1, Maryland	9 461	663 097	15.2	25.0	13.4	27.3	51 918	7.3	3.9	248 619	78.5
Anne Arundel County (part)	205	101 788	8.2	26.6	10.2	41.0	76 571	3.1	2.5	35 677	88.7
Baltimore County (part)	258	59 152	7.8	23.4	15.8	43.3	70 984	2.4	2.3	22 304	89.5
Caroline County	829	29 772	19.3	26.8	13.6	12.1	38 832	11.7	4.8	11 097	74.0
Cecil County (part)	902	85 951	7.2	27.7	10.4	16.4	50 510	7.2	4.1	31 223	74.9
Dorchester County (part)	1 444	30 674	31.2	23.3	17.9	12.0	34 077	13.8	5.8	12 706	70.1
Harford County (part)	389	106 254	6.9	27.7	10.6	34.1	65 178	2.5	2.3	38 051	85.9
Kent County (part)	724	19 197	21.5	20.9	19.2	21.7	39 869	13.0	4.4	7 666	70.3
Queen Anne's County (part)	964	40 563	11.7	25.3	12.8	25.4	57 037	6.3	2.8	15 315	83.2
Somerset County (part)	847	24 747	44.3	18.5	14.3	11.6	29 903	20.1	9.7	8 361	69.7
Talbot County (part)	697	33 812	18.7	21.6	20.5	27.8	43 532	8.3	3.4	14 307	71.6
Wicomico County (part)	977	84 644	28.3	24.7	12.8	21.9	39 035	12.8	5.5	32 218	66.5
Worcester County (part)	1 226	46 543	19.5	20.5	20.2	21.6	40 650	9.6	6.8	19 694	75.0
Congressional District 2, Maryland	919	661 945	33.8	25.6	12.3	20.3	44 309	9.8	5.0	260 455	62.4
Anne Arundel County (part)	134	106 857	27.6	28.4	8.2	18.1	52 488	6.6	3.6	38 041	68.1
Baltimore County (part)	430	359 278	26.1	23.5	14.7	23.0	45 810	7.6	4.5	145 768	63.2
Harford County (part)	305	83 190	27.0	28.1	9.5	19.3	48 129	8.5	4.2	31 509	65.0
Baltimore city (part)	50	112 620	69.2	28.1	10.6	13.9	31 554	20.6	8.7	45 137	53.0
Congressional District 3, Maryland	758	661 068	24.2	23.0	12.6	36.5	52 906	7.7	4.0	262 186	67.5
Anne Arundel County (part)	392	232 055	24.3	23.1	10.5	32.2	59 889	5.6	3.4	86 886	70.4
Baltimore County (part)	193	185 149	17.9	23.1	15.0	39.9	53 473	6.1	3.8	74 370	68.1
Howard County (part)	99	76 164	31.4	27.6	5.4	52.1	69 770	4.5	2.8	28 403	72.6
Baltimore city (part)	74	167 700	27.7	20.8	16.1	31.8	38 091	13.6	5.9	72 527	61.4
Congressional District 4, Maryland	816	661 651	72.5	28.4	7.3	32.7	57 727	7.3	5.3	236 464	62.8
Montgomery County (part)	438	251 141	45.5	27.4	7.6	49.9	70 345	5.3	3.1	88 955	69.0
Prince George's County (part)	379	410 510	89.0	28.9	7.0	21.7	51 500	8.6	6.7	147 509	59.1
Congressional District 5, Maryland	3 896	662 203	39.5	26.2	8.7	28.7	62 661	5.6	4.1	234 188	74.8
Anne Arundel County (part)	346	48 956	9.9	25.0	10.7	26.8	68 938	4.1	2.4	18 066	89.3
Calvert County (part)	557	74 563	16.9	29.6	8.9	22.5	65 945	4.4	3.0	25 447	85.2
Charles County (part)	1 194	120 546	32.7	28.8	7.8	20.0	62 199	5.5	3.4	41 668	78.2
Prince George's County (part)	863	331 927	56.5	24.3	8.5	35.2	63 983	5.6	4.7	118 365	70.0
St. Mary's County (part)	936	86 211	19.6	27.9	9.0	22.6	54 706	7.2	4.5	30 642	71.8
Congressional District 6, Maryland	7 931	661 559	8.4	25.9	12.0	23.7	50 957	6.7	3.6	240 769	75.7
Allegany County	1 102	74 930	7.6	20.5	17.9	14.1	30 821	14.8	8.9	29 322	70.1
Baltimore County (part)	546	30 610	4.3	26.0	11.5	41.8	70 962	2.7	2.2	11 426	83.6
Carroll County	1 163	150 897	5.0	27.7	10.8	24.8	60 021	3.8	2.7	52 503	82.0
Frederick County	1 717	195 277	11.9	27.5	9.6	30.0	60 276	4.5	3.1	70 060	75.8
Garrett County	1 678	29 846	1.0	25.1	14.9	13.8	32 238	13.3	5.6	11 476	77.9
Harford County (part)	447	29 146	4.1	27.1	10.4	24.6	59 570	3.6	2.5	10 107	88.6
Montgomery County (part)	92	18 930	10.9	32.6	6.0	41.8	72 440	4.0	1.9	6 149	88.3
Washington County	1 187	131 923	10.7	23.4	14.2	14.6	40 617	9.5	3.3	49 726	65.6
Congressional District 7, Maryland	762	662 615	65.8	26.0	11.7	27.5	38 885	17.6	8.6	247 981	55.5
Baltimore County (part)	123	120 103	55.8	24.5	14.0	29.3	50 118	6.6	5.2	46 009	65.9
Howard County (part)	554	171 678	25.8	28.1	8.2	53.3	77 245	3.6	2.2	61 640	74.3
Baltimore city (part)	85	370 834	87.6	25.5	12.7	14.4	25 564	28.0	14.0	140 332	43.7

[1]Dry land or land partially or temporarily covered by water.
[2]Persons who do not identify themselves as White alone, not of Hispanic origin.
[3]Persons 25 years old and over.

Table B. 109th Congressional Districts by Counties, 2000—*Continued*

(Number, percent.)

STATE Congressional district County	Land area,[1] (sq km)	Population Total	Percent minority[2]	Percent under 18 years old	Percent 65 years old and over	Percent with bachelor's degree or more[3]	Median income, 1999 (dollars)	Percent living in poverty	Percent unemployed	Households Total	Percent owner occupied
	1	2	3	4	5	6	7	8	9	10	11
Congressional District 8, Maryland	769	662 348	44.1	24.3	12.4	53.7	68 306	6.2	3.6	250 197	65.3
Montgomery County (part)	753	603 270	39.6	24.1	12.8	56.8	72 040	5.6	3.2	229 461	68.1
Prince George's County (part)	16	59 078	90.1	25.8	7.7	18.3	38 924	12.9	7.7	20 736	34.9
MASSACHUSETTS	20 306	6 349 097	18.1	23.6	13.5	33.2	50 502	9.3	4.6	2 443 580	61.7
Congressional District 1, Massachusetts	8 032	634 484	11.1	24.2	13.9	25.4	42 570	10.5	5.0	245 029	65.5
Berkshire County	2 412	134 953	5.9	22.5	18.0	26.0	39 047	9.5	5.1	56 006	66.9
Franklin County	1 818	71 535	5.2	23.4	14.3	29.1	40 768	9.4	4.5	29 466	67.0
Hampden County (part)	804	123 424	20.3	25.8	14.4	21.1	40 253	15.6	5.2	47 450	59.1
Hampshire County (part)	1 175	101 284	10.7	20.2	10.2	36.0	46 988	10.0	5.5	35 630	66.6
Middlesex County (part)	205	23 190	3.0	30.2	7.3	30.1	62 885	4.4	3.3	7 931	82.8
Worcester County (part)	1 617	180 098	12.3	26.1	13.4	20.3	44 201	9.2	4.9	68 546	65.7
Congressional District 2, Massachusetts	2 387	634 444	17.6	25.5	13.7	23.1	44 386	10.8	4.7	242 706	65.8
Hampden County (part)	797	332 804	27.6	26.0	14.5	20.2	39 456	14.4	5.8	127 838	63.0
Hampshire County (part)	195	50 967	10.2	18.1	15.6	41.2	44 325	8.2	4.4	20 361	62.1
Norfolk County (part)	48	15 314	3.6	26.9	9.5	22.0	64 496	2.5	3.6	5 557	83.9
Worcester County (part)	1 346	235 359	6.0	26.2	12.3	23.3	51 230	6.8	3.3	88 950	69.7
Congressional District 3, Massachusetts	1 505	634 466	13.9	25.5	12.9	30.8	50 223	9.0	4.4	240 491	62.9
Bristol County (part)	386	180 528	8.1	24.8	14.2	20.1	44 649	8.7	4.8	70 009	61.4
Middlesex County (part)	204	78 076	10.3	26.4	9.9	43.6	67 302	4.4	3.2	29 460	73.3
Norfolk County (part)	185	60 245	4.2	29.6	9.6	40.3	70 723	3.1	3.1	20 745	81.2
Worcester County (part)	730	315 617	20.1	24.8	13.6	32.1	46 433	11.5	4.7	120 277	58.1
Congressional District 4, Massachusetts	1 895	634 697	12.2	23.9	13.7	36.9	53 169	8.4	4.9	241 784	65.1
Bristol County (part)	981	331 851	12.3	24.4	14.5	18.5	41 561	11.3	6.5	127 913	60.5
Middlesex County (part)	88	88 029	13.0	21.7	14.9	68.4	87 167	4.2	3.0	32 624	70.6
Norfolk County (part)	266	141 248	14.4	22.9	11.6	65.5	77 103	5.6	3.1	53 913	65.1
Plymouth County (part)	561	73 569	6.7	25.9	13.2	25.3	52 322	6.0	3.9	27 334	80.0
Congressional District 5, Massachusetts	1 465	635 223	20.4	27.2	11.0	33.6	56 217	8.9	3.9	227 344	67.2
Essex County (part)	243	206 048	31.4	28.0	12.1	25.3	44 992	13.3	5.0	75 276	56.4
Middlesex County (part)	998	409 286	15.2	26.9	10.5	36.8	62 230	6.9	3.5	145 914	71.9
Worcester County (part)	225	19 889	12.1	25.3	8.8	49.5	83 498	2.9	2.6	6 154	86.0
Congressional District 6, Massachusetts	1 244	636 554	10.2	24.2	14.4	35.1	57 826	6.3	4.0	243 310	68.9
Essex County (part)	1 054	517 371	11.1	24.0	14.5	33.4	54 513	7.2	4.5	200 143	66.2
Middlesex County (part)	190	119 183	6.5	25.1	13.7	42.5	74 105	2.3	2.2	43 167	81.5
Congressional District 7, Massachusetts	441	634 385	16.5	20.4	15.5	39.5	56 110	6.7	3.5	255 260	57.1
Middlesex County (part)	421	568 799	16.4	20.5	15.4	42.0	58 143	6.1	3.3	227 954	57.9
Suffolk County (part)	20	65 586	17.3	20.1	16.6	17.9	41 650	12.1	5.3	27 306	50.9
Congressional District 8, Massachusetts	105	635 185	51.2	18.3	9.4	39.8	39 300	19.9	7.1	254 471	28.4
Middlesex County (part)	27	178 833	32.0	13.8	9.7	54.1	47 159	12.7	5.0	74 170	31.5
Suffolk County (part)	78	456 352	58.7	20.1	9.2	33.6	35 880	22.6	8.1	180 301	27.0
Congressional District 9, Massachusetts	811	633 846	20.5	23.8	14.1	33.8	55 407	7.5	4.2	238 738	64.4
Bristol County (part)	74	22 299	5.8	24.4	9.5	39.6	69 144	2.0	3.1	7 489	81.7
Norfolk County (part)	423	284 227	11.6	24.2	16.3	40.2	65 899	3.6	3.0	105 028	76.7
Plymouth County (part)	261	159 451	27.2	26.8	11.0	18.4	46 976	10.2	5.7	55 106	63.6
Suffolk County (part)	53	167 869	31.0	20.1	14.0	35.5	47 152	12.4	4.9	71 115	44.9
Congressional District 10, Massachusetts	2 420	635 813	7.8	22.7	16.7	33.5	51 928	5.9	3.9	254 447	73.6
Barnstable County	1 024	222 230	6.6	20.4	23.1	33.6	45 933	6.9	5.2	94 822	77.8
Bristol County (part)	0	0	X	X	X	X	X	X	X	0	X
Dukes County	269	14 987	10.6	22.7	14.2	38.4	45 559	7.3	2.7	6 421	71.3
Nantucket County	124	9 520	14.0	19.3	10.4	38.4	55 522	7.5	4.3	3 699	63.1
Norfolk County (part)	113	149 274	14.9	19.6	15.9	31.1	49 891	6.5	3.5	63 584	56.9
Plymouth County (part)	890	239 802	4.1	26.9	11.8	34.4	62 857	4.5	3.2	85 921	81.8
MICHIGAN	147 121	9 938 444	21.5	26.1	12.3	21.8	44 667	10.5	5.8	3 785 661	73.8
Congressional District 1, Michigan	64 458	662 583	6.2	23.1	17.0	15.6	34 076	11.2	8.0	266 115	80.1
Alcona County (part)	1 747	11 719	3.0	19.2	24.5	10.9	31 362	12.6	10.0	5 132	89.5
Alger County (part)	2 377	9 862	12.7	20.4	17.1	14.7	35 892	10.3	8.6	3 785	82.4
Alpena County (part)	1 487	31 314	2.6	23.7	17.1	13.2	34 177	10.5	7.3	12 818	79.3
Antrim County (part)	1 235	23 110	3.5	24.4	17.6	19.4	38 107	9.0	6.4	9 222	85.0
Arenac County (part)	950	17 269	5.6	23.2	16.5	9.1	32 805	13.9	8.4	6 710	84.3
Baraga County (part)	2 341	8 746	21.7	22.8	16.3	10.9	33 673	11.1	7.9	3 353	77.7
Bay County (part)	803	30 855	4.0	25.3	12.7	12.2	45 034	7.4	5.8	11 436	90.0
Charlevoix County (part)	1 080	26 090	4.1	26.0	14.8	19.8	39 788	8.0	6.0	10 400	81.2
Cheboygan County (part)	1 853	26 448	5.7	23.6	17.9	13.9	33 417	12.2	14.3	10 835	82.8
Chippewa County (part)	4 043	38 543	25.0	21.3	12.7	15.0	34 464	12.8	10.0	13 474	74.0

[1]Dry land or land partially or temporarily covered by water.
[2]Persons who do not identify themselves as White alone, not of Hispanic origin.
[3]Persons 25 years old and over.

Table B. 109th Congressional Districts by Counties, 2000—*Continued*

(Number, percent.)

STATE Congressional district County	Land area,[1] (sq km)	Population Total	Population Percent minority[2]	Population Percent under 18 years old	Population Percent 65 years old and over	Percent with bachelor's degree or more[3]	Median income, 1999 (dollars)	Percent living in poverty	Percent unemployed	Households Total	Households Percent owner occupied
	1	2	3	4	5	6	7	8	9	10	11
Congressional District 1, Michigan—*Continued*											
Crawford County	1 446	14 273	4.6	24.4	16.6	12.9	33 364	12.7	7.5	5 625	82.8
Delta County (part)	3 030	38 520	4.7	23.8	17.1	17.1	35 511	9.5	7.5	15 836	79.6
Dickinson County	1 985	27 472	2.5	25.1	18.1	16.7	34 825	9.1	5.6	11 386	80.1
Emmet County (part)	1 212	31 437	5.8	25.3	14.3	26.2	40 222	7.4	7.3	12 577	75.5
Gladwin County	1 313	26 023	2.9	23.2	18.3	9.2	32 019	13.8	8.4	10 561	85.6
Gogebic County (part)	2 854	17 370	6.0	20.5	22.6	15.8	27 405	14.4	9.4	7 425	78.7
Houghton County (part)	2 620	36 016	4.9	21.9	15.5	23.0	28 817	16.8	7.9	13 793	71.5
Iosco County (part)	1 422	27 339	3.7	22.3	21.5	11.3	31 321	12.7	9.0	11 727	82.0
Iron County	3 021	13 138	4.0	20.6	25.1	13.7	28 560	11.3	9.4	5 748	82.5
Keweenaw County (part)	1 401	2 301	5.0	22.5	20.2	19.1	28 140	12.7	11.1	998	89.3
Luce County (part)	2 339	7 024	18.0	21.4	15.4	11.8	32 031	14.9	8.7	2 481	79.6
Mackinac County (part)	2 646	11 943	20.7	22.3	18.3	14.9	33 356	10.5	14.8	5 067	79.1
Marquette County (part)	4 717	64 634	5.1	21.4	13.5	23.7	35 548	10.9	6.2	25 767	69.8
Menominee County (part)	2 703	25 326	4.1	24.1	17.3	11.0	32 888	11.5	5.1	10 529	79.5
Montmorency County	1 418	10 315	2.3	20.4	23.8	8.2	30 005	12.8	12.4	4 455	86.1
Ogemaw County	1 462	21 645	3.4	23.5	18.7	9.6	30 474	14.0	8.5	8 842	85.0
Ontonagon County (part)	3 397	7 818	3.5	20.2	21.6	13.0	29 552	10.4	9.6	3 456	84.9
Oscoda County	1 463	9 418	2.7	23.3	20.3	8.0	28 228	14.6	8.8	3 921	85.3
Otsego County	1 333	23 301	3.2	26.7	13.8	17.4	40 876	6.8	5.6	8 995	81.9
Presque Isle County (part)	1 710	14 411	1.9	20.9	22.5	11.5	31 656	10.3	10.9	6 155	85.5
Schoolcraft County (part)	3 051	8 903	11.5	22.9	18.6	11.3	31 140	12.2	12.4	3 606	81.8
Congressional District 2, Michigan	13 895	663 003	12.6	27.6	12.3	18.3	42 589	8.9	5.0	242 071	80.0
Allegan County (part)	733	38 872	10.8	28.9	11.5	19.0	49 223	5.9	2.2	14 061	83.6
Benzie County (part)	832	15 998	4.9	23.3	17.5	20.0	37 350	7.0	6.2	6 500	85.8
Kent County (part)	340	30 254	8.9	27.5	9.8	14.6	43 603	7.6	4.4	11 347	70.3
Lake County	1 470	11 333	16.0	22.0	19.6	7.8	26 622	19.4	8.4	4 704	82.9
Manistee County (part)	1 408	24 527	7.3	22.8	18.1	14.2	34 208	10.3	6.5	9 860	81.0
Mason County (part)	1 282	28 274	6.5	24.2	16.9	15.9	34 704	11.0	7.3	11 406	78.3
Muskegon County (part)	1 319	170 200	20.4	27.4	12.9	13.9	38 008	11.4	5.4	63 330	77.7
Newaygo County	2 182	47 874	7.0	29.1	12.8	11.4	37 130	11.6	5.8	17 599	84.5
Oceana County (part)	1 400	26 873	14.3	28.1	13.9	12.6	35 307	14.7	7.9	9 778	82.7
Ottawa County (part)	1 465	238 314	11.5	28.7	10.1	26.0	52 347	5.5	4.0	81 662	80.8
Wexford County	1 465	30 484	3.4	26.8	14.0	15.3	35 363	10.3	6.9	11 824	79.2
Congressional District 3, Michigan	4 803	662 354	17.8	28.1	10.5	23.9	45 936	8.6	4.4	243 184	72.5
Barry County	1 440	56 755	3.4	27.2	11.7	14.7	46 820	5.5	4.7	21 035	85.9
Ionia County	1 485	61 518	9.0	26.9	10.0	10.8	43 074	8.7	4.6	20 606	80.1
Kent County (part)	1 878	544 081	20.3	28.3	10.4	26.4	46 128	8.9	4.4	201 543	70.3
Congressional District 4, Michigan	19 299	662 497	7.1	24.6	13.6	18.6	39 020	10.5	6.2	252 141	77.8
Clare County	1 468	31 252	3.4	24.5	17.3	8.8	28 845	16.0	8.6	12 686	82.2
Grand Traverse County (part)	1 205	77 654	4.5	25.4	13.1	26.1	43 169	5.9	4.6	30 396	77.3
Gratiot County	1 477	42 285	10.0	23.8	13.5	12.9	37 262	10.3	5.7	14 501	77.5
Isabella County	1 487	63 351	9.5	20.4	9.0	23.9	34 262	20.4	7.2	22 425	63.3
Kalkaska County	1 453	16 571	3.0	25.6	13.8	9.7	36 072	10.5	6.4	6 428	85.4
Leelanau County (part)	903	21 119	7.7	24.4	17.4	31.4	47 062	5.4	5.0	8 436	84.7
Mecosta County	1 439	40 553	7.9	22.5	13.1	19.1	33 849	16.1	11.6	14 915	73.6
Midland County	1 350	82 874	5.6	26.9	12.0	29.3	45 674	8.4	5.1	31 769	78.4
Missaukee County	1 468	14 478	2.5	27.1	14.9	10.2	35 224	10.7	6.5	5 450	83.5
Montcalm County	1 834	61 266	6.6	27.2	12.1	10.8	37 218	10.9	5.5	22 079	81.6
Osceola County	1 466	23 197	3.3	27.1	14.1	11.3	34 102	12.7	6.6	8 861	81.3
Roscommon County	1 350	25 469	2.7	19.9	23.7	10.9	30 029	12.4	8.8	11 250	85.8
Saginaw County (part)	1 661	121 164	12.5	24.0	14.1	18.2	45 084	7.1	5.4	46 830	77.9
Shiawassee County (part)	739	41 264	4.0	25.9	13.6	11.6	38 650	9.1	6.2	16 115	76.1
Congressional District 5, Michigan	4 543	662 584	25.0	27.3	12.3	15.1	39 675	13.7	7.5	257 373	73.8
Bay County (part)	348	79 302	8.5	24.0	15.4	14.9	36 570	10.6	6.5	32 494	75.6
Genesee County	1 657	436 141	25.8	27.4	11.6	16.2	41 951	13.1	7.1	169 825	73.2
Saginaw County (part)	434	88 875	48.4	30.1	12.5	12.4	30 523	23.1	11.1	33 600	68.2
Tuscola County (part)	2 104	58 266	5.3	26.9	12.8	10.6	40 174	8.2	6.2	21 454	84.1
Congressional District 6, Michigan	8 628	662 305	15.7	25.9	12.5	21.1	40 943	11.4	5.8	253 892	72.9
Allegan County (part)	1 410	66 793	8.6	28.7	10.8	14.0	44 040	8.2	5.4	24 104	82.4
Berrien County (part)	1 479	162 453	21.8	25.9	14.5	19.6	38 567	12.7	5.5	63 569	72.2
Calhoun County (part)	123	4 667	3.9	28.0	13.0	15.5	48 939	7.8	4.9	1 701	90.1
Cass County	1 275	51 104	11.3	25.6	13.6	12.1	41 264	9.9	5.0	19 676	81.9
Kalamazoo County	1 455	238 603	16.6	24.0	11.3	31.2	42 022	12.0	6.6	93 479	65.8
St. Joseph County	1 305	62 422	8.8	27.4	13.0	12.7	40 355	11.3	4.6	23 381	76.9
Van Buren County (part)	1 582	76 263	15.6	28.1	12.3	14.3	39 365	11.1	5.8	27 982	79.5

[1] Dry land or land partially or temporarily covered by water.
[2] Persons who do not identify themselves as White alone, not of Hispanic origin.
[3] Persons 25 years old and over.

Table B. 109th Congressional Districts by Counties, 2000—*Continued*

(Number, percent.)

STATE Congressional district County	Land area,[1] (sq km)	Population				Percent with bachelor's degree or more[3]	Median income, 1999 (dollars)	Percent living in poverty	Percent unem-ployed	Households	
		Total	Percent minority[2]	Percent under 18 years old	Percent 65 years old and over					Total	Percent owner occupied
	1	2	3	4	5	6	7	8	9	10	11
Congressional District 7, Michigan	11 125	662 535	11.5	26.0	12.5	19.1	45 181	7.9	4.9	248 411	76.7
Branch County	1 314	45 787	7.8	25.6	13.0	10.6	38 760	9.3	4.8	16 349	78.9
Calhoun County (part)	1 713	133 318	18.0	25.9	13.8	16.0	38 579	11.4	5.8	52 399	72.4
Eaton County	1 493	103 655	11.4	26.1	11.3	21.7	49 588	5.8	4.3	40 167	74.1
Hillsdale County	1 551	46 527	3.2	26.3	13.3	12.0	40 396	8.2	5.3	17 335	79.9
Jackson County	1 830	158 422	12.5	25.6	12.9	16.3	43 171	9.0	5.5	58 168	76.5
Lenawee County	1 944	98 890	10.7	25.9	12.7	16.3	45 739	6.7	4.7	35 930	78.2
Washtenaw County (part)	1 280	75 936	6.5	27.0	9.8	39.8	68 241	3.0	2.9	28 063	83.9
Congressional District 8, Michigan	5 837	662 349	12.4	26.3	8.8	29.0	52 510	8.4	4.4	245 099	75.2
Clinton County	1 480	64 753	5.4	28.1	10.8	21.2	52 806	4.6	3.0	23 653	85.2
Ingham County	1 448	279 320	23.1	23.4	9.4	33.0	40 774	14.6	5.7	108 593	60.7
Livingston County	1 472	156 951	3.9	28.7	8.2	28.2	67 400	3.4	3.3	55 384	88.1
Oakland County (part)	780	130 902	5.1	28.5	7.1	28.9	68 788	4.3	3.5	46 688	86.1
Shiawassee County (part)	656	30 423	3.5	28.2	9.8	16.8	49 047	6.2	4.3	10 781	86.2
Congressional District 9, Michigan	806	662 892	18.6	24.4	12.4	43.5	65 358	5.4	3.6	264 060	74.3
Oakland County (part)	806	662 892	18.6	24.4	12.4	43.5	65 358	5.4	3.6	264 060	74.3
Congressional District 10, Michigan	9 193	662 510	6.4	26.6	11.1	16.9	52 690	6.0	4.5	244 523	82.1
Huron County (part)	2 167	36 079	3.2	24.3	19.5	10.9	35 315	10.2	5.9	14 597	83.5
Lapeer County	1 694	87 904	5.2	28.2	9.5	12.7	51 717	5.4	5.5	30 729	85.0
Macomb County (part)	960	329 745	7.3	26.4	9.4	21.8	63 412	4.1	3.5	120 254	82.5
St. Clair County (part)	1 876	164 235	6.4	26.6	12.3	12.6	46 313	7.8	5.2	62 072	79.6
Sanilac County (part)	2 496	44 547	4.3	26.9	15.4	10.0	36 870	10.4	6.0	16 871	81.9
Congressional District 11, Michigan	1 032	662 505	10.4	25.4	11.6	28.5	59 177	4.3	3.4	257 783	78.5
Oakland County (part)	543	196 207	6.9	27.5	8.2	34.0	65 085	3.7	3.0	74 584	80.6
Wayne County (part)	489	466 298	11.9	24.5	13.0	26.3	56 594	4.6	3.5	183 199	77.7
Congressional District 12, Michigan	415	662 559	18.4	22.6	15.7	19.5	46 784	7.3	4.7	274 732	73.0
Macomb County (part)	285	458 404	9.5	22.4	16.7	14.7	46 258	6.7	4.6	188 949	76.6
Oakland County (part)	131	204 155	38.4	23.2	13.3	30.6	48 099	8.5	4.7	85 783	64.9
Congressional District 13, Michigan	280	662 844	71.1	30.0	11.5	14.1	31 165	24.4	12.9	239 745	55.7
Wayne County (part)	280	662 844	71.1	30.0	11.5	14.1	31 165	24.4	12.9	239 745	55.7
Congressional District 14, Michigan	318	662 468	67.8	28.9	12.4	14.2	36 099	19.7	9.8	243 452	64.9
Wayne County (part)	318	662 468	67.8	28.9	12.4	14.2	36 099	19.7	9.8	243 452	64.9
Congressional District 15, Michigan	2 490	662 456	20.8	24.5	10.0	27.5	48 963	10.3	4.5	253 080	68.4
Monroe County (part)	1 427	145 945	5.8	27.3	11.1	14.3	51 743	7.0	3.5	53 772	80.9
Washtenaw County (part)	559	246 959	29.4	20.4	7.5	51.0	47 703	13.7	4.1	97 264	52.7
Wayne County (part)	503	269 552	21.0	26.7	11.6	15.0	48 313	9.1	5.6	102 044	76.7
MINNESOTA	206 189	4 919 479	11.8	26.2	12.1	27.4	47 111	7.9	4.1	1 895 127	74.5
Congressional District 1, Minnesota	34 503	614 952	6.7	25.5	15.1	21.6	40 941	8.5	4.0	237 886	76.9
Blue Earth County	1 949	55 941	5.7	21.3	12.1	26.6	38 940	12.9	4.6	21 062	66.4
Brown County	1 582	26 911	3.5	25.3	17.5	16.5	39 800	6.4	5.4	10 598	80.1
Cottonwood County	1 658	12 167	5.0	25.0	22.0	14.2	31 943	11.7	3.8	4 917	80.4
Dodge County	1 138	17 731	4.3	30.3	12.1	17.1	47 437	5.8	3.5	6 420	84.4
Faribault County	1 848	16 181	5.0	24.4	22.3	13.8	34 440	8.6	4.6	6 652	80.6
Fillmore County	2 231	21 122	1.4	26.1	19.3	15.1	36 651	10.1	3.5	8 228	80.7
Freeborn County	1 833	32 584	7.9	23.9	18.9	12.8	36 964	8.4	4.3	13 356	78.7
Houston County	1 446	19 718	1.9	27.2	16.0	20.5	40 680	6.5	3.9	7 633	81.1
Jackson County	1 817	11 268	3.4	24.6	20.5	14.2	36 746	8.6	3.5	4 556	79.1
Le Sueur County (part)	9	586	0.0	27.3	12.3	14.8	38 500	7.4	5.2	240	84.2
Martin County	1 837	21 802	3.0	25.0	19.8	16.1	34 810	10.5	4.1	9 067	77.4
Mower County	1 843	38 603	6.6	25.0	19.5	14.7	36 654	9.2	3.9	15 582	78.3
Murray County	1 824	9 165	2.8	24.9	21.3	11.9	34 966	8.3	3.7	3 722	84.5
Nicollet County	1 171	29 771	4.5	24.7	10.9	29.3	46 170	7.5	4.5	10 642	75.6
Nobles County	1 853	20 832	16.9	26.6	17.3	13.5	35 684	11.7	3.9	7 939	75.1
Olmsted County	1 691	124 277	10.8	27.0	10.8	34.7	51 316	6.4	3.7	47 807	76.0
Pipestone County	1 207	9 895	3.7	25.7	21.4	13.9	31 909	9.5	2.5	4 069	77.5
Rock County	1 250	9 721	3.1	26.3	20.5	15.4	38 102	8.0	1.7	3 843	78.0
Steele County	1 113	33 680	6.5	27.8	13.1	20.1	46 106	6.2	3.4	12 846	80.2
Wabasha County	1 360	21 610	2.9	27.1	14.9	16.9	42 117	6.0	2.9	8 277	82.5
Waseca County	1 096	19 526	7.2	25.8	14.2	16.2	42 440	6.5	2.5	7 059	80.0
Watonwan County	1 125	11 876	17.1	27.7	18.6	13.7	35 441	9.8	3.5	4 627	77.0
Winona County	1 622	49 985	4.9	22.8	13.1	23.2	38 700	12.0	5.3	18 744	71.0
Congressional District 2, Minnesota	7 861	615 117	8.1	29.8	7.5	31.2	61 344	3.9	3.0	217 641	82.2
Carver County	925	70 205	5.6	31.6	7.3	34.3	65 540	3.5	3.2	24 356	83.5
Dakota County (part)	1 411	295 704	9.5	30.2	5.9	36.4	64 973	3.3	2.4	106 239	80.9
Goodhue County	1 964	44 127	4.1	26.4	15.0	19.1	46 972	5.7	3.1	16 983	78.9
Hennepin County (part)	1	0	X	X	X	X	X	X	X	0	X
Le Sueur County (part)	1 153	24 840	5.4	27.4	14.1	16.9	46 089	6.9	3.8	9 390	82.9

[1]Dry land or land partially or temporarily covered by water.
[2]Persons who do not identify themselves as White alone, not of Hispanic origin.
[3]Persons 25 years old and over.

Table B. 109th Congressional Districts by Counties, 2000—*Continued*

(Number, percent.)

STATE Congressional district County	Land area,[1] (sq km)	Population				Percent with bachelor's degree or more[3]	Median income, 1999 (dollars)	Percent living in poverty	Percent unem- ployed	Households	
		Total	Percent minority[2]	Percent under 18 years old	Percent 65 years old and over					Total	Percent owner occupied
	1	2	3	4	5	6	7	8	9	10	11
Congressional District 2, Minnesota—*Continued*											
Rice County	1 289	56 665	9.6	25.2	11.3	22.4	48 651	6.9	6.3	18 888	77.9
Scott County	924	89 498	7.4	31.2	6.1	29.4	66 612	3.4	2.6	30 692	86.6
Washington County (part)	195	34 078	7.2	32.3	5.1	25.7	66 839	2.6	2.6	11 093	92.2
Congressional District 3, Minnesota	1 211	614 979	11.3	26.6	10.2	40.1	63 816	3.5	2.8	237 651	77.4
Anoka County (part)	55	58 414	7.7	28.5	7.3	21.1	54 656	5.0	3.9	21 485	79.4
Hennepin County (part)	1 156	556 565	11.7	26.4	10.5	41.9	65 160	3.4	2.6	216 166	77.2
Congressional District 4, Minnesota	523	614 911	22.2	25.8	11.7	33.0	46 811	9.6	4.2	242 046	65.3
Dakota County (part)	64	60 200	11.9	24.0	15.1	27.9	49 052	5.1	3.6	24 912	66.8
Ramsey County (part)	401	508 730	24.7	25.6	11.6	34.3	45 791	10.6	4.4	199 981	63.7
Washington County (part)	57	45 981	8.1	29.7	8.5	25.8	56 072	3.8	2.8	17 153	81.8
Congressional District 5, Minnesota	321	614 874	28.7	21.5	11.7	34.9	41 569	12.7	4.8	263 486	57.2
Anoka County (part)	41	53 402	13.1	21.8	14.3	20.8	44 838	6.9	3.4	22 437	69.8
Hennepin County (part)	279	559 167	30.2	21.5	11.4	36.3	41 328	13.3	5.0	239 794	56.2
Ramsey County (part)	2	2 305	19.5	12.5	21.1	33.1	37 458	7.1	3.9	1 255	33.1
Congressional District 6, Minnesota	7 979	614 793	5.1	29.2	7.6	24.5	56 862	4.7	3.0	214 072	82.8
Anoka County (part)	1 001	186 268	5.6	31.1	4.8	21.5	62 871	3.1	3.1	62 506	89.7
Benton County	1 057	34 226	4.7	27.0	11.1	17.2	41 968	7.1	3.4	13 065	67.1
Hennepin County (part)	6	468	5.6	23.9	6.0	12.3	70 417	1.9	0.7	169	97.6
Ramsey County (part)	0	0	X	X	X	X	X	X	X	0	X
Sherburne County	1 130	64 417	3.8	30.9	7.1	19.4	57 014	4.4	2.6	21 581	84.0
Stearns County (part)	2 310	118 357	4.6	25.4	10.1	23.3	43 407	8.8	3.7	42 070	72.8
Washington County (part)	762	121 071	7.4	28.6	7.8	39.0	70 419	2.6	2.5	43 216	85.8
Wright County	1 711	89 986	2.7	31.2	8.8	17.9	53 945	4.7	3.0	31 465	84.3
Congressional District 7, Minnesota	82 353	615 129	6.8	26.1	16.9	16.4	36 453	10.3	5.0	238 530	77.8
Becker County	3 394	30 000	10.9	26.6	16.3	16.7	34 797	12.2	6.3	11 844	80.4
Beltrami County (part)	5 459	29 293	27.3	28.5	12.0	22.5	31 069	20.2	8.3	10 520	69.4
Big Stone County	1 287	5 820	1.5	24.9	24.2	11.4	30 721	12.0	5.3	2 377	85.1
Chippewa County	1 509	13 088	3.7	25.3	20.0	13.7	35 582	8.6	5.6	5 361	76.5
Clay County	2 707	51 229	7.7	25.0	13.0	24.7	37 889	13.2	5.3	18 670	71.6
Clearwater County	2 576	8 423	9.8	26.1	17.3	14.7	30 517	15.1	10.3	3 330	81.6
Douglas County	1 643	32 821	1.8	24.0	17.9	17.3	37 703	8.5	3.9	13 276	77.2
Grant County	1 415	6 289	1.5	23.7	23.0	15.7	33 775	8.4	4.8	2 534	82.2
Kandiyohi County	2 062	41 203	9.5	26.6	15.0	18.3	39 772	9.2	3.6	15 936	75.5
Kittson County	2 841	5 285	3.4	25.1	21.6	14.8	32 515	10.2	5.0	2 167	82.7
Lac qui Parle County	1 981	8 067	1.3	24.5	23.3	13.0	32 626	8.5	3.3	3 316	80.7
Lake of the Woods County	3 358	4 522	3.2	24.5	17.3	17.2	32 861	9.8	4.8	1 903	85.4
Lincoln County	1 391	6 429	0.9	23.7	24.3	14.1	31 607	9.7	3.5	2 653	80.4
Lyon County	1 850	25 425	8.1	26.1	14.6	21.4	38 996	10.1	5.1	9 715	68.4
McLeod County	1 274	34 898	4.6	27.8	13.9	15.4	45 953	4.8	3.8	13 449	78.5
Mahnomen County	1 440	5 190	37.3	29.4	16.9	12.4	30 053	16.7	6.7	1 969	77.3
Marshall County	4 590	10 155	4.4	25.3	18.6	12.0	34 804	9.8	8.7	4 101	83.8
Meeker County	1 576	22 644	2.8	27.1	16.3	13.9	40 908	7.1	4.8	8 590	81.5
Norman County	2 270	7 442	6.0	25.6	21.0	13.1	32 535	10.3	6.1	3 010	81.1
Otter Tail County	5 127	57 159	3.5	25.0	18.9	17.2	35 395	10.1	5.2	22 671	80.0
Pennington County	1 597	13 584	2.9	24.3	15.9	14.9	34 216	11.1	7.6	5 525	74.6
Polk County	5 103	31 369	7.6	25.9	17.3	17.6	35 105	10.9	5.9	12 070	74.0
Pope County	1 736	11 236	1.1	24.8	21.6	14.7	35 633	8.8	3.6	4 513	80.8
Red Lake County	1 120	4 299	3.5	25.4	19.0	10.7	32 052	10.8	9.1	1 727	79.4
Redwood County	2 278	16 815	5.3	26.5	19.3	13.4	37 352	7.7	3.1	6 674	80.0
Renville County	2 546	17 154	6.3	26.6	19.8	12.6	37 652	8.8	3.8	6 779	81.0
Roseau County	4 306	16 338	4.7	29.8	12.6	14.9	39 852	6.6	3.3	6 190	84.1
Sibley County	1 525	15 356	6.5	27.6	16.5	11.6	41 458	8.1	2.7	5 772	80.9
Stearns County (part)	1 172	14 809	3.6	28.4	18.2	12.6	36 845	8.4	3.6	5 534	81.0
Stevens County	1 456	10 053	4.3	21.6	16.9	20.6	37 267	13.6	5.3	3 751	70.2
Swift County	1 926	11 956	9.5	23.0	18.7	14.0	34 820	8.4	4.3	4 353	77.1
Todd County	2 440	24 426	3.8	27.4	16.1	10.0	32 281	12.9	5.2	9 342	82.9
Traverse County	1 487	4 134	4.2	25.5	26.5	10.7	30 617	12.0	5.2	1 717	80.5
Wilkin County	1 946	7 138	3.1	27.9	16.1	14.0	38 093	8.1	3.7	2 752	80.6
Yellow Medicine County	1 963	11 080	5.4	25.8	20.4	14.4	34 393	10.4	5.5	4 439	79.3
Congressional District 8, Minnesota	71 439	614 724	5.4	24.8	15.8	17.7	37 911	10.4	6.0	243 815	80.1
Aitkin County	4 712	15 301	4.2	20.9	23.0	11.3	31 139	11.6	7.7	6 644	85.3
Beltrami County (part)	1 029	10 357	13.8	29.5	10.4	26.1	39 544	10.5	5.2	3 817	88.3
Carlton County	2 228	31 671	8.7	25.4	15.1	14.9	40 021	7.9	5.8	12 064	82.0
Cass County	5 226	27 150	13.5	25.1	18.0	16.6	34 332	13.6	6.8	10 893	86.0
Chisago County	1 082	41 101	3.7	30.1	9.8	15.3	52 012	5.1	3.4	14 454	87.0

[1]Dry land or land partially or temporarily covered by water.
[2]Persons who do not identify themselves as White alone, not of Hispanic origin.
[3]Persons 25 years old and over.

Table B. 109th Congressional Districts by Counties, 2000—*Continued*

(Number, percent.)

STATE Congressional district County	Land area,[1] (sq km)	Population Total	Percent minority[2]	Percent under 18 years old	Percent 65 years old and over	Percent with bachelor's degree or more[3]	Median income, 1999 (dollars)	Percent living in poverty	Percent unem- ployed	Households Total	Percent owner occupied
	1	2	3	4	5	6	7	8	9	10	11
Congressional District 8, Minnesota—*Continued*											
Cook County	3 757	5 168	10.6	20.1	17.3	28.8	36 640	10.1	6.2	2 350	78.2
Crow Wing County	2 581	55 099	2.7	24.8	17.1	18.4	37 589	9.8	5.5	22 250	79.6
Hubbard County	2 389	18 376	3.7	24.6	17.9	20.2	35 321	9.7	6.6	7 435	83.4
Isanti County	1 137	31 287	2.9	28.6	10.9	14.5	50 127	5.7	4.3	11 236	85.2
Itasca County	6 902	43 992	5.6	24.3	16.8	17.6	36 234	10.6	6.7	17 789	82.9
Kanabec County	1 360	14 996	2.8	27.5	14.1	10.5	38 520	9.5	6.2	5 759	84.0
Koochiching County	8 035	14 355	4.4	23.9	17.9	15.1	36 262	12.1	5.5	6 040	80.4
Lake County	5 437	11 058	2.5	22.3	20.1	19.5	40 402	7.4	5.3	4 646	84.0
Mille Lacs County	1 488	22 330	6.8	27.0	16.1	12.2	36 977	9.6	5.4	8 638	79.8
Morrison County	2 912	31 712	1.8	28.0	15.6	12.6	37 047	11.1	5.7	11 816	82.0
Pine County	3 655	26 530	7.2	25.5	15.1	10.3	37 379	11.3	6.8	9 939	83.7
St. Louis County	16 123	200 528	5.6	22.4	16.1	21.9	36 306	12.1	6.8	82 619	74.7
Wadena County	1 386	13 713	3.2	25.8	19.7	13.4	30 651	14.1	5.6	5 426	77.4
MISSISSIPPI	121 488	2 844 658	39.2	27.2	12.1	16.9	31 330	19.9	7.4	1 046 434	72.4
Congressional District 1, Mississippi	29 559	711 113	28.7	26.6	12.4	13.9	32 535	16.4	6.1	267 649	75.1
Alcorn County	1 036	34 558	13.1	23.8	14.8	11.7	29 041	16.6	4.7	14 224	73.5
Benton County	1 054	8 026	38.0	26.9	15.4	7.8	24 149	23.2	7.1	2 999	84.3
Calhoun County	1 519	15 069	31.5	25.3	16.6	10.2	27 113	18.1	6.5	6 019	76.2
Chickasaw County	1 299	19 440	44.1	28.6	13.1	9.5	26 364	20.0	5.2	7 253	77.8
Choctaw County	1 085	9 758	32.3	27.8	14.8	11.2	27 020	24.7	11.7	3 686	81.3
Clay County	1 058	21 979	57.5	28.8	13.4	14.6	27 372	23.5	8.1	8 152	73.4
DeSoto County	1 238	107 199	15.2	28.1	8.9	14.3	48 206	7.1	3.6	38 792	79.2
Grenada County	1 092	23 263	42.3	27.2	14.5	13.5	27 385	20.9	6.0	8 820	69.1
Itawamba County	1 379	22 770	8.2	24.3	14.1	8.8	31 156	14.0	7.2	8 773	82.5
Lafayette County	1 635	38 744	28.8	19.6	9.9	31.1	28 517	21.3	6.6	14 373	60.6
Lee County	1 164	75 755	27.0	27.6	11.5	18.1	36 165	13.4	4.9	29 200	69.2
Lowndes County	1 301	61 586	44.0	28.5	11.3	20.5	32 123	21.3	7.9	22 849	66.6
Marshall County	1 829	34 993	52.1	26.5	11.4	9.0	28 756	21.9	8.9	12 163	80.5
Monroe County	1 979	38 014	32.4	27.2	13.8	10.9	30 307	17.2	6.7	14 603	79.0
Panola County	1 772	34 274	50.2	29.5	12.4	10.8	26 785	25.3	7.8	12 232	77.9
Pontotoc County	1 288	26 726	16.4	27.5	12.7	11.4	32 055	13.8	5.5	10 097	78.1
Prentiss County	1 075	25 556	14.1	25.1	13.6	9.9	28 446	16.5	5.6	9 821	78.0
Tate County	1 048	25 370	32.5	27.2	11.3	12.3	35 836	13.5	10.3	8 850	78.3
Tippah County	1 186	20 826	18.9	25.0	14.5	9.0	29 300	16.9	5.3	8 108	78.1
Tishomingo County	1 098	19 163	5.2	22.9	17.0	8.7	28 315	14.1	5.7	7 917	78.7
Union County	1 076	25 362	17.3	26.0	14.4	13.2	32 682	12.6	4.8	9 786	77.6
Webster County (part)	1 052	9 485	21.9	25.8	16.9	13.3	28 639	17.9	6.1	3 609	77.8
Winston County (part)	86	146	15.8	19.9	21.2	42.7	27 083	30.1	0.0	63	100.0
Yalobusha County	1 210	13 051	39.9	25.6	16.1	9.6	26 315	21.8	7.0	5 260	79.0
Congressional District 2, Mississippi	35 288	710 996	65.5	29.4	11.5	16.8	26 894	27.3	10.4	245 770	65.7
Attala County	1 904	19 661	42.0	26.0	17.3	11.6	24 794	21.8	7.0	7 567	77.7
Bolivar County	2 270	40 633	66.9	29.5	11.0	18.8	23 428	33.3	15.1	13 776	61.1
Carroll County	1 626	10 769	38.3	24.3	14.1	10.9	28 878	16.0	7.4	4 071	84.8
Claiborne County	1 261	11 831	84.8	26.3	10.5	18.9	22 615	32.4	18.0	3 685	80.3
Coahoma County	1 435	30 622	70.8	33.0	12.3	16.2	22 338	35.9	10.1	10 553	57.3
Copiah County	2 011	28 757	52.6	26.9	13.2	11.6	26 358	25.1	11.0	10 142	79.8
Hinds County (part)	2 207	219 002	69.2	29.1	9.9	21.4	31 423	21.9	8.7	76 996	62.9
Holmes County	1 958	21 609	79.8	32.1	12.5	11.2	17 235	41.1	17.3	7 314	73.2
Humphreys County	1 083	11 206	73.0	32.8	12.2	11.6	20 566	38.2	11.4	3 765	61.4
Issaquena County	1 070	2 274	63.9	27.6	10.7	7.1	19 936	33.2	13.5	726	67.4
Jefferson County	1 345	9 740	86.8	28.6	11.1	10.6	18 447	36.0	14.2	3 308	80.4
Leake County (part)	734	11 397	53.5	27.4	14.7	13.7	24 922	25.9	7.4	3 972	76.5
Leflore County	1 533	37 947	70.4	29.8	12.1	15.9	21 518	34.8	15.9	12 956	53.3
Madison County (part)	1 223	27 393	75.0	31.5	11.4	18.2	31 162	28.6	10.9	8 271	70.9
Montgomery County	1 054	12 189	46.1	26.8	16.7	11.0	25 270	24.3	6.9	4 690	76.9
Quitman County	1 049	10 117	69.7	31.9	13.3	10.6	20 636	33.1	8.4	3 565	68.8
Sharkey County	1 108	6 580	71.2	33.1	11.1	12.6	22 285	38.3	14.5	2 163	65.7
Sunflower County	1 797	34 369	71.6	27.9	9.7	12.0	24 970	30.0	12.9	9 637	61.9
Tallahatchie County	1 668	14 903	60.7	30.1	13.3	10.9	22 229	32.2	9.6	5 263	76.1
Tunica County	1 178	9 227	73.1	31.5	9.8	9.1	23 270	33.1	9.3	3 258	51.8
Warren County	1 519	49 644	45.4	28.5	11.8	20.8	35 056	18.7	6.7	18 756	68.3
Washington County	1 875	62 977	66.3	31.4	11.7	16.4	25 757	29.2	11.9	22 158	59.5
Yazoo County	2 381	28 149	59.0	28.4	12.6	11.8	24 795	31.9	10.7	9 178	68.9

[1]Dry land or land partially or temporarily covered by water.
[2]Persons who do not identify themselves as White alone, not of Hispanic origin.
[3]Persons 25 years old and over.

Table B. 109th Congressional Districts by Counties, 2000—*Continued*

(Number, percent.)

STATE Congressional district County	Land area,[1] (sq km)	Population				Percent with bachelor's degree or more[3]	Median income, 1999 (dollars)	Percent living in poverty	Percent unem-ployed	Households	
		Total	Percent minority[2]	Percent under 18 years old	Percent 65 years old and over					Total	Percent owner occupied
	1	2	3	4	5	6	7	8	9	10	11
Congressional District 3, Mississippi	34 106	711 409	36.3	26.4	12.8	20.2	31 907	19.2	6.7	269 154	75.7
Adams County	1 192	34 340	54.4	26.7	15.6	17.5	25 234	25.9	9.1	13 677	70.2
Amite County	1 890	13 599	44.0	25.8	15.6	9.4	26 033	22.6	8.9	5 271	85.9
Covington County	1 072	19 407	36.9	28.6	12.9	11.4	26 669	23.5	7.7	7 126	84.9
Franklin County	1 462	8 448	37.5	27.5	15.2	10.5	24 885	24.1	8.7	3 211	86.1
Hinds County (part)	45	31 798	19.2	19.5	18.3	59.5	52 885	6.9	3.1	14 034	69.3
Jasper County (part)	628	7 293	54.6	27.9	15.3	10.3	22 260	25.4	7.6	2 713	83.9
Jefferson Davis County	1 058	13 962	58.8	28.2	13.8	10.4	21 834	28.2	12.9	5 177	84.5
Jones County (part)	136	2 126	37.5	27.0	13.5	10.9	29 612	17.1	5.2	797	84.7
Kemper County	1 984	10 453	60.6	25.3	15.1	10.3	23 998	26.0	12.6	3 909	83.9
Lauderdale County	1 822	78 161	40.3	26.6	14.2	16.2	30 768	20.8	7.5	29 990	67.8
Lawrence County	1 115	13 258	33.7	27.5	13.1	12.0	28 495	19.6	6.3	5 040	84.3
Leake County (part)	775	9 543	33.2	26.8	14.3	9.2	28 541	20.4	6.7	3 639	88.0
Lincoln County	1 517	33 166	30.8	26.8	13.9	12.4	27 279	19.2	7.1	12 538	78.1
Madison County (part)	634	47 281	20.4	26.9	8.8	47.7	54 559	6.0	2.6	18 948	70.8
Marion County (part)	676	9 800	24.7	28.3	11.8	7.8	25 995	23.4	6.3	3 608	87.4
Neshoba County	1 476	28 684	34.3	28.4	14.2	11.4	28 300	21.0	7.4	10 694	79.5
Newton County	1 497	21 838	34.9	26.2	14.8	12.1	28 735	19.9	5.2	8 221	81.8
Noxubee County	1 799	12 548	70.8	30.7	12.9	10.9	22 330	32.8	9.4	4 470	79.7
Oktibbeha County	1 185	42 902	41.4	21.1	8.8	34.8	24 899	28.2	11.7	15 945	55.6
Pike County	1 059	38 940	49.0	27.7	14.3	12.5	24 562	25.3	9.4	14 792	74.3
Rankin County	2 006	115 327	19.8	25.8	9.1	23.8	44 946	9.5	3.8	42 089	77.2
Scott County	1 578	28 423	45.2	28.6	12.3	8.6	26 686	20.7	6.0	10 183	78.4
Simpson County	1 525	27 639	36.2	27.9	13.0	10.9	28 343	21.6	6.3	10 076	81.2
Smith County	1 647	16 182	24.2	27.5	14.2	9.1	30 840	16.9	5.9	6 046	87.0
Walthall County	1 046	15 156	45.8	28.5	14.0	10.4	22 945	27.8	9.8	5 571	83.2
Webster County (part)	42	809	36.1	28.2	13.0	9.3	30 962	27.6	12.1	296	85.5
Wilkinson County	1 753	10 312	68.9	25.9	13.9	10.0	18 929	37.7	10.4	3 578	83.1
Winston County (part)	1 486	20 014	45.4	26.8	15.1	13.6	28 261	23.7	7.4	7 515	79.4
Congressional District 4, Mississippi	22 535	711 140	26.5	26.5	11.7	16.7	33 023	16.9	6.7	263 861	72.4
Clarke County	1 790	17 955	36.3	26.8	15.4	9.6	26 610	23.0	8.5	6 978	84.2
Forrest County	1 208	72 604	36.5	24.4	11.2	22.8	27 420	22.5	7.9	27 183	60.4
George County	1 239	19 144	11.3	28.9	11.2	9.1	34 730	16.7	9.1	6 742	86.2
Greene County	1 846	13 299	27.6	24.0	10.3	8.0	28 336	19.6	10.4	4 148	86.9
Hancock County	1 235	42 967	10.7	25.2	14.0	17.3	35 202	14.4	6.9	16 897	79.6
Harrison County	1 505	189 601	28.2	26.0	11.1	18.4	35 624	14.6	6.1	71 538	62.7
Jackson County	1 883	131 420	25.8	27.6	10.3	16.5	39 118	12.7	6.7	47 676	74.6
Jasper County (part)	1 123	10 856	53.4	27.9	13.4	9.4	25 737	20.9	8.7	3 995	88.8
Jones County (part)	1 661	62 832	29.3	25.7	14.2	14.1	28 760	19.9	5.7	23 478	76.6
Lamar County	1 287	39 070	15.0	28.1	9.8	26.8	37 628	13.3	4.3	14 396	75.8
Marion County (part)	728	15 795	38.8	27.5	15.4	13.8	23 577	25.6	7.5	5 728	76.0
Pearl River County	2 101	48 621	15.5	27.0	12.5	13.9	30 912	18.4	7.3	18 078	79.8
Perry County	1 676	12 138	24.0	28.6	11.1	7.7	27 189	22.0	7.1	4 420	84.6
Stone County	1 153	13 622	21.0	27.0	11.2	12.4	30 495	17.5	6.8	4 747	81.3
Wayne County	2 099	21 216	38.9	29.2	11.9	9.5	25 918	25.4	7.8	7 857	84.9
MISSOURI	178 414	5 595 211	16.2	25.5	13.5	21.6	37 934	11.7	5.3	2 194 594	70.3
Congressional District 1, Missouri	562	621 497	54.0	26.4	13.9	22.4	36 314	15.8	8.3	249 256	62.1
St. Louis County (part)	469	458 398	43.0	26.4	13.6	24.1	41 598	10.1	5.8	182 789	70.0
St. Louis city (part)	93	163 099	85.1	26.7	14.5	17.4	21 802	32.2	16.8	66 467	40.2
Congressional District 2, Missouri	3 232	621 422	6.8	27.3	11.3	38.3	61 416	3.6	3.1	230 452	81.6
Lincoln County	1 633	38 944	4.6	30.0	10.8	9.7	42 592	8.3	4.8	13 851	80.8
St. Charles County (part)	913	245 678	6.5	28.9	8.6	25.4	55 881	4.1	3.8	88 279	80.8
St. Louis County (part)	686	336 800	7.2	25.8	13.4	50.0	69 833	2.8	2.4	128 322	82.1
Congressional District 3, Missouri	3 230	622 148	14.3	24.8	13.0	23.2	41 091	10.1	5.6	251 895	68.9
Jefferson County	1 701	198 099	3.1	27.9	9.2	12.1	46 338	6.8	4.6	71 499	83.4
Ste. Genevieve County	1 301	17 842	2.4	26.5	14.6	8.1	39 200	8.2	3.2	6 586	82.3
St. Louis County (part)	160	221 117	10.1	21.8	16.3	35.7	47 476	6.5	5.4	93 201	71.2
St. Louis city (part)	67	185 090	32.3	24.8	13.0	20.5	31 100	18.0	7.3	80 609	52.4
Congressional District 4, Missouri	37 669	621 882	7.6	25.5	14.4	15.6	34 541	12.1	4.6	238 497	73.7
Barton County	1 539	12 541	3.7	27.4	16.5	10.6	29 275	13.0	3.0	4 895	73.4
Bates County	2 198	16 653	3.0	26.6	17.4	10.1	30 731	14.5	5.0	6 511	75.0
Benton County	1 827	17 180	2.9	20.5	22.4	8.8	26 646	15.7	6.1	7 420	82.2
Camden County (part)	1 487	35 020	2.8	20.4	18.9	17.8	35 808	11.5	4.8	14 911	82.1
Cass County (part)	1 559	39 076	3.7	27.6	12.2	16.5	49 199	5.2	2.7	14 424	80.4
Cedar County	1 233	13 733	3.6	24.6	20.8	10.0	26 694	17.4	4.3	5 685	78.3
Cole County	1 014	71 397	13.5	24.1	11.3	27.4	42 924	8.7	3.7	27 040	67.8
Dade County	1 270	7 923	3.2	24.3	20.3	9.9	29 097	13.4	5.2	3 202	78.8
Dallas County	1 403	15 661	3.2	27.2	15.2	9.5	27 346	17.9	4.9	6 030	79.2
Henry County	1 819	21 997	3.8	23.7	18.3	11.7	30 949	14.3	5.0	9 133	73.0

[1]Dry land or land partially or temporarily covered by water.
[2]Persons who do not identify themselves White, not of Hispanic origin.
[3]Persons 25 years old and over.

Table B. 109th Congressional Districts by Counties, 2000—*Continued*

(Number, percent.)

STATE Congressional district County	Land area,[1] (sq km)	Population Total	Population Percent minority[2]	Population Percent under 18 years old	Population Percent 65 years old and over	Percent with bachelor's degree or more[3]	Median income, 1999 (dollars)	Percent living in poverty	Percent unemployed	Households Total	Households Percent owner occupied
	1	2	3	4	5	6	7	8	9	10	11
Congressional District 4, Missouri—*Continued*											
Hickory County	1 032	8 940	4.2	19.9	26.0	7.7	25 346	19.7	8.1	3 911	84.5
Jackson County (part)	74	18 952	6.7	28.2	10.3	17.5	46 265	7.0	3.3	7 231	66.2
Johnson County	2 151	48 258	11.4	25.2	9.4	23.2	35 391	14.9	6.1	17 410	61.5
Laclede County	1 984	32 513	3.8	26.7	14.2	11.3	29 562	14.3	4.8	12 760	72.8
Lafayette County	1 630	32 960	5.1	26.0	15.4	13.8	38 235	8.8	3.7	12 569	75.4
Moniteau County	1 079	14 827	7.6	25.8	14.0	13.0	37 168	9.9	3.0	5 259	77.7
Morgan County	1 547	19 309	3.5	23.8	19.6	10.7	30 659	16.2	4.8	7 850	82.9
Pettis County	1 774	39 403	8.8	26.3	15.5	15.0	31 822	12.8	5.1	15 568	72.5
Polk County (part)	753	6 113	3.3	24.4	19.2	8.4	27 688	15.9	4.3	2 418	83.4
Pulaski County	1 417	41 165	24.3	27.5	7.9	18.8	34 247	10.3	6.8	13 433	58.0
Ray County	1 475	23 354	3.9	27.6	12.7	10.8	41 886	6.8	5.5	8 743	79.5
St. Clair County	1 753	9 652	4.0	23.1	21.2	9.0	25 321	19.6	6.3	4 040	79.5
Saline County	1 957	23 756	11.6	24.4	16.2	15.8	32 743	13.2	4.6	9 015	69.1
Vernon County	2 160	20 454	3.4	26.6	16.3	14.2	30 021	14.9	4.4	7 966	72.3
Webster County	1 537	31 045	4.6	28.9	11.5	11.0	31 929	14.8	4.0	11 073	78.0
Congressional District 5, Missouri	1 325	621 496	33.7	25.5	13.0	22.9	38 311	12.4	5.9	254 560	62.3
Cass County (part)	251	43 016	7.9	28.9	11.3	18.8	49 903	6.3	3.4	15 744	78.8
Jackson County (part)	1 073	578 480	35.6	25.3	13.1	23.2	37 462	12.9	6.0	238 816	61.3
Congressional District 6, Missouri	33 753	621 790	7.6	25.3	13.3	21.2	41 225	8.7	3.8	241 504	72.0
Andrew County	1 127	16 492	2.6	26.2	14.4	18.8	40 688	8.2	3.1	6 273	80.0
Atchison County	1 411	6 430	3.5	24.1	21.1	16.6	30 959	11.6	3.7	2 722	69.2
Buchanan County	1 061	85 998	8.8	24.3	15.0	16.9	34 704	12.2	5.9	33 557	67.5
Caldwell County	1 112	8 969	2.2	27.1	16.9	11.7	31 240	11.9	3.1	3 523	77.4
Carroll County	1 799	10 285	3.9	25.1	20.1	14.0	30 643	13.7	4.1	4 169	74.0
Chariton County	1 958	8 438	3.7	23.8	22.4	11.4	32 285	11.6	4.0	3 469	80.5
Clay County	1 027	184 006	9.5	25.8	10.8	24.9	48 347	5.5	3.3	72 558	70.7
Clinton County	1 085	18 979	4.2	26.8	14.1	14.5	41 629	9.3	4.4	7 152	79.0
Cooper County	1 463	16 670	11.7	22.8	15.4	13.7	35 343	10.7	3.4	5 932	74.2
Daviess County	1 468	8 016	1.2	27.1	17.6	12.0	30 855	15.2	4.3	3 178	76.8
DeKalb County	1 099	11 597	11.5	20.6	14.0	10.7	31 654	10.8	3.8	3 528	73.4
Gentry County	1 273	6 861	1.3	26.0	21.7	14.5	28 750	12.0	5.3	2 747	74.5
Grundy County	1 129	10 432	4.0	23.2	20.5	12.5	27 333	15.8	4.8	4 382	71.8
Harrison County	1 878	8 850	2.0	23.9	22.1	9.3	28 707	13.5	3.8	3 658	74.7
Holt County	1 196	5 351	1.6	23.7	21.5	11.7	29 461	13.0	2.2	2 237	74.4
Howard County	1 206	10 212	9.3	23.9	16.2	17.9	31 614	11.6	5.2	3 836	75.2
Jackson County (part)	419	57 448	7.4	29.5	7.2	28.2	57 265	4.3	2.8	20 247	80.7
Linn County	1 607	13 754	2.7	25.2	20.5	10.8	28 242	14.9	3.4	5 697	77.0
Livingston County	1 384	14 558	4.3	24.0	19.0	13.1	32 290	12.4	3.2	5 736	70.8
Mercer County	1 176	3 757	0.7	22.8	21.9	12.2	29 640	13.3	3.8	1 600	76.8
Nodaway County	2 270	21 912	3.6	19.3	13.8	23.6	31 781	16.5	5.6	8 138	63.8
Platte County	1 089	73 781	10.2	25.7	8.8	33.3	55 849	4.8	2.6	29 278	67.4
Putnam County	1 341	5 223	1.5	24.0	20.6	11.2	26 282	16.0	4.6	2 228	77.2
Schuyler County	797	4 170	1.4	24.6	19.8	11.6	27 385	17.0	4.8	1 725	75.2
Sullivan County	1 686	7 219	9.4	25.2	18.3	8.4	26 107	16.5	5.2	2 925	71.7
Worth County	690	2 382	1.4	24.2	22.5	11.3	27 471	14.3	5.9	1 009	76.8
Congressional District 7, Missouri	14 192	621 746	7.1	24.5	13.9	18.8	32 929	13.0	5.6	246 008	68.9
Barry County	2 018	34 010	7.6	26.2	16.1	10.7	28 906	16.6	4.8	13 398	75.7
Christian County	1 459	54 285	3.5	27.8	10.6	20.9	38 085	9.1	3.2	20 425	75.9
Greene County	1 748	240 391	7.5	22.2	13.7	24.2	34 157	12.1	5.5	97 859	63.6
Jasper County	1 657	104 686	8.9	25.7	13.8	16.5	31 323	14.5	6.6	41 412	67.0
Lawrence County	1 588	35 204	5.8	27.2	15.6	12.1	31 239	14.1	4.4	13 568	74.3
McDonald County	1 397	21 681	15.9	28.8	11.2	7.0	27 010	20.7	4.2	8 113	71.5
Newton County	1 622	52 636	7.4	26.2	14.1	16.1	35 041	11.6	4.6	20 140	76.6
Polk County (part)	898	20 879	3.3	26.0	14.1	16.8	30 165	16.4	4.7	7 499	69.6
Stone County	1 200	28 658	2.8	21.4	18.9	14.2	32 637	12.8	9.6	11 822	81.2
Taney County (part)	606	29 316	5.7	22.4	14.4	16.5	31 598	12.1	10.1	11 772	64.6
Congressional District 8, Missouri	48 384	621 746	7.6	25.1	15.8	11.9	27 865	18.2	6.5	245 519	72.0
Bollinger County	1 608	12 029	2.8	26.2	14.7	6.9	30 462	13.8	6.2	4 576	81.6
Butler County	1 807	40 867	8.2	24.1	16.7	11.6	27 228	18.6	6.6	16 718	68.9
Cape Girardeau County	1 499	68 693	8.3	23.4	13.7	24.2	36 458	11.1	5.0	26 980	68.4
Carter County	1 315	5 941	5.3	25.2	15.9	10.8	22 863	25.2	8.1	2 378	76.7
Dent County	1 952	14 927	3.1	24.7	17.8	10.1	27 193	17.2	7.1	5 982	74.1
Douglas County	2 110	13 084	3.6	25.8	17.0	9.9	25 918	17.5	4.7	5 201	79.0
Dunklin County	1 413	33 155	12.5	26.0	16.6	9.1	24 878	24.5	6.2	13 411	65.9
Howell County	2 403	37 238	4.4	25.9	16.8	10.9	25 628	18.7	6.4	14 762	73.5
Iron County	1 428	10 697	3.9	24.9	17.1	8.4	26 080	19.0	6.7	4 197	75.9
Madison County	1 287	11 800	2.4	24.5	18.0	7.8	25 601	17.2	6.8	4 711	76.0

[1]Dry land or land partially or temporarily covered by water.
[2]Persons who do not identify themselves White, not of Hispanic origin.
[3]Persons 25 years old and over.

Table B. 109th Congressional Districts by Counties, 2000—*Continued*

(Number, percent.)

STATE Congressional district County	Land area,[1] (sq km)	Population Total	Population Percent minority[2]	Population Percent under 18 years old	Population Percent 65 years old and over	Percent with bachelor's degree or more[3]	Median income, 1999 (dollars)	Percent living in poverty	Percent unem-ployed	Households Total	Households Percent owner occupied
	1	2	3	4	5	6	7	8	9	10	11
Congressional District 8, Missouri—*Continued*											
Mississippi County	1 070	13 427	22.7	26.4	15.9	9.6	23 012	23.7	8.8	5 383	63.5
New Madrid County	1 756	19 760	17.2	26.4	15.4	9.6	26 826	22.1	6.0	7 824	66.1
Oregon County	2 050	10 344	6.3	24.2	17.9	9.1	22 359	22.0	7.3	4 263	78.3
Ozark County	1 922	9 542	3.5	21.9	19.5	8.3	25 861	21.6	5.9	3 950	81.6
Pemiscot County	1 277	20 047	29.4	29.9	15.1	8.4	21 911	30.4	8.6	7 855	58.4
Perry County	1 229	18 132	3.0	26.0	15.7	9.9	36 632	9.0	3.0	6 904	79.9
Phelps County	1 743	39 825	7.5	23.9	13.9	21.1	29 378	16.4	6.5	15 683	65.6
Reynolds County	2 101	6 689	5.8	23.9	16.3	7.5	25 867	20.1	10.2	2 721	77.1
Ripley County	1 630	13 509	3.2	24.8	17.3	7.8	22 761	22.0	8.4	5 416	78.0
St. Francois County	1 164	55 641	4.4	23.9	15.0	10.2	31 199	14.9	7.5	20 793	73.2
Scott County	1 090	40 422	12.6	27.4	13.8	10.6	31 352	16.1	6.3	15 626	69.3
Shannon County	2 600	8 324	4.1	26.2	14.9	7.6	20 878	26.9	6.7	3 319	79.7
Stoddard County	2 142	29 705	3.4	23.8	17.2	10.1	26 987	16.5	6.0	12 064	72.3
Taney County (part)	1 032	10 387	4.2	22.4	21.1	10.7	28 940	13.2	10.1	4 386	80.3
Texas County	3 052	23 003	4.9	24.9	17.9	10.8	24 545	21.4	6.5	9 378	76.6
Washington County	1 967	23 344	5.2	26.6	11.7	7.5	27 112	20.8	7.8	8 406	79.9
Wayne County	1 971	13 259	2.6	23.3	19.9	6.8	24 007	21.9	9.3	5 551	78.2
Wright County	1 767	17 955	3.6	27.0	16.5	9.8	24 691	21.7	5.9	7 081	73.1
Congressional District 9, Missouri	36 067	621 484	7.3	25.1	13.0	19.9	36 693	11.8	4.6	236 903	72.6
Adair County	1 469	24 977	5.0	19.2	12.2	28.5	26 677	23.3	4.8	9 669	60.4
Audrain County	1 795	25 853	9.3	24.6	17.2	12.7	32 057	14.8	4.0	9 844	74.1
Boone County	1 775	135 454	15.3	22.8	8.6	41.7	37 485	14.5	5.3	53 094	57.5
Callaway County	2 173	40 766	8.7	25.4	10.9	16.5	39 110	8.5	3.9	14 416	76.8
Camden County (part)	210	2 031	3.4	16.7	19.5	17.2	36 313	8.7	2.2	868	85.7
Clark County	1 314	7 416	1.6	25.0	16.7	10.7	29 457	14.1	5.3	2 966	78.5
Crawford County	1 923	22 804	2.7	26.1	15.8	8.4	30 860	16.3	6.0	8 858	76.7
Franklin County	2 390	93 807	3.2	27.4	12.1	12.8	43 474	7.0	3.5	34 945	78.0
Gasconade County	1 349	15 342	1.6	24.7	18.9	10.4	35 047	9.5	4.1	6 171	80.3
Knox County	1 310	4 361	1.7	24.8	21.3	12.8	27 124	18.0	4.7	1 791	77.1
Lewis County	1 308	10 494	4.4	25.1	16.1	13.0	30 651	16.1	4.8	3 956	76.5
Macon County	2 082	15 762	3.8	24.1	19.1	13.0	30 195	12.5	3.9	6 501	75.9
Maries County	1 367	8 903	3.2	26.0	15.9	11.0	31 925	13.1	3.6	3 519	81.5
Marion County	1 135	28 289	6.9	25.8	16.7	15.6	31 774	12.1	6.7	11 066	70.4
Miller County	1 534	23 564	3.3	26.3	15.3	11.4	30 977	14.2	5.4	9 284	75.0
Monroe County	1 673	9 311	5.5	25.9	17.7	9.5	30 871	11.9	4.5	3 656	78.5
Montgomery County	1 392	12 136	4.6	25.3	17.4	9.9	32 772	11.8	6.1	4 775	78.7
Osage County	1 570	13 062	1.5	26.4	14.7	10.4	39 565	8.3	2.7	4 922	83.0
Pike County	1 743	18 351	12.2	23.5	14.6	10.2	32 373	15.5	4.8	6 451	74.1
Ralls County	1 220	9 626	2.3	25.2	14.3	12.3	37 094	8.7	4.9	3 736	82.3
Randolph County	1 249	24 663	10.3	23.8	14.9	11.7	31 464	12.5	4.6	9 199	72.0
St. Charles County (part)	538	38 205	4.2	29.2	9.4	32.2	68 525	3.5	3.7	13 384	89.5
Scotland County	1 136	4 983	2.1	28.7	18.9	11.2	27 409	16.8	4.6	1 902	76.7
Shelby County	1 297	6 799	2.0	25.3	19.9	12.5	29 448	16.3	4.8	2 745	75.1
Warren County	1 117	24 525	5.4	26.8	13.0	11.1	41 016	8.6	4.3	9 185	83.1
MONTANA	376 979	902 195	10.5	25.5	13.4	24.4	33 024	14.6	6.3	358 667	69.1
Congressional District (At Large), Montana	376 979	902 195	10.5	25.5	13.4	24.4	33 024	14.6	6.3	358 667	69.1
Beaverhead County	14 355	9 202	5.9	24.5	13.4	26.4	28 962	17.1	3.8	3 684	63.7
Big Horn County	12 936	12 671	64.7	35.9	8.2	14.3	27 684	29.2	14.0	3 924	64.9
Blaine County	10 946	7 009	47.3	32.5	12.9	17.4	25 247	28.1	10.9	2 501	61.0
Broadwater County	3 086	4 385	4.1	25.3	16.4	15.0	32 689	10.8	4.6	1 752	79.3
Carbon County	5 304	9 552	3.0	24.0	16.9	23.3	32 139	11.6	4.7	4 065	74.2
Carter County	8 649	1 360	1.4	26.4	17.8	13.6	26 313	18.1	0.5	543	74.6
Cascade County	6 988	80 357	10.5	26.0	14.1	21.5	32 971	13.5	6.3	32 547	64.9
Chouteau County	10 291	5 970	15.7	28.8	17.4	20.5	29 150	20.5	5.7	2 226	68.6
Custer County	9 798	11 696	4.6	24.9	17.1	18.8	30 000	15.1	5.4	4 768	70.1
Daniels County	3 694	2 017	3.8	22.3	23.6	14.1	27 306	16.9	3.1	892	77.9
Dawson County	6 146	9 059	2.7	23.3	17.6	15.1	31 393	14.9	4.4	3 625	74.0
Deer Lodge County	1 909	9 417	5.6	22.2	18.8	14.7	26 305	15.8	10.3	3 995	73.9
Fallon County	4 197	2 837	1.5	25.7	17.9	14.4	29 944	12.5	3.1	1 140	77.3
Fergus County	11 238	11 893	3.6	24.5	19.9	19.1	30 409	15.4	5.3	4 860	73.7
Flathead County	13 205	74 471	4.7	25.8	12.9	22.4	34 466	13.0	6.4	29 588	73.3
Gallatin County	6 749	67 831	5.0	21.8	8.5	41.0	38 120	12.8	6.1	26 323	62.4
Garfield County	12 090	1 279	0.7	24.9	19.3	16.8	25 917	21.5	3.1	532	73.3
Glacier County	7 756	13 247	64.1	35.2	9.5	16.5	27 921	27.3	15.4	4 304	62.0
Golden Valley County	3 044	1 042	1.3	27.8	16.4	16.2	27 308	25.8	1.9	365	77.5
Granite County	4 474	2 830	6.1	24.5	15.7	22.1	27 813	16.8	5.4	1 200	74.0

[1]Dry land or land partially or temporarily covered by water.
[2]Persons who do not identify themselves White, not of Hispanic origin.
[3]Persons 25 years old and over.

Table B. 109th Congressional Districts by Counties, 2000—*Continued*

(Number, percent.)

STATE Congressional district County	Land area,[1] (sq km)	Population				Percent with bachelor's degree or more[3]	Median income, 1999 (dollars)	Percent living in poverty	Percent unemployed	Households	
		Total	Percent minority[2]	Percent under 18 years old	Percent 65 years old and over					Total	Percent owner occupied
	1	2	3	4	5	6	7	8	9	10	11
Congressional District (At Large), **Montana**—*Continued*											
Hill County	7 502	16 673	21.0	28.1	12.8	20.0	30 781	18.4	10.0	6 457	64.4
Jefferson County	4 291	10 049	4.8	27.8	10.2	27.7	41 506	9.0	5.1	3 747	83.2
Judith Basin County	4 843	2 329	2.1	27.0	17.2	23.6	29 241	21.1	2.5	951	77.2
Lake County	3 869	26 507	29.0	28.0	14.5	22.2	28 740	18.7	8.0	10 192	71.5
Lewis and Clark County	8 964	55 716	5.8	25.6	11.7	31.6	37 360	10.9	5.1	22 850	70.0
Liberty County	3 703	2 158	0.8	26.0	19.5	17.6	30 284	20.3	3.5	833	71.9
Lincoln County	9 357	18 837	4.7	25.2	15.1	13.7	26 754	19.2	13.8	7 764	76.5
McCone County	6 844	1 977	4.2	24.7	18.9	16.4	29 718	16.8	2.2	810	77.7
Madison County	9 289	6 851	4.3	22.9	17.2	25.5	30 233	12.1	5.2	2 956	70.4
Meagher County	6 195	1 932	2.8	25.2	18.3	18.7	29 375	18.9	5.4	803	73.2
Mineral County	3 159	3 884	5.7	24.1	14.1	12.3	27 143	15.8	7.4	1 584	73.0
Missoula County	6 729	95 802	7.1	22.8	10.1	32.8	34 454	14.8	6.2	38 439	61.9
Musselshell County	4 836	4 497	4.2	23.6	17.5	16.7	25 527	19.9	7.6	1 878	76.9
Park County	7 258	15 694	4.2	23.4	14.8	23.1	31 739	11.4	5.0	6 828	66.4
Petroleum County	4 284	493	2.0	25.8	16.4	17.4	24 107	23.2	2.1	211	74.4
Phillips County	13 311	4 601	11.6	27.1	17.4	17.1	28 702	18.3	4.2	1 848	70.5
Pondera County	4 208	6 424	16.7	29.5	16.1	19.8	30 464	18.8	6.9	2 410	70.2
Powder River County	8 540	1 858	3.4	26.8	18.3	16.0	28 398	12.9	3.6	737	72.9
Powell County	6 024	7 180	8.4	21.3	14.3	13.1	30 625	12.6	5.6	2 422	71.3
Prairie County	4 498	1 199	1.8	19.2	24.2	14.8	25 451	17.2	3.8	537	77.7
Ravalli County	6 201	36 070	4.2	25.7	15.4	22.5	31 992	13.8	5.9	14 289	75.7
Richland County	5 398	9 667	4.8	27.3	15.7	17.2	32 110	12.2	6.1	3 878	72.3
Roosevelt County	6 101	10 620	58.5	34.6	11.6	15.6	24 834	32.4	15.7	3 581	65.3
Rosebud County	12 982	9 383	36.4	33.5	8.7	17.6	35 898	22.4	8.4	3 307	67.2
Sanders County	7 154	10 227	9.0	23.7	16.9	15.5	26 852	17.2	9.8	4 273	76.5
Sheridan County	4 342	4 105	5.5	22.4	23.5	18.4	29 518	14.7	3.5	1 741	80.1
Silver Bow County	1 860	34 606	6.4	23.7	15.9	21.7	30 402	14.9	6.8	14 432	70.4
Stillwater County	4 649	8 195	4.6	25.2	14.5	17.8	39 205	9.8	6.8	3 234	76.0
Sweet Grass County	4 805	3 609	3.4	25.8	17.6	23.6	32 422	11.4	2.3	1 476	74.1
Teton County	5 886	6 445	4.5	27.3	16.9	20.8	30 197	16.6	3.7	2 538	75.7
Toole County	4 949	5 267	6.6	25.6	15.7	16.8	30 169	12.9	4.3	1 962	71.5
Treasure County	2 535	861	4.9	27.4	16.7	18.2	29 830	14.7	4.2	357	71.4
Valley County	12 745	7 675	11.9	25.2	19.0	15.7	30 979	13.5	5.4	3 150	75.9
Wheatland County	3 686	2 259	3.5	26.6	19.1	13.5	24 492	20.4	5.9	853	72.2
Wibaux County	2 303	1 068	2.7	25.9	21.3	16.0	28 224	15.3	4.9	421	73.2
Yellowstone County	6 825	129 352	9.0	25.6	13.3	26.4	36 727	11.1	4.5	52 084	69.2
NEBRASKA	199 099	1 711 263	12.6	26.3	13.6	23.7	39 250	9.7	3.5	666 184	67.4
Congressional District 1, Nebraska	30 952	570 423	9.5	25.4	13.4	23.9	40 021	9.2	3.6	220 835	67.4
Burt County	1 276	7 791	3.0	25.7	21.7	14.2	33 954	8.9	2.8	3 155	75.9
Butler County	1 511	8 767	1.8	27.9	17.7	13.6	36 331	8.2	4.0	3 426	75.5
Cass County	1 448	24 334	3.3	27.9	12.3	18.7	46 515	5.2	2.6	9 161	79.7
Cedar County (part)	662	3 092	1.1	27.4	21.8	16.0	33 138	7.5	3.0	1 199	75.5
Colfax County	1 070	10 441	27.3	29.0	16.0	11.5	35 849	10.8	3.5	3 682	75.4
Cuming County	1 481	10 203	6.1	27.1	20.3	12.3	33 186	9.0	2.0	3 945	71.5
Dakota County	683	20 253	28.4	30.6	9.9	12.4	38 834	11.4	3.9	7 095	67.5
Dixon County	1 234	6 339	7.0	27.4	18.2	14.1	34 201	10.0	3.1	2 413	76.3
Dodge County	1 384	36 160	5.6	24.7	17.6	15.0	37 188	8.6	3.3	14 433	67.9
Gage County	2 215	22 993	2.7	24.2	19.1	15.4	34 908	8.7	2.8	9 316	71.4
Johnson County	974	4 488	8.1	24.1	22.1	14.7	32 460	8.9	4.6	1 887	75.0
Lancaster County	2 173	250 291	11.3	23.5	10.4	32.6	41 850	9.5	3.6	99 187	60.5
Madison County	1 483	35 226	11.5	26.8	14.4	17.0	35 807	11.2	4.7	13 436	65.8
Nemaha County	1 060	7 576	2.0	23.1	18.4	22.9	32 588	12.6	6.2	3 047	72.5
Otoe County	1 595	15 396	4.2	26.3	18.4	18.1	37 302	8.1	4.0	6 060	74.0
Pawnee County	1 118	3 087	0.9	22.5	27.1	14.4	29 000	11.0	3.4	1 339	81.0
Richardson County	1 433	9 531	4.4	25.5	21.5	13.6	29 884	10.1	4.9	3 993	74.7
Sarpy County (part)	417	15 872	4.2	29.3	7.8	31.5	60 609	2.4	1.8	5 621	87.6
Saunders County	1 953	19 830	2.4	27.9	15.2	16.9	42 173	6.6	2.4	7 498	79.6
Seward County	1 489	16 496	2.5	24.9	15.2	22.6	42 700	7.0	3.0	6 013	72.0
Stanton County	1 113	6 455	3.3	29.7	13.5	13.7	36 676	6.8	2.7	2 297	80.1
Thurston County	1 020	7 171	54.2	37.0	13.2	12.0	28 170	25.6	12.6	2 255	60.8
Washington County	1 011	18 780	2.7	27.1	13.1	22.7	48 500	6.0	3.3	6 940	77.3
Wayne County	1 148	9 851	3.6	21.7	13.6	28.0	32 366	14.5	2.9	3 437	64.8
Congressional District 2, Nebraska	1 063	570 308	20.3	27.3	10.1	30.5	45 235	8.8	3.8	219 999	63.8
Douglas County	857	463 585	21.8	26.5	11.0	30.6	43 209	9.8	3.9	182 194	63.2
Sarpy County (part)	206	106 723	14.0	30.7	6.4	30.1	52 682	4.5	3.1	37 805	66.5

[1]Dry land or land partially or temporarily covered by water.
[2]Persons who do not identify themselves White, not of Hispanic origin.
[3]Persons 25 years old and over.

Table B. 109th Congressional Districts by Counties, 2000—*Continued*

(Number, percent.)

STATE Congressional district County	Land area,[1] (sq km)	Population				Percent with bachelor's degree or more[3]	Median income, 1999 (dollars)	Percent living in poverty	Percent unem- ployed	Households	
		Total	Percent minority[2]	Percent under 18 years old	Percent 65 years old and over					Total	Percent owner occupied
	1	2	3	4	5	6	7	8	9	10	11
Congressional District 3, Nebraska	167 083	570 532	8.0	26.2	17.3	17.1	33 866	11.1	3.3	225 350	71.0
Adams County	1 459	31 151	7.8	24.3	15.9	19.9	37 160	9.3	3.5	12 141	66.8
Antelope County	2 220	7 452	1.3	27.5	19.9	14.3	30 114	13.6	2.2	2 953	76.4
Arthur County	1 853	444	2.7	24.3	17.3	15.7	27 375	13.8	1.2	185	63.8
Banner County	1 933	819	3.5	28.0	16.5	19.6	31 339	13.6	1.7	311	64.6
Blaine County	1 841	583	0.3	26.9	16.5	12.3	25 278	19.4	1.4	238	65.1
Boone County	1 779	6 259	1.5	29.1	20.6	13.1	31 444	10.4	1.5	2 454	75.2
Box Butte County	2 785	12 158	12.1	28.2	14.4	15.3	39 366	10.7	5.1	4 780	70.1
Boyd County	1 399	2 438	1.0	24.8	24.2	12.8	26 075	15.2	2.0	1 014	80.4
Brown County	3 163	3 525	1.5	24.5	22.5	17.2	28 356	11.1	1.6	1 530	74.4
Buffalo County	2 507	42 259	6.5	24.8	11.6	30.2	36 782	11.2	2.7	15 930	63.6
Cedar County (part)	1 255	6 523	1.3	30.5	19.2	11.4	33 573	9.9	2.5	2 424	82.6
Chase County	2 317	4 068	3.6	25.4	21.0	16.6	32 351	9.6	1.4	1 662	77.1
Cherry County	15 438	6 148	6.2	26.7	17.2	19.4	29 268	12.3	1.8	2 508	62.2
Cheyenne County	3 099	9 830	5.8	26.4	17.2	16.8	33 438	10.0	2.1	4 071	72.8
Clay County	1 484	7 039	4.5	27.4	18.2	16.2	34 259	10.4	2.8	2 756	77.8
Custer County	6 671	11 793	2.3	26.2	21.0	16.1	30 677	12.4	2.5	4 826	73.2
Dawes County	3 616	9 060	7.4	21.2	14.9	28.4	29 476	18.9	4.1	3 512	62.6
Dawson County	2 623	24 365	27.1	29.3	14.3	14.4	36 132	10.8	3.8	8 824	69.1
Deuel County	1 139	2 098	3.9	23.3	23.0	17.4	32 981	9.1	2.2	908	78.0
Dundy County	2 382	2 292	3.9	23.2	22.3	16.7	27 010	13.6	1.5	961	72.4
Fillmore County	1 493	6 634	2.5	26.2	21.4	15.7	35 162	7.8	2.2	2 689	74.7
Franklin County	1 492	3 574	1.3	24.5	23.7	15.8	29 304	13.2	2.5	1 485	81.3
Frontier County	2 524	3 099	2.6	26.0	16.6	17.9	33 038	12.2	2.0	1 192	73.0
Furnas County	1 860	5 324	2.0	24.2	23.8	16.1	30 498	10.6	3.6	2 278	76.6
Garden County	4 414	2 292	3.8	21.8	24.1	14.2	26 458	14.8	1.9	1 020	70.8
Garfield County	1 476	1 902	1.5	23.3	24.9	13.4	27 407	12.6	1.8	813	72.6
Gosper County	1 187	2 143	2.1	23.6	20.7	17.6	36 827	7.9	0.8	863	75.6
Grant County	2 010	747	1.9	29.2	13.9	24.7	34 821	9.7	1.0	292	67.8
Greeley County	1 476	2 714	1.1	26.9	23.4	13.5	28 375	14.6	2.1	1 077	78.4
Hall County	1 415	53 534	16.3	27.1	14.1	15.9	36 972	12.0	4.5	20 356	65.9
Hamilton County	1 408	9 403	1.2	29.0	15.3	18.6	40 277	7.5	2.5	3 503	75.2
Harlan County	1 432	3 786	1.8	24.3	22.7	15.3	30 679	10.1	2.6	1 597	80.2
Hayes County	1 847	1 068	3.3	26.5	20.3	11.6	26 667	18.4	2.1	430	71.9
Hitchcock County	1 839	3 111	3.8	24.1	22.1	13.8	28 287	14.9	2.6	1 287	78.0
Holt County	6 249	11 551	1.2	27.0	19.8	14.5	30 738	13.0	2.2	4 608	73.5
Hooker County	1 868	783	2.8	23.9	26.7	15.7	27 868	6.9	1.3	335	74.0
Howard County	1 475	6 567	1.8	28.1	17.2	14.2	33 305	11.7	2.9	2 546	77.2
Jefferson County	1 484	8 333	2.2	23.3	22.7	14.4	32 629	8.9	3.6	3 527	75.7
Kearney County	1 337	6 882	4.0	26.8	16.6	21.3	39 247	8.5	4.1	2 643	74.0
Keith County	2 749	8 875	6.1	25.3	18.4	16.8	32 325	9.3	3.3	3 707	73.1
Keya Paha County	2 003	983	2.4	24.0	20.5	15.7	24 911	26.9	1.7	409	71.4
Kimball County	2 465	4 089	6.0	24.7	21.2	13.5	30 586	11.1	2.0	1 727	76.5
Knox County	2 870	9 374	8.5	25.6	23.1	14.4	27 564	15.6	3.7	3 811	74.9
Lincoln County	6 641	34 632	6.9	26.1	15.3	16.2	36 568	9.7	4.0	14 076	69.2
Logan County	1 478	774	5.2	27.6	17.6	10.5	33 125	10.5	1.8	316	71.5
Loup County	1 476	712	2.0	27.2	19.4	13.3	26 250	17.7	0.9	289	77.5
McPherson County	2 225	533	2.3	27.4	18.4	22.2	25 750	16.2	0.0	202	67.3
Merrick County	1 256	8 204	2.4	27.6	17.4	14.9	34 961	8.9	3.0	3 209	74.3
Morrill County	3 687	5 440	12.2	27.3	16.8	14.3	30 235	14.7	5.1	2 138	71.4
Nance County	1 143	4 038	2.1	27.6	19.6	11.4	31 267	13.1	2.8	1 577	74.8
Nuckolls County	1 490	5 057	1.4	23.7	24.5	13.1	28 958	11.2	2.4	2 218	80.0
Perkins County	2 287	3 200	3.0	26.6	19.4	17.6	34 205	13.6	2.5	1 275	75.6
Phelps County	1 399	9 747	4.1	26.4	18.2	20.4	37 319	8.9	3.0	3 844	73.2
Pierce County	1 486	7 857	2.4	29.1	17.1	13.3	32 239	11.8	2.3	2 979	77.8
Platte County	1 756	31 662	7.7	29.0	13.8	17.2	39 359	7.7	2.5	12 076	73.3
Polk County	1 137	5 639	1.2	25.1	21.3	13.5	37 819	5.8	1.8	2 259	76.9
Red Willow County	1 856	11 448	3.4	24.9	19.0	15.2	32 293	9.6	2.8	4 710	70.6
Rock County	2 612	1 756	2.6	22.7	22.1	12.2	25 795	21.8	2.3	763	73.1
Saline County	1 490	13 843	9.2	24.7	17.2	14.0	35 914	9.4	2.5	5 188	70.8
Scotts Bluff County	1 915	36 951	20.2	25.9	17.4	17.3	32 016	14.5	5.8	14 887	66.2
Sheridan County	6 322	6 198	12.0	25.4	21.6	17.2	29 484	13.2	2.7	2 549	69.9
Sherman County	1 466	3 318	2.1	24.5	22.9	10.8	28 646	12.9	2.9	1 394	80.6
Sioux County	5 352	1 475	3.4	24.5	16.3	21.5	29 851	15.4	4.1	605	66.8
Thayer County	1 488	6 055	1.7	24.0	24.6	15.0	30 740	10.7	2.2	2 541	80.0
Thomas County	1 846	729	2.9	23.9	20.6	17.2	27 292	14.3	2.0	325	73.5
Valley County	1 471	4 647	2.1	24.7	24.1	16.4	27 926	12.8	3.2	1 965	75.8
Webster County	1 489	4 061	2.5	23.6	24.3	13.7	30 026	11.2	5.9	1 708	78.3
Wheeler County	1 490	886	1.8	28.9	16.9	14.9	26 771	20.9	3.2	352	70.2
York County	1 491	14 598	3.6	25.3	17.4	17.0	37 093	8.5	3.5	5 722	69.6

[1]Dry land or land partially or temporarily covered by water.
[2]Persons who do not identify themselves White, not of Hispanic origin.
[3]Persons 25 years old and over.

Table B. 109th Congressional Districts by Counties, 2000—*Continued*

(Number, percent.)

STATE Congressional district County	Land area,[1] (sq km)	Population				Percent with bachelor's degree or more[3]	Median income, 1999 (dollars)	Percent living in poverty	Percent unem- ployed	Households	
		Total	Percent minority[2]	Percent under 18 years old	Percent 65 years old and over					Total	Percent owner occupied
	1	2	3	4	5	6	7	8	9	10	11
NEVADA	284 448	1 998 257	34.9	25.5	10.9	18.2	44 581	10.5	6.2	751 165	60.9
Congressional District 1, Nevada	459	666 442	48.5	26.5	9.9	14.6	39 480	13.9	7.8	244 538	51.8
Clark County (part)	459	666 442	48.5	26.5	9.9	14.6	39 480	13.9	7.8	244 538	51.8
Congressional District 2, Nevada	272 153	666 470	25.1	25.8	11.3	19.3	43 879	10.1	5.6	253 503	63.6
Churchill County	12 766	23 982	20.1	28.9	11.8	16.7	40 808	8.7	5.9	8 912	65.8
Clark County (part)	8 193	43 978	44.1	28.8	7.1	9.3	36 455	14.4	7.0	14 591	47.6
Douglas County	1 839	41 259	12.0	23.9	15.2	23.2	51 849	7.3	5.9	16 401	74.2
Elko County	44 493	45 291	27.4	32.4	6.2	14.8	48 383	8.9	5.7	15 638	69.8
Esmeralda County	9 294	971	18.6	20.2	17.2	9.6	33 203	15.3	3.3	455	66.4
Eureka County	10 815	1 651	14.7	27.9	12.5	13.6	41 417	12.6	4.0	666	74.0
Humboldt County	24 988	16 106	25.9	31.4	7.4	14.2	47 147	9.7	8.3	5 733	73.0
Lander County	14 228	5 794	24.9	32.1	6.9	10.8	46 067	12.5	7.8	2 093	77.1
Lincoln County	27 541	4 165	9.9	30.2	15.9	15.1	31 979	16.5	5.2	1 540	74.7
Lyon County	5 164	34 501	16.6	27.0	13.8	11.3	40 699	10.4	6.9	13 007	75.9
Mineral County	9 729	5 071	29.6	24.2	20.4	10.1	32 891	15.2	12.9	2 197	72.7
Nye County	47 000	32 485	14.8	23.4	18.3	10.1	36 024	10.7	7.1	13 309	76.4
Pershing County	15 635	6 693	30.3	25.4	7.8	8.7	40 670	11.4	7.6	1 962	69.4
Storey County	682	3 399	10.2	19.2	13.4	18.0	45 490	5.8	5.2	1 462	79.7
Washoe County	16 426	339 486	27.0	24.8	10.5	23.7	45 815	10.0	5.0	132 084	59.3
White Pine County	22 989	9 181	20.6	24.1	13.5	11.8	36 688	11.0	7.6	3 282	76.5
Carson City	371	52 457	21.6	23.3	14.9	18.5	41 809	10.0	4.6	20 171	63.1
Congressional District 3, Nevada	11 836	665 345	30.9	24.2	11.6	20.4	50 749	7.5	5.4	253 124	66.9
Clark County (part)	11 836	665 345	30.9	24.2	11.6	20.4	50 749	7.5	5.4	253 124	66.9
NEW HAMPSHIRE	23 227	1 235 786	4.9	25.0	12.0	28.7	49 467	6.5	3.8	474 606	69.7
Congressional District 1, New Hampshire	6 342	617 575	5.0	25.0	11.7	28.5	50 135	6.7	3.4	238 422	68.6
Belknap County (part)	887	50 267	3.4	23.6	15.2	23.7	43 421	6.2	3.3	20 130	74.2
Carroll County (part)	2 418	43 666	2.1	22.6	17.8	26.5	39 990	7.9	3.8	18 351	77.7
Hillsborough County (part)	351	167 328	8.0	24.9	11.7	27.4	49 447	7.8	3.4	64 971	58.6
Merrimack County (part)	94	11 721	4.6	24.4	9.0	29.4	61 491	4.0	8.8	4 147	79.7
Rockingham County (part)	1 638	232 360	3.9	26.4	10.1	31.5	56 894	4.7	2.7	88 242	74.2
Strafford County	955	112 233	4.4	23.6	11.2	26.4	44 803	9.2	4.1	42 581	64.4
Congressional District 2, New Hampshire	16 885	618 211	4.9	25.0	12.3	28.9	48 762	6.4	4.2	236 184	70.9
Belknap County (part)	153	6 058	2.6	23.9	14.2	19.7	44 985	5.1	4.1	2 329	73.3
Carroll County (part)	0	0	X	X	X	X	X	X	X	0	X
Cheshire County	1 832	73 825	2.6	23.1	13.7	26.6	42 382	8.0	7.0	28 299	70.9
Coos County	4 663	33 111	2.1	22.8	18.5	11.9	33 593	10.0	5.4	13 961	71.1
Grafton County	4 438	81 743	5.1	21.9	13.5	32.7	41 962	8.6	4.8	31 598	68.6
Hillsborough County (part)	1 919	213 513	7.5	27.4	9.8	32.2	57 504	5.1	3.4	79 484	70.2
Merrimack County (part)	2 326	124 504	3.5	24.9	12.7	29.1	47 391	6.1	3.9	47 696	68.6
Rockingham County (part)	162	44 999	4.7	26.0	10.3	32.5	66 458	3.4	2.8	16 287	83.1
Sullivan County	1 392	40 458	2.2	23.8	15.8	19.7	40 938	8.5	3.3	16 530	72.1
NEW JERSEY	19 211	8 414 350	34.0	24.7	13.2	29.8	55 146	8.5	5.8	3 064 645	65.6
Congressional District 1, New Jersey	867	647 392	28.7	26.5	12.0	20.7	47 473	9.9	6.2	236 875	70.0
Burlington County (part)	17	28 929	17.7	20.5	15.2	23.0	47 002	4.9	3.7	12 532	56.9
Camden County (part)	419	428 482	35.3	27.2	11.7	20.3	45 151	11.6	6.4	155 992	67.4
Gloucester County (part)	431	189 981	15.7	25.6	12.1	21.3	52 864	6.6	6.2	68 351	78.1
Congressional District 2, New Jersey	5 133	647 080	28.3	25.2	14.1	17.9	44 173	10.3	7.7	238 517	71.1
Atlantic County	1 453	252 552	36.3	25.3	13.5	18.7	43 933	10.5	7.5	95 024	66.3
Burlington County (part)	373	6 302	5.2	30.2	7.6	33.9	72 659	3.3	2.6	2 016	93.5
Camden County (part)	94	10 485	9.0	25.5	8.8	12.8	59 075	5.6	7.5	3 525	87.8
Cape May County	661	102 326	9.8	22.3	20.3	22.0	41 591	8.6	8.2	42 148	74.3
Cumberland County	1 267	146 438	41.5	25.4	12.9	11.7	39 150	15.0	9.9	49 143	67.9
Gloucester County (part)	410	64 692	10.1	28.4	10.1	24.0	58 440	4.8	5.3	22 366	85.3
Salem County	875	64 285	20.5	25.6	14.4	15.2	45 573	9.5	6.6	24 295	73.0
Congressional District 3, New Jersey	2 397	647 300	16.6	24.0	17.0	27.2	55 282	5.1	4.4	243 939	82.4
Burlington County (part)	1 414	320 738	24.1	25.7	12.2	30.0	60 577	4.6	3.9	115 608	79.5
Camden County (part)	63	69 965	16.7	23.5	18.0	46.2	69 421	4.0	3.7	26 227	82.9
Ocean County (part)	921	256 597	7.1	21.8	22.8	18.9	46 769	5.9	5.3	102 104	85.6
Congressional District 4, New Jersey	1 862	647 357	18.8	25.0	16.3	25.4	54 073	6.6	4.5	241 042	77.7
Burlington County (part)	281	67 425	25.7	23.6	13.8	22.6	56 132	5.2	4.3	24 215	76.6
Mercer County (part)	205	165 333	29.6	24.1	13.4	24.7	54 124	7.1	4.3	62 444	68.7
Monmouth County (part)	649	160 280	13.5	27.0	12.1	35.7	69 801	4.4	4.0	56 085	83.0
Ocean County (part)	727	254 319	13.2	24.7	21.5	20.1	46 108	8.0	5.0	98 298	80.7

[1] Dry land or land partially or temporarily covered by water.
[2] Persons who do not identify themselves White, not of Hispanic origin.
[3] Persons 25 years old and over.
X = Not applicable.

Table B. 109th Congressional Districts by Counties, 2000—*Continued*

(Number, percent.)

STATE Congressional district County	Land area,[1] (sq km)	Population				Percent with bachelor's degree or more[3]	Median income, 1999 (dollars)	Percent living in poverty	Percent unemployed	Households	
		Total	Percent minority[2]	Percent under 18 years old	Percent 65 years old and over					Total	Percent owner occupied
	1	2	3	4	5	6	7	8	9	10	11
Congressional District 5, New Jersey	2 846	647 338	13.7	26.1	13.3	38.6	72 781	3.6	3.3	229 150	81.6
Bergen County (part)	417	390 710	18.0	25.6	14.9	47.1	82 753	2.8	3.0	136 653	83.7
Passaic County (part)	298	52 974	8.5	26.4	9.0	29.1	73 561	3.4	3.8	18 246	87.1
Sussex County (part)	1 205	101 217	6.0	27.7	9.8	24.4	61 469	4.8	3.7	35 591	80.1
Warren County	927	102 437	7.7	26.0	12.9	24.4	56 100	5.4	3.8	38 660	72.8
Congressional District 6, New Jersey	509	647 121	38.3	23.7	11.7	29.7	55 681	9.1	5.8	234 071	61.3
Middlesex County (part)	236	286 000	42.0	22.5	10.4	33.5	59 293	8.2	5.7	99 394	59.0
Monmouth County (part)	245	295 032	25.0	24.3	13.4	27.7	53 418	9.0	5.7	113 027	64.8
Somerset County (part)	12	18 260	66.0	24.5	11.7	31.1	58 693	8.3	3.7	6 513	59.6
Union County (part)	16	47 829	88.1	27.5	9.3	18.5	46 683	15.9	7.9	15 137	50.1
Congressional District 7, New Jersey	1 541	647 269	20.9	24.7	13.1	41.5	74 823	3.4	3.2	233 383	78.7
Hunterdon County (part)	730	97 985	8.4	26.3	9.5	43.1	82 017	2.5	2.5	34 355	84.8
Middlesex County (part)	96	144 317	36.6	23.1	13.1	31.9	66 436	4.6	4.4	50 046	74.6
Somerset County (part)	558	182 890	21.5	26.2	10.4	45.2	78 062	3.6	2.9	65 941	78.4
Union County (part)	158	222 077	15.8	23.8	16.9	44.1	75 532	3.0	3.1	83 041	78.8
Congressional District 8, New Jersey	277	647 130	46.4	25.0	13.4	28.0	51 954	10.7	6.5	225 542	56.7
Essex County (part)	110	232 981	29.9	22.8	15.3	41.1	64 691	5.2	4.2	88 535	66.1
Passaic County (part)	167	414 149	55.7	26.2	12.3	19.9	45 390	13.9	8.1	137 007	50.7
Congressional District 9, New Jersey	241	647 477	38.9	21.2	14.8	29.5	52 437	7.6	5.4	251 055	52.8
Bergen County (part)	189	493 408	35.7	20.7	15.5	31.5	55 180	6.7	4.8	194 164	55.5
Hudson County (part)	43	135 851	54.4	22.8	12.3	22.7	44 208	11.6	7.8	49 631	40.3
Passaic County (part)	9	18 218	10.8	21.7	15.7	25.6	55 340	3.4	2.9	7 260	65.2
Congressional District 10, New Jersey	171	647 109	78.6	27.0	10.9	18.3	38 177	17.5	10.9	228 419	38.6
Essex County (part)	92	375 695	88.2	28.4	10.0	18.5	34 094	21.9	13.5	132 369	31.7
Hudson County (part)	8	69 234	78.9	26.8	11.3	22.1	39 391	17.0	10.6	24 007	39.4
Union County (part)	70	202 180	60.8	24.5	12.5	16.9	45 468	9.6	6.8	72 043	50.9
Congressional District 11, New Jersey	1 580	647 127	17.1	25.0	11.9	45.2	79 009	3.5	3.4	233 258	77.9
Essex County (part)	104	66 561	13.8	24.6	15.8	53.8	94 184	2.3	2.4	23 276	83.9
Morris County	1 215	470 212	18.0	24.7	11.6	44.1	77 340	3.9	3.5	169 711	76.0
Passaic County (part)	6	3 708	9.2	18.6	15.2	23.1	68 929	5.9	5.2	1 343	81.5
Somerset County (part)	110	63 697	20.9	25.7	13.3	52.8	84 106	3.2	3.3	23 688	78.1
Sussex County (part)	145	42 949	7.8	28.2	7.2	33.8	74 721	2.2	3.3	15 240	88.6
Congressional District 12, New Jersey	1 640	647 253	27.7	24.8	12.6	42.3	69 668	5.2	5.5	233 010	75.1
Hunterdon County (part)	384	24 004	4.0	22.9	12.2	36.9	72 451	3.0	2.5	9 323	79.5
Mercer County (part)	380	185 428	41.4	23.7	11.7	42.8	60 716	10.2	10.5	63 363	65.4
Middlesex County (part)	438	245 189	26.5	24.1	14.3	39.0	66 973	3.5	3.8	92 358	74.4
Monmouth County (part)	329	159 989	15.2	28.2	11.5	46.3	84 481	3.4	3.2	55 124	86.0
Somerset County (part)	109	32 643	38.5	21.7	11.2	49.5	72 305	3.2	3.4	12 842	78.3
Congressional District 13, New Jersey	147	647 397	67.7	23.4	10.9	20.5	37 129	18.0	9.5	236 384	28.9
Essex County (part)	21	118 396	71.7	25.0	9.5	8.6	30 563	23.6	12.4	39 556	24.0
Hudson County (part)	70	403 890	65.8	21.6	11.2	26.7	38 907	16.6	8.6	156 908	26.3
Middlesex County (part)	32	74 656	64.8	27.2	11.9	11.2	42 046	14.5	9.7	24 017	52.9
Union County (part)	24	50 455	77.5	27.7	9.9	8.4	32 549	21.0	10.6	15 903	31.5
NEW MEXICO	314 309	1 819 046	55.3	27.9	11.7	23.5	34 133	18.4	7.3	677 971	70.0
Congressional District 1, New Mexico	12 216	606 729	51.5	25.7	11.3	29.5	38 413	14.0	5.8	238 379	65.4
Bernalillo County (part)	1 889	543 181	51.6	25.1	11.6	30.6	38 589	13.7	5.8	216 172	63.3
Sandoval County (part)	565	16 784	54.5	27.2	9.1	29.1	46 691	11.6	4.8	6 170	86.3
Santa Fe County (part)	137	4 876	18.6	31.0	6.1	32.8	55 875	6.5	2.7	1 721	93.3
Torrance County	8 663	16 911	42.6	30.3	10.1	14.4	30 446	19.0	6.0	6 024	83.9
Valencia County (part)	962	24 977	59.8	32.7	9.2	13.2	32 468	19.5	7.5	8 292	87.4
Congressional District 2, New Mexico	179 986	606 110	55.8	28.8	13.1	16.9	29 269	22.4	8.7	218 546	72.0
Bernalillo County (part)	1 106	3 742	98.0	36.3	6.9	4.2	23 083	29.4	13.8	1 133	92.1
Catron County	17 943	3 543	23.8	20.9	18.8	18.4	23 892	24.5	8.9	1 584	80.4
Chaves County	15 723	61 382	48.1	29.0	14.8	16.2	28 513	21.3	9.0	22 561	70.9
Cibola County	11 757	25 595	75.3	30.7	11.1	12.0	27 774	24.8	11.5	8 327	77.1
De Baca County	6 021	2 240	35.5	23.9	26.3	16.2	25 441	17.7	5.4	922	77.8
Dona Ana County	9 861	174 682	67.5	29.7	10.7	22.3	29 808	25.4	9.2	59 556	67.5
Eddy County	10 831	51 658	42.6	28.7	14.7	13.5	31 998	17.2	6.8	19 379	74.3
Grant County	10 272	31 002	51.4	26.2	16.4	20.5	29 134	18.7	8.0	12 146	74.5
Guadalupe County	7 849	4 680	83.7	24.4	13.1	10.3	24 783	21.6	7.7	1 655	74.1
Hidalgo County	8 924	5 932	57.3	31.8	13.5	9.9	24 819	27.3	9.7	2 152	67.8
Lea County	11 378	55 511	45.9	30.1	12.5	11.6	29 799	21.1	9.1	19 699	72.6
Lincoln County	12 512	19 411	29.1	22.7	18.0	22.8	33 886	14.9	3.9	8 202	77.2
Luna County	7 680	25 016	60.1	29.9	18.2	10.4	20 784	32.9	17.1	9 397	75.0
McKinley County (part)	1 123	6 895	94.0	34.5	7.2	6.5	23 145	41.7	17.9	1 672	88.6
Otero County	17 163	62 298	44.8	29.5	11.5	15.4	30 861	19.3	8.1	22 984	66.9
Sierra County	10 827	13 270	29.4	20.0	27.9	13.1	24 152	20.9	6.6	6 113	74.8
Socorro County	17 214	18 078	62.3	28.2	11.1	19.4	23 439	31.7	9.1	6 675	71.0
Valencia County (part)	1 803	41 175	60.8	28.3	11.0	15.7	35 027	15.0	5.6	14 389	81.9

[1]Dry land or land partially or temporarily covered by water.
[2]Persons who do not identify themselves White, not of Hispanic origin.
[3]Persons 25 years old and over.

Table B. 109th Congressional Districts by Counties, 2000—*Continued*

(Number, percent.)

STATE Congressional district County	Land area,[1] (sq km)	Population				Percent with bachelor's degree or more[3]	Median income, 1999 (dollars)	Percent living in poverty	Percent unem- ployed	Households	
		Total	Percent minority[2]	Percent under 18 years old	Percent 65 years old and over					Total	Percent owner occupied
	1	2	3	4	5	6	7	8	9	10	11
Congressional District 3, New Mexico	122 108	606 207	58.6	29.2	10.7	23.7	35 058	19.0	7.7	221 046	72.9
Bernalillo County (part)	25	9 755	40.8	28.1	9.0	33.9	56 728	6.3	3.2	3 631	78.0
Colfax County	9 730	14 189	49.8	25.1	17.4	18.5	30 744	14.8	6.4	5 821	72.7
Curry County	3 641	45 044	41.3	30.1	11.4	15.3	28 917	19.0	6.9	16 766	59.4
Harding County	5 505	810	49.1	20.1	29.4	18.1	26 111	16.3	3.2	371	75.2
Los Alamos County	283	18 343	17.8	25.9	12.4	60.5	78 993	2.9	2.0	7 497	78.6
McKinley County (part)	12 989	67 903	87.3	38.3	6.8	12.6	25 184	35.5	17.1	19 804	71.0
Mora County	5 002	5 180	82.5	26.9	17.1	15.5	24 518	25.4	13.2	2 017	82.5
Quay County	7 446	10 155	41.1	24.9	19.4	13.7	24 894	20.9	5.2	4 201	70.5
Rio Arriba County	15 171	41 190	86.3	28.5	10.8	15.4	29 429	20.3	8.2	15 044	81.7
Roosevelt County	6 342	18 018	37.2	27.9	12.1	22.6	26 586	22.7	8.0	6 639	62.7
Sandoval County (part)	9 043	73 124	48.6	30.1	10.8	23.8	44 526	12.3	6.5	25 241	83.0
San Juan County	14 281	113 801	53.8	32.6	9.0	13.5	33 762	21.5	9.1	37 711	75.3
San Miguel County	12 217	30 126	81.0	27.6	11.8	21.2	26 524	24.4	8.7	11 134	73.2
Santa Fe County (part)	4 808	124 416	56.0	23.7	10.9	37.1	41 735	12.2	4.8	50 761	67.7
Taos County	5 706	29 979	65.8	24.5	12.2	25.9	26 762	20.9	8.9	12 675	75.5
Union County	9 920	4 174	37.1	27.4	17.8	13.0	28 080	18.1	1.9	1 733	72.9
NEW YORK	122 283	18 976 457	38.0	24.6	12.9	27.4	43 393	14.6	7.1	7 056 860	53.0
Congressional District 1, New York	1 674	654 458	15.6	25.6	12.1	27.2	61 884	6.0	4.1	223 885	79.4
Suffolk County (part)	1 674	654 458	15.6	25.6	12.1	27.2	61 884	6.0	4.1	223 885	79.4
Congressional District 2, New York	620	654 346	28.6	26.6	11.6	30.6	71 147	5.9	3.8	206 854	81.7
Nassau County (part)	36	48 498	10.6	25.2	17.0	53.5	97 897	3.2	2.7	16 079	93.1
Suffolk County (part)	584	605 848	30.1	26.8	11.1	28.7	69 556	6.1	3.8	190 775	80.8
Congressional District 3, New York	475	653 934	13.1	24.3	14.6	31.3	70 561	4.3	3.4	225 221	81.7
Nassau County (part)	370	494 871	13.8	24.1	15.1	33.6	72 514	4.1	3.4	170 582	82.9
Suffolk County (part)	105	159 063	11.0	25.2	13.1	23.9	64 665	5.1	3.4	54 639	78.0
Congressional District 4, New York	233	654 691	37.7	25.1	14.3	31.0	66 799	6.4	4.0	212 562	77.3
Nassau County (part)	233	654 691	37.7	25.1	14.3	31.0	66 799	6.4	4.0	212 562	77.3
Congressional District 5, New York	172	654 253	55.8	21.8	14.8	33.6	51 156	12.1	6.0	228 362	53.3
Nassau County (part)	103	136 484	20.5	23.9	17.2	55.6	93 381	4.4	3.6	48 164	80.0
Queens County (part)	68	517 769	65.1	21.2	14.2	27.8	44 954	14.0	6.6	180 198	46.1
Congressional District 6, New York	102	654 946	87.2	26.8	10.6	18.0	43 546	14.5	9.5	204 235	52.7
Queens County (part)	102	654 946	87.2	26.8	10.6	18.0	43 546	14.5	9.5	204 235	52.7
Congressional District 7, New York	68	652 943	72.4	23.5	13.0	19.8	36 990	17.7	8.8	238 573	32.3
Bronx County (part)	48	372 882	71.5	25.2	14.0	17.6	35 164	18.9	9.3	141 322	31.4
Queens County (part)	20	280 061	73.5	21.1	11.6	22.5	40 003	16.1	8.1	97 251	33.5
Congressional District 8, New York	39	654 429	31.2	17.7	13.8	47.8	47 061	18.7	6.7	303 343	26.1
Kings County (part)	22	318 887	35.0	26.7	16.4	20.4	27 604	27.1	8.3	112 290	26.1
New York County (part)	16	335 542	27.5	9.3	11.2	68.2	63 630	10.4	5.9	191 053	26.1
Congressional District 9, New York	96	654 916	36.0	21.0	16.7	31.0	45 426	12.2	5.9	255 970	46.2
Kings County (part)	35	203 549	22.8	22.1	17.9	30.3	39 554	15.5	5.8	77 830	43.4
Queens County (part)	60	451 367	42.0	20.5	16.2	31.2	47 400	10.7	6.0	178 140	47.4
Congressional District 10, New York	46	655 668	83.7	30.0	9.6	17.5	30 212	29.0	13.5	226 363	28.6
Kings County (part)	46	655 668	83.7	30.0	9.6	17.5	30 212	29.0	13.5	226 363	28.6
Congressional District 11, New York	31	654 134	78.5	27.0	9.2	25.0	34 082	23.2	11.6	238 213	21.6
Kings County (part)	31	654 134	78.5	27.0	9.2	25.0	34 082	23.2	11.6	238 213	21.6
Congressional District 12, New York	49	653 346	76.9	25.6	9.5	17.1	29 195	28.3	11.0	224 653	18.8
Kings County (part)	31	422 197	77.2	27.0	8.3	17.8	29 288	29.7	11.3	141 983	20.4
New York County (part)	3	110 526	88.2	20.6	14.2	15.3	21 476	33.6	11.5	41 048	6.2
Queens County (part)	14	120 623	65.8	25.1	9.2	16.2	35 904	18.8	9.1	41 622	25.9
Congressional District 13, New York	168	654 619	29.2	23.5	13.4	24.0	50 092	11.9	6.1	240 389	54.0
Kings County (part)	16	210 891	30.4	19.5	17.1	25.6	40 425	15.8	6.6	84 048	35.7
Richmond County	151	443 728	28.6	25.4	11.6	23.2	55 039	10.0	5.9	156 341	63.8
Congressional District 14, New York	33	654 165	33.9	13.2	13.2	56.9	57 152	12.4	5.2	340 543	25.8
New York County (part)	17	449 552	24.0	10.2	14.0	69.3	66 908	8.8	4.3	259 325	27.5
Queens County (part)	16	204 613	55.7	19.7	11.5	25.0	35 658	20.2	7.8	81 218	20.1
Congressional District 15, New York	27	654 355	83.7	23.9	10.8	25.0	27 934	30.5	14.5	247 218	10.0
Bronx County (part)	2	12 780	91.5	3.9	0.0	0.0	X	X	X	0	X
New York County (part)	24	641 575	83.5	24.3	11.0	25.6	27 934	30.5	14.5	247 218	10.0
Queens County (part)	1	0	X	X	X	X	X	X	X	0	X
Congressional District 16, New York	31	654 400	97.1	34.5	6.7	7.8	19 311	42.2	20.3	211 904	7.1
Bronx County (part)	31	654 400	97.1	34.5	6.7	7.8	19 311	42.2	20.3	211 904	7.1

[1]Dry land or land partially or temporarily covered by water.
[2]Persons who do not identify themselves White, not of Hispanic origin.
[3]Persons 25 years old and over.
X = Not applicable.

Table B. 109th Congressional Districts by Counties, 2000—*Continued*

(Number, percent.)

STATE Congressional district County	Land area,[1] (sq km)	Population Total	Percent minority[2]	Percent under 18 years old	Percent 65 years old and over	Percent with bachelor's degree or more[3]	Median income, 1999 (dollars)	Percent living in poverty	Percent unem- ployed	Households Total	Percent owner occupied
	1	2	3	4	5	6	7	8	9	10	11
Congressional District 17, New York	328	654 283	58.9	26.6	12.8	28.5	44 868	16.0	7.6	235 347	41.2
Bronx County (part)	29	292 588	76.8	25.8	13.3	24.2	37 370	19.9	10.3	109 986	28.1
Rockland County (part)	267	197 862	28.9	28.9	11.9	38.4	65 836	11.1	3.8	63 450	68.5
Westchester County (part)	33	163 833	63.2	25.1	13.0	24.4	41 769	15.0	7.6	61 911	36.3
Congressional District 18, New York	575	654 696	32.9	24.7	14.4	43.8	68 887	7.8	3.9	235 623	63.7
Rockland County (part)	65	60 981	31.7	26.6	11.7	38.2	75 412	6.5	3.7	19 368	77.6
Westchester County (part)	510	593 715	33.1	24.5	14.6	44.4	68 099	8.0	3.9	216 255	62.5
Congressional District 19, New York	3 629	653 397	16.5	26.8	10.9	32.3	64 337	6.4	4.2	223 647	75.2
Dutchess County (part)	699	151 102	19.6	25.1	11.2	28.2	58 590	5.3	5.5	52 633	71.7
Orange County (part)	1 634	212 729	14.8	29.1	10.0	25.0	56 957	9.2	4.8	69 478	72.6
Putnam County	599	95 745	10.4	26.3	9.6	33.9	72 279	4.4	3.5	32 703	82.2
Rockland County (part)	119	27 910	18.1	24.7	10.5	30.0	68 190	4.9	3.1	9 857	80.5
Westchester County (part)	578	165 911	19.3	26.1	12.8	43.9	78 200	5.2	3.1	58 976	76.6
Congressional District 20, New York	18 176	655 277	6.6	24.4	13.7	24.7	44 239	7.9	4.7	250 312	73.8
Columbia County	1 647	63 094	8.8	23.9	16.5	22.6	41 915	9.0	4.3	24 796	70.5
Delaware County (part)	2 968	41 851	4.8	22.8	18.7	17.5	32 724	12.7	5.9	16 749	75.7
Dutchess County (part)	1 364	99 177	10.7	24.4	12.7	29.0	54 387	6.1	5.3	34 889	75.8
Essex County (part)	1 740	14 279	12.4	19.9	15.7	20.7	34 907	10.1	3.8	5 241	67.4
Greene County	1 678	48 195	11.4	22.8	15.6	16.4	36 493	12.2	6.1	18 256	72.2
Otsego County (part)	823	12 037	2.8	24.1	16.4	20.4	35 924	10.6	7.2	4 743	81.5
Rensselaer County (part)	1 456	60 179	3.0	25.9	12.5	23.9	50 251	5.4	3.6	22 786	81.2
Saratoga County (part)	2 086	192 120	5.2	25.1	11.3	31.4	49 584	5.7	3.9	74 668	72.7
Warren County	2 251	63 303	3.1	24.0	15.1	23.2	39 198	9.7	5.3	25 726	69.9
Washington County	2 164	61 042	6.1	24.6	14.0	14.3	37 668	9.4	4.9	22 458	74.3
Congressional District 21, New York	5 012	654 374	14.5	23.3	15.5	27.0	40 254	11.2	6.5	265 380	60.8
Albany County	1 356	294 565	18.2	22.4	14.6	33.3	42 935	10.6	6.8	120 512	57.7
Fulton County	208	31 090	6.0	23.9	17.9	13.8	30 808	15.4	6.7	12 550	62.6
Montgomery County	1 048	49 708	9.2	24.5	19.1	13.6	32 128	12.0	5.8	20 038	67.1
Rensselaer County (part)	238	92 359	13.8	23.1	14.3	23.6	38 025	12.3	7.7	37 108	54.9
Saratoga County (part)	17	8 515	3.3	23.6	14.2	18.9	46 362	5.7	4.0	3 497	59.0
Schenectady County	534	146 555	13.7	24.3	16.6	26.3	41 739	10.9	5.1	59 684	65.4
Schoharie County	1 611	31 582	4.8	24.0	14.9	17.3	36 585	11.4	7.2	11 991	75.3
Congressional District 22, New York	8 407	654 522	20.0	23.8	13.6	23.9	38 586	14.3	6.5	248 893	61.2
Broome County (part)	933	155 671	11.2	22.1	17.1	24.0	33 772	14.2	5.6	63 783	60.3
Delaware County (part)	779	6 204	4.1	24.4	18.1	10.9	30 958	13.8	8.0	2 521	75.8
Dutchess County (part)	13	29 871	50.2	25.8	13.7	19.5	29 389	22.7	8.2	12 014	36.8
Orange County (part)	481	128 638	35.0	28.8	10.9	18.4	46 138	12.6	5.7	45 310	58.4
Sullivan County	2 512	73 966	20.1	24.8	14.3	16.7	36 998	16.3	9.2	27 661	68.1
Tioga County (part)	544	31 890	3.5	26.9	13.8	21.6	40 561	8.6	5.1	12 224	75.4
Tompkins County (part)	228	50 533	23.0	12.5	9.0	61.9	31 376	27.4	7.5	17 881	39.0
Ulster County	2 918	177 749	14.4	23.4	13.3	25.0	42 551	11.4	6.3	67 499	68.0
Congressional District 23, New York	34 278	654 216	7.1	25.1	12.5	16.0	35 434	13.5	8.2	240 431	71.0
Clinton County	2 691	79 894	7.7	23.0	11.9	17.8	37 028	13.9	6.2	29 423	68.5
Essex County (part)	2 913	24 572	3.3	24.4	16.3	16.8	34 773	12.3	8.5	9 787	77.3
Franklin County	4 226	51 134	16.5	22.6	12.8	13.0	31 517	14.6	10.6	17 931	70.3
Fulton County (part)	1 077	23 983	3.4	25.9	14.2	13.1	37 436	8.9	5.8	9 334	85.0
Hamilton County	4 456	5 379	2.2	19.8	20.1	18.4	32 287	10.4	9.7	2 362	79.3
Jefferson County	3 295	111 738	12.8	26.4	11.4	16.0	34 006	13.3	9.1	40 068	59.8
Lewis County	3 303	26 944	1.9	27.7	13.8	11.7	34 361	13.2	7.8	10 040	77.0
Madison County	1 699	69 441	4.5	25.0	12.5	21.6	40 184	9.8	7.1	25 368	74.9
Oneida County (part)	1 193	26 823	2.5	27.2	12.9	12.3	37 069	10.6	5.7	10 090	80.0
Oswego County	2 469	122 377	3.6	26.8	11.3	14.4	36 598	14.0	9.3	45 522	72.8
St. Lawrence County	6 956	111 931	6.3	23.4	13.0	16.4	32 356	16.9	8.5	40 506	70.6
Congressional District 24, New York	15 964	654 390	7.9	24.3	15.2	19.3	36 082	12.6	6.5	251 360	69.8
Broome County (part)	898	44 865	3.6	26.0	14.1	18.2	40 290	8.3	4.5	16 966	83.1
Cayuga County (part)	1 374	70 664	8.5	24.4	15.1	16.2	37 213	11.3	5.1	26 475	70.1
Chenango County	2 316	51 401	3.2	26.2	14.9	14.4	33 679	14.4	5.6	19 926	75.3
Cortland County	1 294	48 599	3.7	23.6	12.5	18.8	34 364	15.5	8.5	18 210	64.3
Herkimer County	3 655	64 427	2.5	24.3	16.9	15.7	32 924	12.5	6.7	25 734	71.2
Oneida County (part)	1 948	208 646	12.7	23.5	17.0	19.1	35 765	13.4	5.9	80 406	65.6
Ontario County (part)	60	16 945	18.6	23.4	16.5	22.3	34 078	14.4	7.3	6 425	57.5
Otsego County (part)	1 774	49 639	5.5	22.3	14.8	22.5	32 728	16.0	14.1	18 548	70.9
Seneca County	842	33 342	6.4	24.9	15.1	17.5	37 140	11.5	6.0	12 630	73.7
Tioga County (part)	799	19 894	3.3	27.0	12.0	16.5	39 780	8.0	5.0	7 501	81.6
Tompkins County (part)	1 005	45 968	8.3	26.3	10.2	36.5	42 433	9.0	4.0	18 539	68.0
Congressional District 25, New York	4 195	654 484	13.4	25.9	13.8	27.8	43 188	10.4	5.0	255 813	69.1
Cayuga County (part)	422	11 299	3.1	28.9	10.5	11.5	40 015	9.5	5.6	4 083	84.2
Monroe County (part)	188	91 084	6.2	24.8	16.1	36.6	56 497	3.6	3.3	35 669	82.5
Onondaga County	2 021	458 336	16.3	25.8	13.8	28.5	40 847	12.2	5.4	181 153	64.5
Wayne County	1 565	93 765	7.2	27.4	12.1	17.0	44 157	8.6	5.1	34 908	77.6

[1]Dry land or land partially or temporarily covered by water.
[2]Persons who do not identify themselves White, not of Hispanic origin.
[3]Persons 25 years old and over.

Table B. 109th Congressional Districts by Counties, 2000—*Continued*

(Number, percent.)

STATE Congressional district County	Land area,[1] (sq km)	Population Total	Population Percent minority[2]	Population Percent under 18 years old	Population Percent 65 years old and over	Percent with bachelor's degree or more[3]	Median income, 1999 (dollars)	Percent living in poverty	Percent unem-ployed	Households Total	Households Percent owner occupied
	1	2	3	4	5	6	7	8	9	10	11
Congressional District 26, New York	7 073	654 343	7.6	24.6	14.1	25.5	46 653	6.9	5.7	243 482	75.0
Erie County (part)	544	193 269	8.6	23.4	16.7	39.2	54 225	5.2	7.1	73 202	76.6
Genesee County	1 280	60 370	5.5	25.9	14.3	16.3	40 542	7.6	4.3	22 770	72.9
Livingston County	1 637	64 328	7.0	23.3	11.4	19.2	42 066	10.4	6.1	22 150	74.5
Monroe County (part)	630	144 491	7.0	25.8	12.8	26.2	51 370	5.3	4.6	53 671	76.2
Niagara County (part)	728	112 598	5.4	24.9	14.1	18.8	42 252	7.9	4.9	44 419	72.0
Orleans County (part)	718	35 863	14.5	25.8	12.6	12.3	36 788	11.5	6.9	12 364	73.3
Wyoming County	1 536	43 424	9.4	24.0	12.1	11.5	39 895	8.4	6.1	14 906	76.9
Congressional District 27, New York	4 740	654 200	11.1	23.9	15.8	19.9	36 884	12.0	6.3	261 614	66.2
Chautauqua County	2 751	139 750	8.0	24.4	16.0	16.9	33 458	13.8	6.3	54 515	69.3
Erie County (part)	1 990	514 450	11.9	23.8	15.7	20.7	37 904	11.5	6.3	207 099	65.4
Congressional District 28, New York	1 383	654 464	38.1	26.1	14.3	21.2	31 751	18.7	8.7	268 193	55.4
Erie County (part)	171	242 546	42.9	25.9	15.9	20.9	30 531	19.1	9.6	100 572	57.0
Monroe County (part)	290	296 362	43.3	26.8	12.1	23.6	31 827	20.5	8.4	121 195	48.9
Niagara County (part)	626	107 248	15.2	24.4	16.9	15.9	33 653	13.4	7.4	43 427	67.7
Orleans County (part)	295	8 308	3.8	28.1	11.5	15.8	42 452	7.9	6.8	2 999	84.9
Congressional District 29, New York	14 660	654 208	7.4	25.0	14.1	26.1	41 875	9.9	6.2	248 477	74.0
Allegany County	2 668	49 927	3.5	24.3	14.0	17.2	32 106	15.5	9.0	18 009	73.9
Cattaraugus County	3 393	83 955	5.9	26.1	14.7	14.9	33 404	13.7	7.4	32 023	74.4
Chemung County	1 057	91 070	10.1	24.3	15.6	18.6	36 415	13.0	7.8	35 049	68.9
Monroe County (part)	599	203 406	12.1	23.9	13.2	42.6	58 588	5.1	5.1	75 977	74.9
Ontario County (part)	1 609	83 279	3.3	25.8	12.6	25.1	46 411	6.0	4.0	31 945	76.8
Schuyler County	851	19 224	4.3	25.3	14.7	15.5	36 010	11.8	7.4	7 374	77.2
Steuben County	3 607	98 726	3.7	25.9	15.2	17.9	35 479	13.2	7.0	39 071	73.2
Yates County	876	24 621	3.2	26.7	15.6	18.2	34 640	13.1	6.4	9 029	77.0
NORTH CAROLINA	126 161	8 049 313	29.8	24.4	12.0	22.5	39 184	12.3	5.3	3 132 013	69.4
Congressional District 1, North Carolina	18 645	619 249	55.6	26.0	14.1	12.0	28 410	21.1	8.5	236 646	63.4
Beaufort County (part)	806	16 351	46.4	25.8	15.5	10.5	24 848	25.3	7.9	6 767	66.0
Bertie County	1 811	19 773	64.0	26.1	16.0	8.8	25 177	23.5	7.1	7 743	74.9
Chowan County	447	14 526	39.8	24.1	18.1	16.4	30 928	17.6	6.7	5 580	72.3
Craven County (part)	764	38 975	42.5	25.8	10.4	16.2	29 273	16.8	7.0	13 587	54.4
Edgecombe County	1 308	55 606	60.8	27.1	12.6	8.5	30 983	19.6	9.6	20 392	64.0
Gates County	882	10 516	41.4	26.6	14.3	10.5	35 647	17.0	4.4	3 901	82.0
Granville County (part)	182	11 753	54.0	25.1	17.8	17.6	35 260	17.9	5.9	4 512	64.1
Greene County	687	18 974	49.8	25.1	11.9	8.2	32 074	20.2	7.3	6 696	74.7
Halifax County	1 879	57 370	57.7	26.2	14.9	11.1	26 459	23.9	8.1	22 122	67.0
Hertford County	915	22 601	63.0	25.4	16.1	11.1	26 422	18.3	8.7	8 953	70.0
Jones County (part)	721	6 835	49.0	26.7	15.2	10.2	30 211	18.1	5.1	2 627	78.1
Lenoir County (part)	410	30 801	64.6	26.0	16.1	9.4	26 069	22.4	10.7	12 596	58.6
Martin County	1 194	25 593	48.4	25.5	15.4	11.6	28 793	20.2	8.0	10 020	71.8
Nash County (part)	22	14 920	66.6	27.7	15.7	12.1	24 314	27.7	10.4	5 929	43.0
Northampton County	1 389	22 086	61.0	24.4	17.6	10.8	26 652	21.3	8.6	8 691	76.8
Pasquotank County	588	34 897	43.5	24.8	14.1	16.4	30 444	18.4	9.8	12 907	65.7
Perquimans County	640	11 368	29.2	22.9	19.8	12.3	29 538	17.9	5.9	4 645	78.6
Pitt County (part)	918	54 809	59.8	27.1	11.0	14.3	28 242	25.0	8.7	20 998	53.5
Vance County (part)	415	28 373	57.7	26.4	14.7	12.9	30 366	20.8	7.6	10 872	61.9
Warren County	1 110	19 972	61.4	23.5	17.4	11.6	28 351	19.4	8.3	7 708	77.2
Washington County	903	13 723	52.2	25.8	15.5	11.6	28 865	21.8	7.1	5 367	73.5
Wayne County (part)	237	52 666	54.4	27.0	12.1	15.4	31 017	16.4	8.2	20 343	52.2
Wilson County (part)	416	36 761	70.8	27.4	12.2	6.9	23 745	27.8	11.5	13 690	48.7
Congressional District 2, North Carolina	10 246	618 753	40.9	25.5	10.0	15.9	36 510	14.3	7.4	223 122	66.5
Chatham County (part)	1 338	33 094	34.6	23.2	14.8	14.6	37 697	11.5	3.8	12 588	77.9
Cumberland County (part)	264	108 028	59.9	27.2	6.1	18.5	33 101	16.2	14.5	33 612	44.2
Franklin County	1 274	47 260	35.8	25.3	11.1	13.2	38 968	12.6	4.7	17 843	77.8
Harnett County	1 541	91 025	31.3	26.8	10.4	12.8	35 105	14.9	8.3	33 800	70.3
Johnston County	2 051	121 965	24.7	26.2	9.9	15.9	40 872	12.8	4.0	46 549	73.4
Lee County	666	49 040	34.0	25.6	13.0	17.2	38 900	12.8	4.6	18 466	71.7
Nash County (part)	1 088	45 667	41.4	24.6	11.6	14.2	36 824	11.7	5.8	17 262	70.0
Sampson County (part)	1 580	32 741	57.2	26.2	13.7	10.2	28 237	20.5	8.5	12 027	70.6
Vance County (part)	241	14 581	45.7	28.4	9.1	6.2	33 492	19.9	9.5	5 327	75.1
Wake County (part)	201	75 352	54.0	20.6	7.8	24.0	37 554	15.2	10.8	25 602	54.7
Congressional District 3, North Carolina	16 037	618 810	23.6	23.8	11.6	20.1	37 510	12.4	5.2	234 158	70.9
Beaufort County (part)	1 338	28 607	25.3	22.3	16.2	18.9	34 567	16.1	5.5	11 552	80.4
Camden County	623	6 885	19.2	24.7	13.4	16.2	39 493	10.1	3.7	2 662	83.5
Carteret County	1 346	59 383	10.9	20.6	17.1	19.8	38 344	10.7	5.0	25 204	76.6
Craven County (part)	1 071	52 461	23.3	23.4	15.4	21.1	41 199	10.5	4.3	20 995	74.7
Currituck County	678	18 190	10.4	25.2	11.9	13.3	40 822	10.7	3.7	6 902	81.5

[1]Dry land or land partially or temporarily covered by water.
[2]Persons who do not identify themselves White, not of Hispanic origin.
[3]Persons 25 years old and over.

Table B. 109th Congressional Districts by Counties, 2000—*Continued*

(Number, percent.)

STATE Congressional district County	Land area,[1] (sq km)	Population					Percent with bachelor's degree or more[3]	Median income, 1999 (dollars)	Percent living in poverty	Percent unem-ployed	Households	
		Total	Percent minority[2]	Percent under 18 years old	Percent 65 years old and over						Total	Percent owner occupied
	1	2	3	4	5		6	7	8	9	10	11
Congressional District 3, North Carolina—*Continued*												
Dare County	993	29 967	6.5	21.3	13.8		27.7	42 411	8.0	4.9	12 690	74.5
Duplin County (part)	606	14 122	28.7	25.4	11.5		9.9	32 020	16.1	5.5	5 245	76.2
Hyde County	1 587	5 826	38.0	20.4	17.2		10.6	28 444	15.4	5.3	2 185	78.4
Jones County (part)	502	3 546	21.5	23.8	15.5		8.2	32 154	14.7	4.9	1 434	82.2
Lenoir County (part)	625	28 847	23.3	24.6	13.2		17.4	37 872	10.3	5.5	11 266	76.4
Nash County (part)	289	26 833	19.8	25.5	12.5		24.9	47 581	8.4	2.9	10 453	77.8
Onslow County	1 986	150 355	30.5	26.2	6.4		14.8	33 756	12.9	6.9	48 122	58.1
Pamlico County	873	12 934	27.4	21.0	18.7		14.7	34 084	15.3	5.7	5 178	82.1
Pitt County (part)	770	78 989	24.7	21.0	8.7		35.3	37 651	16.9	5.6	31 541	61.2
Tyrrell County	1 010	4 149	44.4	22.5	16.8		10.6	25 684	23.3	6.1	1 537	74.8
Wayne County (part)	1 194	60 663	27.8	25.5	10.9		14.6	37 097	11.6	4.9	22 269	77.3
Wilson County (part)	546	37 053	22.4	23.5	13.4		22.2	43 045	9.5	3.6	14 923	72.7
Congressional District 4, North Carolina	3 246	619 432	31.2	24.6	8.0		48.0	53 847	9.2	3.7	240 099	64.1
Chatham County (part)	430	16 235	15.6	20.7	17.2		52.1	55 371	6.1	1.1	7 153	76.0
Durham County	752	223 314	51.8	22.8	9.6		40.1	43 337	13.4	5.1	89 015	54.2
Orange County	1 036	118 227	24.2	20.3	8.3		51.5	42 372	14.1	3.7	45 863	57.6
Wake County (part)	1 028	261 656	17.7	28.3	5.9		52.8	70 448	3.8	2.6	98 068	75.2
Congressional District 5, North Carolina	11 401	619 433	12.0	23.1	13.5		20.1	39 710	9.5	3.9	249 357	76.8
Alexander County	674	33 603	8.8	24.3	11.8		9.3	38 684	8.5	2.5	13 137	80.5
Alleghany County	608	10 677	7.5	19.3	19.3		11.7	29 244	17.2	4.6	4 593	79.0
Ashe County	1 104	24 384	3.7	19.9	17.9		12.1	28 824	13.5	4.6	10 411	81.0
Davie County	687	34 835	11.3	24.4	13.9		17.6	40 174	8.6	3.7	13 750	83.3
Forsyth County (part)	806	175 683	14.0	23.6	12.9		35.9	51 616	4.7	2.6	73 106	76.0
Iredell County (part)	1 060	68 486	24.8	24.9	13.5		13.6	37 942	10.0	4.9	26 441	72.9
Rockingham County (part)	263	11 160	8.7	25.3	11.1		10.6	42 846	8.3	4.1	4 237	83.9
Stokes County	1 170	44 711	7.5	24.5	11.7		9.3	38 808	9.1	5.9	17 579	82.0
Surry County	1 390	71 219	11.7	23.6	15.4		12.0	33 046	12.4	3.4	28 408	76.3
Watauga County	809	42 695	4.8	16.2	11.1		33.2	32 611	17.9	8.2	16 540	62.9
Wilkes County	1 961	65 632	8.8	22.6	14.2		11.3	34 258	11.9	3.8	26 650	77.9
Yadkin County	869	36 348	10.3	23.9	14.2		10.3	36 660	10.0	3.1	14 505	80.3
Congressional District 6, North Carolina	7 624	619 228	14.6	23.8	13.7		22.7	43 503	8.2	3.6	246 278	76.7
Alamance County (part)	921	90 976	16.3	22.9	13.9		23.7	43 084	8.6	4.4	36 180	75.4
Davidson County (part)	890	73 877	8.4	23.7	13.0		11.6	39 514	8.9	4.0	29 248	77.9
Guilford County (part)	1 248	178 594	14.7	23.7	12.2		37.6	53 919	5.5	2.9	72 626	75.3
Moore County	1 807	74 769	21.1	22.1	22.0		26.8	41 240	11.4	5.5	30 713	78.6
Randolph County	2 039	130 454	13.9	25.1	12.1		11.1	38 348	9.1	3.1	50 659	76.6
Rowan County (part)	719	70 558	13.4	25.1	12.4		11.0	38 382	8.9	3.6	26 852	79.3
Congressional District 7, North Carolina	15 766	619 603	37.0	24.5	12.7		17.8	33 998	16.7	6.7	243 322	73.1
Bladen County	2 266	32 278	44.0	24.7	14.6		11.3	26 877	21.0	5.6	12 897	77.8
Brunswick County	2 214	73 143	19.0	21.2	16.9		16.1	35 888	12.6	4.6	30 438	82.2
Columbus County	2 426	54 749	37.2	25.8	13.9		10.1	26 805	22.7	7.7	21 308	76.4
Cumberland County (part)	1 251	72 063	34.5	26.7	10.4		16.6	38 194	13.3	6.8	27 399	72.5
Duplin County (part)	1 511	34 941	51.2	26.5	13.0		10.7	28 388	20.8	8.2	13 022	74.4
New Hanover County	515	160 307	21.1	20.9	12.8		31.0	40 172	13.1	5.7	68 183	64.7
Pender County	2 255	41 082	28.4	23.2	14.0		13.6	35 902	13.6	5.7	16 054	82.6
Robeson County	2 457	123 339	69.2	29.0	9.9		11.4	28 202	22.8	9.6	43 677	72.8
Sampson County (part)	869	27 420	26.2	25.3	11.8		12.1	35 894	14.0	5.2	10 246	76.9
Scotland County (part)	1	281	10.3	23.8	4.3		53.5	67 188	3.6	4.9	98	100.0
Congressional District 8, North Carolina	8 502	618 465	38.1	26.1	10.6		18.2	38 390	12.4	6.0	233 377	66.2
Anson County	1 377	25 275	50.7	25.2	14.4		9.2	29 849	17.8	6.0	9 204	76.0
Cabarrus County (part)	843	125 451	19.5	25.9	11.8		19.0	45 747	7.2	4.3	47 474	74.0
Cumberland County (part)	175	122 872	44.2	29.2	7.6		21.2	40 462	10.0	5.9	46 347	62.6
Hoke County	1 013	33 646	58.2	29.8	7.8		10.9	33 230	17.7	7.0	11 373	75.0
Mecklenburg County (part)	110	107 178	51.9	21.9	7.9		29.9	39 979	11.4	6.7	43 151	47.1
Montgomery County	1 273	26 822	34.4	24.9	14.0		10.0	32 903	15.4	5.1	9 848	76.5
Richmond County	1 228	46 564	36.4	25.8	13.6		10.1	28 830	19.6	6.9	17 873	72.0
Scotland County (part)	826	35 717	48.9	28.2	11.1		15.6	30 848	20.7	10.0	13 301	68.9
Stanly County	1 023	58 100	16.4	24.9	14.3		12.7	36 898	10.7	4.5	22 223	76.2
Union County (part)	634	36 840	43.4	27.1	11.2		12.8	38 782	16.5	8.4	12 583	62.8
Congressional District 9, North Carolina	2 566	619 705	17.0	25.3	10.0		35.9	55 059	6.2	3.7	243 854	72.8
Gaston County (part)	700	164 160	19.0	24.6	12.6		15.1	39 568	10.9	5.7	63 941	67.6
Mecklenburg County (part)	849	368 708	17.7	24.8	9.2		47.5	62 753	4.4	3.2	149 106	72.0
Union County (part)	1 017	86 837	10.3	28.3	8.2		24.7	55 675	4.7	2.7	30 807	87.8
Congressional District 10, North Carolina	8 552	618 943	15.0	24.3	13.1		14.1	37 649	10.6	4.1	241 060	75.1
Avery County	640	17 167	7.5	19.5	15.7		14.5	30 627	15.3	7.0	6 532	80.5
Burke County	1 312	89 148	15.0	24.0	13.4		12.8	35 629	10.7	4.2	34 528	74.1
Caldwell County	1 221	77 415	9.0	23.3	13.4		10.4	35 739	10.7	3.4	30 768	74.9
Catawba County	1 036	141 685	17.7	24.3	12.2		17.0	40 536	9.1	3.3	55 533	72.6
Cleveland County	1 203	96 287	23.7	25.2	13.7		13.3	35 283	13.3	5.4	37 046	72.9

[1]Dry land or land partially or temporarily covered by water.
[2]Persons who do not identify themselves White, not of Hispanic origin.
[3]Persons 25 years old and over.

Table B. 109th Congressional Districts by Counties, 2000—*Continued*

(Number, percent.)

STATE Congressional district County	Land area,[1] (sq km)	Population Total	Population Percent minority[2]	Population Percent under 18 years old	Population Percent 65 years old and over	Percent with bachelor's degree or more[3]	Median income, 1999 (dollars)	Percent living in poverty	Percent unem- ployed	Households Total	Households Percent owner occupied
	1	2	3	4	5	6	7	8	9	10	11
Congressional District 10, North Carolina—*Continued*											
Gaston County (part)	223	26 205	15.0	24.5	13.4	8.4	38 938	10.8	5.1	9 995	77.1
Iredell County (part)	430	54 174	12.2	26.3	10.8	22.2	47 757	5.8	2.8	20 919	78.4
Lincoln County	774	63 780	13.2	24.8	11.6	13.0	41 421	9.2	3.9	24 041	78.5
Mitchell County	573	15 687	3.0	21.0	18.6	12.2	30 508	13.8	4.1	6 551	80.9
Rutherford County (part)	1 139	37 395	10.8	24.3	15.3	10.8	30 615	14.5	6.3	15 147	76.9
Congressional District 11, North Carolina	15 605	619 224	10.3	21.3	17.8	20.5	34 720	12.0	5.2	257 331	75.4
Buncombe County	1 699	206 330	12.3	21.8	15.4	25.3	36 666	11.4	4.8	85 776	70.3
Cherokee County	1 179	24 298	6.1	20.6	19.8	11.0	27 992	15.3	5.5	10 336	82.1
Clay County	556	8 775	2.2	18.5	22.6	15.4	31 397	11.4	4.0	3 847	84.6
Graham County	756	7 993	9.2	21.9	18.1	11.2	26 645	19.5	5.9	3 354	82.7
Haywood County	1 434	54 033	4.1	20.8	19.1	16.0	33 922	11.5	4.6	23 100	77.3
Henderson County	969	89 173	10.3	20.8	21.7	24.1	38 109	9.7	4.6	37 414	78.8
Jackson County	1 271	33 121	14.8	19.0	14.0	25.5	32 552	15.1	10.2	13 191	72.5
McDowell County	1 144	42 151	9.2	22.9	14.2	9.0	32 396	11.6	4.5	16 604	77.2
Macon County	1 338	29 811	4.4	20.3	22.4	16.2	32 139	12.6	4.9	12 828	81.3
Madison County	1 164	19 635	3.6	21.3	15.9	16.1	30 985	15.4	5.2	8 000	76.5
Polk County	616	18 324	9.9	20.1	23.7	25.7	36 259	10.1	4.1	7 908	78.6
Rutherford County (part)	322	25 504	18.5	23.4	17.1	14.9	32 145	13.0	5.6	10 044	70.8
Swain County	1 368	12 968	32.9	24.3	15.1	13.9	28 608	18.3	10.1	5 137	76.9
Transylvania County	980	29 334	7.4	20.4	21.4	23.7	38 587	9.5	4.9	12 320	79.4
Yancey County	809	17 774	4.0	21.3	18.1	13.1	29 674	15.8	4.5	7 472	80.2
Congressional District 12, North Carolina	2 127	619 269	55.4	25.5	10.8	19.2	35 775	15.9	7.7	235 533	56.8
Cabarrus County (part)	100	5 612	8.6	27.3	8.2	21.8	57 430	4.0	2.5	2 045	89.0
Davidson County (part)	540	73 369	20.7	24.6	12.4	14.0	37 781	11.2	4.2	28 908	70.5
Forsyth County (part)	255	130 384	60.7	24.2	12.6	17.6	30 751	20.0	7.6	50 745	50.6
Guilford County (part)	223	130 554	61.2	25.8	11.2	20.7	35 193	15.9	8.7	49 588	55.8
Mecklenburg County (part)	404	219 568	68.0	26.6	7.7	21.3	37 907	16.3	8.0	81 159	52.6
Rowan County (part)	606	59 782	31.9	24.0	15.9	18.0	36 461	12.7	9.6	23 088	66.9
Congressional District 13, North Carolina	5 842	619 199	36.8	23.1	10.8	27.3	41 060	11.6	4.6	247 876	62.4
Alamance County (part)	193	39 824	53.4	26.0	14.4	8.7	30 193	16.9	6.9	15 404	57.6
Caswell County	1 100	23 501	39.2	23.3	13.1	8.3	35 018	14.4	6.5	8 670	79.4
Granville County (part)	1 193	36 745	36.6	23.5	9.4	11.5	41 384	9.5	4.0	12 142	79.2
Guilford County (part)	210	111 900	44.5	20.9	11.5	28.4	36 370	13.0	6.2	46 453	50.2
Person County	1 016	35 623	31.9	24.1	13.9	10.3	37 159	12.0	4.7	14 085	74.6
Rockingham County (part)	1 204	80 768	26.0	23.0	15.3	10.8	32 609	13.4	6.0	32 752	72.4
Wake County (part)	926	290 838	35.1	23.3	8.5	40.3	48 772	9.8	3.4	118 370	60.6
NORTH DAKOTA	178 647	642 200	8.2	25.1	14.7	22.0	34 604	11.9	4.6	257 152	66.6
Congressional District (At Large), North Dakota	178 647	642 200	8.2	25.1	14.7	22.0	34 604	11.9	4.6	257 152	66.6
Adams County	2 559	2 593	2.6	23.4	24.2	16.6	29 079	10.4	1.9	1 121	70.9
Barnes County	3 863	11 775	2.1	22.2	19.7	22.1	31 166	10.8	4.7	4 884	71.1
Benson County	3 576	6 964	48.9	36.3	13.8	10.9	26 688	29.1	13.0	2 328	68.3
Billings County	2 982	888	0.3	24.5	15.9	18.8	32 667	12.8	2.8	366	76.2
Bottineau County	4 322	7 149	2.9	22.1	21.2	14.9	29 853	10.7	4.7	2 962	80.0
Bowman County	3 010	3 242	1.0	24.0	21.9	17.9	31 906	8.2	2.1	1 358	79.5
Burke County	2 858	2 242	1.7	20.9	24.8	12.0	25 330	15.4	2.6	1 013	84.6
Burleigh County	4 230	69 416	5.1	24.8	12.5	28.7	41 309	7.8	3.5	27 670	68.0
Cass County	4 572	123 138	5.7	23.5	9.6	31.3	38 147	10.1	3.9	51 315	54.4
Cavalier County	3 855	4 831	1.2	24.4	22.9	13.1	31 868	11.5	3.8	2 017	81.5
Dickey County	2 929	5 757	2.8	23.7	21.3	16.6	29 231	14.8	3.8	2 283	71.4
Divide County	3 262	2 283	1.6	20.1	29.4	13.3	30 089	14.6	4.4	1 005	81.9
Dunn County	5 205	3 600	13.3	27.7	17.3	16.3	30 015	17.5	6.4	1 378	79.9
Eddy County	1 632	2 757	2.6	23.6	24.7	15.9	28 642	9.7	4.7	1 164	75.3
Emmons County	3 911	4 331	1.0	24.9	25.6	12.3	26 119	20.1	3.3	1 786	84.2
Foster County	1 645	3 759	1.4	26.2	21.3	19.8	32 019	9.3	3.3	1 540	74.3
Golden Valley County	2 595	1 924	2.2	28.5	21.0	19.8	29 967	15.3	3.9	761	77.8
Grand Forks County	3 724	66 109	8.2	23.8	9.7	27.8	35 785	12.3	4.4	25 435	53.7
Grant County	4 298	2 841	3.1	23.6	24.5	11.2	23 165	20.3	2.3	1 195	79.6
Griggs County	1 835	2 754	0.6	22.7	25.6	15.7	29 572	10.1	3.2	1 178	78.4
Hettinger County	2 933	2 715	1.1	23.3	25.3	14.4	29 209	14.8	4.9	1 152	84.3
Kidder County	3 499	2 753	1.5	23.3	24.1	11.0	25 389	19.8	4.9	1 158	81.9
LaMoure County	2 971	4 701	1.1	24.2	23.3	13.9	29 707	14.7	2.8	1 942	81.0
Logan County	2 571	2 308	1.4	22.9	27.1	12.9	27 986	15.1	2.9	963	85.4
McHenry County	4 854	5 987	1.4	24.0	21.7	13.2	27 274	15.8	5.1	2 526	81.5
McIntosh County	2 526	3 390	1.3	19.3	34.2	9.9	26 389	15.4	2.5	1 467	82.8
McKenzie County	7 102	5 737	22.7	30.7	15.9	15.7	29 342	17.2	6.6	2 151	73.9
McLean County	5 465	9 311	7.9	23.6	20.3	15.1	32 337	13.5	5.6	3 815	82.3
Mercer County	2 708	8 644	4.2	29.0	14.2	14.4	42 269	7.5	5.4	3 346	84.4
Morton County	4 989	25 303	4.4	27.0	14.7	17.0	37 028	9.6	3.8	9 889	75.6

[1]Dry land or land partially or temporarily covered by water.
[2]Persons who do not identify themselves White, not of Hispanic origin.
[3]Persons 25 years old and over.

Table B. 109th Congressional Districts by Counties, 2000—*Continued*

(Number, percent.)

| STATE Congressional district County | Land area,[1] (sq km) | Population | | | | Percent with bachelor's degree or more[3] | Median income, 1999 (dollars) | Percent living in poverty | Percent unem-ployed | Households | |
		Total	Percent minority[2]	Percent under 18 years old	Percent 65 years old and over					Total	Percent owner occupied
	1	2	3	4	5	6	7	8	9	10	11
Congressional District (At Large), North Dakota—*Continued*											
Mountrail County	4 724	6 631	34.5	28.2	17.6	15.6	27 098	19.3	5.9	2 560	72.6
Nelson County	2 542	3 715	1.5	22.3	27.5	17.5	28 892	10.3	3.3	1 628	80.3
Oliver County	1 874	2 065	2.8	27.6	14.6	12.0	36 650	14.9	5.0	791	85.6
Pembina County	2 898	8 585	5.6	24.8	19.5	16.4	36 430	9.2	4.8	3 535	78.3
Pierce County	2 636	4 675	1.5	23.8	24.0	14.7	26 524	12.5	4.1	1 964	73.1
Ramsey County	3 069	12 066	8.2	25.0	18.9	18.8	35 600	12.6	7.0	4 957	64.9
Ransom County	2 235	5 890	2.5	25.1	21.1	15.8	37 672	8.8	3.2	2 350	75.5
Renville County	2 266	2 610	3.2	23.2	21.9	16.1	30 746	11.0	1.8	1 085	77.7
Richland County	3 721	17 998	3.8	24.5	15.4	15.2	36 098	10.4	6.1	6 885	69.5
Rolette County	2 337	13 674	74.4	36.6	9.8	14.7	26 232	31.0	14.3	4 556	67.4
Sargent County	2 224	4 366	1.5	26.3	17.1	12.7	37 213	8.2	1.9	1 786	79.6
Sheridan County	2 517	1 710	1.1	21.2	26.8	9.7	24 450	21.0	7.5	731	84.8
Sioux County	2 834	4 044	83.4	40.7	5.8	11.2	22 483	39.2	23.3	1 095	46.1
Slope County	3 154	767	0.0	25.8	17.9	16.0	24 667	16.9	2.9	313	87.2
Stark County	3 466	22 636	3.1	25.5	15.5	22.3	32 526	12.3	4.9	8 932	70.3
Steele County	1 845	2 258	1.4	27.6	19.6	19.8	35 757	7.1	2.9	923	76.9
Stutsman County	5 753	21 908	2.3	22.9	17.6	19.7	33 848	10.4	3.4	8 954	67.2
Towner County	2 654	2 876	2.9	24.8	23.4	16.1	32 740	8.9	2.3	1 218	74.9
Traill County	2 232	8 477	3.1	24.9	19.2	21.8	37 445	9.2	3.2	3 341	72.4
Walsh County	3 320	12 389	7.0	24.8	19.5	13.3	33 845	10.9	6.2	5 029	76.8
Ward County	5 213	58 795	8.6	26.2	12.5	22.1	33 670	10.8	4.5	23 041	62.7
Wells County	3 293	5 102	1.5	22.5	26.0	13.7	31 894	13.5	6.0	2 215	76.5
Williams County	5 362	19 761	7.4	26.1	16.5	16.5	31 491	11.9	5.7	8 095	71.6
OHIO	106 056	11 353 140	16.0	25.4	13.3	21.1	40 956	10.6	5.0	4 445 773	69.1
Congressional District 1, Ohio	1 078	630 545	31.3	26.4	13.0	22.3	37 414	13.9	5.7	254 914	57.6
Butler County (part)	349	21 619	2.2	26.1	10.5	15.5	55 579	2.7	2.5	7 662	90.6
Hamilton County (part)	729	608 926	32.4	26.4	13.1	22.5	36 927	14.3	5.8	247 252	56.6
Congressional District 2, Ohio	6 764	630 893	8.3	26.1	12.3	29.0	46 813	8.4	4.1	247 290	71.5
Adams County	1 512	27 330	2.4	26.3	13.4	7.2	29 315	17.4	7.6	10 501	73.9
Brown County	1 274	42 285	2.3	27.6	11.6	8.8	38 303	11.6	5.3	15 555	79.5
Clermont County	1 171	177 977	3.4	27.9	9.4	20.8	49 386	7.1	3.5	66 013	74.8
Hamilton County (part)	326	236 377	15.3	24.3	14.5	44.8	52 293	5.5	3.1	99 538	67.9
Pike County	1 143	27 695	4.0	27.1	13.5	9.7	31 649	18.6	9.5	10 444	70.1
Scioto County (part)	860	44 942	5.4	23.5	17.0	10.1	25 638	21.4	9.9	18 589	64.2
Warren County (part)	478	74 287	6.5	28.4	8.9	33.5	60 218	3.9	3.1	26 650	77.2
Congressional District 3, Ohio	4 132	630 804	20.6	24.9	13.6	22.7	41 591	10.2	4.9	252 297	67.4
Clinton County	1 064	40 543	4.7	26.4	12.1	14.1	40 467	8.6	4.4	15 416	68.9
Highland County	1 433	40 875	3.4	27.0	13.7	9.7	35 313	11.8	6.1	15 587	75.3
Montgomery County (part)	1 078	465 290	26.1	24.3	14.4	24.4	40 571	11.1	5.2	191 978	64.7
Warren County (part)	557	84 096	5.9	27.1	9.9	23.9	56 080	4.5	2.9	29 316	79.8
Congressional District 4, Ohio	11 966	630 549	8.3	25.9	13.6	13.1	40 100	9.4	4.2	238 920	73.9
Allen County	1 047	108 473	15.9	25.9	14.1	13.4	37 048	12.1	5.7	40 646	72.1
Auglaize County	1 039	46 611	2.4	27.6	14.4	13.4	43 367	6.2	3.2	17 376	77.9
Champaign County	1 110	38 890	4.3	26.2	12.6	10.6	43 139	7.6	4.3	14 952	76.0
Hancock County	1 376	71 295	6.2	25.7	13.2	21.7	43 856	7.5	3.0	27 898	73.1
Hardin County	1 218	31 945	3.2	24.3	13.0	11.4	34 440	13.2	4.1	11 963	73.0
Logan County	1 187	46 005	4.7	26.6	13.9	11.5	41 479	9.3	3.7	17 956	75.6
Marion County	1 046	66 217	8.2	24.4	13.4	11.1	38 709	9.7	4.5	24 578	72.9
Morrow County	1 052	31 628	1.7	27.3	11.4	9.5	40 882	9.0	4.3	11 499	82.2
Richland County	1 287	128 852	12.2	24.8	14.1	12.6	37 397	10.6	4.8	49 534	71.6
Shelby County	1 060	47 910	4.7	28.6	12.2	12.8	44 507	6.7	3.2	17 636	74.4
Wyandot County (part)	542	12 723	3.2	25.9	15.8	8.0	38 360	6.2	2.8	4 882	74.6
Congressional District 5, Ohio	15 872	630 826	6.3	26.3	13.1	14.6	41 701	7.6	4.6	237 945	76.5
Ashland County (part)	422	11 922	1.2	29.9	10.5	8.0	43 142	9.2	3.4	4 000	88.4
Crawford County	1 041	46 966	2.9	25.0	15.2	9.7	36 227	10.4	5.2	18 957	72.5
Defiance County	1 065	39 500	10.2	26.5	12.8	14.3	44 938	5.6	3.7	15 138	79.6
Fulton County	1 054	42 084	7.3	28.2	12.8	13.2	44 074	5.4	3.3	15 480	80.1
Henry County	1 079	29 210	7.1	27.6	14.0	11.1	42 657	7.0	4.3	10 935	80.5
Huron County	1 276	59 487	6.1	28.2	12.4	10.9	40 558	8.5	5.1	22 307	72.2
Lucas County (part)	186	16 463	3.3	28.1	10.9	26.6	55 792	3.4	3.3	5 868	86.9
Mercer County (part)	671	9 603	1.6	27.1	14.1	9.2	44 138	4.7	2.7	3 414	86.5
Paulding County	1 078	20 293	4.9	26.6	12.5	7.8	40 327	7.7	3.3	7 773	83.9
Putnam County	1 253	34 726	5.2	29.6	13.3	12.9	46 426	5.6	2.9	12 200	84.1

[1]Dry land or land partially or temporarily covered by water.
[2]Persons who do not identify themselves White, not of Hispanic origin.
[3]Persons 25 years old and over.

Table B. 109th Congressional Districts by Counties, 2000—*Continued*

(Number, percent.)

STATE Congressional district County	Land area,[1] (sq km)	Population Total	Population Percent minority[2]	Population Percent under 18 years old	Population Percent 65 years old and over	Percent with bachelor's degree or more[3]	Median income, 1999 (dollars)	Percent living in poverty	Percent unem- ployed	Households Total	Households Percent owner occupied
	1	2	3	4	5	6	7	8	9	10	11
Congressional District 5, Ohio—*Continued*											
Sandusky County (part)	1 060	61 792	10.9	26.1	14.5	11.9	40 584	7.5	4.3	23 717	75.3
Seneca County	1 426	58 683	6.4	25.9	14.1	12.5	38 037	9.0	5.1	22 292	75.1
Van Wert County	1 062	29 659	3.6	26.0	15.4	12.0	39 497	5.5	4.9	11 587	81.7
Williams County	1 092	39 188	4.8	26.2	13.9	10.7	40 735	6.0	3.4	15 105	76.8
Wood County	1 599	121 065	6.7	23.6	10.9	26.2	44 442	9.6	6.2	45 172	70.6
Wyandot County (part)	508	10 185	2.4	25.7	15.1	12.2	39 419	4.7	2.9	4 000	74.9
Congressional District 6, Ohio	13 461	630 529	4.9	23.0	15.4	14.2	32 888	14.0	6.9	246 659	75.1
Athens County (part)	939	43 279	8.7	15.7	8.5	35.1	28 157	28.8	11.2	15 059	57.0
Belmont County (part)	1 169	55 178	3.7	22.7	18.6	9.3	28 068	15.9	7.5	22 996	74.5
Columbiana County	1 379	112 075	4.6	24.4	15.0	10.8	34 226	11.5	4.9	42 973	76.0
Gallia County	1 214	31 069	5.3	25.0	13.4	11.6	30 191	18.1	9.5	12 060	74.8
Jefferson County	1 061	73 894	7.9	21.4	18.6	11.8	30 853	15.1	7.6	30 417	74.3
Lawrence County	1 178	62 319	4.2	24.4	14.4	10.3	29 127	18.9	8.5	24 732	74.8
Mahoning County (part)	825	102 901	4.0	22.7	17.7	23.4	43 504	5.5	3.9	41 202	77.8
Meigs County	1 112	23 072	3.0	23.9	14.8	7.4	27 287	19.8	10.0	9 234	79.4
Monroe County	1 180	15 180	1.7	23.5	16.2	8.4	30 467	13.9	6.8	6 021	80.7
Noble County	1 033	14 058	7.9	22.7	13.1	8.1	32 940	11.4	6.0	4 546	79.8
Scioto County (part)	726	34 253	5.7	25.5	12.2	10.1	32 463	16.4	8.1	12 282	79.1
Washington County	1 645	63 251	3.2	23.5	14.9	15.0	34 275	11.4	7.4	25 137	76.2
Congressional District 7, Ohio	7 377	630 805	11.3	25.4	11.9	18.7	43 248	8.8	4.6	236 171	71.1
Clark County	1 036	144 742	12.4	25.1	14.7	14.9	40 340	10.7	5.9	56 648	71.5
Fairfield County	1 308	122 759	5.5	26.8	11.2	20.8	47 962	5.9	3.3	45 425	76.2
Fayette County	1 053	28 433	4.8	25.3	14.3	10.7	36 735	10.1	4.9	11 054	66.6
Franklin County (part)	201	86 161	24.2	27.4	9.5	14.7	41 729	8.5	3.4	34 182	61.5
Greene County	1 075	147 886	11.6	23.8	11.7	31.1	48 656	8.5	5.2	55 312	69.6
Perry County	1 061	34 078	1.8	28.2	12.0	6.9	34 383	11.8	5.9	12 500	79.4
Pickaway County	1 300	52 727	8.3	24.1	10.8	11.4	42 832	9.5	4.1	17 599	74.6
Ross County (part)	343	14 019	17.2	19.4	6.2	9.5	46 162	9.7	3.4	3 451	83.9
Congressional District 8, Ohio	5 216	630 795	8.3	26.2	11.8	18.7	43 753	8.8	4.2	238 870	71.2
Butler County (part)	861	311 188	10.2	25.9	10.7	24.1	47 340	9.1	4.2	115 420	70.3
Darke County	1 553	53 309	2.3	26.2	15.2	10.1	39 307	8.0	4.2	20 419	76.6
Mercer County (part)	529	31 321	2.3	30.5	14.5	13.8	42 365	6.9	3.4	11 342	78.3
Miami County	1 054	98 868	4.6	25.9	13.3	16.3	44 109	6.7	3.1	38 437	72.3
Montgomery County (part)	118	93 772	14.3	26.5	10.5	14.9	37 906	12.1	6.1	37 251	64.5
Preble County	1 100	42 337	1.8	26.0	13.1	10.1	42 093	6.1	4.3	16 001	78.9
Congressional District 9, Ohio	2 853	630 711	20.4	25.6	13.7	19.8	40 265	12.0	5.7	250 985	68.4
Erie County (part)	660	79 551	12.5	24.6	15.6	16.6	42 746	8.3	4.4	31 727	72.0
Lorain County (part)	837	71 584	7.3	25.0	12.7	18.1	52 137	5.5	3.3	25 805	81.7
Lucas County (part)	695	438 591	25.4	26.1	13.2	21.1	37 376	14.3	6.4	176 979	64.6
Ottawa County (part)	660	40 985	5.5	23.2	16.4	16.0	44 224	5.9	4.1	16 474	80.7
Congressional District 10, Ohio	506	631 003	12.8	23.4	16.2	23.3	41 841	9.1	4.6	262 940	68.0
Cuyahoga County (part)	506	631 003	12.8	23.4	16.2	23.3	41 841	9.1	4.6	262 940	68.0
Congressional District 11, Ohio	348	630 668	60.9	26.2	15.4	23.4	31 998	19.5	8.8	258 965	54.2
Cuyahoga County (part)	348	630 668	60.9	26.2	15.4	23.4	31 998	19.5	8.8	258 965	54.2
Congressional District 12, Ohio	2 632	630 744	27.8	27.3	9.7	32.1	47 289	10.0	4.4	248 615	62.5
Delaware County	1 146	109 989	6.4	28.2	8.1	41.0	67 258	3.8	3.8	39 674	80.4
Franklin County (part)	482	433 332	37.9	27.4	9.5	31.4	42 432	12.5	4.9	175 836	55.7
Knox County (part)	0	0	X	X	X	X	X	X	X	0	X
Licking County (part)	1 004	87 423	5.0	25.4	12.3	24.4	50 660	5.2	3.1	33 105	77.5
Congressional District 13, Ohio	1 374	630 928	18.4	25.8	13.6	22.3	44 524	9.4	4.9	244 563	72.7
Cuyahoga County (part)	182	87 499	6.0	25.2	12.8	36.8	65 554	2.3	3.4	33 176	82.2
Lorain County (part)	438	213 080	21.0	26.6	12.5	16.1	42 702	10.2	4.7	80 031	71.7
Medina County (part)	214	50 648	3.6	27.1	8.8	20.7	59 332	4.1	3.4	17 814	84.7
Summit County (part)	540	279 701	23.1	25.2	15.5	22.5	38 582	12.0	5.9	113 542	68.6
Congressional District 14, Ohio	4 654	630 655	6.0	26.0	13.4	27.1	51 304	5.7	3.5	238 653	79.6
Ashtabula County (part)	1 819	102 728	7.1	26.1	14.6	11.1	35 607	12.1	5.1	39 397	74.1
Cuyahoga County (part)	151	44 808	9.3	27.5	14.7	52.6	79 389	2.8	2.3	16 376	88.3
Geauga County	1 045	90 895	3.0	28.3	11.9	31.7	60 200	4.6	2.8	31 630	87.3
Lake County (part)	591	227 511	5.5	24.2	14.1	21.5	48 763	5.1	3.5	89 700	77.5
Portage County (part)	265	28 047	3.5	25.3	12.9	29.3	57 946	3.9	3.3	10 208	81.8
Summit County (part)	325	124 836	7.9	26.4	11.9	38.7	61 009	3.3	3.1	47 504	79.2
Trumbull County (part)	457	11 830	2.1	32.0	10.7	10.2	40 069	12.0	4.4	3 838	83.5
Congressional District 15, Ohio	3 052	630 607	14.9	23.3	10.0	32.1	43 885	10.8	3.7	256 778	59.1
Franklin County (part)	715	549 485	16.1	22.9	10.0	34.8	43 209	11.5	3.8	228 760	57.1
Madison County	1 205	40 213	8.7	24.7	10.9	13.0	44 212	7.8	3.1	13 672	72.3
Union County	1 131	40 909	4.8	27.5	9.7	15.9	51 743	4.6	2.3	14 346	77.5

[1]Dry land or land partially or temporarily covered by water.
[2]Persons who do not identify themselves White, not of Hispanic origin.
[3]Persons 25 years old and over.
 X = Not applicable.

Table B. 109th Congressional Districts by Counties, 2000—*Continued*

(Number, percent.)

STATE Congressional district County	Land area,[1] (sq km)	Population Total	Percent minority[2]	Percent under 18 years old	Percent 65 years old and over	Percent with bachelor's degree or more[3]	Median income, 1999 (dollars)	Percent living in poverty	Percent unem- ployed	Households Total	Percent owner occupied
	1	2	3	4	5	6	7	8	9	10	11
Congressional District 16, Ohio	4 486	630 710	7.6	25.7	14.0	19.2	41 801	8.3	4.1	241 013	73.6
Ashland County (part)	677	40 601	3.1	24.6	15.0	18.1	38 049	9.5	4.5	15 524	72.3
Medina County (part)	878	100 447	3.8	27.7	11.4	26.8	54 097	4.8	3.3	36 728	79.5
Stark County	1 492	378 098	10.2	24.8	15.1	17.9	39 824	9.2	4.5	148 316	72.4
Wayne County	1 438	111 564	3.7	27.5	12.2	17.2	41 538	8.0	3.2	40 445	73.3
Congressional District 17, Ohio	2 604	630 316	15.5	23.8	14.8	15.8	36 705	12.3	6.0	249 550	70.1
Mahoning County (part)	250	154 654	31.3	24.3	17.8	13.3	30 177	17.3	8.2	61 385	69.5
Portage County (part)	1 010	124 014	6.3	23.3	10.5	19.0	41 602	10.5	4.8	46 241	68.9
Summit County (part)	204	138 362	13.1	23.6	13.5	18.0	37 553	11.7	5.2	56 742	65.9
Trumbull County (part)	1 140	213 286	10.8	23.9	16.0	14.7	38 214	10.2	5.8	85 182	73.8
Congressional District 18, Ohio	17 680	631 052	4.2	26.1	13.7	11.3	34 462	12.6	5.6	240 645	74.3
Athens County (part)	373	18 944	4.0	24.2	11.1	9.2	25 852	24.6	10.9	7 442	67.4
Belmont County (part)	223	15 048	12.2	18.2	17.1	17.6	36 181	9.0	5.5	5 313	77.5
Carroll County	1 022	28 836	1.9	25.2	14.1	9.1	35 509	11.4	4.3	11 126	80.0
Coshocton County	1 461	36 655	3.0	26.2	14.7	9.8	34 701	9.1	5.7	14 356	76.0
Guernsey County	1 352	40 792	4.3	26.2	14.4	10.0	30 110	16.0	6.9	16 094	73.4
Harrison County	1 045	15 856	3.5	23.0	17.7	9.0	30 318	13.3	4.7	6 398	77.5
Hocking County	1 095	28 241	2.5	25.4	13.1	9.8	34 261	13.5	5.7	10 843	75.6
Holmes County	1 096	38 943	1.7	35.6	10.5	8.3	36 944	12.9	2.3	11 337	76.9
Jackson County	1 089	32 641	3.6	26.0	13.6	11.0	30 661	16.5	7.7	12 619	73.8
Knox County (part)	1 365	54 500	2.8	24.8	13.8	16.7	38 877	10.1	6.1	19 975	75.7
Licking County (part)	775	58 068	4.8	26.9	11.2	9.3	36 764	10.8	4.8	22 504	69.9
Morgan County	1 082	14 897	6.2	25.3	15.3	9.1	28 868	18.4	8.4	5 890	78.2
Muskingum County	1 721	84 585	6.5	26.0	14.3	12.6	35 185	12.9	5.8	32 518	73.5
Ross County (part)	1 440	59 326	6.5	25.1	13.5	11.8	35 822	12.3	5.7	23 685	72.0
Tuscarawas County	1 470	90 914	2.7	25.5	15.0	12.2	35 489	9.4	4.1	35 653	75.0
Vinton County	1 072	12 806	2.5	27.1	12.2	6.0	29 465	20.0	9.0	4 892	77.8
OKLAHOMA	177 847	3 450 654	25.9	25.8	13.2	20.3	33 400	14.7	5.3	1 342 293	68.4
Congressional District 1, Oklahoma	4 498	690 419	26.2	26.3	12.0	25.6	38 610	11.3	4.7	275 329	64.8
Creek County (part)	139	5 802	19.0	30.2	9.6	9.7	37 623	10.7	4.3	2 079	80.9
Rogers County (part)	345	14 831	17.5	29.6	9.0	19.9	53 750	6.7	3.4	5 169	87.8
Tulsa County	1 477	563 299	27.5	26.2	11.8	26.9	38 213	11.6	4.8	226 892	61.8
Wagoner County	1 458	57 491	20.9	28.1	10.1	15.4	41 744	8.9	3.7	21 010	81.0
Washington County	1 080	48 996	20.3	25.1	17.7	25.8	35 816	11.9	4.9	20 179	74.0
Congressional District 2, Oklahoma	53 258	689 974	29.8	26.0	15.2	13.2	27 885	18.5	6.5	264 390	74.3
Adair County	1 491	21 038	52.3	30.5	12.1	9.8	24 881	23.2	7.2	7 471	73.3
Atoka County	2 534	13 879	24.7	23.8	14.9	10.1	24 752	19.8	6.6	4 964	76.4
Bryan County	2 354	36 534	21.0	24.7	15.4	17.9	27 888	18.4	6.5	14 422	69.3
Cherokee County	1 945	42 521	44.6	26.2	12.1	22.1	26 536	22.9	8.2	16 175	66.8
Choctaw County	2 004	15 342	32.3	25.9	17.4	9.9	22 743	24.3	7.1	6 220	70.9
Coal County	1 342	6 031	25.5	26.6	17.8	12.4	23 705	23.1	6.9	2 373	75.3
Craig County	1 971	14 950	31.8	24.0	16.5	10.5	30 997	13.7	3.9	5 620	74.9
Delaware County	1 918	37 077	30.6	24.5	17.6	13.3	27 996	18.3	6.6	14 838	79.2
Haskell County	1 495	11 792	22.0	26.0	17.0	10.3	24 553	20.5	4.7	4 624	77.3
Hughes County	2 089	14 154	28.2	22.9	18.5	9.7	22 621	21.9	7.6	5 319	75.8
Johnston County	1 669	10 513	24.4	25.6	15.5	13.3	24 592	22.0	6.1	4 057	73.7
Latimer County	1 870	10 692	27.7	25.6	16.0	12.0	23 962	22.7	7.8	3 951	74.5
Le Flore County	4 107	48 109	21.7	26.1	13.6	11.3	27 278	19.1	6.3	17 861	75.1
McCurtain County	4 797	34 402	30.5	27.9	13.9	10.8	24 162	24.7	7.4	13 216	73.3
McIntosh County	1 606	19 456	27.8	22.6	21.6	13.1	25 964	18.2	6.6	8 085	78.9
Mayes County	1 699	38 369	28.5	26.6	14.7	12.1	31 125	14.3	5.4	14 823	77.0
Muskogee County	2 108	69 451	37.3	25.8	15.5	15.4	28 438	17.9	7.3	26 458	69.6
Nowata County	1 463	10 569	28.5	26.2	17.2	9.5	29 470	14.1	3.9	4 147	77.7
Okfuskee County	1 618	11 814	35.0	24.7	16.3	9.2	24 324	23.0	12.5	4 270	76.0
Okmulgee County	1 805	39 685	31.0	26.9	15.4	11.4	27 652	18.9	7.8	15 300	72.6
Ottawa County	1 221	33 194	26.9	25.7	16.8	12.2	27 507	16.6	6.0	12 984	73.9
Pittsburg County	3 382	43 953	23.7	23.5	17.2	12.9	28 679	17.2	7.2	17 157	76.0
Pushmataha County	3 619	11 667	23.0	26.1	18.3	12.4	22 127	23.2	6.7	4 739	77.8
Rogers County (part)	1 403	55 810	22.2	28.4	11.9	16.1	41 899	9.1	3.8	20 555	79.4
Sequoyah County	1 745	38 972	32.4	27.4	13.6	10.9	27 615	19.8	6.2	14 761	75.2
Congressional District 3, Oklahoma	88 289	689 994	19.0	25.5	14.2	18.1	32 098	15.0	5.1	263 332	72.5
Alfalfa County	2 245	6 105	10.9	19.4	20.7	14.9	30 259	13.7	2.8	2 199	81.7
Beaver County	4 699	5 857	14.8	26.7	17.0	17.6	36 715	11.7	2.6	2 245	79.1
Beckham County	2 336	19 799	15.0	24.3	15.4	15.5	27 402	18.2	6.3	7 356	71.1
Blaine County	2 405	11 976	26.5	24.0	16.6	14.0	28 356	16.9	5.3	4 159	76.9
Caddo County	3 311	30 150	36.1	28.5	14.9	14.2	27 347	21.7	8.0	10 957	73.5

[1]Dry land or land partially or temporarily covered by water.
[2]Persons who do not identify themselves White, not of Hispanic origin.
[3]Persons 25 years old and over.

Table B. 109th Congressional Districts by Counties, 2000—*Continued*

(Number, percent.)

STATE Congressional district County	Land area,[1] (sq km)	Population				Percent with bachelor's degree or more[3]	Median income, 1999 (dollars)	Percent living in poverty	Percent unem-ployed	Households	
		Total	Percent minority[2]	Percent under 18 years old	Percent 65 years old and over					Total	Percent owner occupied
	1	2	3	4	5	6	7	8	9	10	11
Congressional District 3, Oklahoma—*Continued*											
Canadian County (part)	2 133	63 074	15.5	27.2	10.2	20.4	42 061	9.0	3.8	22 895	76.9
Cimarron County	4 753	3 148	17.5	27.4	18.8	17.7	30 625	17.6	2.0	1 257	72.6
Creek County (part)	2 336	61 565	18.7	27.2	13.2	11.9	32 792	13.7	4.8	23 210	77.8
Custer County	2 555	26 142	20.5	24.3	13.7	22.8	28 524	18.5	4.7	10 136	63.7
Dewey County	2 590	4 743	9.1	23.1	21.3	16.6	28 172	15.0	3.3	1 962	79.0
Ellis County	3 183	4 075	5.1	22.0	21.9	19.2	27 951	12.5	2.3	1 769	80.7
Garfield County	2 741	57 813	13.1	25.0	15.9	19.6	33 006	13.9	5.1	23 175	70.2
Grant County	2 591	5 144	4.8	25.4	21.5	16.2	28 977	13.7	2.7	2 089	78.8
Greer County	1 656	6 061	21.1	19.8	20.2	12.6	25 793	19.6	6.9	2 237	74.8
Harmon County	1 393	3 283	34.1	25.7	20.4	12.1	22 365	29.7	6.9	1 266	77.2
Harper County	2 691	3 562	7.0	23.4	21.5	19.2	33 705	10.2	1.4	1 509	78.7
Jackson County	2 079	28 439	28.2	29.2	11.9	18.5	30 737	16.2	5.2	10 590	60.3
Kay County	2 379	48 080	17.3	26.4	16.9	18.3	30 762	16.0	7.7	19 157	71.7
Kingfisher County	2 339	13 926	13.8	27.3	15.4	16.1	36 676	10.8	3.5	5 247	78.2
Kiowa County	2 628	10 227	20.0	24.0	20.3	14.8	26 053	19.3	6.0	4 208	75.2
Lincoln County	2 481	32 080	14.1	27.4	14.0	11.1	31 187	14.5	4.9	12 178	80.1
Logan County	1 928	33 924	19.8	25.4	12.0	19.1	36 784	12.9	5.7	12 389	78.4
Major County	2 478	7 545	6.5	24.6	19.3	14.4	30 949	12.0	3.3	3 046	81.0
Noble County	1 896	11 411	14.1	25.3	15.2	15.8	33 968	12.8	3.7	4 504	75.2
Osage County	5 830	44 437	34.1	26.3	13.1	14.6	34 477	13.2	5.6	16 617	80.5
Pawnee County	1 475	16 612	18.2	26.6	14.7	12.1	31 661	13.0	5.1	6 383	80.0
Payne County	1 778	68 190	16.8	19.5	10.8	34.2	28 733	20.3	4.8	26 680	55.9
Roger Mills County	2 957	3 436	10.1	23.6	18.8	15.8	30 078	16.3	2.4	1 428	78.8
Texas County	5 276	20 107	33.3	28.9	10.3	17.7	35 872	14.1	4.9	7 153	67.1
Washita County	2 599	11 508	9.5	26.1	18.6	15.1	29 563	15.5	4.0	4 506	74.7
Woods County	3 332	9 089	8.6	18.8	19.9	23.7	28 927	15.0	4.1	3 684	69.6
Woodward County	3 218	18 486	9.5	26.0	14.2	15.2	33 581	12.5	6.1	7 141	72.0
Congressional District 4, Oklahoma	26 449	690 400	22.4	25.7	12.1	20.2	35 510	13.1	5.1	262 143	69.7
Canadian County (part)	197	24 623	13.8	29.6	7.5	22.2	52 635	5.2	2.6	8 589	84.4
Carter County	2 134	45 621	23.1	26.2	16.3	15.1	29 405	16.6	5.6	17 992	71.1
Cleveland County	1 389	208 016	18.5	24.4	8.4	28.0	41 846	10.6	4.2	79 186	67.0
Comanche County	2 770	114 996	38.1	27.5	9.7	19.1	33 867	15.6	7.6	39 808	60.3
Cotton County	1 649	6 614	17.1	25.5	18.0	14.0	27 210	18.2	4.8	2 614	76.4
Garvin County	2 091	27 210	16.7	24.7	17.8	12.0	28 070	15.9	5.6	10 865	73.9
Grady County	2 851	45 516	13.9	26.6	13.0	14.4	32 625	13.9	4.8	17 341	75.7
Jefferson County	1 965	6 818	16.4	24.0	20.1	10.6	23 674	19.2	5.5	2 716	74.1
Love County	1 335	8 831	18.6	25.7	16.2	10.8	32 558	11.8	5.2	3 442	81.8
McClain County	1 475	27 740	14.6	26.6	11.9	15.7	37 275	10.5	3.7	10 331	81.3
Marshall County	961	13 184	23.7	23.5	19.4	11.4	26 437	17.9	4.2	5 371	79.2
Murray County	1 083	12 623	20.6	23.7	18.4	14.9	30 294	14.1	5.7	5 003	74.2
Oklahoma County (part)	162	60 996	26.4	26.2	12.6	19.4	39 161	10.5	4.4	23 850	67.3
Pontotoc County	1 864	35 143	25.1	24.7	14.9	21.8	26 955	16.5	6.8	13 978	67.0
Stephens County	2 264	43 182	13.7	24.5	18.4	16.6	30 709	14.6	6.5	17 463	75.6
Tillman County	2 258	9 287	30.3	27.0	19.3	12.5	24 828	21.9	4.3	3 594	77.2
Congressional District 5, Oklahoma	5 353	689 867	32.3	25.5	12.5	24.5	33 893	15.8	5.4	277 099	61.3
Oklahoma County (part)	1 674	599 452	33.6	25.4	12.2	26.0	34 621	15.7	5.3	242 984	59.7
Pottawatomie County	2 040	65 521	21.3	25.8	13.9	15.5	31 573	14.6	5.7	24 540	72.2
Seminole County	1 638	24 894	30.1	26.3	16.8	12.1	25 568	20.8	8.6	9 575	72.3
OREGON	248 631	3 421 399	16.5	24.7	12.8	25.1	40 916	11.6	6.5	1 333 723	64.2
Congressional District 1, Oregon	7 618	684 351	18.9	25.2	10.1	33.3	48 464	8.7	5.2	268 505	59.6
Clatsop County	2 143	35 630	9.4	23.6	15.5	19.1	36 301	13.2	6.6	14 703	64.2
Columbia County	1 701	43 560	6.9	27.3	11.7	14.0	45 797	9.1	6.3	16 375	76.1
Multnomah County (part)	47	74 827	14.3	13.5	12.1	55.2	38 909	14.1	6.8	39 533	40.0
Washington County	1 874	445 342	22.2	26.8	8.8	34.5	52 122	7.4	4.6	169 162	60.5
Yamhill County	1 853	84 992	15.5	26.6	11.7	20.6	44 111	9.2	6.4	28 732	69.6
Congressional District 2, Oregon	179 982	684 184	14.0	25.5	15.1	19.0	35 600	13.0	7.8	264 616	68.2
Baker County	7 946	16 741	4.9	24.3	19.2	16.4	30 367	14.7	8.3	6 883	70.0
Crook County	7 717	19 182	9.0	26.5	14.5	12.6	35 186	11.3	7.7	7 354	74.2
Deschutes County	7 817	115 367	7.1	24.7	13.0	25.0	41 847	9.3	5.2	45 595	72.3
Gilliam County	3 119	1 915	3.6	23.1	19.0	13.4	33 611	9.1	6.8	819	69.6
Grant County	11 729	7 935	5.3	25.9	16.7	15.7	32 560	13.7	11.9	3 246	73.3
Harney County	26 248	7 609	11.2	25.9	14.8	11.9	30 957	11.8	9.4	3 036	72.6
Hood River County	1 353	20 411	29.6	28.0	12.8	23.1	38 326	14.2	6.6	7 248	64.9
Jackson County	7 214	181 269	11.4	24.3	16.0	22.3	36 461	12.5	7.3	71 532	66.5
Jefferson County	4 612	19 009	35.4	29.7	12.4	13.7	35 853	14.6	8.6	6 727	71.3
Josephine County (part)	401	51 363	8.8	23.4	21.0	14.2	31 918	13.7	9.8	21 075	66.9

[1]Dry land or land partially or temporarily covered by water.
[2]Persons who do not identify themselves White, not of Hispanic origin.
[3]Persons 25 years old and over.

Table B. 109th Congressional Districts by Counties, 2000—*Continued*

(Number, percent.)

STATE Congressional district County	Land area,[1] (sq km)	Population Total	Percent minority[2]	Percent under 18 years old	Percent 65 years old and over	Percent with bachelor's degree or more[3]	Median income, 1999 (dollars)	Percent living in poverty	Percent unem- ployed	Households Total	Percent owner occupied
	1	2	3	4	5	6	7	8	9	10	11
Congressional District 2, Oregon—*Continued*											
Klamath County	15 395	63 775	16.1	25.9	14.9	15.9	31 537	16.8	10.0	25 205	68.0
Lake County	21 072	7 422	10.6	24.7	17.7	15.5	29 506	16.1	8.5	3 084	68.8
Malheur County	25 607	31 615	31.3	27.4	13.6	11.1	30 241	18.6	11.1	10 221	63.8
Morrow County	5 264	10 995	28.9	30.7	10.5	11.0	37 521	14.8	10.7	3 776	73.1
Sherman County	2 132	1 934	9.5	26.3	18.1	19.0	35 142	14.6	7.3	797	70.4
Umatilla County	8 327	70 548	22.5	27.8	12.2	16.0	36 249	12.7	7.5	25 195	64.9
Union County	5 275	24 530	6.5	24.6	14.8	21.8	33 738	13.8	7.9	9 740	66.6
Wallowa County	8 146	7 226	2.6	24.1	19.0	20.3	32 129	14.0	11.8	3 029	71.8
Wasco County	6 167	23 791	16.1	25.2	16.7	15.7	35 959	12.9	7.9	9 401	68.4
Wheeler County	4 442	1 547	5.6	22.8	23.0	14.3	28 750	15.6	7.3	653	72.1
Congressional District 3, Oregon	2 644	684 502	22.8	23.9	11.0	24.8	42 063	11.7	6.4	268 551	61.3
Clackamas County (part)	1 588	125 218	12.1	25.3	10.5	21.4	48 638	7.2	5.7	47 332	70.7
Multnomah County (part)	1 056	559 284	25.2	23.6	11.1	25.6	40 925	12.7	6.5	221 219	59.3
Congressional District 4, Oregon	44 498	684 512	10.3	23.3	15.1	21.4	35 796	13.7	6.9	275 607	65.7
Benton County (part)	1 516	49 806	13.2	24.2	11.0	45.2	41 781	12.9	4.6	20 111	59.1
Coos County	4 145	62 779	9.8	21.8	19.1	15.0	31 542	15.0	8.5	26 213	68.2
Curry County	4 215	21 137	9.0	19.0	26.9	16.4	30 117	12.2	7.3	9 543	72.9
Douglas County	13 045	100 399	8.0	23.9	17.8	13.3	33 223	13.1	7.6	39 821	71.7
Josephine County (part)	3 846	24 363	8.2	22.2	18.2	13.8	29 864	17.7	9.8	9 925	76.8
Lane County	11 795	322 959	11.4	22.8	13.3	25.5	36 942	14.4	6.4	130 453	62.3
Linn County	5 937	103 069	8.8	26.0	14.4	13.4	37 518	11.4	7.9	39 541	67.9
Congressional District 5, Oregon	13 889	683 850	16.4	25.6	12.7	27.0	44 409	10.9	6.2	256 444	66.5
Benton County (part)	236	28 347	13.5	16.4	8.7	51.9	42 088	18.0	5.3	10 034	53.6
Clackamas County (part)	3 251	213 173	10.1	26.5	11.4	32.5	54 417	6.2	4.6	80 869	71.3
Lincoln County	2 537	44 479	11.8	21.4	19.4	20.8	32 769	13.9	8.4	19 296	65.7
Marion County	3 066	284 834	23.5	27.3	12.4	19.8	40 314	13.5	7.7	101 641	62.9
Multnomah County (part)	24	26 375	13.4	19.2	9.5	58.2	62 792	6.9	3.6	11 346	69.3
Polk County	1 919	62 380	14.4	25.4	14.7	25.3	42 311	11.5	6.2	23 058	68.4
Tillamook County	2 855	24 262	8.5	22.2	19.6	17.6	34 269	11.4	4.4	10 200	71.9
PENNSYLVANIA	116 074	12 281 054	15.9	23.8	15.6	22.4	40 106	11.0	5.7	4 777 003	71.3
Congressional District 1, Pennsylvania	152	645 422	66.7	28.3	12.1	13.9	28 261	26.9	12.8	238 648	60.3
Delaware County (part)	41	75 324	73.6	29.4	12.8	11.7	31 387	19.8	12.1	26 986	56.0
Philadelphia County (part)	111	570 098	65.8	28.2	12.0	14.2	27 752	27.8	12.9	211 662	60.9
Congressional District 2, Pennsylvania	152	647 350	70.1	24.2	13.9	24.2	30 646	23.8	11.7	259 903	53.4
Montgomery County (part)	23	36 875	34.6	22.7	18.6	49.2	61 713	5.1	7.4	14 346	64.5
Philadelphia County (part)	129	610 475	72.2	24.3	13.6	22.5	29 446	24.9	12.0	245 557	52.8
Congressional District 3, Pennsylvania	10 280	646 332	6.3	24.3	15.4	18.0	35 884	11.6	5.7	247 374	73.5
Armstrong County (part)	1 131	32 386	1.2	23.7	17.0	10.2	32 311	11.4	6.8	12 487	82.5
Butler County (part)	1 613	112 716	2.5	23.1	15.5	16.8	37 056	11.5	5.2	43 189	75.5
Crawford County (part)	2 419	80 015	3.8	24.4	15.3	15.0	34 225	12.4	5.9	30 633	76.6
Erie County	2 077	280 843	10.2	25.0	14.3	20.9	36 627	12.0	5.8	106 507	69.2
Mercer County (part)	1 639	105 658	5.0	23.4	17.4	17.9	35 488	10.6	5.7	40 581	76.7
Venango County (part)	419	6 495	1.9	23.7	16.5	10.5	32 602	12.4	7.4	2 564	81.5
Warren County (part)	981	28 219	1.3	24.8	16.4	15.8	35 449	10.4	4.9	11 413	74.8
Congressional District 4, Pennsylvania	3 373	646 555	5.8	23.9	17.3	27.1	43 547	7.5	4.4	254 233	78.4
Allegheny County (part)	745	274 460	4.4	24.1	16.7	36.2	50 852	5.1	3.5	107 952	80.2
Beaver County (part)	1 065	179 197	8.0	22.6	18.6	15.8	36 880	9.4	5.4	71 783	74.7
Butler County (part)	429	61 367	2.6	27.4	12.1	35.7	54 578	4.8	3.0	22 673	82.1
Lawrence County	934	94 643	5.5	23.1	19.3	15.1	33 152	12.1	6.1	37 091	77.3
Mercer County (part)	101	14 635	24.0	23.3	22.7	13.0	30 193	17.9	8.5	6 131	73.2
Westmoreland County (part)	99	22 253	4.8	24.8	15.5	42.5	58 101	3.5	2.3	8 603	86.4
Congressional District 5, Pennsylvania	28 598	646 326	3.9	22.2	15.4	16.9	33 254	13.5	5.8	250 231	72.9
Cameron County	1 029	5 974	1.0	24.6	19.9	12.1	32 212	9.4	6.3	2 465	75.0
Centre County (part)	2 868	135 758	9.2	17.9	10.3	36.3	36 165	18.8	5.5	49 323	60.2
Clarion County	1 560	41 765	2.1	21.7	15.2	15.3	30 770	15.4	6.6	16 052	72.2
Clearfield County (part)	2 506	75 339	3.2	22.6	17.0	11.6	31 737	12.3	6.8	29 659	78.5
Clinton County	2 307	37 914	2.0	21.5	16.7	13.4	31 064	14.2	5.8	14 773	73.0
Crawford County (part)	204	10 351	1.5	26.7	17.3	12.5	28 427	15.3	6.7	4 045	66.7
Elk County	2 146	35 112	1.4	24.0	17.3	12.3	37 550	7.0	4.5	14 124	79.4
Forest County	1 109	4 946	5.0	22.8	19.5	8.9	27 581	16.4	7.1	2 000	82.6
Jefferson County	1 698	45 932	1.6	23.6	17.9	11.7	31 722	11.8	6.7	18 375	77.2
Juniata County (part)	103	3 253	0.2	25.5	14.2	9.6	30 653	9.5	2.5	1 218	76.4
Lycoming County (part)	1 692	47 222	3.5	23.5	15.8	12.9	36 673	8.1	3.9	18 112	77.4
McKean County	2 542	45 936	4.5	23.8	16.7	14.0	33 040	13.1	6.0	18 024	74.8
Mifflin County (part)	550	30 804	2.0	23.3	16.9	10.5	31 773	12.6	4.7	12 728	70.4
Potter County	2 800	18 080	2.5	25.9	16.6	12.3	32 253	12.7	6.2	7 005	77.4
Tioga County (part)	2 848	41 226	2.3	23.7	16.0	14.2	32 033	13.5	6.0	15 862	76.1
Venango County (part)	1 330	51 070	2.6	24.3	16.8	13.4	32 221	13.5	7.2	20 183	75.8
Warren County (part)	1 307	15 644	1.4	22.8	17.1	11.3	37 435	8.9	5.4	6 283	84.5

[1] Dry land or land partially or temporarily covered by water.
[2] Persons who do not identify themselves White, not of Hispanic origin.
[3] Persons 25 years old and over.

Table B. 109th Congressional Districts by Counties, 2000—*Continued*

(Number, percent.)

STATE Congressional district County	Land area,[1] (sq km)	Population Total	Population Percent minority[2]	Population Percent under 18 years old	Population Percent 65 years old and over	Percent with bachelor's degree or more[3]	Median income, 1999 (dollars)	Percent living in poverty	Percent unem- ployed	Households Total	Households Percent owner occupied
	1	2	3	4	5	6	7	8	9	10	11
Congressional District 6, Pennsylvania	2 107	645 741	13.6	24.5	14.0	34.2	55 611	6.1	5.0	245 016	73.7
Berks County (part)	804	207 176	10.6	23.3	16.3	21.2	46 446	7.0	4.8	80 230	74.3
Chester County (part)	1 004	243 416	11.9	26.7	11.6	40.6	64 453	4.8	3.3	90 293	77.0
Lehigh County (part)	19	2 187	5.9	24.5	10.6	36.2	59 479	1.4	3.8	819	83.4
Montgomery County (part)	280	192 962	19.1	23.1	14.6	39.9	58 274	6.7	7.2	73 674	68.8
Congressional District 7, Pennsylvania	751	646 355	11.6	23.8	15.4	36.1	56 126	5.4	3.6	246 445	74.3
Chester County (part)	163	74 697	7.7	24.6	14.2	54.7	73 989	3.3	2.9	28 832	78.1
Delaware County (part)	436	475 540	12.0	24.0	16.0	32.7	52 554	6.1	3.9	179 334	74.3
Montgomery County (part)	153	96 118	12.3	22.2	13.2	37.9	60 392	3.5	2.9	38 279	71.3
Congressional District 8, Pennsylvania	1 603	644 798	9.1	25.5	12.6	30.7	59 207	4.5	3.5	236 264	77.5
Bucks County	1 573	597 635	8.8	25.7	12.4	31.2	59 727	4.5	3.5	218 725	77.3
Lehigh County (part)	0	0	X	X	X	X	X	X	X	0	X
Montgomery County (part)	13	16 348	19.9	24.2	15.7	37.9	57 652	5.3	3.3	6 354	74.3
Philadelphia County (part)	17	30 815	9.8	22.9	13.7	16.8	52 280	4.4	4.1	11 185	82.4
Congressional District 9, Pennsylvania	18 543	647 032	3.6	23.6	15.9	13.0	34 910	11.1	5.3	250 103	76.6
Bedford County	2 628	49 984	1.6	23.6	16.4	10.2	32 731	10.3	5.7	19 768	80.2
Blair County	1 362	129 144	2.7	22.7	17.3	13.9	32 861	12.6	6.2	51 518	72.9
Cambria County (part)	549	21 696	4.5	21.4	16.7	9.6	28 678	12.8	11.3	7 751	81.0
Clearfield County (part)	466	8 043	0.9	23.9	16.3	6.7	28 272	14.7	8.1	3 126	85.4
Cumberland County (part)	820	40 574	3.9	26.4	11.7	18.7	46 523	5.5	2.4	14 904	82.4
Fayette County (part)	1 028	33 777	1.7	23.7	15.4	9.9	29 408	17.1	7.7	13 040	77.2
Franklin County (part)	1 999	129 313	5.6	24.0	16.0	14.8	40 476	7.6	3.7	50 633	74.0
Fulton County	1 133	14 261	1.8	24.5	14.5	9.3	34 882	10.8	3.9	5 660	79.0
Huntingdon County	2 264	45 586	7.1	21.6	14.9	11.9	33 313	11.3	5.6	16 759	77.6
Indiana County (part)	1 885	66 964	2.6	23.2	15.9	15.1	30 929	14.5	7.1	26 391	75.4
Juniata County (part)	911	19 568	3.0	24.9	15.3	8.7	35 362	9.4	3.7	7 366	77.9
Mifflin County (part)	517	15 682	1.0	27.5	17.2	11.7	33 565	12.4	2.8	5 685	82.3
Perry County (part)	901	21 824	1.9	25.7	12.4	11.4	41 866	7.8	3.3	8 385	81.3
Somerset County (part)	2 055	50 055	4.3	22.5	17.1	10.8	31 089	12.8	5.5	19 027	77.1
Westmoreland County (part)	26	561	28.7	23.0	4.6	23.0	29 107	2.1	0.0	90	92.2
Congressional District 10, Pennsylvania	16 985	646 627	4.4	23.5	16.6	17.1	35 996	10.3	5.2	250 693	75.7
Bradford County	2 980	62 761	2.2	25.5	15.7	14.8	35 038	11.8	5.5	24 453	75.5
Centre County (part)	0	0	X	X	X	X	X	X	X	0	X
Lackawanna County (part)	1 018	85 019	2.1	23.5	17.1	24.1	40 077	7.3	4.3	33 155	79.0
Luzerne County (part)	553	63 018	1.6	21.6	18.9	24.3	39 615	8.0	4.3	25 645	75.1
Lycoming County (part)	1 507	72 822	8.3	23.0	16.1	16.5	32 140	13.8	7.8	28 891	64.5
Montour County	339	18 236	3.4	24.4	17.1	22.1	38 075	8.7	7.2	7 085	72.8
Northumberland County	1 191	94 556	3.5	21.8	19.1	11.1	31 314	11.9	5.2	38 835	73.6
Pike County	1 416	46 302	10.1	26.5	15.1	19.0	44 608	6.9	5.4	17 433	84.8
Snyder County	858	37 546	2.4	24.0	14.0	12.5	35 981	9.9	3.8	13 654	76.5
Sullivan County	1 165	6 556	4.9	20.8	21.8	12.8	30 279	14.5	8.9	2 660	80.4
Susquehanna County	2 131	42 238	1.9	25.5	15.6	13.2	33 622	12.3	4.3	16 529	79.5
Tioga County (part)	89	147	2.7	21.1	16.3	15.5	27 500	15.6	13.6	63	93.7
Union County	820	41 624	12.4	20.0	13.4	18.0	40 336	8.8	3.9	13 178	73.4
Wayne County	1 889	47 722	4.1	24.1	17.5	14.6	34 082	11.3	5.7	18 350	80.5
Wyoming County	1 029	28 080	2.0	25.3	13.3	15.4	36 365	10.2	4.9	10 762	79.0
Congressional District 11, Pennsylvania	5 744	646 148	6.6	22.2	17.9	15.9	34 979	11.3	6.1	256 175	70.2
Carbon County	987	58 802	3.0	22.1	18.5	11.0	35 113	9.5	5.5	23 701	78.2
Columbia County	1 258	64 151	2.7	20.8	15.9	15.8	34 094	13.1	7.3	24 915	72.2
Lackawanna County (part)	170	128 276	5.1	20.6	21.1	16.6	30 867	12.7	6.0	53 063	60.5
Luzerne County (part)	1 754	256 232	4.8	20.9	19.8	14.4	32 348	11.9	5.7	105 042	69.1
Lycoming County (part)	0	0	X	X	X	X	X	X	X	0	X
Monroe County	1 576	138 687	15.0	26.6	12.2	20.5	46 257	9.0	6.6	49 454	78.3
Congressional District 12, Pennsylvania	7 127	646 419	5.0	21.3	19.1	13.7	30 612	13.6	7.4	262 370	73.4
Allegheny County (part)	17	6 586	5.5	22.4	16.4	11.8	27 634	15.7	6.6	2 847	62.1
Armstrong County (part)	563	40 006	2.8	22.2	18.8	10.6	31 020	11.9	5.7	16 518	73.4
Cambria County (part)	1 233	130 902	4.7	20.9	20.2	14.4	30 377	12.4	8.4	52 780	73.8
Fayette County (part)	1 019	114 867	6.0	22.4	19.0	11.9	26 911	18.3	8.4	46 929	72.0
Greene County	1 491	40 672	5.8	22.0	15.2	12.2	30 352	15.9	9.2	15 060	74.1
Indiana County (part)	263	22 641	6.1	14.6	11.9	24.6	27 096	27.0	11.1	7 732	59.4
Somerset County (part)	729	29 968	1.0	22.2	19.7	10.8	30 607	10.2	6.1	12 195	79.5
Washington County (part)	644	103 114	6.9	20.4	19.8	14.5	31 624	12.7	6.8	42 924	71.1
Westmoreland County (part)	1 169	157 663	4.4	21.7	20.0	14.6	33 271	10.4	5.9	65 385	76.3
Congressional District 13, Pennsylvania	660	647 976	14.3	23.3	17.2	28.6	49 319	7.1	4.6	251 044	72.3
Montgomery County (part)	567	341 814	11.9	24.7	15.5	40.4	63 467	3.3	3.3	129 377	76.9
Philadelphia County (part)	93	306 162	17.1	21.8	19.2	15.6	37 196	11.5	6.2	121 667	67.4
Congressional District 14, Pennsylvania	419	645 809	27.0	20.9	18.0	21.4	30 139	17.1	8.4	280 228	57.9
Allegheny County (part)	419	645 809	27.0	20.9	18.0	21.4	30 139	17.1	8.4	280 228	57.9

[1]Dry land or land partially or temporarily covered by water.
[2]Persons who do not identify themselves White, not of Hispanic origin.
[3]Persons 25 years old and over.
X = Not applicable.

Table B. 109th Congressional Districts by Counties, 2000—*Continued*

(Number, percent.)

STATE Congressional district County	Land area,[1] (sq km)	Population				Percent with bachelor's degree or more[3]	Median income, 1999 (dollars)	Percent living in poverty	Percent unem- ployed	Households	
		Total	Percent minority[2]	Percent under 18 years old	Percent 65 years old and over					Total	Percent owner occupied
	1	2	3	4	5	6	7	8	9	10	11
Congressional District 15, Pennsylvania	2 189	646 544	13.6	24.0	15.5	22.2	45 330	8.2	4.4	248 049	71.6
Berks County (part)	126	3 595	1.3	25.9	11.9	20.1	46 650	6.3	2.4	1 353	85.1
Lehigh County (part)	879	309 903	16.8	23.8	15.9	23.2	43 312	9.3	4.4	121 087	68.7
Montgomery County (part)	215	65 980	6.4	27.0	13.1	21.9	54 796	4.6	3.5	24 068	77.9
Northampton County	968	267 066	11.9	23.3	15.7	21.2	45 234	7.9	4.6	101 541	73.3
Congressional District 16, Pennsylvania	3 341	646 602	15.4	26.9	13.2	22.8	45 934	9.4	3.7	233 454	69.9
Berks County (part)	92	60 556	49.0	30.5	12.3	12.6	28 918	24.9	8.6	22 114	56.5
Chester County (part)	791	115 388	17.7	26.1	10.5	37.7	61 123	7.5	4.6	38 780	73.3
Lancaster County	2 458	470 658	10.6	26.6	14.0	20.5	45 507	7.8	3.0	172 560	70.9
Congressional District 17, Pennsylvania	6 048	646 550	12.5	23.3	16.0	17.4	40 473	8.4	4.6	255 934	72.7
Berks County (part)	1 202	102 311	4.2	23.9	15.0	16.2	49 989	5.0	4.0	37 873	83.0
Dauphin County	1 360	251 798	24.3	24.3	14.2	23.5	41 507	9.7	4.5	102 670	65.4
Lebanon County	937	120 327	7.6	23.7	16.4	15.4	40 838	7.5	4.0	46 551	72.7
Perry County (part)	532	21 778	1.8	25.4	12.1	11.3	41 945	7.5	4.2	8 310	77.9
Schuylkill County	2 016	150 336	3.9	20.8	19.9	10.7	32 699	9.5	5.9	60 530	77.9
Congressional District 18, Pennsylvania	3 708	646 325	4.6	22.3	17.6	29.3	44 938	6.3	4.3	260 857	77.3
Allegheny County (part)	711	354 811	5.9	22.0	18.3	34.7	48 174	5.3	4.2	146 123	74.9
Beaver County (part)	60	2 215	3.3	24.9	9.5	14.0	47 500	3.4	5.2	793	92.3
Washington County (part)	1 576	99 783	3.2	24.0	16.0	23.3	45 604	6.9	3.8	38 206	83.9
Westmoreland County (part)	1 362	189 516	2.9	21.8	17.3	22.3	38 934	7.7	4.9	75 735	78.5
Congressional District 19, Pennsylvania	4 294	646 143	7.8	23.7	14.1	21.3	45 345	6.8	3.6	249 982	74.8
Adams County	1 347	91 292	6.3	24.8	13.9	16.7	42 704	7.1	4.2	33 652	76.8
Cumberland County (part)	605	173 100	7.2	20.9	15.7	30.0	46 754	6.8	3.4	68 111	71.0
Franklin County (part)	0	0	X	X	X	X	X	X	X	0	X
York County	2 343	381 751	8.4	24.6	13.5	18.4	45 268	6.7	3.6	148 219	76.1
RHODE ISLAND	2 706	1 048 319	18.1	23.6	14.6	25.6	42 090	11.9	5.6	408 424	60.0
Congressional District 1, Rhode Island	841	524 189	17.4	22.7	15.4	26.0	40 616	11.9	5.5	208 498	55.7
Bristol County	64	50 648	3.9	22.9	16.8	34.3	50 737	6.3	4.8	19 033	71.2
Newport County	269	85 433	9.8	22.5	14.4	38.3	50 448	7.1	5.3	35 228	61.6
Providence County (part)	508	388 108	20.8	22.7	15.5	22.1	37 605	13.8	5.7	154 237	52.4
Congressional District 2, Rhode Island	1 865	524 130	18.8	24.5	13.7	25.2	44 129	11.9	5.7	199 926	64.6
Kent County	441	167 090	5.3	23.1	15.2	24.8	47 617	6.6	4.3	67 320	71.6
Providence County (part)	563	233 494	35.1	26.3	13.3	19.8	35 761	18.3	7.2	85 699	54.5
Washington County	862	123 546	6.1	23.2	12.7	35.5	53 103	7.3	5.1	46 907	72.9
SOUTH CAROLINA	77 983	4 012 012	33.8	25.2	12.1	20.4	37 082	14.1	5.9	1 533 854	72.2
Congressional District 1, South Carolina	6 849	668 462	26.2	24.0	11.8	25.4	40 713	11.5	4.6	263 896	69.4
Berkeley County (part)	809	111 447	27.5	28.0	7.0	15.7	41 826	9.7	4.3	38 978	70.3
Charleston County (part)	1 719	246 044	30.1	22.8	11.7	35.3	42 057	12.5	4.8	100 123	63.8
Dorchester County (part)	309	76 935	24.2	29.7	8.1	24.6	46 901	8.0	4.4	27 849	72.4
Georgetown County (part)	1 076	37 407	32.8	22.6	17.6	25.3	40 056	13.9	5.5	15 146	79.5
Horry County	2 936	196 629	20.1	21.3	15.0	18.7	36 470	12.0	4.6	81 800	73.0
Congressional District 2, South Carolina	12 347	668 374	31.8	25.2	11.2	28.5	42 915	11.0	4.3	254 578	73.4
Aiken County (part)	1 238	26 928	27.7	27.5	10.9	15.7	36 023	13.7	5.7	10 272	81.7
Allendale County	1 057	11 211	73.1	26.4	12.8	9.3	20 898	34.5	10.2	3 915	72.5
Barnwell County	1 420	23 478	45.1	28.2	12.6	11.6	28 591	20.9	7.7	9 021	75.5
Beaufort County	1 520	120 937	32.4	23.1	15.6	33.2	46 992	10.7	4.3	45 532	73.3
Calhoun County (part)	419	6 827	42.0	26.0	9.6	11.1	35 013	13.6	5.6	2 657	88.4
Hampton County	1 450	21 386	58.8	27.7	12.0	10.1	28 771	21.8	6.1	7 444	78.1
Jasper County	1 699	20 678	59.0	26.8	10.9	8.7	30 727	20.7	3.9	7 042	77.8
Lexington County	1 811	216 014	16.9	26.0	10.2	24.6	44 659	9.0	3.7	83 240	77.2
Orangeburg County (part)	766	22 370	44.2	27.1	12.0	20.9	36 616	13.4	5.6	8 520	85.4
Richland County (part)	967	198 545	36.9	24.3	9.4	40.2	46 780	8.2	3.8	76 935	65.4
Congressional District 3, South Carolina	13 966	668 657	24.0	24.3	13.4	17.1	36 092	13.3	5.4	258 800	75.5
Abbeville County	1 316	26 167	31.8	25.2	14.9	12.8	32 635	13.7	5.1	10 131	80.4
Aiken County (part)	1 541	115 624	30.0	25.8	13.3	20.9	38 396	13.9	5.9	45 315	74.3
Anderson County	1 860	165 740	19.1	24.6	13.7	15.9	36 807	12.0	4.3	65 649	76.3
Edgefield County	1 300	24 595	44.4	24.0	10.8	12.5	35 146	15.5	6.4	8 270	80.4
Greenwood County	1 180	66 271	35.9	25.4	13.8	18.9	34 702	14.2	6.3	25 729	69.3
Laurens County (part)	1 760	64 149	29.4	24.7	13.6	12.1	33 333	14.7	7.2	24 432	76.7
McCormick County	931	9 958	55.3	19.4	16.3	16.0	31 577	17.9	5.8	3 558	81.1
Oconee County	1 620	66 215	11.9	22.8	15.5	18.2	36 666	10.8	4.3	27 283	78.4
Pickens County	1 287	110 757	10.6	22.3	11.3	19.1	36 214	13.7	5.4	41 306	73.4
Saluda County	1 172	19 181	37.6	24.9	14.6	11.9	35 774	15.6	5.0	7 127	80.6
Congressional District 4, South Carolina	5 570	668 706	25.3	24.7	12.2	22.3	39 417	11.4	5.1	261 236	70.1
Greenville County	2 046	379 616	24.4	24.6	11.8	26.2	41 149	10.5	4.6	149 556	68.2
Laurens County (part)	92	5 418	24.4	33.0	6.8	6.1	39 245	10.3	6.0	1 858	86.8
Spartanburg County	2 100	253 791	26.0	24.8	12.5	18.2	37 579	12.3	5.5	97 735	72.0
Union County	1 332	29 881	32.5	23.8	15.6	9.8	31 441	14.3	7.3	12 087	76.7

[1]Dry land or land partially or temporarily covered by water.
[2]Persons who do not identify themselves White, not of Hispanic origin.
[3]Persons 25 years old and over.
X = Not applicable.

Table B. 109th Congressional Districts by Counties, 2000—*Continued*

(Number, percent.)

STATE Congressional district County	Land area,[1] (sq km)	Population Total	Population Percent minority[2]	Population Percent under 18 years old	Population Percent 65 years old and over	Percent with bachelor's degree or more[3]	Median income, 1999 (dollars)	Percent living in poverty	Percent unemployed	Households Total	Households Percent owner occupied
	1	2	3	4	5	6	7	8	9	10	11
Congressional District 5, South Carolina	18 221	668 451	35.9	26.3	11.9	14.8	35 416	15.2	6.9	251 219	74.7
Cherokee County	1 017	52 537	23.8	25.9	12.4	11.8	33 787	13.9	6.2	20 495	73.9
Chester County	1 504	34 068	40.4	26.9	12.7	9.6	32 425	15.3	6.8	12 880	78.3
Chesterfield County	2 068	42 768	36.4	26.7	12.2	9.7	29 483	20.3	8.9	16 557	76.2
Darlington County	1 453	67 394	43.4	26.2	12.1	13.5	31 087	20.3	8.0	25 793	77.0
Dillon County	1 049	30 722	50.2	29.1	11.7	9.2	26 630	24.2	8.7	11 199	72.0
Fairfield County	1 778	23 454	60.9	26.2	13.2	11.7	30 376	19.6	6.9	8 774	77.5
Florence County (part)	178	12 487	55.9	25.3	13.8	21.9	35 721	16.7	7.9	4 571	70.3
Kershaw County	1 881	52 647	29.2	26.1	12.8	16.3	38 804	12.8	5.3	20 188	82.0
Lancaster County	1 422	61 351	29.4	25.4	12.3	10.2	34 688	12.8	6.4	23 178	75.2
Lee County (part)	817	17 559	62.6	25.4	12.6	9.2	26 804	20.5	8.9	5 972	79.2
Marlboro County	1 242	28 818	55.6	26.2	12.3	8.3	26 598	21.7	8.2	10 478	70.8
Newberry County	1 634	36 108	38.2	24.1	14.9	14.8	32 867	17.0	7.8	14 026	76.7
Sumter County (part)	409	43 924	43.2	28.5	10.8	22.3	37 691	12.7	6.0	16 057	64.0
York County	1 768	164 614	23.6	26.3	10.3	20.9	44 539	10.0	6.1	61 051	73.1
Congressional District 6, South Carolina	21 030	669 362	59.8	26.3	12.1	14.1	28 967	22.4	9.3	244 125	70.2
Bamberg County	1 019	16 658	63.5	25.4	14.2	15.4	24 007	27.8	11.7	6 123	74.8
Berkeley County (part)	2 034	31 204	53.6	27.7	11.3	10.2	31 662	19.2	7.9	10 944	88.0
Calhoun County (part)	566	8 358	57.6	24.2	17.3	16.6	31 188	18.4	6.1	3 260	80.9
Charleston County (part)	660	63 925	73.3	27.2	12.6	11.6	22 281	32.3	11.9	23 203	49.1
Clarendon County	1 573	32 502	55.6	25.9	14.2	11.4	27 131	23.1	6.7	11 812	79.1
Colleton County	2 736	38 264	45.1	27.3	13.0	11.5	29 733	21.1	6.4	14 470	80.2
Dorchester County (part)	1 179	19 478	52.1	25.3	12.9	9.5	31 095	16.4	6.8	6 860	85.6
Florence County (part)	1 893	113 274	40.2	26.0	11.6	18.3	35 059	16.4	7.9	42 576	73.3
Georgetown County (part)	1 034	18 390	57.5	30.4	10.3	7.4	27 743	23.4	7.9	6 513	85.4
Lee County (part)	245	2 560	85.1	27.6	11.1	9.0	27 944	29.8	16.0	914	80.1
Marion County	1 267	35 466	58.8	27.6	12.4	10.2	26 526	23.2	9.8	13 301	73.4
Orangeburg County (part)	2 099	69 212	69.3	25.6	13.6	14.7	27 355	24.1	9.6	25 598	72.4
Richland County (part)	992	122 132	73.3	24.1	10.1	18.9	29 460	23.1	11.7	43 166	54.3
Sumter County (part)	1 314	60 722	55.8	27.8	11.7	11.3	30 817	18.8	8.7	21 671	73.5
Williamsburg County	2 419	37 217	67.5	28.7	13.1	11.5	24 214	27.9	9.1	13 714	80.7
SOUTH DAKOTA	196 540	754 844	11.9	26.9	14.3	21.5	35 282	13.2	4.4	290 245	68.2
Congressional District (At Large), South Dakota	196 540	754 844	11.9	26.9	14.3	21.5	35 282	13.2	4.4	290 245	68.2
Aurora County	1 834	3 058	5.5	27.5	21.8	12.7	29 783	11.4	1.8	1 165	76.1
Beadle County	3 260	17 023	3.5	24.8	19.4	18.3	30 510	11.9	3.2	7 210	67.7
Bennett County	3 070	3 574	59.1	36.3	11.0	12.7	25 313	39.2	10.5	1 123	59.5
Bon Homme County	1 459	7 260	5.0	23.2	20.8	15.3	30 644	12.9	2.1	2 635	76.1
Brookings County	2 058	28 220	3.9	20.8	11.0	32.2	35 438	14.0	4.9	10 665	58.2
Brown County	4 437	35 460	4.6	23.6	16.1	23.6	35 017	9.9	3.5	14 638	66.3
Brule County	2 121	5 364	10.8	30.6	16.9	20.6	32 370	14.3	6.9	1 998	71.2
Buffalo County	1 219	2 032	83.3	41.7	6.3	5.4	12 692	56.9	21.7	526	43.2
Butte County	5 824	9 094	5.8	28.2	15.0	12.2	29 040	12.8	5.7	3 516	73.4
Campbell County	1 906	1 782	0.9	26.2	21.9	14.8	28 793	14.1	1.5	725	82.1
Charles Mix County	2 843	9 350	31.3	32.2	17.3	14.1	26 060	26.9	8.5	3 343	68.3
Clark County	2 481	4 143	1.4	26.9	22.2	11.4	30 208	14.8	3.0	1 598	80.7
Clay County	1 066	13 537	7.4	18.9	10.2	38.7	27 535	21.2	8.0	4 878	54.4
Codington County	1 781	25 897	3.4	26.8	14.1	18.8	36 257	9.0	3.9	10 357	70.1
Corson County	6 405	4 181	62.6	36.7	10.7	11.3	20 654	41.0	13.2	1 271	59.2
Custer County	4 034	7 275	7.1	24.1	16.4	24.4	36 303	9.4	3.3	2 970	77.0
Davison County	1 128	18 741	3.4	25.4	16.3	20.2	33 476	11.5	2.9	7 585	61.8
Day County	2 664	6 267	9.6	25.3	23.4	15.4	30 227	14.3	4.6	2 586	76.1
Deuel County	1 615	4 498	2.6	25.4	20.6	13.3	31 788	10.3	1.3	1 843	80.0
Dewey County	5 964	5 972	75.8	39.0	8.6	12.2	23 272	33.6	14.3	1 863	55.3
Douglas County	1 123	3 458	1.8	27.6	22.8	14.5	28 478	14.6	1.4	1 321	81.0
Edmunds County	2 967	4 367	0.8	26.7	22.2	15.5	32 205	13.8	2.4	1 681	82.0
Fall River County	4 506	7 453	10.8	22.8	22.3	19.2	29 631	13.6	6.9	3 127	69.5
Faulk County	2 590	2 640	1.4	26.6	22.8	13.1	30 237	18.1	1.8	1 014	81.5
Grant County	1 768	7 847	1.7	26.9	19.1	14.8	33 088	9.9	3.3	3 116	77.4
Gregory County	2 631	4 792	7.4	24.4	24.8	12.0	22 732	20.1	3.8	2 022	74.7
Haakon County	4 696	2 196	3.7	25.3	17.9	15.4	29 894	13.9	3.5	870	76.9
Hamlin County	1 313	5 540	2.3	29.7	19.2	12.8	33 851	12.1	2.6	2 048	81.8
Hand County	3 721	3 741	1.0	24.8	24.4	15.6	32 377	9.2	1.2	1 543	74.1
Hanson County	1 126	3 139	0.7	29.7	15.0	14.0	33 049	16.6	2.1	1 115	79.2
Harding County	6 917	1 353	2.5	32.7	13.5	17.8	25 000	21.1	1.6	525	73.7
Hughes County	1 919	16 481	11.1	27.7	13.6	32.0	42 970	8.0	2.7	6 512	66.2
Hutchinson County	2 105	8 075	1.5	24.8	26.2	14.1	30 026	13.0	1.9	3 190	78.8
Hyde County	2 230	1 671	6.2	25.8	22.3	16.0	31 103	12.3	1.5	679	71.6
Jackson County	4 841	2 930	50.5	36.2	12.0	16.2	23 945	36.5	15.7	945	63.6

[1]Dry land or land partially or temporarily covered by water.
[2]Persons who do not identify themselves White, not of Hispanic origin.
[3]Persons 25 years old and over.

Table B. 109th Congressional Districts by Counties, 2000—*Continued*

(Number, percent.)

STATE Congressional district County	Land area,[1] (sq km)	Population				Percent with bachelor's degree or more[3]	Median income, 1999 (dollars)	Percent living in poverty	Percent unem-ployed	Households	
		Total	Percent minority[2]	Percent under 18 years old	Percent 65 years old and over					Total	Percent owner occupied
	1	2	3	4	5	6	7	8	9	10	11
Congressional District (At Large), South Dakota—*Continued*											
Jerauld County	1 372	2 295	0.5	21.4	25.5	12.3	30 690	20.6	2.5	987	72.1
Jones County	2 514	1 193	4.4	25.7	17.6	17.8	30 288	15.8	3.0	509	72.5
Kingsbury County	2 171	5 815	1.9	24.7	24.3	16.2	31 262	10.0	3.0	2 406	76.1
Lake County	1 459	11 276	3.3	23.7	16.3	21.1	34 087	9.7	3.4	4 372	70.5
Lawrence County	2 072	21 802	5.6	23.2	14.5	24.0	31 755	14.8	9.1	8 881	64.8
Lincoln County	1 497	24 131	2.6	29.7	10.3	25.5	48 338	4.4	1.8	8 782	79.7
Lyman County	4 247	3 895	34.5	32.3	13.6	15.9	28 509	24.3	9.5	1 400	68.8
McCook County	1 488	5 832	1.8	28.4	19.5	16.3	35 396	8.1	1.8	2 204	78.9
McPherson County	2 945	2 904	0.6	22.1	29.3	10.7	22 380	22.6	2.2	1 227	83.2
Marshall County	2 170	4 576	8.1	27.2	21.1	16.2	30 567	13.9	4.4	1 844	77.9
Meade County	8 989	24 253	8.2	28.3	10.5	16.8	36 992	9.4	3.9	8 805	68.2
Mellette County	3 384	2 083	55.4	35.3	12.9	16.6	23 219	35.8	11.5	694	65.0
Miner County	1 477	2 884	1.4	25.6	23.8	13.5	29 519	11.8	1.3	1 212	76.4
Minnehaha County	2 097	148 281	8.0	26.2	11.0	26.0	42 566	7.5	3.0	57 996	64.7
Moody County	1 346	6 595	15.6	29.1	15.2	17.4	35 467	9.6	3.0	2 526	72.5
Pennington County	7 190	88 565	14.5	26.6	11.7	25.0	37 485	11.5	4.5	34 641	66.2
Perkins County	7 437	3 363	3.8	23.9	23.8	14.6	27 750	16.9	3.9	1 429	76.6
Potter County	2 244	2 693	1.2	23.3	25.3	16.2	30 086	12.6	1.4	1 145	79.1
Roberts County	2 852	10 016	31.6	30.0	16.9	13.4	28 322	22.1	7.2	3 683	68.9
Sanborn County	1 474	2 675	3.4	25.6	19.2	14.8	33 375	14.9	2.3	1 043	77.7
Shannon County	5 423	12 466	95.1	45.0	4.7	12.1	20 916	52.3	33.0	2 785	49.6
Spink County	3 895	7 454	2.9	25.9	19.0	14.4	31 717	12.8	3.3	2 847	73.8
Stanley County	3 738	2 772	7.2	27.1	11.0	22.1	41 170	8.7	1.4	1 111	76.6
Sully County	2 608	1 556	2.3	25.4	17.5	16.4	32 500	12.1	2.0	630	75.9
Todd County	3 595	9 050	86.3	43.9	6.2	12.1	20 035	48.3	18.4	2 462	45.0
Tripp County	4 179	6 430	12.3	27.9	19.6	13.5	28 333	19.9	4.2	2 550	75.0
Turner County	1 598	8 849	1.1	25.7	20.6	17.0	36 059	7.2	1.7	3 510	77.4
Union County	1 192	12 584	4.6	27.0	13.5	26.3	44 790	5.5	1.9	4 927	74.5
Walworth County	1 833	5 974	13.6	24.4	21.9	15.8	27 834	18.2	6.1	2 506	71.2
Yankton County	1 351	21 652	6.0	25.7	14.6	23.0	35 374	9.6	2.4	8 187	69.1
Ziebach County	5 082	2 519	73.5	40.5	7.6	12.0	18 063	49.9	17.4	741	59.6
TENNESSEE	106 752	5 689 283	20.8	24.6	12.4	19.6	36 360	13.5	5.5	2 232 905	69.9
Congressional District 1, Tennessee	10 601	632 216	5.0	22.0	14.5	15.0	31 228	14.8	5.5	259 389	74.2
Carter County	883	56 742	2.9	21.3	15.0	12.8	27 371	16.9	5.9	23 486	74.9
Cocke County	1 125	33 565	4.7	22.9	13.6	6.2	25 553	22.5	8.8	13 762	75.5
Greene County	1 610	62 909	4.5	22.3	14.8	12.8	30 382	14.5	5.6	25 756	76.7
Hamblen County	417	58 128	11.2	23.1	13.3	13.3	32 350	14.4	4.2	23 211	72.5
Hancock County	576	6 786	3.1	23.2	15.7	10.2	19 760	29.4	5.7	2 769	78.7
Hawkins County	1 260	53 563	3.1	23.2	13.2	10.0	31 300	15.8	5.1	21 936	78.7
Jefferson County (part)	196	11 136	2.8	23.4	12.7	9.2	32 093	13.1	4.2	4 424	81.5
Johnson County	773	17 499	3.7	19.7	15.0	6.9	23 067	22.6	7.0	6 827	79.7
Sevier County (part)	1 364	53 975	3.9	22.3	13.1	13.4	33 564	11.4	6.6	21 951	70.2
Sullivan County	1 070	153 048	3.9	21.8	15.9	18.1	33 529	12.9	4.6	63 556	75.8
Unicoi County	482	17 667	3.2	20.5	18.1	10.6	29 863	13.1	6.8	7 516	76.6
Washington County	845	107 198	7.1	21.2	13.9	22.9	33 116	13.9	5.4	44 195	68.2
Congressional District 2, Tennessee	6 285	632 112	10.0	22.7	13.2	23.3	36 796	12.2	4.9	258 049	70.9
Blount County	1 447	105 823	5.8	22.8	14.1	17.9	37 862	9.7	4.5	42 667	75.9
Knox County	1 317	382 032	12.6	22.3	12.6	29.0	37 454	12.6	4.8	157 872	66.9
Loudon County	593	39 086	4.8	21.8	16.0	17.0	40 401	10.0	3.6	15 944	79.1
McMinn County	1 114	49 015	7.9	24.0	14.4	10.8	31 919	14.5	5.3	19 721	75.7
Monroe County	1 644	38 961	5.8	24.7	13.2	10.1	30 337	15.5	7.5	15 329	78.3
Sevier County (part)	170	17 195	3.3	25.1	11.0	13.9	38 924	8.4	6.2	6 516	83.9
Congressional District 3, Tennessee	8 834	632 100	14.7	23.4	13.6	18.9	35 434	13.4	5.4	253 042	70.5
Anderson County	874	71 330	7.2	23.1	16.6	20.8	35 483	13.1	5.3	29 780	72.5
Bradley County	851	87 965	7.9	23.7	11.6	15.9	35 034	12.2	5.0	34 281	68.6
Claiborne County	1 125	29 862	2.7	23.6	13.5	8.9	25 782	22.6	7.3	11 799	78.5
Grainger County	726	20 659	2.0	22.9	12.6	7.8	27 997	18.7	4.9	8 270	83.6
Hamilton County	1 405	307 896	24.4	23.2	13.8	23.9	38 930	12.1	5.5	124 444	65.9
Jefferson County (part)	513	33 158	5.7	22.7	12.9	14.1	33 140	13.5	5.8	12 731	76.7
Meigs County	505	11 086	2.3	25.0	11.7	7.0	29 354	18.3	6.3	4 304	81.9
Polk County	1 127	16 050	2.1	22.5	14.4	7.5	29 643	13.0	4.9	6 448	80.8
Rhea County	818	28 400	5.1	23.7	13.7	9.1	30 418	14.7	6.4	11 184	75.4
Roane County (part)	311	7 886	5.9	24.8	12.7	30.2	49 719	6.6	2.8	3 059	85.0
Union County	579	17 808	1.6	25.9	10.9	5.8	27 335	19.6	5.2	6 742	80.9

[1]Dry land or land partially or temporarily covered by water.
[2]Persons who do not identify themselves White, not of Hispanic origin.
[3]Persons 25 years old and over.

Table B. 109th Congressional Districts by Counties, 2000—*Continued*

(Number, percent.)

STATE Congressional district County	Land area,[1] (sq km)	Population Total	Population Percent minority[2]	Population Percent under 18 years old	Population Percent 65 years old and over	Percent with bachelor's degree or more[3]	Median income, 1999 (dollars)	Percent living in poverty	Percent unemployed	Households Total	Households Percent owner occupied
	1	2	3	4	5	6	7	8	9	10	11
Congressional District 4, Tennessee	25 999	631 842	7.3	24.1	14.5	11.3	31 645	15.2	5.6	248 234	76.7
Bledsoe County	1 052	12 367	5.5	23.1	11.6	7.1	28 982	18.1	6.6	4 430	81.7
Campbell County	1 243	39 854	2.8	22.8	15.2	7.0	25 285	22.8	6.7	16 125	73.4
Coffee County	1 111	48 014	7.5	24.8	14.7	17.5	34 898	14.3	6.0	18 885	71.5
Cumberland County	1 765	46 802	2.6	21.3	20.6	13.7	30 901	14.7	5.2	19 508	80.6
Fentress County	1 291	16 625	1.1	24.2	13.6	8.3	23 238	23.1	7.3	6 693	79.1
Franklin County	1 436	39 270	8.5	23.0	15.3	15.3	36 044	13.2	5.0	15 003	78.5
Giles County	1 582	29 447	13.7	24.5	14.5	10.6	34 824	11.7	4.3	11 713	75.4
Grundy County	934	14 332	1.8	25.1	13.9	7.1	22 959	25.8	6.4	5 562	82.1
Hickman County (part)	903	12 938	4.6	25.6	14.1	6.7	29 182	15.2	5.1	5 012	77.4
Lawrence County	1 598	39 926	3.7	26.1	14.7	8.7	30 498	14.6	7.6	15 480	77.1
Lewis County	731	11 367	4.4	25.9	13.6	8.5	30 444	13.4	7.9	4 381	79.5
Lincoln County	1 477	31 340	10.1	23.8	15.5	11.9	33 434	13.6	5.6	12 503	76.2
Marion County	1 291	27 776	5.7	23.7	12.8	9.5	31 419	14.1	5.4	11 037	80.5
Maury County	1 587	69 498	18.8	26.3	12.0	13.6	41 591	10.9	4.2	26 444	72.8
Moore County	335	5 740	5.0	23.3	15.1	11.8	36 591	9.6	4.9	2 211	83.7
Morgan County	1 352	19 757	4.0	23.2	11.6	6.0	27 712	16.0	7.0	6 990	82.8
Pickett County	422	4 945	1.4	21.5	17.8	9.1	24 673	15.6	4.0	2 091	84.3
Roane County (part)	624	44 024	4.9	21.9	16.7	12.0	31 457	15.2	6.2	18 141	76.3
Scott County	1 378	21 127	1.9	26.0	11.4	7.5	24 093	20.2	7.3	8 203	76.5
Sequatchie County	689	11 370	2.2	24.5	12.2	10.2	30 959	16.5	5.1	4 463	76.2
Van Buren County	708	5 508	1.4	23.0	14.0	7.8	28 165	15.2	6.7	2 180	85.6
Warren County	1 121	38 276	9.4	24.0	14.0	9.1	30 920	16.6	4.7	15 181	72.9
White County	975	23 102	4.2	23.6	15.3	7.9	29 383	14.3	6.2	9 229	79.7
Williamson County (part)	392	18 437	15.4	25.8	12.0	22.4	44 787	10.3	3.7	6 769	75.3
Congressional District 5, Tennessee	2 315	632 173	31.7	22.9	10.8	27.9	40 419	12.2	5.0	258 235	58.1
Cheatham County (part)	430	24 333	3.9	27.9	8.2	13.5	45 281	6.9	2.8	8 695	82.2
Davidson County (part)	1 239	542 892	35.8	22.2	11.1	29.1	38 706	13.4	5.4	225 839	54.4
Wilson County (part)	646	64 948	7.9	26.8	8.5	23.1	55 135	4.7	3.0	23 701	84.8
Congressional District 6, Tennessee	14 194	632 118	10.9	25.4	10.9	16.3	39 721	11.1	4.6	238 975	73.3
Bedford County	1 227	37 586	17.2	25.7	12.7	11.1	36 729	13.1	4.4	13 905	73.5
Cannon County	688	12 826	3.5	25.5	13.6	8.4	32 809	12.8	4.6	4 998	78.5
Clay County	612	7 976	3.6	21.3	15.8	6.8	23 958	19.1	7.6	3 379	80.0
DeKalb County	789	17 423	6.3	23.3	14.1	11.3	30 359	17.0	5.2	6 984	75.0
Jackson County	800	10 984	3.2	22.2	15.0	8.4	26 502	18.1	6.3	4 466	80.8
Macon County	795	20 386	3.2	26.1	12.7	5.6	29 867	15.1	5.0	7 916	78.6
Marshall County	972	26 767	11.3	25.6	12.5	10.6	38 457	10.0	4.3	10 307	73.0
Overton County	1 122	20 118	1.9	23.1	15.0	8.3	26 915	16.0	5.5	8 110	80.8
Putnam County	1 039	62 315	6.8	22.2	13.2	20.2	30 914	16.4	5.0	24 865	65.6
Robertson County	1 234	54 433	12.6	26.8	10.8	11.9	43 174	9.0	3.4	19 906	76.5
Rutherford County	1 603	182 023	15.4	26.4	7.5	22.9	46 312	9.0	5.0	66 443	69.8
Smith County	814	17 712	5.0	25.5	13.4	9.3	35 625	12.2	4.4	6 878	78.8
Sumner County	1 371	130 449	9.4	26.2	10.6	18.6	46 030	8.1	3.7	48 941	75.5
Trousdale County	296	7 259	14.0	24.0	14.4	8.9	32 212	13.4	3.4	2 780	76.3
Wilson County (part)	832	23 861	12.8	24.8	12.8	10.1	39 461	12.0	6.5	9 097	72.7
Congressional District 7, Tennessee	16 296	632 793	16.6	27.2	9.7	29.2	50 090	8.0	3.8	229 831	79.3
Cheatham County (part)	354	11 579	4.4	27.2	9.3	18.4	47 273	8.6	2.7	4 183	86.5
Chester County	747	15 540	12.5	24.4	13.8	11.2	34 349	14.4	6.8	5 660	77.3
Davidson County (part)	62	26 999	13.4	22.3	11.2	56.1	64 508	4.7	2.1	11 566	73.4
Decatur County	865	11 731	7.0	21.6	18.1	7.3	28 741	16.0	5.2	4 908	80.1
Dickson County (part)	0	0	X	X	X	X	X	X	X	0	X
Fayette County	1 825	28 806	38.2	25.7	13.1	12.8	40 279	14.3	5.4	10 467	80.3
Hardeman County	1 729	28 105	43.3	24.0	12.7	7.8	29 111	19.7	6.6	9 412	74.1
Hardin County	1 497	25 578	5.5	23.2	16.1	9.8	27 819	18.8	5.3	10 426	77.3
Henderson County	1 347	25 522	10.0	24.3	14.2	9.3	32 057	12.4	4.5	10 306	79.2
Hickman County (part)	683	9 357	9.2	23.2	9.4	6.6	33 548	12.9	3.8	3 069	84.8
McNairy County	1 451	24 653	8.8	23.7	15.8	8.8	30 154	15.9	5.2	9 980	80.0
Montgomery County (part)	885	102 704	30.4	29.4	6.4	20.3	41 022	8.3	5.9	35 762	64.5
Perry County	1 075	7 631	3.7	24.4	16.3	7.1	28 061	15.4	5.4	3 023	85.8
Shelby County (part)	759	189 545	13.1	28.6	8.3	40.2	70 653	3.2	2.4	67 177	86.0
Wayne County	1 901	16 842	8.6	21.4	13.8	8.0	26 576	16.3	7.4	5 936	82.9
Williamson County (part)	1 117	108 201	9.2	30.1	7.0	48.2	74 256	3.8	2.4	37 956	82.6
Congressional District 8, Tennessee	21 398	632 189	25.5	25.9	13.2	12.5	33 001	15.0	6.5	242 466	70.3
Benton County	1 023	16 537	4.4	21.9	17.8	6.3	28 679	15.6	7.3	6 863	80.6
Carroll County	1 551	29 475	12.5	23.2	17.2	11.1	30 463	13.9	8.3	11 779	79.0
Crockett County	687	14 532	20.6	25.2	16.0	9.1	30 015	16.9	5.1	5 632	74.9
Dickson County (part)	1 268	43 156	6.8	26.7	11.6	11.3	39 056	10.2	4.4	16 473	76.1
Dyer County	1 322	37 279	14.9	25.7	13.4	12.0	32 788	15.9	7.6	14 751	65.6

[1]Dry land or land partially or temporarily covered by water.
[2]Persons who do not identify themselves White, not of Hispanic origin.
[3]Persons 25 years old and over.
X = Not applicable.

Table B. 109th Congressional Districts by Counties, 2000—*Continued*

(Number, percent.)

STATE Congressional district County	Land area,[1] (sq km)	Population Total	Percent minority[2]	Percent under 18 years old	Percent 65 years old and over	Percent with bachelor's degree or more[3]	Median income, 1999 (dollars)	Percent living in poverty	Percent unem- ployed	Households Total	Percent owner occupied
	1	2	3	4	5	6	7	8	9	10	11
Congressional District 8, Tennessee—*Continued*											
Gibson County	1 561	48 152	21.6	24.0	17.6	10.1	31 105	12.8	5.8	19 518	72.1
Haywood County	1 381	19 797	54.1	27.0	13.8	11.1	27 671	19.5	6.8	7 558	65.9
Henry County	1 455	31 115	11.4	22.2	18.1	12.1	30 169	14.3	6.1	13 019	77.4
Houston County	519	8 088	5.3	24.3	16.7	10.3	29 968	18.1	3.7	3 216	77.0
Humphreys County	1 378	17 929	5.5	23.8	14.8	9.3	35 786	10.8	4.6	7 238	77.9
Lake County	423	7 954	33.9	18.1	13.3	5.4	21 995	23.6	8.6	2 410	60.0
Lauderdale County	1 218	27 101	36.6	24.9	11.9	7.7	29 751	19.2	6.9	9 567	65.0
Madison County	1 443	91 837	35.6	25.8	12.3	21.5	36 982	14.0	6.9	35 552	67.0
Montgomery County (part)	512	32 064	24.3	25.0	11.9	16.2	31 276	15.4	7.4	12 568	60.7
Obion County	1 411	32 450	12.7	23.4	15.2	10.3	32 764	13.3	5.3	13 182	71.5
Shelby County (part)	365	76 187	60.6	33.7	8.1	10.8	32 555	20.3	8.5	26 505	62.0
Stewart County	1 187	12 370	4.7	23.8	14.9	10.2	32 316	12.4	7.6	4 930	79.3
Tipton County	1 190	51 271	22.7	29.2	9.9	10.8	41 856	12.1	4.9	18 106	76.2
Weakley County	1 503	34 895	10.4	21.6	14.2	15.3	30 008	16.0	6.1	13 599	68.8
Congressional District 9, Tennessee	830	631 740	65.1	27.4	10.7	22.1	33 806	19.4	8.1	244 684	56.9
Shelby County (part)	830	631 740	65.1	27.4	10.7	22.1	33 806	19.4	8.1	244 684	56.9
TEXAS	678 051	20 851 820	47.6	28.2	9.9	23.2	39 927	15.4	6.1	7 393 354	63.8
Congressional District 1, Texas	22 036	651 562	29.4	26.2	14.1	17.6	33 461	16.0	6.9	245 088	71.9
Angelina County	2 076	80 130	30.6	27.5	12.5	14.7	33 806	15.8	6.0	28 685	72.4
Cass County (part)	397	3 035	14.0	27.9	16.8	11.0	31 146	14.8	4.7	1 191	88.3
Gregg County	710	111 379	31.0	26.8	13.5	19.5	35 006	15.1	6.9	42 687	64.1
Harrison County	2 328	62 110	30.8	26.9	13.1	15.4	33 520	16.7	7.4	23 087	77.2
Marion County	987	10 941	28.2	22.4	19.3	8.5	25 347	22.4	8.2	4 610	82.1
Nacogdoches County	2 452	59 203	29.8	23.9	12.0	22.8	28 301	23.3	10.7	22 006	61.5
Panola County	2 074	22 756	22.5	25.4	16.1	13.4	31 909	14.1	6.4	8 821	80.8
Rusk County	2 392	47 372	28.9	24.9	15.6	12.8	32 898	14.6	5.5	17 364	79.9
Sabine County	1 270	10 469	13.0	21.1	24.9	10.6	27 198	15.9	9.2	4 485	86.2
San Augustine County	1 367	8 946	32.4	23.7	21.3	11.8	27 025	21.2	7.0	3 575	81.6
Shelby County	2 057	25 224	30.4	26.5	16.5	12.2	29 112	19.4	5.2	9 595	78.2
Smith County	2 405	174 706	32.0	26.6	14.0	22.5	37 148	13.8	6.5	65 692	69.7
Upshur County	1 522	35 291	15.4	26.9	14.3	11.1	33 347	14.9	5.2	13 290	81.7
Congressional District 2, Texas	5 016	651 605	35.8	27.4	9.9	23.2	47 029	11.4	5.8	233 043	70.1
Harris County (part)	982	349 152	27.3	28.7	7.1	30.3	59 565	6.7	4.2	123 949	72.6
Jefferson County	2 340	252 051	48.2	25.9	13.6	16.3	34 706	17.4	8.1	92 880	65.9
Liberty County (part)	1 693	50 402	32.5	26.9	10.0	8.5	37 288	15.4	7.1	16 214	74.7
Congressional District 3, Texas	686	651 782	36.7	28.5	5.3	41.4	60 878	7.0	3.7	239 947	61.3
Collin County (part)	484	389 809	26.1	28.0	4.8	52.5	73 371	4.7	3.0	147 517	65.0
Dallas County (part)	201	261 973	52.5	29.3	6.1	23.8	45 155	10.5	4.9	92 430	55.5
Congressional District 4, Texas	24 694	651 500	20.7	26.7	13.2	18.0	38 276	12.8	4.9	241 494	74.5
Bowie County	2 300	89 306	29.7	24.9	14.0	16.1	33 001	17.7	6.9	33 058	70.9
Camp County	512	11 549	35.1	26.7	15.6	12.2	31 164	20.9	6.0	4 336	74.8
Cass County (part)	2 031	27 403	23.6	24.5	17.8	12.1	28 073	18.0	5.8	10 999	77.6
Collin County (part)	1 711	101 866	15.5	31.1	6.6	26.7	61 578	5.4	2.9	34 453	84.3
Delta County	718	5 327	13.5	25.5	17.9	13.9	29 094	17.6	5.6	2 094	77.1
Fannin County	2 309	31 242	15.6	23.3	16.0	12.6	34 501	13.9	5.2	11 105	74.7
Franklin County	740	9 458	14.0	24.5	18.3	16.2	31 955	15.6	4.5	3 754	79.0
Grayson County	2 418	110 595	15.7	25.2	15.1	17.2	37 178	11.3	4.7	42 849	70.5
Hopkins County	2 026	31 960	18.7	26.2	15.1	15.1	32 136	14.6	4.8	12 286	71.4
Hunt County	2 179	76 596	20.1	26.5	12.7	16.8	36 752	12.8	5.8	28 742	71.4
Lamar County	2 375	48 499	19.2	26.1	15.8	14.5	31 609	16.4	5.6	19 077	67.2
Morris County	659	13 048	29.6	25.0	18.6	11.2	29 011	18.3	6.5	5 215	77.8
Rains County	601	9 139	10.1	23.9	16.3	11.5	33 712	14.9	6.1	3 617	82.7
Red River County	2 720	14 314	24.2	23.9	19.5	9.0	27 558	17.3	5.9	5 827	75.0
Rockwall County	334	43 080	17.2	30.1	8.4	32.7	65 164	4.7	1.8	14 530	82.7
Titus County	1 063	28 118	40.0	30.4	12.5	13.2	32 452	18.5	5.9	9 552	72.4
Congressional District 5, Texas	14 061	651 919	28.5	26.5	12.0	18.6	41 007	11.0	5.1	237 891	70.4
Anderson County	2 773	55 109	36.8	20.6	11.5	11.1	31 957	16.5	7.5	15 678	73.9
Cherokee County	2 725	46 659	30.6	26.3	15.1	11.4	29 313	17.9	5.6	16 651	73.8
Dallas County (part)	381	320 669	35.1	28.2	8.7	25.7	48 493	7.8	4.2	119 613	63.0
Henderson County	2 264	73 277	15.2	24.4	18.2	12.1	32 533	15.1	6.5	28 804	80.0
Kaufman County	2 036	71 313	23.7	29.0	10.7	12.3	44 783	10.5	4.5	24 367	79.2
Van Zandt County	2 198	48 140	11.6	25.5	17.1	11.6	35 029	13.3	5.9	18 195	80.9
Wood County	1 684	36 752	13.3	21.9	20.9	14.5	32 885	14.3	8.4	14 583	81.4

[1]Dry land or land partially or temporarily covered by water.
[2]Persons who do not identify themselves White, not of Hispanic origin.
[3]Persons 25 years old and over.

Table B. 109th Congressional Districts by Counties, 2000—*Continued*

(Number, percent.)

STATE Congressional district County	Land area,[1] (sq km)	Total	Percent minority[2]	Percent under 18 years old	Percent 65 years old and over	Percent with bachelor's degree or more[3]	Median income, 1999 (dollars)	Percent living in poverty	Percent unemployed	Households Total	Percent owner occupied
	1	2	3	4	5	6	7	8	9	10	11
Congressional District 6, Texas	16 053	651 691	34.0	28.2	8.9	24.4	45 857	10.4	4.6	237 167	64.9
Ellis County	2 434	111 360	28.5	30.1	9.2	17.1	50 350	8.6	5.2	37 020	76.2
Freestone County	2 273	17 867	28.2	23.3	16.4	10.9	31 283	14.2	4.2	6 588	78.6
Houston County	3 188	23 185	36.3	23.2	17.7	12.2	28 119	21.0	6.1	8 259	76.1
Leon County	2 777	15 335	18.8	24.2	20.2	12.1	30 981	15.6	5.4	6 189	82.8
Limestone County (part)	735	11 879	36.3	25.9	16.4	12.4	29 288	18.1	6.6	4 364	73.9
Navarro County	2 610	45 124	34.2	27.6	14.5	12.2	31 268	18.2	7.8	16 491	70.7
Tarrant County (part)	608	421 674	36.2	28.4	6.7	30.1	49 346	8.9	4.1	156 085	59.1
Trinity County (part)	1 430	5 267	15.3	24.5	19.8	8.1	24 220	19.6	5.5	2 171	83.6
Congressional District 7, Texas	512	651 682	32.6	23.5	9.2	50.0	57 846	7.4	3.8	277 148	55.1
Harris County (part)	512	651 682	32.6	23.5	9.2	50.0	57 846	7.4	3.8	277 148	55.1
Congressional District 8, Texas	21 108	651 755	20.1	26.8	11.4	17.7	40 459	12.6	6.0	232 204	78.4
Hardin County	2 316	48 073	11.1	27.7	12.2	13.0	37 612	11.2	5.7	17 805	82.5
Jasper County	2 428	35 604	23.5	26.5	15.7	10.5	30 902	18.1	7.2	13 450	80.6
Liberty County (part)	1 310	19 752	7.0	29.2	11.0	7.0	40 712	11.8	6.4	7 028	89.0
Montgomery County	2 704	293 768	18.8	29.3	8.7	25.3	50 864	9.4	4.5	103 296	78.2
Newton County	2 416	15 072	25.8	26.2	14.1	5.5	28 500	19.1	10.5	5 583	84.5
Orange County	923	84 966	14.2	27.2	12.6	11.0	37 586	13.8	7.9	31 642	77.2
Polk County	2 738	41 133	25.4	22.7	18.0	10.4	30 495	17.4	6.7	15 119	81.6
San Jacinto County	1 478	22 246	19.1	25.4	16.0	9.6	32 220	18.8	7.5	8 651	87.9
Trinity County (part)	364	8 512	19.5	21.9	23.4	10.2	28 438	16.4	7.5	3 552	79.0
Tyler County	2 390	20 871	16.8	23.1	18.0	9.7	29 808	15.8	6.4	7 775	84.0
Walker County	2 039	61 758	39.9	17.7	9.0	18.3	31 468	18.4	8.8	18 303	59.9
Congressional District 9, Texas	399	651 086	82.6	29.5	5.7	24.2	34 870	18.4	7.5	229 350	42.0
Fort Bend County (part)	70	81 175	83.9	33.7	3.6	25.6	52 198	8.0	6.2	24 121	83.1
Harris County (part)	328	569 911	82.4	28.9	6.0	24.0	32 804	19.9	7.7	205 229	37.1
Congressional District 10, Texas	9 851	651 523	33.7	27.4	7.5	35.2	52 465	8.2	4.1	241 672	66.1
Austin County	1 690	23 590	28.2	27.0	14.8	17.3	38 615	12.1	4.4	8 747	77.2
Bastrop County (part)	671	20 605	38.5	27.4	9.4	15.9	43 093	12.5	4.2	6 675	81.1
Burleson County (part)	1 147	12 897	29.4	26.0	16.6	13.2	32 683	17.1	4.9	5 022	79.6
Harris County (part)	1 056	235 146	25.5	33.2	4.7	37.0	69 083	4.5	3.7	76 069	84.3
Lee County	1 628	15 657	31.5	28.8	14.3	13.1	36 280	11.9	2.6	5 663	79.4
Travis County (part)	750	280 592	39.6	23.1	7.1	42.5	50 495	8.7	3.5	117 617	50.2
Waller County	1 330	32 663	49.9	25.6	9.4	16.8	38 136	16.0	13.8	10 557	72.5
Washington County	1 578	30 373	29.3	24.7	16.7	19.0	36 760	12.9	4.3	11 322	73.5
Congressional District 11, Texas	90 636	651 590	35.5	27.3	14.8	17.0	32 711	15.8	6.1	243 501	71.6
Andrews County	3 887	13 004	43.7	31.4	12.1	12.4	34 036	16.4	8.1	4 601	79.7
Brown County	2 445	37 674	20.9	25.7	16.3	15.0	30 974	17.2	7.0	14 306	72.2
Burnet County	2 580	34 147	17.8	24.6	17.7	17.4	37 921	10.9	2.9	13 133	78.4
Coke County	2 328	3 864	19.5	24.2	23.9	14.7	29 085	13.0	4.4	1 544	78.8
Coleman County	3 264	9 235	17.5	23.5	23.0	11.7	25 658	19.9	6.4	3 889	74.6
Comanche County	2 429	14 026	23.1	25.3	20.1	13.0	28 422	17.3	4.4	5 522	76.2
Concho County	2 568	3 966	43.3	16.1	14.0	14.1	31 313	11.9	3.6	1 058	75.0
Crane County	2 035	3 996	47.8	31.6	10.8	12.8	32 194	13.4	8.3	1 360	85.3
Dawson County	2 336	14 985	57.5	25.5	14.4	10.5	28 211	19.7	8.2	4 726	73.4
Ector County	2 334	121 123	48.9	30.4	10.7	12.0	31 152	18.7	7.7	43 846	68.6
Gillespie County	2 748	20 814	17.4	21.4	25.3	22.9	38 109	10.2	3.7	8 521	77.5
Glasscock County	2 333	1 406	31.4	34.1	8.7	18.7	35 655	14.7	3.5	483	67.3
Irion County	2 723	1 771	26.0	26.7	15.8	21.5	37 500	8.4	2.6	694	77.7
Kimble County	3 239	4 468	22.5	23.9	21.2	17.3	29 396	18.8	3.0	1 866	73.6
Lampasas County	1 844	17 762	20.3	27.6	14.6	16.2	36 176	14.1	4.7	6 554	74.0
Llano County	2 421	17 044	6.3	15.9	30.6	21.0	34 830	10.3	2.9	7 879	80.9
Loving County	1 743	67	17.9	20.9	14.9	5.9	40 000	0.0	0.0	31	80.6
McCulloch County	2 769	8 205	28.9	26.5	20.0	14.0	25 705	22.5	6.9	3 277	72.7
Martin County	2 369	4 746	43.8	34.1	13.2	11.8	31 836	18.7	4.9	1 624	74.3
Mason County	2 414	3 738	22.6	22.4	23.5	18.7	30 921	13.2	1.6	1 607	80.5
Menard County	2 336	2 360	34.2	24.4	22.1	17.2	24 762	25.8	3.5	990	75.4
Midland County	2 332	116 009	38.1	30.2	11.7	24.8	39 082	12.9	5.4	42 745	69.5
Mills County	1 938	5 151	13.8	25.6	23.0	20.2	30 579	18.4	2.6	2 001	80.9
Mitchell County	2 357	9 698	45.0	20.1	14.4	10.4	25 399	17.7	3.8	2 837	76.0
Nolan County (part)	339	13 933	36.9	27.3	16.3	12.4	25 336	22.9	6.8	5 417	65.6
Reagan County	3 044	3 326	54.0	34.2	10.8	9.2	33 231	11.8	3.3	1 107	78.4
Runnels County	2 721	11 495	32.6	26.8	20.0	13.1	27 806	19.2	5.7	4 428	77.4
San Saba County	2 938	6 186	26.4	27.9	20.7	15.8	30 104	16.6	3.7	2 289	75.6
Schleicher County	3 394	2 935	46.0	27.7	16.2	17.6	29 746	21.5	1.8	1 115	75.7
Scurry County	2 337	16 361	34.6	25.1	15.3	11.8	31 646	16.0	6.0	5 756	73.9

[1]Dry land or land partially or temporarily covered by water.
[2]Persons who do not identify themselves White, not of Hispanic origin.
[3]Persons 25 years old and over.

Table B. 109th Congressional Districts by Counties, 2000—*Continued*

(Number, percent.)

STATE Congressional district County	Land area,[1] (sq km)	Population Total	Percent minority[2]	Percent under 18 years old	Percent 65 years old and over	Percent with bachelor's degree or more[3]	Median income, 1999 (dollars)	Percent living in poverty	Percent unemployed	Households Total	Percent owner occupied
	1	2	3	4	5	6	7	8	9	10	11
Congressional District 11, Texas—*Continued*											
Sterling County	2 391	1 393	31.6	28.4	14.4	17.1	35 129	16.8	2.0	513	76.2
Sutton County (part)	2 198	1 206	28.4	24.5	19.3	22.9	42 250	12.6	0.7	475	64.8
Tom Green County	3 942	104 010	37.0	26.1	13.5	19.5	33 148	15.2	7.4	39 503	64.1
Upton County	3 216	3 404	45.6	29.1	13.7	11.8	28 977	19.9	5.5	1 256	75.6
Ward County	2 164	10 909	48.2	30.5	14.0	12.4	29 386	17.9	8.4	3 964	78.2
Winkler County	2 178	7 173	46.8	29.9	14.4	10.5	30 591	18.7	8.2	2 584	83.2
Congressional District 12, Texas	5 615	651 770	33.5	27.5	10.0	21.1	41 735	11.3	4.7	236 645	65.1
Parker County	2 340	88 495	10.7	27.6	10.5	18.6	45 497	8.3	4.2	31 131	80.6
Tarrant County (part)	932	514 482	39.3	27.4	9.8	22.3	41 201	12.0	4.8	188 336	61.1
Wise County	2 343	48 793	13.7	28.2	10.6	13.0	41 933	9.9	4.2	17 178	81.3
Congressional District 13, Texas	104 110	651 665	26.3	26.3	14.1	17.2	33 501	14.0	5.3	243 086	69.4
Archer County (part)	461	4 932	5.7	29.4	11.1	18.2	44 145	6.7	3.0	1 790	85.3
Armstrong County	2 366	2 148	5.5	26.0	19.1	20.5	38 194	10.6	3.4	802	79.1
Baylor County	2 255	4 093	13.5	22.9	24.9	12.1	24 627	16.1	4.8	1 791	72.6
Briscoe County	2 332	1 790	26.5	27.3	18.8	17.5	29 917	16.0	3.4	724	77.1
Carson County	2 391	6 516	9.8	27.9	15.4	15.5	40 285	7.3	2.9	2 470	83.6
Childress County	1 840	7 688	36.3	22.2	15.0	8.6	27 457	17.6	5.7	2 474	70.7
Clay County	2 843	11 006	6.0	24.8	16.0	13.9	35 738	10.3	3.5	4 323	83.0
Collingsworth County	2 380	3 206	28.7	26.4	22.0	15.3	25 438	18.7	4.3	1 294	78.9
Cooke County (part)	1 509	9 848	6.7	29.0	12.7	16.9	44 761	8.7	2.3	3 573	79.3
Cottle County	2 334	1 904	28.6	24.2	25.6	15.3	25 446	18.4	5.8	820	71.6
Crosby County	2 330	7 072	53.2	30.7	15.4	10.5	25 769	28.1	8.2	2 512	69.3
Dallam County	3 897	6 222	31.8	32.0	10.4	9.6	27 946	14.1	4.7	2 317	63.0
Dickens County	2 342	2 762	32.2	18.4	18.8	8.4	25 898	17.4	5.1	980	77.7
Donley County	2 408	3 828	11.5	22.6	21.7	15.8	29 006	15.9	9.5	1 578	74.4
Foard County	1 830	1 622	20.2	26.0	23.2	10.5	25 813	14.3	2.2	664	75.0
Gray County	2 404	22 744	22.3	23.8	18.2	11.9	31 368	13.8	5.4	8 793	77.4
Hall County	2 339	3 782	36.4	27.2	21.0	10.3	23 016	26.3	9.0	1 548	74.3
Hansford County	2 382	5 369	33.5	29.1	15.3	18.6	35 438	16.4	4.0	2 005	74.4
Hardeman County	1 801	4 724	22.4	25.1	20.2	12.8	28 312	17.8	4.2	1 943	73.2
Hartley County	3 787	5 537	22.6	20.8	11.8	17.6	46 327	6.6	1.2	1 604	76.4
Haskell County	2 339	6 093	24.8	23.6	25.5	14.4	23 690	22.8	5.2	2 569	78.9
Hemphill County	2 356	3 351	17.9	27.6	14.9	17.9	35 456	12.6	3.1	1 280	77.3
Hutchinson County	2 298	23 857	19.9	27.4	15.4	14.3	36 588	11.1	5.6	9 283	78.9
Jack County	2 374	8 763	15.3	23.5	15.1	12.8	32 500	12.9	4.0	3 047	76.8
Jones County	2 411	20 785	33.8	22.4	13.9	8.2	29 572	16.8	6.1	6 140	79.2
King County	2 363	356	7.0	33.4	10.7	24.6	35 625	20.7	0.0	108	38.9
Knox County	2 199	4 253	34.0	27.9	22.5	11.8	25 453	22.9	6.4	1 690	75.4
Lipscomb County	2 414	3 057	22.0	27.4	18.6	18.9	31 964	16.7	4.2	1 205	77.9
Montague County	2 410	19 117	7.4	24.1	19.8	11.3	31 048	14.0	5.6	7 770	78.7
Moore County	2 330	20 121	50.1	33.6	10.5	11.0	34 852	13.5	4.3	6 774	70.5
Motley County	2 562	1 426	18.0	23.8	24.3	14.7	28 348	19.4	2.2	606	77.4
Ochiltree County	2 376	9 006	33.4	30.7	11.5	16.1	38 013	13.0	4.6	3 261	72.5
Oldham County	3 887	2 185	16.6	35.1	11.0	19.4	33 713	19.8	6.9	735	66.3
Palo Pinto County	2 468	27 026	17.6	25.7	16.4	12.1	31 203	15.9	5.1	10 594	71.9
Potter County	2 355	113 546	42.3	28.0	11.7	13.5	29 492	19.2	7.1	40 760	60.1
Randall County	2 368	104 312	14.3	25.9	11.9	28.9	42 712	8.1	4.2	41 240	70.3
Roberts County	2 393	887	2.6	24.9	14.4	25.4	44 792	7.2	1.3	362	79.6
Sherman County	2 391	3 186	29.2	31.0	13.6	20.4	33 739	16.1	4.5	1 124	74.2
Stonewall County	2 379	1 693	17.6	22.3	24.0	12.6	27 935	19.3	3.0	713	78.5
Swisher County	2 332	8 378	42.2	28.3	15.9	16.2	29 846	17.4	5.8	2 925	70.4
Throckmorton County	2 363	1 850	9.0	25.6	20.6	18.2	28 277	13.5	4.4	765	77.3
Wheeler County	2 368	5 284	16.6	24.9	20.9	13.0	31 029	13.0	1.8	2 152	78.0
Wichita County	1 626	131 664	26.8	25.0	12.7	20.0	33 780	13.2	5.9	48 441	62.3
Wilbarger County	2 515	14 676	31.3	28.0	16.8	17.1	29 500	13.1	3.8	5 537	66.3
Congressional District 14, Texas	18 376	651 837	37.8	28.1	10.9	19.3	41 335	13.3	6.1	234 340	69.3
Aransas County	652	22 497	26.7	23.8	19.9	16.7	30 702	19.9	7.4	9 132	75.1
Brazoria County (part)	3 417	181 250	35.3	28.4	9.0	15.1	43 993	11.8	6.2	60 765	71.1
Calhoun County	1 327	20 647	47.7	28.6	13.4	12.1	35 849	16.4	7.4	7 442	72.8
Chambers County	1 552	26 031	22.0	28.9	8.9	12.1	47 964	11.0	5.0	9 139	83.6
Fort Bend County (part)	627	26 776	25.8	33.6	6.1	47.9	85 820	5.1	3.1	8 760	90.0
Galveston County (part)	657	197 012	36.7	26.5	10.6	25.2	42 976	13.2	6.8	74 995	63.8
Jackson County	2 148	14 391	33.8	27.5	15.7	12.8	35 254	14.7	5.0	5 336	73.7
Matagorda County	2 886	37 957	47.5	29.8	12.9	12.5	32 174	18.5	8.4	13 901	66.8
Victoria County	2 286	84 088	47.1	29.2	11.8	16.2	38 732	12.9	4.7	30 071	67.4
Wharton County	2 823	41 188	46.8	28.7	13.8	14.3	32 208	16.5	6.0	14 799	68.8

[1] Dry land or land partially or temporarily covered by water.
[2] Persons who do not identify themselves White, not of Hispanic origin.
[3] Persons 25 years old and over.

Table B. 109th Congressional Districts by Counties, 2000—*Continued*

(Number, percent.)

STATE Congressional district County	Land area,[1] (sq km)	Population Total	Percent minority[2]	Percent under 18 years old	Percent 65 years old and over	Percent with bachelor's degree or more[3]	Median income, 1999 (dollars)	Percent living in poverty	Percent unemployed	Households Total	Percent owner occupied
	1	2	3	4	5	6	7	8	9	10	11
Congressional District 15, Texas	27 696	651 202	73.0	31.9	12.2	13.3	28 061	28.7	9.1	200 663	73.8
Bastrop County (part)	1 630	37 128	32.4	28.1	10.8	17.7	43 665	11.2	3.8	13 422	79.9
Bee County	2 280	32 359	65.1	23.3	10.4	12.2	28 392	24.0	8.0	9 061	65.5
Brooks County	2 443	7 976	92.2	31.5	15.2	6.8	18 622	40.2	8.5	2 711	73.1
Cameron County (part)	355	87 160	76.5	31.5	14.7	15.1	29 746	26.1	8.9	28 002	67.7
Colorado County	2 494	20 390	35.5	25.5	18.6	14.4	32 425	16.2	5.1	7 641	76.7
DeWitt County	2 355	20 013	39.3	23.7	19.3	11.8	28 714	19.6	5.8	7 207	76.6
Fayette County	2 461	21 804	20.2	23.1	22.1	14.6	34 526	11.4	3.4	8 722	78.2
Goliad County	2 211	6 928	40.6	26.0	17.6	12.3	34 201	16.4	3.2	2 644	80.3
Hidalgo County (part)	3 427	322 028	89.0	35.7	9.4	13.4	24 989	36.2	12.5	88 308	73.9
Jim Wells County	2 239	39 326	77.1	31.3	12.3	10.9	28 843	24.1	6.6	12 961	76.5
Lavaca County	2 512	19 210	19.3	24.1	21.6	11.4	29 132	13.2	2.5	7 669	78.4
Refugio County	1 995	7 828	52.9	26.1	16.9	11.6	29 986	17.8	4.9	2 985	74.7
San Patricio County (part)	1 296	29 052	72.7	31.1	12.5	8.3	27 712	26.3	8.6	9 330	72.9
Congressional District 16, Texas	1 504	652 363	82.7	31.6	10.0	17.0	31 245	23.6	9.4	203 161	62.8
El Paso County (part)	1 504	652 363	82.7	31.6	10.0	17.0	31 245	23.6	9.4	203 161	62.8
Congressional District 17, Texas	19 921	651 509	28.6	25.4	11.9	20.0	35 253	17.0	6.7	236 230	64.5
Bosque County	2 562	17 204	15.5	24.4	20.7	15.4	34 181	12.7	5.2	6 726	77.5
Brazos County	1 517	152 415	33.9	21.5	6.7	37.0	29 104	26.9	8.5	55 202	45.6
Burleson County (part)	576	3 573	37.0	29.8	13.6	13.2	34 390	17.6	3.3	1 341	79.3
Grimes County	2 055	23 552	37.3	24.7	13.8	10.3	32 280	16.6	6.2	7 753	77.8
Hill County	2 493	32 321	22.4	25.7	17.1	12.5	31 600	15.7	4.9	12 204	75.0
Hood County	1 092	41 100	9.5	23.8	17.8	20.5	43 668	8.5	4.8	16 176	81.2
Johnson County	1 889	126 811	16.7	28.7	10.1	13.8	44 621	8.8	4.6	43 636	78.9
Limestone County (part)	1 619	10 172	30.2	24.5	16.3	9.7	29 464	17.3	4.2	3 542	76.1
McLennan County	2 698	213 517	35.3	26.6	13.0	19.1	33 560	17.6	7.6	78 859	60.2
Madison County	1 216	12 940	40.3	21.3	14.2	11.5	29 418	15.8	5.8	3 914	77.0
Robertson County (part)	1 717	11 095	42.1	27.2	18.7	11.4	27 151	21.7	7.4	4 439	69.8
Somervell County	485	6 809	14.7	28.2	13.2	17.2	39 404	8.6	4.7	2 438	74.7
Congressional District 18, Texas	589	651 789	80.2	28.9	8.3	14.4	31 291	23.3	9.5	222 454	48.8
Harris County (part)	589	651 789	80.2	28.9	8.3	14.4	31 291	23.3	9.5	222 454	48.8
Congressional District 19, Texas	65 445	651 610	36.6	27.1	12.9	18.7	31 575	17.5	6.5	239 851	65.3
Archer County (part)	1 895	3 922	7.3	26.4	17.7	13.2	32 146	11.9	3.7	1 555	76.5
Bailey County	2 141	6 594	50.8	30.3	14.8	9.3	27 901	16.7	8.7	2 348	71.3
Borden County	2 328	729	20.3	25.0	15.4	21.4	29 205	14.0	3.7	292	73.3
Callahan County	2 327	12 905	8.1	26.1	17.2	12.3	32 463	12.2	5.0	5 061	80.8
Castro County	2 327	8 285	56.2	33.1	12.2	14.7	30 619	19.0	5.8	2 761	71.0
Cochran County	2 008	3 730	51.0	31.5	14.4	10.2	27 525	27.0	11.1	1 309	74.1
Deaf Smith County	3 878	18 561	60.6	33.4	11.8	11.8	29 601	20.6	8.6	6 180	67.4
Eastland County	2 398	18 297	14.1	23.4	20.7	12.7	26 832	16.8	7.9	7 321	76.7
Fisher County	2 334	4 344	25.3	24.0	22.9	12.4	27 659	17.5	4.4	1 785	76.8
Floyd County	2 570	7 771	50.0	31.3	16.0	12.3	26 851	21.5	6.7	2 730	74.0
Gaines County	3 891	14 467	39.5	34.8	10.2	10.5	30 432	21.7	5.5	4 681	78.6
Garza County	2 319	4 872	44.1	28.0	14.1	10.0	27 206	22.3	5.7	1 663	70.9
Hale County	2 602	36 602	55.3	30.2	12.8	14.4	31 280	18.0	6.7	11 975	64.8
Hockley County	2 352	22 716	42.2	29.1	12.3	13.6	31 085	18.9	6.9	7 994	74.4
Howard County	2 338	33 627	42.9	24.2	14.7	11.1	30 805	18.6	6.7	11 389	69.5
Kent County	2 337	859	11.4	20.5	25.3	15.1	30 433	10.4	3.8	353	78.5
Lamb County	2 632	14 709	49.1	29.6	17.2	11.1	27 898	20.9	5.8	5 360	75.6
Lubbock County	2 330	242 628	37.5	25.6	11.0	24.4	32 198	17.8	5.8	92 516	59.2
Lynn County	2 310	6 550	48.0	31.1	14.2	13.4	26 694	22.6	6.1	2 354	74.6
Nolan County (part)	2 023	1 869	7.8	25.3	19.8	18.6	32 059	13.1	3.5	753	80.5
Parmer County	2 283	10 016	51.5	33.0	12.7	13.4	30 813	17.0	5.3	3 322	72.3
Shackelford County	2 367	3 302	9.1	27.1	18.0	20.8	30 479	13.6	1.8	1 300	78.7
Stephens County	2 317	9 674	19.7	24.4	17.6	13.4	29 583	15.6	3.7	3 661	72.4
Taylor County	2 371	126 555	27.3	26.6	12.3	22.5	34 035	14.5	8.2	47 274	61.5
Terry County	2 305	12 761	50.5	28.3	14.5	9.5	28 090	23.3	5.7	4 278	71.1
Yoakum County	2 071	7 322	47.1	32.2	11.0	10.2	32 672	19.6	9.2	2 469	78.2
Young County	2 389	17 943	13.6	24.9	19.7	14.4	30 499	15.7	5.2	7 167	73.8
Congressional District 20, Texas	476	651 603	76.7	28.7	10.4	15.4	31 937	19.9	7.1	223 059	54.3
Bexar County (part)	476	651 603	76.7	28.7	10.4	15.4	31 937	19.9	7.1	223 059	54.3
Congressional District 21, Texas	6 687	651 297	27.0	24.2	10.1	43.1	55 609	7.0	3.4	254 482	67.1
Bexar County (part)	707	260 583	34.7	25.3	12.0	36.5	52 189	6.0	3.6	101 244	66.0
Blanco County	1 842	8 418	17.9	24.3	16.6	22.2	39 369	11.2	2.9	3 303	78.6
Comal County (part)	1 432	63 865	17.7	25.4	15.1	28.5	49 604	7.3	3.6	24 150	81.2
Hays County (part)	1 454	40 627	14.6	27.7	9.6	40.3	66 231	3.6	2.0	14 496	87.8
Travis County (part)	1 251	277 804	24.0	22.4	7.0	54.3	60 678	8.4	3.3	111 289	62.0

[1]Dry land or land partially or temporarily covered by water.
[2]Persons who do not identify themselves White, not of Hispanic origin.
[3]Persons 25 years old and over.

Table B. 109th Congressional Districts by Counties, 2000—*Continued*

(Number, percent.)

STATE Congressional district County	Land area,[1] (sq km)	Population Total	Population Percent minority[2]	Population Percent under 18 years old	Population Percent 65 years old and over	Percent with bachelor's degree or more[3]	Median income, 1999 (dollars)	Percent living in poverty	Percent unem- ployed	Households Total	Households Percent owner occupied
	1	2	3	4	5	6	7	8	9	10	11
Congressional District 22, Texas	2 516	651 657	39.4	29.1	7.2	32.4	57 932	7.3	4.8	226 585	72.0
Brazoria County (part)	174	60 517	32.7	28.7	8.1	32.6	62 810	5.5	3.6	21 189	82.6
Fort Bend County (part)	1 569	246 501	46.9	31.3	6.3	39.2	66 563	7.1	4.6	78 034	79.1
Galveston County (part)	375	53 146	38.1	27.2	12.4	13.5	41 134	13.3	6.6	19 787	75.5
Harris County (part)	399	291 493	34.7	27.6	6.9	30.2	54 865	6.9	4.9	107 575	64.1
Congressional District 23, Texas	136 287	651 707	59.0	29.6	11.0	25.9	38 081	18.4	6.5	222 061	70.3
Bandera County	2 051	17 645	15.5	24.7	16.1	19.4	39 013	10.8	4.8	7 010	82.9
Bexar County (part)	904	195 144	36.9	25.9	8.2	46.8	61 028	5.9	3.0	75 771	66.6
Brewster County	16 039	8 866	46.3	22.2	14.6	27.7	27 386	18.2	10.7	3 669	59.4
Crockett County	7 271	4 099	55.7	29.1	12.7	10.4	29 355	19.4	6.6	1 524	71.5
Culberson County	9 874	2 975	74.9	32.0	10.6	13.9	25 882	25.1	6.1	1 052	70.4
Dimmit County	3 447	10 248	87.1	33.0	12.9	10.1	21 917	33.2	14.2	3 308	73.9
Edwards County	5 490	2 162	45.9	28.3	16.2	17.3	25 298	31.6	4.9	801	79.7
El Paso County (part)	1 120	27 259	91.2	40.2	4.8	4.8	26 677	28.4	11.1	6 861	86.7
Hudspeth County	11 839	3 344	76.9	34.2	10.0	9.7	21 045	35.8	8.2	1 092	81.0
Jeff Davis County	5 865	2 207	37.9	24.5	16.4	35.1	32 212	15.0	5.8	896	70.2
Kendall County	1 716	23 743	18.9	27.3	13.9	31.4	49 521	10.5	3.3	8 613	79.6
Kerr County	2 865	43 653	22.3	22.7	24.6	23.3	34 283	14.5	4.6	17 813	73.3
Kinney County	3 531	3 379	52.9	25.7	24.7	17.7	28 320	24.0	9.4	1 314	77.9
Maverick County	3 315	47 297	96.8	37.0	9.6	9.1	21 232	34.8	17.6	13 089	69.5
Medina County	3 439	39 304	49.5	29.0	12.3	13.3	36 063	15.4	5.2	12 880	79.7
Pecos County	12 338	16 809	66.7	27.6	11.6	12.9	28 033	20.4	5.7	5 153	74.2
Presidio County	9 986	7 304	85.7	32.9	14.2	11.7	19 860	36.4	13.0	2 530	70.1
Real County	1 813	3 047	23.7	23.7	20.5	17.3	25 118	21.2	3.6	1 245	77.0
Reeves County	6 827	13 137	77.6	29.8	12.7	8.0	23 306	28.9	12.4	4 091	77.6
Sutton County (part)	1 567	2 871	62.7	30.5	12.2	8.4	32 147	20.2	4.7	1 040	75.3
Terrell County	6 106	1 081	52.6	26.5	18.1	19.0	24 219	25.2	5.3	443	77.7
Uvalde County	4 031	25 926	67.4	31.4	13.9	13.8	27 164	24.3	6.7	8 559	72.0
Val Verde County	8 211	44 856	78.3	32.0	10.8	14.1	28 376	26.1	11.3	14 151	66.0
Webb County (part)	3 280	93 751	93.7	33.9	8.0	18.8	33 855	25.1	7.7	25 728	62.8
Zavala County	3 363	11 600	92.6	33.8	11.5	7.6	16 844	41.8	16.7	3 428	73.0
Congressional District 24, Texas	866	651 137	36.1	27.3	5.7	36.2	56 098	6.3	3.3	248 764	57.1
Dallas County (part)	445	333 393	45.5	28.0	6.5	32.1	52 681	7.7	3.9	122 543	59.1
Denton County (part)	118	104 502	32.0	25.0	3.3	42.2	56 183	5.0	2.9	43 564	46.5
Tarrant County (part)	303	213 242	23.5	27.2	5.7	39.5	61 755	4.8	2.7	82 657	59.7
Congressional District 25, Texas	20 759	651 894	78.2	30.2	9.1	15.0	28 348	28.8	8.6	207 233	58.7
Caldwell County	1 413	32 194	51.0	28.4	12.7	13.3	36 573	13.1	5.5	10 816	69.6
Duval County	4 643	13 120	88.9	29.4	14.0	8.9	22 416	27.2	9.5	4 350	80.8
Gonzales County	2 765	18 628	49.2	27.9	16.9	10.7	28 368	18.6	4.8	6 782	69.2
Hidalgo County (part)	639	247 435	90.4	34.6	10.4	12.2	24 690	35.4	11.5	68 516	72.0
Jim Hogg County	2 943	5 281	91.1	31.6	14.1	9.5	25 833	25.9	8.1	1 815	77.6
Karnes County	1 943	15 446	59.3	21.7	14.1	9.4	26 526	21.9	6.5	4 454	74.0
Live Oak County	2 684	12 309	41.9	22.3	16.4	12.0	32 057	16.5	5.8	4 230	81.4
Starr County	3 168	53 597	98.4	37.4	8.1	6.9	16 504	50.9	20.9	14 410	79.4
Travis County (part)	561	253 884	69.6	25.8	5.9	20.9	31 989	21.3	5.8	91 860	40.3
Congressional District 26, Texas	3 346	651 858	33.9	28.7	7.8	26.9	48 714	11.0	5.1	232 209	67.7
Cooke County (part)	754	26 515	18.5	26.8	15.6	15.3	35 539	16.2	5.6	10 070	69.5
Dallas County (part)	16	48	0.0	56.3	0.0	19.0	25 938	0.0	50.0	14	100.0
Denton County (part)	2 183	328 474	21.5	28.4	5.6	34.8	59 106	7.2	4.1	115 339	71.3
Tarrant County (part)	393	296 821	49.1	29.2	9.6	19.5	40 350	14.8	6.3	106 786	63.6
Congressional District 27, Texas	12 225	651 843	72.3	30.9	10.6	16.2	31 327	25.3	9.4	209 011	63.9
Cameron County (part)	1 991	248 067	88.7	34.5	10.0	12.7	24 994	35.5	12.3	69 265	67.7
Kenedy County	3 773	414	86.0	30.2	11.6	20.3	25 000	15.3	6.5	138	40.6
Kleberg County	2 256	31 549	71.6	27.3	10.9	20.4	29 313	26.7	10.6	10 896	58.6
Nueces County	2 165	313 645	62.3	28.3	11.2	18.8	35 959	18.2	7.6	110 365	61.3
San Patricio County (part)	496	38 086	40.0	30.9	8.8	16.7	40 079	11.6	6.3	12 763	64.8
Willacy County	1 545	20 082	88.8	31.6	11.8	7.5	22 114	33.2	13.8	5 584	77.3
Congressional District 28, Texas	26 259	651 295	72.1	31.3	9.9	10.9	31 355	22.6	7.8	203 302	69.4
Atascosa County	3 191	38 628	60.7	31.7	11.0	10.5	33 081	20.2	6.0	12 816	78.5
Bexar County (part)	1 142	285 601	82.4	32.1	10.2	6.8	29 851	22.5	8.1	88 868	68.3
Comal County (part)	22	14 156	60.3	26.7	12.9	14.7	32 471	14.5	4.8	4 916	57.8
Frio County	2 935	16 252	79.2	28.7	11.1	8.4	24 504	29.0	7.3	4 743	69.0
Guadalupe County	1 842	89 023	40.6	28.3	11.1	19.1	43 949	9.8	5.4	30 900	77.0
Hays County (part)	302	56 962	50.4	22.1	6.3	22.2	32 207	22.6	9.2	18 914	47.4
La Salle County	3 856	5 866	81.7	29.1	12.2	6.4	21 857	29.8	7.9	1 819	74.7
McMullen County	2 883	851	35.7	23.0	19.0	16.2	32 500	20.7	1.7	355	80.8
Webb County (part)	5 415	99 366	96.6	38.4	7.4	8.9	24 506	36.8	11.1	25 012	68.6
Wilson County	2 090	32 408	39.2	29.2	11.4	12.8	40 006	11.3	4.9	11 038	85.0
Zapata County	2 582	12 182	85.2	33.0	14.6	8.7	24 635	35.8	11.1	3 921	81.9

[1]Dry land or land partially or temporarily covered by water.
[2]Persons who do not identify themselves White, not of Hispanic origin.
[3]Persons 25 years old and over.

Table B. 109th Congressional Districts by Counties, 2000—*Continued*

(Number, percent.)

STATE Congressional district County	Land area,[1] (sq km)	Population Total	Percent minority[2]	Percent under 18 years old	Percent 65 years old and over	Percent with bachelor's degree or more[3]	Median income, 1999 (dollars)	Percent living in poverty	Percent unem- ployed	Households Total	Percent owner occupied
	1	2	3	4	5	6	7	8	9	10	11
Congressional District 29, Texas	611	651 405	78.2	33.4	7.0	6.5	31 751	21.9	9.3	193 092	55.3
Harris County (part)	611	651 405	78.2	33.4	7.0	6.5	31 751	21.9	9.3	193 092	55.3
Congressional District 30, Texas	822	652 261	78.1	29.5	7.9	16.0	33 505	21.4	8.8	220 701	49.1
Dallas County (part)	822	652 261	78.1	29.5	7.9	16.0	33 505	21.4	8.8	220 701	49.1
Congressional District 31, Texas	18 476	651 868	34.0	28.6	8.8	24.1	43 381	9.6	5.1	225 600	64.8
Bell County	2 745	237 974	42.8	28.9	8.7	19.8	36 872	12.1	6.8	85 507	55.7
Coryell County	2 724	74 978	39.6	26.2	5.6	12.4	35 999	9.5	6.7	19 950	54.8
Erath County	2 814	33 001	17.6	24.6	13.4	25.0	30 708	16.0	10.7	12 568	63.1
Falls County	1 992	18 576	44.3	27.7	16.8	9.6	26 589	22.6	7.4	6 496	71.7
Hamilton County	2 164	8 229	8.4	23.8	23.2	16.8	31 150	14.2	2.6	3 374	77.8
Milam County	2 633	24 238	31.1	27.3	17.0	11.6	33 186	15.9	4.7	9 199	73.0
Robertson County (part)	496	4 905	35.0	30.7	12.2	15.8	31 918	18.2	3.5	1 740	76.1
Williamson County	2 908	249 967	26.5	29.8	7.2	33.6	60 642	4.8	2.8	86 766	74.2
Congressional District 32, Texas	413	650 555	49.8	25.3	9.3	36.4	45 725	12.5	4.5	252 320	46.5
Dallas County (part)	413	650 555	49.8	25.3	9.3	36.4	45 725	12.5	4.5	252 320	46.5
UTAH	212 751	2 233 169	14.7	32.1	8.5	26.1	45 726	9.4	5.0	701 281	71.5
Congressional District 1, Utah	53 790	744 337	16.7	32.3	8.6	24.7	45 058	9.5	5.4	238 384	70.8
Box Elder County	14 823	42 745	9.0	36.1	10.4	19.5	44 630	7.1	5.2	13 144	80.0
Cache County	3 016	91 391	10.1	31.2	7.1	31.9	39 730	13.5	5.1	27 543	64.6
Davis County	789	238 994	10.3	35.2	7.3	28.8	53 726	5.1	4.4	71 201	77.6
Juab County (part)	6 365	1 062	11.4	33.9	10.1	7.9	30 769	15.5	6.8	368	71.5
Morgan County	1 578	7 129	3.0	36.9	8.8	23.3	50 273	5.2	3.8	2 046	88.3
Rich County	2 664	1 961	2.3	34.8	14.1	22.0	39 766	10.2	4.2	645	83.7
Salt Lake County (part)	270	94 051	45.8	26.1	10.1	18.4	30 277	21.0	8.2	34 730	44.9
Summit County	4 846	29 736	10.5	29.8	4.9	45.5	64 962	5.4	2.8	10 332	75.5
Tooele County	17 950	40 735	14.9	35.1	7.5	15.9	45 773	6.7	5.6	12 677	78.3
Weber County	1 491	196 533	17.3	30.9	10.4	19.9	44 014	9.3	6.0	65 698	74.9
Congressional District 2, Utah	118 166	744 287	12.0	29.6	10.8	30.9	45 583	9.0	4.6	252 500	70.6
Carbon County	3 829	20 422	13.8	28.3	13.2	12.3	34 036	13.4	8.9	7 413	77.4
Daggett County	1 809	921	8.7	23.1	13.9	11.9	30 833	5.5	7.7	340	70.6
Duchesne County	8 387	14 371	10.5	36.8	9.3	12.7	31 298	16.8	7.8	4 559	80.8
Emery County	11 530	10 860	7.3	35.4	10.2	11.6	39 850	11.5	6.4	3 468	82.0
Garfield County	13 401	4 735	4.7	32.4	14.1	20.3	35 180	8.1	8.1	1 576	79.0
Grand County	9 535	8 485	11.1	26.8	12.7	22.9	32 387	14.8	8.8	3 434	70.9
Iron County	8 542	33 779	8.4	31.2	8.5	23.8	33 114	19.2	5.3	10 627	66.3
Kane County	10 339	6 046	5.5	29.1	17.0	21.1	34 247	7.9	5.3	2 237	78.1
Piute County	1 963	1 435	4.6	31.1	17.0	14.4	29 625	16.2	6.4	509	87.2
Salt Lake County (part)	924	437 788	12.6	26.6	10.3	37.2	50 962	6.8	3.7	155 607	67.1
San Juan County	20 254	14 413	60.5	39.3	8.4	13.9	28 137	31.4	15.1	4 089	79.3
Uintah County	11 596	25 224	14.5	34.6	9.9	13.2	34 518	14.5	7.7	8 187	77.0
Utah County (part)	351	57 730	5.0	41.0	6.3	32.0	56 861	4.4	3.9	14 882	82.5
Wasatch County	3 049	15 215	7.2	34.2	8.4	26.3	49 612	5.2	4.3	4 743	80.6
Washington County	6 285	90 354	8.6	31.1	17.0	21.0	37 212	11.2	5.5	29 939	74.0
Wayne County	6 372	2 509	3.2	32.4	14.3	20.9	32 000	15.4	3.3	890	77.6
Congressional District 3, Utah	40 795	744 545	15.4	34.4	6.2	22.1	46 568	9.7	4.9	210 397	73.5
Beaver County	6 708	6 005	9.4	33.4	13.9	12.1	34 544	8.3	2.2	1 982	78.9
Juab County (part)	2 420	7 176	3.8	39.2	9.8	12.9	39 063	9.7	3.0	2 088	81.1
Millard County	17 066	12 405	9.5	37.3	12.5	16.8	36 178	13.1	5.9	3 840	79.6
Salt Lake County (part)	716	366 548	20.0	35.8	4.9	16.5	50 718	6.1	4.7	104 804	79.9
Sanpete County	4 113	22 763	9.5	33.2	11.0	17.3	33 042	15.9	6.8	6 547	78.8
Sevier County	4 948	18 842	5.2	34.5	13.0	15.2	35 822	10.8	6.3	6 081	82.0
Utah County (part)	4 824	310 806	11.7	32.7	6.5	31.3	43 890	13.4	4.9	85 055	64.1
VERMONT	23 956	608 827	3.9	24.2	12.7	29.4	40 856	9.4	4.2	240 634	70.6
Congressional District (At Large), Vermont	23 956	608 827	3.9	24.2	12.7	29.4	40 856	9.4	4.2	240 634	70.6
Addison County	1 995	35 974	4.0	24.8	11.3	29.8	43 142	8.6	4.5	13 068	75.0
Bennington County	1 752	36 994	2.9	23.8	16.6	27.1	39 926	10.0	4.6	14 846	71.4
Caledonia County	1 685	29 702	3.1	25.4	14.3	22.5	34 800	12.3	6.2	11 663	72.9
Chittenden County	1 396	146 571	5.6	23.5	9.4	41.2	47 673	8.8	4.0	56 452	66.1
Essex County	1 723	6 459	3.7	25.5	15.0	10.8	30 490	13.7	6.2	2 602	79.7
Franklin County	1 650	45 417	4.2	28.1	10.9	16.6	41 659	9.0	3.7	16 765	75.0
Grand Isle County	214	6 901	2.8	24.9	12.3	25.0	43 033	7.6	3.4	2 761	81.3
Lamoille County	1 194	23 233	3.7	24.3	11.3	31.2	39 356	9.6	4.6	9 221	70.8
Orange County	1 783	28 226	2.6	25.6	12.8	23.9	39 855	9.1	4.4	10 936	78.1
Orleans County	1 807	26 277	3.4	25.1	15.1	16.1	31 084	14.1	6.7	10 446	74.1
Rutland County	2 415	63 400	2.4	23.2	14.9	23.2	36 743	10.9	4.7	25 678	69.8
Washington County	1 785	58 039	3.9	23.5	12.8	32.2	40 972	8.0	3.2	23 659	68.5
Windham County	2 043	44 216	3.9	23.6	14.0	30.5	38 204	9.4	4.0	18 375	67.9
Windsor County	2 515	57 418	2.8	23.4	15.8	30.2	40 688	7.7	3.2	24 162	71.5

[1]Dry land or land partially or temporarily covered by water.
[2]Persons who do not identify themselves White, not of Hispanic origin.
[3]Persons 25 years old and over.

Table B. 109th Congressional Districts by Counties, 2000—*Continued*

(Number, percent.)

STATE Congressional district County	Land area,[1] (sq km)	Population Total	Population Percent minority[2]	Population Percent under 18 years old	Population Percent 65 years old and over	Percent with bachelor's degree or more[3]	Median income, 1999 (dollars)	Percent living in poverty	Percent unemployed	Households Total	Households Percent owner occupied
	1	2	3	4	5	6	7	8	9	10	11
VIRGINIA	102 548	7 078 515	29.9	24.5	11.2	29.5	46 677	9.6	4.2	2 699 173	68.1
Congressional District 1, Virginia	9 771	642 404	25.4	26.4	11.3	26.8	50 257	6.7	4.6	237 490	72.7
Caroline County (part)	1 033	12 074	37.8	24.5	14.7	11.6	38 394	9.6	4.5	4 403	79.1
Essex County	668	9 989	42.6	23.0	17.3	17.4	37 395	11.2	3.2	3 995	77.2
Fauquier County (part)	858	28 479	12.7	28.3	8.6	22.1	60 981	5.4	2.8	9 933	78.6
Gloucester County	561	34 780	14.6	26.2	12.0	17.6	45 421	7.7	4.0	13 127	81.4
James City County (part)	370	48 102	19.1	23.3	16.7	41.5	55 594	6.4	3.6	19 003	77.0
King and Queen County	819	6 630	38.6	22.8	16.9	10.3	35 941	10.9	4.1	2 673	82.3
King George County	466	16 803	23.6	27.7	9.6	23.6	49 882	5.6	4.2	6 091	71.8
King William County	713	13 146	26.7	26.0	11.7	14.8	49 876	5.5	3.1	4 846	85.1
Lancaster County	345	11 567	30.5	19.1	28.6	24.5	33 239	12.5	6.4	5 004	83.0
Mathews County	222	9 207	13.8	19.9	21.3	19.2	43 222	6.0	3.2	3 932	84.7
Middlesex County	337	9 932	22.2	19.3	22.4	18.9	36 875	13.0	3.9	4 253	83.0
Northumberland County	498	12 259	27.9	18.6	26.3	21.7	38 129	12.3	3.9	5 470	87.4
Prince William County (part)	207	37 827	45.8	32.2	3.3	27.5	51 653	6.0	4.2	12 682	53.2
Richmond County	496	8 809	36.7	18.4	17.4	9.9	33 026	15.4	5.0	2 937	77.2
Spotsylvania County (part)	421	71 275	19.5	30.1	8.0	25.9	59 781	3.7	3.2	24 682	81.0
Stafford County	700	92 446	19.9	31.5	5.8	29.6	66 809	3.5	3.0	30 187	80.6
Westmoreland County	594	16 718	35.8	23.0	19.2	13.3	35 797	14.7	4.1	6 846	79.2
York County	274	56 297	21.4	29.1	9.2	37.4	57 956	3.5	2.8	20 000	75.8
Fredericksburg city	27	19 279	28.9	17.7	13.1	30.5	34 585	15.5	9.6	8 102	35.5
Hampton city (part)	38	31 662	47.1	26.9	8.3	23.7	45 774	6.3	4.4	12 034	64.3
Newport News city (part)	62	71 559	29.9	24.4	12.6	27.6	41 533	7.7	3.4	29 505	57.2
Poquoson city	40	11 566	4.9	26.9	11.3	31.6	60 920	4.5	3.2	4 166	84.1
Williamsburg city	22	11 998	22.0	9.9	11.9	45.0	37 093	18.3	41.7	3 619	44.3
Congressional District 2, Virginia	2 489	643 367	32.7	25.5	9.4	25.5	44 193	8.7	5.0	231 653	63.5
Accomack County	1 179	38 305	38.0	24.3	16.9	13.5	30 250	18.0	7.6	15 299	75.0
Northampton County	537	13 093	47.6	23.5	21.6	15.7	28 276	20.5	7.0	5 321	68.7
Hampton city (part)	53	54 637	31.5	21.6	9.9	27.4	45 398	8.6	4.7	18 512	65.6
Norfolk city (part)	77	112 075	37.5	21.0	9.2	19.2	35 022	13.1	8.3	38 066	48.5
Virginia Beach city	643	425 257	30.6	27.4	8.4	28.1	48 705	6.5	4.1	154 455	65.6
Congressional District 3, Virginia	2 895	643 917	62.2	25.9	11.7	17.2	32 238	18.9	7.9	250 417	52.1
Charles City County	473	6 926	64.5	21.9	13.3	10.5	42 745	10.6	3.7	2 670	84.9
Henrico County (part)	351	65 440	54.1	26.3	11.2	13.2	42 016	8.3	3.7	25 755	69.7
Isle of Wight County (part)	0	0	X	X	X	X	X	X	X	0	X
James City County (part)	0	0	X	X	X	X	X	X	X	0	X
New Kent County	543	13 462	20.2	24.9	9.7	16.3	53 595	4.9	3.8	4 925	88.8
Prince George County (part)	395	15 059	37.1	23.2	8.3	17.0	52 079	9.9	3.8	4 810	82.1
Surry County	723	6 829	53.6	25.2	14.1	12.8	37 558	10.8	5.3	2 619	77.0
Hampton city (part)	44	60 138	72.4	25.1	11.9	15.1	31 836	16.2	9.4	23 341	50.1
Newport News city (part)	115	108 591	59.8	29.4	8.4	14.3	32 587	17.9	7.2	40 181	48.9
Norfolk city (part)	62	122 328	67.4	26.8	12.5	19.9	29 365	24.3	9.6	48 144	43.2
Portsmouth city	86	100 565	54.7	25.7	13.8	13.8	33 742	16.2	7.7	38 170	58.5
Richmond city (part)	103	144 579	71.3	23.2	12.4	22.8	27 133	26.1	9.9	59 802	42.5
Congressional District 4, Virginia	11 626	643 670	38.0	26.6	10.6	19.6	45 249	9.5	4.4	231 889	73.5
Amelia County	924	11 400	29.6	25.4	13.2	9.8	40 252	8.4	2.9	4 240	82.0
Brunswick County (part)	412	3 319	53.2	23.5	15.8	7.1	28 167	18.8	7.4	1 304	77.4
Chesterfield County (part)	731	127 191	28.5	27.7	7.4	24.3	55 394	5.5	3.8	45 194	80.5
Dinwiddie County	1 305	24 533	35.5	24.0	12.2	11.0	41 582	9.3	3.8	9 107	79.2
Greensville County	765	11 560	61.5	18.1	11.5	11.0	32 002	14.7	4.4	3 375	78.3
Isle of Wight County (part)	818	29 728	29.2	25.4	12.0	17.5	45 387	8.3	4.1	11 319	80.9
Nottoway County	815	15 725	43.3	23.0	17.0	11.1	30 866	20.1	5.9	5 664	70.9
Powhatan County	677	22 377	18.8	23.9	8.4	19.1	53 992	5.7	1.8	7 258	88.9
Prince George County (part)	292	17 988	44.5	26.9	6.2	21.9	47 846	6.3	4.5	5 349	64.9
Southampton County	1 553	17 482	44.2	22.8	14.4	11.7	33 995	14.6	4.7	6 279	74.3
Sussex County	1 271	12 504	63.5	19.7	13.4	10.0	31 007	16.1	5.3	4 126	69.5
Chesapeake city	882	199 184	34.2	28.8	8.8	24.7	50 743	7.3	4.1	69 900	74.9
Colonial Heights city	19	16 897	10.9	22.5	18.7	19.0	43 224	5.5	2.3	7 027	69.4
Emporia city	18	5 665	59.7	25.3	20.0	14.2	30 333	16.0	6.8	2 226	52.1
Franklin city	22	8 346	54.3	24.9	18.5	16.4	31 687	19.8	7.0	3 384	53.6
Hopewell city	27	22 354	38.8	26.8	14.5	10.2	33 196	14.9	6.7	9 055	55.9
Petersburg city	59	33 740	81.9	24.9	15.6	14.8	28 851	19.6	8.9	13 799	51.5
Suffolk city	1 036	63 677	46.9	27.8	11.6	17.3	41 115	13.2	4.9	23 283	72.2

[1]Dry land or land partially or temporarily covered by water.
[2]Persons who do not identify themselves White, not of Hispanic origin.
[3]Persons 25 years old and over.
X = Not applicable.

Table B. 109th Congressional Districts by Counties, 2000—*Continued*

(Number, percent.)

STATE Congressional district County	Land area,[1] (sq km)	Population Total	Percent minority[2]	Percent under 18 years old	Percent 65 years old and over	Percent with bachelor's degree or more[3]	Median income, 1999 (dollars)	Percent living in poverty	Percent unemployed	Households Total	Percent owner occupied
	1	2	3	4	5	6	7	8	9	10	11
Congressional District 5, Virginia	23 108	643 323	27.5	22.5	14.8	19.0	35 739	13.2	5.1	253 996	72.4
Albemarle County	1 872	79 236	16.4	24.8	12.5	47.7	50 749	6.7	3.1	31 876	65.8
Appomattox County	864	13 705	24.3	24.7	15.0	10.5	36 507	11.4	2.9	5 322	81.0
Bedford County (part)	1 234	35 681	8.0	22.2	14.7	13.9	39 114	7.7	3.3	14 356	87.3
Brunswick County (part)	1 055	15 100	59.6	19.7	14.3	11.6	31 771	15.9	7.2	4 973	77.7
Buckingham County	1 504	15 623	41.0	22.4	13.6	8.5	29 882	20.0	5.5	5 324	77.9
Campbell County	1 307	51 078	17.1	24.0	13.7	14.6	37 280	10.6	3.1	20 639	77.3
Charlotte County	1 230	12 472	35.1	24.4	17.8	10.3	28 929	18.1	5.6	4 951	77.4
Cumberland County	773	9 017	40.2	24.7	15.0	11.8	31 816	15.1	3.5	3 528	77.2
Fluvanna County	744	20 047	21.1	23.7	13.9	24.5	46 372	5.9	2.9	7 387	85.3
Franklin County	1 792	47 286	11.8	22.0	14.3	14.8	38 056	9.7	3.8	18 963	81.2
Greene County	406	15 244	9.8	27.1	9.8	19.8	45 931	6.6	2.7	5 574	81.5
Halifax County	2 122	37 355	40.1	23.3	17.4	9.5	29 929	15.7	7.4	15 018	76.0
Henry County (part)	635	34 868	26.3	22.2	14.4	11.3	34 065	9.9	5.1	14 529	75.7
Lunenburg County	1 118	13 146	41.7	21.4	16.9	9.2	27 899	20.0	5.2	4 998	77.8
Mecklenburg County	1 616	32 380	41.3	21.5	17.8	12.1	31 380	15.5	6.6	12 951	74.3
Nelson County	1 223	14 445	18.5	21.4	16.7	20.8	36 769	12.1	4.8	5 887	80.8
Pittsylvania County	2 514	61 745	25.7	23.0	14.3	9.3	35 153	11.8	4.3	24 684	80.1
Prince Edward County	914	19 720	38.1	20.3	14.1	19.2	31 301	18.9	13.3	6 561	68.5
Bedford city	18	6 299	25.3	21.6	21.8	15.2	28 792	19.7	13.3	2 519	60.3
Charlottesville city	27	45 049	31.4	15.2	10.0	40.8	31 007	25.9	4.3	16 851	40.9
Danville city	112	48 411	46.7	23.3	19.7	13.9	26 900	20.0	10.1	20 607	58.0
Martinsville city	28	15 416	46.0	22.6	20.9	16.6	27 441	19.2	8.7	6 498	60.2
Congressional District 6, Virginia	14 625	643 630	15.1	22.4	15.0	20.8	37 773	11.0	4.4	254 321	69.2
Alleghany County (part)	448	5 085	4.5	24.7	15.7	16.7	41 275	7.0	7.8	2 022	81.2
Amherst County	1 231	31 894	22.8	23.4	13.7	13.1	37 393	10.7	5.0	11 941	78.1
Augusta County	2 513	65 615	5.4	23.6	12.8	15.4	43 045	5.8	2.5	24 818	83.2
Bath County	1 378	5 048	7.8	20.7	17.1	11.1	35 013	7.8	4.2	2 053	79.8
Bedford County (part)	720	24 690	9.2	26.7	10.2	31.8	51 290	6.3	2.4	9 482	85.5
Botetourt County	1 405	30 496	5.4	23.3	13.2	19.6	48 731	5.2	2.7	11 700	87.7
Highland County	1 077	2 536	0.7	19.9	20.2	13.2	29 732	12.6	6.8	1 131	83.7
Roanoke County (part)	330	71 310	6.1	22.6	16.4	29.0	47 380	4.7	2.1	29 112	74.6
Rockbridge County	1 553	20 808	5.0	22.1	15.6	18.7	36 035	9.6	3.6	8 486	77.6
Rockingham County	2 204	67 725	5.3	24.7	13.9	17.6	40 748	8.2	3.4	25 355	78.0
Shenandoah County	1 327	35 075	6.0	22.4	17.2	14.7	39 173	8.2	2.7	14 296	73.1
Buena Vista city	18	6 349	7.0	22.3	16.2	10.5	32 410	10.4	3.9	2 547	70.6
Covington city (part)	2	1 364	13.9	25.1	17.9	5.8	27 798	13.1	5.3	571	55.7
Harrisonburg city	45	40 468	19.6	15.2	9.3	31.2	29 949	30.1	9.3	13 133	39.1
Lexington city	6	6 867	14.3	10.5	16.4	42.6	28 982	21.6	9.9	2 232	55.2
Lynchburg city	128	65 269	34.0	22.2	16.4	25.2	32 234	15.9	6.7	25 477	58.5
Roanoke city	111	94 911	31.4	22.6	16.4	18.7	30 719	15.9	5.8	42 003	56.3
Salem city	38	24 747	8.7	20.8	16.9	19.8	38 997	6.7	3.8	9 954	67.6
Staunton city	51	23 853	16.7	19.9	18.1	20.4	32 941	11.7	3.9	9 676	61.4
Waynesboro city	40	19 520	15.2	23.8	17.5	20.6	32 686	12.8	6.5	8 332	61.2
Congressional District 7, Virginia	9 102	643 583	21.9	25.0	12.1	33.2	50 990	6.1	2.8	252 282	72.9
Caroline County (part)	346	10 047	38.5	25.0	11.1	12.7	42 840	9.0	4.2	3 618	85.6
Chesterfield County (part)	372	132 712	21.0	28.6	8.7	40.4	61 779	3.6	2.6	48 578	81.4
Culpeper County	987	34 262	22.9	25.6	12.0	15.7	45 290	9.2	3.2	12 141	70.5
Goochland County	737	16 863	27.5	21.2	12.3	29.4	56 307	6.9	1.7	6 158	86.7
Hanover County	1 224	86 320	12.3	27.1	10.7	28.7	59 223	3.6	2.2	31 121	84.3
Henrico County (part)	265	196 860	25.0	24.1	12.9	41.9	51 379	5.4	2.7	82 366	64.5
Louisa County	1 288	25 627	23.9	24.4	12.9	14.0	39 402	10.2	3.4	9 945	81.4
Madison County	832	12 520	13.5	23.8	15.2	19.4	39 856	9.6	3.2	4 739	76.9
Orange County	885	25 881	16.6	23.0	17.3	18.5	42 889	9.2	2.9	10 150	77.1
Page County	806	23 177	4.4	22.9	15.8	9.8	33 359	12.5	3.9	9 305	73.9
Rappahannock County	690	6 983	8.3	22.6	13.8	22.9	45 943	7.6	2.2	2 788	75.4
Spotsylvania County (part)	617	19 120	16.2	29.3	8.5	11.8	48 880	8.8	3.1	6 626	86.6
Richmond city (part)	52	53 211	37.5	18.3	16.1	46.0	43 376	8.3	3.5	24 747	55.0
Congressional District 8, Virginia	319	643 764	42.9	19.6	8.8	53.8	63 430	7.5	3.0	277 916	50.1
Arlington County	67	189 453	39.5	16.3	9.1	60.2	63 001	7.8	2.8	86 352	43.3
Fairfax County (part)	207	315 651	44.3	22.6	8.4	49.1	66 992	6.8	3.1	125 204	59.5
Alexandria city	39	128 283	46.3	16.8	8.9	54.3	56 054	8.9	3.2	61 889	40.0
Falls Church city	5	10 377	20.3	23.6	12.3	63.7	74 924	4.2	2.9	4 471	60.5
Congressional District 9, Virginia	22 801	643 561	6.7	20.7	14.6	14.0	29 783	16.2	5.7	259 829	74.2
Alleghany County (part)	704	7 841	3.0	21.7	15.7	11.6	37 228	7.2	3.7	3 127	87.2
Bland County	929	6 871	5.4	19.2	14.8	9.2	30 397	12.4	4.5	2 568	86.1
Buchanan County	1 305	26 978	3.4	21.7	11.4	8.0	22 213	23.2	8.3	10 464	82.9
Carroll County	1 234	29 245	3.1	20.9	17.2	9.5	30 597	12.5	6.1	12 186	81.7
Craig County	856	5 091	1.3	23.6	13.7	10.8	37 314	10.3	2.8	2 060	81.4

[1] Dry land or land partially or temporarily covered by water.
[2] Persons who do not identify themselves White, not of Hispanic origin.
[3] Persons 25 years old and over.

Table B. 109th Congressional Districts by Counties, 2000—*Continued*

(Number, percent.)

STATE Congressional district County	Land area,[1] (sq km)	Population Total	Percent minority[2]	Percent under 18 years old	Percent 65 years old and over	Percent with bachelor's degree or more[3]	Median income, 1999 (dollars)	Percent living in poverty	Percent unem- ployed	Households Total	Percent owner occupied
	1	2	3	4	5	6	7	8	9	10	11
Congressional District 9, Virginia—*Continued*											
Dickenson County	859	16 395	1.4	22.0	14.5	6.7	23 431	21.3	7.2	6 732	82.1
Floyd County	987	13 874	4.2	22.3	15.8	12.5	31 585	11.7	3.6	5 791	81.8
Giles County	925	16 657	3.4	21.9	16.6	12.4	34 927	9.5	5.4	6 994	79.0
Grayson County	1 146	17 917	9.6	19.5	17.0	8.0	28 676	13.6	3.6	7 259	81.3
Henry County (part)	355	23 062	28.8	22.4	15.7	6.6	29 394	14.3	5.9	9 381	78.7
Lee County	1 132	23 589	2.2	22.6	15.5	9.5	22 972	23.9	8.0	9 706	74.4
Montgomery County	1 005	83 629	10.7	17.3	8.6	35.9	32 330	23.2	5.4	30 997	55.1
Patrick County	1 251	19 407	9.2	21.8	16.5	8.6	28 705	13.4	4.0	8 141	80.2
Pulaski County	830	35 127	7.7	20.5	15.4	12.5	33 873	13.1	5.5	14 643	73.6
Roanoke County (part)	320	14 468	9.7	23.3	12.8	24.3	48 962	3.2	2.2	5 574	90.5
Russell County	1 229	30 308	4.5	21.2	13.3	9.4	26 834	16.3	6.9	11 789	81.1
Scott County	1 390	23 403	2.0	20.7	17.7	8.3	27 339	16.8	5.9	9 795	78.3
Smyth County	1 171	33 081	3.6	21.6	16.3	10.6	30 083	13.3	4.7	13 493	74.1
Tazewell County	1 346	44 598	3.9	21.5	15.4	11.0	27 304	15.3	9.1	18 277	77.3
Washington County	1 458	51 103	3.0	20.7	15.3	16.1	32 742	10.9	4.2	21 056	77.3
Wise County	1 046	40 123	3.4	23.0	14.0	10.8	26 149	20.0	7.2	16 013	75.2
Wythe County	1 200	27 599	4.8	21.7	15.8	12.1	32 235	11.0	4.3	11 511	77.4
Bristol city	33	17 367	8.0	20.2	20.4	17.0	27 389	16.2	6.5	7 678	65.0
Clifton Forge city	8	4 289	17.7	21.0	23.8	9.6	26 090	19.4	7.3	1 841	62.7
Covington city (part)	13	4 939	16.9	20.2	21.2	6.5	30 941	12.8	4.6	2 264	73.4
Galax city	21	6 837	18.8	23.2	18.6	11.1	28 236	18.6	2.7	2 950	66.1
Norton city	20	3 904	9.8	22.0	15.7	14.0	22 788	22.8	7.3	1 730	56.0
Radford city	25	15 859	12.0	12.9	9.8	34.1	24 654	31.4	6.4	5 809	44.5
Congressional District 10, Virginia	4 808	643 714	23.0	28.2	7.3	43.1	71 560	4.4	2.4	228 202	75.4
Clarke County	457	12 652	9.5	23.3	14.7	23.9	51 601	6.6	2.1	4 942	75.5
Fairfax County (part)	306	222 465	29.6	28.8	6.0	61.9	96 039	2.7	2.0	75 734	78.5
Fauquier County (part)	825	26 660	13.1	25.3	12.7	32.1	63 871	5.5	2.3	9 909	73.7
Frederick County	1 074	59 209	6.2	26.4	10.7	18.6	46 941	6.4	2.5	22 097	80.3
Loudoun County	1 346	169 599	20.6	29.7	5.5	47.2	80 648	2.8	2.0	59 900	79.4
Prince William County (part)	190	52 535	30.8	27.8	5.5	29.6	61 819	5.9	2.4	18 521	65.0
Warren County	553	31 584	8.7	25.6	12.4	15.0	42 422	8.5	3.4	12 087	74.1
Manassas city	26	35 135	33.7	29.7	5.3	28.1	60 409	6.3	3.7	11 757	69.8
Manassas Park city	6	10 290	33.0	30.9	4.6	20.3	60 794	5.2	2.2	3 254	78.7
Winchester city	24	23 585	20.8	21.8	14.3	23.7	34 335	13.2	4.6	10 001	45.7
Congressional District 11, Virginia	1 004	643 582	33.2	26.9	7.4	48.9	80 397	3.8	2.7	221 178	76.6
Fairfax County (part)	510	431 633	32.6	25.6	8.3	55.6	86 282	3.8	2.5	149 776	76.7
Prince William County (part)	478	190 451	34.6	30.8	4.6	32.7	70 120	3.7	3.0	63 367	77.4
Fairfax city	16	21 498	32.7	20.1	12.6	45.7	67 642	5.7	2.4	8 035	69.1
WASHINGTON	172 348	5 894 121	21.1	25.6	11.2	27.7	45 776	10.6	6.2	2 271 398	64.6
Congressional District 1, Washington	1 138	654 799	18.4	25.4	9.5	36.4	58 565	5.6	3.8	250 775	67.9
King County (part)	217	238 540	18.8	23.3	9.9	45.1	62 694	5.4	3.3	96 035	65.8
Kitsap County (part)	573	109 143	16.1	27.1	10.2	33.8	54 092	5.6	4.6	39 607	72.6
Snohomish County (part)	347	307 116	19.0	26.4	8.9	30.3	56 592	5.7	4.0	115 133	68.1
Congressional District 2, Washington	17 002	654 984	14.4	26.4	11.5	22.4	45 441	10.0	6.4	247 566	67.2
Island County	540	71 558	14.8	25.4	14.3	27.0	45 513	7.0	5.7	27 784	70.1
King County (part)	961	648	6.9	19.4	15.0	14.5	43 661	13.2	10.7	299	78.9
San Juan County	453	14 077	6.1	19.4	19.1	40.2	43 491	9.2	3.2	6 466	73.6
Skagit County	4 494	102 979	17.1	26.2	14.6	20.8	42 381	11.1	6.9	38 852	69.7
Snohomish County (part)	5 064	298 908	14.2	28.3	9.4	18.2	50 224	8.0	6.0	109 719	67.4
Whatcom County	5 490	166 814	13.6	24.1	11.6	27.2	40 005	14.2	7.4	64 446	63.4
Congressional District 3, Washington	19 465	654 992	12.4	27.1	11.4	21.4	44 426	10.5	6.5	249 432	67.9
Clark County	1 627	345 238	13.5	28.7	9.6	22.1	48 376	9.1	5.9	127 208	67.3
Cowlitz County	2 949	92 948	10.2	26.8	13.3	13.3	39 797	14.0	7.7	35 850	67.6
Lewis County	6 236	68 600	9.3	26.5	15.6	12.9	35 511	14.0	9.0	26 306	71.4
Pacific County	2 416	20 984	12.0	21.4	22.4	15.2	31 209	14.4	7.8	9 096	74.7
Skamania County (part)	4 067	7 034	8.3	26.4	10.9	16.7	38 912	13.1	10.3	2 676	72.5
Thurston County (part)	1 485	116 364	13.2	24.5	10.9	32.8	46 868	9.2	5.6	46 743	66.1
Wahkiakum County	684	3 824	6.7	23.4	18.6	14.8	39 444	8.1	8.1	1 553	79.7
Congressional District 4, Washington	49 343	654 851	32.3	30.4	11.2	18.7	37 764	16.2	9.7	228 819	66.0
Adams County (part)	339	11 170	67.2	36.9	8.3	9.9	31 406	20.8	9.7	3 235	67.7
Benton County	4 411	142 475	18.3	29.7	10.3	26.3	47 044	10.3	6.1	52 866	68.8
Chelan County	7 566	66 616	22.6	28.0	14.0	21.9	37 316	12.4	10.4	25 021	64.6
Douglas County	4 715	32 603	22.7	29.4	12.7	16.2	38 464	14.4	9.0	11 726	71.0
Franklin County	3 218	49 347	52.7	34.5	8.4	13.6	38 991	19.2	10.8	14 840	65.7
Grant County	6 944	74 698	34.4	32.1	11.6	13.7	35 276	17.4	11.7	25 204	66.7
Kittitas County	5 950	33 362	10.5	20.6	11.6	26.2	32 546	19.6	9.1	13 382	58.3
Klickitat County	4 849	19 161	15.1	26.8	13.9	16.4	34 267	17.0	10.4	7 473	68.8
Skamania County (part)	223	2 838	8.5	27.6	11.2	17.0	40 610	13.1	13.3	1 079	77.4
Yakima County	11 127	222 581	43.5	31.7	11.2	15.3	34 828	19.7	11.1	73 993	64.4

[1] Dry land or land partially or temporarily covered by water.
[2] Persons who do not identify themselves White, not of Hispanic origin.
[3] Persons 25 years old and over.

Table B. 109th Congressional Districts by Counties, 2000—*Continued*

(Number, percent.)

STATE Congressional district County	Land area,[1] (sq km)	Population Total	Percent minority[2]	Percent under 18 years old	Percent 65 years old and over	Percent with bachelor's degree or more[3]	Median income, 1999 (dollars)	Percent living in poverty	Percent unem- ployed	Households Total	Percent owner occupied
	1	2	3	4	5	6	7	8	9	10	11
Congressional District 5, Washington	59 217	654 935	12.4	25.4	13.0	23.8	35 720	14.4	8.5	253 204	66.0
Adams County (part)	4 646	5 258	12.0	28.6	16.1	15.9	39 271	12.5	6.6	1 994	69.7
Asotin County	1 646	20 551	5.4	25.4	16.2	18.0	33 524	15.4	6.4	8 364	67.1
Columbia County	2 250	4 064	9.8	24.0	18.8	17.5	33 500	12.6	9.0	1 687	69.6
Ferry County	5 708	7 260	24.2	26.9	12.7	13.5	30 388	19.0	18.8	2 823	73.0
Garfield County	1 840	2 397	2.7	26.0	20.7	17.0	33 398	14.2	4.9	987	73.8
Lincoln County	5 986	10 184	5.6	25.2	18.9	18.8	35 255	12.6	6.2	4 151	76.6
Okanogan County	13 644	39 564	28.6	27.7	14.1	15.9	29 726	21.3	12.0	15 027	68.6
Pend Oreille County	3 627	11 732	8.3	26.3	15.1	12.3	31 677	18.1	10.4	4 639	77.4
Spokane County	4 568	417 939	10.3	25.6	12.5	25.0	37 308	12.3	8.0	163 611	65.5
Stevens County	6 419	40 066	10.5	28.7	12.8	15.3	34 673	15.9	9.9	15 017	78.1
Walla Walla County	3 291	55 180	21.2	24.4	14.7	23.3	35 900	15.1	8.2	19 647	65.2
Whitman County	5 593	40 740	13.1	18.1	9.3	44.0	28 584	25.6	9.7	15 257	47.8
Congressional District 6, Washington	17 564	655 068	22.3	25.0	13.9	20.1	39 205	13.2	7.5	259 518	63.5
Clallam County	4 505	64 525	12.7	21.8	21.3	20.8	36 449	12.5	7.7	27 164	72.8
Grays Harbor County	4 965	67 194	13.3	25.7	15.4	12.7	34 160	16.1	8.3	26 808	69.1
Jefferson County	4 699	25 953	8.8	19.7	21.0	28.4	37 869	11.3	6.7	11 645	76.1
Kitsap County (part)	452	122 826	19.8	26.4	10.9	17.6	41 398	11.5	7.3	46 809	63.0
Mason County	2 489	49 405	13.7	23.4	16.4	15.6	39 586	12.2	8.3	18 912	79.0
Pierce County (part)	454	325 165	29.5	25.6	12.3	22.5	40 216	13.7	7.3	128 180	57.0
Congressional District 7, Washington	366	655 016	33.1	16.9	11.9	44.1	45 864	11.5	5.2	292 385	50.5
King County (part)	366	655 016	33.1	16.9	11.9	44.1	45 864	11.5	5.2	292 385	50.5
Congressional District 8, Washington	6 680	655 029	18.1	27.7	8.8	37.4	63 854	5.1	4.0	240 810	75.6
King County (part)	3 670	524 456	19.8	26.9	9.3	42.0	66 039	5.1	3.7	196 233	73.6
Pierce County (part)	3 010	130 573	11.0	30.9	6.6	17.4	57 263	5.3	5.4	44 577	84.1
Congressional District 9, Washington	1 574	654 447	26.8	26.3	9.9	22.3	46 495	9.2	5.6	248 889	59.6
King County (part)	292	318 374	30.8	25.6	9.9	23.0	46 422	9.7	5.1	125 964	55.4
Pierce County (part)	885	245 082	23.7	27.2	9.3	19.7	46 322	9.0	6.0	88 043	62.5
Thurston County (part)	398	90 991	21.1	26.2	11.8	26.0	47 085	8.4	6.5	34 882	67.3
WEST VIRGINIA	62 361	1 808 344	5.5	22.2	15.3	14.8	29 696	17.9	7.3	736 481	75.2
Congressional District 1, West Virginia	16 281	602 545	4.3	21.8	15.8	16.3	30 303	17.0	7.3	245 352	74.0
Barbour County	883	15 557	2.6	23.0	15.6	11.8	24 729	22.6	8.8	6 123	78.5
Brooke County	230	25 447	2.3	20.4	18.3	13.4	32 981	11.7	5.1	10 396	76.6
Doddridge County	830	7 403	2.9	25.4	14.9	10.2	26 744	19.8	8.9	2 845	81.3
Gilmer County	881	7 160	2.9	20.2	15.4	17.1	22 857	25.9	14.9	2 768	72.3
Grant County	1 236	11 299	1.1	22.7	15.3	11.4	28 916	16.3	5.7	4 591	80.8
Hancock County	215	32 667	4.3	20.9	18.4	11.5	33 759	11.1	5.6	13 678	77.0
Harrison County	1 078	68 652	4.3	23.1	16.5	16.3	30 562	17.2	7.6	27 867	74.8
Marion County	802	56 598	5.7	20.5	17.8	16.0	28 626	16.3	7.9	23 652	74.7
Marshall County	795	35 519	2.4	22.9	16.3	10.7	30 989	16.6	7.5	14 207	77.5
Mineral County	849	27 078	4.4	23.4	15.1	11.7	31 149	14.7	5.8	10 784	77.8
Monongalia County	935	81 866	8.3	18.1	10.7	32.4	28 625	22.8	7.3	33 446	61.0
Ohio County	275	47 427	6.1	21.3	18.7	23.1	30 836	15.8	8.7	19 733	68.6
Pleasants County	339	7 514	2.3	24.0	14.9	9.7	32 736	13.7	6.6	2 887	80.5
Preston County	1 679	29 334	1.9	23.7	14.9	10.8	27 927	18.3	6.8	11 544	83.1
Ritchie County	1 175	10 343	2.0	22.9	15.2	7.1	27 332	19.1	7.5	4 184	81.7
Taylor County	448	16 089	3.4	23.0	15.7	11.3	27 124	20.3	7.4	6 320	79.6
Tucker County	1 085	7 321	1.7	21.2	18.1	10.6	26 250	18.1	7.7	3 052	82.5
Tyler County	667	9 592	1.3	23.2	16.6	8.5	29 290	16.6	10.1	3 836	83.7
Wetzel County	930	17 693	1.3	23.7	16.2	10.4	30 935	19.8	10.1	7 164	78.5
Wood County	951	87 986	3.3	23.0	15.5	15.2	33 285	13.9	6.5	36 275	73.4
Congressional District 2, West Virginia	21 909	602 243	6.1	23.0	14.6	16.2	33 198	14.8	5.9	244 587	75.5
Berkeley County	832	75 905	8.1	25.7	11.1	15.1	38 763	11.5	4.3	29 569	74.1
Braxton County	1 330	14 702	1.6	22.6	15.9	9.2	24 412	22.0	8.7	5 771	78.1
Calhoun County	727	7 582	2.5	22.3	16.7	9.3	21 578	25.1	12.1	3 071	79.0
Clay County	887	10 330	2.2	25.5	13.7	7.3	22 120	27.5	11.5	4 020	79.1
Hampshire County	1 662	20 203	2.3	25.0	14.5	11.3	31 666	16.3	5.0	7 955	81.1
Hardy County	1 511	12 669	3.9	23.4	14.8	9.4	31 846	13.1	3.5	5 204	80.5
Jackson County	1 206	28 000	1.2	24.0	15.3	12.4	32 434	15.2	5.9	11 061	79.5
Jefferson County	543	42 190	9.9	23.6	11.2	21.6	44 374	10.3	4.6	16 165	75.9
Kanawha County	2 339	200 073	10.0	21.3	16.5	20.6	33 766	14.4	5.7	86 226	70.3
Lewis County	990	16 919	1.2	22.2	16.4	11.2	27 066	19.9	7.6	6 946	73.0
Mason County	1 118	25 957	2.0	22.6	15.3	8.8	27 134	19.9	10.1	10 587	80.9
Morgan County	593	14 943	2.6	22.4	16.5	11.2	35 016	10.4	4.1	6 145	83.3
Pendleton County	1 807	8 196	3.7	21.8	17.9	10.8	30 429	11.4	7.0	3 350	79.2
Putnam County	897	51 589	2.6	24.9	11.6	19.7	41 892	9.3	4.5	20 028	84.0
Randolph County	2 693	28 262	2.4	22.3	15.1	13.6	27 299	18.0	6.9	11 072	75.8

[1] Dry land or land partially or temporarily covered by water.
[2] Persons who do not identify themselves White, not of Hispanic origin.
[3] Persons 25 years old and over.

Table B. 109th Congressional Districts by Counties, 2000—*Continued*

(Number, percent.)

STATE Congressional district County	Land area,[1] (sq km)	Population Total	Percent minority[2]	Percent under 18 years old	Percent 65 years old and over	Percent with bachelor's degree or more[3]	Median income, 1999 (dollars)	Percent living in poverty	Percent unem- ployed	Households Total	Percent owner occupied
	1	2	3	4	5	6	7	8	9	10	11
Congressional District 2, West Virginia—*Continued*											
Roane County	1 252	15 446	2.4	23.3	14.8	9.0	24 511	22.6	12.6	6 161	79.6
Upshur County	919	23 404	2.5	22.6	14.8	13.8	26 973	20.0	7.0	8 972	76.7
Wirt County	603	5 873	1.2	25.2	12.9	9.9	30 748	19.6	6.2	2 284	83.1
Congressional District 3, West Virginia	24 170	603 556	6.0	21.8	15.6	12.0	25 630	21.9	9.0	246 542	76.0
Boone County	1 303	25 535	1.8	23.3	13.6	7.2	25 669	22.0	8.5	10 291	78.9
Cabell County	729	96 784	7.0	19.9	16.1	20.9	28 479	19.2	7.9	41 180	64.6
Fayette County	1 720	47 579	8.0	21.7	16.2	10.7	24 788	21.7	11.9	18 945	77.2
Greenbrier County	2 645	34 453	5.6	21.6	17.6	13.6	26 927	18.2	8.5	14 571	76.5
Lincoln County	1 133	22 108	1.1	23.4	13.1	5.9	22 662	27.9	10.1	8 664	79.0
Logan County	1 176	37 710	4.4	22.1	14.4	8.8	24 603	24.1	10.5	14 880	76.8
McDowell County	1 385	27 329	12.7	23.3	16.1	5.6	16 931	37.7	14.4	11 169	79.8
Mercer County	1 089	62 980	8.1	21.1	17.5	13.8	26 628	19.7	9.8	26 509	76.9
Mingo County	1 095	28 253	3.9	24.3	12.5	7.3	21 347	29.7	10.8	11 303	77.8
Monroe County	1 226	14 583	7.5	20.1	15.3	8.2	27 575	16.2	5.2	5 447	84.4
Nicholas County	1 680	26 562	1.4	23.3	15.0	9.8	26 974	19.2	7.7	10 722	82.9
Pocahontas County	2 435	9 131	2.2	21.0	17.2	11.8	26 401	17.1	6.3	3 835	80.3
Raleigh County	1 572	79 220	11.0	21.5	15.5	12.7	28 181	18.5	7.7	31 793	76.5
Summers County	935	12 999	3.5	20.4	19.9	10.1	21 147	24.4	12.5	5 530	79.1
Wayne County	1 310	42 903	1.4	23.3	14.9	11.9	27 352	19.6	6.6	17 239	78.1
Webster County	1 440	9 719	0.7	23.0	15.2	8.7	21 055	31.8	14.6	4 010	79.1
Wyoming County	1 297	25 708	1.4	22.4	14.0	7.1	23 932	25.1	9.5	10 454	83.3
WISCONSIN	140 663	5 363 675	12.6	25.5	13.1	22.4	43 791	8.7	4.7	2 084 544	68.4
Congressional District 1, Wisconsin	4 351	670 359	12.4	26.0	12.4	21.5	50 372	6.3	4.6	254 793	70.8
Kenosha County (part)	707	149 577	14.6	27.0	11.5	19.2	46 970	7.5	5.8	56 057	69.1
Milwaukee County (part)	217	115 659	8.7	22.1	14.7	26.4	53 042	3.5	2.7	46 806	65.7
Racine County (part)	863	188 831	20.1	27.0	12.4	20.3	48 059	8.4	6.0	70 819	70.6
Rock County (part)	752	79 212	5.8	26.2	12.6	18.6	47 470	6.1	4.5	30 956	70.2
Walworth County (part)	1 425	81 179	8.4	26.0	13.3	20.9	48 159	6.3	3.8	30 743	73.3
Waukesha County (part)	388	55 901	3.2	28.0	8.6	25.9	66 243	1.8	2.8	19 412	85.5
Congressional District 2, Wisconsin	9 095	670 670	10.9	23.4	10.9	32.1	46 979	8.7	4.3	267 211	62.3
Columbia County	2 004	52 468	4.0	25.1	14.4	16.7	45 064	5.2	3.5	20 439	74.9
Dane County	3 113	426 526	12.5	22.4	9.3	40.6	49 223	9.4	3.8	173 484	57.6
Green County	1 513	33 647	2.2	26.5	14.7	16.7	43 228	5.1	3.2	13 212	73.7
Jefferson County (part)	804	43 886	5.7	25.0	13.5	19.4	47 132	5.9	4.2	17 059	72.0
Rock County (part)	1 114	73 095	16.1	26.7	13.1	14.6	43 175	8.6	6.9	27 661	72.2
Sauk County (part)	534	28 468	4.6	24.8	14.8	20.0	40 585	7.2	4.5	11 577	69.0
Walworth County (part)	13	12 580	9.3	11.6	9.6	33.4	31 824	27.2	13.4	3 779	34.8
Congressional District 3, Wisconsin	35 134	670 473	3.8	25.3	13.5	19.5	40 006	9.8	4.5	254 520	72.1
Buffalo County	1 773	13 804	1.6	25.2	16.7	14.0	37 200	7.5	3.8	5 511	76.5
Clark County (part)	2 303	19 558	2.3	30.1	14.8	10.3	34 679	13.7	4.2	7 028	82.5
Crawford County	1 483	17 243	3.2	26.2	15.9	13.2	34 135	10.2	4.8	6 677	76.9
Dunn County	2 207	39 858	4.3	23.3	11.2	21.1	38 753	12.9	7.2	14 337	69.0
Eau Claire County	1 651	93 142	5.5	23.4	12.2	27.0	39 219	10.9	4.7	35 822	65.0
Grant County	2 973	49 597	2.3	23.6	15.3	17.2	36 268	11.2	4.7	18 465	72.4
Iowa County	1 975	22 780	1.5	27.1	13.4	18.5	42 518	7.3	3.9	8 764	75.8
Jackson County	2 557	19 100	11.1	24.1	15.0	11.3	37 015	9.6	8.3	7 070	75.0
Juneau County	1 988	24 316	4.0	25.5	16.8	10.0	35 335	10.1	6.1	9 696	76.9
La Crosse County	1 173	107 120	6.1	23.6	12.6	25.4	39 472	10.7	4.1	41 599	65.1
Lafayette County	1 641	16 137	1.0	27.2	15.8	13.3	37 220	9.1	2.6	6 211	77.4
Monroe County	2 333	40 899	4.4	28.0	13.9	13.2	37 170	12.0	4.8	15 399	73.7
Pepin County	602	7 213	1.4	26.4	16.9	13.3	37 609	9.1	4.4	2 759	79.6
Pierce County	1 493	36 804	2.6	24.4	9.6	24.6	49 551	7.7	4.7	13 015	73.1
Richland County	1 518	17 924	2.4	25.1	17.2	14.1	33 998	10.1	4.8	7 118	74.5
St. Croix County	1 870	63 155	2.7	27.9	9.8	26.3	54 930	4.0	2.6	23 410	76.4
Sauk County (part)	1 635	26 757	2.2	27.5	14.2	14.9	43 990	7.3	3.8	10 067	78.3
Trempealeau County	1 901	27 010	1.7	25.3	16.4	13.3	37 889	8.3	3.5	10 747	74.3
Vernon County	2 059	28 056	1.3	27.4	17.1	14.0	33 178	14.2	4.2	10 825	79.1
Congressional District 4, Wisconsin	290	670 373	49.3	28.0	11.4	17.8	33 121	19.8	8.8	264 190	46.6
Milwaukee County (part)	290	670 373	49.3	28.0	11.4	17.8	33 121	19.8	8.8	264 190	46.6
Congressional District 5, Wisconsin	3 298	670 392	6.0	25.3	13.7	35.0	58 594	3.4	2.7	261 626	73.4
Jefferson County (part)	411	11 584	4.3	24.7	11.3	13.4	49 004	4.2	3.4	4 377	78.8
Milwaukee County (part)	119	154 132	9.2	22.3	18.2	43.0	51 596	4.5	2.6	66 733	67.2
Ozaukee County (part)	601	82 317	3.9	26.6	12.6	38.6	62 745	2.6	2.2	30 857	76.3
Washington County	1 116	117 493	3.2	26.6	11.2	21.9	57 033	3.6	2.7	43 842	76.0
Waukesha County (part)	1 051	304 866	6.2	25.9	12.6	35.6	62 161	2.9	2.8	115 817	75.0

[1]Dry land or land partially or temporarily covered by water.
[2]Persons who do not identify themselves White, not of Hispanic origin.
[3]Persons 25 years old and over.

Table B. 109th Congressional Districts by Counties, 2000—*Continued*

(Number, percent.)

STATE Congressional district County	Land area,[1] (sq km)	Population Total	Population Percent minority[2]	Population Percent under 18 years old	Population Percent 65 years old and over	Percent with bachelor's degree or more[3]	Median income, 1999 (dollars)	Percent living in poverty	Percent unem- ployed	Households Total	Households Percent owner occupied
	1	2	3	4	5	6	7	8	9	10	11
Congressional District 6, Wisconsin	14 611	670 609	5.8	24.8	14.3	17.1	44 242	6.1	3.7	258 274	73.4
Adams County	1 678	18 643	3.4	20.7	21.0	10.0	33 408	10.4	7.8	7 900	85.4
Calumet County (part)	819	29 723	1.9	27.5	12.4	17.4	51 387	3.4	2.2	11 043	82.4
Dodge County	2 285	85 897	6.1	24.8	14.0	13.2	45 190	5.3	3.3	31 417	73.5
Fond du Lac County (part)	1 872	97 296	4.9	25.2	14.3	16.9	45 578	5.8	4.3	36 931	73.0
Green Lake County	918	19 105	3.1	24.0	18.8	14.5	39 462	7.0	5.1	7 703	77.2
Jefferson County (part)	228	18 551	6.3	26.1	11.3	15.0	45 542	6.1	4.4	6 769	66.4
Manitowoc County (part)	1 532	82 887	4.9	25.4	15.6	15.5	43 286	6.1	3.6	32 721	76.0
Marquette County	1 180	15 832	7.6	21.1	18.1	10.1	35 746	7.7	5.4	5 986	82.3
Outagamie County (part)	11	10 112	2.1	29.2	11.5	21.9	53 095	2.6	1.6	3 766	76.8
Sheboygan County (part)	1 330	112 646	8.9	25.5	14.0	17.9	46 237	5.2	2.6	43 545	71.4
Waushara County	1 621	23 154	4.8	23.6	19.1	11.7	37 000	9.1	6.6	9 336	83.4
Winnebago County (part)	1 136	156 763	6.1	23.8	12.5	22.8	44 445	6.7	3.7	61 157	68.0
Congressional District 7, Wisconsin	48 657	670 432	4.8	25.3	15.2	16.6	39 026	8.6	5.3	263 682	76.1
Ashland County (part)	2 703	16 866	13.0	25.5	16.0	16.5	31 628	11.9	8.1	6 718	70.6
Barron County	2 235	44 963	2.8	25.3	16.4	14.9	37 275	8.8	4.7	17 851	75.9
Bayfield County (part)	3 823	15 013	11.4	24.7	16.4	21.6	33 390	12.5	8.5	6 207	82.6
Burnett County	2 128	15 674	6.9	22.1	20.3	14.0	34 218	8.8	5.8	6 613	84.5
Chippewa County	2 617	55 195	2.4	26.5	14.6	14.7	39 596	8.2	4.7	21 356	75.6
Clark County (part)	846	13 999	2.9	29.7	17.8	10.4	34 440	11.2	4.1	5 019	79.5
Douglas County (part)	3 391	43 287	4.9	23.6	14.5	18.3	35 226	11.0	7.1	17 808	71.5
Iron County (part)	1 961	6 861	1.7	19.4	23.2	13.2	29 580	11.1	8.9	3 083	80.7
Langlade County (part)	1 216	15 852	3.0	23.9	19.6	12.3	32 699	10.5	5.7	6 515	76.2
Lincoln County	2 288	29 641	3.0	25.5	16.3	13.6	39 120	6.9	5.3	11 721	78.3
Marathon County	4 001	125 834	6.2	26.7	13.0	18.3	45 165	6.6	3.8	47 702	75.7
Oneida County (part)	1 445	20 110	2.4	23.5	16.6	18.5	36 067	8.3	7.0	8 228	75.5
Polk County	2 376	41 319	2.9	26.2	15.2	15.6	41 183	7.1	3.9	16 254	80.1
Portage County	2 088	67 182	5.0	24.0	10.9	23.4	43 487	9.5	5.9	25 040	70.9
Price County	3 244	15 822	1.7	23.9	19.0	13.0	35 249	8.9	5.7	6 564	80.8
Rusk County	2 365	15 347	1.9	24.7	18.5	11.2	31 344	11.8	6.3	6 095	78.6
Sawyer County	3 254	16 196	18.6	24.1	18.0	16.5	32 287	12.7	6.6	6 640	76.9
Taylor County	2 525	19 680	2.0	27.1	15.2	11.0	38 502	9.8	5.2	7 529	80.4
Washburn County	2 097	16 036	3.4	23.8	18.6	15.2	33 716	9.9	6.1	6 604	80.9
Wood County	2 053	75 555	4.2	25.7	15.4	16.9	41 595	6.5	5.0	30 135	74.3
Congressional District 8, Wisconsin	25 228	670 367	7.7	25.8	13.5	19.1	43 274	6.8	4.0	260 248	73.4
Brown County (part)	1 369	226 778	10.3	26.0	10.6	22.5	46 447	6.9	3.8	87 295	65.4
Calumet County (part)	9	10 908	8.8	31.7	6.4	30.7	55 879	3.8	2.2	3 867	74.5
Door County (part)	1 250	27 961	2.7	22.0	18.7	21.4	38 813	6.4	5.4	11 828	79.3
Florence County	1 264	5 088	0.8	23.0	17.6	12.4	34 750	9.1	5.7	2 133	85.6
Forest County	2 626	10 024	14.5	25.4	19.3	10.0	32 023	13.1	7.7	4 043	78.9
Kewaunee County (part)	887	20 187	1.9	25.7	15.3	11.4	43 824	5.8	2.6	7 623	81.9
Langlade County (part)	1 044	4 888	2.2	25.4	16.8	9.8	34 455	8.7	6.0	1 937	87.0
Marinette County (part)	3 631	43 384	2.0	23.6	17.6	12.9	35 256	8.3	5.4	17 585	79.5
Menominee County	927	4 562	87.9	39.0	9.2	12.9	29 440	28.8	16.5	1 345	74.5
Oconto County (part)	2 585	35 634	2.5	25.8	15.1	10.6	41 201	7.1	3.9	13 979	82.9
Oneida County (part)	1 468	16 666	2.9	21.1	21.3	21.7	38 721	6.3	4.9	7 105	84.6
Outagamie County (part)	1 647	150 859	7.4	27.5	10.9	22.6	49 349	4.8	3.3	56 764	72.1
Shawano County	2 312	40 664	8.9	25.7	16.8	12.6	38 069	7.9	3.8	15 815	78.2
Vilas County	2 263	21 033	10.6	20.7	23.0	17.6	33 759	8.0	6.1	9 066	82.0
Waupaca County	1 945	51 731	2.6	25.7	16.6	14.8	40 910	6.8	3.6	19 863	76.9
WYOMING	251 489	493 782	11.2	25.9	11.6	21.9	37 892	11.4	5.3	193 608	70.0
Congressional District (At Large), Wyoming	251 489	493 782	11.2	25.9	11.6	21.9	37 892	11.4	5.3	193 608	70.0
Albany County	11 066	32 014	12.3	18.3	8.2	44.1	28 790	21.0	5.4	13 269	51.3
Big Horn County	8 125	11 461	8.5	28.7	16.8	15.9	32 682	14.1	6.3	4 312	74.4
Campbell County	12 424	33 698	6.5	31.1	5.0	15.7	49 536	7.6	4.4	12 207	73.6
Carbon County	20 451	15 639	18.0	24.0	12.0	17.2	36 060	12.9	5.3	6 129	70.9
Converse County	11 020	12 052	7.9	28.3	11.3	14.7	39 603	11.6	4.6	4 694	74.1
Crook County	7 404	5 887	1.8	27.0	14.7	17.5	35 601	9.1	3.3	2 308	80.1
Fremont County	23 782	35 804	25.4	27.4	13.1	19.7	32 503	17.6	8.9	13 545	72.8
Goshen County	5 764	12 538	10.4	22.8	17.3	18.6	32 228	13.9	6.4	5 061	70.7
Hot Springs County	5 190	4 882	5.7	22.1	20.0	17.9	29 888	10.6	1.8	2 108	68.6
Johnson County	10 791	7 075	3.7	24.3	18.1	22.2	34 012	10.1	6.1	2 959	73.7
Laramie County	6 957	81 607	16.9	25.3	11.4	23.4	39 607	9.1	4.9	31 927	69.1
Lincoln County	10 539	14 573	4.2	30.9	12.3	17.2	40 794	9.0	3.8	5 266	81.4
Natrona County	13 830	66 533	8.3	25.9	12.6	20.0	36 619	11.8	5.2	26 819	69.9
Niobrara County	6 801	2 407	2.6	22.4	18.9	15.3	29 701	13.4	3.4	1 011	72.9
Park County	17 981	25 786	5.5	24.4	14.5	23.7	35 829	12.7	5.0	10 312	71.3

[1]Dry land or land partially or temporarily covered by water.
[2]Persons who do not identify themselves White, not of Hispanic origin.
[3]Persons 25 years old and over.

Table B. 109th Congressional Districts by Counties, 2000—*Continued*

(Number, percent.)

STATE Congressional district County	Land area,[1] (sq km)	Population				Percent with bachelor's degree or more[3]	Median income, 1999 (dollars)	Percent living in poverty	Percent unem-ployed	Households	
		Total	Percent minority[2]	Percent under 18 years old	Percent 65 years old and over					Total	Percent owner occupied
	1	2	3	4	5	6	7	8	9	10	11
Congressional District (At Large), **Wyoming**—*Continued*											
Platte County	5 400	8 807	7.2	25.2	16.6	15.2	33 866	11.7	4.3	3 625	75.8
Sheridan County	6 535	26 560	5.4	24.2	15.5	22.4	34 538	10.7	4.5	11 167	68.9
Sublette County	12 646	5 920	3.9	25.9	12.0	21.6	39 044	9.7	4.8	2 371	73.5
Sweetwater County	27 001	37 613	13.4	28.6	8.0	17.0	46 537	7.8	5.7	14 105	75.1
Teton County	10 380	18 251	8.6	19.3	6.9	45.8	54 614	6.0	2.9	7 688	54.8
Uinta County	5 391	19 742	8.2	33.2	7.0	15.0	44 544	9.9	6.4	6 823	75.2
Washakie County	5 802	8 289	12.8	27.2	15.7	18.7	34 943	14.1	8.3	3 278	73.1
Weston County	6 210	6 644	5.2	24.0	15.6	14.5	32 348	9.9	5.6	2 624	78.0
NONVOTING DELEGATES											
AMERICAN SAMOA	200	57 291	98.8	44.6	3.3	7.4	18 219	61.0	21.4	9 349	77.2
Delegate District (At Large), American **Samoa**	200	57 291	98.8	44.6	3.3	7.4	18 219	61.0	21.4	9 349	77.2
Eastern District	67	23 441	99.2	43.9	3.5	6.4	18 271	58.6	21.1	3 845	77.6
Manu'a District	57	1 378	99.1	46.5	8.6	3.9	14 338	65.2	19.5	273	94.1
Rose Island	0	0	X	X	X	X	X	X	X	0	X
Swains Island	2	37	100.0	43.2	2.7	6.3	18 125	52.8	31.8	7	85.7
Western District	75	32 435	98.5	45.0	3.0	8.3	18 445	62.6	21.7	5 224	76.0
GUAM	544	154 805	93.1	35.4	5.2	20.0	39 317	23.0	7.0	38 769	48.4
Delegate District (At Large), Guam	544	154 805	93.1	35.4	5.2	20.0	39 317	23.0	7.0	38 769	48.4
COMMONWEALTH OF THE NORTHERN **MARIANA ISLANDS**	464	69 221	98.2	25.6	1.5	15.5	22 898	46.0	3.2	14 055	32.4
Resident Representative District, Northern Mariana **Islands**	464	69 221	98.2	25.6	1.5	15.5	22 898	46.0	3.2	14 055	32.4
Northern Islands Municipality	155	6	100.0	16.7	0.0	0.0	26 250	83.3	0.0	1	0.0
Rota Municipality	85	3 283	98.4	35.6	2.7	15.7	28 708	34.2	6.6	757	51.8
Saipan Municipality	115	62 392	98.2	24.8	1.4	15.2	22 555	46.9	2.9	12 507	31.0
Tinian Municipality	108	3 540	97.9	30.8	1.8	20.8	23 542	41.2	6.3	790	35.3
PUERTO RICO	8 870	3 808 610	99.0	28.6	11.1	18.3	14 412	48.2	19.2	1 261 325	72.9
Delegate District (At Large), Puerto Rico	8 870	3 808 610	99.0	28.6	11.1	18.3	14 412	48.2	19.2	1 261 325	72.9
Adjuntas Municipio	173	19 143	99.6	32.1	10.4	10.9	9 888	65.4	30.9	5 895	71.8
Aguada Municipio	80	42 042	99.3	29.7	8.7	12.8	11 384	59.3	22.1	13 520	80.6
Aguadilla Municipio	95	64 685	98.5	27.4	11.7	15.7	11 476	55.0	25.3	22 087	66.5
Aguas Buenas Municipio	79	29 032	99.5	29.4	10.0	12.4	12 957	51.7	15.5	9 240	73.5
Aibonito Municipio	81	26 493	99.5	30.5	10.8	14.7	12 725	51.8	23.2	8 408	75.1
Añasco Municipio	102	28 348	99.2	28.3	10.0	12.3	12 620	51.6	23.7	9 398	80.5
Arecibo Municipio	326	100 131	99.3	26.4	12.6	15.7	12 496	50.9	20.7	34 245	75.1
Arroyo Municipio	39	19 117	98.8	31.5	10.0	13.4	11 484	55.1	33.4	6 166	75.1
Barceloneta Municipio	48	22 322	99.4	29.5	11.1	9.1	11 706	56.0	23.8	7 508	79.4
Barranquitas Municipio	89	28 909	99.6	35.3	8.3	14.4	11 322	61.3	25.1	8 663	71.2
Bayamón Municipio	115	224 044	99.0	26.7	12.3	21.7	19 861	34.9	13.1	73 693	73.3
Cabo Rojo Municipio	182	46 911	99.1	25.4	13.8	17.3	13 580	47.1	18.5	17 114	79.3
Caguas Municipio	152	140 502	99.2	27.7	11.4	21.1	16 522	41.7	16.2	46 937	73.4
Camuy Municipio	120	35 244	99.1	29.4	10.4	14.0	13 168	51.9	20.1	11 457	78.9
Canóvanas Municipio	85	43 335	99.1	31.4	8.5	10.9	13 034	54.2	21.1	13 446	82.8
Carolina Municipio	117	186 076	98.7	26.3	11.3	21.5	21 236	33.7	12.6	63 546	73.0
Cataño Municipio	12	30 071	99.4	31.9	10.0	18.2	12 852	50.0	20.9	9 638	64.9
Cayey Municipio	134	47 370	99.3	28.2	11.4	15.0	13 452	50.3	17.9	15 634	69.7
Ceiba Municipio	75	18 004	87.5	28.8	8.7	16.3	16 440	38.6	18.4	5 750	63.8
Ciales Municipio	173	19 811	99.3	33.3	10.0	9.5	10 981	63.1	23.7	6 047	75.3
Cidra Municipio	93	42 753	99.3	30.5	8.6	15.9	15 557	46.9	18.6	13 204	76.0
Coamo Municipio	202	37 597	99.1	32.1	10.5	14.9	12 064	56.1	26.4	11 749	76.9
Comerío Municipio	74	20 002	99.5	31.4	9.2	11.0	10 892	61.6	22.2	6 311	76.0
Corozal Municipio	110	36 867	99.4	31.7	9.2	11.8	11 786	58.2	16.3	11 264	77.7
Culebra Municipio	30	1 868	92.0	25.5	10.9	11.7	17 008	37.0	16.8	699	75.7
Dorado Municipio	60	34 017	98.4	28.9	9.0	19.1	16 460	41.4	14.8	10 887	81.9
Fajardo Municipio	77	40 712	98.2	28.7	12.5	16.2	15 410	42.1	18.6	14 176	76.3
Florida Municipio	39	12 367	99.5	30.8	9.1	10.0	11 123	57.0	26.6	3 962	78.0
Guánica Municipio	96	21 888	99.7	29.8	11.5	9.2	9 721	63.7	35.7	7 291	75.6
Guayama Municipio	169	44 301	99.5	30.4	9.7	14.9	12 112	52.8	27.5	14 225	72.8

[1]Dry land or land partially or temporarily covered by water.
[2]Persons who do not identify themselves White, not of Hispanic origin.
[3]Persons 25 years old and over.
X = Not applicable.

Table B. 109th Congressional Districts by Counties, 2000—*Continued*

(Number, percent.)

STATE Congressional district County	Land area,[1] (sq km)	Population				Percent with bachelor's degree or more[3]	Median income, 1999 (dollars)	Percent living in poverty	Percent unemployed	Households	
		Total	Percent minority[2]	Percent under 18 years old	Percent 65 years old and over					Total	Percent owner occupied
1		2	3	4	5	6	7	8	9	10	11

Delegate District (At Large), Puerto Rico—*Continued*											
Guayanilla Municipio	110	23 072	99.3	29.9	10.9	13.2	11 361	57.0	27.3	7 209	80.8
Guaynabo Municipio	70	100 053	97.9	26.2	12.5	35.9	26 211	31.1	9.4	34 068	77.0
Gurabo Municipio	72	36 743	99.1	29.5	8.5	21.2	16 451	43.1	14.5	11 741	81.4
Hatillo Municipio	108	38 925	98.9	29.2	10.4	14.9	12 378	55.8	22.5	12 685	77.9
Hormigueros Municipio	29	16 614	98.8	23.5	14.6	18.1	16 745	38.4	19.4	5 820	80.3
Humacao Municipio	116	59 035	98.8	28.4	10.7	15.0	14 345	47.2	18.6	19 293	76.0
Isabela Municipio	143	44 444	99.0	27.6	12.0	13.3	11 685	55.5	24.3	14 970	76.3
Jayuya Municipio	115	17 318	99.7	34.2	8.7	10.9	11 220	62.8	31.1	5 083	70.5
Juana Díaz Municipio	156	50 531	99.5	32.6	8.9	15.3	12 892	56.7	27.4	14 954	80.4
Juncos Municipio	69	36 452	99.3	29.5	9.8	13.2	13 072	54.1	22.5	11 933	76.7
Patillas Municipio	156	26 261	99.5	27.3	12.6	13.1	11 384	56.5	26.4	9 007	78.8
Lares Municipio	159	34 415	99.5	30.5	11.4	12.7	9 685	65.5	20.2	10 974	73.3
Las Marías Municipio	120	11 061	99.3	30.0	10.0	9.6	9 472	65.5	30.2	3 564	71.4
Las Piedras Municipio	88	34 485	99.1	29.1	9.2	13.1	14 622	47.3	22.5	11 145	78.1
Loíza Municipio	50	32 537	99.8	35.2	7.0	9.1	11 200	59.7	26.8	9 597	84.2
Luquillo Municipio	67	19 817	98.6	29.2	10.9	17.6	13 631	51.7	23.1	6 573	78.2
Manatí Municipio	117	45 409	99.4	29.7	10.8	14.9	12 796	51.7	24.0	15 266	73.6
Maricao Municipio	95	6 449	99.5	32.3	9.4	6.1	9 243	68.0	28.9	2 013	72.7
Maunabo Municipio	54	12 741	99.8	29.8	11.0	11.5	11 638	59.1	26.1	3 994	77.7
Mayagüez Municipio	201	98 434	99.3	24.0	13.5	18.6	11 775	52.2	23.0	34 742	60.2
Moca Municipio	130	39 697	99.2	30.3	8.8	12.6	11 271	58.7	23.9	12 712	78.0
Morovis Municipio	101	29 965	99.3	34.7	8.1	11.8	12 090	59.5	23.5	8 801	79.2
Naguabo Municipio	134	23 753	98.8	29.0	11.1	12.3	11 461	56.0	21.5	7 872	75.7
Naranjito Municipio	70	29 709	99.2	31.6	9.1	12.0	12 484	55.5	17.4	8 932	80.6
Orocovis Municipio	164	23 844	99.1	34.3	9.3	11.1	9 945	68.0	26.0	7 083	78.0
Patillas Municipio	121	20 152	99.0	30.2	11.3	12.3	12 021	54.6	28.5	6 576	78.5
Peñuelas Municipio	115	26 719	99.3	34.4	8.2	12.8	12 194	59.7	26.3	7 698	81.2
Ponce Municipio	297	186 475	99.1	29.3	11.6	19.8	12 998	52.3	25.1	59 607	69.7
Quebradillas Municipio	59	25 450	99.1	29.9	9.9	11.2	12 210	55.4	22.8	8 280	74.1
Rincón Municipio	37	14 767	98.3	26.1	12.3	11.8	11 460	56.3	22.0	5 147	78.6
Río Grande Municipio	157	52 362	99.2	29.8	9.2	13.6	15 006	46.6	20.4	16 430	82.3
Sabana Grande Municipio	93	25 935	99.4	28.6	11.5	13.3	12 485	52.0	22.3	8 865	79.0
Salinas Municipio	179	31 113	99.4	31.8	10.0	12.8	11 391	58.2	27.8	10 184	78.1
San Germán Municipio	141	37 105	99.3	26.1	13.0	18.3	13 089	49.6	23.5	12 809	74.6
San Juan Municipio	124	434 374	98.6	24.7	14.8	28.9	17 367	40.8	13.7	163 462	55.6
San Lorenzo Municipio	138	40 997	99.4	29.8	10.0	11.7	12 226	54.1	22.0	13 138	78.8
San Sebastián Municipio	183	44 204	99.6	27.9	12.6	12.7	10 962	57.5	25.1	14 970	75.4
Santa Isabel Municipio	88	21 665	99.6	33.3	9.3	13.0	11 895	57.4	23.9	6 781	76.7
Toa Alta Municipio	71	63 929	99.4	32.6	6.7	20.0	20 134	39.0	12.3	19 420	84.4
Toa Baja Municipio	60	94 085	98.9	29.1	9.2	16.6	18 331	39.6	15.1	30 453	79.0
Trujillo Alto Municipio	54	75 728	99.0	29.2	9.0	27.1	21 980	34.0	11.5	24 160	77.5
Utuado Municipio	294	35 336	99.4	30.7	11.8	11.9	9 948	63.6	30.0	11 207	71.5
Vega Alta Municipio	72	37 910	99.4	30.4	9.5	11.9	13 495	51.3	18.5	11 894	80.2
Vega Baja Municipio	119	61 929	99.1	30.4	10.1	14.4	13 933	50.6	20.8	19 758	80.1
Vieques Municipio	132	9 106	98.2	29.8	14.1	10.1	9 331	64.6	28.2	3 319	80.1
Villalba Municipio	92	27 913	99.5	34.5	8.3	12.8	11 728	62.5	28.9	7 722	80.9
Yabucoa Municipio	143	39 246	99.3	29.9	9.4	12.1	12 292	54.5	23.8	12 242	82.1
Yauco Municipio	176	46 384	99.3	29.8	10.8	15.8	11 924	56.6	25.2	15 012	76.9
VIRGIN ISLANDS	346	108 612	88.7	31.6	8.1	16.8	24 704	32.5	5.6	40 648	46.0
Delegate District (At Large), Virgin Islands	346	108 612	88.7	31.6	8.1	16.8	24 704	32.5	5.6	40 648	46.0
St. Croix Island	215	53 234	91.2	34.1	8.2	15.1	21 401	38.7	6.9	19 455	50.4
St. John Island	51	4 197	62.9	24.9	7.0	26.8	32 482	18.5	2.1	1 735	47.7
St. Thomas Island	81	51 181	88.3	29.5	8.2	17.5	26 893	27.2	4.6	19 458	41.4

[1]Dry land or land partially or temporarily covered by water.
[2]Persons who do not identify themselves White, not of Hispanic origin.
[3]Persons 25 years old and over.

SOURCE NOTES AND DEFINITIONS

PART I: MAPS

The U.S. Census Bureau produced maps that reflect the boundaries and geographic relationships for the 108th Congressional Districts. For the most part, these maps also reflect the boundaries of the 109th Congressional Districts. In this volume, the state-level Census Bureau maps of the 108th/109th Congressional Districts have been reprinted for each state, except for the six states with At Large representatives. For these states, the maps are from the U.S. Geological Survey, Department of the Interior's series *National Atlas of the United States*, and have been reproduced at the best possible quality. The *National Atlas* maps are also used for the individual congressional district maps, as well as the county maps for Maine, Pennsylvania, and Texas. The U.S. map of all congressional districts, located in the Introduction, is a product of the U.S. Census Bureau, as is the Northern Mariana Islands map.

The "congressional districts by counties" relationship tables are from the U.S. Census Bureau. The counties are listed alphabetically followed by the congressional district(s) in which they fall. As congressional district boundaries often cross county lines, a county may be split by more than one district, as in the case of Los Angeles County, California, which includes 18 different congressional districts. The Census Bureau also has tables that show the relationships between the congressional districts and counties or county equivalents, incorporated places and census designated places (including consolidated cities), county subdivisions (for 18 states), American Indian areas, census tracts, ZIP Code Tabulation Areas (ZCTAs), urban/rural population and land area, and school districts.

There are no Census Bureau relationship tables for states with At Large representatives, the District of Columbia, or the territories. However, lists of counties, where applicable, for these areas have been included.

For more information on the U.S. Census Bureau maps:
Click on *Maps* under *Geography*.
Click on *Map Products*.
Click on *108th Congressional District Maps and Related Information*.
Listed are the individual, state-based, and national 108th Congressional Districts maps.

For more information on the *National Atlas* maps:
Click on *Printable Maps*.
Click on *Learn More* under the heading *Congressional Districts for the 109th Congress–Printable Maps*.

For more information on the congressional districts by counties relationship tables:

<www.census.gov/geo/www/cd108th/tables108.html>
Click on a state name to find the table included in this volume, as well as seven other relationship tables listed below:
Congressional districts and counties
Congressional districts by counties
Congressional districts by American Indian areas
Congressional districts by places
Congressional districts by census tracts
Congressional districts by ZIP Code Tabulation Areas (ZCTAs)
Congressional districts by school districts
Congressional districts by urban/rural population and land area

PART II: TABLES

The data in this volume are from the 2000 Census of Population and Housing and the 2002 Census of Agriculture. Most of the information can be found on the Internet. The 2000 census data have been tabulated for the congressional districts of the 109th Congress, including changes made in Maine, Pennsylvania, and Texas. The 2002 Census of Agriculture data were tabulated for the congressional districts of the 108th Congress, so they do not reflect the current boundaries in Maine, Pennsylvania, and Texas.

The definitions in this section refer to the United States and the District of Columbia. Some slight variations may apply to data from American Samoa, Guam, the Northern Mariana Islands, Puerto Rico, and the Virgin Islands.

Table A presents 80 items for the United States as a whole; each state, the District of Columbia, and each territory; and each congressional district and delegate district. Table B presents 11 items for the United States as a whole; each state, the District of Columbia, and each territory; and each congressional district and delegate district with its component counties, county equivalents, independent cities, or parts thereof.

2000 Census of Population and Housing

As established by Article 1, Section 2 of the Constitution, the purpose of the decennial census is to enumerate the population for the establishment of 435 congressional districts of approximately equal populations. Each state is assigned at least one congressional seat, and the remaining 385 seats are divided proportionally among the states. Every person and housing unit in the United States is supposed to answer the 100-percent questionnaire with questions on household relationship, sex, age, Hispanic or Latino origin, race, and whether the home is owned or rented. In addition, a longer questionnaire was answered by a sample of the population, with very detailed questions about social and economic characteristics and the physical and financial characteristics of the housing unit.

Because most of the data in this volume are from the sample questionnaire, it is important to remember that small differences between areas may be the result of sampling error. The data are estimates of the actual figures that would have been obtained from a complete count.

Estimates derived from a sample are expected to be different from the 100-percent figures because they are subject to sampling and nonsampling errors. Sampling error in data arises from the selection of people and housing units included in the sample. Nonsampling error affects both sample and 100-percent data and is introduced as a result of errors that may occur during the data collection and processing phases of the census.

For complete details about sampling error and all other technical information, see the Technical Documentation for the 109th Congressional District Sample file at <www.census.gov/prod/cen2000/doc/cd109s.pdf>.

To access the data through American FactFinder:
Click on *American FactFinder*.
Click on *Data Sets*.
Decennial Census Tab
Select *109th Congressional District Summary File (Sample)*
or *109th Congressional District Summary File (100-percent)*.

LAND AREA
Table A, Item 2
Table B, Item 1
On *American FactFinder*:
Geographic Identifiers

Land area measurements are shown to the nearest square kilometer. Land area includes dry land and land temporarily or partially covered by water, such as marshland, swamps, and river floodplains. In Table B, there are some county parts within congressional districts that have no land area and no population. These are unpopulated areas so small that they round to zero square kilometers, or they are water areas where the congressional district boundary is on a river or inlet.

POPULATION AND POPULATION DENSITY
Table A, Items 3 and 4
Table B, Item 2
On *American FactFinder*:
P1 (Sample)

The total population in this volume is the estimate from the sample of the 2000 census, for consistency with other items.

Because the 100-percent population number was used for apportionment, all congressional districts within each state usually have exactly the same official population, which can be found on the 100-percent file. The estimate from the sample includes slight variations among congressional districts as a result of the weighting process.

POPULATION BY RACE AND HISPANIC ORIGIN
Table A, Items 5 through 12
Table B, Item 3
On *American FactFinder*:
P9 (100-Percent) for "alone or in combination" numbers
P4 (Sample) for Hispanic origin by race
P7 (Sample) for "two or more races"

The data on race, which was asked of all people, were derived from answers to long-form (sample) questionnaire Item 6 and short-form (100-percent) questionnaire Item 8. The concept of race, as used by the Census Bureau, reflects self-identification by people according to the race or races with which they most closely identify. These categories are socio-political constructs and should not be interpreted as being scientific or anthropological in nature. Furthermore, the race categories include both racial and national-origin groups.

The racial classifications used by the Census Bureau adhere to the October 30, 1997, Federal Register Notice entitled *Revisions to the Standards for the Classification of Federal Data on Race and Ethnicity*, issued by the Office of Management and Budget (OMB). These standards govern the categories used to collect and present federal data on race and ethnicity. The OMB requires five minimum categories (White, Black or African American, American Indian or Alaska Native, Asian, and Native Hawaiian or Other Pacific Islander) for race. The race categories are described below with a sixth category, "Some other race," added with OMB approval. In addition to the five race groups, the OMB also states that respondents should be offered the option of selecting one or more races.

If an individual did not provide a race response, the race or races of the householder or other household members were assigned using specific rules of precedence of household relationship. For example, if race was missing for a natural-born child in the household, then either the race or races of the householder, another natural-born child, or the spouse of the householder were assigned. If race was not reported for anyone in the household, the race or races of a householder in a previously processed household were assigned.

White. A person having origins in any of the original peoples of Europe, the Middle East, or North Africa. It includes people who indicate their race as "White" or report entries such as Irish, German, Italian, Lebanese, Near Easterner, Arab, or Polish.

Black or African American. A person having origins in any of the Black racial groups of Africa. It includes people who indicate their race as "Black, African Am., or Negro," or provide written entries such as African American, Afro-American, Kenyan, Nigerian, or Haitian.

American Indian or Alaska Native. A person having origins in any of the original peoples of North and South America (including Central America) and who maintain tribal affiliation or community attachment. It includes people who classified themselves as described below:

American Indian. This category includes people who indicated their race as "American Indian," entered the name of an Indian tribe, or reported such entries as Canadian Indian, French American Indian, or Spanish American Indian.

Alaska Native. This category includes written responses of Eskimos, Aleuts, and Alaska Indians as well as entries such as Arctic Slope, Inupiat, Yupik, Alutiiq, Egegik, and Pribilovian. The Alaska tribes are the Alaskan Athabascan, Tlingit, and Haida. The information for the 2000 census is based on the American Indian Tribal Classification List for the 1990 census, which was expanded to list the individual Alaska Native Villages when provided as a written response for race.

Asian. A person having origins in any of the original peoples of the Far East, Southeast Asia, or the Indian subcontinent including, for example, Cambodia, China, India, Japan, Korea, Malaysia, Pakistan, the Philippine Islands, Thailand, and Vietnam. It includes "Asian Indian," "Chinese," "Filipino," "Korean," "Japanese," "Vietnamese," and "Other Asian."

Native Hawaiian or Other Pacific Islander. A person having origins in any of the original peoples of Hawaii, Guam, Samoa, or other Pacific Islands. It includes people who indicate their race as "Native Hawaiian," "Guamanian or Chamorro," "Samoan," and "Other Pacific Islander."

In this volume, the categories **Asian** and **Native Hawaiian or Other Pacific Islander** have been combined into a single category.

Some other race. This category includes all other responses not included in the "White," "Black or African American," "American Indian or Alaska Native," "Asian," and "Native Hawaiian or Other Pacific Islander" race categories described above. Respondents providing write-in entries such as multiracial, mixed, interracial, or a Hispanic/Latino group (for example, Mexican, Puerto Rican, or Cuban) in the "Some other race" write-in space are included in this category.

Two or more races. People may have chosen to provide two or more races either by checking two or more race response check boxes, by providing multiple write-in responses, or by some combination of check boxes and write-in responses. The race response categories shown on the questionnaire are collapsed into the five minimum races identified by the OMB and the Census Bureau "Some other race" category. For data product purposes, "Two or more races" refers to combinations of two or more of the following race categories:

1. White
2. Black or African American
3. American Indian and Alaska Native
4. Asian
5. Native Hawaiian and Other Pacific Islander
6. Some other race

There are 57 possible combinations involving the race categories shown above. Thus, according to this approach, a response of "White" and "Asian" was tallied as two or more races, while a response of "Japanese" and "Chinese" was not because "Japanese" and "Chinese" are both Asian responses.

Hispanic or Latino. The data on the Hispanic or Latino population, which was asked of all people, were derived from answers to long-form questionnaire Item 5. The terms "Spanish," "Hispanic origin," and "Latino" are used interchangeably. Some respondents identify with all three terms, while others may identify with only one of these three specific terms. Hispanics or Latinos who identify with the terms "Spanish," "Hispanic," or "Latino" are those who classify themselves in one of the specific Hispanic or Latino categories listed on the questionnaire—"Mexican," "Puerto Rican," or "Cuban"—as well as those who indicate that they are "other Spanish, Hispanic, or Latino." People who do not identify with one of the specific origins listed on the questionnaire but indicate that they are "other Spanish, Hispanic, or Latino" are those whose origins are from Spain, the Spanish-speaking countries of Central or South America, the Dominican Republic, or people identifying themselves generally as Spanish, Spanish-American, Hispanic, Hispano, Latino, and so on. All write-in responses to the "other Spanish/Hispanic/Latino" category were coded.

Origin can be viewed as the heritage, nationality group, lineage, or country of birth of the person or the person's parents or ancestors before their arrival in the United States. People who identify their origin as Spanish, Hispanic, or Latino may be of any race. If an individual could not provide a Hispanic origin response, his/her origin was assigned using specific rules of precedence of household relationship. For example, if origin was missing for a natural-born daughter in the household, then either the origin of the householder, another natural-born child, or the spouse of the householder was assigned. If Hispanic origin was not reported for anyone in the household, the origin of a householder in a previously processed household with the same race was assigned.

FOREIGN-BORN POPULATION
Table A, Item 13
On *American FactFinder*:
P21 (Sample)

The foreign-born population includes all people who were not U.S. citizens at birth. Foreign-born people are those who indicated they were either a U.S. citizen by naturalization or they were not a citizen of the United States.

The 2000 census did not ask about immigration status. The population surveyed includes all people who indicated that the United States was their usual place of residence on the census date. The foreign-born population includes immigrants (legal permanent residents), temporary migrants (e.g., students), humanitarian migrants (e.g., refugees), and unauthorized migrants (people illegally residing in the United States).

POPULATION BY AGE AND SEX
Table A, Items 14 through 23
Table B, Items 4 and 5
On *American FactFinder*:
P12 (Sample)

The data on age, which was asked of all people, were derived from answers to the long-form questionnaire Item 4. The age classification is based on the age of the person in complete years as of April 1, 2000. The age of the person usually was derived from his/her date-of-birth information. His\her reported age was used only when date of birth information was unavailable. Data on age are used to determine the applicability of some of the sample questions for a person and to classify other characteristics in census tabulations.

The data on sex, which was asked of all people, were derived from answers to long-form questionnaire Item 3. Individuals were asked to mark either "male" or "female" to indicate their sex. For most cases in which sex was not reported, it was determined from the person's given (i.e., first) name and household relationship. Otherwise, sex was imputed according to the relationship to the householder and the age of the person.

HOUSEHOLD CHARACTERISTICS
Table A, Items 24 through 27
Table B, Item 10
On *American FactFinder*:
P26 (Sample) for number of households and household size
H18 (Sample) for persons per household
P34 (Sample) for female-family householders

Household
A household includes all of the people who occupy a housing unit. (People not living in households are classified as living in group quarters.) A housing unit is a house, an apartment, a mobile home, a group of rooms, or a single room occupied (or if vacant, intended for occupancy) as separate living quarters. Separate living quarters are those in which the occupants live separately from any other people in the building and that have direct access from the outside of the building or through a common hall. The occupants may be a single family, one person living alone, two or more families living together, or any other group of related or unrelated people who share living quarters. In 100-percent tabulations, the count of households or householders always equals the count of occupied housing units. In sample tabulations, the numbers may differ as a result of the weighting process.

Persons per household. A measure obtained by dividing the number of people in households by the total number of households (or householders).

Female-family householders. This category includes a family with a female maintaining a household with no husband of the householder present.

A family includes a householder and one or more other people living in the same household who are related to the householder by birth, marriage, or adoption. All people in a household who are related to the householder are regarded as members of his/her family. A family household may contain people not related to the householder, but those people are not included as part of the householder's family in census tabulations. Thus, the number of family households is equal to the number of families, but family households may include more members than do families. A household can contain only one family for purposes of census tabulations. Not all households contain families since a household may comprise a group of unrelated people or one person living alone. Families are classified by type as either a "married-couple family" or "other family" according to the presence of a spouse. "Other family" is further broken out according to the sex of the householder.

One-person households. A householder living alone.

GROUP QUARTERS
Table A, Items 28 through 31
On *American FactFinder*:
PCT16 (100-percent)

The group quarters population includes all people not living in households. Two general categories of people in group quarters are recognized: (1) the institutionalized population and (2) the noninstitutionalized population.

Institutionalized population. The institutionalized population includes people under formally authorized, supervised care or custody in institutions at the time of enumeration, such as **correctional institutions**, **nursing homes**, and juvenile institutions.

Correctional institutions. Includes prisons, federal detention centers, military disciplinary barracks and jails, police lockups, halfway houses used for correctional purposes, local jails, and other confinement facilities, including work farms.

Nursing homes. Comprises a heterogeneous group of places providing continuous nursing and other services to patients. The majority of patients are elderly, although people who require nursing care because of chronic physical conditions may be found in these homes regardless of their age. Included in this category are skilled-nursing facilities, intermediate-care facilities, long-term care rooms in wards or buildings on the grounds of hospitals, or long-term care rooms/nursing wings in congregate housing facilities. Also included are nursing, convalescent, and rest homes such as soldiers', sailors', veterans', and fraternal or religious homes for the aged, with nursing care.

Noninstitutionalized population. The noninstitutionalized population includes all people who live in group quarters other than institutions, such as **college dormitories**, **military quarters**, and group homes. Also included are staff residing at institutional group quarters.

College dormitories. Includes college students in dormitories (provided the dormitory is restricted to students who do not have their families living with them), fraternity and sorority houses, and on-campus residential quarters used exclusively for those in religious orders who are attending college. College dormitory housing includes university-owned, on-campus and off-campus housing for unmarried residents.

Military quarters. Includes military personnel living in barracks and dormitories on base, transient quarters on base for temporary residents (both civilian and military), and military ships. However, patients in military hospitals receiving treatment for chronic diseases or who had no usual home elsewhere, and people being held in military disciplinary barracks, were included as part of the institutionalized population.

SCHOOL ENROLLMENT AND TYPE OF SCHOOL
Table A, Items 32 and 33
On *American FactFinder*:
P36 (Sample)

Data on **school enrollment** were derived from answers to long-form questionnaire Items 8a and 8b, which were asked of a sample of the population. People were classified as enrolled in school if they reported attending a "regular" public or private school or college at any time between February 1, 2000, and the time of enumeration. The question included instructions to "include only nursery school or preschool, kindergarten, elementary school, and schooling which leads to a high school diploma or a college degree" as regular school or college. Respondents who did not answer the enrollment question were assigned the enrollment status and type of school of a person with the same age, sex, and race/Hispanic or Latino origin whose residence was in the same or a nearby area.

Public and private school. Public and private school includes people who attended school in the reference period and indicated they were enrolled by marking one of the questionnaire categories for either "public school, public college" or "private school, private college." Schools supported and controlled primarily by a federal, state, or local government are defined as public (including tribal schools). Those supported and controlled primarily by religious organizations or other private groups are private.

EDUCATIONAL ATTAINMENT
Table A, Items 34 and 35
Table B, Item 8
On *American FactFinder*:
P37 (Sample)

Data on educational attainment were derived from answers to long-form questionnaire Item 9, which was asked of a sample of the population. Data on attainment are tabulated for the population 25 years old and over. People are classified according to the highest degree or level of school completed. The order in which degrees were listed on the questionnaire suggested that doctorate degrees were "higher" than professional school degrees, which were "higher" than master's degrees. The question included instructions for people currently enrolled in school to report the level of the previous grade attended or the highest degree received. Respondents who did not report educational attainment or enrollment level were assigned the attainment of a person of the same age, race, Hispanic or Latino origin, occupation, and sex, where possible, who resided in the same or a nearby area. Respondents who filled more than one box were edited to the highest level or degree reported. The question included a response category that allowed respondents to report completing the 12th grade without receiving a high school diploma. It allowed people who received either a high school diploma or the equivalent, for example, passed the Tests of General Educational Development (GED) and did not attend college, to be reported as "high school graduate(s)."

High school graduate or higher. This category includes people whose highest degree was a high school diploma or its equivalent, people who attended college but did not receive a degree, and people who received a college, university, or professional degree. People who reported completing the 12th grade but not receiving a diploma are not high school graduates.

Bachelor's degree or more. This category includes people whose highest degree was a bachelor's degree, a master's degree, a professional degree, or a doctorate degree. Master's degrees include the traditional MA and MS degrees and field-specific degrees, such as MSW, MEd, MBA, MLS, and MEng. Some examples of professional degrees include medicine, dentistry, chiropractic, optometry, osteopathic medicine, pharmacy, podiatry, veterinary medicine, law, and theology. Vocational and technical training, such as barber school training; business, trade, technical, and vocational schools; or other training for a specific trade, are specifically excluded.

INCOME IN 1999
Table A, Items 36 through 38
Table B, Item 7
On *American FactFinder*:
P82 (Sample) for per capita income
P53 (Sample) for median household income
P52 (Sample) for percent with income over $100,000

The data on income in 1999 were derived from answers to long-form questionnaire Items 31 and 32, which were asked of a sample of the population 15 years old and over. "Total income" is the sum of the amounts reported separately for wage or salary income; net self-employment income; interest, dividends, or net rental or royalty income or income from estates and trusts; social security or railroad retirement income; Supplemental Security Income (SSI); public assistance or welfare payments; retirement, survivor, or disability pensions; and all other income.

Receipts from the following sources are not included as income: capital gains money received from the sale of property (unless the recipient was engaged in the business of selling such property); the value of income "in kind" from food stamps, public housing subsidies, medical care, employer contributions for individuals, etc.; withdrawal of bank deposits; money borrowed; tax refunds; exchange of money between relatives living in the same household; and gifts and lump-sum inheritances, insurance payments, and other types of lump-sum receipts.

Per capita income. Per capita income is the mean income computed for every man, woman, and child in a particular group. It is derived by dividing the total income of a particular group by the total population in that group. Per capita income is rounded to the nearest whole dollar.

Income of households. This includes the income of the householder and all other individuals 15 years old and over in the household, whether they are related to the householder or not. Because many households consist of only one person, average household income is usually less than average family income. Although the household income statistics cover calendar year 1999, the characteristics of individuals and the composition of households refer to the time of enumeration (April 1, 2000). Thus, the income of the household does not include amounts received by individuals who were members of the household during all or part of calendar year 1999 if these individuals no longer resided in the household at the time of enumeration. Similarly, income amounts reported by individuals who did not reside in the household during 1999 but who were members of the household at the time of enumeration are included. However, the composition of most households was the same during 1999 as at the time of enumeration.

Median income. The median divides the income distribution into two equal parts, one-half of the cases falling below the median income and one-half above the median. For households, the median income is based on the distribution of the total number of households including those with no income. Median income is rounded to the nearest whole dollar.

POVERTY STATUS IN 1999
Table A, Items 39 and 40
Table B, Item 6
On *American FactFinder*:
P87 (Sample) for persons in poverty
P90 (Sample) for families in poverty

The poverty data were derived from answers to long-form questionnaire Items 31 and 32, the same questions used to derive income data. The Census Bureau uses the federal government's official poverty definition. The Social Security Administration (SSA) developed the original poverty definition in 1964, which federal interagency committees subsequently revised in 1969 and 1980. The Office of Management and Budget's (OMB's) *Directive 14* prescribes this definition as the official poverty measure for federal agencies to use in their statistical work.

Derivation of the Current Poverty Measure

When the Social Security Administration (SSA) created the poverty definition in 1964, it focused on family food consumption. The U.S. Department of Agriculture (USDA) used its data about the nutritional needs of children and adults to construct food plans for families. Within each food plan, dollar amounts varied according to the total number of people in the family and the family's composition, such as the number of children within each family. The cheapest of these plans, the Economy Food Plan, was designed to address the dietary needs of families on an austere budget. Since the USDA's 1955 Food Consumption Survey showed that families of three or more people across all income levels spent roughly one-third of their income on food, the SSA multiplied the cost of the Economy Food Plan by 3 to obtain dollar figures for the poverty thresholds. Since the Economy Food Plan budgets varied by family size and composition, so too did the poverty thresholds. For two-person families, the thresholds were adjusted by slightly higher factors because those households had higher fixed costs. Thresholds for unrelated individuals were calculated as a fixed proportion of the corresponding thresholds for two-person families. The poverty thresholds are revised annually to allow for changes in the cost of living as reflected in the Consumer Price Index (CPI-U). The poverty thresholds are the same for all parts of the country — they are not adjusted for regional, state, or local variations in the cost of living. For a detailed discussion of the poverty definition, see U.S. Census Bureau, Current Population Reports, *Poverty in the United States: 1999*, P60-210.

How Poverty Status Is Determined

The poverty status of families and unrelated individuals in 1999 was determined using 48 thresholds (income cut-offs) arranged in a two-dimensional matrix. The matrix consists of family size (from one person to nine or more people) cross-classified by presence and number of family members under 18 years old (from no children present to eight or more children present). Unrelated individuals and two-person families were further differentiated by the age of the reference person (RP) (under 65 years old and 65 years old and over).

To determine a person's poverty status, one compares the person's total family income with the poverty threshold appropriate for that person's family size and composition (see table below). If the total income of that person's family is less than the threshold appropriate for that family, then the person is considered "poor," together with every member of his/her family. If a person is not living with anyone related by birth, marriage, or adoption, then the person's own income is compared with his/her poverty threshold.

Weighted average thresholds. Even though the official poverty data are based on the 48 thresholds arranged by family size and number of children within the family, data users often want to get an idea of the "average" threshold for a given family size. The weighted average thresholds provide that summary. They are weighted averages because for any given family size, families with a certain number of children may be more or less common than families with a different number of children. In other words, among three-person families, there are more families with two adults and one child than families with three adults. To get the weighted average threshold for families of a particular size, multiply each threshold by the number of families for whom that threshold applies; then add up those products, and divide by the total number of families who are of that family size. For example, for three-person families, 1999 weighted thresholds were calculated in the following way using information from the 2000 Current Population Survey:

Family type	Number of families		Threshold
No children (three adults)	5,213	*	$13,032 = $67,935,816
One child (two adults)	8,208	*	$13,410 = $110,069,280
Two children (one adult)	2,656	*	$13,423 = $35,651,488
Totals	16,077		$213,656,584

Source: Current Population Survey, March 2000.

Dividing $213,656,584 by 16,077 (the total number of three-person families) yields $13,290, the weighted average threshold for three-person families. Please note that the thresholds are weighted not just by the number of poor families, but by all families for which the thresholds apply: the thresholds are used to determine which families are *at* or *above* poverty, as well as below poverty.

Poverty Thresholds in 1999 by Size of Family

Size of Family Unit	Weighted Average Thresholds
One person (unrelated individual)	$ 8,501
Under 65 years old	8,667
65 years old and over	7,990
Two persons	10,869
Householder under 65 years old	11,214
Householder 65 years old and over	10,075
Three persons	13,290
Four persons	17,029
Five persons	20,127
Six persons	22,727
Seven persons	25,912
Eight persons	28,967
Nine or more persons	34,417

Individuals for whom poverty status is determined.
Poverty status was determined for all people except

institutionalized people, people in military group quarters, people in college dormitories, and unrelated individuals under 15 years old. These groups also were excluded from the numerator and denominator when calculating poverty rates. They are considered neither "poor" nor "nonpoor."

HOUSING UNITS, TENURE, COSTS, AND CONDITION

Table A, Items 41 through 49
Table B, Item 11
On *American FactFinder*:
H1 (Sample) for estimate of total housing units
H7 (Sample) for tenure
H76 (Sample) for median value of owner-occupied units
H95 (Sample) for median owner costs as a percent of income
H63 (Sample) for median rent
H70 (Sample) for median rent as a percent of income
H49 (Sample) for substandard units

Housing units and households

A household includes all of the people who occupy a housing unit. (People not living in households are classified as living in group quarters.) A housing unit is a house, an apartment, a mobile home, a group of rooms, or a single room occupied (or if vacant, intended for occupancy) as separate living quarters. Separate living quarters are those in which the occupants live separately from any other people in the building and that have direct access from the outside of the building or through a common hall. The occupants may be a single family, one person living alone, two or more families living together, or any other group of related or unrelated people who share living quarters. In 100-percent tabulations, the count of households or householders always equals the count of occupied housing units. In sample tabulations, the numbers may differ as a result of the weighting process.

Tenure. The data on tenure, which was asked at all occupied housing units, were obtained from answers to long-form questionnaire Item 33 and short-form questionnaire Item 2. All occupied housing units are classified as either owner occupied or renter occupied.

Owner occupied. A housing unit is owner occupied if the owner or co-owner lives in the unit, even if it is mortgaged or not fully paid for. The owner or co-owner must live in the unit and usually is Person 1 on the questionnaire. The unit is "Owned by you or someone in this household with a mortgage or loan" if it is being purchased with a mortgage or some other debt arrangement, such as a deed of trust, trust deed, contract to purchase, land contract, or purchase agreement. The unit is also considered owned with a mortgage if it is built on leased land and there is a mortgage on the unit. Mobile homes occupied by owners with installment loans balances are also included in this category. A housing unit is "Owned by you or someone in this household free and clear (without a mortgage or loan)" if there is no mortgage or other similar debt on the house, apartment, or mobile home including units built on leased land if the unit is owned outright without a mortgage.

The tenure item on the 2000 census questionnaire distinguishes between units owned with a mortgage or loan and those owned free and clear. In the sample data products, as in the 100-percent products, the tenure item provides data for total owner-occupied units. Detailed information that identifies mortgaged and nonmortgaged units are provided in other sample housing matrices.

Renter occupied. All occupied housing units that are not owner occupied, whether they are rented for cash rent or occupied without payment of cash rent, are classified as renter occupied. "No cash rent" units are separately identified in the rent tabulations. Such units are generally provided free by friends or relatives or in exchange for services, such as resident manager, caretaker, minister, or tenant farmer. Housing units on military bases also are classified in the "No cash rent" category. "Rented for cash rent" includes units in continuing care, sometimes called "life care arrangements." These arrangements usually involve a contract between one or more individuals and a service provider guaranteeing the individual shelter, usually a house or apartment, and services, such as meals or transportation to shopping or recreation.

Value. The data on value (also referred to as "price asked" for vacant units) were obtained from answers to long-form questionnaire Item 51, which was asked on a sample basis at owner-occupied housing units and units that were being bought, or vacant for sale at the time of enumeration. Value is the respondent's estimate of how much the property (house and lot, mobile home and lot, or condominium unit) would sell for if it were for sale. If the house or mobile home was owned or being bought, but the land on which it sits was not, the respondent was asked to estimate the combined value of the house or mobile home and the land. For vacant units, value was the price asked for the property. Value was tabulated separately for all owner-occupied and vacant-for-sale housing units, owner-occupied and vacant-for-sale mobile homes, and specified owner-occupied and specified vacant-for-sale housing units.

Specified owner-occupied and specified vacant-for-sale units. Specified owner-occupied and specified vacant-for-sale housing units include only one-family houses on less than 10 acres without a business or medical office on the property. The data for "specified units" exclude mobile homes, houses with a business or medical office, houses on 10 or more acres, and housing units in multiunit buildings.

Selected monthly owner costs. The data on selected monthly owner costs were obtained from answers to long-form questionnaire Items 45a-d, 47b, 48b, 49, 50, 52, and 53b, which were asked on a sample basis at owner-occupied housing units. Selected monthly owner costs are the sum of payments for mortgages, deeds of trust, contracts to purchase, or similar debts on the property (including payments for the first mortgage, second mortgage, home equity loans, and other junior mortgages); real estate taxes; fire, hazard, and flood insurance on the property; utilities (electricity, gas, water, and sewer); and fuels (oil, coal, kerosene, wood, etc.). It also includes, where appropriate, the monthly condominium fees or mobile home costs (installment loan payments, personal property taxes, site rent, registration fees, and license fees). Selected monthly owner costs were tabulated separately for all owner-occupied units, specified owner-occupied units, and owner-occupied mobile homes, and usually are shown separately for units "with a mortgage" and for units "not mortgaged."

Selected monthly owner costs as a percentage of household income in 1999. The information on selected monthly owner costs as a percentage of household income in 1999 is the computed ratio of selected monthly owner costs to monthly household income in 1999. The ratio was computed separately for each unit and rounded to the nearest whole percentage. It is based on questions asked of a sample of households. The data are tabulated separately for all owner-occupied units housing units and specified owner-occupied housing units. Separate distributions are often shown for units "with a mortgage" and for units "not mortgaged." Units occupied by households reporting no income or a net loss in 1999 are included in the "not computed" category.

Median selected monthly owner costs as a percentage of household income. This measure divides the selected monthly owner costs as a percentage of household income distribution into two equal parts, one-half of the cases falling below the median selected monthly owner costs as a percentage of household income and one-half above the median. Median selected monthly owner costs as a percentage of household income is computed on the basis of a standard distribution. Median selected monthly owner costs as a percentage of household income is rounded to the nearest tenth.

Gross rent. The data on gross rent were obtained from answers to long-form questionnaire Items 45a-d, which were asked on a sample basis. Gross rent is the contract rent plus the estimated average monthly cost of utilities (electricity, gas, water, and sewer) and fuels (oil, coal, kerosene, wood, etc.) if these are paid by the renter (or paid for the renter by someone else). Gross rent is intended to eliminate differentials that result from varying practices with respect to the inclusion of utilities and fuels as part of the rental payment. The estimated costs of utilities and fuels are reported on an annual basis but are converted to monthly figures for the tabulations. Renter units occupied without payment of cash rent are shown separately as "No cash rent" in the tabulations.

Median gross rent. Median gross rent divides the gross rent distribution into two equal parts, one-half of the cases falling below the median gross rent and one-half above the median. Median gross rent is computed on the basis of a standard distribution. Median gross rent is rounded to the nearest whole dollar.

Gross rent as a percentage of household income in 1999. Gross rent as a percentage of household income in 1999 is a computed ratio of monthly gross rent to monthly household income (total household income in 1999 divided by 12). The ratio is computed separately for each unit and is rounded to the nearest tenth. Units for which no cash rent is paid and units occupied by households that reported no income or a net loss in 1999 comprise the category "Not computed."

Median gross rent as a percentage of household income in 1999. This measure divides the gross rent as a percentage of household income distribution into two equal parts, one-half of the cases falling below the median gross rent as a percentage of household income and one-half above the median. Median gross rent as a percentage of household income is computed on the basis of a standard distribution. Median gross rent as a percentage of household income is rounded to the nearest tenth.

Substandard housing units. In this volume, "substandard housing units" includes overcrowded units (1.01 or more occupants per room) and units lacking complete plumbing facilities.

Occupants per room. Occupants per room is obtained by dividing the number of people in each occupied housing unit by the number of rooms in the unit. The figures show the number of occupied housing units having the specified ratio of people per room. Although the Census Bureau has no official definition of crowded units, many users consider units with more than one occupant per room to be crowded. Occupants per room is rounded to the nearest hundredth. This item was derived from questions asked on a sample basis.

Plumbing facilities. The data on plumbing facilities were obtained from answers to long-form questionnaire Item 39, which was asked on a sample basis at both occupied and vacant housing units. Complete plumbing facilities include (1) hot and cold piped water, (2) a flush toilet, and (3) a bathtub or shower. All three facilities must be located inside the house, apartment, or mobile home, but not necessarily in the same room. Housing units are classified as lacking complete plumbing facilities when any of the three facilities is not present.

CIVILIAN LABOR FORCE
Table A, Items 50 through 52
Table B, Item 9
On *American FactFinder*:
P43 (Sample)

NOTE: The Census Bureau is aware that there may be a problem or problems in the employment-status data of Census 2000. The labor force data for some places where colleges are located appear to overstate the number in the labor force, the number unemployed, and the percent unemployed. Research into this "college-town" issue indicates that the problem extended beyond places with colleges to the country in general. It stems from the tendency of many working-age people living in civilian noninstitutional group quarters (GQ), such as college dormitories, worker dormitories, and group homes (for the mentally ill or physically handicapped), to exhibit a particular pattern of entries to the employment questions in Census 2000. They now estimate that the pattern affected the employment data for about 15 percent of the civilian noninstitutional GQ population 16 years of age and over in the United States, or around 500,000 people. It had an impact on the Census 2000 labor force statistics for the entire country, but its effects were most visible and substantial for places such as college towns, with high concentrations of people living in civilian noninstitutional group quarters.

The data on employment status (referred to as labor force status in previous censuses) were derived from answers to long-form questionnaire Items 21 and 25, which were asked of a sample of the population 15 years old and over. The series of questions on employment status was designed to identify, in this sequence: (1) people who worked at any time during the reference week; (2) people who did not work during the reference week, but who had jobs or businesses from which they were temporarily absent (excluding people on layoff); (3) people on temporary layoff who expected to be recalled to work within the next 6 months or who had been given a date to return to work, and who were available for work during the reference week; and (4) people who did not work during the reference week, who had looked for work during the reference week or the three previous weeks, and who were available for work during the reference week. The employment status data shown in the 2000 census tabulations relate to people 16 years old and over.

Civilian labor force. Consists of people classified as employed or unemployed in accordance with the criteria described below.

Labor force. All people classified in the civilian labor force (i.e., "employed" and "unemployed" people), plus members of the United States Armed Forces (people on active duty with the United States Army, Air Force, Navy, Marine Corps, or Coast Guard).

Not in labor force. All people 16 years old and over who are not classified as members of the labor force. This category consists mainly of students, individuals taking care of home or family, retired workers, seasonal workers enumerated in an off-season who were not looking for work, institutionalized people (all institutionalized people are placed in this category regardless of any work activities they may have done in the reference week), and people doing only incidental unpaid family work (fewer than 15 hours during the reference week).

Employed. All civilians 16 years old and over who were either (1) "at work"—those who did any work at all during the reference week as paid employees, worked in their own business or profession, worked on their own farm, or worked 15 hours or more as unpaid workers on a family farm or in a family business; or (2) were "with a job but not at work"—those who did not work during the reference week, but who had jobs or businesses from which they were temporarily absent because of illness, bad weather, industrial dispute, vacation, or other personal reasons. Excluded from the employed are people whose only activity consisted of work around their own house (painting, repairing, or own home housework) or unpaid volunteer work for religious, charitable, and similar organizations. Also excluded are all institutionalized people and people on active duty in the United States Armed Forces.

Civilian employed. This term is defined exactly the same as the term "employed" above.

Unemployed. All civilians 16 years old and over were classified as unemployed if they were neither "at work" nor "with a job but not at work" during the reference week, were looking for work during the last 4 weeks, and were available to start a job. Also included as unemployed were civilians 16 years old and over who (1) did not work at all during the reference week, (2) were on temporary layoff from a job, (3) had been informed that they would be recalled to work within the next 6 months or had been given a date to return to work, and (4) were available to return to work during the reference week, except for temporary illness. Examples of job-seeking activities were:

- Registering at a public or private employment office
- Meeting with prospective employers
- Investigating possibilities for starting a professional practice or opening a business
- Placing or answering advertisements
- Writing letters of application
- Being on a union or professional register

Unemployment rate. The unemployment rate is the number of unemployed persons as a percentage of the civilian labor force.

CIVILIAN EMPLOYMENT AND OCCUPATIONS
Table A, Items 53 through 56
On *American FactFinder*:
P50 (Sample)

Occupation. The occupational classification system used during the 2000 census consists of 509 specific occupational categories for employed people arranged into 23 major occupational groups. This classification was developed based on the *Standard Occupational Classification (SOC) Manual: 2000*, which includes a hierarchical structure showing 23 major occupational groups divided into 96 minor groups, 449 broad groups, and 821 detailed occupations.

This volume includes three combined groupings of the major categories. **Management, Professional, and Related** occupations include managers, business and financial specialists, computer specialists, doctors, lawyers, teachers, and similar occupations. **Service, Sales, and Office** occupations include healthcare support workers, firefighting and law enforcement workers, food preparation workers, building maintenance workers, sales, and administrative support occupations. **Construction and Production** occupations include construction trades supervisors and workers; extraction workers; installation, maintenance, and repair workers; production workers; and transportation and material-moving workers such as traffic controllers and motor vehicle operators.

2002 Census of Agriculture

The census of agriculture is the leading source of facts and statistics about the nation's agricultural production. It provides a detailed picture of U.S. farms and ranches every 5 years and is the only source of uniform, comprehensive agricultural data for every state and county or county equivalent in the United States.

The first agriculture census was taken in 1840 as part of the sixth decennial census of population. The agriculture census continued to be taken as part of the decennial census through 1950. A separate mid-decade census of agriculture was conducted in 1925, 1935, and 1945. From 1954 to 1974, the census was taken for the years ending in 4 and 9. In 1976, Congress authorized the census of agriculture to be taken for 1978 and 1982 to adjust the data reference year so that it coincided with other economic censuses. This adjustment in timing established the agriculture census on a 5-year cycle, with data being collected for years ending in 2 and 7.

For 156 years (1840–1996), the U.S. Department of Commerce, Bureau of the Census was responsible for collecting census of agriculture data. The 1997 Appropriations Act contained a provision that transferred the responsibility for the census of agriculture

from the Bureau of the Census to the U.S. Department of Agriculture (USDA), National Agricultural Statistics Service (NASS). The 2002 Census of Agriculture is the 26th federal census of agriculture and the second conducted by NASS.

To access the data on the Internet:

The main page for the 2002 Census of Agriculture is <www.nass.usda.gov/census/>
Under *Query and Downloadable Options,* click on *Congressional District Tabulations.*
Select data items and geographic areas:
"2002 Census of Agriculture - Volume 1 Geographic Area Series; Congressional District Tabulations of Selected Items."

Additional items can by found be returning to the main page.
Under *Congressional Districts,* click on *Profiles* or *Rankings.*

FARMS
Table A, Item 57

The census definition of a farm is any place from which $1,000 or more of agricultural products were produced and sold, or normally would have been sold, during the census year.

FARMS BY SIZE
Table A, Items 58 through 62

All **farms** were classified into size groups according to the total land area in the farm. The land area of a farm is an operating unit concept and includes land owned and operated as well as land rented from others. Land rented to or assigned to a tenant was considered part of the tenant's farm and not part of the owner's.

The approximate land area represents the total land area as determined by records and calculations as of January 1, 2000. The proportion of land area in farms may exceed 100 percent because some operations have land in two or more counties, but all acres are tabulated in the principal county of operation.

The **acreage** designated as "land in farms" consists primarily of agricultural land used for crops, pasture, or grazing. It also includes woodland and wasteland not actually under cultivation or used for pasture or grazing, provided it was part of the farm operator's total operation. Large acreages of woodland or wasteland held for nonagricultural purposes were deleted from individual reports during the edit process. Land in farms includes acres in the Conservation Reserve and Wetlands Reserve Programs.

Land in farms is an operating unit concept and includes land owned and operated as well as land rented from others. Land used rent free was reported as land rented from others. All grazing land, except land used under government permits on a per-head basis, was included as "land in farms" provided it was part of a farm or ranch. Land under the exclusive use of a grazing association was reported by the grazing association and included as land in farms. All land in American Indian reservations used for growing crops or grazing livestock was included as land in farms. Land in reservations not reported by individual American Indians or non-Native Americans was reported in the name of the cooperative group that used the land. In many instances, an entire American Indian reservation was reported as one farm.

CROPLAND HARVESTED
Table A, Items 63 and 64

This category includes land from which crops were harvested and hay was cut, land used to grow short-rotation woody crops, land in orchards, citrus groves, Christmas trees, vineyards, nurseries, and greenhouses. Land from which two or more crops were harvested was counted only once. Land in tapped maple trees was included in woodland not pastured.

PRINCIPAL OPERATOR
Table A, Items 65 and 66

The **Principal Operator** is the person primarily responsible for the on-site, day-to-day operation of the farm or ranch business. This person may be a hired manager or business manager.

The term "operator" designates a person who operates a farm, either doing the work or making day-to-day decisions about such things as planting, harvesting, feeding, and marketing. The operator may be the owner, a member of the owner's household, a hired manager, a tenant, a renter, or a sharecropper. If a person rents land to others or has land worked on shares by others, he/she is considered the operator only of the land which is retained for his/her own operation.

The primary occupation classifications used were:

• *Farming*. The operator spent 50 percent or more of his/her work time during 2002 at farming or ranching.
• *Other*. The operator spent more than 50 percent of his/her work time during 2002 at occupations other than farming or ranching. Also, operators who spent the majority of their work time working for another agricultural operation for wages were included in this classification.

All farms were classified by tenure of operators in the 2002 census.
The classifications used were:

• Full owners operated only land they owned.
• Part owners operated land they owned and also land they rented from others.
• Tenants operated only land they rented from others or worked on shares for others.

Farms with hired managers are classified according to the land ownership characteristics reported. For example, a corporation owns all the land used on the farm and hires a manager to run the farm. The hired manager is considered the farm operator, and the farm is classified with a tenure type of "full owner" even though the hired manager owns none of the land he/she operates.

TYPE OF ORGANIZATION
Table A, Items 67 through 69

All farms were classified by type of organization in the 2002 census.
The classifications used were:

• **Individual or family** (sole proprietorship), excluding partnership and corporation
• **Partnership**, including family partnership (further subclassified into two categories: registered under state law or not registered under state law)
• **Corporation**, including family corporations (further subclassified into two categories: family held or other than family held; or more than 10 stockholders)
• **Other**, cooperative, estate or trust, institutional, etc.

VALUE OF AGRICULTURAL PRODUCTS SOLD
Table A, Items 70 through 74

This category represents the gross market value before taxes and production expenses of all agricultural products sold or removed from the farm in 2002 regardless of who received the payment. It is equivalent to total sales. It includes sales by the operators as well as the value of any shares received by partners, landlords, contractors, or others associated with the operation. The value of commodities placed in the Commodity Credit Corporation (CCC) loan program is included in this figure. Market value of agricultural products sold does not include payments received for participation in other federal farm programs. Also, it does not include income from farm-related sources such as "customwork" and other agricultural services, or income from nonfarm sources. The value of crops sold in 2002 does not necessarily represent the sales from crops harvested in 2002. Data may include sales from crops produced in earlier years and may exclude some crops produced in 2002 but held in storage and not sold. For commodities such as sugarbeets and wool sold through a co-op that made payments in several installments, respondents were requested to report the total value received in 2002.

The value of agricultural products sold was requested of all operators. If the operators failed to report this information, estimates were made based on the amount of crops harvested, livestock or poultry inventory, or number sold.

PAYMENTS RECEIVED FROM FEDERAL FARM PROGRAMS
Table A, Items 75 through 80

This category consists of direct cash payments received by the farm operators in 2002. It includes disaster payments, loan deficiency payments from prior participation, payments from the Conservation Reserve Program (CRP), the Wetlands Reserve Program (WRP), other conservation programs, and all other federal farm programs under which payments were made directly to farm operators. Commodity Credit Corporation (CCC) proceeds and federal crop insurance payments were not tabulated in this category.